Collins
Italian
Dictionary

HarperCollins Publishers
Westerhill Road
Bishopbriggs
Glasgow
G64 2QT
Great Britain

First Edition 2005

Previously published as Collins Pocket
Italian Dictionary

Latest Reprint 2005

© William Collins Sons & Co. Ltd. 1990
© HarperCollins Publishers 1996, 1999,
2002

ISBN 0–00–719640–7

Collins® and Bank of English® are
registered trademarks of HarperCollins
Publishers Limited

www.collins.co.uk

A catalogue record for this book is
available from the British Library

HarperCollins Publishers, Inc.
10 East 53rd Street, New York, NY 10022

ISBN 0-06-008452-9

Library of Congress Cataloging-in-
Publication Data has been applied for

www.harpercollins.com

First HarperCollins edition published
2000

HarperCollins books may be purchased
for educational, business, or sales
promotional use. For information,
please write to: Special Markets
Department, HarperCollins Publishers
Inc., 10 East 53rd Street, New York,
NY 10022

Typeset by Morton Word Processing Ltd,
Scarborough

Printed in Italy by Rotolito Lombarda
SpA

Acknowledgements
We would like to thank those authors
and publishers who kindly gave
permission for copyright material to be
used in the Collins Word Web. We
would also like to thank Times
Newspapers Ltd for providing valuable
data.

general editors/a cura di
Catherine E. Love • Michela Clari

with/hanno collaborato
Gabriella Bacchelli • Loredana Riu
Bob Grossmith

editorial staff/segreteria di redazione
Joyce Littlejohn • Isobel Gordon

series editor/collana a cura di
Lorna Sinclair Knight

INDICE/CONTENTS

I marchi registrati

I termini che a nostro parere costituiscono un marchio registrato sono stati designati come tali. In ogni caso, né la presenza né l'assenza di tale designazione implicano alcuna valutazione del loro reale stato giuridico.

Note on trademarks

Words which we have reason to believe constitute trademarks have been designated as such. However, neither the presence nor the absence of such designation should be regarded as affecting the legal status of any trademark.

INTRODUZIONE

Questo dizionario è stato concepito e scritto per chi vuole imparare l'inglese per motivi di studio, lavoro o turismo.

La modernità e la ricchezza del lemmario e della fraseologia, l'elegante presentazione delle voci, l'uso del colore e il pratico formato fanno di questo dizionario un'opera unica nel suo genere.

Grazie ai giochi e agli esercizi che troverete nell'originale supplemento vi riuscirà facile e divertente imparare ad usare il dizionario così da trarne il massimo vantaggio.

I dizionari Collins sono sinonimo di qualità e modernità: vi ringraziamo di aver scelto il dizionario inglese Tascabile che siamo certi si rivelerà uno strumento di lavoro utile e piacevole da usarsi in ogni occasione.

COME USARE IL DIZIONARIO

Per imparare ad usare in modo efficace il dizionario è importante comprendere la funzione delle differenziazioni tipografiche, dei simboli e delle abbreviazioni usati nel testo. Vi forniamo pertanto qui di seguito alcuni chiarimenti in merito a tali convenzioni.

I lemmi
Sono le parole a colori elencate in ordine alfabetico. Il primo e l'ultimo lemma di ciascuna pagina appaiono al margine superiore.

Dove opportuno, informazioni sull'ambito d'uso o sul livello di formalità di certe parole vengono fornite tra parentesi in corsivo e spesso in forma abbreviata dopo la trascrizione fonetica (es. (COMM), (inf)).

In certi casi più parole con radice comune sono raggruppate sotto lo stesso lemma. Tali parole appaiono a colori ma in un carattere leggermente ridotto (es. **dolce, dolcezza; accept, acceptance**).

Esempi d'uso del lemma sono a loro volta in neretto ma in un carattere diverso dal lemma (es. **to be cold**).

La trascrizione fonetica

La trascrizione fonetica che illustra la corretta pronuncia del lemma è in parentesi quadra e segue immediatamente il lemma (es. **mezzo** ['mɛddzo]; **knead** [niːd]). L'elenco dei simboli fonetici è alle pagine xiv-xv.

Le traduzioni

Le traduzioni sono in carattere tondo e se si riferiscono a diversi significati del lemma sono separate da un punto e virgola. Spesso diverse traduzioni di un lemma sono introdotte da una o più parole in corsivo in parentesi tonda: la loro funzione è di chiarire a quale significato del lemma si riferisce la traduzione. Possono essere sinonimi, indicazioni di ambito d'uso o di registro del lemma (es. **party** (*POL*) (*team*) o (*celebration*), **laid back** (*inf*) etc.).

Le "parole chiave"

Un trattamento particolare è stato riservato a quelle parole che, per frequenza d'uso o complessità, necessitano una strutturazione più chiara ed esauriente (es. **da, di, avere** in italiano, **at, to, be, this** in inglese). Il simbolo ♦ e i numeri sono usati per guidarvi attraverso le varie distinzioni grammaticali e di significato. Dove necessario, ulteriori informazioni sono fornite in corsivo tra parentesi.

Informazioni grammaticali

Le parti del discorso (noun, adjective ecc.) sono espresse da abbreviazioni convenzionali in corsivo (*n, adj* ecc) e seguono la trascrizione fonetica del lemma.

Eventuali ulteriori informazioni grammaticali, come ad esempio le forme di un verbo irregolare o il plurale irregolare di un sostantivo, precedono tra parentesi la parte del discorso (es. **fall** (*pt* **fell**, *pp* **fallen**) *n*; **man** (*pl* **men**) *n*).

INTRODUCTION

We are delighted that you have decided to buy the Collins Italian Dictionary, and hope you will enjoy and benefit from using it at home, at school, on holiday or at work.

The innovative use of colour guides you quickly and efficiently to the word you want, and the comprehensive wordlist provides a wealth of modern and idiomatic phrases not normally found in a dictionary this size.

In addition, the supplement provides you with guidance on using the dictionary, along with entertaining ways of improving your dictionary skills.

We hope that you will enjoy using it and that it will significantly enhance your language studies.

USING YOUR COLLINS ITALIAN DICTIONARY

A wealth of information is presented in the dictionary, using various typefaces, sizes of type, symbols, abbreviations and brackets. The conventions and symbols used are explained in the following sections.

Headwords
The words you look up in a dictionary — "headwords" — are listed alphabetically. They are printed in **colour** for rapid identification. The two headwords appearing at the top of each page indicate the first and last word dealt with on the page in question.

Information about the usage or form of certain headwords is given in brackets after the phonetic spelling. This usually appears in abbreviated form and in italics (e.g. (*fam*), (*COMM*)).

Where appropriate, words related to headwords are grouped in the same entry (**illustrare, illustrazione; accept, acceptance**) in a slightly smaller type than the headword.

Common expressions in which the headword appears are shown in a different bold roman type (e.g. **aver freddo**).

Phonetic spellings
Where the phonetic spelling of headwords (indicating their pronunciation) is given, it will appear in square brackets immediately after the headword (e.g. **calza** ['kaltsa]; **knead** [ni:d]). A list of these symbols is given on pages xiv-xv.

Translations
Headword translations are given in ordinary type and, where more than one meaning or usage exists, these are separated by a semi-colon. You will often find other words in italics in brackets before the translations. These offer suggested contexts in which the headword might appear (e.g. **duro** (*pietra*) or (*lavoro*)) or provide synonyms (e.g. **duro** (*ostinato*)).

"Key" words
Special status is given to certain Italian and English words which are considered as "key" words in each language. They may, for example, occur very frequently or have several types of usage (e.g. **da, di, avere; at, to, be, this**). A combination of lozenges and numbers helps you to distinguish different parts of speech and different meanings. Further helpful information is provided in brackets and in italics.

Grammatical information
Parts of speech are given in abbreviated form in italics after the phonetic spellings of headwords (e.g. *vt, av, cong*).

Genders of Italian nouns are indicated as follows: *sm* for a masculine and *sf* for a feminine noun. Feminine and irregular plural forms of nouns are also shown (**dottore, essa; droga, ghe**).

Feminine adjective endings are given as are plural forms (**opaco, a, chi, che**).

ABBREVIAZIONI

ABBREVIATIONS

abbreviazione	abbr	abbreviation
aggettivo	adj	adjective
amministrazione	ADMIN	administration
avverbio	adv	adverb
aeronautica, viaggi aerei	AER	flying, air travel
aggettivo	ag	adjective
agricoltura	AGR	agriculture
amministrazione	AMM	administration
anatomia	ANAT	anatomy
architettura	ARCHIT	architecture
articolo indeterminativo	art indet	indefinite article
attributivo	attrib	attributive
ausiliare	aus, aux	auxiliary
l'automobile	AUT	the motor car and motoring
avverbio	av	adverb
aeronautica, viaggi aerei	AVIAT	flying, air travel
biologia	BIOL	biology
botanica	BOT	botany
inglese della Gran Bretagna	BRIT	British English
consonante	C	consonant
chimica	CHIM, CHEM	chemistry
commercio, finanza, banca	COMM	commerce, finance, banking
comparativo	compar	comparative
informatica	COMPUT	computers
congiunzione	cong, conj	conjunction
edilizia	CONSTR	building
sostantivo usato come aggettivo, non può essere usato né come attributo, né dopo il sostantivo qualificato	cpd	compound element: noun used as adjective and which cannot follow the noun it qualifies
cucina	CUC, CULIN	cookery
davanti a	dav	before
articolo determinativo	def art	definite article
determinativo: articolo, aggettivo dimostrativo o indefinito etc	det	determiner: article, demonstrative etc
diminutivo	dimin	diminutive
diritto	DIR	law
economia	ECON	economics
edilizia	EDIL	building
elettricità, elettronica	ELETTR, ELEC	electricity, electronics
esclamazione	escl, excl	exclamation
femminile	f	feminine
familiare (! da evitare)	fam(!)	informal usage (! particularly offensive)
ferrovia	FERR	railways
figurato	fig	figurative use

fisiologia	FISIOL	physiology
fotografia	FOT	photography
(verbo inglese) la cui particella è inseparabile dal verbo	fus	(phrasal verb) where the particle cannot be separated from main verb
nella maggior parte dei sensi; generalmente	gen	in most or all senses; generally
geografia, geologia	GEO	geography, geology
geometria	GEOM	geometry
impersonale	impers	impersonal
articolo indeterminativo	indef art	indefinite article
familiare (! da evitare)	inf(!)	informal usage (! particularly offensive)
infinito	infin	infinitive
informatica	INFORM	computers
insegnamento, sistema scolastico e universitario	INS	schooling, schools and universities
invariabile	inv	invariable
irregolare	irreg	irregular
grammatica, linguistica	LING	grammar, linguistics
maschile	m	masculine
matematica	MAT(H)	mathematics
termine medico, medicina	MED	medical term, medicine
il tempo, meteorologia	METEOR	the weather, meteorology
maschile o femminile, secondo il sesso	m/f	either masculine or feminine depending on sex
esercito, linguaggio militare	MIL	military matters
musica	MUS	music
sostantivo	n	noun
nautica	NAUT	sailing, navigation
numerale (aggettivo, sostantivo)	num	numeral adjective or noun
	o.s.	oneself
peggiorativo	peg, pej	derogatory, pejorative
fotografia	PHOT	photography
fisiologia	PHYSIOL	physiology
plurale	pl	plural
politica	POL	politics
participio passato	pp	past participle
preposizione	prep	preposition
pronome	pron	pronoun
psicologia, psichiatria	PSIC, PSYCH	psychology, psychiatry
tempo passato	pt	past tense
qualcosa	qc	
qualcuno	qn	
religione, liturgia	REL	religions, church service
sostantivo	s	noun
	sb	somebody

ABBREVIAZIONI

ABBREVIATIONS

insegnamento, sistema scolastico e universitario	SCOL	schooling, schools and universities
singolare	sg	singular
soggetto (grammaticale)	sog	(grammatical) subject
	sth	something
congiuntivo	sub	subjunctive
soggetto (grammaticale)	subj	(grammatical) subject
superlativo	superl	superlative
termine tecnico, tecnologia	TECN, TECH	technical term, technology
telecomunicazioni	TEL	telecommunications
tipografia	TIP	typography, printing
televisione	TV	television
tipografia	TYP	typography, printing
inglese degli Stati Uniti	US	American English
vocale	V	vowel
verbo	vb	verb
verbo o gruppo verbale con funzione intransitiva	vi	verb or phrasal verb used intransitively
verbo riflessivo	vr	reflexive verb
verbo o gruppo verbale con funzione transitiva	vt	verb or phrasal verb used transitively
zoologia	ZOOL	zoology
marchio registrato	®	registered trademark
introduce un'equivalenza culturale	≈	introduces a cultural equivalent

TRASCRIZIONE FONETICA

PHONETIC TRANSCRIPTION

Consonants   Consonanti

NB p, b, t, d, k, g are not aspirated in Italian/sono seguite da un'aspirazione in inglese.

*pu*ppy	p	*p*adre
*b*aby	b	*b*ambino
*t*en*t*	t	*t*u*tt*o
*d*a*dd*y	d	*d*a*d*o
*c*ork *k*iss	k	*c*ane *ch*e
*ch*ord		
*g*a*g* *gu*ess	g	*g*ola *gh*iro
*s*o ri*c*e ki*ss*	s	*s*ano
cou*s*in bu*zz*	z	*s*vago e*s*ame
*sh*eep *s*ugar	ʃ	*sc*ena
plea*s*ure bei*g*e	ʒ	*g*arage
*ch*urch	tʃ	pe*c*e lan*c*iare
*j*udge *g*eneral	dʒ	*g*iro *gi*oco
*f*arm ra*ff*le	f	a*f*a *f*aro
*v*ery re*v*	v	*v*ero *b*ravo
*th*in ma*th*s	θ	
*th*at o*th*er	ð	
*l*ittle ba*ll*	l	*l*etto a*l*a
	ʎ	*gl*i
*r*at b*r*at	r	*r*ete a*r*co
*m*ummy co*mb*	m	*r*a*m*o *m*adre
*n*o ra*n*	n	*n*o fuma*n*te
	ɲ	*gn*omo
si*ng*ing ba*n*k	ŋ	
*h*at re*h*eat	h	
*y*et	j	bu*i*o *pi*acere
*w*all be*w*ail	w	*u*omo g*u*aio
lo*ch*	x	

Vowels   Vocali

NB The pairing of some vowel sounds only indicates approximate equivalence./La messa in equivalenza di certi suoni indica solo un rassomiglianza approssimativa.

h*ee*l b*ea*d	iː i	v*i*no *i*dea
h*i*t p*i*ty	ɪ	
	e	st*e*lla *e*dera
s*e*t t*e*nt	ɛ	*e*poca e*cce*tto
*a*pple b*a*t	æ a	m*a*mma
		am*o*re
*a*fter c*a*r c*a*lm	ɑː	
f*u*n c*ou*sin	ʌ	
*o*ver *a*bove	ə	
*u*rn f*e*rn w*o*rk	əː	
w*a*sh p*o*t	ɔ	r*o*sa *o*cchio
b*o*rn c*o*rk	ɔː	
	o	p*o*nte *o*gnuno
	ø	f*ö*hn
f*u*ll s*oo*t	u	*u*tile z*u*cca
b*oo*n l*ew*d	uː	

Diphthongs   Dittonghi

	ɪə	b*ee*r t*ie*r
	ɛə	t*ea*r f*ai*r th*e*re
	eɪ	d*a*te pl*ai*ce
		d*ay*
	aɪ	l*i*fe b*uy* cr*y*
	au	*ow*l f*ou*l n*ow*
	əu	l*ow* n*o*
	ɔɪ	b*oi*l b*oy* *oi*ly
	uə	p*oo*r t*ou*r

Miscellaneous   Varie

* per l'inglese: la "r" finale viene pronunciata se seguita da una vocale.

' precedes the stressed syllable/precede la sillaba accentata.

ITALIAN PRONUNCIATION

Vowels

Where the vowel **e** or the vowel **o** appears in a stressed syllable it can be either open [ɛ], [ɔ] or closed [e], [o]. As the open or closed pronunciation of these vowels is subject to regional variation, the distinction is of little importance to the user of this dictionary. Phonetic transcription for headwords containing these vowels will therefore only appear where other pronunciation difficulties are present.

Consonants

c before "e" or "i" is pronounced *tch*.

ch is pronounced like the "k" in "kit".

g before "e" or "i" is pronounced like the "j" in "jet".

gh is pronounced like the "g" in "get".

gl before "e" or "i" is normally pronounced like the "lli" in "million", and in a few cases only like the "gl" in "glove".

gn is pronounced like the "ny" in "canyon".

sc before "e" or "i" is pronounced *sh*.

z is pronounced like the "ts" in "stetson", or like the "d's" in "bird's-eye".

Headwords containing the above consonants and consonantal groups have been given full phonetic transcription in this dictionary.

NB All double written consonants in Italian are fully sounded: e.g. the "tt" in "tutto" is pronounced as in "ha*t t*rick".

ITALIANO – INGLESE
ITALIAN – ENGLISH

A, a

A *abbr* (= *autostrada*) ≈ M (= *motorway*)

a (*a+il* = **al**, *a+lo* = **allo**, *a+l'* = **all'**, *a+la* = **alla**, *a+i* = **ai**, *a+gli* = **agli**, *a+le* = **alle**) *prep* **1** (*stato in luogo*) at; (: *in*) in; **essere alla stazione** to be at the station; **essere ~ casa/~ scuola/~ Roma** to be at home/at school/in Rome; **è ~ 10 km da qui** it's 10 km from here, it's 10 km away
2 (*moto a luogo*) to; **andare ~ casa/~ scuola** to go home/to school
3 (*tempo*) at; (*epoca, stagione*) in; **alle cinque** at five (o'clock); **~ mezzanotte/Natale** at midnight/Christmas; **al mattino** in the morning; **~ maggio/primavera** in May/spring; **~ cinquant'anni** at fifty (years of age); **~ domani!** see you tomorrow!
4 (*complemento di termine*) to; **dare qc ~ qn** to give sth to sb
5 (*mezzo, modo*) with, by; **~ piedi/cavallo** on foot/horseback; **fatto ~ mano** made by hand, handmade; **una barca ~ motore** a motorboat; **~ uno ~ uno** one by one; **all'italiana** the Italian way, in the Italian fashion
6 (*rapporto*) a, per; (: *con prezzi*) at; **prendo 500.000 lire al mese** I get 500,000 lire a *o* per month; **pagato ~ ore** paid by the hour; **vendere qc ~ 2500 lire il chilo** to sell sth at 2,500 lire a *o* per kilo

abbacchi'ato, a [abbak'kjato] *ag* downhearted, in low spirits
abbagli'ante [abbaʎˈʎante] *ag* dazzling; **~i** *smpl* (AUT): **accendere gli ~i** to put one's headlights on full (BRIT) *o* high (US) beam
abbagli'are [abbaʎˈʎare] *vt* to dazzle; (*illudere*) to delude; **ab'baglio** *sm* blunder; **prendere un abbaglio** to

blunder, make a blunder
abbai'are *vi* to bark
abba'ino *sm* dormer window; (*soffitta*) attic room
abbando'nare *vt* to leave, abandon, desert; (*trascurare*) to neglect; (*rinunciare a*) to abandon, give up; **~rsi** *vr* to let o.s. go; **~rsi a** (*ricordi, vizio*) to give o.s. up to; **abban'dono** *sm* abandonment; neglect; (SPORT) withdrawal; (*fig*) abandon; **in abbandono** (*edificio, giardino*) neglected
abbas'sare *vt* to lower; (*radio*) to turn down; **~rsi** *vr* (*chinarsi*) to stoop; (*livello, sole*) to go down; (*fig: umiliarsi*) to demean o.s.; **~ i fari** (AUT) to dip *o* dim (US) one's lights
ab'basso *escl*: **~ il re!** down with the king!
abbas'tanza [abbas'tantsa] *av* (*a sufficienza*) enough; (*alquanto*) quite, rather, fairly; **non è ~ furbo** he's not shrewd enough; **un vino ~ dolce** quite a sweet wine; **averne ~ di qn/qc** to have had enough of sb/sth
ab'battere *vt* (*muro, casa*) to pull down; (*ostacolo*) to knock down; (*albero*) to fell; (: *sog: vento*) to bring down; (*bestie da macello*) to slaughter; (*cane, cavallo*) to destroy, put down; (*selvaggina, aereo*) to shoot down; (*fig: sog: malattia, disgrazia*) to lay low; **~rsi** *vr* (*avvilirsi*) to lose heart; **abbat'tuto, a** *ag* (*fig*) depressed
abba'zia [abbat'tsia] *sf* abbey
abbece'dario [abbetʃe'darjo] *sm* primer
abbel'lire *vt* (*ornare*) to embellish
abbeve'rare *vt* to water; **~rsi** *vr* to drink
'abbia *etc vb vedi* **avere**
abbicci [abbit'tʃi] *sm inv* alphabet; (*sillabario*) primer; (*fig*) rudiments *pl*
abbi'enti *smpl*: **gli ~** the well-to-do
abbiglia'mento [abbiʎʎa'mento] *sm* dress

no pl; (indumenti) clothes pl; (industria) clothing industry

abbigli'are [abbiλ'λare] vt to dress up

abbi'nare vt: ~ (a) to combine (with)

abbindo'lare vt (fig) to cheat, trick

abbocca'mento sm talks pl, meeting

abboc'care vi (pesce) to bite; (tubi) to join; ~ (all'amo) (fig) to swallow the bait

abboc'cato, a ag (vino) sweetish

abbona'mento sm subscription; (alle ferrovie etc) season ticket; **fare l'~** to take out a subscription (o season ticket)

abbo'narsi vr: ~ **a un giornale** to take out a subscription to a newspaper; ~ **al teatro/alle ferrovie** to take out a season ticket for the theatre/the train; **abbo'nato, a** sm/f subscriber; season-ticket holder

abbon'dante ag abundant, plentiful; (giacca) roomy

abbon'danza [abbon'dantsa] sf abundance, plenty

abbon'dare vi to abound, be plentiful; ~ **in** o **di** to be full of, abound in

abbor'dabile ag (persona) approachable; (prezzo) reasonable

abbor'dare vt (nave) to board; (persona) to approach; (argomento) to tackle

abbotto'nare vt to button up, do up

abboz'zare [abbot'tsare] vt to sketch, outline; (SCULTURA) to rough-hew; ~ **un sorriso** to give a hint of a smile; **ab'bozzo** sm sketch, outline; (DIR) draft

abbracci'are [abbrat'tʃare] vt to embrace; (persona) to hug, embrace; (professione) to take up; (contenere) to include; **~rsi** vr to hug o embrace (one another); **ab'braccio** sm hug, embrace

abbrevi'are vt to shorten; (parola) to abbreviate

abbreviazi'one [abbrevjat'tsjone] sf abbreviation

abbron'zante [abbron'dzante] ag tanning, sun cpd

abbron'zare [abbron'dzare] vt (pelle) to tan; (metalli) to bronze; **~rsi** vr to tan, get a tan; **abbronza'tura** sf tan, suntan

abbrusto'lire vt (pane) to toast; (caffè) to roast

abbru'tire vt to exhaust; to degrade

abbu'ono sm (COMM) allowance, discount; (SPORT) handicap

abdi'care vi to abdicate; ~ **a** to give up, renounce

aberrazi'one [aberrat'tsjone] sf aberration

a'bete sm fir (tree); ~ **rosso** spruce

abi'etto, a ag despicable, abject

'abile ag (idoneo): ~ **(a qc/a fare qc)** fit (for sth/to do sth); (capace) able; (astuto) clever; (accorto) skilful; ~ **al servizio militare** fit for military service; **abilità** sf inv ability; cleverness; skill

abili'tato, a ag qualified; (TEL) which has an outside line; **abilitazi'one** sf qualification

a'bisso sm abyss, gulf

abi'tacolo sm (AER) cockpit; (AUT) inside; (: di camion) cab

abi'tante sm/f inhabitant

abi'tare vt to live in, dwell in ♦ vi: ~ **in campagna/a Roma** to live in the country/in Rome; **abi'tato, a** ag inhabited; lived in ♦ sm (anche: **centro abitato**) built-up area; **abitazi'one** sf residence; house

'abito sm dress no pl; (da uomo) suit; (da donna) dress; (abitudine, disposizione, REL) habit; **~i** smpl (vestiti) clothes; **in ~ da sera** in evening dress

abitu'ale ag usual, habitual; (cliente) regular

abitu'are vt: ~ **qn a** to get sb used o accustomed to; **~rsi a** to get used to, accustom o.s. to

abitudi'nario, a ag of fixed habits ♦ sm/f regular customer

abi'tudine sf habit; **aver l'~ di fare qc** to be in the habit of doing sth; **d'~** usually; **per ~** from o out of habit

abo'lire vt to abolish; (DIR) to repeal

abomi'nevole ag abominable

abo'rigeno [abo'ridʒeno] sm aborigine

abor'rire vt to abhor, detest

abor'tire vi (MED) to miscarry, have a

miscarriage; (: *deliberatamente*) to have an abortion; (*fig*) to miscarry, fail; **a'borto** *sm* miscarriage; abortion

abrasi'one *sf* abrasion; **abra'sivo, a** *ag*, *sm* abrasive

abro'gare *vt* to repeal, abrogate

A'bruzzo *sm*: **l'~, gli ~i** the Abruzzi

ABS [abɪˈɛse] *sigla m* (= *Anti-Blockier System*) ABS

'abside *sf* apse

a'bulico, a, ci, che *ag* lacking in will power

abu'sare *vi*: **~ di** to abuse, misuse; (*alcool*) to take to excess; (*approfittare, violare*) to take advantage of; **a'buso** *sm* abuse, misuse; excessive use

a.C. *av abbr* (= *avanti Cristo*) B.C.

a'cacia, cie [aˈkatʃa] *sf* (BOT) acacia

'acca *sf* letter H; **non capire un'~** not to understand a thing

acca'demia *sf* (*società*) learned society; (*scuola: d'arte, militare*) academy; **acca'demico, a, ci, che** *ag* academic ♦ *sm* academician

acca'dere *vb impers* to happen, occur; **acca'duto** *sm*: **raccontare l'accaduto** to describe what has happened

accalappi'are *vt* to catch

accal'carsi *vr*: **~ (in)** to crowd (into)

accal'darsi *vr* to grow hot

accalo'rarsi *vr* (*fig*) to get excited

accampa'mento *sm* camp

accam'pare *vt* to encamp; (*fig*) to put forward, advance; **~rsi** *vr* to camp

accani'mento *sm* fury; (*tenacia*) tenacity, perseverance

acca'nirsi *vr* (*infierire*) to rage; (*ostinarsi*) to persist; **acca'nito, a** *ag* (*odio, gelosia*) fierce, bitter; (*lavoratore*) assiduous, dogged; (*fumatore*) inveterate

ac'canto *av* near, nearby; **~ a** *prep* near, beside, close to

accanto'nare *vt* (*problema*) to shelve; (*somma*) to set aside

accapar'rare *vt* (COMM) to corner, buy up; **~rsi qc** (*fig: simpatia, voti*) to secure sth (for o.s.)

accapigli'arsi [akkapiʎˈʎarsi] *vr* to come to

blows; (*fig*) to quarrel

accappa'toio *sm* bathrobe

accappo'nare *vi*: **far ~ la pelle a qn** to bring sb out in goose pimples

accarez'zare [akkaretˈtsare] *vt* to caress, stroke, fondle; (*fig*) to toy with

acca'sarsi *vr* to set up house; to get married

accasci'arsi [akkaʃˈʃarsi] *vr* to collapse; (*fig*) to lose heart

accat'tone, a *sm/f* beggar

accaval'lare *vt* (*gambe*) to cross; **~rsi** *vr* (*sovrapporsi*) to overlap; (*addensarsi*) to gather

acce'care [attʃeˈkare] *vt* to blind ♦ *vi* to go blind

ac'cedere [atˈtʃedere] *vi*: **~ a** to enter; (*richiesta*) to grant, accede to

accele'rare [attʃeleˈrare] *vt* to speed up ♦ *vi* (AUT) to accelerate; **~ il passo** to quicken one's pace; **accele'rato** *sm* (FERR) slow train; **accelera'tore** *sm* (AUT) accelerator; **accelerazi'one** *sf* acceleration

ac'cendere [atˈtʃendere] *vt* (*fuoco, sigaretta*) to light; (*luce, televisione*) to put on, switch on, turn on; (AUT: *motore*) to switch on; (COMM: *conto*) to open; (*fig: suscitare*) to inflame, stir up; **~rsi** *vr* (*luce*) to come o go on; (*legna*) to catch fire, ignite; **accen'dino** *sm*, **accendi'sigaro** *sm* (cigarette) lighter

accen'nare [attʃenˈnare] *vt* (MUS) to pick out the notes of; to hum ♦ *vi*: **~ a** (*fig: alludere a*) to hint at; (: *far atto di*) to make as if; **~ un saluto** (*con la mano*) to make as if to wave; (*col capo*) to half nod; **accenna a piovere** it looks as if it's going to rain

ac'cenno [atˈtʃenno] *sm* (*cenno*) sign; nod; (*allusione*) hint

accensi'one [attʃenˈsjone] *sf* (*vedi verbo*) lighting; switching on; opening; (AUT) ignition

accen'tare [attʃenˈtare] *vt* (*parlando*) to stress; (*scrivendo*) to accent

ac'cento [atˈtʃento] *sm* accent; (FONETICA, *fig*) stress; (*inflessione*) tone (of voice)

accen'trare [attʃenˈtrare] *vt* to centralize

accentu'are [attʃentu'are] *vt* to stress, emphasize; **~rsi** *vr* to become more noticeable

accerchi'are [attʃer'kjare] *vt* to surround, encircle

accerta'mento [attʃerta'mento] *sm* check; assessment

accer'tare [attʃer'tare] *vt* to ascertain; (*verificare*) to check; (*reddito*) to assess; **~rsi** *vr*: **~rsi (di)** to make sure (of)

ac'ceso, a [at'tʃeso] *pp di* **accendere ♦** *ag* lit; on; open; (*colore*) bright

acces'sibile [attʃes'sibile] *ag* (*luogo*) accessible; (*persona*) approachable; (*prezzo*) reasonable

ac'cesso [at'tʃesso] *sm* (*anche INFORM*) access; (*MED*) attack, fit; (*impulso violento*) fit, outburst

acces'sorio, a [attʃes'sɔrjo] *ag* secondary, of secondary importance; **~i** *smpl* accessories

ac'cetta [at'tʃetta] *sf* hatchet

accet'tabile [attʃet'tabile] *ag* acceptable

accet'tare [attʃet'tare] *vt* to accept; **~ di fare qc** to agree to do sth; **accettazi'one** *sf* acceptance; (*locale di servizio pubblico*) reception; **accettazione bagagli** (*AER*) check-in (desk)

ac'cetto, a [at'tʃetto] *ag*: **(ben) ~** welcome; (*persona*) well-liked

accezi'one [attʃet'tsjone] *sf* meaning

acchiap'pare [akkjap'pare] *vt* to catch

acci'acco, chi [at'tʃakko] *sm* ailment

acciaie'ria [attʃaje'ria] *sf* steelworks *sg*

acci'aio [at'tʃajo] *sm* steel

acciden'tale [attʃiden'tale] *ag* accidental

acciden'tato, a [attʃiden'tato] *ag* (*terreno etc*) uneven

acci'dente [attʃi'dɛnte] *sm* (*caso imprevisto*) accident; (*disgrazia*) mishap; **non si capisce un ~** it's as clear as mud; **~i!** (*fam: per rabbia*) damn (it)!; (*: per meraviglia*) good heavens!

accigli'ato, a [attʃiʎ'ʎato] *ag* frowning

ac'cingersi [at'tʃindʒersi] *vr*: **~ a fare qc** to be about to do sth

acciuf'fare [attʃuf'fare] *vt* to seize, catch

acci'uga, ghe [at'tʃuga] *sf* anchovy

accla'mare *vt* (*applaudire*) to applaud; (*eleggere*) to acclaim; **acclamazi'one** *sf* applause; acclamation

acclima'tare *vt* to acclimatize; **~rsi** *vr* to become acclimatized

ac'cludere *vt* to enclose; **ac'cluso, a** *pp di* **accludere ♦** *ag* enclosed

accocco'larsi *vr* to crouch

accogli'ente [akkoʎ'ʎɛnte] *ag* welcoming, friendly; **accogli'enza** *sf* reception; welcome

ac'cogliere [ak'kɔʎʎere] *vt* (*ricevere*) to receive; (*dare il benvenuto*) to welcome; (*approvare*) to agree to, accept; (*contenere*) to hold, accommodate

accol'lato, a *ag* (*vestito*) high-necked

accoltel'lare *vt* to knife, stab

ac'colto, a *pp di* **accogliere**

accoman'dita *sf* (*DIR*) limited partnership

accomia'tare *vt* to dismiss; **~rsi** *vr*: **~rsi (da)** to take one's leave (of)

accomoda'mento *sm* agreement, settlement

accomo'dante *ag* accommodating

accomo'dare *vt* (*aggiustare*) to repair, mend; (*riordinare*) to tidy; (*conciliare*) to settle; **~rsi** *vr* (*sedersi*) to sit down; **s'accomodi!** (*venga avanti*) come in!; (*si sieda*) take a seat!

accompagna'mento [akkompaɲɲa'mento] *sm* (*MUS*) accompaniment

accompa'gnare [akkompaɲ'ɲare] *vt* to accompany, come *o* go with; (*MUS*) to accompany; (*unire*) to couple; **~ la porta** to close the door gently

accompagna'tore, trice *sm/f* companion; **~ turistico** courier

accomu'nare *vt* to pool, share; (*avvicinare*) to unite

acconcia'tura [akkontʃa'tura] *sf* hairstyle

accondi'scendere [akkondiʃ'ʃɛndere] *vi*: **~ a** to agree *o* consent to; **accondi'sceso, a** *pp di* **accondiscendere**

acconsen'tire *vi*: **~ (a)** to agree *o* consent (to)

acconten'tare *vt* to satisfy; **~rsi di** to be satisfied with, content o.s. with

ac'conto *sm* part payment; **pagare una somma in ~** to pay a sum of money as a deposit

accoppi'are *vt* to couple, pair off; (*BIOL*) to mate; **~rsi** *vr* to pair off; to mate

acco'rato, a *ag* heartfelt

accorci'are [akkor'tʃare] *vt* to shorten; **~rsi** *vr* to become shorter

accor'dare *vt* to reconcile; (*colori*) to match; (*MUS*) to tune; (*LING*): **~ qc con qc** to make sth agree with sth; (*DIR*) to grant; **~rsi** *vr* to agree, come to an agreement; (*colori*) to match

ac'cordo *sm* agreement; (*armonia*) harmony; (*MUS*) chord; **essere d'~** to agree; **andare d'~** to get on well together; **d'~!** all right!, agreed!

ac'corgersi [ak'kordʒersi] *vr*: **~ di** to notice; (*fig*) to realize; **accorgi'mento** *sm* shrewdness *no pl*; (*espediente*) trick, device

ac'correre *vi* to run up

ac'corso, a *pp di* **accorrere**

ac'corto, a *pp di* **accorgersi** ♦ *ag* shrewd; **stare ~** to be on one's guard

accos'tare *vt* (*avvicinare*): **~ qc a** to bring sth near to, put sth near to; (*avvicinarsi a*) to approach; (*socchiudere: imposte*) to half-close; (*: porta*) to leave ajar ♦ *vi* (*NAUT*) to come alongside; **~rsi a** to draw near, approach; (*fig*) to support

accovacci'arsi [akkovat'tʃarsi] *vr* to crouch down

accoz'zaglia [akkot'tsaʎʎa] (*peg*) *sf* (*di idee, oggetti*) jumble, hotchpotch

accredi'tare *vt* (*notizia*) to confirm the truth of; (*COMM*) to credit; (*diplomatico*) to accredit; **~rsi** *vr* (*fig*) to gain credit

ac'crescere [ak'kreʃʃere] *vt* to increase; **~rsi** *vr* to increase, grow; **accresci'tivo, a** *ag, sm* (*LING*) augmentative; **accresci'uto, a** *pp di* **accrescere**

accucci'arsi [akkut'tʃarsi] *vr* (*cane*) to lie down

accu'dire *vt* (*anche: vi*): **~ a** to attend to

accumu'lare *vt* to accumulate

accumula'tore *sm* (*ELETTR*) accumulator

accura'tezza [akkura'tettsa] *sf* care; accuracy

accu'rato, a *ag* (*diligente*) careful; (*preciso*) accurate

ac'cusa *sf* accusation; (*DIR*) charge; **la pubblica ~** the prosecution

accu'sare *vt*: **~ qn di qc** to accuse sb of sth; (*DIR*) to charge sb with sth; **~ ricevuta di** (*COMM*) to acknowledge receipt of

accu'sato, a *sm/f* accused; defendant

accusa'tore, 'trice *sm/f* accuser ♦ *sm* (*DIR*) prosecutor

a'cerbo, a [a'tʃerbo] *ag* bitter; (*frutta*) sour, unripe; (*persona*) immature

'acero ['atʃero] *sm* maple

a'cerrimo, a [a'tʃerrimo] *ag* very fierce

a'ceto [a'tʃeto] *sm* vinegar

ace'tone [atʃe'tone] *sm* nail varnish remover

A.C.I. ['atʃi] *sigla m = Automobile Club d'Italia*

'acido, a ['atʃido] *ag* (*sapore*) acid, sour; (*CHIM*) acid ♦ *sm* (*CHIM*) acid

'acino ['atʃino] *sm* berry; **~ d'uva** grape

'acne *sf* acne

'acqua *sf* water; (*pioggia*) rain; **~e** *sfpl* (*di mare, fiume etc*) waters; **fare ~** (*NAUT*) to leak, take in water; **~ in bocca!** mum's the word!; **~ corrente** running water; **~ dolce** fresh water; **~ minerale** mineral water; **~ potabile** drinking water; **~ salata** salt water; **~ tonica** tonic water

acqua'forte (*pl* **acque'forti**) *sf* etching

a'cquaio *sm* sink

acqua'ragia [akkwa'radʒa] *sf* turpentine

a'cquario *sm* aquarium; (*dello zodiaco*): **A~** Aquarius

acqua'santa *sf* holy water

ac'quatico, a, ci, che *ag* aquatic; (*SPORT, SCIENZA*) water *cpd*

acqua'vite *sf* brandy

acquaz'zone [akkwat'tsone] *sm* cloudburst, heavy shower

acque'dotto *sm* aqueduct; waterworks *pl*, water system

'acqueo, a *ag*: **vapore ~** water vapour

acque'rello *sm* watercolour

acqui'rente *sm/f* purchaser, buyer

acqui'sire *vt* to acquire

acquis'tare *vt* to purchase, buy; (*fig*) to gain; **a'cquisto** *sm* purchase; **fare acquisti** to go shopping

acqui'trino *sm* bog, marsh

acquo'lina *sf*: **far venire l'~ in bocca a qn** to make sb's mouth water

a'cquoso, a *ag* watery

'acre *ag* acrid, pungent; (*fig*) harsh, biting

a'crobata, i, e *sm/f* acrobat

acu'ire *vt* to sharpen

a'culeo *sm* (*ZOOL*) sting; (*BOT*) prickle

a'cume *sm* acumen, perspicacity

a'custica *sf* (*scienza*) acoustics *sg*; (*di una sala*) acoustics *pl*

a'cuto, a *ag* (*appuntito*) sharp, pointed; (*suono, voce*) shrill, piercing; (*MAT, LING, MED*) acute; (*MUS*) high-pitched; (*fig: dolore, desiderio*) intense; (: *perspicace*) acute, keen

ad (*before V*) *prep* = **a**

adagi'are [ada'dʒare] *vt* to lay *o* set down carefully; **~rsi** *vr* to lie down, stretch out

a'dagio [a'dadʒo] *av* slowly ♦ *sm* (*MUS*) adagio; (*proverbio*) adage, saying

adatta'mento *sm* adaptation

adat'tare *vt* to adapt; (*sistemare*) to fit; **~rsi (a)** (*ambiente, tempi*) to adapt (to); (*essere adatto*) to be suitable (for)

a'datto, a *ag*: **~ (a)** suitable (for), right (for)

addebi'tare *vt*: **~ qc a qn** to debit sb with sth

ad'debito *sm* (*COMM*) debit

adden'sare *vt* to thicken; **~rsi** *vr* to thicken; (*nuvole*) to gather

adden'tare *vt* to bite into

adden'trarsi *vr*: **~ in** to penetrate, go into

ad'dentro *av*: **essere molto ~ in qc** to be well-versed in sth

addestra'mento *sm* training

addes'trare *vt* to train; **~rsi** *vr* to train; **~rsi in qc** to practise (*BRIT*) *o* practice (*US*) sth

ad'detto, a *ag*: **~ a** (*persona*) assigned to; (*oggetto*) intended for ♦ *sm* employee; (*funzionario*) attaché; **~ commerciale/**stampa commercial/press attaché; **gli ~i ai lavori** authorized personnel; (*fig*) those in the know

addì *av* (*AMM*): **~ 3 luglio 1999** on the 3rd of July 1999 (*BRIT*), on July 3rd 1999 (*US*)

addi'accio [ad'djattʃo] *sm* (*MIL*) bivouac; **dormire all'~** to sleep in the open

addi'etro *av* (*indietro*) behind; (*nel passato, prima*) before, ago

ad'dio *sm, escl* goodbye, farewell

addirit'tura *av* (*veramente*) really, absolutely; (*perfino*) even; (*direttamente*) directly, right away

ad'dirsi *vr*: **~ a** to suit, be suitable for

addi'tare *vt* to point out; (*fig*) to expose

addi'tivo *sm* additive

addizio'nare [additts jo'nare] *vt* (*MAT*) to add (up); **addizi'one** *sf* addition

addob'bare *vt* to decorate; **ad'dobbo** *sm* decoration

addol'cire [addol'tʃire] *vt* (*caffè etc*) to sweeten; (*acqua, fig: carattere*) to soften; **~rsi** *vr* (*fig*) to mellow, soften

addolo'rare *vt* to pain, grieve; **~rsi (per)** to be distressed (by)

ad'dome *sm* abdomen

addomesti'care *vt* to tame

addormen'tare *vt* to put to sleep; **~rsi** *vr* to fall asleep, go to sleep

addos'sare *vt* (*appoggiare*): **~ qc a qc** to lean sth against sth; (*fig*): **~ la colpa a qn** to lay the blame on sb; **~rsi qc** (*responsabilità etc*) to shoulder sth

ad'dosso *av* on; **mettersi ~ il cappotto** to put one's coat on; **~ a** (*sopra*) on; (*molto vicino*) right next to; **stare ~ a qn** (*fig*) to breathe down sb's neck; **dare ~ a qn** (*fig*) to attack sb

ad'dotto, a *pp di* **addurre**

ad'durre *vt* (*DIR*) to produce; (*citare*) to cite

adegu'are *vt*: **~ qc a** to adjust *o* relate sth to; **~rsi** *vr* to adapt; **adegu'ato, a** *ag* adequate; (*conveniente*) suitable; (*equo*) fair

a'dempiere *vt* to fulfil, carry out

adem'pire *vt* = **adempiere**

ade'rente *ag* adhesive; (*vestito*) close-fitting ♦ *sm/f* follower; **ade'renza** *sf* adhesion; **aderenze** *sfpl* connections, contacts

ade'rire *vi* (*stare attaccato*) to adhere, stick; ~ **a** to adhere to, stick to; (*fig: società, partito*) to join; (: *opinione*) to support; (*richiesta*) to agree to

ades'care *vt* to lure, entice

adesi'one *sf* adhesion; (*fig*) agreement, acceptance; **ade'sivo, a** *ag, sm* adhesive

a'desso *av* (*ora*) now; (*or ora, poco fa*) just now; (*tra poco*) any moment now

adia'cente [adja'tʃɛnte] *ag* adjacent

adi'bire *vt* (*usare*): ~ **qc a** to turn sth into

adi'rarsi *vr*: ~ (**con** *o* **contro qn per qc**) to get angry (with sb over sth)

a'dire *vt* (*DIR*): ~ **le vie legali** to take legal proceedings

'adito *sm*: **dare ~ a** to give rise to

adocchi'are [adok'kjare] *vt* (*scorgere*) to catch sight of; (*occhieggiare*) to eye

adole'scente [adoleʃ'ʃɛnte] *ag, sm/f* adolescent; **adole'scenza** *sf* adolescence

adope'rare *vt* to use; ~**rsi** *vr* to strive; ~**rsi per qn/qc** to do one's best for sb/sth

ado'rare *vt* to adore; (*REL*) to adore, worship

adot'tare *vt* to adopt; (*decisione, provvedimenti*) to pass; **adot'tivo, a** *ag* (*genitori*) adoptive; (*figlio, patria*) adopted; **adozi'one** *sf* adoption

adri'atico, a, ci, che *ag* Adriatic ♦ *sm*: **l'A~, il mare A~** the Adriatic, the Adriatic Sea

adu'lare *vt* to adulate, flatter

adulte'rare *vt* to adulterate

adul'terio *sm* adultery

a'dulto, a *ag* adult; (*fig*) mature ♦ *sm* adult, grown-up

adu'nanza [adu'nantsa] *sf* assembly, meeting

adu'nare *vt* to assemble, gather; ~**rsi** *vr* to assemble, gather; **adu'nata** *sf* (*MIL*) parade, muster

a'dunco, a, chi, che *ag* hooked

a'ereo, a *ag* air *cpd*; (*radice*) aerial ♦ *sm* aerial; (*aeroplano*) plane; ~ **a reazione** jet (plane); ~ **da caccia** fighter (plane); ~ **di**

linea airliner; **ae'robica** *sf* aerobics *sg*;

aerodi'namica *sf* aerodynamics *sg*;

aerodi'namico, a, ci, che *ag* aerodynamic; (*affusolato*) streamlined;

aero'nautica *sf* (*scienza*) aeronautics *sg*;

aeronautica militare air force;

aero'plano *sm* (aero)plane (*BRIT*), (air)plane (*US*)

aero'porto *sm* airport

aero'sol *sm inv* aerosol

'afa *sf* sultriness

af'fabile *ag* affable

affacen'dato, a [affatffen'dato] *ag* (*persona*) busy

affacci'arsi [affatt'tfarsi] *vr*: ~ (**a**) to appear (at)

affa'mato, a *ag* starving; (*fig*): ~ (**di**) eager (for)

affan'nare *vt* to leave breathless; (*fig*) to worry; ~**rsi** *vr*: ~**rsi per qn/qc** to worry about sb/sth; af'fanno *sm* breathlessness; (*fig*) anxiety, worry; **affan'noso, a** *ag* (*respiro*) difficult; (*fig*) troubled, anxious

af'fare *sm* (*faccenda*) matter, affair; (*COMM*) piece of business, (business) deal; (*occasione*) bargain; (*DIR*) case; (*fam: cosa*) thing; ~**i** *smpl* (*COMM*) business *sg*; **Ministro degli A~i esteri** Foreign Secretary (*BRIT*), Secretary of State (*US*); **affa'rista, i** *sm* profiteer, unscrupulous businessman

affasci'nante [affaʃʃi'nante] *ag* fascinating

affasci'nare [affaʃʃi'nare] *vt* to bewitch; (*fig*) to charm, fascinate

affati'care *vt* to tire; ~**rsi** *vr* (*durar fatica*) to tire o.s. out

af'fatto *av* completely; **non ... ~** not ... at all; **niente ~** not at all

affer'mare *vt* (*dichiarare*) to maintain, affirm; ~**rsi** *vr* to assert o.s., make one's name known; **affermazi'one** *sf* affirmation, assertion; (*successo*) achievement

affer'rare *vt* to seize, grasp; (*fig: idea*) to grasp; ~**rsi** *vr*: ~**rsi a** to cling to

affet'tare *vt* (*tagliare a fette*) to slice; (*ostentare*) to affect; **affet'tato, a** *ag* sliced; affected ♦ *sm* sliced cold meat

affet'tivo, a *ag* emotional, affective
af'fetto *sm* affection; **affettu'oso, a** *ag* affectionate
affezio'narsi [affettsjo'narsi] *vr*: ~ **a** to grow fond of
affian'care *vt* to place side by side; (*MIL*) to flank; (*fig*) to support; ~ **qc a qc** to place sth next to *o* beside sth; **~rsi a qn** to stand beside sb
affia'tato, a *ag*: **essere molto ~i** to get on very well
affibbi'are *vt* (*fig: dare*) to give
affi'dabile *ag* reliable
affida'mento *sm* (*DIR: di bambino*) custody; (*fiducia*): **fare ~ su qn** to rely on sb; **non dà nessun ~** he's not to be trusted
affi'dare *vt*: ~ **qc** *o* **qn a qn** to entrust sth *o* sb to sb; **~rsi** *vr*: **~rsi a** to place one's trust in
affievo'lirsi *vr* to grow weak
af'figgere [af'fiddʒere] *vt* to stick up, post up
affi'lare *vt* to sharpen
affili'arsi *vr*: ~ **a** to become affiliated to
affi'nare *vt* to sharpen
affinché [affin'ke] *cong* in order that, so that
af'fine *ag* similar; **affinità** *sf inv* affinity
affio'rare *vi* to emerge
affissi'one *sf* billposting
af'fisso, a *pp di* **affiggere** ♦ *sm* bill, poster; (*LING*) affix
affit'tare *vt* (*dare in affitto*) to let, rent (out); (*prendere in affitto*) to rent; **af'fitto** *sm* rent; (*contratto*) lease
af'fliggere [af'fliddʒere] *vt* to torment; **~rsi** *vr* to grieve; **af'flitto, a** *pp di* **affliggere**; **afflizi'one** *sf* distress, torment
afflosci'arsi [affloʃ'farsi] *vr* to go limp
afflu'ente *sm* tributary; **afflu'enza** *sf* flow; (*di persone*) crowd
afflu'ire *vi* to flow; (*fig: merci, persone*) to pour in; **af'flusso** *sm* influx
affo'gare *vt, vi* to drown; **~rsi** *vr* to drown; (*deliberatamente*) to drown o.s.
affol'lare *vt* to crowd; **~rsi** *vr* to crowd;

affol'lato, a *ag* crowded
affon'dare *vt* to sink
affran'care *vt* to free, liberate; (*AMM*) to redeem; (*lettera*) to stamp; (: *meccanicamente*) to frank (*BRIT*), meter (*US*); **~rsi** *vr* to free o.s.; **affranca'tura** *sf* (*di francobollo*) stamping; franking (*BRIT*), metering (*US*); (*tassa di spedizione*) postage
af'franto, a *ag* (*esausto*) worn out; (*abbattuto*) overcome
af'fresco, schi *sm* fresco
affret'tare *vt* to quicken, speed up; **~rsi** *vr* to hurry; **~rsi a fare qc** to hurry *o* hasten to do sth
affron'tare *vt* (*pericolo etc*) to face; (*nemico*) to confront; **~rsi** *vr* (*reciproco*) to come to blows
af'fronto *sm* affront, insult
affumi'care *vt* to fill with smoke; to blacken with smoke; (*alimenti*) to smoke
affuso'lato, a *ag* tapering
a'foso, a *ag* sultry, close
'Africa *sf*: **l'~** Africa; **afri'cano, a** *ag, sm/f* African
afrodi'siaco, a, ci, che *ag, sm* aphrodisiac
a'genda [a'dʒenda] *sf* diary
a'gente [a'dʒente] *sm* agent; ~ **di cambio** stockbroker; ~ **di polizia** police officer; **agen'zia** *sf* agency; (*succursale*) branch; **agenzia di collocamento** employment agency; **agenzia immobiliare** estate agent's (office) (*BRIT*), real estate office (*US*); **agenzia pubblicitaria/viaggi** advertising/travel agency
agevo'lare [adʒevo'lare] *vt* to facilitate, make easy
a'gevole [a'dʒevole] *ag* easy; (*strada*) smooth
aggan'ciare [aggan'tʃare] *vt* to hook up; (*FERR*) to couple
ag'geggio [ad'dʒeddʒo] *sm* gadget, contraption
agget'tivo [addʒet'tivo] *sm* adjective
agghiacci'ante [aggjat'tʃante] *ag* chilling
agghin'darsi [aggin'darsi] *vr* to deck o.s. out

aggior'nare [addʒor'nare] *vt* (*opera, manuale*) to bring up-to-date; (*seduta etc*) to postpone; **~rsi** *vr* to bring (*o* keep) o.s. up-to-date; **aggior'nato, a** *ag* up-to-date

aggi'rare [addʒi'rare] *vt* to go round; (*fig: ingannare*) to trick; **~rsi** *vr* to wander about; **il prezzo s'aggira sul milione** the price is around the million mark

aggiudi'care [addʒudi'kare] *vt* to award; (*all'asta*) to knock down; **~rsi qc** to win sth

aggi'ungere [ad'dʒundʒere] *vt* to add; **aggi'unta** *sf* addition; **aggi'unto, a** *pp di* **aggiungere** ♦ *ag* assistant *cpd* ♦ *sm* assistant

aggius'tare [addʒus'tare] *vt* (*accomodare*) to mend, repair; (*riassettare*) to adjust; (*fig: lite*) to settle; **~rsi** *vr* (*arrangiarsi*) to make do; (*con senso reciproco*) to come to an agreement

agglome'rato *sm* (*di rocce*) conglomerate; (*di legno*) chipboard; **~ urbano** built-up area

aggrap'parsi *vr*: **~ a** to cling to

aggra'vare *vt* (*aumentare*) to increase; (*appesantire: anche fig*) to weigh down, make heavy; (*pena*) to make worse; **~rsi** *vr* to worsen, become worse

aggrazi'ato, a [aggrat'tsjato] *ag* graceful

aggre'dire *vt* to attack, assault

aggre'gare *vt*: **~ qn a qc** to admit sb to sth; **~rsi** *vr* to join; **~rsi a** to join, become a member of

aggressi'one *sf* aggression; (*atto*) attack, assault

aggres'sivo, a *ag* aggressive

aggrot'tare *vt*: **~ le sopracciglia** to frown

aggrovigli'are [aggroviʎ'ʎare] *vt* to tangle; **~rsi** *vr* (*fig*) to become complicated

agguan'tare *vt* to catch, seize

aggu'ato *sm* trap; (*imboscata*) ambush; **tendere un ~ a qn** to set a trap for sb

agguer'rito, a *ag* fierce

agi'ato, a [a'dʒato] *ag* (*vita*) easy; (*persona*) well-off, well-to-do

'agile ['adʒile] *ag* agile, nimble; **agilità** *sf* agility, nimbleness

'agio ['adʒo] *sm* ease, comfort; **mettersi a proprio ~** to make o.s. at home *o* comfortable

a'gire [a'dʒire] *vi* to act; (*esercitare un'azione*) to take effect; (*TECN*) to work, function; **~ contro qn** (*DIR*) to take action against sb

agi'tare [adʒi'tare] *vt* (*bottiglia*) to shake; (*mano, fazzoletto*) to wave; (*fig: turbare*) to disturb; (: *incitare*) to stir (up); (: *dibattere*) to discuss; **~rsi** *vr* (*mare*) to be rough; (*malato, dormitore*) to toss and turn; (*bambino*) to fidget; (*emozionarsi*) to get upset; (*POL*) to agitate; **agi'tato, a** *ag* rough; restless; fidgety; upset, perturbed; **agitazi'one** *sf* agitation; (*POL*) unrest, agitation; **mettere in agitazione qn** to upset *o* distress sb

'agli ['aʎʎi] *prep + det vedi* **a**

'aglio ['aʎʎo] *sm* garlic

a'gnello [aɲ'ɲello] *sm* lamb

'ago (*pl* **'aghi**) *sm* needle

ago'nia *sf* agony

ago'nistico, a, ci, che *ag* athletic; (*fig*) competitive

agoniz'zare [agonid'dzare] *vi* to be dying

agopun'tura *sf* acupuncture

a'gosto *sm* August

a'graria *sf* agriculture

a'grario, a *ag* agrarian, agricultural; (*riforma*) land *cpd*

a'gricolo, a *ag* agricultural, farm *cpd*; **agricol'tore** *sm* farmer; **agricol'tura** *sf* agriculture, farming

agri'foglio [agri'foʎʎo] *sm* holly

agrimen'sore *sm* land surveyor

agritu'rismo *sm* farm holidays *pl*

'agro, a *ag* sour, sharp; **~dolce** *ag* bittersweet; (*salsa*) sweet and sour

a'grume *sm* (*spesso al pl: pianta*) citrus; (: *frutto*) citrus fruit

aguz'zare [agut'tsare] *vt* to sharpen; **~ gli orecchi** to prick up one's ears

a'guzzo, a [a'guttso] *ag* sharp

'ai *prep + det vedi* **a**

'Aia *sf*: **l'~** the Hague

'aia *sf* threshing floor

AIDS *sigla f o m* AIDS

ai'rone *sm* heron

aiu'ola *sf* flower bed

aiu'tante *sm/f* assistant ♦ *sm* (MIL) adjutant; (NAUT) master-at-arms; ~ **di campo** aide-de-camp

aiu'tare *vt* to help; ~ **qn (a fare)** to help sb (to do)

ai'uto *sm* help, assistance, aid; (aiutante) assistant; **venire in ~ di qn** to come to sb's aid; ~ **chirurgo** assistant surgeon

aiz'zare [ait'tsare] *vt* to incite; ~ **i cani contro qn** to set the dogs on sb

al *prep* + *det vedi* **a**

'ala (*pl* **'ali**) *sf* wing; **fare ~** to fall back, make way; ~ **destra/sinistra** (SPORT) right/left wing

a'lacre *ag* quick, brisk

a'lano *sm* Great Dane

a'lare *ag* wing *cpd*

'alba *sf* dawn

Alba'nia *sf*: **l'~** Albania

al'batro *sm* albatross

albeggi'are [albed'dʒare] *vi*, *vb impers* to dawn

alberghi'ero, a [alber'gjero] *ag* hotel *cpd*

al'bergo, ghi *sm* hotel; ~ **della gioventù** youth hostel

'albero *sm* tree; (NAUT) mast; (TECN) shaft; ~ **genealogico** family tree; ~ **a gomiti** crankshaft; ~ **di Natale** Christmas tree; ~ **maestro** mainmast; ~ **di trasmissione** transmission shaft

albi'cocca, che *sf* apricot; **albi'cocco, chi** *sm* apricot tree

'albo *sm* (registro) register, roll; (AMM) notice board

'album *sm* album; ~ **da disegno** sketch book

al'bume *sm* albumen

'alce ['altʃe] *sm* elk

al'colico, a, ci, che *ag* alcoholic ♦ *sm* alcoholic drink

alcoliz'zato, a [alkolid'dzato] *sm/f* alcoholic

'alcool *sm* alcohol; **alco'olico** *etc* = **alcolico** *etc*

al'cuno, a (*det: dav sm:* **alcun** +C, V,

alcuno +*s impura, gn, pn, ps, x, z; dav sf:* **alcuna** +C, **alcun'** +V) *det* (nessuno): **non ... ~** no, not any; **~i, e** *det pl* some, a few; **non c'è ~a fretta** there's no hurry, there isn't any hurry; **senza alcun riguardo** without any consideration ♦ *pron pl:* **~i, e** some, a few

aldilà *sm*: **l'~** the after-life

alfa'beto *sm* alphabet

alfi'ere *sm* standard-bearer; (MIL) ensign; (SCACCHI) bishop

'alga, ghe *sf* seaweed *no pl*, alga

'algebra ['aldʒebra] *sf* algebra

Alge'ria [aldʒe'ria] *sf*: **l'~** Algeria

ali'ante *sm* (AER) glider

'alibi *sm inv* alibi

a'lice [a'litʃe] *sf* anchovy

alie'nare *vt* (DIR) to alienate, transfer; (rendere ostile) to alienate; **~rsi qn** to alienate sb; **alie'nato, a** *ag* alienated; transferred; (fuor di senno) insane ♦ *sm* lunatic, insane person; **alienazi'one** *sf* alienation; transfer; insanity

ali'eno, a *ag* (avverso): ~ **(da)** opposed (to), averse (to) ♦ *sm/f* alien

alimen'tare *vt* to feed; (TECN) to feed; supply; (fig) to sustain ♦ *ag* food *cpd*; **~i** *smpl* foodstuffs; (anche: **negozio di ~i**) grocer's shop; **alimentazi'one** *sf* feeding; supplying; sustaining; (gli alimenti) diet

ali'mento *sm* food; **~i** *smpl* (cibo) food *sg*; (DIR) alimony

a'liquota *sf* share; (d'imposta) rate

alis'cafo *sm* hydrofoil

'alito *sm* breath

all. *abbr* (= allegato) encl.

'alla *prep* + *det vedi* **a**

allacci'are [allat'tʃare] *vt* (scarpe) to tie, lace (up); (cintura) to do up, fasten; (luce, gas) to connect; (amicizia) to form

alla'gare *vt* to flood; **~rsi** *vr* to flood

allar'gare *vt* to widen; (vestito) to let out; (aprire) to open; (fig: dilatare) to extend

allar'mare *vt* to alarm

al'larme *sm* alarm; ~ **aereo** air-raid warning

allar'mismo *sm* scaremongering

allat'tare *vt* to feed

'alle *prep + det vedi* **a**

alle'anza [alle'antsa] *sf* alliance

alle'arsi *vr* to form an alliance; **alle'ato, a** *ag* allied ♦ *sm/f* ally

alle'gare *vt (accludere)* to enclose; *(DIR: citare)* to cite, adduce; *(denti)* to set on edge; **alle'gato, a** *ag* enclosed ♦ *sm* enclosure; *(di email)* attachment; **in allegato** enclosed

allegge'rire [alledd͡ʒe'rire] *vt* to lighten, make lighter; *(fig: lavoro, tasse)* to reduce

alle'gria [alle'dʒia] *sf* gaiety, cheerfulness

al'legro, a *ag* cheerful, merry; *(un po' brillo)* merry, tipsy; *(vivace: colore)* bright ♦ *sm (MUS)* allegro

allena'mento *sm* training

alle'nare *vt* to train; **~rsi** *vr* to train; **allena'tore** *sm (SPORT)* trainer, coach

allen'tare *vt* to slacken; *(disciplina)* to relax; **~rsi** *vr* to become slack; *(ingranaggio)* to work loose

aller'gia, 'gie [aller'dʒia] *sf* allergy; **al'lergico, a, ci, che** *ag* allergic

alles'tire *vt (cena)* to prepare; *(esercito, nave)* to equip, fit out; *(spettacolo)* to stage

allet'tare *vt* to lure, entice

alleva'mento *sm* breeding, rearing; *(luogo)* stock farm

alle'vare *vt (animale)* to breed, rear; *(bambino)* to bring up

allevi'are *vt* to alleviate

alli'bito, a *ag* astounded

allibra'tore *sm* bookmaker

allie'tare *vt* to cheer up, gladden

alli'evo *sm* pupil; *(apprendista)* apprentice; *(MIL)* cadet

alliga'tore *sm* alligator

alline'are *vt (persone, cose)* to line up; *(TIP)* to align; *(fig: economia, salari)* to adjust, align; **~rsi** *vr* to line up; *(fig: a idee)*: **~rsi a** to come into line with

'allo *prep + det vedi* **a**

al'locco, a, chi, che *sm* tawny owl ♦ *sm/f* oaf

allocuzi'one [allokut'tsjone] *sf* address

al'lodola *sf* (sky)lark

alloggi'are [allod'dʒare] *vt* to accommodate ♦ *vi* to live; **al'loggio** *sm* lodging, accommodation *(BRIT)*, accommodations *(US)*

allontana'mento *sm* removal; dismissal

allonta'nare *vt* to send away, send off; *(impiegato)* to dismiss; *(pericolo)* to avert, remove; *(estraniare)* to alienate; **~rsi** *vr*: **~rsi (da)** to go away (from); *(estraniarsi)* to become estranged (from)

al'lora *av (in quel momento)* then ♦ *cong (in questo caso)* well then; *(dunque)* well then, so; **la gente d'~** people then *o* in those days; **da ~ in poi** from then on

allor'ché [allor'ke] *cong (formale)* when, as soon as

al'loro *sm* laurel

'alluce ['allutʃe] *sm* big toe

alluci'nante [allutʃi'nante] *ag* awful; *(fam)* amazing

allucinazi'one [allutʃinat'tsjone] *sf* hallucination

al'ludere *vi*: **~ a** to allude to, hint at

allu'minio *sm* aluminium *(BRIT)*, aluminum *(US)*

allun'gare *vt* to lengthen; *(distendere)* to prolong, extend; *(diluire)* to water down; **~rsi** *vr* to lengthen; *(ragazzo)* to stretch, grow taller; *(sdraiarsi)* to lie down, stretch out

allusi'one *sf* hint, allusion

al'luso, a *pp di* **alludere**

alluvi'one *sf* flood

al'meno *av* at least ♦ *cong*: **(se) ~** if only; **(se) ~ piovesse!** if only it would rain!

a'logeno, a [a'lɔdʒeno] *ag*: **lampada ~a** halogen lamp

a'lone *sm* halo

'Alpi *sfpl*: **le ~** the Alps

alpi'nismo *sm* mountaineering, climbing; **alpi'nista, i, e** *sm/f* mountaineer, climber

al'pino, a *ag* Alpine; mountain *cpd*

al'quanto *av* rather, a little; **~, a** *det* a certain amount of, some ♦ *pron* a certain amount, some; **~i, e** *det pl, pron pl* several, quite a few

alt *escl* halt!, stop!
alta'lena *sf (a funi)* swing; *(in bilico, anche fig)* seesaw
al'tare *sm* altar
alte'rare *vt* to alter, change; *(cibo)* to adulterate; *(registro)* to falsify; *(persona)* to irritate; **~rsi** *vr* to alter; *(cibo)* to go bad; *(persona)* to lose one's temper
al'terco, chi *sm* altercation, wrangle
alter'nare *vt* to alternate; **~rsi** *vr* to alternate; **alterna'tiva** *sf* alternative; **alterna'tivo, a** *ag* alternative; **alter'nato, a** *ag* alternate; *(ELETTR)* alternating; **alterna'tore** *sm* alternator
al'terno, a *ag* alternate; **a giorni ~i** on alternate days, every other day
al'tezza [al'tettsa] *sf* height; width, breadth; depth; pitch; *(GEO)* latitude; *(titolo)* highness; *(fig: nobiltà)* greatness; **essere all'~ di** to be on a level with; *(fig)* to be up to *o* equal to; **altez'zoso, a** *ag* haughty
al'ticcio, a, ci, ce [al'tittʃo] *ag* tipsy
altipi'ano *sm* = **altopiano**
alti'tudine *sf* altitude
'alto, a *ag* high; *(persona)* tall; *(tessuto)* wide, broad; *(sonno, acque)* deep; *(suono)* high(-pitched); *(GEO)* upper; *(: setten-trionale)* northern ♦ *sm* top (part) ♦ *av* high; *(parlare)* aloud, loudly; **il palazzo è ~ 20 metri** the building is 20 metres high; **ad ~a voce** aloud; **a notte ~a** in the dead of night; **in ~** up, upwards; at the top; **dall'~ in** *o* **al basso** up and down; **degli ~i e bassi** *(fig)* ups and downs; **~a fedeltà** high fidelity, hi-fi; **~a finanza** high finance; **~a moda** haute couture; **~a società** high society
alto'forno *sm* blast furnace
altolo'cato, a *ag* of high rank
altopar'lante *sm* loudspeaker
altopi'ano *(pl* **altipi'ani)** *sm* plateau, upland plain
altret'tanto, a *ag, pron* as much; *(pl)* as many ♦ *av* equally; **tanti auguri! – grazie, ~** all the best! — thank you, the same to you
'altri *pron inv (qualcuno)* somebody; *(: in espressioni negative)* anybody; *(un'altra persona)* another (person)
altri'menti *av* otherwise

PAROLA CHIAVE

'altro, a *det* **1** *(diverso)* other, different; **questa è un'~a cosa** that's another *o* a different thing
2 *(supplementare)* other; **prendi un ~ cioccolatino** have another chocolate; **hai avuto ~e notizie?** have you had any more *o* any other news?
3 *(nel tempo)*: **l'~ giorno** the other day; **l'altr'anno** last year; **l'~ ieri** the day before yesterday; **domani l'~** the day after tomorrow; **quest'~ mese** next month
4: **d'~a parte** on the other hand
♦ *pron* **1** *(persona, cosa diversa o supplementare)*: **un ~, un'~a** another (one); **lo farà un ~** someone else will do it; **~i, e others**; **gli ~i** *(la gente)* others, other people; **l'uno e l'~** both (of them); **aiutarsi l'un l'~** to help one another; **da un giorno all'~** from day to day; *(nel giro di 24 ore)* from one day to the next; *(da un momento all'altro)* any day now
2 *(sostantivato: solo maschile)* something else; *(: in espressioni interrogative)* anything else; **non ho ~ da dire** I have nothing else *o* I don't have anything else to say; **più che ~** above all; **se non ~** at least; **tra l'~** among other things; **ci mancherebbe ~!** that's all we need!; **non faccio ~ che lavorare** I do nothing but work; **contento? – ~ che!** are you pleased? — and how!; *vedi* **senza; noialtri; voialtri; tutto**

---

al'tronde *av*: **d'~** on the other hand
al'trove *av* elsewhere, somewhere else
al'trui *ag inv* other people's ♦ *sm*: **l'~** other people's belongings *pl*
altru'ista, i, e *ag* altruistic
al'tura *sf (rialto)* height, high ground; *(alto mare)* open sea; **pesca d'~** deep-sea fishing
a'lunno, a *sm/f* pupil

alve'are *sm* hive

'alveo *sm* riverbed

al'zare [al'tsare] *vt* to raise, lift; (*issare*) to hoist; (*costruire*) to build, erect; ~rsi *vr* to rise; (*dal letto*) to get up; (*crescere*) to grow tall (*o* taller); ~ le spalle to shrug one's shoulders; ~rsi in piedi to stand up, get to one's feet; al'zata *sf* lifting, raising; un'alzata di spalle a shrug

a'mabile *ag* lovable; (*vino*) sweet

a'maca, che *sf* hammock

amalga'mare *vt* to amalgamate

a'mante *ag*: ~ di (*musica etc*) fond of ♦ *sm/f* lover/mistress

a'mare *vt* to love; (*amico, musica, sport*) to like

amareggi'ato, a [amared'dʒato] *ag* upset, saddened

ama'rena *sf* sour black cherry

ama'rezza [ama'rettsa] *sf* bitterness

a'maro, a *ag* bitter ♦ *sm* bitterness; (*liquore*) bitters *pl*

ambasci'ata [ambaʃ'ʃata] *sf* embassy; (*messaggio*) message; ambascia'tore, 'trice *sm/f* ambassador/ambassadress

ambe'due *ag inv*: ~ i ragazzi both boys ♦ *pron inv* both

ambien'tare *vt* to acclimatize; (*romanzo, film*) to set; ~rsi *vr* to get used to one's surroundings

ambi'ente *sm* environment; (*fig: insieme di persone*) milieu; (*stanza*) room

am'biguo, a *ag* ambiguous

am'bire *vt* (*anche: vi*: ~ a) to aspire to

'ambito *sm* sphere, field

ambizi'one [ambit'tsjone] *sf* ambition; ambizi'oso, a *ag* ambitious

'ambo *ag inv* both ♦ (*al gioco*) double

'ambra *sf* amber; ~ grigia ambergris

ambu'lante *ag* itinerant ♦ *sm* peddler

ambu'lanza [ambu'lantsa] *sf* ambulance

ambula'torio *sm* (*studio medico*) surgery

a'meno, a *ag* pleasant; (*strano*) funny

A'merica *sf*: l'~ America; l'~ latina Latin America; ameri'cano, a *ag, sm/f* American

ami'anto *sm* asbestos

a'mica *sf vedi* amico

ami'chevole [ami'kevole] *ag* friendly

ami'cizia [ami'tʃittsja] *sf* friendship; ~e *sfpl* (*amici*) friends

a'mico, a, ci, che *sm/f* friend; (*fidanzato*) boyfriend/girlfriend; ~ del cuore *o* intimo bosom friend

'amido *sm* starch

ammac'care *vt* (*pentola*) to dent; (*persona*) to bruise; ~rsi *vr* to bruise

ammaes'trare *vt* (*animale*) to train

ammai'nare *vt* to lower, haul down

amma'larsi *vr* to fall ill; amma'lato, a *ag* ill, sick ♦ *sm/f* sick person; (*paziente*) patient

ammali'are *vt* (*fig*) to enchant, charm

am'manco, chi *sm* deficit

ammanet'tare *vt* to handcuff

ammas'sare *vt* (*ammucchiare*) to amass; (*raccogliere*) to gather together; ~rsi *vr* to pile up; to gather; am'masso *sm* mass; (*mucchio*) pile, heap; (ECON) stockpile

ammat'tire *vi* to go mad

ammaz'zare [ammat'tsare] *vt* to kill; ~rsi *vr* (*uccidersi*) to kill o.s.; (*rimanere ucciso*) to be killed; ~rsi di lavoro to work o.s. to death

am'menda *sf* amends *pl*; (DIR, SPORT) fine

am'messo, a *pp di* ammettere ♦ *cong*: ~ che supposing that

am'mettere *vt* to admit; (*riconoscere: fatto*) to acknowledge, admit; (*permettere*) to allow, accept; (*supporre*) to suppose

ammez'zato [ammed'dzato] *sm* (*anche*: piano ~) mezzanine, entresol

ammic'care *vi*: ~ (a) to wink (at)

amminis'trare *vt* to run, manage; (REL, DIR) to administer; amministra'tivo, a *ag* administrative; amministra'tore *sm* administrator; (*di condominio*) flats manager; amministratore delegato managing director; amministrazi'one *sf* management; administration

ammiragli'ato [ammira'ʎ'ʎato] *sm* admiralty

ammi'raglio [ammi'raʎʎo] *sm* admiral

ammi'rare *vt* to admire; ammira'tore, 'trice *sm/f* admirer; ammirazi'one *sf* admiration

ammissi'one *sf* admission

ammobili'ato, a *ag* furnished

am'modo *av* properly ♦ *ag inv* respectable, nice

am'mollo *sm*: **lasciare in ~** to leave to soak

ammo'niaca *sf* ammonia

ammoni'mento *sm* warning; admonishment

ammo'nire *vt* (*avvertire*) to warn; (*rimproverare*) to admonish; (*DIR*) to caution

ammon'tare *vi*: **~ a** to amount to ♦ *sm* (total) amount

ammorbi'dente *sm* fabric conditioner

ammorbi'dire *vt* to soften

ammortiz'zare [ammortid'dzare] *vt* (*ECON*) to pay off, amortize; (: *spese d'impianto*) to write off; (*AUT, TECN*) to absorb, deaden; **ammortizza'tore** *sm* (*AUT, TECN*) shock-absorber

ammucchi'are [ammuk'kjare] *vt* to pile up, accumulate

ammuf'fire *vi* to go mouldy (*BRIT*) *o* moldy (*US*)

ammutina'mento *sm* mutiny

ammuto'lire *vi* to be struck dumb

amnis'tia *sf* amnesty

'amo *sm* (*PESCA*) hook; (*fig*) bait

a'modo *av* = **ammodo**

a'more *sm* love; **~i** *smpl* love affairs; **il tuo bambino è un ~** your baby's a darling; **fare l'~** *o* **all'~** to make love; **per ~ o per forza** by hook or by crook; **amor proprio** self-esteem, pride; **amo'revole** *ag* loving, affectionate

a'morfo, a *ag* amorphous; (*fig: persona*) lifeless

amo'roso, a *ag* (*affettuoso*) loving, affectionate; (*d'amore: sguardo*) amorous; (: *poesia, relazione*) love *cpd*

ampi'ezza [am'pjettsa] *sf* width, breadth; spaciousness; (*fig: importanza*) scale, size

'ampio, a *ag* wide, broad; (*spazioso*) spacious; (*abbondante: vestito*) loose; (: *gonna*) full; (: *spiegazione*) ample, full

am'plesso *sm* intercourse

ampli'are *vt* (*ingrandire*) to enlarge; (*allargare*) to widen

amplifi'care *vt* to amplify; **amplifica'tore** *sm* (*TECN, MUS*) amplifier

am'polla *sf* (*vasetto*) cruet

ampu'tare *vt* (*MED*) to amputate

amu'leto *sm* lucky charm

anabbagli'ante [anabbáʎ'ʎante] *ag* (*AUT*) dipped (*BRIT*), dimmed (*US*); **~i** *smpl* dipped (*BRIT*) *o* dimmed (*US*) headlights

a'nagrafe *sf* (*registro*) register of births, marriages and deaths; (*ufficio*) registry office (*BRIT*), office of vital statistics (*US*)

anal'colico, a, ci, che *ag* non-alcoholic ♦ *sm* soft drink

analfa'beta, i, e *ag, sm/f* illiterate

anal'gesico, a, ci, che [anal'dʒɛziko] *ag, sm* analgesic

a'nalisi *sf inv* analysis; (*MED: esame*) test; **~ grammaticale** parsing; **ana'lista, i, e** *sm/f* analyst; (*PSIC*) (psycho)analyst

analiz'zare [analid'dzare] *vt* to analyse; (*MED*) to test

analo'gia, 'gie [analo'dʒia] *sf* analogy

a'nalogo, a, ghi, ghe *ag* analogous

'ananas *sm inv* pineapple

anar'chia [anar'kia] *sf* anarchy; **a'narchico, a, ci, che** *ag* anarchic(al) ♦ *sm/f* anarchist

'ANAS *sigla f* (= *Azienda Nazionale Autonoma delle Strade*) national roads department

anato'mia *sf* anatomy; **ana'tomico, a, ci, che** *ag* anatomical; (*sedile*) contoured

'anatra *sf* duck

'anca, che *sf* (*ANAT*) hip

'anche ['anke] *cong* (*inoltre, pure*) also, too; (*perfino*) even; **vengo anch'io** I'm coming too; **~ se** even if

an'cora[1] *av* still; (*di nuovo*) again; (*di più*) some more; (*persino*): **~ più forte** even stronger; **non ~** not yet; **~ una volta** once more, once again; **~ un po'** a little more; (*di tempo*) a little longer

'ancora[2] *sf* anchor; **gettare/levare l'~** to cast/weigh anchor; **anco'raggio** *sm* anchorage; **anco'rare** *vt* to anchor;

ancorarsi *vr* to anchor

anda'mento *sm* progress, movement; course; state

an'dante *ag* (*corrente*) current; (*di poco pregio*) cheap, second-rate ♦ *sm* (*MUS*) andante

an'dare *sm*: **a lungo ~** in the long run ♦ *vi* to go; (*essere adatto*): **~ a** to suit; (*piacere*): **il suo comportamento non mi va** I don't like the way he behaves; **ti va di andare al cinema?** do you feel like going to the cinema?; **andarsene** to go away; **questa camicia va lavata** this shirt needs a wash ♦ should be washed; **~ a cavallo** to ride; **~ in macchina/aereo** to go by car/plane; **~ a fare qc** to go and do sth; **~ a pescare/sciare** to go fishing/skiing; **~ a male** to go bad; **come va?** (*lavoro, progetto*) how are things?; **come va? — bene, grazie!** how are you? — fine, thanks!; **va fatto entro oggi** it's got to be done today; **ne va della nostra vita** our lives are at stake; **an'data** *sf* going; (*viaggio*) outward journey; **biglietto di sola andata** single (*BRIT*) *o* one-way ticket; **biglietto di andata e ritorno** return (*BRIT*) *o* round-trip (*US*) ticket; **anda'tura** *sf* (*modo di andare*) walk, gait; (*SPORT*) pace; (*NAUT*) tack

an'dazzo [an'dattso] (*peg*) *sm*: **prendere un brutto ~** to take a turn for the worse

andirivi'eni *sm inv* coming and going

'andito *sm* corridor, passage

an'drone *sm* entrance hall

a'neddoto *sm* anecdote

ane'lare *vi*: **~ a** to long for, yearn for

a'nelito *sm* (*fig*): **~ di** longing *o* yearning for

a'nello *sm* ring; (*di catena*) link

a'nemico, a, ci, che *ag* anaemic

a'nemone *sm* anemone

aneste'sia *sf* anaesthesia; **anes'tetico, a, ci, che** *ag, sm* anaesthetic

anfite'atro *sm* amphitheatre

an'fratto *sm* ravine

an'gelico, a, ci, che [an'dʒɛliko] *ag* angelic(al)

'angelo ['andʒelo] *sm* angel; **~ custode** guardian angel

anghe'ria [ange'ria] *sf* vexation

an'gina [an'dʒina] *sf* tonsillitis; **~ pectoris** angina

angli'cano, a *ag* Anglican

angli'cismo [angli'tʃizmo] *sm* anglicism

anglo'sassone *ag* Anglo-Saxon

ango'lare *ag* angular

angolazi'one [angolat'tsjone] *sf* (*FOT etc, fig*) angle

'angolo *sm* corner; (*MAT*) angle

an'goscia, sce [an'gɔʃʃa] *sf* deep anxiety, anguish *no pl*; **angosci'oso, a** *ag* (*d'angoscia*) anguished; (*che dà angoscia*) distressing, painful

angu'illa *sf* eel

an'guria *sf* watermelon

an'gustia *sf* (*ansia*) anguish, distress; (*povertà*) poverty, want

angusti'are *vt* to distress; **~rsi** *vr*: **~rsi (per)** to worry (about)

an'gusto, a *ag* (*stretto*) narrow

'anice ['anitʃe] *sm* (*CUC*) aniseed; (*BOT*) anise

a'nidride *sf* (*CHIM*): **~ carbonica/solforosa** carbon/sulphur dioxide

'anima *sf* soul; (*abitante*) inhabitant; **non c'era ~ viva** there wasn't a living soul

ani'male *sm, ag* animal; **~ domestico** pet

ani'mare *vt* to give life to, liven up; (*incoraggiare*) to encourage; **~rsi** *vr* to become animated, come to life; **ani'mato, a** *ag* animate; (*vivace*) lively, animated; (*: strada*) busy; **anima'tore, 'trice** *sm/f* guiding spirit; (*CINEMA*) animator; (*di festa*) life and soul; **animazi'one** *sf* liveliness; (*di strada*) bustle; (*CINEMA*) animation; **animazione teatrale** amateur dramatics

'animo *sm* (*mente*) mind; (*cuore*) heart; (*coraggio*) courage; (*disposizione*) character, disposition; **avere in ~ di fare qc** to intend *o* have a mind to do sth; **perdersi d'~** to lose heart

'anitra *sf* = **anatra**

anna'cquare *vt* to water down, dilute

annaffi'are *vt* to water; **annaffia'toio** *sm* watering can an'nali *smpl* annals

annas'pare *vi* to flounder

an'nata *sf* year; (*importo annuo*) annual amount; **vino d'~** vintage wine

annebbi'are *vt* (*fig*) to cloud; **~rsi** *vr* to become foggy; (*vista*) to become dim

annega'mento *sm* drowning

anne'gare *vt, vi* to drown; **~rsi** *vr* (*accidentalmente*) to drown; (*deliberatamente*) to drown o.s.

anne'rire *vt* to blacken ♦ *vi* to become black

an'nesso, a *pp di* **annettere** ♦ *ag* attached; (*POL*) annexed; **... e tutti gli ~i e connessi** and so on and so forth

an'nettere *vt* (*POL*) to annex; (*accludere*) to attach

annichi'lire [anniki'lire] *vt* = **annichilare**

anni'darsi *vr* to nest

annien'tare *vt* to annihilate, destroy

anniver'sario *sm* anniversary

'anno *sm* year; **ha 8 ~i** he's 8 (years old)

anno'dare *vt* to knot, tie; (*fig: rapporto*) to form

annoi'are *vt* to bore; (*seccare*) to annoy; **~rsi** *vr* to be bored; to be annoyed

an'noso, a *ag* (*problema etc*) age-old

anno'tare *vt* (*registrare*) to note, note down; (*commentare*) to annotate; **annotazi'one** *sf* note; annotation

annove'rare *vt* to number

annu'ale *ag* annual

annu'ario *sm* yearbook

annu'ire *vi* to nod; (*acconsentire*) to agree

annul'lare *vt* to annihilate, destroy; (*contratto, francobollo*) to cancel; (*matrimonio*) to annul; (*sentenza*) to quash; (*risultati*) to declare void

annunci'are [annun'tʃare] *vt* to announce; (*dar segni rivelatori*) to herald; **annuncia'tore, 'trice** *sm/f* (*RADIO, TV*) announcer; **l'Annunciazi'one** *sf* the Annunciation

an'nuncio [an'nuntʃo] *sm* announcement; (*fig*) sign; **~ pubblicitario** advertisement; **~i economici** classified advertisements, small ads

'annuo, a *ag* annual, yearly

annu'sare *vt* to sniff, smell; **~ tabacco** to take snuff

'ano *sm* anus

anoma'lia *sf* anomaly

a'nomalo, a *ag* anomalous

a'nonimo, a *ag* anonymous ♦ *sm* (*autore*) anonymous writer (*o* painter *etc*); **società ~a** (*COMM*) joint stock company

anores'sia *sf* anorexia

anor'male *ag* abnormal ♦ *sm/f* subnormal person

ANSA *sigla f* (= *Agenzia Nazionale Stampa Associata*) press agency

'ansa *sf* (*manico*) handle; (*di fiume*) bend, loop

'ansia *sf* anxiety

ansietà *sf* = **ansia**

ansi'mare *vi* to pant

ansi'oso, a *ag* anxious

'anta *sf* (*di finestra*) shutter; (*di armadio*) door

antago'nismo *sm* antagonism

an'tartico, a, ci, che *ag* Antarctic ♦ *sm*: **l'A~** the Antarctic

An'tartide *sf*: **l'~** Antarctica

antece'dente [antetʃe'dɛnte] *ag* preceding, previous

ante'fatto *sm* previous events *pl*; previous history

antegu'erra *sm* pre-war period

ante'nato *sm* ancestor, forefather

an'tenna *sf* (*RADIO, TV*) aerial; (*ZOOL*) antenna, feeler; (*NAUT*) yard; **~ parabolica** satellite dish

ante'prima *sf* preview

anteri'ore *ag* (*ruota, zampa*) front; (*fatti*) previous, preceding

antia'ereo, a *ag* anti-aircraft

antia'tomico, a, ci, che *ag* antinuclear; **rifugio ~** fallout shelter

antibi'otico, a, ci, che *ag, sm* antibiotic

anti'camera *sf* anteroom; **fare ~** to wait (for an audience)

antichità [antiki'ta] *sf inv* antiquity; (*oggetto*) antique

antici'pare [antitʃi'pare] *vt* (*consegna,*

visita) to bring forward, anticipate; (*somma di denaro*) to pay in advance; (*notizia*) to disclose ♦ *vi* to be ahead of time; **anticipazi'one** *sf* anticipation; (*di notizia*) advance information; (*somma di denaro*) advance; **an'ticipo** *sm* anticipation; (*di denaro*) advance; **in anticipo** early, in advance

an'tico, a, chi, che *ag* (*quadro, mobili*) antique; (*dell'antichità*) ancient; **all'~a** old-fashioned

anticoncezio'nale [antikontʃettsjo'nale] *sm* contraceptive

anticonfor'mista, i, e *ag, sm/f* nonconformist

anti'corpo *sm* antibody

antidepres'sivo *sm* antidepressant

an'tidoto *sm* antidote

anti'furto *sm* anti-theft device

anti'gelo [anti'dʒelo] *ag inv*: **(liquido)** ~ (*per motore*) antifreeze; (*per cristalli*) de-icer

An'tille *sfpl*: **le** ~ the West Indies

antin'cendio [antin'tʃendjo] *ag inv* fire *cpd*

antio'rario [antio'rarjo] *ag*: **in senso** ~ anticlockwise

anti'pasto *sm* hors d'œuvre

antipa'tia *sf* antipathy, dislike;

anti'patico, a, ci, che *ag* unpleasant

antiquari'ato *sm* antique trade; **un oggetto d'~** an antique

anti'quario *sm* antique dealer

anti'quato, a *ag* antiquated, old-fashioned

antise'mita, i, e *ag* anti-Semitic

anti'settico, a, ci, che *ag, sm* antiseptic

antista'minico, a, ci, che *ag, sm* antihistamine

antolo'gia, 'gie [antolo'dʒia] *sf* anthology

antra'ce *sm* anthrax

anu'lare *ag* ring *cpd* ♦ *sm* third finger

'anzi ['antsi] *av* (*invece*) on the contrary; (*o meglio*) or rather, or better still

anzianità [antsjani'ta] *sf* old age; (*AMM*) seniority

anzi'ano, a [an'tsjano] *ag* old; (*AMM*) senior ♦ *sm/f* old person; senior member

anziché [antsi'ke] *cong* rather than

anzi'tutto [antsi'tutto] *av* first of all

apa'tia *sf* apathy, indifference

a'patico, a, ci, che *ag* apathetic

'ape *sf* bee

aperi'tivo *sm* apéritif

a'perto, a *pp di* aprire ♦ *ag* open; **all'~** in the open (air)

aper'tura *sf* opening; (*ampiezza*) width; (*FOT*) aperture; ~ **alare** wing span

'apice ['apitʃe] *sm* apex; (*fig*) height

ap'nea *sf*: **immergersi in** ~ to dive without breathing apparatus

a'postolo *sm* apostle

a'postrofo *sm* apostrophe

appa'gare *vt* to satisfy

ap'palto *sm* (*COMM*) contract; **dare/ prendere in** ~ **un lavoro** to let out/ undertake a job on contract

appan'nare *vt* (*vetro*) to mist; (*vista*) to dim; ~**rsi** *vr* to mist over; to grow dim

appa'rato *sm* equipment, machinery; (*ANAT*) apparatus; ~ **scenico** (*TEATRO*) props *pl*

apparecchi'are [apparek'kjare] *vt* to prepare; (*tavola*) to set ♦ *vi* to set the table; **apparecchia'tura** *sf* equipment; (*macchina*) machine, device

appa'recchio [appa'rekkjo] *sm* device; (*aeroplano*) aircraft *inv*; ~ **televisivo/ telefonico** television set/telephone

appa'rente *ag* apparent; **appa'renza** *sf* appearance; **in** *o* **all'apparenza** apparently

appa'rire *vi* to appear; (*sembrare*) to seem, appear; **appari'scente** *ag* (*colore*) garish, gaudy; (*bellezza*) striking

ap'parso, a *pp di* apparire

apparta'mento *sm* flat (*BRIT*), apartment (*US*)

appar'tarsi *vr* to withdraw; **appar'tato, a** *ag* (*luogo*) secluded

apparte'nere *vi*: ~ **a** to belong to

appassio'nare *vt* to thrill; (*commuovere*) to move; ~**rsi a qc** to take a great interest in sth; **appassio'nato, a** *ag* passionate; (*entusiasta*): **appassionato (di)** keen (on)

appas'sire *vi* to wither

appel'larsi *vr* (*ricorrere*): ~ **a** to appeal to; (*DIR*): ~ **contro** to appeal against; **ap'pello** *sm* roll-call; (*implorazione, DIR*) appeal; **fare**

appello a to appeal to

ap'pena *av* (*a stento*) hardly, scarcely; (*solamente, da poco*) just ♦ *cong* as soon as; **(non) ~ furono arrivati ...** as soon as they had arrived ...; **~ ... che** *o* **quando** no sooner ... than

ap'pendere *vt* to hang (up)

appen'dice [appen'ditʃe] *sf* appendix; **romanzo d'~** popular serial

appendi'cite [appendi'tʃite] *sf* appendicitis

Appen'nini *smpl*: **gli ~** the Apennines

appesan'tire *vt* to make heavy; **~rsi** *vr* to grow stout

ap'peso, a *pp di* **appendere**

appe'tito *sm* appetite; **appeti'toso, a** *ag* appetising; (*fig*) attractive, desirable

appia'nare *vt* to level; (*fig*) to smooth away, iron out

appiat'tire *vt* to flatten; **~rsi** *vr* to become flatter; (*farsi piatto*) to flatten o.s.; **~rsi al suolo** to lie flat on the ground

appic'care *vt*: **~ il fuoco a** to set fire to, set on fire

appicci'care [appittʃi'kare] *vt* to stick; **~rsi** *vr* to stick; (*fig: persona*) to cling

appi'eno *av* fully

appigli'arsi [appiʎ'ʎarsi] *vr*: **~ a** (*afferrarsi*) to take hold of; (*fig*) to cling to; **ap'piglio** *sm* hold; (*fig*) pretext

appiso'larsi *vr* to doze off

applau'dire *vt, vi* to applaud; **ap'plauso** *sm* applause

appli'care *vt* to apply; (*regolamento*) to enforce; **~rsi** *vr* to apply o.s.; **applicazi'one** *sf* application; enforcement

appoggi'are [appod'dʒare] *vt* (*mettere contro*): **~ qc a qc** to lean *o* rest sth against sth; (*fig: sostenere*) to support; **~rsi** *vr*: **~rsi a** to lean against; (*fig*) to rely upon; **ap'poggio** *sm* support

appollai'arsi *vr* (*anche fig*) to perch

ap'porre *vt* to affix

appor'tare *vt* to bring

apposita'mente *av* specially; (*apposta*) on purpose

ap'posito, a *ag* appropriate

ap'posta *av* on purpose, deliberately

appos'tarsi *vr* to lie in wait

ap'prendere *vt* (*imparare*) to learn

appren'dista, i, e *sm/f* apprentice

apprensi'one *sf* apprehension; **appren'sivo, a** *ag* apprehensive

ap'presso *av* (*accanto, vicino*) close by, near; (*dietro*) behind; (*dopo, più tardi*) after, later ♦ *ag inv* (*dopo*): **il giorno ~** the next day; **~ a** (*vicino a*) near, close to

appres'tare *vt* to prepare, get ready; **~rsi** *vr*: **~rsi a fare qc** to prepare *o* get ready to do sth

ap'pretto *sm* starch

apprezza'mento [apprettsa'mento] *sm* appreciation; (*giudizio*) opinion

apprez'zare [appret'tsare] *vt* to appreciate

ap'proccio [ap'prɔttʃo] *sm* approach

appro'dare *vi* (NAUT) to land; (*fig*): **non ~ a nulla** to come to nothing; **ap'prodo** *sm* landing; (*luogo*) landing-place

approfit'tare *vi*: **~ di** to make the most of; (*peg*) to take advantage of

approfon'dire *vt* to deepen; (*fig*) to study in depth

appropri'ato, a *ag* appropriate

approssi'marsi *vr*: **~ a** to approach

approssima'tivo, a *ag* approximate, rough; (*impreciso*) inexact, imprecise

appro'vare *vt* (*condotta, azione*) to approve of; (*candidato*) to pass; (*progetto di legge*) to approve; **approvazi'one** *sf* approval

approvvigio'nare [approvvidʒo'nare] *vt* to supply

appunta'mento *sm* appointment; (*amoroso*) date; **darsi ~** to arrange to meet (one another)

appun'tato *sm* (CARABINIERI) corporal

ap'punto *sm* note; (*rimprovero*) reproach ♦ *av* (*proprio*) exactly, just; **per l'~!, ~!** exactly!

appu'rare *vt* to check, verify

apribot'tiglie [apribot'tiʎʎe] *sm inv* bottle opener

a'prile *sm* April

a'prire *vt* to open; (*via, cadavere*) to open

up; (*gas, luce, acqua*) to turn on ♦ *vi* to open; **~rsi** *vr* to open; **~rsi a qn** to confide in sb, open one's heart to sb

apris'catole *sm inv* tin (*BRIT*) *o* can opener

a'quario *sm* = **acquario**

'aquila *sf* (*ZOOL*) eagle; (*fig*) genius

aqui'lone *sm* (*giocattolo*) kite; (*vento*) North wind

A'rabia Sau'dita *sf:* **l'~** Saudi Arabia

'arabo, a *ag, sm/f* Arab ♦ *sm* (*LING*) Arabic

a'rachide [a'rakide] *sf* peanut

ara'gosta *sf* crayfish; lobster

a'rancia, ce [a'rantʃa] *sf* orange; **aranci'ata** *sf* orangeade; **a'rancio** *sm* (*BOT*) orange tree; (*colore*) orange ♦ *ag inv* (*colore*) orange; **aranci'one** *ag inv:* **(color) arancione** bright orange

a'rare *vt* to plough (*BRIT*), plow (*US*)

a'ratro *sm* plough (*BRIT*), plow (*US*)

a'razzo [a'rattso] *sm* tapestry

arbi'trare *vt* (*SPORT*) to referee; to umpire; (*DIR*) to arbitrate

arbi'trario, a *ag* arbitrary

ar'bitrio *sm* will; (*abuso, sopruso*) arbitrary act

'arbitro *sm* arbiter, judge; (*DIR*) arbitrator; (*SPORT*) referee; (*: TENNIS, CRICKET*) umpire

ar'busto *sm* shrub

'arca, che *sf* (*sarcofago*) sarcophagus; **l'~ di Noè** Noah's ark

ar'cangelo [ar'kandʒelo] *sm* archangel

ar'cata *sf* (*ARCHIT, ANAT*) arch; (*ordine di archi*) arcade

archeolo'gia [arkeolo'dʒia] *sf* arch(a)eology; **arche'ologo, a, gi, ghe** *sm/f* arch(a)eologist

ar'chetto [ar'ketto] *sm* (*MUS*) bow

architet'tare [arkitet'tare] *vt* (*fig: ideare*) to devise; (*: macchinare*) to plan, concoct

archi'tetto [arki'tetto] *sm* architect; **architet'tura** *sf* architecture

ar'chivio [ar'kivjo] *sm* archives *pl*; (*INFORM*) file

arci'ere [ar'tʃere] *sm* archer

ar'cigno, a [ar'tʃiɲɲo] *ag* grim, severe

arci'vescovo [artʃi'veskovo] *sm* archbishop

'arco *sm* (*arma, MUS*) bow; (*ARCHIT*) arch;

(*MAT*) arc

arcoba'leno *sm* rainbow

arcu'ato, a *ag* curved, bent

ar'dente *ag* burning; (*fig*) burning, ardent

'ardere *vt, vi* to burn

ar'desia *sf* slate

ar'dire *vi* to dare ♦ *sm* daring; **ar'dito, a** *ag* brave, daring, bold; (*sfacciato*) bold

ar'dore *sm* blazing heat; (*fig*) ardour, fervour

'arduo, a *ag* arduous, difficult

'area *sf* area; (*EDIL*) land, ground

a'rena *sf* arena; (*per corride*) bullring; (*sabbia*) sand

are'narsi *vr* to run aground

areo'plano *sm* = **aeroplano**

'argano *sm* winch

argente'ria [ardʒente'ria] *sf* silverware, silver

Argen'tina [ardʒen'tina] *sf:* **l'~** Argentina; **argen'tino, a** *ag, sm/f* Argentinian

ar'gento [ar'dʒento] *sm* silver; **~ vivo** quicksilver

ar'gilla [ar'dʒilla] *sf* clay

'argine ['ardʒine] *sm* embankment, bank; (*diga*) dyke, dike

argo'mento *sm* argument; (*motivo*) motive; (*materia, tema*) subject

argu'ire *vt* to deduce

ar'guto, a *ag* sharp, quick-witted; **ar'guzia** *sf* wit; (*battuta*) witty remark

'aria *sf* air; (*espressione, aspetto*) air, look; (*MUS: melodia*) tune; (*: di opera*) aria; **mandare all'~ qc** to ruin *o* upset sth; **all'~ aperta** in the open (air)

'arido, a *ag* arid

arieggi'are [arjed'dʒare] *vt* (*cambiare aria*) to air; (*imitare*) to imitate

ari'ete *sm* ram; (*MIL*) battering ram; (*dello zodiaco*): **A~** Aries

a'ringa, ghe *sf* herring *inv*

'arista *sf* (*CUC*) chine of pork

aristo'cratico, a, ci, che *ag* aristocratic

arit'metica *sf* arithmetic

arlec'chino [arlek'kino] *sm* harlequin

'arma, i *sf* weapon, arm; (*parte dell'esercito*) arm; **chiamare alle ~i** to call up (BRIT), draft (US); **sotto le ~i** in the army (o forces); **alle ~i!** to arms!; **~ da fuoco** firearm

ar'madio sm cupboard; (*per abiti*) wardrobe; **~ a muro** built-in cupboard

armamen'tario sm equipment

arma'mento sm (MIL) armament; (: *materiale*) arms pl, weapons pl; (NAUT) fitting out; manning

ar'mare vt to arm; (*arma da fuoco*) to cock; (NAUT: *nave*) to rig, fit out; to man; (EDIL: *volta, galleria*) to prop up, shore up; **~rsi** vr to arm o.s.; (MIL) to take up arms; ar'mata sf (MIL) army; (NAUT) fleet; arma'tore sm shipowner; arma'tura sf (*struttura di sostegno*) framework; (*impalcatura*) scaffolding; (STORIA) armour no pl, suit of armour

armeggi'are [armed'dʒare] vi: **~ (intorno a qc)** to mess about (with sth)

armis'tizio [armis'tittsjo] sm armistice

armo'nia sf harmony; ar'monica, che sf (MUS) harmonica; **~ a bocca** mouth organ; ar'monico, a, ci, che ag harmonic; (*fig*) harmonious; armoni'oso, a ag harmonious

armoniz'zare [armonid'dzare] vt to harmonize; (*colori, abiti*) to match ♦ vi to be in harmony; to match

ar'nese sm tool, implement; (*oggetto indeterminato*) thing, contraption; **male in ~** (*malvestito*) badly dressed; (*di salute malferma*) in poor health; (*di condizioni economiche*) down-at-heel

'arnia sf hive

a'roma, i sm aroma; fragrance; **~i** smpl (CUC) herbs and spices; aromatera'pia sf aromatherapy; aro'matico, a, ci, che ag aromatic; (*cibo*) spicy

'arpa sf (MUS) harp

ar'peggio [ar'peddʒo] sm (MUS) arpeggio

ar'pia sf (*anche fig*) harpy

arpi'one sm (*gancio*) hook; (*cardine*) hinge; (PESCA) harpoon

arrabat'tarsi vr to do all one can, strive

arrabbi'are vi (*cane*) to be affected with rabies; **~rsi** vr (*essere preso dall'ira*) to get angry, fly into a rage; arrabbi'ato, a ag rabid, with rabies; furious, angry

arraf'fare vt to snatch, seize; (*sottrarre*) to pinch

arrampi'carsi vr to climb (up)

arran'care vi to limp, hobble

arran'giare [arran'dʒare] vt to arrange; **~rsi** vr to manage, do the best one can

arre'care vt to bring; (*causare*) to cause

arreda'mento sm (*studio*) interior design; (*mobili etc*) furnishings pl

arre'dare vt to furnish; arreda'tore, 'trice sm/f interior designer; ar'redo sm fittings pl, furnishings pl

ar'rendersi vr to surrender

arres'tare vt (*fermare*) to stop, halt; (*catturare*) to arrest; **~rsi** vr (*fermarsi*) to stop; ar'resto sm (*cessazione*) stopping; (*fermata*) stop; (*cattura, MED*) arrest; **subire un arresto** to come to a stop o standstill; **mettere agli arresti** to place under arrest; **arresti domiciliari** house arrest sg

arre'trare vt, vi to withdraw; arre'trato, a ag (*lavoro*) behind schedule; (*paese, bambino*) backward; (*numero di giornale*) back cpd; **arretrati** smpl arrears

arric'chire [arrik'kire] vt to enrich; **~rsi** vr to become rich

arricci'are [arrit'tʃare] vt to curl

ar'ringa, ghe sf harangue; (DIR) address by counsel

arrischi'are [arris'kjare] vt to risk; **~rsi** vr to venture, dare; arrischi'ato, a ag risky; (*temerario*) reckless, rash

arri'vare vi to arrive; (*accadere*) to happen, occur; **~ a** (*livello, grado etc*) to reach; **lui arriva a Roma alle 7** he gets to o arrives at Rome at 7; **non ci arrivo** I can't reach it; (*fig: non capisco*) I can't understand it

arrive'derci [arrive'dertʃi] escl goodbye!

arrive'derla escl (*forma di cortesia*) goodbye!

arri'vista, i, e sm/f go-getter

ar'rivo sm arrival; (SPORT) finish, finishing line

arro'gante ag arrogant

arro'lare vb = arruolare

arros'sire *vi* (*per vergogna, timidezza*) to blush, flush; (*per gioia, rabbia*) to flush

arros'tire *vt* to roast; (*pane*) to toast; (*ai ferri*) to grill

ar'rosto *sm, ag inv* roast

arro'tare *vt* to sharpen; (*investire con un veicolo*) to run over

arroto'lare *vt* to roll up

arroton'dare *vt* (*forma, oggetto*) to round; (*stipendio*) to add to; (*somma*) to round off

arrovel'larsi *vr* to rack one's brains

arruf'fare *vt* to ruffle; (*fili*) to tangle; (*fig: questione*) to confuse

arruggi'nire [arruddʒi'nire] *vt* to rust; **~rsi** *vr* to rust; (*fig*) to become rusty

arruo'lare *vt* (MIL) to enlist; **~rsi** *vr* to enlist, join up

arse'nale *sm* (MIL) arsenal; (*cantiere navale*) dockyard

'arso, a *pp di* **ardere** ♦ *ag* (*bruciato*) burnt; (*arido*) dry; **ar'sura** *sf* (*calore opprimente*) burning heat; (*siccità*) drought

'arte *sf* art; (*abilità*) skill

arte'fatto, a *ag* (*cibo*) adulterated; (*fig: modi*) artificial

ar'tefice [ar'tefitʃe] *sm/f* craftsman/woman; (*autore*) author

ar'teria *sf* artery

'artico, a, ci, che *ag* Arctic

artico'lare *ag* (ANAT) of the joints, articular ♦ *vt* to articulate; (*suddividere*) to divide, split up; **articolazi'one** *sf* articulation; (ANAT, TECN) joint

ar'ticolo *sm* article; **~ di fondo** (STAMPA) leader, leading article

'Artide *sm*: **l'~** the Arctic

artifici'ale [artifi'tʃale] *ag* artificial

arti'ficio [arti'fitʃo] *sm* (*espediente*) trick, artifice; (*ricerca di effetto*) artificiality

artigia'nato [artidʒa'nato] *sm* craftsmanship; craftsmen *pl*

artigi'ano, a [arti'dʒano] *sm/f* craftsman/woman

artiglie'ria [artiʎʎe'ria] *sf* artillery

ar'tiglio [ar'tiʎʎo] *sm* claw; (*di rapaci*) talon

ar'tista, i, e *sm/f* artist; **ar'tistico, a, ci, che** *ag* artistic

'arto *sm* (ANAT) limb

ar'trite *sf* (MED) arthritis

ar'trosi *sf* osteoarthritis

ar'zillo, a [ar'dzillo] *ag* lively, sprightly

a'scella [aʃ'ʃella] *sf* (ANAT) armpit

ascen'dente [aʃʃen'dente] *sm* ancestor; (*fig*) ascendancy; (ASTR) ascendant

ascensi'one [aʃʃen'sjone] *sf* (ALPINISMO) ascent; (REL): **l'A~** the Ascension

ascen'sore [aʃʃen'sore] *sm* lift

a'scesa [aʃ'ʃesa] *sf* ascent; (*al trono*) accession

a'scesso [aʃ'ʃesso] *sm* (MED) abscess

'ascia ['aʃʃa] (*pl* **'asce**) *sf* axe

asciugaca'pelli [aʃʃugaka'pelli] *sm* hair-dryer

asciuga'mano [aʃʃuga'mano] *sm* towel

asciu'gare [aʃʃu'gare] *vt* to dry; **~rsi** *vr* to dry o.s.; (*diventare asciutto*) to dry

asci'utto, a [aʃ'ʃutto] *ag* dry; (*fig: magro*) lean; (*: burbero*) curt; **restare a bocca ~a** (*fig*) to be disappointed

ascol'tare *vt* to listen to; **ascolta'tore, 'trice** *sm/f* listener; **as'colto** *sm*: **essere** *o* **stare in ascolto** to be listening; **dare** *o* **prestare ascolto (a)** to pay attention (to)

as'falto *sm* asphalt

asfissi'are *vt* to suffocate

'Asia *sf*: **l'~** Asia; **asi'atico, a, ci, che** *ag, sm/f* Asiatic, Asian

a'silo *sm* refuge, sanctuary; **~ (d'infanzia)** nursery(-school); **~ nido** crèche; **~ politico** political asylum

'asino *sm* donkey, ass

A. S. L. *sigla f* (= *Azienda Sanitaria Locale*) *local health centre*

'asma *sf* asthma

'asola *sf* buttonhole

as'parago, gi *sm* asparagus *no pl*

aspet'tare *vt* to wait for; (*anche* COMM) to await; (*aspettarsi*) to expect ♦ *vi* to wait; **~rsi** *vr* to expect; **~ un bambino** to be expecting (a baby); **questo non me l'aspettavo** I wasn't expecting this; **aspetta'tiva** *sf* wait; expectation; **inferiore all'aspettativa** worse than expected; **essere in aspettativa** (AMM) to be on leave of absence as'petto sm (apparenza) aspect, appearance, look; (punto di vista) point of view; **di bell'~** good-looking

aspi'rante ag (attore etc) aspiring ♦ sm/f candidate, applicant

aspira'polvere sm inv vacuum cleaner

aspi'rare vt (respirare) to breathe in, inhale; (sog: apparecchi) to suck (up) ♦ vi: **~ a** to aspire to; **aspira'tore** sm extractor fan

aspi'rina sf aspirin

aspor'tare vt (anche MED) to remove, take away

'aspro, a ag (sapore) sour, tart; (odore) acrid, pungent; (voce, clima, fig) harsh; (superficie) rough; (paesaggio) rugged

assaggi'are [assad'dʒare] vt to taste

assag'gini [assad'dʒini] smpl (CUC) selection of first courses

as'sai av (molto) a lot, much; (: con ag) very; (a sufficienza) enough ♦ ag inv (quantità) a lot of, much; (numero) a lot of, many; **~ contento** very pleased

assa'lire vt to attack, assail

as'salto sm attack, assault

assapo'rare vt to savour

assassi'nare vt to murder; to assassinate; (fig) to ruin; **assas'sinio** sm murder; assassination; **assas'sino, a** ag murderous ♦ sm/f murderer; assassin

'asse sm (TECN) axle; (MAT) axis ♦ sf board; **~ sf da stiro** ironing board

assedi'are vt to besiege; **as'sedio** sm siege

asse'gnare [assen'ɲare] vt to assign, allot; (premio) to award

as'segno [as'seɲɲo] sm allowance; (anche: **~ bancario**) cheque (BRIT), check (US); **contro ~** cash on delivery; **~ circolare** bank draft; **~ sbarrato** crossed cheque; **~ di viaggio** traveller's cheque; **~ a vuoto** dud cheque; **~i familiari** ≈ child benefit no pl

assem'blea sf assembly

assen'nato, a ag sensible

as'senso sm assent, consent

as'sente ag absent; (fig) faraway, vacant;

as'senza sf absence

asses'sore sm (POL) councillor

asses'tare vt (mettere in ordine) to put in order, arrange; **~rsi** vr to settle in; **~ un colpo a qn** to deal sb a blow

asse'tato, a ag thirsty, parched

as'setto sm order, arrangement; (NAUT, AER) trim; **in ~ di guerra** on a war footing

assicu'rare vt (accertare) to ensure; (infondere certezza) to assure; (fermare, legare) to make fast, secure; (fare un contratto di assicurazione) to insure; **~rsi** vr (accertarsi): **~rsi (di)** to make sure (of); (contro il furto etc): **~rsi (contro)** to insure o.s. (against); **assicu'rata** sf (anche: **lettera assicurata**) registered letter; **assicu'rato, a** ag insured; **assicurazi'one** sf assurance; insurance

assidera'mento sm exposure

as'siduo, a ag (costante) assiduous; (frequentatore etc) regular

assi'eme av (insieme) together; **~ a** (together) with

assil'lare vt to pester, torment

as'sillo sm (fig) worrying thought

as'sise sfpl (DIR) assizes; **Corte** sf **d'A~** Court of Assizes, ≈ Crown Court (BRIT)

assis'tente sm/f assistant; **~ sociale** social worker; **~ di volo** (AER) steward/stewardess

assis'tenza [assis'tɛntsa] sf assistance; **~ ospedaliera** free hospital treatment; **~ sanitaria** health service; **~ sociale** welfare services pl

as'sistere vt (aiutare) to assist, help; (curare) to treat ♦ vi: **~ (a qc)** (essere presente) to be present (at sth), to attend (sth)

'asso sm ace; **piantare qn in ~** to leave sb in the lurch

associ'are [asso'tʃare] vt to associate; **~rsi** vr to enter into partnership; **~rsi a** to become a member of, join; (dolori, gioie) to share in; **~ qn alle carceri** to take sb to prison

associazi'one [assotʃat'tsjone] sf association; (COMM) association, society; **~ a delinquere** (DIR) criminal association

asso'dato, a *ag* well-founded
assogget'tare [assoddʒet'tare] *vt* to subject, subjugate
asso'lato, a *ag* sunny
assol'dare *vt* to recruit
as'solto, a *pp di* assolvere
assoluta'mente *av* absolutely
asso'luto, a *ag* absolute
assoluzi'one [assolut'tsjone] *sf* (*DIR*) acquittal; (*REL*) absolution
as'solvere *vt* (*DIR*) to acquit; (*REL*) to absolve; (*adempiere*) to carry out, perform
assomigli'are [assomiʎ'ʎare] *vi*: ~ a to resemble, look like
asson'nato, a *ag* sleepy
asso'pirsi *vr* to doze off
assor'bente *ag* absorbent ♦ *sm*: ~ igienico sanitary towel; ~ interno tampon
assor'bire *vt* to absorb
assor'dare *vt* to deafen
assorti'mento *sm* assortment
assor'tito, a *ag* assorted; matched, matching
as'sorto, a *ag* absorbed, engrossed
assottigli'are [assottiʎ'ʎare] *vt* to make thin, to thin; (*aguzzare*) to sharpen; (*ridurre*) to reduce; ~rsi *vr* to grow thin; (*fig: ridursi*) to be reduced
assue'fare *vt* to accustom; ~rsi a to get used to, accustom o.s. to
as'sumere *vt* (*impiegato*) to take on, engage; (*responsabilità*) to assume, take upon o.s.; (*contegno, espressione*) to assume, put on; (*droga*) to consume; as'sunto, a *pp di* assumere ♦ *sm* (*tesi*) proposition
assurdità *sf inv* absurdity; dire delle ~ to talk nonsense
as'surdo, a *ag* absurd
'asta *sf* pole; (*vendita*) auction
astan'te'ria *sf* casualty department
as'temio, a *ag* teetotal ♦ *sm/f* teetotaller
aste'nersi *vr*: ~ (da) to abstain (from), refrain (from); (*POL*) to abstain (from)
aste'risco, schi *sm* asterisk
'astice ['astitʃe] *sm* lobster
asti'nenza [asti'nɛntsa] *sf* abstinence;

essere in crisi di ~ to suffer from withdrawal symptoms
'astio *sm* rancour, resentment
as'tratto, a *ag* abstract
'astro *sm* star
'astro... *prefisso*: astrolo'gia [astrolo'dʒia] *sf* astrology; as'trologo, a, ghi, ghe *sm/f* astrologer; astro'nauta, i, e *sm/f* astronaut; astro'nave *sf* space ship; astrono'mia *sf* astronomy; astro'nomico, a, ci, che *ag* astronomic(al)
as'tuccio [as'tuttʃo] *sm* case, box, holder
as'tuto, a *ag* astute, cunning, shrewd; as'tuzia *sf* astuteness, shrewdness; (*azione*) trick
A'tene *sf* Athens
ate'neo *sm* university
'ateo, a *ag, sm/f* atheist
at'lante *sm* atlas
at'lantico, a, ci, che *ag* Atlantic ♦ *sm*: l'A~, l'Oceano A~ the Atlantic, the Atlantic Ocean
at'leta, i, e *sm/f* athlete; at'letica *sf* athletics *sg*; atletica leggera track and field events *pl*; atletica pesante weightlifting and wrestling
atmos'fera *sf* atmosphere
a'tomico, a, ci, che *ag* atomic; (*nucleare*) atomic, atom *cpd*, nuclear
'atomo *sm* atom
'atrio *sm* entrance hall, lobby
a'troce [a'trotʃe] *ag* (*che provoca orrore*) dreadful; (*terribile*) atrocious
attacca'mento *sm* (*fig*) attachment, affection
attacca'panni *sm* hook, peg; (*mobile*) hall stand
attac'care *vt* (*unire*) to attach; (*cucendo*) to sew on; (*far aderire*) to stick (on); (*appendere*) to hang (up); (*assalire: anche fig*) to attack; (*iniziare*) to begin, start; (*fig: contagiare*) to pass on ♦ *vi* to stick, adhere; ~rsi *vr* to stick, adhere; (*trasmettersi per contagio*) to be contagious; (*afferrarsi*): ~rsi (a) to cling (to); (*fig: affezionarsi*): ~rsi (a) to become attached (to); ~ discorso to

start a conversation; **at'tacco, chi** *sm* (*azione offensiva: anche fig*) attack; (*MED*) attack, fit; (*SCI*) binding; (*ELETTR*) socket

atteggia'mento [atteddʒaˈmento] *sm* attitude

atteggi'arsi [attedˈdʒarsi] *vr*: ~ **a** to pose as

attem'pato, a *ag* elderly

at'tendere *vt* to wait for, await ♦ *vi*: ~ **a** to attend to

atten'dibile *ag* (*storia*) credible; (*testimone*) reliable

atte'nersi *vr*: ~ **a** to keep *o* stick to

atten'tare *vi*: ~ **a** to make an attempt on; **atten'tato** *sm* attack; **attentato alla vita di qn** attempt on sb's life

at'tento, a *ag* attentive; (*accurato*) careful, thorough; **stare ~ a qc** to pay attention to sth; **~!** be careful!

attenu'ante *sf* (*DIR*) extenuating circumstance

attenu'are *vt* to attenuate; (*dolore, rumore*) to lessen, deaden; (*pena, tasse*) to alleviate; **~rsi** *vr* to ease, abate

attenzi'one [attenˈtsjone] *sf* attention; **~!** watch out!, be careful!

atter'raggio [atterˈraddʒo] *sm* landing

atter'rare *vt* to bring down ♦ *vi* to land

atter'rire *vt* to terrify

at'tesa *sf* waiting; (*tempo trascorso aspettando*) wait; **essere in attesa di qc** to be waiting for sth

at'teso, a *pp di* **attendere**

attes'tato *sm* certificate

'attico, ci *sm* attic

at'tiguo, a *ag* adjacent, adjoining

attil'lato, a *ag* (*vestito*) close-fitting

'attimo *sm* moment; **in un ~** in a moment

atti'nente *ag*: ~ **a** relating to, concerning

atti'rare *vt* to attract

atti'tudine *sf* (*disposizione*) aptitude; (*atteggiamento*) attitude

atti'vare *vt* to activate; (*far funzionare*) to set going, start

attività *sf inv* activity; (*COMM*) assets *pl*

at'tivo, a *ag* active; (*COMM*) profit-making, credit *cpd* ♦ *sm* (*COMM*) assets *pl*; **in ~** in credit

attiz'zare [attitˈtsare] *vt* (*fuoco*) to poke

'atto *sm* act; (*azione, gesto*) action, act, deed; (*DIR: documento*) deed, document; **~i** *smpl* (*di congressi etc*) proceedings; **mettere in ~** to put into action; **fare ~ di fare qc** to make as if to do sth

at'tonito, a *ag* dumbfounded, astonished

attorcigli'are [attortʃiʎˈʎare] *vt* to twist; **~rsi** *vr* to twist

at'tore, 'trice *sm/f* actor/actress

at'torno *av* round, around, about; ~ **a** round, around, about

at'tracco, chi *sm* (*NAUT*) docking *no pl*; berth

attra'ente *ag* attractive

at'trarre *vt* to attract; **attrat'tiva** *sf* (*fig: fascino*) attraction, charm; **at'tratto, a** *pp di* **attrarre**

attraversa'mento *sm*: ~ **pedonale** pedestrian crossing

attraver'sare *vt* to cross; (*città, bosco, fig: periodo*) to go through; (*sog: fiume*) to run through

attra'verso *prep* through; (*da una parte all'altra*) across

attrazi'one [attratˈtsjone] *sf* attraction

attrez'zare [attretˈtsare] *vt* to equip; (*NAUT*) to rig; **attrezza'tura** *sf* equipment *no pl*; rigging; **at'trezzo** *sm* tool, instrument; (*SPORT*) piece of equipment

attribu'ire *vt*: ~ **qc a qn** (*assegnare*) to give *o* award sth to sb; (*quadro etc*) to attribute sth to sb; **attri'buto** *sm* attribute

at'trice [atˈtritʃe] *sf vedi* **attore**

at'trito *sm* (*anche fig*) friction

attu'ale *ag* (*presente*) present; (*di attualità*) topical; (*che è in atto*) actual; **attualità** *sf inv* topicality; (*avvenimento*) current event; **attual'mente** *av* at the moment, at present

attu'are *vt* to carry out; **~rsi** *vr* to be realized

attu'tire *vt* to deaden, reduce

au'dace [auˈdatʃe] *ag* audacious, daring, bold; (*provocante*) provocative; (*sfacciato*) impudent, bold; **au'dacia** *sf* audacity, daring; boldness; provocativeness;

impudence

audiovi'sivo, a *ag* audiovisual

audizi'one [audit'tsjone] *sf* hearing; (*MUS*) audition

'auge ['audʒe] *sf*: **in ~** popular

augu'rare *vt* to wish; **~rsi qc** to hope for sth

au'gurio *sm* (*presagio*) omen; (*voto di benessere etc*) (good) wish; **essere di buon/cattivo ~** to be of good omen/be ominous; **fare gli ~i a qn** to give sb one's best wishes; **tanti ~i!** all the best!

'aula *sf* (*scolastica*) classroom; (*universitaria*) lecture theatre; (*di edificio pubblico*) hall

aumen'tare *vt, vi* to increase; **au'mento** *sm* increase

au'reola *sf* halo

au'rora *sf* dawn

ausili'are *ag, sm, sm/f* auxiliary

aus'picio [aus'pitʃo] *sm* omen; (*protezione*) patronage; **sotto gli ~i di** under the auspices of

aus'tero, a *ag* austere

Aus'tralia *sf*: **l'~** Australia; **australi'ano, a** *ag, sm/f* Australian

'Austria *sf*: **l'~** Austria; **aus'triaco, a, ci, che** *ag, sm/f* Austrian

au'tentico, a, ci, che *ag* authentic, genuine

au'tista, i *sm* driver

'auto *sf inv* car

autoabbronzante *sm, ag* self-tan

autoade'sivo, a *ag* self-adhesive ♦ *sm* sticker

autobiogra'fia *sf* autobiography

auto'botte *sf* tanker

'autobus *sm inv* bus

auto'carro *sm* lorry (*BRIT*), truck

autocorri'era *sf* coach, bus

au'tografo, a *ag, sm* autograph

auto'grill ® *sm inv* motorway restaurant

autogrù *sf inv* breakdown van

auto'linea *sf* bus company

au'toma, i *sm* automaton

auto'matico, a, ci, che *ag* automatic ♦ *sm* (*bottone*) snap fastener; (*fucile*) automatic

automazi'one [automat'tsjone] *sf* automation

auto'mezzo [auto'mɛddzo] *sm* motor vehicle

auto'mobile *sf* (motor) car

automobi'lista, i, e *sm/f* motorist

autono'leggio *sm* car hire

autono'mia *sf* autonomy; (*di volo*) range

au'tonomo, a *ag* autonomous, independent

autop'sia *sf* post-mortem, autopsy

auto'radio *sf inv* (*apparecchio*) car radio; (*autoveicolo*) radio car

au'tore, 'trice *sm/f* author

auto'revole *ag* authoritative; (*persona*) influential

autori'messa *sf* garage

autorità *sf inv* authority

autoriz'zare [autorid'dzare] *vt* (*permettere*) to authorize; (*giustificare*) to allow, sanction; **autorizzazi'one** *sf* authorization

autoscu'ola *sf* driving school

autos'top *sm* hitchhiking; **autostop'pista, i, e** *sm/f* hitchhiker

autos'trada *sf* motorway (*BRIT*), highway (*US*)

auto'treno *sm* articulated lorry (*BRIT*), semi (trailer) (*US*)

autove'icolo *sm* motor vehicle

auto'velox ® *sm inv* (police) speed camera

autovet'tura *sf* (motor) car

au'tunno *sm* autumn

avam'braccio [avam'brattʃo] (*pl* (*f*) **-cia**) *sm* forearm

avangu'ardia *sf* vanguard

a'vanti *av* (*stato in luogo*) in front; (*moto: andare, venire*) forward; (*tempo: prima*) before ♦ *prep* (*luogo*): **~ a** before, in front of; (*tempo*): **~ Cristo** before Christ ♦ *escl* (*entrate*) come (o *go*) in!; (*MIL*) forward!; (*coraggio*) come on! ♦ *sm inv* (*SPORT*) forward; **~ e indietro** backwards and forwards; **andare ~** to go forward; (*continuare*) to go on; (*precedere*) to go (on) ahead; (*orologio*) to be fast; **essere ~ negli studi** to be well advanced with one's studies

avanza'mento [avantsa'mento] *sm* progress; promotion

avan'zare [avan'tsare] *vt* (*spostare in avanti*) to move forward, advance; (*domanda*) to put forward; (*promuovere*) to promote; (*essere creditore*): ~ **qc da qn** to be owed sth by sb ♦ *vi* (*andare avanti*) to move forward, advance; (*progredire*) to make progress; (*essere d'avanzo*) to be left, remain; **avan'zata** *sf* (MIL) advance; a'**vanzo** *sm* (*residuo*) remains *pl*, left-overs *pl*; (MAT) remainder; (COMM) surplus; **averne d'avanzo di qc** to have more than enough of sth; **avanzo di galera** jailbird

ava'ria *sf* (*guasto*) damage; (: *meccanico*) breakdown

a'varo, a *ag* avaricious, miserly ♦ *sm* miser

a'vena *sf* oats *pl*

PAROLA CHIAVE

a'vere *sm* (COMM) credit; **gli ~i** (*ricchezze*) wealth *sg*

♦ *vt* **1** (*possedere*) to have; **ha due bambini/una bella casa** she has (got) two children/a lovely house; **ha i capelli lunghi** he has (got) long hair; **non ho da mangiare/bere** I've (got) nothing to eat/drink, I don't have anything to eat/drink

2 (*indossare*) to wear, have on; **aveva una maglietta rossa** he was wearing *o* he had on a red tee-shirt; **ha gli occhiali** he wears *o* has glasses

3 (*ricevere*) to get; **hai avuto l'assegno?** did you get *o* have you had the cheque?

4 (*età, dimensione*) to be; **ha 9 anni** he is 9 (years old); **la stanza ha 3 metri di lunghezza** the room is 3 metres in length; *vedi* **fame**; **paura** *etc*

5 (*tempo*): **quanti ne abbiamo oggi?** what's the date today?; **ne hai per molto?** will you be long?

6 (*fraseologia*): **avercela con qn** to be angry with sb; **cos'hai?** what's wrong *o* what's the matter (with you)?; **non ha niente a che vedere *o* fare con me** it's got nothing to do with me

♦ *vb aus* **1** to have; **aver bevuto/**

mangiato to have drunk/eaten

2 (+*da* +*infinito*): ~ **da fare qc** to have to do sth; **non hai che da chiederlo** you only have to ask him

---

'avi *smpl* ancestors, forefathers

aviazi'one [avjat'tsjone] *sf* aviation; (MIL) air force

avidità *sf* eagerness; greed

'avido, a *ag* eager; (*peg*) greedy

avo'cado *sm* avocado

a'vorio *sm* ivory

Avv. *abbr* = **avvocato**

avvalla'mento *sm* sinking *no pl*; (*effetto*) depression

avvalo'rare *vt* to confirm

avvam'pare *vi* (*incendio*) to flare up

avvantaggi'are [avvantad'dʒare] *vt* to favour; **~rsi** *vr*: **~rsi negli affari/sui concorrenti** to get ahead in business/of one's competitors

avvele'nare *vt* to poison

avve'nente *ag* attractive, charming

avveni'mento *sm* event

avve'nire *vi, vb impers* to happen, occur ♦ *sm* future

avven'tarsi *vr*: ~ **su** *o* **contro qn/qc** to hurl o.s. *o* rush at sb/sth

avven'tato, a *ag* rash, reckless

avven'tizio, a [avven'tittsjo] *ag* (*impiegato*) temporary; (*guadagno*) casual

av'vento *sm* advent, coming; (REL): **l'A~** Advent

avven'tore *sm* (regular) customer

avven'tura *sf* adventure; (*amorosa*) affair

avventu'rarsi *vr* to venture

avventu'roso, a *ag* adventurous

avve'rarsi *vr* to come true

av'verbio *sm* adverb

avver'sario, a *ag* opposing ♦ *sm* opponent, adversary

av'verso, a *ag* (*contrario*) contrary; (*sfavorevole*) unfavourable

avver'tenza [avver'tentsa] *sf* (*ammonimento*) warning; (*cautela*) care; (*premessa*) foreword; **~e** *sfpl* (*istruzioni per l'uso*) instructions

avverti'mento *sm* warning

avver'tire *vt* (*avvisare*) to warn; (*rendere consapevole*) to inform, notify; (*percepire*) to feel

av'vezzo, a [av'vettso] *ag*: ~ **a** used to

avvia'mento *sm* (*atto*) starting; (*effetto*) start; (*AUT*) starting; (*: dispositivo*) starter; (*COMM*) goodwill

avvi'are *vt* (*mettere sul cammino*) to direct; (*impresa, trattative*) to begin, start; (*motore*) to start; ~**rsi** *vr* to set off, set out

avvicen'darsi [avvitʃen'darsi] *vr* to alternate

avvici'nare [avvitʃi'nare] *vt* to bring near; (*trattare con: persona*) to approach; ~**rsi** *vr*: ~**rsi (a qn/qc)** to approach (sb/sth), draw near (to sb/sth)

avvi'lire *vt* (*umiliare*) to humiliate; (*degradare*) to disgrace; (*scoraggiare*) to dishearten, discourage; ~**rsi** *vr* (*abbattersi*) to lose heart

avvilup'pare *vt* (*avvolgere*) to wrap up

avvinaz'zato, a [avvinat'tsato] *ag* drunk

avvin'cente *ag* captivating

av'vincere [av'vintʃere] *vt* to charm, enthral

avvinghi'are [avvin'gjare] *vt* to clasp; ~**rsi** *vr*: ~**rsi a** to cling to

avvi'sare *vt* (*far sapere*) to inform; (*mettere in guardia*) to warn; **av'viso** *sm* warning; (*annuncio*) announcement; (*: affiso*) notice; (*inserzione pubblicitaria*) advertisement; **a mio avviso** in my opinion; **avviso di chiamata** (*TEL*) call waiting service

avvis'tare *vt* to sight

avvi'tare *vt* to screw down (*o* in)

avviz'zire [avvit'tsire] *vi* to wither

avvo'cato, 'essa *sm/f* (*DIR*) barrister (*BRIT*), lawyer; (*fig*) defender, advocate

av'volgere [av'voldʒere] *vt* to roll up; (*avviluppare*) to wrap up; ~**rsi** *vr* (*avvilupparsi*) to wrap o.s. up; **avvol'gibile** *sm* roller blind (*BRIT*), blind

avvol'toio *sm* vulture

azi'enda [ad'dzjɛnda] *sf* business, firm, concern; ~ **agricola** farm

azio'nare [attsjo'nare] *vt* to activate

azi'one [at'tsjone] *sf* action; (*COMM*) share; **azio'nista, i, e** *sm/f* (*COMM*) shareholder

a'zoto [ad'dzɔto] *sm* nitrogen

azzan'nare [attsan'nare] *vt* to sink one's teeth into

azzar'darsi [addzar'darsi] *vr*: ~ **a fare** to dare (to) do; **azzar'dato, a** *ag* (*impresa*) risky; (*risposta*) rash

az'zardo [ad'dzardo] *sm* risk

azzec'care [attsek'kare] *vt* (*risposta etc*) to get right

azzuf'farsi [attsuf'farsi] *vr* to come to blows

az'zurro, a [ad'dzurro] *ag* blue ♦ *sm* (*colore*) blue; **gli ~i** (*SPORT*) the Italian national team

B, b

bab'beo *sm* simpleton

'babbo *sm* (*fam*) dad, daddy; **B~ Natale** Father Christmas

bab'buccia, ce [bab'buttʃa] *sf* slipper; (*per neonati*) bootee

ba'bordo *sm* (*NAUT*) port side

ba'cato, a *ag* worm-eaten, rotten

'bacca, che *sf* berry

baccalà *sm* dried salted cod; (*fig: peg*) dummy

bac'cano *sm* din, clamour

bac'cello [bat'tʃello] *sm* pod

bac'chetta [bak'ketta] *sf* (*verga*) stick, rod; (*di direttore d'orchestra*) baton; (*di tamburo*) drumstick; ~ **magica** magic wand

baci'are [ba'tʃare] *vt* to kiss; ~**rsi** *vr* to kiss (one another)

baci'nella [batʃi'nɛlla] *sf* basin

ba'cino [ba'tʃino] *sm* basin; (*MINERALOGIA*) field, bed; (*ANAT*) pelvis; (*NAUT*) dock

'bacio ['batʃo] *sm* kiss

'baco, chi *sm* worm; ~ **da seta** silkworm

ba'dare *vi* (*fare attenzione*) to take care, be careful; (*occuparsi di*): ~ **a** to look after, take care of; (*dar ascolto*): ~ **a** to pay attention to; **bada ai fatti tuoi!** mind your

own business!
ba'dia *sf* abbey
ba'dile *sm* shovel
'baffi *smpl* moustache *sg*; (*di animale*) whiskers; **ridere sotto i ~** to laugh up one's sleeve; **leccarsi i ~** to lick one's lips
ba'gagli [ba'gaʎʎi] *smpl* luggage *sg*; **fare i ~** to pack
bagagli'aio [bagaʎ'ʎajo] *sm* luggage van (*BRIT*) *o* car (*US*); (*AUT*) boot (*BRIT*), trunk (*US*)
bagli'ore [baʎ'ʎore] *sm* flash, dazzling light; **un ~ di speranza** a ray of hope
ba'gnante [baɲ'ɲante] *sm/f* bather
ba'gnare [baɲ'ɲare] *vt* to wet; (*inzuppare*) to soak; (*innaffiare*) to water; (*sog: fiume*) to flow through; (*: mare*) to wash, bathe; **~rsi** *vr* to get wet; (*al mare*) to go swimming *o* bathing; (*in vasca*) to have a bath
ba'gnato, a [baɲ'ɲato] *ag* wet
ba'gnino [baɲ'ɲino] *sm* lifeguard
'bagno ['baɲɲo] *sm* bath; (*locale*) bathroom; **~i** *smpl* (*stabilimento*) baths; **fare il ~** to have a bath; (*nel mare*) to go swimming *o* bathing; **fare il ~ a qn** to give sb a bath; **mettere a ~** to soak; **~ schiuma** bubble bath
bagnoma'ria [baɲɲoma'ria] *sm*: **cuocere a ~** to cook in a double saucepan
'baia *sf* bay
baio'netta *sf* bayonet
balbet'tare *vi* to stutter, stammer; (*bimbo*) to babble ♦ *vt* to stammer out
balbuzi'ente [balbut'tsjente] *ag* stuttering, stammering
bal'cone *sm* balcony
baldac'chino [baldak'kino] *sm* canopy
bal'danza [bal'dantsa] *sf* self-confidence
'baldo, a *ag* bold, daring
bal'doria *sf*: **fare ~** to have a riotous time
ba'lena *sf* whale
bale'nare *vb impers*: **balena** there's lightning ♦ *vi* to flash; **mi balenò un'idea** an idea flashed through my mind; **ba'leno** *sm* flash of lightning; **in un baleno** in a flash

ba'lestra *sf* crossbow
ba'lia *sf*: **in ~ di** at the mercy of
'balla *sf* (*di merci*) bale; (*fandonia*) (tall) story
bal'lare *vt, vi* to dance; **bal'lata** *sf* ballad
balle'rina *sf* dancer; ballet dancer; (*scarpa*) ballet shoe
balle'rino *sm* dancer; ballet dancer
bal'letto *sm* ballet
'ballo *sm* dance; (*azione*) dancing *no pl*; **essere in ~** (*fig: persona*) to be involved; (*: cosa*) to be at stake
ballot'taggio [ballot'taddʒo] *sm* (*POL*) second ballot
balne'are *ag* seaside *cpd*; (*stagione*) bathing
balneazi'one *sf* bathing; **è vietata la ~** bathing strictly prohibited
ba'locco, chi *sm* toy
ba'lordo, a *ag* stupid, senseless
'balsamo *sm* (*aroma*) balsam; (*lenimento, fig*) balm
balu'ardo *sm* bulwark
'balza ['baltsa] *sf* (*dirupo*) crag; (*di stoffa*) frill
bal'zare [bal'tsare] *vi* to bounce; (*lanciarsi*) to jump, leap; **'balzo** *sm* bounce; jump, leap; (*del terreno*) crag
bam'bagia [bam'baddʒa] *sf* (*ovatta*) cotton wool (*BRIT*), absorbent cotton (*US*); (*cascame*) cotton waste
bam'bina *ag, sf vedi* **bambino**
bambi'naia *sf* nanny, nurse(maid)
bam'bino, a *sm/f* child
bam'boccio [bam'bɔttʃo] *sm* plump child; (*pupazzo*) rag doll
'bambola *sf* doll
bambù *sm* bamboo
ba'nale *ag* banal, commonplace
ba'nana *sf* banana; **ba'nano** *sm* banana tree
'banca, che *sf* bank; **~ dei dati** data bank
banca'rella *sf* stall
ban'cario, a *ag* banking, bank *cpd* ♦ *sm* bank clerk
banca'rotta *sf* bankruptcy; **fare ~** to go bankrupt

ban'chetto [ban'ketto] *sm* banquet

banchi'ere [ban'kjere] *sm* banker

ban'china [ban'kina] *sf* (*di porto*) quay; (*per pedoni, ciclisti*) path; (*di stazione*) platform; **~ cedevole** (*AUT*) soft verge (*BRIT*) *o* shoulder (*US*)

'banco, chi *sm* bench; (*di negozio*) counter; (*di mercato*) stall; (*di officina*) (work-)bench; (*GEO, banca*) bank; **~ di corallo** coral reef; **~ degli imputati** dock; **~ dei pegni** pawnshop; **~ di prova** (*fig*) testing ground; **~ dei testimoni** witness box

'Bancomat ® *sm inv* automated banking; (*tessera*) cash card

banco'nota *sf* banknote

'banda *sf* band; (*di stoffa*) band, stripe; (*lato, parte*) side; **~ perforata** punch tape

banderu'ola *sf* (*METEOR*) weathercock

bandi'era *sf* flag, banner

ban'dire *vt* to proclaim; (*esiliare*) to exile; (*fig*) to dispense with

ban'dito *sm* outlaw, bandit

bandi'tore *sm* (*di aste*) auctioneer

'bando *sm* proclamation; (*esilio*) exile, banishment; **~ alle chiacchiere!** that's enough talk!

'bandolo *sm*: **il ~ della matassa** (*fig*) the key to the problem

bar *sm inv* bar

'bara *sf* coffin

ba'racca, che *sf* shed, hut; (*peg*) hovel; **mandare avanti la ~** to keep things going

bara'onda *sf* hubbub, bustle

ba'rare *vi* to cheat

'baratro *sm* abyss

barat'tare *vt*: **~ qc con** to barter sth for, swap sth for; **ba'ratto** *sm* barter

ba'rattolo *sm* (*di latta*) tin; (*di vetro*) jar; (*di coccio*) pot

'barba *sf* beard; **farsi la ~** to shave; **farla in ~ a qn** (*fig*) to do sth to sb's face; **che ~!** what a bore!

barbabi'etola *sf* beetroot (*BRIT*), beet (*US*); **~ da zucchero** sugar beet

bar'barico, a, ci, che *ag* barbarian; barbaric

'barbaro, a *ag* barbarous; **~i** *smpl* barbarians

barbi'ere *sm* barber

bar'bone *sm* (*cane*) poodle; (*vagabondo*) tramp

bar'buto, a *ag* bearded

'barca, che *sf* boat; **~ a remi** rowing boat; **~ a vela** sail(ing) boat; **barcai'olo** *sm* boatman

barcol'lare *vi* to stagger

bar'cone *sm* (*per ponti di barche*) pontoon

ba'rella *sf* (*lettiga*) stretcher

ba'rile *sm* barrel, cask

ba'rista, i, e *sm/f* barman/maid; (*proprietario*) bar owner

ba'ritono *sm* baritone

bar'lume *sm* glimmer, gleam

ba'rocco, a, chi, che *ag, sm* baroque

ba'rometro *sm* barometer

ba'rone *sm* baron; **baro'nessa** *sf* baroness

'barra *sf* bar; (*NAUT*) helm; (*linea grafica*) line, stroke; (*obliqua*) slash

barri'care *vt* to barricade; **barri'cata** *sf* barricade

barri'era *sf* barrier; (*GEO*) reef

ba'ruffa *sf* scuffle

barzel'letta [bardzel'letta] *sf* joke, funny story

ba'sare *vt* to base, found; **~rsi** *vr*: **~rsi su** (*sog: fatti, prove*) to be based *o* founded on; (*: persona*) to base one's arguments on

'basco, a, schi, sche *ag* Basque ♦ *sm* (*copricapo*) beret

'base *sf* base; (*fig: fondamento*) basis; (*POL*) rank and file; **di ~** basic; **in ~ a** on the basis of, according to; **a ~ di caffè** coffee-based

ba'setta *sf* sideburn

ba'silica, che *sf* basilica

ba'silico *sm* basil

bassi'fondi *smpl*: **i ~** the slums

bas'sista *sm/f* bass player

'basso, a *ag* low; (*di statura*) short; (*meridionale*) southern ♦ *sm* bottom, lower part; (*MUS*) bass; **la ~a Italia** southern Italy

bassorili'evo *sm* bas-relief

'basta *escl* (that's) enough!, that will do!

bas'tardo, a *ag* (*animale, pianta*) hybrid,

crossbreed; (*persona*) illegitimate, bastard (*peg*) ♦ *sm/f* illegitimate child, bastard (*peg*)

bas'tare *vi, vb impers* to be enough, be sufficient; **~ a qn** to be enough for sb; **basta chiedere** *o* **che chieda a un vigile** you have only to *o* need only ask a policeman

basti'mento *sm* ship, vessel

basto'nare *vt* to beat, thrash

baston'cino [baston't∫ino] *sm* (*SCI*) ski pole; **~i di pesce** fish fingers

bas'tone *sm* stick; **~ da passeggio** walking stick

bat'taglia [bat'taʎʎa] *sf* battle; fight

bat'taglio [bat'taʎʎo] *sm* (*di campana*) clapper; (*di porta*) knocker

battagli'one [battaʎ'ʎone] *sm* battalion

bat'tello *sm* boat

bat'tente *sm* (*imposta: di porta*) wing, flap; (*: di finestra*) shutter; (*batacchio: di porta*) knocker; (*: di orologio*) hammer; **chiudere i ~i** (*fig*) to shut up shop

'battere *vt* to beat; (*grano*) to thresh; (*percorrere*) to scour ♦ *vi* (*bussare*) to knock; (*urtare*): **~ contro** to hit *o* strike against; (*pioggia, sole*) to beat down; (*cuore*) to beat; (*TENNIS*) to serve; **~rsi** *vr* to fight; **~ le mani** to clap; **~ i piedi** to stamp one's feet; **~ a macchina** to type; **~ bandiera italiana** to fly the Italian flag; **~ in testa** (*AUT*) to knock; **in un batter d'occhio** in the twinkling of an eye

bat'teri *smpl* bacteria

batte'ria *sf* battery; (*MUS*) drums *pl*

batte'rista *sm/f* drummer

bat'tesimo *sm* (*rito*) baptism; christening

battez'zare [batted'dzare] *vt* to baptize; to christen

batticu'ore *sm* palpitations *pl*

batti'mano *sm* applause

batti'panni *sm inv* carpet-beater

battis'tero *sm* baptistry

battis'trada *sm inv* (*di pneumatico*) tread; (*di gara*) pacemaker

battitap'peto *sm* vacuum cleaner

'battito *sm* beat, throb; **~ cardiaco** heartbeat

bat'tuta *sf* blow; (*di macchina da scrivere*) stroke; (*MUS*) bar; beat; (*TEATRO*) cue; (*frase spiritosa*) witty remark; (*di caccia*) beating; (*POLIZIA*) combing, scouring; (*TENNIS*) service

ba'ule *sm* trunk; (*AUT*) boot (*BRIT*), trunk (*US*)

'bava *sf* (*di animale*) slaver, slobber; (*di lumaca*) slime; (*di vento*) breath

bava'glino [bavaʎ'ʎino] *sm* bib

ba'vaglio [ba'vaʎʎo] *sm* gag

'bavero *sm* collar

Bavi'era *sf* Bavaria

ba'zar [bad'dzar] *sm inv* bazaar

baz'zecola [bad'dzekola] *sf* trifle

bazzi'care [battsi'kare] *vt* to frequent ♦ *vi*: **~ in/con** to frequent

BCE *sigla f* (= *Banca Centrale Europa*) ECB

be'ato, a *ag* blessed; (*fig*) happy; **~ te!** lucky you!

bebè *sm inv* baby

bec'caccia, ce [bek'katt∫a] *sf* woodcock

bec'care *vt* to peck; (*fig: raffreddore*) to catch; **~rsi qc** to catch sth

bec'cata *sf* peck

beccheggi'are [bekked'dʒare] *vi* to pitch

bec'chino [bek'kino] *sm* gravedigger

'becco, chi *sm* beak, bill; (*di caffettiera etc*) spout; lip

Be'fana *sf see box*; (*Epifania*) Epiphany; (*donna brutta*): **b~** hag, witch

---

Befana

i The **Befana** *is a national holiday on the feast of the Epiphany. It takes its name from a legendary old woman,* la Befana, *who comes down the chimney during the night leaving gifts for children who have been good, and coal for those who have not.*

'beffa *sf* practical joke; **farsi ~e di qn** to make a fool of sb; **bef'fardo, a** *ag* scornful, mocking; **bef'fare** *vt* (*anche*: **beffarsi di**) to make a fool of, mock

'bega, ghe *sf* quarrel

'**begli** ['beʎʎi] *ag vedi* **bello**
'**bei** *ag vedi* **bello**
bel *ag vedi* **bello**
be'lare *vi* to bleat
'**belga, gi, ghe** *ag, sm/f* Belgian
'**Belgio** ['bɛldʒo] *sm*: **il ~** Belgium
bel'lezza [bel'lettsa] *sf* beauty
'**bella** *sf* (SPORT) decider; *vedi anche* **bello**

PAROLA CHIAVE

'**bello, a** (*ag: dav sm* **bel** +C, **bell'** +V,
bello +s *impura, gn, pn, ps, x, z, pl* **bei** +C,
begli +s *impura etc o V*) *ag* **1** (*oggetto,
donna, paesaggio*) beautiful, lovely; (*uomo*)
handsome; (*tempo*) beautiful, fine, lovely;
le belle arti fine arts
2 (*quantità*): **una ~a cifra** a considerable
sum of money; **un bel niente** absolutely
nothing
3 (*rafforzativo*): **è una truffa ~a e buona!**
it's a real fraud!; **è bell'e finito** it's already
finished
♦ *sm* **1** (*bellezza*) beauty; (*tempo*) fine
weather
2: **adesso viene il ~** now comes the best
bit; **sul più ~** at the crucial point; **cosa fai
di ~?** are you doing anything interesting?
♦ *av*: **fa ~** the weather is fine, it's fine

'**belva** *sf* wild animal
belve'dere *sm inv* panoramic viewpoint
benché [ben'ke] *cong* although
'**benda** *sf* bandage; (*per gli occhi*) blindfold;
ben'dare *vt* to bandage; to blindfold
'**bene** *av* well; (*completamente, affatto*): **è
ben difficile** it's very difficult ♦ *ag inv*:
gente ~ well-to-do people ♦ *sm* good; **~i**
smpl (*averi*) property *sg*, estate *sg*; **io sto
~/poco ~** I'm well/not very well; **va ~** all
right; **volere un ~ dell'anima a qn** to love
sb very much; **un uomo per ~** a
respectable man; **fare ~** to do the right
thing; **fare ~ a** (*salute*) to be good for; **fare
del ~ a qn** to do sb a good turn; **~i di
consumo** consumer goods
bene'detto, a *pp di* **benedire** ♦ *ag*
blessed, holy

bene'dire *vt* to bless; to consecrate;
benedizi'one *sf* blessing
benedu'cato, a *ag* well-mannered
benefi'cenza [benefi'tʃɛntsa] *sf* charity
bene'ficio [bene'fitʃo] *sm* benefit; **con ~
d'inventario** (*fig*) with reservations
be'nefico, a, ci, che *ag* beneficial;
charitable
beneme'renza [beneme'rɛntsa] *sf* merit
bene'merito, a *ag* meritorious
be'nessere *sm* well-being
benes'tante *ag* well-to-do
benes'tare *sm* consent, approval
be'nevolo, a *ag* benevolent
be'nigno, a [be'niɲɲo] *ag* kind, kindly;
(*critica etc*) favourable; (MED) benign
benin'teso *av* of course
bensì *cong* but (rather)
benve'nuto, a *ag, sm* welcome; **dare il ~
a qn** to welcome sb
ben'zina [ben'dzina] *sf* petrol (BRIT), gas
(US); **fare ~** to get petrol (BRIT) o gas (US); **~
verde** unleaded (petrol); **benzi'naio** *sm*
petrol (BRIT) o gas (US) pump attendant
'**bere** *vt* to drink; **darla a ~ a qn** (*fig*) to
fool sb
ber'lina *sf* (AUT) saloon (car) (BRIT), sedan
(US)
Ber'lino *sf* Berlin
ber'noccolo *sm* bump; (*inclinazione*) flair
ber'retto *sm* cap
bersagli'are [bersaʎ'ʎare] *vt* to shoot at;
(*colpire ripetutamente, fig*) to bombard
ber'saglio [ber'saʎʎo] *sm* target
bes'temmia *sf* curse; (REL) blasphemy
bestemmi'are *vi* to curse, swear; to
blaspheme ♦ *vt* to curse, swear at; to
blaspheme
'**bestia** *sf* animal; **andare in ~** (*fig*) to fly
into a rage; **besti'ale** *ag* beastly; animal
cpd; (*fam*): **fa un freddo bestiale** it's
bitterly cold; **besti'ame** *sm* livestock;
(*bovino*) cattle *pl*
'**bettola** (*peg*) *sf* dive
be'tulla *sf* birch
be'vanda *sf* drink, beverage
bevi'tore, 'trice *sm/f* drinker

be'vuta *sf* drink
be'vuto, a *pp di* **bere**
bi'ada *sf* fodder
bianche'ria [bjanke'ria] *sf* linen; **~ intima**
underwear; **~ da donna** ladies' underwear,
lingerie
bi'anco, a, chi, che *ag* white; (*non
scritto*) blank ♦ *sm* white; (*intonaco*)
whitewash ♦ *sm/f* white, white man/
woman; **in ~** (*foglio, assegno*) blank; (*notte*)
sleepless; **in ~ e nero** (*TV, FOT*) black and
white; **mangiare in ~** to follow a bland
diet; **pesce in ~** boiled fish; **andare in ~**
(*non riuscire*) to fail; **~ dell'uovo** egg-white
biasi'mare *vt* to disapprove of, censure;
bi'asimo *sm* disapproval, censure
'bibbia *sf* (*anche fig*) bible
bibe'ron *sm inv* feeding bottle
'bibita *sf* (soft) drink
biblio'teca, che *sf* library; (*mobile*)
bookcase; **bibliote'cario, a** *sm/f* librarian
bicarbo'nato *sm*: **~ (di sodio)**
bicarbonate (of soda)
bicchi'ere [bik'kjɛre] *sm* glass
bici'cletta [bitʃi'kletta] *sf* bicycle; **andare in
~** to cycle
bidé *sm inv* bidet
bi'dello, a *sm/f* (*INS*) janitor
bi'done *sm* drum, can; (*anche: ~
dell'immondizia*) (dust)bin; (*fam: truffa*)
swindle; **fare un ~ a qn** (*fam*) to let sb
down; to cheat sb
bien'nale *ag* biennial

Biennale di Venezia

ⓘ The **Biennale di Venezia** *is an
international contemporary art festival,
which takes place every two years at
Giardini. In its current form, it includes
exhibits from the countries taking part, a
thematic exhibition and a section for young
artists.*

---

bi'ennio *sm* period of two years
bi'etola *sf* beet
bifor'carsi *vr* to fork; **biforcazi'one** *sf*
fork

bighello'nare [bigello'nare] *vi* to loaf
(about)
bigiotte'ria [bidʒotte'ria] *sf* costume
jewellery; (*negozio*) jeweller's (*selling only
costume jewellery*)
bigli'ardo [biʎ'ʎardo] *sm* = **biliardo**
bigliet'taio, a *sm/f* (*in treno*) ticket
inspector; (*in autobus*) conductor
bigliette'ria [biʎʎette'ria] *sf* (*di stazione*)
ticket office; booking office; (*di teatro*) box
office
bigli'etto [biʎ'ʎetto] *sm* (*per viaggi,
spettacoli etc*) ticket; (*cartoncino*) card;
(*anche: ~ di banca*) (bank)note; **~
d'auguri/da visita** greetings/visiting card;
~ d'andata e ritorno return (ticket),
round-trip ticket (*US*)
bignè [biɲ'ɲe] *sm inv* cream puff
bigo'dino *sm* roller, curler
bi'gotto, a *ag* over-pious ♦ *sm/f* church
fiend
bi'lancia, ce [bi'lantʃa] *sf* (*pesa*) scales *pl*;
(: *di precisione*) balance; (*dello zodiaco*): **B~**
Libra; **~ commerciale/dei pagamenti**
balance of trade/payments; **bilanci'are** *vt*
(*pesare*) to weigh; (: *fig*) to weigh up;
(*pareggiare*) to balance
bi'lancio [bi'lantʃo] *sm* (*COMM*) balance
(-sheet); (*statale*) budget; **fare il ~ di** (*fig*)
to assess; **~ consuntivo** (final) balance; **~
preventivo** budget
'bile *sf* bile; (*fig*) rage, anger
bili'ardo *sm* billiards *sg*; billiard table
'bilico, chi *sm*: **essere in ~** to be
balanced; **tenere qn in ~** (*fig*) to keep sb in
suspense
bi'lingue *ag* bilingual
bili'one *sm* (*mille milioni*) thousand million;
(*milione di milioni*) billion (*BRIT*), trillion (*US*)
'bimbo, a *sm/f* little boy/girl
bimen'sile *ag* fortnightly
bimes'trale *ag* two-monthly, bimonthly
bi'nario, a *ag* (*sistema*) binary ♦ *sm*
(*railway*) track *o* line; (*piattaforma*)
platform; **~ morto** dead-end track
bi'nocolo *sm* binoculars *pl*
bio... *prefisso*: **bio'chimica** [bio'kimika] *sf*

biochemistry; **biodegra'dabile** *ag* biodegradable; **biogra'fia** *sf* biography; **biolo'gia** *sf* biology; **bio'logico, a, ci, che** *ag* biological

bi'ondo, a *ag* blond, fair

bir'bante *sm* rogue, rascal

biri'chino, a [biri'kino] *ag* mischievous ♦ *sm/f* scamp, little rascal

bi'rillo *sm* skittle (*BRIT*), pin (*US*); **~i** *smpl* (*gioco*) skittles *sg* (*BRIT*), bowling (*US*)

'biro ® *sf inv* biro ®

'birra *sf* beer; **a tutta ~** (*fig*) at top speed; **birra chiara** ≈ lager; **birra scura** ≈ stout; **birre'ria** *sf* ≈ bierkeller

bis *escl, sm inv* encore

bis'betico, a, ci, che *ag* ill-tempered, crabby

bisbigli'are [bisbiʎ'ʎare] *vt, vi* to whisper

'bisca, sche *sf* gambling-house

'biscia, sce ['biʃʃa] *sf* snake; **~ d'acqua** grass snake

bis'cotto *sm* biscuit

bises'tile *ag*: **anno ~** leap year

bis'lungo, a, ghi, ghe *ag* oblong

bis'nonno, a *sm/f* great grandfather/ grandmother

biso'gnare [bizoɲ'ɲare] *vb impers*: **bisogna che tu parta/lo faccia** you'll have to go/ do it; **bisogna parlargli** we'll (*o* I'll) have to talk to him

bi'sogno [bi'zoɲɲo] *sm* need; **~i** *smpl*: **fare i propri ~i** to relieve o.s.; **avere ~ di qc/di fare qc** to need sth/to do sth; **al ~, in caso di ~** if need be; **biso'gnoso, a** *ag* needy, poor; **bisognoso di** in need of, needing

bis'tecca, che *sf* steak, beefsteak

bisticci'are [bistit'tʃare] *vi* to quarrel, bicker, **~rsi** *vr* to quarrel, bicker; **bis'ticcio** *sm* quarrel, squabble; (*gioco di parole*) pun

'bisturi *sm* scalpel

bi'sunto, a *ag* very greasy

'bitter *sm inv* bitters *pl*

bi'vacco, chi *sm* bivouac

'bivio *sm* fork; (*fig*) dilemma

'bizza ['biddza] *sf* tantrum; **fare le ~e**

(*bambino*) to be naughty

biz'zarro, a [bid'dzarro] *ag* bizarre, strange

biz'zeffe [bid'dzɛffe]: **a ~** *av* in plenty, galore

blan'dire *vt* to soothe; to flatter

'blando, a *ag* mild, gentle

bla'sone *sm* coat of arms

blate'rare *vi* to chatter

blin'dato, a *ag* armoured

bloc'care *vt* to block; (*isolare*) to isolate, cut off; (*porto*) to blockade; (*prezzi, beni*) to freeze; (*meccanismo*) to jam; **~rsi** *vr* (*motore*) to stall; (*freni, porta*) to jam, stick; (*ascensore*) to stop, get stuck

bloc'chetto [blok'ketto] *sm* notebook; (*di biglietti*) book

'blocco, chi *sm* block; (*MIL*) blockade; (*dei fitti*) restriction; (*quadernetto*) pad; (*fig: unione*) coalition; (*il bloccare*) blocking; isolating, cutting-off; blockading; freezing; jamming; **in ~** (*nell'insieme*) as a whole; (*COMM*) in bulk; **~ cardiaco** cardiac arrest

blu *ag inv, sm* dark blue

'blusa *sf* (*camiciotto*) smock; (*camicetta*) blouse

'boa *sm inv* (*ZOOL*) boa constrictor; (*sciarpa*) feather boa ♦ *sf* buoy

bo'ato *sm* rumble, roar

bo'bina *sf* reel, spool; (*di pellicola*) spool; (*di film*) reel; (*ELETTR*) coil

'bocca, che *sf* mouth; **in ~ al lupo!** good luck!

boc'caccia, ce [bok'kattʃa] *sf* (*malalingua*) gossip; **fare le ~ce** to pull faces

boc'cale *sm* jug; **~ da birra** tankard

boc'cetta [bot'tʃetta] *sf* small bottle

boccheggi'are [bokked'dʒare] *vi* to gasp

boc'chino [bok'kino] *sm* (*di sigaretta, sigaro: cannella*) cigarette-holder; cigar-holder; (*di pipa, strumenti musicali*) mouthpiece

'boccia, ce ['bottʃa] *sf* bottle; (*da vino*) decanter, carafe; (*palla*) bowl; **gioco delle ~ce** bowls *sg*

bocci'are [bot'tʃare] *vt* (*proposta, progetto*) to reject; (*INS*) to fail; (*BOCCE*) to hit; **boccia'tura** *sf* failure

bocci'olo [bot'tʃɔlo] *sm* bud

boc'cone *sm* mouthful, morsel

boc'coni *av* face downwards

'boia *sm inv* executioner; hangman

boi'ata *sf* botch

boicot'tare *vt* to boycott

'bolide *sm* meteor; **come un ~** like a flash, at top speed

'bolla *sf* bubble; (*MED*) blister; **~ papale** papal bull; **~ di consegna** (*COMM*) delivery note

bol'lare *vt* to stamp; (*fig*) to brand

bol'lente *ag* boiling; boiling hot

bol'letta *sf* bill; (*ricevuta*) receipt; **essere in ~** to be hard up

bollet'tino *sm* bulletin; (*COMM*) note; **~ meteorologico** weather report; **~ di spedizione** consignment note

bol'lire *vt, vi* to boil; **bol'lito** *sm* (*CUC*) boiled meat

bolli'tore *sm* (*CUC*) kettle; (*per riscaldamento*) boiler

'bollo *sm* stamp; **~ per patente** driving licence tax

'bomba *sf* bomb; **~ atomica** atom bomb

bombarda'mento *sm* bombardment; bombing

bombar'dare *vt* to bombard; (*da aereo*) to bomb

bombardi'ere *sm* bomber

bom'betta *sf* bowler (hat)

'bombola *sf* cylinder

bo'naccia, ce [bo'nattʃa] *sf* dead calm

bo'nario, a *ag* good-natured, kind

bo'nifica, che *sf* reclamation; reclaimed land

bo'nifico, ci *sm* (*riduzione, abbuono*) discount; (*versamento a terzi*) credit transfer

bontà *sf* goodness; (*cortesia*) kindness; **aver la ~ di fare qc** to be good *o* kind enough to do sth

borbot'tare *vi* to mumble

'borchia ['bɔrkja] *sf* stud

borda'tura *sf* (*SARTORIA*) border, trim

bor'deaux [bɔr'dɔ] *ag inv, sm inv* maroon

'bordo *sm* (*NAUT*) ship's side; (*orlo*) edge; (*striscia di guarnizione*) border, trim; **a ~ di** (*nave, aereo*) aboard, on board; (*macchina*) in

bor'gata *sf* (*in campagna*) hamlet

bor'ghese [bor'geze] *ag* (*spesso peg*) middle-class; bourgeois; **abito ~** civilian dress; **borghe'sia** *sf* middle classes *pl*; bourgeoisie

'borgo, ghi *sm* (*paesino*) village; (*quartiere*) district; (*sobborgo*) suburb

'boria *sf* self-conceit, arrogance

boro'talco *sm* talcum powder

bor'raccia, ce [bor'rattʃa] *sf* canteen, water-bottle

'borsa *sf* bag; (*anche: ~ da signora*) handbag; (*ECON*): **la B~ (valori)** the Stock Exchange; **~ nera** black market; **~ della spesa** shopping bag; **~ di studio** grant; **borsai'olo** *sm* pickpocket; **borsel'lino** *sm* purse; **bor'setta** *sf* handbag; **bor'sista, i, e** *sm/f* (*ECON*) speculator; (*INS*) grant-holder

bos'caglia [bos'kaʎʎa] *sf* woodlands *pl*

boscai'olo *sm* woodcutter; forester

'bosco, schi *sm* wood; **bos'coso, a** *ag* wooded

'bossolo *sm* cartridge-case

bo'tanica *sf* botany

bo'tanico, a, ci, che *ag* botanical ♦ *sm* botanist

'botola *sf* trap door

'botta *sf* blow; (*rumore*) bang

'botte *sf* barrel, cask

bot'tega, ghe *sf* shop; (*officina*) workshop; **botte'gaio, a** *sm/f* shopkeeper; **botte'ghino** *sm* ticket office; (*del lotto*) public lottery office

bot'tiglia [bot'tiʎʎa] *sf* bottle; **bottiglie'ria** *sf* wine shop

bot'tino *sm* (*di guerra*) booty; (*di rapina, furto*) loot

'botto *sm* bang; crash; **di ~** suddenly

bot'tone *sm* button; **attaccare ~ a qn** (*fig*) to buttonhole sb

bo'vino, a *ag* bovine; **~i** *smpl* cattle

boxe [bɔks] *sf* boxing

'bozza ['bɔttsa] *sf* draft; sketch; (*TIP*) proof; **boz'zetto** *sm* sketch

'**bozzolo** ['bɔttsolo] *sm* cocoon
BR *sigla fpl* = **Brigate Rosse**
brac'care *vt* to hunt
brac'cetto [brat'tʃetto] *sm*: **a ~** arm in arm
bracci'ale [brat'tʃale] *sm* bracelet; (*distintivo*) armband; **braccia'letto** *sm* bracelet, bangle
bracci'ante [brat'tʃante] *sm* (*AGR*) day labourer
bracci'ata [brat'tʃata] *sf* (*nel nuoto*) stroke
'**braccio** ['brattʃo] (*pl(f)* **braccia**) *sm* (*ANAT*) arm; (*pl(m)* **bracci**: *di gru, fiume*) arm; (*: di edificio*) wing; **~ di mare** sound; **bracci'olo** *sm* (*appoggio*) arm
'**bracco, chi** *sm* hound
bracconi'ere *sm* poacher
'**brace** ['bratʃe] *sf* embers *pl*; **braci'ere** *sm* brazier
braci'ola [bra'tʃɔla] *sf* (*CUC*) chop
bra'mare *vt*: **~ qc/di fare** to long for sth/ to do
'**branca, che** *sf* branch
'**branchia** ['brankja] *sf* (*ZOOL*) gill
'**branco, chi** *sm* (*di cani, lupi*) pack; (*di pecore*) flock; (*peg: di persone*) gang, pack
branco'lare *vi* to grope, feel one's way
'**branda** *sf* camp bed
bran'dello *sm* scrap, shred; **a ~i** in tatters, in rags
bran'dire *vt* to brandish
'**brano** *sm* piece; (*di libro*) passage
bra'sato *sm* braised beef
Bra'sile *sm*: **il ~** Brazil; **brasili'ano, a** *ag, sm/f* Brazilian
'**bravo, a** *ag* (*abile*) clever, capable, skilful; (*buono*) good, honest; (*: bambino*) good; (*coraggioso*) brave; **~!** well done!; (*a teatro*) bravo!
bra'vura *sf* cleverness, skill
'**breccia, ce** ['brettʃa] *sf* breach
bre'tella *sf* (*AUT*) link; **~e** *sfpl* (*di calzoni*) braces
'**breve** *ag* brief, short; **in ~** in short
brevet'tare *vt* to patent
bre'vetto *sm* patent; **~ di pilotaggio** pilot's licence (*BRIT*) o license (*US*)
'**brezza** ['breddza] *sf* breeze

'**bricco, chi** *sm* jug; **~ del caffè** coffeepot
bric'cone, a *sm/f* rogue, rascal
briciola ['britʃola] *sf* crumb
briciolo ['britʃolo] *sm* (*specie fig*) bit
'**briga, ghe** *sf* (*fastidio*) trouble, bother; **pigliarsi la ~ di fare qc** to take the trouble to do sth
brigadi'ere *sm* (*dei carabinieri etc*) ≈ sergeant
bri'gante *sm* bandit
bri'gata *sf* (*MIL*) brigade; (*gruppo*) group, party; **B~e Rosse** (*POL*) Red Brigades
'**briglia** ['briʎʎa] *sf* rein; **a ~ sciolta** at full gallop; (*fig*) at full speed
bril'lante *ag* bright; (*anche fig*) brilliant; (*che luccica*) shining ♦ *sm* diamond
bril'lare *vi* to shine; (*mina*) to blow up ♦ *vt* (*mina*) to set off
'**brillo, a** *ag* merry, tipsy
'**brina** *sf* hoarfrost
brin'dare *vi*: **~ a qn/qc** to drink to *o* toast sb/sth
'**brindisi** *sm inv* toast
'**brio** *sm* liveliness, go
bri'oche [bri'ɔʃ] *sf inv* brioche
bri'oso, a *ag* lively
bri'tannico, a, ci, che *ag* British
'**brivido** *sm* shiver; (*di ribrezzo*) shudder; (*fig*) thrill
brizzo'lato, a [brittso'lato] *ag* (*persona*) going grey; (*barba, capelli*) greying
'**brocca, che** *sf* jug
broc'cato *sm* brocade
'**broccolo** *sm* broccoli *sg*
'**brodo** *sm* broth; (*per cucinare*) stock; **~ ristretto** consommé
brogli'accio [broʎ'ʎattʃo] *sm* scribbling pad
'**broglio** ['brɔʎʎo] *sm*: **~ elettorale** gerrymandering
bron'chite [bron'kite] *sf* (*MED*) bronchitis
'**broncio** ['brontʃo] *sm* sulky expression; **tenere il ~** to sulk
'**bronco, chi** *sm* bronchial tube
bronto'lare *vi* to grumble; (*tuono, stomaco*) to rumble
'**bronzo** ['brondzo] *sm* bronze

'browser ['brauzer] *sm inv* (*INFORM*)
browser

bru'care *vt* to browse on, nibble at

brucia'pelo [brutʃa'pelo]: **a ~** *av* point-blank

bruci'are [bru'tʃare] *vt* to burn; (*scottare*) to scald ♦ *vi* to burn; **brucia'tore** *sm* burner; **brucia'tura** *sf* (*atto*) burning *no pl*; (*segno*) burn; (*scottatura*) scald; **bruci'ore** *sm* burning *o* smarting sensation; **bruciore di stomaco** heartburn

'bruco, chi *sm* caterpillar; grub

brughi'era [bru'gjera] *sf* heath, moor

bruli'care *vi* to swarm

'brullo, a *ag* bare, bleak

'bruma *sf* mist

'bruno, a *ag* brown, dark; (*persona*) dark(-haired)

'brusco, a, schi, sche *ag* (*sapore*) sharp; (*modi, persona*) brusque, abrupt; (*movimento*) abrupt, sudden

bru'sio *sm* buzz, buzzing

bru'tale *ag* brutal

'bruto, a *ag* (*forza*) brute *cpd* ♦ *sm* brute

brut'tezza [brut'tettsa] *sf* ugliness

'brutto, a *ag* ugly; (*cattivo*) bad; (*malattia, strada, affare*) nasty, bad; **~ tempo** bad weather; **brut'tura** *sf* (*cosa brutta*) ugly thing; (*sudiciume*) filth; (*azione meschina*) mean action

Bru'xelles [bry'sɛl] *sf* Brussels

BSE [biɛsse'e] *sigla f* (= *encefalopatia spongiforme bovina*) BSE

bub'bone *sm* swelling

'buca, che *sf* hole; (*avvallamento*) hollow; **~ delle lettere** letterbox

buca'neve *sm inv* snowdrop

bu'care *vt* (*forare*) to make a hole (*o* holes) in; (*pungere*) to pierce; (*biglietto*) to punch; **~rsi** *vr* (*di eroina*) to mainline; **~ una gomma** to have a puncture

bu'cato *sm* (*operazione*) washing; (*panni*) wash, washing

'buccia, ce ['buttʃa] *sf* skin, peel

bucherel'lare [bukerel'lare] *vt* to riddle with holes

'buco, chi *sm* hole

bu'dello *sm* (*ANAT*: *pl(f)* **~a**) bowel, gut; (*fig: tubo*) tube; (*vicolo*) alley

bu'dino *sm* pudding

'bue *sm* ox; **carne di ~** beef

'bufalo *sm* buffalo

bu'fera *sf* storm

'buffo, a *ag* funny; (*TEATRO*) comic

buf'fone *sm* buffoon; (*peg*) clown

bu'gia, 'gie [bu'dʒia] *sf* lie; **dire una ~** to tell a lie; **bugi'ardo, a** *ag* lying, deceitful ♦ *sm/f* liar

bugi'gattolo [budʒi'gattolo] *sm* poky little room

'buio, a *ag* dark ♦ *sm* dark, darkness

'bulbo *sm* (*BOT*) bulb; **~ oculare** eyeball

Bulga'ria *sf*: **la ~** Bulgaria

bul'lone *sm* bolt

buona'notte *escl* good night! ♦ *sf*: **dare la ~ a** to say good night to

buona'sera *escl* good evening!

buongi'orno [bwon'dʒorno] *escl* good morning (*o* afternoon)!

buongus'taio, a *sm/f* gourmet

buon'gusto *sm* good taste

PAROLA CHIAVE
---

bu'ono, a (*ag*: *dav sm* **buon** +*C o V*, **buono** +*s impura, gn, pn, ps, x, z*; *dav sf* **buon'** +*V*) *ag* **1** (*gen*) good; **un buon pranzo** a good lunch; **(stai) ~!** behave!
2 (*benevolo*): **~ (con)** good (to), kind (to)
3 (*giusto, valido*) right; **al momento ~** at the right moment
4 (*adatto*): **~ a/da** fit for/to; **essere ~ a nulla** to be no good *o* use at anything
5 (*auguri*): **buon anno!** happy New Year!; **buon appetito!** enjoy your meal!; **buon compleanno!** happy birthday!; **buon divertimento!** have a nice time!; **~a fortuna!** good luck!; **buon riposo!** sleep well!; **buon viaggio!** bon voyage!, have a good trip!
6: **a buon mercato** cheap; **di buon'ora** early; **buon senso** common sense; **alla ~a** *ag* simple ♦ *av* without any fuss
♦ *sm* **1** (*bontà*) goodness, good
2 (*COMM*) voucher, coupon; **~ di cassa**

cash voucher; **~ di consegna** delivery note; **~ del Tesoro** Treasury bill

buontem'pone, a *sm/f* jovial person
burat'tino *sm* puppet
'burbero, a *ag* surly, gruff
'burla *sf* prank, trick; **bur'lare** *vt*: **burlare qc/qn, burlarsi di qc/qn** to make fun of sth/sb
burocra'zia [burokrat'tsia] *sf* bureaucracy
bur'rasca, sche *sf* storm
'burro *sm* butter
bur'rone *sm* ravine
bus'care *vt* (*anche*: **~rsi**: *raffreddore*) to get, catch; **buscarle** (*fam*) to get a hiding
bus'sare *vi* to knock
'bussola *sf* compass
'busta *sf* (*da lettera*) envelope; (*astuccio*) case; **in ~ aperta/chiusa** in an unsealed/sealed envelope; **~ paga** pay packet
busta'rella *sf* bribe, backhander
'busto *sm* bust; (*indumento*) corset, girdle; **a mezzo ~** (*foto*) half-length
buttafu'ori *sm inv* bouncer
but'tare *vt* to throw; (*anche*: **~ via**) to throw away; **~ giù** (*scritto*) to scribble down; (*cibo*) to gulp down; (*edificio*) to pull down, demolish; (*pasta, verdura*) to put into boiling water

C, c

ca'bina *sf* (*di nave*) cabin; (*da spiaggia*) beach hut; (*di autocarro, treno*) cab; (*di aereo*) cockpit; (*di ascensore*) cage; **~ telefonica** call *o* (tele)phone box; **cabi'nato** *sm* cabin cruiser
ca'cao *sm* cocoa
'caccia ['kattʃa] *sf* hunting; (*con fucile*) shooting; (*inseguimento*) chase; (*cacciagione*) game ♦ *sm inv* (*aereo*) fighter; (*nave*) destroyer; **~ grossa** big-game hunting; **~ all'uomo** manhunt
cacciabombardi'ere [kattʃabombar'djere] *sm* fighter-bomber
cacciagi'one [kattʃa'dʒone] *sf* game

cacci'are [kat'tʃare] *vt* to hunt; (*mandar via*) to chase away; (*ficcare*) to shove, stick ♦ *vi* to hunt; **~rsi** *vr*: **dove s'è cacciata la mia borsa?** where has my bag got to?; **~rsi nei guai** to get into trouble; **~ fuori qc** to whip *o* pull sth out; **~ un urlo** to let out a yell; **caccia'tore** *sm* hunter; **cacciatore di frodo** poacher
caccia'vite [kattʃa'vite] *sm inv* screwdriver
'cactus *sm inv* cactus
ca'davere *sm* (dead) body, corpse
ca'dente *ag* falling; (*casa*) tumbledown
ca'denza [ka'dentsa] *sf* cadence; (*ritmo*) rhythm; (*MUS*) cadenza
ca'dere *vi* to fall; (*denti, capelli*) to fall out; (*tetto*) to fall in; **questa gonna cade bene** this skirt hangs well; **lasciar ~** (*anche fig*) to drop; **~ dal sonno** to be falling asleep on one's feet; **~ dalle nuvole** (*fig*) to be taken aback
ca'detto, a *ag* younger; (*squadra*) junior *cpd* ♦ *sm* cadet
ca'duta *sf* fall; **la ~ dei capelli** hair loss
caffè *sm inv* coffee; (*locale*) café; **~ macchiato** coffee with a dash of milk; **~ macinato** ground coffee
caffel'latte *sm inv* white coffee
caffetti'era *sf* coffeepot
cagio'nare [kadʒo'nare] *vt* to cause
cagio'nevole [kadʒo'nevole] *ag* delicate, weak
cagli'are [kaʎ'ʎare] *vi* to curdle
'cagna ['kaɲɲa] *sf* (*ZOOL, peg*) bitch
ca'gnesco, a, schi, sche [kaɲ'ɲesko] *ag* (*fig*): **guardare qn in ~** to scowl at sb
cala'brone *sm* hornet
cala'maio *sm* inkpot; inkwell
cala'maro *sm* squid
cala'mita *sf* magnet
calamità *sf inv* calamity, disaster
ca'lare *vt* (*far discendere*) to lower; (*MAGLIA*) to decrease ♦ *vi* (*discendere*) to go (*o* come) down; (*tramontare*) to set, go down; **~ di peso** to lose weight
'calca *sf* throng, press
cal'cagno [kal'kaɲɲo] *sm* heel
cal'care *sm* limestone ♦ *vt* (*premere coi*

piedi) to tread, press down; (*premere con forza*) to press down; (*mettere in rilievo*) to stress; **~ la mano** to overdo it, exaggerate

'**calce** ['kaltʃe] *sm*: **in ~** at the foot of the page ♦ *sf* lime; **~ viva** quicklime

calces'truzzo [kaltʃes'truttso] *sm* concrete

calci'are [kal'tʃare] *vt, vi* to kick; **calcia'tore** *sm* footballer

'**calcio** ['kaltʃo] *sm* (*pedata*) kick; (*sport*) football, soccer; (*di pistola, fucile*) butt; (*CHIM*) calcium; **~ d'angolo** (*SPORT*) corner (kick); **~ di punizione** (*SPORT*) free kick

'**calco, chi** *sm* (*ARTE*) casting, moulding; cast, mould

calco'lare *vt* to calculate, work out, reckon; (*ponderare*) to weigh (up); **calcola'tore, 'trice** *ag* calculating ♦ *sm* calculator; (*fig*) calculating person; **calcolatore elettronico** computer; **calcola'trice** *sf* calculator

'**calcolo** *sm* (*anche MAT*) calculation; (*infinitesimale etc*) calculus; (*MED*) stone; **fare i propri ~i** (*fig*) to weigh the pros and cons; **per ~** out of self-interest

cal'daia *sf* boiler

caldeggi'are [kalded'dʒare] *vt* to support

'**caldo, a** *ag* warm; (*molto ~*) hot; (*fig: appassionato*) keen; hearty ♦ *sm* heat; **ho ~** I'm warm; I'm hot; **fa ~** it's warm; it's hot

calen'dario *sm* calendar

'**calibro** *sm* (*di arma*) calibre, bore; (*TECN*) callipers *pl*; (*fig*) calibre; **di grosso ~** (*fig*) prominent

'**calice** ['kalitʃe] *sm* goblet; (*REL*) chalice

ca'ligine [ka'lidʒine] *sf* fog; (*mista con fumo*) smog

'**callo** *sm* callus; (*ai piedi*) corn

'**calma** *sf* calm

cal'mante *sm* tranquillizer

cal'mare *vt* to calm; (*lenire*) to soothe; **~rsi** *vr* to grow calm, calm down; (*vento*) to abate; (*dolori*) to ease

calmi'ere *sm* controlled price

'**calmo, a** *ag* calm, quiet

'**calo** *sm* (*COMM: di prezzi*) fall; (*: di volume*) shrinkage; (*: di peso*) loss

ca'lore *sm* warmth; heat; **in ~** (*ZOOL*) on heat

calo'ria *sf* calorie

calo'roso, a *ag* warm

calpes'tare *vt* to tread on, trample on; **"è vietato ~ l'erba"** "keep off the grass"

ca'lunnia *sf* slander; (*scritta*) libel

cal'vario *sm* (*fig*) affliction, cross

cal'vizie [kal'vittsje] *sf* baldness

'**calvo, a** *ag* bald

'**calza** ['kaltsa] *sf* (*da donna*) stocking; (*da uomo*) sock; **fare la ~** to knit; **~e di nailon** nylons, (nylon) stockings

cal'zare [kal'tsare] *vt* (*scarpe, guanti: mettersi*) to put on; (*: portare*) to wear ♦ *vi* to fit; **calza'tura** *sf* footwear

calzet'tone [kaltset'tone] *sm* heavy knee-length sock

cal'zino [kal'tsino] *sm* sock

calzo'laio [kaltso'lajo] *sm* shoemaker; (*che ripara scarpe*) cobbler; **calzole'ria** *sf* (*negozio*) shoe shop

calzon'cini [kaltson'tʃini] *smpl* shorts

cal'zone [kal'tsone] *sm* trouser leg; (*CUC*) savoury turnover made with pizza dough; **~i** *smpl* (*pantaloni*) trousers (*BRIT*), pants (*US*)

cambi'ale *sf* bill (of exchange); (*pagherò cambiario*) promissory note

cambia'mento *sm* change

cambi'are *vt* to change; (*modificare*) to alter, change; (*barattare*): **~ (qc con qn/ qc)** to exchange (sth with sb/for sth) ♦ *vi* to change, alter; **~rsi** *vr* (*d'abito*) to change; **~ casa** to move (house); **~ idea** to change one's mind; **~ treno** to change trains

'**cambio** *sm* change; (*modifica*) alteration, change; (*scambio, COMM*) exchange; (*corso dei cambi*) rate (of exchange); (*TECN, AUT*) gears *pl*; **in ~ di** in exchange for; **dare il ~ a qn** to take over from sb

'**camera** *sf* room; (*anche: ~ da letto*) bedroom; (*POL*) chamber, house; **~ ardente** mortuary chapel; **~ d'aria** inner tube; (*di pallone*) bladder; **C~ di Commercio** Chamber of Commerce; **C~ dei Deputati** Chamber of Deputies, ≈ House of

Commons (*BRIT*), ≈ House of Representatives (*US*); **~ a gas** gas chamber; **~ a un letto/a due letti/matrimoniale** single/twin-bedded/double room; **~ oscura** (*FOT*) dark room

came'rata, i, e *sm/f* companion, mate
  ♦ *sf* dormitory

cameri'era *sf* (*domestica*) maid; (*che serve a tavola*) waitress; (*che fa le camere*) chambermaid

cameri'ere *sm* (man)servant; (*di ristorante*) waiter

came'rino *sm* (*TEATRO*) dressing room

'camice ['kamitʃe] *sm* (*REL*) alb; (*per medici etc*) white coat

cami'cetta [kami'tʃetta] *sf* blouse

ca'micia, cie [ka'mitʃa] *sf* (*da uomo*) shirt; (*da donna*) blouse; **~ di forza** straitjacket

cami'netto *sm* hearth, fireplace

ca'mino *sm* chimney; (*focolare*) fireplace, hearth

'camion *sm inv* lorry (*BRIT*), truck (*US*); **camion'cino** *sm* van

cam'mello *sm* (*ZOOL*) camel; (*tessuto*) camel hair

cammi'nare *vi* to walk; (*funzionare*) to work, go; **cammi'nata** *sf* walk

cam'mino *sm* walk; (*sentiero*) path; (*itinerario, direzione, tragitto*) way; **mettersi in ~** to set *o* start off

camo'milla *sf* camomile; (*infuso*) camomile tea

ca'morra *sf* camorra; racket

ca'moscio [ka'moʃʃo] *sm* chamois; **di ~** (*scarpe, borsa*) suede *cpd*

cam'pagna [kam'paɲɲa] *sf* country, countryside; (*POL, COMM, MIL*) campaign; **in ~** in the country; **andare in ~** to go to the country; **fare una ~** to campaign; **campa'gnola** *sf* (*AUT*) cross-country vehicle; **campa'gnolo, a** *ag* country *cpd*

cam'pale *ag* field *cpd*; (*fig*): **una giornata ~** a hard day

cam'pana *sf* bell; (*anche:* **~ di vetro**) bell jar; **campa'nella** *sf* small bell; (*di tenda*) curtain ring; **campa'nello** *sm* (*all'uscio, da tavola*) bell

campa'nile *sm* bell tower, belfry; **campani'lismo** *sm* parochialism

cam'pare *vi* to live; (*tirare avanti*) to get by, manage

cam'pato, a *ag*: **~ in aria** unfounded

campeggi'are [kamped'dʒare] *vi* to camp; (*risaltare*) to stand out; **campeggia'tore, 'trice** *sm/f* camper; **cam'peggio** *sm* camping; (*terreno*) camp site; **fare (del) campeggio** to go camping

cam'pestre *ag* country *cpd*, rural

Campidoglio

i The **Campidoglio**, one of the Seven Hills of Rome, is the site of the Comune di Roma.

---

campio'nario, a *ag*: **fiera ~a** trade fair
  ♦ *sm* collection of samples

campio'nato *sm* championship

campi'one, 'essa *sm/f* (*SPORT*) champion
  ♦ *sm* (*COMM*) sample

'campo *sm* field; (*MIL*) field; (*: accampamento*) camp; (*spazio delimitato: sportivo etc*) ground; field; (*di quadro*) background; **i ~i** (*campagna*) the countryside; **~ da aviazione** airfield; **~ di battaglia** (*MIL, fig*) battlefield; **~ di golf** golf course; **~ da tennis** tennis court; **~ visivo** field of vision

campo'santo (*pl* **campisanti**) *sm* cemetery

camuf'fare *vt* to disguise

'Canada *sm*: **il ~** Canada; **cana'dese** *ag, sm/f* Canadian ♦ *sf* (*anche:* **tenda canadese**) ridge tent

ca'naglia [ka'naʎʎa] *sf* rabble, mob; (*persona*) scoundrel, rogue

ca'nale *sm* (*anche fig*) channel; (*artificiale*) canal

'canapa *sf* hemp; **~ indiana** (*droga*) cannabis

cana'rino *sm* canary

cancel'lare [kantʃel'lare] *vt* (*con la gomma*) to rub out, erase; (*con la penna*) to strike out; (*annullare*) to annul, cancel; (*disdire*) to cancel

cancelle'ria [kantʃelle'ria] *sf* chancery; (*materiale per scrivere*) stationery

cancelli'ere [kantʃel'ljere] *sm* chancellor; (*di tribunale*) clerk of the court

can'cello [kan'tʃɛllo] *sm* gate

can'crena *sf* gangrene

'cancro *sm* (*MED*) cancer; (*dello zodiaco*): **C~** Cancer

candeg'gina [kanded'dʒina] *sf* bleach

can'dela *sf* candle; **~ (di accensione)** (*AUT*) spark(ing) plug

cande'labro *sm* candelabra

candeli'ere *sm* candlestick

candi'dato, a *sm/f* candidate; (*aspirante a una carica*) applicant

'candido, a *ag* white as snow; (*puro*) pure; (*sincero*) sincere, candid

can'dito, a *ag* candied

can'dore *sm* brilliant white; purity; sincerity, candour

'cane *sm* dog; (*di pistola, fucile*) cock; **fa un freddo ~** it's bitterly cold; **non c'era un ~** there wasn't a soul; **~ da caccia/uardia** hunting/guard dog; **~ lupo** alsatian

ca'nestro *sm* basket

'canfora *sf* camphor

cangi'ante [kan'dʒante] *ag* iridescent

can'guro *sm* kangaroo

ca'nile *sm* kennel; (*di allevamento*) kennels *pl*; **~ municipale** dog pound

ca'nino, a *ag, sm* canine

'canna *sf* (*pianta*) reed; (: *indica, da zucchero*) cane; (*bastone*) stick, cane; (*di fucile*) barrel; (*di organo*) pipe; (*fam: droga*) joint; **~ da pesca** (fishing) rod; **~ da zucchero** sugar cane

can'nella *sf* (*CUC*) cinnamon

cannel'loni *smpl* pasta tubes stuffed with sauce and baked

cannocchi'ale [kannok'kjale] *sm* telescope

can'none *sm* (*MIL*) gun; (: *STORIA*) cannon; (*tubo*) pipe, tube; (*piega*) box pleat; (*fig*) ace

can'nuccia, ce [kan'nuttʃa] *sf* (drinking) straw

ca'noa *sf* canoe

'canone *sm* canon, criterion; (*mensile, annuo*) rent; fee

ca'nonico, ci *sm* (*REL*) canon

ca'noro, a *ag* (*uccello*) singing, song *cpd*

canot'taggio [kanot'taddʒo] *sm* rowing

canotti'era *sf* vest

ca'notto *sm* small boat, dinghy; canoe

cano'vaccio [kano'vattʃo] *sm* (*tela*) canvas; (*strofinaccio*) duster; (*trama*) plot

can'tante *sm/f* singer

can'tare *vt, vi* to sing; **cantau'tore, 'trice** *sm/f* singer-composer

canti'ere *sm* (*EDIL*) (building) site; (*anche:* **~ navale**) shipyard

canti'lena *sf* (*filastrocca*) lullaby; (*fig*) sing-song voice

can'tina *sf* cellar; (*bottega*) wine shop

'canto *sm* song; (*arte*) singing; (*REL*) chant; chanting; (*poesia*) poem, lyric; (*parte di una poesia*) canto; (*parte, lato*): **da un ~** on the one hand; **d'altro ~** on the other hand

canto'nata *sf* corner; **prendere una ~** (*fig*) to blunder

can'tone *sm* (*in Svizzera*) canton

can'tuccio [kan'tuttʃo] *sm* corner, nook

canzo'nare [kantso'nare] *vt* to tease

can'zone [kan'tsone] *sf* song; (*POESIA*) canzone; **canzoni'ere** *sm* (*MUS*) songbook; (*LETTERATURA*) collection of poems

'caos *sm inv* chaos; **ca'otico, a, ci, che** *ag* chaotic

C.A.P. *sigla m* = **codice di avviamento postale**

ca'pace [ka'patʃe] *ag* able, capable; (*ampio, vasto*) large, capacious; **sei ~ di farlo?** can you *o* are you able to do it?; **capacità** *sf inv* ability; (*DIR, di recipiente*) capacity; **capaci'tarsi** *vr* to understand

ca'panna *sf* hut

capan'none *sm* (*AGR*) barn; (*fabbricato industriale*) factory) shed

ca'parbio, a *ag* stubborn

ca'parra *sf* deposit, down payment

ca'pello *sm* hair; **~i** *smpl* (*capigliatura*) hair *sg*

capez'zale [kapet'tsale] *sm* bolster; (*fig*)

bedside
ca'pezzolo [ka'pettsolo] *sm* nipple
capi'enza [ka'pjentsa] *sf* capacity
capiglia'tura [kapiʎʎa'tura] *sf* hair
ca'pire *vt* to understand
capi'tale *ag* (*mortale*) capital; (*fondamentale*) main, chief ♦ *sf* (*città*) capital ♦ *sm* (ECON) capital; **capita'lismo** *sm* capitalism; **capita'lista, i, e** *ag, sm/f* capitalist
capitane'ria *sf*: **~ di porto** port authorities *pl*
capi'tano *sm* captain
capi'tare *vi* (*giungere casualmente*) to happen to go, find o.s.; (*accadere*) to happen; (*presentarsi: cosa*) to turn up, present itself ♦ *vb impers* to happen; **mi è capitato un guaio** I've had a spot of trouble
capi'tello *sm* (ARCHIT) capital
ca'pitolo *sm* chapter
capi'tombolo *sm* headlong fall, tumble
'capo *sm* head; (*persona*) head, leader; (: *in ufficio*) head, boss; (: *in tribù*) chief; (*di oggetti*) head; top; end; (GEO) cape; **andare a ~ a** to start a new paragraph; **da ~** over again; **~ di bestiame** head *inv* of cattle; **~ di vestiario** item of clothing
'capo... *prefisso*: **capocu'oco, chi** *sm* head cook; **Capo'danno** *sm* New Year; **capo'fitto: a capofitto** *av* headfirst, headlong; **capo'giro** *sm* dizziness *no pl*; **capola'voro, i** *sm* masterpiece; **capo'linea** (*pl* **capi'linea**) *sm* terminus; **capo'lino** *sm*: **fare capolino** to peep out (*o in etc*); **capolu'ogo** (*pl* **-ghi** *o* **capilu'oghi**) *sm* chief town, administrative centre
capo'rale *sm* (MIL) lance corporal (BRIT), private first class (US)
'capo... *prefisso*: **capostazi'one** (*pl* **capistazi'one**) *sm* station master; **capo'treno** (*pl* **capi'treno** *o* **capo'treni**) *sm* guard
capo'volgere [kapo'voldʒere] *vt* to overturn; (*fig*) to reverse; **~rsi** *vr* to overturn; (*barca*) to capsize; (*fig*) to be

reversed; **capo'volto, a** *pp di* **capovolgere**
'cappa *sf* (*mantello*) cape, cloak; (*del camino*) hood
cap'pella *sf* (REL) chapel; **cappel'lano** *sm* chaplain
cap'pello *sm* hat
'cappero *sm* caper
cap'pone *sm* capon
cap'potto *sm* (over)coat
cappuc'cino [kapput'tʃino] *sm* (*frate*) Capuchin monk; (*bevanda*) cappuccino, frothy white coffee
cap'puccio [kap'puttʃo] *sm* (*copricapo*) hood; (*della biro*) cap
'capra *sf* (she-)goat; **ca'pretto** *sm* kid
ca'priccio [ka'prittʃo] *sm* caprice, whim; (*bizza*) tantrum; **fare i ~i** to be very naughty; **capricci'oso, a** *ag* capricious, whimsical; naughty
Capri'corno *sm* Capricorn
capri'ola *sf* somersault
capri'olo *sm* roe deer
'capro *sm*: **~ espiatorio** scapegoat
'capsula *sf* capsule; (*di arma, per bottiglie*) cap
cap'tare *vt* (RADIO, TV) to pick up; (*cattivarsi*) to gain, win
cara'bina *sf* rifle
carabini'ere *sm* member of Italian military police force

---

carabinieri

i Originally part of the armed forces, the **carabinieri** are police who now perform both military and civil duties and include paratroop units and mounted divisions.

---

ca'raffa *sf* carafe
cara'mella *sf* sweet
ca'rattere *sm* character; (*caratteristica*) characteristic, trait; **avere un buon ~** to be good-natured; **caratte'ristica, che** *sf* characteristic, trait, peculiarity; **caratte'ristico, a, ci, che** *ag* characteristic; **caratteriz'zare** *vt* to characterize

car'bone *sm* coal
carbu'rante *sm* (motor) fuel
carbura'tore *sm* carburettor
car'cassa *sf* carcass; (*fig: peg: macchina etc*) (old) wreck
carce'rato, a [kartʃe'rato] *sm/f* prisoner
'carcere ['kartʃere] *sm* prison; (*pena*) imprisonment
carci'ofo [kar'tʃɔfo] *sm* artichoke
car'diaco, a, ci, che *ag* cardiac, heart *cpd*
cardi'nale *ag, sm* cardinal
'cardine *sm* hinge
'cardo *sm* thistle
ca'renza [ka'rentsa] *sf* lack, scarcity; (*vitaminica*) deficiency
cares'tia *sf* famine; (*penuria*) scarcity, dearth
ca'rezza [ka'rettsa] *sf* caress; **carez'zare** *vt* to caress, stroke
'carica, che *sf* (*mansione ufficiale*) office, position; (*MIL, TECN, ELETTR*) charge; **ha una forte ~ di simpatia** he's very likeable; *vedi anche* **carico**
caricabatte'ria *sm inv* battery charger
cari'care *vt* (*merce, INFORM*) to load; (*orologio*) to wind up; (*batteria, MIL*) to charge
'carico, a, chi, che *ag* (*che porta un peso*): **~ di** loaded *o* laden with; (*fucile*) loaded; (*orologio*) wound up; (*batteria*) charged; (*colore*) deep; (*caffè, tè*) strong ♦ *sm* (*il caricare*) loading; (*ciò che si carica*) load; (*fig: peso*) burden, weight; **persona a ~** dependent; **essere a ~ di qn** (*spese etc*) to be charged to sb
'carie *sf* (*dentaria*) decay
ca'rino, a *ag* (*grazioso*) lovely, pretty, nice; (*riferito a uomo, anche simpatico*) nice
carità *sf* charity; **per ~!** (*escl di rifiuto*) good heavens, no!
carnagi'one [karna'dʒone] *sf* complexion
car'nale *ag* (*amore*) carnal
'carne *sf* flesh; (*bovina, ovina etc*) meat; **~ di manzo/maiale/pecora** beef/pork/mutton; **~ tritata** mince (*BRIT*), hamburger meat (*US*), minced *o* ground (*US*) meat
car'nefice [kar'nefitʃe] *sm* executioner; (*alla*

forca) hangman
carne'vale *sm* carnival

| **carnevale** |

ⓘ **Carnevale** *is the period between Epiphany and the start of Lent. People wear fancy dress, and there are parties, processions of floats and bonfires. It culminates immediately before Lent in the festivities of* **martedì grasso** *(Shrove Tuesday).*

---

car'noso, a *ag* fleshy
'caro, a *ag* (*amato*) dear; (*costoso*) dear, expensive
ca'rogna [ka'roɲɲa] *sf* carrion; (*fig: fam*) swine
ca'rota *sf* carrot
caro'vana *sf* caravan
caro'vita *sm* high cost of living
carpenti'ere *sm* carpenter
car'pire *vt*: **~ qc a qn** (*segreto etc*) to get sth out of sb
car'poni *av* on all fours
car'rabile *ag* suitable for vehicles; **"passo ~"** "keep clear"
car'raio, a *ag*: **passo ~** driveway
carreggi'ata [karred'dʒata] *sf* carriageway (*BRIT*), (road)way
car'rello *sm* trolley; (*AER*) undercarriage; (*CINEMA*) dolly; (*di macchina da scrivere*) carriage
carri'era *sf* career; **fare ~** to get on; **a gran ~** at full speed
carri'ola *sf* wheelbarrow
'carro *sm* cart, wagon; **~ armato** tank; **~ attrezzi** breakdown van
car'rozza [kar'rɔttsa] *sf* carriage, coach
carrozze'ria [karrottse'ria] *sf* body, coachwork (*BRIT*); (*officina*) coachbuilder's workshop (*BRIT*), body shop
carroz'zina [karrot'tsina] *sf* pram (*BRIT*), baby carriage (*US*)
'carta *sf* paper; (*al ristorante*) menu; (*GEO*) map; plan; (*documento, da gioco*) card; (*costituzione*) charter; **~e** *sfpl* (*documenti*) papers, documents; **alla ~** (*al ristorante*) à

la carte; ~ **assegni** bank card; ~ **assorbente** blotting paper; ~ **bollata** o **da bollo** official stamped paper; ~ **di credito** credit card; ~ **(geografica)** map; ~ **d'identità** identity card; ~ **igienica** toilet paper; ~ **ria** (AER, NAUT) boarding card; ~ **d'imbarco** (CINEMA) boarding card; ~ **da lettere** writing paper; ~ **libera** (AMM) unstamped paper; ~ **da parati** wallpaper; ~ **stradale** road map; ~ **verde** (AUT) green card; ~ **vetrata** sandpaper; ~ **da visita** visiting card

carta**car'bone** (pl **cartecar'bone**) sf carbon paper

car**'taccia, ce** [kar'tattʃa] sf waste paper

carta**'pecora** sf parchment

carta**'pesta** sf papier-mâché

car**'teggio** [kar'teddʒo] sm correspondence

car**'tella** sf (scheda) card; (INFORM; custodia: di cartone) folder; (: di uomo d'affari etc) briefcase; (: di scolaro) schoolbag, satchel; ~ **clinica** (MED) case sheet

car**'tello** sm sign; (pubblicitario) poster; (stradale) sign, signpost; (ECON) cartel; (in dimostrazioni) placard; **cartel'lone** sm (pubblicitario) advertising poster; (della tombola) scoring frame; (TEATRO) playbill; **tenere il cartellone** (spettacolo) to have a long run

carti**'era** sf paper mill

car**'tina** sf (AUT, GEO) map

car**'toccio** [kar'tɔttʃo] sm paper bag

cartole**'ria** sf stationer's (shop)

carto**'lina** sf postcard; ~ **postale** ready-stamped postcard

car**'tone** sm cardboard; (ARTE) cartoon; ~**i animati** smpl (CINEMA) cartoons

car**'tuccia, ce** [kar'tuttʃa] sf cartridge

'casa sf house; (in senso astratto) home; (COMM) firm, house; **essere a** ~ to be at home; **vado a** ~ **mia/tua** I'm going home/to your house; ~ **di cura** nursing home; ~ **dello studente** student hostel; ~**e popolari** ≈ council houses (o flats) (BRIT), ≈ public housing units (US); **vino della** ~ house wine

ca**'sacca, che** sf military coat; (di fantino) blouse

casa**'linga, ghe** sf housewife

casa**'lingo, a, ghi, ghe** ag household, domestic; (fatto a casa) home-made; (semplice) homely; (amante della casa) home-loving; ~**ghi** smpl household articles; **cucina** ~**a** plain home cooking

cas**'care** vi to fall; cas**'cata** sf fall; (d'acqua) cascade, waterfall

ca**'scina** [kaʃ'ʃina] sf farmstead

'casco, schi sm helmet; (del parrucchiere) hair-dryer; (di banane) bunch

casei**'ficio** [kazei'fitʃo] sm creamery

ca**'sella** sf pigeon-hole; ~ **postale** post office box

casel**'lario** sm filing cabinet; ~ **giudiziale** court records pl

ca**'sello** sm (di autostrada) toll-house

ca**'serma** sf barracks pl

ca**'sino** (fam) sm brothel; (confusione) row, racket

casi**nò** sm inv casino

'caso sm chance; (fatto, vicenda) event, incident; (possibilità) possibility; (MED, LING) case; **a** ~ at random; **per** ~ by chance, by accident; **in ogni** ~, **in tutti i** ~**i** in any case, at any rate; **al** ~ should the opportunity arise; **nel** ~ **che** in case; ~ **mai** if by chance; ~ **limite** borderline case

caso**'lare** sm cottage

'cassa sf case, crate, box; (bara) coffin; (mobile) chest; (involucro: di orologio etc) case; (macchina) cash register, till; (luogo di pagamento) checkout (counter); (fondo) fund; (istituto bancario) bank; ~ **automatica prelievi** cash dispenser; ~ **continua** night safe; ~ **integrazione: mettere in** ~ **integrazione** ≈ to lay off; ~ **mutua** o **malattia** health insurance scheme; ~ **di risparmio** savings bank; ~ **toracica** (ANAT) chest

cassa**'forte** (pl **casse'forti**) sf safe

cassa**'panca** (pl **cassa'panche** o **casse'panche**) sf settle

casse**'rola** sf = **casseruola**

casseru**'ola** sf saucepan

cas**'setta** sf box; (per registratore) cassette; (CINEMA, TEATRO) box-office takings pl; **film**

di ~ box-office draw; ~ **di sicurezza** strongbox; ~ **delle lettere** letterbox
cas'setto *sm* drawer; casset'tone *sm* chest of drawers
cassi'ere, a *sm/f* cashier; (*di banca*) teller
casso'netto *sm* wheelie-bin
'casta *sf* caste
cas'tagna [kas'taɲɲa] *sf* chestnut
cas'tagno [kas'taɲɲo] *sm* chestnut (tree)
cas'tano, a *ag* chestnut (brown)
cas'tello *sm* castle; (*TECN*) scaffolding
casti'gare *vt* to punish; cas'tigo, ghi *sm* punishment
castità *sf* chastity
cas'toro *sm* beaver
cas'trare *vt* to castrate; to geld; to doctor (*BRIT*), fix (*US*)
casu'ale *ag* chance *cpd*; (*INFORM*) random *cpd*
cata'comba *sf* catacomb
ca'talogo, ghi *sm* catalogue
catarifran'gente [katarifran'dʒɛnte] *sm* (*AUT*) reflector
ca'tarro *sm* catarrh
ca'tasta *sf* stack, pile
ca'tasto *sm* land register; land registry office
ca'tastrofe *sf* catastrophe, disaster
catego'ria *sf* category
ca'tena *sf* chain; ~ **di montaggio** assembly line; ~e **da neve** (*AUT*) snow chains; cate'naccio *sm* bolt
cate'ratta *sf* cataract; (*chiusa*) sluice-gate
cati'nella *sf*: **piovere a ~e** to pour
ca'tino *sm* basin
ca'trame *sm* tar
'cattedra *sf* teacher's desk; (*di docente*) chair
catte'drale *sf* cathedral
catti'veria *sf* malice, spite; naughtiness; (*atto*) spiteful act; (*parole*) malicious *o* spiteful remark
cattività *sf* captivity
cat'tivo, a *ag* bad; (*malvagio*) bad, wicked; (*turbolento: bambino*) bad, naughty; (: *mare*) rough; (*odore, sapore*) nasty, bad
cat'tolico, a, ci, che *ag, sm/f* (Roman)
Catholic
cat'tura *sf* capture
cattu'rare *vt* to capture
caucciù [kaut'tʃu] *sm* rubber
'causa *sf* cause; (*DIR*) lawsuit, case, action; **a ~ di, per ~ di** because of; **fare** *o* **muovere ~ a qn** to take legal action against sb
cau'sare *vt* to cause
cau'tela *sf* caution, prudence
caute'lare *vt* to protect; ~rsi *vr*: ~rsi (da) to take precautions (against)
'cauto, a *ag* cautious, prudent
cauzi'one [kaut'tsjone] *sf* security; (*DIR*) bail
cav. *abbr* = cavaliere
'cava *sf* quarry
caval'care *vt* (*cavallo*) to ride; (*muro*) to sit astride; (*sog: ponte*) to span; caval'cata *sf* ride; (*gruppo di persone*) riding party
cavalca'via *sm inv* flyover
cavalci'oni [kaval'tʃoni] *sm*: **a ~ di** *prep* astride
cavali'ere *sm* rider; (*feudale, titolo*) knight; (*soldato*) cavalryman; (*al ballo*) partner; cavalle'resco, a, schi, sche *ag* chivalrous; cavalle'ria *sf* (*di persona*) chivalry; (*milizia a cavallo*) cavalry
cavalle'rizzo, a [kavalle'rittso] *sm/f* riding instructor; circus rider
caval'letta *sf* grasshopper
caval'letto *sm* (*FOT*) tripod; (*da pittore*) easel
ca'vallo *sm* horse; (*SCACCHI*) knight; (*AUT: anche:* ~ **vapore**) horsepower; (*dei pantaloni*) crotch; **a** ~ on horseback; **a** ~ **di** astride, straddling; ~ **di battaglia** (*fig*) hobby-horse; ~ **da corsa** racehorse
ca'vare *vt* (*togliere*) to draw out, extract, take out; (: *giacca, scarpe*) to take off; (: *fame, sete, voglia*) to satisfy; **cavarsela** to manage, get on all right; (*scamparla*) to get away with it
cava'tappi *sm inv* corkscrew
ca'verna *sf* cave
'cavia *sf* guinea pig
cavi'ale *sm* caviar
ca'viglia [ka'viʎʎa] *sf* ankle
ca'villo *sm* quibble

'cavo, a *ag* hollow ♦ *sm* (*ANAT*) cavity; (*corda, ELETTR, TEL*) cable

cavolfi'ore *sm* cauliflower

'cavolo *sm* cabbage; (*fam*): non m'importa un ~ I don't give a damn; ~ di Bruxelles Brussels sprout

cazzu'ola [katˈtswɔla] *sf* trowel

c/c *abbr* = conto corrente

CCD *sigla m* = Centro Cristiano Democratico

CD *sm inv* CD

CD-ROM [tʃidiˈrɔm] *sm inv* CD-ROM

C. d. u. *sigla m* = Cristiano Democratici Uniti

C.E. [tʃe] *sigla f* (= Comunità Europea) EC

ce [tʃe] *pron, av vedi* ci

'cece [ˈtʃetʃe] *sm* chickpea

cecità [tʃetʃiˈta] *sf* blindness

'ceco, a [ˈtʃɛko] *ag, sm/f* Czech; la Repubblica ~a the Czech Republic

Cecoslo'vacchia [tʃekozloˈvakkja] *sf*: la ~ Czechoslovakia

'cedere [ˈtʃedere] *vt* (*concedere: posto*) to give up; (*DIR*) to transfer, make over ♦ *vi* (*cadere*) to give way, subside; ~ (a) to surrender (to), yield (to), give in (to); ce'devole *ag* (*terreno*) soft; (*fig*) yielding

'cedola [ˈtʃedola] *sf* coupon; voucher

'cedro [ˈtʃedro] *sm* cedar; (*albero da frutto, frutto*) citron

'ceffo [ˈtʃeffo] (*peg*) *sm* ugly mug

cef'fone [tʃefˈfone] *sm* slap, smack

ce'lare [tʃeˈlare] *vt* to conceal; ~rsi to hide

cele'brare [tʃeleˈbrare] *vt* to celebrate; celebrazi'one *sf* celebration

'celebre [ˈtʃelebre] *ag* famous, celebrated; celebrità *sf inv* fame; (*persona*) celebrity

'celere [ˈtʃelere] *ag* fast, swift; (*corso*) crash *cpd*

ce'leste [tʃeˈlɛste] *ag* celestial; heavenly; (*colore*) sky-blue

'celibe [ˈtʃelibe] *ag* single, unmarried

'cella [ˈtʃella] *sf* cell

'cellula [ˈtʃellula] *sf* (*BIOL, ELETTR, POL*) cell; cellu'lare *sm* cellphone

cellu'lite [tʃelluˈlite] *sf* cellulite

cemen'tare [tʃemenˈtare] *vt* (*anche fig*) to

cement

ce'mento [tʃeˈmento] *sm* cement

'cena [ˈtʃena] *sf* dinner; (*leggera*) supper

ce'nare [tʃeˈnare] *vi* to dine, have dinner

'cencio [ˈtʃentʃo] *sm* piece of cloth, rag; (*per spolverare*) duster

'cenere [ˈtʃenere] *sf* ash

'cenno [ˈtʃenno] *sm* (*segno*) sign, signal; (*gesto*) gesture; (*col capo*) nod; (*con la mano*) wave; (*allusione*) hint, mention; (*breve esposizione*) short account; far ~ di sì/no to nod (one's head)/shake one's head

censi'mento [tʃensiˈmento] *sm* census

cen'sura [tʃenˈsura] *sf* censorship; censor's office; (*fig*) censure

cente'nario, a [tʃenteˈnarjo] *ag* (*che ha cento anni*) hundred-year-old; (*che ricorre ogni cento anni*) centennial, centenary *cpd* ♦ *sm/f* centenarian ♦ *sm* centenary

cen'tesimo, a [tʃenˈtezimo] *ag, sm* hundredth

cen'tigrado, a [tʃenˈtigrado] *ag* centigrade; 20 gradi ~i 20 degrees centigrade

cen'timetro [tʃenˈtimetro] *sm* centimetre

centi'naio [tʃentiˈnajo] (*pl(f)* -aia) *sm*: un ~ (di) a hundred; about a hundred

'cento [ˈtʃento] *num* a hundred, one hundred

cen'trale [tʃenˈtrale] *ag* central ♦ *sf*: ~ telefonica (telephone) exchange; ~ elettrica electric power station; centrali'nista *sm/f* operator; centra'lino *sm* (telephone) exchange; (*di albergo etc*) switchboard

cen'trare [tʃenˈtrare] *vt* to hit the centre of; (*TECN*) to centre

cen'trifuga [tʃenˈtrifuga] *sf* spin-dryer

'centro [ˈtʃentro] *sm* centre; ~ civico civic centre; ~ commerciale shopping centre; (*città*) commercial centre

'ceppo [ˈtʃeppo] *sm* (*di albero*) stump; (*pezzo di legno*) log

'cera [ˈtʃera] *sf* wax; (*aspetto*) appearance

ce'ramica, che [tʃeˈramika] *sf* ceramic; (*ARTE*) ceramics *sg*

cerbi'atto [tʃerˈbjatto] *sm* (*ZOOL*) fawn

'cerca [ˈtʃerka] *sf*: in o alla ~ di in search of

cer'care [tʃerˈkare] *vt* to look for, search for

♦ *vi*: ~ **di fare qc** to try to do sth
'**cerchia** ['tʃerkja] *sf* circle
'**cerchio** ['tʃerkjo] *sm* circle; (*giocattolo, di botte*) hoop
cere'**ale** [tʃere'ale] *sm* cereal
ceri'**monia** [tʃeri'mɔnja] *sf* ceremony
ce'**rino** [tʃe'rino] *sm* wax match
'**cernia** ['tʃernja] *sf* (ZOOL) stone bass
cerni'**era** [tʃer'njɛra] *sf* hinge; ~ **lampo** zip (fastener) (BRIT), zipper (US)
'**cernita** ['tʃernita] *sf* selection
'**cero** ['tʃero] *sm* (church) candle
ce'**rotto** [tʃe'rɔtto] *sm* sticking plaster
certa'**mente** [tʃerta'mente] *av* certainly
cer'**tezza** [tʃer'tettsa] *sf* certainty
certifi'**cato** *sm* certificate; ~ **medico/di nascita** medical/birth certificate

---
PAROLA CHIAVE

'**certo, a** ['tʃerto] *ag* (*sicuro*): ~ **(di/che)** certain *o* sure (of/that)
♦ *det* 1 (*tale*) certain; **un ~ signor Smith** a (certain) Mr Smith
2 (*qualche; con valore intensivo*) some; **dopo un ~ tempo** after some time; **un fatto di una ~a importanza** a matter of some importance; **di una ~a età** past one's prime, not so young
♦ *pron*: ~**i, e** *pl* some
♦ *av* (*certamente*) certainly; (*senz'altro*) of course; **di ~** certainly; **no (di) ~!, ~ che no!** certainly not!; **sì ~** yes indeed, certainly

cer'**vello, i** [tʃer'vello] (ANAT: *pl(f)* **-a**) *sm* brain
'**cervo, a** ['tʃervo] *sm/f* stag/doe ♦ *sm* deer
ce'**sello** [tʃe'zello] *sm* chisel
ce'**soie** [tʃe'zoje] *sfpl* shears
ces'**puglio** [tʃes'puʎʎo] *sm* bush
ces'**sare** [tʃes'sare] *vi, vt* to stop, cease; ~ **di fare qc** to stop doing sth
'**cesso** ['tʃesso] (*fam*) *sm* (*gabinetto*) bog
'**cesta** ['tʃesta] *sf* (large) basket
ces'**tino** [tʃes'tino] *sm* basket; (*per la carta straccia*) wastepaper basket; ~ **da viaggio** (FERR) packed lunch (*o* dinner)
'**cesto** ['tʃesto] *sm* basket

'**ceto** ['tʃeto] *sm* (social) class
cetri'**olino** [tʃetrio'lino] *sm* gherkin
cetri'**olo** [tʃetri'ɔlo] *sm* cucumber
CFC *sm inv* (= *clorofluorocarburo*) CFC
cfr. *abbr* (= *confronta*) cf
CGIL *sigla f* (= *Confederazione Generale Italiana del Lavoro*) *trades union organization*
chat line *sf inv* chatline
chattare *vi* (INFORM) to chat

PAROLA CHIAVE
---

che [ke] *pron* 1 (*relativo: persona: soggetto*) who; (: *oggetto*) whom, that; (: *cosa, animale*) which, that; **il ragazzo ~ è venuto** the boy who came; **l'uomo ~ io vedo** the man (whom) I see; **il libro ~ è sul tavolo** the book which *o* that is on the table; **il libro ~ vedi** the book (which *o* that) you see; **la sera ~ ti ho visto** the evening I saw you
2 (*interrogativo, esclamativo*) what; ~ **(cosa) fai?** what are you doing?; **a ~ (cosa) pensi?** what are you thinking about?; **non sa ~ (cosa) fare** he doesn't know what to do
3 (*indefinito*): **quell'uomo ha un ~ di losco** there's something suspicious about that man; **un certo non so ~** an indefinable something
♦ *det* 1 (*interrogativo: tra tanti*) what; (: *tra pochi*) which; ~ **tipo di film preferisci?** what sort of film do you prefer?; ~ **vestito ti vuoi mettere?** what (*o* which) dress do you want to put on?
2 (*esclamativo: seguito da aggettivo*) how; (: *seguito da sostantivo*) what; ~ **buono!** how delicious!; ~ **bel vestito!** what a lovely dress!
♦ *cong* 1 (*con proposizioni subordinate*) that; **credo ~ verrà** I think he'll come; **voglio ~ tu studi** I want you to study; **so ~ tu c'eri** I know (that) you were there; **non ~**: **non ~ sia sbagliato, ma ...** not that it's wrong, but ...
2 (*finale*) so that; **vieni qua, ~ ti veda** come here, so (that) I can see you

3 (*temporale*): **arrivai ~ eri già partito** you had already left when I arrived; **sono anni ~ non lo vedo** I haven't seen him for years **4** (*in frasi imperative, concessive*): **~ venga pure!** let him come by all means!; **~ tu sia benedetto!** may God bless you! **5** (*comparativo: con più, meno*) than; *vedi anche* **più; meno; così** *etc*

cheti'chella [keti'kella]: **alla ~** *av* stealthily, unobtrusively

---
PAROLA CHIAVE
---

chi [ki] *pron* **1** (*interrogativo: soggetto*) who; (: *oggetto*) who, whom; **~ è?** who is it?; **di ~ è questo libro?** whose book is this?, whose is this book?; **con ~ parli?** who are you talking to?; **a ~ pensi?** who are you thinking about?; **~ di voi?** which of you?; **non so a ~ rivolgermi** I don't know who to ask **2** (*relativo*) whoever, anyone who; **dillo a ~ vuoi** tell whoever you like **3** (*indefinito*): **~ ... ~ ...** some ... others ...; **~ dice una cosa, ~ dice un'altra** some say one thing, others say another

---

chiacchie'rare [kjakkje'rare] *vi* to chat; (*discorrere futilmente*) to chatter; (*far pettegolezzi*) to gossip; **chiacchie'rata** *sf* chat; **chi'acchiere** *sfpl*: **fare due** *o* **quattro chiacchiere** to have a chat; **chiacchie'rone, a** *ag* talkative, chatty; gossipy ♦ *sm/f* chatterbox; gossip

chia'mare [kja'mare] *vt* (*rivolgersi a qn*) to call (in), send for; **~rsi** *vr* (*aver nome*) to be called; **mi chiamo Paolo** my name is Paolo, I'm called Paolo; **~ alle armi** to call up; **~ in giudizio** to summon; **chia'mata** *sf* (*TEL*) call; (*MIL*) call-up

chia'rezza [kja'rettsa] *sf* clearness; clarity

chia'rire [kja'rire] *vt* to make clear; (*fig: spiegare*) to clear up, explain; **~rsi** *vr* to become clear

chi'aro, a [kjaro] *ag* clear; (*luminoso*) clear, bright; (*colore*) pale, light

chiaroveg'gente [kjaroved'dʒɛnte] *sm/f* clairvoyant

chi'asso [kjasso] *sm* uproar, row; **chias'soso, a** *ag* noisy, rowdy; (*vistoso*) showy, gaudy

chi'ave [kjave] *sf* key ♦ *ag inv* key *cpd*; **~ d'accensione** (*AUT*) ignition key; **~ inglese** monkey wrench; **~ di volta** keystone; **chiavis'tello** *sm* bolt

chi'azza [kjattsa] *sf* stain; splash

'chicco, chi [kikko] *sm* grain; (*di caffè*) bean; **~ d'uva** grape

chi'edere [kjedere] *vt* (*per sapere*) to ask; (*per avere*) to ask for ♦ *vi*: **~ di qn** to ask after sb; (*al telefono*) to ask for *o* want sb; **~ qc a qn** to ask sb sth; to ask sb for sth

chi'erico, ci [kjeriko] *sm* cleric; altar boy

chi'esa [kjeza] *sf* church

chi'esto, a *pp di* **chiedere**

'chiglia [kiʎʎa] *sf* keel

'chilo [kilo] *sm* kilo; **chilo'grammo** *sm* kilogram(me); **chilome'traggio** *sm* ≈ mileage; **~metraggio illimitato** unlimited mileage; **chi'lometro** *sm* kilometre

'chimica [kimika] *sf* chemistry

'chimico, a, ci, che [kimiko] *ag* chemical ♦ *sm/f* chemist

'china [kina] *sf* (*pendio*) slope, descent; (*inchiostro*) Indian ink

chi'nare [ki'nare] *vt* to lower, bend; **~rsi** *vr* to stoop, bend

chi'nino [ki'nino] *sm* quinine

chi'occiola [kjɔttʃola] *sf* snail; **scala a ~** spiral staircase

chi'odo [kjɔdo] *sm* nail; (*fig*) obsession

chi'oma [kjɔma] *sf* (*capelli*) head of hair

chi'osco, schi [kjɔsko] *sm* kiosk, stall

chi'ostro [kjɔstro] *sm* cloister

chiro'mante [kiro'mante] *sm/f* palmist

chirur'gia [kirur'dʒia] *sf* surgery; **~ estetica** cosmetic surgery; **chi'rurgo, ghi** *o* **gi** *sm* surgeon

chissà [kis'sa] *av* who knows, I wonder

chi'tarra [ki'tarra] *sf* guitar

chi'udere [kjudere] *vt* to close, shut; (*luce, acqua*) to put off, turn off; (*definitivamente: fabbrica*) to close down, shut down;

(*strada*) to close; (*recingere*) to enclose; (*porre termine a*) to end ♦ *vi* to close, shut; to close down, shut down; to end; **~rsi** *vr* to shut, close; (*ritirarsi: anche fig*) to shut o.s. away; (*ferita*) to close up

chi'unque [ki'unkwe] *pron* (*relativo*) whoever; (*indefinito*) anyone, anybody; **~ sia** whoever it is

chi'uso, a ['kjuzo] *pp di* **chiudere** ♦ *sf* (*di corso d'acqua*) sluice, lock; (*recinto*) enclosure; (*di discorso etc*) conclusion, ending; **chiu'sura** *sf* (*vedi* **chiudere**) closing; shutting; enclosing; putting *o* turning off; ending; (*dispositivo*) catch; fastening; fastener

---

PAROLA CHIAVE

---

ci [tʃi] (*dav lo, la, li, le, ne diventa* **ce**) *pron*
1 (*personale: complemento oggetto*) us; (*: a noi: complemento di termine*) (to) us; (*: riflessivo*) ourselves; (*: reciproco*) each other, one another; (*impersonale*): **~ si veste** we get dressed; **~ ha visti** he's seen us; **non ~ ha dato niente** he gave us nothing; **~ vestiamo** we get dressed; **~ amiamo** we love one another *o* each other
2 (*dimostrativo: di ciò, su ciò, in ciò etc*) about (*o* on *o* of) it; **non so cosa far~** I don't know what to do about it; **che c'entro io?** what have I got to do with it? ♦ *av* (*qui*) here; (*lì*) there; (*moto attraverso luogo*): **~ passa sopra un ponte** a bridge passes over it; **non ~ passa più nessuno** nobody comes this way any more; **esser~** *vedi* **essere**

---

cia'batta [tʃa'batta] *sf* slipper; (*pane*) ciabatta

ci'alda ['tʃalda] *sf* (*CUC*) wafer

ciam'bella [tʃam'bella] *sf* (*CUC*) ring-shaped cake; (*salvagente*) rubber ring

ci'ao ['tʃao] *escl* (*all'arrivo*) hello!; (*alla partenza*) cheerio! (*BRIT*), bye!

cias'cuno, a [tʃas'kuno] (*det: dav sm:* **ciascun** +*C, V*, **ciascuno** +*s impura, gn, pn, ps, x, z*; *dav sf:* **ciascuna** +*C*, **ciascun'** +*V*) *det* every, each; (*ogni*) every ♦ *pron* each

(one); (*tutti*) everyone, everybody

ci'barie [tʃi'barje] *sfpl* foodstuffs

'cibo ['tʃibo] *sm* food

ci'cala [tʃi'kala] *sf* cicada

cica'trice [tʃika'tritʃe] *sf* scar

'cicca ['tʃikka] *sf* cigarette end

'ciccia ['tʃittʃa] (*fam*) *sf* fat

cice'rone [tʃitʃe'rone] *sm* guide

ci'clismo [tʃi'klizmo] *sm* cycling; **ci'clista, i, e** *sm/f* cyclist

'ciclo ['tʃiklo] *sm* cycle; (*di malattia*) course

ciclomo'tore [tʃiklomo'tore] *sm* moped

ci'clone [tʃi'klone] *sm* cyclone

ci'cogna [tʃi'koɲɲa] *sf* stork

ci'coria [tʃi'kɔrja] *sf* chicory

ci'eco, a, ci, che ['tʃɛko] *ag* blind ♦ *sm/f* blind man/woman

ci'elo ['tʃɛlo] *sm* sky; (*REL*) heaven

'cifra ['tʃifra] *sf* (*numero*) figure; numeral; (*somma di denaro*) sum, figure; (*monogramma*) monogram, initials *pl*; (*codice*) code, cipher

'ciglio, i ['tʃiʎʎo] (*delle palpebre: pl(f)* **ciglia**) *sm* (*margine*) edge, verge; (*eye*)lash; (*eye*)lid; (*sopracciglio*) eyebrow

'cigno ['tʃiɲɲo] *sm* swan

cigo'lare [tʃigo'lare] *vi* to squeak, creak

'Cile ['tʃile] *sm*: **il ~** Chile

ci'lecca [tʃi'lekka] *sf*: **far ~** to fail

cili'egia, gie *o* **ge** [tʃi'ljɛdʒa] *sf* cherry; **cili'egio** *sm* cherry tree

cilin'drata [tʃilin'drata] *sf* (*AUT*) (cubic) capacity; **una macchina di grossa ~** a big-engined car

ci'lindro [tʃi'lindro] *sm* cylinder; (*cappello*) top hat

'cima ['tʃima] *sf* (*sommità*) top; (*di monte*) top, summit; (*estremità*) end; **in ~ a** at the top of; **da ~ a fondo** from top to bottom; (*fig*) from beginning to end

'cimice ['tʃimitʃe] *sf* (*ZOOL*) bug; (*puntina*) drawing pin (*BRIT*), thumbtack (*US*)

cimini'era [tʃimi'njera] *sf* chimney; (*di nave*) funnel

cimi'tero [tʃimi'tero] *sm* cemetery

'Cina ['tʃina] *sf*: **la ~** China

cin'cin [tʃin'tʃin] *escl* cheers!

cin cin [tʃin'tʃin] *escl* = **cincin**

'**cinema** ['tʃinema] *sm inv* cinema; **cine'presa** *sf* cine-camera

ci'**nese** [tʃi'nese] *ag, sm/f, sm* Chinese *inv*

'**cingere** ['tʃindʒere] *vt* (*attorniare*) to surround, encircle

'**cinghia** ['tʃingja] *sf* strap; (*cintura, TECN*) belt

cinghi'ale [tʃin'gjale] *sm* wild boar

cinguet'tare [tʃingwet'tare] *vi* to twitter

'**cinico, a, ci, che** ['tʃiniko] *ag* cynical ♦ *sm/f* cynic; **ci'nismo** *sm* cynicism

cin'quanta [tʃin'kwanta] *num* fifty; **cinquan'tesimo, a** *num* fiftieth

cinquan'tina [tʃinkwan'tina] *sf* (*serie*): **una ~ (di)** about fifty; (*età*): **essere sulla ~** to be about fifty

'**cinque** ['tʃinkwe] *num* five; **avere ~ anni** to be five (years old); **il ~ dicembre 1999** the fifth of December 1999; **alle ~** (*ora*) at five (o'clock)

cinque'cento [tʃinkwe'tʃento] *num* five hundred ♦ *sm*: **il C~** the sixteenth century

'**cinto, a** ['tʃinto] *pp di* **cingere**

cin'tura [tʃin'tura] *sf* belt; **~ di salvataggio** lifebelt (*BRIT*), life preserver (*US*); **~ di sicurezza** (*AUT, AER*) safety *o* seat belt

ciò [tʃɔ] *pron* this; that; **~ che** what; **~ nonostante** *o* **nondimeno** nevertheless, in spite of that

ci'occa, che ['tʃɔkka] *sf* (*di capelli*) lock

ciocco'lata [tʃokko'lata] *sf* chocolate; (*bevanda*) (hot) chocolate; **cioccola'tino** *sm* chocolate; **ciocco'lato** *sm* chocolate

cioè [tʃo'ɛ] *av* that is (to say)

ciondo'lare [tʃondo'lare] *vi* to dangle; (*fig*) to loaf (about); **ci'ondolo** *sm* pendant

ci'otola ['tʃɔtola] *sf* bowl

ci'ottolo ['tʃɔttolo] *sm* pebble; (*di strada*) cobble(stone)

ci'polla [tʃi'polla] *sf* onion; (*di tulipano etc*) bulb

ci'presso [tʃi'presso] *sm* cypress (tree)

'**cipria** ['tʃiprja] *sf* (face) powder

'**Cipro** ['tʃipro] *sm* Cyprus

'**circa** ['tʃirka] *av* about, roughly ♦ *prep* about, concerning; **a mezzogiorno ~** about midday

'**circo, chi** ['tʃirko] *sm* circus

circo'lare [tʃirko'lare] *vi* to circulate; (*AUT*) to drive (along), move (along) ♦ *ag* circular ♦ *sf* (*AMM*) circular; (*di autobus*) circle (line); **circolazi'one** *sf* circulation; (*AUT*): **la circolazione** (the) traffic

'**circolo** ['tʃirkolo] *sm* circle

circon'dare [tʃirkon'dare] *vt* to surround

circonfe'renza [tʃirkonfe'rentsa] *sf* circumference

circonvallazi'one [tʃirkonvallat'tsjone] *sf* ring road (*BRIT*), beltway (*US*); (*per evitare una città*) by-pass

circos'critto, a [tʃirkos'kritto] *pp di* **circoscrivere**

circos'crivere [tʃirkos'krivere] *vt* to circumscribe; (*fig*) to limit, restrict; **circoscrizi'one** *sf* (*AMM*) district, area; **circoscrizione elettorale** constituency

circos'petto, a [tʃirkos'petto] *ag* circumspect, cautious

circos'tante [tʃirkos'tante] *ag* surrounding, neighbouring

circos'tanza [tʃirkos'tantsa] *sf* circumstance; (*occasione*) occasion

cir'cuito [tʃir'kuito] *sm* circuit

CISL *sigla f* (= *Confederazione Italiana Sindacati Lavoratori*) *trades union organization*

'**ciste** ['tʃiste] *sf* = **cisti**

cis'terna [tʃis'terna] *sf* tank, cistern

'**cisti** ['tʃisti] *sf* cyst

C.I.T. [tʃit] *sigla f* = **Compagnia Italiana Turismo**

ci'tare [tʃi'tare] *vt* (*DIR*) to summon; (*autore*) to quote; (*a esempio, modello*) to cite; **citazi'one** *sf* summons *sg*; quotation; (*di persona*) mention

ci'tofono [tʃi'tɔfono] *sm* entry phone; (*in uffici*) intercom

città [tʃit'ta] *sf inv* town; (*importante*) city; **~ universitaria** university campus

cittadi'nanza [tʃittadi'nantsa] *sf* citizens *pl*; (*DIR*) citizenship

citta'dino, a [tʃitta'dino] *ag* town *cpd*; city *cpd* ♦ *sm/f* (*di uno Stato*) citizen; (*abitante*

di città) townsman, city dweller
ci'uco, a, chi, che ['tʃuko] *sm/f* ass
ci'uffo ['tʃuffo] *sm* tuft
ci'vetta [tʃi'vetta] *sf* (*ZOOL*) owl; (*fig: donna*) flirt ♦ *ag inv*: **auto/nave ~** decoy car/ship
'civico, a, ci, che ['tʃiviko] *ag* civic; (*museo*) municipal, town *cpd*; city *cpd*
ci'vile [tʃi'vile] *ag* civil; (*non militare*) civilian; (*nazione*) civilized ♦ *sm* civilian
civilizzazi'one [tʃiviliddzat'tsjone] *sf* civilization
civiltà [tʃivil'ta] *sf* civilization; (*cortesia*) civility
'clacson *sm inv* (*AUT*) horn
cla'more *sm* (*frastuono*) din, uproar, clamour; (*fig*) outcry; **clamo'roso, a** *ag* noisy; (*fig*) sensational
clandes'tino, a *ag* clandestine; (*POL*) underground, clandestine; (*immigrato*) illegal ♦ *sm/f* stowaway
clari'netto *sm* clarinet
'classe *sf* class; **di ~** (*fig*) with class; of excellent quality
'classico, a, ci, che *ag* classical; (*tradizionale: moda*) classic(al) ♦ *sm* classic; classical author
clas'sifica *sf* classification; (*SPORT*) placings *pl*
classifi'care *vt* to classify; (*candidato, compito*) to grade; **~rsi** *vr* to be placed
'clausola *sf* (*DIR*) clause
'clava *sf* club
clavi'cembalo [klavi'tʃembalo] *sm* harpsichord
cla'vicola *sf* (*ANAT*) collar bone
cle'mente *ag* merciful; (*clima*) mild; **cle'menza** *sf* mercy, clemency; mildness
'clero *sm* clergy
clic'care *vi* (*INFORM*): **~ su** to click on
cli'ente *sm/f* customer, client; **clien'tela** *sf* customers *pl*, clientèle
'clima, i *sm* climate; **cli'matico, a, ci, che** *ag* climatic; **stazione climatica** health resort; **climatizzatore** *sm* air conditioning system; **climatizzazi'one** *sf* (*TECN*) air conditioning
'clinica, che *sf* (*scienza*) clinical medicine;

(*casa di cura*) clinic, nursing home; (*settore d'ospedale*) clinic
'clinico, a, ci, che *ag* clinical ♦ *sm* (*medico*) clinician
clo'aca, che *sf* sewer
'cloro *sm* chlorine
cloro'formio *sm* chloroform
club *sm inv* club
c.m. *abbr* = **corrente mese**
coabi'tare *vi* to live together
coagu'lare *vt* to coagulate ♦ *vi* to coagulate; (*latte*) to curdle; **~rsi** *vr* to coagulate; to curdle
coalizi'one [koalit'tsjone] *sf* coalition
co'atto, a *ag* (*DIR*) compulsory, forced
'COBAS *sigla mpl* (= *Comitati di base*) *independent trades unions*
Coca'Cola ® *sf* Coca-Cola ®
coca'ina *sf* cocaine
cocci'nella [kottʃi'nella] *sf* ladybird (*BRIT*), ladybug (*US*)
'coccio ['kɔttʃo] *sm* earthenware; (*vaso*) earthenware pot; **~i** *smpl* (*frammenti*) fragments (of pottery)
cocci'uto, a [kot'tʃuto] *ag* stubborn, pigheaded
'cocco, chi *sm* (*pianta*) coconut palm; (*frutto*): **noce di ~** coconut ♦ *sm/f* (*fam*) darling
cocco'drillo *sm* crocodile
cocco'lare *vt* to cuddle, fondle
co'cente [ko'tʃente] *ag* (*anche fig*) burning
co'comero *sm* watermelon
co'cuzzolo [ko'kuttsolo] *sm* top; (*di capo, cappello*) crown
'coda *sf* tail; (*fila di persone, auto*) queue (*BRIT*), line (*US*); (*di abiti*) train; **con la ~ dell'occhio** out of the corner of one's eye; **mettersi in ~** to queue (up) (*BRIT*), line up (*US*); to join the queue (*BRIT*) o line (*US*); **~ di cavallo** (*acconciatura*) ponytail
co'dardo, a *ag* cowardly ♦ *sm/f* coward
'codice ['kɔditʃe] *sm* code; **~ di avviamento postale** postcode (*BRIT*), zip code (*US*); **~ fiscale** tax code; **~ della strada** highway code
coe'rente *ag* coherent; **coe'renza** *sf*

coherence

'coe'taneo, a *ag, sm/f* contemporary

'cofano *sm* (*AUT*) bonnet (*BRIT*), hood (*US*); (*forziere*) chest

'cogli ['kɔʎʎi] *prep* + *det* = con + gli; *vedi* con

'cogliere ['kɔʎʎere] *vt* (*fiore, frutto*) to pick, gather; (*sorprendere*) to catch, surprise; (*bersaglio*) to hit; (*fig: momento opportuno etc*) to grasp, seize, take; (*: capire*) to grasp; ~ qn in flagrante *o* in fallo to catch sb red-handed

co'gnato, a [koɲ'ɲato] *sm/f* brother-/sister-in-law

co'gnome [koɲ'ɲome] *sm* surname

'coi *prep* + *det* = con + i; *vedi* con

coinci'denza [kointʃi'dentsa] *sf* coincidence; (*FERR, AER, di autobus*) connection

coin'cidere [koin'tʃidere] *vi* to coincide; coin'ciso, a *pp di* coincidere

coin'volgere [koin'vɔldʒere] *vt*: ~ in to involve in; coin'volto, a *pp di* coinvolgere

col *prep* + *det* = con + il; *vedi* con

cola'brodo *sm inv* strainer

cola'pasta *sm inv* colander

co'lare *vt* (*liquido*) to strain; (*pasta*) to drain; (*oro fuso*) to pour ♦ *vi* (*sudore*) to drip; (*botte*) to leak; (*cera*) to melt; ~ a picco *vt, vi* (*nave*) to sink

co'lata *sf* (*di lava*) flow; (*FONDERIA*) casting

colazi'one [kolat'tsjone] *sf* (*anche: prima* ~) breakfast; (*anche: seconda* ~) lunch; fare ~ to have breakfast (*o* lunch)

co'lei *pron vedi* colui

co'lera *sm* (*MED*) cholera

'colica *sf* (*MED*) colic

'colla *sf* glue; (*di farina*) paste

collabo'rare *vi* to collaborate; ~ a to collaborate on; (*giornale*) to contribute to; collabora'tore, 'trice *sm/f* collaborator; contributor

col'lana *sf* necklace; (*collezione*) collection, series

col'lant [kɔ'lã] *sm inv* tights *pl*

col'lare *sm* collar

col'lasso *sm* (*MED*) collapse

collau'dare *vt* to test, try out; col'laudo *sm* testing *no pl*; test

'colle *sm* hill

col'lega, ghi, ghe *sm/f* colleague

collega'mento *sm* connection; (*MIL*) liaison

colle'gare *vt* to connect, join, link; ~rsi *vr* (*RADIO, TV*) to link up; ~rsi con (*TEL*) to get through to

col'legio [kol'lɛdʒo] *sm* college; (*convitto*) boarding school; ~ elettorale (*POL*) constituency

'collera *sf* anger

col'lerico, a, ci, che *ag* quick-tempered, irascible

col'letta *sf* collection

collettività *sf* community

collet'tivo, a *ag* collective; (*interesse*) general, everybody's; (*biglietto, visita etc*) group *cpd* ♦ *sm* (*POL*) (political) group

col'letto *sm* collar

collezio'nare [kollettsjo'nare] *vt* to collect

collezi'one [kollet'tsjone] *sf* collection

colli'mare *vi* to correspond, coincide

collisi'one *sf* collision

'collo *sm* neck; (*di abito*) neck, collar; (*pacco*) parcel; ~ del piede instep

colloca'mento *sm* (*impiego*) employment; (*disposizione*) placing, arrangement

collo'care *vt* (*libri, mobili*) to place; (*COMM: merce*) to find a market for

col'loquio *sm* conversation, talk; (*ufficiale, per un lavoro*) interview; (*INS*) preliminary oral exam

col'mare *vt*: ~ di (*anche fig*) to fill with; (*dare in abbondanza*) to load *o* overwhelm with; 'colmo, a *ag*: colmo (di) full (of) ♦ *sm* summit, top; (*fig*) height; al colmo della disperazione in the depths of despair; è il colmo! it's the last straw!

co'lombo, a *sm/f* dove; pigeon

co'lonia *sf* colony; (*per bambini*) holiday camp; (acqua di) ~ (eau de) cologne; coloni'ale *ag* colonial ♦ *sm/f* colonist, settler

co'lonna *sf* column; **~ vertebrale** spine, spinal column

colon'nello *sm* colonel

co'lono *sm* (*coltivatore*) tenant farmer

colo'rante *sm* colouring

colo'rare *vt* to colour; (*disegno*) to colour in

co'lore *sm* colour; **a ~i** in colour, colour *cpd*; **farne di tutti i ~i** to get up to all sorts of mischief

colo'rito, a *ag* coloured; (*viso*) rosy, pink; (*linguaggio*) colourful ♦ *sm* (*tinta*) colour; (*carnagione*) complexion

co'loro *pron pl vedi* **colui**

co'losso *sm* colossus

'colpa *sf* fault; (*biasimo*) blame; (*colpevolezza*) guilt; (*azione colpevole*) offence; (*peccato*) sin; **di chi è la ~?** whose fault is it?; **è ~ sua** it's his fault; **per ~ di** through, owing to; **col'pevole** *ag* guilty

col'pire *vt* to hit, strike; (*fig*) to strike; **rimanere colpito da qc** to be amazed *o* struck by sth

'colpo *sm* (*urto*) knock; (: *affettivo*) blow, shock; (: *aggressivo*) blow; (*di pistola*) shot; (*MED*) stroke; (*rapina*) raid; **di ~** suddenly; **fare ~** to make a strong impression; **~ di grazia** coup de grâce; **~ di scena** (*TEATRO*) coup de théâtre; (*fig*) dramatic turn of events; **~ di sole** sunstroke; **~ di Stato** coup d'état; **~ di telefono** phone call; **~ di testa** (sudden) impulse *o* whim; **~ di vento** gust (of wind)

coltel'lata *sf* stab

col'tello *sm* knife; **~ a serramanico** clasp knife

colti'vare *vt* to cultivate; (*verdura*) to grow, cultivate; **coltiva'tore** *sm* farmer; **coltivazi'one** *sf* cultivation; growing

'colto, a *pp di* **cogliere** ♦ *ag* (*istruito*) cultured, educated

'coltre *sf* blanket

col'tura *sf* cultivation

co'lui (*f* **co'lei**, *pl* **co'loro**) *pron* the one; **~ che parla** the one *o* the man *o* the person who is speaking; **colei che amo** the one *o*

the woman *o* the person (whom) I love

'coma *sm inv* coma

comanda'mento *sm* (*REL*) commandment

coman'dante *sm* (*MIL*) commander, commandant; (*di reggimento*) commanding officer; (*NAUT, AER*) captain

coman'dare *vi* to be in command ♦ *vt* to command; (*imporre*) to order, command; **~ a qn di fare** to order sb to do; **co'mando** *sm* (*ingiunzione*) order, command; (*autorità*) command; (*TECN*) control

co'mare *sf* (*madrina*) godmother

combaci'are [kombaˈtʃare] *vi* to meet; (*fig: coincidere*) to coincide

com'battere *vt, vi* to fight; **combatti'mento** *sm* fight; fighting *no pl*; (*di pugilato*) match

combi'nare *vt* to combine; (*organizzare*) to arrange; (*fam: fare*) to make, cause; **combinazi'one** *sf* combination; (*caso fortuito*) coincidence; **per combinazione** by chance

combus'tibile *ag* combustible ♦ *sm* fuel

com'butta (*peg*) *sf*: **in ~** in league

PAROLA CHIAVE

'come *av* **1** (*alla maniera di*) like; **ti comporti ~ lui** you behave like him *o* like he does; **bianco ~ la neve** (as) white as snow; **~ se** as if, as though

2 (*in qualità di*) as a; **lavora ~ autista** he works as a driver

3 (*interrogativo*) how; **~ ti chiami?** what's your name?; **~ sta?** how are you?; **com'è il tuo amico?** what is your friend like?; **~?** (*prego?*) pardon?, sorry?; **~ mai?** how come?; **~ mai non ci hai avvertiti?** why on earth didn't you warn us?

4 (*esclamativo*): **~ sei bravo!** how clever you are!; **~ mi dispiace!** I'm terribly sorry!

♦ *cong* **1** (*in che modo*) how; **mi ha spiegato ~ l'ha conosciuto** he told me how he met him

2 (*correlativo*) as; (*con comparativi di maggioranza*) than; **non è bravo ~ pensavo** he isn't as clever as I thought; **è meglio di ~ pensassi** it's better than I thought

3 (*appena che, quando*) as soon as; **~ arrivò, iniziò a lavorare** as soon as he arrived, he set to work; *vedi* **così; tanto**

comico, a, ci, che *ag* (*TEATRO*) comic; (*buffo*) comical ♦ *sm* (*attore*) comedian, comic actor

co'mignolo [ko'miɲɲolo] *sm* chimney top

cominci'are [komin'tʃare] *vt, vi* to begin, start; **~ a fare/col fare** to begin to do/by doing

comi'tato *sm* committee

comi'tiva *sf* party, group

co'mizio [ko'mittsjo] *sm* (*POL*) meeting, assembly

com'mando *sm inv* commando (squad)

com'media *sf* comedy; (*opera teatrale*) play; (*: che fa ridere*) comedy; (*fig*) playacting *no pl*; **commedi'ante** (*peg*) *sm/f* third-rate actor/actress; (*fig*) sham

ommemo'rare *vt* to commemorate

ommenda'tore *sm* official title awarded for services to one's country

ommen'tare *vt* to comment on; (*testo*) to annotate; (*RADIO, TV*) to give a commentary on; **commenta'tore, 'trice** *sm/f* commentator; **com'mento** *sm* comment; (*a un testo, RADIO, TV*) commentary

ommerci'ale [kommer'tʃale] *ag* commercial, trading; (*peg*) commercial

ommerci'ante [kommer'tʃante] *sm/f* trader, dealer; (*negoziante*) shopkeeper

ommerci'are [kommer'tʃare] *vt, vi*: **~ in** to deal or trade in

om'mercio [kom'mertʃo] *sm* trade, commerce; **essere in ~** (*prodotto*) to be on the market *o* on sale; **essere nel ~** (*persona*) to be in business

om'messa *sf* (*COMM*) order

om'messo, a *pp di* **commettere** ♦ *sm/f* shop assistant (*BRIT*), sales clerk (*US*) ♦ *sm* (*impiegato*) clerk; **~ viaggiatore** commercial traveller

ommes'tibile *ag* edible; **~i** *smpl* foodstuffs

com'mettere *vt* to commit

com'miato *sm* leave-taking

commi'nare *vt* (*DIR*) to threaten; to inflict

commissari'ato *sm* (*AMM*) commissionership; (*: sede*) commissioner's office; (*: di polizia*) police station

commis'sario *sm* commissioner; (*di pubblica sicurezza*) ≈ (police) superintendent (*BRIT*), (police) captain (*US*); (*SPORT*) steward; (*membro di commissione*) member of a committee *o* board

commissio'nario *sm* (*COMM*) agent, broker

commissi'one *sf* (*incarico*) errand; (*comitato, percentuale*) commission; (*COMM: ordinazione*) order

commit'tente *sm/f* (*COMM*) purchaser, customer

com'mosso, a *pp di* **commuovere**

commo'vente *ag* moving

commozi'one [kommot'tsjone] *sf* emotion, deep feeling; **~ cerebrale** (*MED*) concussion

commu'overe *vt* to move, affect; **~rsi** *vr* to be moved

commu'tare *vt* (*pena*) to commute; (*ELETTR*) to change *o* switch over

comò *sm inv* chest of drawers

como'dino *sm* bedside table

comodità *sf inv* comfort; convenience

'comodo, a *ag* comfortable; (*facile*) easy; (*conveniente*) convenient; (*utile*) useful, handy ♦ *sm* comfort; convenience; **con ~** at one's convenience *o* leisure; **fare il proprio ~** to do as one pleases; **far ~** to be useful *o* handy

compae'sano, a *sm/f* fellow countryman; person from the same town

com'pagine [kom'padʒine] *sf* (*squadra*) team

compa'gnia [kompaɲ'ɲia] *sf* company; (*gruppo*) gathering

com'pagno, a [kom'paɲɲo] *sm/f* (*di classe, gioco*) companion; (*POL*) comrade

compa'rare *vt* to compare

compara'tivo, a *ag, sm* comparative

compa'rire *vi* to appear; **com'parsa** *sf* appearance; (*TEATRO*) walk-on; (*CINEMA*)

extra; **comparso, a** *pp di* **comparire**
compartecipazi'one [kompar-
tetʃipat'tsjone] *sf* sharing; (*quota*) share; **~
agli utili** profit-sharing
comparti'mento *sm* compartment;
(*AMM*) district
compas'sato, a *ag* (*persona*) composed
compassi'one *sf* compassion, pity; **avere
~ di qn** to feel sorry for sb, to pity sb
com'passo *sm* (pair of) compasses *pl*;
callipers *pl*
compa'tibile *ag* (*scusabile*) excusable;
(*conciliabile, INFORM*) compatible
compa'tire *vt* (*aver compassione di*) to
sympathize with, feel sorry for; (*scusare*) to
make allowances for
com'patto, a *ag* compact; (*roccia*) solid;
(*folla*) dense; (*fig: gruppo, partito*) united
com'pendio *sm* summary; (*libro*)
compendium
compen'sare *vt* (*equilibrare*) to
compensate for, make up for; **~ qn di**
(*rimunerare*) to pay *o* remunerate sb for;
(*risarcire*) to pay compensation to sb for;
(*fig: fatiche, dolori*) to reward sb for;
com'penso *sm* compensation; payment;
remuneration; reward; **in compenso**
(*d'altra parte*) on the other hand
'compera *sf* (*acquisto*) purchase; **fare le
~e** to do the shopping
compe'rare *vt* = **comprare**
compe'tente *ag* competent; (*mancia*) apt,
suitable; **compe'tenza** *sf* competence;
competenze *sfpl* (*onorari*) fees
com'petere *vi* to compete, vie; (*DIR:
spettare*) **~ a** to lie within the competence
of; **competizi'one** *sf* competition
compia'cente [kompja'tʃente] *ag*
courteous, obliging; **compia'cenza** *sf*
courtesy
compia'cere [kompja'tʃere] *vi:* **~ a** to
gratify, please ♦ *vt* to please; **~rsi** *vr*
(*provare soddisfazione*): **~rsi** *o* **per qc** to
be delighted at sth; (*rallegrarsi*): **~rsi con
qn** to congratulate sb; (*degnarsi*): **~rsi di
fare** to be so good as to do;
compiaci'uto, a *pp di* **compiacere**

compi'angere [kom'pjandʒere] *vt* to
sympathize with, feel sorry for;
compi'anto, a *pp di* **compiangere**
'compiere *vt* (*concludere*) to finish,
complete; (*adempiere*) to carry out, fulfil;
~rsi *vr* (*avverarsi*) to be fulfilled, come true;
~ gli anni to have one's birthday
compi'lare *vt* (*modulo*) to fill in;
(*dizionario, elenco*) to compile
com'pire *vt* = **compiere**
compi'tare *vt* to spell out
'compito *sm* (*incarico*) task, duty; (*dovere*)
duty; (*INS*) exercise; (*: a casa*) piece of
homework; **fare i ~i** to do one's homework
com'pito, a *ag* well-mannered, polite
comple'anno *sm* birthday
complemen'tare *ag* complementary;
(*INS: materia*) subsidiary
comple'mento *sm* complement; (*MIL*)
reserve (troops); **~ oggetto** (*LING*) direct
object
complessità *sf* complexity
comples'sivo, a *ag* (*globale*)
comprehensive, overall; (*totale: cifra*) total
com'plesso, a *ag* complex ♦ *sm* (*PSIC,
EDIL*) complex; (*MUS: corale*) ensemble;
(*: orchestrina*) band; (*: di musica pop*)
group; **in** *o* **nel ~** on the whole
comple'tare *vt* to complete
com'pleto, a *ag* complete; (*teatro,
autobus*) full ♦ *sm* suit; **al ~** full; (*tutti
presenti*) all present
compli'care *vt* to complicate; **~rsi** *vr* to
become complicated; **complicazi'one** *sf*
complication
'complice ['kɔmplitʃe] *sm/f* accomplice
complimen'tarsi *vr:* **~ con** to
congratulate
compli'mento *sm* compliment; **~i** *smpl*
(*cortesia eccessiva*) ceremony *sg*; (*ossequi*)
regards, compliments; **~i!** congratulations!;
senza ~i! don't stand on ceremony!; **make
yourself at home!; help yourself!**
complot'tare *vi* to plot, conspire
com'plotto *sm* plot, conspiracy
compo'nente *sm/f* member ♦ *sm*
component

componi'mento sm (DIR) settlement; (INS) composition; (poetico, teatrale) work

com'porre vt (musica, testo) to compose; (mettere in ordine) to arrange; (DIR: lite) to settle; (TIP) to set; (TEL) to dial

comporta'mento sm behaviour

compor'tare vt (implicare) to involve; ~rsi vr to behave

composi'tore, 'trice sm/f composer; (TIP) compositor, typesetter

composizi'one [kompozit'tsjone] sf composition; (DIR) settlement

com'posta sf (CUC) stewed fruit no pl; (AGR) compost; vedi anche composto

compos'tezza [kompos'tettsa] sf composure; decorum

com'posto, a pp di comporre ♦ ag (persona) composed, self-possessed; (: decoroso) dignified; (formato da più elementi) compound cpd ♦ sm compound

com'prare vt to buy; compra'tore, 'trice sm/f buyer, purchaser

com'prendere vt (contenere) to comprise, consist of; (capire) to understand

comprensi'one sf understanding

compren'sivo, a ag (prezzo): ~ di inclusive of; (indulgente) understanding

com'preso, a pp di comprendere ♦ ag (incluso) included

com'pressa sf (MED: garza) compress; (: pastiglia) tablet; vedi anche compresso

compressi'one sf compression

com'presso, a pp di comprimere ♦ ag (vedi comprimere) pressed; compressed; repressed

com'primere vt (premere) to press; (FISICA) to compress; (fig) to repress

compro'messo, a pp di compromettere ♦ sm compromise

compro'mettere vt to compromise

compro'vare vt to confirm

com'punto, a ag contrite

compu'tare vt to calculate

com'puter sm inv computer

computiste'ria sf accounting, book-keeping

'computo sm calculation

comu'nale ag municipal, town cpd, ≈ borough cpd

co'mune ag common; (consueto) common, everyday; (di livello medio) average; (ordinario) ordinary ♦ sm (AMM) town council; (: sede) town hall ♦ sf (di persone) commune; fuori del ~ out of the ordinary; avere in ~ to have in common, share; mettere in ~ to share

comuni'care vt (notizia) to pass on, convey; (malattia) to pass on; (ansia etc) to communicate; (trasmettere: calore etc) to transmit, communicate; (REL) to administer communion to ♦ vi to communicate; ~rsi vr (propagarsi): ~rsi a to spread to; (REL) to receive communion

comuni'cato sm communiqué; ~ stampa press release

comunicazi'one [komunikat'tsjone] sf communication; (annuncio) announcement; (TEL): ~ (telefonica) (telephone) call; dare la ~ a qn to put sb through; ottenere la ~ to get through

comuni'one sf communion; ~ di beni (DIR) joint ownership of property

comu'nismo sm communism; comu'nista, i, e ag, sm/f communist

comunità sf inv community; C~ Europea European Community

co'munque cong however, no matter how ♦ av (in ogni modo) in any case; (tuttavia) however, nevertheless

con prep with; partire col treno to leave by train; ~ mio grande stupore to my great astonishment; ~ tutto ciò for all that

co'nato sm: ~ di vomito retching

'conca, che sf (GEO) valley

con'cedere [kon'tʃedere] vt (accordare) to grant; (ammettere) to admit, concede; ~rsi qc to treat o.s. to sth, to allow o.s. sth

concentra'mento [kontʃentra'mento] sm concentration

concen'trare [kontʃen'trare] vt to concentrate; ~rsi vr to concentrate; concentrazi'one sf concentration

conce'pire [kontʃe'pire] vt (bambino) to conceive; (progetto, idea) to conceive (of);

(*metodo, piano*) to devise
con'cernere [kon'tʃernere] vt to concern
concer'tare [kontʃer'tare] vt (*MUS*) to harmonize; (*ordire*) to devise, plan; **~rsi** vr to agree
con'certo [kon'tʃerto] sm (*MUS*) concert; (*: componimento*) concerto
concessio'nario [kontʃessjo'narjo] sm (*COMM*) agent, dealer
con'cesso, a [kon'tʃesso] pp di concedere
con'cetto [kon'tʃetto] sm (*pensiero, idea*) concept; (*opinione*) opinion
concezi'one [kontʃet'tsjone] sf conception
con'chiglia [kon'kiʎʎa] sf shell
'concia ['kontʃa] sf (*di pelle*) tanning; (*di tabacco*) curing; (*sostanza*) tannin
conci'are [kon'tʃare] vt (*pelli*) to tan; (*tabacco*) to cure; (*fig: ridurre in cattivo stato*) to beat up; **~rsi** vr (*sporcarsi*) to get in a mess; (*vestirsi male*) to dress badly
concili'are [kontʃi'ljare] vt to reconcile; (*contravvenzione*) to pay on the spot; (*sonno*) to be conducive to, induce; **~rsi qc** to gain o win sth (for o.s.); **~rsi qn** to win sb over; **~rsi con** to be reconciled with; conciliazi'one sf reconciliation; (*DIR*) settlement
con'cilio [kon'tʃiljo] sm (*REL*) council
con'cime [kon'tʃime] sm manure; (*chimico*) fertilizer
con'ciso, a [kon'tʃizo] ag concise, succinct
conci'tato, a [kontʃi'tato] ag excited, emotional
concitta'dino, a [kontʃitta'dino] sm/f fellow citizen
con'cludere vt to conclude; (*portare a compimento*) to conclude, finish, bring to an end; (*operare positivamente*) to achieve ♦ vi (*essere convincente*) to be conclusive; **~rsi** vr to come to an end, close; conclusi'one sf conclusion; (*risultato*) result; conclu'sivo, a ag conclusive; (*finale*) final; con'cluso, a pp di concludere
concor'danza [konkor'dantsa] sf (*anche LING*) agreement
concor'dare vt (*tregua, prezzo*) to agree

on; (*LING*) to make agree ♦ vi to agree; concor'dato sm agreement; (*REL*) concordat
con'corde ag (*d'accordo*) in agreement; (*simultaneo*) simultaneous
concor'rente sm/f competitor; (*INS*) candidate; concor'renza sf competition
con'correre vi: ~ (**in**) (*MAT*) to converge o meet (in); ~ (**a**) (*competere*) to compete (for); (*: INS: a una cattedra*) to apply (for); (*partecipare: a un'impresa*) to take part (in), contribute (to); con'corso, a pp di concorrere ♦ sm competition; (*INS*) competitive examination; **concorso di colpa** (*DIR*) contributory negligence
con'creto, a ag concrete
concussi'one sf (*DIR*) extortion
con'danna sf sentence; conviction; condemnation
condan'nare vt (*DIR*): ~ **a** to sentence to; ~ **per** to convict of; (*disapprovare*) to condemn; condan'nato, a sm/f convict
conden'sare vt to condense; **~rsi** vr to condense; condensazi'one sf condensation
condi'mento sm seasoning; dressing
con'dire vt to season; (*insalata*) to dress
condi'videre vt to share; condi'viso, a pp di condividere
condizio'nale [kondittsjo'nale] ag conditional ♦ sm (*LING*) conditional ♦ sf (*DIR*) suspended sentence
condizio'nare [kondittsjo'nare] vt to condition; **ad aria condizionata** air-conditioned; condiziona'tore sm air conditioner
condizi'one [kondit'tsjone] sf condition; **~i** sfpl (*di pagamento etc*) terms, conditions; **a ~ che** on condition that, provided that
condogli'anze [kondoʎʎ'ʎantse] sfpl condolences
condo'minio sm joint ownership; (*edificio*) jointly-owned building
condo'nare vt (*DIR*) to remit; con'dono sm remission; **condono fiscale** *conditional amnesty for people evading tax*
con'dotta sf (*modo di comportarsi*)

conduct, behaviour; (*di un affare etc*) handling; (*di acqua*) piping; (*incarico sanitario*) country medical practice controlled by a local authority

con'dotto, a *pp di* condurre ♦ *ag*: medico ~ local authority doctor (*in country district*) ♦ *sm* (*canale, tubo*) pipe, conduit; (*ANAT*) duct

condu'cente [kondu'tʃɛnte] *sm* driver

con'durre *vt* to conduct; (*azienda*) to manage; (*accompagnare: bambino*) to take; (*automobile*) to drive; (*trasportare: acqua, gas*) to convey, conduct; (*fig*) to lead ♦ *vi* to lead; condursi *vr* to behave, conduct o.s.

con'farsi *vr*: ~ a to suit, agree with

confederazi'one [konfederat'tsjone] *sf* confederation

confe'renza [konfe'rɛntsa] *sf* (*discorso*) lecture; (*riunione*) conference; ~ stampa press conference; conferenzi'ere, a *sm/f* lecturer

confe'rire *vt*: ~ qc a qn to give sth to sb, bestow sth on sb ♦ *vi* to confer

con'ferma *sf* confirmation

confer'mare *vt* to confirm

confes'sare *vt* to confess; ~rsi *vr* to confess; andare a ~rsi (*REL*) to go to confession; confessio'nale *ag, sm* confessional; confessi'one *sf* confession; (*setta religiosa*) denomination; confes'sore *sm* confessor

con'fetto *sm* sugared almond; (*MED*) pill

confezio'nare [konfettsjo'nare] *vt* (*vestito*) to make (up); (*merci, pacchi*) to package

confezi'one [konfet'tsjone] *sf* (*di abiti: da uomo*) tailoring; (*: da donna*) dressmaking; (*imballaggio*) packaging; ~ regalo gift pack; ~i per signora ladies' wear; ~i da uomo menswear

confic'care *vt*: ~ qc in to hammer o drive sth into; ~rsi *vr* to stick

confi'dare *vi*: ~ in to confide in, rely on ♦ *vt* to confide; ~rsi con qn to confide in sb; confi'dente *sm/f* (*persona amica*) confidant/confidante; (*informatore*) informer; confi'denza *sf* (*familiarità*) intimacy, familiarity; (*fiducia*) trust, confidence; (*rivelazione*) confidence; confidenzi'ale *ag* familiar, friendly; (*segreto*) confidential

configu'rarsi *vr*: ~ a to assume the shape o form of

confi'nare *vi*: ~ con to border on ♦ *vt* (*POL*) to intern; (*fig*) to confine; ~rsi *vr* (*isolarsi*): ~rsi in to shut o.s. up in

Confin'dustria *sigla f* (= *Confederazione Generale dell'Industria Italiana*) employers' association, ≈ CBI (*BRIT*)

con'fine *sm* boundary; (*di paese*) border, frontier

con'fino *sm* internment

confis'care *vt* to confiscate

con'flitto *sm* conflict

conflu'enza [konflu'ɛntsa] *sf* (*di fiumi*) confluence; (*di strade*) junction

conflu'ire *vi* (*fiumi*) to flow into each other, meet; (*strade*) to meet

con'fondere *vt* to mix up, confuse; (*imbarazzare*) to embarrass; (*fig*) (*mescolarsi*) to mingle; (*turbarsi*) to be confused; (*sbagliare*) to get mixed up

confor'mare *vt* (*adeguare*): ~ a to adapt o conform to; ~rsi *vr*: ~rsi (a) to conform (to)

confor'tare *vt* to comfort, console; confor'tevole *ag* (*consolante*) comforting; (*comodo*) comfortable; con'forto *sm* comfort, consolation

confron'tare *vt* to compare

con'fronto *sm* comparison; in o a ~ di in comparison with, compared to; nei miei (o tuoi *etc*) ~i towards me (o you *etc*)

confusi'one *sf* confusion; (*chiasso*) racket, noise; (*imbarazzo*) embarrassment

con'fuso, a *pp di* confondere ♦ *ag* (*vedi* confondere) confused; embarrassed

confu'tare *vt* to refute

conge'dare [kondʒe'dare] *vt* to dismiss; (*MIL*) to demobilize; ~rsi *vr* to take one's leave; con'gedo *sm* (*anche MIL*) leave; prendere congedo da qn to take one's leave of sb; **congedo assoluto** (*MIL*) discharge

conge'gnare [kondʒeŋ'ɲare] *vt* to construct, put together; con'gegno *sm* device, mechanism

conge'lare [kondʒe'lare] *vt* to freeze; ~rsi *vr* to freeze; congela'tore *sm* freezer

congestio'nare [kondʒestjo'nare] *vt* to congest

congesti'one [kondʒes'tjone] *sf* congestion

conget'tura [kondʒet'tura] *sf* conjecture

con'giungere [kon'dʒundʒere] *vt* to join (together); ~rsi *vr* to join (together)

congiunti'vite [kondʒunti'vite] *sf* conjunctivitis

congiun'tivo [kondʒun'tivo] *sm* (*LING*) subjunctive

congi'unto, a [kon'dʒunto] *pp di* **congiungere** ♦ *ag* (*unito*) joined ♦ *sm/f* relative

congiun'tura [kondʒun'tura] *sf* (*giuntura*) junction, join; (*ANAT*) joint; (*circostanza*) juncture; (*ECON*) economic situation

congiunzi'one [kondʒun'tsjone] *sf* (*LING*) conjunction

congi'ura [kon'dʒura] *sf* conspiracy; congiu'rare *vi* to conspire

conglome'rato *sm* (*GEO*) conglomerate; (*fig*) conglomeration; (*EDIL*) concrete

congratu'larsi *vr*: ~ **con qn per qc** to congratulate sb on sth

congratulazi'oni [kongratulat'tsjoni] *sfpl* congratulations

con'grega, ghe *sf* band, bunch

con'gresso *sm* congress

congu'aglio [kon'gwaʎʎo] *sm* balancing, adjusting; (*somma di denaro*) balance

coni'are *vt* to mint, coin; (*fig*) to coin

co'niglio [ko'niʎʎo] *sm* rabbit

coniu'gare *vt* (*LING*) to conjugate; ~rsi *vr* to get married; coniu'gato, a *ag* (*sposato*) married; coniugazi'one *sf* (*LING*) conjugation

'coniuge ['kɔnjudʒe] *sm/f* spouse

connazio'nale [konnattsjo'nale] *sm/f* fellow-countryman/woman

connessi'one *sf* connection

con'nesso, a *pp di* **connettere**

con'nettere *vt* to connect, join ♦ *vi* (*fig*) to think straight

conni'vente *ag* conniving

conno'tati *smpl* distinguishing marks

'cono *sm* cone; ~ **gelato** ice-cream cone

cono'scente [konoʃ'ʃente] *sm/f* acquaintance

cono'scenza [konoʃ'ʃentsa] *sf* (*il sapere*) knowledge *no pl*; (*persona*) acquaintance; (*facoltà sensoriale*) consciousness *no pl*; **perdere ~** to lose consciousness

co'noscere [ko'noʃʃere] *vt* to know; **ci siamo conosciuti a Firenze** we (first) met in Florence; conosci'tore, 'trice *sm/f* connoisseur; conosci'uto, a *pp di* **conoscere** ♦ *ag* well-known

con'quista *sf* conquest

conquis'tare *vt* to conquer; (*fig*) to gain, win

consa'crare *vt* (*REL*) to consecrate; (: *sacerdote*) to ordain; (*dedicare*) to dedicate; (*fig: uso etc*) to sanction; ~rsi a to dedicate o.s. to

consangu'ineo, a *sm/f* blood relation

consa'pevole *ag*: ~ **di** aware *o* conscious of; consapevo'lezza *sf* awareness, consciousness

'conscio, a, sci, sce ['kɔnʃo] *ag*: ~ **di** aware *o* conscious of

consecu'tivo, a *ag* consecutive; (*successivo: giorno*) following, next

con'segna [kon'seɲɲa] *sf* delivery; (*merce consegnata*) consignment; (*custodia*) care, custody; (*MIL: ordine*) orders *pl*; (: *punizione*) confinement to barracks; **pagamento alla ~** cash on delivery; **dare qc in ~ a qn** to entrust sth to sb

conse'gnare [konseɲ'ɲare] *vt* to deliver; (*affidare*) to entrust, hand over; (*MIL*) to confine to barracks

consegu'enza [konse'gwentsa] *sf* consequence; **per** *o* **di ~** consequently

consegu'ire *vt* to achieve ♦ *vi* to follow

con'senso *sm* approval, consent

consen'tire *vi*: ~ **a** to consent *o* agree to ♦ *vt* to allow, permit con'serva *sf* (CUC) preserve; ~ **di frutta** jam; ~ **di pomodoro** tomato purée

conser'vare *vt* (CUC) to preserve; (*custodire*) to keep; (: **dalla distruzione etc**) to preserve, conserve; **~rsi** *vr* to keep

conserva'tore, 'trice *sm/f* (POL) conservative

conservazi'one [konservat'tsjone] *sf* preservation; conservation

conside'rare *vt* to consider; (*reputare*) to consider, regard; **considerazi'one** *sf* consideration; (*stima*) regard, esteem; **prendere in considerazione** to take into consideration; **conside'revole** *ag* considerable

consigli'are [konsiʎ'ʎare] *vt* (*persona*) to advise; (*metodo, azione*) to recommend, advise, suggest; **~rsi** *vr*: **~rsi con qn** to ask sb for advice; **consigli'ere, a** *sm/f* adviser ♦ *sm*: **consigliere d'amministrazione** board member; **consigliere comunale** town councillor; **con'siglio** *sm* (*suggerimento*) advice *no pl*, piece of advice; (*assemblea*) council; **consiglio d'amministrazione** board; **il Consiglio dei Ministri** (POL) ≈ the Cabinet; **Consiglio d'Europa** Council of Europe

consis'tente *ag* thick; solid; (*fig*) sound, valid; **consis'tenza** *sf* consistency, thickness; solidity; validity

consis'tere *vi*: ~ **in** to consist of; **consis'tito, a** *pp di* **consistere**

conso'lare *ag* consular ♦ *vt* (*confortare*) to console, comfort; (*rallegrare*) to cheer up; **~rsi** *vr* to be comforted; to cheer up

conso'lato *sm* consulate

consolazi'one [konsolat'tsjone] *sf* consolation, comfort

'console[1] *sm* consul

con'sole[2] [kon'sɔl] *sf* (*quadro di comando*) console

conso'nante *sf* consonant

'consono, a *ag*: ~ **a** consistent with, consonant with

con'sorte *sm/f* consort

con'sorzio [kon'sɔrtsjo] *sm* consortium

con'stare *vi*: ~ **di** to consist of ♦ *vb impers*: **mi consta che** it has come to my knowledge that, it appears that

consta'tare *vt* to establish, verify; **constatazi'one** *sf* observation; **constatazione amichevole** *jointly-agreed statement for insurance purposes*

consu'eto, a *ag* habitual, usual; **consue'tudine** *sf* habit, custom; (*usanza*) custom

consu'lente *sm/f* consultant; **consu'lenza** *sf* consultancy

consul'tare *vt* to consult; **~rsi** *vr*: **~rsi con qn** to seek the advice of sb; **consultazi'one** *sf* consultation; **consultazioni** *sfpl* (POL) talks, consultations

consul'torio *sm*: ~ **familiare** family planning clinic

consu'mare *vt* (*logorare: abiti, scarpe*) to wear out; (*usare*) to consume, use up; (*mangiare, bere*) to consume; (DIR) to consummate; **~rsi** *vr* to wear out; to be used up; (*anche fig*) to be consumed; (*combustibile*) to burn out; **consuma'tore** *sm* consumer; **consumazi'one** *sf* (*bibita*) drink; (*spuntino*) snack; (DIR) consummation; **consu'mismo** *sm* consumerism; **con'sumo** *sm* consumption; wear; use

consun'tivo *sm* (ECON) final balance

con'tabile *ag* accounts *cpd*, accounting ♦ *sm/f* accountant; **contabilità** *sf* (*attività, tecnica*) accounting, accountancy; (*insieme dei libri etc*) books *pl*, accounts *pl*; (*ufficio*) accounts department

contachi'lometri [kontaki'lɔmetri] *sm inv* ≈ mileometer

conta'dino, a *sm/f* countryman/woman; farm worker; (*peg*) peasant

contagi'are [konta'dʒare] *vt* to infect

con'tagio [kon'tadʒo] *sm* infection; (*per contatto diretto*) contagion; (*epidemia*) epidemic; **contagi'oso, a** *ag* infectious; contagious

conta'gocce [konta'gottʃe] *sm inv* (MED) dropper

contami'nare *vt* to contaminate

con'tante *sm* cash; **pagare in ~i** to pay cash

con'tare *vt* to count; (*considerare*) to consider ♦ *vi* to count, be of importance; **~ su qn** to count *o* rely on sb; **~ di fare qc** to intend to do sth; **conta'tore** *sm* meter

contat'tare *vt* to contact

con'tatto *sm* contact

'conte *sm* count

conteggi'are [konted'dʒare] *vt* to charge, put on the bill; **con'teggio** *sm* calculation

con'tegno [kon'teɲɲo] *sm* (*comportamento*) behaviour; (*atteggiamento*) attitude; **darsi un ~** to act nonchalant; to pull o.s. together

contem'plare *vt* to contemplate, gaze at; (*DIR*) to make provision for

contemporanea'mente *av* simultaneously; at the same time

contempo'raneo, a *ag*, *sm/f* contemporary

con'tendente *sm/f* opponent, adversary

con'tendere *vi* (*competere*) to compete; (*litigare*) to quarrel ♦ *vt*: **~ qc a qn** to contend with *o* be in competition with sb for sth

conte'nere *vt* to contain; **conteni'tore** *sm* container

conten'tare *vt* to please, satisfy; **~rsi di** to be satisfied with, content o.s. with

conten'tezza [konten'tettsa] *sf* contentment

con'tento, a *ag* pleased, glad; **~ di** pleased with

conte'nuto *sm* contents *pl*; (*argomento*) content

con'tesa *sf* dispute, argument

con'teso, a *pp di* **contendere**

con'tessa *sf* countess

contes'tare *vt* (*DIR*) to notify; (*fig*) to dispute; **contestazi'one** *sf* (*DIR*) notification; dispute; (*protesta*) protest

con'testo *sm* context

con'tiguo, a *ag*: **~ (a)** adjacent (to)

continen'tale *ag*, *sm/f* continental

conti'nente *ag* continent ♦ *sm* (*GEO*) continent; (: *terra ferma*) mainland

contin'gente [kontin'dʒente] *ag* contingent ♦ *sm* (*COMM*) quota; (*MIL*) contingent; contin'genza *sf* circumstance; (*ECON*): **(indennità di) contingenza** cost-of-living allowance

continu'are *vt* to continue (with), go on with ♦ *vi* to continue, go on; **~ a fare qc** to go on *o* continue doing sth; continuazi'one *sf* continuation

continuità *sf* continuity

con'tinuo, a *ag* (*numerazione*) continuous; (*pioggia*) continual, constant; (*ELETTR*): **corrente ~a** direct current; **di ~** continually

'conto *sm* (*calcolo*) calculation; (*COMM*, *ECON*) account; (*di ristorante, albergo*) bill; (*fig: stima*) consideration, esteem; **fare i ~i con qn** to settle one's account with sb; **fare ~ su qn/qc** to count *o* rely on sb; **rendere ~ a qn di qc** to be accountable to sb for sth; **tener ~ di qn/qc** to take sb/sth into account; **per ~ di** on behalf of; **per ~ mio** as far as I'm concerned; **a ~i fatti, in fin dei ~i** all things considered; **~ corrente** current account; **~ alla rovescia** countdown

con'torcere [kon'tortʃere] *vt* to twist; **~rsi** *vr* to twist, writhe

contor'nare *vt* to surround

con'torno *sm* (*linea*) outline, contour; (*ornamento*) border; (*CUC*) vegetables *pl*

con'torto, a *pp di* **contorcere**

contrabbandi'ere, a *sm/f* smuggler

contrab'bando *sm* smuggling, contraband; **merce di ~** contraband, smuggled goods *pl*

contrab'basso *sm* (*MUS*) (double) bass

contraccambi'are *vt* (*favore etc*) to return

contraccet'tivo, a [kontratt∫et'tivo] *ag*, *sm* contraceptive

contrac'colpo *sm* rebound; (*di arma da fuoco*) recoil; (*fig*) repercussion

con'trada *sf* street; district

contrad'detto, a *pp di* **contraddire**

contrad'dire *vt* to contradict; **contraddit'torio, a** *ag* contradictory; (*sentimenti*) conflicting ♦ *sm* (*DIR*) cross-examination; **contraddizi'one** sf contradiction

contraf'fare vt (persona) to mimic; (alterare: voce) to disguise; (firma) to forge, counterfeit; **contraf'fatto, a** pp di **contraffare ♦** ag counterfeit; **contraffazi'one** sf mimicking no pl; disguising no pl; forging no pl; (cosa contraffatta) forgery

contrap'peso sm counterbalance, counterweight

contrap'porre vt: ~ **qc a qc** to counter sth with sth; (paragonare) to compare sth with sth; **contrap'posto, a** pp di **contrapporre**

contraria'mente av: ~ **a** contrary to

contrari'are vt (contrastare) to thwart, oppose; (irritare) to annoy, bother; **~rsi** vr to get annoyed

contrarietà sf adversity; (fig) aversion

con'trario, a ag opposite; (sfavorevole) unfavourable ♦ sm opposite; **essere ~ a qc** (persona) to be against sth; **in caso ~** otherwise; **avere qc in ~** to have some objection; **al ~** on the contrary

con'trarre vt to contract; **contrarsi** vr to contract

contrasse'gnare [kontrassen'ɲare] vt to mark; **contras'segno** sm (distintivo) distinguishing mark; **spedire in contrassegno** to send C.O.D.

contras'tare vt (avversare) to oppose; (impedire) to bar; (negare: diritto) to contest, dispute ♦ vi: ~ **(con)** (essere in disaccordo) to contrast (with); (lottare) to struggle (with); **con'trasto** sm contrast; (conflitto) conflict; (litigio) dispute

contrat'tacco sm counterattack

contrat'tare vt, vi to negotiate

contrat'tempo sm hitch

con'tratto, a pp di **contrarre ♦** sm contract; **contrattu'ale** ag contractual

contravvenzi'one [kontravven'tsjone] sf contravention; (ammenda) fine

contrazi'one [kontrat'tsjone] sf contraction; (di prezzi etc) reduction

contribu'ente sm/f taxpayer; ratepayer

(BRIT), property tax payer (US)

contribu'ire vi to contribute; **contri'buto** sm contribution; (tassa) tax

'contro prep against; ~ **di me/lui** against me/him; **pastiglie ~ la tosse** throat lozenges; ~ **pagamento** (COMM) on payment ♦ prefisso: **contro'battere** vt (fig: a parole) to answer back; (: confutare) to refute; **controfi'gura** sf (CINEMA) double; **controfir'mare** vt to countersign

control'lare vt (accertare) to check; (sorvegliare) to watch, control; (tenere nel proprio potere, fig: dominare) to control; **con'trollo** sm check; watch; control; **controllo delle nascite** birth control; **control'lore** sm (FERR, AUTOBUS) (ticket) inspector

controprodu'cente [kontroprodu'tʃente] ag counterproductive

contro'senso sm (contraddizione) contradiction in terms; (assurdità) nonsense

controspio'naggio [kontrospio'naddʒo] sm counterespionage

contro'versia sf controversy; (DIR) dispute

contro'verso, a ag controversial

contro'voglia [kontro'vɔʎʎa] av unwillingly

contu'macia [kontu'matʃa] sf (DIR) default

contusi'one sf (MED) bruise

convale'scente [konvaleʃ'ʃente] ag, sm/f convalescent; **convale'scenza** sf convalescence

convali'dare vt (AMM) to validate; (fig: sospetto, dubbio) to confirm

con'vegno [kon'veɲɲo] sm (incontro) meeting; (congresso) convention, congress; (luogo) meeting place

conve'nevoli smpl civilities

conveni'ente ag suitable; (vantaggioso) profitable; (: prezzo) cheap; **conveni'enza** sf suitability; advantage; cheapness; **le convenienze** sfpl social conventions

conve'nire vi (riunirsi) to gather, assemble; (concordare) to agree; (tornare utile) to be worthwhile ♦ vb impers: **conviene fare questo** it is advisable to do this; **conviene andarsene** we should go; **ne convengo** I agree

con'vento *sm* (*di frati*) monastery; (*di suore*) convent

convenzio'nale [konventsjo'nale] *ag* conventional

convenzi'one [konven'tsjone] *sf* (*DIR*) agreement; (*nella società*) convention; **le ~i** *sfpl* social conventions

conver'sare *vi* to have a conversation, converse

conversazi'one [konversat'tsjone] *sf* conversation; **fare ~** to chat, have a chat

conversi'one *sf* conversion; **~ ad U** (*AUT*) U-turn

conver'tire *vt* (*trasformare*) to change; (*POL, REL*) to convert; **~rsi** *vr*: **~rsi (a)** to be converted (to)

con'vesso, a *ag* convex

con'vincere [kon'vintʃere] *vt* to convince; **~ qn di qc** to convince sb of sth; **~ qn a fare qc** to persuade sb to do sth; con'vinto, a *pp di* **convincere**; convinzi'one *sf* conviction, firm belief

convis'suto, a *pp di* **convivere**

con'vivere *vi* to live together

convo'care *vt* to call, convene; (*DIR*) to summon; convocazi'one *sf* meeting; summons *sg*

convogli'are [konvoʎ'ʎare] *vt* to convey; (*dirigere*) to direct, send; con'voglio *sm* (*di veicoli*) convoy; (*FERR*) train

convulsi'one *sf* convulsion

con'vulso, a *ag* (*pianto*) violent, convulsive; (*attività*) feverish

coope'rare *vi*: **~ (a)** to cooperate (in); coopera'tiva *sf* cooperative; cooperazi'one *sf* cooperation

coordi'nare *vt* to coordinate; coordi'nate *sfpl* (*MAT, GEO*) coordinates; coordi'nati *smpl* (*MODA*) coordinates

co'perchio [ko'perkjo] *sm* cover; (*di pentola*) lid

co'perta *sf* cover; (*di lana*) blanket; (*da viaggio*) rug; (*NAUT*) deck

coper'tina *sf* (*STAMPA*) cover, jacket

co'perto, a *pp di* **coprire** ♦ *ag* covered; (*cielo*) overcast ♦ *sm* place setting; (*posto a tavola*) place; (*al ristorante*) cover charge; **~ di** covered in *o*

coper'tone *sm* (*AUT*) rubber tyre

coper'tura *sf* (*anche ECON, MIL*) cover; (*di edificio*) roofing

'copia *sf* copy; **brutta / bella ~** rough / final copy

copi'are *vt* to copy; copia'trice *sf* copier, copying machine

copi'one *sm* (*CINEMA, TEATRO*) script

'coppa *sf* (*bicchiere*) goblet; (*per frutta, gelato*) dish; (*trofeo*) cup, trophy; **~ dell'olio** oil sump (*BRIT*) *o* pan (*US*)

'coppia *sf* (*di persone*) couple; (*di animali, SPORT*) pair

coprifu'oco, chi *sm* curfew

copri'letto *sm* bedspread

co'prire *vt* to cover; (*occupare: carica, posto*) to hold; **~rsi** *vr* (*cielo*) to cloud over; (*vestirsi*) to wrap up, cover up; (*ECON*) to cover o.s.; **~rsi di** (*macchie, muffa*) to become covered in

co'raggio [ko'raddʒo] *sm* courage, bravery; **~!** (*forza!*) come on!; (*animo!*) cheer up!; coraggi'oso, a *ag* courageous, brave

co'rallo *sm* coral

co'rano *sm* (*REL*) Koran

co'razza [ko'rattsa] *sf* armour; (*di animali*) carapace, shell; (*MIL*) armour(-plating); coraz'zata *sf* battleship

corbelle'ria *sf* stupid remark; **~e** *sfpl* nonsense *no pl*

'corda *sf* cord; (*fune*) rope; (*spago, MUS*) string; **dare ~ a qn** to let sb have his (*o* her) way; **tenere sulla ~ qn** to keep sb on tenterhooks; **tagliare la ~** to slip away, sneak off; **~e vocali** vocal cords

cordi'ale *ag* cordial, warm ♦ *sm* (*bevanda*) cordial

cor'doglio [kor'dɔʎʎo] *sm* grief; (*lutto*) mourning

cor'done *sm* cord, string; (*linea: di polizia*) cordon; **~ ombelicale** umbilical cord

Co'rea *sf*: **la ~** Korea

coreogra'fia *sf* choreography

cori'andolo *sm* (*BOT*) coriander; **~i** *smpl* confetti *sg* cori'carsi vr to go to bed

'corna sfpl vedi corno

cor'nacchia [kor'nakkja] sf crow

corna'musa sf bagpipes pl

cor'netta sf (MUS) cornet; (TEL) receiver

cor'netto sm (CUC) croissant; (gelato) cone

cor'nice [kor'nitʃe] sf frame; (fig) setting, background

cornici'one [korni'tʃone] sm (di edificio) ledge; (ARCHIT) cornice

'corno (pl(f) -a) sm (ZOOL) horn; (pl(m) -i: MUS) horn; fare le ~a a qn to be unfaithful to sb

Corno'vaglia [korno'vaʎʎa] sf: la ~ Cornwall

cor'nuto, a ag (con corna) horned; (fam!: marito) cuckolded ♦ sm (fam!) cuckold; (: insulto) bastard (!)

'coro sm chorus; (REL) choir

co'rona sf crown; (di fiori) wreath; coro'nare vt to crown

'corpo sm body; (militare, diplomatico) corps inv; prendere ~ to take shape; a ~ a ~ hand-to-hand; ~ di ballo corps de ballet; ~ insegnante teaching staff

corpo'rale ag bodily; (punizione) corporal

corpora'tura sf build, physique

corporazi'one [korporat'tsjone] sf corporation

corpu'lento, a ag stout

corre'dare vt: ~ di to provide o furnish with; cor'redo sm equipment; (di sposa) trousseau

cor'reggere [kor'reddʒere] vt to correct; (compiti) to correct, mark

cor'rente ag (acqua: di fiume) flowing; (: di rubinetto) running; (moneta, prezzo) current; (comune) everyday ♦ sm: essere al ~ (di) to be well-informed (about); mettere al ~ (di) to inform (of) ♦ sf (d'acqua) current, stream; (spiffero) draught; (ELETTR, METEOR) current; (fig) trend, tendency; la vostra lettera del 5 ~ mese (COMM) your letter of the 5th of this month; corrente'mente av commonly; parlare una lingua correntemente to speak a language fluently

'correre vi to run; (precipitarsi) to rush; (partecipare a una gara) to race, run; (fig: diffondersi) to go round ♦ vt (SPORT: gara) to compete in; (rischio) to run; (pericolo) to face; ~ dietro a qn to run after sb; corre voce che ... it is rumoured that ...

cor'retto, a pp di correggere ♦ ag (comportamento) correct, proper; caffè ~ al cognac coffee laced with brandy

correzi'one [korret'tsjone] sf correction; marking; ~ di bozze proofreading

corri'doio sm corridor

corri'dore sm (SPORT) runner; (: su veicolo) racer

corri'era sf coach (BRIT), bus

corri'ere sm (diplomatico, di guerra, postale) courier; (COMM) carrier

corrispet'tivo sm (somma) amount due

corrispon'dente ag corresponding ♦ sm/f correspondent

corrispon'denza [korrispon'dɛntsa] sf correspondence

corris'pondere vi (equivalere): ~ (a) to correspond (to) ♦ vt (stipendio) to pay; (fig: amore) to return; corris'posto, a pp di corrispondere

corrobo'rare vt to strengthen, fortify; (fig) to corroborate, bear out

cor'rodere vt to corrode; ~rsi vr to corrode

cor'rompere vt to corrupt; (comprare) to bribe

corrosi'one sf corrosion

cor'roso, a pp di corrodere

cor'rotto, a pp di corrompere ♦ ag corrupt

corrucci'arsi [korrut'tʃarsi] vr to grow angry o vexed

corru'gare vt to wrinkle; ~ la fronte to knit one's brows

corruzi'one [korrut'tsjone] sf corruption; bribery

'corsa sf running no pl; (gara) race; (di autobus, taxi) journey, trip; fare una ~ to run, dash; (SPORT) to run a race

cor'sia sf (AUT, SPORT) lane; (di ospedale) ward

cor'sivo *sm* cursive (writing); (*TIP*) italics *pl*

'corso, a *pp di* correre ♦ *sm* course; (*strada cittadina*) main street; (*di unità monetaria*) circulation; (*di titoli, valori*) rate, price; in ~ in progress, under way; (*annata*) current; ~ d'acqua river, stream; (*artificiale*) waterway; ~ d'aggiornamento refresher course; ~ serale evening class

'corte *sf* (court)yard; (*DIR, regale*) court; fare la ~ a qn to court sb; ~ marziale court-martial

cor'teccia, ce [kor'tettʃa] *sf* bark

corteggi'are [korted'dʒare] *vt* to court

cor'teo *sm* procession

cor'tese *ag* courteous; corte'sia *sf* courtesy; per cortesia ... excuse me, please ...

cortigi'ana [korti'dʒana] *sf* courtesan

cortigi'ano, a [korti'dʒano] *sm/f* courtier

cor'tile *sm* (court)yard

cor'tina *sf* curtain; (*anche fig*) screen

'corto, a *ag* short; essere a ~ di qc to be short of sth; ~ circuito short-circuit

'corvo *sm* raven

'cosa *sf* (*faccenda*) affair, matter, business *no pl*; (che) ~? what?; (che) cos'è? what is it?; a ~ pensi? what are you thinking about?

'coscia, sce ['kɔʃʃa] *sf* thigh; ~ di pollo (*CUC*) chicken leg

cosci'ente [koʃ'ʃɛnte] *ag* conscious; ~ di conscious *o* aware of; cosci'enza *sf* conscience; (*consapevolezza*) consciousness; coscienzi'oso, a *ag* conscientious

cosci'otto [koʃ'ʃɔtto] *sm* (*CUC*) leg

cos'critto *sm* (*MIL*) conscript

<u>**PAROLA CHIAVE**</u>

così *av* 1 (*in questo modo*) like this, (in) this way; (*in tal modo*) so; le cose stanno ~ this is the way things stand; non ho detto ~! I didn't say that!; come stai? – (e) ~ how are you? — so-so; e ~ via and so on; per ~ dire so to speak
2 (*tanto*) so; ~ lontano so far away; un ragazzo ~ intelligente such an intelligent boy

♦ *ag inv* (*tale*): non ho mai visto un film ~ I've never seen such a film

♦ *cong* 1 (*perciò*) so, therefore
2: ~ ... come as ... as; non è ~ bravo come te he's not as good as you; ~ ... che so ... that

---

cosid'detto, a *ag* so-called

cos'metico, a, ci, che *ag, sm* cosmetic

cos'pargere [kos'pardʒere] *vt*: ~ di to sprinkle with; cos'parso, a *pp di* cospargere

cos'petto *sm*: al ~ di in front of; in the presence of

cos'picuo, a *ag* considerable, large

cospi'rare *vi* to conspire; cospirazi'one *sf* conspiracy

'costa *sf* (*tra terra e mare*) coast(line); (*litorale*) shore; (*ANAT*) rib; la C~ Azzurra the French Riviera

cos'tante *ag* constant; (*persona*) steadfast ♦ *sf* constant

cos'tare *vi, vt* to cost; ~ caro to be expensive, cost a lot

cos'tata *sf* (*CUC*) large chop

cos'tato *sm* (*ANAT*) ribs *pl*

costeggi'are [kosted'dʒare] *vt* to be close to; to run alongside

cos'tei *pron vedi* costui

costi'era *sf* stretch of coast

costi'ero, a *ag* coastal, coast *cpd*

costitu'ire *vt* (*comitato, gruppo*) to set up, form; (*sog: elementi, parti: comporre*) to make up, constitute; (*rappresentare*) to constitute; (*DIR*) to appoint; ~rsi alla polizia to give o.s. up to the police

costituzio'nale [kostituttsjo'nale] *ag* constitutional

costituzi'one [kostitut'tsjone] *sf* setting up; building up; constitution

'costo *sm* cost; a ogni *o* qualunque ~, a tutti i ~i at all costs

'costola *sf* (*ANAT*) rib

cos'toro *pron pl vedi* costui

cos'toso, a *ag* expensive, costly

cos'tretto, a *pp di* costringere

cos'tringere [kos'trindʒere] *vt*: ~ qn a fare

qc to force sb to do sth; **costrizi'one** *sf* coercion

costru'ire *vt* to construct, build; **costruzi'one** *sf* construction, building

cos'tui (*f* **cos'tei**, *pl* **cos'toro**) *pron* (*soggetto*) he/she; *pl* they; (*complemento*) him/her; *pl* them; **si può sapere chi è ~?** (*peg*) just who is that fellow?

cos'tume *sm* (*uso*) custom; (*foggia di vestire, indumento*) costume; **~i** *smpl* (*condotta morale*) morals, morality *sg*; **~ da bagno** bathing *o* swimming costume (*BRIT*), swimsuit; (*da uomo*) bathing *o* swimming trunks *pl*

co'tenna *sf* bacon rind

co'togna [ko'toɲɲa] *sf* quince

coto'letta *sf* (*di maiale, montone*) chop; (*di vitello, agnello*) cutlet

co'tone *sm* cotton; **~ idrofilo** cotton wool (*BRIT*), absorbent cotton (*US*)

'cotta *sf* (*fam: innamoramento*) crush

'cottimo *sm*: **lavorare a ~** to do piecework

'cotto, a *pp di* **cuocere** ♦ *ag* cooked; (*fam: innamorato*) head-over-heels in love; **ben ~** (*carne*) well done

cot'tura *sf* cooking; (*in forno*) baking; (*in umido*) stewing

co'vare *vt* to hatch; (*fig: malattia*) to be sickening for; (: *odio, rancore*) to nurse ♦ *vi* (*fuoco, fig*) to smoulder

'covo *sm* den

co'vone *sm* sheaf

'cozza ['kottsa] *sf* mussel

coz'zare [kot'tsare] *vi*: **~ contro** to bang into, collide with

C.P. *abbr* (= *casella postale*) P.O. Box

crack [kræk] *sm inv* (*droga*) crack

'crampo *sm* cramp

'cranio *sm* skull

cra'tere *sm* crater

cra'vatta *sf* tie

cre'anza [kre'antsa] *sf* manners *pl*

cre'are *vt* to create; **cre'ato** *sm* creation; **crea'tore, 'trice** *ag* creative ♦ *sm* creator; **crea'tura** *sf* creature; (*bimbo*) baby, infant; **creazi'one** *sf* creation; (*fondazione*) foundation, establishment

cre'dente *sm/f* (*REL*) believer

cre'denza [kre'dentsa] *sf* belief; (*armadio*) sideboard

credenzi'ali [kreden'tsjali] *sfpl* credentials

'credere *vt* to believe ♦ *vi*: **~ in, ~ a** to believe in; **~ qn onesto** to believe sb (to be) honest; **~ che** to believe *o* think that; **~rsi furbo** to believe one is clever

'credito *sm* (*anche COMM*) credit; (*reputazione*) esteem, repute; **comprare a ~** to buy on credit

'credo *sm inv* creed

'crema *sf* cream; (*con uova, zucchero etc*) custard; **~ solare** sun cream

cre'mare *vt* to cremate

Crem'lino *sm*: **il ~** the Kremlin

'crepa *sf* crack

cre'paccio [kre'pattʃo] *sm* large crack, fissure; (*di ghiacciaio*) crevasse

crepacu'ore *sm* broken heart

cre'pare *vi* (*fam: morire*) to snuff it, kick the bucket; **~ dalle risa** to split one's sides laughing

crepi'tare *vi* (*fuoco*) to crackle; (*pioggia*) to patter

cre'puscolo *sm* twilight, dusk

'crescere ['kreʃʃere] *vi* to grow ♦ *vt* (*figli*) to raise; **'crescita** *sf* growth; **cresci'uto, a** *pp di* **crescere**

cre'sima (*REL*) confirmation

'crespo, a *ag* (*capelli*) frizzy; (*tessuto*) puckered ♦ *sm* crêpe

'cresta *sf* crest; (*di polli, uccelli*) crest, comb

'creta *sf* chalk; clay

cre'tino, a *ag* stupid ♦ *sm/f* idiot, fool

cric *sm inv* (*TECN*) jack

'cricca, che *sf* clique

cri'ceto [kri'tʃeto] *sm* hamster

crimi'nale *ag, sm/f* criminal

'crimine *sm* (*DIR*) crime

'crine *sm* horsehair; **crini'era** *sf* mane

crisan'temo *sm* chrysanthemum

'crisi *sf inv* crisis; (*MED*) attack, fit; **~ di nervi** attack *o* fit of nerves

cristalliz'zare [kristalid'dzare] *vi* to crystallize; (*fig*) to become fossilized; **~rsi**

vr to crystallize; to become fossilized
cris'tallo *sm* crystal
cristia'nesimo *sm* Christianity
cristi'ano, a *ag, sm/f* Christian
'Cristo *sm* Christ
cri'terio *sm* criterion; (*buon senso*) (common) sense
'critica, che *sf* criticism; **la ~** (*attività*) criticism; (*persone*) the critics *pl*; *vedi anche* **critico**
criti'care *vt* to criticize
'critico, a, ci, che *ag* critical ♦ *sm* critic
Croa'zia [kroa'ttsja] *sf* Croatia
croc'cante *ag* crisp, crunchy
'croce ['krotʃe] *sf* cross; **in ~** (*di traverso*) crosswise; (*fig*) on tenterhooks; **la C~ Rossa** the Red Cross
croce'figgere etc [krotʃe'fiddʒere] = **crocifiggere** etc
croce'via *sm inv* crossroads *sg*
croci'ata [kro'tʃata] *sf* crusade
cro'cicchio [kro'tʃikkjo] *sm* crossroads *sg*
cro'ciera [kro'tʃera] *sf* (*viaggio*) cruise; (*ARCHIT*) transept
croci'figgere [krotʃi'fiddʒere] *vt* to crucify; **crocifissi'one** *sf* crucifixion; **croci'fisso, a** *pp di* **crocifiggere**
crogi'olo [kro'dʒɔlo] *sm* (*fig*) melting pot
crol'lare *vi* to collapse; **'crollo** *sm* collapse; (*di prezzi*) slump, sudden fall
cro'mato, a *ag* chromium-plated
'cromo *sm* chrome, chromium
'cronaca, che *sf* (*STAMPA*) news *sg*; (: *rubrica*) column; (*TV, RADIO*) commentary; **fatto** *o* **episodio di ~** news item; **~ nera** crime news *sg*; crime column
'cronico, a, ci, che *ag* chronic
cro'nista, i *sm* (*STAMPA*) reporter
cronolo'gia [kronolo'dʒia] *sf* chronology
cro'nometro *sm* chronometer; (*a scatto*) stopwatch
'crosta *sf* crust
cros'tacei [kros'tatʃei] *smpl* shellfish
cros'tata *sf* (*CUC*) tart
cros'tino *sm* (*CUC*) croûton; (: *da antipasto*) canapé
'cruccio ['kruttʃo] *sm* worry, torment

cruci'verba *sm inv* crossword (puzzle)
cru'dele *ag* cruel; **crudeltà** *sf* cruelty
'crudo, a *ag* (*non cotto*) raw; (*aspro*) harsh, severe
cru'miro (*peg*) *sm* blackleg (*BRIT*), scab
'crusca *sf* bran
crus'cotto *sm* (*AUT*) dashboard
CSI *sigla f inv* (= *Comunità Stati Indipendenti*) CIS
'Cuba *sf* Cuba
cu'betto *sm*: **~ di ghiaccio** ice cube
'cubico, a, ci, che *ag* cubic
'cubo, a *ag* cubic ♦ *sm* cube; **elevare al ~** (*MAT*) to cube
cuc'cagna [kuk'kaɲɲa] *sf*: **paese della ~** land of plenty; **albero della ~** greasy pole (*fig*)
cuc'cetta [kut'tʃetta] *sf* (*FERR*) couchette; (*NAUT*) berth
cucchiai'ata [kukja'jata] *sf* spoonful
cucchia'ino [kukkja'ino] *sm* teaspoon; coffee spoon
cucchi'aio [kuk'kjajo] *sm* spoon
'cuccia, ce ['kuttʃa] *sf* dog's bed; **a ~!** down!
'cucciolo ['kuttʃolo] *sm* cub; (*di cane*) puppy
cu'cina [ku'tʃina] *sf* (*locale*) kitchen; (*arte culinaria*) cooking, cookery; (*le vivande*) food, cooking; (*apparecchio*) cooker; **~ componibile** fitted kitchen; **cuci'nare** *vt* to cook
cu'cire [ku'tʃire] *vt* to sew, stitch; **cuci'trice** *sf* stapler; **cuci'tura** *sf* sewing, stitching; (*costura*) seam
cucù *sm inv* = **cuculo**
cu'culo *sm* cuckoo
'cuffia *sf* bonnet, cap; (*da infermiera*) cap; (*da bagno*) (bathing) cap; (*per ascoltare*) headphones *pl*, headset
cu'gino, a [ku'dʒino] *sm/f* cousin

PAROLA CHIAVE

'cui *pron* **1** (*nei complementi indiretti: persona*) whom; (: *oggetto, animale*) which; **la persona/le persone a ~ accennavi** the person/people you were referring to *o* to whom you were referring; **i libri di ~ parlavo** the books I was talking about *o* about which I was talking; **il quartiere in ~ abito** the district where I live; **la ragione per ~** the reason why

2 (*inserito tra articolo e sostantivo*) whose; **la donna i ~ figli sono scomparsi** the woman whose children have disappeared; **il signore, dal ~ figlio ho avuto il libro** the man from whose son I got the book

culi'naria *sf* cookery

culla *sf* cradle

cul'lare *vt* to rock

culmi'nare *vi:* **~ con** to culminate in

culmine *sm* top, summit

culo (*fam!*) *sm* arse (*Brit!*), ass (*US!*); (*fig: fortuna*): **aver ~** to have the luck of the devil

culto *sm* (*religione*) religion; (*adorazione*) worship; (*venerazione: anche fig*) cult

cul'tura *sf* culture; education, learning; **cultu'rale** *ag* cultural

cumula'tivo, a *ag* cumulative; (*prezzo*) inclusive; (*biglietto*) group *cpd*

cumulo *sm* (*mucchio*) pile, heap; (*METEOR*) cumulus

cuneo *sm* wedge

cu'netta *sf* (*avvallamento*) dip; (*di scolo*) gutter

cu'oca *sf vedi* **cuoco**

cu'ocere ['kwɔtʃere] *vt* (*alimenti*) to cook; (*mattoni etc*) to fire ♦ *vi* to cook; **~ al forno** (*pane*) to bake; (*arrosto*) to roast; **cu'oco, a, chi, che** *sm/f* cook; (*di ristorante*) chef

cu'oio *sm* leather; **~ capelluto** scalp

cu'ore *sm* heart; **~i** *smpl* (*CARTE*) hearts; **avere buon ~** to be kind-hearted; **stare a ~ a qn** to be important to sb

cupi'digia [kupi'didʒa] *sf* greed, covetousness

cupo, a *ag* dark; (*suono*) dull; (*fig*) gloomy, dismal

cupola *sf* dome; cupola

cura *sf* care; (*MED: trattamento*) (course of) treatment; **aver ~ di** (*occuparsi di*) to look after; **a ~ di** (*libro*) edited by; **~**

dimagrante diet

cu'rare *vt* (*malato, malattia*) to treat; (*: guarire*) to cure; (*aver cura di*) to take care of; (*testo*) to edit; **~rsi** *vr* to take care of o.s.; (*MED*) to follow a course of treatment; **~rsi di** to pay attention to

cu'rato *sm* parish priest; (*protestante*) vicar, minister

cura'tore, 'trice *sm/f* (*DIR*) trustee; (*di antologia etc*) editor

curio'sare *vi* to look round, wander round; (*tra libri*) to browse; **~ nei negozi** to look *o* wander round the shops

curiosità *sf inv* curiosity; (*cosa rara*) curio, curiosity

curi'oso, a *ag* curious; **essere ~ di** to be curious about

cur'sore *sm* (*INFORM*) cursor

curva *sf* curve; (*stradale*) bend, curve

cur'vare *vt* to bend ♦ *vi* (*veicolo*) to take a bend; (*strada*) to bend, curve; **~rsi** *vr* to bend; (*legno*) to warp

curvo, a *ag* curved; (*piegato*) bent

cusci'netto [kuʃʃi'netto] *sm* pad; (*TECN*) bearing ♦ *ag inv:* **stato ~** buffer state; **~ a sfere** ball bearing

cu'scino [kuʃʃino] *sm* cushion; (*guanciale*) pillow

cuspide *sf* (*ARCHIT*) spire

cus'tode *sm/f* keeper, custodian

cus'todia *sf* care; (*DIR*) custody; (*astuccio*) case, holder

custo'dire *vt* (*conservare*) to keep; (*assistere*) to look after, take care of; (*fare la guardia*) to guard

cute *sf* (*ANAT*) skin

C.V. *abbr* (= *cavallo vapore*) h.p.

cybercaffè [tʃiberka'fe] *sm inv* cybercafé

D, d

---

da (*da+il* = **dal**, *da+lo* = **dallo**, *da+l'* = **dall'**, *da+la* = **dalla**, *da+i* = **dai**, *da+gli* = **dagli**, *da+le* = **dalle**) *prep* **1** (*agente*) by;

dipinto ~ un grande artista painted by a great artist

2 (*causa*) with; **tremare dalla paura** to tremble with fear

3 (*stato in luogo*) at; **abito ~ lui** I'm living at his house *o* with him; **sono dal giornalaio/~ Francesco** I'm at the newsagent's/Francesco's (house)

4 (*moto a luogo*) to; (*moto per luogo*) through; **vado ~ Pietro/dal giornalaio** I'm going to Pietro's (house)/to the newsagent's; **sono passati dalla finestra** they came in through the window

5 (*provenienza, allontanamento*) from; **arrivare/partire ~ Milano** to arrive/depart from Milan; **scendere dal treno/dalla macchina** to get off the train/out of the car; **si trova a 5 km ~ qui** it's 5 km from here

6 (*tempo: durata*) for; (: *a partire da: nel passato*) since; (: *nel futuro*) from; **vivo qui ~ un anno** I've been living here for a year; **è dalle 3 che ti aspetto** I've been waiting for you since 3 (o'clock); **~ oggi in poi** from today onwards; **~ bambino** as a child, when I (*o* he *etc*) was a child

7 (*modo, maniera*) like; **comportarsi ~ uomo** to behave like a man; **l'ho fatto ~ me** I did it (by) myself

8 (*descrittivo*): **una macchina ~ corsa** a racing car; **una ragazza dai capelli biondi** a girl with blonde hair; **un vestito ~ 100.000 lire** a 100,000 lire dress

da 'capo *av* = **daccapo**

dac'capo *av* (*di nuovo*) (once) again; (*dal principio*) all over again, from the beginning

'dado *sm* (*da gioco*) dice *o* die; (*CUC*) stock (*BRIT*) *o* bouillon (*US*) cube; (*TECN*) (screw)nut; **giocare a ~i** to play dice

daf'fare *sm* work, toil

'dagli ['daʎʎi] *prep + det vedi* **da**

'dai *prep + det vedi* **da**

'daino *sm* (fallow) deer *inv*; (*pelle*) buckskin

dal *prep + det vedi* **da**

dall' *prep + det vedi* **da**

'dalla *prep + det vedi* **da**

'dalle *prep + det vedi* **da**

'dallo *prep + det vedi* **da**

dal'tonico, a, ci, che *ag* colour-blind

'dama *sf* lady; (*nei balli*) partner; (*gioco*) draughts *sg* (*BRIT*), checkers *sg* (*US*)

damigi'ana [dami'dʒana] *sf* demijohn

da'naro *sm* = **denaro**

da'nese *ag* Danish ♦ *sm/f* Dane ♦ *sm* (*LING*) Danish

Dani'marca *sf*: **la ~** Denmark

dan'nare *vt* (*REL*) to damn; **~rsi** *vr* (*fig: tormentarsi*) to be worried to death; **far ~ qn** to drive sb mad; **dannazi'one** *sf* damnation

danneggi'are [danned'dʒare] *vt* to damage; (*rovinare*) to spoil; (*nuocere*) to harm

'danno *sm* damage; (*a persona*) harm, injury; **~i** *smpl* (*DIR*) damages; **dan'noso, a** *ag*: **dannoso (a, per)** harmful (to), bad (for)

Da'nubio *sm*: **il ~** the Danube

'danza ['dantsa] *sf*: **la ~** dancing; **una ~** a dance

dan'zare [dan'tsare] *vt, vi* to dance

dapper'tutto *av* everywhere

dap'poco *ag inv* inept, worthless

dap'prima *av* at first

'dare *sm* (*COMM*) debit ♦ *vt* to give; (*produrre: frutti, suono*) to produce ♦ *vi* (*guardare*): **~ su** to look (out) onto; **~rsi** *vr*: **~rsi a** to dedicate o.s. to; **~rsi al commercio** to go into business; **~rsi al bere** to take to drink; **~ da mangiare a qn** to give sb sth to eat; **~ per certo qc** to consider sth certain; **~ per morto qn** to give sb up for dead; **~rsi per vinto** to give in

'darsena *sf* dock; dockyard

'data *sf* date; **~ di nascita** date of birth

da'tare *vt* to date ♦ *vi*: **~ da** to date from

'dato, a *ag* (*stabilito*) given ♦ *sm* datum; **~i** *smpl* data *pl*; **~ che** given that; **un ~ di fatto** a fact; **~ sensibili** personal information

da'tore, trice *sm/f*: **~ di lavoro** employer

'dattero *sm* date

dattilogra'fare vt to type; **dattilogra'fia** sf typing; **datti'lografo, a** sm/f typist

da'vanti av in front; (dirimpetto) opposite ♦ ag inv front ♦ sm front; **~ a** in front of; facing, opposite; (in presenza di) before, in front of

davan'zale [davan'tsale] sm windowsill

a'vanzo [da'vantso] av more than enough

av'vero av really, indeed

dazio ['dattsjo] sm (somma) duty; (luogo) customs pl

DC sigla f = **Democrazia Cristiana**

d. C. ad abbr (= dopo Cristo) A.D.

dea sf goddess

debito, a ag due, proper ♦ sm debt; (COMM: dare) debit; **a tempo ~** at the right time; **debi'tore, 'trice** sm/f debtor

debole ag weak, feeble; (suono) faint; (luce) dim ♦ sm weakness; **debo'lezza** sf weakness

debut'tare vi to make one's début; **de'butto** sm début

deca'denza [deka'dɛntsa] sf decline; (DIR) loss, forfeiture

decaffei'nato, a ag decaffeinated

decan'tare vt to praise, sing the praises of

decapi'tare vt to decapitate

decappot'tabile ag, sf convertible

dece'duto, a [detʃe'duto] ag deceased

de'cennio [de'tʃɛnnjo] sm decade

de'cente [de'tʃɛnte] ag decent, respectable, proper; (accettabile) satisfactory, decent

de'cesso [de'tʃɛsso] sm death

de'cidere [de'tʃidere] vt: **~ qc** to decide on sth; (questione, lite) to settle sth; **~ di fare/che** to decide to do/that; **~ di qc** (sog: cosa) to determine sth; **~rsi (a fare)** to decide (to do), make up one's mind (to do)

deci'frare [detʃi'frare] vt to decode; (fig) to decipher, make out

deci'male [detʃi'male] ag decimal

decimo, a ['dɛtʃimo] num tenth

de'cina [de'tʃina] sf ten; (circa dieci): **una ~ (di)** about ten

deci'sione [detʃi'zjone] sf decision;

prendere una ~ to make a decision

de'ciso, a [de'tʃizo] pp di **decidere**

declas'sare vt to downgrade; to lower in status

decli'nare vi (pendio) to slope down; (fig: diminuire) to decline ♦ vt to decline

declinazi'one sf (LING) declension

de'clino sm decline

decodifica'tore sm (TEL) decoder

decol'lare vi (AER) to take off; **de'collo** sm take-off

decolo'rare vt to bleach

decom'porre vt to decompose; **decomporsi** vr to decompose; **decom'posto, a** pp di **decomporre**

deconge'lare [dekondʒe'lare] vt to defrost

deco'rare vt to decorate; **decora'tore, 'trice** sm/f (interior) decorator; **decorazi'one** sf decoration

de'coro sm decorum; **deco'roso, a** ag decorous, dignified

de'correre vi to pass, elapse; (avere effetto) to run, have effect; **de'corso, a** pp di **decorrere** ♦ sm (evoluzione: anche MED) course

de'crepito, a ag decrepit

de'crescere [de'kreʃʃere] vi (diminuire) to decrease, diminish; (acque) to subside, go down; (prezzi) to go down; **decresci'uto, a** pp di **decrescere**

de'creto sm decree; **~ legge** decree with the force of law

'dedalo sm maze, labyrinth

'dedica, che sf dedication

dedi'care vt to dedicate

'dedito, a ag: **~ a** (studio etc) dedicated o devoted to; (vizio) addicted to

de'dotto, a pp di **dedurre**

de'durre vt (concludere) to deduce; (defalcare) to deduct; **deduzi'one** sf deduction

defal'care vt to deduct

defe'rente ag respectful, deferential

defe'rire vt: **~ a** (DIR) to refer to

defezi'one [defet'tsjone] sf defection, desertion

defici'ente [defi'tʃɛnte] ag (mancante): **~ di**

deficient in; (*insufficiente*) insufficient
♦ *sm/f* mental defective; (*peg: cretino*) idiot

'deficit ['dɛfitʃit] *sm inv* (ECON) deficit

defi'nire *vt* to define; (*risolvere*) to settle;
defini'tivo, a *ag* definitive, final;
definizi'one *sf* definition; settlement

deflet'tore *sm* (AUT) quarter-light

de'flusso *sm* (*della marea*) ebb

defor'mare *vt* (*alterare*) to put out of
shape; (*corpo*) to deform; (*pensiero, fatto*)
to distort; **~rsi** *vr* to lose its shape

de'forme *ag* deformed; disfigured;
deformità *sf inv* deformity

defrau'dare *vt*: **~ qn di qc** to defraud sb
of sth, cheat sb out of sth

de'funto, a *ag* late *cpd* ♦ *sm/f* deceased

degene'rare [dedʒene'rare] *vi* to
degenerate; **de'genere** *ag* degenerate

de'gente [de'dʒɛnte] *sm/f* (*in ospedale*) in-
patient

'degli ['deʎʎi] *prep + det vedi* **di**

de'gnarsi [deɲ'ɲarsi] *vr*: **~ di fare** to deign
o condescend to do

'degno, a *ag* dignified; **~ di** worthy of; **~
di lode** praiseworthy

degra'dare *vt* (MIL) to demote; (*privare
della dignità*) to degrade; **~rsi** *vr* to
demean o.s.

degustazi'one [degustat'tsjone] *sf*
sampling, tasting

'dei *prep + det vedi* **di**

.**del** *prep + det vedi* **di**

dela'tore, 'trice *sm/f* police informer

'delega, ghe *sf* (*procura*) proxy

dele'gare *vt* to delegate; **dele'gato** *sm*
delegate

dele'terio, a *ag* damaging; (*per salute etc*)
harmful

del'fino *sm* (ZOOL) dolphin; (STORIA)
dauphin; (*fig*) probable successor

delibe'rare *vt* to come to a decision on
♦ *vi* (DIR): **~ (su qc)** to rule (on sth)

delica'tezza [delika'tettsa] *sf* delicacy;
frailty; thoughtfulness; tactfulness

deli'cato, a *ag* delicate; (*salute*) delicate,
frail; (*fig: gentile*) thoughtful, considerate;
(: *che dimostra tatto*) tactful

deline'are *vt* to outline; **~rsi** *vr* to be
outlined; (*fig*) to emerge

delin'quente *sm/f* criminal, delinquent; **~
abituale** regular offender, habitual
offender; **delin'quenza** *sf* criminality,
delinquency; **delinquenza minorile**
juvenile delinquency

deli'rare *vi* to be delirious, rave; (*fig*) to
rave

de'lirio *sm* delirium; (*ragionamento
insensato*) raving; (*fig*): **andare / mandare
in ~** to go/send into a frenzy

de'litto *sm* crime

de'lizia [de'littsja] *sf* delight; **delizi'oso, a**
ag delightful; (*cibi*) delicious

dell' *prep + det vedi* **di**

'della *prep + det vedi* **di**

'delle *prep + det vedi* **di**

'dello *prep + det vedi* **di**

delta'plano *sm* hang-glider; **volo col ~**
hang-gliding

de'ludere *vt* to disappoint; **delusi'one** *sf*
disappointment; **de'luso, a** *pp di*
deludere

de'manio *sm* state property

de'menza [de'mɛntsa] *sf* dementia;
(*stupidità*) foolishness

demo'cratico, a, ci, che *ag* democratic

democra'zia [demokrat'tsia] *sf* democracy

democristi'ano, a *ag, sm/f* Christian
Democrat

demo'lire *vt* to demolish

de'mone *sm* demon

de'monio *sm* demon, devil; **il D~** the Devil

de'naro *sm* money

denomi'nare *vt* to name;
denominazi'one *sf* name;
denomination; **denominazione d'origine
controllata** label guaranteeing the quality
and origin of a wine

densità *sf inv* density

'denso, a *ag* thick, dense

den'tale *ag* dental

'dente *sm* tooth; (*di forchetta*) prong; **al ~**
(CUC: *pasta*) al dente; **~i del giudizio**
wisdom teeth; **denti'era** *sf* (set of) false
teeth *pl*

denti'fricio [denti'fritʃo] *sm* toothpaste
den'tista, i, e *sm/f* dentist
'dentro *av* inside; (*in casa*) indoors; (*fig: nell'intimo*) inwardly ♦ *prep*: ~ **(a)** in; **piegato in** ~ folded over; **qui/là** ~ in here/there; ~ **di sé** (*pensare, brontolare*) to oneself
de'nuncia, ce *o* **cie** [de'nuntʃa] *sf* denunciation; declaration; ~ **dei redditi** (income) tax return
denunci'are [denun'tʃare] *vt* to denounce; (*dichiarare*) to declare
de'nunzia *etc* [de'nuntsja] = **denuncia** *etc*
denutrizi'one [denutrit'tsjone] *sf* malnutrition
deodo'rante *sm* deodorant
depe'rire *vi* to waste away
depila'torio, a *ag* hair-removing *cpd*, depilatory
dépli'ant [depli'ɑ̃] *sm inv* leaflet; (*opuscolo*) brochure
deplo'revole *ag* deplorable
de'porre *vt* (*depositare*) to put down; (*rimuovere: da una carica*) to remove; (: *re*) to depose; (*DIR*) to testify
depor'tare *vt* to deport
deposi'tare *vt* (*gen, GEO, ECON*) to deposit; (*lasciare*) to leave; (*merci*) to store
de'posito *sm* deposit; (*luogo*) warehouse; depot; (: *MIL*) depot; ~ **bagagli** left-luggage office
deposizi'one [depozit'tsjone] *sf* deposition; (*da una carica*) removal
de'posto, a *pp di* **deporre**
depra'vato, a *ag* depraved ♦ *sm/f* degenerate
depre'dare *vt* to rob, plunder
depressi'one *sf* depression
de'presso, a *pp di* **deprimere** ♦ *ag* depressed
deprez'zare [depret'tsare] *vt* (*ECON*) to depreciate
de'primere *vt* to depress
depu'rare *vt* to purify
depu'tato *sm* (*POL*) deputy, ≈ Member of Parliament (*BRIT*), ≈ Member of Congress (*US*)

deragli'are [deraʎ'ʎare] *vi* to be derailed; **far** ~ to derail
dere'litto, a *ag* derelict
dere'tano (*fam*) *sm* bottom, buttocks *pl*
de'ridere *vt* to mock, deride; **de'riso, a** *pp di* **deridere**
de'riva *sf* (*NAUT, AER*) drift; **andare alla** ~ (*anche fig*) to drift
deri'vare *vi*: ~ **da** to derive from ♦ *vt* to derive; (*corso d'acqua*) to divert; **derivazi'one** *sf* derivation; diversion
derma'tologo, a, gi, ghe *sm/f* dermatologist
der'rate *sfpl*: ~ **alimentari** foodstuffs
deru'bare *vt* to rob
des'critto, a *pp di* **descrivere**
des'crivere *vt* to describe; **descrizi'one** *sf* description
de'serto, a *ag* deserted ♦ *sm* (*GEO*) desert; **isola** ~**a** desert island
deside'rare *vt* to want, wish for; (*sessualmente*) to desire; ~ **fare/che qn faccia** to want *o* wish to do/sb to do; **desidera fare una passeggiata?** would you like to go for a walk?
desi'derio *sm* wish; (*più intenso, carnale*) desire
deside'roso, a *ag*: ~ **di** longing *o* eager for
desi'nenza [dezi'nɛntsa] *sf* (*LING*) ending, inflexion
de'sistere *vi*: ~ **da** to give up, desist from; **desis'tito, a** *pp di* **desistere**
deso'lato, a *ag* (*paesaggio*) desolate; (*persona: spiacente*) sorry
des'tare *vt* to wake (up); (*fig*) to awaken, arouse; ~**rsi** *vr* to wake (up)
desti'nare *vt* to destine; (*assegnare*) to appoint, assign; (*indirizzare*) to address; ~ **qc a qn** to intend to give sth to sb, intend sb to have sth; **destina'tario, a** *sm/f* (*di lettera*) addressee
destinazi'one [destinat'tsjone] *sf* destination; (*uso*) purpose
des'tino *sm* destiny, fate
destitu'ire *vt* to dismiss, remove
'desto, a *ag* (wide) awake

'**destra** *sf* (*mano*) right hand; (*parte*) right (side); (*POL*): **la ~** the Right; **a ~** (*essere*) on the right; (*andare*) to the right

destreggi'arsi [destred'dʒarsi] *vr* to manoeuvre (*BRIT*), maneuver (*US*)

des'trezza [des'trettsa] *sf* skill, dexterity

'**destro, a** *ag* right, right-hand

dete'nere *vt* (*incarico, primato*) to hold; (*proprietà*) to have, possess; (*in prigione*) to detain, hold; **dete'nuto, a** *sm/f* prisoner; **detenzi'one** *sf* holding; possession; detention

deter'gente [deter'dʒɛnte] *ag* detergent; (*crema, latte*) cleansing ♦ *sm* detergent

deterio'rare *vt* to damage; **~rsi** *vr* to deteriorate

determi'nare *vt* to determine; **determinazi'one** *sf* determination; (*decisione*) decision

deter'sivo *sm* detergent

detes'tare *vt* to detest, hate

de'trarre *vt*: **~ (da)** to deduct (from), take away (from); **de'tratto, a** *pp di* **detrarre**; **detrazi'one** *sf* deduction; **detrazione d'imposta** tax allowance

de'trito *sm* (*GEO*) detritus

'**detta** *sf*: **a ~ di** according to

dettagli'are [detta'ʎʎare] *vt* to detail, give full details of

det'taglio [det'taʎʎo] *sm* detail; (*COMM*): **il ~** retail; **al ~** (*COMM*) retail; separately

det'tare *vt* to dictate; **~ legge** (*fig*) to lay down the law; **det'tato** *sm* dictation; **detta'tura** *sf* dictation

'**detto, a** *pp di* **dire** ♦ *ag* (*soprannominato*) called, known as; (*già nominato*) above-mentioned ♦ *sm* saying; **~ fatto** no sooner said than done

detur'pare *vt* to disfigure; (*moralmente*) to sully

devas'tare *vt* to devastate; (*fig*) to ravage

devi'are *vi*: **~ (da)** to turn off (from) ♦ *vt* to divert; **deviazi'one** *sf* (*anche AUT*) diversion

devo'luto, a *pp di* **devolvere**

devoluzi'one [devolut'tsjone] *sf* (*DIR*) devolution, transfer

de'volvere *vt* (*DIR*) to transfer, devolve

de'voto, a *ag* (*REL*) devout, pious; (*affezionato*) devoted

devozi'one [devot'tsjone] *sf* devoutness; (*anche REL*) devotion

---

PAROLA CHIAVE

---

di (*di+il* = **del**, *di+lo* = **dello**, *di+l'* = **dell'**, *di+la* = **della**, *di+i* = **dei**, *di+gli* = **degli**, *di+le* = **delle**) *prep* **1** (*possesso, specificazione*) of; (*composto da, scritto da*) by; **la macchina ~ Paolo/mio fratello** Paolo's/my brother's car; **un amico ~ mio fratello** a friend of my brother's, one of my brother's friends; **un quadro ~ Botticelli** a painting by Botticelli

2 (*caratterizzazione, misura*) of; **una casa ~ mattoni** a brick house, a house made of bricks; **un orologio d'oro** a gold watch; **un bimbo ~ 3 anni** a child of 3, a 3-year-old child

3 (*causa, mezzo, modo*) with; **tremare ~ paura** to tremble with fear; **morire ~ cancro** to die of cancer; **spalmare ~ burro** to spread with butter

4 (*argomento*) about, of; **discutere ~ sport** to talk about sport

5 (*luogo: provenienza*) from; out of; **essere ~ Roma** to be from Rome; **uscire ~ casa** to come out of *o* leave the house

6 (*tempo*) in; **d'estate/d'inverno** in (the) summer/winter; **~ notte** by night, at night; **~ mattina/sera** in the morning/evening; **~ lunedì** on Mondays

♦ *det* (*una certa quantità di*) some; (: *negativo*) any; (: *interrogativo*) any, some; **del pane** (some) bread; **delle caramelle** (some) sweets; **degli amici miei** some friends of mine; **vuoi del vino?** do you want some *o* any wine?

---

dia'bete *sm* diabetes *sg*

di'acono *sm* (*REL*) deacon

dia'dema, i *sm* diadem; (*di donna*) tiara

dia'framma, i *sm* (*divisione*) screen; (*ANAT, FOT, contraccettivo*) diaphragm

di'agnosi [di'aɲɲozi] *sf* diagnosis *sg*

diago'nale *ag, sf* diagonal

dia'gramma, i *sm* diagram

dia'letto *sm* dialect

di'alisi *sf* dialysis *sg*

di'alogo, ghi *sm* dialogue

dia'mante *sm* diamond

di'ametro *sm* diameter

di'amine *escl:* **che ~ ...?** what on earth ...?

diaposi'tiva *sf* transparency, slide

di'ario *sm* diary

diar'rea *sf* diarrhoea

di'avolo *sm* devil

di'battere *vt* to debate, discuss; **~rsi** *vr* to struggle; **di'battito** *sm* debate, discussion

dicas'tero *sm* ministry

di'cembre [di'tʃɛmbre] *sm* December

dice'ria [ditʃe'ria] *sf* rumour, piece of gossip

dichia'rare [dikja'rare] *vt* to declare; **dichiarazi'one** *sf* declaration

dician'nove [ditʃan'nɔve] *num* nineteen

dicias'sette [ditʃas'sette] *num* seventeen

dici'otto [di'tʃɔtto] *num* eighteen

dici'tura [ditʃi'tura] *sf* words *pl*, wording

di'eci ['djɛtʃi] *num* ten; **die'cina** *sf* = **decina**

'diesel ['dizəl] *sm inv* diesel engine

di'eta *sf* diet; **essere a ~** to be on a diet

di'etro *av* behind; (*in fondo*) at the back ♦ *prep* behind; (*tempo: dopo*) after ♦ *sm* back, rear ♦ *ag inv* back *cpd*; **le zampe di ~** the hind legs; **~ richiesta** on demand; (*scritta*) on application

di'fatti *cong* in fact, as a matter of fact

di'fendere *vt* to defend; **difen'sivo, a** *ag* defensive ♦ *sf:* **stare sulla difensiva** (*anche fig*) to be on the defensive; **difen'sore, a** *sm/f* defender; **avvocato difensore** counsel for the defence; **di'fesa** *sf* defence; **di'feso, a** *pp di* **difendere**

difet'tare *vi* to be defective; **~ di** to be lacking in, lack; **difet'tivo, a** *ag* defective

di'fetto *sm* (*mancanza*): **~ di** lack of; shortage of; (*di fabbricazione*) fault, flaw, defect; (*morale*) fault, failing, defect; (*fisico*) defect; **far ~** to be lacking; **in ~** at fault; in the wrong; **difet'toso, a** *ag* defective, faulty

diffa'mare *vt* to slander; to libel

diffe'rente *ag* different

diffe'renza [diffe'rentsa] *sf* difference; **a ~ di** unlike

differenzi'are [differen'tsjare] *vt* to differentiate; **~rsi da** to differentiate o.s. from; to differ from

diffe'rire *vt* to postpone, defer ♦ *vi* to be different

dif'ficile [dif'fitʃile] *ag* difficult; (*persona*) hard to please, difficult (to please); (*poco probabile*): **è ~ che sia libero** it is unlikely that he'll be free ♦ *sm* difficult part; difficulty; **difficoltà** *sf inv* difficulty

dif'fida *sf* (*DIR*) warning, notice

diffi'dare *vi:* **~ di** to be suspicious *o* distrustful of ♦ *vt* (*DIR*) to warn; **~ qn dal fare qc** to warn sb not to do sth, caution sb against doing sth; **diffi'dente** *ag* suspicious, distrustful; **diffi'denza** *sf* suspicion, distrust

dif'fondere *vt* (*luce, calore*) to diffuse; (*notizie*) to spread, circulate; **~rsi** *vr* to spread; **diffusi'one** *sf* diffusion; spread; (*anche di giornale*) circulation; (*FISICA*) scattering; **dif'fuso, a** *pp di* **diffondere** ♦ *ag* (*malattia, fenomeno*) widespread

difi'lato *av* (*direttamente*) straight, directly; (*subito*) straight away

difte'rite *sf* (*MED*) diphtheria

'diga, ghe *sf* dam; (*portuale*) breakwater

dige'rente [didʒe'rente] *ag* (*apparato*) digestive

dige'rire [didʒe'rire] *vt* to digest; **digesti'one** *sf* digestion; **diges'tivo, a** *ag* digestive ♦ *sm* (*after-dinner*) liqueur

digi'tale [didʒi'tale] *ag* digital; (*delle dita*) finger *cpd*, digital ♦ *sf* (*BOT*) foxglove

digi'tare [didʒi'tare] *vt, vi* (*INFORM*) to key (in)

digiu'nare [didʒu'nare] *vi* to starve o.s.; (*REL*) to fast; **digi'uno, a** *ag:* **essere digiuno** not to have eaten ♦ *sm* fast; **a digiuno** on an empty stomach

dignità [diɲɲi'ta] *sf inv* dignity; **digni'toso, a** *ag* dignified

'DIGOS ['digɔs] *sigla f* (= *Divisione*

Investigazioni Generali e Operazioni Speciali) police department dealing with political security

digri'gnare [digriɲ'ɲare] vt: ~ **i denti** to grind one's teeth

dila'gare vi to flood; (*fig*) to spread

dilani'are vt (*preda*) to tear to pieces

dilapi'dare vt to squander, waste

dila'tare vt to dilate; (*gas*) to cause to expand; (*passaggio, cavità*) to open (up); **~rsi** vr to dilate; (*FISICA*) to expand

dilazio'nare [dilattsjo'nare] vt to delay, defer; **dilazi'one** sf delay; (*COMM: di pagamento etc*) extension; (*rinvio*) postponement

dilegu'are vi to vanish, disappear; **~rsi** vr to vanish, disappear

di'lemma, i sm dilemma

dilet'tante sm/f dilettante; (*anche SPORT*) amateur

dilet'tare vt to give pleasure to, delight; **~rsi** vr: **~rsi di** to take pleasure in, enjoy

di'letto, a ag dear, beloved ♦ sm pleasure, delight

dili'gente [dili'dʒɛnte] ag (*scrupoloso*) diligent; (*accurato*) careful, accurate; **dili'genza** sf diligence; care; (*carrozza*) stagecoach

dilu'ire vt to dilute

dilun'garsi vr (*fig*): ~ **su** to talk at length on o about

diluvi'are vb impers to pour (down)

di'luvio sm downpour; (*inondazione, fig*) flood

dima'grire vi to get thinner, lose weight

dime'nare vt to wave, shake; **~rsi** vr to toss and turn; (*fig*) to struggle; ~ **la coda** (*sog: cane*) to wag its tail

dimensi'one sf dimension; (*grandezza*) size

dimenti'canza [dimenti'kantsa] sf forgetfulness; (*errore*) oversight, slip; **per ~** inadvertently

dimenti'care vt to forget; **~rsi di qc** to forget sth

di'messo, a pp di **dimettere** ♦ ag (*voce*) subdued; (*uomo, abito*) modest, humble

dimesti'chezza [dimesti'kettsa] sf familiarity

di'mettere vt: ~ **qn da** to dismiss sb from; (*dall'ospedale*) to discharge sb from; **~rsi (da)** to resign (from)

dimez'zare [dimed'dzare] vt to halve

diminu'ire vt to reduce, diminish; (*prezzi*) to bring down, reduce ♦ vi to decrease, diminish; (*rumore*) to die down, die away; (*prezzi*) to fall, go down; **diminuzi'one** sf decreasing, diminishing

dimissi'oni sfpl resignation sg; **dare o presentare le ~** to resign, hand in one's resignation

di'mora sf residence

dimo'rare vi to reside

dimos'trare vt to demonstrate, show; (*provare*) to prove, demonstrate; **~rsi** vr: **~rsi molto abile** to show o.s. o prove to be very clever; **dimostra 30 anni** he looks about 30 (years old); **dimostrazi'one** sf demonstration; proof

di'namica sf dynamics sg

di'namico, a, ci, che ag dynamic

dina'mite sf dynamite

'dinamo sf inv dynamo

di'nanzi [di'nantsi]: ~ **a** prep in front of

dini'ego, ghi sm refusal; denial

dinocco'lato, a ag lanky

din'torno av round, (round) about; **~i** smpl outskirts; **nei ~i di** in the vicinity o neighbourhood of

'dio (*pl* **'dei**) sm god; **D~** God; **gli dei** the gods; **D~ mio!** my goodness!, my God!

di'ocesi [di'ɔtʃezi] sf inv diocese

dipa'nare vt (*lana*) to wind into a ball; (*fig*) to disentangle, sort out

diparti'mento sm department

dipen'dente ag dependent ♦ sm/f employee; **dipen'denza** sf dependence; **essere alle dipendenze di qn** to be employed by sb o in sb's employ

di'pendere vi: ~ **da** to depend on; (*finanziariamente*) to be dependent on; (*derivare*) to come from, be due to; **di'peso, a** pp di **dipendere**

di'pingere [di'pindʒere] vt to paint;

di'pinto, a *pp di* dipingere ♦ *sm* painting
di'ploma, i *sm* diploma
diplo'mare *vt* to award a diploma to, graduate (*US*); ~rsi *vr* to obtain a diploma, graduate (*US*)
diplo'matico, a, ci, che *ag* diplomatic ♦ *sm* diplomat
diploma'zia [diplomat'tsia] *sf* diplomacy
di'porto: imbarcazione da ~ *sf* pleasure craft
dira'dare *vt* to thin (out); (*visite*) to reduce, make less frequent; ~rsi *vr* to disperse; (*nebbia*) to clear (up)
dira'mare *vt* to issue ♦ *vi* (*strade*) to branch; ~rsi *vr* to branch
'dire *vt* to say; (*segreto, fatto*) to tell; ~ qc a qn to tell sb sth; ~ a qn di fare qc to tell sb to do sth; ~ di sì/no to say yes/no; si dice che ... they say that ...; si direbbe che ... it looks (*o* sounds) as though ...; dica, signora? (*in un negozio*) yes, Madam, can I help you?
di'retto, a *pp di* dirigere ♦ *ag* direct ♦ *sm* (*FERR*) through train
diret'tore, 'trice *sm/f* (*di azienda*) director; manager/ess; (*di scuola elementare*) head (teacher) (*BRIT*), principal (*US*); ~ d'orchestra conductor; ~ vendite sales director *o* manager
direzi'one [diret'tsjone] *sf* board of directors; management; (*senso di movimento*) direction; in ~ di in the direction of, towards
diri'gente [diri'dʒente] *sm/f* executive; (*POL*) leader ♦ *ag*: classe ~ ruling class
di'rigere [di'ridʒere] *vt* to direct; (*impresa*) to run, manage; (*MUS*) to conduct; ~rsi *vr*: ~rsi verso *o* a to make *o* head for
dirim'petto *av* opposite; ~ a opposite, facing
di'ritto, a *ag* straight; (*onesto*) straight, upright ♦ *av* straight, directly; andare ~ to go straight on ♦ *sm* right hand side; (*TENNIS*) forehand; (*MAGLIA*) plain stitch; (*prerogativa*) right; (*leggi, scienza*): il ~ law; ~i *smpl* (*tasse*) duty *sg*; stare ~ to stand up straight; aver ~ a qc to be entitled to sth;

~i d'autore royalties
dirit'tura *sf* (*SPORT*) straight; (*fig*) rectitude
diroc'cato, a *ag* tumbledown, in ruins
dirot'tare *vt* (*nave, aereo*) to change the course of; (*aereo: sotto minaccia*) to hijack; (*traffico*) to divert ♦ *vi* (*nave, aereo*) to change course; dirotta'tore, 'trice *sm/f* hijacker
di'rotto, a *ag* (*pioggia*) torrential; (*pianto*) unrestrained; piovere a ~ to pour; piangere a ~ to cry one's heart out
di'rupo *sm* crag, precipice
disabi'tato, a *ag* uninhabited
disabitu'arsi *vr*: ~ a to get out of the habit of
disac'cordo *sm* disagreement
disadat'tato, a *ag* (*PSIC*) maladjusted
disa'dorno, a *ag* plain, unadorned
disagi'ato, a [diza'dʒato] *ag* poor, needy; (*vita*) hard
di'sagio [di'zadʒo] *sm* discomfort; (*disturbo*) inconvenience; (*fig: imbarazzo*) embarrassment; essere a ~ to be ill at ease
disappro'vare *vt* to disapprove of; disapprovazi'one *sf* disapproval
disap'punto *sm* disappointment
disar'mare *vt, vi* to disarm; di'sarmo *sm* (*MIL*) disarmament
di'sastro *sm* disaster
disat'tento, a *ag* inattentive; disattenzi'one *sf* carelessness, lack of attention
disa'vanzo [diza'vantso] *sm* (*ECON*) deficit
disavven'tura *sf* misadventure, mishap
dis'brigo, ghi *sm* (*prompt*) clearing up *o* settlement
dis'capito *sm*: a ~ di to the detriment of
dis'carica, che *sf* (*di rifiuti*) rubbish tip *o* dump
discen'dente [diʃʃen'dɛnte] *ag* descending ♦ *sm/f* descendant
di'scendere [diʃʃendere] *vt* to go (*o* come) down ♦ *vi* to go (*o* come) down; (*strada*) to go down; (*smontare*) to get off; ~ da (*famiglia*) to be descended from; ~ dalla macchina/dal treno to get out of the car/out of *o* off the train; ~ da cavallo to

dismount, get off one's horse

di'scepolo, a [diʃʃepolo] *sm/f* disciple

di'scernere [diʃʃernere] *vt* to discern

di'scesa [diʃʃesa] *sf* descent; (*pendio*) slope; **in ~** (*strada*) downhill *cpd*, sloping; **~ libera** (*SCI*) downhill (race)

di'sceso, a [diʃʃeso] *pp di* **discendere**

disci'ogliere [diʃʃɔʎʎere] *vt* to dissolve; (*fondere*) to melt; **~rsi** *vr* to dissolve; to melt; **disci'olto, a** *pp di* **disciogliere**

disci'plina [diʃʃiplina] *sf* discipline; **discipli'nare** *ag* disciplinary ♦ *vt* to discipline

'disco, schi *sm* disc; (*SPORT*) discus; (*fonografico*) record; (*INFORM*) disk; **~ orario** (*AUT*) parking disc; **~ rigido** (*INFORM*) hard disk; **~ volante** flying saucer

discol'pare *vt* to clear of blame

disco'noscere [diskonoʃʃere] *vt* (*figlio*) to disown; (*meriti*) to ignore, disregard; **disconosci'uto, a** *pp di* **disconoscere**

dis'corde *ag* conflicting, clashing; **dis'cordia** *sf* discord; (*dissidio*) disagreement, clash

dis'correre *vi:* **~ (di)** to talk (about)

dis'corso, a *pp di* **discorrere** ♦ *sm* speech; (*conversazione*) conversation, talk

dis'costo, a *ag* faraway, distant ♦ *av* far away; **~ da** far from

disco'teca, che *sf* (*raccolta*) record library; (*locale*) disco

discre'panza [diskre'pantsa] *sf* disagreement

dis'creto, a *ag* discreet; (*abbastanza buono*) reasonable, fair; **discrezi'one** *sf* discretion; (*giudizio*) judgment, discernment; **a discrezione di** at the discretion of

discriminazi'one [diskriminat'tsjone] *sf* discrimination

discussi'one *sf* discussion; (*litigio*) argument; **fuori ~** out of the question

dis'cusso, a *pp di* **discutere**

dis'cutere *vt* to discuss, debate; (*contestare*) to question ♦ *vi* (*conversare*): **~ (di)** to discuss; (*litigare*) to argue

disde'gnare [disdeɲˈɲare] *vt* to scorn

dis'detta *sf* (*di prenotazione etc*) cancellation; (*sfortuna*) bad luck

dis'detto, a *pp di* **disdire**

dis'dire *vt* (*prenotazione*) to cancel; (*DIR*): **~ un contratto d'affitto** to give notice (to quit)

dise'gnare [diseɲˈɲare] *vt* to draw; (*progettare*) to design; (*fig*) to outline

disegna'tore, 'trice *sm/f* designer

di'segno [di'seɲɲo] *sm* drawing; design; outline; **~ di legge** (*DIR*) bill

diser'bante *sm* weed-killer

diser'tare *vt, vi* to desert; **diser'tore** *sm* (*MIL*) deserter

dis'fare *vt* to undo; (*valigie*) to unpack; (*meccanismo*) to take to pieces; (*neve*) to melt; **~rsi** *vr* to come undone; (*neve*) to melt; **~ il letto** to strip the bed; **~rsi di qn** (*liberarsi*) to get rid of sb; **dis'fatta** *sf* (*sconfitta*) rout; **dis'fatto, a** *pp di* **disfare**

dis'gelo [diz'dʒelo] *sm* thaw

dis'grazia [diz'grattsja] *sf* (*sventura*) misfortune; (*incidente*) accident, mishap; **disgrazi'ato, a** *ag* unfortunate ♦ *sm/f* wretch

disgre'gare *vt* to break up; **~rsi** *vr* to break up

disgu'ido *sm* hitch; **~ postale** error in postal delivery

disgus'tare *vt* to disgust; **~rsi** *vr:* **~rsi di** to be disgusted by

dis'gusto *sm* disgust; **disgus'toso, a** *ag* disgusting

disidra'tare *vt* to dehydrate

disil'ludere *vt* to disillusion, disenchant

disimpa'rare *vt* to forget

disinfet'tante *ag, sm* disinfectant

disinfet'tare *vt* to disinfect

disini'bito, a *ag* uninhibited

disinte'grare *vt, vi* to disintegrate

disinteres'sarsi *vr:* **~ di** to take no interest in

disinte'resse *sm* indifference; (*generosità*) unselfishness

disintossi'care *vt* (*alcolizzato, drogato*) to treat for alcoholism (*o* drug addiction); **~ l'organismo** to clear out one's system disin'volto, a *ag* casual, free and easy; disinvol'tura *sf* casualness, ease

disles'sia *sf* dyslexia

dislo'care *vt* to station, position

dismi'sura *sf* excess; **a ~** to excess, excessively

disobbe'dire *etc* = **disubbidire** *etc*

disoccu'pato, a *ag* unemployed ♦ *sm/f* unemployed person; disoccupazi'one *sf* unemployment

diso'nesto, a *ag* dishonest

diso'nore *sm* dishonour, disgrace

di'sopra *av* (*con contatto*) on top; (*senza contatto*) above; (*al piano superiore*) upstairs ♦ *ag inv* (*superiore*) upper ♦ *sm inv* top, upper part

disordi'nato, a *ag* untidy; (*privo di misura*) irregular, wild

di'sordine *sm* (*confusione*) disorder, confusion; (*sregolatezza*) debauchery

disorien'tare *vt* to disorientate; **~rsi** *vr* (*fig*) to get confused, lose one's bearings

di'sotto *av* below, underneath; (*in fondo*) at the bottom; (*al piano inferiore*) downstairs ♦ *ag inv* (*inferiore*) lower; bottom *cpd* ♦ *sm inv* (*parte inferiore*) lower part; bottom

dis'paccio [dis'pattʃo] *sm* dispatch

'dispari *ag inv* odd, uneven

dis'parte: **in ~** *av* (*da lato*) aside, apart; **tenersi** *o* **starsene in ~** to keep to o.s., hold o.s. aloof

dispendi'oso, a *ag* expensive

dis'pensa *sf* pantry, larder; (*mobile*) sideboard; (*DIR*) exemption; (*REL*) dispensation; (*fascicolo*) number, issue

dispen'sare *vt* (*elemosine, favori*) to distribute; (*esonerare*) to exempt

dispe'rare *vi*: **~ (di)** to despair (of); **~rsi** *vr* to despair; dispe'rato, a *ag* (*persona*) in despair; (*caso, tentativo*) desperate; disperazi'one *sf* despair

dis'perdere *vt* (*disseminare*) to disperse; (*MIL*) to scatter, rout; (*fig: consumare*) to waste, squander; **~rsi** *vr* to disperse; to scatter; dis'perso, a *pp di* **disperdere** ♦ *sm/f* missing person

dis'petto *sm* spite *no pl*, spitefulness *no pl*; **fare un ~ a qn** to play a (nasty) trick on sb; **a ~ di** in spite of; dispet'toso, a *ag* spiteful

dispia'cere [dispja'tʃere] *sm* (*rammarico*) regret, sorrow; (*dolore*) grief; **~i** *smpl* (*preoccupazioni*) troubles, worries ♦ *vi*: **~ a** to displease ♦ *vb impers*: **mi dispiace (che)** I am sorry (that); **se non le dispiace, me ne vado adesso** if you don't mind, I'll go now; dispiaci'uto, a *pp di* **dispiacere** ♦ *ag* sorry

dispo'nibile *ag* available; disponibilità *sf inv* (*di biglietti, camere*) availability; (*gentilezza*) helpfulness; (*spec pl: FIN*) liquid assets *pl*

dis'porre *vt* (*sistemare*) to arrange; (*preparare*) to prepare; (*DIR*) to order; (*persuadere*): **~ qn a** to incline *o* dispose sb towards ♦ *vi* (*decidere*) to decide; (*usufruire*): **~ di** to use, have at one's disposal; (*essere dotato*): **~ di** to have; **disporsi** *vr* (*ordinarsi*) to place o.s., arrange o.s.

disposi'tivo *sm* (*meccanismo*) device

disposizi'one [dispozit'tsjone] *sf* arrangement, layout; (*stato d'animo*) mood; (*tendenza*) bent, inclination; (*comando*) order; (*DIR*) provision, regulation; **a ~ di qn** at sb's disposal

dis'posto, a *pp di* **disporre**

disprez'zare [dispret'tsare] *vt* to despise

dis'prezzo [dis'prettso] *sm* contempt

'disputa *sf* dispute, quarrel

dispu'tare *vt* (*contendere*) to dispute, contest; (*gara*) to take part in ♦ *vi* to quarrel; **~ di** to discuss; **~rsi qc** to fight for sth

dissan'guare *vt* (*fig: persona*) to bleed white; (*: patrimonio*) to suck dry; **~rsi** *vr* (*MED*) to lose blood; (*fig: rovinarsi*) to ruin o.s.

dissec'care *vt* to dry up; **~rsi** *vr* to dry up

dissemi'nare *vt* to scatter; (*fig: notizie*) to spread

dis'senso *sm* dissent; (*disapprovazione*) disapproval

dissente'ria *sf* dysentery
dissen'tire *vi*: ~ **(da)** to disagree (with)
dissertazi'one [dissertat'tsjone] *sf* dissertation
disser'vizio [disser'vittsjo] *sm* inefficiency
disses'tare *vt* (ECON) to ruin; **dis'sesto** *sm* (financial) ruin
disse'tante *ag* refreshing
dis'sidio *sm* disagreement
dis'simile *ag* different, dissimilar
dissimu'lare *vt* (*fingere*) to dissemble; (*nascondere*) to conceal
dissi'pare *vt* to dissipate; (*scialacquare*) to squander, waste
dis'solto, a *pp di* **dissolvere**
disso'luto, a *pp di* **dissolvere** ♦ *ag* dissolute, licentious
dis'solvere *vt* to dissolve; (*neve*) to melt; (*fumo*) to disperse; **~rsi** *vr* to dissolve; to melt; to disperse
dissu'adere *vt*: ~ **qn da** to dissuade sb from; **dissu'aso, a** *pp di* **dissuadere**
distac'care *vt* to detach, separate; (SPORT) to leave behind; **~rsi** *vr* to be detached; (*fig*) to stand out; **~rsi da** (*fig: allontanarsi*) to grow away from
dis'tacco, chi *sm* (*separazione*) separation; (*fig: indifferenza*) detachment; (SPORT): **vincere con un ~ di ...** to win by a distance of ...
dis'tante *av* far away ♦ *ag*: ~ **(da)** distant (from), far away (from)
dis'tanza [dis'tantsa] *sf* distance
distanzi'are [distan'tsjare] *vt* to space out, place at intervals; (SPORT) to outdistance; (*fig: superare*) to outstrip, surpass
dis'tare *vi*: **distiamo pochi chilometri da Roma** we are only a few kilometres (away) from Rome
dis'tendere *vt* (*coperta*) to spread out; (*gambe*) to stretch (out); (*mettere a giacere*) to lay; (*rilassare: muscoli, nervi*) to relax; **~rsi** *vr* (*rilassarsi*) to relax; (*sdraiarsi*) to lie down; **disten'sione** *sf* stretching; relaxation; (POL) détente
dis'tesa *sf* expanse, stretch
dis'teso, a *pp di* **distendere**

distil'lare *vt* to distil
distille'ria *sf* distillery
dis'tinguere *vt* to distinguish
dis'tinta *sf* (*nota*) note; (*elenco*) list
distin'tivo, a *ag* distinctive; distinguishing ♦ *sm* badge
dis'tinto, a *pp di* **distinguere** ♦ *ag* (*dignitoso ed elegante*) distinguished; **~i saluti** (*in lettera*) yours faithfully
distinzi'one [distin'tsjone] *sf* distinction
dis'togliere [dis'tɔʎʎere] *vt*: ~ **da** to take away from; (*fig*) to dissuade from; **dis'tolto, a** *pp di* **distogliere**
distorsi'one *sf* (MED) sprain; (FISICA, OTTICA) distortion
dis'trarre *vt* to distract; (*divertire*) to entertain, amuse; **distrarsi** *vr* (*non fare attenzione*) to be distracted, let one's mind wander; (*svagarsi*) to amuse *o* enjoy o.s.; **dis'tratto, a** *pp di* **distrarre** ♦ *ag* absent-minded; (*disattento*) inattentive; **distrazi'one** *sf* absent-mindedness; inattention; (*svago*) distraction, entertainment
dis'tretto *sm* district
distribu'ire *vt* to distribute; (CARTE) to deal (out); (*posta*) to deliver; (*lavoro*) to allocate, assign; (*ripartire*) to share out; **distribu'tore** *sm* (*di benzina*) petrol (BRIT) *o* gas (US) pump; (AUT, ELETTR) distributor; (*automatico*) vending machine; **distribuzi'one** *sf* distribution; delivery
distri'care *vt* to disentangle, unravel
dis'truggere [dis'truddʒere] *vt* to destroy; **dis'trutto, a** *pp di* **distruggere**; **distruzi'one** *sf* destruction
distur'bare *vt* to disturb, trouble; (*sonno, lezioni*) to disturb, interrupt; **~rsi** *vr* to put o.s. out
dis'turbo *sm* trouble, bother, inconvenience; (*indisposizione*) (slight) disorder, ailment; **~i** *smpl* (RADIO, TV) static *sg*
disubbidi'ente *ag* disobedient; **disubbidi'enza** *sf* disobedience
disubbi'dire *vi*: ~ **(a qn)** to disobey (sb)
disugu'ale *ag* unequal; (*diverso*) different;

(*irregolare*) uneven

disu'mano, a *ag* inhuman

di'suso *sm*: **andare** *o* **cadere in ~** to fall into disuse

'dita *fpl di* **dito**

di'tale *sm* thimble

'dito (*pl(f)* **'dita**) *sm* finger; (*misura*) finger, finger's breadth; **~ (del piede)** toe

'ditta *sf* firm, business

ditta'tore *sm* dictator

ditta'tura *sf* dictatorship

dit'tongo, ghi *sm* diphthong

di'urno, a *ag* day *cpd*, daytime *cpd*

'diva *sf vedi* **divo**

diva'gare *vi* to digress

divam'pare *vi* to flare up, blaze up

di'vano *sm* sofa; divan

divari'care *vt* to open wide

di'vario *sm* difference

dive'nire *vi* = **diventare**

diven'tare *vi* to become; **~ famoso/ professore** to become famous/a teacher

dive'nuto, a *pp di* **divenire**

di'verbio *sm* altercation

di'vergere [di'vɛrdʒere] *vi* to diverge

diversifi'care *vt* to diversify, vary; to differentiate

diversi'one *sf* diversion

diversità *sf inv* difference, diversity; (*varietà*) variety

diver'sivo *sm* diversion, distraction

di'verso, a *ag* (*differente*): **~ (da)** different (from); **~i, e** *det pl* several, various; (*COMM*) sundry ♦ *pron pl* several (people), many (people)

diver'tente *ag* amusing

diverti'mento *sm* amusement, pleasure; (*passatempo*) pastime, recreation

diver'tire *vt* to amuse, entertain; **~rsi** *vr* to amuse *o* enjoy o.s.

divi'dendo *sm* dividend

di'videre *vt* (*anche MAT*) to divide; (*distribuire, ripartire*) to divide (up), split (up); **~rsi** *vr* (*separarsi*) to separate; (*strade*) to fork

divi'eto *sm* prohibition; **"~ di sosta"** (*AUT*) "no parking"

divinco'larsi *vr* to wriggle, writhe

divinità *sf inv* divinity

di'vino, a *ag* divine

di'visa *sf* (*MIL etc*) uniform; (*COMM*) foreign currency

divisi'one *sf* division

di'viso, a *pp di* **dividere**

'divo, a *sm/f* star

divo'rare *vt* to devour

divorzi'are [divor'tsjare] *vi*: **~ (da qn)** to divorce (sb); **divorzi'ato, a** *sm/f* divorcee

di'vorzio [di'vɔrtsjo] *sm* divorce

divul'gare *vt* to divulge, disclose; (*rendere comprensibile*) to popularize; **~rsi** *vr* to spread

dizio'nario [ditsjo'narjo] *sm* dictionary

dizi'one [dit'tsjone] *sf* diction; pronunciation

do *sm* (*MUS*) C; (: *solfeggiando*) do(h)

DOC [dɔk] *abbr* (= *denominazione di origine controllata*) *label guaranteeing the quality of wine*

'doccia, ce ['dɔttʃa] *sf* (*bagno*) shower; **fare la ~** to have a shower

do'cente [do'tʃɛnte] *ag* teaching ♦ *sm/f* teacher; (*di università*) lecturer

'docile ['dɔtʃile] *ag* docile

documen'tare *vt* to document; **~rsi** *vr*: **~rsi (su)** to gather information *o* material (about)

documen'tario *sm* documentary

docu'mento *sm* document; **~i** *smpl* (*d'identità etc*) papers

'dodici ['doditʃi] *num* twelve

do'gana *sf* (*ufficio*) customs *pl*; (*tassa*) (customs) duty; **passare la ~** to go through customs; **doga'nale** *ag* customs *cpd*; **dogani'ere** *sm* customs officer

'doglie ['dɔʎʎe] *sfpl* (*MED*) labour *sg*, labour pains

'dolce ['doltʃe] *ag* sweet; (*carattere, persona*) gentle, mild; (*fig: mite: clima*) mild; (*non ripido: pendio*) gentle ♦ *sm* (*sapore dolce*) sweetness, sweet taste; (*CUC: portata*) sweet, dessert; (: *torta*) cake; **dol'cezza** *sf* sweetness; softness; mildness; gentleness; **dolcifi'cante** *sm* sweetener; **dolci'umi**

smpl sweets

do'lente *ag* sorrowful, sad

do'lere *vi* to be sore, hurt, ache; **~rsi** *vr* to complain; (*essere spiacente*): **~rsi di** to be sorry for; **mi duole la testa** my head aches, I've got a headache

'dollaro *sm* dollar

'dolo *sm* (*DIR*) malice

Dolo'miti *sfpl*: **le ~** the Dolomites

do'lore *sm* (*fisico*) pain; (*morale*) sorrow, grief; dolo'roso, a *ag* painful; sorrowful, sad

do'loso, a *ag* (*DIR*) malicious

do'manda *sf* question; (*richiesta*) demand; (*: cortese*) request; (*DIR: richiesta scritta*) application; (*ECON*): **la ~** demand; **fare una ~ a qn** to ask sb a question; **fare ~ (per un lavoro)** to apply (for a job)

doman'dare *vt* (*per avere*) to ask for; (*per sapere*) to ask; (*esigere*) to demand; **~rsi** *vr* to wonder; to ask o.s.; **~ qc a qn** to ask sb for sth; to ask sb sth

do'mani *av* tomorrow ♦ *sm*: **il ~** (*il futuro*) the future; (*il giorno successivo*) the next day; **~ l'altro** the day after tomorrow

do'mare *vt* to tame

domat'tina *av* tomorrow morning

do'menica, che *sf* Sunday; **di** *o* **la ~** on Sundays; domeni'cale *ag* Sunday *cpd*

do'mestica, che *sf vedi* **domestico**

do'mestico, a, ci, che *ag* domestic ♦ *sm/f* servant, domestic

domi'cilio [domi'tʃiljo] *sm* (*DIR*) domicile, place of residence

domi'nare *vt* to dominate; (*fig: sentimenti*) to control, master ♦ *vi* to be in the dominant position; **~rsi** *vr* (*controllarsi*) to control o.s.; **~ su** (*fig*) to surpass, outclass; dominazi'one *sf* domination

do'minio *sm* dominion; (*fig: campo*) field, domain

do'nare *vt* to give, present; (*per beneficenza etc*) to donate ♦ *vi* (*fig*): **~ a** to suit, become; **~ sangue** to give blood; dona'tore, 'trice *sm/f* donor; **donatore di sangue/di organi** blood/organ donor

dondo'lare *vt* (*cullare*) to rock; **~rsi** *vr* to

swing, sway; 'dondolo *sm*: **sedia/cavallo a dondolo** rocking chair/horse

'donna *sf* woman; **~ di casa** housewife; home-loving woman; **~ di servizio** maid

donnai'olo *sm* ladykiller

'donnola *sf* weasel

'dono *sm* gift

'doping *sm inv* drug abuse

'dopo *av* (*tempo*) afterwards; (*: più tardi*) later; (*luogo*) after, next ♦ *prep* after ♦ *cong* (*temporale*): **~ mangiato va a dormire** after having eaten *o* after a meal he goes for a sleep ♦ *ag inv*: **il giorno ~** the following day; **un anno ~** a year later; **~ di me/lui** after me/him

dopo'barba *sm inv* after-shave

dopodo'mani *av* the day after tomorrow

dopogu'erra *sm* postwar years *pl*

dopo'pranzo [dopo'prandzo] *av* after lunch (*o* dinner)

doposcì [dopoʃ'ʃi] *sm inv* après-ski outfit

doposcu'ola *sm inv* school club offering extra tuition and recreational facilities

dopo'sole *sm inv* aftersun (lotion) ♦ *ag inv* aftersun

dopo'tutto *av* (*tutto considerato*) after all

doppi'aggio [dop'pjaddʒo] *sm* (*CINEMA*) dubbing

doppi'are *vt* (*NAUT*) to round; (*SPORT*) to lap; (*CINEMA*) to dub

'doppio, a *ag* double; (*fig: falso*) double-dealing, deceitful ♦ *sm* (*quantità*): **il ~ (di)** twice as much (*o* many), double the amount (*o* number) of; (*SPORT*) doubles *pl* ♦ *av* double

doppi'one *sm* duplicate (copy)

doppio'petto *sm* double-breasted jacket

do'rare *vt* to gild; (*CUC*) to brown; do'rato, a *ag* golden; (*ricoperto d'oro*) gilt, gilded; dora'tura *sf* gilding

dormicchi'are [dormik'kjare] *vi* to doze

dormigli'one, a [dormiʎ'ʎone] *sm/f* sleepyhead

dor'mire *vt, vi* to sleep; **andare a ~** to go to bed; dor'mita *sf*: **farsi una dormita** to have a good sleep

dormi'torio *sm* dormitory

dormi'veglia [dormi'veʎʎa] *sm* drowsiness

'dorso *sm* back; (*di montagna*) ridge, crest; (*di libro*) spine; **a ~ di cavallo** on horseback

do'sare *vt* to measure out; (*MED*) to dose

'dose *sf* quantity, amount; (*MED*) dose

'dosso *sm* (*rilievo*) rise; (*di strada*) bump; (*dorso*): **levarsi di ~ i vestiti** to take one's clothes off

do'tare *vt*: **~ di** to provide *o* supply with; **dotazi'one** *sf* (*insieme di beni*) endowment; (*di macchine etc*) equipment

'dote *sf* (*di sposa*) dowry; (*assegnata a un ente*) endowment; (*fig*) gift, talent

Dott. *abbr* (= *dottore*) Dr.

'dotto, a *ag* (*colto*) learned ♦ *sm* (*sapiente*) scholar; (*ANAT*) duct

dotto'rato *sm* degree; **~ di ricerca** doctorate, doctor's degree

dot'tore, essa *sm/f* doctor

dot'trina *sf* doctrine

Dott.ssa *abbr* (= *dottoressa*) Dr.

'dove *av* (*gen*) where; (*in cui*) where, in which; (*dovunque*) wherever ♦ *cong* (*mentre, laddove*) whereas; **~ sei?/vai?** where are you?/are you going?; **dimmi dov'è** tell me where it is; **di ~ sei?** where are you from?; **per ~ si passa?** which way should we go?; **la città ~ abito** the town where *o* in which I live; **siediti ~ vuoi** sit wherever you like

do'vere *sm* (*obbligo*) duty ♦ *vt* (*essere debitore*): **~ qc (a qn)** to owe (sb) sth ♦ *vi* (*seguito dall'infinito: obbligo*) to have to; **rivolgersi a chi di ~** to apply to the appropriate authority *o* person; **lui deve farlo** he has to do it, he must do it; **è dovuto partire** he had to leave; **ha dovuto pagare** he had to pay; (: *intenzione*): **devo partire domani** I'm (due) to leave tomorrow; (: *probabilità*): **dev'essere tardi** it must be late; **come si deve** (*lavorare, comportarsi*) properly; **una persona come si deve** a respectable person

dove'roso, a *ag* (right and) proper

do'vunque *av* (*in qualunque luogo*) wherever; (*dappertutto*) everywhere; **~ io**

vada wherever I go

do'vuto, a *ag* (*causato*): **~ a** due to

doz'zina [dod'dzina] *sf* dozen; **una ~ di uova** a dozen eggs

dozzi'nale [doddzi'nale] *ag* cheap, second-rate

dra'gare *vt* to dredge

'drago, ghi *sm* dragon

'dramma, i [dra'nadd3o] *sm* drama; **dram'matico, a, ci, che** *ag* dramatic; **drammatiz'zare** *vt* to dramatize; **dramma'turgo, ghi** *sm* playwright, dramatist

drappeggi'are [draped'dʒare] *vt* to drape

drap'pello *sm* (*MIL*) squad; (*gruppo*) band, group

'drastico, a, ci, che *ag* drastic

dre'naggio [dre'nadd3o] *sm* drainage

dre'nare *vt* to drain

'dritto, a *ag, av* = **diritto**

driz'zare [drit'tsare] *vt* (*far tornare dritto*) to straighten; (*innalzare: antenna, muro*) to erect; **~rsi** *vr*: **~rsi (in piedi)** to stand up; **~ le orecchie** to prick up one's ears

'droga, ghe *sf* (*sostanza aromatica*) spice; (*stupefacente*) drug; **dro'gare** *vt* to season, spice; to drug, dope; **drogarsi** *vr* to take drugs; **dro'gato, a** *sm/f* drug addict

droghe'ria [droge'ria] *sf* grocer's shop (*BRIT*), grocery (store) (*US*)

DS *sigla mpl* = **Democratici di Sinistra**

'dubbio, a *ag* (*incerto*) doubtful, dubious; (*ambiguo*) dubious ♦ *sm* (*incertezza*) doubt; **avere il ~ che** to be afraid that, suspect that; **mettere in ~ qc** to question sth; **dubbi'oso, a** *ag* doubtful, dubious

dubi'tare *vi*: **~ di** to doubt; (*risultato*) to be doubtful of

Dub'lino *sf* Dublin

'duca, chi *sm* duke

du'chessa [du'kessa] *sf* duchess

'due *num* two

due'cento [due'tʃento] *num* two hundred

due'pezzi [due'pettsi] *sm* (*costume da bagno*) two-piece swimsuit; (*abito femminile*) two-piece suit

du'etto *sm* duet

'**dunque** *cong* (*perciò*) so, therefore; (*riprendendo il discorso*) well (then) ♦ *sm inv*: **venire al ~** to come to the point

du'**omo** *sm* cathedral

'**duplex** *sm inv* (*TEL*) party line

dupli'**cato** *sm* duplicate

'**duplice** ['duplitʃe] *ag* double, twofold; **in ~ copia** in duplicate

du'**rante** *prep* during

du'**rare** *vi* to last; **~ fatica a** to have difficulty in; **du'rata** *sf* length (of time); duration; **dura'turo, a** *ag* lasting

du'**rezza** [du'rettsa] *sf* hardness; stubbornness; harshness; toughness

'**duro, a** *ag* (*pietra, lavoro, materasso, problema*) hard; (*persona: ostinato*) stubborn, obstinate; (*: severo*) harsh, hard; (*voce*) harsh; (*carne*) tough ♦ *sm* hardness; (*difficoltà*) hard part; (*persona*) tough guy; **tener ~** to stand firm, hold out; **~ d'orecchi** hard of hearing

du'**rone** *sm* hard skin

DVD *sigla m* (= *digital versatile* (or) *video disc*) DVD

E, e

e (*dav V spesso* **ed**) *cong* and; **~ lui?** what about him?; **~ compralo!** well buy it then!

E. *abbr* (= *est*) E

è *vb vedi* **essere**

'**ebano** *sm* ebony

eb'**bene** *cong* well (then)

eb'**brezza** [eb'brettsa] *sf* intoxication

'**ebbro, a** *ag* drunk; **~ di** (*gioia etc*) beside o.s. ♦ wild with

'**ebete** *ag* stupid, idiotic

ebolli'**zione** [ebollit'tsjone] *sf* boiling; **punto di ~** boiling point

e'**braico, a, ci, che** *ag* Hebrew, Hebraic ♦ *sm* (*LING*) Hebrew

e'**breo, a** *ag* Jewish ♦ *sm/f* Jew/Jewess

'**Ebridi** *sfpl*: **le** (**isole**) **~** the Hebrides

ecc *av abbr* (= *eccetera*) etc

ecce'**denza** [ettʃe'dɛntsa] *sf* excess, surplus

ec'**cedere** [et'tʃɛdere] *vt* to exceed ♦ *vi* to go too far; **~ nel bere/mangiare** to indulge in drink/food to excess

eccel'**lente** [ettʃel'lɛnte] *ag* excellent; **eccel'lenza** *sf* excellence; (*titolo*) Excellency

ec'**cellere** [et'tʃɛllere] *vi*: **~ (in)** to excel (at); **ec'celso, a** *pp di* **eccellere**

ec'**centrico, a, ci, che** [et'tʃɛntriko] *ag* eccentric

ecces'**sivo, a** [ettʃes'sivo] *ag* excessive

ec'**cesso** [et'tʃɛsso] *sm* excess; **all'~** (*gentile, generoso*) to excess, excessively; **~ di velocità** (*AUT*) speeding

ec'**cetera** [et'tʃɛtera] *av* et cetera, and so on

ec'**cetto** [et'tʃɛtto] *prep* except, with the exception of; **~ che** except, other than; **~ che (non)** unless

eccettu'**are** [ettʃettu'are] *vt* to except

eccezio'**nale** [ettʃettsjo'nale] *ag* exceptional

eccezi'**one** [ettʃet'tsjone] *sf* exception; (*DIR*) objection; **a ~ di** with the exception of, except for; **d'~** exceptional

ec'**cidio** [et'tʃidio] *sm* massacre

ecci'**tare** [ettʃi'tare] *vt* (*curiosità, interesse*) to excite, arouse; (*folla*) to incite; **~rsi** *vr* to get excited; (*sessualmente*) to become aroused; **eccitazi'one** *sf* excitement

'**ecco** *av* (*per dimostrare*): **~ il treno!** here's o here comes the train!; (*dav pron*): **~mi!** here I am!; **~ne uno!** here's one (of them)!; (*dav pp*): **~ fatto!** there, that's it done!

echeg'**gia** [eked'dʒare] *vi* to echo

e'**clissi** *sf* eclipse

'**eco** (*pl*(*m*) '**echi**) *sm o f* echo

ecogra'**fia** *sf* (*MED*) scan

ecolo'**gia** [ekolo'dʒia] *sf* ecology

econo'**mia** *sf* economy; (*scienza*) economics *sg*; (*risparmio: azione*) saving; **fare ~** to economize, make economies; **eco'nomico, a, ci, che** *ag* economic; (*poco costoso*) economical; **econo'mista, i** *sm* economist; **economiz'zare** *vt, vi* to save; **e'conomo, a** *ag* thrifty ♦ *sm/f* (*INS*) bursar

E'CU [e'ku] *sm inv* (= *Unità monetaria europea*) ECU *n*

ed *cong vedi* **e**

'**edera** *sf* ivy

e'dicola sf newspaper kiosk o stand (US)
edifi'care vt to build; (fig: teoria, azienda)
to establish; (indurre al bene) to edify
edi'ficio [edi'fitʃo] sm building
e'dile ag building cpd; edi'lizia sf building,
building trade; edi'lizio, a ag building
cpd
Edim'burgo sf Edinburgh
edi'tore, 'trice ag publishing cpd ♦ sm/f
publisher; (curatore) editor; edito'ria sf
publishing; editori'ale ag publishing cpd
♦ sm editorial, leader
edizi'one [edit'tsjone] sf edition; (tiratura)
printing
edu'care vt to educate; (gusto, mente) to
train; ~ qn a fare to train sb to do;
edu'cato, a ag polite, well-mannered;
educazi'one sf education; (familiare)
upbringing; (comportamento) (good)
manners pl; educazione fisica (INS)
physical training o education
effemi'nato, a ag effeminate
effet'tivo, a ag (reale) real, actual;
(impiegato, professore) permanent; (MIL)
regular ♦ sm (MIL) strength; (di patrimonio
etc) sum total
ef'fetto sm effect; (COMM: cambiale) bill;
(fig: impressione) impression; in ~ in fact,
actually; ~ serra greenhouse effect;
effettu'are vt to effect, carry out
effi'cace [effi'katʃe] ag effective
effici'ente [effi'tʃɛnte] ag efficient;
effici'enza sf efficiency
ef'fimero, a ag ephemeral
E'geo [e'dʒɛo] sm: l'~, il mare ~ the Aegean
(Sea)
E'gitto [e'dʒitto] sm: l'~ Egypt
egizi'ano, a [edʒit'tsjano] ag, sm/f
Egyptian
'egli ['eʎʎi] pron he; ~ stesso he himself
ego'ismo sm selfishness, egoism;
ego'ista, i, e ag selfish, egoistic ♦ sm/f
egoist
egr, abbr = egregio
e'gregio, a, gi, gie [e'grɛdʒo] ag (nelle
lettere): E~ Signore Dear Sir
eguagli'anza etc [egwaʎ'ʎantsa]

= uguaglianza etc
E.I. abbr = Esercito Italiano
elabo'rare vt (progetto) to work out,
elaborate; (dati) to process; elabora'tore
sm (INFORM): elaboratore elettronico
computer; elaborazi'one sf elaboration;
elaborazione dei dati data processing
elasticiz'zato, a [elastitʃid'dzato] ag
stretch cpd
e'lastico, a, ci, che ag elastic; (fig:
andatura) springy; (: decisione, vedute)
flexible ♦ sm (di gomma) rubber band; (per
il cucito) elastic no pl
ele'fante sm elephant
ele'gante ag elegant
e'leggere [e'leddʒere] vt to elect
elemen'tare ag elementary; le (scuole) ~i
sfpl primary (BRIT) o grade (US) school
ele'mento sm element; (parte componente)
element, component, part; ~i smpl (della
scienza etc) elements, rudiments
ele'mosina sf charity, alms pl; chiedere
l'~ to beg
elen'care vt to list
e'lenco, chi sm list; ~ telefonico
telephone directory
e'letto, a pp di eleggere ♦ sm/f
(nominato) elected member; elet'torale
ag electoral, election cpd; eletto'rato sm
electorate; elet'tore, 'trice sm/f voter,
elector
elet'trauto sm inv workshop for car
electrical repairs; (tecnico) car electrician
elettri'cista, i [elettri'tʃista] sm electrician
elettricità [elettritʃi'ta] sf electricity
e'lettrico, a, ci, che ag electric(al)
elettriz'zare [elettrid'dzare] vt to electrify
e'lettro... prefisso: elettrocar-
dio'gramma, i sm electrocardiogram;
elettrodo'mestico, a, ci, che ag:
apparecchi elettrodomestici domestic
(electrical) appliances; elet'trone sm
electron; elet'tronica sf electronics
sg; elet'tronico, a, ci, che ag
electronic
ele'vare vt to raise; (edificio) to erect;
(multa) to impose

elezi'one [elet'tsjone] *sf* election; **~i** *sfpl* (*POL*) election(s)

'elica, che *sf* propeller

eli'cottero *sm* helicopter

elimi'nare *vt* to eliminate; **elimina'toria** *sf* eliminating round

'elio *sm* helium

elisoc'corso *sm* helicopter ambulance

'ella *pron* she; (*forma di cortesia*) you; **~ stessa** she herself; you yourself

el'metto *sm* helmet

e'logio [e'lɔdʒo] *sm* (*discorso, scritto*) eulogy; (*lode*) praise (*di solito no pl*)

elo'quente *ag* eloquent

e'ludere *vt* to evade; **elu'sivo, a** *ag* evasive

e-mail *sf inv* e-mail

ema'nare *vt* to send out, give off; (*fig: leggi, decreti*) to issue ♦ *vi:* **~ da** to come from

emanci'pare [emantʃi'pare] *vt* to emancipate; **~rsi** *vr* (*fig*) to become liberated *o* emancipated

embri'one *sm* embryo

emenda'mento *sm* amendment

emen'dare *vt* to amend

emer'genza [emer'dʒentsa] *sf* emergency; **in caso di ~** in an emergency

e'mergere [e'mɛrdʒere] *vi* to emerge; (*sommergibile*) to surface; (*fig: distinguersi*) to stand out; **e'merso, a** *pp di* **emergere**

e'messo, a *pp di* **emettere**

e'mettere *vt* (*suono, luce*) to give out, emit; (*onde radio*) to send out; (*assegno, francobollo, ordine*) to issue

emi'crania *sf* migraine

emi'grare *vi* to emigrate; **emigrazi'one** *sf* emigration

emi'nente *ag* eminent, distinguished

emis'fero *sm* hemisphere; **~ boreale/ australe** northern/southern hemisphere

emissi'one *sf* (*vedi* emettere) emission; sending out; issue; (*RADIO*) broadcast

emit'tente *ag* (*banca*) issuing; (*RADIO*) broadcasting, transmitting ♦ *sf* (*RADIO*) transmitter

emorra'gia, 'gie [emorra'dʒia] *sf* haemorrhage

emor'roidi *sfpl* haemorrhoids *pl* (*BRIT*), hemorrhoids *pl* (*US*)

emo'tivo, a *ag* emotional

emozio'nante [emottsjo'nante] *ag* exciting, thrilling

emozio'nare [emottsjo'nare] *vt* (*appassionare*) to thrill, excite; (*commuovere*) to move; (*innervosire*) to upset; **~rsi** *vr* to be excited; to be moved; to be upset

emozi'one [emot'tsjone] *sf* emotion; (*agitazione*) excitement

'empio, a *ag* (*sacrilego*) impious; (*spietato*) cruel, pitiless; (*malvagio*) wicked, evil

emulsi'one *sf* emulsion

enciclope'dia [entʃiklope'dia] *sf* encyclopaedia

endove'noso, a *ag* (*MED*) intravenous

'ENEL ['enel] *sigla m* (= *Ente Nazionale per l'Energia Elettrica*) *national electricity company*

ener'gia, 'gie [ener'dʒia] *sf* (*FISICA*) energy; (*fig*) energy, strength, vigour; **~ eolica** wind power; **~ solare** solar energy, solar power; **e'nergico, a, ci, che** *ag* energetic, vigorous

'enfasi *sf* emphasis; (*peg*) bombast, pomposity; **en'fatico, a, ci, che** *ag* emphatic; pompous

en'nesimo, a *ag* (*MAT, fig*) nth; **per l'~a volta** for the umpteenth time

e'norme *ag* enormous, huge; **enormità** *sf inv* enormity, huge size; (*assurdità*) absurdity; **non dire enormità!** don't talk nonsense!

'ente *sm* (*istituzione*) body, board, corporation; (*FILOSOFIA*) being

en'trambi, e *pron pl* both (of them) ♦ *ag pl:* **~ i ragazzi** both boys, both of the boys

en'trare *vi* to go (*o* come) in; **~ in** (*luogo*) to enter, go (*o* come) into; (*trovar posto, poter stare*) to fit into; (*essere ammesso a: club etc*) to join, become a member of; **~ in automobile** to get into the car; **far ~ qn** (*visitatore etc*) to show sb in; **questo non c'entra** (*fig*) that's got nothing to do with it; **en'trata** *sf* entrance, entry; **entrate** *sfpl* (*COMM*) receipts, takings; (*ECON*) income *sg*

'entro prep (temporale) within

entusias'mare vt to excite, fill with enthusiasm; ~rsi (per qc/qn) to become enthusiastic (about sth/sb); entusi'asmo sm enthusiasm; entusi'asta, i, e ag enthusiastic ♦ sm/f enthusiast; entusi'astico, a, ci, che ag enthusiastic

enunci'are [enun'tʃare] vt (teoria) to set out

epa'tite sf hepatitis

'epico, a, ci, che ag epic

epide'mia sf epidemic

epi'dermide sf skin, epidermis

Epifa'nia sf Epiphany

epiles'sia sf epilepsy

e'pilogo, ghi sm conclusion

epi'sodio sm episode

e'piteto sm epithet

'epoca, che sf (periodo storico) age, era; (tempo) time; (GEO) age

ep'pure cong and yet, nevertheless

equa'tore sm equator

equazi'one [ekwat'tsjone] sf (MAT) equation

e'questre ag equestrian

equi'latero, a ag equilateral

equili'brare vt to balance; equi'librio sm balance, equilibrium; perdere l'~ to lose one's balance

e'quino, a ag horse cpd, equine

equipaggi'are [ekwipad'dʒare] vt (di persone) to man; (di mezzi) to equip; equi'paggio sm crew

equipa'rare vt to make equal

equità sf equity, fairness

equitazi'one [ekwitat'tsjone] sf (horse-)riding

equiva'lente ag, sm equivalent; equiva'lenza sf equivalence

equivo'care vi to misunderstand; e'quivoco, a, ci, che ag equivocal, ambiguous; (sospetto) dubious ♦ sm misunderstanding; a scanso di equivoci to avoid any misunderstanding; giocare sull'equivoco to equivocate

'equo, a ag fair, just

'era sf era

'erba sf grass; (aromatica, medicinale) herb; in ~ (fig) budding; er'baccia, ce sf weed

e'rede sm/f heir; eredità sf (DIR) inheritance; (BIOL) heredity; lasciare qc in eredità a qn to leave o bequeath sth to sb; eredi'tare vt to inherit; eredi'tario, a ag hereditary

ere'mita, i sm hermit

ere'sia sf heresy; e'retico, a, ci, che ag heretical ♦ sm/f heretic

e'retto, a pp di erigere ♦ ag erect, upright; erezi'one sf (FISIOL) erection

er'gastolo sm (DIR: pena) life imprisonment

'erica sf heather

e'rigere [e'ridʒere] vt to erect, raise; (fig: fondare) to found

ERM sigla (= Meccanismo dei tassi di cambio) ERM n

ermel'lino sm ermine

er'metico, a, ci, che ag hermetic

'ernia sf (MED) hernia

e'roe sm hero

ero'gare vt (somme) to distribute; (gas, servizi) to supply

e'roico, a, ci, che ag heroic

ero'ina sf heroine; (droga) heroin

ero'ismo sm heroism

erosi'one sf erosion

e'rotico, a, ci, che ag erotic

er'rare vi (vagare) to wander, roam; (sbagliare) to be mistaken

er'rore sm error, mistake; (morale) error; per ~ by mistake

'erta sf steep slope; stare all'~ to be on the alert

erut'tare vt (sog: vulcano) to throw out, belch

eruzi'one [erut'tsjone] sf eruption

esacer'bare [ezatʃer'bare] vt to exacerbate

esage'rare [ezadʒe'rare] vt to exaggerate ♦ vi to exaggerate; (eccedere) to go too far; esagerazi'one sf exaggeration

e'sagono sm hexagon

esal'tare vt to exalt; (entusiasmare) to excite, stir; esal'tato, a sm/f fanatic

e'same sm examination; (INS) exam, examination; fare o dare un ~ to sit o take

an exam; ~ **del sangue** blood test
esami'nare _vt_ to examine
e'sanime _ag_ lifeless
esaspe'rare _vt_ to exasperate; to exacerbate; **~rsi** _vr_ to become annoyed _o_ exasperated; **esasperazi'one** _sf_ exasperation
esatta'mente _av_ exactly; accurately, precisely
esat'tezza [ezat'tettsa] _sf_ exactitude, accuracy, precision
e'satto, a _pp di_ **esigere** ♦ _ag_ (_calcolo, ora_) correct, right, exact; (_preciso_) accurate, precise; (_puntuale_) punctual
esat'tore _sm_ (_di imposte etc_) collector
esau'dire _vt_ to grant, fulfil
esauri'ente _ag_ exhaustive
esauri'mento _sm_ exhaustion; ~ **nervoso** nervous breakdown
esau'rire _vt_ (_stancare_) to exhaust, wear out; (_provviste, miniera_) to exhaust; **~rsi** _vr_ to exhaust o.s., wear o.s. out; (_provviste_) to run out; **esau'rito, a** _ag_ exhausted; (_merci_) sold out; **registrare il tutto esaurito** (_TEATRO_) to have a full house; **e'sausto, a** _ag_ exhausted
'**esca** (_pl_ '**esche**) _sf_ bait
escande'scenza [eskandeʃʃentsa] _sf_: **dare in ~e** to lose one's temper, fly into a rage
'**esce** _etc_ ['eʃe] _vb vedi_ **uscire**
eschi'mese [eski'mese] _ag, sm/f_ Eskimo
escla'mare _vi_ to exclaim, cry out; **esclamazi'one** _sf_ exclamation
es'cludere _vt_ to exclude
esclu'siva _sf_ (_DIR, COMM_) exclusive _o_ sole rights _pl_
esclu'sivo, a _ag_ exclusive
es'cluso, a _pp di_ **escludere**
'**esco** _etc_ _vb vedi_ **uscire**
escogi'tare [eskodʒi'tare] _vt_ to devise, think up
escursi'one _sf_ (_gita_) excursion, trip; (: _a piedi_) hike, walk; (_METEOR_) range
ese'crare _vt_ to loathe, abhor
esecu'tivo, a _ag, sm_ executive
esecu'tore, 'trice _sm/f_ (_MUS_) performer; (_DIR_) executor

esecuzi'one [ezekut'tsjone] _sf_ execution, carrying out; (_MUS_) performance; ~ **capitale** execution
esegu'ire _vt_ to carry out, execute; (_MUS_) to perform, execute
e'sempio _sm_ example; **per ~** for example, for instance; **fare un ~** to give an example; **esem'plare** _ag_ exemplary ♦ _sm_ example; (_copia_) copy; **esemplifi'care** _vt_ to exemplify
esen'tare _vt_: ~ **qn/qc da** to exempt sb/ sth from
e'sente _ag_: ~ **da** (_dispensato da_) exempt from; (_privo di_) free from; **esenzi'one** _sf_ exemption
e'sequie _sfpl_ funeral rites; funeral service _sg_
eser'cente [ezer'tʃente] _sm/f_ trader, dealer; shopkeeper
eserci'tare [ezertʃi'tare] _vt_ (_professione_) to practise (_BRIT_), practice (_US_); (_allenare: corpo, mente_) to exercise, train; (_diritto_) to exercise; (_influenza, pressione_) to exert; **~rsi** _vr_ to practise; **~rsi alla lotta** to practise fighting; **esercitazi'one** _sf_ (_scolastica, militare_) exercise
e'sercito [e'zertʃito] _sm_ army
eser'cizio [ezer'tʃittsjo] _sm_ practice; exercising; (_fisico, di matematica_) exercise; (_ECON_) financial year; (_azienda_) business, concern; **in ~** (_medico etc_) practising
esi'bire _vt_ to exhibit, display; (_documenti_) to produce, present; **~rsi** _vr_ (_attore_) to perform; (_fig_) to show off; **esibizi'one** _sf_ exhibition; (_di documento_) presentation; (_spettacolo_) show, performance
esi'gente [ezi'dʒente] _ag_ demanding; **esi'genza** _sf_ demand, requirement
e'sigere [e'zidʒere] _vt_ (_pretendere_) to demand; (_richiedere_) to demand, require; (_imposte_) to collect
e'siguo, a _ag_ small, slight
'**esile** _ag_ (_persona_) slender, slim; (_stelo_) thin; (_voce_) faint
esili'are _vt_ to exile; **e'silio** _sm_ exile
e'simere _vt_: ~ **qn/qc da** to exempt sb/sth from; **~rsi** _vr_: **~rsi da** to get out of

esis'tenza [ezis'tentsa] *sf* existence
e'sistere *vi* to exist
esis'tito, a *pp di* **esistere**
esi'tare *vi* to hesitate; **esitazi'one** *sf* hesitation
'esito *sm* result, outcome
'esodo *sm* exodus
esone'rare *vt* to exempt
e'sordio *sm* début
esor'tare *vt*: **~ qn a fare** to urge sb to do
e'sotico, a, ci, che *ag* exotic
es'pandere *vt* to expand; (*confini*) to extend; (*influenza*) to extend, spread; **~rsi** *vr* to expand; **espansi'one** *sf* expansion; **espan'sivo, a** *ag* expansive, communicative
espatri'are *vi* to leave one's country
espedi'ente *sm* expedient
es'pellere *vt* to expel
esperi'enza [espe'rjɛntsa] *sf* experience
esperi'mento *sm* experiment
es'perto, a *ag*, *sm* expert
espi'are *vt* to atone for
espi'rare *vt*, *vi* to breathe out
espli'care *vt* (*attività*) to carry out, perform
es'plicito, a [es'plitʃito] *ag* explicit
es'plodere *vi* (*anche fig*) to explode ♦ *vt* to fire
esplo'rare *vt* to explore; **esplora'tore** *sm* explorer; **giovane esploratore** (boy) scout
esplosi'one *sf* explosion; **esplo'sivo, a** *ag*, *sm* explosive; **es'ploso, a** *pp di* **esplodere**
espo'nente *sm/f* (*rappresentante*) representative
es'porre *vt* (*merci*) to display; (*quadro*) to exhibit, show; (*fatti, idee*) to explain, set out; (*porre in pericolo, FOT*) to expose
espor'tare *vt* to export; **esportazi'one** *sf* exportation; export
esposizi'one [espozit'tsjone] *sf* displaying; exhibiting; setting out; (*anche FOT*) exposure; (*mostra*) exhibition; (*narrazione*) explanation, exposition
es'posto, a *pp di* **esporre** ♦ *ag*: **~ a nord**

facing north ♦ *sm* (*AMM*) statement, account; (: *petizione*) petition
espressi'one *sf* expression
espres'sivo, a *ag* expressive
es'presso, a *pp di* **esprimere** ♦ *ag* express ♦ *sm* (*lettera*) express letter; (*anche*: **treno ~**) express train; (*anche*: **caffè ~**) espresso
es'primere *vt* to express
espulsi'one *sf* expulsion; **es'pulso, a** *pp di* **espellere**
'essa (*pl* **'esse**) *pron f vedi* **esso**
es'senza [es'sentsa] *sf* essence; **essenzi'ale** *ag* essential; **l'essenziale** the main *o* most important thing

┌─────────────────┐
│ *PAROLA CHIAVE* │
└─────────────────┘

'essere *sm* being; **~ umano** human being
♦ *vb copulativo* **1** (*con attributo, sostantivo*) to be; **sei giovane/simpatico** you are *o* you're young/nice; **è medico** he is *o* he's a doctor
2 (*+di: appartenere*) to be; **di chi è la penna?** whose pen is it?; **è di Carla** it is *o* it's Carla's, it belongs to Carla
3 (*+di: provenire*) to be; **è di Venezia** he is *o* he's from Venice
4 (*data, ora*): **è il 15 agosto/lunedì** it is *o* it's the 15th of August/Monday; **che ora è?, che ore sono?** what time is it?; **è l'una** it is *o* it's one o'clock; **sono le due** it is *o* it's two o'clock
5 (*costare*): **quant'è?** how much is it?; **sono 20.000 lire** it's 20,000 lire
♦ *vb aus* **1** (*attivo*): **~ arrivato/venuto** to have arrived/come; **è già partita** she has already left
2 (*passivo*) to be; **~ fatto da** to be made by; **è stata uccisa** she has been killed
3 (*riflessivo*): **si sono lavati** they washed, they got washed
4 (*+da +infinito*): **è da farsi subito** it must be *o* is to be done immediately
♦ *vi* **1** (*esistere, trovarsi*) to be; **sono a casa** I'm at home; **~ in piedi/seduto** to be standing/sitting
2: **esserci**: **c'è** there is; **ci sono** there are;

che c'è? what's the matter?, what is it?; **ci sono!** (*fig: ho capito*) I get it!; *vedi anche* **ci ♦** *vb impers:* **è tardi/Pasqua** it's late/Easter; **è possibile che venga** he may come; **è così** that's the way it is

'**esso, a** *pron* it; (*riferito a persona: soggetto*) he/she; (: *complemento*) him/her; **~i, e** *pron pl* they; (*complemento*) them

est *sm* east

'**estasi** *sf* ecstasy

es'**tate** *sf* summer

es'**tendere** *vt* to extend; **~rsi** *vr* (*diffondersi*) to spread; (*territorio, confini*) to extend; **estensi'one** *sf* extension; (*di superficie*) expanse; (*di voce*) range

esteri'**ore** *ag* outward, external

ester'**nare** *vt* to express

es'**terno, a** *ag* (*porta, muro*) outer, outside; (*scala*) outside; (*alunno, impressione*) external **♦** *sm* outside, exterior **♦** *sm/f* (*allievo*) day pupil; **per uso ~** for external use only

'**estero, a** *ag* foreign **♦** *sm:* **all'~** abroad

es'**teso, a** *pp di* **estendere ♦** *ag* extensive, large; **scrivere per ~** to write in full

es'**tetico, a, ci, che** *ag* aesthetic **♦** *sf* (*disciplina*) aesthetics *sg*; (*bellezza*) attractiveness; **este'tista, i, e** *sm/f* beautician

'**estimo** *sm* valuation; (*disciplina*) surveying

es'**tinguere** *vt* to extinguish, put out; (*debito*) to pay off; **~rsi** *vr* to go out; (*specie*) to become extinct; **es'tinto, a** *pp di* **estinguere; estin'tore** *sm* (*fire*) extinguisher; **estinzi'one** *sf* putting out; (*di specie*) extinction

estir'**pare** *vt* (*pianta*) to uproot, pull up; (*fig: vizio*) to eradicate

es'**tivo, a** *ag* summer *cpd*

es'**torcere** [es'tɔrtʃere] *vt:* **~ qc (a qn)** to extort sth (from sb); **es'torto, a** *pp di* **estorcere**

estradizi'**one** [estradit'tsjone] *sf* extradition

es'**traneo, a** *ag* foreign **♦** *sm/f* stranger; **rimanere ~ a qc** to take no part in sth

es'**trarre** *vt* to extract; (*minerali*) to mine; (*sorteggiare*) to draw; **es'tratto, a** *pp di* **estrarre ♦** *sm* extract; (*di documento*)

abstract; **estratto conto** statement of account; **estratto di carne** (*CUC*) meat extract; **estratto di nascita** birth certificate; **estrazi'one** *sf* extraction; mining; drawing *no pl*; draw

estre'**mità** *sf inv* extremity, end **♦** *sfpl* (*ANAT*) extremities

es'**tremo, a** *ag* extreme; (*ultimo: ora, tentativo*) final, last **♦** *sm* extreme; (*di pazienza, forze*) limit, end; **~i** *smpl* (*AMM: dati essenziali*) details, particulars; **l'~ Oriente** the Far East

'**estro** *sm* (*capriccio*) whim, fancy; (*ispirazione creativa*) inspiration; **es'troso, a** *ag* whimsical, capricious; inspired

estro'**verso, a** *ag, sm* extrovert

'**esule** *sm/f* exile

età *sf inv* age; **all'~ di 8 anni** at the age of 8, at 8 years of age; **ha la mia ~** he (*o* she) is the same age as me *o* as I am; **raggiungere la maggiore ~** to come of age; **essere in ~ minore** to be under age

'**etere** *sm* ether; **e'tereo, a** *ag* ethereal

eterni'**tà** *sf* eternity

e'**terno, a** *ag* eternal

etero'**geneo, a** [etero'dʒɛneo] *ag* heterogeneous

'**etica** *sf* ethics *sg*; *vedi anche* **etico**

eti'**chetta** [eti'ketta] *sf* label; (*cerimoniale*): **l'~** etiquette

'**etico, a, ci, che** *ag* ethical

etimolo'**gia, 'gie** [etimolo'dʒia] *sf* etymology

Eti'**opia** *sf:* **l'~** Ethiopia

'**Etna** *sm:* **l'~** Etna

'**etnico, a, ci, che** *ag* ethnic

e'**trusco, a, schi, sche** *ag, sm/f* Etruscan

'**ettaro** *sm* hectare (= 10,000 m^2)

'**etto** *sm abbr* = **ettogrammo**

etto'**grammo** *sm* hectogram(me) (= 100 grams)

Eucaris'**tia** *sf:* **l'~** the Eucharist

'**euro** *sm inv* (*divisa*) euro

euro'**city** [euro'siti] *sm* international express train

Euro'**landia** *sf* Euroland

train

Eu'ropa *sf*: **l'~** Europe; **euro'peo, a** *ag, sm/f* European

evacu'are *vt* to evacuate

e'vadere *vi* (*fuggire*): **~ da** to escape from ♦ *vt* (*sbrigare*) to deal with, dispatch; (*tasse*) to evade

evan'gelico, a, ci, che [evan'dʒɛliko] *ag* evangelical

evapo'rare *vi* to evaporate; **evaporazi'one** *sf* evaporation

evasi'one *sf* (*vedi evadere*) escape; dispatch; **~ fiscale** tax evasion

eva'sivo, a *ag* evasive

e'vaso, a *pp di* **evadere** ♦ *sm* escapee

eveni'enza [eve'njentsa] *sf*: **pronto(a) per ogni ~** ready for any eventuality

e'vento *sm* event

eventu'ale *ag* possible

eventual'mente *av* if necessary

evi'dente *ag* evident, obvious; **evi'denza** *sf* obviousness; **mettere in evidenza** to point out, highlight; **evidenzi'are** *vt* to emphasize; (*con evidenziatore*) to highlight; **evidenzia'tore** *sm* highlighter

evi'tare *vt* to avoid; **~ di fare** to avoid doing; **~ qc a qn** to spare sb sth

'evo *sm* age, epoch

evo'care *vt* to evoke

evo'luto, a *pp di* **evolvere** ♦ *ag* (*civiltà*) (highly) developed, advanced; (*persona*) independent

evoluzi'one [evolut'tsjone] *sf* evolution

e'volversi *vr* to evolve

ev'viva *escl* hurrah!; **~ il re!** long live the king!, hurrah for the king!

ex *prefisso* ex, former

'extra *ag inv* first-rate; top-quality ♦ *sm inv* extra; **extracomuni'tario, a** *ag* from outside the EC ♦ *sm/f* non-EC citizen; **extraconiu'gale** *ag* extramarital

F, f

fa *vb vedi* **fare** ♦ *sm inv* (*MUS*) F; (: *solfeggiando la scala*) fa ♦ *av*: **10 anni ~** 10 years ago

fabbi'sogno [fabbi'zoɲɲo] *sm* needs *pl*, requirements *pl*

'fabbrica, che ['fabbrika] *sf* factory; **fabbri'cante** *sm* manufacturer, maker; **fabbri'care** *vt* to build; (*produrre*) to manufacture, make; (*fig*) to fabricate, invent

'fabbro *sm* (black)smith

fac'cenda [fat'tʃɛnda] *sf* matter, affair; (*cosa da fare*) task, chore

fac'chino [fak'kino] *sm* porter

'faccia, ce ['fattʃa] *sf* face; (*di moneta, medaglia*) side; **~ a ~** face to face

facci'ata [fat'tʃata] *sf* façade; (*di pagina*) side

'faccio ['fattʃo] *vb vedi* **fare**

'facile ['fatʃile] *ag* easy; (*disposto*): **~ a** inclined to, prone to; (*probabile*): **è ~ che piova** it's likely to rain; **facilità** *sf* easiness; (*disposizione, dono*) aptitude; **facili'tare** *vt* to make easier

facino'roso, a [fatʃino'roso] *ag* violent

facoltà *sf inv* faculty; (*autorità*) power

facolta'tivo, a *ag* optional; (*fermata d'autobus*) request *cpd*

fac'simile *sm* facsimile

'faggio ['faddʒo] *sm* beech

fagi'ano [fa'dʒano] *sm* pheasant

fagio'lino [fadʒo'lino] *sm* French (*BRIT*) *o* string bean

fagi'olo [fa'dʒolo] *sm* bean

fa'gotto *sm* bundle; (*MUS*) bassoon; **far ~** (*fig*) to pack up and go

'fai *vb vedi* **fare**

'falce ['faltʃe] *sf* scythe; **falci'are** *vt* to cut; (*fig*) to mow down

'falco, chi *sm* hawk

fal'cone *sm* falcon

'falda *sf* layer, stratum; (*di cappello*) brim; (*di cappotto*) tails *pl*; (*di monte*) lower slope; (*di tetto*) pitch

fale'gname [falɲˈɲame] *sm* joiner

fal'lace [falˈlatʃe] *ag* misleading

falli'mento *sm* failure; bankruptcy

fal'lire *vi* (*non riuscire*): ~ **(in)** to fail (in); (*DIR*) to go bankrupt ♦ *vt* (*colpo, bersaglio*) to miss; **fal'lito, a** *ag* unsuccessful; bankrupt ♦ *sm/f* bankrupt

'fallo *sm* error, mistake; (*imperfezione*) defect, flaw; (*SPORT*) foul; fault; **senza ~** without fail

falò *sm inv* bonfire

fal'sare *vt* to distort, misrepresent; **fal'sario** *sm* forger; counterfeiter; **falsifi'care** *vt* to forge; (*monete*) to forge, counterfeit

'falso, a *ag* false; (*errato*) wrong; (*falsificato*) forged; fake; (*: oro, gioielli*) imitation *cpd* ♦ *sm* forgery; **giurare il ~** to commit perjury

'fama *sf* fame; (*reputazione*) reputation, name

'fame *sf* hunger; **aver ~** to be hungry; **fa'melico, a, ci, che** *ag* ravenous

fa'miglia [faˈmiʎʎa] *sf* family

famili'are *ag* (*della famiglia*) family *cpd*; (*ben noto*) familiar; (*rapporti, atmosfera*) friendly; (*LING*) informal, colloquial ♦ *sm/f* relative, relation; **familiarità** *sf* familiarity; friendliness; informality

fa'moso, a *ag* famous, well-known

fa'nale *sm* (*AUT*) light, lamp (*BRIT*); (*luce stradale, NAUT*) light; (*di faro*) beacon

fa'natico, a, ci, che *ag* fanatical; (*del teatro, calcio etc*): ~ **di** *o* **per** mad *o* crazy about ♦ *sm/f* fanatic; (*tifoso*) fan

fanci'ullo, a [fanˈtʃullo] *sm/f* child

fan'donia *sf* tall story; **~e** *sfpl* (*assurdità*) nonsense *sg*

fan'fara *sf* (*musica*) fanfare

'fango, ghi *sm* mud; **fan'goso, a** *ag* muddy

'fanno *vb vedi* **fare**

fannul'lone, a *sm/f* idler, loafer

fantasci'enza [fantaʃˈʃɛntsa] *sf* science fiction

fanta'sia *sf* fantasy, imagination; (*capriccio*) whim, caprice ♦ *ag inv*: **vestito ~**

patterned dress

fan'tasma, i *sm* ghost, phantom

fan'tastico, a, ci, che *ag* fantastic; (*potenza, ingegno*) imaginative

'fante *sm* infantryman; (*CARTE*) jack, knave (*BRIT*); **fante'ria** *sf* infantry

fan'toccio [fanˈtɔttʃo] *sm* puppet

fara'butto *sm* crook

fard *sm inv* blusher

far'dello *sm* bundle; (*fig*) burden

PAROLA CHIAVE

'fare *sm* **1** (*modo di fare*): **con ~ distratto** absent-mindedly; **ha un ~ simpatico** he has a pleasant manner

2: **sul far del giorno/della notte** at daybreak/nightfall

♦ *vt* **1** (*fabbricare, creare*) to make; (*: casa*) to build; (*: assegno*) to make out; ~ **un pasto/una promessa/un film** to make a meal/a promise/a film; ~ **rumore** to make a noise

2 (*effettuare: lavoro, attività, studi*) to do; (*: sport*) to play; **cosa fa?** (*adesso*) what are you doing?; (*di professione*) what do you do?; ~ **psicologia/italiano** (*INS*) to do psychology/Italian; ~ **un viaggio** to go on a trip *o* journey; ~ **una passeggiata** to go for a walk; ~ **la spesa** to do the shopping

3 (*funzione*) to be; (*TEATRO*) to play, be; ~ **il medico** to be a doctor; ~ **il malato** (*fingere*) to act the invalid

4 (*suscitare: sentimenti*): ~ **paura a qn** to frighten sb; **(non) fa niente** (*non importa*) it doesn't matter

5 (*ammontare*): **3 più 3 fa 6** 3 and 3 are *o* make 6; **fanno 6.000 lire** that's 6,000 lire; **Roma fa 2.000.000 di abitanti** Rome has 2,000,000 inhabitants; **che ora fai?** what time do you make it?

6 (*+infinito*): **far ~ qc a qn** (*obbligare*) to make sb do sth; (*permettere*) to let sb do sth; **fammi vedere** let me see; **far partire il motore** to start (up) the engine; **far riparare la macchina/costruire una casa** to get *o* have the car repaired/a house built

7: **~rsi**: **~rsi una gonna** to make o.s. a

skirt; **~rsi un nome** to make a name for o.s.; **~rsi la permanente** to get a perm; **~rsi tagliare i capelli** to get one's hair cut; **~rsi operare** to have an operation
8 (*fraseologia*): **farcela** to succeed, manage; **non ce la faccio più** I can't go on; **ce la faremo** we'll make it; **me l'hanno fatta!** (*imbrogliare*) I've been done!; **lo facevo più giovane** I thought he was younger; **fare sì/no con la testa** to nod/shake one's head
♦ *vi* **1** (*agire*) to act, do; **fate come volete** do as you like; **~ presto** to be quick; **~ da** to act as; **non c'è niente da ~** it's no use; **saperci ~ con qn/qc** to know how to deal with sb/sth; **faccia pure!** go ahead!
2 (*dire*) to say; **"davvero?" fece** "really?" he said
3: **~ per** (*essere adatto*) to be suitable for; **~ per ~ qc** to be about to do sth; **fece per andarsene** he made as if to leave
4: **~rsi: si fa così** you do it like this, this is the way it's done; **non si fa così!** (*rimprovero*) that's no way to behave!; **la festa non si fa** the party is off
5: **~ a gara con qn** to compete *o* vie with sb; **~ a pugni** to come to blows; **~ in tempo a ~** to be in time to do
♦ *vb impers*: **fa caldo/freddo** it's hot/cold; **fa bel tempo** the weather is fine; **fa notte** it's getting dark
♦ *vr*: **~rsi 1** (*diventare*) to become; **~rsi prete** to become a priest; **~rsi grande/vecchio** to grow tall/old
2 (*spostarsi*): **~rsi avanti/indietro** to move forward/back
3 (*fam: drogarsi*) to be a junkie

far'falla *sf* butterfly
fa'rina *sf* flour
farma'cia, 'cie [farma'tʃia] *sf* pharmacy; (*negozio*) chemist's (shop) (*BRIT*), pharmacy; **farma'cista, i, e** *sm/f* chemist (*BRIT*), pharmacist
'farmaco, ci *o* **chi** *sm* drug, medicine
'faro *sm* (*NAUT*) lighthouse; (*AER*) beacon; (*AUT*) headlight

'farsa *sf* farce
'fascia, sce ['faʃʃa] *sf* band, strip; (*MED*) bandage; (*di sindaco, ufficiale*) sash; (*parte di territorio*) strip, belt; (*di contribuenti etc*) group, band; **essere in ~sce** (*anche fig*) to be in one's infancy; **~ oraria** time band
fasci'are [faʃ'ʃare] *vt* to bind; (*MED*) to bandage
fa'scicolo [faʃ'ʃikolo] *sm* (*di documenti*) file, dossier; (*di rivista*) issue, number; (*opuscolo*) booklet, pamphlet
fa'scino ['faʃʃino] *sm* charm, fascination
'fascio ['faʃʃo] *sm* bundle, sheaf; (*di fiori*) bunch; (*di luce*) beam; (*POL*): **il F~** the Fascist Party
fa'scismo [faʃ'ʃizmo] *sm* fascism
'fase *sf* phase; (*TECN*) stroke; **fuori ~** (*motore*) rough
fas'tidio *sm* bother, trouble; **dare ~ a qn** to bother *o* annoy sb; **sento ~ allo stomaco** my stomach's upset; **avere ~i con la polizia** to have trouble *o* bother with the police; **fastidi'oso, a** *ag* annoying, tiresome
'fasto *sm* pomp, splendour
'fata *sf* fairy
fa'tale *ag* fatal; (*inevitabile*) inevitable; (*fig*) irresistible; **fatalità** *sf inv* inevitability; (*avversità*) misfortune; (*fato*) fate, destiny
fa'tica, che *sf* hard work; (*sforzo*) effort; (*di metalli*) fatigue; **a ~** with difficulty; **fare ~ a fare qc** to have a job doing sth; **fati'care** *vi* to toil; **faticare a fare qc** to have difficulty doing sth; **fati'coso, a** *ag* tiring, exhausting; (*lavoro*) laborious
'fato *sm* fate, destiny
'fatto, a *pp di* **fare** ♦ *ag*: **un uomo ~** a grown man; **~ a mano/in casa** hand-/home-made ♦ *sm* fact; (*azione*) deed; (*avvenimento*) event, occurrence; (*di romanzo, film*) action, story; **cogliere qn sul ~** to catch sb red-handed; **il ~ sta o è che** the fact remains *o* is that; **in ~ di** as for, as far as ... is concerned
fat'tore *sm* (*AGR*) farm manager; (*MAT, elemento costitutivo*) factor; **~ di protezione** (*di lozione solare*) factor

fatto'ria *sf* farm; farmhouse
fatto'rino *sm* errand-boy; (*di ufficio*) office-boy; (*d'albergo*) porter
fat'tura *sf* (COMM) invoice; (*di abito*) tailoring; (*malia*) spell
fattu'rare *vt* (COMM) to invoice
fattu'rato *sm* (COMM) turnover
'fatuo, a *ag* vain, fatuous
'fauna *sf* fauna
fau'tore, trice *sm/f* advocate, supporter
fa'villa *sf* spark
'favola *sf* (*fiaba*) fairy tale; (*d'intento morale*) fable; (*fandonia*) yarn; **favo'loso, a** *ag* fabulous; (*incredibile*) incredible
fa'vore *sm* favour; **per ~** please; **fare un ~ a qn** to do sb a favour; **favo'revole** *ag* favourable
favo'rire *vt* to favour; (*il commercio, l'industria, le arti*) to promote, encourage; **vuole ~?** won't you help yourself?; **favorisca in salotto** please come into the sitting room; **favo'rito, a** *ag, sm/f* favourite
fazzo'letto [fattso'letto] *sm* handkerchief; (*per la testa*) (head)scarf; **~ di carta** tissue
feb'braio *sm* February
'febbre *sf* fever; **aver la ~** to have a high temperature; **~ da fieno** hay fever; **feb'brile** *ag* (*anche fig*) feverish
'feccia, ce ['fɛttʃa] *sf* dregs *pl*
'fecola *sf* potato flour
fecondazi'one [fekondat'tsjone] *sf* fertilization; **~ artificiale** artificial insemination
fe'condo, a *ag* fertile
'fede *sf* (*credenza*) belief, faith; (REL) faith; (*fiducia*) faith, trust; (*fedeltà*) loyalty; (*anello*) wedding ring; (*attestato*) certificate; **aver ~ in qn** to have faith in sb; **in buona/cattiva ~** in good/bad faith; **"in ~"** (DIR) "in witness whereof"; **fe'dele** *ag*: **fedele (a)** faithful (to) ♦ *sm/f* follower; **i fedeli** (REL) the faithful; **fedeltà** *sf* faithfulness; (*coniugale*) fidelity; **alta fedeltà** high fidelity
'federa *sf* pillowslip, pillowcase
fede'rale *ag* federal

'fegato *sm* liver; (*fig*) guts *pl*, nerve
'felce ['fɛltʃe] *sf* fern
fe'lice [fe'litʃe] *ag* happy; (*fortunato*) lucky; **felicità** *sf* happiness
felici'tarsi [felitʃi'tarsi] *vr* (*congratularsi*): **~ con qn per qc** to congratulate sb on sth
fe'lino, a *ag, sm* feline
'felpa *sf* sweatshirt
'feltro *sm* felt
'femmina *sf* (ZOOL, TECN) female; (*figlia*) girl, daughter; (*spesso peg*) woman; **femmi'nile** *ag* feminine; (*sesso*) female; (*lavoro, giornale, moda*) woman's ♦ *sm* (LING) feminine; **femmi'nismo** *sm* feminism
'fendere *vt* to cut through; **fendi'nebbia** *sm inv* (AUT) fog lamp
fe'nomeno *sm* phenomenon
'feretro *sm* coffin
feri'ale *ag*: **giorno ~** weekday
'ferie *sfpl* holidays (BRIT), vacation *sg* (US); **andare in ~** to go on holiday *o* vacation
fe'rire *vt* to injure; (*deliberatamente*: MIL *etc*) to wound; (*colpire*) to hurt; **fe'rita** *sf* injury, wound; **fe'rito, a** *sm/f* wounded *o* injured man/woman
'ferma *sf* (MIL) (period of) service; (CACCIA): **cane da ~** pointer
fer'maglio [fer'maʎʎo] *sm* clasp; (*per documenti*) clip
fer'mare *vt* to stop, halt; (POLIZIA) to detain, hold ♦ *vi* to stop; **~rsi** *vr* to stop, halt; **~rsi a fare qc** to stop to do sth
fer'mata *sf* stop; **~ dell'autobus** bus stop
fer'mento *sm* (*anche fig*) ferment; (*lievito*) yeast
fer'mezza [fer'mettsa] *sf* (*fig*) firmness, steadfastness
'fermo, a *ag* still, motionless; (*veicolo*) stationary; (*orologio*) not working; (*saldo: anche fig*) firm; (*voce, mano*) steady ♦ *escl* stop!; keep still! ♦ *sm* (*chiusura*) catch, lock; (DIR): **~ di polizia** police detention
'fermo 'posta *av, sm inv* poste restante (BRIT), general delivery (US)
fe'roce [fe'rɔtʃe] *ag* (*animale*) fierce, ferocious; (*persona*) cruel, fierce; (*fame,*

dolore) raging; **le bestie ~i** wild animals
ferra'gosto *sm (festa)* feast of the
Assumption; *(periodo)* August holidays *pl*

---

ferragosto

ℹ️ **Ferragosto** *is a national holiday which falls on 15 August and is the most important holiday of the summer season. Most people extend it by taking the days around the 15th off too. Consequently during this period, most of industry and commerce is at a standstill.*

---

ferra'menta *sfpl:* **negozio di ~**
ironmonger's *(BRIT)*, hardware shop *o* store
(US)
fer'rato, a *ag (FERR):* **strada ~a** railway
(BRIT) o railroad *(US)* line; *(fig):* **essere ~ in**
to be well up in
'ferro *sm* iron; **una bistecca ai ~i** a grilled
steak; **~ battuto** wrought iron; **~ da calza**
knitting needle; **~ di cavallo** horseshoe; **~
da stiro** iron
ferro'via *sf* railway *(BRIT)*, railroad *(US)*;
ferrovi'ario, a *ag* railway *cpd (BRIT)*,
railroad *cpd (US)*; **ferrovi'ere** *sm*
railwayman *(BRIT)*, railroad man *(US)*
'fertile *ag* fertile; **fertiliz'zante** *sm*
fertilizer
'fervido, a *ag* fervent
fer'vore *sm* fervour, ardour
'fesso, a *pp di* **fendere** ♦ *ag (fam: sciocco)*
crazy, cracked
fes'sura *sf* crack, split; *(per gettone,
moneta)* slot
'festa *sf (religiosa)* feast; *(pubblica)* holiday;
(compleanno) birthday; *(onomastico)* name
day; *(ricevimento)* celebration, party; **far ~**
to have a holiday; (to live it up); **far ~ a qn**
to give sb a warm welcome

---

festa della Repubblica

ℹ️ *The* **festa della Repubblica**, *which takes place on 2 June, celebrates the founding of the Italian Republic after the fall of the monarchy and the subsequent referendum in 1946. It is marked by*

military parades and political speeches.

---

festeggi'are [fisted'dʒare] *vt* to celebrate;
(persona) to have a celebration for
fes'tino *sm* party; *(con balli)* ball
fes'tivo, a *ag (atmosfera)* festive; **giorno ~**
holiday
fes'toso, a *ag* merry, joyful
fe'ticcio [fe'tittʃo] *sm* fetish
'feto *sm* foetus *(BRIT)*, fetus *(US)*
'fetta *sf* slice
fettuc'cine [fettut'tʃine] *sfpl (CUC)* ribbon-
shaped pasta
FF.SS. *abbr =* **Ferrovie dello Stato**
fi'aba *sf* fairy tale
fi'acca *sf* weariness; *(svogliatezza)*
listlessness
fiac'care *vt* to weaken
fi'acco, a, chi, che *ag (stanco)* tired,
weary; *(svogliato)* listless; *(debole)* weak;
(mercato) slack
fi'accola *sf* torch
fi'ala *sf* phial
fi'amma *sf* flame
fiam'mante *ag (colore)* flaming; **nuovo ~**
brand new
fiam'mifero *sm* match
fiam'mingo, a, ghi, ghe *ag* Flemish
♦ *sm/f* Fleming ♦ *sm (LING)* Flemish; **i
F~ghi** the Flemish
fiancheggi'are [fjanked'dʒare] *vt* to
border; *(fig)* to support, back (up); *(MIL)* to
flank
fi'anco, chi *sm* side; *(MIL)* flank; **di ~**
sideways, from the side; **a ~ a ~** side by
side
fi'asco, schi *sm* flask; *(fig)* fiasco; **fare ~**
to fail
fi'ato *sm* breath; *(resistenza)* stamina; **avere
il ~ grosso** to be out of breath; **prendere
~** to catch one's breath; **~i** *smpl (MUS)*
wind instruments; **strumento a ~** wind
instrument
'fibbia *sf* buckle
'fibra *sf* fibre; *(fig)* constitution
fic'care *vt* to push, thrust, drive; **~rsi** *vr*
(andare a finire) to get to

'**fico, chi** *sm* (*pianta*) fig tree; (*frutto*) fig; **~ d'India** prickly pear; **~ secco** dried fig

fidanza'mento [fidantsa'mento] *sm* engagement

fidan'zarsi [fidan'tsarsi] *vr* to get engaged; **fidan'zato, a** *sm/f* fiancé/fiancée

fi'darsi *vr*: **~ di** to trust; **fi'dato, a** *ag* reliable, trustworthy

'**fido, a** *ag* faithful, loyal ♦ *sm* (COMM) credit

fi'ducia [fi'dutʃa] *sf* confidence, trust; **incarico di ~** position of trust, responsible position; **persona di ~** reliable person

fi'ele *sm* (*fig*) bitterness

fie'nile *sm* barn; hayloft

fi'eno *sm* hay

fi'era *sf* fair

fie'rezza [fje'rettsa] *sf* pride

fi'ero, a *ag* proud; (*audace*) bold

'**fifa** (*fam*) *sf*: **aver ~** to have the jitters

'**figlia** ['fiʎʎa] *sf* daughter

figli'astro, a [fiʎ'ʎastro] *sm/f* stepson/daughter

'**figlio** ['fiʎʎo] *sm* son; (*senza distinzione di sesso*) child; **~ di papà** spoilt, wealthy young man; **~ unico** only child; **figli'occio, a, ci, ce** *sm/f* godchild, godson/daughter

fi'gura *sf* figure; (*forma, aspetto esterno*) form, shape; (*illustrazione*) picture, illustration; **far ~** to look smart; **fare una brutta ~** to make a bad impression

figu'rare *vi* to appear ♦ *vt*: **~rsi qc** to imagine sth; **~rsi** *vr*: **figurati!** imagine that!; **ti do noia? — ma figurati!** am I disturbing you? — not at all!

figura'tivo, a *ag* figurative

figu'rina *sf* figurine; (*cartoncino*) picture card

'**fila** *sf* row, line; (*coda*) queue; (*serie*) series, string; **di ~** in succession; **fare la ~** to queue; **in ~ indiana** in single file

filantro'pia *sf* philanthropy

fi'lare *vt* to spin ♦ *vi* (*baco, ragno*) to spin; (*formaggio fuso*) to go stringy; (*discorso*) to hang together; (*fam: amoreggiare*) to go steady; (*muoversi a forte velocità*) to go at full speed; **~ diritto** (*fig*) to toe the line; **~ via** to dash off

filas'trocca, che *sf* nursery rhyme

filate'lia *sf* philately, stamp collecting

fi'lato, a *ag* spun ♦ *sm* yarn; **3 giorni ~i** 3 days running *o* on end

fi'letto *sm* (*di vite*) thread; (*di carne*) fillet

fili'ale *ag* filial ♦ *sf* (*di impresa*) branch

fili'grana *sf* (*in oreficeria*) filigree; (*su carta*) watermark

film *sm inv* film; **fil'mare** *vt* to film

'**filo** *sm* (*anche fig*) thread; (*filato*) yarn; (*metallico*) wire; (*di lama, rasoio*) edge; **per ~ e per segno** in detail; **~ d'erba** blade of grass; **~ interdentale** dental floss; **~ di perle** string of pearls; **~ spinato** barbed wire; **con un ~ di voce** in a whisper

'**filobus** *sm inv* trolley bus

filon'cino [filon'tʃino] *sm* ≈ French stick

fi'lone *sm* (*di minerali*) seam, vein; (*pane*) ≈ Vienna loaf; (*fig*) trend

filoso'fia *sf* philosophy; **fi'losofo, a** *sm/f* philosopher

fil'trare *vt, vi* to filter

'**filtro** *sm* filter; **~ dell'olio** (AUT) oil filter

fin *av, prep* = **fino**

fi'nale *ag* final ♦ *sm* (*di opera*) end, ending; (: MUS) finale ♦ *sf* (SPORT) final; **finalità** *sf* (*scopo*) aim, purpose; **final'mente** *av* finally, at last

fi'nanza [fi'nantsa] *sf* finance; **~e** *sfpl* (*di individuo, Stato*) finances; **finanzi'ario, a** *ag* financial; **finanzi'ere** *sm* financier; (*doganale*) customs officer; (*della tributaria*) inland revenue official

finché [fin'ke] *cong* (*per tutto il tempo che*) as long as; (*fino al momento in cui*) until; **aspetta ~ io (non) sia ritornato** wait until I get back

'**fine** *ag* (*lamina, carta*) thin; (*capelli, polvere*) fine; (*vista, udito*) keen, sharp; (*persona: raffinata*) refined, distinguished; (*osservazione*) subtle ♦ *sf* end ♦ *sm* aim, purpose; (*esito*) result, outcome; **secondo ~** ulterior motive; **in** *o* **alla ~** in the end, finally; **~ settimana** *sm o f inv* weekend

fi'nestra *sf* window; **fines'trino** *sm* (*di*

treno, auto) window

'fingere ['findʒere] *vt* to feign; (*supporre*) to imagine, suppose; **~rsi** *vr*: **~rsi ubriaco/pazzo** to pretend to be drunk/mad; **~ di fare** to pretend to do

fini'mondo *sm* pandemonium

fi'nire *vt* to finish ♦ *vi* to finish, end; **~ di fare** (*compiere*) to finish doing; (*smettere*) to stop doing; **~ in galera** to end up *o* finish up in prison; **fini'tura** *sf* finish

finlan'dese *ag, sm* (*LING*) Finnish ♦ *sm/f* Finn

Fin'landia *sf*: **la ~** Finland

'fino, a *ag* (*capelli, seta*) fine; (*oro*) pure; (*fig: acuto*) shrewd ♦ *av* (*spesso troncato in* **fin**: *pure, anche*) even ♦ *prep* (*spesso troncato in* **fin**: *tempo*): **fin quando?** till when?; (: *luogo*): **fin qui** as far as here; **~ a** (*tempo*) until, till; (*luogo*) as far as, (up) to; **fin da domani** from tomorrow onwards; **fin da ieri** since yesterday; **fin dalla nascita** from *o* since birth

fi'nocchio [fi'nɔkkjo] *sm* fennel; (*fam: peg: omosessuale*) queer

fi'nora *av* up till now

'finta *sf* pretence, sham; (*SPORT*) feint; **far ~a (di fare)** to pretend (to do)

'finto, a *pp di* **fingere** ♦ *ag* false; artificial

finzi'one [fin'tsjone] *sf* pretence, sham

fi'occo, chi *sm* (*di nastro*) bow; (*di stoffa, lana*) flock; (*di neve*) flake; (*NAUT*) jib; **coi ~chi** (*fig*) first-rate; **~chi di granoturco** cornflakes

fi'ocina ['fjɔtʃina] *sf* harpoon

fi'oco, a, chi, che *ag* faint, dim

fi'onda *sf* catapult

fio'raio, a *sm/f* florist

fi'ore *sm* flower; **~i** *smpl* (*CARTE*) clubs; **a fior d'acqua** on the surface of the water; **avere i nervi a fior di pelle** to be on edge

fioren'tino, a *ag* Florentine

fio'retto *sm* (*SCHERMA*) foil

fio'rire *vi* (*rosa*) to flower; (*albero*) to blossom; (*fig*) to flourish

Fi'renze [fi'rɛntse] *sf* Florence

'firma *sf* signature

fir'mare *vt* to sign; **un abito firmato** a designer suit

fisar'monica, che *sf* accordion

fis'cale *ag* fiscal, tax *cpd*; **medico ~** doctor *employed by Social Security to verify cases of sick leave*

fischi'are [fis'kjare] *vi* to whistle ♦ *vt* to whistle; (*attore*) to boo, hiss

'fischio ['fiskjo] *sm* whistle

'fisco *sm* tax authorities *pl*, ≈ Inland Revenue (*BRIT*), ≈ Internal Revenue Service (*US*)

'fisica *sf* physics *sg*

'fisico, a, ci, che *ag* physical ♦ *sm/f* physicist ♦ *sm* physique

fisiolo'gia [fizjolo'dʒia] *sf* physiology

fisiono'mia *sf* face, physiognomy

fisiotera'pia *sf* physiotherapy

fis'sare *vt* to fix, fasten; (*guardare intensamente*) to stare at; (*data, condizioni*) to fix, establish, set; (*prenotare*) to book; **~rsi su** (*sog: sguardo, attenzione*) to focus on; (*fig: idea*) to become obsessed with; **fissazi'one** *sf* (*PSIC*) fixation

'fisso, a *ag* fixed; (*stipendio, impiego*) regular ♦ *av*: **guardare ~ qc/qn** to stare at sth/sb

'fitta *sf* sharp pain; *vedi anche* **fitto**

fit'tizio, a *ag* fictitious, imaginary

'fitto, a *ag* thick, dense; (*pioggia*) heavy ♦ *sm* depths *pl*, middle; (*affitto, pigione*) rent

fi'ume *sm* river

fiu'tare *vt* to smell, sniff; (*sog: animale*) to scent; (*fig: inganno*) to get wind of, smell; **~ tabacco/cocaina** to take snuff/cocaine; **fi'uto** *sm* (*sense of*) smell; (*fig*) nose

fla'gello [fla'dʒello] *sm* scourge

fla'grante *ag*: **cogliere qn in ~** to catch sb red-handed

fla'nella *sf* flannel

flash [flaʃ] *sm inv* (*FOT*) flash; (*giornalistico*) newsflash

'flauto *sm* flute

'flebile *ag* faint, feeble

'flemma *sf* (*calma*) coolness, phlegm

fles'sibile *ag* pliable; (*fig: che si adatta*) flexible '**flesso, a** *pp di* **flettere**

flessu'oso, a *ag* supple, lithe

'**flettere** *vt* to bend

'**flipper** *sm inv* pinball machine

F.lli *abbr* (= **fratelli**) Bros.

'**flora** *sf* flora

'**florido, a** *ag* flourishing; (*fig*) glowing with health

'**floscio, a, sci, sce** ['flɔʃʃo] *ag* (*cappello*) floppy, soft; (*muscoli*) flabby

'**flotta** *sf* fleet

'**fluido, a** *ag, sm* fluid

flu'ire *vi* to flow

flu'oro *sm* fluorine

fluo'ruro *sm* fluoride

'**flusso** *sm* flow; (*FISICA, MED*) flux; **~ e riflusso** ebb and flow

fluttu'are *vi* (*mare*) to rise and fall; (*ECON*) to fluctuate

fluvi'ale *ag* river *cpd*, fluvial

'**foca, che** (*ZOOL*) *sf* seal

fo'caccia, ce [fo'kattʃa] *sf kind of pizza;* (*dolce*) bun

'**foce** ['fotʃe] *sf* (*GEO*) mouth

foco'laio *sm* (*MED*) centre of infection; (*fig*) hotbed

foco'lare *sm* hearth, fireside; (*TECN*) furnace

'**fodera** *sf* (*di vestito*) lining; (*di libro, poltrona*) cover; **fode'rare** *vt* to line; to cover

'**fodero** *sm* (*di spada*) scabbard; (*di pugnale*) sheath; (*di pistola*) holster

'**foga** *sf* enthusiasm, ardour

'**foggia, ge** ['fɔddʒa] *sf* (*maniera*) style; (*aspetto*) form, shape

'**foglia** ['fɔʎʎa] *sf* leaf; **~ d'argento/d'oro** silver/gold leaf; **fogli'ame** *sm* foliage, leaves *pl*

'**foglio** ['fɔʎʎo] *sm* (*di carta*) sheet (of paper); (*di metallo*) sheet; **~ rosa** (*AUT*) provisional licence; **~ di via** (*DIR*) expulsion order; **~ volante** pamphlet

'**fogna** ['fɔɲɲa] *sf* drain, sewer; **fogna'tura** *sf* drainage, sewerage

'**föhn** [føːn] *sm inv* hair dryer

folgo'rare *vt* (*sog: fulmine*) to strike down;

(: *alta tensione*) to electrocute

'**folla** *sf* crowd, throng

'**folle** *ag* mad, insane; (*TECN*) idle; **in ~** (*AUT*) in neutral

fol'lia *sf* folly, foolishness; foolish act; (*pazzia*) madness, lunacy

'**folto, a** *ag* thick

fomen'tare *vt* to stir up, foment

fon *sm inv* hair dryer

fondamen'tale *ag* fundamental, basic

fonda'mento *sm* foundation; **~a** *sfpl* (*EDIL*) foundations

fon'dare *vt* to found; (*fig: dar base*): **~ qc su** to base sth on; **fondazi'one** *sf* foundation

'**fondere** *vt* (*neve*) to melt; (*metallo*) to fuse, melt; (*fig: colori*) to merge, blend; (: *imprese, gruppi*) to merge ♦ *vi* to melt; **~rsi** *vr* to melt; (*fig: partiti, correnti*) to unite, merge; **fonde'ria** *sf* foundry

'**fondo, a** *ag* deep ♦ *sm* (*di recipiente, pozzo*) bottom; (*di stanza*) back; (*quantità di liquido che resta, deposito*) dregs *pl*; (*sfondo*) background; (*unità immobiliare*) property, estate; (*somma di denaro*) fund; (*SPORT*) long-distance race; **~i** *smpl* (*denaro*) funds; **a notte ~a** at dead of night; **in ~ a** at the bottom of; (*strada*) at the back of; (*strada*) at the end of; **andare a ~** (*nave*) to sink; **conoscere a ~** to know inside out; **dar ~ a** (*fig: provviste, soldi*) to use up; **in ~** (*fig*) after all, all things considered; **andare fino in ~ a** (*fig*) to examine thoroughly; **a ~ perduto** (*COMM*) without security; **~i di caffè** coffee grounds; **~i di magazzino** old *o* unsold stock *sg*

fo'netica *sf* phonetics *sg*

fon'tana *sf* fountain

'**fonte** *sf* spring, source; (*fig*) source ♦ *sm*: **~ battesimale** (*REL*) font

fon'tina *sm sweet full-fat hard cheese from Val d'Aosta*

fo'raggio [fo'raddʒo] *sm* fodder, forage

fo'rare *vt* to pierce, make a hole in; (*pallone*) to burst; (*biglietto*) to punch; **~ una gomma** to burst a tyre (*BRIT*) *o* tire (*US*)

'forbici ['fɔrbitʃi] *sfpl* scissors

'forca, che *sf* (*AGR*) fork, pitchfork; (*patibolo*) gallows *sg*

for'cella [for'tʃella] *sf* (*TECN*) fork; (*di monte*) pass

for'chetta [for'ketta] *sf* fork

for'cina [for'tʃina] *sf* hairpin

'forcipe ['fɔrtʃipe] *sm* forceps *pl*

fo'resta *sf* forest

foresti'ero, a *ag* foreign ♦ *sm/f* foreigner

'forfora *sf* dandruff

forgi'are *vt* to forge

'forma *sf* form; (*aspetto esteriore*) form, shape; (*DIR: procedura*) procedure; (*per calzature*) last; (*stampo da cucina*) mould; **~e** *sfpl* (*del corpo*) figure, shape; **le ~e** (*convenzioni*) appearances; **essere in ~** to be in good shape

formag'gino [formad'dʒino] *sm* processed cheese

for'maggio [for'maddʒo] *sm* cheese

for'male *ag* formal; **formalità** *sf inv* formality

for'mare *vt* to form, shape, make; (*numero di telefono*) to dial; (*fig: carattere*) to form, mould; **~rsi** *vr* to form, take shape; **for'mato** *sm* format, size; **formazi'one** *sf* formation; (*fig: educazione*) training

for'mica, che *sf* ant; **formi'caio** *sm* anthill

formico'lare *vi* (*anche fig*): **~ di** to be swarming with; **mi formicola la gamba** I've got pins and needles in my leg; **formico'lio** *sm* pins and needles *pl*; swarming

formi'dabile *ag* powerful, formidable; (*straordinario*) remarkable

'formula *sf* formula; **~ di cortesia** courtesy form

formu'lare *vt* to formulate; to express

for'nace [for'natʃe] *sf* (*per laterizi etc*) kiln; (*per metalli*) furnace; **~ a microonde** microwave oven

for'naio *sm* baker

for'nello *sm* (*elettrico, a gas*) ring; (*di pipa*) bowl

for'nire *vt*: **~ qn di qc, ~ qc a qn** to provide *o* supply sb with sth, to supply sth to sb

'forno *sm* (*di cucina*) oven; (*panetteria*) bakery; (*TECN: per calce etc*) kiln; (: *per metalli*) furnace; **~ a microonde** microwave oven

'foro *sm* (*buco*) hole; (*STORIA*) forum; (*tribunale*) (law) court

'forse *av* perhaps, maybe; (*circa*) about; **essere in ~** to be in doubt

forsen'nato, a *ag* mad, insane

'forte *ag* strong; (*suono*) loud; (*spesa*) considerable, great; (*passione, dolore*) great, deep ♦ *av* strongly; (*velocemente*) fast; (*a voce alta*) loud(ly); (*violentemente*) hard ♦ *sm* (*edificio*) fort; (*specialità*) forte, strong point; **essere ~ in qc** to be good at sth

for'tezza [for'tettsa] *sf* (*morale*) strength; (*luogo fortificato*) fortress

for'tuito, a *ag* fortuitous, chance

for'tuna *sf* (*destino*) fortune, luck; (*buona sorte*) success, fortune; (*eredità, averi*) fortune; **per ~** luckily, fortunately; **di ~** makeshift, improvised; **atterraggio di ~** emergency landing; **fortu'nato, a** *ag* lucky, fortunate; (*coronato da successo*) successful

'forza ['fɔrtsa] *sf* strength; (*potere*) power; (*FISICA*) force; **~e** *sfpl* (*fisiche*) strength *sg*; (*MIL*) forces ♦ *escl* come on!; **per ~** against one's will; (*naturalmente*) of course; **a viva ~** by force; **a ~ di** by dint of; **~ maggiore** circumstances beyond one's control; **la ~ pubblica** the police *pl*; **le ~e armate** the armed forces; **~e dell'ordine** the forces of law and order

for'zare [for'tsare] *vt* to force; **~ qn a fare** to force sb to do; **for'zato, a** *ag* forced ♦ *sm* (*DIR*) prisoner sentenced to hard labour

fos'chia [fos'kia] *sf* mist, haze

'fosco, a, schi, sche *ag* dark, gloomy

'fosforo *sm* phosphorous

'fossa *sf* pit; (*di cimitero*) grave; **~ biologica** septic tank

fos'sato *sm* ditch; (*di fortezza*) moat

fos'setta *sf* dimple

'fossile *ag, sm* fossil

'fosso *sm* ditch; (*MIL*) trench

'foto *sf* photo ♦ *prefisso:* **foto'copia** *sf* photocopy; **fotocopi'are** *vt* to photocopy; **fotogra'fare** *vt* to photograph; **fotogra'fia** *sf* (*procedimento*) photography; (*immagine*) photograph; **fare una fotografia** to take a photograph; **una fotografia a colori/in bianco e nero** a colour/black and white photograph; **fo'tografo, a** *sm/f* photographer; **fotoro'manzo** *sm* romantic picture story; **foto'tessera** *sf* passport-size photo

fra *prep* = **tra**

fracas'sare *vt* to shatter, smash; **~rsi** *vr* to shatter, smash; (*veicolo*) to crash; **fra'casso** *sm* smash; crash; (*baccano*) din, racket

'fradicio, a, ci, ce ['fraditʃo] *ag* (*molto bagnato*) soaking (wet); **ubriaco ~** blind drunk

'fragile ['fradʒile] *ag* fragile; (*fig: salute*) delicate

'fragola *sf* strawberry

fra'gore *sm* roar; (*di tuono*) rumble

frago'roso, a *ag* deafening

fra'grante *ag* fragrant

frain'tendere *vt* to misunderstand; **frain'teso, a** *pp di* **fraintendere**

fram'mento *sm* fragment

'frana *sf* landslide; (*fig: persona*): **essere una ~** to be useless; **fra'nare** *vi* to slip, slide down

fran'cese [fran'tʃeze] *ag* French ♦ *sm/f* Frenchman/woman ♦ *sm* (*LING*) French; **i F~i** the French

fran'chezza [fran'kettsa] *sf* frankness, openness

'Francia ['frantʃa] *sf:* **la ~** France

'franco, a, chi, che (*COMM*) free; (*sincero*) frank, open, sincere ♦ *sm* (*moneta*) franc; **farla ~a** (*fig*) to get off scot-free; **~ di dogana** duty-free; **prezzo ~ fabbrica** ex-works price; **~ tiratore** *sm* sniper

franco'bollo *sm* (*postage*) stamp

fran'gente [fran'dʒente] *sm* (*onda*) breaker; (*scoglio emergente*) reef; (*circostanza*) situation, circumstance

'frangia, ge ['frandʒa] *sf* fringe

frantu'mare *vt* to break into pieces, shatter; **~rsi** *vr* to break into pieces, shatter

frap'pé *sm* milk shake

'frasca, sche *sf* (*leafy*) branch

'frase *sf* (*LING*) sentence; (*locuzione, espressione, MUS*) phrase; **~ fatta** set phrase

'frassino *sm* ash (tree)

frastagli'ato, a [frastaʎ'ʎato] *ag* (*costa*) indented, jagged

frastor'nare *vt* to daze; to befuddle

frastu'ono *sm* hubbub, din

'frate *sm* friar, monk

fratel'lanza [fratel'lantsa] *sf* brotherhood; (*associazione*) fraternity

fratel'lastro *sm* stepbrother

fra'tello *sm* brother; **~i** *smpl* brothers; (*nel senso di fratelli e sorelle*) brothers and sisters

fra'terno, a *ag* fraternal, brotherly

frat'tanto *av* in the meantime, meanwhile

frat'tempo *sm:* **nel ~** in the meantime, meanwhile

frat'tura *sf* fracture; (*fig*) split, break

frazi'one [frat'tsjone] *sf* fraction; (*di comune*) small town

'freccia, ce ['frettʃa] *sf* arrow; **~ di direzione** (*AUT*) indicator

fred'dare *vt* to shoot dead

fred'dezza [fred'dettsa] *sf* coldness

'freddo, a *ag, sm* cold; **fa ~** it's cold; **aver ~** to be cold; **a ~** (*fig*) deliberately; **freddo'loso, a** *ag* sensitive to the cold

fred'dura *sf* pun

fre'gare *vt* to rub; (*fam: truffare*) to take in, cheat; (: *rubare*) to swipe, pinch; **fregarsene** (*fam!*): **chi se ne frega?** who gives a damn (about it)?

fre'gata *sf* rub; (*fam*) swindle; (*NAUT*) frigate

'fregio ['fredʒo] *sm* (*ARCHIT*) frieze; (*ornamento*) decoration

'fremere *vi:* **~ di** to tremble *o* quiver with;

'fremito *sm* tremor, quiver

fre'nare *vt* (*veicolo*) to slow down; (*cavallo*) to rein in; (*lacrime*) to restrain, hold back

♦ *vi* to brake; **~rsi** *vr* (*fig*) to restrain o.s., control o.s.; **fre'nata** *sf*: **fare una frenata** to brake

frene'sia *sf* frenzy

'**freno** *sm* brake; (*morso*) bit; **~ a disco** disc brake; **~ a mano** handbrake; **tenere a ~** to restrain

frequen'tare *vt* (*scuola, corso*) to attend; (*locale, bar*) to go to, frequent; (*persone*) to see (often)

fre'quente *ag* frequent; **di ~** frequently; **fre'quenza** *sf* frequency; (*INS*) attendance

fres'chezza [fres'kettsa] *sf* freshness

'**fresco, a, schi, sche** *ag* fresh; (*temperatura*) cool; (*notizia*) recent, fresh ♦ *sm*: **godere il ~** to enjoy the cool air; **stare ~** (*fig*) to be in for it; **mettere al ~** to put in a cool place

'**fretta** *sf* hurry, haste; **in ~** in a hurry; **in ~ e furia** in a mad rush; **aver ~** to be in a hurry; **fretto'loso, a** *ag* (*persona*) in a hurry; (*lavoro etc*) hurried, rushed

fri'abile *ag* (*terreno*) friable; (*pasta*) crumbly

'**friggere** ['friddʒere] *vt* to fry ♦ *vi* (*olio etc*) to sizzle

'**frigido, a** ['fridʒido] *ag* (*MED*) frigid

'**frigo** *sm* fridge

frigo'rifero, a *ag* refrigerating ♦ *sm* refrigerator

fringu'ello *sm* chaffinch

frit'tata *sf* omelette; **fare una ~** (*fig*) to make a mess of things

frit'tella *sf* (*CUC*) fritter

'**fritto, a** *pp di* **friggere** ♦ *ag* fried ♦ *sm* fried food; **~ misto** mixed fry

frit'tura *sf* (*CUC*): **~ di pesce** mixed fried fish

'**frivolo, a** *ag* frivolous

frizi'one [frit'tsjone] *sf* friction; (*di pelle*) rub, rub-down; (*AUT*) clutch

friz'zante [frid'dzante] *ag* (*anche fig*) sparkling

fro'dare *vt* to defraud, cheat

'**frode** *sf* fraud; **~ fiscale** tax evasion

'**frollo, a** *ag* (*carne*) tender; (*: di selvaggina*) high; **pasta ~a** short(crust) pastry

'**fronda** *sf* (leafy) branch; (*di partito politico*) internal opposition

fron'tale *ag* frontal; (*scontro*) head-on

'**fronte** *sf* (*ANAT*) forehead; (*di edificio*) front, façade ♦ *sm* (*MIL, POL, METEOR*) front; **a ~, di ~** facing, opposite; **di ~ a** (*posizione*) opposite, facing, in front of; (*a paragone di*) compared with

fronteggi'are [fronted'dʒare] *vt* (*avversari, difficoltà*) to face, stand up to; (*spese*) to cope with

fronti'era *sf* border, frontier

'**fronzolo** ['frondzolo] *sm* frill

'**frottola** *sf* fib; **~e** *sfpl* (*assurdità*) nonsense *sg*

fru'gare *vi* to rummage ♦ *vt* to search

frul'lare *vt* (*CUC*) to whisk ♦ *vi* (*uccelli*) to flutter; **frul'lato** *sm* milk shake; fruit drink; **frulla'tore** *sm* electric mixer; **frul'lino** *sm* whisk

fru'mento *sm* wheat

fru'scio [fruʃ'ʃio] *sm* rustle; rustling; (*di acque*) murmur

'**frusta** *sf* whip; (*CUC*) whisk

frus'tare *vt* to whip

frus'tino *sm* riding crop

frus'trare *vt* to frustrate

'**frutta** *sf* fruit; (*portata*) dessert; **~ candita/secca** candied/dried fruit

frut'tare *vi* to bear dividends, give a return

frut'teto *sm* orchard

frutti'vendolo, a *sm/f* greengrocer (*BRIT*), produce dealer (*US*)

'**frutto** *sm* fruit; (*fig: risultato*) result(s); (*ECON: interesse*) interest; (*: reddito*) income; **~i di mare** seafood *sg*

FS *abbr* = **Ferrovie dello Stato**

fu *vb vedi* **essere** ♦ *ag inv*: **il ~ Paolo Bianchi** the late Paolo Bianchi

fuci'lare [futʃi'lare] *vt* to shoot; **fuci'lata** *sf* rifle shot

fu'cile [fu'tʃile] *sm* rifle, gun; (*da caccia*) shotgun, gun

fu'cina [fu'tʃina] *sf* forge

'**fuga** *sf* escape, flight; (*di gas, liquidi*) leak; (*MUS*) fugue; **~ di cervelli** brain drain

fu'gace [fu'gatʃe] *ag* fleeting, transient

fug'gevole [fud'dʒevole] *ag* fleeting

fuggi'asco, a, schi, sche [fud'dʒasko] *ag, sm/f* fugitive

fuggi'fuggi [fuddʒi'fuddʒi] *sm* scramble, stampede

fug'gire [fud'dʒire] *vi* to flee, run away; (*fig: passar veloce*) to fly ♦ *vt* to avoid; **fuggi'tivo, a** *sm/f* fugitive, runaway

ful'gore *sm* brilliance, splendour

fu'liggine [fu'liddʒine] *sf* soot

fulmi'nare *vt* (*sog: fulmine*) to strike; (*: elettricità*) to electrocute; (*con arma da fuoco*) to shoot dead; (*fig: con lo sguardo*) to look daggers at

'fulmine *sm* thunderbolt; lightning *no pl*

fu'mare *vi* to smoke; (*emettere vapore*) to steam ♦ *vt* to smoke; **fu'mata** *sf* (*segnale*) smoke signal; **farsi una fumata** to have a smoke; **fuma'tore, 'trice** *sm/f* smoker

fu'metto *sm* comic strip; **giornale** *sm* **a ~i** comic

'fumo *sm* smoke; (*vapore*) steam; (*il fumare tabacco*) smoking; **~i** *smpl* (*industriali etc*) fumes; **i ~i dell'alcool** the after-effects of drink; **vendere ~** to deceive, cheat; **~ passivo** passive smoking; **fu'moso, a** *ag* smoky; (*fig*) muddled

fu'nambolo, a *sm/f* tightrope walker

'fune *sf* rope, cord; (*più grossa*) cable

'funebre *ag* (*rito*) funeral; (*aspetto*) gloomy, funereal

fune'rale *sm* funeral

'fungere ['fundʒere] *vi*: **~ da** to act as

'fungo, ghi *sm* fungus; (*commestibile*) mushroom; **~ velenoso** toadstool

funico'lare *sf* funicular railway

funi'via *sf* cable railway

funzio'nare [funtsjo'nare] *vi* to work, function; (*fungere*): **~ da** to act as

funzio'nario [funtsjo'narjo] *sm* official

funzi'one [fun'tsjone] *sf* function; (*carica*) post, position; (*REL*) service; **in ~** (*meccanismo*) in operation; **in ~ di** (*come*) as; **fare la ~ di qn** (*farne le veci*) to take sb's place

fu'oco, chi *sm* fire; (*fornello*) ring; (*FOT, FISICA*) focus; **dare ~ a qc** to set fire to sth;

far ~ (*sparare*) to fire; **~ d'artificio** firework

fuorché [fwor'ke] *cong, prep* except

fu'ori *av* outside; (*all'aperto*) outdoors, outside; (*fuori di casa, SPORT*) out; (*esclamativo*) get out! ♦ *prep*: **~ (di)** out of, outside ♦ *sm* outside; **lasciar ~ qc/qn** to leave sth/sb out; **far ~ qn** (*fam*) to kill sb, do sb in; **essere ~ di sé** to be beside o.s.; **~ luogo** (*inopportuno*) out of place, uncalled for; **~ mano** out of the way, remote; **~ pericolo** out of danger; **~ uso** old-fashioned; obsolete

fu'ori... *prefisso*: **fuori'bordo** *sm inv* speedboat (with outboard motor); outboard motor; **fuori'classe** *sm/f inv* (undisputed) champion; **fuorigi'oco** *sm* offside; **fuori'legge** *sm/f inv* outlaw; **fuori'serie** *ag inv* (*auto etc*) custom-built ♦ *sf* custom-built car; **fuori'strada** *sm* (*AUT*) cross-country vehicle; **fuor(i)u'scito, a** *sm/f* exile; **fuorvi'are** *vt* to mislead; (*fig*) to lead astray ♦ *vi* to go astray

'furbo, a *ag* clever, smart; (*peg*) cunning

fu'rente *ag*: **~ (contro)** furious (with)

fur'fante *sm* rascal, scoundrel

fur'gone *sm* van

'furia *sf* (*ira*) rage; (*fig: impeto*) fury, violence; (*fretta*) rush; **a ~ di** by dint of; **andare su tutte le ~e** to get into a towering rage; **furi'bondo, a** *ag* furious

furi'oso, a *ag* furious

fu'rore *sm* fury; (*esaltazione*) frenzy; **far ~** to be all the rage

fur'tivo, a *ag* furtive

'furto *sm* theft; **~ con scasso** burglary

'fusa *sfpl*: **fare le ~** to purr

fu'sibile *sm* (*ELETTR*) fuse

fusi'one *sf* (*di metalli*) fusion, melting; (*colata*) casting; (*COMM*) merger; (*fig*) merging

'fuso, a *pp di* **fondere** ♦ *sm* (*FILATURA*) spindle; **~ orario** time zone

fus'tagno [fus'taɲɲo] *sm* corduroy

fus'tino *sm* (*di detersivo*) tub

'fusto *sm* stem; (*ANAT, di albero*) trunk; (*recipiente*) drum, can

fu'turo, a *ag*, *sm* future

G, g

gab'bare *vt* to take in, dupe; ~rsi *vr*: ~rsi di qn to make fun of sb

'gabbia *sf* cage; (*da imballaggio*) crate; ~ dell'ascensore lift (*BRIT*) *o* elevator (*US*) shaft; ~ toracica (*ANAT*) rib cage

gabbi'ano *sm* (sea)gull

gabi'netto *sm* (*MED etc*) consulting room; (*POL*) ministry; (*WC*) toilet, lavatory; (*INS: di fisica etc*) laboratory

'gaffe [gaf] *sf inv* blunder

gagli'ardo, a [gaʎ'ʎardo] *ag* strong, vigorous

'gaio, a *ag* cheerful, gay

'gala *sf* (*sfarzo*) pomp; (*festa*) gala

ga'lante *ag* gallant, courteous; (*avventura*) amorous; galante'ria *sf* gallantry

galantu'omo (*pl* galantu'omini) *sm* gentleman

ga'lassia *sf* galaxy

gala'teo *sm* (good) manners *pl*

gale'otto *sm* (*rematore*) galley slave; (*carcerato*) convict

ga'lera *sf* (*NAUT*) galley; (*prigione*) prison

'galla *sf*: a ~ afloat; venire a ~ to surface, come to the surface; (*fig: verità*) to come out

galleggi'ante [galled'dʒante] *ag* floating ♦ *sm* (*di pescatore, lenza, TECN*) float

galleggi'are [galled'dʒare] *vi* to float

galle'ria *sf* (*traforo*) tunnel; (*ARCHIT, d'arte*) gallery; (*TEATRO*) circle; (*strada coperta con negozi*) arcade

'Galles *sm*: il ~ Wales; gal'lese *ag*, *sm* (*LING*) Welsh ♦ *sm/f* Welshman/woman

gal'letta *sf* cracker

gal'lina *sf* hen

'gallo *sm* cock

gal'lone *sm* piece of braid; (*MIL*) stripe; (*unità di misura*) gallon

galop'pare *vi* to gallop

ga'loppo *sm* gallop; al *o* di ~ at a gallop

'gamba *sf* leg; (*asta: di lettera*) stem; in ~

(*in buona salute*) well; (*bravo, sveglio*) bright, smart; prendere qc sotto ~ (*fig*) to treat sth too lightly

gambe'retto *sm* shrimp

'gambero *sm* (*di acqua dolce*) crayfish; (*di mare*) prawn

'gambo *sm* stem; (*di frutta*) stalk

'gamma *sf* (*MUS*) scale; (*di colori, fig*) range

ga'nascia, sce [ga'naʃʃa] *sf* jaw; ~sce del freno (*AUT*) brake shoes

'gancio ['gantʃo] *sm* hook

'gangheri ['gangeri] *smpl*: uscire dai ~ (*fig*) to fly into a temper

'gara *sf* competition; (*SPORT*) competition; contest; match; (: *corsa*) race; fare a ~ to compete, vie

ga'rage [ga'raʒ] *sm inv* garage

garan'tire *vt* to guarantee; (*debito*) to stand surety for; (*dare per certo*) to assure

garan'zia [garan'tsia] *sf* guarantee; (*pegno*) security

gar'bato, a *ag* courteous, polite

'garbo *sm* (*buone maniere*) politeness, courtesy; (*di vestito etc*) grace, style

gareggi'are [gared'dʒare] *vi* to compete

garga'rismo *sm* gargle; fare i ~ to gargle

ga'rofano *sm* carnation; chiodo di ~ clove

'garza ['gardza] *sf* (*per bende*) gauze

gar'zone [gar'dzone] *sm* (*di negozio*) boy

gas *sm inv* gas; a tutto ~ at full speed; dare ~ (*AUT*) to accelerate

ga'solio *sm* diesel (oil)

ga's(s)ato, a *ag* (*bibita*) aerated, fizzy

gas'sosa *sf* fizzy drink

gas'soso, a *ag* gaseous; gassy

gastrono'mia *sf* gastronomy

gat'tino *sm* kitten

'gatto, a *sm/f* cat, tomcat/she-cat; ~ selvatico wildcat; ~ delle nevi (*AUT*, *SCI*) snowcat

gatto'pardo *sm*: ~ africano serval; ~ americano ocelot

'gaudio *sm* joy, happiness

ga'vetta *sf* (*MIL*) mess tin; venire dalla ~ (*MIL*, *fig*) to rise from the ranks

'gazza ['gaddza] *sf* magpie

gaz'zella [gad'dzɛlla] sf gazelle

gaz'zetta [gad'dzetta] sf news sheet; **G~ Ufficiale** *official publication containing details of new laws*

gel [dʒɛl] sm inv gel

ge'lare [dʒe'lare] vt, vi, vb impers to freeze; **ge'lata** sf frost

gelate'ria [dʒelate'ria] sf ice-cream shop

gela'tina [dʒela'tina] sf gelatine; ~ **esplosiva** dynamite; ~ **di frutta** fruit jelly

ge'lato, a [dʒe'lato] ag frozen ♦ sm ice cream

'gelido, a ['dʒɛlido] ag icy, ice-cold

'gelo ['dʒɛlo] sm (temperatura) intense cold; (brina) frost; (fig) chill; **ge'lone** sm chilblain

gelo'sia [dʒelo'sia] sf jealousy

ge'loso, a [dʒe'loso] ag jealous

'gelso ['dʒɛlso] sm mulberry (tree)

gelso'mino [dʒelso'mino] sm jasmine

ge'mello, a [dʒe'mɛllo] ag, sm/f twin; **~i** smpl (di camicia) cufflinks; (dello zodiaco): **G~i** Gemini sg

'gemere ['dʒɛmere] vi to moan, groan; (cigolare) to creak; **'gemito** sm moan, groan

'gemma ['dʒɛmma] sf (BOT) bud; (pietra preziosa) gem

gene'rale [dʒene'rale] ag, sm general; **in ~** (per sommi capi) in general terms; (di solito) usually, in general; **generalità** sfpl (dati d'identità) particulars; **generaliz'zare** vt, vi to generalize; **general'mente** av generally

gene'rare [dʒene'rare] vt (dar vita) to give birth to; (produrre) to produce; (causare) to arouse; (TECN) to produce, generate; **genera'tore** sm (TECN) generator; **generazi'one** sf generation

'genere ['dʒɛnere] sm kind, type, sort; (BIOL) genus; (merce) article, product; (LING) gender; (ARTE, LETTERATURA) genre; **in ~** generally, as a rule; **il ~ umano** mankind; **~i alimentari** foodstuffs

ge'nerico, a, ci, che [dʒe'nɛriko] ag generic; (vago) vague, imprecise

'genero ['dʒɛnero] sm son-in-law

generosità [dʒenerosi'ta] sf generosity

gene'roso, a [dʒene'roso] ag generous

ge'netica [dʒe'nɛtika] sf genetics sg

ge'netico, a, ci, che [dʒe'nɛtiko] ag genetic

gen'giva [dʒen'dʒiva] sf (ANAT) gum

geni'ale [dʒen'jale] ag (persona) of genius; (idea) ingenious, brilliant

'genio ['dʒɛnjo] sm genius; **andare a ~ a qn** to be to sb's liking, appeal to sb

geni'tale [dʒeni'tale] ag genital; **~i** smpl genitals

geni'tore [dʒeni'tore] sm parent, father o mother; **i miei ~i** my parents, my father and mother

gen'naio [dʒen'najo] sm January

'Genova ['dʒɛnova] sf Genoa

gen'taglia [dʒen'taʎʎa] (peg) sf rabble

'gente ['dʒɛnte] sf people pl

gen'tile [dʒen'tile] ag (persona, atto) kind; (: garbato) courteous, polite; (nelle lettere): **G~ Signore** Dear Sir; (: sulla busta): **G~ Signor Fernando Villa** Mr Fernando Villa; **genti'lezza** sf kindness; courtesy, politeness; **per gentilezza** (per favore) please

gentilu'omo [dʒenti'lwɔmo] (pl gentilu'omini) sm gentleman

genu'ino, a [dʒenu'ino] ag (prodotto) natural; (persona, sentimento) genuine, sincere

geogra'fia [dʒeogra'fia] sf geography

geolo'gia [dʒeolo'dʒia] sf geology

ge'ometra, i, e [dʒe'ɔmetra] sm/f (professionista) surveyor

geome'tria [dʒeome'tria] sf geometry; **geo'metrico, a, ci, che** ag geometric(al)

gerar'chia [dʒerar'kia] sf hierarchy

ge'rente [dʒe'rɛnte] sm/f manager/ manageress

'gergo, ghi ['dʒɛrgo] sm jargon; slang

geria'tria [dʒerja'tria] sf geriatrics sg

Ger'mania [dʒer'manja] sf: **la ~** Germany; **la ~ occidentale/orientale** West/East Germany

'germe ['dʒɛrme] sm germ; (fig) seed

germogli'are [dʒermoʎˈʎare] *vi* to sprout; to germinate; **ger'moglio** *sm* shoot; bud

gero'glifico, ci [dʒeroˈglifiko] *sm* hieroglyphic

'gesso [ˈdʒɛsso] *sm* chalk; (*SCULTURA, MED, EDIL*) plaster; (*statua*) plaster figure; (*minerale*) gypsum

gesti'one [dʒesˈtjone] *sf* management

ges'tire [dʒesˈtire] *vt* to run, manage

'gesto [ˈdʒɛsto] *sm* gesture

ges'tore [dʒesˈtore] *sm* manager

Gesù [dʒeˈzu] *sm* Jesus

gesu'ita, i [dʒezuˈita] *sm* Jesuit

get'tare [dʒetˈtare] *vt* to throw; (*anche:* ~ **via**) to throw away *o* out; (*SCULTURA*) to cast; (*EDIL*) to lay; (*acqua*) to spout; (*grido*) to utter; **~rsi** *vr*: **~rsi in** (*sog: fiume*) to flow into; **~ uno sguardo su** to take a quick look at; **get'tata** *sf* (*di cemento, gesso, metalli*) cast; (*diga*) jetty

'getto [ˈdʒɛtto] *sm* (*di gas, liquido, AER*) jet; **a ~ continuo** uninterruptedly; **di ~** (*fig*) straight off, in one go

get'tone [dʒetˈtone] *sm* token; (*per giochi*) counter; (: *roulette etc*) chip; **~ telefonico** telephone token

ghiacci'aio [gjatˈtʃajo] *sm* glacier

ghiacci'are [gjatˈtʃare] *vt* to freeze; (*fig*): **~ qn** to make sb's blood run cold ♦ *vi* to freeze, ice over; **ghiacci'ato, a** *ag* frozen; (*bevanda*) ice-cold

ghi'accio [ˈgjattʃo] *sm* ice

ghiacci'olo [gjatˈtʃolo] *sm* icicle; (*tipo di gelato*) ice lolly (*BRIT*), popsicle (*US*)

ghi'aia [ˈgjaja] *sf* gravel

ghi'anda [ˈgjanda] *sf* (*BOT*) acorn

ghi'andola [ˈgjandola] *sf* gland

ghigliot'tina [giʎʎotˈtina] *sf* guillotine

ghi'gnare [giɲˈɲare] *vi* to sneer

ghi'otto, a [ˈgjotto] *ag* greedy; (*cibo*) delicious, appetizing; **ghiot'tone, a** *sm/f* glutton

ghiri'goro [giriˈgoro] *sm* scribble, squiggle

ghir'landa [girˈlanda] *sf* garland, wreath

'ghiro [ˈgiro] *sm* dormouse

'ghisa [ˈgiza] *sf* cast iron

già [dʒa] *av* already; (*ex, in precedenza*) formerly ♦ *escl* of course!, yes indeed!

gi'acca, che [ˈdʒakka] *sf* jacket; **~ a vento** windcheater (*BRIT*), windbreaker (*US*)

giacché [dʒakˈke] *cong* since, as

giac'chetta [dʒakˈketta] *sf* (light) jacket

gia'cenza [dʒaˈtʃɛntsa] *sf*: **merce in ~** goods in stock; **~e di magazzino** unsold stock

gia'cere [dʒaˈtʃere] *vi* to lie; **giaci'mento** *sm* deposit

gia'cinto [dʒaˈtʃinto] *sm* hyacinth

gi'ada [ˈdʒada] *sf* jade

giaggi'olo [dʒadˈdʒɔlo] *sm* iris

giagu'aro [dʒaˈgwaro] *sm* jaguar

gi'allo [ˈdʒallo] *ag* yellow; (*carnagione*) sallow ♦ *sm* yellow; (*anche:* **romanzo ~**) detective novel; (*anche:* **film ~**) detective film; **~ dell'uovo** yolk

giam'mai [dʒamˈmai] *av* never

Giap'pone [dʒapˈpone] *sm* Japan; **giappo'nese** *ag, sm/f, sm* Japanese *inv*

gi'ara [ˈdʒara] *sf* jar

giardi'naggio [dʒardiˈnaddʒo] *sm* gardening

giardini'era [dʒardiˈnjera] *sf* (*misto di sottaceti*) mixed pickles *pl*

giardini'ere, a [dʒardiˈnjere] *sm/f* gardener

giar'dino [dʒarˈdino] *sm* garden; **~ d'infanzia** nursery school; **~ pubblico** public gardens *pl*, (public) park; **~ zoologico** zoo

giarretti'era [dʒarretˈtjera] *sf* garter

giavel'lotto [dʒavelˈlɔtto] *sm* javelin

gi'gante, 'essa [dʒiˈgante] *sm/f* giant ♦ *ag* giant, gigantic; (*COMM*) giant-size; **gigan'tesco, a, schi, sche** *ag* gigantic

'giglio [ˈdʒiʎʎo] *sm* lily

gilè [dʒiˈle] *sm inv* waistcoat

gin [dʒin] *sm inv* gin

gine'cologo, a, gi, ghe [dʒineˈkɔlogo] *sm/f* gynaecologist

gi'nepro [dʒiˈnepro] *sm* juniper

gi'nestra [dʒiˈnestra] *sf* (*BOT*) broom

Gi'nevra [dʒiˈnevra] *sf* Geneva

gingil'larsi [dʒindʒilˈlarsi] *vr* to fritter away one's time; (*giocare*): **~ con** to fiddle with

gin'gillo [dʒin'dʒillo] *sm* plaything

gin'nasio [dʒin'nazjo] *sm* the 4th and 5th year of secondary school in Italy

gin'nasta, i, e [dʒin'nasta] *sm/f* gymnast; **gin'nastica** *sf* gymnastics *sg*; (*esercizio fisico*) keep-fit exercises; (*INS*) physical education

gi'nocchio [dʒi'nɔkkjo] (*pl(m)* **gi'nocchi** *o pl(f)* **gi'nocchia**) *sm* knee; **stare in ~** to kneel, be on one's knees; **mettersi in ~** to kneel (down); **ginocchi'oni** *av* on one's knees

gio'care [dʒo'kare] *vt* to play; (*scommettere*) to stake, wager, bet; (*ingannare*) to take in ♦ *vi* to play; (*a roulette etc*) to gamble; (*fig*) to play a part, be important; **~ a** (*gioco, sport*) to play; (*cavalli*) to bet on; **~rsi la carriera** to put one's career at risk; **gioca'tore, 'trice** *sm/f* player; gambler

gio'cattolo [dʒo'kattolo] *sm* toy

gio'chetto [dʒo'ketto] *sm* (*tranello*) trick; (*fig*): **è un ~** it's child's play

gi'oco, chi ['dʒɔko] *sm* game; (*divertimento, TECN*) play; (*al casinò*) gambling; (*CARTE*) hand; (*insieme di pezzi etc necessari per un gioco*) set; **per ~** for fun; **fare il doppio ~ con qn** to double-cross sb; **~ d'azzardo** game of chance; **~ degli scacchi** chess set; **i Giochi Olimpici** the Olympic Games

giocoli'ere [dʒoko'ljere] *sm* juggler

gio'coso, a [dʒo'koso] *ag* playful, jesting

gi'ogo, ghi ['dʒɔgo] *sm* yoke

gi'oia ['dʒɔja] *sf* joy, delight; (*pietra preziosa*) jewel, precious stone

gioielle'ria [dʒojelle'ria] *sf* jeweller's craft; jeweller's (shop)

gioielli'ere, a [dʒojel'ljere] *sm/f* jeweller

gioi'ello [dʒo'jello] *sm* jewel, piece of jewellery; **i miei ~i** my jewels *o* jewellery

gioi'oso, a [dʒo'joso] *ag* joyful

Gior'dania [dʒor'danja] *sf*: **la ~** Jordan

giorna'laio, a [dʒorna'lajo] *sm/f* newsagent (*BRIT*), newsdealer (*US*)

gior'nale [dʒor'nale] *sm* newspaper; (*diario*) journal, diary; (*COMM*) journal; **~ di bordo** log; **~ radio** radio news *sg*

giornali'ero, a [dʒorna'ljero] *ag* daily; (*che varia: umore*) changeable ♦ *sm* day labourer

giorna'lismo [dʒorna'lizmo] *sm* journalism

giorna'lista, i, e [dʒorna'lista] *sm/f* journalist

gior'nata [dʒor'nata] *sf* day; **~ lavorativa** working day

gi'orno ['dʒorno] *sm* day; (*opposto alla notte*) day, daytime; (*luce del ~*) daylight; **al ~** per day; **di ~** by day; **al ~ d'oggi** nowadays

---
giorno dei morti
---

i **Il giorno dei Morti**, All Souls' Day, falls on 2 November. On that day, relatives make a special visit to the graves of loved ones, to lay flowers.

---

gi'ostra ['dʒɔstra] *sf* (*per bimbi*) merry-go-round; (*torneo storico*) joust

gio'vane ['dʒovane] *ag* young; (*aspetto*) youthful ♦ *sm/f* youth/girl, young man/woman; **i ~i** young people; **giova'nile** *ag* youthful; (*scritti*) early; (*errore*) of youth; **giova'notto** *sm* young man

gio'vare [dʒo'vare] *vi*: **~ a** (*essere utile*) to be useful to; (*far bene*) to be good for ♦ *vb impers* (*essere bene, utile*) to be useful; **~rsi di qc** to make use of sth

giovedì [dʒove'di] *sm inv* Thursday; **di** *o* **il ~** on Thursdays

gioven'tù [dʒoven'tu] *sf* (*periodo*) youth; (*i giovani*) young people *pl*, youth

giovi'ale [dʒo'vjale] *ag* jovial, jolly

giovi'nezza [dʒovi'nettsa] *sf* youth

gira'dischi [dʒira'diski] *sm inv* record player

gi'raffa [dʒi'raffa] *sf* giraffe

gi'randola [dʒi'randola] *sf* (*fuoco d'artificio*) Catherine wheel; (*giocattolo*) toy windmill; (*banderuola*) weather vane, weathercock

gi'rare [dʒi'rare] *vt* (*far ruotare*) to turn; (*percorrere, visitare*) to go round; (*CINEMA*) to shoot; to make; (*COMM*) to endorse ♦ *vi* to turn; (*più veloce*) to spin; (*andare in giro*) to wander, go around; **~rsi** *vr* to turn; **~**

attorno a to go round; to revolve round; **far ~ la testa a qn** to make sb dizzy; (*fig*) to turn sb's head

girar'rosto [dʒirar'rɔsto] *sm* (*CUC*) spit

gira'sole [dʒira'sole] *sm* sunflower

gi'rata [dʒi'rata] *sf* (*passeggiata*) stroll; (*con veicolo*) drive; (*COMM*) endorsement

gira'volta [dʒira'vɔlta] *sf* twirl, turn; (*curva*) sharp bend; (*fig*) about-turn

gi'revole [dʒi'revole] *ag* revolving, turning

gi'rino [dʒi'rino] *sm* tadpole

'giro ['dʒiro] *sm* (*circuito, cerchio*) circle; (*di chiave, manovella*) turn; (*viaggio*) tour, excursion; (*passeggiata*) stroll, walk; (*in macchina*) drive; (*in bicicletta*) ride; (*SPORT: della pista*) lap; (*di denaro*) circulation; (*CARTE*) hand; (*TECN*) revolution; **prendere in ~ qn** (*fig*) to pull sb's leg; **fare un ~** to go for a walk (*o* a drive *o* a ride); **andare in ~** to go about, walk around; **a stretto ~ di posta** by return of post; **nel ~ di un mese** in a month's time; **essere nel ~** (*fig*) to belong to a circle (of friends); **~ d'affari** (*COMM*) turnover; **~ di parole** circumlocution; **~ di prova** (*AUT*) test drive; **~ turistico** sightseeing tour; **giro'collo** *sm*: **a girocollo** crew-neck *cpd*

gironzo'lare [dʒirondzo'lare] *vi* to stroll about

'gita ['dʒita] *sf* excursion, trip; **fare una ~** to go for a trip, go on an outing

gi'tano, a [dʒi'tano] *sm/f* gipsy

giù [dʒu] *av* down; (*dabbasso*) downstairs; **in ~** downwards, down; **~ di lì** (*pressappoco*) thereabouts; **bambini dai 6 anni in ~** children aged 6 and under; **~ per: cadere ~ per le scale** to fall down the stairs; **essere ~** (*fig: di salute*) to be run down; (*: di spirito*) to be depressed

giub'botto [dʒub'bɔtto] *sm* jerkin; **~ antiproiettile** bulletproof vest

gi'ubilo ['dʒubilo] *sm* rejoicing

giudi'care [dʒudi'kare] *vt* to judge; (*accusato*) to try; (*lite*) to arbitrate in; **~ qn/qc bello** to consider sb/sth (to be) beautiful

gi'udice ['dʒuditʃe] *sm* judge; **~ conciliatore** justice of the peace; **~ istruttore** examining (*BRIT*) *o* committing (*US*) magistrate; **~ popolare** member of a jury

giu'dizio [dʒu'dittsjo] *sm* judgment; (*opinione*) opinion; (*DIR*) judgment, sentence; (*: processo*) trial; (*: verdetto*) verdict; **aver ~** to be wise *o* prudent; **citare in ~** to summons; **giudizi'oso, a** *ag* prudent, judicious

gi'ugno ['dʒuɲɲo] *sm* June

giul'lare [dʒul'lare] *sm* jester

giu'menta [dʒu'menta] *sf* mare

gi'unco, chi ['dʒunko] *sm* rush

gi'ungere ['dʒundʒere] *vi* to arrive ♦ *vt* (*mani etc*) to join; **~ a** to arrive at, reach

gi'ungla ['dʒungla] *sf* jungle

gi'unta ['dʒunta] *sf* addition; (*organo esecutivo, amministrativo*) council, board; **per ~a** into the bargain, in addition; **~a militare** military junta

gi'unto, a ['dʒunto] *pp di* **giungere** ♦ *sm* (*TECN*) coupling, joint; **giun'tura** *sf* joint

giuo'care [dʒwo'kare] *etc* = **giocare** *etc*

giura'mento [dʒura'mento] *sm* oath; **~ falso** perjury

giu'rare [dʒu'rare] *vt* to swear ♦ *vi* to swear, take an oath; **giu'rato, a** *ag*: **nemico giurato** sworn enemy ♦ *sm/f* juror, juryman/woman

giu'ria [dʒu'ria] *sf* jury

giu'ridico, a, ci, che [dʒu'ridiko] *ag* legal

giustifi'care [dʒustifi'kare] *vt* to justify; **giustificazi'one** *sf* justification; (*INS*) (note of) excuse

gius'tizia [dʒus'tittsja] *sf* justice; **giustizi'are** *vt* to execute, put to death; **giustizi'ere** *sm* executioner

gi'usto, a ['dʒusto] *ag* (*equo*) fair, just; (*vero*) true, correct; (*adatto*) right, suitable; (*preciso*) exact, correct ♦ *av* (*esattamente*) exactly, precisely; (*per l'appunto, appena*) just; **arrivare ~** to arrive just in time; **ho ~ bisogno di te** you're just the person I need

glaci'ale [gla'tʃale] *ag* glacial

gli [ʎi] (*dav V, s impura, gn, pn, ps, x, z*) *det mpl* the ♦ *pron* (*a lui*) to him; (*a esso*) to it; (in coppia con lo, la, li, le, ne: a lui, a lei, a loro etc): **gliele do** I'm giving them to him (o her o them); vedi anche **il**

gli'ela ['ʎela] etc vedi **gli**

glo'bale ag overall

'globo sm globe

'globulo sm (ANAT): ~ **rosso/bianco** red/white corpuscle

'gloria sf glory; **glori'oso, a** ag glorious

glos'sario sm glossary

'gnocchi ['ɲɔkki] smpl (CUC) small dumplings made of semolina pasta or potato

'gobba sf (ANAT) hump; (protuberanza) bump

'gobbo, a ag hunchbacked; (ricurvo) round-shouldered ♦ sm/f hunchback

'goccia, ce ['gottʃa] sf drop; **goccio'lare** vi, vt to drip

go'dere vi (compiacersi): ~ **(di)** to be delighted (at), rejoice (at); (trarre vantaggio): ~ **di** to benefit from ♦ vt to enjoy; ~**rsi la vita** to enjoy life; ~**sela** to have a good time, enjoy o.s.; **godi'mento** sm enjoyment

'goffo, a ag clumsy, awkward

'gola sf (ANAT) throat; (golosità) gluttony, greed; (di camino) flue; (di monte) gorge; **fare ~** (anche fig) to tempt

golf sm inv (SPORT) golf; (maglia) cardigan

'golfo sm gulf

go'loso, a ag greedy

go'mito sm elbow; (di strada etc) sharp bend

go'mitolo sm ball

'gomma sf rubber; (per cancellare) rubber, eraser; (di veicolo) tyre (BRIT), tire (US); ~ **americana** o **da masticare** chewing gum; ~ **a terra** flat tyre (BRIT) o tire (US); **gommapi'uma** ® sf foam rubber; **gom'mone** sm rubber dinghy

'gondola sf gondola; **gondoli'ere** sm gondolier

gonfa'lone sm banner

gonfi'are vt (pallone) to blow up, inflate; (dilatare, ingrossare) to swell; (fig: notizia) to exaggerate; ~**rsi** vr to swell; (fiume) to

rise; **'gonfio, a** ag swollen; (stomaco) bloated; (vela) full; **gonfi'ore** sm swelling

gongo'lare vi to look pleased with o.s.; ~ **di gioia** to be overjoyed

'gonna sf skirt; ~ **pantalone** culottes pl

'gonzo ['gondzo] sm simpleton, fool

gorgheggi'are [gorged'dʒare] vi to warble; to trill

'gorgo, ghi sm whirlpool

gorgogli'are [gorgoʎ'ʎare] vi to gurgle

go'rilla sm inv gorilla; (guardia del corpo) bodyguard

'gotta sf gout

gover'nante sm/f ruler ♦ sf (di bambini) governess; (donna di servizio) housekeeper

gover'nare vt (stato) to govern, rule; (pilotare, guidare) to steer; (bestiame) to tend, look after; **governa'tivo, a** ag government cpd; **governa'tore** sm governor

go'verno sm government

gozzovigli'are [gottsoviʎ'ʎare] vi to make merry, carouse

gpl sigla m (= gas di petrolio liquefatto) lpg

gracchi'are [grak'kjare] vi to caw

graci'dare [gratʃi'dare] vi to croak

'gracile ['gratʃile] ag frail, delicate

gra'dasso sm boaster

gradazi'one [gradat'tsjone] sf (sfumatura) gradation; ~ **alcolica** alcoholic content, strength

gra'devole ag pleasant, agreeable

gradi'mento sm pleasure, satisfaction; **è di suo ~?** is it to your liking?

gradi'nata sf flight of steps; (in teatro, stadio) tiers pl

gra'dino sm step; (ALPINISMO) foothold

gra'dire vt (accettare con piacere) to accept; (desiderare) to wish, like; **gradisce una tazza di tè?** would you like a cup of tea?; **gra'dito, a** ag pleasing; welcome

'grado sm (MAT, FISICA etc) degree; (stadio) degree, level; (MIL, sociale) rank; **essere in ~ di fare** to be in a position to do

gradu'ale ag gradual

gradu'are vt to grade; **gradu'ato, a** ag (esercizi) graded; (scala, termometro) graduated ♦ sm (MIL) non-commissioned officer

'graffa *sf* (*gancio*) clip; (*segno grafico*) brace

graffi'are *vt* to scratch

'graffio *sm* scratch

gra'fia *sf* spelling; (*scrittura*) handwriting

'grafica *sf* graphic arts *pl*

'grafico, a, ci, che *ag* graphic ♦ *sm* graph; (*persona*) graphic designer

gra'migna [gra'miɲɲa] *sf* weed; couch grass

gram'matica, che *sf* grammar; grammati'cale *ag* grammatical

'grammo *sm* gram(me)

gran *ag vedi* grande

'grana *sf* (*granello, di minerali, corpi spezzati*) grain; (*fam: seccatura*) trouble; (: *soldi*) cash ♦ *sm inv* Parmesan (cheese)

gra'naio *sm* granary, barn

gra'nata *sf* (*proiettile*) grenade

Gran Bre'tagna [-bre'taɲɲa] *sf*: la ~ Great Britain

'granchio ['grankjo] *sm* crab; (*fig*) blunder; prendere un ~ (*fig*) to blunder

grandango'lare *sm* wide-angle lens *sg*

'grande (*qualche volta* gran +C, grand' +V) *ag* (*grosso, largo, vasto*) big, large; (*alto*) tall; (*lungo*) long; (*in sensi astratti*) great ♦ *sm/f* (*persona adulta*) adult, grown-up; (*chi ha ingegno e potenza*) great man/ woman; fare le cose in ~ to do things in style; una gran bella donna a very beautiful woman; non è una gran cosa *o* un gran che it's nothing special; non ne so gran che I don't know very much about it

grandeggi'are [granded'dʒare] *vi* (*emergere per grandezza*): ~ su to tower over; (*darsi arie*) to put on airs

gran'dezza [gran'dettsa] *sf* (*dimensione*) size; magnitude; (*fig*) greatness; in ~ naturale lifesize

grandi'nare *vb impers* to hail

'grandine *sf* hail

gran'duca, chi *sm* grand duke

gra'nello *sm* (*di cereali, uva*) seed; (*di frutta*) pip; (*di sabbia, sale etc*) grain

gra'nita *sf* kind of water ice

gra'nito *sm* granite

'grano *sm* (*in quasi tutti i sensi*) grain; (*frumento*) wheat; (*di rosario, collana*) bead; ~ di pepe peppercorn

gran'turco *sm* maize

'grappa *sf* rough, strong brandy

'grappolo *sm* bunch, cluster

gras'setto *sm* (*TIP*) bold (type)

'grasso, a *ag* fat; (*cibo*) fatty; (*pelle*) greasy; (*terreno*) rich; (*fig: guadagno, annata*) plentiful ♦ *sm* (*di persona, animale*) fat; (*sostanza che unge*) grease; gras'soccio, a, ci, ce *ag* plump

'grata *sf* grating

gra'ticola *sf* grill

gra'tifica, che *sf* bonus

'gratis *av* free, for nothing

grati'tudine *sf* gratitude

'grato, a *ag* grateful; (*gradito*) pleasant, agreeable

gratta'capo *sm* worry, headache

grattaci'elo [gratta'tʃɛlo] *sm* skyscraper

grat'tare *vt* (*pelle*) to scratch; (*raschiare*) to scrape; (*pane, formaggio, carote*) to grate; (*fam: rubare*) to pinch ♦ *vi* (*stridere*) to grate; (*AUT*) to grind; ~rsi *vr* to scratch o.s.; gratta e vinci ≈ scratch card

grat'tugia, gie [grat'tudʒa] *sf* grater; grattugi'are *vt* to grate; pane grattugiato breadcrumbs *pl*

gra'tuito, a *ag* free; (*fig*) gratuitous

gra'vare *vt* to burden ♦ *vi*: ~ su to weigh on

'grave *ag* (*danno, pericolo, peccato etc*) grave, serious; (*responsabilità*) heavy, grave; (*contegno*) grave, solemn; (*voce, suono*) deep, low-pitched; (*LING*): accento ~ grave accent; un malato ~ a person who is seriously ill

gravi'danza [gravi'dantsa] *sf* pregnancy

'gravido, a *ag* pregnant

gravità *sf* seriousness; (*anche FISICA*) gravity

gra'voso, a *ag* heavy, onerous

'grazia ['grattsja] *sf* grace; (*favore*) favour; (*DIR*) pardon; grazi'are *vt* (*DIR*) to pardon

'grazie ['grattsje] *escl* thank you!; ~ mille! *o* tante! *o* infinite! thank you very much!; ~

a thanks to

grazi'oso, a [grat'tsjoso] *ag* charming, delightful; (*gentile*) gracious

'Grecia ['grɛtʃa] *sf:* **la ~** Greece; **'greco, a, ci, che** *ag, sm/f, sm* Greek

'gregge ['greddʒe] (*pl(f)* **-i**) *sm* flock

'greggio, gi ['greddʒo] *sm* (*anche:* **petrolio ~**) crude (oil)

grembi'ule *sm* apron; (*sopravveste*) overall

'grembo *sm* lap; (*ventre della madre*) womb

gre'mito, a *ag:* **~ (di)** packed *o* crowded (with)

'gretto, a *ag* mean, stingy; (*fig*) narrow-minded

'greve *ag* heavy

'grezzo, a ['greddzo] *ag* raw, unrefined; (*diamante*) rough, uncut; (*tessuto*) unbleached

gri'dare *vi* (*per chiamare*) to shout, cry (out); (*strillare*) to scream, yell ♦ *vt* to shout (out), yell (out); **~ aiuto** to cry *o* shout for help

'grido (*pl(m)* **-i** *o pl(f)* **-a**) *sm* shout, cry; scream, yell; (*di animale*) cry; **di ~** famous

'grigio, a, gi, gie ['gridʒo] *ag, sm* grey

'griglia ['griʎʎa] *sf* (*per arrostire*) grill; (*ELETTR*) grid; (*inferriata*) grating; **alla ~** (*CUC*) grilled; **grigli'ata** *sf* (*CUC*) grill

gril'letto *sm* trigger

'grillo *sm* (*ZOOL*) cricket; (*fig*) whim

grimal'dello *sm* picklock

'grinta *sf* grim expression; (*SPORT*) fighting spirit

'grinza ['grintsa] *sf* crease, wrinkle; (*ruga*) wrinkle; **non fare una ~** (*fig: ragionamento*) to be faultless; **grin'zoso, a** *ag* creased, wrinkled

gris'sino *sm* bread-stick

'gronda *sf* eaves *pl*

gron'daia *sf* gutter

gron'dare *vi* to pour; (*essere bagnato*): **~ di** to be dripping with ♦ *vt* to drip with

'groppa *sf* (*di animale*) back, rump; (*fam: dell'uomo*) back, shoulders *pl*

'groppo *sm* tangle; **avere un ~ alla gola** (*fig*) to have a lump in one's throat

gros'sezza [gros'settsa] *sf* size; thickness

gros'sista, i, e *sm/f* (*COMM*) wholesaler

'grosso, a *ag* big, large; (*di spessore*) thick; (*grossolano: anche fig*) coarse; (*grave, insopportabile*) serious, great; (*tempo, mare*) rough ♦ *sm:* **il ~ di** the bulk of; **un pezzo ~** (*fig*) a VIP, a bigwig; **farla ~a** to do something very stupid; **dirle ~e** to tell tall stories; **sbagliarsi di ~** to be completely wrong

grosso'lano, a *ag* rough, coarse; (*fig*) coarse, crude; (*: errore*) stupid

grosso'modo *av* roughly

'grotta *sf* cave; grotto

grot'tesco, a, schi, sche *ag* grotesque

grovi'era *sm o f* gruyère (cheese)

gro'viglio [gro'viʎʎo] *sm* tangle; (*fig*) muddle

gru *sf inv* crane

'gruccia, ce ['gruttʃa] *sf* (*per camminare*) crutch; (*per abiti*) coat-hanger

gru'gnire [grun'ɲire] *vi* to grunt; **gru'gnito** *sm* grunt

'grugno ['gruɲɲo] *sm* snout; (*fam: faccia*) mug

'grullo, a *ag* silly, stupid

'grumo *sm* (*di sangue*) clot; (*di farina etc*) lump

'gruppo *sm* group; **~ sanguigno** blood group

gruvi'era *sm o f* = **groviera**

guada'gnare [gwadaɲ'ɲare] *vt* (*ottenere*) to gain; (*soldi, stipendio*) to earn; (*vincere*) to win; (*raggiungere*) to reach

gua'dagno [gwa'daɲɲo] *sm* earnings *pl*; (*COMM*) profit; (*vantaggio, utile*) advantage, gain; **~ lordo/netto** gross/net earnings *pl*

gu'ado *sm* ford; **passare a ~** to ford

gu'ai *escl:* **~ a te** (*o lui etc*)! woe betide you (*o him etc*)!

gua'ina *sf* (*fodero*) sheath; (*indumento per donna*) girdle

gu'aio *sm* trouble, mishap; (*inconveniente*) trouble, snag

gua'ire *vi* to whine, yelp

gu'ancia, ce ['gwantʃa] *sf* cheek

guanci'ale [gwan'tʃale] *sm* pillow

gu'anto *sm* glove

gu'arda... *prefisso*: ~'**boschi** *sm inv* forester; ~'**caccia** *sm inv* gamekeeper; ~'**coste** *sm inv* coastguard; (*nave*) coastguard patrol vessel; ~'**linee** *sm inv* (*SPORT*) linesman

guar'dare *vt* (*con lo sguardo: osservare*) to look at; (*film, televisione*) to watch; (*custodire*) to look after, take care of ♦ *vi* to look; (*badare*): ~ **a** to pay attention to; (*luoghi: esser orientato*): ~ **a** to face; ~**rsi** *vr* to look at o.s.; ~**rsi da** (*astenersi*) to refrain from; (*stare in guardia*) to beware of; ~**rsi dal fare** to take care not to do; **guarda di non sbagliare** try not to make a mistake; ~ **a vista qn** to keep a close watch on sb

guarda'roba *sm inv* wardrobe; (*locale*) cloakroom; **guardarobi'ere, a** *sm/f* cloakroom attendant

gu'ardia *sf* (*individuo, corpo*) guard; (*sorveglianza*) watch; **fare la ~ a qc/qn** to guard sth/sb; **stare in ~** (*fig*) to be on one's guard; **di ~** (*medico*) on call; ~ **carceraria** (*prison*) warder; ~ **del corpo** bodyguard; ~ **di finanza** (*corpo*) customs *pl*; (*persona*) customs officer; ~ **medica** emergency doctor service

---

Guardia di finanza

ℹ️ The **Guardia di finanza** is a military body which deals with infringements of the laws relating to income tax and monopolies. It reports to the Ministers of Finance, Justice or Agriculture.

---

guardi'ano, a *sm/f* (*di carcere*) warder; (*di villa etc*) caretaker; (*di museo*) custodian; (*di zoo*) keeper; ~ **notturno** night watchman

guar'dingo, a, ghi, ghe *ag* wary, cautious

guardi'ola *sf* porter's lodge; (*MIL*) look-out tower

guard'rail [ga:dreil] *sm inv* crash barrier

guarigi'one [gwari'dʒone] *sf* recovery

gua'rire *vt* (*persona, malattia*) to cure; (*ferita*) to heal ♦ *vi* to recover, be cured; to heal (up)

guarnigi'one [gwarni'dʒone] *sf* garrison

guar'nire *vt* (*ornare: abiti*) to trim; (*CUC*) to garnish; **guarnizi'one** *sf* trimming; garnish; (*TECN*) gasket

guasta'feste *sm/f inv* spoilsport

guas'tare *vt* to spoil, ruin; (*meccanismo*) to break; ~**rsi** *vr* (*cibo*) to go bad; (*meccanismo*) to break down; (*tempo*) to change for the worse

gu'asto, a *ag* (*non funzionante*) broken; (: *telefono etc*) out of order; (*andato a male*) bad, rotten; (: *cibo*) decayed, bad; (*fig: corrotto*) depraved ♦ *sm* breakdown; (*avaria*) failure; ~ **al motore** engine failure

gu'ercio, a, ci, ce ['gwertʃo] *ag* cross-eyed

gu'erra *sf* war; (*tecnica: atomica, chimica etc*) warfare; **fare la ~ (a)** to wage war (against); ~ **mondiale** world war; **guerri'ero, a** *ag* warlike ♦ *sm* warrior; **guer'riglia** *sf* guerrilla warfare; **guerrigli'ero** *sm* guerrilla

'gufo *sm* owl

gu'ida *sf* guidebook; (*comando, direzione*) guidance, direction; (*AUT*) driving; (*tappeto, di tenda, cassetto*) runner; ~ **a destra/sinistra** (*AUT*) right-/left-hand drive; ~ **telefonica** telephone directory; ~ **turistica** tourist guide

gui'dare *vt* to guide; (*squadra, rivolta*) to lead; (*auto*) to drive; (*aereo, nave*) to pilot; **sai ~?** can you drive?; **guida'tore, trice** *sm/f* (*conducente*) driver

guin'zaglio [gwin'tsaʎʎo] *sm* leash, lead

gu'isa *sf*: **a ~ di** like, in the manner of

guiz'zare [gwit'tsare] *vi* to dart; to flicker; to leap

'guscio ['guʃʃo] *sm* shell

gus'tare *vt* (*cibi*) to taste; (: *assaporare con piacere*) to enjoy, savour; (*fig*) to enjoy, appreciate ♦ *vi*: ~ **a** to please; **non mi gusta affatto** I don't like it at all

'gusto *sm* taste; (*sapore*) flavour; (*godimento*) enjoyment; **al ~ di fragola** strawberry-flavoured; **mangiare di ~** to eat heartily; **prenderci ~: ci ha preso ~** he's

acquired a taste for it, he's got to like it;
gus'toso, a *ag* tasty; *(fig)* agreeable

H, h

h *abbr* = **ora; altezza**
ha *etc* [a] *vb vedi* **avere**
ha'cker ['hækə*] *sm inv* hacker
hall [hɔl] *sf inv* hall, foyer
'handicap ['handikap] *sm inv* handicap;
handicap'pato, a *ag* handicapped
♦ *sm/f* handicapped person, disabled
person
'hanno ['anno] *vb vedi* **avere**
'hascisc ['haʃiʃ] *sm* hashish
'herpes ['ɛrpes] *sm (MED)* herpes *sg;* ~
zoster shingles *sg*
ho [ɔ] *vb vedi* **avere**
'hobby ['hɔbi] *sm inv* hobby
'hockey ['hɔki] *sm* hockey; ~ **su ghiaccio**
ice hockey
'hostess ['houstis] *sf inv* air hostess *(BRIT)* o
stewardess
ho'tel *sm inv* hotel

I, i

i *det mpl* the
i'ato *sm* hiatus
ibernazi'one [ibernat'tsjone] *sf* hibernation
'ibrido, a *ag, sm* hybrid
i'cona *sf (REL, INFORM, fig)* icon
Id'dio *sm* God
i'dea *sf* idea; *(opinione)* opinion, view;
(ideale) ideal; **dare l'~ di** to seem, look like;
~ **fissa** obsession; **neanche** *o* **neppure per**
~! certainly not!
ide'ale *ag, sm* ideal
ide'are *vt (immaginare)* to think up,
conceive; *(progettare)* to plan
i'dentico, a, ci, che *ag* identical
identifi'care *vt* to identify;
identificazi'one *sf* identification
identità *sf inv* identity
ideolo'gia, 'gie [ideolo'dʒia] *sf* ideology

idi'oma, i *sm* idiom, language;
idio'matico, a, ci, che *ag* idiomatic;
frase idiomatica idiom
idi'ota, i, e *ag* idiotic ♦ *sm/f* idiot
idola'trare *vt* to worship; *(fig)* to idolize
'idolo *sm* idol
idoneità *sf* suitability
i'doneo, a *ag*: ~ **a** suitable for, fit for; *(MIL)*
fit for; *(qualificato)* qualified for
i'drante *sm* hydrant
idra'tante *ag* moisturizing ♦ *sm*
moisturizer
i'draulica *sf* hydraulics *sg*
i'draulico, a, ci, che *ag* hydraulic ♦ *sm*
plumber
idroe'lettrico, a, ci, che *ag*
hydroelectric
i'drofilo, a *ag vedi* **cotone**
i'drogeno [i'drɔdʒeno] *sm* hydrogen
idros'calo *sm* seaplane base
idrovo'lante *sm* seaplane
i'ena *sf* hyena
i'eri *av, sm* yesterday; **il giornale di** ~
yesterday's paper; ~ **l'altro** the day before
yesterday; ~ **sera** yesterday evening
igi'ene [i'dʒene] *sf* hygiene; ~ **pubblica**
public health; **igi'enico, a, ci, che** *ag*
hygienic; *(salubre)* healthy
i'gnaro, a [iɲ'ɲaro] *ag*: ~ **di** unaware of,
ignorant of
i'gnobile [iɲ'ɲɔbile] *ag* despicable, vile
igno'rante [iɲɲo'rante] *ag* ignorant
igno'rare [iɲɲo'rare] *vt (non sapere, conoscere)*
to be ignorant o unaware of, not to know;
(fingere di non vedere, sentire) to ignore
i'gnoto, a [iɲ'ɲɔto] *ag* unknown

PAROLA CHIAVE

il *(pl (m)* **i**; *diventa* **lo** *(pl* **gli)** *davanti a s
impura, gn, pn, ps, x, z; f* **la** *(pl* **le))** *det m*
1 the; ~ **libro/lo studente/l'acqua** the
book/the student/the water; **gli scolari** the
pupils
2 *(astrazione):* ~ **coraggio/l'amore/la
giovinezza** courage/love/youth
3 *(tempo):* ~ **mattino/la sera** in the
morning/evening; ~ **venerdì** *etc*

(*abitualmente*) on Fridays *etc*; (*quel giorno*) on (the) Friday *etc*; **la settimana prossima** next week

4 (*distributivo*) a, an; **2.500 lire ~ chilo/ paio** 2,500 lire a *o* per kilo/pair

5 (*partitivo*) some, any; **hai messo lo zucchero?** have you added sugar?; **hai comprato ~ latte?** did you buy (some *o* any) milk?

6 (*possesso*): **aprire gli occhi** to open one's eyes; **rompersi la gamba** to break one's leg; **avere i capelli neri/~ naso rosso** to have dark hair/a red nose

7 (*con nomi propri*): **~ Petrarca** Petrarch; **~ Presidente Clinton** President Clinton; **dov'è la Francesca?** where's Francesca?

8 (*con nomi geografici*): **~ Tevere** the Tiber; **l'Italia** Italy; **~ Regno Unito** the United Kingdom; **l'Everest** Everest

'**ilare** *ag* cheerful; **ilarità** *sf* hilarity, mirth

illazi'one [illat'tsjone] *sf* inference, deduction

ille'gale *ag* illegal

illeg'gibile [illed'dʒibile] *ag* illegible

ille'gittimo, a [ille'dʒittimo] *ag* illegitimate

il'leso, a *ag* unhurt, unharmed

illi'bato, a *ag*: **donna ~a** virgin

illimi'tato, a *ag* boundless; unlimited

ill.mo *abbr* = **illustrissimo**

il'ludere *vt* to deceive, delude; **~rsi** *vr* to deceive o.s., delude o.s.

illumi'nare *vt* to light up, illuminate; (*fig*) to enlighten; **~rsi** *vr* to light up; **~ a giorno** to floodlight; **illuminazi'one** *sf* lighting; illumination; floodlighting; (*fig*) flash of inspiration

illusi'one *sf* illusion; **farsi delle ~i** to delude o.s.

illusio'nismo *sm* conjuring

il'luso, a *pp di* **illudere**

illus'trare *vt* to illustrate; **illustra'tivo, a** *ag* illustrative; **illustrazi'one** *sf* illustration

il'lustre *ag* eminent, renowned; **illus'trissimo, a** *ag* (*negli indirizzi*) very revered

imbacuc'care *vt* to wrap up; **~rsi** *vr* to

wrap up

imbal'laggio [imbal'laddʒo] *sm* packing *no pl*

imbal'lare *vt* to pack; (*AUT*) to race; **~rsi** *vr* (*AUT*) to race

imbalsa'mare *vt* to embalm

imbambo'lato, a *ag* (*sguardo*) vacant, blank

imban'dire *vt*: **~ un pranzo** to prepare a lavish meal

imbaraz'zare [imbarat'tsare] *vt* (*mettere a disagio*) to embarrass; (*ostacolare: movimenti*) to hamper

imba'razzo [imba'rattso] *sm* (*disagio*) embarrassment; (*perplessità*) puzzlement, bewilderment; **~ di stomaco** indigestion

imbarca'dero *sm* landing stage

imbar'care *vt* (*passeggeri*) to embark; (*merci*) to load; **~rsi** *vr*: **~rsi su** to board; **~rsi per l'America** to sail for America; **~rsi in** (*fig: affare etc*) to embark on

imbarcazi'one [imbarkat'tsjone] *sf* (small) boat, (small) craft *inv*; **~ di salvataggio** lifeboat

im'barco, chi *sm* embarkation; loading; boarding; (*banchina*) landing stage

imbas'tire *vt* (*cucire*) to tack; (*fig: abbozzare*) to sketch, outline

im'battersi *vr*: **~ in** (*incontrare*) to bump *o* run into

imbat'tibile *ag* unbeatable, invincible

imbavagli'are [imbavaʎ'ʎare] *vt* to gag

imbec'ata *sf* (*TEATRO*) prompt

imbe'cille [imbe'tʃille] *ag* idiotic ♦ *sm/f* idiot; (*MED*) imbecile

imbel'lire *vt* to adorn, embellish ♦ *vi* to grow more beautiful

im'berbe *ag* beardless

im'bevere *vt* to soak; **~rsi** *vr*: **~rsi di** to soak up, absorb

imbian'care *vt* to whiten; (*muro*) to whitewash ♦ *vi* to become *o* turn white

imbian'chino [imbjan'kino] *sm* (house) painter, painter and decorator

imboc'care *vt* (*bambino*) to feed; (*entrare: strada*) to enter, turn into

imbocca'tura *sf* mouth; (*di strada, porto*)

entrance; (MUS, *del morso*) mouthpiece

im'bocco, chi *sm* entrance

imbos'care *vt* to hide; ~rsi *vr* (MIL) to evade military service

imbos'cata *sf* ambush

imbottigli'are [imbottiʎ'ʎare] *vt* to bottle; (NAUT) to blockade; (MIL) to hem in; ~rsi *vr* to be stuck in a traffic jam

imbot'tire *vt* to stuff; (*giacca*) to pad; imbot'tita *sf* quilt; imbot'tito, a *ag* stuffed; (*giacca*) padded; panino imbottito filled roll; imbotti'tura *sf* stuffing; padding

imbrat'tare *vt* to dirty, smear, daub

imbrigli'are [imbriʎ'ʎare] *vt* to bridle

imbroc'care *vt* (*fig*) to guess correctly

imbrogli'are [imbroʎ'ʎare] *vt* to mix up; (*fig: raggirare*) to deceive, cheat; (: *confondere*) to confuse, mix up; ~rsi *vr* to get tangled; (*fig*) to become confused; im'broglio *sm* (*groviglio*) tangle; (*situazione confusa*) mess; (*truffa*) swindle, trick; imbrogli'one, a *sm/f* cheat, swindler

imbronci'ato, a *ag* sulky

imbru'nire *vi*, *vb impers* to grow dark; all'~ at dusk

imbrut'tire *vt* to make ugly ♦ *vi* to become ugly

imbu'care *vt* to post

imbur'rare *vt* to butter

im'buto *sm* funnel

imi'tare *vt* to imitate; (*riprodurre*) to copy; (*assomigliare*) to look like; imitazi'one *sf* imitation

immaco'lato, a *ag* spotless; immaculate

immagazzi'nare [immagaddzi'nare] *vt* to store

immagi'nare [immadʒi'nare] *vt* to imagine; (*supporre*) to suppose; (*inventare*) to invent; s'immagini! don't mention it!, not at all!; immagi'nario, a *ag* imaginary; immaginazi'one *sf* imagination; (*cosa immaginata*) fancy

im'magine [im'madʒine] *sf* image; (*rappresentazione grafica, mentale*) picture

imman'cabile *ag* certain; unfailing

im'mane *ag* (*smisurato*) enormous; (*spaventoso*) terrible

immangi'abile [imman'dʒabile] *ag* inedible

immatrico'lare *vt* to register; ~rsi *vr* (INS) to matriculate, enrol; immatricolazi'one *sf* registration; matriculation, enrolment

imma'turo, a *ag* (*frutto*) unripe; (*persona*) immature; (*prematuro*) premature

immedesi'marsi *vr*: ~ in to identify with

immediata'mente *av* immediately, at once

immedi'ato, a *ag* immediate

im'memore *ag*: ~ di forgetful of

im'menso, a *ag* immense

im'mergere [im'mɛrdʒere] *vt* to immerse, plunge; ~rsi *vr* to plunge; (*sommergibile*) to dive, submerge; (*dedicarsi a*): ~rsi in to immerse o.s. in

immeri'tato, a *ag* undeserved

immeri'tevole *ag* undeserving, unworthy

immersi'one *sf* immersion; (*di sommergibile*) submersion, dive; (*di palombaro*) dive

im'merso, a *pp di* immergere

im'mettere *vt*: ~ (in) to introduce (into); ~ dati in un computer to enter data on a computer

immi'grato, a *sm/f* immigrant; immigrazi'one *sf* immigration

immi'nente *ag* imminent

immischi'are [immis'kjare] *vt*: ~ qn in to involve sb in; ~rsi in to interfere *o* meddle in

immissi'one *sf* (*di aria, gas*) intake; ~ di dati (INFORM) data entry

im'mobile *ag* motionless, still; ~i *smpl* (*anche*: beni ~i) real estate *sg*; immobili'are *ag* (DIR) property *cpd*; immobilità *sf* stillness; immobility

immo'desto, a *ag* immodest

immo'lare *vt* to sacrifice, immolate

immon'dizia [immon'dittsja] *sf* dirt, filth; (*spesso al pl: spazzatura, rifiuti*) rubbish *no pl*, refuse *no pl*

im'mondo, a *ag* filthy, foul

immo'rale *ag* immoral

immor'tale *ag* immortal

im'mune *ag* (*esente*) exempt; (*MED, DIR*) immune; immunità *sf* immunity; **immunità parlamentare** parliamentary privilege

immu'tabile *ag* immutable; unchanging

impacchet'tare [impakket'tare] *vt* to pack up

impacci'are [impat'tʃare] *vt* to hinder, hamper; impacci'ato, a *ag* awkward, clumsy; (*imbarazzato*) embarrassed; im'paccio *sm* obstacle; (*imbarazzo*) embarrassment; (*situazione imbarazzante*) awkward situation

im'pacco, chi *sm* (*MED*) compress

impadro'nirsi *vr*: ~ di to seize, take possession of; (*fig: apprendere a fondo*) to master

impa'gabile *ag* priceless

impagi'nare [impadʒi'nare] *vt* (*TIP*) to paginate, page (up)

impagli'are [impaʎ'ʎare] *vt* to stuff (with straw)

impa'lato, a *ag* (*fig*) stiff as a board

impalca'tura *sf* scaffolding

impalli'dire *vi* to turn pale; (*fig*) to fade

impa'nare *vt* (*CUC*) to dip in breadcrumbs

impanta'narsi *vr* to sink (in the mud); (*fig*) to get bogged down

impappi'narsi *vr* to stammer, falter

impa'rare *vt* to learn

imparen'tarsi *vr*: ~ con to marry into

'impari *ag inv* (*disuguale*) unequal; (*dispari*) odd

impar'tire *vt* to bestow, give

imparzi'ale [impar'tsjale] *ag* impartial, unbiased

impas'sibile *ag* impassive

impas'tare *vt* (*pasta*) to knead

im'pasto *sm* (*l'impastare: di pane*) kneading; (: *di cemento*) mixing; (*pasta*) dough; (*anche fig*) mixture

im'patto *sm* impact

impau'rire *vt* to scare, frighten ♦ *vi* (*anche*: ~rsi) to become scared *o* frightened

im'pavido, a *ag* intrepid, fearless

impazi'ente [impat'tsjɛnte] *ag* impatient; impazi'enza *sf* impatience

impaz'zata [impat'tsata] *sf*: all'~ (*precipitosamente*) at breakneck speed

impaz'zire [impat'tsire] *vi* to go mad; ~ per qn/qc to be crazy about sb/sth

impec'cabile *ag* impeccable

impedi'mento *sm* obstacle, hindrance

impe'dire *vt* (*vietare*): ~ a qn di fare to prevent sb from doing; (*ostruire*) to obstruct; (*impacciare*) to hamper, hinder

impe'gnare [impeɲ'ɲare] *vt* (*dare in pegno*) to pawn; (*onore etc*) to pledge; (*prenotare*) to book, reserve; (*obbligare*) to oblige; (*occupare*) to keep busy; (*MIL: nemico*) to engage; ~rsi *vr* (*vincolarsi*): ~rsi a fare to undertake to do; (*mettersi risolutamente*): ~rsi in qc to devote o.s. to sth; ~rsi con qn (*accordarsi*) to come to an agreement with sb; impegna'tivo, a *ag* binding; (*lavoro*) demanding, exacting; impe'gnato, a *ag* (*occupato*) busy; (*fig: romanzo, autore*) committed, engagé

im'pegno [im'peɲɲo] *sm* (*obbligo*) obligation; (*promessa*) promise, pledge; (*zelo*) diligence, zeal; (*compito, d'autore*) commitment

impel'lente *ag* pressing, urgent

impene'trabile *ag* impenetrable

impen'narsi *vr* (*cavallo*) to rear up; (*AER*) to nose up; (*fig*) to bridle

impen'sato, a *ag* unforeseen, unexpected

impensie'rire *vt* to worry; ~rsi *vr* to worry

impe'rare *vi* (*anche fig*) to reign, rule

impera'tivo, a *ag, sm* imperative

impera'tore, 'trice *sm/f* emperor/empress

imperdo'nabile *ag* unforgivable, unpardonable

imper'fetto, a *ag* imperfect ♦ *sm* (*LING*) imperfect (tense); imperfezi'one *sf* imperfection

imperi'ale *ag* imperial

imperi'oso, a *ag* (*persona*) imperious; (*motivo, esigenza*) urgent, pressing

impe'rizia [impe'rittsja] *sf* lack of experience

imperma'lirsi *vr* to take offence

imperme'abile *ag* waterproof ♦ *sm* raincoat

imperni'are *vt*: ~ **qc su** to hinge sth on; (*fig*) to base sth on; ~**rsi** *vr* (*fig*): ~**rsi su** to be based on

im'pero *sm* empire; (*forza, autorità*) rule, control

imperscru'tabile *ag* inscrutable

imperso'nale *ag* impersonal

imperso'nare *vt* to personify; (*TEATRO*) to play, act (the part of)

imperter'rito, a *ag* fearless, undaunted; impassive

imperti'nente *ag* impertinent

imperver'sare *vi* to rage

'impeto *sm* (*moto, forza*) force, impetus; (*assalto*) onslaught; (*fig: impulso*) impulse; (: *slancio*) transport; **con ~** energetically, vehemently

impet'tito, a *ag* stiff, erect

impetu'oso, a *ag* (*vento*) strong, raging; (*persona*) impetuous

impian'tare *vt* (*motore*) to install; (*azienda, discussione*) to establish, start

impi'anto *sm* (*installazione*) installation; (*apparecchiature*) plant; (*sistema*) system; ~ **elettrico** wiring; ~ **sportivo** sports complex; ~**i di risalita** (*SCI*) ski lifts

impiastricci'are [impjastrit't∫are] *vt* = **impiastrare**

impi'astro *sm* poultice

impic'care *vt* to hang; ~**rsi** *vr* to hang o.s.

impicci'are [impit't∫are] *vt* to hinder, hamper; ~**rsi** *vr* to meddle, interfere; **im'piccio** *sm* (*ostacolo*) hindrance; (*seccatura*) trouble, bother; (*affare imbrogliato*) mess; **essere d'impiccio** to be in the way

impie'gare *vt* (*usare*) to use, employ; (*spendere: denaro, tempo*) to spend; (*investire*) to invest; **impie'gato, a** *sm/f* employee

impi'ego, ghi *sm* (*uso*) use; (*occupazione*) employment; (*posto di lavoro*) (regular) job, post; (*ECON*) investment

impieto'sire *vt* to move to pity; ~**rsi** *vr* to be moved to pity

impie'trire *vt* (*fig*) to petrify

impigli'are [impiʎ'ʎare] *vt* to catch, entangle; ~**rsi** *vr* to get caught up *o* entangled

impi'grire *vt* to make lazy ♦ *vi* (*anche*: ~**rsi**) to grow lazy

impli'care *vt* to imply; (*coinvolgere*) to involve; **implicazi'one** *sf* implication

im'plicito, a [im'plit∫ito] *ag* implicit

implo'rare *vt* to implore; (*pietà etc*) to beg for

impolve'rare *vt* to cover with dust; ~**rsi** *vr* to get dusty

impo'nente *ag* imposing, impressive

impo'nibile *ag* taxable ♦ *sm* taxable income

impopo'lare *ag* unpopular

im'porre *vt* to impose; (*costringere*) to force, make; (*far valere*) to impose, enforce; **imporsi** *vr* (*persona*) to assert o.s.; (*cosa: rendersi necessario*) to become necessary; (*aver successo: moda, attore*) to become popular; ~ **a qn di fare** to force sb to do, make sb do

impor'tante *ag* important; **impor'tanza** *sf* importance; **dare importanza a qc** to attach importance to sth; **darsi importanza** to give o.s. airs

impor'tare *vt* (*introdurre dall'estero*) to import ♦ *vi* to matter, be important ♦ *vb impers* (*essere necessario*) to be necessary; (*interessare*) to matter; **non importa!** it doesn't matter!; **non me ne importa!** I don't care!; **importazi'one** *sf* importation; (*merci importate*) imports *pl*

im'porto *sm* (*total*) amount

importu'nare *vt* to bother

impor'tuno, a *ag* irksome, annoying

imposizi'one [impozit'tsjone] *sf* imposition; order, command; (*onere, imposta*) tax

imposses'sarsi *vr*: ~ **di** to seize, take possession of

impos'sibile *ag* impossible; **fare l'~** to do one's utmost, do all one can; **impossibilità** *sf* impossibility; **essere nell'impossibilità di fare qc** to be unable to do sth

im'posta *sf* (*di finestra*) shutter; (*tassa*) tax; ~ **sul reddito** income tax; ~ **sul valore aggiunto** value added tax (*BRIT*), sales tax (*US*)

impos'tare *vt* (*imbucare*) to post; (*preparare*) to plan, set out; (*avviare*) to begin, start off; (*voce*) to pitch

im'posto, a *pp di* **imporre**

impo'tente *ag* weak, powerless; (*anche MED*) impotent

impove'rire *vt* to impoverish ♦ *vi* (*anche*: ~rsi) to become poor

imprati'cabile *ag* (*strada*) impassable; (*campo da gioco*) unplayable

imprati'chirsi [imprati'kirsi] *vr*: ~rsi in qc to practise (*BRIT*) *o* practice (*US*) sth

impre'gnare [impren'nare] *vt*: ~ (di) (*imbevere*) to soak *o* impregnate (with); (*riempire: anche fig*) to fill (with)

imprendi'tore *sm* (*industriale*) entrepreneur; (*appaltatore*) contractor; **piccolo ~** small businessman

im'presa *sf* (*iniziativa*) enterprise; (*azione*) exploit; (*azienda*) firm, concern

impre'sario *sm* (*TEATRO*) manager, impresario; ~ **di pompe funebri** funeral director

imprescin'dibile [impreʃʃin'dibile] *ag* not to be ignored

impressio'nante *ag* impressive; upsetting

impressio'nare *vt* to impress; (*turbare*) to upset; (*FOT*) to expose; ~rsi *vr* to be easily upset

impressi'one *sf* impression; (*fig: sensazione*) sensation, feeling; (*stampa*) printing; **fare ~** (*colpire*) to impress; (*turbare*) to frighten, upset; **fare buona/ cattiva ~ a** to make a good/bad impression on

im'presso, a *pp di* **imprimere**

impres'tare *vt*: ~ **qc a qn** to lend sth to sb

impreve'dibile *ag* unforeseeable; (*persona*) unpredictable

imprevi'dente *ag* lacking in foresight

impre'visto, a *ag* unexpected, unforeseen ♦ *sm* unforeseen event; **salvo ~i** unless anything unexpected happens

imprigio'nare [impridʒo'nare] *vt* to imprison

im'primere *vt* (*anche fig*) to impress, stamp; (*comunicare: movimento*) to transmit, give

impro'babile *ag* improbable, unlikely

im'pronta *sf* imprint, impression, sign; (*di piede, mano*) print; (*fig*) mark, stamp; ~ **digitale** fingerprint

impro'perio *sm* insult

im'proprio, a *ag* improper; **arma ~a** offensive weapon

improvvisa'mente *av* suddenly; unexpectedly

improvvi'sare *vt* to improvise; ~rsi *vr*: ~rsi cuoco to (decide to) act as cook; improvvi'sata *sf* (pleasant) surprise

improv'viso, a *ag* (*imprevisto*) unexpected; (*subitaneo*) sudden; **all'~** unexpectedly; suddenly

impru'dente *ag* unwise, rash

impu'dente *ag* impudent

impu'dico, a, chi, che *ag* immodest

impu'gnare [impun'nare] *vt* to grasp, grip; (*DIR*) to contest

impul'sivo, a *ag* impulsive

im'pulso *sm* impulse

impun'tarsi *vr* to stop dead, refuse to budge; (*fig*) to be obstinate

impu'tare *vt* (*ascrivere*): ~ **qc a** to attribute sth to; (*DIR: accusare*): ~ **qn di** to charge sb with, accuse sb of; **impu'tato, a** *sm/f* (*DIR*) accused, defendant; **imputazi'one** *sf* (*DIR*) charge

imputri'dire *vi* to rot

PAROLA CHIAVE
---

in (*in+il* = **nel**, *in+lo* = **nello**, *in+l'* = **nell'**, *in+la* = **nella**, *in+i* = **nei**, *in+gli* = **negli**, *in+le* = **nelle**) *prep* **1** (*stato in luogo*) in; **vivere ~ Italia/città** to live in Italy/town; **essere ~ casa/ufficio** to be at home/the office; **se fossi ~ te** if I were you

2 (*moto a luogo*) to; (*: dentro*) into; **andare ~ Germania/città** to go to Germany/

town; **andare ~ ufficio** to go to the office;
entrare ~ macchina/casa to get into the
car/go into the house
3 (*tempo*) in; **nel 1999** in 1999; **~
giugno/estate** in June/summer
4 (*modo, maniera*) in; **~ silenzio** in silence;
~ abito da sera in evening dress; **~
guerra** at war; **~ vacanza** on holiday;
Maria Bianchi ~ Rossi Maria Rossi née
Bianchi
5 (*mezzo*) by; **viaggiare ~ autobus/treno**
to travel by bus/train
6 (*materia*) made of; **~ marmo** made of
marble, marble *cpd*; **una collana ~ oro** a
gold necklace
7 (*misura*) in; **siamo ~ quattro** there are
four of us; **~ tutto** in all
8 (*fine*): **dare ~ dono** to give as a gift;
spende tutto ~ alcool he spends all his
money on drink; **~ onore di** in honour of

---

inabi'tabile *ag* uninhabitable
inacces'sibile [inattʃes'sibile] *ag* (*luogo*)
inaccessible; (*persona*) unapproachable
inaccet'tabile [inattʃet'tabile] *ag*
unacceptable
ina'datto, a *ag*: **~ (a)** unsuitable *o* unfit
(for)
inadegu'ato, a *ag* inadequate
inadempi'enza [inadem'pjɛntsa] *sf*: **~ (a)**
non-fulfilment (of)
inaffer'rabile *ag* elusive; (*concetto, senso*)
difficult to grasp
inalbe'rarsi *vr* (*fig*) to flare up, fly off the
handle
inalte'rabile *ag* unchangeable; (*colore*)
fast, permanent; (*affetto*) constant
inalte'rato, a *ag* unchanged
inami'dato, a *ag* starched
inani'mato, a *ag* inanimate; (*senza vita*:
corpo) lifeless
inappa'gabile *ag* insatiable
inappel'labile *ag* (*decisione*) final,
irrevocable; (*DIR*) final, not open to appeal
inappe'tenza [inappe'tɛntsa] *sf* (*MED*) lack
of appetite
inappun'tabile *ag* irreproachable

inar'care *vt* (*schiena*) to arch; (*sopracciglia*)
to raise; **~rsi** *vr* to arch
inari'dire *vt* to make arid, dry up ♦ *vi*
(*anche*: **~rsi**) to dry up, become arid
inaspet'tato, a *ag* unexpected
inas'prire *vt* (*disciplina*) to tighten up,
make harsher; (*carattere*) to embitter; **~rsi**
vr to become harsher; to become bitter; to
become worse
inattac'cabile *ag* (*anche fig*) unassailable;
(*alibi*) cast-iron
inatten'dibile *ag* unreliable
inat'teso, a *ag* unexpected
inattu'abile *ag* impracticable
inau'dito, a *ag* unheard of
inaugu'rare *vt* to inaugurate, open;
(*monumento*) to unveil
inavver'tenza [inavver'tɛntsa] *sf*
carelessness, inadvertence
incagli'are [inkaʎ'ʎare] *vi* (*NAUT: anche*:
~rsi) to run aground
incal'lito, a *ag* calloused; (*fig*) hardened,
inveterate; (: *insensibile*) hard
incal'zare [inkal'tsare] *vt* to follow *o* pursue
closely; (*fig*) to press ♦ *vi* (*urgere*) to be
pressing; (*essere imminente*) to be
imminent
incammi'nare *vt* (*fig: avviare*) to start up;
~rsi *vr* to set off
incande'scente [inkandeʃ'ʃɛnte] *ag*
incandescent, white-hot
incan'tare *vt* to enchant, bewitch; **~rsi** *vr*
(*rimanere intontito*) to be spellbound; to be
in a daze; (*meccanismo: bloccarsi*) to jam;
incanta'tore, 'trice *ag* enchanting,
bewitching ♦ *sm/f* enchanter/enchantress;
incan'tesimo *sm* spell, charm;
incan'tevole *ag* charming, enchanting
in'canto *sm* spell, charm, enchantment;
(*asta*) auction; **come per ~** as if by magic;
mettere all'~ to put up for auction
inca'pace [inka'patʃe] *ag* incapable;
incapacità *sf* inability; (*DIR*) incapacity
incapo'nirsi *vr* to be stubborn, be
determined
incap'pare *vi*: **~ in qc/qn** (*anche fig*) to
run into sth/sb

incapricci'arsi [inkaprit't∫arsi] *vr*: ~ **di** to take a fancy to *o* for

incapsu'lare *vt* (*dente*) to crown

incarce'rare [inkart∫e'rare] *vt* to imprison

incari'care *vt*: ~ **qn di fare** to give sb the responsibility of doing; **~rsi di** to take care *o* charge of; **incari'cato, a** *ag*: **incaricato (di)** in charge (of), responsible (for) ♦ *sm/f* delegate, representative; **professore incaricato** *teacher with a temporary appointment*

in'carico, chi *sm* task, job

incar'nare *vt* to embody; **~rsi** *vr* to be embodied; (*REL*) to become incarnate

incarta'mento *sm* dossier, file

incar'tare *vt* to wrap (in paper)

incas'sare *vt* (*merce*) to pack (in cases); (*gemma: incastonare*) to set; (*ECON: riscuotere*) to collect; (*PUGILATO: colpi*) to take, stand up to; **in'casso** *sm* cashing, encashment; (*introito*) takings *pl*

incasto'nare *vt* to set; **incastona'tura** *sf* setting

incas'trare *vt* to fit in, insert; (*fig: intrappolare*) to catch; **~rsi** *vr* (*combaciare*) to fit together; (*restare bloccato*) to become stuck; **in'castro** *sm* slot, groove; (*punto di unione*) joint

incate'nare *vt* to chain up

incatra'mare *vt* to tar

incatti'vire *vt* to make wicked; **~rsi** *vr* to turn nasty

in'cauto, a *ag* imprudent, rash

inca'vare *vt* to hollow out; **in'cavo** *sm* hollow; (*solco*) groove

incendi'are [int∫en'djare] *vt* to set fire to; **~rsi** *vr* to catch fire, burst into flames

incendi'ario, a [int∫en'djarjo] *ag* incendiary ♦ *sm/f* arsonist

in'cendio [in't∫endjo] *sm* fire

incene'rire [int∫ene'rire] *vt* to burn to ashes, incinerate; (*cadavere*) to cremate; **~rsi** *vr* to be burnt to ashes

in'censo [in't∫enso] *sm* incense

incensu'rato, a [int∫ensu'rato] *ag* (*DIR*): **essere ~** to have a clean record

incen'tivo [int∫en'tivo] *sm* incentive

incep'pare [int∫ep'pare] *vt* to obstruct, hamper; **~rsi** *vr* to jam

ince'rata [int∫e'rata] *sf* (*tela*) tarpaulin; (*impermeabile*) oilskins *pl*

incer'tezza [int∫er'tettsa] *sf* uncertainty

in'certo, a [in't∫erto] *ag* uncertain; (*irresoluto*) undecided, hesitating ♦ *sm* uncertainty

in'cetta [in't∫etta] *sf* buying up; **fare ~ di qc** to buy up sth

inchi'esta [in'kjesta] *sf* investigation, inquiry

inchi'nare [inki'nare] *vt* to bow; **~rsi** *vr* to bend down; (*per riverenza*) to bow; (*: donna*) to curtsy; **in'chino** *sm* bow; curtsy

inchio'dare [inkjo'dare] *vt* to nail (down); **~ la macchina** (*AUT*) to jam on the brakes

inchi'ostro [in'kjɔstro] *sm* ink; **~ simpatico** invisible ink

inciam'pare [int∫am'pare] *vi* to trip, stumble

inci'ampo [in't∫ampo] *sm* obstacle; **essere d'~ a qn** (*fig*) to be in sb's way

inci'dente [int∫i'dɛnte] *sm* accident; **~ d'auto** car accident

inci'denza [int∫i'dɛntsa] *sf* incidence; **avere una forte ~ su qc** to affect sth greatly

in'cidere [in't∫idere] *vi*: ~ **su** to bear upon, affect ♦ *vt* (*tagliare incavando*) to cut into; (*ARTE*) to engrave; to etch; (*canzone*) to record

in'cinta [in't∫inta] *ag f* pregnant

incipri'are [int∫i'prjare] *vt* to powder

in'circa [in't∫irka] *av*: **all'~** more or less, very nearly

incisi'one [int∫i'zjone] *sf* cut; (*disegno*) engraving; etching; (*registrazione*) recording; (*MED*) incision

in'ciso, a [in't∫izo] *pp di* **incidere** ♦ *sm*: **per ~** incidentally, by the way

inci'tare [int∫i'tare] *vt* to incite

inci'vile [int∫i'vile] *ag* uncivilized; (*villano*) impolite

incl. *abbr* (= *incluso*) encl.

incli'nare *vt* to tilt; **~rsi** *vr* (*barca*) to list; (*aereo*) to bank; **incli'nato, a** *ag* sloping; **inclinazi'one** *sf* slope; (*fig*) inclination,

tendency; in'cline *ag*: **incline a** inclined
to
in'cludere *vt* to include; (*accludere*) to
enclose; in'cluso, a *pp di* includere ♦ *ag*
included; enclosed
incoe'rente *ag* incoherent; (*contraddittorio*) inconsistent
in'cognita [in'koɲɲita] *sf* (MAT, *fig*)
unknown quantity
in'cognito, a [in'koɲɲito] *ag* unknown
♦ *sm*: **in ~** incognito
incol'lare *vt* to glue, gum; (*unire con colla*)
to stick together
incolon'nare *vt* to draw up in columns
inco'lore *ag* colourless
incol'pare *vt*: **~ qn di** to charge sb with
in'colto, a *ag* (*terreno*) uncultivated;
(*trascurato: capelli*) neglected; (*persona*)
uneducated
in'columne *ag* safe and sound, unhurt
incom'benza [inkom'bentsa] *sf* duty, task
in'combere *vi* (*sovrastare minacciando*): **~
su** to threaten, hang over
incominci'are [inkomin'tʃare] *vi*, *vt* to
begin, start
in'comodo *sm* inconvenience
incompe'tente *ag* incompetent
incompi'uto, a *ag* unfinished, incomplete
incom'pleto, a *ag* incomplete
incompren'sibile *ag* incomprehensible
incom'preso, a *ag* not understood;
misunderstood
inconce'pibile [inkontʃe'pibile] *ag*
inconceivable
inconcili'abile [inkontʃi'ljabile] *ag*
irreconcilable
inconclu'dente *ag* inconclusive; (*persona*)
ineffectual
incondizio'nato, a [inkondittsjo'nato] *ag*
unconditional
inconfu'tabile *ag* irrefutable
incongru'ente *ag* inconsistent
inconsa'pevole *ag*: **~ di** unaware of,
ignorant of
in'conscio, a, sci, sce [in'kɔnʃo] *ag*
unconscious ♦ *sm* (PSIC): **l'~** the
unconscious

inconsis'tente *ag* insubstantial;
unfounded
inconsu'eto, a *ag* unusual
incon'sulto, a *ag* rash
incon'trare *vt* to meet; (*difficoltà*) to meet
with; **~rsi** *vr* to meet
incontras'tabile *ag* incontrovertible,
indisputable
in'contro *av*: **~ a** (*verso*) towards ♦ *sm*
meeting; (SPORT) match; meeting; **~ di
calcio** football match
inconveni'ente *sm* drawback, snag
incoraggia'mento [inkoraddʒa'mento] *sm*
encouragement
incoraggi'are [inkorad'dʒare] *vt* to
encourage
incornici'are [inkorni'tʃare] *vt* to frame
incoro'nare *vt* to crown;
incoronazi'one *sf* coronation
incorpo'rare *vt* to incorporate; (*fig:
annettere*) to annex
in'correre *vi*: **~ in** to meet with, run into
incosci'ente [inkoʃ'ʃɛnte] *ag* (*inconscio*)
unconscious; (*irresponsabile*) reckless,
thoughtless; incosci'enza *sf*
unconsciousness; recklessness,
thoughtlessness
incre'dibile *ag* incredible, unbelievable
in'credulo, a *ag* incredulous, disbelieving
incremen'tare *vt* to increase; (*dar
sviluppo a*) to promote
incre'mento *sm* (*sviluppo*) development;
(*aumento numerico*) increase, growth
incresci'oso, a [inkreʃ'ʃoso] *ag* (*incidente
etc*) regrettable
incres'parsi *vr* (*acqua*) to ripple; (*capelli*)
to go frizzy; (*pelle, tessuto*) to wrinkle
incrimi'nare *vt* (DIR) to charge
incri'nare *vt* to crack; (*fig: rapporti,
amicizia*) to cause to deteriorate; **~rsi** *vr* to
crack; to deteriorate; incrina'tura *sf*
crack; (*fig*) rift
incroci'are [inkro'tʃare] *vt* to cross;
(*incontrare*) to meet ♦ *vi* (NAUT, AER) to
cruise; **~rsi** *vr* (*strade*) to cross, intersect;
(*persone, veicoli*) to pass each other; **~ le
braccia/le gambe** to fold one's arms/cross

one's legs; **incrocia'tore** sm cruiser
in'crocio [in'krotʃo] sm (anche FERR) crossing; (di strade) crossroads
incros'tare vt to encrust
incuba'trice [inkuba'tritʃe] sf incubator
'incubo sm nightmare
in'cudine sf anvil
incu'rante ag: **~ (di)** heedless (of), careless (of)
incurio'sire vt to make curious; **~rsi** vr to become curious
incursi'one sf raid
incur'vare vt to bend, curve; **~rsi** vr to bend, curve
in'cusso, a pp di **incutere**
incusto'dito, a ag unguarded, unattended
in'cutere vt: **~ timore/rispetto a qn** to strike fear into sb/command sb's respect
'indaco sm indigo
indaffa'rato, a ag busy
inda'gare vt to investigate
in'dagine [in'dadʒine] sf investigation, inquiry; (ricerca) research, study
indebi'tarsi vr to run o get into debt
in'debito, a ag undue; undeserved
indebo'lire vt, vi (anche: **~rsi**) to weaken
inde'cente [inde'tʃɛnte] ag indecent; **inde'cenza** sf indecency
inde'ciso, a [inde'tʃizo] ag indecisive; (irresoluto) undecided
inde'fesso, a ag untiring, indefatigable
indefi'nito, a ag (anche LING) indefinite; (impreciso, non determinato) undefined
in'degno, a [in'deɲɲo] ag (atto) shameful; (persona) unworthy
indeli'catezza [indelika'tettsa] sf tactlessness
indemoni'ato, a ag possessed (by the devil)
in'denne ag unhurt, uninjured; **indennità** sf inv (rimborso: di spese) allowance; (: di perdita) compensation, indemnity; **indennità di contingenza** cost-of-living allowance; **indennità di trasferta** travel expenses pl
indenniz'zare [indennid'dzare] vt to

compensate; **inden'nizzo** sm (somma) compensation, indemnity
indero'gabile ag binding
'India sf: **l'~** India; **indi'ano, a** ag Indian ♦ sm/f (d'India) Indian; (d'America) Native American, (American) Indian
indiavo'lato, a ag possessed (by the devil); (vivace, violento) wild
indi'care vt (mostrare) to show, indicate; (: col dito) to point to, point out; (consigliare) to suggest, recommend; **indica'tivo, a** ag indicative ♦ sm (LING) indicative (mood); **indica'tore** sm (elenco) guide; directory; (TECN) gauge; indicator; **indicatore di velocità** (AUT) speedometer; **indicatore della benzina** fuel gauge; **indicazi'one** sf indication; (informazione) piece of information
'indice ['inditʃe] sm index; (fig) sign; (dito) index finger, forefinger; **~ di gradimento** (RADIO, TV) popularity rating
indi'cibile [indi'tʃibile] ag inexpressible
indietreggi'are [indietred'dʒare] vi to draw back, retreat
indi'etro av back; (guardare) behind, back; (andare, cadere: anche: **all'~**) backwards; **rimanere ~** to be left behind; **essere ~** (col lavoro) to be behind; (orologio) to be slow; **rimandare qc ~** to send sth back
indi'feso, a ag (città etc) undefended; (persona) defenceless
indiffe'rente ag indifferent; **indiffe'renza** sf indifference
in'digeno, a [in'didʒeno] ag indigenous, native ♦ sm/f native
indi'gente [indi'dʒɛnte] ag poverty-stricken, destitute; **indi'genza** sf extreme poverty
indigesti'one [indidʒes'tjone] sf indigestion
indi'gesto, a [indi'dʒɛsto] ag indigestible
indi'gnare [indiɲ'ɲare] vt to fill with indignation; **~rsi** vr to get indignant
indimenti'cabile ag unforgettable
indipen'dente ag independent; **indipen'denza** sf independence
in'dire vt (concorso) to announce; (elezioni) to call

indi'retto, a *ag* indirect

indiriz'zare [indirit'tsare] *vt* (*dirigere*) to direct; (*mandare*) to send; (*lettera*) to address

indi'rizzo [indi'rittso] *sm* address; (*direzione*) direction; (*avvio*) trend, course

indis'creto, a *ag* indiscreet

indis'cusso, a *ag* unquestioned

indispen'sabile *ag* indispensable, essential

indispet'tire *vt* to irritate, annoy ♦ *vi* (*anche: ~rsi*) to get irritated o annoyed

in'divia *sf* endive

individu'ale *ag* individual; individualità *sf* individuality

individu'are *vt* (*dar forma distinta a*) to characterize; (*determinare*) to locate; (*riconoscere*) to single out

indi'viduo *sm* individual

indizi'ato, a *ag* suspected ♦ *sm/f* suspect

in'dizio [in'dittsjo] *sm* (*segno*) sign, indication; (*POLIZIA*) clue; (*DIR*) piece of evidence

'indole *sf* nature, character

indolen'zito, a [indolen'tsito] *ag* stiff, aching; (*intorpidito*) numb

indo'lore *ag* painless

indo'mani *sm*: l'~ the next day, the following day

Indo'nesia *sf*: l'~ Indonesia

indos'sare *vt* (*mettere indosso*) to put on; (*avere indosso*) to have on; indossa'tore, 'trice *sm/f* model

in'dotto, a *pp di* indurre

indottri'nare *vt* to indoctrinate

indovi'nare *vt* (*scoprire*) to guess; (*immaginare*) to imagine, guess; (*il futuro*) to foretell; indovi'nato, a *ag* successful; (*scelta*) inspired; indovi'nello *sm* riddle; indo'vino, a *sm/f* fortuneteller

indubbia'mente *av* undoubtedly

in'dubbio, a *ag* certain, undoubted

indugi'are [indu'dʒare] *vi* to take one's time, delay

in'dugio [in'dudʒo] *sm* (*ritardo*) delay; senza ~ without delay

indul'gente [indul'dʒɛnte] *ag* indulgent;

(*giudice*) lenient; indul'genza *sf* indulgence; leniency

in'dulgere [in'duldʒere] *vi*: ~ a (*accondiscendere*) to comply with; (*abbandonarsi*) to indulge in; in'dulto, a *pp di* indulgere ♦ *sm* (*DIR*) pardon

indu'mento *sm* article of clothing, garment; ~i *smpl* (*vestiti*) clothes

indu'rire *vt* to harden ♦ *vi* (*anche: ~rsi*) to harden, become hard

in'durre *vt*: ~ qn a fare qc to induce o persuade sb to do sth; ~ qn in errore to mislead sb

in'dustria *sf* industry; industri'ale *ag* industrial ♦ *sm* industrialist

industri'arsi *vr* to do one's best, try hard

industri'oso, a *ag* industrious, hard-working

induzi'one [indut'tsjone] *sf* induction

inebe'tito, a *ag* dazed, stunned

inebri'are *vt* (*anche fig*) to intoxicate; ~rsi *vr* to become intoxicated

inecce'pibile [inettʃe'pibile] *ag* unexceptionable

i'nedia *sf* starvation

i'nedito, a *ag* unpublished

ineffi'cace [ineffi'katʃe] *ag* ineffective

ineffici'ente [ineffi'tʃɛnte] *ag* inefficient

inegu'ale *ag* unequal; (*irregolare*) uneven

ine'rente *ag*: ~ a concerning, regarding

i'nerme *ag* unarmed; defenceless

inerpi'carsi *vr*: ~ (su) to clamber (up)

i'nerte *ag* inert; (*inattivo*) indolent, sluggish; i'nerzia *sf* inertia; indolence, sluggishness

ine'satto, a *ag* (*impreciso*) inexact; (*erroneo*) incorrect; (*AMM: non riscosso*) uncollected

inesis'tente *ag* non-existent

inesperi'enza [inespe'rjɛntsa] *sf* inexperience

ines'perto, a *ag* inexperienced

i'netto, a *ag* (*incapace*) inept; (*che non ha attitudine*): ~ (a) unsuited (to)

ine'vaso, a *ag* (*ordine, corrispondenza*) outstanding

inevi'tabile *ag* inevitable

i'nezia [i'nettsja] *sf* trifle, thing of no

importance

infagot'tare *vt* to bundle up, wrap up; **~rsi** *vr* to wrap up

infal'libile *ag* infallible

infa'mante *ag* defamatory

in'fame *ag* infamous; *(fig: cosa, compito)* awful, dreadful

infan'gare *vt* to cover with mud; *(fig: reputazione)* to sully

infan'tile *ag* child *cpd*; childlike; *(adulto, azione)* childish; **letteratura ~** children's books *pl*

in'fanzia [in'fantsja] *sf* childhood; *(bambini)* children *pl*; **prima ~** babyhood, infancy

infari'nare *vt* to cover with *(o* sprinkle with *o* dip in) flour; **infarina'tura** *sf (fig)* smattering

in'farto *sm (MED)* heart attack

infasti'dire *vt* to annoy, irritate; **~rsi** *vr* to get annoyed *o* irritated

infati'cabile *ag* tireless, untiring

in'fatti *cong* as a matter of fact, in fact, actually

infatu'arsi *vr*: **~ di** to become infatuated with, fall for; **infatuazi'one** *sf* infatuation

in'fausto, a *ag* unpropitious, unfavourable

infe'condo, a *ag* infertile

infe'dele *ag* unfaithful; **infedeltà** *sf* infidelity

infe'lice [infe'litʃe] *ag* unhappy; *(sfortunato)* unlucky, unfortunate; *(inopportuno)* inopportune, ill-timed; *(mal riuscito: lavoro)* bad, poor; **infelicità** *sf* unhappiness

inferi'ore *ag* lower; *(per intelligenza, qualità)* inferior ♦ *sm/f* inferior; **~ a** *(numero, quantità)* less *o* smaller than; *(meno buono)* inferior to; **~ alla media** below average; **inferiorità** *sf* inferiority

inferme'ria *sf* infirmary; *(di scuola, nave)* sick bay

infermi'ere, a *sm/f* nurse

infermità *sf inv* illness; infirmity

in'fermo, a *ag (ammalato)* ill; *(debole)* infirm

infer'nale *ag* infernal; *(proposito, complotto)* diabolical

in'ferno *sm* hell

inferri'ata *sf* grating

infervo'rarsi *vr* to get excited, get carried away

infes'tare *vt* to infest

infet'tare *vt* to infect; **~rsi** *vr* to become infected; **infet'tivo, a** *ag* infectious; **in'fetto, a** *ag* infected; *(acque)* polluted, contaminated; **infezi'one** *sf* infection

infiac'chire [infjak'kire] *vt* to weaken ♦ *vi (anche: ~rsi)* to grow weak

infiam'mabile *ag* inflammable

infiam'mare *vt* to set alight; *(fig, MED)* to inflame; **~rsi** *vr* to catch fire; *(MED)* to become inflamed; **infiammazi'one** *sf (MED)* inflammation

in'fido, a *ag* unreliable, treacherous

infie'rire *vi*: **~ su** *(fisicamente)* to attack furiously; *(verbalmente)* to rage at

in'figgere [in'fiddʒere] *vt*: **~ qc in** to thrust *o* drive sth into

infi'lare *vt (ago)* to thread; *(mettere: chiave)* to insert; *(: anello, vestito)* to slip *o* put on; *(strada)* to turn into, take; **~rsi** *vr*: **~rsi in** to slip into; *(indossare)* to slip on; **~ l'uscio** to slip in; to slip out

infil'trarsi *vr* to penetrate, seep through; *(MIL)* to infiltrate; **infiltrazi'one** *sf* infiltration

infil'zare [infil'tsare] *vt (infilare)* to string together; *(trafiggere)* to pierce

'infimo, a *ag* lowest

in'fine *av* finally; *(insomma)* in short

infinità *sf* infinity; *(in quantità)*: **un'~ di** an infinite number of

infi'nito, a *ag* infinite; *(LING)* infinitive ♦ *sm* infinity; *(LING)* infinitive; **all'~** *(senza fine)* endlessly

infinocchi'are [infinok'kjare] *(fam) vt* to hoodwink

infischi'arsi [infis'kjarsi] *vr*: **~ di** not to care about

in'fisso, a *pp di* **infiggere** ♦ *sm* fixture; *(di porta, finestra)* frame

infit'tire *vt, vi (anche: ~rsi)* to thicken

inflazi'one [inflat'tsjone] *sf* inflation

in'fliggere [in'fliddʒere] *vt* to inflict; **in'flitto, a** *pp di* **infliggere**

influ'ente *ag* influential; **influ'enza** *sf* influence; (*MED*) influenza, flu
influ'ire *vi*: ~ **su** to influence
in'flusso *sm* influence
infol'tire *vt, vi* to thicken
infon'dato, a *ag* unfounded, groundless
in'fondere *vt*: ~ **qc in qn** to instill sth in sb
infor'care *vt* to fork (up); (*bicicletta, cavallo*) to get on; (*occhiali*) to put on
infor'mare *vt* to inform, tell; **~rsi** *vr*: **~rsi (di** *o* **su)** to inquire (about)
infor'matica *sf* computer science
informa'tivo, a *ag* informative
informa'tore *sm* informer
informazi'one [informat'tsjone] *sf* piece of information; **prendere ~i sul conto di qn** to get information about sb; **chiedere un'~** to ask for (some) information
in'forme *ag* shapeless
informico'larsi *vr* = **informicolirsi**
informico'lirsi *vr* to have pins and needles
infor'tunio *sm* accident; ~ **sul lavoro** industrial accident, accident at work
infos'sarsi *vr* (*terreno*) to sink; (*guance*) to become hollow; **infos'sato, a** *ag* hollow; (*occhi*) deep-set; (*: per malattia*) sunken
in'frangere [in'frandʒere] *vt* to smash; (*fig: legge, patti*) to break; **~rsi** *vr* to smash, break; **infran'gibile** *ag* unbreakable; **in'franto, a** *pp di* **infrangere** ♦ *ag* broken
infrazi'one [infrat'tsjone] *sf*: ~ **a** breaking of, violation of
infredda'tura *sf* slight cold
infreddo'lito, a *ag* cold, chilled
infruttu'oso, a *ag* fruitless
infu'ori *av* out; **all'~** outwards; **all'~ di** (*eccetto*) except, with the exception of
infuri'are *vi* to rage; **~rsi** *vr* to fly into a rage
infusi'one *sf* infusion
in'fuso, a *pp di* **infondere** ♦ *sm* infusion
Ing. *abbr* = **ingegnere**
ingabbi'are *vt* to cage
ingaggi'are [ingad'dʒare] *vt* (*assumere con compenso*) to take on, hire; (*SPORT*) to sign on; (*MIL*) to engage; **in'gaggio** *sm* hiring;

signing on
ingan'nare *vt* to deceive; (*fisco*) to cheat; (*eludere*) to dodge, elude; (*fig: tempo*) to while away ♦ *vi* (*apparenza*) to be deceptive; **~rsi** *vr* to be mistaken, be wrong; **ingan'nevole** *ag* deceptive
in'ganno *sm* deceit, deception; (*azione*) trick; (*menzogna, frode*) cheat, swindle; (*illusione*) illusion
ingarbugli'are [ingarbuʎ'ʎare] *vt* to tangle; (*fig*) to confuse, muddle; **~rsi** *vr* to become confused *o* muddled
inge'gnarsi [indʒeŋ'narsi] *vr* to do one's best, try hard; ~ **per vivere** to live by one's wits
inge'gnere [indʒeŋ'nɛre] *sm* engineer; ~ **civile/navale** civil/naval engineer; **ingegne'ria** *sf* engineering; ~ **genetica** genetic engineering
in'gegno [in'dʒeŋno] *sm* (*intelligenza*) intelligence, brains *pl*; (*capacità creativa*) ingenuity; (*disposizione*) talent; **inge'gnoso, a** *ag* ingenious, clever
ingelo'sire [indʒelo'zire] *vt* to make jealous ♦ *vi* (*anche*: **~rsi**) to become jealous
in'gente [in'dʒɛnte] *ag* huge, enormous
ingenuità [indʒenui'ta] *sf* ingenuousness
in'genuo, a [in'dʒɛnuo] *ag* ingenuous, naïve
inge'rire [indʒe'rire] *vt* to ingest
inges'sare [indʒes'sare] *vt* (*MED*) to put in plaster; **ingessa'tura** *sf* plaster
Inghil'terra [ingil'tɛrra] *sf*: **l'~** England
inghiot'tire [ingjot'tire] *vt* to swallow
ingial'lire [indʒal'lire] *vi* to go yellow
ingigan'tire [indʒigan'tire] *vt* to enlarge, magnify ♦ *vi* to become gigantic *o* enormous
inginocchi'arsi [indʒinok'kjarsi] *vr* to kneel (down)
ingiù [in'dʒu] *av* down, downwards
ingiunzi'one [indʒun'tsjone] *sf* injunction
ingi'uria [in'dʒurja] *sf* insult; (*fig: danno*) damage; **ingiuri'are** *vt* to insult, abuse; **ingiuri'oso, a** *ag* insulting, abusive
ingius'tizia [indʒus'tittsja] *sf* injustice
ingi'usto, a [in'dʒusto] *ag* unjust, unfair

in'glese *ag* English ♦ *sm/f* Englishman/ woman ♦ *sm* (LING) English; **gli I~i** the English; **andarsene** *o* **filare all'~** to take French leave

ingoi'are *vt* to gulp (down); (*fig*) to swallow (up)

ingol'fare *vt* (*motore*) to flood; **~rsi** *vr* to flood

ingom'brante *ag* cumbersome

ingom'brare *vt* (*strada*) to block; (*stanza*) to clutter up; **in'gombro, a** *ag* (*strada, passaggio*) blocked ♦ *sm* obstacle; **essere d'ingombro** to be in the way

in'gordo, a *ag*: **~ di** greedy for

in'gorgo, ghi *sm* blockage, obstruction; (*anche*: **~ stradale**) traffic jam

ingoz'zare [ingot'tsare] *vt* (*animali*) to fatten; (*fig: persona*) to stuff; **~rsi** *vr*: **~rsi (di)** to stuff o.s. (with)

ingra'naggio [ingra'naddʒo] *sm* (TECN) gear; (*di orologio*) mechanism; **gli ~i della burocrazia** the bureaucratic machinery

ingra'nare *vi* to mesh, engage ♦ *vt* to engage; **~ la marcia** to get into gear

ingrandi'mento *sm* enlargement; extension

ingran'dire *vt* (*anche* FOT) to enlarge; (*estendere*) to extend; (OTTICA, *fig*) to magnify ♦ *vi* (*anche*: **~rsi**) to become larger *o* bigger; (*aumentare*) to grow, increase; (*espandersi*) to expand

ingras'sare *vt* to make fat; (*animali*) to fatten; (*lubrificare*) to oil, lubricate ♦ *vi* (*anche*: **~rsi**) to get fat, put on weight

in'grato, a *ag* ungrateful; (*lavoro*) thankless, unrewarding

ingredi'ente *sm* ingredient

in'gresso *sm* (*porta*) entrance; (*atrio*) hall; (*l'entrare*) entrance, entry; (*facoltà di entrare*) admission; **"~ libero"** "admission free"

ingros'sare *vt* to increase; (*folla, livello*) to swell ♦ *vi* (*anche*: **~rsi**) to increase; to swell

in'grosso *av*: **all'~** (COMM) wholesale; (*all'incirca*) roughly, about

ingua'ribile *ag* incurable

'inguine *sm* (ANAT) groin

ini'bire *vt* to forbid, prohibit; (PSIC) to inhibit; **inibizi'one** *sf* prohibition; inhibition

iniet'tare *vt* to inject; **~rsi** *vr*: **~rsi di sangue** (*occhi*) to become bloodshot; **iniezi'one** *sf* injection

inimi'carsi *vr*: **~ con qn** to fall out with sb

ininter'rotto, a *ag* unbroken; uninterrupted

iniquità *sf inv* iniquity; (*atto*) wicked action

inizi'ale [init'tsjale] *ag, sf* initial

inizi'are [init'tsjare] *vi, vt* to begin, start; **~ qn a** to initiate sb into; (*pittura etc*) to introduce sb to; **~ a fare qc** to start doing sth

inizia'tiva [inittsja'tiva] *sf* initiative; **~ privata** private enterprise

i'nizio [i'nittsjo] *sm* beginning; **all'~** at the beginning, at the start; **dare ~ a qc** to start sth, get sth going

innaffi'are *vt* = **annaffiare** *etc*

innal'zare [innal'tsare] *vt* (*sollevare, alzare*) to raise; (*rizzare*) to erect; **~rsi** *vr* to rise

innamo'rarsi *vr*: **~ (di qn)** to fall in love (with sb); **innamo'rato, a** *ag* (*che nutre amore*): **innamorato (di)** in love (with); (*appassionato*): **innamorato di** very fond of ♦ *sm/f* lover; sweetheart

in'nanzi [in'nantsi] *av* (*stato in luogo*) in front, ahead; (*moto a luogo*) forward, on; (*tempo: prima*) before ♦ *prep* (*prima*) before; **~ a** in front of; **innanzi'tutto** *av* first of all

in'nato, a *ag* innate

innatu'rale *ag* unnatural

inne'gabile *ag* undeniable

innervo'sire *vt*: **~ qn** to get on sb's nerves; **~rsi** *vr* to get irritated *o* upset

innes'care *vt* to prime

innes'tare *vt* (BOT, MED) to graft; (TECN) to engage; (*inserire: presa*) to insert; **in'nesto** *sm* graft; grafting *no pl*; (TECN) clutch; (ELETTR) connection

'inno *sm* hymn; **~ nazionale** national anthem

inno'cente [inno'tʃɛnte] *ag* innocent;

inno'cenza *sf* innocence

in'nocuo, a *ag* innocuous, harmless

innova'tivo, a *ag* innovative

innume'revole *ag* innumerable

ino'doro, a *ag* odourless

inol'trare *vt* (AMM) to pass on, forward; **~rsi** *vr* (addentrarsi) to advance, go forward

i'noltre *av* besides, moreover

inon'dare *vt* to flood; **inondazi'one** *sf* flooding *no pl*; flood

inope'roso, a *ag* inactive, idle

inoppor'tuno, a *ag* untimely, ill-timed; (inappropriato) inappropriate; (momento) inopportune

inorgo'glire [inorgoʎˈʎire] *vt* to make proud ♦ *vi* (anche: **~rsi**) to become proud; **~rsi di qc** to pride o.s. on sth

inorri'dire *vt* to horrify ♦ *vi* to be horrified

inospi'tale *ag* inhospitable

inosser'vato, a *ag* (non notato) unobserved; (non rispettato) not observed, not kept

inossi'dabile *ag* stainless

inqua'drare *vt* (foto, immagine) to frame; (fig) to situate, set

inquie'tare *vt* (turbare) to disturb, worry; **~rsi** *vr* to worry, become anxious; (impazientirsi) to get upset

inqui'eto, a *ag* restless; (preoccupato) worried, anxious; **inquie'tudine** *sf* anxiety, worry

inqui'lino, a *sm/f* tenant

inquina'mento *sm* pollution

inqui'nare *vt* to pollute

inqui'sire *vt, vi* to investigate; **inquisi'tore, 'trice** *ag* (sguardo) inquiring; **inquisizi'one** *sf* (STORIA) inquisition

insabbi'are *vt* (fig: pratica) to shelve; **~rsi** *vr* (arenarsi: barca) to run aground; (fig: pratica) to be shelved

insac'cati *smpl* (CUC) sausages

insa'lata *sf* salad; **~ mista** mixed salad; **insalati'era** *sf* salad bowl

insa'lubre *ag* unhealthy

insa'nabile *ag* (piaga) which cannot be healed; (situazione) irremediable; (odio) implacable

insangui'nare *vt* to stain with blood

insa'puta *sf*: **all'~ di qn** without sb knowing

insce'nare [inʃeˈnare] *vt* (TEATRO) to stage, put on; (fig) to stage

insedi'are *vt* to install; **~rsi** *vr* to take up office; (popolo, colonia) to settle

in'segna [inˈseɲɲa] *sf* sign; (emblema) sign, emblem; (bandiera) flag, banner; **~e** *sfpl* (decorazioni) insignia *pl*

insegna'mento [inseɲɲaˈmento] *sm* teaching

inse'gnante [inseɲˈɲante] *ag* teaching ♦ *sm/f* teacher

inse'gnare [inseɲˈɲare] *vt, vi* to teach; **~ a qn qc** to teach sb sth; **~ a qn a fare qc** to teach sb (how) to do sth

insegui'mento *sm* pursuit, chase

insegu'ire *vt* to pursue, chase

inselvati'chire [inselvatiˈkire] *vi* (anche: **~rsi**) to grow wild

insena'tura *sf* inlet, creek

insen'sato, a *ag* senseless, stupid

insen'sibile *ag* (nervo) insensible; (persona) indifferent

inse'rire *vt* to insert; (ELETTR) to connect; (allegare) to enclose; (annuncio) to put in, place; **~rsi** *vr* (fig): **~rsi in** to become part of; **in'serto** *sm* (pubblicazione) insert

inservi'ente *sm/f* attendant

inserzi'one [inserˈtsjone] *sf* insertion; (avviso) advertisement; **fare un'~ sul giornale** to put an advertisement in the paper

insetti'cida, i [insettiˈtʃida] *sm* insecticide

in'setto *sm* insect

insi'curo, a *ag* insecure

in'sidia *sf* snare, trap; (pericolo) hidden danger; **insidi'are** *vt*: **~ la vita di qn** to make an attempt on sb's life

insi'eme *av* together ♦ *prep*: **~ a o con** together with ♦ *sm* whole; (MAT, servizio, assortimento) set; (MODA) ensemble, outfit; **tutti ~** all together; **tutto ~** all together; (in una volta) at one go; **nell'~** on the whole; **d'~** (veduta etc) overall

in'signe [in'siɲɲe] *ag* (*persona*) famous, distinguished; (*città, monumento*) notable

insignifi'cante [insiɲɲifi'kante] *ag* insignificant

insi'gnire [insiɲ'ɲire] *vt*: ~ qn di to honour *o* decorate sb with

insin'cero, a [insin'tʃero] *ag* insincere

insinda'cabile *ag* unquestionable

insinu'are *vt* (*introdurre*): ~ qc in to slip *o* slide sth into; (*fig*) to insinuate, imply; ~rsi *vr*: ~rsi in to seep into; (*fig*) to creep into; to worm one's way into

in'sipido, a *ag* insipid

insis'tente *ag* insistent; persistent

in'sistere *vi*: ~ su qc to insist on sth; ~ in qc/a fare (*perseverare*) to persist in sth/in doing; insis'tito, a *pp di* insistere

insoddis'fatto, a *ag* dissatisfied

insoffe'rente *ag* intolerant

insolazi'one [insolat'tsjone] *sf* (*MED*) sunstroke

inso'lente *ag* insolent; insolen'tire *vi* to grow insolent ♦ *vt* to insult, be rude to

in'solito, a *ag* unusual, out of the ordinary

inso'luto, a *ag* (*non risolto*) unsolved

in'somma *av* (*in conclusione*) in short; (*dunque*) well ♦ *escl* for heaven's sake!

in'sonne *ag* sleepless; in'sonnia *sf* insomnia, sleeplessness

insonno'lito, a *ag* sleepy, drowsy

insoppor'tabile *ag* unbearable

in'sorgere [in'sordʒere] *vi* (*ribellarsi*) to rise up, rebel; (*apparire*) to come up, arise

in'sorto, a *pp di* insorgere ♦ *sm/f* rebel, insurgent

insospet'tire *vt* to make suspicious ♦ *vi* (*anche*: ~rsi) to become suspicious

inspi'rare *vt* to breathe in, inhale

in'stabile *ag* (*carico, indole*) unstable; (*tempo*) unsettled; (*equilibrio*) unsteady

instal'lare *vt* to install; ~rsi *vr* (*sistemarsi*): ~rsi in to settle in; installazi'one *sf* installation

instan'cabile *ag* untiring, indefatigable

instau'rare *vt* to introduce, institute

instra'dare *vt*: ~ (verso) to direct (towards)

insuc'cesso [insut'tʃɛsso] *sm* failure, flop

insudici'are [insudi'tʃare] *vt* to dirty; ~rsi *vr* to get dirty

insuffici'ente [insuffi'tʃɛnte] *ag* insufficient; (*compito, allievo*) inadequate; insuffici'enza *sf* insufficiency; inadequacy; (*INS*) fail

insu'lare *ag* insular

insu'lina *sf* insulin

in'sulso, a *ag* (*sciocco*) inane, silly; (*persona*) dull, insipid

insul'tare *vt* to insult, affront

in'sulto *sm* insult, affront

insussis'tente *ag* non-existent

intac'care *vt* (*fare tacche*) to cut into; (*corrodere*) to corrode; (*fig: cominciare ad usare: risparmi*) to break into; (: *ledere*) to damage

intagli'are [intaʎ'ʎare] *vt* to carve; in'taglio *sm* carving

intan'gibile [intan'dʒibile] *ag* untouchable; inviolable

in'tanto *av* (*nel frattempo*) meanwhile, in the meantime; (*per cominciare*) just to begin with; ~ che while

in'tarsio *sm* inlaying *no pl*, marquetry *no pl*; inlay

inta'sare *vt* to choke (up), block (up); (*AUT*) to obstruct, block; ~rsi *vr* to become choked *o* blocked

intas'care *vt* to pocket

in'tatto, a *ag* intact; (*puro*) unsullied

intavo'lare *vt* to start, enter into

inte'grale *ag* complete; (*pane, farina*) wholemeal (*BRIT*), whole-wheat (*US*); (*MAT*): calcolo ~ integral calculus

inte'grante *ag*: parte ~ integral part

inte'grare *vt* to complete; (*MAT*) to integrate; ~rsi *vr* (*persona*) to become integrated

integrità *sf* integrity

'integro, a *ag* (*intatto, intero*) complete, whole; (*retto*) upright

intelaia'tura *sf* frame; (*fig*) structure, framework

intel'letto *sm* intellect; intellettu'ale *ag*, *sm/f* intellectual

intelli'gente [intelli'dʒɛnte] *ag* intelligent; **intelli'genza** *sf* intelligence

intem'perie *sfpl* bad weather *sg*

intempes'tivo, a *ag* untimely

inten'dente *sm*: ~ **di Finanza** inland (*BRIT*) *o* internal (*US*) revenue officer; **inten'denza** *sf*: **intendenza di Finanza** inland (*BRIT*) *o* internal (*US*) revenue office

in'tendere *vt* (*avere intenzione*): ~ **fare qc** to intend *o* mean to do sth; (*comprendere*) to understand; (*udire*) to hear; (*significare*) to mean; **~rsi** *vr* (*conoscere*): **~rsi di** to know a lot about, be a connoisseur of; (*accordarsi*) to get on (well); **intendersela con qn** (*avere una relazione amorosa*) to have an affair with sb; **intendi'mento** *sm* (*intelligenza*) understanding; (*proposito*) intention; **intendi'tore, 'trice** *sm/f* connoisseur, expert

intene'rire *vt* (*fig*) to move (to pity); **~rsi** *vr* (*fig*) to be moved

inten'sivo, a *ag* intensive

in'tenso, a *ag* intense

in'tento, a *ag* (*teso, assorto*): ~ **(a)** intent (on), absorbed (in) ♦ *sm* aim, purpose

intenzio'nale [intentsjo'nale] *ag* intentional

intenzi'one [inten'tsjone] *sf* intention; (*DIR*) intent; **avere ~ di fare qc** to intend *o* have the intention of doing sth

interat'tivo, a *ag* interactive

interca'lare *sm* pet phrase, stock phrase ♦ *vt* to insert

interca'pedine *sf* gap, cavity

intercet'tare [intertʃet'tare] *vt* to intercept

intercity [ɪntəsɪ'tɪ] *sm inv* (*FERR*) ≈ intercity (train)

inter'detto, a *pp di* **interdire** ♦ *ag* forbidden, prohibited; (*sconcertato*) dumbfounded ♦ *sm* (*REL*) interdict

inter'dire *vt* to forbid, prohibit, ban; (*REL*) to interdict; (*DIR*) to deprive of civil rights; **interdizi'one** *sf* prohibition, ban

interessa'mento *sm* interest

interes'sante *ag* interesting; **essere in stato ~** to be expecting (a baby)

interes'sare *vt* to interest; (*concernere*) to concern, be of interest to; (*far intervenire*): ~ **qn a** to draw sb's attention to ♦ *vi*: ~ **a** to interest, matter to; **~rsi** *vr* (*mostrare interesse*): **~rsi a** to take an interest in, be interested in; (*occuparsi*): **~rsi di** to take care of

inte'resse *sm* (*anche COMM*) interest

inter'faccia, ce [inter'fattʃa] *sf* (*INFORM*) interface

interfe'renza [interfe'rɛntsa] *sf* interference

interfe'rire *vi* to interfere

interiezi'one [interjet'tsjone] *sf* exclamation, interjection

interi'ora *sfpl* entrails

interi'ore *ag* interior, inner, inside, internal; (*fig*) inner

inter'ludio *sm* (*MUS*) interlude

inter'medio, a *ag* intermediate

inter'mezzo [inter'mɛddzo] *sm* (*intervallo*) interval; (*breve spettacolo*) intermezzo

inter'nare *vt* (*arrestare*) to intern; (*MED*) to commit (to a mental institution)

inter'nauta *sm/f* (Inter)net surfer

internazio'nale [internattsjo'nale] *ag* international

'Internet ['internet] *sf* Internet; **in ~** on the Internet

in'terno, a *ag* (*di dentro*) internal, interior, inner; (*: mare*) inland; (*nazionale*) domestic; (*allievo*) boarding ♦ *sm* inside, interior; (*di paese*) interior; (*fodera*) lining; (*di appartamento*) flat (number); (*TEL*) extension ♦ *sm/f* (*INS*) boarder; **~i** *smpl* (*CINEMA*) interior shots; **all'~** inside; **Ministero degli I~i** Ministry of the Interior, ≈ Home Office (*BRIT*), Department of the Interior (*US*)

in'tero, a *ag* (*integro, intatto*) whole, entire; (*completo, totale*) complete; (*numero*) whole; (*non ridotto: biglietto*) full; (*latte*) full-cream

interpel'lare *vt* to consult

inter'porre *vt* (*ostacolo*): ~ **qc a qc** to put sth in the way of sth; (*influenza*) to use; **interporsi** *vr* to intervene; **interporsi fra** (*mettersi in mezzo*) to come between; **inter'posto, a** *pp di* **interporre**

interpre'tare *vt* to interpret; **in'terprete** *sm/f* interpreter; (*TEATRO*) actor/actress, performer; (*MUS*) performer

interregio'nale [interredʒo'nale] *sm* long

distance train (*stopping frequently*)

interro'gare *vt* to question; (*INS*) to test; **interroga'tivo, a** *ag* (*occhi, sguardo*) questioning, inquiring; (*LING*) interrogative ♦ *sm* question; (*fig*) mystery; **interroga'torio, a** *ag* interrogatory, questioning ♦ *sm* (*DIR*) questioning *no pl*; **interrogazi'one** *sf* questioning *no pl*; (*INS*) oral test

inter'rompere *vt* to interrupt; (*studi, trattative*) to break off, interrupt; **~rsi** *vr* to break off, stop; **inter'rotto, a** *pp di* **interrompere**

interrut'tore *sm* switch

interruzi'one [interrut'tsjone] *sf* interruption; break

interse'care *vt* to intersect; **~rsi** *vr* to intersect

inter'stizio [inter'stittsjo] *sm* interstice, crack

interur'bana *sf* trunk *o* long-distance call

interur'bano, a *ag* inter-city; (*TEL: chiamata*) trunk *cpd*, long-distance; (*: telefono*) long-distance

inter'vallo *sm* interval; (*spazio*) space, gap

interve'nire *vi* (*partecipare*): **~ a** to take part in; (*intromettersi: anche POL*) to intervene; (*MED: operare*) to operate; **inter'vento** *sm* participation; (*intromissione*) intervention; (*MED*) operation; **fare un intervento nel corso di** (*dibattito, programma*) to take part in

inter'vista *sf* interview; **intervis'tare** *vt* to interview

in'tesa *sf* understanding; (*accordo*) agreement, understanding

in'teso, a *pp di* **intendere** ♦ *ag* agreed; **siamo ~i?** OK?

intes'tare *vt* (*lettera*) to address; (*proprietà*): **~ a** to register in the name of; **~ un assegno a qn** to make out a cheque to sb; **intestazi'one** *sf* heading; (*su carta da lettere*) letterhead

intes'tino, a *ag* (*lotte*) internal, civil ♦ *sm* (*ANAT*) intestine

inti'mare *vt* to order, command; **intimazi'one** *sf* order, command

intimidazi'one [intimidat'tsjone] *sf* intimidation

intimi'dire *vt* to intimidate ♦ *vi* (*anche: ~rsi*) to grow shy

intimità *sf* intimacy; privacy; (*familiarità*) familiarity

'intimo, a *ag* intimate; (*affetti, vita*) private; (*fig: profondo*) inmost ♦ *sm* (*persona*) intimate *o* close friend; (*dell'animo*) bottom, depths *pl*; **parti ~e** (*ANAT*) private parts

intimo'rire *vt* to frighten; **~rsi** *vr* to become frightened

in'tingolo *sm* sauce; (*pietanza*) stew

intiriz'zire [intirid'dzire] *vt* to numb ♦ *vi* (*anche: ~rsi*) to go numb

intito'lare *vt* to give a title to; (*dedicare*) to dedicate

intolle'rabile *ag* intolerable

intolle'rante *ag* intolerant

in'tonaco, ci *o* **chi** *sm* plaster

into'nare *vt* (*canto*) to start to sing; (*armonizzare*) to match; **~rsi** *vr* (*colori*) to go together; **~rsi a** (*carnagione*) to suit; (*abito*) to go with, match

inton'tire *vt* to stun, daze ♦ *vi* (*anche: ~rsi*) to be stunned *o* dazed

in'toppo *sm* stumbling block, obstacle

in'torno *av* around; **~ a** (*attorno a*) around; (*riguardo, circa*) about

intorpi'dire *vt* to numb; (*fig*) to make sluggish ♦ *vi* (*anche: ~rsi*) to grow numb; (*fig*) to become sluggish

intossi'care *vt* to poison; **intossicazi'one** *sf* poisoning

intralci'are [intral'tʃare] *vt* to hamper, hold up

intransi'tivo, a *ag, sm* intransitive

intrapren'dente *ag* enterprising, go-ahead

intra'prendere *vt* to undertake

intrat'tabile *ag* intractable

intratte'nere *vt* to entertain; to engage in conversation; **~rsi** *vr* to linger; **~rsi su qc** to dwell on sth

intrave'dere *vt* to catch a glimpse of; (*fig*) to foresee

intrecci'are [intret'tʃare] *vt* (*capelli*) to plait, braid; (*intessere: anche fig*) to weave, interweave, intertwine; **~rsi** *vr* to intertwine, become interwoven; **~ le mani** to clasp one's hands; **in'treccio** *sm* (*fig: trama*) plot, story

intri'gare *vi* to manoeuvre (*BRIT*), maneuver (*US*); scheme; **in'trigo, ghi** *sm* plot, intrigue

in'trinseco, a, ci, che *ag* intrinsic

in'triso, a *ag*: **~ (di)** soaked (in)

intro'durre *vt* to introduce; (*chiave etc*): **~ qc in** to insert sth into; (*persone: far entrare*) to show in; **introdursi** *vr* (*moda, tecniche*) to be introduced; **introdursi in** (*persona: penetrare*) to enter; (*: entrare furtivamente*) to steal *o* slip into; **introduzi'one** *sf* introduction

in'troito *sm* income, revenue

intro'mettersi *vr* to interfere, meddle; (*interporsi*) to intervene

in'truglio [in'truʎʎo] *sm* concoction

intrusi'one *sf* intrusion; interference

in'truso, a *sm/f* intruder

intu'ire *vt* to perceive by intuition; (*rendersi conto*) to realize; **in'tuito** *sm* intuition; (*perspicacia*) perspicacity; **intuizi'one** *sf* intuition

inu'mano, a *ag* inhuman

inumi'dire *vt* to dampen, moisten; **~rsi** *vr* to become damp *o* wet

i'nutile *ag* useless; (*superfluo*) pointless, unnecessary; **inutilità** *sf* uselessness; pointlessness

inutil'mente *av* unnecessarily; (*senza risultato*) in vain

inva'dente *ag* (*fig*) interfering, nosey

in'vadere *vt* to invade; (*affollare*) to swarm into, overrun; (*sog: acque*) to flood

inva'ghirsi [inva'girsi] *vr*: **~ di** to take a fancy to

invalidità *sf* infirmity; disability; (*DIR*) invalidity

in'valido, a *ag* (*infermo*) infirm, invalid; (*al lavoro*) disabled; (*DIR: nullo*) invalid ♦ *sm/f* invalid; disabled person

in'vano *av* in vain

invasi'one *sf* invasion

in'vaso, a *pp di* **invadere**

inva'sore, invadi'trice [invadi'tritʃe] *ag* invading ♦ *sm* invader

invecchi'are [invek'kjare] *vi* (*persona*) to grow old; (*vino, popolazione*) to age; (*moda*) to become dated ♦ *vt* to age; (*far apparire più vecchio*) to make look older

in'vece [in'vetʃe] *av* instead; (*al contrario*) on the contrary; **~ di** instead of

inve'ire *vi*: **~ contro** to rail against

inven'tare *vt* to invent; (*pericoli, pettegolezzi*) to make up, invent

inven'tario *sm* inventory; (*COMM*) stocktaking *no pl*

inven'tivo, a *ag* inventive ♦ *sf* inventiveness

inven'tore *sm* inventor

invenzi'one [inven'tsjone] *sf* invention; (*bugia*) lie, story

inver'nale *ag* winter *cpd*; (*simile all'inverno*) wintry

in'verno *sm* winter

invero'simile *ag* unlikely

inversi'one *sf* inversion; reversal; **"divieto d'~"** (*AUT*) "no U-turns"

in'verso, a *ag* opposite; (*MAT*) inverse ♦ *sm* contrary, opposite; **in senso ~** in the opposite direction; **in ordine ~** in reverse order

inver'tire *vt* to invert, reverse; **~ la marcia** (*AUT*) to do a U-turn; **inver'tito, a** *sm/f* homosexual

investi'gare *vt, vi* to investigate; **investiga'tore, trice** *sm/f* investigator, detective; **investigazi'one** *sf* investigation, inquiry

investi'mento *sm* (*ECON*) investment

inves'tire *vt* (*denaro*) to invest; (*sog: veicolo: pedone*) to knock down; (*: altro veicolo*) to crash into; (*apostrofare*) to assail; (*incaricare*): **~ qn di** to invest sb with

invi'are *vt* to send; **invi'ato, a** *sm/f* envoy; (*STAMPA*) correspondent

in'vidia *sf* envy; **invidi'are** *vt*: **invidiare qn (per qc)** to envy sb for sth; **invidiare qc a qn** to envy sb sth; **invidi'oso, a** *ag* envious

in'vio, 'vii *sm* sending; (*insieme di merci*) consignment; (*tasto*) return

invipe'rito, a *ag* furious

invischi'are [invis'kjare] *vt* (*fig*): ~ **qn in** to involve sb in; **~rsi** *vr*: **~rsi (con qn/in qc)** to get mixed up *o* involved (with sb/in sth)

invi'sibile *ag* invisible

invi'tare *vt* to invite; ~ **qn a fare** to invite sb to do; **invi'tato, a** *sm/f* guest; **in'vito** *sm* invitation

invo'care *vt* (*chiedere: aiuto, pace*) to cry out for; (*appellarsi: la legge, Dio*) to appeal to, invoke

invogli'are [invoʎ'ʎare] *vt*: ~ **qn a fare** to tempt sb to do, induce sb to do

involon'tario, a *ag* (*errore*) unintentional; (*gesto*) involuntary

invol'tino *sm* (*CUC*) roulade

in'volto *sm* (*pacco*) parcel; (*fagotto*) bundle

in'volucro *sm* cover, wrapping

involuzi'one [involut'tsjone] *sf* (*di stile*) convolutedness; (*regresso*): **subire un'~** to regress

inzacche'rare [intsakke'rare] *vt* to spatter with mud

inzup'pare [intsup'pare] *vt* to soak; **~rsi** *vr* to get soaked

'io *pron* **I ♦** *sm inv*: **l'~** the ego, the self; ~ **stesso(a)** I myself

i'odio *sm* iodine

l'onio *sm*: **lo ~, il mar ~** the Ionian (Sea)

ipermer'cato *sm* hypermarket

ipertensi'one *sf* high blood pressure

iper'testo *sm* hypertext; **ipertestuale** *ag* hypertext(ual)

ip'nosi *sf* hypnosis; **ipno'tismo** *sm* hypnotism; **ipnotiz'zare** *vt* to hypnotize

ipocri'sia *sf* hypocrisy

i'pocrita, i, e *ag* hypocritical ♦ *sm/f* hypocrite

ipo'teca, che *sf* mortgage; **ipote'care** *vt* to mortgage

i'potesi *sf inv* hypothesis; **ipo'tetico, a, ci, che** *ag* hypothetical

'ippica *sf* horseracing

'ippico, a, ci, che *ag* horse *cpd*

ippocas'tano *sm* horse chestnut

ip'podromo *sm* racecourse

ippo'potamo *sm* hippopotamus

'ira *sf* anger, wrath

l'ran *sm*: **l'~** Iran

l'raq *sm*: **l'~** Iraq

'iride *sf* (*arcobaleno*) rainbow; (*ANAT, BOT*) iris

Ir'landa *sf*: **l'~** Ireland; **l'~ del Nord** Northern Ireland, Ulster; **la Repubblica d'~** Eire, the Republic of Ireland; **irlan'dese** *ag* Irish ♦ *sm/f* Irishman/woman; **gli Irlandesi** the Irish

iro'nia *sf* irony; **i'ronico, a, ci, che** *ag* ironic(al)

irradi'are *vt* to radiate; (*sog: raggi di luce: illuminare*) to shine on ♦ *vi* (*diffondersi: anche:* **~rsi**) to radiate

irragio'nevole [irradʒo'nevole] *ag* irrational; unreasonable

irrazio'nale [irrattsjo'nale] *ag* irrational

irre'ale *ag* unreal

irrecupe'rabile *ag* irretrievable; (*fig: persona*) irredeemable

irrecu'sabile *ag* (*offerta*) not to be refused; (*prova*) irrefutable

irrego'lare *ag* irregular; (*terreno*) uneven

irremo'vibile *ag* (*fig*) unyielding

irrepa'rabile *ag* irreparable; (*fig*) inevitable

irrepe'ribile *ag* nowhere to be found

irrequi'eto, a *ag* restless

irresis'tibile *ag* irresistible

irrespon'sabile *ag* irresponsible

irridu'cibile [irridu'tʃibile] *ag* irreducible; (*fig*) indomitable

irri'gare *vt* (*annaffiare*) to irrigate; (*sog: fiume etc*) to flow through; **irrigazi'one** *sf* irrigation

irrigi'dire [irridʒi'dire] *vt* to stiffen; **~rsi** *vr* to stiffen

irri'sorio, a *ag* derisory

irri'tare *vt* (*mettere di malumore*) to irritate, annoy; (*MED*) to irritate; **~rsi** *vr* (*stizzirsi*) to become irritated *o* annoyed; (*MED*) to become irritated; **irritazi'one** *sf* irritation; annoyance

ir'rompere *vi*: ~ **in** to burst into

irro'rare *vt* to sprinkle; (*AGR*) to spray
irru'ente *ag* (*fig*) impetuous, violent
irruzi'one [irrut'tsjone] *sf*: **fare ~ in** to burst into; (*sog: polizia*) to raid
'irto, a *ag* bristly; **~ di** bristling with
is'critto, a *pp di* **iscrivere** ♦ *sm/f* member; **per** *o* **in ~** in writing
is'crivere *vt* to register, enter; (*persona*): **~ (a)** to register (in), enrol (in); **~rsi** *vr*: **~rsi (a)** (*club, partito*) to join; (*università*) to register *o* enrol (at); (*esame, concorso*) to register *o* enter (for); **iscrizi'one** *sf* (*epigrafe etc*) inscription; (*a scuola, società*) enrolment, registration; (*registrazione*) registration
Is'lam *sm*: **l'~** Islam
Is'landa *sf*: **l'~** Iceland
'isola *sf* island; **~ pedonale** (*AUT*) pedestrian precinct
isola'mento *sm* isolation; (*TECN*) insulation
iso'lante *ag* insulating ♦ *sm* insulator
iso'lare *vt* to isolate; (*TECN*) to insulate; (*: acusticamente*) to soundproof; **iso'lato, a** *ag* isolated; insulated ♦ *sm* (*gruppo di edifici*) block
ispetto'rato *sm* inspectorate
ispet'tore *sm* inspector
ispezio'nare [ispettsjo'nare] *vt* to inspect; **ispezi'one** *sf* inspection
'ispido, a *ag* bristly, shaggy
ispi'rare *vt* to inspire; **~rsi** *vr*: **~rsi a** to draw one's inspiration from
Isra'ele *sm*: **l'~** Israel; **israeli'ano, a** *ag, sm/f* Israeli
is'sare *vt* to hoist
istan'taneo, a *ag* instantaneous ♦ *sf* (*FOT*) snapshot
is'tante *sm* instant, moment; **all'~, sull'~** instantly, immediately
is'tanza [is'tantsa] *sf* petition, request
is'terico, a, ci, che *ag* hysterical
iste'rismo *sm* hysteria
isti'gare *vt* to incite; **istigazi'one** *sf* incitement; **istigazione a delinquere** (*DIR*) incitement to crime
is'tinto *sm* instinct
istitu'ire *vt* (*fondare*) to institute, found;

(*porre: confronto*) to establish; (*intraprendere: inchiesta*) to set up
isti'tuto *sm* institute; (*di università*) department; (*ente, DIR*) institution; **~ di bellezza** beauty salon
istituzi'one [istitut'tsjone] *sf* institution
'istmo *sm* (*GEO*) isthmus
'istrice ['istritʃe] *sm* porcupine
istri'one (*peg*) *sm* ham actor
istru'ire *vt* (*insegnare*) to teach; (*ammaestrare*) to train; (*informare*) to instruct, inform; (*DIR*) to prepare; **istrut'tore, 'trice** *sm/f* instructor ♦ *ag*: **giudice istruttore** *vedi* **giudice**; **istrut'toria** *sf* (*DIR*) (preliminary) investigation and hearing; **istruzi'one** *sf* education; training; (*direttiva*) instruction
l'talia *sf*: **l'~** Italy
itali'ano, a *ag* Italian ♦ *sm/f* Italian ♦ *sm* (*LING*) Italian; **gli I~i** the Italians
itine'rario *sm* itinerary
itte'rizia [itte'rittsja] *sf* (*MED*) jaundice
'ittico, a, ci, che *ag* fish *cpd*; fishing *cpd*
lugos'lavia *etc* = **Jugoslavia** *etc*
i'uta *sf* jute
I.V.A. ['iva] *sigla f* (= *imposta sul valore aggiunto*) VAT

J, j

jazz [dʒaz] *sm* jazz
jeans [dʒinz] *smpl* jeans
Jugos'lavia [jugoz'lavja] *sf*: **la ~** Yugoslavia; **la ex-~** former Yugoslavia; **jugos'lavo, a** *ag, sm/f* Yugoslav(ian)
'juta ['juta] *sf* = **iuta**

K, k

K *abbr* (*INFORM*) K
k *abbr* (= *kilo*) k
karatè *sm* karate
Kg *abbr* (= *chilogrammo*) kg
'killer *sm inv* gunman, hired gun
'kiwi ['kiwi] *sm inv* kiwi fruit

km *abbr* (= *chilometro*) km
koso'varo, a *sm/f, ag* Kosovar
'krapfen *sm inv* (*CUC*) doughnut

L, l

l' *det vedi* **la; lo; il**
la[1] (*dav V* **l'**) *det f* the ♦ *pron* (*oggetto: persona*) her; (: *cosa*) it; (: *forma di cortesia*) you; *vedi anche* **il**
la[2] *sm inv* (*MUS*) A; (: *solfeggiando*) la
là *av* there; (: *da quel luogo*) from there; (*in quel luogo*) in there; (*dall'altra parte*) over there; **di ~ di** beyond; **per di ~** that way; **più in ~** further on; (*tempo*) later on; **fatti in ~** move up; **~ dentro/sopra/sotto** in/up (*o* on)/under there; *vedi anche* **quello**
'labbro (*pl(f)*: **labbra**: *solo nel senso ANAT*) *sm* lip
labi'rinto *sm* labyrinth, maze
labora'torio *sm* (*di ricerca*) laboratory; (*di arti, mestieri*) workshop
labori'oso *ag* (*faticoso*) laborious; (*attivo*) hard-working
labu'rista, i, e *ag* Labour (*BRIT*) *cpd* ♦ *sm/f* Labour Party member (*BRIT*)
'lacca, che *sf* lacquer
'laccio ['lattʃo] *sm* noose; (*legaccio, tirante*) lasso; (*di scarpa*) lace; **~ emostatico** tourniquet
lace'rare [latʃe'rare] *vt* to tear to shreds, lacerate; **~rsi** *vr* to tear; **'lacero, a** *ag* (*logoro*) torn, tattered; (*MED*) lacerated
'lacrima *sf* tear; **in ~e** in tears; **lacri'mare** *vi* to water; **lacri'mogeno, a** *ag*: **gas lacrimogeno** tear gas
la'cuna *sf* (*fig*) gap
'ladro *sm* thief; **ladro'cinio** *sm* theft, larceny
laggiù [lad'dʒu] *av* down there; (*di là*) over there
la'gnarsi [laɲ'ɲarsi] *vr*: **~ (di)** to complain (about)
'lago, ghi *sm* lake
la'guna *sf* lagoon

'laico, a, ci, che *ag* (*apostolato*) lay; (*vita*) secular; (*scuola*) non-denominational ♦ *sm/f* layman/woman
'lama *sm inv* (*ZOOL*) llama; (*REL*) lama ♦ *sf* blade
lam'bire *vt* to lick; to lap
lamen'tare *vt* to lament; **~rsi** *vr* (*emettere lamenti*) to moan, groan; (*rammaricarsi*): **~rsi (di)** to complain (about); **lamen'tela** *sf* complaining *no pl*; **lamen'tevole** *ag* (*voce*) complaining, plaintive; (*destino*) pitiful; **la'mento** *sm* moan, groan; wail; **lamen'toso, a** *ag* plaintive
la'metta *sf* razor blade
lami'era *sf* sheet metal
'lamina *sf* (*lastra sottile*) thin sheet (*o* layer *o* plate); **~ d'oro** gold leaf; gold foil; **lami'nare** *vt* to laminate; **lami'nato, a** *ag* laminated; (*tessuto*) lamé ♦ *sm* laminate
'lampada *sf* lamp; **~ a gas** gas lamp; **~ da tavolo** table lamp
lampa'dario *sm* chandelier
lampa'dina *sf* light bulb; **~ tascabile** pocket torch (*BRIT*) *o* flashlight (*US*)
lam'pante *ag* (*fig: evidente*) crystal clear, evident
lampeggi'are [lamped'dʒare] *vi* (*luce, fari*) to flash ♦ *vb impers*: **lampeggia** there's lightning; **lampeggia'tore** *sm* (*AUT*) indicator
lampi'one *sm* street light *o* lamp (*BRIT*)
'lampo *sm* (*METEOR*) flash of lightning; (*di luce, fig*) flash; **~i** *smpl* lightning *no pl* ♦ *ag inv*: **cerniera ~** zip (fastener) (*BRIT*), zipper (*US*); **guerra ~** blitzkrieg
lam'pone *sm* raspberry
'lana *sf* wool; **~ d'acciaio** steel wool; **pura ~ vergine** pure new wool; **~ di vetro** glass wool
lan'cetta [lan'tʃetta] *sf* (*indice*) pointer, needle; (*di orologio*) hand
'lancia ['lantʃa] *sf* (*arma*) lance; (: *picca*) spear; (*di pompa antincendio*) nozzle; (*imbarcazione*) launch
lanciafi'amme [lantʃa'fjamme] *sm inv* flamethrower
lanci'are [lan'tʃare] *vt* to throw, hurl, fling;

(SPORT) to throw; (*far partire: automobile*) to get up to full speed; (*bombe*) to drop; (*razzo, prodotto, moda*) to launch; **~rsi** *vr*: **~rsi contro/su** to throw *o* hurl *o* fling o.s. against/on; **~rsi in** (*fig*) to embark on

lanci'nante [lantʃi'nante] *ag* (*dolore*) shooting, throbbing; (*grido*) piercing

'**lancio** ['lantʃo] *sm* throwing *no pl*; throw; dropping *no pl*; drop; launching *no pl*; launch; **~ del peso** putting the shot

'**landa** *sf* (GEO) moor

'**languido, a** *ag* (*fiacco*) languid, weak; (*tenero, malinconico*) languishing

langu'ore *sm* weakness, languor

lani'ficio [lani'fitʃo] *sm* woollen mill

la'noso, a *ag* woolly

lan'terna *sf* lantern; (*faro*) lighthouse

la'nugine [la'nudʒine] *sf* down

lapi'dario, a *ag* (*fig*) terse

'**lapide** *sf* (*di sepolcro*) tombstone; (*commemorativa*) plaque

'**lapis** *sm inv* pencil

Lap'ponia *sf* Lapland

'**lapsus** *sm inv* slip

'**laptop** ['læptɔp] *sm inv* laptop (computer)

'**lardo** *sm* bacon fat, lard

lar'ghezza [lar'gettsa] *sf* width; breadth; looseness; generosity; (*mare aperto*) broad-mindedness

'**largo, a, ghi, ghe** *ag* wide; broad; (*maniche*) wide; (*abito: troppo ampio*) loose; (*fig*) generous ♦ *sm* width; breadth; (*mare aperto*): **il ~** the open sea ♦ *sf*: **stare** *o* **tenersi alla ~a (da qn/qc)** to keep one's distance (from sb/sth), keep away (from sb/sth); **~ due metri** two metres wide; **~ di spalle** broad-shouldered; **di ~ghe vedute** broad-minded; **su ~a scala** on a large scale; **di manica ~a** generous, open-handed; **al ~ di Genova** off (the coast of) Genoa; **farsi ~ tra la folla** to push one's way through the crowd

'**larice** ['laritʃe] *sm* (BOT) larch

larin'gite [larin'dʒite] *sf* laryngitis

'**larva** *sf* larva; (*fig*) shadow

la'sagne [la'zaɲɲe] *sfpl* lasagna *sg*

lasci'are [laʃ'ʃare] *vt* to leave;

(*abbandonare*) to leave, abandon, give up; (*cessare di tenere*) to let go of ♦ *vb aus*: **~ fare qn** to let sb do; **~ andare** *o* **correre** *o* **perdere** to let things go their own way; **~ stare qc/qn** to leave sth/sb alone; **~rsi** *vr* (*persone*) to part; (*coppia*) to split up; **~rsi andare** to let o.s. go

'**lascito** [la'ʃʃito] *sm* (DIR) legacy

'**laser** ['lazer] *ag, sm inv*: **(raggio) ~** laser (beam)

lassa'tivo, a *ag, sm* laxative

'**lasso** *sm*: **~ di tempo** interval, lapse of time

las'sù *av* up there

'**lastra** *sf* (*di pietra*) slab; (*di metallo, FOT*) plate; (*di ghiaccio, vetro*) sheet; (*radiografica*) X-ray (plate)

lastri'cato *sm* paving

late'rale *ag* lateral, side *cpd*; (*uscita, ingresso etc*) side *cpd* ♦ *sm* (CALCIO) half-back

late'rizio [late'rittsjo] *sm* (perforated) brick

lati'fondo *sm* large estate

la'tino, a *ag, sm* Latin; **~-ameri'cano, a** *ag* Latin-American

lati'tante *sm/f* fugitive (from justice)

lati'tudine *sf* latitude

'**lato, a** *ag* (*fig*) wide, broad ♦ *sm* side; (*fig*) aspect, point of view; **in senso ~** broadly speaking

la'trare *vi* to bark

la'trina *sf* public lavatory

'**latta** *sf* tin (plate); (*recipiente*) tin, can

lat'taio, a *sm/f* milkman/woman; dairyman/woman

lat'tante *ag* unweaned

'**latte** *sm* milk; **~ detergente** cleansing milk *o* lotion; **~ in polvere** dried *o* powdered milk; **~ scremato** skimmed milk; **latte'ria** *sf* dairy; **latti'cini** *smpl* dairy products

lat'tina *sf* (*di birra etc*) can

lat'tuga, ghe *sf* lettuce

la'urea *sf* degree; **laurearsi** *vr* to graduate; **laure'ato, a** *ag, sm/f* graduate

'**lauro** *sm* laurel

'**lauto, a** *ag* (*pranzo, mancia*) lavish

'**lava** *sf* lava

la'vabo *sm* washbasin

la'vaggio [la'vaddʒo] *sm* washing *no pl*; ~ **del cervello** brainwashing *no pl*

la'vagna [la'vaɲɲa] *sf* (*GEO*) slate; (*di scuola*) blackboard

la'vanda *sf* (*anche MED*) wash; (*BOT*) lavender; lavan'daia *sf* washerwoman; lavande'ria *sf* laundry; **lavanderia automatica** launderette; **lavanderia a secco** dry-cleaner's; lavan'dino *sm* sink

lavapi'atti *sm/f* dishwasher

la'vare *vt* to wash; ~rsi *vr* to wash, have a wash; ~ **a secco** to dry-clean; ~rsi le **mani/i denti** to wash one's hands/clean one's teeth

lava'secco *sm o f inv* drycleaner's

lavasto'viglie [lavasto'viʎʎe] *sm o f inv* (*macchina*) dishwasher

lava'trice [lava'tritʃe] *sf* washing machine

lava'tura *sf* washing *no pl*; ~ **di piatti** dishwater

lavo'rante *sm/f* worker

lavo'rare *vi* to work; (*fig: bar, studio etc*) to do good business ♦ *vt* to work; ~rsi qn (*persuaderlo*) to work on sb; ~ **a** to work on; ~ **a maglia** to knit; lavora'tivo, a *ag* working; lavora'tore, 'trice *sm/f* worker ♦ *ag* working; lavorazi'one *sf* (*gen*) working; (*di legno, pietra*) carving; (*di film*) making; (*di prodotto*) manufacture; (*modo di esecuzione*) workmanship; lavo'rio *sm* intense activity

la'voro *sm* work; (*occupazione*) job, work *no pl*; (*opera*) piece of work, job; (*ECON*) labour; ~i forzati hard labour *sg*; ~i pubblici public works

le *det fpl* the ♦ *pron* (*oggetto*) them; (: *a lei, a essa*) (to) her; (: *forma di cortesia*) (to) you; *vedi anche* il

le'ale *ag* loyal; (*sincero*) sincere; (*onesto*) fair; lealtà *sf* loyalty; sincerity; fairness

'lebbra *sf* leprosy

'lecca 'lecca *sm inv* lollipop

leccapi'edi (*peg*) *sm/f inv* toady, bootlicker

lec'care *vt* to lick; (*sog: gatto: latte etc*) to lick *o* lap up; (*fig*) to flatter; ~rsi i baffi to lick one's lips

'leccio ['lettʃo] *sm* holm oak, ilex

leccor'nia *sf* titbit, delicacy

'lecito, a ['lɛtʃito] *ag* permitted, allowed

'ledere *vt* to damage, injure

'lega, ghe *sf* league; (*di metalli*) alloy

le'gaccio [le'gattʃo] *sm* string, lace

le'gale *ag* legal ♦ *sm* lawyer; legaliz'zare *vt* to authenticate; (*regolarizzare*) to legalize

le'game *sm* (*corda, fig: affettivo*) tie, bond; (*nesso logico*) link, connection

le'gare *vt* (*prigioniero, capelli, cane*) to tie (up); (*libro*) to bind; (*CHIM*) to alloy; (*fig: collegare*) to bind, join ♦ *vi* (*far lega*) to unite; (*fig*) to get on well

le'gato *sm* (*REL*) legate; (*DIR*) legacy, bequest

lega'tura *sf* (*di libro*) binding; (*MUS*) ligature

le'genda [le'dʒɛnda] *sf* (*di carta geografica etc*) = leggenda

'legge ['leddʒe] *sf* law

leg'genda [led'dʒɛnda] *sf* (*narrazione*) legend; (*di carta geografica etc*) key, legend

'leggere ['leddʒere] *vt, vi* to read

legge'rezza [leddʒe'rettsa] *sf* lightness; thoughtlessness; fickleness

leg'gero, a [led'dʒɛro] *ag* light; (*agile, snello*) nimble, agile, light; (*tè, caffè*) weak; (*fig: non grave, piccolo*) slight; (: *spensierato*) thoughtless; (: *incostante*) fickle; free and easy; alla ~a thoughtlessly

leggi'adro, a [led'dʒadro] *ag* pretty, lovely; (*movimenti*) graceful

leg'gio, 'gii [led'dʒio] *sm* lectern; (*MUS*) music stand

legisla'tura [ledʒizla'tura] *sf* legislature

legislazi'one [ledʒizlat'tsjone] *sf* legislation

le'gittimo, a [le'dʒittimo] *ag* legitimate; (*fig: giustificato, lecito*) justified, legitimate; ~a difesa (*DIR*) self-defence

'legna ['leɲɲa] *sf* firewood; le'gname *sm* wood, timber

'legno ['leɲɲo] *sm* wood; (*pezzo di ~*) piece of wood; di ~ wooden; ~ compensato plywood; **le'gnoso, a** *ag* wooden; woody; (*carne*) tough

le'gumi *smpl* (*BOT*) pulses

'lei *pron* (*soggetto*) she; (*oggetto: per dare rilievo, con preposizione*) her; (*forma di cortesia: anche:* **L~**) you ♦ *sm*: **dare del ~ a qn** to address sb as "lei"; **~ stessa** she herself; you yourself

'lembo *sm* (*di abito, strada*) edge; (*striscia sottile: di terra*) strip

'lemma, i *sm* headword

'lemme 'lemme *av* (very) very slowly

'lena *sf* (*fig*) energy, stamina

le'nire *vt* to soothe

lenta'mente *av* slowly

'lente *sf* (*OTTICA*) lens *sg*; **~ d'ingrandimento** magnifying glass; **~i a contatto** *o* **corneali** contact lenses

len'tezza [len'tettsa] *sf* slowness

len'ticchia [len'tikkja] *sf* (*BOT*) lentil

len'tiggine [len'tiddʒine] *sf* freckle

'lento, a *ag* slow; (*molle: fune*) slack; (*non stretto: vite, abito*) loose ♦ *sm* (*ballo*) slow dance

'lenza ['lentsa] *sf* fishing-line

lenzu'olo [len'tswɔlo] *sm* sheet; **~a** *sfpl* pair of sheets

le'one *sm* lion; (*dello zodiaco*): **L~** Leo

lepo'rino, a *ag*: **labbro ~** harelip

'lepre *sf* hare

'lercio, a, ci, cie ['lɛrtʃo] *ag* filthy

'lesbica, che *sf* lesbian

lesi'nare *vt* to be stingy with ♦ *vi*: **~ (su)** to skimp (on), be stingy (with)

lesi'one (*MED*) lesion; (*DIR*) injury, damage; (*EDIL*) crack

'leso, a *pp di* **ledere** ♦ *ag* (*offeso*) injured; **parte ~a** (*DIR*) injured party

les'sare *vt* (*CUC*) to boil

'lessico, ci *sm* vocabulary; lexicon

'lesso, a *ag* boiled ♦ *sm* boiled meat

'lesto, a *ag* quick; (*agile*) nimble; **~ di mano** (*per rubare*) light-fingered; (*per picchiare*) free with one's fists

le'tale *ag* lethal; fatal

leta'maio *sm* dunghill

le'tame *sm* manure, dung

le'targo, ghi *sm* lethargy; (*ZOOL*) hibernation

le'tizia [le'tittsja] *sf* joy, happiness

'lettera *sf* letter; **~e** *sfpl* (*letteratura*) literature *sg*; (*studi umanistici*) arts (subjects); **alla ~** literally; **in ~e** in words, in full; **lette'rale** *ag* literal

lette'rario, a *ag* literary

lette'rato, a *ag* well-read, scholarly

lettera'tura *sf* literature

let'tiga, ghe *sf* (*barella*) stretcher

let'tino *sm* cot (*BRIT*), crib (*US*)

'letto, a *pp di* **leggere** ♦ *sm* bed; **andare a ~** to go to bed; **~ a castello** bunk beds *pl*; **~ a una piazza/a due piazze** *o* **matrimoniale** single/double bed

let'tore, 'trice *sm/f* reader; (*INS*) (foreign language) assistant (*BRIT*), (foreign) teaching assistant (*US*) ♦ *sm* (*TECN*): **~ ottico** optical character reader

let'tura *sf* reading

leuce'mia [leutʃe'mia] *sf* leukaemia

'leva *sf* lever; (*MIL*) conscription; **far ~ su qn** to work on sb; **~ del cambio** (*AUT*) gear lever

le'vante *sm* east; (*vento*) East wind; **il L~** the Levant

le'vare *vt* (*occhi, braccio*) to raise; (*sollevare, togliere: tassa, divieto*) to lift; (*indumenti*) to take off, remove; (*rimuovere*) to take away; (: *dal di sopra*) to take off; (: *dal di dentro*) to take out; **~rsi** *vr* to get up; (*sole*) to rise; **le'vata** *sf* (*di posta*) collection

leva'toio, a *ag*: **ponte ~** drawbridge

leva'tura *sf* intelligence, mental capacity

levi'gare *vt* to smooth; (*con carta vetrata*) to sand

levri'ere *sm* greyhound

lezi'one [let'tsjone] *sf* lesson; (*UNIV*) lecture; **fare ~** to teach; to lecture; **dare una ~ a qn** to teach sb a lesson

lezi'oso, a [let'tsjoso] *ag* affected; simpering

'lezzo ['leddzo] *sm* stench, stink

li *pron pl* (*oggetto*) them

lì *av* there; **di** *o* **da ~** from there; **per di ~** that way; **di ~ a pochi giorni** a few days later; **~ per ~** there and then; at first; **essere ~ (~) per fare** to be on the point of doing, be about to do; **~ dentro** in there; **~ sotto** under there; **~ sopra** on there; up there; *vedi anche* **quello**

liba'nese *ag, sm/f* Lebanese *inv*

Li'bano *sm*: **il ~** the Lebanon

'libbra *sf (peso)* pound

li'beccio [li'bettʃo] *sm* south-west wind

li'bello *sm* libel

li'bellula *sf* dragonfly

libe'rale *ag, sm/f* liberal

liberaliz'zare [liberalid'dzare] *vt* to liberalize

libe'rare *vt (rendere libero: prigioniero)* to release; *(: popolo)* to free, liberate; *(sgombrare: passaggio)* to clear; *(: stanza)* to vacate; *(produrre: energia)* to release; **~rsi** *vr*: **~rsi di qc/qn** to get rid of sth/sb; **libera'tore, 'trice** *ag* liberating ♦ *sm/f* liberator; **liberazi'one** *sf* liberation, freeing; release; rescuing

---

Liberazione

ⓘ The **Liberazione** *is a national holiday which falls on 25 April. It commemorates the liberation of Italy at the end of the Second World War.*

'libero, a *ag* free; *(strada)* clear; *(non occupata: posto etc)* vacant; not taken; empty; not engaged; **~ di fare qc** free to do sth; **~ da** free from; **~ arbitrio** free will; **~ professionista** self-employed professional person; **~ scambio** free trade; **libertà** *sf inv* freedom; *(tempo disponibile)* free time ♦ *sfpl (licenza)* liberties; **in libertà provvisoria/vigilata** released without bail/on probation

'Libia *sf*: **la ~** Libya; **'libico, a, ci, che** *ag, sm/f* Libyan

li'bidine *sf* lust

li'braio *sm* bookseller

li'brarsi *vr* to hover

libre'ria *sf (bottega)* bookshop; *(stanza)* library; *(mobile)* bookcase

li'bretto *sm* booklet; *(taccuino)* notebook; *(MUS)* libretto; **~ degli assegni** cheque book; **~ di circolazione** *(AUT)* logbook; **~ di risparmio** *(savings)* bank-book, passbook; **~ universitario** student's report book

'libro *sm* book; **~ di cassa** cash book; **~ mastro** ledger; **~ paga** payroll; **~ di testo** textbook

li'cenza [li'tʃɛntsa] *sf (permesso)* permission, leave; *(di pesca, caccia, circolazione)* permit, licence; *(MIL)* leave; *(INS)* school leaving certificate; *(libertà)* liberty; licence; licentiousness; **andare in ~** *(MIL)* to go on leave

licenzia'mento [litʃentsja'mento] *sm* dismissal

licenzi'are [litʃen'tsjare] *vt (impiegato)* to dismiss; *(COMM: per eccesso di personale)* to make redundant; *(INS)* to award a certificate to; **~rsi** *vr (impiegato)* to resign, hand in one's notice; *(INS)* to obtain one's school-leaving certificate

li'ceo [li'tʃɛo] *sm (INS)* secondary *(BRIT)* or high *(US)* school *(for 14- to 19-year-olds)*

'lido *sm* beach, shore

li'eto, a *ag* happy, glad; **"molto ~"** *(nelle presentazioni)* "pleased to meet you"

li'eve *ag* light; *(di poco conto)* slight; *(sommesso: voce)* faint, soft

lievi'tare *vi (anche fig)* to rise ♦ *vt* to leaven

li'evito *sm* yeast; **~ di birra** brewer's yeast

'ligio, a, gi, gie ['lidʒo] *ag* faithful, loyal

'lilla *sm inv* lilac

'lillà *sm inv* lilac

'lima *sf* file

limacci'oso, a [limat'tʃoso] *ag* slimy; muddy

li'mare *vt* to file (down); *(fig)* to polish

'limbo *sm (REL)* limbo

li'metta *sf* nail file

limi'tare *vt* to limit, restrict; *(circoscrivere)* to bound, surround; **limita'tivo, a** *ag* limiting, restricting; **limi'tato, a** *ag* limited, restricted

'limite *sm* limit; *(confine)* border, boundary; **~ di velocità** speed limit

li'mitrofo, a *ag* neighbouring

limo'nata *sf* lemonade (*BRIT*), (lemon) soda (*US*); lemon squash (*BRIT*), lemonade (*US*)

li'mone *sm* (*pianta*) lemon tree; (*frutto*) lemon

'limpido, a *ag* clear; (*acqua*) limpid, clear

'lince ['lintʃe] *sf* lynx

linci'are *vt* to lynch

'lindo, a *ag* tidy, spick and span; (*biancheria*) clean

'linea *sf* line; (*di mezzi pubblici di trasporto: itinerario*) route; (: *servizio*) service; **a grandi ~e** in outline; **mantenere la ~** to look after one's figure; **aereo di ~** airliner; **nave di ~** liner; **volo di ~** scheduled flight; **~ aerea** airline; **~ cortesia ~ di partenza/ d'arrivo** (*SPORT*) starting/finishing line; **~ di tiro** line of fire

linea'menti *smpl* features; (*fig*) outlines

line'are *ag* linear; (*fig*) coherent, logical

line'etta *sf* (*trattino*) dash; (*d'unione*) hyphen

lin'gotto *sm* ingot, bar

'lingua *sf* (*ANAT, CUC*) tongue; (*idioma*) language; **mostrare la ~** to stick out one's tongue; **di ~ italiana** Italian-speaking; **~ madre** mother tongue; **una ~ di terra** a spit of land

lingu'aggio [lin'gwaddʒo] *sm* language

lingu'etta *sf* (*di strumento*) reed; (*di scarpa, TECN*) tongue; (*di busta*) flap

lingu'istica *sf* linguistics *sg*

'lino *sm* (*pianta*) flax; (*tessuto*) linen

li'noleum *sm inv* linoleum, lino

liposuzi'one [liposut'tsjone] *sf* liposuction

lique'fare *vt* (*render liquido*) to liquefy; (*fondere*) to melt; **~rsi** *vr* to liquefy; to melt

liqui'dare *vt* (*società, beni, persona: uccidere*) to liquidate; (*persona: sbarazzarsene*) to get rid of; (*conto, problema*) to settle; (*COMM: merce*) to sell off, clear; **liquidazi'one** *sf* liquidation; settlement; clearance sale

liquidità *sf* liquidity

'liquido, a *ag, sm* liquid; **~ per freni** brake fluid

liqui'rizia [likwi'rittsja] *sf* liquorice

li'quore *sm* liqueur

'lira *sf* (*unità monetaria*) lira; (*MUS*) lyre; **~ sterlina** pound sterling

'lirica, che *sf* (*poesia*) lyric poetry; (*componimento poetico*) lyric; (*MUS*) opera

'lirico, a, ci, che *ag* lyric(al); (*MUS*) lyric; **cantante/teatro ~** opera singer/house

'lisca, sche *sf* (*di pesce*) fishbone

lisci'are [liʃ'ʃare] *vt* to smooth; (*fig*) to flatter

'liscio, a, sci, sce ['liʃʃo] *ag* smooth; (*capelli*) straight; (*mobile*) plain; (*bevanda alcolica*) neat; (*fig*) straightforward, simple ♦ *av*: **andare ~** to go smoothly; **passarla ~a** to get away with it

'liso, a *ag* worn out, threadbare

'lista *sf* (*elenco*) list; **~ elettorale** electoral roll; **~ delle vivande** menu; **~ delle spese** shopping list

lis'tino *sm* list; **~ dei cambi** (foreign) exchange rate; **~ dei prezzi** price list

Lit. *abbr* = **lire italiane**

'lite *sf* quarrel, argument; (*DIR*) lawsuit

liti'gare *vi* to quarrel; (*DIR*) to litigate

li'tigio [li'tidʒo] *sm* quarrel; **litigi'oso, a** *ag* quarrelsome; (*DIR*) litigious

litogra'fia *sf* (*sistema*) lithography; (*stampa*) lithograph

lito'rale *ag* coastal, coast *cpd* ♦ *sm* coast

'litro *sm* litre

livel'lare *vt* to level, make level; **~rsi** *vr* to become level; (*fig*) to level out, balance out

li'vello *sm* level; (*fig*) level, standard; **ad alto ~** (*fig*) high-level; **~ del mare** sea level

'livido, a *ag* livid; (*per percosse*) bruised, black and blue; (*cielo*) leaden ♦ *sm* bruise

li'vore *sm* malice, spite

Li'vorno *sf* Livorno, Leghorn

li'vrea *sf* livery

'lizza ['littsa] *sf* lists *pl*; **scendere in ~** (*anche fig*) to enter the lists

lo (*dav s impura, gn, pn, ps, x, z; dav V* **l'**) *det m* the ♦ *pron* (*oggetto: persona*) him; (: *cosa*) it; **~ sapevo** I knew it; **~ so** I know; **sii buono, anche se lui non ~ è** be good, even if he isn't; *vedi anche* **il**

lo'cale *ag* local ♦ *sm* room; (*luogo pubblico*) premises *pl*; **~ notturno** nightclub;

località *sf inv* locality; **localiz'zare** *vt* (*circoscrivere*) to confine, localize; (*accertare*) to locate, place

lo'canda *sf* inn; **locandi'ere, a** *sm/f* innkeeper

loca'tario, a *sm/f* tenant

loca'tore, 'trice *sm/f* landlord/lady

locazi'one [lokat'tsjone] *sf* (*da parte del locatario*) renting *no pl*; (*da parte del locatore*) renting out *no pl*, letting *no pl*; **(contratto di)** ~ lease; **(canone di)** ~ rent; **dare in** ~ to rent out, let

locomo'tiva *sf* locomotive

locomo'tore *sm* electric locomotive

locomozi'one [lokomot'tsjone] *sf* locomotion; **mezzi di** ~ vehicles, means of transport

lo'custa *sf* locust

locuzi'one [lokut'tsjone] *sf* phrase, expression

lo'dare *vt* to praise

'lode *sf* praise; (*INS*): **laurearsi con 110 e** ~ ≈ to graduate with a first-class honours degree (*BRIT*), graduate summa cum laude (*US*)

'loden *sm inv* (*stoffa*) loden; (*cappotto*) loden overcoat

lo'devole *ag* praiseworthy

loga'ritmo *sm* logarithm

'loggia, ge ['lɔddʒa] *sf* (*ARCHIT*) loggia; (*circolo massonico*) lodge; **loggi'one** *sm* (*di teatro*): **il loggione** the Gods *sg*

'logica *sf* logic

'logico, a, ci, che ['lɔdʒiko] *ag* logical

logo'rare *vt* to wear out; (*sciupare*) to waste; **~rsi** *vr* to wear out; (*fig*) to wear o.s. out

logo'rio *sm* wear and tear; (*fig*) strain

'logoro, a *ag* (*stoffa*) worn out, threadbare; (*persona*) worn out

lom'baggine [lom'baddʒine] *sf* lumbago

Lombar'dia *sf*: **la** ~ Lombardy

lom'bata *sf* (*taglio di carne*) loin

'lombo *sm* (*ANAT*) loin

lom'brico, chi *sm* earthworm

londi'nese *ag* London *cpd* ♦ *sm/f* Londoner

'Londra *sf* London

lon'gevo, a [lon'dʒevo] *ag* long-lived

longi'tudine [londʒi'tudine] *sf* longitude

lonta'nanza [lonta'nantsa] *sf* distance; absence

lon'tano, a *ag* (*distante*) distant, faraway; (*assente*) absent; (*vago: sospetto*) slight, remote; (*tempo: remoto*) far-off, distant; (*parente*) distant, remote ♦ *av* far; **è ~a la casa?** is it far to the house?, is the house far from here?; **è ~ un chilometro** it's a kilometre away *o* a kilometre from here; **più** ~ farther; **da** *o* **di** ~ from a distance; ~ **da** a long way from; **alla ~a** slightly, vaguely

'lontra *sf* otter

lo'quace [lo'kwatʃe] *ag* talkative, loquacious; (*gesto etc*) eloquent

'lordo, a *ag* dirty, filthy; (*peso, stipendio*) gross

'loro *pron pl* (*oggetto, con preposizione*) them; (*complemento di termine*) to them; (*soggetto*) they; (*forma di cortesia: anche:* **L~**) you; to you; **il(la)** ~, **i(le)** ~ *det* their; (*forma di cortesia: anche:* **L~**) your ♦ *pron* theirs; (*forma di cortesia: anche:* **L~**) yours; ~ **stessi(e)** they themselves; you yourselves

'losco, a, schi, sche *ag* (*fig*) shady, suspicious

'lotta *sf* struggle, fight; (*SPORT*) wrestling; ~ **libera** all-in wrestling; **lot'tare** *vi* to fight, struggle; to wrestle; **lotta'tore, trice** *sm/f* wrestler

lotte'ria *sf* lottery; (*di gara ippica*) sweepstake

'lotto *sm* (*gioco*) (state) lottery; (*parte*) lot; (*EDIL*) site

lozi'one [lot'tsjone] *sf* lotion

lubrifi'cante *sm* lubricant

lubrifi'care *vt* to lubricate

luc'chetto [luk'ketto] *sm* padlock

lucci'care [luttʃi'kare] *vi* to sparkle, glitter, twinkle

'luccio ['luttʃo] *sm* (*ZOOL*) pike

'lucciola ['luttʃola] *sf* (*ZOOL*) firefly; glowworm

'luce ['lutʃe] *sf* light; (*finestra*) window; **alla**

~ di by the light of; **fare ~ su qc** (*fig*) to shed *o* throw light on sth; **~ del sole/della luna** sun/moonlight; **lu'cente** *ag* shining

lucer'nario [lutʃer'narjo] *sm* skylight

lu'certola [lu'tʃertola] *sf* lizard

luci'dare [lutʃi'dare] *vt* to polish

lucida'trice [lutʃida'tritʃe] *sf* floor polisher

'lucido, a ['lutʃido] *ag* shining, bright; **.(***lucidato***)** polished; (*fig*) lucid ♦ *sm* shine, lustre; (*per scarpe etc*) polish; (*disegno*) tracing

'lucro *sm* profit, gain; **lu'croso, a** *ag* lucrative, profitable

'luglio ['luʎʎo] *sm* July

'lugubre *ag* gloomy

'lui *pronome* (*soggetto*) he; (*oggetto: per dare rilievo, con preposizione*) him; **~ stesso** he himself

lu'maca, che *sf* slug; (*chiocciola*) snail

'lume *sm* light; (*lampada*) lamp; (*fig*): **chiedere ~i a qn** to ask sb for advice; **a ~ di naso** (*fig*) by rule of thumb

lumi'naria *sf* (*per feste*) illuminations *pl*

lumi'noso, a *ag* (*che emette luce*) luminous; (*cielo, colore, stanza*) bright; (*sorgente*) of light, light *cpd*; (*fig: sorriso*) bright, radiant

'luna *sf* moon; **~ nuova/piena** new/full moon; **~ di miele** honeymoon

'luna park *sm inv* amusement park, funfair

lu'nare *ag* lunar, moon *cpd*

lu'nario *sm* almanac; **sbarcare il ~** to make ends meet

lu'natico, a, ci, che *ag* whimsical, temperamental

lunedì *sm inv* Monday; **di** *o* **il ~** on Mondays

lun'gaggine [lun'gaddʒine] *sf* slowness; **~i della burocrazia** red tape

lun'ghezza [lun'gettsa] *sf* length; **~ d'onda** (*FISICA*) wavelength

'lungi ['lundʒi]: **~ da** *prep* far from

'lungo, a, ghi, ghe *ag* long; (*lento: persona*) slow; (*diluito: caffè, brodo*) weak, watery, thin ♦ *sm* length ♦ *prep* along; **~ 3 metri** 3 metres long; **a ~** for a long time; **a ~ andare** in the long run; **di gran ~a**

(*molto*) by far; **andare in ~** *o* **per le lunghe** to drag on; **saperla ~a** to know what's what; **in ~ e in largo** far and wide, all over; **~ il corso dei secoli** throughout the centuries

lungo'mare *sm* promenade

lu'notto *sm* (*AUT*) rear *o* back window; **~ termico** heated rear window

lu'ogo, ghi *sm* place; (*posto: di incidente etc*) scene, site; (*punto, passo di libro*) passage; **in ~ di** instead of; **in primo ~** in the first place; **aver ~** to take place; **dar ~ a** to give rise to; **~ comune** commonplace; **~ di nascita** birthplace; (*AMM*) place of birth; **~ di provenienza** place of origin

luogote'nente *sm* (*MIL*) lieutenant

lu'para *sf* sawn-off shotgun

'lupo, a *sm/f* wolf

'luppolo *sm* (*BOT*) hop

'lurido, a *ag* filthy

lu'singa, ghe *sf* (*spesso al pl*) flattery *no pl*

lusin'gare *vt* to flatter; **lusinghi'ero, a** *ag* flattering, gratifying

lus'sare *vt* (*MED*) to dislocate

Lussem'burgo *sm* (*stato*): **il ~** Luxembourg ♦ *sf* (*città*) Luxembourg

'lusso *sm* luxury; **di ~** luxury *cpd*; **lussu'oso, a** *ag* luxurious

lussureggi'ante [lussured'dʒante] *ag* luxuriant

lus'suria *sf* lust

lus'trare *vt* to polish, shine

lustras'carpe *sm/f inv* shoeshine

lus'trino *sm* sequin

'lustro, a *ag* shiny; (*pelo*) glossy ♦ *sm* shine, gloss; (*fig*) prestige, glory; (*quinquennio*) five-year period

'lutto *sm* mourning; **essere in/portare il ~** to be in/wear mourning; **luttu'oso, a** *ag* mournful, sad

M, m

ma *cong* but; **~ insomma!** for goodness sake!; **~ no!** of course not!

'macabro, a *ag* gruesome, macabre

macché [mak'ke] *escl* not at all!, certainly not!

macche'roni [makke'roni] *smpl* macaroni *sg*

'macchia ['makkja] *sf* stain, spot; (*chiazza di diverso colore*) spot; splash, patch; (*tipo di boscaglia*) scrub; **alla ~** (*fig*) in hiding; **macchi'are** *vt* (*sporcare*) to stain, mark; **macchiarsi** *vr* (*persona*) to get o.s. dirty; (*stoffa*) to stain; to get stained *o* marked

'macchina ['makkina] *sf* machine; (*motore, locomotiva*) engine; (*automobile*) car; (*fig: meccanismo*) machinery; **andare in ~** (*AUT*) to go by car; (*STAMPA*) to go to press; **~ da cucire** sewing machine; **~ fotografica** camera; **~ da presa** cine *o* movie camera; **~ da scrivere** typewriter; **~ a vapore** steam engine

macchi'nare [makki'nare] *vt* to plot

macchi'nario [makki'narjo] *sm* machinery

macchi'netta [makki'netta] (*fam*) *sf* (*caffettiera*) percolator; (*accendino*) lighter

macchi'nista, i [makki'nista] *sm* (*di treno*) engine-driver; (*di nave*) engineer

macchi'noso, a [makki'noso] *ag* complex, complicated

mace'donia [matʃe'dɔnja] *sf* fruit salad

macel'laio [matʃel'lajo] *sm* butcher

macel'lare [matʃel'lare] *vt* to slaughter, butcher; **macelle'ria** *sf* butcher's (shop); **ma'cello** *sm* (*mattatoio*) slaughterhouse, abattoir (*BRIT*); (*fig*) slaughter, massacre; (*: disastro*) shambles *sg*

mace'rare [matʃe'rare] *vt* to macerate; (*CUC*) to marinate; **~rsi** *vr* (*fig*): **~rsi in** to be consumed with

ma'cerie [ma'tʃerje] *sfpl* rubble *sg*, debris *sg*

ma'cigno [ma'tʃinno] *sm* (*masso*) rock, boulder

'macina ['matʃina] *sf* (*pietra*) millstone; (*macchina*) grinder; **macinacaffè** *sm inv* coffee grinder; **macina'pepe** *sm inv* peppermill

maci'nare [matʃi'nare] *vt* to grind; (*carne*) to mince (*BRIT*), grind (*US*); **maci'nato** *sm* meal, flour; (*carne*) minced (*BRIT*) *o* ground (*US*) meat

maci'nino [matʃi'nino] *sm* coffee grinder; peppermill

'madido, a *ag*: **~ (di)** wet *o* moist (with)

Ma'donna *sf* (*REL*) Our Lady

mador'nale *ag* enormous, huge

'madre *sf* mother; (*matrice di bolletta*) counterfoil ♦ *ag inv* mother *cpd*; **ragazza ~** unmarried mother; **scena ~** (*TEATRO*) principal scene; (*fig*) terrible scene

madre'lingua *sf* mother tongue, native language

madre'perla *sf* mother-of-pearl

ma'drina *sf* godmother

maestà *sf inv* majesty; **maes'toso, a** *ag* majestic

ma'estra *sf vedi* **maestro**

maes'trale *sm* north-west wind, mistral

maes'tranze [maes'trantse] *sfpl* workforce *sg*

maes'tria *sf* mastery, skill

ma'estro, a *sm/f* (*INS: anche:* **~ di scuola** *o* **elementare**) primary (*BRIT*) *o* grade school (*US*) teacher; (*esperto*) expert ♦ *sm* (*artigiano, fig: guida*) master; (*MUS*) maestro ♦ *ag* (*principale*) main; (*di grande abilità*) masterly, skilful; **~a d'asilo** nursery teacher; **~ di cerimonie** master of ceremonies

'mafia *sf* Mafia; **mafi'oso** *sm* member of the Mafia

'maga *sf* sorceress

ma'gagna [ma'ganna] *sf* defect, flaw, blemish; (*noia, guaio*) problem

ma'gari *escl* (*esprime desiderio*): **~ fosse vero!** if only it were true!; **ti piacerebbe andare in Scozia?** — **~!** would you like to go to Scotland? — and how! ♦ *av* (*anche*) even; (*forse*) perhaps

magaz'zino [magad'dzino] *sm* warehouse; **grande ~** department store

'maggio ['maddʒo] *sm* May

maggio'rana [maddʒo'rana] *sf* (*BOT*) (sweet) marjoram

maggio'ranza [maddʒo'rantsa] *sf* majority

maggio'rare [maddʒo'rare] *vt* to increase, raise

maggior'domo [maddʒor'dɔmo] *sm* butler

maggi'ore [mad'dʒore] *ag* (*comparativo: più grande*) bigger, larger; taller; greater; (*: più vecchio: sorella, fratello*) older, elder; (*: di grado superiore*) senior; (*: più importante, MIL, MUS*) major; (*superlativo*) biggest, largest; tallest; greatest; oldest, eldest ♦ *sm/f* (*di grado*) superior; (*di età*) elder; (*MIL*) major; (*: AER*) squadron leader; **la maggior parte** the majority; **andare per la ~** (*cantante etc*) to be very popular; **maggio'renne** *ag* of age ♦ *sm/f* person who has come of age; **maggior'mente** *av* much more; (*con senso superlativo*) most

ma'gia [ma'dʒia] *sf* magic; **'magico, a, ci, che** *ag* magic; (*fig*) fascinating, charming, magical

'magio ['madʒo] *sm* (*REL*): **i re Magi** the Magi, the Three Wise Men

magis'tero [madʒis'tero] *sm*: **facoltà di M~** ≈ teachers' training college; **magis'trale** *ag* primary (*BRIT*) *o* grade school (*US*) teachers', primary (*BRIT*) *o* grade school (*US*) teaching *cpd*; skilful

magis'trato [madʒis'trato] *sm* magistrate; **magistra'tura** *sf* magistrature; (*magistrati*): **la magistratura** the Bench

'maglia ['maʎʎa] *sf* stitch; (*lavoro ai ferri*) knitting *no pl*; (*tessuto, SPORT*) jersey; (*maglione*) jersey, sweater; (*di catena*) link; (*di rete*) mesh; **~ diritta/rovescia** plain/purl; **maglie'ria** *sf* knitwear; (*negozio*) knitwear shop; **magli'etta** *sf* (*canottiera*) vest; (*tipo camicia*) T-shirt; **magli'ficio** *sm* knitwear factory

'maglio ['maʎʎo] *sm* mallet; (*macchina*) power hammer

magli'one *sm* sweater, jumper

ma'gnanimo, a [maɲ'ɲanimo, a] *ag* magnanimous

ma'gnete [maɲ'ɲete] *sm* magnet; **ma'gnetico, a, ci, che** *ag* magnetic

magne'tofono [maɲɲe'tɔfono] *sm* tape recorder

ma'gnifico, a, ci, che [maɲ'ɲifiko] *ag* magnificent, splendid; (*ospite*) generous

'magno, a ['maɲɲo] *ag*: **aula ~a** main hall

ma'gnolia [maɲ'ɲɔlja] *sf* magnolia

'mago, ghi *sm* (*stregone*) magician, wizard; (*illusionista*) magician

ma'grezza [ma'grettsa] *sf* thinness

'magro, a *ag* (*very*) thin, skinny; (*carne*) lean; (*formaggio*) low-fat; (*fig: scarso, misero*) meagre, poor; (*: meschino: scusa*) poor, lame; **mangiare di ~** not to eat meat

'mai *av* (*nessuna volta*) never; (*talvolta*) ever; **non ... ~** never; **~ più** never again; **come ~?** why (*o* how) on earth?; **chi/dove/quando ~?** whoever/wherever/whenever?

mai'ale *sm* (*ZOOL*) pig; (*carne*) pork

mail *sf inv* e-mail

maio'nese *sf* mayonnaise

'mais *sm inv* maize

mai'uscola *sf* capital letter

mai'uscolo, a *ag* (*lettera*) capital; (*fig*) enormous, huge

mal *av, sm vedi* **male**

malac'corto, a *ag* rash, careless

mala'fede *sf* bad faith

mala'lingua (*pl* **male'lingue**) *sf* gossip(monger)

mala'mente *av* badly; dangerously

malan'dato, a *ag* (*persona: di salute*) in poor health; (*: di condizioni finanziarie*) badly off; (*trascurato*) shabby

ma'lanno *sm* (*disgrazia*) misfortune; (*malattia*) ailment

mala'pena *sf*: **a ~** hardly, scarcely

mala'sorte *sf* bad luck

mala'ticcio, a [mala'tittʃo] *ag* sickly

ma'lato, a *ag* ill, sick; (*gamba*) bad; (*pianta*) diseased ♦ *sm/f* sick person; (*in ospedale*) patient; **malat'tia** *sf* (*infettiva etc*) illness, disease; (*cattiva salute*) illness, sickness; (*di pianta*) disease

malau'gurio *sm* bad *o* ill omen

mala'vita *sf* underworld

mala'voglia [mala'vɔʎʎa] *sf*: **di ~** unwillingly, reluctantly

mal'concio, a, ci, ce [mal'kontʃo] *ag* in a sorry state

malcon'tento *sm* discontent

malcos'tume *sm* immorality

mal'destro, a *ag* (*inabile*) inexpert, inexperienced; (*goffo*) awkward

maldi'cenza [maldi'tʃentsa] *sf* malicious gossip

maldis'posto, a *ag*: ~ **(verso)** ill-disposed (towards)

'male *av* badly ♦ *sm* (*ciò che è ingiusto, disonesto*) evil; (*danno, svantaggio*) harm; (*sventura*) misfortune; (*dolore fisico, morale*) pain, ache; **di ~ in peggio** from bad to worse; **sentirsi ~** to feel ill; **far ~** (*dolere*) to hurt; **far ~ alla salute** to be bad for one's health; **far del ~ a qn** to hurt *o* harm sb; **restare** *o* **rimanere ~** to be sorry; to be disappointed; to be hurt; **andare a ~** to go bad; **come va? — non c'è ~** how are you? — not bad; **avere mal di cuore** heart trouble; **~ di dente** toothache; **mal di mare** seasickness; **avere mal di gola/testa** to have a sore throat/a headache; **aver ~ ai piedi** to have sore feet

male'detto, a *pp di* maledire ♦ *ag* cursed, damned; (*fig: fam*) damned, blasted

male'dire *vt* to curse; maledizi'one *sf* curse; **maledizione!** damn it!

maledu'cato, a *ag* rude, ill-mannered

male'fatta *sf* misdeed

male'ficio [male'fitʃo] *sm* witchcraft

ma'lefico, a, ci, che *ag* (*influsso, azione*) evil

ma'lessere *sm* indisposition, slight illness; (*fig*) uneasiness

ma'levolo, a *ag* malevolent

malfa'mato, a *ag* notorious

mal'fatto, a *ag* (*persona*) deformed; (*oggetto*) badly made; (*lavoro*) badly done

malfat'tore, 'trice *sm/f* wrongdoer

mal'fermo, a *ag* unsteady, shaky; (*salute*) poor, delicate

malformazi'one [malformat'tsjone] *sf* malformation

malgo'verno *sm* maladministration

mal'grado *prep* in spite of, despite ♦ *cong* although; **mio** (*o* **tuo** *etc*) ~ against my (*o* your *etc*) will

mali'gnare [malin'nare] *vi*: ~ **su** to malign, speak ill of

ma'ligno, a [ma'linno] *ag* (*malvagio*) malicious, malignant; (*MED*) malignant

malinco'nia *sf* melancholy, gloom; malin'conico, a, ci, che *ag* melancholy

malincu'ore: **a ~** *av* reluctantly, unwillingly

malintenzio'nato, a [malintentsjo'nato] *ag* ill-intentioned

malin'teso, a *ag* misunderstood; (*riguardo, senso del dovere*) mistaken, wrong ♦ *sm* misunderstanding

ma'lizia [ma'littsja] *sf* (*malignità*) malice; (*furbizia*) cunning; (*espediente*) trick; malizi'oso, a *ag* malicious; cunning; (*vivace, birichino*) mischievous

mal'loppo *sm* (*involto*) bundle; (*fam: refurtiva*) loot

malme'nare *vt* to beat up

mal'messo, a *ag* shabby

malnu'trito, a *ag* undernourished

ma'locchio [ma'lɔkkjo] *sm* evil eye

ma'lora *sf*: **andare in ~** to go to the dogs

ma'lore *sm* (sudden) illness

mal'sano, a *ag* unhealthy

malsi'curo, a *ag* unsafe

'Malta *sf* Malta

'malta *sf* (*EDIL*) mortar

mal'tempo *sm* bad weather

'malto *sm* malt

maltrat'tare *vt* to ill-treat

malu'more *sm* bad mood; (*irritabilità*) bad temper; (*discordia*) ill feeling; **di ~** in a bad mood

mal'vagio, a, gi, gie [mal'vadʒo] *ag* wicked, evil

malversazi'one [malversat'tsjone] *sf* (*DIR*) embezzlement

mal'visto, a *ag*: ~ **(da)** disliked (by), unpopular (with)

malvi'vente *sm* criminal

malvolenti'eri *av* unwillingly, reluctantly

'mamma *sf* mummy, mum; ~ **mia!** my

goodness!

mam'mella *sf* (*ANAT*) breast; (*di vacca, capra etc*) udder

mam'mifero *sm* mammal

'mammola *sf* (*BOT*) violet

ma'nata *sf* (*colpo*) slap; (*quantità*) handful

'manca *sf* left (hand); **a destra e a ~** left, right and centre, on all sides

man'canza [man'kantsa] *sf* lack; (*carenza*) shortage, scarcity; (*fallo*) fault; (*imperfezione*) failing, shortcoming; **per ~ di tempo** through lack of time; **in ~ di meglio** for lack of anything better

man'care *vi* (*essere insufficiente*) to be lacking; (*venir meno*) to fail; (*sbagliare*) to be wrong, make a mistake; (*non esserci*) to be missing, not to be there; (*essere lontano*): **~ (da)** to be away (from) ♦ *vt* to miss; **~ di** to lack; **~ a** (*promessa*) to fail to keep; **tu mi manchi** I miss you; **mancò poco che morisse** he very nearly died; **mancano ancora 10 sterline** we're still £10 short; **manca un quarto alle 6** it's a quarter to 6; **man'cato, a** *ag* (*tentativo*) unsuccessful; (*artista*) failed

'mancia, ce ['mantʃa] *sf* tip; **~ competente** reward

manci'ata [man'tʃata] *sf* handful

man'cino, a [man'tʃino] *ag* (*braccio*) left; (*persona*) left-handed; (*fig*) underhand

'manco *av* (*nemmeno*): **~ per sogno** *o* **per idea!** not on your life!

man'dante *sm/f* (*di delitto*) instigator

manda'rancio [manda'rantʃo] *sm* clementine

man'dare *vt* to send; (*far funzionare: macchina*) to drive; (*emettere*) to send out; (*: grido*) to give, utter, let out; **~ a chiamare qn** to send for sb; **~ avanti** (*fig: famiglia*) to provide for; (*: fabbrica*) to run, look after; **~ giù** to send down; (*anche fig*) to swallow; **~ via** to send away; (*licenziare*) to fire

manda'rino *sm* mandarin (orange); (*cinese*) mandarin

man'data *sf* (*quantità*) lot, batch; (*di chiave*) turn; **chiudere a doppia ~** to

double-lock

man'dato *sm* (*incarico*) commission; (*DIR: provvedimento*) warrant; (*di deputato etc*) mandate; (*ordine di pagamento*) postal *o* money order; **~ d'arresto** warrant for arrest

man'dibola *sf* mandible, jaw

'mandorla *sf* almond; **'mandorlo** *sm* almond tree

'mandria *sf* herd

maneggi'are [maned'dʒare] *vt* (*creta, cera*) to mould, work, fashion; (*arnesi, utensili*) to handle; (: *adoperare*) to use; (*fig: persone, denaro*) to handle, deal with; **ma'neggio** *sm* moulding; handling; use; (*intrigo*) plot, scheme; (*per cavalli*) riding school

ma'nesco, a, schi, sche *ag* free with one's fists

ma'nette *sfpl* handcuffs

manga'nello *sm* club

manga'nese *sm* manganese

mange'reccio, a, ci, ce [mandʒe'rettʃo] *ag* edible

mangi'are [man'dʒare] *vt* to eat; (*intaccare*) to eat into *o* away; (*CARTE, SCACCHI etc*) to take ♦ *vi* to eat ♦ *sm* eating; (*cibo*) food; (*cucina*) cooking; **~rsi le parole** to mumble; **~rsi le unghie** to bite one's nails; **mangia'toia** *sf* feeding-trough

man'gime [man'dʒime] *sm* fodder

'mango, ghi *sm* mango

ma'nia *sf* (*PSIC*) mania; (*fig*) obsession, craze; **ma'niaco, a, ci, che** *ag* suffering from a mania; **maniaco (di)** obsessed (by), crazy (about)

'manica *sf* sleeve; (*fig: gruppo*) gang, bunch; (*GEO*): **la M~, il Canale della M~** the (English) Channel; **essere di ~ larga/ stretta** to be easy-going/strict; **~ a vento** (*AER*) wind sock

mani'chino [mani'kino] *sm* (*di sarto, vetrina*) dummy

'manico, ci *sm* handle; (*MUS*) neck

mani'comio *sm* mental hospital; (*fig*) madhouse

mani'cotto *sm* muff; (*TECN*) coupling; sleeve

mani'cure *sm o f inv* manicure ♦ *sf inv* manicurist

mani'era *sf* way, manner; (*stile*) style, manner; **~e** *sfpl* (*comportamento*) manners; **in ~ che** so that; **in ~ da** so as to; **in tutte le ~e** at all costs

manie'rato, a *ag* affected

manifat'tura *sf* (*lavorazione*) manufacture; (*stabilimento*) factory

manifes'tare *vt* to show, display; (*esprimere*) to express; (*rivelare*) to reveal, disclose ♦ *vi* to demonstrate; **~rsi** *vr* to show o.s.; **~rsi amico** to prove o.s. (to be) a friend; **manifestazi'one** *sf* show, display; expression; (*sintomo*) sign, symptom; (*dimostrazione pubblica*) demonstration; (*cerimonia*) event

mani'festo, a *ag* obvious, evident ♦ *sm* poster, bill; (*scritto ideologico*) manifesto

ma'niglia [maˈniʎʎa] *sf* handle; (*sostegno: negli autobus etc*) strap

manipo'lare *vt* to manipulate; (*alterare: vino*) to adulterate; **manipolazi'one** *sf* manipulation; adulteration

---

mani pulite

🛈 **Mani pulite** is a term used to describe the judicial operation which identified, gathered evidence against, and brought to trial a number of politicians and industrialists implicated in bribery and corruption scandals. See also **Tangentopoli**.

'manna *sf* (*REL*) manna; (*fig*) godsend

man'naia *sf* (*del boia*) (executioner's) axe; (*per carni*) cleaver

man'naro: lupo ~ *sm* werewolf

'mano, i *sf* hand; (*strato: di vernice etc*) coat; **di prima ~** (*notizia*) first-hand; **di seconda ~** second-hand; **man ~** little by little, gradually; **man ~ che** as; **darsi o stringersi la ~** to shake hands; **mettere le ~i avanti** (*fig*) to safeguard o.s.; **restare a ~i vuote** to be left empty-handed; **venire alle ~i** to come to blows; **a ~** by hand; **~i in alto!** hands up!

mano'dopera *sf* labour

mano'messo, a *pp di* **manomettere**

ma'nometro *sm* gauge, manometer

mano'mettere *vt* (*alterare*) to tamper with; (*aprire indebitamente*) to break open illegally

ma'nopola *sf* (*dell'armatura*) gauntlet; (*guanto*) mitt; (*di impugnatura*) hand-grip; (*pomello*) knob

manos'critto, a *ag* handwritten ♦ *sm* manuscript

mano'vale *sm* labourer

mano'vella *sf* handle; (*TECN*) crank

ma'novra *sf* manoeuvre (*BRIT*), maneuver (*US*); (*FERR*) shunting; **mano'vrare** *vt* (*veicolo*) to manoeuvre (*BRIT*), maneuver (*US*); (*macchina, congegno*) to operate; (*fig: persona*) to manipulate ♦ *vi* to manoeuvre

manro'vescio [manroˈveʃʃo] *sm* slap (with back of hand)

man'sarda *sf* attic

mansi'one *sf* task, duty, job

mansu'eto, a *ag* gentle, docile

man'tello *sm* cloak; (*fig: di neve etc*) blanket, mantle; (*ZOOL*) coat

mante'nere *vt* to maintain; (*adempiere: promesse*) to keep, abide by; (*provvedere a*) to support, maintain; **~rsi** *vr*: **~rsi calmo/ giovane** to stay calm/young; **manteni'mento** *sm* maintenance

'mantice [ˈmantitʃe] *sm* bellows *pl*

'manto *sm* cloak; **~ stradale** road surface

manu'ale *ag* manual ♦ *sm* (*testo*) manual, handbook

ma'nubrio *sm* handle; (*di bicicletta etc*) handlebars *pl*; (*SPORT*) dumbbell

manu'fatto *sm* manufactured article

manutenzi'one [manutenˈtsjone] *sf* maintenance, upkeep; (*d'impianti*) maintenance, servicing

'manzo [ˈmandzo] *sm* (*ZOOL*) steer; (*carne*) beef

'mappa *sf* (*GEO*) map; **mappa'mondo** *sm* map of the world; (*globo girevole*) globe

mara'tona *sf* marathon

'marca, che *sf* (*COMM: di prodotti*) brand; (*contrassegno, scontrino*) ticket, check;

prodotto di ~ (*di buona qualità*) high-class product; **~ da bollo** official stamp

mar'care *vt* (*munire di contrassegno*) to mark; (*a fuoco*) to brand; (SPORT: *gol*) to score; (: *avversario*) to mark; (*accentuare*) to stress; **~ visita** (MIL) to report sick

'Marche ['marke] *sfpl*: **le ~** the Marches (*region of central Italy*)

mar'chese, a [mar'keze] *sm/f* marquis *o* marquess/marchioness

marchi'are [mar'kjare] *vt* to brand; 'marchio *sm* (*di bestiame*, COMM, *fig*) brand; **marchio depositato** registered trademark; **marchio di fabbrica** trademark

'marcia, ce ['martʃa] *sf* (*anche* MUS, MIL) march; (*funzionamento*) running; (*il camminare*) walking; (AUT) gear; **mettere in ~** to start; **mettersi in ~** to get moving; **far ~ indietro** (AUT) to reverse; (*fig*) to back-pedal

marciapi'ede [martʃa'pjɛde] *sm* (*di strada*) pavement (BRIT), sidewalk (US); (FERR) platform

marci'are [mar'tʃare] *vi* to march; (*andare: treno, macchina*) to go; (*funzionare*) to run, work

'marcio, a, ci, ce ['martʃo] *ag* (*frutta, legno*) rotten, bad; (MED) festering; (*fig*) corrupt, rotten

mar'cire [mar'tʃire] *vi* (*andare a male*) to go bad, rot; (*suppurare*) to fester; (*fig*) to rot, waste away

'marco, chi *sm* (*unità monetaria*) mark

'mare *sm* sea; **in ~** at sea; **andare al ~** (*in vacanza etc*) to go to the seaside; **il M~ del Nord** the North Sea

ma'rea *sf* tide; **alta/bassa ~** high/low tide

mareggi'ata [mared'dʒata] *sf* heavy sea

mare'moto *sm* seaquake

maresci'allo [mareʃ'ʃallo] *sm* (MIL) marshal; (: *sottufficiale*) warrant officer

marga'rina *sf* margarine

marghe'rita [marge'rita] *sf* (ox-eye) daisy, marguerite; (*di stampante*) daisy wheel

'margine ['mardʒine] *sm* margin; (*di bosco, via*) edge, border

ma'rina *sf* navy; (*costa*) coast; (*quadro*)

seascape; **~ militare/mercantile** navy/merchant navy (BRIT) *o* marine (US)

mari'naio *sm* sailor

mari'nare *vt* (CUC) to marinate; **~ la scuola** to play truant; **mari'nata** *sf* marinade

ma'rino, a *ag* sea *cpd*, marine

mario'netta *sf* puppet

mari'tare *vt* to marry; **~rsi** *vr*: **~rsi a** *o* **con qn** to marry sb, get married to sb

ma'rito *sm* husband

ma'rittimo, a *ag* maritime, sea *cpd*

mar'maglia [mar'maʎʎa] *sf* mob, riff-raff

marmel'lata *sf* jam; (*di agrumi*) marmalade

mar'mitta *sf* (*recipiente*) pot; (AUT) silencer; **~ catalitica** catalytic converter

'marmo *sm* marble

mar'mocchio [mar'mɔkkjo] (*fam*) *sm* tot, kid

mar'motta *sf* (ZOOL) marmot

Ma'rocco *sm*: **il ~** Morocco

mar'rone *ag inv* brown ♦ *sm* (BOT) chestnut

mar'sala *sm inv* (*vino*) Marsala

mar'sina *sf* tails *pl*, tail coat

mar'supio *sm* pouch; (*per denaro*) bum bag; (*per neonato*) sling

martedì *sm inv* Tuesday; **di** *o* **il ~ on** Tuesdays; **~ grasso** Shrove Tuesday

martel'lare *vt* to hammer ♦ *vi* (*pulsare*) to throb; (: *cuore*) to thump

mar'tello *sm* hammer; (*di uscio*) knocker

marti'netto *sm* (TECN) jack

'martire *sm/f* martyr; mar'tirio *sm* martyrdom; (*fig*) agony, torture

'martora *sf* marten

martori'are *vt* to torment, torture

mar'xista, i, e [mar'ksista] *ag, sm/f* Marxist

marza'pane [martsa'pane] *sm* marzipan

'marzo ['martso] *sm* March

mascal'zone [maskal'tsone] *sm* rascal, scoundrel

ma'scella [maʃ'ʃɛlla] *sf* (ANAT) jaw

'maschera ['maskera] *sf* mask; (*travestimento*) disguise; (: *per un ballo etc*) fancy dress; (TEATRO, CINEMA) usher/

usherette; (*personaggio del teatro*) stock character; **masche'rare** *vt* to mask; (*travestire*) to disguise; to dress up; (*celare*) to hide, conceal; (*MIL*) to camouflage; **~rsi da** to disguise o.s. as; to dress up as; (*fig*) to masquerade as

mas'chile [mas'kile] *ag* masculine; (*sesso, popolazione*) male; (*abiti*) men's; (*per ragazzi: scuola*) boys'

'**maschio, a** ['maskjo] *ag* (*BIOL*) male; (*virile*) manly ♦ *sm* (*anche ZOOL, TECN*) male; (*uomo*) man; (*ragazzo*) boy; (*figlio*) son

masco'lino, a *ag* masculine

'**massa** *sf* mass; (*di errori etc*): **una ~ di** heaps of, masses of; (*di gente*) mass, multitude; (*ELETTR*) earth; **in ~** (*COMM*) in bulk; (*tutti insieme*) en masse; **adunata in ~** mass meeting; **di ~** (*cultura, manifestazione*) mass *cpd*

mas'sacro *sm* massacre, slaughter; (*fig*) mess, disaster

mas'saggio [mas'saddʒo] *sm* massage

mas'saia *sf* housewife

masse'rizie [masse'rittsje] *sfpl* (household) furnishings

mas'siccio, a, ci, ce [mas'sittʃo] *ag* (*oro, legno*) solid; (*palazzo*) massive; (*corporatura*) stout ♦ *sm* (*GEO*) massif

'**massima** *sf* (*sentenza, regola*) maxim; (*METEOR*) maximum temperature; **in linea di ~** generally speaking; *vedi anche* **massimo**

massi'male *sm* maximum

'**massimo, a** *ag, sm* maximum; **al ~** at (the) most

'**masso** *sm* rock, boulder

mas'sone *sm* freemason; **massone'ria** *sf* freemasonry

mas'tello *sm* tub

masti'care *vt* to chew

'**mastice** ['mastitʃe] *sm* mastic; (*per vetri*) putty

mas'tino *sm* mastiff

ma'tassa *sf* skein

mate'matica *sf* mathematics *sg*

mate'matico, a, ci, che *ag* mathematical ♦ *sm/f* mathematician

materas'sino *sm* mat; (*gonfiabile*) air bed

mate'rasso *sm* mattress; **~ a molle** spring *o* interior-sprung mattress

ma'teria *sf* (*FISICA*) matter; (*TECN, COMM*) material, matter *no pl*; (*disciplina*) subject; (*argomento*) subject matter, material; **~e prime** raw materials; **in ~ di** (*per quanto concerne*) on the subject of

materi'ale *ag* material; (*fig: grossolano*) rough, rude ♦ *sm* material; (*insieme di strumenti etc*) equipment *no pl*, materials *pl*

maternità *sf* motherhood, maternity; (*reparto*) maternity ward

ma'terno, a *ag* (*amore, cura etc*) maternal, motherly; (*nonno*) maternal; (*lingua, terra*) mother *cpd*

ma'tita *sf* pencil

ma'trice [ma'tritʃe] *sf* matrix; (*COMM*) counterfoil; (*fig: origine*) background

ma'tricola *sf* (*registro*) register; (*numero*) registration number; (*nell'università*) freshman, fresher

ma'trigna [ma'triɲɲa] *sf* stepmother

matrimoni'ale *ag* matrimonial, marriage *cpd*

matri'monio *sm* marriage, matrimony; (*durata*) marriage, married life; (*cerimonia*) wedding

ma'trona *sf* (*fig*) matronly woman

mat'tina *sf* morning; **matti'nata** *sf* morning; (*spettacolo*) matinée, afternoon performance; **mattini'ero, a** *ag*: **essere mattiniero** to be an early riser

mat'tino *sm* morning

'**matto, a** *ag* mad, crazy; (*fig: falso*) false, imitation ♦ *sm/f* madman/woman; **avere una voglia ~a di qc** to be dying for sth

mat'tone *sm* brick; (*fig*): **questo libro/film è un ~** this book/film is heavy going

matto'nella *sf* tile

matu'rare *vi* (*anche: ~rsi*) (*frutta, grano*) to ripen; (*ascesso*) to come to a head; (*fig: persona, idea, ECON*) to mature ♦ *vt* to ripen; to (make) mature

maturità *sf* maturity; (*di frutta*) ripeness, maturity; (*INS*) school-leaving examination,

≈ GCE A-levels (*BRIT*)

ma'turo, a *ag* mature; (*frutto*) ripe, mature

maxiprocesso *n* criminal trial involving large numbers of co-accused

'mazza ['mattsa] *sf* (*bastone*) club; (*martello*) sledge-hammer; (*SPORT: da golf*) club; (: *da baseball, cricket*) bat

maz'zata [mat'tsata] *sf* (*anche fig*) heavy blow

'mazzo ['mattso] *sm* (*di fiori, chiavi etc*) bunch; (*di carte da gioco*) pack

me *pron* me; ~ stesso(a) myself; sei bravo quanto ~ you are as clever as I (am) *o* as me

me'andro *sm* meander

mec'canica, che *sf* mechanics *sg*; (*attività tecnologica*) mechanical engineering; (*meccanismo*) mechanism

mec'canico, a, ci, che *ag* mechanical ♦ *sm* mechanic

mecca'nismo *sm* mechanism

me'daglia [me'daʎʎa] *sf* medal; medagli'one *sm* (*ARCHIT*) medallion; (*gioiello*) locket

me'desimo, a *ag* same; (*in persona*): io ~ I myself

'media *sf* average; (*MAT*) mean; (*INS: voto*) end-of-term average; in ~ on average; *vedi anche* medio

medi'ano, a *ag* median; (*valore*) mean ♦ *sm* (*CALCIO*) half-back

medi'ante *prep* by means of

medi'are *vt* (*fare da mediatore*) to act as mediator in; (*MAT*) to average

media'tore, 'trice *sm/f* mediator; (*COMM*) middle man, agent

medica'mento *sm* medicine, drug

medi'care *vt* to treat; (*ferita*) to dress; medicazi'one *sf* treatment, medication; dressing

medi'cina [medi'tʃina] *sf* medicine; ~ legale forensic medicine; medici'nale *ag* medicinal ♦ *sm* drug, medicine

'medico, a, ci, che *ag* medical ♦ *sm* doctor; ~ generico general practitioner, GP

medie'vale *ag* medieval

'medio, a *ag* average; (*punto, ceto*) middle; (*altezza, statura*) medium ♦ *sm* (*dito*) middle finger; licenza ~a *leaving certificate awarded at the end of 3 years of secondary education*; scuola ~a *first 3 years of secondary school*

medi'ocre *ag* mediocre, poor

medioe'vale *ag* = medievale

medio'evo *sm* Middle Ages *pl*

medi'tare *vt* to ponder over, meditate on; (*progettare*) to plan, think out ♦ *vi* to meditate

mediter'raneo, a *ag* Mediterranean; il (mare) M~ the Mediterranean (Sea)

me'dusa *sf* (*ZOOL*) jellyfish

me'gafono *sm* megaphone

'meglio ['meʎʎo] *av, ag inv* better; (*con senso superlativo*) best ♦ *sm* (*la cosa migliore*): il ~ the best (thing); faresti ~ ad andartene you had better leave; alla ~ as best one can; andar di bene in ~ to get better and better; fare del proprio ~ to do one's best; per il ~ for the best; aver la ~ su qn to get the better of sb

'mela *sf* apple; ~ cotogna quince

mela'grana *sf* pomegranate

melan'zana [melan'dzana] *sf* aubergine (*BRIT*), eggplant (*US*)

me'lenso, a *ag* dull, stupid

mel'lifluo, a (*peg*) *ag* sugary, honeyed

'melma *sf* mud, mire

'melo *sm* apple tree

melo'dia *sf* melody

me'lone *sm* (musk)melon

'membro *sm* member; (*pl*(~a: *arto*) limb

memo'randum *sm inv* memorandum

me'moria *sf* memory; ~e *sfpl* (*opera autobiografica*) memoirs; a ~ (*imparare, sapere*) by heart; a ~ d'uomo within living memory; memori'ale *sm* (*raccolta di memorie*) memoirs *pl*; (*DIR*) memorial

mena'dito: a ~ *av* perfectly, thoroughly; sapere qc a ~ to have sth at one's fingertips

me'nare *vt* to lead; (*picchiare*) to hit, beat; (*dare: colpi*) to deal; ~ la coda (*cane*) to wag its tail

mendi'cante *sm/f* beggar

mendi'care *vt* to beg for ♦ *vi* to beg

PAROLA CHIAVE

'**meno** *av* 1 (*in minore misura*) less; **dovresti mangiare ~** you should eat less, you shouldn't eat so much
2 (*comparativo*): **~ ... di** not as ... as, less ... than; **sono ~ alto di te** I'm not as tall as you (are), I'm less tall than you (are); **~ ... che** not as ... as, less ... than; **~ che mai** less than ever; **è ~ intelligente che ricco** he's more rich than intelligent; **~ fumo più mangio** the less I smoke the more I eat
3 (*superlativo*) least; **il ~ dotato degli studenti** the least gifted of the students; **è quello che compro ~ spesso** it's the one I buy least often
4 (*MAT*) minus; **8 ~ 5** 8 minus 5, 8 take away 5; **sono le 8 ~ un quarto** it's a quarter to 8; **~ 5 gradi** 5 degrees below zero, minus 5 degrees; **mille lire in ~** a thousand lire less
5 (*fraseologia*): **quanto ~ poteva telefonare** he could at least have phoned; **non so se accettare o ~** I don't know whether to accept or not; **fare a ~ di qc/ qn** to do without sth/sb; **non potevo fare a ~ di ridere** I couldn't help laughing; **~ male!** thank goodness!; **~ male che sei arrivato** it's a good job that you've come
♦ *ag inv* (*tempo, denaro*) less; (*errori, persone*) fewer; **ha fatto ~ errori di tutti** he made fewer mistakes than anyone, he made the fewest mistakes of all
♦ *sm inv* 1: **il ~** (*il minimo*) the least; **parlare del più e del ~** to talk about this and that
2 (*MAT*) minus
♦ *prep* (*eccetto*) except (for), apart from; **a ~ che, a ~ di** unless; **a ~ che non piova** unless it rains; **non posso, a ~ di prendere ferie** I can't, unless I take some leave

meno'mare *vt* (*danneggiare*) to maim, disable
meno'pausa *sf* menopause

'**mensa** *sf* (*locale*) canteen; (: *MIL*) mess; (: *nelle università*) refectory
men'sile *ag* monthly ♦ *sm* (*periodico*) monthly (magazine); (*stipendio*) monthly salary
'**mensola** *sf* bracket; (*ripiano*) shelf; (*ARCHIT*) corbel
'**menta** *sf* mint; (*anche*: **~ piperita**) peppermint; (*bibita*) peppermint cordial; (*caramella*) mint, peppermint
men'tale *ag* mental; **mentalità** *sf inv* mentality
'**mente** *sf* mind; **imparare/sapere qc a ~** to learn/know sth by heart; **avere in ~ qc** to have sth in mind; **passare di ~ a qn** to slip sb's mind
men'tire *vi* to lie
'**mento** *sm* chin
men'tolo *sm* menthol
'**mentre** *cong* (*temporale*) while; (*avversativo*) whereas
menù *sm inv* menu; **~ turistico** set menu
menzio'nare [mentsjo'nare] *vt* to mention
menzi'one [men'tsjone] *sf* mention; **fare ~ di** to mention
men'zogna [men'tsɔɲɲa] *sf* lie
mera'viglia [mera'viʎʎa] *sf* amazement, wonder; (*persona, cosa*) marvel, wonder; **a ~** perfectly, wonderfully; **meravigli'are** *vt* to amaze, astonish; **meravigliarsi (di)** to marvel (at); (*stupirsi*) to be amazed (at), be astonished (at); **meravigli'oso, a** *ag* wonderful, marvellous
mer'cante *sm* merchant; **~ d'arte** art dealer; **mercanteggi'are** *vt* (*onore, voto*) to sell ♦ *vi* to bargain, haggle; **mercan'tile** *ag* commercial, mercantile; (*nave, marina*) merchant *cpd* ♦ *sm* (*nave*) merchantman; **mercan'zia** *sf* merchandise, goods *pl*
mer'cato *sm* market; **~ dei cambi** exchange market; **~ nero** black market
'**merce** ['mertʃe] *sf* goods *pl*, merchandise; **~ deperibile** perishable goods *pl*
mercé [mer'tʃe] *sf* mercy
merce'nario, a [mertʃe'narjo] *ag, sm* mercenary

merce'ria [mertʃe'ria] *sf* (*articoli*) haberdashery (*BRIT*), notions *pl* (*US*); (*bottega*) haberdasher's shop (*BRIT*), notions store (*US*)

mercoledì *sm inv* Wednesday; **di** *o* **il ~** on Wednesdays; **~ delle Ceneri** Ash Wednesday

---
mercoledì delle ceneri

i Mercoledì delle ceneri, in the Catholic Church, marks the beginning of Lent. On that day, people go to church and are marked on the forehead with ash from the burning of the blessed olive branch. Ash Wednesday is a day of fasting, abstinence and penitence.

---

mer'curio *sm* mercury

'merda (*fam!*) *sf* shit (!)

me'renda *sf* afternoon snack

meridi'ana *sf* (*orologio*) sundial

meridi'ano, a *ag* meridian; midday *cpd*, noonday ♦ *sm* meridian

meridio'nale *ag* southern ♦ *sm/f* southerner

meridi'one *sm* south

me'ringa, ghe *sf* (*CUC*) meringue

meri'tare *vt* to deserve, merit ♦ *vb impers*: **merita andare** it's worth going

meri'tevole *ag* worthy

'merito *sm* merit; (*valore*) worth; **in ~ a** as regards, with regard to; **dare ~ a qn di** to give sb credit for; **finire a pari ~** to finish joint first (*o* second *etc*); to tie; **meri'torio, a** *ag* praiseworthy

mer'letto *sm* lace

'merlo *sm* (*ZOOL*) blackbird; (*ARCHIT*) battlement

mer'luzzo [mer'luttso] *sm* (*ZOOL*) cod

mes'chino, a [mes'kino] *ag* wretched; (*scarso*) scanty, poor; (*persona: gretta*) mean; (*: limitata*) narrow-minded, petty

mesco'lanza [mesko'lantsa] *sf* mixture

mesco'lare *vt* to mix; (*vini, colori*) to blend; (*mettere in disordine*) to mix up, muddle up; (*carte*) to shuffle; **~rsi** *vr* to mix; to blend; to get mixed up; (*fig*): **~rsi**

in to get mixed up in, meddle in

'mese *sm* month

'messa *sf* (*REL*) mass; (*il mettere*): **~ in moto** starting; **~ in piega** set; **~ a punto** (*TECN*) adjustment; (*AUT*) tuning; (*fig*) clarification; **~ in scena = messinscena**

messag'gero [messad'dʒero] *sm* messenger

mes'saggio [mes'saddʒo] *sm* message

mes'sale *sm* (*REL*) missal

'messe *sf* harvest

Mes'sia *sm inv* (*REL*): **il ~** the Messiah

'Messico *sm*: **il ~** Mexico

messin'scena [messin'ʃena] *sf* (*TEATRO*) production

'messo, a *pp di* **mettere** ♦ *sm* messenger

mesti'ere *sm* (*professione*) job; (*: manuale*) trade; (*: artigianale*) craft; (*fig: abilità nel lavoro*) skill, technique; **essere del ~** to know the tricks of the trade

'mesto, a *ag* sad, melancholy

'mestolo *sm* (*CUC*) ladle

mestruazi'one [mestruat'tsjone] *sf* menstruation

'meta *sf* destination; (*fig*) aim, goal

metà *sf inv* half; (*punto di mezzo*) middle; **dividere qc a** *o* **per ~** to divide sth in half, halve sth; **fare a ~ (di qc con qn)** to go halves (with sb in sth); **a ~ prezzo** at half price; **a ~ strada** halfway

me'tafora *sf* metaphor

me'tallico, a, ci, che *ag* (*di metallo*) metal *cpd*; (*splendore, rumore etc*) metallic

me'tallo *sm* metal

metalmec'canico, a, ci, che *ag* engineering *cpd* ♦ *sm* engineering worker

me'tano *sm* methane

meteorolo'gia [meteorolo'dʒia] *sf* meteorology; **meteoro'logico, a, ci, che** *ag* meteorological, weather *cpd*

me'ticcio, a, ci, ce [me'tittʃo] *sm/f* half-caste, half-breed

me'todico, a, ci, che *ag* methodical

'metodo *sm* method

'metrica *sf* metrics *sg*; **'metrico, a, ci, che** *ag* metric; (*POESIA*) metrical

'metro *sm* metre; (*nastro*) tape measure;

(*asta*) (metre) rule

metropoli'tana *sf* underground, subway

metropoli'tano, a *ag* metropolitan

'**mettere** *vt* to put; (*abito*) to put on; (: *portare*) to wear; (*installare: telefono*) to put in; (*fig: provocare*): ~ **fame/allegria a qn** to make sb hungry/happy; (*supporre*): **mettiamo che ...** let's suppose *o* say that ... ; ~**rsi** *vr* (*persona*) to put o.s.; (*oggetto*) to go; (*disporsi: faccenda*) to turn out; ~**rsi a sedere** *o* **a letto** to sit down; ~**rsi a letto** to get into bed; (*per malattia*) to take to one's bed; ~**rsi il cappello** to put on one's hat; ~**rsi a** (*cominciare*) to begin to, start to; ~**rsi al lavoro** to set to work; ~**rsi con qn** (*in società*) to team up with sb; (*in coppia*) to start going out with sb; ~**rci:** ~**rci molta cura/molto tempo** to take a lot of care/a lot of time; **ci ho messo 3 ore per venire** it's taken me 3 hours to get here; ~**rcela tutta** to do one's best; ~ **a tacere qn/qc** to keep sb/sth quiet; ~ **su casa** to set up house; ~ **su un negozio** to start a shop; ~ **via** to put away

'**mezza** ['mɛddza] *sf*: **la** ~ half-past twelve (*in the afternoon*); *vedi anche* **mezzo**

mez'zadro [med'dzadro] *sm* (*AGR*) sharecropper

mezza'luna [meddza'luna] *sf* half-moon; (*dell'islamismo*) crescent; (*coltello*) (*semicircular*) chopping knife

mezza'nino [meddza'nino] *sm* mezzanine (floor)

mez'zano, a [med'dzano] *ag* (*medio*) average, medium; (*figlio*) middle *cpd* ♦ *sm/f* (*ruffiano*) pimp

mezza'notte [meddza'nɔtte] *sf* midnight

'**mezzo, a** ['mɛddzo] *ag* half; **un** ~ **litro/panino** half a litre/roll ♦ *av* half-; ~ **morto** half-dead ♦ *sm* (*metà*) half; (*parte centrale: di strada etc*) middle; (*per raggiungere un fine*) means *sg*; (*veicolo*) vehicle; (*nell'indicare l'ora*): **le nove e** ~ half past nine; **mezzogiorno e** ~ half past twelve; ~**i** *smpl* (*possibilità economiche*) means; **di** ~**a età** middle-aged; **un soprabito di** ~**a stagione** a spring (*o* autumn) coat; **di** ~

middle, in the middle; **andarci di** ~ (*patir danno*) to suffer; **levarsi** *o* **togliersi di** ~ to get out of the way; **in** ~ **a** in the middle of; **per** *o* **a** ~ **di** by means of; ~**i di comunicazione di massa** mass media *pl*; ~**i pubblici** public transport *sg*; ~**i di trasporto** means of transport

mezzogi'orno [meddzo'dʒorno] *sm* midday, noon; **a** ~ at 12 (o'clock) *o* midday *o* noon; **il** ~ **d'Italia** southern Italy

mez'z'ora [med'dzora] *sf* half-hour, half an hour

mi (*dav lo, la, li, le, ne diventa* **me**) *pron* (*oggetto*) me; (*complemento di termine*) to me; (*riflessivo*) myself ♦ *sm* (*MUS*) E; (: *solfeggiando la scala*) mi

'**mia** *vedi* **mio**

miago'lare *vi* to miaow, mew

'**mica** *av* (*fam*): **non ...** ~ not ... at all; **non sono** ~ **stanco** I'm not a bit tired; **non sarà** ~ **partito?** he wouldn't have left, would he?; ~ **male** not bad

'**miccia, ce** ['mittʃa] *sf* fuse

micidi'ale [mitʃi'djale] *ag* fatal; (*dannosissimo*) deadly

mi'crofono *sm* microphone

micros'copio *sm* microscope

mi'dollo (*pl(f)* ~**a**) *sm* (*ANAT*) marrow; ~ **osseo** bone marrow

'**mie** *vedi* **mio**

mi'ei *vedi* **mio**

mi'ele *sm* honey

mi'etere *vt* (*AGR*) to reap, harvest; (*fig: vite*) to take, claim

'**miglia** ['miʎʎa] *sfpl di* **miglio**

migli'aio [miʎ'ʎajo] (*pl(f)* ~**a**) *sm* thousand; **un** ~ **(di)** about a thousand; **a** ~**a** by the thousand, in thousands

'**miglio** ['miʎʎo] *sm* (*BOT*) millet; (*pl(f)* ~**a**: *unità di misura*) mile; ~ **marino** *o* **nautico** nautical mile

migliora'mento [miʎʎora'mento] *sm* improvement

miglio'rare [miʎʎo'rare] *vt, vi* to improve

migli'ore [miʎ'ʎore] *ag* (*comparativo*) better; (*superlativo*) best ♦ *sm*: **il** ~ the best (thing) ♦ *sm/f*: **il(la)** ~ the best (person); **il**

miglior vino di questa regione the best wine in this area

'mi**gnolo** ['miɲɲolo] *sm* (ANAT) little finger, pinkie; (*: dito del piede*) little toe

mi'**grare** *vi* to migrate

'**mila** *pl di* **mille**

Mi'**lano** *sf* Milan

miliar'**dario, a** *sm/f* millionaire

mili'**ardo** *sm* thousand million, billion (US)

mili'**are** *ag*: **pietra ~** milestone

mili'**one** *sm* million; **due ~i di lire** two million lire

mili'**tante** *ag, sm/f* militant

mili'**tare** *vi* (MIL) to be a soldier, serve; (*fig: in un partito*) to be a militant ♦ *ag* military ♦ *sm* serviceman; **fare il ~** to do one's military service

mi'**lite** *sm* soldier

millanta'**tore, 'trice** *sm/f* boaster

'**mille** (*pl* **mila**) *num* a *o* one thousand; **dieci mila** ten thousand

mille'**foglie** [mille'fɔʎʎe] *sm inv* (CUC) cream *o* vanilla slice

mil'**lennio** *sm* millennium

millepi'**edi** *sm inv* centipede

mil'**lesimo, a** *ag, sm* thousandth

milli'**grammo** *sm* milligram(me)

mil'**limetro** *sm* millimetre

'**milza** ['miltsa] *sf* (ANAT) spleen

mimetiz'**zare** [mimetid'dzare] *vt* to camouflage; **~rsi** *vr* to camouflage o.s.

'**mimica** *sf* (*arte*) mime

'**mimo** *sm* (*attore, componimento*) mime

mi'**mosa** *sf* mimosa

'**mina** *sf* (*esplosiva*) mine; (*di matita*) lead

mi'**naccia, ce** [mi'nattʃa] *sf* threat; **minacci'are** *vt* to threaten; **minacciare qn di morte** to threaten to kill sb; **minacciare di fare qc** to threaten to do sth; **minacci'oso, a** *ag* threatening

mi'**nare** *vt* (MIL) to mine; (*fig*) to undermine

mina'**tore** *sm* miner

mina'**torio, a** *ag* threatening

mine'**rale** *ag, sm* mineral

mine'**rario, a** *ag* (*delle miniere*) mining; (*dei minerali*) ore *cpd*

mi'**nestra** *sf* soup; **~ in brodo/di verdure** noodle/vegetable soup; **mines'trone** *sm* thick vegetable and pasta soup

mingher'**lino, a** [minger'lino] *ag* thin, slender

'**mini** *ag inv* mini ♦ *sf inv* miniskirt

minia'**tura** *sf* miniature

mini'**disc** *sm inv* Minidisc ®

mini'**era** *sf* mine

mini'**gonna** *sf* miniskirt

'**minimo, a** *ag* minimum, least, slightest; (*piccolissimo*) very small, slight; (*il più basso*) lowest, minimum ♦ *sm* minimum; **al ~** at least; **girare al ~** (AUT) to idle

minis'**tero** *sm* (POL, REL) ministry; (*governo*) government; **M~ delle Finanze** Ministry of Finance, ≈ Treasury

mi'**nistro** *sm* (POL, REL) minister

mino'**ranza** [mino'rantsa] *sf* minority

mino'**rato, a** *ag* handicapped ♦ *sm/f* physically (*o* mentally) handicapped person

mi'**nore** *ag* (*comparativo*) less; (*più piccolo*) smaller; (*numero*) lower; (*inferiore*) lower, inferior; (*meno importante*) minor; (*più giovane*) younger; (*superlativo*) least; smallest; lowest; youngest ♦ *sm/f* = **minorenne**

mino'**renne** *ag* under age ♦ *sm/f* minor, person under age

mi'**nuscolo, a** *ag* (*scrittura, carattere*) small; (*piccolissimo*) tiny ♦ *sf* small letter

mi'**nuta** *sf* rough copy, draft

mi'**nuto, a** *ag* tiny, minute; (*pioggia*) fine; (*corporatura*) delicate, fine ♦ *sm* (*unità di misura*) minute; **al ~** (COMM) retail

'**mio** (*f* '**mia**, *pl* **mi'ei, 'mie**) *det*: **il ~, la mia** *etc* my ♦ *pron*: **il ~, la mia** *etc* mine; **i miei** my family; **un ~ amico** a friend of mine

'**miope** *ag* short-sighted

'**mira** *sf* (*anche fig*) aim; **prendere la ~** to take aim; **prendere di ~ qn** (*fig*) to pick on sb

mi'**rabile** *ag* admirable, wonderful

mi'**racolo** *sm* miracle

mi'**raggio** [mi'raddʒo] *sm* mirage

mi'**rare** *vi*: **~ a** to aim at

mi'**rino** *sm* (TECN) sight; (FOT) viewer, viewfinder

mir'tillo *sm* bilberry (*BRIT*), blueberry (*US*), whortleberry

mi'scela [miʃʃela] *sf* mixture; (*di caffè*) blend

miscel'lanea [miʃʃelˈlanea] *sf* miscellany

'mischia [ˈmiskja] *sf* scuffle; (*RUGBY*) scrum, scrummage

mischi'are [misˈkjare] *vt* to mix, blend; **~rsi** *vr* to mix, blend

mis'cuglio [misˈkuʎʎo] *sm* mixture, hotchpotch, jumble

mise'rabile *ag* (*infelice*) miserable, wretched; (*povero*) poverty-stricken; (*di scarso valore*) miserable

mi'seria *sf* extreme poverty; (*infelicità*) misery; **~e** *sfpl* (*del mondo etc*) misfortunes, troubles; **porca ~!** (*fam*) blast!, damn!

miseri'cordia *sf* mercy, pity

'misero, a *ag* miserable, wretched; (*povero*) poverty-stricken; (*insufficiente*) miserable

mis'fatto *sm* misdeed, crime

mi'sogino [miˈzɔdʒino] *sm* misogynist

'missile *sm* missile

missio'nario, a *ag, sm/f* missionary

missi'one *sf* mission

misteri'oso, a *ag* mysterious

mis'tero *sm* mystery

'misto, a *ag* mixed; (*scuola*) mixed, coeducational ♦ *sm* mixture

mis'tura *sf* mixture

mi'sura *sf* measure; (*misurazione, dimensione*) measurement; (*taglia*) size; (*provvedimento*) measure, step; (*moderazione*) moderation; (*MUS*) time; (: *divisione*) bar; (*fig: limite*) bounds *pl*, limit; **nella ~ in cui** inasmuch as, insofar as; **(fatto) su ~** made to measure

misu'rare *vt* (*ambiente, stoffa*) to measure; (*terreno*) to survey; (*abito*) to try on; (*pesare*) to weigh; (*fig: parole etc*) to weigh up; (: *spese, cibo*) to limit ♦ *vi* to measure; **~rsi** *vr*: **~rsi con qn** to have a confrontation with sb; to compete with sb; **misu'rato, a** *ag* (*ponderato*) measured; (*moderato*) moderate

'mite *ag* mild

miti'gare *vt* to mitigate, lessen; (*lenire*) to soothe, relieve; **~rsi** *vr* (*odio*) to subside; (*tempo*) to become milder

'mito *sm* myth; **mitolo'gia, 'gie** *sf* mythology

'mitra *sf* (*REL*) mitre ♦ *sm inv* (*arma*) sub-machine gun

mitraglia'trice [mitraʎʎaˈtritʃe] *sf* machine gun

mit'tente *sm/f* sender

'mobile *ag* mobile; (*parte di macchina*) moving; (*DIR: bene*) movable, personal ♦ *sm* (*arredamento*) piece of furniture; **~i** *smpl* (*mobilia*) furniture *sg*

mo'bilia *sf* furniture

mobili'are *ag* (*DIR*) personal, movable

mo'bilio *sm* = **mobilia**

mobili'tare *vt* to mobilize

mocas'sino *sm* moccasin

mocci'oso, a [mottˈʃoso, a] *sm/f* (*peg*) snotty(-nosed) kid

'moccolo *sm* (*di candela*) candle-end; (*fam: bestemmia*) oath; (: *moccio*) snot; **reggere il ~** to play gooseberry (*BRIT*), act as chaperon

'moda *sf* fashion; **alla ~, di ~** fashionable, in fashion

modalità *sf inv* formality

mo'della *sf* model

model'lare *vt* (*creta*) to model, shape; **~rsi** *vr*: **~rsi su** to model o.s. on

mo'dello *sm* model; (*stampo*) mould ♦ *ag inv* model *cpd*

'modem *sm inv* modem

mode'rare *vt* to moderate; **~rsi** *vr* to restrain o.s.; **mode'rato, a** *ag* moderate

modera'tore, 'trice *sm/f* moderator

mo'derno, a *ag* modern

mo'destia *sf* modesty

mo'desto, a *ag* modest

'modico, a, ci, che *ag* reasonable, moderate

mo'difica, che *sf* modification

modifi'care *vt* to modify, alter; **~rsi** *vr* to alter, change

mo'dista *sf* milliner

'modo *sm* way, manner; (*mezzo*) means,

way; (*occasione*) opportunity; (*LING*) mood; (*MUS*) mode; **~i** *smpl* (*comportamento*) manners; **a suo ~, a ~ suo** in his own way; **ad** *o* **in ogni ~** anyway; **di** *o* **in ~ che** so that; **in ~ da** so as to; **in tutti i ~i** at all costs; (*comunque sia*) anyway; (*in ogni caso*) in any case; **in qualche ~** somehow or other; **~ di dire** turn of phrase; **per ~ di dire** so to speak

modu'lare *vt* to modulate; **modulazi'one** *sf* modulation; **modulazione di frequenza** frequency modulation

'**modulo** *sm* (*modello*) form; (*ARCHIT, lunare, di comando*) module

'**mogano** *sm* mahogany

'**mogio, a, gi, gie** ['mɔdʒo] *ag* down in the dumps, dejected

'**moglie** ['moʎʎe] *sf* wife

mo'**ine** *sfpl* cajolery *sg*; (*leziosità*) affectation *sg*

'**mola** *sf* millstone; (*utensile abrasivo*) grindstone

mo'**lare** *sm* (*dente*) molar

'**mole** *sf* mass; (*dimensioni*) size; (*edificio grandioso*) massive structure

moles'**tare** *vt* to bother, annoy; mo'**lestia** *sf* annoyance, bother; **recar molestia a qn** to bother sb; mo'**lesto, a** *ag* annoying

'**molla** *sf* spring; **~e** *sfpl* (*per camino*) tongs

mol'**lare** *vt* to release, let go; (*NAUT*) to ease; (*fig: ceffone*) to give ♦ *vi* (*cedere*) to give in

'**molle** *ag* soft; (*muscoli*) flabby

mol'**letta** *sf* (*per capelli*) hairgrip; (*per panni stesi*) clothes peg

'**mollica, che** *sf* crumb, soft part

mol'**lusco, schi** *sm* mollusc

'**molo** *sm* mole, breakwater; jetty

mol'**teplice** [mol'teplitʃe] *ag* (*formato di più elementi*) complex; **~i** *pl* (*svariati: interessi, attività*) numerous, various

moltipli'**care** *vt* to multiply; **~rsi** *vr* to multiply; to increase in number; **moltiplicazi'one** *sf* multiplication

---

PAROLA CHIAVE

'**molto, a** *det* (*quantità*) a lot of, much; (*numero*) a lot of, many; **~ pane/carbone** a lot of bread/coal; **~a gente** a lot of people, many people; **~i libri** a lot of books, many books; **non ho ~ tempo** I haven't got much time; **per ~ (tempo)** for a long time

♦ *av* **1** a lot, (very) much; **viaggia ~** he travels a lot; **non viaggia ~** he doesn't travel much *o* a lot

2 (*intensivo: con aggettivi, avverbi*) very; (: *con participio passato*) (very) much; **~ buono** very good; **~ migliore, ~ meglio** much *o* a lot better

♦ *pron* much, a lot; **~i, e** *pron pl* many, a lot; **~i pensano che ...** many (people) think ...

---

momen'**taneo, a** *ag* momentary, fleeting

mo'**mento** *sm* moment; **da un ~ all'altro** at any moment; (*all'improvviso*) suddenly; **al ~ di fare** just as I was (*o* you were *o* he was *etc*) doing; **per il ~** for the time being; **dal ~ che** ever since; (*dato che*) since; **a ~i** (*da un ~ all'altro*) any time *o* moment now; (*quasi*) nearly

'**monaca, che** *sf* nun

'**Monaco** *sf* Monaco; **~ (di Baviera)** Munich

'**monaco, ci** *sm* monk

mo'**narca, chi** *sm* monarch; monar'**chia** *sf* monarchy

monas'**tero** *sm* (*di monaci*) monastery; (*di monache*) convent; mo'**nastico, a, ci, che** *ag* monastic

'**monco, a, chi, che** *ag* maimed; (*fig*) incomplete

mon'**dano, a** *ag* (*anche fig*) worldly; (*dell'alta società*) society *cpd*; fashionable

mon'**dare** *vt* (*frutta, patate*) to peel; (*piselli*) to shell; (*pulire*) to clean

mondi'**ale** *ag* (*campionato, popolazione*) world *cpd*; (*influenza*) world-wide

'**mondo** *sm* world; (*grande quantità*): **un ~ di** lots of, a host of; **il bel ~** high society mo'nello, a *sm/f* street urchin; (*ragazzo vivace*) scamp, imp

mo'neta *sf* coin; (*ECON: valuta*) currency; (*denaro spicciolo*) (small) change; ~ **estera** foreign currency; ~ **legale** legal tender; **mone'tario, a** *ag* monetary

mongo'loide *ag, sm/f* (*MED*) mongol

'monito *sm* warning

'monitor *sm inv* (*TECN, TV*) monitor

monolo'cale *sm* studio flat

mono'polio *sm* monopoly

mo'notono, a *ag* monotonous

monsi'gnore [monsiɲ'ɲore] *sm* (*REL: titolo*) Your (*o* His) Grace

mon'sone *sm* monsoon

monta'carichi [monta'kariki] *sm inv* hoist, goods lift

mon'taggio [mon'taddʒo] *sm* (*TECN*) assembly; (*CINEMA*) editing

mon'tagna [mon'taɲɲa] *sf* mountain; (*zona montuosa*): **la** ~ the mountains *pl*; **andare in** ~ to go to the mountains; **~e russe** roller coaster *sg*, big dipper *sg* (*BRIT*); **monta'gnoso, a** *ag* mountainous

monta'naro, a *ag* mountain *cpd* ♦ *sm/f* mountain dweller

mon'tano, a *ag* mountain *cpd*; alpine

mon'tare *vt* to go (*o* come) up; (*cavallo*) to ride; (*apparecchiatura*) to set up, assemble; (*CUC*) to whip; (*ZOOL*) to cover; (*incastonare*) to mount, set; (*CINEMA*) to edit; (*FOT*) to mount ♦ *vi* to go (*o* come) up; (*a cavallo*): **~ bene/male** to ride well/badly; (*aumentare di livello, volume*) to rise; **~rsi** *vr* to become big-headed; **~ qc** to exaggerate sth; **~ qn** *o* **la testa a qn** to turn sb's head; **~ in bicicletta/macchina/treno** to get on a bicycle/into a car/on a train; **~ a cavallo** to get on *o* mount a horse

monta'tura *sf* assembling *no pl*; (*di occhiali*) frames *pl*; (*di gioiello*) mounting, setting; (*fig*): ~ **pubblicitaria** publicity stunt

'monte *sm* mountain; **a** ~ upstream; **mandare a** ~ **qc** to upset sth, cause sth to fail; **il M~ Bianco** Mont Blanc; ~ **di pietà** pawnshop

mon'tone *sm* (*ZOOL*) ram; **carne di** ~ mutton

montu'oso, a *ag* mountainous

monu'mento *sm* monument

mo'quette [mɔ'kɛt] *sf inv* fitted carpet

'mora *sf* (*del rovo*) blackberry; (*del gelso*) mulberry; (*DIR*) delay; (: *somma*) arrears *pl*

mo'rale *ag* moral ♦ *sf* (*scienza*) ethics *sg*, moral philosophy; (*complesso di norme*) moral standards *pl*, morality; (*condotta*) morals *pl*; (*insegnamento morale*) moral ♦ *sm* morale; **essere giù di** ~ to be feeling down; **moralità** *sf* morality; (*condotta*) morals *pl*

'morbido, a *ag* soft; (*pelle*) soft, smooth

mor'billo *sm* (*MED*) measles *sg*

'morbo *sm* disease

mor'boso, a *ag* (*fig*) morbid

mor'dace [mor'datʃe] *ag* biting, cutting

mor'dente *sm* (*fig: di satira, critica*) bite; (: *di persona*) drive

'mordere *vt* to bite; (*addentare*) to bite into

mori'bondo, a *ag* dying, moribund

morige'rato, a [moridʒe'rato] *ag* of good morals

mo'rire *vi* to die; (*abitudine, civiltà*) to die out; ~ **di fame** to die of hunger; (*fig*) to be starving; ~ **di noia/paura** to be bored/scared to death; **fa un caldo da** ~ it's terribly hot

mormo'rare *vi* to murmur; (*brontolare*) to grumble

'moro, a *ag* dark(-haired); dark(-complexioned); **i M~i** *smpl* (*STORIA*) the Moors

mo'roso, a *ag* in arrears ♦ *sm/f* (*fam: innamorato*) sweetheart

'morsa *sf* (*TECN*) vice; (*fig: stretta*) grip

morsi'care *vt* to nibble (at), gnaw (at); (*sog: insetto*) to bite

'morso, a *pp di* **mordere** ♦ *sm* bite; (*di insetto*) sting; (*parte della briglia*) bit; **~i della fame** pangs of hunger

mor'taio *sm* mortar

mor'tale *ag, sm* mortal; **mortalità** *sf* mortality, death rate 'morte *sf* death

mortifi'care *vt* to mortify

'morto, a *pp di* morire ♦ *ag* dead ♦ *sm/f* dead man/woman; **i ~i** the dead; **fare il ~** (*nell'acqua*) to float on one's back; **il Mar M~** the Dead Sea

mor'torio *sm* (*anche fig*) funeral

mo'saico, ci *sm* mosaic

'Mosca *sf* Moscow

'mosca, sche *sf* fly; **~ cieca** blind-man's-buff

mos'cato *sm* muscatel (wine)

mosce'rino [moʃʃe'rino] *sm* midge, gnat

mos'chea [mos'kea] *sf* mosque

mos'chetto [mos'ketto] *sm* musket

'moscio, a, sci, sce ['moʃʃo] *ag* (*fig*) lifeless

mos'cone *sm* (*ZOOL*) bluebottle; (*barca*) pedalo; (: *a remi*) *kind of pedalo with oars*

'mossa *sf* movement; (*nel gioco*) move

'mosso, a *pp di* muovere ♦ *ag* (*mare*) rough; (*capelli*) wavy; (*FOT*) blurred

mos'tarda *sf* mustard

'mostra *sf* exhibition, show; (*ostentazione*) show; **in ~** on show; **far ~ di** (*fingere*) to pretend; **far ~ di sé** to show off

mos'trare *vt* to show; **~rsi** *vr* to appear

'mostro *sm* monster; mostru'oso, a *ag* monstrous

mo'tel *sm inv* motel

moti'vare *vt* (*causare*) to cause; (*giustificare*) to justify, account for; motivazi'one *sf* justification; motive; (*PSIC*) motivation

mo'tivo *sm* (*causa*) reason, cause; (*movente*) motive; (*letterario*) (central) theme; (*disegno*) motif, design, pattern; (*MUS*) motif; **per quale ~?** why?, for what reason?

'moto *sm* (*anche FISICA*) motion; (*movimento, gesto*) movement; (*esercizio fisico*) exercise; (*sommossa*) rising, revolt; (*commozione*) feeling, impulse ♦ *sf inv* (*motocicletta*) motorbike; **mettere in ~** to set in motion; (*AUT*) to start up

motoci'cletta [mototʃi'kletta] *sf* motorcycle; motoci'clismo *sm* motorcycling, motorcycle racing;

motoci'clista, i, e *sm/f* motorcyclist

mo'tore, 'trice *ag* motor; (*TECN*) driving ♦ *sm* engine, motor; **a ~** motor *cpd*, power-driven; **~ a combustione interna/a reazione** internal combustion/jet engine; **~ di ricerca** search engine; moto'rino *sm* moped; **motorino di avviamento** (*AUT*) starter; motoriz'zato, a *ag* (*truppe*) motorized; (*persona*) having a car *o* transport

motos'cafo *sm* motorboat

'motto *sm* (*battuta scherzosa*) witty remark; (*frase emblematica*) motto, maxim

'mouse ['maus] *sm inv* (*INFORM*) mouse

mo'vente *sm* motive

movimen'tare *vt* to liven up

movi'mento *sm* movement; (*fig*) activity, hustle and bustle; (*MUS*) tempo, movement

mozi'one [mot'tsjone] *sf* (*POL*) motion

moz'zare [mot'tsare] *vt* to cut off; (*coda*) to dock; **~ il fiato *o* il respiro a qn** (*fig*) to take sb's breath away

mozza'rella [mottsa'rella] *sf* mozzarella

mozzi'cone [mottsi'kone] *sm* stub, butt, end; (*anche*: **~ di sigaretta**) cigarette end

'mozzo ['mottso] *sm* (*NAUT*) ship's boy

'mucca, che *sf* cow

'mucchio ['mukkjo] *sm* pile, heap; (*fig*): **un ~ di** lots of, heaps of

'muco, chi *sm* mucus

'muffa *sf* mould, mildew

mug'gire [mud'dʒire] *vi* (*vacca*) to low, moo; (*toro*) to bellow; (*fig*) to roar; mug'gito *sm* low, moo; bellow; roar

mu'ghetto [mu'getto] *sm* lily of the valley

mu'gnaio, a [muɲ'najo] *sm/f* miller

mugo'lare *vi* (*cane*) to whimper, whine; (*fig: persona*) to moan

muli'nare *vi* to whirl, spin (round and round)

muli'nello *sm* (*moto vorticoso*) eddy, whirl; (*di canna da pesca*) reel

mu'lino *sm* mill; **~ a vento** windmill

'mulo *sm* mule

'multa *sf* fine; mul'tare *vt* to fine

'multiplo, a *ag*, *sm* multiple

multiproprietà *sf inv* time-share

'mummia *sf* mummy

'mungere ['mundʒere] *vt* (*anche fig*) to milk

munici'pale [munitʃi'pale] *ag* municipal; town *cpd*

muni'cipio [muni'tʃipjo] *sm* town council, corporation; (*edificio*) town hall

mu'nire *vt*: ~ **qc/qn di** to equip sth/sb with

munizi'oni [munit'tsjoni] *sfpl* (*MIL*) ammunition *sg*

'munto, a *pp di* **mungere**

mu'overe *vt* to move; (*ruota, macchina*) to drive; (*sollevare: questione, obiezione*) to raise, bring up; (: *accusa*) to make, bring forward; (~**rsi** *vr*) to move; **muoviti!** hurry up!, get a move on!

'mura *sfpl vedi* **muro**

mu'raglia [mu'raʎʎa] *sf* (high) wall

mu'rale *ag* wall *cpd*; mural

mu'rare *vt* (*persona, porta*) to wall up

mura'tore *sm* mason; bricklayer

'muro *sm* wall; ~**a** *sfpl* (*cinta cittadina*) walls; **a ~** *wall cpd*; (*armadio etc*) built-in; ~ **del suono** sound barrier; **mettere al ~** (*fucilare*) to shoot *o* execute (by firing squad)

'muschio ['muskjo] *sm* (*ZOOL*) musk; (*BOT*) moss

musco'lare *ag* muscular, muscle *cpd*

'muscolo *sm* (*ANAT*) muscle

mu'seo *sm* museum

museru'ola *sf* muzzle

'musica *sf* music; ~ **da ballo/camera** dance/chamber music; **musi'cale** *ag* musical; **musi'cista, i, e** *sm/f* musician

'muso *sm* muzzle; (*di auto, aereo*) nose; **tenere il ~** to sulk; **mu'sone, a** *sm/f* sulky person

'muta *sf* (*di animali*) moulting; (*di serpenti*) sloughing; (*per immersioni subacquee*) diving suit; (*gruppo di cani*) pack

muta'mento *sm* change

mu'tande *sfpl* (*da uomo*) (under) pants; **mutan'dine** *sfpl* (*da donna, bambino*) pants (*BRIT*), briefs

mu'tare *vt, vi* to change, alter; **mutazi'one** *sf* change, alteration; (*BIOL*)

mutation; **mu'tevole** *ag* changeable

muti'lare *vt* to mutilate, maim; (*fig*) to mutilate, deface; **muti'lato, a** *sm/f* disabled person (*through loss of limbs*)

mu'tismo *sm* (*MED*) mutism; (*atteggiamento*) (stubborn) silence

'muto, a *ag* (*MED*) dumb; (*emozione, dolore, CINEMA*) silent; (*LING*) silent, mute; (*carta geografica*) blank; ~ **per lo stupore** *etc* speechless with amazement *etc*

'mutua *sf* (*anche*: **cassa ~**) health insurance scheme

mutu'are *vt* (*fig*) to borrow

mutu'ato, a *sm/f* member of a health insurance scheme

'mutuo, a *ag* (*reciproco*) mutual ♦ *sm* (*ECON*) (long-term) loan

N, n

N. *abbr* (= *nord*) N

'nacchere ['nakkere] *sfpl* castanets

'nafta *sf* naphtha; (*per motori diesel*) diesel oil

nafta'lina *sf* (*CHIM*) naphthalene; (*tarmicida*) mothballs *pl*

'naia *sf* (*MIL*) slang term for national service

'nailon *sm* nylon

'nanna *sf* (*linguaggio infantile*): **andare a ~** to go to beddy-byes

'nano, a *ag, sm/f* dwarf

napole'tano, a *ag, sm/f* Neapolitan

'Napoli *sf* Naples

'nappa *sf* tassel

nar'ciso [nar'tʃizo] *sm* narcissus

nar'cosi *sf* narcosis

nar'cotico, ci *sm* narcotic

na'rice [na'ritʃe] *sf* nostril

nar'rare *vt* to tell the story of, recount; **narra'tiva** *sf* (*branca letteraria*) fiction; **narra'tivo, a** *ag* narrative; **narra'tore, 'trice** *sm/f* narrator; **narrazi'one** *sf* narration; (*racconto*) story, tale

na'sale *ag* nasal

'nascere ['naʃʃere] *vi* (*bambino*) to be born; (*pianta*) to come *o* spring up; (*fiume*) to rise, have its source; (*sole*) to rise; (*dente*) to come through; (*fig: derivare, conseguire*): ~ **da** to arise from, be born out of; **è nata nel 1952** she was born in 1952; **'nascita** *sf* birth

nas'condere *vt* to hide, conceal; **~rsi** *vr* to hide; **nascon'diglio** *sm* hiding place; **nascon'dino** *sm* (*gioco*) hide-and-seek; **nas'costo, a** *pp di* **nascondere** ♦ *ag* hidden; **di nascosto** secretly

na'sello *sm* (*ZOOL*) hake

'naso *sm* nose

'nastro *sm* ribbon; (*magnetico, isolante, SPORT*) tape; **~ adesivo** adhesive tape; **~ trasportatore** conveyor belt

nas'turzio [nas'turtsjo] *sm* nasturtium

na'tale *ag* of one's birth ♦ *sm* (*REL*): **N~** Christmas; (*giorno della nascita*) birthday; **natalità** *sf* birth rate; **nata'lizio, a** *ag* (*del Natale*) Christmas *cpd*

na'tante *sm* craft *inv*, boat

'natica, che *sf* (*ANAT*) buttock

na'tio, a, 'tii, 'tie *ag* native

Nativ'ità *sf* (*REL*) Nativity

na'tivo, a *ag, sm/f* native

'nato, a *pp di* **nascere** ♦ *ag*: **un attore ~** a born actor; **~a Pieri** née Pieri

na'tura *sf* nature; **pagare in ~** to pay in kind; **~ morta** still life

natu'rale *ag* natural; **natura'lezza** *sf* naturalness; **natura'lista, i, e** *sm/f* naturalist

naturaliz'zare [naturalid'dzare] *vt* to naturalize

natural'mente *av* naturally; (*certamente, sì*) of course

naufra'gare *vi* (*nave*) to be wrecked; (*persona*) to be shipwrecked; (*fig*) to fall through; **nau'fragio** *sm* shipwreck; (*fig*) ruin, failure; **'naufrago, ghi** *sm* castaway, shipwreck victim

'nausea *sf* nausea; **nausea'bondo, a** *ag* nauseating, sickening; **nause'are** *vt* to nauseate, make (feel) sick

'nautica *sf* (art of) navigation

'nautico, a, ci, che *ag* nautical

na'vale *ag* naval

na'vata *sf* (*anche:* ~ **centrale**) nave; (*anche:* ~ **laterale**) aisle

'nave *sf* ship, vessel; **~ cisterna** tanker; **~ da guerra** warship; **~ passeggeri** passenger ship

na'vetta *sf* shuttle; (*servizio di collegamento*) shuttle (service)

navi'cella [navi'tʃella] *sf* (*di aerostato*) gondola; **~ spaziale** spaceship

navi'gare *vi* to sail; **~ in Internet** to surf the Net; **navigazi'one** *sf* navigation

na'viglio [na'viʎʎo] *sm* (*canale artificiale*) canal; **~ da pesca** fishing fleet

nazio'nale [nattsjo'nale] *ag* national ♦ *sf* (*SPORT*) national team; **naziona'lismo** *sm* nationalism; **nazionalità** *sf inv* nationality

nazi'one [nat'tsjone] *sf* nation

PAROLA CHIAVE

ne *pron* **1** (*di lui, lei, loro*) of him/her/them; about him/her/them; **~ riconosco la voce** I recognize his (*o* her) voice
2 (*di questa, quella cosa*) of it; about it; **~ voglio ancora** I want some more (of it *o* them); **non parliamone più!** let's not talk about it any more!
3 (*con valore partitivo*): **hai dei libri? – sì, ~ ho** have you any books? — yes, I have (some); **hai del pane? — no, non ~ ho** have you any bread? — no, I haven't any; **quanti anni hai? – ~ ho 17** how old are you? — I'm 17
♦ *av* (*moto da luogo: da lì*) from there; **~ vengo ora** I've just come from there

---

né *cong*: **~ ... ~** neither ... nor; **~ l'uno ~ l'altro lo vuole** neither of them wants it; **non parla ~ l'italiano ~ il tedesco** he speaks neither Italian nor German, he doesn't speak either Italian or German; **non piove ~ nevica** it isn't raining or snowing

ne'anche [ne'anke] *av, cong* not even; **non ... ~** not even; **~ se volesse potrebbe venire** he couldn't come even if he wanted to; **non l'ho visto — ~ io** I didn't see him — neither did I *o* I didn't either; **~ per idea** *o* **sogno!** not on your life!

'**nebbia** *sf* fog; *(foschia)* mist; **nebbi'oso,
a** *ag* foggy; misty

nebu'loso, a *ag (atmosfera)* hazy; *(fig)*
hazy, vague

necessaria'mente [netʃessarja'mente] *av*
necessarily

neces'sario, a [netʃes'sarjo] *ag* necessary

necessità [netʃessi'ta] *sf inv* necessity;
(povertà) need, poverty; **necessi'tare** *vt*
to require ♦ *vi (aver bisogno):* **necessitare
di** to need

necro'logio [nekro'lɔdʒo] *sm* obituary
notice

ne'fando, a *ag* infamous, wicked

ne'fasto, a *ag* inauspicious, ill-omened

ne'gare *vt* to deny; *(rifiutare)* to deny,
refuse; **~ di aver fatto/che** to deny having
done/that; **nega'tivo, a** *ag, sf, sm*
negative; **negazi'one** *sf* negation

ne'gletto, a *ag (trascurato)* neglected

'negli ['neʎʎi] *prep +det vedi* **in**

negli'gente [negli'dʒente] *ag* negligent,
careless; **negli'genza** *sf* negligence,
carelessness

negozi'ante [negot'tsjante] *sm/f* trader,
dealer; *(bottegaio)* shopkeeper *(BRIT)*,
storekeeper *(US)*

negozi'are [negot'tsjare] *vt* to negotiate
♦ *vi:* **~ in** to trade *o* deal in; **negozi'ato**
sm negotiation

ne'gozio [ne'gɔttsjo] *sm (locale)* shop *(BRIT)*,
store *(US)*

'**negro, a** *ag, sm/f* Negro

'**nei** *prep +det vedi* **in**

nel *prep +det vedi* **in**

nell' *prep +det vedi* **in**

'**nella** *prep +det vedi* **in**

'**nelle** *prep +det vedi* **in**

'**nello** *prep +det vedi* **in**

'**nembo** *sm (METEOR)* nimbus

ne'mico, a, ci, che *ag* hostile; *(MIL)*
enemy *cpd* ♦ *sm/f* enemy; **essere ~ di** to
be strongly averse *o* opposed to

nem'meno *av, cong* = **neanche**

ne'nia *sf* dirge; *(motivo monotono)*
monotonous tune

'**neo** *sm* mole; *(fig)* (slight) flaw

'**neo...** *prefisso* neo...

'**neon** *sm (CHIM)* neon

neo'nato, a *ag* newborn ♦ *sm/f* newborn
baby

neozelan'dese [neoddzelan'dese] *ag* New
Zealand *cpd* ♦ *sm/f* New Zealander

nep'pure *av, cong* = **neanche**

'**nerbo** *sm* lash; *(fig)* strength, backbone;
nerbo'ruto, a *ag* muscular; robust

ne'retto *sm (TIP)* bold type

'**nero, a** *ag* black; *(scuro)* dark ♦ *sm* black;
il Mar N~ the Black Sea

nerva'tura *sf (ANAT)* nervous system; *(BOT)*
veining; *(ARCHIT, TECN)* rib

'**nervo** *sm (ANAT)* nerve; *(BOT)* vein; **avere i
~i** to be on edge; **dare sui ~i a qn** to get
on sb's nerves; **ner'voso, a** *ag* nervous;
(irritabile) irritable ♦ *sm (fam):* **far venire il
nervoso a qn** to get on sb's nerves

'**nespola** *sf (BOT)* medlar; *(fig)* blow,
punch; '**nespolo** *sm* medlar tree

'**nesso** *sm* connection, link

PAROLA CHIAVE

nes'suno, a *(det: dav sm* **nessun** *+C, V,*
nessuno *+s impura, gn, pn, ps, x, z; dav sf*
nessuna *+C,* **nessun'** *+V) det* **1** *(non uno)*
no, *espressione negativa +any;* **non c'è
nessun libro** there isn't any book, there is
no book; **nessun altro** no one else,
nobody else; **nessun'altra cosa** nothing
else; **in nessun luogo** nowhere

2 *(qualche)* any; **hai ~a obiezione?** do you
have any objections?

♦ *pron* **1** *(non uno)* no one, nobody,
espressione negativa +any(one); (: *cosa)*
none, *espressione negativa +any;* **~ è
venuto, non è venuto ~** nobody came

2 *(qualcuno)* anyone, anybody; **ha
telefonato ~?** did anyone phone?

---

net'tare[1] *vt* to clean

'**nettare**[2] *sm* nectar

net'tezza [net'tettsa] *sf* cleanness,
cleanliness; **~ urbana** cleansing department

'**netto, a** *ag (pulito)* clean; *(chiaro)* clear,
clear-cut; *(deciso)* definite; *(ECON)* net

nettur'bino *sm* dustman (*BRIT*), garbage collector (*US*)

neu'rosi *sf* = **nevrosi**

neu'trale *ag* neutral; **neutralità** *sf* neutrality; **neutraliz'zare** *vt* to neutralize

'neutro, a *ag* neutral; (*LING*) neuter ♦ *sm* (*LING*) neuter

'neve *sf* snow; **nevi'care** *vb impers* to snow; **nevi'cata** *sf* snowfall

ne'vischio [ne'viskjo] *sm* sleet

ne'voso, a *ag* snowy; snow-covered

nevral'gia [nevral'dʒia] *sf* neuralgia

nevras'tenico, a, ci, che *ag* (*MED*) neurasthenic; (*fig*) hot-tempered

ne'vrosi *sf* neurosis

'nibbio *sm* (*ZOOL*) kite

'nicchia ['nikkja] *sf* niche; (*naturale*) cavity, hollow

nicchi'are [nik'kjare] *vi* to shilly-shally, hesitate

'nichel ['nikel] *sm* nickel

nico'tina *sf* nicotine

'nido *sm* nest; **a ~ d'ape** (*tessuto etc*) honeycomb *cpd*

PAROLA CHIAVE
---

ni'ente *pron* **1** (*nessuna cosa*) nothing; **~ può fermarlo** nothing can stop him; **~ di ~** absolutely nothing; **nient'altro** nothing else; **nient'altro che** nothing but, just, only; **~ affatto** not at all, not in the least; **come se ~ fosse** as if nothing had happened; **cose da ~** trivial matters; **per ~** (*gratis, invano*) for nothing

2 (*qualcosa*): **hai bisogno di ~?** do you need anything?

3: **non ... ~** nothing, *espressione negativa* +anything; **non ho visto ~** I saw nothing, I didn't see anything; **non ho ~ da dire** I have nothing *o* haven't anything to say ♦ *sm* nothing; **un bel ~** absolutely nothing; **basta un ~ per farla piangere** the slightest thing is enough to make her cry ♦ *av* (*in nessuna misura*): **non ... ~** not ... at all; **non è (per) ~ buono** it isn't good at all

nientedi'meno *av* actually, even ♦ *escl* really!, I say!

niente'meno *av, escl* = **nientedimeno**

'Nilo *sm*: **il ~** the Nile

'ninfa *sf* nymph

nin'fea *sf* water lily

ninna-'nanna *sf* lullaby

'ninnolo *sm* (*gingillo*) knick-knack

ni'pote *sm/f* (*di zii*) nephew/niece; (*di nonni*) grandson/daughter, grand-child

'nitido, a *ag* clear; (*specchio*) bright

ni'trato *sm* nitrate

'nitrico, a, ci, che *ag* nitric

ni'trire *vi* to neigh

ni'trito *sm* (*di cavallo*) neighing *no pl*; neigh; (*CHIM*) nitrite

nitroglice'rina [nitroglitʃe'rina] *sf* nitroglycerine

no *av* (*risposta*) no; **vieni o ~?** are you coming or not?; **perché ~?** why not?; **lo conosciamo? — tu ~ ma io sì** do we know him? — you don't but I do; **verrai, ~?** you'll come, won't you?

'nobile *ag* noble ♦ *sm/f* noble, nobleman/woman; **nobili'are** *ag* noble; **nobiltà** *sf* nobility; (*di azione*) nobleness

'nocca, che *sf* (*ANAT*) knuckle

nocci'ola [not'tʃɔla] *ag inv* (*colore*) hazel, light brown ♦ *sf* hazelnut

noccio'lina [nottʃo'lina] *sf*: **~ americana** peanut

'nocciolo¹ ['nɔttʃolo] *sm* (*di frutto*) stone; (*fig*) heart, core

noc'ciolo² [not'tʃɔlo] *sm* (*albero*) hazel

'noce ['notʃe] *sm* (*albero*) walnut tree ♦ *sf* (*frutto*) walnut; **~ moscata** nutmeg

no'civo, a [no'tʃivo] *ag* harmful, noxious

'nodo *sm* (*di cravatta, legname, NAUT*) knot; (*AUT, FERR*) junction; (*MED, ASTR, BOT*) node; (*fig: legame*) bond, tie; (*: punto centrale*) heart, crux; **avere un ~ alla gola** to have a lump in one's throat; **no'doso, a** *ag* (*tronco*) gnarled

'noi *pron* (*soggetto*) we; (*oggetto: per dare rilievo, con preposizione*) us; **~ stessi(e)** we ourselves; (*oggetto*) ourselves 'noia *sf* boredom; (*disturbo, impaccio*) bother *no pl*, trouble *no pl*; avere qn/qc a ~ not to like sb/sth; mi è venuto a ~ I'm tired of it; dare ~ a to annoy; avere delle ~e con qn to have trouble with sb

noi'altri *pron* we

noi'oso, a *ag* boring; (*fastidioso*) annoying, troublesome

noleggi'are [noled'dʒare] *vt* (*prendere a noleggio*) to hire (*BRIT*), rent; (*dare a noleggio*) to hire out (*BRIT*), rent (out); (*aereo, nave*) to charter; no'leggio *sm* hire (*BRIT*), rental; charter

'nolo *sm* hire (*BRIT*), rental; charter; (*per trasporto merci*) freight; prendere/dare a ~ qc to hire/hire out sth

'nomade *ag* nomadic ♦ *sm/f* nomad

'nome *sm* name; (*LING*) noun; in/a ~ di in the name of; di o per ~ (*chiamato*) called, named; conoscere qn di ~ to know sb by name; ~ d'arte stage name; ~ di battesimo Christian name; ~ di famiglia surname

no'mea *sf* notoriety

no'mignolo [no'miɲɲolo] *sm* nickname

'nomina *sf* appointment

nomi'nale *ag* nominal; (*LING*) noun *cpd*

nomi'nare *vt* to name; (*eleggere*) to appoint; (*citare*) to mention

nomina'tivo, a *ag* (*LING*) nominative; (*ECON*) registered ♦ *sm* (*LING: anche:* caso ~) nominative (case); (*AMM*) name

non *av* not ♦ *prefisso* non-; *vedi* affatto; appena *etc*

nonché [non'ke] *cong* (*tanto più, tanto meno*) let alone; (*e inoltre*) as well as

noncu'rante *ag*: ~ (di) careless (of), indifferent (to); noncu'ranza *sf* carelessness, indifference

nondi'meno *cong* (*tuttavia*) however; (*nonostante*) nevertheless

'nonno, a *sm/f* grandfather/mother; (*in senso più familiare*) grandma/grandpa; ~i *smpl* grandparents

non'nulla *sm inv*: un ~ nothing, a trifle

'nono, a *ag, sm* ninth

nonos'tante *prep* in spite of,

notwithstanding ♦ *cong* although, even though

nontiscordardimé *sm inv* (*BOT*) forget-me-not

nord *sm* North ♦ *ag inv* north; northern; il Mare del N~ the North Sea; nor'dest *sm* north-east; 'nordico, a, ci, che *ag* nordic, northern European; nor'dovest *sm* north-west

'norma *sf* (*principio*) norm; (*regola*) regulation, rule; (*consuetudine*) custom, rule; a ~ di legge according to law, as laid down by law

nor'male *ag* normal; standard *cpd*; normalità *sf* normality; normaliz'zare *vt* to normalize, bring back to normal

normal'mente *av* normally

norve'gese [norve'dʒese] *ag, sm/f, sm* Norwegian

Nor'vegia [nor'vedʒa] *sf*: la ~ Norway

nostal'gia [nostal'dʒia] *sf* (*di casa, paese*) homesickness; (*del passato*) nostalgia; nos'talgico, a, ci, che *ag* homesick; nostalgic

nos'trano, a *ag* local; national; home-produced

'nostro, a *det*: il(la) ~(a) *etc* our ♦ *pron*: il(la) ~(a) *etc* ours ♦ *sm*: il ~ our money; our belongings; i ~i our family; our own people; è dei ~i he's one of us

'nota *sf* (*segno*) mark; (*comunicazione scritta, MUS*) note; (*fattura*) bill; (*elenco*) list; degno di ~ noteworthy, worthy of note

no'tabile *ag* notable ♦ *sm* prominent citizen

no'taio *sm* notary

no'tare *vt* (*segnare: errori*) to mark; (*registrare*) to note (down), write down; (*rilevare, osservare*) to note, notice; farsi ~ to get o.s. noticed

no'tevole *ag* (*talento*) notable, remarkable; (*peso*) considerable

no'tifica, che *sf* notification

notifi'care *vt* (*DIR*): ~ qc a qn to notify sb of sth, give sb notice of sth

no'tizia [no'tittsja] *sf* (*piece of*) news *sg*; (*informazione*) piece of information; ~e *sfpl*

(*informazioni*) news *sg*; information *sg*;
notizi'ario *sm* (RADIO, TV, STAMPA) news *sg*
'**noto, a** *ag* (well-)known
notorietà *sf* fame; notoriety
no'torio, a *ag* well-known; (*peg*) notorious
not'tambulo, a *sm/f* night-bird (*fig*)
not'tata *sf* night
'**notte** *sf* night; **di ~** at night; (*durante la
notte*) in the night, during the night; ~
bianca sleepless night; **notte'tempo** *av*
at night; during the night
not'turno, a *ag* nocturnal; (*servizio,
guardiano*) night *cpd*
no'vanta *num* ninety; **novan'tesimo, a**
num ninetieth; **novan'tina** *sf*: **una
novantina (di)** about ninety
'**nove** *num* nine
nove'cento [nove'tʃɛnto] *num* nine
hundred ♦ *sm*: **il N~** the twentieth century
no'vella *sf* (LETTERATURA) short story
novel'lino, a *ag* (*pivello*) green,
inexperienced
no'vello, a *ag* (*piante, patate*) new;
(*insalata, verdura*) early; (*sposo*) newly-
married
no'vembre *sm* November
novi'lunio *sm* (ASTR) new moon
novità *sf inv* novelty; (*innovazione*)
innovation; (*cosa originale, insolita*)
something new; (*notizia*) (piece of) news
sg; **le ~ della moda** the latest fashions
no'vizio, a [no'vittsjo] *sm/f* (REL) novice;
(*tirocinante*) beginner, apprentice
nozi'one [not'tsjone] *sf* notion, idea; **~i** *sfpl*
(*rudimenti*) basic knowledge *sg*, rudiments
'**nozze** ['nɔttse] *sfpl* wedding *sg*, marriage
sg; **~ d'argento/d'oro** silver/golden
wedding *sg*
ns. *abbr* (COMM) = **nostro**
'**nube** *sf* cloud; **nubi'fragio** *sm* cloudburst
'**nubile** *ag* (*donna*) unmarried, single
'**nuca** *sf* nape of the neck
nucle'are *ag* nuclear
'**nucleo** *sm* nucleus; (*gruppo*) team, unit,
group; (MIL, POLIZIA) squad; **il ~ familiare**
the family unit
nu'dista, i, e *sm/f* nudist

'**nudo, a** *ag* (*persona*) bare, naked, nude;
(*membra*) bare, naked; (*montagna*) bare
♦ *sm* (ARTE) nude
'**nugolo** *sm*: **un ~ di** a whole host of
'**nulla** *pron, av* = **niente** ♦ *sm*: **il ~** nothing
nulla'osta *sm inv* authorization
nullità *sf inv* nullity; (*persona*) nonentity
'**nullo, a** *ag* useless, worthless; (DIR) null
(and void); (SPORT): **incontro ~** draw
nume'rale *ag, sm* numeral
nume'rare *vt* to number; **numerazi'one**
sf numbering; (*araba, decimale*) notation
nu'merico, a, ci, che *ag* numerical
'**numero** *sm* number; (*romano, arabo*)
numeral; (*di spettacolo*) act, turn; **~ civico**
house number; **~ di telefono** telephone
number; **nume'roso, a** *ag* numerous,
many; (*con sostantivo sg*) large
'**nunzio** ['nuntsjo] *sm* (REL) nuncio
nu'ocere ['nwɔtʃere] *vi*: **~ a** to harm,
damage; **nuoci'uto, a** *pp di* **nuocere**
nu'ora *sf* daughter-in-law
nuo'tare *vi* to swim; (*galleggiare: oggetti*)
to float; **nuota'tore, 'trice** *sm/f*
swimmer; **nu'oto** *sm* swimming
nu'ova *sf* (*notizia*) (piece of) news *sg*; *vedi
anche* **nuovo**
nuova'mente *av* again
Nu'ova Ze'landa [-dze'landa] *sf*: **la ~**
New Zealand
nu'ovo, a *ag* new; **di ~** again; ~
fiammante *o* **di zecca** brand-new
nutri'ente *ag* nutritious, nourishing
nutri'mento *sm* food, nourishment
nu'trire *vt* to feed; (*fig: sentimenti*) to
harbour, nurse; **nutri'tivo, a** *ag*
nutritional; (*alimento*) nutritious;
nutrizi'one *sf* nutrition
'**nuvola** *sf* cloud; **nuvo'loso, a** *ag* cloudy
nuzi'ale [nut'tsjale] *ag* nuptial; wedding *cpd*

O, o

o (*dav V spesso* **od**) *cong* or; **~ ... ~** either ... or; **~ l'uno ~ l'altro** either (of them)

O. *abbr* (= *ovest*) W

'oasi *sf inv* oasis

obbedi'ente *etc* = **ubbidiente** *etc*

obbli'gare *vt* (*costringere*): **~ qn a fare** to force *o* oblige sb to do; (*DIR*) to bind; **~rsi** *vr*: **~rsi a fare** to undertake to do; **obbli'gato, a** *ag* (*costretto, grato*) obliged; (*percorso, tappa*) set, fixed; **obbliga'torio, a** *ag* compulsory, obligatory; **obbligazi'one** *sf* (*COMM*) bond, debenture; **'obbligo, ghi** *sm* obligation; (*dovere*) duty; **avere l'obbligo di fare** to be obliged to do; **essere d'obbligo** (*discorso, applauso*) to be called for

ob'brobrio *sm* disgrace; (*fig*) eyesore

o'beso, a *ag* obese

obiet'tare *vt*: **~ che** to object that; **~ su qc** to object to sth, raise objections concerning sth

obiet'tivo, a *ag* objective ♦ *sm* (*OTTICA, FOT*) lens *sg*, objective; (*MIL, fig*) objective

obiet'tore *sm* objector; **~ di coscienza** conscientious objector

obiezi'one *sf* [objet'tsjone] *sf* objection

obi'torio *sm* morgue, mortuary

o'bliquo, a *ag* oblique; (*inclinato*) slanting; (*fig*) devious, underhand

oblite'rare *vt* (*biglietto*) to stamp; (*francobollo*) to cancel

oblò *sm inv* porthole

o'blungo, a, ghi, ghe *ag* oblong

'oboe *sm* (*MUS*) oboe

'oca (*pl* **'oche**) *sf* goose

occasi'one *sf* (*caso favorevole*) opportunity; (*causa, motivo, circostanza*) occasion; (*COMM*) bargain; **d'~** (*a buon prezzo*) bargain *cpd*; (*usato*) secondhand

occhi'aia [ok'kjaja] *sf* eye socket; **avere le ~e** to have shadows under one's eyes

occhi'ali [ok'kjali] *smpl* glasses, spectacles;

~ da sole sunglasses; **~ da vista** (prescription) glasses

occhi'ata [ok'kjata] *sf* look, glance; **dare un'~ a** to have a look at

occhi'ello [ok'kjɛllo] *sm* buttonhole; (*asola*) eyelet

'occhio ['ɔkkjo] *sm* eye; **~!** careful!, watch out!; **a ~ nudo** with the naked eye; **a quattr'~i** privately, tête-à-tête; **dare all'~** *o* **nell'~ a qn** to catch sb's eye; **fare l'~ a qc** to get used to sth; **tenere d'~ qn** to keep an eye on sb; **vedere di buon/mal ~ qc** to look favourably/unfavourably on sth

occhio'lino [okkjo'lino] *sm*: **fare l'~ a qn** to wink at sb

occiden'tale [ottʃiden'tale] *ag* western ♦ *sm/f* Westerner

occi'dente [ottʃi'dɛnte] *sm* west; (*POL*): **l'O~** the West; **a ~** in the west

oc'cipite [ot'tʃipite] *sm* back of the head, occiput

oc'cludere *vt* to block; **occlusi'one** *sf* blockage, obstruction; **oc'cluso, a** *pp di* **occludere**

occor'rente *ag* necessary ♦ *sm* all that is necessary

occor'renza [okkor'rɛntsa] *sf* necessity, need; **all'~** in case of need

oc'correre *vi* to be needed, be required ♦ *vb impers*: **occorre farlo** it must be done; **occorre che tu parta** you must leave, you'll have to leave; **mi occorrono i soldi** I need the money; **oc'corso, a** *pp di* **occorrere**

occul'tare *vt* to hide, conceal

oc'culto, a *ag* hidden, concealed; (*scienze, forze*) occult

occu'pare *vt* to occupy; (*manodopera*) to employ; (*ingombrare*) to occupy, take up; **~rsi** *vr* to occupy o.s., keep o.s. busy; (*impiegarsi*) to get a job; **~rsi di** (*interessarsi*) to take an interest in; (*prendersi cura di*) to look after, take care of; **occu'pato, a** *ag* (*MIL, POL*) occupied; (*persona: affaccendato*) busy; (*posto, sedia*) taken; (*toilette, TEL*) engaged; **occupazi'one** *sf* occupation; (*impiego,* *lavoro*) job; (*ECON*) employment

o'ceano [o'tʃeano] *sm* ocean

'ocra *sf* ochre

ocu'lare *ag* ocular, eye *cpd*; **testimone ~** eye witness

ocu'lato, a *ag* (*attento*) cautious, prudent; (*accorto*) shrewd

ocu'lista, i, e *sm/f* eye specialist, oculist

'ode *sf* ode

odi'are *vt* to hate, detest

odi'erno, a *ag* today's, of today; (*attuale*) present

'odio *sm* hatred; **avere in ~ qc/qn** to hate *o* detest sth/sb; **odi'oso, a** *ag* hateful, odious

odo'rare *vt* (*annusare*) to smell; (*profumare*) to perfume, scent ♦ *vi*: **~ (di)** to smell (of); **odo'rato** *sm* sense of smell

o'dore *sm* smell; **gli ~i** *smpl* (*CUC*) (aromatic) herbs; **odo'roso, a** *ag* sweet-smelling

of'fendere *vt* to offend; (*violare*) to break, violate; (*insultare*) to insult; (*ferire*) to hurt; **~rsi** *vr* (*con senso reciproco*) to insult one another; (*risentirsi*): **~rsi (di)** to take offence (at), be offended (by); **offen'sivo, a** *ag*, *sf* offensive

offe'rente *sm* (*in aste*): **al maggior ~** to the highest bidder

of'ferta *sf* offer; (*donazione, anche REL*) offering; (*in gara d'appalto*) tender; (*in aste*) bid; (*ECON*) supply; **''~e d'impiego''** ''situations vacant''; **fare un'~a** to make an offer; to tender; to bid

of'ferto, a *pp di* offrire

of'fesa *sf* insult, affront; (*MIL*) attack; (*DIR*) offence; *vedi anche* offeso

of'feso, a *pp di* offendere ♦ *ag* offended; (*fisicamente*) hurt, injured ♦ *sm/f* offended party; **essere ~ con qn** to be annoyed with sb; **parte ~a** (*DIR*) plaintiff

offi'cina [offi'tʃina] *sf* workshop

of'frire *vt* to offer; **~rsi** *vr* (*proporsi*) to offer (o.s.); (*occasione*) to present itself; (*esporsi*): **~rsi a** to expose o.s. to; **ti offro da bere** I'll buy you a drink

offus'care *vt* to obscure, darken; (*fig:*

intelletto) to dim, cloud; (: *fama*) to obscure, overshadow; **~rsi** *vr* to grow dark; to cloud, grow dim; to be obscured

ogget'tivo, a [oddʒet'tivo] *ag* objective

og'getto [od'dʒetto] *sm* object; (*materia, argomento*) subject (matter); **~i smarriti** lost property *sg*

'oggi ['oddʒi] *av*, *sm* today; **~ a otto** a week today; **oggigi'orno** *av* nowadays

OGM *sigla m* (= *organismo geneticamente modificato*) GMO

'ogni ['oɲɲi] *det* every, each; (*tutti*) all; (*con valore distributivo*) every; **~ uomo è mortale** all men are mortal; **viene ~ due giorni** he comes every two days; **~ cosa** everything; **ad ~ costo** at all costs, at any price; **in ~ luogo** everywhere; **~ tanto** every so often; **~ volta che** every time that

Ognis'santi [oɲɲis'santi] *sm* All Saints' Day

o'gnuno [oɲ'ɲuno] *pron* everyone, everybody

'ohi *escl* oh!; (*esprimere dolore*) ow!

ohimè *escl* oh dear!

O'landa *sf*: **l'~** Holland; **olan'dese** *ag* Dutch ♦ *sm* (*LING*) Dutch ♦ *sm/f* Dutchman/woman; **gli Olandesi** the Dutch

oleo'dotto *sm* oil pipeline

ole'oso, a *ag* oily; (*che contiene olio*) oil-yielding

ol'fatto *sm* sense of smell

oli'are *vt* to oil

oli'era *sf* oil cruet

olim'piadi *sfpl* Olympic games; **o'limpico, a, ci, che** *ag* Olympic

'olio *sm* oil; **sott'~** (*CUC*) in oil; **~ di fegato di merluzzo** cod liver oil; **~ d'oliva** olive oil; **~ di semi** vegetable oil

o'liva *sf* olive; **oli'vastro, a** *ag* olive-(coloured); (*carnagione*) sallow; **oli'veto** *sm* olive grove; **o'livo** *sm* olive tree

'olmo *sm* elm

oltraggi'are [oltrad'dʒare] *vt* to outrage

ol'traggio [ol'traddʒo] *sm* outrage; offence, insult; **~ al pudore** (*DIR*) indecent behaviour; **oltraggi'oso, a** *ag* offensive

ol'tralpe *av* beyond the Alps

ol'tranza [ol'trantsa] *sf*: **a ~** to the last, to

the bitter end

'**oltre** *av* (*più in là*) further; (*di più: aspettare*) longer, more ♦ *prep* (*di là da*) beyond, over, on the other side of; (*più di*) more than, over; (*in aggiunta a*) besides; (*eccetto*): ~ **a** except, apart from; **oltre'mare** *av* overseas; **oltre'modo** *av* extremely; **oltrepas'sare** *vt* to go beyond, exceed

o'**maggio** [o'maddʒo] *sm* (*dono*) gift; (*segno di rispetto*) homage, tribute; **~i** *smpl* (*complimenti*) respects; **rendere ~ a** to pay homage *o* tribute to; **in ~** (*copia, biglietto*) complimentary

ombe'lico, chi *sm* navel

'**ombra** *sf* (*zona non assolata, fantasma*) shade; (*sagoma scura*) shadow; **sedere all'~** to sit in the shade; **restare nell'~** (*fig*) to remain in obscurity

om'brello *sm* umbrella; **ombrel'lone** *sm* beach umbrella

om'bretto *sm* eyeshadow

om'broso, a *ag* shady, shaded; (*cavallo*) nervous, skittish; (*persona*) touchy, easily offended

ome'lia *sf* (*REL*) homily, sermon

omeopa'tia *sf* homoeopathy

omertà *sf* conspiracy of silence

o'**messo, a** *pp di* **omettere**

o'**mettere** *vt* to omit, leave out; ~ **di fare** to omit *o* fail to do

omi'cida, i, e [omi'tʃida] *ag* homicidal, murderous ♦ *sm/f* murderer/eress

omi'cidio [omi'tʃidjo] *sm* murder; ~ **colposo** culpable homicide

omissi'one *sf* omission; ~ **di soccorso** (*DIR*) failure to stop and give assistance

omogeneiz'zato [omodʒeneid'dzato] *sm* baby food

omo'geneo, a [omo'dʒɛneo] *ag* homogeneous

omolo'gare *vt* to approve, recognize; to ratify

o'**monimo, a** *sm/f* namesake ♦ *sm* (*LING*) homonym

omosessu'ale *ag, sm/f* homosexual

'**oncia, ce** ['ontʃa] *sf* ounce

'**onda** *sf* wave; **mettere** *o* **mandare in ~** (*RADIO, TV*) to broadcast; **andare in ~** (*RADIO, TV*) to go on the air; **~e corte/ medie/lunghe** short/medium/long wave; **on'data** *sf* wave, billow; (*fig*) wave, surge; **a ondate** in waves; **ondata di caldo** heatwave

ondeggi'are [onded'dʒare] *vi* (*acqua*) to ripple; (*muoversi sulle onde: barca*) to rock, roll; (*fig: muoversi come le onde, barcollare*) to sway; (: *essere incerto*) to waver

'**onere** *sm* burden; **~i fiscali** taxes; **one'roso, a** *ag* (*fig*) heavy, onerous

onestà *sf* honesty

o'**nesto, a** *ag* (*probo, retto*) honest; (*giusto*) fair; (*casto*) chaste, virtuous

'**onice** ['ɔnitʃe] *sf* onyx

onnipo'tente *ag* omnipotent

ono'mastico, ci *sm* name-day

ono'ranze [ono'rantse] *sfpl* honours; ~ **funebri** funeral (service)

ono'rare *vt* to honour; (*far onore a*) to do credit to; **~rsi** *vr*: **~rsi di** to feel honoured at, be proud of

ono'rario, a *ag* honorary ♦ *sm* fee

o'**nore** *sm* honour; **in ~ di** in honour of; **fare gli ~i di casa** to play host (*o* hostess); **fare ~ a** to honour; (*pranzo*) to do justice to; (*famiglia*) to be a credit to; **farsi ~** to distinguish o.s.; **ono'revole** *ag* honourable ♦ *sm/f* (*POL*) ≈ Member of Parliament (*BRIT*); ≈ Congressman/woman (*US*); **onorifi'cenza** *sf* honour; decoration; **ono'rifico, a, ci, che** *ag* honorary

'**onta** *sf* shame, disgrace

on'tano *sm* (*BOT*) alder

'**O.N.U.** ['ɔnu] *sigla f* (= *Organizzazione delle Nazioni Unite*) UN, UNO

o'**paco, a, chi, che** *ag* (*vetro*) opaque; (*metallo*) dull, matt

o'**pale** *sm o f* opal

'**opera** *sf* work; (*azione rilevante*) action, deed, work; (*MUS*) work; opus; (: *melodramma*) opera; (: *teatro*) opera house; (*ente*) institution, organization; ~ **d'arte** work of art; ~ **lirica** (grand) opera;

~e pubbliche public works
ope'raio, a *ag* working-class; workers'
♦ *sm/f* worker; **classe ~a** working class
ope'rare *vt* to carry out, make; (*MED*) to
operate on ♦ *vi* to operate, work; (*rimedio*)
to act, work; (*MED*) to operate; **~rsi** *vr*
(*MED*) to have an operation; **~rsi
d'appendicite** to have one's appendix out;
opera'tivo, a *ag* operative, operating;
opera'tore, 'trice *sm/f* operator; (*TV,
CINEMA*) cameraman; **operatore
economico** agent, broker; **operatore
turistico** tour operator; **opera'torio, a** *ag*
(*MED*) operating; **operazi'one** *sf*
operation
ope'retta *sf* (*MUS*) operetta, light opera
ope'roso, a *ag* busy, active, hard-working
opini'one *sf* opinion; **~ pubblica** public
opinion
'**oppio** *sm* opium
oppo'nente *ag* opposing ♦ *sm/f* opponent
op'porre *vt* to oppose; **opporsi** *vr*:
opporsi (a qc) to oppose (sth); to object
(to sth); **~ resistenza/un rifiuto** to offer
resistance/refuse
opportu'nista, i, e *sm/f* opportunist
opportunità *sf inv* opportunity;
(*convenienza*) opportuneness, timeliness
oppor'tuno, a *ag* timely, opportune
opposi'tore, 'trice *sm/f* opposer,
opponent
opposizi'one [oppozit'tsjone] *sf*
opposition; (*DIR*) objection
op'posto, a *pp di* **opporre** ♦ *ag* opposite;
(*opinioni*) conflicting ♦ *sm* opposite,
contrary; **all'~** on the contrary
oppressi'one *sf* oppression
oppres'sivo, a *ag* oppressive
op'presso, a *pp di* **opprimere**
oppres'sore *sm* oppressor
op'primere *vt* (*premere, gravare*) to weigh
down; (*estenuare: sog: caldo*) to suffocate,
oppress; (*tiranneggiare: popolo*) to oppress
op'pure *cong* or (else)
op'tare *vi*: **~ per** to opt for
o'puscolo *sm* booklet, pamphlet
opzi'one [op'tsjone] *sf* option

'**ora**[1] *sf* (*60 minuti*) hour; (*momento*) time;
che ~ è?, che ~e sono? what time is it?;
non veder l'~ di fare to long to do, look
forward to doing; **di buon'~** early; **alla
buon'~!** at last!; **~ di cena** dinner time; **~
legale** *o* **estiva** summer time (*BRIT*),
daylight saving time (*US*); **~ locale** local
time; **~ di pranzo** lunchtime; **~ di punta**
(*AUT*) rush hour
ora[2] *av* (*adesso*) now; (*poco fa*): **è uscito
proprio ~** he's just gone out; (*tra poco*)
presently, in a minute; (*correlativo*): **~ ... ~**
now ... now; **d'~ in avanti** *o* **poi** from now
on; **or ~** now, a moment ago; **5 anni
or sono** 5 years ago; **~ come ~** right now,
at present
o'racolo *sm* oracle
'**orafo** *sm* goldsmith
ora'mai *av* = **ormai**
o'rario, a *ag* hourly; (*fuso, segnale*) time
cpd; (*velocità*) per hour ♦ *sm* timetable,
schedule; (*di ufficio, visite etc*) hours *pl*,
time(s *pl*); **in ~** on time
o'rata *sf* (*ZOOL*) sea bream
ora'tore, 'trice *sm/f* speaker; orator
ora'toria *sf* (*arte*) oratory
ora'torio, a *ag* oratorical ♦ *sm* (*REL*)
oratory; (*MUS*) oratorio
ora'zione [orat'tsjone] *sf* (*REL*) prayer;
(*discorso*) speech, oration
or'bene *cong* so, well (then)
'**orbita** *sf* (*ASTR, FISICA*) orbit; (*ANAT*)
(eye-)socket
or'chestra [or'kestra] *sf* orchestra;
orches'trare *vt* to orchestrate; (*fig*) to
mount, stage-manage
orchi'dea [orki'dɛa] *sf* orchid
'**orco, chi** *sm* ogre
'**orda** *sf* horde
or'digno [or'diɲɲo] *sm* (*esplosivo*) explosive
device
ordi'nale *ag, sm* ordinal
ordina'mento *sm* order, arrangement;
(*regolamento*) regulations *pl*, rules *pl*; **~
scolastico/giuridico** education/legal
system

ordi'nanza [ordi'nantsa] *sf* (DIR, MIL) order; (*persona:* MIL) orderly, batman; **d'~** (MIL) regulation *cpd*

ordi'nare *vt* (*mettere in ordine*) to arrange, organize; (COMM) to order; (*prescrivere: medicina*) to prescribe; (*comandare*): **~ a qn di fare qc** to order *o* command sb to do sth; (REL) to ordain

ordi'nario, a *ag* (*comune*) ordinary; everyday; standard; (*grossolano*) coarse, common ♦ *sm* ordinary; (INS: *di università*) full professor

ordi'nato, a *ag* tidy, orderly

ordinazi'one [ordinat'tsjone] *sf* (COMM) order; (REL) ordination; **eseguire qc su ~** to make sth to order

'ordine *sm* order; (*carattere*): **d'~ pratico** of a practical nature; **all'~** (COMM: *assegno*) to order; **di prim'~** first-class; **fino a nuovo ~** until further notice; **essere in ~** (*documenti*) to be in order; (*stanza, persona*) to be tidy; **mettere in ~** to put in order, tidy (up); **~ del giorno** (*di seduta*) agenda; (MIL) order of the day; **~ di pagamento** (COMM) order for payment; **l'~ pubblico** law and order; **~i (sacri)** (REL) holy orders

or'dire *vt* (*fig*) to plot, scheme; **or'dito** *sm* (*di tessuto*) warp

orec'chino [orek'kino] *sm* earring

o'recchio [o'rekkjo] (*pl(f)* **o'recchie**) *sm* (ANAT) ear

orecchi'oni [orek'kjoni] *smpl* (MED) mumps *sg*

o'refice [o'refitʃe] *sm* goldsmith; jeweller; **orefice'ria** *sf* (*arte*) goldsmith's art; (*negozio*) jeweller's (shop)

'orfano, a *ag* orphan(ed) ♦ *sm/f* orphan; **~ di padre/madre** fatherless/motherless; **orfano'trofio** *sm* orphanage

orga'netto *sm* barrel organ; (*fam: armonica a bocca*) mouth organ; (: *fisarmonica*) accordion

or'ganico, a, ci, che *ag* organic ♦ *sm* personnel, staff

organi'gramma, i *sm* organization chart

orga'nismo *sm* (BIOL) organism; (*corpo umano*) body; (AMM) body, organism

organiz'zare [organid'dzare] *vt* to organize; **~rsi** *vr* to get organized; **organizza'tore, 'trice** *ag* organizing ♦ *sm/f* organizer; **organizzazi'one** *sf* organization

'organo *sm* organ; (*di congegno*) part; (*portavoce*) spokesman, mouthpiece

or'gasmo *sm* (FISIOL) orgasm; (*fig*) agitation, anxiety

'orgia, ge ['ɔrdʒa] *sf* orgy

or'goglio [or'gɔʎʎo] *sm* pride; **orgogli'oso, a** *ag* proud

orien'tale *ag* oriental; eastern; east

orienta'mento *sm* positioning; orientation; direction; (*senso di* **~** sense of direction; **perdere l'~** to lose one's bearings; **~ professionale** careers guidance

orien'tare *vt* (*situare*) to position; (*fig*) to direct, orientate; **~rsi** *vr* to find one's bearings; (*fig: tendere*) to tend, lean; (: *indirizzarsi*): **~rsi verso** to take up, go in for

ori'ente *sm* east; **l'O~** the East, the Orient; **a ~** in the east

o'rigano *sm* oregano

origi'nale [oridʒi'nale] *ag* original; (*bizzarro*) eccentric ♦ *sm* original; **originalità** *sf* originality; eccentricity

origi'nare [oridʒi'nare] *vt* to bring about, produce ♦ *vi*: **~ da** to arise *o* spring from

origi'nario, a [oridʒi'narjo] *ag* original; **essere ~ di** to be a native of; (*provenire da*) to originate from; to be native to

o'rigine [o'ridʒine] *sf* origin; **all'~** originally; **d'~ inglese** of English origin; **dare ~ a** to give rise to

origli'are [oriʎ'ʎare] *vi*: **~ (a)** to eavesdrop (on)

o'rina *sf* urine

ori'nare *vi* to urinate ♦ *vt* to pass; **orina'toio** *sm* (*public*) urinal

ori'undo, a *ag*: **essere ~ di Milano** *etc* to be of Milanese *etc* extraction *o* origin ♦ *sm/f* person of foreign extraction *o* origin

orizzon'tale [oriddzon'tale] *ag* horizontal

oriz'zonte [orid'dzonte] *sm* horizon

or'lare *vt* to hem

'orlo *sm* edge, border; (*di recipiente*) rim, brim; (*di vestito etc*) hem

'orma *sf* (*di persona*) footprint; (*di animale*) track; (*impronta, traccia*) mark, trace

or'mai *av* by now, by this time; (*adesso*) now; (*quasi*) almost, nearly

ormeggi'are [ormed'dʒare] *vt* (NAUT) to moor; or'meggio *sm* (*atto*) mooring *no pl*; (*luogo*) moorings *pl*

or'mone *sm* hormone

ornamen'tale *ag* ornamental, decorative

orna'mento *sm* ornament, decoration

or'nare *vt* to adorn, decorate; ~rsi *vr*: ~rsi (di) to deck o.s. (out) (with); or'nato, a *ag* ornate

ornitolo'gia [ornitolo'dʒia] *sf* ornithology

'oro *sm* gold; d'~, in ~ gold *cpd*; d'~ (*colore, occasione*) golden; (*persona*) marvellous

oroge'ria [orolodʒe'ria] *sf* watchmaking *no pl*; watchmaker's (shop); clockmaker's (shop); **bomba a ~** time bomb

orologi'aio [orolo'dʒajo] *sm* watchmaker; clockmaker

oro'logio [oro'lɔdʒo] *sm* clock; (*da tasca, da polso*) watch; **~ da polso** wristwatch; **~ al quarzo** quartz watch

o'roscopo *sm* horoscope

or'rendo, a *ag* (*spaventoso*) horrible, awful; (*bruttissimo*) hideous

or'ribile *ag* horrible

'orrido, a *ag* fearful, horrid

orripi'lante *ag* hair-raising, horrifying

or'rore *sm* horror; **avere in ~ qn/qc** to loathe *o* detest sb/sth; **mi fanno ~** I loathe *o* detest them

orsacchi'otto [orsak'kjɔtto] *sm* teddy bear

'orso *sm* bear; **~ bruno/bianco** brown/ polar bear

or'taggio [or'taddʒo] *sm* vegetable

or'tensia *sf* hydrangea

or'tica, che *sf* (stinging) nettle

orti'caria *sf* nettle rash

'orto *sm* vegetable garden, kitchen garden; (AGR) market garden (BRIT), truck farm (US)

orto'dosso, a *ag* orthodox

ortogra'fia *sf* spelling

orto'lano, a *sm/f* (*venditore*) greengrocer (BRIT), produce dealer (US)

orto'pedia *sf* orthopaedics *sg*; orto'pedico, a, ci, che *ag* orthopaedic ♦ *sm* orthopaedic specialist

orzai'olo [ordza'jɔlo] *sm* (MED) stye

or'zata [or'dzata] *sf* barley water

'orzo ['ordzo] *sm* barley

o'sare *vt, vi* to dare; **~ fare** to dare (to) do

oscenità [offeni'ta] *sf inv* obscenity

o'sceno, a [oʃ'ʃɛno] *ag* obscene; (*ripugnante*) ghastly

oscil'lare [offil'lare] *vi* (*pendolo*) to swing; (*dondolare: al vento etc*) to rock; (*variare*) to fluctuate; (TECN) to oscillate; (*fig*): **~ fra** to waver *o* hesitate between; **oscillazi'one** *sf* oscillation; (*di prezzi, temperatura*) fluctuation

oscura'mento *sm* darkening; obscuring; (*in tempo di guerra*) blackout

oscu'rare *vt* to darken, obscure; (*fig*) to obscure; **~rsi** *vr* to darken, cloud over; (*persona*): **si oscurò in volto** his face clouded over

os'curo, a *ag* dark; (*fig*) obscure; humble, lowly ♦ *sm*: **all'~** in the dark; **tenere qn all'~ di qc** to keep sb in the dark about sth

ospe'dale *sm* hospital; **ospedali'ero, a** *ag* hospital *cpd*

ospi'tale *ag* hospitable; **ospitalità** *sf* hospitality

ospi'tare *vt* to give hospitality to; (*sog: albergo*) to accommodate

'ospite *sm/f* (*persona che ospita*) host/ hostess; (*persona ospitata*) guest

os'pizio [os'pittsjo] *sm* (*per vecchi etc*) home

'ossa *sfpl vedi* osso

ossa'tura *sf* (ANAT) skeletal structure, frame; (TECN, *fig*) framework

'osseo, a *ag* bony; (*tessuto etc*) bone *cpd*

os'sequio *sm* deference, respect; **~i** *smpl* (*saluto*) respects, regards; **ossequi'oso, a** *ag* obsequious

osser'vanza [osser'vantsa] *sf* observance

osser'vare *vt* to observe, watch; (*esaminare*) to examine; (*notare, rilevare*) to notice, observe; (DIR: la legge) to observe, respect; (mantenere: silenzio) to keep, observe; **far ~ qc a qn** to point sth out to sb; **osserva'tore, 'trice** ag observant, perceptive ♦ sm/f observer;

osserva'torio sm (ASTR) observatory; (MIL) observation post; osservazi'one sf observation; (di legge etc) observance; (considerazione critica) observation, remark; (rimprovero) reproof; **in osservazione** under observation

ossessio'nare vt to obsess, haunt; (tormentare) to torment, harass

ossessi'one sf obsession

os'sesso, a ag (spiritato) possessed

os'sia cong that is, to be precise

ossi'buchi [ossi'buki] smpl di **ossobuco**

ossi'dare vt to oxidize; **~rsi** vr to oxidize

'ossido sm oxide; **~ di carbonio** carbon monoxide

ossige'nare [ossidʒe'nare] vt to oxygenate; (decolorare) to bleach; **acqua ossigenata** hydrogen peroxide

os'sigeno sm oxygen

'osso (pl(f) **ossa** nel senso ANAT) sm bone; **d'~** (bottone etc) of bone, bone cpd

osso'buco (pl **ossi'buchi**) sm (CUC) marrowbone; (: piatto) stew made with knuckle of veal in tomato sauce

os'suto, a ag bony

ostaco'lare vt to block, obstruct

os'tacolo sm obstacle; (EQUITAZIONE) hurdle, jump

os'taggio [os'taddʒo] sm hostage

'oste, os'tessa sm/f innkeeper

osteggi'are [osted'dʒare] vt to oppose, be opposed to

os'tello sm: **~ della gioventù** youth hostel

osten'tare vt to make a show of, flaunt; ostentazi'one sf ostentation, show

oste'ria sf inn

os'tessa sf vedi **oste**

os'tetrica sf midwife; os'tetrico, a, ci, che ag obstetric ♦ sm obstetrician

'ostia sf (REL) host; (per medicinali) wafer

'ostico, a, ci, che ag (fig) harsh; hard, difficult; unpleasant

os'tile ag hostile; ostilità sf inv hostility ♦ sfpl (MIL) hostilities

osti'narsi vr to insist, dig one's heels in; **~ a fare** to persist (obstinately) in doing; osti'nato, a ag (caparbio) obstinate; (tenace) persistent, determined; ostinazi'one sf obstinacy; persistence

'ostrica, che sf oyster

ostru'ire vt to obstruct, block; ostruzi'one sf obstruction, blockage

'otre sm (recipiente) goatskin

ottago'nale ag octagonal

ot'tagono sm octagon

ot'tanta num eighty; ottan'tesimo, a num eightieth; ottan'tina sf: **una ottantina (di)** about eighty

ot'tava sf octave

ot'tavo, a num eighth

ottempe'rare vi: **~ a** to comply with, obey

otte'nere vt to obtain, get; (risultato) to achieve, obtain

'ottica sf (scienza) optics sg; (FOT: lenti, prismi etc) optics pl

'ottico, a, ci, che ag (della vista: nervo) optic; (dell'ottica) optical ♦ sm optician

ottima'mente av excellently, very well

otti'mismo sm optimism; otti'mista, i, e sm/f optimist

'ottimo, a ag excellent, very good

'otto num eight

ot'tobre sm October

otto'cento [otto'tʃento] num eight hundred ♦ sm: **l'O~** the nineteenth century

ot'tone sm brass; **gli ~i** (MUS) the brass

ottu'rare vt to close (up); (dente) to fill; ottura'tore sm (FOT) shutter; (nelle armi) breechblock; otturazi'one sf closing (up); (dentaria) filling

ot'tuso, a ag (MAT, fig) obtuse; (suono) dull

o'vaia sf (ANAT) ovary

o'vale ag, sm oval

o'vatta sf cotton wool; (per imbottire) padding, wadding; ovat'tare vt (fig: smorzare) to muffle

ovazi'one [ovat'tsjone] sf ovation

over'dose ['ouvadous] sf inv overdose

'ovest *sm* west

o'vile *sm* pen, enclosure

o'vino, a *ag* sheep *cpd*, ovine

ovulazi'one [ovulat'tsjone] *sf* ovulation

'ovulo *sm* (FISIOL) ovum

o'vunque *av* = dovunque

ov'vero *cong* (ossia) that is, to be precise; (oppure) or (else)

ovvi'are *vi*: ~ a to obviate

'ovvio, a *ag* obvious

ozi'are [ot'tsjare] *vi* to laze, idle

'ozio ['ɔttsjo] *sm* idleness; (tempo libero) leisure; ore d'~ leisure time; stare in ~ to be idle; ozi'oso, a *ag* idle

o'zono [o'dzɔno] *sm* ozone

P, p

P *abbr* (= parcheggio) P; (AUT: = principiante) L

pa'cato, a *ag* quiet, calm

'pacca *sf* pat

pac'chetto [pak'ketto] *sm* packet; ~ azionario (COMM) shareholding

pacchi'ano, a [pak'kjano] *ag* vulgar

'pacco, chi *sm* parcel; (involto) bundle

'pace ['patʃe] *sf* peace; darsi ~ to resign o.s.; fare la ~ con to make it up with

pacifi'care [patʃifi'kare] *vt* (riconciliare) to reconcile, make peace between; (mettere in pace) to pacify

pa'cifico, a, ci, che [pa'tʃifiko] *ag* (persona) peaceable; (vita) peaceful; (fig: indiscusso) indisputable; (: ovvio) obvious, clear *♦ sm*: il P~, l'Oceano P~ the Pacific (Ocean)

paci'fista, i, e [patʃi'fista] *sm/f* pacifist

pa'della *sf* frying pan; (per infermi) bedpan

padigli'one [padiʎ'ʎone] *sm* pavilion

'Padova *sf* Padua

'padre *sm* father; ~i *smpl* (antenati) forefathers

pa'drino *sm* godfather

padro'nanza [padro'nantsa] *sf* command, mastery

pa'drone, a *sm/f* master/mistress; (proprietario) owner; (datore di lavoro) employer; essere ~ di sé to be in control of o.s.; ~ di casa (ospite) host/hostess; (per gli inquilini) landlord/lady; padroneggi'are *vt* (fig: sentimenti) to master, control; (: materia) to master, know thoroughly; padroneggiarsi *vr* to control o.s.

pae'saggio [pae'zaddʒo] *sm* landscape

pae'sano, a *ag* country *cpd ♦ sm/f* villager; countryman/woman

pa'ese *sm* (nazione) country, nation; (terra) country, land; (villaggio) village; (small) town; ~ di provenienza country of origin; i P~i Bassi the Netherlands

paf'futo, a *ag* chubby, plump

'paga, ghe *sf* pay, wages *pl*

paga'mento *sm* payment

pa'gano, a *ag, sm/f* pagan

pa'gare *vt* to pay; (acquisto, fig: colpa) to pay for; (contraccambiare) to repay, pay back *♦ vi* to pay; quanto l'hai pagato? how much did you pay for it?; ~ con carta di credito to pay by credit card; ~ in contanti to pay cash

pa'gella [pa'dʒella] *sf* (INS) report card

'paggio ['paddʒo] *sm* page(boy)

paghe'rò [page'rɔ] *sm inv* acknowledgement of a debt, IOU

'pagina ['padʒina] *sf* page; ~e gialle Yellow Pages

'paglia ['paʎʎa] *sf* straw

pagliac'cetto [paʎʎat'tʃetto] *sm* (per bambini) rompers *pl*

pagli'accio [paʎ'ʎattʃo] *sm* clown

pagli'etta [paʎ'ʎetta] *sf* (cappello per uomo) (straw) boater; (per tegami etc) steel wool

pa'gnotta [pap'ɲɔtta] *sf* round loaf

'paio (*pl*(f) 'paia) *sm* pair; un ~ di (alcuni) a couple of

pai'olo *sm* (copper) pot

'pala *sf* shovel; (di remo, ventilatore, elica) blade; (di ruota) paddle

pa'lato *sm* palate

pa'lazzo [pa'lattso] *sm* (reggia) palace; (edificio) building; ~ di giustizia courthouse; ~ dello sport sports stadium

---
palazzi

---

*Rome has a number of **palazzi**, which are now associated with various government departments and political figures or groups. Palazzo Chigi, in Piazza Colonna, dates from the 16th century and has, since 1961, been the Prime Minister's office and the place where the cabinet meets. **Palazzo Madama**, also built in the 16th century, has been the seat of the Senate since 1871. **Palazzo di Montecitorio**, which was completed in 1694, has housed the **Camera dei deputati** since 1870. **Palazzo Viminale**, which takes its name from the hill in Rome on which it stands, is the home of the Ministry of the Interior.*

'**palco, chi** sm (*TEATRO*) box; (*tavolato*) platform, stand; (*ripiano*) layer

palco'scenico, ci [palkoʃ'ʃeniko] sm (*TEATRO*) stage

pale'sare vt to reveal, disclose; **~rsi** vr to reveal o reveal o.s.

pa'lese ag clear, evident

Pales'tina sf: **la ~** Palestine

pa'lestra sf gymnasium; (*esercizio atletico*) exercise; (*fig*) training ground, school

pa'letta sf spade; (*per il focolare*) shovel; (*del capostazione*) signalling disc

pa'letto sm stake, peg; (*spranga*) bolt

'**palio** sm (*gara*): **il P~** horse race run at Siena; **mettere qc in ~** to offer sth as a prize

---
palio

---

*The **palio** is a horse race which takes place in a number of Italian towns, the most famous being the one in Siena. This is usually held twice a year on 2 July and 16 August in the Piazza del Campo, Siena. 10 of the 17 **contrade** or districts take part, each represented by a horse and rider. The winner is the first horse to complete the course, whether it has a rider or not.*

'**palla** sf ball; (*pallottola*) bullet; **~ canestro** sm basketball; **~ nuoto** sm water polo; **~ ovale** rugby ball; **~ volo** sm volleyball

palleggi'are [palled'dʒare] vi (*CALCIO*) to practise with the ball; (*TENNIS*) to knock up

pallia'tivo sm palliative; (*fig*) stopgap measure

'**pallido, a** ag pale

pal'lina sf (*bilia*) marble

pallon'cino [pallon'tʃino] sm balloon; (*lampioncino*) Chinese lantern

pal'lone sm (*palla*) ball; (*CALCIO*) football; (*aerostato*) balloon; **gioco del ~** football

pal'lore sm pallor, paleness

pal'lottola sf pellet; (*proiettile*) bullet

'**palma** sf (*ANAT*) = **palmo**; (*BOT, simbolo*) palm; **~ da datteri** date palm

'**palmo** sm (*ANAT*) palm; **restare con un ~ di naso** to be badly disappointed

'**palo** sm (*legno appuntito*) stake; (*sostegno*) pole; **fare da** o **il ~** (*fig*) to act as look-out

palom'baro sm diver

pa'lombo sm (*pesce*) dogfish

pal'pare vt to feel, finger

'**palpebra** sf eyelid

palpi'tare vi (*cuore, polso*) to beat; (: *più forte*) to pound, throb; (*fremere*) to quiver; '**palpito** sm (*del cuore*) beat; (*fig: d'amore etc*) throb

paltò sm inv overcoat

pa'lude sf marsh, swamp; **palu'doso, a** ag marshy, swampy

pa'lustre ag marsh cpd, swamp cpd

'**pampino** sm vine leaf

'**panca, che** sf bench

pancar'rè sm sliced square bread

pan'cetta [pan'tʃetta] sf (*CUC*) bacon

pan'chetto [pan'ketto] sm stool; footstool

pan'china [pan'kina] sf garden seat; (*di giardino pubblico*) (park) bench

'**pancia, ce** ['pantʃa] sf belly, stomach; **mettere** o **fare ~** to be getting a paunch; **avere mal di ~** to have stomachache o a sore stomach

panci'otto [pan'tʃɔtto] sm waistcoat

'pancreas *sm inv* pancreas
'panda *sm inv* panda
pande'monio *sm* pandemonium
'pane *sm* bread; (*pagnotta*) loaf (of bread); (*forma*): un ~ di burro a pat of butter; guadagnarsi il ~ to earn one's living; ~ a cassetta sliced bread; ~ di Spagna sponge cake; ~ integrale wholemeal bread; ~ tostato toast
panette'ria *sf* (*forno*) bakery; (*negozio*) baker's (shop), bakery
panetti'ere, a *sm/f* baker
panet'tone *sm a kind of spiced brioche with sultanas, eaten at Christmas*
'panfilo *sm* yacht
pangrat'tato *sm* breadcrumbs *pl*
'panico, a, ci, che *ag, sm* panic
pani'ere *sm* basket
pani'ficio [pani'fitʃo] *sm* (*forno*) bakery; (*negozio*) baker's (shop), bakery
pa'nino *sm* roll; ~ caldo toasted sandwich; ~ imbottito filled roll; sandwich; panino'teca *sf* sandwich bar
'panna *sf* (*CUC*) cream; (*TECN*) = panne; ~ da cucina cooking cream; ~ montata whipped cream
'panne *sf inv*: essere in ~ (*AUT*) to have broken down
pan'nello *sm* panel; ~ solare solar panel
'panno *sm* cloth; ~i *smpl* (*abiti*) clothes; mettiti nei miei ~i (*fig*) put yourself in my shoes
pan'nocchia [pan'nɔkkja] *sf* (*di mais etc*) ear
panno'lino *sm* (*per bambini*) nappy (*BRIT*), diaper (*US*)
pano'rama *sm* panorama; pano'ramico, a, ci, che *ag* panoramic; strada panoramica scenic route
panta'loni *smpl* trousers (*BRIT*), pants (*US*), pair *sg* of trousers *o* pants
pan'tano *sm* bog
pan'tera *sf* panther
pan'tofola *sf* slipper
panto'mima *sf* pantomime
pan'zana [pan'tsana] *sf* fib, tall story
pao'nazzo, a [pao'nattso] *ag* purple

'papa, i *sm* pope
papà *sm inv* dad(dy)
pa'pale *ag* papal
pa'pato *sm* papacy
pa'pavero *sm* poppy
'papera *sf* (*fig*) slip of the tongue, blunder; *vedi anche* papero
'papero, a *sm/f* (*ZOOL*) gosling
pa'piro *sm* papyrus
'pappa *sf* baby cereal
pappa'gallo *sm* parrot; (*fig: uomo*) Romeo, wolf
pappa'gorgia, ge [pappa'gɔrdʒa] *sf* double chin
pap'pare *vt* (*fam: anche*: ~rsi) to gobble up
'para *sf*: suole di ~ crepe soles
pa'rabola *sf* (*MAT*) parabola; (*REL*) parable
para'brezza [para'breddza] *sm inv* (*AUT*) windscreen (*BRIT*), windshield (*US*)
paraca'dute *sm inv* parachute
para'carro *sm* kerbstone (*BRIT*), curbstone (*US*)
para'diso *sm* paradise
parados'sale *ag* paradoxical
para'dosso *sm* paradox
para'fango, ghi *sm* mudguard
paraf'fina *sf* paraffin, paraffin wax
para'fulmine *sm* lightning conductor
pa'raggi [pa'raddʒi] *smpl*: nei ~ in the vicinity, in the neighbourhood
parago'nare *vt*: ~ con/a to compare with/to
para'gone *sm* comparison; (*esempio analogo*) analogy, parallel; reggere al ~ to stand comparison
pa'ragrafo *sm* paragraph
pa'ralisi *sf* paralysis; para'litico, a, ci, che *ag, sm/f* paralytic
paraliz'zare [paralid'dzare] *vt* to paralyze
paral'lela *sf* parallel (line); ~e *sfpl* (*attrezzo ginnico*) parallel bars
paral'lelo, a *ag* parallel ♦ *sm* (*GEO*) parallel; (*comparazione*): fare un ~ tra to draw a parallel between
para'lume *sm* lampshade
pa'rametro *sm* parameter

para'noia *sf* paranoia; **para'noico, a, ci, che** *ag*, *sm/f* paranoid

para'occhi [para'ɔkki] *smpl* blinkers

para'petto *sm* balustrade

para'piglia [para'piʎʎa] *sm* commotion, uproar

pa'rare *vt* (*addobbare*) to adorn, deck; (*proteggere*) to shield, protect; (*scansare: colpo*) to parry; (*CALCIO*) to save ♦ *vi*: **dove vuole andare a ~?** what are you driving at?; **~rsi** *vr* (*presentarsi*) to appear, present o.s.

para'sole *sm inv* parasol, sunshade

paras'sita, i *sm* parasite

pa'rata *sf* (*SPORT*) save; (*MIL*) review, parade

para'tia *sf* (*di nave*) bulkhead

para'urti *sm inv* (*AUT*) bumper

para'vento *sm* folding screen; **fare da ~ a qn** (*fig*) to shield sb

par'cella [par'tʃɛlla] *sf* account, fee (*of lawyer etc*)

parcheggi'are [parked'dʒare] *vt* to park; **par'cheggio** *sm* parking *no pl*; (*luogo*) car park; (*singolo posto*) parking space

par'chimetro [par'kimetro] *sm* parking meter

'parco¹, chi *sm* park; (*spazio per deposito*) depot; (*complesso di veicoli*) fleet

'parco², a, chi, che *ag*: **~ (in)** (*sobrio*) moderate (in); (*avaro*) sparing (with)

pa'recchio, a [pa'rekkjo] *det* quite a lot of; (*tempo*) quite a lot of, a long; **~i, e** *det pl* quite a lot of, several ♦ *pron* quite a lot, quite a bit; (*tempo*) quite a while, a long time; **~i, e** *pron pl* quite a lot, several ♦ *av* (*con ag*) quite, rather; (*con vb*) quite a lot, quite a bit

pareggi'are [pared'dʒare] *vt* to make equal; (*terreno*) to level, make level; (*bilancio, conti*) to balance ♦ *vi* (*SPORT*) to draw; **pa'reggio** *sm* (*ECON*) balance; (*SPORT*) draw

pa'rente *sm/f* relative, relation

paren'tela *sf* (*vincolo di sangue, fig*) relationship

pa'rentesi *sf* (*segno grafico*) bracket, parenthesis; (*frase incisa*) parenthesis; (*digressione*) parenthesis, digression

pa'rere *sm* (*opinione*) opinion; (*consiglio*) advice, opinion; **a mio ~** in my opinion ♦ *vi* to seem, appear ♦ *vb impers*: **pare che** it seems *o* appears that, they say that; **mi pare che** it seems to me that; **mi pare di sì** I think so; **fai come ti pare** do as you like; **che ti pare del mio libro?** what do you think of my book?

pa'rete *sf* wall

'pari *ag inv* (*uguale*) equal, same; (*in giochi*) equal; drawn, tied; (*MAT*) even ♦ *sm inv* (*POL: di Gran Bretagna*) peer ♦ *sm/f inv* peer, equal; **copiato ~ ~** copied word for word; **alla ~** on the same level; **ragazza alla ~** au pair girl; **mettersi alla ~ con** to place o.s. on the same level as; **mettersi in ~ con** to catch up with; **andare di ~ passo con qn** to keep pace with sb

Pa'rigi [pa'ridʒi] *sf* Paris

pa'riglia [pa'riʎʎa] *sf* pair; **rendere la ~** to give tit for tat

parità *sf* parity, equality; (*SPORT*) draw, tie

parlamen'tare *ag* parliamentary ♦ *sm/f* ≈ Member of Parliament (*BRIT*), ≈ Congressman/woman (*US*) ♦ *vi* to negotiate, parley

parla'mento *sm* parliament

parlan'tina (*fam*) *sf* talkativeness; **avere ~** to have the gift of the gab

par'lare *vi* to speak, talk; (*confidare cose segrete*) to talk ♦ *vt* to speak; **~ (a qn) di** to speak *o* talk (to sb) about; **parla'torio** *sm* (*di carcere etc*) visiting room; (*REL*) parlour

parmigi'ano [parmi'dʒano] *sm* (*grana*) Parmesan (cheese)

paro'dia *sf* parody

pa'rola *sf* word; (*facoltà*) speech; **~e** *sfpl* (*chiacchiere*) talk *sg*; **chiedere la ~** to ask permission to speak; **prendere la ~** to take the floor; **~ d'onore** word of honour; **~ d'ordine** (*MIL*) password; **~e incrociate** crossword (puzzle) *sg*; **paro'laccia, ce** *sf* bad word, swearword

par'rocchia [par'rɔkkja] *sf* parish; parish church

'parroco, ci *sm* parish priest

par'rucca, che *sf* wig
parrucchi'ere, a [parruk'kjɛre] *sm/f* hairdresser ♦ *sm* barber
parsi'monia *sf* frugality, thrift
'parso, a *pp di* **parere**
'parte *sf* part; (*lato*) side; (*quota spettante a ciascuno*) share; (*direzione*) direction; (*POL*) party; faction; (*DIR*) party; **a ~** *ag* separate ♦ *av* separately; **scherzi a ~** joking aside; **a ~ ciò** apart from that; **da ~** (*in disparte*) to one side, aside; **d'altra ~** on the other hand; **da ~ di** (*per conto di*) on behalf of; **da ~ mia** as far as I'm concerned, as for me; **da ~ a ~** right through; **da ogni ~** on all sides, everywhere; (*moto da luogo*) from all sides; **da nessuna ~** nowhere; **da questa ~** (*in questa direzione*) this way; **prendere ~ a qc** to take part in sth; **mettere da ~** to put aside; **mettere qn a ~ di** to inform sb of
parteci'pare [partetʃi'pare] *vi*: **~ a** to take part in, participate in; (*utili etc*) to share in; (*spese etc*) to contribute to; (*dolore, successo di qn*) to share (in);
partecipazi'one *sf* participation; sharing; (*ECON*) interest; **partecipazione agli utili** profit-sharing; **partecipazioni di nozze** *wedding announcement card*; **par'tecipe** *ag* participating; **essere partecipe di** to take part in, participate in; to share (in); (*consapevole*) to be aware of
parteggi'are [parted'dʒare] *vi*: **~ per** to side with, be on the side of
par'tenza [par'tentsa] *sf* departure; (*SPORT*) start; **essere in ~** to be about to leave, be leaving
parti'cella [parti'tʃɛlla] *sf* particle
parti'cipio [parti'tʃipjo] *sm* participle
partico'lare *ag* (*specifico*) particular; (*proprio*) personal, private; (*speciale*) special, particular; (*caratteristico*) distinctive, characteristic; (*fuori dal comune*) peculiar ♦ *sm* detail, particular; **in ~** in particular, particularly; **particolarità** *sf inv* particularity; detail; characteristic, feature
partigi'ano, a [parti'dʒano] *ag* partisan ♦ *sm* (*MIL*) partisan

par'tire *vi* to go, leave; (*allontanarsi*) to go (*o drive etc*) away *o* off; (*petardo, colpo*) to go off; (*fig: avere inizio, SPORT*) to start; **sono partita da Roma alle 7** I left Rome at 7; **il volo parte da Ciampino** the flight leaves from Ciampino; **a ~ da** from
par'tita *sf* (*COMM*) lot, consignment; (*ECON: registrazione*) entry, item; (*CARTE, SPORT: gioco*) game; (: *competizione*) match, game; **~ di caccia** hunting party; **~ IVA** VAT registration number
par'tito *sm* (*POL*) party; (*decisione*) decision, resolution; (*persona da maritare*) match
parti'tura *sf* (*MUS*) score
'parto *sm* (*MED*) delivery, (child)birth; labour; **parto'rire** *vt* to give birth to; (*fig*) to produce
parzi'ale [par'tsjale] *ag* (*limitato*) partial; (*non obiettivo*) biased, partial
'pascere ['paʃʃere] *vt* (*brucare*) to graze on; (*far pascolare*) to graze, pasture; **pasci'uto, a** *pp di* **pascere**
pasco'lare *vt, vi* to graze
'pascolo *sm* pasture
'Pasqua *sf* Easter; **pas'quale** *ag* Easter *cpd*; **Pas'quetta** *sf* Easter Monday
pas'sabile *ag* fairly good, passable
pas'saggio [pas'saddʒo] *sm* passing *no pl*, passage; (*traversata*) crossing *no pl*, passage; (*luogo, prezzo della traversata, brano di libro etc*) passage; (*su veicolo altrui*) lift (*BRIT*), ride; (*SPORT*) pass; **di ~** (*persona*) passing through; **~ pedonale/a livello** pedestrian/level (*BRIT*) *o* grade (*US*) crossing
passamon'tagna [passamon'taɲɲa] *sm inv* balaclava
pas'sante *sm/f* passer-by ♦ *sm* loop
passa'porto *sm* passport
pas'sare *vi* (*andare*) to go; (*veicolo, pedone*) to pass (by), go by; (*fare una breve sosta: postino etc*) to come, call; (: *amico: per fare una visita*) to call *o* drop in; (*sole, aria, luce*) to get through; (*trascorrere: giorni, tempo*) to pass, go by; (*fig: proposta di legge*) to be passed; (: *dolore*) to pass, go away; (*CARTE*) to pass ♦ *vt* (*attraversare*) to cross; (*trasmettere: messaggio*): **~ qc a qn**

to pass sth on to sb; (*dare*): **~ qc a qn** to pass sth to sb, give sb sth; (*trascorrere: tempo*) to spend; (*superare: esame*) to pass; (*triturare: verdura*) to strain; (*approvare*) to pass, approve; (*oltrepassare, sorpassare: anche fig*) to go beyond, pass; (*fig: subire*) to go through; **~ da ... a** to pass from ... to; **~ di padre in figlio** to be handed down *o* to pass from father to son; **~ per** (*anche fig*) to go through; **~ per stupido/un genio** to be taken for a fool/a genius; **~ sopra** (*anche fig*) to pass over; **~ attraverso** (*anche fig*) to go through; **~ alla storia** to pass into history; **~ a un esame** to go up (to the next class) after an exam; **~ inosservato** to go unnoticed; **~ di moda** to go out of fashion; **le passo il Signor X** (*al telefono*) here is Mr X; I'm putting you through to Mr X; **lasciar ~ qn/qc** to let sb/sth through; **come te la passi?** how are you getting on *o* along?

pas'sata *sf*: **dare una ~ di vernice a qc** to give sth a coat of paint; **dare una ~ al giornale** to have a look at the paper, skim through the paper

passa'tempo *sm* pastime, hobby

pas'sato, a *ag* past; (*sfiorito*) faded ♦ *sm* past; (*LING*) past (tense); **~ prossimo** (*LING*) present perfect; **~ remoto** (*LING*) past historic; **~ di verdura** (*CUC*) vegetable purée

passaver'dura *sm inv* vegetable mill

passeg'gero, a [passed'dʒero] *ag* passing ♦ *sm/f* passenger

passeggi'are [passed'dʒare] *vi* to go for a walk; (*in veicolo*) to go for a drive; **passeggi'ata** *sf* walk; drive; (*luogo*) promenade; **fare una passeggiata** to go for a walk *o* drive; **passeg'gino** *sm* pushchair (*BRIT*), stroller (*US*); **pas'seggio** *sm* walk, stroll; (*luogo*) promenade

passe'rella *sf* footbridge; (*di nave, aereo*) gangway; (*pedana*) catwalk

'passero *sm* sparrow

pas'sibile *ag*: **~ di** liable to

passi'one *sf* passion

pas'sivo, a *ag* passive ♦ *sm* (*LING*) passive;

(*ECON*) debit; (: *complesso dei debiti*) liabilities *pl*

'passo *sm* step; (*andatura*) pace; (*rumore*) (foot)step; (*orma*) footprint; (*passaggio, fig: brano*) passage; (*valico*) pass; **a ~ d'uomo** at walking pace; **~ (a)** ~ step by step; **fare due** *o* **quattro ~i** to go for a walk *o* a stroll; **di questo ~** at this rate; **"~ carraio"** "vehicle entrance — keep clear"

'pasta *sf* (*CUC*) dough; (: *impasto per dolce*) pastry; (: *anche*: **~ alimentare**) pasta; (*massa molle di materia*) paste; (*fig: indole*) nature; **~e** *sfpl* (*pasticcini*) pastries; **~ in brodo** noodle soup

pastasci'utta [pastaʃ'ʃutta] *sf* pasta

pas'tella *sf* batter

pas'tello *sm* pastel

pas'ticca, che *sf* = **pastiglia**

pasticce'ria [pastittʃe'ria] *sf* (*pasticcini*) pastries *pl*, cakes *pl*; (*negozio*) cake shop; (*arte*) confectionery

pasticci'are [pastit'tʃare] *vt* to mess up, make a mess of ♦ *vi* to make a mess

pasticci'ere, a [pastit'tʃere] *sm/f* pastrycook; confectioner

pas'ticcio [pas'tittʃo] *sm* (*CUC*) pie; (*lavoro disordinato, imbroglio*) mess; **trovarsi nei ~i** to get into trouble

pasti'ficio [pasti'fitʃo] *sm* pasta factory

pas'tiglia [pas'tiʎʎa] *sf* pastille, lozenge

pas'tina *sf* small pasta shapes used in soup

'pasto *sm* meal

pas'tore *sm* shepherd; (*REL*) pastor, minister; (*anche*: **cane ~**) sheepdog; **~ tedesco** (*ZOOL*) Alsatian, German shepherd

pastoriz'zare [pastorid'dzare] *vt* to pasteurize

pas'toso, a *ag* doughy; pasty; (*fig: voce, colore*) mellow, soft

pas'trano *sm* greatcoat

pa'tata *sf* potato; **~e fritte** chips (*BRIT*), French fries; **pata'tine** *sfpl* (*potato*) crisps; **~ fritte** chips

pata'trac *sm* (*crollo: anche fig*) crash

paté *sm inv* pâté

pa'tella *sf* (*ZOOL*) limpet

pa'tema, i sm anxiety, worry

pa'tente sf licence; (*anche*: ~ **di guida**) driving licence (*BRIT*), driver's license (*US*)

paternità sf paternity, fatherhood

pa'terno, a ag (*affetto, consigli*) fatherly; (*casa, autorità*) paternal

pa'tetico, a, ci, che ag pathetic; (*commovente*) moving, touching

pa'tibolo sm gallows sg, scaffold

'patina sf (*su rame etc*) patina; (*sulla lingua*) fur, coating

pa'tire vt, vi to suffer

pa'tito, a sm/f enthusiast, fan, lover

patolo'gia [patolo'dʒia] sf pathology; pato'logico, a, ci, che ag pathological

'patria sf homeland

patri'arca, chi sm patriarch

pa'trigno [pa'triɲɲo] sm stepfather

patri'monio sm estate, property; (*fig*) heritage

patri'ota, i, e sm/f patriot; patri'ottico, a, ci, che ag patriotic; patriot'tismo sm patriotism

patroci'nare [patrotʃi'nare] vt (*DIR: difendere*) to defend; (*sostenere*) to sponsor, support; patro'cinio sm defence; support, sponsorship

patro'nato sm patronage; (*istituzione benefica*) charitable institution o society

pa'trono sm (*REL*) patron saint; (*socio di patronato*) patron; (*DIR*) counsel

'patta sf flap; (*dei pantaloni*) fly

patteggia'mento [patteddʒa'mento] sm (*DIR*) plea bargaining

patteggi'are [patted'dʒare] vt, vi to negotiate; (*DIR*) to plea-bargain

patti'naggio [patti'naddʒo] sm skating

patti'nare vi to skate; ~ **sul ghiaccio** to ice-skate; patti'na'tore, 'trice sm/f skater; 'pattino[1] sm skate; (*di slitta*) runner; (*AER*) skid; (*TECN*) sliding block; **pattini (da ghiaccio)** (ice) skates; **pattini a rotelle** roller skates; pat'tino[2] sm (*barca*) kind of pedalo with oars

'patto sm (*accordo*) pact, agreement; (*condizione*) term, condition; **a ~ che** on condition that

pat'tuglia [pat'tuʎʎa] sf (*MIL*) patrol

pattu'ire vt to reach an agreement on

pattumi'era sf (dust)bin (*BRIT*), ashcan (*US*)

pa'ura sf fear; **aver ~ di/di fare/che** to be frightened o afraid of/of doing/that; **far ~ a** to frighten; **per ~ di/che** for fear of/that; pau'roso, a ag (*che fa paura*) frightening; (*che ha paura*) fearful, timorous

'pausa sf (*sosta*) break; (*nel parlare, MUS*) pause

pavi'mento sm floor

pa'vone sm peacock; pavoneggi'arsi vr to strut about, show off

pazien'tare [pattsjen'tare] vi to be patient

pazi'ente [pat'tsjente] ag, sm/f patient; pazi'enza sf patience

paz'zesco, a, schi, sche [pat'tsesko] ag mad, crazy

paz'zia [pat'tsia] sf (*MED*) madness, insanity; (*azione*) folly; (*di azione, decisione*) madness, folly

'pazzo, a ['pattso] ag (*MED*) mad, insane; (*strano*) wild, mad ♦ sm/f madman/woman; ~ **di** (*gioia, amore etc*) mad o crazy with; ~ **per qc/qn** mad o crazy about sth/sb

PCI sigla m = **Partito Comunista Italiano**

'pecca, che sf defect, flaw, fault

peccami'noso, a ag sinful

pec'care vi to sin; (*fig*) to err

pec'cato sm sin; **è un ~** it's a pity that; **che ~!** what a shame o pity!

pecca'tore, 'trice sm/f sinner

'pece ['petʃe] sf pitch

Pe'chino [pe'kino] sf Beijing

'pecora sf sheep; peco'raio sm shepherd; peco'rino sm sheep's milk cheese

peculi'are ag: ~ **di** peculiar to

pe'daggio [pe'daddʒo] sm toll

pedago'gia [pedago'dʒia] sf pedagogy, educational methods pl

peda'lare vi to pedal; (*andare in bicicletta*) to cycle

pe'dale sm pedal

pe'dana sf footboard; (*SPORT: nel salto*) springboard; (: *nella scherma*) piste

pe'dante ag pedantic ♦ sm/f pedant

pe'data *sf* (*impronta*) footprint; (*colpo*) kick; **prendere a ~e qn/qc** to kick sb/sth

pede'rasta, i *sm* pederast; homosexual

pedi'atra, i, e *sm/f* paediatrician; pedia'tria *sf* paediatrics *sg*

pedi'cure *sm/f inv* chiropodist

pe'dina *sf* (*della dama*) draughtsman (*BRIT*), draftsman (*US*); (*fig*) pawn

pedi'nare *vt* to shadow, tail

pedo'nale *ag* pedestrian

pe'done, a *sm/f* pedestrian ♦ *sm* (*SCACCHI*) pawn

'peggio ['peddʒo] *av, ag inv* worse ♦ *sm o f*: **il o la ~** the worst; **alla ~** at worst, if the worst comes to the worst; peggiora'mento *sm* worsening; peggio'rare *vt* to make worse, worsen ♦ *vi* to grow worse, worsen; peggiora'tivo, a *ag* pejorative; peggi'ore *ag* (*comparativo*) worse; (*superlativo*) worst ♦ *sm/f*: **il(la) peggiore** the worst (person)

'pegno ['peɲɲo] *sm* (*DIR*) security, pledge; (*nei giochi di società*) forfeit; (*fig*) pledge, token; **dare in ~ qc** to pawn sth

pe'lare *vt* (*spennare*) to pluck; (*spellare*) to skin; (*sbucciare*) to peel; (*fig*) to make pay through the nose; **~rsi** *vr* to go bald

pe'lato, a *ag*: **pomodori ~i** tinned tomatoes

pel'lame *sm* skins *pl*, hides *pl*

'pelle *sf* skin; (*di animale*) skin, hide; (*cuoio*) leather; **avere la ~ d'oca** to have goose pimples *o* goose flesh

pellegri'naggio [pellegri'naddʒo] *sm* pilgrimage

pelle'grino, a *sm/f* pilgrim

pelle'rossa (*pl* pelli'rosse) *sm/f* Red Indian

pellette'ria *sf* leather goods *pl*; (*negozio*) leather goods shop

pelli'cano *sm* pelican

pellicce'ria [pellittʃe'ria] *sf* (*negozio*) furrier's (shop)

pel'liccia, ce [pel'littʃa] *sf* (*mantello di animale*) coat, fur; (*indumento*) fur coat

pel'licola *sf* (*membrana sottile*) film, layer;

(*FOT, CINEMA*) film

'pelo *sm* hair; (*pelame*) coat, hair; (*pelliccia*) fur; (*di tappeto*) pile; (*di liquido*) surface; **per un ~: per un ~ non ho perduto il treno** I very nearly missed the train; **c'è mancato un ~ che affogasse** he escaped drowning by the skin of his teeth; pe'loso, a *ag* hairy

'peltro *sm* pewter

pe'luria *sf* down

'pena *sf* (*DIR*) sentence; (*punizione*) punishment; (*sofferenza*) sadness *no pl*, sorrow; (*fatica*) trouble *no pl*, effort; (*difficoltà*) difficulty; **far ~** to be pitiful; **mi fai ~** I feel sorry for you; **prendersi o darsi la ~ di fare** to go to the trouble of doing; **~ di morte** death sentence; **~ pecuniaria** fine; pe'nale *ag* penal; penalità *sf inv* penalty; penaliz'zare *vt* (*SPORT*) to penalize

pe'nare *vi* (*patire*) to suffer; (*faticare*) to struggle

pen'dente *ag* hanging; leaning ♦ *sm* (*ciondolo*) pendant; (*orecchino*) drop earring; pen'denza *sf* slope, slant; (*grado d'inclinazione*) gradient; (*ECON*) outstanding account

'pendere *vi* (*essere appeso*): **~ da** to hang from; (*essere inclinato*) to lean; (*fig: incombere*): **~ su** to hang over

pen'dice [pen'ditʃe] *sf*: **alle ~i del monte** at the foot of the mountain

pen'dio, 'dii *sm* slope, slant; (*luogo in pendenza*) slope

'pendola *sf* pendulum clock

pendo'lare *sm/f* commuter

pendo'lino *sm* high-speed train

'pendolo *sm* (*peso*) pendulum; (*anche*: **orologio a ~**) pendulum clock

'pene *sm* penis

pene'trante *ag* piercing, penetrating

pene'trare *vi* to come *o* get in ♦ *vt* to penetrate; **~ in** to enter; (*sog: proiettile*) to penetrate; (*: acqua, aria*) to go *o* come into

penicil'lina [penitʃil'lina] *sf* penicillin

pe'nisola *sf* peninsula

peni'tenza [peni'tentsa] *sf* penitence;

(*punizione*) penance

penitenzi'ario [peniten'tsjarjo] *sm* prison

'penna *sf* (*di uccello*) feather; (*per scrivere*) pen; **~e** *sfpl* (*CUC*) quills (*type of pasta*); **~ stilografica/a sfera** fountain/ballpoint pen

penna'rello *sm* felt(-tip) pen

pennel'lare *vi* to paint

pen'nello *sm* brush; (*per dipingere*) (paint)brush; **a ~** (*perfettamente*) to perfection, perfectly; **~ per la barba** shaving brush

pen'nino *sm* nib

pen'none *sm* (*NAUT*) yard; (*stendardo*) banner, standard

pe'nombra *sf* half-light, dim light

pe'noso, a *ag* painful, distressing; (*faticoso*) tiring, laborious

pen'sare *vi* to think ♦ *vt* to think; (*inventare, escogitare*) to think out; **~ a** to think of; (*amico, vacanze*) to think of *o* about; (*problema*) to think about; **~ di fare qc** to think of doing sth; **ci penso io** I'll see to *o* take care of it

pensi'ero *sm* thought; (*modo di pensare, dottrina*) thinking *no pl*; (*preoccupazione*) worry, care, trouble; **stare in ~ per qn** to be worried about sb; **pensie'roso, a** *ag* thoughtful

'pensile *ag* hanging

pensi'lina *sf* (*per autobus*) bus shelter

pensio'nante *sm/f* (*presso una famiglia*) lodger; (*di albergo*) guest

pensio'nato, a *sm/f* pensioner

pensi'one *sf* (*al prestatore di lavoro*) pension; (*vitto e alloggio*) board and lodging; (*albergo*) boarding house; **andare in ~** to retire; **mezza ~** half board; **~ completa** full board

pen'soso, a *ag* thoughtful, pensive, lost in thought

pentapar'tito *sm* five-party government

Pente'coste *sf* Pentecost, Whit Sunday (*BRIT*)

penti'mento *sm* repentance, contrition

pen'tirsi *vr*: **~ di** to repent of; (*rammaricarsi*) to regret, be sorry for

'pentola *sf* pot; **~ a pressione** pressure

cooker

pe'nultimo, a *ag* last but one (*BRIT*), next to last, penultimate

pe'nuria *sf* shortage

penzo'lare [pendzo'lare] *vi* to dangle, hang loosely; **penzo'loni** *av* dangling, hanging down; **stare penzoloni** to dangle, hang down

'pepe *sm* pepper; **~ macinato/in grani** ground/whole pepper

pepero'nata *sf* (*CUC*) stewed peppers, tomatoes and onions

pepe'rone *sm* pepper, capsicum; (*piccante*) chili

pe'pita *sf* nugget

PAROLA CHIAVE

---

per *prep* **1** (*moto attraverso luogo*) through; **i ladri sono passati ~ la finestra** the thieves got in (*o* out) through the window; **l'ho cercato ~ tutta la casa** I've searched the whole house *o* all over the house for it

2 (*moto a luogo*) for, to; **partire ~ la Germania/il mare** to leave for Germany/ the sea; **il treno ~ Roma** the Rome train, the train for *o* to Rome

3 (*stato in luogo*): **seduto/sdraiato ~ terra** sitting/lying on the ground

4 (*tempo*) for; **~ anni/lungo tempo** for years/a long time; **~ tutta l'estate** throughout the summer, all summer long; **lo rividi ~ Natale** I saw him again at Christmas; **lo faccio ~ lunedì** I'll do it for Monday

5 (*mezzo, maniera*) by; **~ lettera/via aerea/ferrovia** by letter/airmail/rail; **prendere qn ~ un braccio** to take sb by the arm

6 (*causa, scopo*) for; **assente ~ malattia** absent because of *o* through *o* owing to illness; **ottimo ~ il mal di gola** excellent for sore throats

7 (*limitazione*) for; **è troppo difficile ~ lui** it's too difficult for him; **~ quel che mi riguarda** as far as I'm concerned; **~ poco che sia** however little it may be; **~ questa volta ti perdono** I'll forgive you this time

8 (*prezzo, misura*) for; (*distributivo*) a, per; **venduto ~ 3 milioni** sold for 3 million; **1000 lire ~ persona** 1000 lire a *o* per person; **uno ~ volta** one at a time; **uno ~ uno** one by one; **5 ~ cento** 5 per cent; **3 ~ 4 fa 12** 3 times 4 equals 12; **dividere/ moltiplicare 12 ~ 4** to divide/multiply 12 by 4

9 (*in qualità di*) as; (*al posto di*) for; **avere qn ~ professore** to have sb as a teacher; **ti ho preso ~ Mario** I mistook you for Mario, I thought you were Mario; **dare ~ morto qn** to give sb up for dead

10 (*seguito da vb: finale*): **~ fare qc** (so as) to do sth, in order to do sth; (*: causale*): **~ aver fatto qc** for having done sth; (*: consecutivo*): **è abbastanza grande ~ andarci da solo** he's big enough to go on his own

'**pera** *sf* pear

pe'**raltro** *av* moreover, what's more

per'**bene** *ag inv* respectable, decent ♦ *av* (*con cura*) properly, well

percentu'ale [pertʃentu'ale] *sf* percentage

perce'**pire** [pertʃe'pire] *vt* (*sentire*) to perceive; (*ricevere*) to receive; **percezi'one** *sf* perception

---

PAROLA CHIAVE

---

perché [per'ke] *av* why; **~ no?** why not?; **~ non vuoi andarci?** why don't you want to go?; **spiegami ~ l'hai fatto** tell me why you did it

♦ *cong* **1** (*causale*) because; **non posso uscire ~ ho da fare** I can't go out because *o* as I've a lot to do

2 (*finale*) in order that, so that; **te lo do ~ tu lo legga** I'm giving it to you so (that) you can read it

3 (*consecutivo*): **è troppo forte ~ si possa batterlo** he's too strong to be beaten

♦ *sm inv* reason; **il ~ di** the reason for

---

perciò [per'tʃɔ] *cong* so, for this (*o* that) reason

per'**correre** *vt* (*luogo*) to go all over;

(*: paese*) to travel up and down, go all over; (*distanza*) to cover

per'**corso, a** *pp di* **percorrere** ♦ *sm* (*tragitto*) journey; (*tratto*) route

per'**cossa** *sf* blow

per'**cosso, a** *pp di* **percuotere**

percu'**otere** *vt* to hit, strike

percussi'one *sf* percussion; **strumenti a ~** (*MUS*) percussion instruments

'**perdere** *vt* to lose; (*lasciarsi sfuggire*) to miss; (*sprecare: tempo, denaro*) to waste ♦ *vi* to lose; (*serbatoio etc*) to leak; **~rsi** *vr* (*smarrirsi*) to get lost; (*svanire*) to disappear, vanish; **saper ~** to be a good loser; **lascia ~!** forget it!, never mind!

perdigi'orno [perdi'dʒorno] *sm/f inv* idler, waster

'**perdita** *sf* loss; (*spreco*) waste; (*fuoriuscita*) leak; **siamo in ~** (*COMM*) we are running at a loss; **a ~ d'occhio** as far as the eye can see

perdo'**nare** *vt* to pardon, forgive; (*scusare*) to excuse, pardon

per'**dono** *sm* forgiveness; (*DIR*) pardon

perdu'**rare** *vi* to go on, last

perduta'**mente** *av* desperately, passionately

per'**duto, a** *pp di* **perdere**

peregri'**nare** *vi* to wander, roam

pe'**renne** *ag* eternal, perpetual, perennial; (*BOT*) perennial

peren'**torio, a** *ag* peremptory; (*definitivo*) final

per'**fetto, a** *ag* perfect ♦ *sm* (*LING*) perfect (tense)

perfezio'**nare** [perfettsjo'nare] *vt* to improve, perfect; **~rsi** *vr* to improve

perfezi'one [perfet'tsjone] *sf* perfection

'**perfido, a** *ag* perfidious, treacherous

per'**fino** *av* even

perfo'**rare** *vt* to perforate; to punch a hole (*o* holes) in; (*banda, schede*) to punch; (*trivellare*) to drill; **perfora'trice** *sf* (*TECN*) boring *o* drilling machine; (*INFORM*) card punch; **perforazi'one** *sf* perforation; punching; drilling; (*INFORM*) punch; (*MED*) perforation

perga'mena *sf* parchment
'pergola *sf* (*per rampicanti*) pergola
perico'lante *ag* precarious
pe'ricolo *sm* danger; **mettere in ~** to endanger, put in danger; **perico'loso, a** *ag* dangerous
perife'ria *sf* (*di città*) outskirts *pl*
pe'rifrasi *sf* circumlocution
pe'rimetro *sm* perimeter
peri'odico, a, ci, che *ag* periodic(al); (*MAT*) recurring ♦ *sm* periodical
pe'riodo *sm* period
peripe'zie [peripet'tsie] *sfpl* ups and downs, vicissitudes
pe'rire *vi* to perish, die
pe'rito, a *ag* expert, skilled ♦ *sm/f* expert; (*agronomo, navale*) surveyor; **un ~ chimico** a qualified chemist
pe'rizia [pe'rittsja] *sf* (*abilità*) ability; (*giudizio tecnico*) expert opinion; expert's report
'perla *sf* pearl; **per'lina** *sf* bead
perlus'trare *vt* to patrol
perma'loso, a *ag* touchy
perma'nente *ag* permanent ♦ *sf* permanent wave, perm; **perma'nenza** *sf* permanence; (*soggiorno*) stay
perma'nere *vi* to remain
perme'are *vt* to permeate
per'messo, a *pp di* **permettere** ♦ *sm* (*autorizzazione*) permission, leave; (*dato a militare, impiegato*) leave; (*licenza*) licence, permit; (*MIL: foglio*) pass; **~?, è ~?** (*posso entrare?*) may I come in?; (*posso passare?*) excuse me; **~ di lavoro/pesca** work/fishing permit; **~ di soggiorno** residence permit
per'mettere *vt* to allow, permit; **~ a qn qc/di fare** to allow sb sth/to do; **~rsi qc/di fare** to allow o.s. sth/to do; (*avere la possibilità*) to afford sth/to do
per'nacchia [per'nakkja] (*fam*) *sf:* **fare una ~** to blow a raspberry
per'nice [per'nitʃe] *sf* partridge
'perno *sm* pivot
pernot'tare *vi* to spend the night, stay overnight

'pero *sm* pear tree
però *cong* (*ma*) but; (*tuttavia*) however, nevertheless
pero'rare *vt* (*DIR, fig*): **~ la causa di qn** to plead sb's case
perpendico'lare *ag, sf* perpendicular
perpe'trare *vt* to perpetrate
perpetu'are *vt* to perpetuate
per'petuo, a *ag* perpetual
per'plesso, a *ag* perplexed; uncertain, undecided
perqui'sire *vt* to search; **perquisizi'one** *sf* (*police*) search
persecu'tore *sm* persecutor
persecuzi'one [persekut'tsjone] *sf* persecution
persegu'ire *vt* to pursue
persegui'tare *vt* to persecute
perseve'rante *ag* persevering
perseve'rare *vi* to persevere
'Persia *sf*: **la ~** Persia
persi'ana *sf* shutter; **~ avvolgibile** roller shutter
persi'ano, a *ag, sm/f* Persian
'persico, a, ci, che *ag*: **il golfo P~** the Persian Gulf
per'sino *av* = **perfino**
persis'tente *ag* persistent
per'sistere *vi* to persist; **~ a fare** to persist in doing; **persis'tito, a** *pp di* **persistere**
'perso, a *pp di* **perdere**
per'sona *sf* person; (*qualcuno*): **una ~** someone, somebody, *espressione interrogativa* +anyone *o* anybody; **~e** *sfpl* people; **non c'è ~ che ...** there's nobody who ..., there isn't anybody who ...
perso'naggio [perso'naddʒo] *sm* (*persona ragguardevole*) personality, figure; (*tipo*) character, individual; (*LETTERATURA*) character
perso'nale *ag* personal ♦ *sm* staff; personnel; (*figura fisica*) build
personalità *sf inv* personality
personifi'care *vt* to personify; to embody
perspi'cace [perspi'katʃe] *ag* shrewd, discerning
persu'adere *vt*: **~ qn (di qc/a fare)** to

persuade sb (of sth/to do); **persuasi'one**
sf persuasion; **persua'sivo, a** ag
persuasive; **persu'aso, a** pp di
persuadere

per'tanto cong (quindi) so, therefore

'pertica, che sf pole

perti'nente ag: ~ **(a)** relevant (to),
pertinent (to)

per'tosse sf whooping cough

per'tugio [per'tudʒo] sm hole, opening

perturbazi'one [perturbat'tsjone] sf
disruption; perturbation; ~ **atmosferica**
atmospheric disturbance

per'vadere vt to pervade; **per'vaso, a**
pp di **pervadere**

perve'nire vi: ~ **a** to reach, arrive at, come
to; (venire in possesso): **gli pervenne una
fortuna** he inherited a fortune; **far ~ qc a**
to have sth sent to; **perve'nuto, a** pp di
pervenire

per'verso, a ag depraved; perverse

p. es. abbr (= per esempio) e.g.

'pesa sf weighing no pl; weighbridge

pe'sante ag heavy

pe'sare vt to weigh ♦ vi (avere un peso) to
weigh; (essere pesante) to be heavy; (fig) to
carry weight; ~ **su** (fig) to lie heavy on; to
influence; to have weight

'pesca (pl pesche: frutto) sf peach; (il
pescare) fishing; **andare a ~** to go fishing;
~ **di beneficenza** (lotteria) lucky dip; ~ **con
la lenza** angling

pes'care vt (pesce) to fish for; to catch; (qc
nell'acqua) to fish out; (fig: trovare) to get
hold of, find; **andare a ~** to go fishing

pesca'tore sm fisherman; angler

'pesce ['peʃʃe] sm fish gen inv; **P~i** (dello
zodiaco) Pisces; ~ **d'aprile!** April Fool!; ~
spada swordfish; **pesce'cane** sm shark

┌─────────────────┐
│ **pesce d'aprile** │
└─────────────────┘

i **Il pesce d'aprile** is a practical joke
played on 1 April. It takes its name from
the traditional prank of surreptitiously
sticking a paper fish on someone's back.

pesche'reccio [peske'rettʃo] sm fishing

boat

pesche'ria [peske'ria] sf fishmonger's
(shop) (BRIT), fish store (US)

pesci'vendolo, a [peʃʃi'vendolo] sm/f
fishmonger (BRIT), fish merchant (US)

'pesco, schi sm peach tree

pes'coso, a ag abounding in fish

'peso sm weight; (SPORT) shot; **rubare sul
~** to give short weight; **essere di ~ a qn**
(fig) to be a burden to sb; ~ **lordo/netto**
gross/net weight; ~ **piuma/mosca/gallo/
medio/massimo** (PUGILATO) feather/fly/
bantam/middle/heavyweight

pessi'mismo sm pessimism;
pessi'mista, i, e ag pessimistic ♦ sm/f
pessimist

'pessimo, a ag very bad, awful

pes'tare vt to tread on, trample on; (sale,
pepe) to grind; (uva, aglio) to crush; (fig:
picchiare): ~ **qn** to beat sb up

'peste sf plague; (persona) nuisance, pest

pes'tello sm pestle

pesti'lenza [pesti'lentsa] sf pestilence;
(fetore) stench

'pesto, a ag: **c'è buio ~** it's pitch-dark;
occhio ~ black eye ♦ sm (CUC) sauce made
with basil, garlic, cheese and oil

'petalo sm (BOT) petal

pe'tardo sm firecracker, banger (BRIT)

petizi'one [petit'tsjone] sf petition

'peto (fam!) sm fart (!)

petrol'chimica [petrol'kimika] sf
petrochemical industry

petroli'era sf (nave) oil tanker

petro'lifero, a ag oil-bearing; oil cpd

pe'trolio sm oil, petroleum; (per lampada,
fornello) paraffin

petteg'lare vi to gossip

petteg'lezzo [pettego'leddzo] sm gossip
no pl; **fare ~i** to gossip

pet'tegolo, a ag gossipy ♦ sm/f gossip

petti'nare vt to comb (the hair of); **~rsi** vr
to comb one's hair; **pettina'tura** sf
(acconciatura) hairstyle

'pettine sm comb; (ZOOL) scallop

petti'rosso sm robin

'petto sm chest; (seno) breast, bust; (CUC: di

carne bovina) brisket; (: *di pollo etc*) breast; **a doppio ~** (*abito*) double-breasted; **petto'ruto, a** *ag* broad-chested; full-breasted

petu'lante *ag* insolent

pe'tunia *sf* (BOT) petunia

'pezza ['pɛttsa] *sf* piece of cloth; (*toppa*) patch; (*cencio*) rag, cloth

pez'zato, a [pet'tsato] *ag* piebald

pez'zente [pet'tsɛnte] *sm/f* beggar

'pezzo ['pɛttso] *sm* (*gen*) piece; (*brandello, frammento*) piece, bit; (*di macchina, arnese etc*) part; (STAMPA) article; (*di tempo*): **aspettare un ~** to wait quite a while *o* some time; **in** *o* **a ~i** in pieces; **andare in ~i** to break into pieces; **un bel ~ d'uomo** a fine figure of a man; **abito a due ~i** two-piece suit; **~ di cronaca** (STAMPA) report; **~ grosso** (*fig*) bigwig; **~ di ricambio** spare part

pia'cente [pja'tʃɛnte] *ag* attractive

pia'cere [pja'tʃere] *vi* to please; **una ragazza che piace** a likeable girl; an attractive girl; **~ a: mi piace** I like it; **quei ragazzi non mi piacciono** I don't like those boys; **gli piacerebbe andare al cinema** he would like to go to the cinema ♦ *sm* pleasure; (*favore*) favour; **"~!"** (*nelle presentazioni*) "pleased to meet you!"; **con ~** certainly, with pleasure; **per ~!** please; **fare un ~ a qn** to do sb a favour; **pia'cevole** *ag* pleasant, agreeable; **piaci'uto, a** *pp di* **piacere**

pi'aga, ghe *sf* (*lesione*) sore; (*ferita: anche fig*) wound; (*fig: flagello*) scourge, curse; (: *persona*) pest, nuisance

piagnis'teo [pjaɲɲis'teo] *sm* whining, whimpering

piagnuco'lare [pjaɲɲuko'lare] *vi* to whimper

pi'alla *sf* (*arnese*) plane; **pial'lare** *vt* to plane

pi'ana *sf* stretch of level ground; (*più estesa*) plain

pianeggi'ante [pjaned'dʒante] *ag* flat, level

piane'rottolo *sm* landing

pia'neta *sm* (ASTR) planet

pi'angere ['pjandʒere] *vi* to cry, weep; (*occhi*) to water ♦ *vt* to cry, weep; (*lamentare*) to bewail, lament; **~ la morte di qn** to mourn sb's death

pianifi'care *vt* to plan; **pianificazi'one** *sf* planning

pia'nista, i, e *sm/f* pianist

pi'ano, a *ag* (*piatto*) flat, level; (MAT) plane; (*chiaro*) clear, plain ♦ *av* (*adagio*) slowly; (*a bassa voce*) softly; (*con cautela*) slowly, carefully ♦ *sm* (MAT) plane; (GEO) plain; (*livello*) level, plane; (*di edificio*) floor; (*programma*) plan; (MUS) piano; **pian ~** very slowly; (*poco a poco*) little by little; **in primo/secondo ~** in the foreground/ background; **di primo ~** (*fig*) prominent, high-ranking

piano'forte *sm* piano, pianoforte

pi'anta *sf* (BOT) plant; (ANAT: *anche*: **~ del piede**) sole (of the foot); (*grafico*) plan; (*topografica*) map; **in ~ stabile** on the permanent staff; **piantagi'one** *sf* plantation; **pian'tare** *vt* to plant; (*conficcare*) to drive *o* hammer in; (*tenda*) to put up, pitch; (*fig: lasciare*) to leave, desert; **~rsi** *vr*: **~rsi davanti a qn** to plant o.s. in front of sb; **piantala!** (*fam*) cut it out!

pianter'reno *sm* ground floor

pian'tina *sf* (*carta*) map

pi'anto, a *pp di* **piangere** ♦ *sm* tears *pl*, crying

pian'tone *sm* (*vigilante*) sentry, guard; (*soldato*) orderly; (AUT) steering column

pia'nura *sf* plain

pi'astra *sf* plate; (*di pietra*) slab; (*di fornello*) hotplate; **~ di registrazione** tape deck; **panino alla ~** ≈ toasted sandwich

pias'trella *sf* tile

pias'trina *sf* (MIL) identity disc

piatta'forma *sf* (*anche fig*) platform

piat'tino *sm* saucer

pi'atto, a *ag* flat; (*fig: scialbo*) dull ♦ *sm* (*recipiente, vivanda*) dish; (*portata*) course; (*parte piana*) flat (part); **~i** *smpl* (MUS) cymbals; **~ fondo** soup dish; **~ forte** main course; **~ del giorno** dish of the day, plat du jour; **~ del giradischi** turntable

pi'azza ['pjattsa] *sf* square; (*COMM*) market; **far ~ pulita** to make a clean sweep; **~ d'armi** (*MIL*) parade ground; **piaz'zale** *sm* (large) square

piaz'zare [pjat'tsare] *vt* to place; (*COMM*) to market, sell; **~rsi** *vr* (*SPORT*) to be placed

piaz'zista, i [pjat'tsista] *sm* (*COMM*) commercial traveller

piaz'zola [pjat'tsɔla] *sf* (*AUT*) lay-by

'picca, che *sf* pike; **~che** *sfpl* (*CARTE*) spades

pic'cante *ag* hot, pungent; (*fig*) racy; biting

pic'carsi *vr*: **~ di fare** to pride o.s. on one's ability to do; **~ per qc** to take offence at sth

pic'chetto [pik'ketto] *sm* (*MIL, di scioperanti*) picket; (*di tenda*) peg

picchi'are [pik'kjare] *vt* (*persona: colpire*) to hit, strike; (: *prendere a botte*) to beat (up); (*battere*) to beat; (*sbattere*) to bang ♦ *vi* (*bussare*) to knock; (: *con forza*) to bang; (*colpire*) to hit, strike; (*sole*) to beat down; **picchi'ata** (*AER*) dive

picchiet'tare [pikkjet'tare] *vt* (*punteggiare*) to spot, dot; (*colpire*) to tap

'picchio ['pikkjo] *sm* woodpecker

pic'cino, a [pit'tʃino] *ag* tiny, very small

piccio'naia [pittʃo'naja] *sf* pigeon-loft; (*TEATRO*): **la ~** the gods *sg*

picci'one [pit'tʃone] *sm* pigeon

'picco, chi *sm* peak; **a ~** vertically

'piccolo, a *ag* small; (*oggetto, mano, di età: bambino*) small, little (*dav sostantivo*); (*di breve durata: viaggio*) short; (*fig*) mean, petty ♦ *sm/f* child, little one; **~i** *smpl* (*di animale*) young *pl*; **in ~** in miniature

pic'cone *sm* pick(-axe)

pic'cozza [pik'kɔttsa] *sf* ice-axe

'pic'nic *sm inv* picnic

pi'docchio [pi'dɔkkjo] *sm* louse

pi'ede *sm* foot; (*di mobile*) leg; **in ~i** standing; **a ~i** on foot; **a ~i nudi** barefoot; **su due ~i** (*fig*) at once; **prendere ~** (*fig*) to gain ground, catch on; **sul ~ di guerra** (*MIL*) ready for action; **~ di porco** crowbar

piedes'tallo *sm* pedestal

piedipi'atti *sm inv* (*peg*) cop

pi'ega, ghe *sf* (*piegatura, GEO*) fold; (*di gonna*) pleat; (*di pantaloni*) crease; (*grinza*) wrinkle, crease; **prendere una brutta ~** (*fig*) to take a turn for the worse

pie'gare *vt* to fold; (*braccia, gambe, testa*) to bend ♦ *vi* to bend; **~rsi** *vr* to bend; (*fig*): **~rsi (a)** to yield (to), submit (to); **pieghet'tare** *vt* to pleat; **pie'ghevole** *ag* pliable, flexible; (*porta*) folding

Pie'monte *sm*: **il ~** Piedmont

pi'ena *sf* (*di fiume*) flood, spate

pi'eno, a *ag* full; (*muro, mattone*) solid ♦ *sm* (*colmo*) height, peak; (*carico*) full load; **~ di** full of; **in ~ giorno** in broad daylight; **fare il ~ (di benzina)** to fill up (with petrol)

pietà *sf* pity; (*REL*) piety; **senza ~** pitiless, merciless; **avere ~ di** (*compassione*) to pity, feel sorry for; (*misericordia*) to have pity *o* mercy on

pie'tanza [pje'tantsa] *sf* dish, course

pie'toso, a *ag* (*compassionevole*) pitying, compassionate; (*che desta pietà*) pitiful

pi'etra *sf* stone; **~ preziosa** precious stone, gem; **pie'traia** *sf* (*terreno*) stony ground; **pietrifi'care** *vt* to petrify; (*fig*) to transfix, paralyze

'piffero *sm* (*MUS*) pipe

pigi'ama, i [pi'dʒama] *sm* pyjamas *pl*

'pigia 'pigia ['pidʒa'pidʒa] *sm* crowd, press

pigi'are [pi'dʒare] *vt* to press

pigi'one [pi'dʒone] *sf* rent

pigli'are [piʎ'ʎare] *vt* to take, grab; (*afferrare*) to catch

'piglio ['piʎʎo] *sm* look, expression

pig'meo, a *sm/f* pygmy

'pigna ['pinna] *sf* pine cone

pi'gnolo, a [pin'nɔlo] *ag* pernickety

pigno'rare [pinno'rare] *vt* to distrain

pigo'lare *vi* to cheep, chirp

pi'grizia [pi'grittsja] *sf* laziness

'pigro, a *ag* lazy

'pila *sf* (*catasta, di ponte*) pile; (*ELETTR*) battery; (*torcia*) torch (*BRIT*), flashlight

pi'lastro *sm* pillar

'pile ['pail] sm inv fleece

'pillola sf pill; **prendere la ~** to be on the pill

pi'lone sm (di ponte) pier; (di linea elettrica) pylon

pi'lota, i, e sm/f pilot; (AUT) driver ♦ ag inv pilot cpd; **~ automatico** automatic pilot; **pilo'tare** vt to pilot; to drive

pinaco'teca, che sf art gallery

pi'neta sf pinewood

ping-'pong [piŋ'pɔŋ] sm table tennis

'pingue ag fat, corpulent

pingu'ino sm (ZOOL) penguin

'pinna sf (di pesce) fin; (di cetaceo, per nuotare) flipper

'pino sm pine (tree); pi'nolo sm pine kernel

'pinza ['pintsa] sf pliers pl; (MED) forceps pl; (ZOOL) pincer

pin'zette [pin'tsette] sfpl tweezers

'pio, a, 'pii, 'pie ag pious; (opere, istituzione) charitable, charity cpd

pi'oggia, ge ['pjɔddʒa] sf rain; **~ acida** acid rain

pi'olo sm peg; (di scala) rung

piom'bare vi to fall heavily; (gettarsi con impeto): **~ su** to fall upon, assail ♦ vt (dente) to fill; piomba'tura sf (di dente) filling

piom'bino sm (sigillo) (lead) seal; (del filo a piombo) plummet; (PESCA) sinker

pi'ombo sm (CHIM) lead; **a ~** (cadere) straight down; **senza ~** (benzina) unleaded

pioni'ere, a sm/f pioneer

pi'oppo sm poplar

pi'overe vb impers to rain ♦ vi (fig: scendere dall'alto) to rain down; (lettere, regali) to pour into; **pioviggi'nare** vb impers to drizzle; **pio'voso, a** ag rainy

pi'ovra sf octopus

'pipa sf pipe

pipì (fam) sf: **fare ~** to have a wee (wee)

pipis'trello sm (ZOOL) bat

pi'ramide sf pyramid

pi'rata, i sm pirate; **~ della strada** hit-and-run driver

Pire'nei smpl: **i ~** the Pyrenees

'pirico, a, ci, che ag: **polvere ~a** gunpowder

pi'rofilo, a ag heat-resistant; pi'rofila sf heat-resistant dish

pi'roga, ghe sf dug-out canoe

pi'romane sm/f pyromaniac; arsonist

pi'roscafo sm steamer, steamship

pisci'are [piʃ'ʃare] (fam!) vi to piss (!), pee (!)

pi'scina [piʃ'ʃina] sf (swimming) pool; (stabilimento) (swimming) baths pl

pi'sello sm pea

piso'lino sm nap

'pista sf (traccia) track, trail; (di stadio) track; (di pattinaggio) rink; (da sci) run; (AER) runway; (di circo) ring; **~ da ballo** dance floor

pis'tacchio [pis'takkjo] sm pistachio (tree); pistachio (nut)

pis'tola sf pistol, gun

pis'tone sm piston

pi'tone sm python

pit'tore, 'trice sm/f painter; pitto'resco, a, schi, sche ag picturesque

pit'tura sf painting; pittu'rare vt to paint

PAROLA CHIAVE

più av 1 (in maggiore quantità) more; **~ del solito** more than usual; **in ~, di ~** more; **ne voglio di ~** I want some more; **ci sono 3 persone in o di ~** there are 3 more o extra people; **~ o meno** more or less; **per di ~** (inoltre) what's more, moreover

2 (comparativo) more, aggettivo corto +...er; **~ ... di/che** more ... than; **lavoro ~ di te/Paola** I work harder than you/Paola; **è ~ intelligente che ricco** he's more intelligent than rich

3 (superlativo) most, aggettivo corto +...est; **il ~ grande/intelligente** the biggest/most intelligent; **è quello che compro ~ spesso** that's the one I buy most often; **al ~ presto** as soon as possible; **al ~ tardi** at the latest

4 (negazione): **non ... ~** no more, no longer; **non ho ~ soldi** I've got no more money, I don't have any more money; **non**

lavoro ~ I'm no longer working, I don't work any more; **a ~ non posso** (*gridare*) at the top of one's voice; (*correre*) as fast as one can

5 (*MAT*) plus; **4 ~ 5 fa 9** 4 plus 5 equals 9; **~ 5 gradi** 5 degrees above freezing, plus 5
♦ *prep* plus
♦ *ag inv* 1: **~ ... (di)** more ... (than); **~ denaro/tempo** more money/time; **~ persone di quante ci aspettassimo** more people than we expected
2 (*numerosi, diversi*) several; **l'aspettai per ~ giorni** I waited for it for several days
♦ *sm* 1 (*la maggior parte*): **il ~ è fatto** most of it is done
2 (*MAT*) plus (sign)
3: **i ~** the majority

---

piucchepper'fetto [pjukkepper'fetto] *sm* (*LING*) pluperfect, past perfect
pi'uma *sf* feather; **piu'maggio** *sm*-plumage, feathers *pl*; **piu'mino** *sm* (eider)down; (*per letto*) eiderdown; (: *tipo danese*) duvet, continental quilt; (*giacca*) quilted jacket (*with goose-feather padding*); (*per cipria*) powder puff; (*per spolverare*) feather duster
piut'tosto *av* rather; **~ che** (*anziché*) rather than
pi'vello, a *sm/f* greenhorn
'pizza ['pittsa] *sf* pizza; **pizze'ria** *sf* place where pizzas are made, sold or eaten
pizzi'cagnolo, a [pittsi'kaɲɲolo] *sm/f* specialist grocer
pizzi'care [pittsi'kare] *vt* (*stringere*) to nip, pinch; (*pungere*) to sting; to bite; (*MUS*) to pluck ♦ *vi* (*prudere*) to itch, be itchy; (*cibo*) to be hot o spicy
pizziche'ria [pittsike'ria] *sf* delicatessen (shop)
'pizzico, chi ['pittsiko] *sm* (*pizzicotto*) pinch, nip; (*piccola quantità*) pinch, dash; (*d'insetto*) sting; bite
pizzi'cotto [pittsi'kɔtto] *sm* pinch, nip
'pizzo ['pittso] *sm* (*merletto*) lace; (*barbetta*) goatee beard
pla'care *vt* to placate, soothe; **~rsi** *vr* to

calm down
'placca, che *sf* plate; (*con iscrizione*) plaque; (*anche:* **~ dentaria**) (dental) plaque; **plac'care** *vt* to plate; **placcato in oro/argento** gold-/silver-plated
'placido, a ['platʃido] *ag* placid, calm
plagi'are [pla'dʒare] *vt* (*copiare*) to plagiarize; **'plagio** *sm* plagiarism
pla'nare *vi* (*AER*) to glide
'plancia, ce ['plantʃa] *sf* (*NAUT*) bridge
plane'tario, a *ag* planetary ♦ *sm* (*locale*) planetarium
'plasma *sm* plasma
plas'mare *vt* to mould, shape
'plastica, che *sf* (*arte*) plastic arts *pl*; (*MED*) plastic surgery; (*sostanza*) plastic
'plastico, a, ci, che *ag* plastic ♦ *sm* (*rappresentazione*) relief model; (*esplosivo*): **bomba al ~** plastic bomb
plasti'lina ® *sf* plasticine ®
'platano *sm* plane tree
pla'tea *sf* (*TEATRO*) stalls *pl*
'platino *sm* platinum
pla'tonico, a, ci, che *ag* platonic
plau'sibile *ag* plausible
'plauso *sm* (*fig*) approval
ple'baglia [ple'baʎʎa] (*peg*) *sf* rabble, mob
'plebe *sf* common people; **ple'beo, a** *ag* plebeian; (*volgare*) coarse, common
ple'nario, a *ag* plenary
pleni'lunio *sm* full moon
'plettro *sm* plectrum
pleu'rite *sf* pleurisy
'plico, chi *sm* (*pacco*) parcel; **in ~ a parte** (*COMM*) under separate cover
plo'tone *sm* (*MIL*) platoon; **~ d'esecuzione** firing squad
'plumbeo, a *ag* leaden
plu'rale *ag, sm* plural; **pluralità** *sf* plurality; (*maggioranza*) majority
plusva'lore *sm* (*ECON*) surplus
pneu'matico, a, ci, che *ag* inflatable; pneumatic ♦ *sm* (*AUT*) tyre (*BRIT*), tire (*US*)
po' *av, sm vedi* **poco**

PAROLA CHIAVE

'poco, a, chi, che *ag* (*quantità*) little, not

much; (*numero*) few, not many; ~ **pane/denaro/spazio** little *o* not much bread/money/space; **~che persone/idee** few *o* not many people/ideas; **ci vediamo tra ~** (*sottinteso: tempo*) see you soon

♦ *av* 1 (*in piccola quantità*) little, not much; (*numero limitato*) few, not many; **guadagna ~** he doesn't earn much, he earns little

2 (*con ag, av*) (a) little, not very; **sta ~ bene** he isn't very well; **è ~ più vecchia di lui** she's a little *o* slightly older than him

3 (*tempo*): **~ dopo/prima** shortly afterwards/before; **il film dura ~** the film doesn't last very long; **ci vediamo molto ~** we don't see each other very often, we hardly ever see each other

4: **un po'** a little, a bit; **è un po' corto** it's a little *o* a bit short; **arriverà fra un po'** he'll arrive shortly *o* in a little while

5: **a dir ~** to say the least; **a ~ a ~** little by little; **per ~ non cadevo** I nearly fell; **è una cosa da ~** it's nothing, it's of no importance; **una persona da ~** a worthless person

♦ *pron* (a) little; **~chi, che** *pron pl* (*persone*) few (people); (*cose*) few

♦ *sm* 1 little; **vive del ~ che ha** he lives on the little he has

2: **un po'** a little; **un po' di zucchero** a little sugar; **un bel po' di denaro** quite a lot of money; **un po' per ciascuno** a bit each

po'dere *sm* (*AGR*) farm
pode'roso, a *ag* powerful
podestà *sm inv* (*nel fascismo*) podesta, mayor
'podio *sm* dais, platform; (*MUS*) podium
po'dismo *sm* (*SPORT*) track events *pl*
po'ema, i *sm* poem
poe'sia *sf* (*arte*) poetry; (*componimento*) poem
po'eta, 'essa *sm/f* poet/poetess;
po'etico, a, ci, che *ag* poetic(al)
poggi'are [pod'dʒare] *vt* to lean, rest; (*posare*) to lay, place; **poggia'testa** *sm*

inv (*AUT*) headrest
'poggio ['pɔddʒo] *sm* hillock, knoll
poggi'olo [pod'dʒɔlo] *sm* balcony
'poi *av* then; (*alla fine*) finally, at last; **e ~** (*inoltre*) and besides; **questa ~ (è bella)!** (*ironico*) that's a good one!
poiché [poi'ke] *cong* since, as
'poker *sm* poker
po'lacco, a, chi, che *ag* Polish ♦ *sm/f* Pole
po'lare *ag* polar
po'lemica, che *sf* controversy
po'lemico, a, ci, che *ag* polemic(al), controversial
po'lenta *sf* (*CUC*) sort of thick porridge *made with maize flour*
poliambula'torio *sm* health centre
poli'clinico, ci *sm* general hospital, polyclinic
poli'estere *sm* polyester
'polio(mie'lite) *sf* polio(myelitis)
'polipo *sm* polyp
polisti'rolo *sm* polystyrene
poli'tecnico, ci *sm* postgraduate technical college
po'litica, che *sf* politics *sg*; (*linea di condotta*) policy; *vedi anche* **politico**
politiciz'zare [politit ʃid'dzare] *vt* to politicize
po'litico, a, ci, che *ag* political ♦ *sm/f* politician
poli'zia [polit'tsia] *sf* police; **~ giudiziaria** ≈ Criminal Investigation Department (*BRIT*), ≈ Federal Bureau of Investigation (*US*); **~ stradale** traffic police; **polizi'esco, a, schi, sche** *ag* police *cpd*; (*film, romanzo*) detective *cpd*; **polizi'otto** *sm* policeman; **cane poliziotto** police dog; **donna poliziotto** policewoman

---
polizia di stato
---

i The function of the **polizia di stato** is to maintain public order, to uphold the law and prevent and investigate crime. They are a civil body, reporting to the Minister of the Interior.

'polizza ['polittsa] *sf* (*COMM*) bill; ~ di assicurazione insurance policy; ~ di carico bill of lading
pol'laio *sm* henhouse
pol'lame *sm* poultry
pol'lastro *sm* (*ZOOL*) cockerel
'pollice ['pollitʃe] *sm* thumb
'polline *sm* pollen
'pollo *sm* chicken
pol'mone *sm* lung; ~ d'acciaio (*MED*) iron lung; polmo'nite *sf* pneumonia
'polo *sm* (*GEO, FISICA*) pole; (*gioco*) polo; il ~ sud/nord the South/North Pole
Po'lonia *sf*: la ~ Poland
'polpa *sf* flesh, pulp; (*carne*) lean meat
pol'paccio [pol'pattʃo] *sm* (*ANAT*) calf
polpas'trello *sm* fingertip
pol'petta *sf* (*CUC*) meatball; polpet'tone *sm* (*CUC*) meatloaf
'polpo *sm* octopus
pol'poso, a *ag* fleshy
pol'sino *sm* cuff
'polso *sm* (*ANAT*) wrist; (*pulsazione*) pulse; (*fig: forza*) drive, vigour
pol'tiglia [pol'tiʎʎa] *sf* (*composto*) mash, mush; (*di fango e neve*) slush
pol'trire *vi* to laze about
pol'trona *sf* armchair; (*TEATRO: posto*) seat in the front stalls (*BRIT*) o orchestra (*US*)
pol'trone *ag* lazy, slothful
'polvere *sf* dust; (*anche*: ~ da sparo) (gun)powder; (*sostanza ridotta minutissima*) powder, dust; latte in ~ dried o powdered milk; caffè in ~ instant coffee; sapone in ~ soap powder; polveri'era *sf* (*MIL*) (gun)-powder magazine; polveriz'zare *vt* to pulverize; (*nebulizzare*) to atomize; (*fig*) to crush, pulverize; to smash; polve'rone *sm* thick cloud of dust; polve'roso, a *ag* dusty
po'mata *sf* ointment, cream
po'mello *sm* knob
pomeridi'ano, a *ag* afternoon *cpd*; nelle ore ~ in the afternoon
pome'riggio [pome'riddʒo] *sm* afternoon
'pomice ['pomitʃe] *sf* pumice
'pomo *sm* (*mela*) apple; (*ornamentale*) knob; (*di sella*) pommel; ~ d'Adamo (*ANAT*) Adam's apple
pomo'doro *sm* tomato
'pompa *sf* pump; (*sfarzo*) pomp (and ceremony); ~e funebri funeral parlour *sg* (*BRIT*), undertaker's *sg*; pom'pare *vt* to pump; (*trarre*) to pump out; (*gonfiare d'aria*) to pump up
pom'pelmo *sm* grapefruit
pompi'ere *sm* fireman
pom'poso, a *ag* pompous
ponde'rare *vt* to ponder over, consider carefully
ponde'roso, a *ag* (*anche fig*) weighty
po'nente *sm* west
'ponte *sm* bridge; (*di nave*) deck; (: *anche*: ~ di comando) bridge; (*impalcatura*) scaffold; fare il ~ (*fig*) to take the extra day off (*between 2 public holidays*); governo ~ interim government; ~ aereo airlift; ~ sospeso suspension bridge
pon'tefice [pon'tefitʃe] *sm* (*REL*) pontiff
pontifi'care *vi* (*anche fig*) to pontificate
ponti'ficio, a, ci, cie [ponti'fitʃo] *ag* papal
popo'lano, a *ag* popular, of the people
popo'lare *ag* popular; (*quartiere, clientela*) working-class ♦ *vt* (*rendere abitato*) to populate; ~rsi *vr* to fill with people, get crowded; popolarità *sf* popularity; popolazi'one *sf* population
'popolo *sm* people; popo'loso, a *ag* densely populated
'poppa *sf* (*di nave*) stern; (*seno*) breast
pop'pare *vt* to suck
poppa'toio *sm* (*feeding*) bottle
porcel'lana [portʃel'lana] *sf* porcelain, china; piece of china
porcel'lino, a [portʃel'lino] *sm/f* piglet
porche'ria [porke'ria] *sf* filth, muck; (*fig: oscenità*) obscenity; (: *azione disonesta*) dirty trick; (: *cosa mal fatta*) rubbish
por'cile [por'tʃile] *sm* pigsty
por'cino, a [por'tʃino] *ag* of pigs, pork *cpd* ♦ *sm* (*fungo*) type of edible mushroom
'porco, ci *sm* pig; (*carne*) pork
porcos'pino *sm* porcupine

'porgere ['pɔrdʒere] vt to hand, give; (*tendere*) to hold out

pornogra'fia sf pornography; porno'grafico, a, ci, che ag pornographic

'poro sm pore; po'roso, a ag porous

'porpora sf purple

'porre vt (*mettere*) to put; (*collocare*) to place; (*posare*) to lay (down), put (down); (*fig: supporre*): poniamo (il caso) che ... let's suppose that ...; porsi vr (*mettersi*): porsi a sedere/in cammino to sit down/set off; ~ una domanda a qn to ask sb a question, put a question to sb

'porro sm (BOT) leek; (MED) wart

'porta sf door; (SPORT) goal; ~e sfpl (*di città*) gates; a ~e chiuse (DIR) in camera

'porta... prefisso: portaba'gagli sm inv (*facchino*) porter; (AUT, FERR) luggage rack; porta'cenere sm inv ashtray; portachi'avi sm inv keyring; porta'cipria sm inv powder compact; portae'rei sf inv (*nave*) aircraft carrier; portafi'nestra (pl portefi'nestre) sf French window; porta'foglio sm wallet; (POL, BORSA) portfolio; portafor'tuna sm inv lucky charm; mascot; portagi'oie sm inv jewellery box

por'tale sm (*di chiesa*, INFORM) portal

porta'lettere sm/f inv postman/woman (BRIT), mailman/woman (US)

porta'mento sm carriage, bearing

portamo'nete sm inv purse

por'tante ag (*muro etc*) supporting, load-bearing

portan'tina sf sedan chair; (*per ammalati*) stretcher

por'tare vt (*sostenere, sorreggere: peso, bambino, pacco*) to carry; (*indossare: abito, occhiali, ecc: nome, titolo*) to wear; (*: capelli lunghi*) to have; (*avere: nome, titolo*) to have, bear; (*recare*): ~ qc a qn to take (o bring) sth to sb; (*fig: sentimenti*) to bear; ~rsi vr (*recarsi*) to go; ~ avanti (*discorso, idea*) to pursue; ~ via to take away; (*rubare*) to take; ~ i bambini a spasso to take the children for a walk; ~ fortuna to bring good luck

portasiga'rette sm inv cigarette case

por'tata sf (*vivanda*) course; (AUT) carrying (o loading) capacity; (*di arma*) range; (*volume d'acqua*) (rate of) flow; (*fig: limite*) scope, capability; (*: importanza*) impact, import; alla ~ di tutti (*conoscenza*) within everybody's capabilities; (*prezzo*) within everybody's means; a/fuori ~ (di) within/out of reach (of); a ~ di mano within (arm's) reach

por'tatile ag portable

por'tato, a ag: ~ a inclined o apt to

porta'tore, 'trice sm/f (*anche* COMM) bearer; (MED) carrier

portau'ovo sm inv eggcup

porta'voce [porta'votʃe] sm/f inv spokesman/woman

por'tento sm wonder, marvel

porticci'olo [portit'tʃolo] sm marina

'portico, ci sm portico

porti'era sf (AUT) door

porti'ere sm (*portinaio*) concierge, caretaker; (*di hotel*) porter; (*nel calcio*) goalkeeper

porti'naio, a sm/f concierge, caretaker

portine'ria sf caretaker's lodge

'porto, a pp di porgere ♦ sm (NAUT) harbour, port ♦ sm inv port (wine); ~ d'armi (*documento*) gun licence

Porto'gallo sm: il ~ Portugal; porto'ghese ag, sm/f, sm Portuguese inv

por'tone sm main entrance, main door

portu'ale ag harbour cpd, port cpd ♦ sm dock worker

porzi'one [por'tsjone] sf portion, share; (*di cibo*) portion, helping

'posa sf (FOT) exposure; (*atteggiamento, di modello*) pose

posa'cenere [posa'tʃenere] sm inv ashtray

po'sare vt to put (down), lay (down) ♦ vi (*ponte, edificio, teoria*) to rest on; (FOT, *atteggiarsi*) to pose; ~rsi vr (*aereo*) to land; (*uccello*) to alight; (*sguardo*) to settle

po'sata sf piece of cutlery; ~e sfpl (*servizio*) cutlery sg

po'sato, a ag serious

pos'critto sm postscript

posi'tivo, a *ag* positive

posizi'one [pozit'tsjone] *sf* position; **prendere ~** (*fig*) to take a stand; **luci di ~** (*AUT*) sidelights

posolo'gia, 'gie [pozolo'dʒia] *sf* dosage, directions *pl* for use

pos'porre *vt* to place after; (*differire*) to postpone, defer; **pos'posto, a** *pp di* **posporre**

posse'dere *vt* to own, possess; (*qualità, virtù*) to have, possess; **possedi'mento** *sm* possession

posses'sivo, a *ag* possessive

pos'sesso *sm* ownership *no pl*; possession

posses'sore *sm* owner

pos'sibile *ag* possible ♦ *sm*: **fare tutto il ~** to do everything possible; **nei limiti del ~** as far as possible; **al più tardi ~** as late as possible; **possibilità** *sf inv* possibility ♦ *sfpl* (*mezzi*) means; **aver la possibilità di fare** to be in a position to do; to have the opportunity to do

possi'dente *sm/f* landowner

'posta *sf* (*servizio*) post, postal service; (*corrispondenza*) post, mail; (*ufficio postale*) post office; (*nei giochi d'azzardo*) stake; **~e** *sfpl* (*amministrazione*) post office; **~ aerea** airmail; **~ elettronica** E-mail, e-mail, electronic mail; **ministro delle P~e e Telecomunicazioni** Postmaster General; **posta'giro** *sm* post office cheque, postal giro (*BRIT*); **pos'tale** *ag* postal, post office *cpd*

post'bellico, a, ci, che *ag* postwar

posteggi'are [posted'dʒare] *vt, vi* to park; **posteggia'tore, trice** *sm/f* car park attendant; **pos'teggio** *sm* car park (*BRIT*), parking lot (*US*); (*di taxi*) rank (*BRIT*), stand (*US*)

postelegra'fonico, a, ci, che *ag* postal and telecommunications *cpd*

'poster *sm inv* poster

posteri'ore *ag* (*dietro*) back; (*dopo*) later ♦ *sm* (*fam: sedere*) behind

pos'ticcio, a, ci, ce [pos'tittʃo] *ag* false ♦ *sm* hairpiece

postici'pare [postitʃi'pare] *vt* to defer,

postpone

pos'tilla *sf* marginal note

pos'tino *sm* postman (*BRIT*), mailman (*US*)

'posto, a *pp di* **porre** ♦ *sm* (*sito, posizione*) place; (*impiego*) job; (*spazio libero*) room, space; (*di parcheggio*) space; (*sedile: al teatro, in treno etc*) seat; (*MIL*) post; **a ~** (*in ordine*) in place, tidy; (*fig*) settled; (: *persona*) reliable; **al ~ di** in place of; **sul ~** on the spot; **mettere a ~** to tidy (up), put in order; (*faccende*) to straighten out; **~ di blocco** roadblock; **~ di polizia** police station

pos'tribolo *sm* brothel

'postumo, a *ag* posthumous; (*tardivo*) belated; **~i** *smpl* (*conseguenze*) after-effects, consequences

po'tabile *ag* drinkable; **acqua ~** drinking water

po'tare *vt* to prune

po'tassio *sm* potassium

po'tente *ag* (*nazione*) strong, powerful; (*veleno, farmaco*) potent, strong; **po'tenza** *sf* power; (*forza*) strength

potenzi'ale [poten'tsjale] *ag, sm* potential

PAROLA CHIAVE

---

po'tere *sm* power; **al ~** (*partito etc*) in power; **~ d'acquisto** purchasing power ♦ *vb aus* **1** (*essere in grado di*) can, be able to; **non ha potuto ripararlo** he couldn't *o* he wasn't able to repair it; **non è potuto venire** he couldn't *o* he wasn't able to come; **spiacente di non poter aiutare** sorry not to be able to help

2 (*avere il permesso*) can, may, be allowed to; **posso entrare?** can *o* may I come in?; **si può sapere dove sei stato?** where on earth have you been?

3 (*eventualità*) may, might, could; **potrebbe essere vero** it might *o* could be true; **può aver avuto un incidente** he may *o* might *o* could have had an accident; **può darsi** perhaps; **può darsi** *o* **essere che non venga** he may *o* might not come

4 (*augurio*): **potessi almeno parlargli!** if only I could speak to him!

5 (*suggerimento*): **potresti almeno scusarti!** you could at least apologize! ♦ *vt* can, be able to; **può molto per noi** he can do a lot for us; **non ne posso più** (*per stanchezza*) I'm exhausted; (*per rabbia*) I can't take any more

potestà *sf* (*potere*) power; (*DIR*) authority

'povero, a *ag* poor; (*disadorno*) plain, bare ♦ *sm/f* poor man/woman; **i ~i** the poor; **~ di** lacking in, having little; **povertà** *sf* poverty

'pozza ['pottsa] *sf* pool

poz'zanghera [pot'tsangera] *sf* puddle

'pozzo ['pottso] *sm* well; (*cava: di carbone*) pit; (*di miniera*) shaft; **~ petrolifero** oil well

pran'zare [pran'dzare] *vi* to dine, have dinner; to lunch, have lunch

'pranzo ['prandzo] *sm* dinner; (*a mezzogiorno*) lunch

'prassi *sf* usual procedure

'pratica, che *sf* practice; (*esperienza*) experience; (*conoscenza*) knowledge, familiarity; (*tirocinio*) training, practice; (*AMM: affare*) matter, case; (: *incartamento*) file, dossier; **in ~** (*praticamente*) in practice; **mettere in ~** to put into practice

prati'cabile *ag* (*progetto*) practicable, feasible; (*luogo*) passable, practicable

prati'cante *sm/f* apprentice, trainee; (*REL*) (regular) churchgoer

prati'care *vt* to practise; (*SPORT: tennis etc*) to play; (: *nuoto, scherma etc*) to go in for; (*eseguire: apertura, buco*) to make; **~ uno sconto** to give a discount

'pratico, a, ci, che *ag* practical; **~ di** (*esperto*) experienced *o* skilled in; (*familiare*) familiar with

'prato *sm* meadow; (*di giardino*) lawn

preav'viso *sm* notice; **telefonata con ~** personal *o* person to person call

pre'cario, a *ag* precarious; (*INS*) temporary

precauzi'one [prekaut'tsjone] *sf* caution, care; (*misura*) precaution

prece'dente [pretʃe'dɛnte] *ag* previous ♦ *sm* precedent; **il discorso/film ~** the previous *o* preceding speech/film; **senza ~i**

unprecedented; **~i penali** criminal record *sg*; **prece'denza** *sf* priority, precedence; (*AUT*) right of way

pre'cedere [pre'tʃɛdere] *vt* to precede, go (*o* come) before

pre'cetto [pre'tʃɛtto] *sm* precept; (*MIL*) call-up notice

precet'tore [pretʃet'tore] *sm* (private) tutor

precipi'tare [pretʃipi'tare] *vi* (*cadere*) to fall headlong; (*fig: situazione*) to get out of control ♦ *vt* (*gettare dall'alto in basso*) to hurl, fling; (*fig: affrettare*) to rush; **~rsi** *vr* (*gettarsi*) to hurl *o* fling o.s.; (*affrettarsi*) to rush; **precipitazi'one** *sf* (*METEOR*) precipitation; (*fig*) haste; **precipi'toso, a** *ag* (*caduta, fuga*) headlong; (*fig: avventato*) rash, reckless; (: *affrettato*) hasty, rushed

preci'pizio [pretʃi'pittsjo] *sm* precipice; **a ~** (*fig: correre*) headlong

preci'sare [pretʃi'zare] *vt* to state, specify; (*spiegare*) to explain (in detail)

precisi'one [pretʃi'zjone] *sf* precision; accuracy

pre'ciso, a [pre'tʃizo] *ag* (*esatto*) precise; (*accurato*) accurate, precise; (*deciso: idee*) precise, definite; (*uguale*): **2 vestiti ~i** 2 dresses exactly the same; **sono le 9 ~e** it's exactly 9 o'clock

pre'cludere *vt* to block, obstruct; **pre'cluso, a** *pp di* **precludere**

pre'coce [pre'kɔtʃe] *ag* early; (*bambino*) precocious; (*vecchiaia*) premature

precon'cetto [prekon'tʃɛtto] *sm* preconceived idea, prejudice

precur'sore *sm* forerunner, precursor

'preda *sf* (*bottino*) booty; (*animale, fig*) prey; **essere ~ di** to fall prey to; **essere in ~ a** to be prey to; **preda'tore** *sm* predator

predeces'sore, a [predetʃes'sore] *sm/f* predecessor

predesti'nare *vt* to predestine

pre'detto, a *pp di* **predire**

'predica, che *sf* sermon; (*fig*) lecture, talking-to

predi'care *vt, vi* to preach

predi'cato *sm* (*LING*) predicate

predi'letto, a *pp di* prediligere ♦ *ag, sm/f* favourite

predilezi'one [predilet'tsjone] *sf* fondness, partiality; **avere una ~ per qc/qn** to be partial to sth/fond of sb

predi'ligere [predi'lidʒere] *vt* to prefer, have a preference for

pre'dire *vt* to foretell, predict

predis'porre *vt* to get ready, prepare; **~ qn a qc** to predispose sb to sth; predis'posto, a *pp di* predisporre

predizi'one [predit'tsjone] *sf* prediction

predomi'nare *vi* to predominate; predo'minio *sm* predominance; supremacy

prefabbri'cato, a *ag* (EDIL) prefabricated

prefazi'one [prefat'tsjone] *sf* preface, foreword

prefe'renza [prefe'rentsa] *sf* preference; preferenzi'ale *ag* preferential; **corsia ~** bus and taxi lane

prefe'rire *vt* to prefer, like better; **~ il caffè al tè** to prefer coffee to tea, like coffee better than tea; prefe'rito, a *ag* favourite

pre'fetto *sm* prefect; prefet'tura *sf* prefecture

pre'figgersi [pre'fiddʒersi] *vr*: **~ uno scopo** to set o.s. a goal

pre'fisso, a *pp di* prefiggere ♦ *sm* (LING) prefix; (TEL) dialling (BRIT) *o* dial (US) code

pre'gare *vi* to pray ♦ *vt* (REL) to pray to; (implorare) to beg; (chiedere): **~ qn di fare** to ask sb to do; **farsi ~** to need coaxing *o* persuading

pre'gevole [pre'dʒevole] *ag* valuable

preghi'era [pre'gjera] *sf* (REL) prayer; (domanda) request

pregi'ato, a [pre'dʒato] *ag* (di valore) valuable; **vino ~** vintage wine

'pregio ['predʒo] *sm* (stima) esteem, regard; (qualità) (good) quality, merit; (valore) value, worth

pregiudi'care [predʒudi'kare] *vt* to prejudice, harm, be detrimental to; pregiudi'cato, a *sm/f* (DIR) previous offender

pregiu'dizio [predʒu'dittsjo] *sm* (idea errata) prejudice; (danno) harm *no pl*

'pregno, a ['preɲɲo] *ag* (saturo): **~ di** full of, saturated with

'prego *escl* (a chi ringrazia) don't mention it!; (invitando qn ad accomodarsi) please sit down!; (invitando qn ad andare prima) after you!

pregus'tare *vt* to look forward to

preis'torico, a, ci, che *ag* prehistoric

pre'lato *sm* prelate

prele'vare *vt* (denaro) to withdraw; (campione) to take; (sog: polizia) to take, capture

preli'evo *sm* (di denaro) withdrawal; (MED): **fare un ~ (di)** to take a sample (of)

prelimi'nare *ag* preliminary; **~i** *smpl* preliminary talks; preliminaries

pre'ludio *sm* prelude

pré-ma'man [prema'mã] *sm inv* maternity dress

prema'turo, a *ag* premature

premeditazi'one [premeditat'tsjone] *sf* (DIR) premeditation; **con ~** *ag* premeditated ♦ *av* with intent

'premere *vt* to press ♦ *vi*: **~ su** to press down on; (fig) to put pressure on; **~ a** (fig: importare) to matter to

pre'messa *sf* introductory statement, introduction

pre'messo, a *pp di* premettere

pre'mettere *vt* to put before; (dire prima) to start by saying, state first

premi'are *vt* to give a prize to; (fig: merito, onestà) to reward

'premio *sm* prize; (ricompensa) reward; (COMM) premium; (AMM: indennità) bonus

premu'nirsi *vr*: **~ di** to provide o.s. with; **~ contro** to protect o.s. from, guard o.s. against

pre'mura *sf* (fretta) haste, hurry; (riguardo) attention, care; premu'roso, a *ag* thoughtful, considerate

prena'tale *ag* antenatal

'prendere *vt* to take; (andare a prendere) to get, fetch; (ottenere) to get; (guadagnare) to get, earn; (catturare: ladro, *pesce*) to catch; (*collaboratore, dipendente*) to take on; (*passeggero*) to pick up; (*chiedere: somma, prezzo*) to charge, ask; (*trattare: persona*) to handle ♦ *vi* (*colla, cemento*) to set; (*pianta*) to take; (*fuoco: nel camino*) to catch; (*voltare*): ~ **a destra** to turn (to the) right; ~**rsi** *vr* (*azzuffarsi*): ~**rsi a pugni** to come to blows; **prendi qualcosa?** (*da bere, da mangiare*) would you like something to eat (*o* drink)?; **prendo un caffè** I'll have a coffee; ~ **qn/ qc per** (*scambiare*) to take sb/sth for; ~ **fuoco** to catch fire; ~ **parte a** to take part in; ~**rsi cura di qn/qc** to look after sb/sth; **prendersela** (*adirarsi*) to get annoyed; (*preoccuparsi*) to get upset, worry

prendi'sole *sm inv* sundress

preno'tare *vt* to book, reserve; **prenotazi'one** *sf* booking, reservation

preoccu'pare *vt* to worry; to preoccupy; ~**rsi** *vr*: ~**rsi di qn/qc** to worry about sb/ sth; ~**rsi per qn** to be anxious for sb; **preoccupazi'one** *sf* worry, anxiety

prepa'rare *vt* to prepare; (*esame, concorso*) to prepare for; ~**rsi** *vr* (*vestirsi*) to get ready; ~**rsi a qc/a fare** to get ready *o* prepare (o.s.) for sth/to do; ~ **da mangiare** to prepare a meal; **prepara'tivi** *smpl* preparations; **prepa'rato** *sm* (*prodotto*) preparation; **preparazi'one** *sf* preparation

preposizi'one [prepozit'tsjone] *sf* (*LING*) preposition

prepo'tente *ag* (*persona*) domineering, arrogant; (*bisogno, desiderio*) overwhelming, pressing ♦ *sm/f* bully; **prepo'tenza** *sf* arrogance; arrogant behaviour

'presa *sf* taking *no pl*; catching *no pl*; (*di città*) capture; (*indurimento: di cemento*) setting; (*appiglio, SPORT*) hold; (*di acqua, gas*) (supply) point; (*ELETTR*): ~ **(di corrente)** socket; (: *al muro*) point; (*piccola quantità: di sale etc*) pinch; (*CARTE*) trick; **far ~** (*colla*) to set; **far ~ sul pubblico** to catch the public's imagination; ~ **d'aria** air inlet; **essere alle ~e con** (*fig*) to be struggling

with

pre'sagio [pre'zadʒo] *sm* omen

presa'gire [preza'dʒire] *vt* to foresee

'presbite *ag* long-sighted

presbi'terio *sm* presbytery

pre'scindere [preʃ'ʃindere] *vi*: ~ **da** to leave out of consideration; **a ~ da** apart from

pres'critto, a *pp di* **prescrivere**

pres'crivere *vt* to prescribe; **prescrizi'one** *sf* (*MED, DIR*) prescription; (*norma*) rule, regulation

presen'tare *vt* to present; (*far conoscere*): ~ **qn (a)** to introduce sb (to); (*AMM: inoltrare*) to submit; ~**rsi** *vr* (*recarsi, farsi vedere*) to present o.s., appear; (*farsi conoscere*) to introduce o.s.; (*occasione*) to arise; ~**rsi come candidato** (*POL*) to stand as a candidate; ~**rsi bene/male** to have a good/poor appearance; **presentazi'one** *sf* presentation; introduction

pre'sente *ag* present; (*questo*) this ♦ *sm* present; **i ~i** those present; **aver ~ qc/qn** to remember sth/sb

presenti'mento *sm* premonition

pre'senza [pre'zentsa] *sf* presence; (*aspetto esteriore*) appearance; ~ **di spirito** presence of mind

pre'sepe, pre'sepio *sm* crib

preser'vare *vt* to protect; to save; **preserva'tivo** *sm* sheath, condom

'preside *sm/f* (*INS*) head (teacher) (*BRIT*), principal (*US*); (*di facoltà universitaria*) dean

presi'dente *sm* (*POL*) president; (*di assemblea, COMM*) chairman; ~ **del consiglio** prime minister; **presiden'tessa** *sf* president; president's wife; chairwoman; **presi'denza** *sf* presidency; office of president; chairmanship

presidi'are *vt* to garrison; **pre'sidio** *sm* garrison

presi'edere *vt* to preside over ♦ *vi*: ~ **a** to direct, be in charge of

'preso, a *pp di* **prendere**

'pressa *sf* (*TECN*) press

pressap'poco *av* about, roughly

pres'sare *vt* to press

pressi'one *sf* pressure; **far ~ su qn** to put pressure on sb; **~ sanguigna** blood pressure

'presso *av* (*vicino*) nearby, close at hand
♦ *prep* (*vicino a*) near; (*accanto a*) beside, next to; (*in casa di*): **~ qn** at sb's home; (*nelle lettere*) care of, c/o; (*alle dipendenze di*): **lavora ~ di noi** he works for *o* with us
♦ *smpl*: **nei ~i di** near, in the vicinity of

pressuriz'zare [pressurid'dzare] *vt* to pressurize

presta'nome (*peg*) *sm/f inv* figurehead

pres'tante *ag* good-looking

pres'tare *vt*: **~ (qc a qn)** to lend (sb sth *o* sth to sb); (*di buon'ora*): **~rsi a fare** to offer to do; (*essere adatto*): **~rsi a** to lend itself to, be suitable for; **~ aiuto** to lend a hand; **~ attenzione** to pay attention; **~ fede a qc/qn** to give credence to sth/sb; **~ orecchio** to listen; **prestazi'one** *sf* (*TECN, SPORT*) performance; **prestazioni** *sfpl* (*di persona: servizi*) services

prestigia'tore, **'trice** [prestidʒa'tore] *sm/f* conjurer

pres'tigio [pres'tidʒo] *sm* (*fama*) prestige; (*illusione*): **gioco di ~** conjuring trick

'prestito *sm* lending *no pl*; loan; **dar in ~** to lend; **prendere in ~** to borrow

'presto *av* (*tra poco*) soon; (*in fretta*) quickly; (*di buon'ora*) early; **a ~** see you soon; **fare ~ a fare qc** to hurry up and do sth; (*non costare fatica*) to have no trouble doing sth; **si fa ~ a criticare** it's easy to criticize

pre'sumere *vt* to presume, assume; **pre'sunto**, **a** *pp di* **presumere**

presuntu'oso, **a** *ag* presumptuous

presunzi'one [prezun'tsjone] *sf* presumption

presup'porre *vt* to suppose; to presuppose

'prete *sm* priest

preten'dente *sm/f* pretender ♦ *sm* (*corteggiatore*) suitor

pre'tendere *vt* (*esigere*) to demand, require; (*sostenere*): **~ che** to claim that; **pretende di aver sempre ragione** he thinks he's always right

pretenzi'oso, **a** [preten'tsjoso] *ag* pretentious

pre'tesa *sf* (*esigenza*) claim, demand; (*presunzione, sfarzo*) pretentiousness; **senza ~e** unpretentious

pre'teso, **a** *pp di* **pretendere**

pre'testo *sm* pretext, excuse

pre'tore *sm* magistrate; **pre'tura** *sf* magistracy; (*sede*) magistrate's court

preva'lente *ag* prevailing; **preva'lenza** *sf* predominance

preva'lere *vi* to prevail; **pre'valso**, **a** *pp di* **prevalere**

preve'dere *vt* (*indovinare*) to foresee; (*presagire*) to foretell; (*considerare*) to make provision for

preven'dita *sf* advance booking

preve'nire *vt* (*anticipare*) to forestall; to anticipate; (*evitare*) to avoid, prevent

preven'tivo, **a** *ag* preventive ♦ *sm* (*COMM*) estimate

prevenzi'one [preven'tsjone] *sf* prevention; (*preconcetto*) prejudice

previ'dente *ag* showing foresight; prudent; **previ'denza** *sf* foresight; **istituto di previdenza** provident institution; **previdenza sociale** social security (*BRIT*), welfare (*US*)

previsi'one *sf* forecast, prediction; **~i meteorologiche** *o* **del tempo** weather forecast *sg*

pre'visto, **a** *pp di* **prevedere** ♦ *sm*: **più/ meno del ~** more/less than expected

prezi'oso, **a** [pret'tsjoso] *ag* precious; invaluable ♦ *sm* jewel; valuable

prez'zemolo [pret'tsemolo] *sm* parsley

'prezzo ['prettso] *sm* price; **~ d'acquisto / di vendita** buying/selling price

prigi'one [pri'dʒone] *sf* prison; **prigio'nia** *sf* imprisonment; **prigioni'ero**, **a** *ag* captive ♦ *sm/f* prisoner

'prima *sf* (*TEATRO*) first night; (*CINEMA*) première; (*AUT*) first gear; *vedi anche* **primo**
♦ *av* before; (*in anticipo*) in advance,

beforehand; *(per l'addietro)* at one time, formerly; *(più presto)* sooner, earlier; *(in primo luogo)* first ♦ *cong*: **~ di fare/che parta** before doing/he leaves; **~ di** before; **~ o poi** sooner or later

pri'mario, a *ag* primary; *(principale)* chief, leading, primary ♦ *sm (MED)* chief physician

pri'mato *sm* supremacy; *(SPORT)* record

prima'vera *sf* spring; **primave'rile** *ag* spring *cpd*

primeggi'are [primed'dʒare] *vi* to excel, be one of the best

primi'tivo, a *ag* primitive; original

pri'mizie [pri'mittsje] *sfpl* early produce *sg*

'primo, a *ag* first; *(fig)* initial; basic; prime ♦ *sm/f* first (one) ♦ *sm (CUC)* first course; *(in date)*: **il ~ luglio** the first of July; **le ~e ore del mattino** the early hours of the morning; **ai ~i di maggio** at the beginning of May; **viaggiare in ~a** to travel first-class; **in ~ luogo** first of all, in the first place; **di prim'ordine** *o* **~a qualità** first-class, first-rate; **in un ~ tempo** at first; **~a donna** leading lady; *(di opera lirica)* prima donna

primo'genito, a [primo'dʒenito] *ag, sm/f* firstborn

'primula *sf* primrose

princi'pale [printʃi'pale] *ag* main, principal ♦ *sm* manager, boss

princi'pato [printʃi'pato] *sm* principality

'principe ['printʃipe] *sm* prince; **~ ereditario** crown prince; **princi'pessa** *sf* princess

principi'ante [printʃi'pjante] *sm/f* beginner

prin'cipio [prin'tʃipjo] *sm (inizio)* beginning, start; *(origine)* origin, cause; *(concetto, norma)* principle; **al** *o* **in ~** at first; **per ~** on principle

pri'ore *sm (REL)* prior

priorità *sf* priority

priori'tario, a *ag* priority; **posta prioritaria** first-class mail

'prisma, i *sm* prism

pri'vare *vt*: **~ qn di** to deprive sb of; **~rsi di** to go *o* do without

pri'vato, a *ag* private ♦ *sm/f* private citizen; **in ~** in private

privazi'one [privat'tsjone] *sf* privation, hardship

privilegi'are [privile'dʒare] *vt* to grant a privilege to

privi'legio [privi'lɛdʒo] *sm* privilege

'privo, a *ag*: **~ di** without, lacking

pro *prep* for, on behalf of ♦ *sm inv (utilità)* advantage, benefit; **a che ~?** what's the use?; **il ~ e il contro** the pros and cons

pro'babile *ag* probable, likely; **probabilità** *sf inv* probability

pro'blema, i *sm* problem

pro'boscide [pro'bɔʃʃide] *sf (di elefante)* trunk

procacci'are [prokat'tʃare] *vt* to get, obtain

pro'cedere [pro'tʃedere] *vi* to proceed; *(comportarsi)* to behave; *(iniziare)*: **~ a** to start; **~ contro** *(DIR)* to start legal proceedings against; **procedi'mento** *sm* procedure; *(di avvenimenti)* course; *(TECN)* process; **procedimento penale** *(DIR)* criminal proceedings; **proce'dura** *sf (DIR)* procedure

proces'sare [protʃes'sare] *vt (DIR)* to try

processi'one [protʃes'sjone] *sf* procession

pro'cesso [pro'tʃɛsso] *sm (DIR)* trial; proceedings *pl*; *(metodo)* process

pro'cinto [pro'tʃinto] *sm*: **in ~ di fare** about to do, on the point of doing

pro'clama, i *sm* proclamation

procla'mare *vt* to proclaim

procre'are *vt* to procreate

pro'cura *sf (DIR)* proxy; power of attorney; *(ufficio)* attorney's office

procu'rare *vt*: **~ qc a qn** *(fornire)* to get *o* obtain sth for sb; *(causare: noie etc)* to bring *o* give sb sth

procura'tore, 'trice *sm/f (DIR)* ≈ solicitor; *(: chi ha la procura)* attorney; proxy; **~ generale** *(in corte d'appello)* public prosecutor; *(in corte di cassazione)* Attorney General; **~ della Repubblica** *(in corte d'assise, tribunale)* public prosecutor

prodi'gare *vt* to be lavish with; **~rsi per qn** to do all one can for sb

pro'digio [pro'didʒo] *sm* marvel, wonder; *(persona)* prodigy; **prodigi'oso, a** *ag* prodigious; phenomenal

'**prodigo, a, ghi, ghe** *ag* lavish, extravagant

pro'**dotto, a** *pp di* **produrre** ♦ *sm* product; **~i agricoli** farm produce *sg*

pro'**durre** *vt* to produce; **produttività** *sf* productivity; **produt'tivo, a** *ag* productive; **produt'tore, 'trice** *sm/f* producer; **produzi'one** *sf* production; (*rendimento*) output

pro'**emio** *sm* introduction, preface

Prof. *abbr* (= *professore*) Prof

profa'**nare** *vt* to desecrate

pro'**fano, a** *ag* (*mondano*) secular; profane; (*sacrilego*) profane

profe'**rire** *vt* to utter

profes'**sare** *vt* to profess; (*medicina etc*) to practise

professio'**nale** *ag* professional

professi'**one** *sf* profession; **professio'nista, i, e** *sm/f* professional

profes'**sore, 'essa** *sm/f* (*INS*) teacher; (*: di università*) lecturer; (*: titolare di cattedra*) professor

pro'**feta, i** *sm* prophet; **profe'zia** *sf* prophecy

pro'**ficuo, a** *ag* useful, profitable

profi'**larsi** *vr* to stand out, be silhouetted; to loom up

profi'**lattico** *sm* condom

pro'**filo** *sm* profile; (*breve descrizione*) sketch, outline; **di ~** in profile

pro'**fitto** *sm* advantage, profit, benefit; (*fig: progresso*) progress; (*COMM*) profit

profondità *sf inv* depth

pro'**fondo, a** *ag* deep; (*rancore, meditazione*) profound ♦ *sm* depth(s *pl*), bottom; **~ 8 metri** 8 metres deep

'**profugo, a, ghi, ghe** *sm/f* refugee

profu'**mare** *vt* to perfume ♦ *vi* to be fragrant; **~rsi** *vr* to put on perfume *o* scent

profume'**ria** *sf* perfumery; (*negozio*) perfume shop

pro'**fumo** *sm* (*prodotto*) perfume, scent; (*fragranza*) scent, fragrance

profusi'**one** *sf* profusion; **a ~** in plenty

proget'**tare** [prodʒet'tare] *vt* to plan;

(*edificio*) to plan, design; **pro'getto** *sm* plan; (*idea*) plan, project; **progetto di legge** bill

pro'**gramma, i** *sm* programme; (*TV, RADIO*) programmes *pl*; (*INS*) syllabus, curriculum; (*INFORM*) program; **program'mare** *vt* (*TV, RADIO*) to put on; (*INFORM*) to program; (*ECON*) to plan; **programma'tore, 'trice** *sm/f* (*INFORM*) computer programmer

progre'**dire** *vi* to progress, make progress

progres'**sivo, a** *ag* progressive

pro'**gresso** *sm* progress *no pl*; **fare ~i** to make progress

proi'**bire** *vt* to forbid, prohibit; **proibi'tivo, a** *ag* prohibitive; **proibizi'one** *sf* prohibition

proiet'**tare** *vt* (*gen, GEOM, CINEMA*) to project; (*: presentare*) to show, screen; (*luce, ombra*) to throw, cast, project; **proi'ettile** *sm* projectile, bullet (*o* shell *etc*); **proiet'tore** *sm* (*CINEMA*) projector; (*AUT*) headlamp; (*MIL*) searchlight; **proiezi'one** *sf* (*CINEMA*) projection; showing

'**prole** *sf* children *pl*, offspring

prole'**tario, a** *ag, sm* proletarian

prolife'**rare** *vi* (*fig*) to proliferate

pro'**lisso, a** *ag* verbose

'**prologo, ghi** *sm* prologue

pro'**lunga, ghe** *sf* (*di cavo etc*) extension

prolun'**gare** *vt* (*discorso, attesa*) to prolong; (*linea, termine*) to extend

prome'**moria** *sm inv* memorandum

pro'**messa** *sf* promise

pro'**messo, a** *pp di* **promettere**

pro'**mettere** *vt* to promise ♦ *vi* to be *o* look promising; **~ a qn di fare** to promise sb that one will do

promi'**nente** *ag* prominent

promiscuità *sf* promiscuousness

promon'**torio** *sm* promontory, headland

pro'**mosso, a** *pp di* **promuovere**

promo'**tore, trice** *sm/f* promoter, organizer

promozi'**one** [promot'tsjone] *sf* promotion

promul'**gare** *vt* to promulgate

promu'overe *vt* to promote

proni'pote *sm/f* (*di nonni*) great-grandchild, great-grandson/granddaughter; (*di zii*) great-nephew/niece; **~i** *smpl* (*discendenti*) descendants

pro'nome *sm* (*LING*) pronoun

pro'nostico, ci *sm* forecast, prediction

pron'tezza [pron'tettsa] *sf* readiness; quickness, promptness

'pronto, a *ag* ready; (*rapido*) fast, quick, prompt; **~!** (*TEL*) hello!; **~ all'ira** quick-tempered; **~ soccorso** first aid

prontu'ario *sm* manual, handbook

pro'nuncia [pro'nuntʃa] *sf* pronunciation

pronunci'are [pronun'tʃare] *vt* (*parola, sentenza*) to pronounce; (*dire*) to utter; (*discorso*) to deliver; **~rsi** *vr* to declare one's opinion; **pronunci'ato, a** *ag* (*spiccato*) pronounced, marked; (*sporgente*) prominent

pro'nunzia *etc* [pro'nuntsja] = **pronuncia** *etc*

propa'ganda *sf* propaganda

propa'gare *vt* (*notizia, malattia*) to spread; (*REL, BIOL*) to propagate; **~rsi** *vr* to spread; (*BIOL*) to propagate; (*FISICA*) to be propagated

pro'pendere *vi*: **~ per** to favour, lean towards; **propensi'one** *sf* inclination, propensity; **pro'penso, a** *pp di* **propendere**

propi'nare *vt* to administer

pro'pizio, a [pro'pittsjo] *ag* favourable

pro'porre *vt* (*suggerire*): **~ qc (a qn)** to suggest sth (to sb); (*candidato*) to put forward; (*legge, brindisi*) to propose; **~ di fare** to suggest *o* propose doing; **proporsi di fare** to propose *o* intend to do; **proporsi una meta** to set o.s. a goal

proporzio'nale [proportsjo'nale] *ag* proportional

proporzio'nare [proportsjo'nare] *vt*: **~ qc a** to proportion *o* adjust sth to

proporzi'one [propor'tsjone] *sf* proportion; **in ~ a** in proportion to

pro'posito *sm* (*intenzione*) intention, aim; (*argomento*) subject, matter; **a ~ di**

regarding, with regard to; **di ~** (*apposta*) deliberately, on purpose; **a ~** by the way; **capitare a ~** (*cosa, persona*) to turn up at the right time

proposizi'one [propozit'tsjone] *sf* (*LING*) clause; (: *periodo*) sentence

pro'posta *sf* proposal; (*suggerimento*) suggestion; **~a di legge** bill

pro'posto, a *pp di* **proporre**

proprietà *sf inv* (*ciò che si possiede*) property *gen no pl*, estate; (*caratteristica*) property; (*correttezza*) correctness; **proprie'tario, a** *sm/f* owner; (*di albergo etc*) proprietor, owner; (*per l'inquilino*) landlord/lady

'proprio, a *ag* (*possessivo*) own; (: *impersonale*) one's; (*esatto*) exact, correct, proper; (*senso, significato*) literal; (*LING: nome*) proper; (*particolare*): **~ di** characteristic of, peculiar to ♦ *av* (*precisamente*) just, exactly; (*davvero*) really; (*affatto*): **non ... ~** not ... at all; **l'ha visto con i (suoi) ~i occhi** he saw it with his own eyes

'prora *sf* (*NAUT*) bow(s *pl*), prow

'proroga, ghe *sf* extension; postponement; **proro'gare** *vt* to extend; (*differire*) to postpone, defer

pro'rompere *vi* to burst out; **pro'rotto, a** *pp di* **prorompere**

'prosa *sf* prose; **pro'saico, a, ci, che** *ag* (*fig*) prosaic, mundane

pro'sciogliere [proʃ'ʃɔʎʎere] *vt* to release; (*DIR*) to acquit; **prosci'olto, a** *pp di* **prosciogliere**

prosciu'gare [proʃʃu'gare] *vt* (*terreni*) to drain, reclaim; **~rsi** *vr* to dry up

prosci'utto [proʃ'ʃutto] *sm* ham; **~ cotto/crudo** cooked/cured ham

prosegui'mento *sm* continuation; **buon ~!** all the best!; (*a chi viaggia*) enjoy the rest of your journey!

prosegu'ire *vt* to carry on with, continue ♦ *vi* to carry on, go on

prospe'rare *vi* to thrive; **prosperità** *sf* prosperity; **'prospero, a** *ag* (*fiorente*) flourishing, thriving, prosperous;

prospe'roso, a ag (robusto) hale and hearty; (: ragazza) buxom
prospet'tare vt (esporre) to point out, show; **~rsi** vr to look, appear
prospet'tiva sf (ARTE) perspective; (veduta) view; (fig: previsione, possibilità) prospect
pros'petto sm (DISEGNO) elevation; (veduta) view, prospect; (facciata) façade, front; (tabella) table; (sommario) summary
prospici'ente [prospi'tʃɛnte] ag: **~ qc** facing o overlooking sth
prossimità sf nearness, proximity; **in ~ di** near (to), close to
'prossimo, a ag (vicino): **~ a** near (to), close to; (che viene subito dopo) next; (parente) close ♦ sm neighbour, fellow man
prosti'tuta sf prostitute; **prostituzi'one** sf prostitution
pros'trare vt (fig) to exhaust, wear out; **~rsi** vr (fig) to humble o.s.
protago'nista, i, e sm/f protagonist
pro'teggere [pro'teddʒere] vt to protect
proteggi'slip [proteddʒi'zlip] sm inv panty liner
prote'ina sf protein
pro'tendere vt to stretch out; **pro'teso, a** pp di **protendere**
pro'testa sf protest
protes'tante ag, sm/f Protestant
protes'tare vt, vi to protest; **~rsi** vr: **~rsi innocente** etc to protest one's innocence o that one is innocent etc
protet'tivo, a ag protective
pro'tetto, a pp di **proteggere**
protet'tore, 'trice sm/f protector; (sostenitore) patron
protezi'one [protet'tsjone] sf protection; (patrocinio) patronage
protocol'lare vt to register ♦ ag formal; of protocol; **proto'collo** sm protocol; (registro) register of documents
pro'totipo sm prototype
pro'trarre vt (prolungare) to prolong; **pro'tratto, a** pp di **protrarre**
protube'ranza [protube'rantsa] sf protuberance, bulge
'prova sf (esperimento, cimento) test, trial;

(tentativo) attempt, try; (MAT, testimonianza, documento etc) proof; (DIR) evidence no pl, proof; (INS) exam, test; (TEATRO) rehearsal; (di abito) fitting; **a ~ di** (in testimonianza di) as proof of; **a ~ di fuoco** fireproof; **fino a ~ contraria** until it is proved otherwise; **mettere alla ~** to put to the test; **giro di ~** test o trial run; **~ generale** (TEATRO) dress rehearsal
pro'vare vt (sperimentare) to test; (tentare) to try, attempt; (assaggiare) to try, taste; (sperimentare in sé) to experience; (sentire) to feel; (cimentare) to put to the test; (dimostrare) to prove; (abito) to try on; **~ a fare** to try o attempt to do
proveni'enza [prove'njentsa] sf origin, source
prove'nire vi: **~ da** to come from
pro'venti smpl revenue sg
prove'nuto, a pp di **provenire**
pro'verbio sm proverb
pro'vetta sf test tube; **bambino in ~** test-tube baby
pro'vetto, a ag skilled, experienced
pro'vincia, ce o **cie** [pro'vintʃa] sf province; **provinci'ale** ag provincial; **(strada) provinciale** main road (BRIT), highway (US)
pro'vino sm (CINEMA) screen test; (campione) specimen
provo'cante ag (attraente) provocative
provo'care vt (causare) to cause, bring about; (eccitare: riso, pietà) to arouse; (irritare, sfidare) to provoke; **provoca'torio, a** ag provocative; **provocazi'one** sf provocation
provve'dere vi (disporre): **~ (a)** to provide (for); (prendere un provvedimento) to take steps, act; **provvedi'mento** sm measure; (di previdenza) precaution
provvi'denza [provvi'dentsa] sf: **la ~** providence; **provvidenzi'ale** ag providential
provvigi'one [provvi'dʒone] sf (COMM) commission
provvi'sorio, a ag temporary
prov'vista sf provision, supply

'**prua** *sf* (NAUT) = **prora**

pru'**dente** *ag* cautious, prudent; (*assennato*) sensible, wise; pru'**denza** *sf* prudence, caution; wisdom

'**prudere** *vi* to itch, be itchy

'**prugna** ['pruɲɲa] *sf* plum; ~ **secca** prune

prurigi'**noso**, a [pruridʒi'noso] *ag* itchy

pru'**rito** *sm* itchiness *no pl*; itch

P.S. *abbr* (= *postscriptum*) P.S.; (POLIZIA) = **Pubblica Sicurezza**

pseu'**donimo** *sm* pseudonym

PSI *sigla m* = **Partito Socialista Italiano**

psicana'**lista**, i, e *sm/f* psychoanalyst

'**psiche** ['psike] *sf* (PSIC) psyche

psichi'**atra**, i, e [psi'kjatra] *sm/f* psychiatrist; **psichi'atrico**, a, ci, che *ag* psychiatric

'**psichico**, a, ci, che ['psikiko] *ag* psychological

psicolo'**gia** [psikolo'dʒia] *sf* psychology; **psico'logico**, a, ci, che *ag* psychological; **psi'cologo**, a, gi, ghe *sm/f* psychologist

psico'**patico**, a, ci, che *ag* psychopathic ♦ *sm/f* psychopath

P.T. *abbr* = **Posta e Telegrafi**

pubbli'**care** *vt* to publish

pubblicazi'**one** [pubblikat'tsjone] *sf* publication; ~**i (matrimoniali)** *sfpl* (marriage) banns

pubbli'**cista**, i, e [pubbli'tʃista] *sm/f* (STAMPA) occasional contributor

pubbli'**cità** [pubblitʃi'ta] *sf* (*diffusione*) publicity; (*attività*) advertising; (*annunci nei giornali*) advertisements *pl*; **pubblici'tario**, a *ag* advertising *cpd*; (*trovata, film*) publicity *cpd*

'**pubblico**, a, ci, che *ag* public; (*statale: scuola etc*) state *cpd* ♦ *sm* public; (*spettatori*) audience; **in** ~ in public; ~ **funzionario** civil servant; **P~ Ministero** Public Prosecutor's Office; **la P~a Sicurezza** the police

'**pube** *sm* (ANAT) pubis

puber'**tà** *sf* puberty

'**pudico**, a, ci, che *ag* modest

pu'**dore** *sm* modesty

puericul'**tura** *sf* paediatric nursing; infant care

pue'**rile** *ag* childish

pugi'**lato** [pudʒi'lato] *sm* boxing

'**pugile** ['pudʒile] *sm* boxer

pugna'**lare** [puɲɲa'lare] *vt* to stab

pu'**gnale** [puɲ'ɲale] *sm* dagger

'**pugno** ['puɲɲo] *sm* fist; (*colpo*) punch; (*quantità*) fistful

'**pulce** ['pultʃe] *sf* flea

pul'**cino** [pul'tʃino] *sm* chick

pu'**ledro**, a *sm/f* colt/filly

pu'**leggia**, ge [pu'leddʒa] *sf* pulley

pu'**lire** *vt* to clean; (*lucidare*) to polish; **pu'lita** *sf* quick clean; **pu'lito**, a *ag* (*anche fig*) clean; (*ordinato*) neat, tidy; **puli'tura** *sf* cleaning; **pulitura a secco** dry cleaning; **puli'zia** *sf* cleaning; cleanness; **fare le pulizie** to do the cleaning *o* the housework

'**pullman** *sm inv* coach

pul'**lover** *sm inv* pullover, jumper

pullu'**lare** *vi* to swarm, teem

pul'**mino** *sm* minibus

'**pulpito** *sm* pulpit

pul'**sante** *sm* (push-)button

pul'**sare** *vi* to pulsate, beat; **pulsazi'one** *sf* beat

pul'**viscolo** *sm* fine dust

'**puma** *sm inv* puma

pun'**gente** [pun'dʒɛnte] *ag* prickly; stinging; (*anche fig*) biting

'**pungere** ['pundʒere] *vt* to prick; (*sog: insetto, ortica*) to sting; (: *freddo*) to bite

pungigli'**one** [pundʒiʎ'ʎone] *sm* sting

pu'**nire** *vt* to punish; **punizi'one** *sf* punishment; (SPORT) penalty

'**punta** *sf* point; (*parte terminale*) tip, end; (*di monte*) peak; (*di costa*) promontory; (*minima parte*) touch, trace; **in ~ di piedi** on tip-toe; **ore di ~** peak hours; **uomo di ~** front-rank *o* leading man

pun'**tare** *vt* (*piedi a terra, gomiti sul tavolo*) to plant; (*dirigere: pistola*) to point; (*scommettere*) to bet ♦ *vi* (*mirare*): ~ **a** to aim at; ~ **su** (*dirigersi*) to head *o* make for; (*fig: contare*) to count *o* rely on

pun'tata *sf* (*gita*) short trip; (*scommessa*) bet; (*parte di opera*) instalment; **romanzo a ~e** serial

punteggia'tura [punteddʒa'tura] *sf* (*LING*) punctuation

pun'teggio [pun'teddʒo] *sm* score

puntel'lare *vt* to support

pun'tello *sm* prop, support

puntigli'oso, a [puntiʎ'ʎoso] *ag* punctilious

pun'tina *sf*: **~ da disegno** drawing pin

pun'tino *sm* dot; **fare qc a ~** to do sth properly

'punto, a *pp di* **pungere** ♦ *sm* (*segno, macchiolina*) dot; (*LING*) full stop; (*MAT, momento, di punteggio, fig: argomento*) point; (*posto*) spot; (*a scuola*) mark; (*nel cucire, nella maglia, MED*) stitch ♦ *av*: **non ... ~** not at all; **due ~i** *sm* (*LING*) colon; **sul ~ di fare** (just) about to do; **fare il ~** (*NAUT*) to take a bearing; (*fig*): **fare il ~ della situazione** to take stock of the situation; to sum up the situation; **alle 6 in ~** at 6 o'clock sharp *o* on the dot; **essere a buon ~** to have reached a satisfactory stage; **mettere a ~** to adjust; (*motore*) to tune; (*cannocchiale*) to focus; (*fig*) to settle; **di ~ in bianco** point-blank; **~ cardinale** point of the compass, cardinal point; **~ debole** weak point; **~ esclamativo/interrogativo** exclamation/question mark; **~ di riferimento** landmark; (*fig*) point of reference; **~ di vendita** retail outlet; **~ e virgola** semicolon; **~ di vista** (*fig*) point of view; **~i di sospensione** suspension points

puntu'ale *ag* punctual; **puntualità** *sf* punctuality

pun'tura *sf* (*di ago*) prick; (*di insetto*) sting, bite; (*MED*) puncture; (: *iniezione*) injection; (*dolore*) sharp pain

punzecchi'are [puntsek'kjare] *vt* to prick; (*fig*) to tease

'pupa *sf* doll

pu'pazzo [pu'pattso] *sm* puppet

pu'pilla *sf* (*ANAT*) pupil

pu'pillo, a *sm/f* (*DIR*) ward; (*prediletto*) favourite, pet

purché [pur'ke] *cong* provided that, on condition that

'pure *cong* (*tuttavia*) and yet, nevertheless; (*anche se*) even if ♦ *av* (*anche*) too, also; **pur di** (*al fine di*) just to; **faccia ~!** go ahead!, please do!

purè *sm* (*CUC*) purée; (: *di patate*) mashed potatoes

pu'rea *sf* = **purè**

pu'rezza [pu'rettsa] *sf* purity

'purga, ghe *sf* (*MED*) purging *no pl*; purge; (*POL*) purge

pur'gante *sm* (*MED*) purgative, purge

pur'gare *vt* (*MED, POL*) to purge; (*pulire*) to clean

purga'torio *sm* purgatory

purifi'care *vt* to purify; (*metallo*) to refine

puri'tano, a *ag, sm/f* puritan

'puro, a *ag* pure; (*acqua*) clear, limpid; (*vino*) undiluted; **puro'sangue** *sm/f inv* thoroughbred

pur'troppo *av* unfortunately

'pustola *sf* pimple

puti'ferio *sm* rumpus, row

putre'fare *vi* to putrefy, rot; **putre'fatto, a** *pp di* **putrefare**

'putrido, a *ag* putrid, rotten

put'tana (*fam!*) *sf* whore (!)

'puzza ['puttsa] *sf* = **puzzo**

puz'zare [put'tsare] *vi* to stink

'puzzo ['puttso] *sm* stink, foul smell

'puzzola ['puttsola] *sf* polecat

puzzo'lente [puttso'lente] *ag* stinking

Q, q

qua *av* here; **in ~** (*verso questa parte*) this way; **da un anno in ~** for a year now; **da quando in ~?** since when?; **per di ~** (*passare*) this way; **al di ~ di** (*fiume, strada*) on this side of; **~ dentro/fuori** *etc* in/out here *etc*; *vedi anche* **questo**

qua'derno *sm* notebook; (*per scuola*) exercise book

qua'drante *sm* quadrant; (*di orologio*) face

qua'drare *vi* (*bilancio*) to balance, tally;

(*descrizione*) to correspond ♦ *vt* (*MAT*) to square; **non mi quadra** I don't like it; **qua'drato, a** *ag* square; (*fig: equilibrato*) level-headed, sensible; (: *peg*) square ♦ *sm* (*MAT*) square; (*PUGILATO*) ring; **5 al quadrato** 5 squared

qua'dretto *sm*: **a ~i** (*tessuto*) checked; (*foglio*) squared

quadri'foglio [kwadri'fɔʎʎo] *sm* four-leaf clover

'quadro *sm* (*pittura*) painting, picture; (*quadrato*) square; (*tabella*) table, chart; (*TECN*) board, panel; (*TEATRO*) scene; (*fig: scena, spettacolo*) sight; (: *descrizione*) outline, description; **~i** *smpl* (*POL*) party organizers; (*MIL*) cadres; (*COMM*) managerial staff; (*CARTE*) diamonds

'quadruplo, a *ag, sm* quadruple

quaggiù [kwad'dʒu] *av* down here

'quaglia ['kwaʎʎa] *sf* quail

'qualche ['kwalke] *det* **1** some, a few; (*in interrogative*) any; **ho comprato ~ libro** I've bought some *o* a few books; **~ volta** sometimes; **hai ~ sigaretta?** have you any cigarettes?

2 (*uno*): **c'è ~ medico?** is there a doctor?; **in ~ modo** somehow

3 (*un certo, parecchio*) some; **un personaggio di ~ rilievo** a figure of some importance

4: **~ cosa = qualcosa**

qualche'duno [kwalke'duno] *pron* = **qualcuno**

qual'cosa *pron* something; (*in espressioni interrogative*) anything; **qualcos'altro** something else; anything else; **~ di nuovo** something new; anything new; **~ da mangiare** something to eat; anything to eat; **c'è ~ che non va?** is there something *o* anything wrong?

qual'cuno *pron* (*persona*) someone, somebody; (: *in espressioni interrogative*) anyone, anybody; (*alcuni*) some; **~ è favorevole a noi** some are on our side;

qualcun altro someone *o* somebody else; anyone *o* anybody else

'quale (*spesso troncato in* **qual**) *det* **1** (*interrogativo*) what; (: *scegliendo tra due o più cose o persone*) which; **~ uomo/denaro?** what man/money?; which man/money?; **~i sono i tuoi programmi?** what are your plans?; **~ stanza preferisci?** which room do you prefer?

2 (*relativo: come*): **il risultato fu ~ ci si aspettava** the result was as expected

3 (*esclamativo*) what; **~ disgrazia!** what bad luck!

♦ *pron* **1** (*interrogativo*) which; **~ dei due scegli?** which of the two do you want?

2 (*relativo*): **il(la) ~** (*persona: soggetto*) who; (: *oggetto, con preposizione*) whom; (*cosa*) which; (*possessivo*) whose; **suo padre, il ~ è avvocato, ...** his father, who is a lawyer, ...; **il signore con il ~ parlavo** the gentleman to whom I was speaking; **l'albergo al ~ ci siamo fermati** the hotel where we stayed *o* which we stayed at; **la signora della ~ ammiriamo la bellezza** the lady whose beauty we admire

3 (*relativo: in elenchi*) such as, like; **piante ~i l'edera** plants like *o* such as ivy; **~ sindaco di questa città** as mayor of this town

qua'lifica, che *sf* qualification; (*titolo*) title

qualifi'care *vt* to qualify; (*definire*): **~ qn/qc come** to describe sb/sth as; **~rsi** *vr* (*anche SPORT*) to qualify; **qualifica'tivo, a** *ag* qualifying; **qualificazi'one** *sf*: **gara di qualificazione** (*SPORT*) qualifying event

qualità *sf inv* quality; **in ~ di** in one's capacity as

qua'lora *cong* in case, if

qual'siasi *det inv* = **qualunque**

qua'lunque *det inv* any; (*quale che sia*) whatever; (*discriminativo*) whichever; (*posposto: mediocre*) poor, indifferent; ordinary; **mettiti un vestito ~** put on any old dress; **~ cosa** anything; **~ cosa**

accada whatever happens; **a ~ costo** at any cost, whatever the cost; **l'uomo ~** the man in the street; **~ persona** anyone, anybody

'**quando** *cong, av* when; **~ sarò ricco** when I'm rich; **da ~** (*dacché*) since; (*interrogativo*): **da ~ sei qui?** how long have you been here?; **quand'anche** even if

quantità *sf inv* quantity; (*gran numero*): **una ~ di** a great deal of; a lot of; **in grande ~** in large quantities; **quantita'tivo** *sm* (*COMM*) amount, quantity

PAROLA CHIAVE

'**quanto, a** *det* 1 (*interrogativo: quantità*) how much; (: *numero*) how many; **~ pane/denaro?** how much bread/money?; **~i libri/ragazzi?** how many books/boys?; **~ tempo?** how long?; **~i anni hai?** how old are you?

2 (*esclamativo*): **~e storie!** what a lot of nonsense!; **~ tempo sprecato!** what a waste of time!

3 (*relativo: quantità*) as much ... as; (: *numero*) as many ... as; **ho ~ denaro mi occorre** I have as much money as I need; **prendi ~i libri vuoi** take as many books as you like

♦ *pron* 1 (*interrogativo: quantità*) how much; (: *numero*) how many; (: *tempo*) how long; **~ mi dai?** how much will you give me?; **~i me ne hai portati?** how many did you bring me?; **da ~ sei qui?** how long have you been here?; **~i ne abbiamo oggi?** what's the date today?

2 (*relativo: quantità*) as much as; (: *numero*) as many as; **farò ~ posso** I'll do as much as I can; **possono venire ~i sono stati invitati** all those who have been invited can come

♦ *av* 1 (*interrogativo: con ag, av*) how; (: *con vb*) how much; **~ stanco ti sembrava?** how tired did he seem to you?; **~ corre la tua moto?** how fast can your motorbike go?; **~ costa?** how much

does it cost?; **quant'è?** how much is it?

2 (*esclamativo: con ag, av*) how; (: *con vb*) how much; **~ sono felice!** how happy I am!; **sapessi ~ abbiamo camminato!** if you knew how far we've walked!; **studierò ~ posso** I'll study as much as *o* all I can; **~ prima** as soon as possible

3: **in ~** (*in qualità di*) as; (*perché, per il fatto che*) as, since; **(in) ~ a** (*per ciò che riguarda*) as for, as regards

4: **per ~** (*nonostante, anche se*) however; **per ~ si sforzi, non ce la farà** try as he may, he won't manage it; **per ~ sia brava, fa degli errori** however good she may be, she makes mistakes; **per ~ io sappia** as far as I know

quan'tunque *cong* although, though
qua'ranta *num* forty
quaran'tena *sf* quarantine
quaran'tesimo, a *num* fortieth
quaran'tina *sf*: **una ~ (di)** about forty
qua'resima *sf*: **la ~** Lent
'**quarta** *sf* (*AUT*) fourth (gear); *vedi anche* **quarto**
quar'tetto *sm* quartet(te)
quarti'ere *sm* district, area; (*MIL*) quarters *pl*; **~ generale** headquarters *pl*
'**quarto, a** *ag* fourth ♦ *sm* fourth; (*quarta parte*) quarter; **le 6 e un ~** a quarter past six; **~ d'ora** quarter of an hour; **~i di finale** quarter final
'**quarzo** ['kwartso] *sm* quartz
'**quasi** *av* almost, nearly ♦ *cong* (*anche*: **~ che**) as if; **(non) ... ~ mai** hardly ever; **~ ~ me ne andrei** I've half a mind to leave
quas'sù *av* up here
'**quatto, a** *ag* crouched, squatting; (*silenzioso*) silent; **~ ~** very quietly; stealthily
quat'tordici [kwat'torditʃi] *num* fourteen
quat'trini *smpl* money *sg*, cash *sg*
'**quattro** *num* four; **in ~ e quatt'otto** in less than no time; **quattro'cento** *num* four hundred ♦ *sm*: **il Quattrocento** the fifteenth century; **quattro'mila** *num* four thousand

---

PAROLA CHIAVE

'**quello, a** (*dav sm* **quel** +*C*, **quell'** +*V*, **quello** +*s impura, gn, pn, ps, x, z; pl* **quei** +*C*, **quegli** +*V o s impura, gn, pn, ps, x, z; dav sf* **quella** +*C*, **quell'** +*V; pl* **quelle**) *det* that; those *pl*; ~ **casa** that house; **quegli uomini** those men; **voglio ~ camicia (lì** *o* **là)** I want that shirt

♦ *pron* 1 (*dimostrativo*) that (one); those (ones) *pl*; (*ciò*) that; **conosci ~a?** do you know that woman?; **prendo ~ bianco** I'll take the white one; **chi è ~?** who's that?; **prendi ~ (lì** *o* **là)** take that one (there)
2 (*relativo*): **~(a) che** (*persona*) the one (who); (*cosa*) the one (which), the one (that); **~i(e) che** (*persone*) those who; (*cose*) those which; **è lui ~ che non voleva venire** he's the one who didn't want to come; **ho fatto ~ che potevo** I did what I could

---

'**quercia, ce** ['kwertʃa] *sf* oak (tree); (*legno*) oak
que'rela *sf* (*DIR*) (legal) action; **quere'lare** *vt* to bring an action against
que'sito *sm* question, query; problem
questio'nario *sm* questionnaire
questi'one *sf* problem, question; (*controversia*) issue; (*litigio*) quarrel; **in ~** in question; **è ~ di tempo** it's a matter *o* question of time

---

PAROLA CHIAVE

'**questo, a** *det* 1 (*dimostrativo*) this; these *pl*; ~ **libro (qui** *o* **qua)** this book; **io prendo ~ cappotto, tu quello** I'll take this coat, you take that one; **quest'oggi** today; ~**a sera** this evening
2 (*enfatico*): **non fatemi più prendere di ~e paure** don't frighten me like that again
♦ *pron* (*dimostrativo*) this (one); these (ones) *pl*; (*ciò*) this; **prendo ~ (qui** *o* **qua)** I'll take this one; **preferisci ~i o quelli?** do you prefer these (ones) or those (ones)?; ~ **intendevo io** this is what I meant; **vengono Paolo e Luca: ~ da Roma,**

quello da Palermo Paolo and Luca are coming: the former from Palermo, the latter from Rome

---

ques'tore *sm* ≈ chief constable (*BRIT*), ≈ police commissioner (*US*)
ques'tua *sf* collection (of alms)
ques'tura *sf* police headquarters *pl*
qui *av* here; **da** *o* **di ~** from here; **di ~ in avanti** from now on; **di ~ a poco/una settimana** in a little while/a week's time; ~ **dentro/sopra/vicino** in/up/near here; *vedi anche* **questo**
quie'tanza [kwje'tantsa] *sf* receipt
quie'tare *vt* to calm, soothe
qui'ete *sf* quiet, quietness; calmness; stillness; peace
qui'eto, a *ag* quiet; (*notte*) calm, still; (*mare*) calm
'**quindi** *av* then ♦ *cong* therefore, so
'**quindici** ['kwinditʃi] *num* fifteen; ~ **giorni** a fortnight (*BRIT*), two weeks
quindi'cina [kwindi'tʃina] *sf* (*serie*): **una ~ (di)** about fifteen; **fra una ~ di giorni** in a fortnight
quin'quennio *sm* period of five years
quin'tale *sm* quintal (*100 kg*)
'**quinte** *sfpl* (*TEATRO*) wings
'**quinto, a** *num* fifth

Quirinale

ⓘ *The* **Quirinale**, *which takes its name from the hill in Rome on which it stands, is the official residence of the Presidente della Repubblica.*

'**quota** *sf* (*parte*) quota, share; (*AER*) height, altitude; (*IPPICA*) odds *pl*; **prendere/ perdere ~** (*AER*) to gain/lose height *o* altitude; ~ **d'iscrizione** enrolment fee; (*a club*) membership fee
quo'tare *vt* (*BORSA*) to quote; **quotazi'one** *sf* quotation
quotidi'ano, a *ag* daily; (*banale*) everyday ♦ *sm* (*giornale*) daily (paper)
quozi'ente [kwot'tsjente] *sm* (*MAT*) quotient; ~ **d'intelligenza**

intelligence quotient, IQ

R, r

ra'barbaro *sm* rhubarb

'rabbia *sf* (*ira*) anger, rage; (*accanimento, furia*) fury; (MED: *idrofobia*) rabies *sg*

rab'bino *sm* rabbi

rabbi'oso, a *ag* angry, furious; (*facile all'ira*) quick-tempered; (*forze, acqua etc*) furious, raging; (MED) rabid, mad

rabbo'nire *vt* to calm down; **~rsi** *vr* to calm down

rabbrivi'dire *vi* to shudder, shiver

rabbui'arsi *vr* to grow dark

raccapez'zarsi [rakkapet'tsarsi] *vr*: **non ~** to be at a loss

raccapricci'ante [rakkaprit'tʃante] *ag* horrifying

raccatta'palle *sm inv* (SPORT) ballboy

raccat'tare *vt* to pick up

rac'chetta [rak'ketta] *sf* (*per tennis*) racket; (*per ping-pong*) bat; **~ da neve** snowshoe; **~ da sci** ski stick

racchi'udere [rak'kjudere] *vt* to contain;

racchi'uso, a *pp di* **racchiudere**

rac'cogliere [rak'kɔʎʎere] *vt* to collect; (*raccattare*) to pick up; (*frutti, fiori*) to pick, pluck; (AGR) to harvest; (*approvazione, voti*) to win; **~rsi** *vr* to gather; (*fig*) to gather one's thoughts; to meditate;

raccogli'mento *sm* meditation;

raccogli'tore *sm* (*cartella*) folder, binder; **raccoglitore ad anelli** ring binder

rac'colta *sf* collecting *no pl*; collection; (AGR) harvesting *no pl*, gathering *no pl*; harvest, crop; (*adunata*) gathering

rac'colto, a *pp di* **raccogliere** ♦ *ag* (*persona: pensoso*) thoughtful; (*luogo: appartato*) secluded, quiet ♦ *sm* (AGR) crop, harvest

raccoman'dare *vt* to recommend; (*affidare*) to entrust; (*esortare*): **~ a qn di non fare** to tell *o* warn sb not to do; **~rsi** *vr*: **~rsi a qn** to commend o.s. to sb; **mi raccomando!** don't forget!;

raccoman'data *sf* (*anche:* **lettera raccomandata**) recorded-delivery letter; **raccomandazi'one** *sf* recommendation

raccon'tare *vt*: **~ (a qn)** (*dire*) to tell (sb); (*narrare*) to relate (to sb), tell sb about; **rac'conto** *sm* telling *no pl*, relating *no pl*; (*fatto raccontato*) story, tale

raccorci'are [rakkor'tʃare] *vt* to shorten

rac'cordo *sm* (TECN: *giunto*) connection, joint; (AUT: *di autostrada*) slip road (BRIT), entrance (*o* exit) ramp (US); **~ anulare** (AUT) ring road (BRIT), beltway (US)

ra'chitico, a, ci, che [ra'kitiko] *ag* suffering from rickets; (*fig*) scraggy, scrawny

racimo'lare [ratʃimo'lare] *vt* (*fig*) to scrape together, glean

'rada *sf* (natural) harbour

'radar *sm* radar

raddol'cire [raddol'tʃire] *vt* (*persona, carattere*) to soften; **~rsi** *vr* (*tempo*) to grow milder; (*persona*) to soften, mellow

raddoppi'are *vt, vi* to double

raddriz'zare [raddrit'tsare] *vt* to straighten; (*fig: correggere*) to put straight, correct

'radere *vt* (*barba*) to shave off; (*mento*) to shave; (*fig: rasentare*) to graze; to skim; **~rsi** *vr* to shave (o.s.); **~ al suolo** to raze to the ground

radi'are *vt* to strike off

radia'tore *sm* radiator

radiazi'one [radjat'tsjone] *sf* (FISICA) radiation; (*cancellazione*) striking off

radi'cale *ag* radical ♦ *sm* (LING) root

ra'dicchio [ra'dikkjo] *sm* chicory

ra'dice [ra'ditʃe] *sf* root

'radio *sf inv* radio ♦ *sm* (CHIM) radium; **radioat'tivo, a** *ag* radioactive; **radiodiffusi'one** *sf* (radio) broadcasting; **radiogra'fare** *vt* to X-ray; **radiogra'fia** *sf* radiography; (*foto*) X-ray photograph

radi'oso, a *ag* radiant

'rado, a *ag* (*capelli*) sparse, thin; (*visite*) infrequent; **di ~** rarely

radu'nare *vt, vi* to gather, assemble; **~rsi** *vr* to gather, assemble; **ra'duno** *sm* meeting

ra'dura *sf* clearing

raffazzo'nato [raffattso'nato] *ag* patched up

raf'fermo, a *ag* stale

'raffica, che *sf (METEOR)* gust (of wind); *(di colpi: scarica)* burst of gunfire

raffigu'rare *vt* to represent

raffi'nare *vt* to refine; **raffina'tezza** *sf* refinement; **raffi'nato, a** *ag* refined; **raffine'ria** *sf* refinery

raffor'zare [raffor'tsare] *vt* to reinforce

raffredda'mento *sm* cooling

raffred'dare *vt* to cool; *(fig)* to dampen, have a cooling effect on; **~rsi** *vr* to grow cool *o* cold; *(prendere un raffreddore)* to catch a cold; *(fig)* to cool (off)

raffred'dato, a *ag (MED)*: **essere ~** to have a cold

raffred'dore *sm (MED)* cold

raf'fronto *sm* comparison

'rafia *sf (fibra)* raffia

ra'gazzo, a [ra'gattso] *sm/f* boy/girl; *(fam: fidanzato)* boyfriend/girlfriend

raggi'ante [rad'dʒante] *ag* radiant, shining

'raggio ['raddʒo] *sm (di sole etc)* ray; *(MAT, distanza)* radius; *(di ruota etc)* spoke; **~ d'azione** range; **~i X** X-rays

raggi'rare [raddʒi'rare] *vt* to take in, trick; **rag'giro** *sm* trick

raggi'ungere [rad'dʒundʒere] *vt* to reach; *(persona: riprendere)* to catch up (with); *(bersaglio)* to hit; *(fig: meta)* to achieve; **raggi'unto, a** *pp di* **raggiungere**

raggomito'larsi *vr* to curl up

raggranel'lare *vt* to scrape together

raggrup'pare *vt* to group (together)

raggu'aglio [rag'gwaʎʎo] *sm (informazione)* piece of information

ragguar'devole *ag (degno di riguardo)* distinguished, notable; *(notevole: somma)* considerable

ragiona'mento [radʒona'mento] *sm* reasoning *no pl*; arguing *no pl*; argument

ragio'nare [radʒo'nare] *vi* to reason; **~ di** *(discorrere)* to talk about

ragi'one [ra'dʒone] *sf* reason; *(dimostrazione, prova)* argument, reason; *(diritto)* right; **aver ~** to be right; **aver ~ di**

qn to get the better of sb; **dare ~ a qn** to agree with sb; to prove sb right; **perdere la ~** to become insane; *(fig)* to take leave of one's senses; **in ~ di** at the rate of; to the amount of; according to; **a *o* con ~** rightly, justly; **~ sociale** *(COMM)* corporate name; **a ragion veduta** after due consideration

ragione'ria [radʒone'ria] *sf* accountancy; accounts department

ragio'nevole [radʒo'nevole] *ag* reasonable

ragioni'ere, a [radʒo'njere] *sm/f* accountant

ragli'are [raʎ'ʎare] *vi* to bray

ragna'tela [raɲɲa'tela] *sf* cobweb, spider's web

'ragno ['raɲɲo] *sm* spider

ragù *sm inv (CUC)* meat sauce; stew

RAI-TV [raiti'vu] *sigla f* = **Radio televisione italiana**

rallegra'menti *smpl* congratulations

ralle'grare *vt* to cheer up; **~rsi** *vr* to cheer up; *(provare allegrezza)* to rejoice; **~rsi con qn** to congratulate sb

rallen'tare *vt* to slow down; *(fig)* to lessen, slacken ♦ *vi* to slow down

raman'zina [raman'dzina] *sf* lecture, telling-off

'rame *sm (CHIM)* copper

rammari'carsi *vr*: **~ (di)** *(rincrescersi)* to be sorry (about), regret; *(lamentarsi)* to complain (about); **ram'marico, chi** *sm* regret

rammen'dare *vt* to mend; *(calza)* to darn; **ram'mendo** *sm* mending *no pl*; darning *no pl*; mend; darn

rammen'tare *vt* to remember, recall; *(richiamare alla memoria)*: **~ qc a qn** to remind sb of sth; **~rsi** *vr*: **~rsi (di qc)** to remember (sth)

rammol'lire *vt* to soften ♦ *vi (anche: ~rsi)* to go soft

'ramo *sm* branch

ramo'scello [ramoʃ'ʃello] *sm* twig

'rampa *sf* flight (of stairs); **~ di lancio** launching pad

rampi'cante *ag (BOT)* climbing

ram'pone *sm* harpoon; (*ALPINISMO*) crampon

'**rana** *sf* frog

'**rancido, a** ['rantʃido] *ag* rancid

ran'core *sm* rancour, resentment

ran'dagio, a, gi, gie *o* **ge** [ran'dadʒo] *ag* (*gatto, cane*) stray

ran'dello *sm* club, cudgel

'**rango, ghi** *sm* (*condizione sociale, MIL: riga*) rank

rannicchi'arsi [rannik'kjarsi] *vr* to crouch, huddle

rannuvo'larsi *vr* to cloud over, become overcast

ra'nocchio [ra'nɔkkjo] *sm* (edible) frog

'**rantolo** *sm* wheeze; (*di agonizzanti*) death rattle

'**rapa** *sf* (*BOT*) turnip

ra'pace [ra'patʃe] *ag* (*animale*) predatory; (*fig*) rapacious, grasping ♦ *sm* bird of prey

ra'pare *vt* (*capelli*) to crop, cut very short

'**rapida** *sf* (*di fiume*) rapid; *vedi anche* **rapido**

rapida'mente *av* quickly, rapidly

rapidità *sf* speed

'**rapido, a** *ag* fast; (*esame, occhiata*) quick, rapid ♦ *sm* (*FERR*) express (train)

rapi'mento *sm* kidnapping; (*fig*) rapture

ra'pina *sf* robbery; ~ **a mano armata** armed robbery; **rapi'nare** *vt* to rob; **rapina'tore, 'trice** *sm/f* robber

ra'pire *vt* (*cose*) to steal; (*persone*) to kidnap; (*fig*) to enrapture, delight; **rapi'tore, 'trice** *sm/f* kidnapper

rappor'tare *vt* (*confrontare*) to compare; (*riprodurre*) to reproduce

rap'porto *sm* (*resoconto*) report; (*legame*) relationship; (*MAT, TECN*) ratio; ~**i** *smpl* (*fra persone, paesi*) relations; ~**i sessuali** sexual intercourse *sg*

rap'prendersi *vr* to coagulate, clot; (*latte*) to curdle

rappre'saglia [rappre'saʎʎa] *sf* reprisal, retaliation

rappresen'tante *sm/f* representative; **rappresen'tanza** *sf* delegation, deputation; (*COMM: ufficio, sede*) agency

rappresen'tare *vt* to represent; (*TEATRO*) to perform; **rappresentazi'one** *sf* representation; performing *no pl*; (*spettacolo*) performance

rap'preso, a *pp di* **rapprendere**

rapso'dia *sf* rhapsody

rara'mente *av* seldom, rarely

rare'fatto, a *ag* rarefied

'**raro, a** *ag* rare

ra'sare *vt* (*barba etc*) to shave off; (*siepi, erba*) to trim, cut; ~**rsi** *vr* to shave (o.s.)

raschi'are [ras'kjare] *vt* to scrape; (*macchia, fango*) to scrape off ♦ *vi* to clear one's throat

rasen'tare *vt* (*andar rasente*) to keep close to; (*sfiorare*) to skim along (*o* over); (*fig*) to border on

ra'sente *prep*: ~ **(a)** close to, very near

'**raso, a** *pp di* **radere** ♦ *ag* (*barba*) shaved; (*capelli*) cropped; (*con misure di capacità*) level; (*pieno: bicchiere*) full to the brim ♦ *sm* (*tessuto*) satin; ~ **terra** close to the ground; **un cucchiaio** ~ a level spoonful

ra'soio *sm* razor; ~ **elettrico** electric shaver *o* razor

ras'segna [ras'seɲɲa] *sf* (*MIL*) inspection, review; (*esame*) inspection; (*resoconto*) review, survey; (*pubblicazione letteraria etc*) review; (*mostra*) exhibition, show; **passare in** ~ (*MIL, fig*) to review

rasse'gnare [rasseɲ'ɲare] *vt*: ~ **le dimissioni** to resign, hand in one's resignation; ~**rsi** *vr* (*accettare*): ~**rsi (a qc/ a fare)** to resign o.s. (to sth/to doing); **rassegnazi'one** *sf* resignation

rasse'renarsi *vr* (*tempo*) to clear up

rasset'tare *vt* to tidy, put in order; (*aggiustare*) to repair, mend

rassicu'rare *vt* to reassure

rasso'dare *vt* to harden, stiffen

rassomigli'anza [rassomiʎ'ʎantsa] *sf* resemblance

rassomigli'are [rassomiʎ'ʎare] *vi*: ~ **a** to resemble, look like

rastrel'lare *vt* to rake; (*fig: perlustrare*) to comb

rastrelli'era *sf* rack; (*per piatti*) dish rack

ras'trello *sm* rake

'rata *sf* (*quota*) instalment; **pagare a ~e** to pay by instalments *o* on hire purchase (*BRIT*)

ratifi'care *vt* (*DIR*) to ratify

'ratto *sm* (*DIR*) abduction; (*ZOOL*) rat

rattop'pare *vt* to patch; **rat'toppo** *sm* patching *no pl*; patch

rattrap'pirsi *vr* to get stiff

rattris'tare *vt* to sadden; **~rsi** *vr* to become sad

'rauco, a, chi, che *ag* hoarse

rava'nello *sm* radish

ravi'oli *smpl* ravioli *sg*

ravve'dersi *vr* to mend one's ways

ravvici'nare [ravvitʃi'nare] *vt* (*avvicinare*): **~ qc a** to bring sth nearer to; (*: due tubi*) to bring closer together; (*riconciliare*) to reconcile, bring together

ravvi'sare *vt* to recognize

ravvi'vare *vt* to revive; (*fig*) to brighten up, enliven; **~rsi** *vr* to revive; to brighten up

razio'cinio [ratsjo'tʃinjo] *sm* reasoning *no pl*; reason; (*buon senso*) common sense

razio'nale [rattsjo'nale] *ag* rational

razio'nare [rattsjo'nare] *vt* to ration

razi'one [rat'tsjone] *sf* ration; (*porzione*) portion, share

'razza ['rattsa] *sf* race; (*ZOOL*) breed; (*discendenza, stirpe*) stock, race; (*sorta*) sort, kind

raz'zia [rat'tsia] *sf* raid, foray

razzi'ale [rat'tsjale] *ag* racial

raz'zismo [rat'tsizmo] *sm* racism, racialism

raz'zista, i, e [rat'tsista] *ag, sm/f* racist, racialist

'razzo ['raddzo] *sm* rocket

razzo'lare [rattso'lare] *vi* (*galline*) to scratch about

re *sm inv* king; (*MUS*) D; (*: solfeggiando*) re

rea'gire [rea'dʒire] *vi* to react

re'ale *ag* real; (*di, da re*) royal ♦ *sm*: **il ~** reality; **rea'lismo** *sm* realism; **rea'lista, i, e** *sm/f* realist; (*POL*) royalist

realiz'zare [realid'dzare] *vt* (*progetto etc*) to realize, carry out; (*sogno, desiderio*) to realize, fulfil; (*scopo*) to achieve; (*COMM: titoli etc*) to realize; (*CALCIO etc*) to score; **~rsi** *vr* to be realized; **realizzazi'one** *sf* realization; fulfilment; achievement

real'mente *av* really, actually

realtà *sf inv* reality

re'ato *sm* offence

reat'tore *sm* (*FISICA*) reactor; (*AER: aereo*) jet; (*: motore*) jet engine

reazio'nario, a [reattsjo'narjo] *ag* (*POL*) reactionary

reazi'one [reat'tsjone] *sf* reaction

recapi'tare *vt* to deliver

re'capito *sm* (*indirizzo*) address; (*consegna*) delivery

re'care *vt* (*portare*) to bring; (*avere su di sé*) to carry, bear; (*cagionare*) to cause, bring; **~rsi** *vr* to go

re'cedere [re'tʃedere] *vi* to withdraw

recensi'one [retʃen'sjone] *sf* review; **recen'sire** *vt* to review

re'cente [re'tʃɛnte] *ag* recent; **di ~** recently; **recente'mente** *av* recently

recessi'one [retʃes'sjone] *sf* (*ECON*) recession

re'cidere [re'tʃidere] *vt* to cut off, chop off

reci'divo, a [retʃi'divo] *sm/f* (*DIR*) second (*o* habitual) offender, recidivist

re'cinto [re'tʃinto] *sm* enclosure; (*ciò che recinge*) fence; surrounding wall

recipi'ente [retʃi'pjɛnte] *sm* container

re'ciproco, a, ci, che [re'tʃiproko] *ag* reciprocal

re'ciso, a [re'tʃizo] *pp di* **recidere**

'recita ['rɛtʃita] *sf* performance

reci'tare [retʃi'tare] *vt* (*poesia, lezione*) to recite; (*dramma*) to perform; (*ruolo*) to play *o* act (the part of); **recitazi'one** *sf* recitation; (*di attore*) acting

recla'mare *vi* to complain ♦ *vt* (*richiedere*) to demand

ré'clame [re'klam] *sf inv* advertising *no pl*; advertisement, advert (*BRIT*), ad (*fam*)

re'clamo *sm* complaint

reclusi'one *sf* (*DIR*) imprisonment

'recluta *sf* recruit; **reclu'tare** *vt* to recruit

re'condito, a *ag* secluded; (*fig*) secret,

hidden

recriminazi'one [rekriminat'tsjone] *sf* recrimination

recrude'scenza [rekrudeʃʃentsa] *sf* fresh outbreak

recupe'rare *vt* = **ricuperare**

redargu'ire *vt* to rebuke

re'datto, a *pp di* **redigere; redat'tore, 'trice** *sm/f* (*STAMPA*) editor; (: *di articolo*) writer; (*di dizionario etc*) compiler; **redattore capo** chief editor; **redazi'one** *sf* editing; writing; (*sede*) editorial office(s); (*personale*) editorial staff; (*versione*) version

reddi'tizio, a [reddi'tittsjo] *ag* profitable

'reddito *sm* income; (*dello Stato*) revenue; (*di un capitale*) yield

re'dento, a *pp di* **redimere**

redenzi'one [reden'tsjone] *sf* redemption

re'digere [re'didʒere] *vt* to write; (*contratto*) to draw up

'redini *sfpl* reins

re'duce ['rɛdutʃe] *ag*: ~ **da** returning from, back from ♦ *sm/f* survivor

refe'rendum *sm inv* referendum

refe'renza [refe'rɛntsa] *sf* reference

re'ferto *sm* medical report

refet'torio *sm* refectory

refrat'tario, a *ag* refractory

refrige'rare [refridʒe'rare] *vt* to refrigerate; (*rinfrescare*) to cool, refresh

rega'lare *vt* to give (as a present), make a present of

re'gale *ag* regal

re'galo *sm* gift, present

re'gata *sf* regatta

reg'gente [red'dʒɛnte] *sm/f* regent

'reggere ['rɛddʒere] *vt* (*tenere*) to hold; (*sostenere*) to support, bear, hold up; (*portare*) to carry, bear; (*resistere*) to withstand; (*dirigere: impresa*) to manage, run; (*governare*) to rule, govern; (*LING*) to take, be followed by ♦ *vi* (*resistere*): ~ **a** to stand up to, hold out against; (*sopportare*): ~ **a** to stand; (*durare*) to last; (*fig: teoria etc*) to hold water; **~rsi** *vr* (*stare ritto*) to stand

'reggia, ge ['rɛddʒa] *sf* royal palace

reggi'calze [reddʒi'kaltse] *sm inv*

suspender belt

reggi'mento [reddʒi'mento] *sm* (*MIL*) regiment

reggi'petto [reddʒi'petto] *sm* bra

reggi'seno [reddʒi'seno] *sm* bra

re'gia, 'gie [re'dʒia] *sf* (*TV, CINEMA etc*) direction

re'gime [re'dʒime] *sm* (*POL*) regime; (*DIR: aureo, patrimoniale etc*) system; (*MED*) diet; (*TECN*) (engine) speed

re'gina [re'dʒina] *sf* queen

'regio, a, gi, gie ['rɛdʒo] *ag* royal

regio'nale [redʒo'nale] *ag* regional ♦ *sm* local train (*stopping frequently*)

regi'one [re'dʒone] *sf* region; (*territorio*) region, district, area

re'gista, i, e [re'dʒista] *sm/f* (*TV, CINEMA etc*) director

regis'trare [redʒis'trare] *vt* (*AMM*) to register; (*COMM*) to enter; (*notare*) to note, take note of; (*canzone, conversazione, sog: strumento di misura*) to record; (*mettere a punto*) to adjust, regulate; (*bagagli*) to check in; **registra'tore** *sm* (*strumento*) recorder, register; (*magnetofono*) tape recorder; **registratore di cassa** cash register; **registrazi'one** *sf* recording; (*AMM*) registration; (*COMM*) entry; (*di bagagli*) check-in

re'gistro [re'dʒistro] *sm* (*libro, MUS, TECH*) register; ledger; logbook; (*DIR*) registry

re'gnare [ren'nare] *vi* to reign, rule

'regno ['renno] *sm* kingdom; (*periodo*) reign; (*fig*) realm; **il ~ animale/vegetale** the animal/vegetable kingdom; **il R~ Unito** the United Kingdom

'regola *sf* rule; **a ~ d'arte** duly; perfectly; **in ~** in order

rego'labile *ag* adjustable

regola'mento *sm* (*complesso di norme*) regulations *pl*; (*di debito*) settlement; **~ di conti** (*fig*) settling of scores

rego'lare *ag* regular; (*in regola: domanda*) in order, lawful ♦ *vt* to regulate, control; (*apparecchio*) to adjust, regulate; (*questione, conto, debito*) to settle; **~rsi** *vr* (*moderarsi*): **~rsi nel bere/nello spendere** to control one's drinking/spending; (*comportarsi*) to behave, act; **regolarità** *sf inv* regularity

'**regolo** *sm* ruler; **~ calcolatore** slide rule

reinte'grare *vt* (*energie*) to recover; (*in una carica*) to reinstate

rela'tivo, a *ag* relative

relazi'one [relat'tsjone] *sf* (*fra cose, persone*) relation(ship); (*resoconto*) report, account; **~i** *sfpl* (*conoscenze*) connections

rele'gare *vt* to banish; (*fig*) to relegate

religi'one [reli'dʒone] *sf* religion; **religi'oso, a** *ag* religious ♦ *sm/f* monk/nun

re'liquia *sf* relic

re'litto *sm* wreck; (*fig*) down-and-out

re'mare *vi* to row

remini'scenze [reminif'ʃentse] *sfpl* reminiscences

remissi'one *sf* remission

remis'sivo, a *ag* submissive, compliant

'**remo** *sm* oar

re'moto, a *ag* remote

'**rendere** *vt* (*ridare*) to return, give back; (*: saluto etc*) to return; (*produrre*) to yield, bring in; (*esprimere, tradurre*) to render; **~ qc possibile** to make sth possible; **~rsi utile** to make o.s. useful; **~rsi conto di qc** to realize sth

rendi'conto *sm* (*rapporto*) report, account; (*AMM, COMM*) statement of account

rendi'mento *sm* (*reddito*) yield; (*di manodopera, TECN*) efficiency; (*capacità di produrre*) output; (*di studenti*) performance

'**rendita** *sf* (*di individuo*) private *o* unearned income; (*COMM*) revenue; **~ annua** annuity

'**rene** *sm* kidney

'**reni** *sfpl* back *sg*

reni'tente *ag* reluctant, unwilling; **~ ai consigli di qn** unwilling to follow sb's advice; **essere ~ alla leva** (*MIL*) to fail to report for military service

'**renna** *sf* reindeer *inv*

'**Reno** *sm*: **il ~** the Rhine

'**reo, a** *sm/f* (*DIR*) offender

re'parto *sm* department, section; (*MIL*) detachment

repel'lente *ag* repulsive

repen'taglio [repen'taʎʎo] *sm*: **mettere a ~** to jeopardize, risk

repen'tino, a *ag* sudden, unexpected

repe'rire *vt* to find, trace

re'perto *sm* (*ARCHEOLOGIA*) find; (*MED*) report; (*DIR: anche:* **~ giudiziario**) exhibit

reper'torio *sm* (*TEATRO*) repertory; (*elenco*) index, (alphabetical) list

'**replica, che** *sf* repetition; reply, answer; (*obiezione*) objection; (*TEATRO, CINEMA*) repeat performance; (*copia*) replica

repli'care *vt* (*ripetere*) to repeat; (*rispondere*) to answer, reply

repressi'one *sf* repression

re'presso, a *pp di* **reprimere**

re'primere *vt* to suppress, repress

re'pubblica, che *sf* republic; **repubbli'cano, a** *ag, sm/f* republican

repu'tare *vt* to consider, judge

reputazi'one [reputat'tsjone] *sf* reputation

'**requie** *sf*: **senza ~** unceasingly

requi'sire *vt* to requisition

requi'sito *sm* requirement

'**resa** *sf* (*l'arrendersi*) surrender; (*restituzione, rendimento*) return; **~ dei conti** rendering of accounts; (*fig*) day of reckoning

resi'dente *ag* resident; **resi'denza** *sf* residence; **residenzi'ale** *ag* residential

re'siduo, a *ag* residual, remaining ♦ *sm* remainder; (*CHIM*) residue

'**resina** *sf* resin

resis'tente *ag* (*che resiste*): **~ a** resistant to; (*forte*) strong; (*duraturo*) long-lasting, durable; **~ al caldo** heat-resistant; **resis'tenza** *sf* resistance; (*di persona: fisica*) stamina, endurance; (*: mentale*) endurance, resistance

---

Resistenza

ⓘ The **Resistenza** in Italy fought against the Nazis and the Fascists during the Second World War. Members of the Resistance spanned a wide political spectrum and played a vital role in the Liberation and in the formation of the new democratic government at the end

of the war.

re'sistere *vi* to resist; **~ a** (*assalto, tentazioni*) to resist; (*dolore, sog: pianta*) to withstand; (*non patir danno*) to be resistant to; **resis'tito, a** *pp di* **resistere**

'reso, a *pp di* **rendere**

reso'conto *sm* report, account

res'pingere [res'pindʒere] *vt* to drive back, repel; (*rifiutare*) to reject; (*INS: bocciare*) to fail; **res'pinto, a** *pp di* **respingere**

respi'rare *vi* to breathe; (*fig*) to get one's breath; to breathe again ♦ *vt* to breathe (in), inhale; **respira'tore** *sm* respirator; **respirazi'one** *sf* breathing; **respirazione artificiale** artificial respiration; **res'piro** *sm* breathing *no pl*; (*singolo atto*) breath; (*fig*) respite, rest; **mandare un respiro di sollievo** to give a sigh of relief

respon'sabile *ag* responsible ♦ *sm/f* person responsible; (*capo*) person in charge; **~ di** responsible for; (*DIR*) liable for; **responsabilità** *sf inv* responsibility; (*legale*) liability

res'ponso *sm* answer

'ressa *sf* crowd, throng

res'tare *vi* (*rimanere*) to remain, stay; (*avanzare*) to be left, remain; **~ orfano/ cieco** to become *o* be left an orphan/ become blind; **~ d'accordo** to agree; **non resta più niente** there's nothing left; **restano pochi giorni** there are only a few days left

restau'rare *vt* to restore; **restaurazi'one** *sf* (*POL*) restoration; **res'tauro** *sm* (*di edifici etc*) restoration

res'tio, a, 'tii, 'tie *ag*: **~ a** reluctant to

restitu'ire *vt* to return, give back; (*energie, forze*) to restore

'resto *sm* remainder, rest; (*denaro*) change; (*MAT*) remainder; **~i** *smpl* (*di cibo*) leftovers; (*di città*) remains; **del ~** moreover, besides; **~i mortali** (*mortal*) remains

res'tringere [res'trindʒere] *vt* to reduce; (*vestito*) to take in; (*stoffa*) to shrink; (*fig*) to restrict, limit; **~rsi** *vr* (*strada*) to narrow; (*stoffa*) to shrink; **restrizi'one** *sf* restriction

'rete *sf* net; (*fig*) trap, snare; (*di recinzione*) wire netting; (*AUT, FERR, di spionaggio etc*) network; **segnare una ~** (*CALCIO*) to score a goal; **~ del letto** (sprung) bed base

reti'cente [reti'tʃɛnte] *ag* reticent

retico'lato *sm* grid; (*rete*) wire netting; (*di filo spinato*) barbed wire (fence)

'retina *sf* (*ANAT*) retina

re'torica *sf* rhetoric

re'torico, a, ci, che *ag* rhetorical

retribu'ire *vt* to pay; **retribuzi'one** *sf* payment

'retro *sm inv* back ♦ *av* (*dietro*): **vedi ~** see over(leaf)

retro'cedere [retro'tʃɛdere] *vi* to withdraw ♦ *vt* (*CALCIO*) to degrade

re'trogrado, a *ag* (*fig*) reactionary, backward-looking

retro'marcia [retro'martʃa] *sf* (*AUT*) reverse; (*: dispositivo*) reverse gear

retro'scena [retro'ʃɛna] *sm inv* (*TEATRO*) backstage; **i ~** (*fig*) the behind-the-scenes activities

retrospet'tivo, a *ag* retrospective

retrovi'sore *sm* (*AUT*) (rear-view) mirror

'retta *sf* (*MAT*) straight line; (*di convitto*) charge for bed and board; (*fig: ascolto*): **dar ~ a** to listen to, pay attention to

rettango'lare *ag* rectangular

ret'tangolo, a *ag* right-angled ♦ *sm* rectangle

retti'fica, che *sf* rectification, correction

rettifi'care *vt* (*curva*) to straighten; (*fig*) to rectify, correct

'rettile *sm* reptile

retti'lineo, a *ag* rectilinear

retti'tudine *sf* rectitude, uprightness

'retto, a *pp di* **reggere** ♦ *ag* straight; (*MAT*): **angolo ~** right angle; (*onesto*) honest, upright; (*giusto, esatto*) correct, proper, right

ret'tore *sm* (*REL*) rector; (*di università*) ≈ chancellor

reuma'tismo *sm* rheumatism

reve'rendo, a *ag*: **il ~ padre Belli** the Reverend Father Belli

rever'sibile *ag* reversible

revisio'nare *vt* (*conti*) to audit; (*TECN*) to overhaul, service; (*DIR: processo*) to review

revisi'one *sf* auditing *no pl*; audit; servicing *no pl*; overhaul; review; revision

revi'sore *sm*: ~ **di conti/bozze** auditor/proofreader

'revoca *sf* revocation

revo'care *vt* to revoke

re'volver *sm inv* revolver

riabili'tare *vt* to rehabilitate

riagganci'are [riaggan'tʃare] *vt* (*TEL*) to hang up

rial'zare [rial'tsare] *vt* to raise, lift; (*alzare di più*) to heighten, raise; (*aumentare: prezzi*) to increase, raise ♦ *vi* (*prezzi*) to rise, increase; **ri'alzo** *sm* (*di prezzi*) increase, rise; (*sporgenza*) rise

rianimazi'one [rianimat'tsjone] *sf* (*MED*) resuscitation; **centro di ~** intensive care unit

riap'pendere *vt* to rehang; (*TEL*) to hang up

ria'prire *vt* to reopen, open again; **~rsi** *vr* to reopen, open again

ri'armo *sm* (*MIL*) rearmament

rias'setto *sm* (*di stanza etc*) rearrangement; (*ordinamento*) reorganization

rias'sumere *vt* (*riprendere*) to resume; (*impiegare di nuovo*) to re-employ; (*sintetizzare*) to summarize; **rias'sunto, a** *pp di* **riassumere** ♦ *sm* summary

ria'vere *vt* to have again; (*avere indietro*) to get back; (*riacquistare*) to recover; **~rsi** *vr* to recover

riba'dire *vt* (*fig*) to confirm

ri'balta *sf* flap; (*TEATRO: proscenio*) front of the stage; (*fig*) limelight; **luci della ~** footlights *pl*

ribal'tabile *ag* (*sedile*) tip-up

ribal'tare *vt, vi* (*anche:* **~rsi**) to turn over, tip over

ribas'sare *vt* to lower, bring down ♦ *vi* to come down, fall; **ri'basso** *sm* reduction, fall

ri'battere *vt* to return, hit back; (*confutare*) to refute; ~ **che** to retort that

ribel'larsi *vr*: ~ **(a)** to rebel (against); **ri'belle** *ag* (*soldati*) rebel; (*ragazzo*) rebellious ♦ *sm/f* rebel; **ribelli'one** *sf* rebellion

'ribes *sm inv* currant; ~ **nero** blackcurrant; ~ **rosso** redcurrant

ribol'lire *vi* (*fermentare*) to ferment; (*fare bolle*) to bubble, boil; (*fig*) to seethe

ri'brezzo [ri'breddzo] *sm* disgust, loathing; **far ~ a** to disgust

ribut'tante *ag* disgusting, revolting

rica'dere *vi* to fall again; (*scendere a terra, fig: nel peccato etc*) to fall back; (*vestiti, capelli etc*) to hang (down); (*riversarsi: fatiche, colpe*): ~ **su** to fall on; **rica'duta** *sf* (*MED*) relapse

rical'care *vt* (*disegni*) to trace; (*fig*) to follow faithfully

rica'mare *vt* to embroider

ricambi'are *vt* to change again; (*contraccambiare*) to repay, return; **ri'cambio** *sm* exchange, return; (*FISIOL*) metabolism; **ricambi** *smpl* (*TECN*) spare parts

ri'camo *sm* embroidery

ricapito'lare *vt* to recapitulate, sum up

ricari'care *vt* (*arma, macchina fotografica*) to reload; (*pipa*) to refill; (*orologio*) to rewind; (*batteria*) to recharge

ricat'tare *vt* to blackmail; **ricatta'tore, 'trice** *sm/f* blackmailer; **ri'catto** *sm* blackmail

rica'vare *vt* (*estrarre*) to draw out, extract; (*ottenere*) to obtain, gain; **ri'cavo** *sm* proceeds *pl*

ric'chezza [rik'kettsa] *sf* wealth; (*fig*) richness; **~e** *sfpl* (*beni*) wealth *sg*, riches

'riccio, a ['rittʃo] *ag* curly ♦ *sm* (*ZOOL*) hedgehog; (*: anche:* ~ **di mare**) sea urchin; **'ricciolo** *sm* curl; **ricci'uto, a** *ag* curly

'ricco, a, chi, che *ag* rich; (*persona, paese*) rich, wealthy ♦ *sm/f* rich man/woman; **i ~chi** the rich; ~ **di** full of; rich in

ri'cerca, che [ri'tʃerka] *sf* search; (*indagine*) investigation, inquiry; (*studio*): **la ~** research; **una ~** piece of research

ricer'care [ritʃer'kare] *vt* (*motivi, cause*) to look for, try to determine; (*successo, piacere*) to pursue; (*onore, gloria*) to seek; **ricer'cato, a** *ag* (*apprezzato*) much sought-after; (*affettato*) studied, affected ♦ *sm/f* (*POLIZIA*) wanted man/woman

ri'cetta [ri'tʃetta] *sf* (*MED*) prescription; (*CUC*) recipe

ricettazi'one [ritʃettat'tsjone] *sf* (*DIR*) receiving (stolen goods)

ri'cevere [ri'tʃevere] *vt* to receive; (*stipendio, lettera*) to get, receive; (*accogliere: ospite*) to welcome; (*vedere: cliente, rappresentante etc*) to see; **ricevi'mento** *sm* receiving *no pl*; (*festa*) reception; **ricevi'tore** *sm* (*TECN*) receiver; **ricevito'ria** *sf* lottery *o* pools office; **rice'vuta** *sf* receipt; **ricevuta fiscale** receipt for tax purposes; **ricezi'one** *sf* (*RADIO, TV*) reception

richia'mare [rikja'mare] *vt* (*chiamare indietro, ritelefonare*) to call back; (*ambasciatore, truppe*) to recall; (*rimproverare*) to reprimand; (*attirare*) to attract, draw; **~rsi a** (*riferirsi a*) to refer to; **richi'amo** *sm* call; recall; reprimand; attraction

richi'edere [ri'kjɛdere] *vt* to ask again for; (*chiedere indietro*): **~ qc** to ask for sth back; (*chiedere: per sapere*) to ask; (*: per avere*) to ask for; (*AMM: documenti*) to apply for; (*esigere*) to need, require; **richi'esta** *sf* (*domanda*) request; (*AMM*) application, request; (*esigenza*) demand, request; **a richiesta** on request; **richi'esto, a** *pp di* **richiedere**

rici'clare [ritʃi'klare] *vt* to recycle

'ricino ['ritʃino] *sm*: **olio di ~** castor oil

ricogni'one [rikoɲɲit'tsjone] *sf* (*MIL*) reconnaissance; (*DIR*) recognition, acknowledgement

ricomincia're [rikomin'tʃare] *vt, vi* to start again, begin again

ricom'pensa *sf* reward

ricompen'sare *vt* to reward

riconcili'are [rikontʃi'ljare] *vt* to reconcile; **~rsi** *vr* to be reconciled; **riconciliazi'one** *sf* reconciliation

ricono'scente [rikonoʃ'ʃente] *ag* grateful; **ricono'scenza** *sf* gratitude

rico'noscere [riko'noʃʃere] *vt* to recognize; (*DIR: figlio, debito*) to acknowledge; (*ammettere: errore*) to admit, acknowledge; **riconosci'mento** *sm* recognition; acknowledgement; (*identificazione*) identification; **riconosci'uto, a** *pp di* **riconoscere**

ricopi'are *vt* to copy

rico'prire *vt* (*coprire*) to cover; (*occupare: carica*) to hold

ricor'dare *vt* to remember, recall; (*richiamare alla memoria*): **~ qc a qn** to remind sb of sth; **~rsi** *vr*: **~rsi (di)** to remember; **~rsi di qc/di aver fatto** to remember sth/having done

ri'cordo *sm* memory; (*regalo*) keepsake, souvenir; (*di viaggio*) souvenir; **~i** *smpl* (*memorie*) memoirs

ricor'rente *ag* recurrent, recurring; **ricor'renza** *sf* recurrence; (*festività*) anniversary

ri'correre *vi* (*ripetersi*) to recur; **~ a** (*rivolgersi*) to turn to; (*: DIR*) to appeal to; (*servirsi di*) to have recourse to; **ri'corso, a** *pp di* **ricorrere** ♦ *sm* recurrence; (*DIR*) appeal; **far ricorso a** = **ricorrere a**

ricostitu'ente *ag* (*MED*): **cura ~** tonic

ricostru'ire *vt* (*casa*) to rebuild; (*fatti*) to reconstruct; **ricostruzi'one** *sf* rebuilding *no pl*; reconstruction

ri'cotta *sf* soft white unsalted cheese made from sheep's milk

ricove'rare *vt* to give shelter to; **~ qn in ospedale** to admit sb to hospital

ri'covero *sm* shelter, refuge; (*MIL*) shelter; (*MED*) admission (to hospital)

ricre'are *vt* to recreate; (*fig: distrarre*) to amuse

ricreazi'one *sf* recreation, entertainment; (*INS*) break

ri'credersi *vr* to change one's mind

ricupe'rare *vt* (*rientrare in possesso di*) to recover, get back; (*tempo perduto*) to make up for; (*NAUT*) to salvage; (*: naufraghi*) to rescue; (*delinquente*) to rehabilitate; **~ lo**

svantaggio (*SPORT*) to close the gap
ridacchi'are [ridak'kjare] *vi* to snigger
ri'dare *vt* to return, give back
'**ridere** *vi* to laugh; (*deridere, beffare*): **~ di** to laugh at, make fun of
ri'detto, a *pp di* **ridire**
ri'dicolo, a *ag* ridiculous, absurd
ridimensio'nare *vt* to reorganize; (*fig*) to see in the right perspective
ri'dire *vt* to repeat; (*criticare*) to find fault with; to object to; **trova sempre qualcosa da ~** he always manages to find fault
ridon'dante *ag* redundant
ri'dotto, a *pp di* **ridurre ♦** *ag* (*biglietto*) reduced; (*formato*) small
ri'durre *vt* (*anche CHIM, MAT*) to reduce; (*prezzo, spese*) to cut, reduce; (*accorciare: opera letteraria*) to abridge; (: *RADIO, TV*) to adapt; **ridursi** *vr* (*diminuirsi*) to be reduced, shrink; **ridursi a** to be reduced to; **ridursi pelle e ossa** to be reduced to skin and bone; **ridut'tore** *sm* (*ELEC*) adaptor; **riduzi'one** *sf* reduction; abridgement; adaptation
riem'pire *vt* to fill (up); (*modulo*) to fill in *o* out; **~rsi** *vr* to fill (up); **~ qc di** to fill sth (up) with
rien'tranza [rien'trantsa] *sf* recess; indentation
rien'trare *vi* (*entrare di nuovo*) to go (*o* come) back in; (*tornare*) to return; (*fare una rientranza*) to go in, curve inwards; to be indented; (*riguardare*): **~ in** to be included among, form part of; **ri'entro** *sm* (*ritorno*) return; (*di astronave*) re-entry
riepilo'gare *vt* to summarize ♦ *vi* to recapitulate
ri'fare *vt* to do again; (*ricostruire*) to make again; (*nodo*) to tie again, do up again; (*imitare*) to imitate, copy; **~rsi** *vr* (*risarcirsi*): **~rsi di** to make up for; (*vendicarsi*): **~rsi di qc su qn** to get one's own back on sb for sth; (*riferirsi*): **~rsi a** to go back to; to follow; **~ il letto** to make the bed; **~rsi una vita** to make a new life for o.s.; **ri'fatto, a** *pp di* **rifare**
riferi'mento *sm* reference; **in** *o* **con ~ a** with reference to

rife'rire *vt* (*riportare*) to report ♦ *vi* to do a report; **~rsi** *vr*: **~rsi a** to refer to
rifi'nire *vt* to finish off, put the finishing touches to; **rifini'tura** *sf* finishing touch; **rifiniture** *sfpl* (*di mobile, auto*) finish *sg*
rifiu'tare *vt* to refuse; **~ di fare** to refuse to do; **rifi'uto** *sm* refusal; **rifiuti** *smpl* (*spazzatura*) rubbish *sg*, refuse *sg*
riflessi'one *sf* (*FISICA, meditazione*) reflection; (*il pensare*) thought, reflection; (*osservazione*) remark
rifles'sivo, a *ag* (*persona*) thoughtful, reflective; (*LING*) reflexive
ri'flesso, a *pp di* **riflettere ♦** *sm* (*di luce, allo specchio*) reflection; (*FISIOL*) reflex; **di** *o* **per ~** indirectly
ri'flettere *vt* to reflect ♦ *vi* to think; **~rsi** *vr* to be reflected; **~ su** to think over
riflet'tore *sm* reflector; (*proiettore*) floodlight; searchlight
ri'flusso *sm* flowing back; (*della marea*) ebb; **un'epoca di ~** an era of nostalgia
ri'fondere *vt* to refund, repay
ri'forma *sf* reform; **la R~** (*REL*) the Reformation
rifor'mare *vt* to re-form; (*REL, POL*) to reform; (*MIL: recluta*) to declare unfit for service; (: *soldato*) to invalid out, discharge; **riforma'torio** *sm* (*DIR*) community home (*BRIT*), reformatory (*US*)
riforni'mento *sm* supplying, providing; restocking; **~i** *smpl* (*provviste*) supplies, provisions
rifor'nire *vt* (*provvedere*): **~ di** to supply *o* provide with; (*fornire di nuovo: casa etc*) to restock
rifrazi'one [rifrat'tsjone] *sf* refraction
rifu'gire [rifud'ʒire] *vi* to escape again; (*fig*): **~ da** to shun
rifugi'arsi [rifu'dʒarsi] *vr* to take refuge; **rifugi'ato, a** *sm/f* refugee
ri'fugio [ri'fudʒo] *sm* refuge, shelter; (*in montagna*) shelter; **~ antiaereo** air-raid shelter
'**riga, ghe** *sf* line; (*striscia*) stripe; (*di persone, cose*) line, row; (*regolo*) ruler;

(*scriminatura*) parting; **mettersi in ~** to line up; **a ~ghe** (*foglio*) lined; (*vestito*) striped

ri'**gagnolo** [ri'ɡaɲɲolo] *sm* rivulet

ri'**gare** *vt* (*foglio*) to rule ♦ *vi*: **~ diritto** (*fig*) to toe the line

rigatti'**ere** *sm* junk dealer

riget'**tare** [ridʒet'tare] *vt* (*gettare indietro*) to throw back; (*fig: respingere*) to reject; (*vomitare*) to bring *o* throw up; ri'**getto** *sm* (*anche MED*) rejection

rigidità [ridʒidi'ta] *sf* rigidity; stiffness; severity, rigours *pl*; strictness

'**rigido, a** [ˈridʒido] *ag* rigid, stiff; (*membra etc: indurite*) stiff; (*METEOR*) harsh, severe; (*fig*) strict

rigi'**rare** [ridʒi'rare] *vt* to turn; **~rsi** *vr* to turn round; (*nel letto*) to turn over; **~ qc tra le mani** to turn sth over in one's hands; **~ il discorso** to change the subject

'**rigo, ghi** *sm* line; (*MUS*) staff, stave

rigogli'**oso, a** [riɡoʎ'ʎoso] *ag* (*pianta*) luxuriant; (*fig: commercio, sviluppo*) thriving

ri'**gonfio, a** *ag* swollen

ri'**gore** *sm* (*METEOR*) harshness, rigours *pl*; (*fig*) severity, strictness; (*anche:* **calcio di ~**) penalty; **di ~** compulsory; **a rigor di termini** strictly speaking; **rigo'roso, a** *ag* (*severo: persona, ordine*) strict; (*preciso*) rigorous

rigover'**nare** *vt* to wash (up)

riguar'**dare** *vt* to look at again; (*considerare*) to regard, consider; (*concernere*) to regard, concern; **~rsi** *vr* (*aver cura di sé*) to look after o.s.

rigu'**ardo** *sm* (*attenzione*) care; (*considerazione*) regard, respect; **~ a** concerning, with regard to; **non aver ~i nell'agire/nel parlare** to act/speak freely

rilasci'**are** [rilaʃ'ʃare] *vt* (*rimettere in libertà*) to release; (*AMM: documenti*) to issue; ri'**lascio** *sm* release; issue

rilas'**sare** *vt* to relax; **~rsi** *vr* to relax; (*fig: disciplina*) to become slack

rile'**gare** *vt* (*libro*) to bind; **rilega'tura** *sf* binding

ri'**leggere** [ri'lɛddʒere] *vt* to reread, read again; (*rivedere*) to read over

ri'**lento: a ~** *av* slowly

rileva'**mento** *sm* (*topografico, statistico*) survey; (*NAUT*) bearing

rile'**vante** *ag* considerable; important

rile'**vare** *vt* (*ricavare*) to find; (*notare*) to notice; (*mettere in evidenza*) to point out; (*venire a conoscere: notizia*) to learn; (*raccogliere: dati*) to gather, collect; (*TOPOGRAFIA*) to survey; (*MIL*) to relieve; (*COMM*) to take over

ri'**lievo** *sm* (*ARTE, GEO*) relief; (*fig: rilevanza*) importance; (*TOPOGRAFIA*) survey; **dar ~ a** *o* **mettere in ~ qc** (*fig*) to bring sth out, highlight sth

rilut'**tante** *ag* reluctant; **rilut'tanza** *sf* reluctance

'**rima** *sf* rhyme; (*verso*) verse

riman'**dare** *vt* to send again; (*restituire, rinviare*) to send back, return; (*differire*): **~ qc (a)** to postpone sth *o* put sth off (till); (*fare riferimento*): **~ qn a** to refer sb to; **essere rimandato** (*INS*) to have to repeat one's exams

ri'**mando** *sm* (*rinvio*) return; (*dilazione*) postponement; (*riferimento*) cross-reference

rima'**nente** *ag* remaining ♦ *sm* rest, remainder; **i ~i** (*persone*) the rest of them, the others; **rima'nenza** *sf* rest, remainder; **rimanenze** *sfpl* (*COMM*) unsold stock *sg*

rima'**nere** *vi* (*restare*) to remain, stay; (*avanzare*) to be left, remain; (*restare stupito*) to be amazed; (*restare, mancare*): **rimangono poche settimane a Pasqua** there are only a few weeks left till Easter; **rimane da vedere se** it remains to be seen whether; (*diventare*): **~ vedovo** to be left a widower; (*trovarsi*): **~ sorpreso** to be surprised

ri'**mare** *vt, vi* to rhyme

rimargi'**nare** [rimardʒi'nare] *vt, vi* (*anche:* **~rsi**) to heal

ri'**masto, a** *pp di* **rimanere**

rima'**sugli** [rima'suʎʎi] *smpl* leftovers

rimbal'**zare** [rimbal'tsare] *vi* to bounce back, rebound; (*proiettile*) to ricochet; rim'**balzo** *sm* rebound; ricochet

rimbam'**bito, a** *ag* senile, in one's dotage

rimboc'care vt (coperta) to tuck in; (maniche, pantaloni) to turn o roll up

rimbom'bare vi to resound

rimbor'sare vt to pay back, repay; **rim'borso** sm repayment

rimedi'are vi: ~ **a** to remedy ♦ vt (fam: procurarsi) to get o scrape together

ri'medio sm (medicina) medicine; (cura, fig) remedy, cure

rimesco'lare vt to mix well, stir well; (carte) to shuffle; **sentirsi ~ il sangue** (per paura) to feel one's blood run cold; (per rabbia) to feel one's blood boil

ri'messa sf (locale: per veicoli) garage; (: per aerei) hangar; (COMM: di merce) consignment; (: di denaro) remittance; (TENNIS) return; (CALCIO: anche: ~ **in gioco**) throw-in

ri'messo, a pp di **rimettere**

ri'mettere vt (mettere di nuovo) to put back; (indossare di nuovo): ~ **qc** to put sth back on, put sth on again; (affidare) to entrust; (: decisione) to refer; (condonare) to remit; (COMM: merci) to deliver; (: denaro) to remit; (vomitare) to bring up; (perdere: anche: **rimetterci**) to lose; **~rsi al bello** (tempo) to clear up; **~rsi in salute** to get better, recover one's health

'rimmel ® sm inv mascara

rimoder'nare vt to modernize

rimon'tare vt (meccanismo) to reassemble; (: tenda) to put up again ♦ vi (salire di nuovo): ~ **in** (macchina, treno) to get back into; (SPORT) to close the gap

rimorchi'are [rimor'kjare] vt to tow; (fig: ragazza) to pick up; **rimorchia'tore** sm (NAUT) tug(boat)

ri'morchio [ri'mɔrkjo] sm tow; (veicolo) trailer

ri'morso sm remorse

rimozi'one [rimot'tsjone] sf removal; (da un impiego) dismissal; (PSIC) repression

rim'pasto sm (POL) reshuffle

rimpatri'are vi to return home ♦ vt to repatriate; **rim'patrio** sm repatriation

rimpi'angere [rim'pjandʒere] vt to regret; (persona) to miss; **rimpi'anto, a** pp di

rimpiangere ♦ sm regret

rimpiat'tino sm hide-and-seek

rimpiaz'zare [rimpjat'tsare] vt to replace

rimpiccio'lire [rimpittʃo'lire] vt to make smaller ♦ vi (anche: ~**rsi**) to become smaller

rimpin'zare [rimpin'tsare] vt: ~ **di** to cram o stuff with

rimprove'rare vt to rebuke, reprimand; **rim'provero** sm rebuke, reprimand

rimugi'nare [rimudʒi'nare] vt (fig) to turn over in one's mind

rimunerazi'one [rimunerat'tsjone] sf remuneration; (premio) reward

rimu'overe vt to remove; (destituire) to dismiss

Rinasci'mento [rinaʃʃi'mento] sm: **il ~** the Renaissance

ri'nascita [ri'naʃʃita] sf rebirth, revival

rinca'rare vt to increase the price of ♦ vi to go up, become more expensive

rinca'sare vi to go home

rinchi'udere [rin'kjudere] vt to shut (o lock) up; **~rsi** vr: **~rsi in** to shut o.s. up in; **~rsi in se stesso** to withdraw into o.s.; **rinchi'uso, a** pp di **rinchiudere**

rin'correre vt to chase, run after; **rin'corsa** sf short run; **rin'corso, a** pp di **rincorrere**

rin'crescere [rin'kreʃʃere] vb impers: **mi rincresce che/di non poter fare** I'm sorry that/I can't do, I regret that/being unable to do; **rincresci'mento** sm regret; **rincresci'uto, a** pp di **rincrescere**

rincu'lare vi (arma) to recoil

rinfacci'are [rinfat'tʃare] vt (fig): ~ **qc a qn** to throw sth in sb's face

rinfor'zare [rinfor'tsare] vt to reinforce, strengthen ♦ vi (anche: ~**rsi**) to grow stronger; **rin'forzo** sm: **mettere un rinforzo a** to strengthen; **di rinforzo** (asse, sbarra) strengthening; (esercito) supporting; (personale) extra, additional; **rinforzi** smpl (MIL) reinforcements

rinfran'care vt to encourage, reassure

rinfres'care vt (atmosfera, temperatura) to cool (down); (abito, pareti) to freshen up

♦ vi (tempo) to grow cooler; ~rsi vr (ristorarsi) to refresh o.s.; (lavarsi) to freshen up; rin'fresco, schi sm (festa) party; rinfreschi smpl refreshments

rin'fusa sf: alla ~ in confusion, higgledy-piggledy

ringhi'are [rin'gjare] vi to growl, snarl

ringhi'era [rin'gjɛra] sf railing; (delle scale) banister(s pl)

ringiova'nire [rindʒova'nire] vt (sog: vestito, acconciatura etc): ~ qn to make sb look younger; (: vacanze etc) to rejuvenate ♦ vi (anche: ~rsi) to become (o look) younger

ringrazia'mento [ringrattsja'mento] sm thanks pl

ringrazi'are [ringrat'tsjare] vt to thank; ~ qn di qc to thank sb for sth

rinne'gare vt (fede) to renounce; (figlio) to disown, repudiate; rinne'gato, a sm/f renegade

rinnova'mento sm renewal; (economico) revival

rinno'vare vt to renew; (ripetere) to repeat, renew; rin'novo sm (di contratto) renewal; "chiuso per rinnovo dei locali" "closed for alterations"

rinoce'ronte [rinotʃe'ronte] sm rhinoceros

rino'mato, a ag renowned, celebrated

rinsal'dare vt to strengthen

rintoc'care vi (campana) to toll; (orologio) to strike

rintracci'are [rintrat'tʃare] vt to track down

rintro'nare vi to boom, roar ♦ vt (assordare) to deafen; (stordire) to stun

ri'nuncia [ri'nuntʃa] etc = rinunzia etc

ri'nunzia [ri'nuntsja] sf renunciation

rinunzi'are [rinun'tsjare] vi: ~ a to give up, renounce

rinve'nire vt to find, recover; (scoprire) to discover, find out ♦ vi (riprendere i sensi) to come round; (fiori) to revive

rinvi'are vt (rimandare indietro) to send back, return; (differire): ~ qc (a) to postpone sth o put sth off (till); to adjourn sth (till); (fare un rimando): ~ qn a to refer sb to

rinvigo'rire vt to strengthen

rin'vio, 'vii sm (rimando) return; (differimento) postponement; (: di seduta) adjournment; (in un testo) cross-reference

ri'one sm district, quarter

riordi'nare vt (rimettere in ordine) to tidy; (riorganizzare) to reorganize

riorganiz'zare [riorganid'dzare] vt to reorganize

ripa'gare vt to repay

ripa'rare vt (proteggere) to protect, defend; (correggere: male, torto) to make up for; (: errore) to put right; (aggiustare) to repair ♦ vi (mettere rimedio): ~ a to make up for; ~rsi vr (rifugiarsi) to take refuge o shelter; riparazi'one sf (di un torto) reparation; (di guasto, scarpe) repairing no pl; repair; (risarcimento) compensation

ri'paro sm (protezione) shelter, protection; (rimedio) remedy

ripar'tire vt (dividere) to divide up; (distribuire) to share out ♦ vi to set off again; to leave again

ripas'sare vi to come (o go) back ♦ vt (scritto, lezione) to go over (again); ri'passo sm revision (BRIT), review (US)

ripen'sare vi to think; (cambiare pensiero) to change one's mind; (tornare col pensiero): ~ a to recall

ripercu'otersi vr: ~ su (fig) to have repercussions on

ripercussi'one sf (fig): avere una ~ o delle ~i su to have repercussions on

ripes'care vt (pesce) to catch again; (persona, cosa) to fish out; (fig: ritrovare) to dig out

ri'petere vt to repeat; (ripassare) to go over; ripetizi'one sf repetition; (di lezione) revision; ripetizioni sfpl (INS) private tutoring o coaching sg

ripi'ano sm (di mobile) shelf

ri'picca sf: per ~ out of spite

'ripido, a ag steep

ripie'gare vt to refold; (piegare più volte) to fold (up) ♦ vi (MIL) to retreat, fall back; (fig: accontentarsi): ~ su to make do with; ~rsi vr to bend; ripi'ego, ghi sm expedient ripi'eno, a *ag* full; (*CUC*) stuffed; (: *panino*) filled ♦ *sm* (*CUC*) stuffing

ri'porre *vt* (*porre al suo posto*) to put back, replace; (*mettere via*) to put away; (*fiducia, speranza*): ~ **qc in qn** to place *o* put sth in sb

ripor'tare *vt* (*portare indietro*) to bring (*o* take) back; (*riferire*) to report; (*citare*) to quote; (*vittoria*) to gain; (*successo*) to have; (*MAT*) to carry; ~**rsi a** (*anche fig*) to go back to; (*riferirsi a*) to refer to; ~ **danni** to suffer damage

ripo'sare *vt, vi* to rest; ~**rsi** *vr* to rest; ri'poso *sm* rest; (*MIL*): **riposo!** at ease!; **a riposo** (*in pensione*) retired; **giorno di riposo** day off

ripos'tiglio [ripos'tiʎʎo] *sm* lumber-room

ri'posto, a *pp di* riporre

ri'prendere *vt* (*prigioniero, fortezza*) to recapture; (*prendere indietro*) to take back; (*ricominciare: lavoro*) to resume; (*andare a prendere*) to fetch, come back for; (*riassumere: impiegati*) to take on again, re-employ; (*rimproverare*) to tell off; (*restringere: abito*) to take in; (*CINEMA*) to shoot; ~**rsi** *vr* to recover; (*correggersi*) to correct o.s.; ri'presa *sf* recapture; resumption; (*economica, da malattia, emozione*) recovery; (*AUT*) acceleration *no pl*; (*TEATRO, CINEMA*) rerun; (*CINEMA: presa*) shooting *no pl*; shot; (*SPORT*) second half; (: *PUGILATO*) round; **a più riprese** on several occasions, several times; ri'preso, a *pp di* riprendere

ripristi'nare *vt* to restore

ripro'durre *vt* to reproduce; **riprodursi** *vr* (*BIOL*) to reproduce; (*riformarsi*) to form again; riprodu'zione *sf* reproduction; **riproduzione vietata** all rights reserved

ripudi'are *vt* to repudiate, disown

ripu'gnante [ripuɲ'ɲante] *ag* disgusting, repulsive

ripu'gnare [ripuɲ'ɲare] *vi*: ~ **a qn** to repel *o* disgust sb

ripu'lire *vt* to clean up; (*sog: ladri*) to clean out; (*perfezionare*) to polish, refine

ri'quadro *sm* square; (*ARCHIT*) panel

ri'saia *sf* paddy field

risa'lire *vi* (*ritornare in su*) to go back up; ~ **a** (*ritornare con la mente*) to go back to; (*datare da*) to date back to, go back to

risal'tare *vi* (*fig: distinguersi*) to stand out; (*ARCHIT*) to project, jut out; ri'salto *sm* prominence; (*sporgenza*) projection; **mettere** *o* **porre in risalto qc** to make sth stand out

risa'nare *vt* (*guarire*) to heal, cure; (*palude*) to reclaim; (*economia*) to improve; (*bilancio*) to reorganize

risa'puto, a *ag*: **è ~ che ...** everyone knows that ..., it is common knowledge that ...

risarci'mento [risartʃi'mento] *sm*: ~ **(di)** compensation (for)

risar'cire [risar'tʃire] *vt* (*cose*) to pay compensation for; (*persona*): ~ **qn di qc** to compensate sb for sth

ri'sata *sf* laugh

riscalda'mento *sm* heating; ~ **centrale** central heating

riscal'dare *vt* (*scaldare*) to heat; (: *mani, persona*) to warm; (*minestra*) to reheat; ~**rsi** *vr* to warm up

riscat'tare *vt* (*prigioniero*) to ransom, pay a ransom for; (*DIR*) to redeem; ~**rsi** *vr* (*da disonore*) to redeem o.s.; ris'catto *sm* ransom; redemption

rischia'rare [riskja'rare] *vt* (*illuminare*) to light up; (*colore*) to make lighter; ~**rsi** *vr* (*tempo*) to clear up; (*cielo*) to clear; (*fig: volto*) to brighten up; ~**rsi la voce** to clear one's throat

rischi'are [ris'kjare] *vt* to risk ♦ *vi*: ~ **di fare qc** to run the risk of doing sth

'rischio ['riskjo] *sm* risk; rischi'oso, a *ag* risky, dangerous

riscia'cquare [riʃʃa'kware] *vt* to rinse

riscon'trare *vt* (*rilevare*) to find; ris'contro *sm* confirmation; (*lettera di risposta*) reply

ris'cossa *sf* (*riconquista*) recovery, reconquest; *vedi anche* **riscosso**

riscossi'one *sf* collection

ris'cosso, a *pp di* riscuotere

ris'cuotere *vt* (*ritirare: somma*) to collect; (*: stipendio*) to draw, collect; (*assegno*) to cash; (*fig: successo etc*) to win, earn; **~rsi** *vr*: **~rsi (da)** to shake o.s. (out of), rouse o.s. (from)

risenti'mento *sm* resentment

risen'tire *vt* to hear again; (*provare*) to feel ♦ *vi*: **~ di** to feel (*o* show) the effects of; **~rsi** *vr*: **~rsi di** *o* **per** to take offence at, resent

risen'tito, a *ag* resentful

ri'serbo *sm* reserve

ri'serva *sf* reserve; (*di caccia, pesca*) preserve; (*restrizione, di indigeni*) reservation; **di ~** (*provviste etc*) in reserve

riser'vare *vt* (*tenere in serbo*) to keep, put aside; (*prenotare*) to book, reserve; **~rsi** *vr*: **~rsi di fare qc** to intend to do sth

riserva'tezza *sf* reserve

riser'vato, a *ag* (*prenotato, fig: persona*) reserved; (*confidenziale*) confidential

risi'edere *vi*: **~ a** *o* **in** to reside in

'risma *sf* (*di carta*) ream; (*fig*) kind, sort

'riso (*pl(f)* **~a**: *il ridere*) *sm*: **il ~** laughter; (*pianta*) rice ♦ *pp di* **ridere**

riso'lino *sm* snigger

ri'solto, a *pp di* **risolvere**

risolu'tezza [risolu'tettsa] *sf* determination

riso'luto, a *ag* determined, resolute

risoluzi'one [risolut'tsjone] *sf* solving *no pl*; (*MAT*) solution; (*decisione, di immagine*) resolution

ri'solvere *vt* (*difficoltà, controversia*) to resolve; (*problema*) to solve; (*decidere*): **~ di fare** to resolve to do; **~rsi** *vr* (*decidersi*): **~rsi a fare** to make up one's mind to do; (*andare a finire*): **~rsi in** to end up, turn out; **~rsi in nulla** to come to nothing

riso'nanza [riso'nantsa] *sf* resonance; **aver vasta ~** (*fig: fatto etc*) to be known far and wide

riso'nare *vt, vi* = **risuonare**

ri'sorgere [ri'sordʒere] *vi* to rise again; **risorgi'mento** *sm* revival; **il Risorgimento** (*STORIA*) the Risorgimento

🛈 *The* **Risorgimento** *was the political movement which led to the proclamation of the Kingdom of Italy in 1861, and eventually to unification (1871).*

ri'sorsa *sf* expedient, resort; **~e** *sfpl* (*naturali, finanziarie etc*) resources; **persona piena di ~e** resourceful person

ri'sorto, a *pp di* **risorgere**

ri'sotto *sm* (*CUC*) risotto

risparmi'are *vt* to save; (*non uccidere*) to spare ♦ *vi* to save; **~ qc a qn** to spare sb sth

ris'parmio *sm* saving *no pl*; (*denaro*) savings *pl*

rispec'chiare [rispek'kjare] *vt* to reflect

rispet'tabile *ag* respectable

rispet'tare *vt* to respect; **farsi ~** to command respect

rispet'tivo, a *ag* respective

ris'petto *sm* respect; **~i** *smpl* (*saluti*) respects, regards; **~ a** (*in paragone a*) compared to; (*in relazione a*) as regards, as for; **rispet'toso, a** *ag* respectful

ris'plendere *vi* to shine

ris'pondere *vi* to answer, reply; (*freni*) to respond; **~ a** (*domanda*) to answer, reply to; (*persona*) to answer; (*invito*) to reply to; (*provocazione, sog: veicolo, apparecchio*) to respond to; (*corrispondere a*) to correspond to; (*: speranze, bisogno*) to answer; **~ di** to answer for; **ris'posta** *sf* answer, reply; **in risposta a** in reply to; **risposto, a** *pp di* **rispondere**

'rissa *sf* brawl

ristabi'lire *vt* to re-establish, restore; (*persona: sog: riposo etc*) to restore to health; **~rsi** *vr* to recover

rista'gnare [ristaɲ'ɲare] *vi* (*acqua*) to become stagnant; (*sangue*) to cease flowing; (*fig: industria*) to stagnate; **ris'tagno** *sm* stagnation

ris'tampa *sf* reprinting *no pl*; reprint

risto'rante *sm* restaurant

risto'rarsi *vr* to have something to eat and

drink; (*riposarsi*) to rest, have a rest; **ris'toro** *sm* (*bevanda, cibo*) refreshment; **servizio di ristoro** (FERR) refreshments *pl*

ristret'tezza [ristret'tettsa] *sf* (*strettezza*) narrowness; (*fig: scarsezza*) scarcity, lack; (: *meschinità*) meanness; **~e** *sfpl* (*povertà*) financial straits

ris'tretto, a *pp di* **restringere** ♦ *ag* (*racchiuso*) enclosed, hemmed in; (*angusto*) narrow; (*limitato*): **~ (a)** restricted *o* limited (to); (CUC: *brodo*) thick; (: *caffè*) extra strong

risucchi'are [risuk'kjare] *vt* to suck in

risul'tare *vi* (*dimostrarsi*) to prove (to be), turn out (to be); (*riuscire*): **~ vincitore** to emerge as the winner; **~ da** (*provenire*) to result from, be the result of; **mi risulta che ...** I understand that ...; **non mi risulta** not as far as I know; **risul'tato** *sm* result

risuo'nare *vi* (*rimbombare*) to resound

risurrezi'one [risurret'tsjone] *sf* (REL) resurrection

risusci'tare [risuʃʃi'tare] *vt* to resuscitate, restore to life; (*fig*) to revive, bring back ♦ *vi* to rise (from the dead)

ris'veglio [riz'veʎʎo] *sm* waking up; (*fig*) revival

ris'volto *sm* (*di giacca*) lapel; (*di pantaloni*) turn-up; (*di manica*) cuff; (*di tasca*) flap; (*di libro*) inside flap; (*fig*) implication

ritagli'are [ritaʎ'ʎare] *vt* (*tagliar via*) to cut out; **ri'taglio** *sm* (*di giornale*) cutting, clipping; (*di stoffa etc*) scrap; **nei ritagli di tempo** in one's spare time

ritar'dare *vi* (*persona, treno*) to be late; (*orologio*) to be slow ♦ *vt* (*rallentare*) to slow down; (*impedire*) to delay, hold up; (*differire*) to postpone, delay; **ritarda'tario, a** *sm/f* latecomer

ri'tardo *sm* delay; (*di persona aspettata*) lateness *no pl*; (*fig: mentale*) backwardness; **in ~** late

ri'tegno [ri'teɲɲo] *sm* restraint

rite'nere *vt* (*trattenere*) to hold back; (: *somma*) to deduct; (*giudicare*) to consider, believe; **rite'nuta** *sf* (*sul salario*) deduction

riti'rare *vt* to withdraw; (POL: *richiamare*) to recall; (*andare a prendere: pacco etc*) to collect, pick up; **~rsi** *vr* to withdraw; (*da un'attività*) to retire; (*stoffa*) to shrink; (*marea*) to recede; **riti'rata** *sf* (MIL) retreat; (*latrina*) lavatory; **ri'tiro** *sm* withdrawal; recall; collection; (*luogo appartato*) retreat

'ritmo *sm* rhythm; (*fig*) rate; (: *della vita*) pace, tempo

'rito *sm* rite; **di ~** usual, customary

ritoc'care *vt* (*disegno, fotografia*) to touch up; (*testo*) to alter; **ri'tocco, chi** *sm* touching up *no pl*; alteration

ritor'nare *vi* to return, go (*o* come) back; (*ripresentarsi*) to recur; (*ridiventare*): **~ ricco** to become rich again ♦ *vt* (*restituire*) to return, give back

ritor'nello *sm* refrain

ri'torno *sm* return; **essere di ~** to be back; **avere un ~ di fiamma** (AUT) to backfire; (*fig: persona*) to be back in love again

ritorsi'one *sf* retaliation

ri'trarre *vt* (*trarre indietro, via*) to withdraw; (*distogliere: sguardo*) to turn away; (*rappresentare*) to portray, depict; (*ricavare*) to get, obtain

ritrat'tare *vt* (*disdire*) to retract, take back; (*trattare nuovamente*) to deal with again

ri'tratto, a *pp di* **ritrarre** ♦ *sm* portrait

ri'troso, a *ag* (*restio*): **~ (a)** reluctant (to); (*schivo*) shy; **andare a ~** to go backwards

ritro'vare *vt* to find; (*salute*) to regain; (*persona*) to find; to meet again; **~rsi** *vr* (*essere, capitare*) to find o.s.; (*raccapezzarsi*) to find one's way; (*con senso reciproco*) to meet (again); **ri'trovo** *sm* meeting place; **ritrovo notturno** night club

'ritto, a *ag* (*in piedi*) standing, on one's feet; (*levato in alto*) erect, raised; (: *capelli*) standing on end; (*posto verticalmente*) upright

ritu'ale *ag, sm* ritual

riuni'one *sf* (*adunanza*) meeting; (*riconciliazione*) reunion

riu'nire *vt* (*ricongiungere*) to join (together); (*riconciliare*) to reunite, bring together (again); **~rsi** *vr* (*adunarsi*) to meet; (*tornare insieme*) to be reunited

riu'scire [riuʃʃire] *vi* (*uscire di nuovo*) to go out again, go back out; (*aver esito: fatti, azioni*) to go, turn out; (*aver successo*) to succeed, be successful; (*essere, apparire*) to be, prove; (*raggiungere il fine*) to manage, succeed; **~ a fare qc** to manage to do *o* succeed in doing *o* be able to do sth; **riu'scita** *sf* (*esito*) result, outcome; (*buon esito*) success

'riva *sf* (*di fiume*) bank; (*di lago, mare*) shore

ri'vale *sm/f* rival; **rivalità** *sf* rivalry

ri'valsa *sf* (*rivincita*) revenge

rivalu'tare *vt* (*ECON*) to revalue

rivan'gare *vt* (*ricordi etc*) to dig up (again)

rive'dere *vt* to see again; (*ripassare*) to revise; (*verificare*) to check

rive'lare *vt* to reveal; (*divulgare*) to reveal, disclose; (*dare indizio*) to reveal, show; **~rsi** *vr* (*manifestarsi*) to be revealed; **~rsi onesto** *etc* to prove to be honest *etc*; **rivela'tore, 'trice** *sf* retailer; **~ autorizzato** (*COMM*) authorized dealer

ri'verbero *sm* (*di luce, calore*) reflection; (*di suono*) reverberation

rive'renza [rive'rɛntsa] *sf* reverence; (*inchino*) bow; curtsey

rive'rire *vt* (*rispettare*) to revere; (*salutare*) to pay one's respects to

river'sare *vt* (*anche fig*) to pour; **~rsi** *vr* (*fig: persone*) to pour out

rivesti'mento *sm* covering; coating

rives'tire *vt* to dress again; (*ricoprire*) to cover; to coat; (*fig: carica*) to hold; **~rsi** *vr* to get dressed again; to change (one's clothes)

rivi'era *sf* coast; **la ~ ligure** the Italian Riviera

ri'vincita [ri'vintʃita] *sf* (*SPORT*) return match; (*fig*) revenge

rivis'suto, a *pp di* **rivivere**

ri'vista *sf* review; (*periodico*) magazine, review; (*TEATRO*) revue; variety show

ri'vivere *vi* (*riacquistare forza*) to come alive again; (*tornare in uso*) to be revived
♦ *vt* to relive

ri'volgere [ri'vɔldʒere] *vt* (*attenzione, sguardo*) to turn, direct; (*parole*) to address; **~rsi** *vr* to turn round; (*fig: dirigersi per informazioni*): **~rsi a** to go and see, go and speak to; (*: ufficio*) to enquire at

ri'volta *sf* revolt, rebellion

rivol'tare *vt* to turn over; (*con l'interno all'esterno*) to turn inside out; (*disgustare: stomaco*) to upset, turn; **~rsi** *vr* (*ribellarsi*): **~rsi (a)** to rebel (against)

rivol'tella *sf* revolver

ri'volto, a *pp di* **rivolgere**

rivoluzio'nare [rivoluttsjo'nare] *vt* to revolutionize

rivoluzio'nario, a [rivoluttsjo'narjo] *ag, sm/f* revolutionary

rivoluzi'one [rivolut'tsjone] *sf* revolution

riz'zare [rit'tsare] *vt* to raise, erect; **~rsi** *vr* to stand up; (*capelli*) to stand on end

'roba *sf* stuff, things *pl*; (*possessi, beni*) belongings *pl*, things *pl*, possessions *pl*; **~ da mangiare** things *pl* to eat, food; **~ da matti** sheer madness *o* lunacy

'robot *sm inv* robot

ro'busto, a *ag* robust, sturdy; (*solido: catena*) strong

'rocca, che *sf* fortress

rocca'forte *sf* stronghold

roc'chetto [rok'ketto] *sm* reel, spool

'roccia, ce ['rɔttʃa] *sf* rock; **fare ~** (*SPORT*) to go rock climbing; **roc'cioso, a** *ag* rocky

ro'daggio [ro'daddʒo] *sm* running (*BRIT*) *o* breaking (*US*) in; **in ~** running (*BRIT*) *o* breaking (*US*) in

'Rodano *sm*: **il ~** the Rhone

'rodere *vt* to gnaw (at); (*distruggere poco a poco*) to eat into

rodi'tore *sm* (*ZOOL*) rodent

rodo'dendro *sm* rhododendron

'rogna ['rɔɲɲa] *sf* (*MED*) scabies *sg*; (*fig*) bother, nuisance ro'gnone [ron'none] sm (CUC) kidney

'rogo, ghi sm (per cadaveri) (funeral) pyre; (supplizio): il ~ the stake

rol'lio sm roll(ing)

'Roma sf Rome

Roma'nia sf: la ~ Romania

ro'manico, a, ci, che ag Romanesque

ro'mano, a ag, sm/f Roman

romanti'cismo [romanti'tʃizmo] sm romanticism

ro'mantico, a, ci, che ag romantic

ro'manza [ro'mandza] sf (MUS, LETTERATURA) romance

roman'zesco, a, schi, sche [roman'dzesko] ag (stile, personaggi) fictional; (fig) storybook cpd

romanzi'ere [roman'dzjere] sm novelist

ro'manzo, a [ro'mandzo] ag (LING) romance cpd ♦ sm novel; ~ d'appendice serial (story)

rom'bare vi to rumble, thunder, roar

'rombo sm rumble, thunder, roar; (MAT) rhombus; (ZOOL) turbot; brill

ro'meno, a ag, sm/f, sm = rumeno, a

'rompere vt to break; (fidanzamento) to break off ♦ vi to break; ~rsi vr to break; mi rompe le scatole (fam) he (o she) is a pain in the neck; ~rsi un braccio to break an arm; rompi'capo sm worry, headache; (indovinello) puzzle; (in enigmistica) brainteaser; rompighi'accio sm (NAUT) icebreaker; rompis'catole (fam) sm/f inv pest, pain in the neck

'ronda sf (MIL) rounds pl, patrol

ron'della sf (TECN) washer

'rondine sf (ZOOL) swallow

ron'done sm (ZOOL) swift

ron'zare [ron'dzare] vi to buzz, hum

ron'zino [ron'dzino] sm (peg: cavallo) nag

ron'zio [ron'dzio] sm buzzing

'rosa sf rose ♦ ag inv, sm pink; ro'saio sm (pianta) rosebush, rose tree; (giardino) rose garden; ro'sario sm (REL) rosary; ro'sato, a ag pink, rosy ♦ sm (vino) rosé (wine); ro'seo, a ag (anche fig) rosy

rosicchi'are [rosik'kjare] vt to gnaw (at); (mangiucchiare) to nibble (at)

rosma'rino sm rosemary

'roso, a pp di rodere

roso'lare vt to brown

roso'lia sf (MED) German measles sg, rubella

ro'sone sm rosette; (vetrata) rose window

'rospo sm (ZOOL) toad

ros'setto sm (per labbra) lipstick

'rosso, a ag, sm, sm/f red; il mar R~ the Red Sea; ~ d'uovo egg yolk; ros'sore sm flush, blush

rosticce'ria [rostittʃe'ria] sf shop selling roast meat and other cooked food

ro'tabile ag (percorribile): strada ~ roadway; (FERR): materiale ~ rolling stock

ro'taia sf rut, track; (FERR) rail

ro'tare vt, vi to rotate; rotazi'one sf rotation

rote'are vt, vi to whirl; ~ gli occhi to roll one's eyes

ro'tella sf small wheel; (di mobile) castor

roto'lare vt, vi to roll; ~rsi vr to roll (about)

'rotolo sm roll; andare a ~i (fig) to go to rack and ruin

ro'tonda sf rotunda

ro'tondo, a ag round

'rotta sf (AER, NAUT) course, route; (MIL) rout; a ~ di collo at breakneck speed; essere in ~ con qn to be on bad terms with sb

rot'tame sm fragment, scrap, broken bit; ~i smpl (di nave, aereo etc) wreckage sg

'rotto, a pp di rompere ♦ ag broken; (calzoni) torn, split; per il ~ della cuffia by the skin of one's teeth

rot'tura sf breaking no pl; break; breaking off; (MED) fracture, break

rou'lotte [ru'lɔt] sf caravan

ro'vente ag red-hot

'rovere sm oak

rovesci'are [roveʃ'ʃare] vt (versare in giù) to pour; (: accidentalmente) to spill; (capovolgere) to turn upside down; (gettare a terra) to knock down; (: fig: governo) to overthrow; (piegare all'indietro: testa) to throw back; ~rsi vr (sedia, macchina) to overturn; (*barca*) to capsize; (*liquido*) to spill; (*fig: situazione*) to be reversed

ro'vescio, sci [ro'veʃʃo] *sm* other side, wrong side; (*della mano*) back; (*di moneta*) reverse; (*pioggia*) sudden downpour; (*fig*) setback; (MAGLIA: anche: **punto ~**) purl (stitch); (TENNIS) backhand (stroke); **a ~** upside-down; inside-out; **capire qc a ~** to misunderstand sth

ro'vina *sf* ruin; **andare in ~** (*andare a pezzi*) to collapse; (*fig*) to go to rack and ruin

rovi'nare *vi* to collapse, fall down ♦ *vt* (*danneggiare, fig*) to ruin; rovi'noso, a *ag* disastrous; damaging; violent

rovis'tare *vt* (*casa*) to ransack; (*tasche*) to rummage in (*o* through)

'rovo *sm* (BOT) blackberry bush, bramble bush

'rozzo, a ['roddzo] *ag* rough, coarse

'ruba *sf*: **andare a ~** to sell like hot cakes

ru'bare *vt* to steal; **~ qc a qn** to steal sth from sb

rubi'netto *sm* tap, faucet (US)

ru'bino *sm* ruby

ru'brica, che *sf* (STAMPA) column; (*quadernetto*) index book; address book

'rude *ag* tough, rough

'rudere *sm* (*rovina*) ruins *pl*

rudimen'tale *ag* rudimentary, basic

rudi'menti *smpl* rudiments; basic principles; basic knowledge *sg*

ruffi'ano *sm* pimp

'ruga, ghe *sf* wrinkle

'ruggine ['ruddʒine] *sf* rust

rug'gire [rud'dʒire] *vi* to roar

rugi'ada [ru'dʒada] *sf* dew

ru'goso, a *ag* wrinkled

rul'lare *vi* (*tamburo, nave*) to roll; (*aereo*) to taxi

rul'lino *sm* (FOT) spool; (: *pellicola*) film

'rullo *sm* (*di tamburi*) roll; (*arnese cilindrico*, TIP) roller; **~ compressore** steam roller; **~ di pellicola** roll of film

rum *sm* rum

ru'meno, a *ag, sm/f, sm* Romanian

rumi'nare *vt* (ZOOL) to ruminate

ru'more *sm*: **un ~** a noise, a sound; (*fig*) a rumour; **il ~** noise; rumo'roso, a *ag* noisy

ru'olo *sm* (TEATRO, *fig*) role, part; (*elenco*) roll, register, list; **di ~** permanent, on the permanent staff

ru'ota *sf* wheel; **~ anteriore/posteriore** front/back wheel; **~ di scorta** spare wheel

ruo'tare *vt, vi* = **rotare**

'rupe *sf* cliff

ru'rale *ag* rural, country *cpd*

ru'scello [ruʃ'ʃɛllo] *sm* stream

'ruspa *sf* excavator

rus'sare *vi* to snore

'Russia *sf*: **la ~** Russia; 'russo, a *ag, sm/f, sm* Russian

'rustico, a, ci, che *ag* rustic; (*fig*) rough, unrefined

rut'tare *vi* to belch; 'rutto *sm* belch

'ruvido, a *ag* rough, coarse

ruzzo'lare [ruttso'lare] *vi* to tumble down; ruzzo'loni *av*: **cadere ruzzoloni** to tumble down

S, s

S. *abbr* (= *sud*) S

sa *vb vedi* **sapere**

'sabato *sm* Saturday; **di *o* il ~** on Saturdays

'sabbia *sf* sand; **~e mobili** quicksand(s); sabbi'oso, a *ag* sandy

sabo'taggio [sabo'taddʒo] *sm* sabotage

sabo'tare *vt* to sabotage

'sacca, che *sf* bag; (*bisaccia*) haversack; **~ da viaggio** travelling bag

sacca'rina *sf* saccharin(e)

sac'cente [sat'tʃente] *sm/f* know-all (BRIT), know-it-all (US)

saccheggi'are [sakked'dʒare] *vt* to sack, plunder; sac'cheggio *sm* sack(ing)

sac'chetto [sak'ketto] *sm* (small) bag; (small) sack

'sacco, chi *sm* bag; (*per carbone etc*) sack; (ANAT, BIOL) sac; (*tela*) sacking; (*saccheggio*) sack(ing); (*fig: grande quantità*): **un ~ di** lots of, heaps of; **~ a pelo** sleeping bag; **~ per i rifiuti** bin bag

sacer'dote [satʃer'dɔte] *sm* priest; **sacer'dozio** *sm* priesthood

sacra'mento *sm* sacrament

sacrifi'care *vt* to sacrifice; **~rsi** *vr* to sacrifice o.s.; (*privarsi di qc*) to make sacrifices

sacri'ficio [sakri'fitʃo] *sm* sacrifice

sacri'legio [sakri'lɛdʒo] *sm* sacrilege

'sacro, a *ag* sacred

'sadico, a, ci, che *ag* sadistic ♦ *sm/f* sadist

sa'etta *sf* arrow; (*fulmine: anche fig*) thunderbolt; flash of lightning

sa'fari *sm inv* safari

sa'gace [sa'gatʃe] *ag* shrewd, sagacious

sag'gezza [sad'dʒettsa] *sf* wisdom

saggi'are [sad'dʒare] *vt* (*metalli*) to assay; (*fig*) to test

'saggio, a, gi, ge ['saddʒo] *ag* wise ♦ *sm* (*persona*) sage; (*esperimento*) test; (*fig: prova*) proof; (*campione*) sample; (*scritto*) essay

Sagit'tario [sadʒit'tarjo] *sm* Sagittarius

'sagoma *sf* (*profilo*) outline, profile; (*forma*) form, shape; (*TECN*) template; (*bersaglio*) target; (*fig: persona*) character

'sagra *sf* festival

sagres'tano *sm* sacristan; sexton

sagres'tia *sf* sacristy

Sa'hara [sa'ara] *sm*: **il (deserto del) ~** the Sahara (Desert)

'sai *vb vedi* **sapere**

'sala *sf* hall; (*stanza*) room; **~ d'aspetto** waiting room; **~ da ballo** ballroom; **~ per concerti** concert hall; **~ da gioco** gaming room; **~ operatoria** operating theatre; **~ da pranzo** dining room

sa'lame *sm* salami *no pl*, salami sausage

sala'moia *sf* (*CUC*) brine

sa'lare *vt* to salt

sa'lario *sm* pay, wages *pl*

sa'lato, a *ag* (*sapore*) salty; (*CUC*) salted, salt *cpd*; (*fig: prezzo*) steep, stiff

sal'dare *vt* (*congiungere*) to join, bind; (*parti metalliche*) to solder; (*: con saldatura autogena*) to weld; (*conto*) to settle, pay; **salda'tura** *sf* soldering; welding; (*punto*

saldato) soldered joint; weld

sal'dezza [sal'dettsa] *sf* firmness; strength

'saldo, a *ag* (*resistente, forte*) strong, firm; (*fermo*) firm, steady, stable; (*fig*) firm, steadfast ♦ *sm* (*svendita*) sale; (*di conto*) settlement; (*ECON*) balance

'sale *sm* salt; (*fig*): **ha poco ~ in zucca** he doesn't have much sense; **~ fino/grosso** table/cooking salt

'salice ['salitʃe] *sm* willow; **~ piangente** weeping willow

sali'ente *ag* (*fig*) salient, main

sali'era *sf* salt cellar

sa'lina *sf* saltworks *sg*

sa'lino, a *ag* saline

sa'lire *vi* to go (*o come*) up; (*aereo etc*) to climb, go up; (*passeggero*) to get on; (*sentiero, prezzi, livello*) to go up, rise ♦ *vt* (*scale, gradini*) to go (*o come*) up; **~ su** to climb (up); **~ sul treno/sull'autobus** to board the train/the bus; **~ in macchina** to get into the car; **sa'lita** *sf* climb, ascent; (*erta*) hill, slope; **in salita** *ag, av* uphill

sa'liva *sf* saliva

'salma *sf* corpse

'salmo *sm* psalm

sal'mone *sm* salmon

sa'lone *sm* (*stanza*) sitting room, lounge; (*in albergo*) lounge; (*su nave*) lounge, saloon; (*mostra*) show, exhibition; **~ di bellezza** beauty salon

sa'lotto *sm* lounge, sitting room; (*mobilio*) lounge suite

sal'pare *vi* (*NAUT*) to set sail; (*anche: ~ l'ancora*) to weigh anchor

'salsa *sf* (*CUC*) sauce; **~ di pomodoro** tomato sauce

sal'siccia, ce [sal'sittʃa] *sf* pork sausage

sal'tare *vi* to jump, leap; (*esplodere*) to blow up, explode; (*: valvola*) to blow; (*venir via*) to pop off; (*non aver luogo: corso etc*) to be cancelled ♦ *vt* to jump (over), leap (over); (*fig: pranzo, capitolo*) to skip, miss (out); (*CUC*) to sauté; **far ~** to blow up; to burst open; **~ fuori** (*fig: apparire all'improvviso*) to turn up

saltel'lare *vi* to skip; to hop

saltim'banco *sm* acrobat

'salto *sm* jump; (*SPORT*) jumping; **fare un ~** to jump, leap; **fare un ~ da qn** to pop over to sb's (place); **~ in alto/lungo** high/long jump; **~ con l'asta** pole vaulting; **~ mortale** somersault

saltu'ario, a *ag* occasional, irregular

sa'lubre *ag* healthy, salubrious

salume'ria *sf* delicatessen

sa'lumi *smpl* salted pork meats

salu'tare *ag* healthy; (*fig*) salutary, beneficial ♦ *vt* (*incontrandosi*) to greet; (*congedandosi*) to say goodbye to; (*MIL*) to salute

sa'lute *sf* health; **~!** (*a chi starnutisce*) bless you!; (*nei brindisi*) cheers!; **bere alla ~ di qn** to drink (to) sb's health

sa'luto *sm* (*gesto*) wave; (*parola*) greeting; (*MIL*) salute; **~i** *smpl* (*formula di cortesia*) greetings; **cari ~i** best regards; **vogliate gradire i nostri più distinti ~i** Yours faithfully

salvacon'dotto *sm* (*MIL*) safe-conduct

salva'gente [salva'dʒɛnte] *sm* (*NAUT*) lifebuoy; (*ciambella*) life belt; (*giubbotto*) lifejacket; (*stradale*) traffic island

salvaguar'dare *vt* to safeguard

sal'vare *vt* to save; (*trarre da un pericolo*) to rescue; (*proteggere*) to protect; **~rsi** *vr* to save o.s.; to escape; **salva'taggio** *sm* rescue; **salva'tore, 'trice** *sm/f* saviour

'salve (*fam*) *escl* hi!

sal'vezza [sal'vettsa] *sf* salvation; (*sicurezza*) safety

'salvia *sf* (*BOT*) sage

salvi'etta *sf* napkin; **~ umidificata** baby wipe

'salvo, a *ag* safe, unhurt, unharmed; (*fuori pericolo*) safe, out of danger ♦ *sm*: **in ~** safe ♦ *prep* (*eccetto*) except; **mettere qc in ~** to put sth in a safe place; **~ che** (*a meno che*) unless; (*eccetto che*) except (that); **~ imprevisti** barring accidents

sam'buco *sm* elder (tree)

san *ag vedi* santo

sa'nare *vt* to heal, cure; (*economia*) to put right

san'cire [san'tʃire] *vt* to sanction

'sandalo *sm* (*BOT*) sandalwood; (*calzatura*) sandal

'sangue *sm* blood; **farsi cattivo ~** to fret, get in a state; (*fig*) sang-froid, calm; **a ~ freddo** in cold blood; **sangu'igno, a** *ag* blood *cpd*; (*colore*) blood-red; **sangui'nare** *vi* to bleed; **sangui'noso, a** *ag* bloody; **sangui'suga** *sf* leech

sanità *sf* health; (*salubrità*) healthiness; **Ministero della S~** Department of Health; **~ mentale** sanity

sani'tario, a *ag* health *cpd*; (*condizioni*) sanitary ♦ *sm* (*AMM*) doctor; (**impianti**) **~i** *smpl* bathroom *o* sanitary fittings

'sanno *vb vedi* sapere

'sano, a *ag* healthy; (*denti, costituzione*) healthy, sound; (*integro*) whole, unbroken; (*fig: politica, consigli*) sound; **~ di mente** sane; **di ~a pianta** completely, entirely; **~ e salvo** safe and sound

sant' *ag vedi* santo

santifi'care *vt* to sanctify; (*feste*) to observe

santità *sf* sanctity; holiness; **Sua/Vostra ~** (*titolo di Papa*) His/Your Holiness

'santo, a *ag* holy; (*fig*) saintly; (*seguito da nome proprio*) saint ♦ *sm/f* saint; **la S~a Sede** the Holy See

santu'ario *sm* sanctuary

sanzio'nare [santsjo'nare] *vt* to sanction

sanzi'one [san'tsjone] *sf* sanction; (*penale, civile*) sanction, penalty

sa'pere *vt* to know; (*essere capace di*): **so nuotare** I know how to swim, I can swim ♦ *vi*: **~ di** (*aver sapore*) to taste of; (*aver odore*) to smell of ♦ *sm* knowledge; **far ~ qc a qn** to inform sb about sth, let sb know sth; **mi sa che non sia vero** I don't think that's true

sapi'enza [sa'pjɛntsa] *sf* wisdom

sa'pone *sm* soap; **~ da bucato** washing soap; **sapo'netta** *sf* cake *o* bar *o* tablet of soap

sa'pore *sm* taste, flavour; **sapo'rito, a** *ag* tasty

sappi'amo vb vedi **sapere**

saraci'nesca [saratʃi'neska] sf (serranda) rolling shutter

sar'casmo sm sarcasm no pl; sarcastic remark

Sar'degna [sar'deɲɲa] sf: **la ~** Sardinia

sar'dina sf sardine

'sardo, a ag, sm/f Sardinian

'sarto, a sm/f tailor/dressmaker; **sarto'ria** sf tailor's (shop); dressmaker's (shop); (casa di moda) fashion house; (arte) couture

'sasso sm stone; (ciottolo) pebble; (masso) rock

sas'sofono sm saxophone

sas'soso, a ag stony; pebbly

Satana sm Satan; **sa'tanico, a, ci, che** ag satanic, fiendish

sa'tellite sm, ag satellite

satira sf satire

'saturo, a ag saturated; (fig): **~ di** full of

'sauna sf sauna

Sa'voia sf Savoy

savoi'ardo, a ag of Savoy, Savoyard ♦ sm (biscotto) sponge finger

sazi'are [sat'tsjare] vt to satisfy, satiate; **~rsi** vr: **~rsi (di)** to eat one's fill (of); (fig): **~rsi di** to grow tired o weary of

'sazio, a ['sattsjo] ag: **~ (di)** sated (with), full (of); (fig: stufo) fed up (with), sick (of)

sba'dato, a ag careless, inattentive

sbadigli'are [zbadiʎ'ʎare] vi to yawn; **sba'diglio** sm yawn

sbagli'are [zbaʎ'ʎare] vt to make a mistake in, get wrong ♦ vi to make a mistake, be mistaken, be wrong; (operare in modo non giusto) to err; **~rsi** vr to make a mistake, be mistaken, be wrong; **~ la mira/strada** to miss one's aim/take the wrong road; **'sbaglio** sm mistake, error; (morale) error; **fare uno sbaglio** to make a mistake

sbal'lare vt (merce) to unpack ♦ vi (nel fare un conto) to overestimate; (fam: gergo della droga) to get high

sballot'tare vt to toss (about)

sbalor'dire vt to stun, amaze ♦ vi to be stunned, be amazed; **sbalordi'tivo, a** ag amazing; (prezzo) incredible, absurd

sbal'zare [zbal'tsare] vt to throw, hurl ♦ vi (balzare) to bounce; (saltare) to leap, bound; **'sbalzo** sm (spostamento improvviso) jolt, jerk; **a sbalzi** jerkily; (fig) in fits and starts; **uno sbalzo di temperatura** a sudden change in temperature

sban'dare vi (NAUT) to list; (AER) to bank; (AUT) to skid; **~rsi** vr (folla) to disperse

sbandie'rare vt (bandiera) to wave; (fig) to parade, show off

sbaragli'are [zbaraʎ'ʎare] vt (MIL) to rout; (in gare sportive etc) to beat, defeat

sba'raglio [zbara'ʎʎo] sm rout; defeat; **gettarsi allo ~** to risk everything

sbaraz'zarsi [zbarat'tsarsi] vr: **~ di** to get rid of, rid o.s. of

sbar'care vt (passeggeri) to disembark; (merci) to unload ♦ vi to disembark; **'sbarco** sm disembarkation; unloading; (MIL) landing

'sbarra sf bar; (di passaggio a livello) barrier; (DIR): **presentarsi alla ~** to appear before the court

sbarra'mento sm (stradale) barrier; (diga) dam, barrage; (MIL) barrage

sbar'rare vt (strada etc) to block, bar; (assegno) to cross; **~ il passo** to bar the way; **~ gli occhi** to open one's eyes wide

'sbattere vt (porta) to slam, bang; (tappeti, ali, CUC) to beat; (urtare) to knock, hit ♦ vi (porta, finestra) to bang; (agitarsi: ali, vele etc) to flap; **me ne sbatto!** (fam) I don't give a damn!; **sbat'tuto, a** ag (viso, aria) dejected, worn out; (uovo) beaten

sba'vare vi to dribble; (colore) to smear, smudge

sbia'dire vi, vt to fade; **~rsi** vr to fade, **sbia'dito, a** ag faded; (fig) colourless, dull

sbian'care vt to whiten; (tessuto) to bleach ♦ vi (impallidire) to grow pale o white

sbi'eco, a, chi, che ag (storto) squint, askew; **di ~: guardare qn di ~** (fig) to look askance at sb; **tagliare una stoffa di ~** to cut a material on the bias

sbigot'tire vt to dismay, stun ♦ vi (anche: **~rsi**) to be dismayed

sbilanci'are [zbilan'tʃare] *vt* to throw off balance; **~rsi** *vr* (*perdere l'equilibrio*) to overbalance, lose one's balance; (*fig: compromettersi*) to compromise o.s.

sbirci'are [zbir'tʃare] *vt* to cast sidelong glances at, eye

'sbirro (*peg*) *sm* cop

sbizzar'rirsi [zbiddzar'rirsi] *vr* to indulge one's whims

sbloc'care *vt* to unblock, free; (*freno*) to release; (*prezzi, affitti*) to decontrol

sboc'care *vi*: **~ in** (*fiume*) to flow into; (*strada*) to lead into; (*persona*) to come (out) into; (*fig: concludersi*) to end (up) in

sboc'cato, a *ag* (*persona*) foul-mouthed; (*linguaggio*) foul

sbocci'are [zbot'tʃare] *vi* (*fiore*) to bloom, open (out)

'sbocco, chi *sm* (*di fiume*) mouth; (*di strada*) end; (*di tubazione, COMM*) outlet; (*uscita: anche fig*) way out; **siamo in una situazione senza ~chi** there's no way out of this for us

sbol'lire *vi* (*fig*) to cool down, calm down

'sbornia (*fam*) *sf*: **prendersi una ~** to get plastered

sbor'sare *vt* (*denaro*) to pay out

sbot'tare *vi*: **~ in una risata/per la collera** to burst out laughing/explode with anger

sbotto'nare *vt* to unbutton, undo

sbrai'tare *vi* to yell, bawl

sbra'nare *vt* to tear to pieces

sbricio'lare [zbritʃo'lare] *vt* to crumble; **~rsi** *vr* to crumble

sbri'gare *vt* to deal with; **~rsi** *vr* to hurry (up); **sbriga'tivo, a** *ag* (*persona, modo*) quick, expeditious; (*giudizio*) hasty

sbrindel'lato, a *ag* tattered, in tatters

sbrodo'lare *vt* to stain, dirty

'sbronza ['zbrontsa] (*fam*) *sf* (*ubriaco*): **prendersi una ~** to get plastered

'sbronzo, a ['zbrontso] (*fam*) *ag* plastered

sbruf'fone, a *sm/f* boaster

sbu'care *vi* to come out, emerge; (*improvvisamente*) to pop out (*o* up)

sbucci'are [zbut'tʃare] *vt* (*arancia, patata*)

to peel; (*piselli*) to shell; **~rsi un ginocchio** to graze one's knee

sbudel'larsi *vr*: **~ dalle risa** to split one's sides laughing

sbuf'fare *vi* (*persona, cavallo*) to snort; (: *ansimare*) to puff, pant; (*treno*) to puff; **'sbuffo** *sm* (*di aria, fumo, vapore*) puff; **maniche a sbuffo** puff(ed) sleeves

'scabbia *sf* (*MED*) scabies *sg*

sca'broso, a *ag* (*fig: difficile*) difficult, thorny; (: *imbarazzante*) embarrassing; (: *sconcio*) indecent

scacchi'era [skak'kjera] *sf* chessboard

scacci'are [skat'tʃare] *vt* to chase away *o* out, drive away *o* out

'scacco, chi *sm* (*pezzo del gioco*) chessman; (*quadretto di scacchiera*) square; (*fig*) setback, reverse; **~chi** *smpl* (*gioco*) chess *sg*; **a ~chi** (*tessuto*) check(ed); **scacco'matto** *sm* checkmate

sca'dente *ag* shoddy, of poor quality

sca'denza [ska'dentsa] *sf* (*di cambiale, contratto*) maturity; (*di passaporto*) expiry date; **a breve/lunga ~** short-/long-term; **data di ~** expiry date

sca'dere *vi* (*contratto etc*) to expire; (*debito*) to fall due; (*valore, forze, peso*) to decline, go down

sca'fandro *sm* (*di palombaro*) diving suit; (*di astronauta*) space-suit

scaf'fale *sm* shelf; (*mobile*) set of shelves

'scafo *sm* (*NAUT, AER*) hull

scagio'nare [skadʒo'nare] *vt* to exonerate, free from blame

'scaglia ['skaʎʎa] *sf* (*ZOOL*) scale; (*scheggia*) chip, flake

scagli'are [skaʎ'ʎare] *vt* (*lanciare: anche fig*) to hurl, fling; **~rsi** *vr*: **~rsi su *o* contro** to hurl *o* fling o.s. at; (*fig*) to rail at

scaglio'nare [skaʎʎo'nare] *vt* (*pagamenti*) to space out, spread out; (*MIL*) to echelon; **scagli'one** *sm* echelon; (*GEO*) terrace; **a scaglioni** in groups

'scala *sf* (*a gradini etc*) staircase, stairs *pl*; (*a pioli, di corda*) ladder; (*MUS, GEO, di colori, valori, fig*) scale; **~e** *sfpl* (*scalinata*) stairs; **su vasta ~/~ ridotta** on a large/small scale; ~ **a libretto** stepladder; ~ **mobile** escalator; (ECON) sliding scale; ~ **mobile (dei salari)** index-linked pay scale

---
Scala

ℹ️ Milan's world-famous **la Scala** *theatre first opened its doors in 1778 with a performance of Salieri's opera, "L'Europa riconosciuta". It suffered serious damage in the bombing of Milan in 1943 and reopened in 1946 with a concert conducted by Toscanini. It also has a famous classical dance school.*

---

sca'lare vt (ALPINISMO, muro) to climb, scale; (debito) to scale down, reduce; sca'lata sf scaling no pl, climbing no pl; (arrampicata, fig) climb; scala'tore, 'trice sm/f climber

scalda'bagno [skalda'baɲɲo] sm water-heater

scal'dare vt to heat; ~rsi vr to warm up, heat up; (al fuoco, al sole) to warm o.s.; (fig) to get excited

scal'fire vt to scratch

scali'nata sf staircase

sca'lino sm (anche fig) step; (di scala a pioli) rung

'scalo sm (NAUT) slipway; (: porto d'approdo) port of call; (AER) stopover; **fare ~ (a)** (NAUT) to call (at), put in (at); (AER) to land a stop (at); ~ **merci** (FERR) goods (BRIT) o freight yard

scalop'pina sf (CUC) escalope

scal'pello sm chisel

scal'pore sm noise, row; **far ~** (notizia) to cause a sensation o a stir

'scaltro, a ag cunning, shrewd

'scalzo, a ['skaltso] ag barefoot

scambi'are vt to exchange; (confondere): ~ **qn/qc per** to take o mistake sb/sth for; **mi hanno scambiato il cappello** they've given me the wrong hat

scambi'evole ag mutual, reciprocal

'scambio sm exchange; (FERR) points pl; **fare (uno) ~** to make a swap

scampa'gnata [skampaɲ'ɲata] sf trip to

the country

scam'pare vt (salvare) to rescue, save; (evitare: morte, prigione) to escape ♦ vi: ~ **(a qc)** to survive (sth), escape (sth); **scamparla bella** to have a narrow escape

'scampo sm (salvezza) escape; (ZOOL) prawn; **cercare ~ nella fuga** to seek safety in flight

'scampolo sm remnant

scanala'tura sf (incavo) channel, groove

scandagli'are [skandaʎ'ʎare] vt (NAUT) to sound; (fig) to sound out; to probe

scandaliz'zare [skandalid'dzare] vt to shock, scandalize; ~rsi vr to be shocked

'scandalo sm scandal

Scandi'navia sf: **la ~** Scandinavia; scandi'navo, a ag, sm/f Scandinavian

scan'dire vt (versi) to scan; (parole) to articulate, pronounce distinctly; ~ **il tempo** (MUS) to beat time

scan'nare vt (animale) to butcher, slaughter; (persona) to cut o slit the throat of

'scanno sm seat, bench

scansafa'tiche [skansafa'tike] sm/f inv idler, loafer

scan'sare vt (rimuovere) to move (aside), shift; (schivare: schiaffo) to dodge; (sfuggire) to avoid; ~rsi vr to move aside

scan'sia sf shelves pl; (per libri) bookcase

'scanso sm: **a ~ di** in order to avoid, as a precaution against

scanti'nato sm basement

scanto'nare vi to turn the corner; (svignarsela) to sneak off

scapacci'one [skapat'tʃone] sm clout

scapes'trato, a ag dissolute

'scapito sm: **a ~ di** to the detriment of

'scapola sf shoulder blade

'scapolo sm bachelor

scappa'mento sm (AUT) exhaust

scap'pare vi (fuggire) to escape; (andare via in fretta) to rush off; **lasciarsi ~ un'occasione** to let an opportunity go by; ~ **di prigione** to escape from prison; ~ **di mano** (oggetto) to slip out of one's hands; ~ **di mente a qn** to slip sb's mind; **mi**

scappò detto I let it slip; **scap'pata** *sf* quick visit *o* call; **scappa'tella** *sf* escapade; **scappa'toia** *sf* way out

scara'beo *sm* beetle

scarabocchi'are [skarabok'kjare] *vt* to scribble, scrawl; **scara'bocchio** *sm* scribble, scrawl

scara'faggio [skara'faddʒo] *sm* cockroach

scaraven'tare *vt* to fling, hurl

scarce'rare [skartʃe'rare] *vt* to release (from prison)

scardi'nare *vt*: **~ una porta** to take a door off its hinges

'scarica, che *sf* (*di più armi*) volley of shots; (*di sassi, pugni*) hail, shower; (*ELETTR*) discharge; **~ di mitra** burst of machine-gun fire

scari'care *vt* (*merci, camion etc*) to unload; (*passeggeri*) to set down, put off; (*arma*) to unload; (: *sparare, ELETTR*) to discharge; (*sog: corso d'acqua*) to empty, pour; (*fig: liberare da un peso*) to unburden, relieve; **~rsi** *vr* (*orologio*) to run *o* wind down; (*batteria, accumulatore*) to go flat *o* dead; (*fig: rilassarsi*) to unwind; (: *sfogarsi*) to let off steam; **scarica'tore** *sm* (*di porto*) docker

'scarico, a, chi, che *ag* unloaded; (*orologio*) run down; (*accumulatore*) dead, flat ♦ *sm* (*di merci, materiali*) unloading; (*di immondizie*) dumping, tipping (*BRIT*); (*TECN: deflusso*) draining; (: *dispositivo*) drain; (*AUT*) exhaust

scarlat'tina *sf* scarlet fever

scar'latto, a *ag* scarlet

'scarno, a *ag* thin, bony

'scarpa *sf* shoe; **~e da ginnastica/tennis** gym/tennis shoes

scar'pata *sf* escarpment

scar'pone *sm* boot; **~i da sci** ski-boots

scarseggi'are [skarsed'dʒare] *vi* to be scarce; **~ di** to be short of, lack

scar'sezza [skar'settsa] *sf* scarcity, lack

'scarso, a *ag* (*insufficiente*) insufficient, meagre; (*povero: annata*) poor, lean; (*INS: voto*) poor; **~ di** lacking in; **3 chili ~i** just under 3 kilos, barely 3 kilos

scarta'mento *sm* (*FERR*) gauge; **~ normale/ridotto** standard/narrow gauge

scar'tare *vt* (*pacco*) to unwrap; (*idea*) to reject; (*MIL*) to declare unfit for military service; (*carte da gioco*) to discard; (*CALCIO*) to dodge (past) ♦ *vi* to swerve

'scarto *sm* (*cosa scartata, anche COMM*) reject; (*di veicolo*) swerve; (*differenza*) gap, difference

scassi'nare *vt* to break, force

'scasso *sm vedi* **furto**

scate'nare *vt* (*fig*) to incite, stir up; **~rsi** *vr* (*temporale*) to break; (*rivolta*) to break out; (*persona: infuriarsi*) to rage

'scatola *sf* box; (*di latta*) tin (*BRIT*), can; **cibi in ~** tinned (*BRIT*) *o* canned foods; **~ cranica** cranium

scat'tare *vt* (*fotografia*) to take ♦ *vi* (*congegno, molla etc*) to be released; (*balzare*) to spring up; (*SPORT*) to put on a spurt; (*fig: per l'ira*) to fly into a rage; **~ in piedi** to spring to one's feet

'scatto *sm* (*dispositivo*) release; (: *di arma da fuoco*) trigger mechanism; (*rumore*) click; (*balzo*) jump, start; (*SPORT*) spurt; (*fig: di ira etc*) fit; (: *di stipendio*) increment; **di ~** suddenly

scatu'rire *vi* to gush, spring

scaval'care *vt* (*ostacolo*) to pass (*o* climb) over; (*fig*) to get ahead of, overtake

sca'vare *vt* (*terreno*) to dig; (*legno*) to hollow out; (*pozzo, galleria*) to bore; (*città sepolta etc*) to excavate

'scavo *sm* excavating *no pl*; excavation

'scegliere ['ʃeʎʎere] *vt* to choose, select

sce'icco, chi [ʃe'ikko] *sm* sheik

scelle'rato, a [ʃelle'rato] *ag* wicked, evil

scel'lino [ʃel'lino] *sm* shilling

'scelta ['ʃelta] *sf* choice; selection; **di prima ~** top grade *o* quality; **frutta o formaggi a ~** choice of fruit or cheese

'scelto, a ['ʃelto] *pp di* **scegliere** ♦ *ag* (*gruppo*) carefully selected; (*frutta, verdura*) choice, top quality; (*MIL: specializzato*) crack *cpd*, highly skilled

sce'mare [ʃe'mare] *vt, vi* to diminish

'scemo, a ['ʃemo] *ag* stupid, silly

'**scempio** ['ʃempjo] *sm* slaughter, massacre; (*fig*) ruin; **far ~ di** (*fig*) to play havoc with, ruin

'**scena** ['ʃena] *sf* (*gen*) scene; (*palcoscenico*) stage; **le ~e** (*fig: teatro*) the stage; **fare una ~** to make a scene; **andare in ~** to be staged *o* put on *o* performed; **mettere in ~** to stage

sce'**nario** [ʃe'narjo] *sm* scenery; (*di film*) scenario

sce'**nata** [ʃe'nata] *sf* row, scene

'**scendere** ['ʃendere] *vi* to go (*o* come) down; (*strada, sole*) to go down; (*notte*) to fall; (*passeggero: fermarsi*) to get out, alight; (*fig: temperatura, prezzi*) to go *o* come down, fall, drop ♦ *vt* (*scale, pendio*) to go (*o* come) down; **~ dalle scale** to go (*o* come) down the stairs; **~ dal treno** to get off *o* out of the train; **~ dalla macchina** to get out of the car; **~ da cavallo** to dismount, get off one's horse

'**scenico, a, ci, che** ['ʃeniko] *ag* stage *cpd*, scenic

scervel'**lato, a** [ʃervel'lato] *ag* featherbrained, scatterbrained

'**sceso, a** ['ʃeso] *pp di* **scendere**

'**scettico, a, ci, che** ['ʃettiko] *ag* sceptical

'**scettro** ['ʃettro] *sm* sceptre

'**scheda** ['skeda] *sf* (index) card; **~ elettorale** ballot paper; **~ telefonica** phone card; **sche'dare** *vt* (*dati*) to file; (*libri*) to catalogue; (*registrare: anche POLIZIA*) to put on one's files; **sche'dario** *sm* file; (*mobile*) filing cabinet

'**scheggia, ge** ['skeddʒa] *sf* splinter, sliver

'**scheletro** ['skeletro] *sm* skeleton

'**schema, i** ['skema] *sm* (*diagramma*) diagram, sketch; (*progetto, abbozzo*) outline, plan

'**scherma** ['skerma] *sf* fencing

scher'**maglia** [sker'maʎʎa] *sf* (*fig*) skirmish

'**schermo** ['skermo] *sm* shield, screen; (*CINEMA, TV*) screen

scher'**nire** [sker'nire] *vt* to mock, sneer at; '**scherno** *sm* mockery, derision

scher'**zare** [sker'tsare] *vi* to joke

'**scherzo** ['skertso] *sm* joke; (*tiro*) trick; (*MUS*) scherzo; **è uno ~!** (*una cosa facile*) it's child's play!, it's easy!; **per ~** in jest; for a joke *o* a laugh; **fare un brutto ~ a qn** to play a nasty trick on sb; **scher'zoso, a** *ag* (*tono, gesto*) playful; (*osservazione*) facetious; **è un tipo scherzoso** he likes a joke

schiaccia'**noci** [skjattʃa'notʃi] *sm inv* nutcracker

schiacci'**are** [skjat'tʃare] *vt* (*dito*) to crush; (*noci*) to crack; **~ un pisolino** to have a nap

schiaffeggi'**are** [skjaffed'dʒare] *vt* to slap

schi'**affo** ['skjaffo] *sm* slap

schiamaz'**zare** [skjamat'tsare] *vi* to squawk, cackle

schian'**tare** [skjan'tare] *vt* to break, tear apart; **~rsi** *vr* to break (up), shatter; **schi'anto** *sm* (*rumore*) crash; tearing sound; **è uno schianto!** (*fam*) it's (*o* he's *o* she's) terrific!; **di schianto** all of a sudden

schia'**rire** [skja'rire] *vt* to lighten, make lighter ♦ *vi* (*anche:* **~rsi**) to grow lighter; (*tornar sereno*) to clear, brighten up; **~rsi la voce** to clear one's throat

schiavi'**tù** [skjavi'tu] *sf* slavery

schi'**avo, a** ['skjavo] *sm/f* slave

schi'**ena** ['skjena] *sf* (*ANAT*) back; **schie'nale** *sm* (*di sedia*) back

schi'**era** ['skjera] *sf* (*MIL*) rank; (*gruppo*) group, band

schiera'**mento** [skjera'mento] *sm* (*MIL, SPORT*) formation; (*fig*) alliance

schie'**rare** [skje'rare] *vt* (*esercito*) to line up, draw up, marshal; **~rsi** *vr* to line up; (*fig*): **~rsi con** *o* **dalla parte di / contro qn** to side with / oppose sb

schi'**etto, a** ['skjetto] *ag* (*puro*) pure; (*fig*) frank, straightforward; sincere

'**schifo** ['skifo] *sm* disgust; **fare ~** (*essere fatto male, dare pessimi risultati*) to be awful; **mi fa ~** it makes me sick, it's disgusting; **quel libro è uno ~** that book's rotten; **schi'foso, a** *ag* disgusting, revolting; (*molto scadente*) rotten, lousy

schioc'**care** [skjok'kare] *vt* (*frusta*) to crack; (*dita*) to snap; (*lingua*) to click; **~ le labbra** to smack one's lips

schi'udere [ˈskjudere] *vt* to open; **~rsi** *vr* to open

schi'uma [ˈskjuma] *sf* foam; (*di sapone*) lather; (*di latte*) froth; (*fig: feccia*) scum; **schiu'mare** *vt* to skim ♦ *vi* to foam

schi'uso, a [ˈskjuso] *pp di* **schiudere**

schi'vare [skiˈvare] *vt* to dodge, avoid

'schivo, a [ˈskivo] *ag* (*ritroso*) stand-offish, reserved; (*timido*) shy

schiz'zare [skitˈtsare] *vt* (*spruzzare*) to spurt, squirt; (*sporcare*) to splash, spatter; (*fig: abbozzare*) to sketch ♦ *vi* to spurt, squirt; (*saltar fuori*) to dart up (*o* off *etc*)

schizzi'noso, a [skittsiˈnoso] *ag* fussy, finicky

'schizzo [ˈskittso] *sm* (*di liquido*) spurt; splash, spatter; (*abbozzo*) sketch

sci [ʃi] *sm* (*attrezzo*) ski; (*attività*) skiing; **~ nautico** water-skiing

'scia [ˈʃia] (*pl* **'scie**) *sf* (*di imbarcazione*) wake; (*di profumo*) trail

scià [ʃa] *sm inv* shah

sci'abola [ˈʃabola] *sf* sabre

scia'callo [ʃaˈkallo] *sm* jackal

sciac'quare [ʃakˈkware] *vt* to rinse

scia'gura [ʃaˈgura] *sf* disaster, calamity; misfortune; **sciagu'rato, a** *ag* unfortunate; (*malvagio*) wicked

scialac'quare [ʃalakˈkware] *vt* to squander

scia'lare [ʃaˈlare] *vi* to lead a life of luxury

sci'albo, a [ˈʃalbo] *ag* pale, dull; (*fig*) dull, colourless

sci'alle [ˈʃalle] *sm* shawl

scia'luppa [ʃaˈluppa] *sf* (*anche:* **~ di salvataggio**) lifeboat

sci'ame [ˈʃame] *sm* swarm

scian'cato, a [ʃanˈkato] *ag* lame

sci'are [ʃiˈare] *vi* to ski

sci'arpa [ˈʃarpa] *sf* scarf; (*fascia*) sash

scia'tore, 'trice [ʃiaˈtore] *sm/f* skier

sci'atto, a [ˈʃatto] *ag* (*persona*) slovenly, unkempt

scien'tifico, a, ci, che [ʃenˈtifiko] *ag* scientific

sci'enza [ˈʃentsa] *sf* science; (*sapere*) knowledge; **~e** *sfpl* (*INS*) science *sg*; **~e**

naturali natural sciences; **scienzi'ato, a** *sm/f* scientist

'scimmia [ˈʃimmja] *sf* monkey; **scimmiot'tare** *vt* to ape, mimic

scimpanzé [ʃimpanˈtse] *sm inv* chimpanzee

scimu'nito, a [ʃimuˈnito] *ag* silly, idiotic

'scindere [ˈʃindere] *vt* to split (up); **~rsi** *vr* to split (up)

scin'tilla [ʃinˈtilla] *sf* spark; **scintil'lare** *vi* to spark; (*acqua, occhi*) to sparkle

scioc'chezza [ʃokˈkettsa] *sf* stupidity *no pl*; stupid *o* foolish thing; **dire ~e** to talk nonsense

sci'occo, a, chi, che [ˈʃokko] *ag* stupid, foolish

sci'ogliere [ˈʃɔʎʎere] *vt* (*nodo*) to untie; (*capelli*) to loosen; (*persona, animale*) to untie, release; (*fig: persona*): **~ da** to release from; (*neve*) to melt; (*nell'acqua: zucchero etc*) to dissolve; (*fig: mistero*) to solve; (*porre fine a: contratto*) to cancel; (: *società, matrimonio*) to dissolve; (: *riunione*) to bring to an end; **~rsi** *vr* to loosen, come untied; to melt; to dissolve; (*assemblea etc*) to break up; **~ i muscoli** to limber up

sciol'tezza [ʃolˈtettsa] *sf* agility; suppleness; ease

sci'olto, a [ˈʃɔlto] *pp di* **sciogliere** ♦ *ag* loose; (*agile*) agile, nimble; supple; (*disinvolto*) free and easy; **versi ~i** (*POESIA*) blank verse

sciope'rante [ʃopeˈrante] *sm/f* striker

sciope'rare [ʃopeˈrare] *vi* to strike, go on strike

sci'opero [ˈʃɔpero] *sm* strike; **fare ~** to strike; **~ bianco** work-to-rule (*BRIT*), slowdown (*US*); **~ selvaggio** wildcat strike; **~ a singhiozzo** on-off strike

scip'pare [ʃipˈpare] *vt*: **~ qn** to snatch sb's bag; **mi hanno scippato** they snatched my bag

sci'rocco [ʃiˈrɔkko] *sm* sirocco

sci'roppo [ʃiˈrɔppo] *sm* syrup

'scisma, i [ˈʃizma] *sm* (*REL*) schism

scissi'one [ʃisˈsjone] *sf* (*anche fig*) split, division; (*FISICA*) fission

'scisso, a [ˈʃisso] *pp di* **scindere**

sciu'pare [ʃu'pare] vt (abito, libro, appetito) to spoil, ruin; (tempo, denaro) to waste; ~**rsi** vr to get spoilt o ruined; (rovinarsi la salute) to ruin one's health

scivo'lare [ʃivo'lare] vi to slide o glide along; (involontariamente) to slip, slide; '**scivolo** sm slide; (TECN) chute; **scivo'loso, a** ag slippery

scle'rosi sf sclerosis

scoc'care vt (freccia) to shoot ♦ vi (guizzare) to shoot up; (battere: ora) to strike

scocci'are [skot'tʃare] (fam) vt to bother, annoy; ~**rsi** vr to be bothered o annoyed

sco'della sf bowl

scodinzo'lare [skodintso'lare] vi to wag its tail

scogli'era [skoʎ'ʎera] sf reef; cliff

'**scoglio** ['skoʎʎo] sm (al mare) rock

scoi'attolo sm squirrel

scolapi'atti sm inv drainer (for plates)

sco'lare ag: **età** ~ school age ♦ vt to drain ♦ vi to drip

scola'resca sf schoolchildren pl, pupils pl

sco'laro, a sm/f pupil, schoolboy/girl

sco'lastico, a, ci, che ag school cpd; scholastic

scol'lare vt (staccare) to unstick; ~**rsi** vr to come unstuck

scolla'tura sf neckline

'**scolo** sm drainage

scolo'rire vt to fade; to discolour ♦ vi (anche: ~**rsi**) to fade; to become discoloured; (impallidire) to turn pale

scol'pire vt to carve, sculpt

scombi'nare vt to mess up, upset

scombusso'lare vt to upset

scom'messa sf bet, wager

scom'messo, a pp di **scommettere**

scom'mettere vt, vi to bet

scomo'dare vt to trouble, bother; to disturb; ~**rsi** vr to put o.s. out; ~**rsi a fare** to go to the bother o trouble of doing

'**scomodo, a** ag uncomfortable; (sistemazione, posto) awkward, inconvenient

scompa'rire vi (sparire) to disappear,

vanish; (fig) to be insignificant; **scom'parsa** sf disappearance; **scom'parso, a** pp di **scomparire**

scomparti'mento sm compartment

scom'parto sm compartment, division

scompigli'are [skompiʎ'ʎare] vt (cassetto, capelli) to mess up, disarrange; (fig: piani) to upset; **scom'piglio** sm mess, confusion

scom'porre vt (parola, numero) to break up; (CHIM) to decompose; **scomporsi** vr (fig) to get upset, lose one's composure; **scom'posto, a** pp di **scomporre** ♦ ag (gesto) unseemly; (capelli) ruffled, dishevelled

sco'munica sf excommunication

scomuni'care vt to excommunicate

sconcer'tare [skontʃer'tare] vt to disconcert, bewilder

'**sconcio, a, ci, ce** ['skontʃo] ag (osceno) indecent, obscene ♦ sm disgrace

sconfes'sare vt to renounce, disavow; to repudiate

scon'figgere [skon'fiddʒere] vt to defeat, overcome

sconfi'nare vi to cross the border; (in proprietà privata) to trespass; (fig): ~ **da** to stray o digress from; **sconfi'nato, a** ag boundless, unlimited

scon'fitta sf defeat

scon'fitto, a pp di **sconfiggere**

scon'forto sm despondency

scongiu'rare [skondʒu'rare] vt (implorare) to entreat, beseech, implore; (eludere: pericolo) to ward off, avert; **scongi'uro** sm entreaty; (esorcismo) exorcism; **fare gli scongiuri** to touch wood (BRIT), knock on wood (US)

scon'nesso, a ag incoherent

sconosci'uto, a [skonoʃ'ʃuto] ag unknown; new, strange ♦ sm/f stranger; unknown person

sconquas'sare vt to shatter, smash

sconside'rato, a ag thoughtless, rash

sconsigli'are [skonsiʎ'ʎare] vt: ~ **qc a qn** to advise sb against sth; ~ **qn dal fare qc** to advise sb not to do o against doing sth

sconso'lato, a ag inconsolable; desolate

scon'tare vt (COMM: detrarre) to deduct; (: debito) to pay off; (: cambiale) to discount; (pena) to serve; (colpa, errori) to pay for, suffer for

scon'tato, a ag (previsto) foreseen, taken for granted; **dare per ~ che** to take it for granted that

scon'tento, a ag: **~ (di)** dissatisfied (with) ♦ sm dissatisfaction

'sconto sm discount; **fare uno ~** to give a discount

scon'trarsi vr (treni etc) to crash, collide; (venire ad uno scontro, fig) to clash; **~ con** to crash into, collide with

scon'trino sm ticket

'scontro sm clash, encounter; crash, collision

scon'troso, a ag sullen, surly; (permaloso) touchy

sconveni'ente ag unseemly, improper

scon'volgere [skon'vɔldʒere] vt to throw into confusion, upset; (turbare) to shake, disturb, upset; **scon'volto, a** pp di **sconvolgere**

'scopa sf broom; (CARTE) Italian card game; **sco'pare** vt to sweep

sco'perta sf discovery

sco'perto, a pp di **scoprire** ♦ ag uncovered; (capo) uncovered, bare; (macchina) open; (MIL) exposed, without cover; (conto) overdrawn

'scopo sm aim, purpose; **a che ~?** what for?

scoppi'are vi (spaccarsi) to burst; (esplodere) to explode; (fig) to break out; **~ in pianto** o **a piangere** to burst out crying; **~ dalle risa** o **dal ridere** to split one's sides laughing

scoppiet'tare vi to crackle

'scoppio sm explosion; (di tuono, arma etc) crash, bang; (fig: di risa, ira) outburst; (: di guerra) outbreak; **a ~ ritardato** delayed-action

sco'prire vt to discover; (liberare da ciò che copre) to uncover; (: monumento) to unveil; **~rsi** vr to put on lighter clothes; (fig) to give o.s. away

scoraggi'are [skorad'dʒare] vt to discourage; **~rsi** vr to become discouraged, lose heart

scorcia'toia [skortʃa'toja] sf short cut

'scorcio ['skortʃo] sm (ARTE) foreshortening; (di secolo, periodo) end, close

scor'dare vt to forget; **~rsi** vr: **~rsi di qc/ di fare** to forget sth/to do

'scorgere ['skɔrdʒere] vt to make out, distinguish, see

sco'ria sf (di metalli) slag; (vulcanica) scoria; **~e radioattive** (FISICA) radioactive waste sg

'scorno sm ignominy, disgrace

scorpacci'ata [skorpat'tʃata] sf: **fare una ~ (di)** to stuff o.s. (with), eat one's fill (of)

scorpi'one sm scorpion; (dello zodiaco): **S~** Scorpio

scorraz'zare [skorrat'tsare] vi to run about

'scorrere vt (giornale, lettera) to run o skim through ♦ vi (liquido, fiume) to run, flow; (fune) to run; (cassetto, porta) to slide easily; (tempo) to pass (by)

scor'retto, a ag incorrect; (sgarbato) impolite; (sconveniente) improper

scor'revole ag (porta) sliding; (fig: stile) fluent, flowing

scorri'banda sf (MIL) raid; (escursione) trip, excursion

'scorsa sf quick look, glance

'scorso, a pp di **scorrere** ♦ ag last

scor'soio, a ag: **nodo ~** noose

'scorta sf (di personalità, convoglio) escort; (provvista) supply, stock; **scor'tare** vt to escort

scor'tese ag discourteous, rude; **scorte'sia** sf discourtesy, rudeness; (azione) discourtesy

scorti'care vt to skin

'scorto, a pp di **scorgere**

'scorza ['skɔrdza] sf (di albero) bark; (di agrumi) peel, skin

sco'sceso, a [skoʃ'feso] ag steep

'scossa sf jerk, jolt, shake; (ELETTR, fig) shock

'scosso, a pp di **scuotere** ♦ ag (turbato) shaken, upset

scos'tante *ag* (*fig*) off-putting (*BRIT*), unpleasant

scos'tare *vt* to move (away), shift; **~rsi** *vr* to move away

scostu'mato, a *ag* immoral, dissolute

scot'tare *vt* (*ustionare*) to burn; (: *con liquido bollente*) to scald ♦ *vi* to burn; (*caffè*) to be too hot; **scotta'tura** *sf* burn; scald

'scotto, a *ag* overcooked ♦ *sm* (*fig*): **pagare lo ~ (di)** to pay the penalty (for)

sco'vare *vt* to drive out, flush out; (*fig*) to discover

'Scozia ['skɔttsja] *sf*: **la ~** Scotland; **scoz'zese** *ag* Scottish ♦ *sm/f* Scot

scredi'tare *vt* to discredit

screpo'lare *vt* to crack; **~rsi** *vr* to crack; **screpola'tura** *sf* cracking *no pl*; crack

screzi'ato, a [skret'tsjato] *ag* streaked

'screzio ['skrettsjo] *sm* disagreement

scricchio'lare [skrikkjo'lare] *vi* to creak, squeak

'scricciolo ['skrittʃolo] *sm* wren

'scrigno ['skriɲɲo] *sm* casket

scrimina'tura *sf* parting

'scritta *sf* inscription

'scritto, a *pp di* **scrivere** ♦ *ag* written ♦ *sm* writing; (*lettera*) letter, note; **~i** *smpl* (*letterari etc*) writing *sg*

scrit'toio *sm* writing desk

scrit'tore, 'trice *sm/f* writer

scrit'tura *sf* writing; (*COMM*) entry; (*contratto*) contract; (*REL*): **la Sacra S~** the Scriptures *pl*; **~e** *sfpl* (*COMM*) accounts, books

scrittu'rare *vt* (*TEATRO, CINEMA*) to sign up, engage; (*COMM*) to enter

scriva'nia *sf* desk

'scrivere *vt* to write; **come si scrive?** how is it spelt?, how do you write it?

scroc'cone, a *sm/f* scrounger

'scrofa *sf* (*ZOOL*) sow

scrol'lare *vt* to shake; **~rsi** *vr* (*anche fig*) to give o.s. a shake; **~ le spalle/il capo** to shrug one's shoulders/shake one's head

scrosci'are [skroʃ'ʃare] *vi* (*pioggia*) to pour down, pelt down; (*torrente, fig: applausi*) to thunder, roar; **'scroscio** *sm* pelting; thunder, roar; (*di applausi*) burst

scros'tare *vt* (*intonaco*) to scrape off, strip; **~rsi** *vr* to peel off, flake off

'scrupolo *sm* scruple; (*meticolosità*) care, conscientiousness

scru'tare *vt* to scrutinize; (*intenzioni, causa*) to examine, scrutinize

scruti'nare *vt* (*voti*) to count; **scru'tinio** *sm* (*votazione*) ballot; (*insieme delle operazioni*) poll; (*INS*) (*meeting for*) assignment of marks at end of a term or year

scu'cire [sku'tʃire] *vt* (*orlo etc*) to unpick, undo

scude'ria *sf* stable

scu'detto *sm* (*SPORT*) (championship) shield; (*distintivo*) badge

'scudo *sm* shield

scul'tore, 'trice *sm/f* sculptor

scul'tura *sf* sculpture

scu'ola *sf* school; **~ elementare/ materna/media** primary (*BRIT*) *o* grade (*US*)/nursery/secondary (*BRIT*) *o* high (*US*) school; **~ guida** driving school; **~ dell'obbligo** compulsory education; **~e serali** evening classes, night school *sg*; **~ tecnica** technical college

scu'otere *vt* to shake; **~rsi** *vr* to jump, be startled; (*fig: muoversi*) to rouse o.s., stir o.s. (: *turbarsi*) to be shaken

'scure *sf* axe

'scuro, a *ag* dark; (*fig: espressione*) grim ♦ *sm* darkness; dark colour; (*imposta*) (window) shutter; **verde/rosso** *etc* **~** dark green/red *etc*

scur'rile *ag* scurrilous

'scusa *sf* apology; (*pretesto*) excuse; **chiedere ~ a qn (per)** to apologize to sb (for); **chiedo ~** I'm sorry; (*disturbando etc*) excuse me

scu'sare *vt* to excuse; **~rsi** *vr*: **~rsi (di)** to apologize (for); **(mi) scusi** I'm sorry; (*per richiamare l'attenzione*) excuse me

sde'gnato, a [zdeɲ'ɲato] *ag* indignant, angry

'sdegno ['zdeɲɲo] *sm* scorn, disdain;

sde'gnoso, a *ag* scornful, disdainful

sdoga'nare *vt (merci)* to clear through customs

sdolci'nato, a [zdoltʃi'nato] *ag* mawkish, oversentimental

sdrai'arsi *vr* to stretch out, lie down

'sdraio *sm*: **sedia a ~** deck chair

sdruccio'levole [zdruttʃo'levole] *ag* slippery

PAROLA CHIAVE

se *pron vedi* **si**

♦ *cong* **1** *(condizionale, ipotetica)* if; **~ nevica non vengo** I won't come if it snows; **sarei rimasto ~ me l'avessero chiesto** I would have stayed if they'd asked me; **non puoi fare altro ~ non telefonare** all you can do is phone; **~ mai** if, if ever; **siamo noi ~ mai che ti siamo grati** it is we who should be grateful to you; **~ no** *(altrimenti)* or (else), otherwise

2 *(in frasi dubitative, interrogative indirette)* if, whether; **non so ~ scrivere o telefonare** I don't know whether *o* if I should write or phone

---

sé *pron (gen)* oneself; *(esso, essa, lui, lei, loro)* itself; himself; herself; themselves; **~ stesso(a)** *pron* oneself; itself; himself; herself; **~ stessi(e)** *pron pl* themselves

seb'bene *cong* although, though

sec. *abbr* (= *secolo*) c

'secca *sf (del mare)* shallows *pl*; *vedi anche* **secco**

sec'care *vt* to dry; *(prosciugare)* to dry up; *(fig: importunare)* to annoy, bother ♦ *vi* to dry; to dry up; **~rsi** *vr* to dry; to dry up; *(fig)* to grow annoyed; **secca'tura** *sf (fig)* bother *no pl*, trouble *no pl*

secchi'ello *sm* bucket; **~ del ghiaccio** ice bucket

'secchio ['sekkjo] *sm* bucket, pail

'secco, a, chi, che *ag* dry; *(fichi, pesce)* dried; *(foglie, ramo)* withered; *(magro: persona)* thin, skinny; *(fig: risposta, modo di fare)* curt, abrupt; (: *colpo)* clean, sharp ♦ *sm (siccità)* drought; **restarci ~** *(fig:*

morire sul colpo)* to drop dead; **mettere in ~ *(barca)* to beach; **rimanere a ~** *(fig)* to be left in the lurch

seco'lare *ag* age-old, centuries-old; *(laico, mondano)* secular

'secolo *sm* century; *(epoca)* age

se'conda *sf (AUT)* second (gear); **viaggiare in ~** to travel second-class; *vedi anche* **secondo**

secon'dario, a *ag* secondary

se'condo, a *ag* second ♦ *sm* second; *(di pranzo)* main course ♦ *prep* according to; *(nel modo prescritto)* in accordance with; **~ me** in my opinion, to my mind; **di ~a classe** second-class; **di ~a mano** second-hand; **a ~a di** according to; in accordance with

'sedano *sm* celery

seda'tivo, a *ag, sm* sedative

'sede *sf* seat; *(di ditta)* head office; *(di organizzazione)* headquarters *pl*; **~ sociale** registered office

seden'tario, a *ag* sedentary

se'dere *vi* to sit, be seated; **~rsi** *vr* to sit down ♦ *sm (deretano)* behind, bottom

'sedia *sf* chair

sedi'cente [sedi'tʃɛnte] *ag* self-styled

'sedici ['seditʃi] *num* sixteen

se'dile *sm* seat; *(panchina)* bench

se'dotto, a *pp di* **sedurre**

sedu'cente [sedu'tʃɛnte] *ag* seductive; *(proposta)* very attractive

se'durre *vt* to seduce

se'duta *sf* session, sitting; *(riunione)* meeting; **~ spiritica** séance; **~ stante** *(fig)* immediately

seduzi'one [sedut'tsjone] *sf* seduction; *(fascino)* charm, appeal

'sega, ghe *sf* saw

'segale *sf* rye

se'gare *vt* to saw; *(recidere)* to saw off; **sega'tura** *sf (residuo)* sawdust

'seggio ['seddʒo] *sm* seat; **~ elettorale** polling station

'seggiola ['seddʒola] *sf* chair; **seggio'lino** *sm* seat; *(per bambini)* child's chair; **seggio'lone** *sm (per bambini)* highchair

seggio'via [seddʒo'via] *sf* chairlift

seghe'ria [sege'ria] *sf* sawmill

segna'lare [senɲa'lare] *vt* (*manovra etc*) to signal; to indicate; (*annunciare*) to announce; to report; (*fig: far conoscere*) to point out; (: *persona*) to single out; **~rsi** *vr* (*distinguersi*) to distinguish o.s.

se'gnale [sen'ɲale] *sm* signal; (*cartello*): **~ stradale** road sign; **~ d'allarme** alarm; (*FERR*) communication cord; **~ orario** (*RADIO*) time signal; **segna'letica** *sf* signalling, signposting; **segnaletica stradale** road signs *pl*

segna'libro [senɲa'libro] *sm* bookmark

se'gnare [sen'ɲare] *vt* to mark; (*prendere nota*) to note; (*indicare*) to indicate, mark; (*SPORT: goal*) to score; **~rsi** *vr* (*REL*) to make the sign of the cross, cross o.s.

'segno ['seɲɲo] *sm* sign; (*impronta, contrassegno*) mark; (*limite*) limit, bounds *pl*; (*bersaglio*) target; **fare ~ di sì/no** to nod (one's head)/shake one's head; **fare ~ a qn di fermarsi** to motion (to) sb to stop; **cogliere** *o* **colpire nel ~** (*fig*) to hit the mark

segre'gare *vt* to segregate, isolate; **segregazi'one** *sf* segregation

segre'tario, a *sm/f* secretary; **~ comunale** town clerk; **S~ di Stato** Secretary of State

segrete'ria *sf* (*di ditta, scuola*) (secretary's) office; (*d'organizzazione internazionale*) secretariat; (*POL etc: carica*) office of Secretary; **~ telefonica** answering service

segre'tezza [segre'tettsa] *sf* secrecy

se'greto, a *ag* secret ♦ *sm* secret; secrecy *no pl*; **in ~** in secret, secretly

segu'ace [se'gwatʃe] *sm/f* follower, disciple

segu'ente *ag* following, next

segu'ire *vt* to follow; (*frequentare: corso*) to attend ♦ *vi* to follow; (*continuare: testo*) to continue

segui'tare *vt* to continue, carry on with ♦ *vi* to continue, carry on

'seguito *sm* (*scorta*) suite, retinue; (*discepoli*) followers *pl*; (*favore*) following; (*continuazione*) continuation; (*conseguenza*) result; **di ~** at a stretch, on end; **in ~** later on; **in ~ a, a ~ di** following; (*a causa di*) as a result of, owing to

'sei *vb vedi* **essere** ♦ *num* six

sei'cento [sei'tʃɛnto] *num* six hundred ♦ *sm*: **il S~** the seventeenth century

selci'ato [sel'tʃato] *sm* cobbled surface

selezio'nare [selettsjo'nare] *vt* to select

selezi'one [selet'tsjone] *sf* selection

'sella *sf* saddle; **sel'lare** *vt* to saddle

selvag'gina [selvad'dʒina] *sf* (*animali*) game

sel'vaggio, a, gi, ge [sel'vaddʒo] *ag* wild; (*tribù*) savage, uncivilized; (*fig*) savage, brutal ♦ *sm/f* savage

sel'vatico, a, ci, che *ag* wild

se'maforo *sm* (*AUT*) traffic lights *pl*

sem'brare *vi* to seem ♦ *vb impers*: **sembra che** it seems that; **mi sembra che** it seems to me that; I think (that); **~ di essere** to seem to be

'seme *sm* seed; (*sperma*) semen; (*CARTE*) suit

se'mestre *sm* half-year, six-month period

'semi... *prefisso* semi...; **semi'cerchio** *sm* semicircle; **semifi'nale** *sf* semifinal; **semi'freddo** *sm* ice-cream cake

'semina *sf* (*AGR*) sowing

semi'nare *vt* to sow

semi'nario *sm* seminar; (*REL*) seminary

seminter'rato *sm* basement; (*appartamento*) basement flat

sem'mai = **se mai**; *vedi* **se**

'semola *sf*: **~ di grano duro** durum wheat

semo'lino *sm* semolina

'semplice ['semplitʃe] *ag* simple; (*di un solo elemento*) single; **semplice'mente** *av* simply; **semplicità** *sf* simplicity

'sempre *av* always; (*ancora*) still; **posso ~ tentare** I can always *o* still try; **da ~** always; **per ~** forever; **una volta per ~** once and for all; **~ che** provided (that); **~ più** more and more; **~ meno** less and less

sempre'verde *ag, sm o f* (*BOT*) evergreen

'senape *sf* (*CUC*) mustard

se'nato *sm* senate; **sena'tore, 'trice**

sm/f senator

'**senno** *sm* judgment, (common) sense; **col ~ di poi** with hindsight

sennò *av* = **se no**; *vedi* **se**

'**seno** *sm* (ANAT: *petto, mammella*) breast; (: *grembo, fig*) womb; (: *cavità*) sinus

sen'sato, a *ag* sensible

sensazio'nale [sensattsjo'nale] *ag* sensational

sensazi'one [sensat'tsjone] *sf* feeling, sensation; **avere la ~ che** to have a feeling that; **fare ~** to cause a sensation, create a stir

sen'sibile *ag* sensitive; (*ai sensi*) perceptible; (*rilevante, notevole*) appreciable, noticeable; **~ a** sensitive to; **sensibilità** *sf* sensitivity

senso *sm* (FISIOL, *istinto*) sense; (*impressione, sensazione*) feeling, sensation; (*significato*) meaning, sense; (*direzione*) direction; **~i** *smpl* (*coscienza*) consciousness *sg*; (*sensualità*) senses; **ciò non ha ~** that doesn't make sense; **fare ~ a** (*ripugnare*) to disgust, repel; **~ comune** common sense; **in ~ orario/antiorario** clockwise/anticlockwise; **a ~ unico** (*strada*) one-way

sensu'ale *ag* sensual; sensuous; **sensualità** *sf* sensuality; sensuousness

sen'tenza [sen'tentsa] *sf* (DIR) sentence; (*massima*) maxim; **sentenzi'are** *vi* (DIR) to pass judgment

senti'ero *sm* path

sentimen'tale *ag* sentimental; (*vita, avventura*) love *cpd*

senti'mento *sm* feeling

senti'nella *sf* sentry

sen'tire *vt* (*percepire al tatto, fig*) to feel; (*udire*) to hear; (*ascoltare*) to listen to; (*odore*) to smell; (*avvertire con il gusto, assaggiare*) to taste ♦ *vi*: **~ di** (*avere sapore*) to taste of; (*avere odore*) to smell of; **~rsi** *vr* (*uso reciproco*) to be in touch; **~rsi bene/male** to feel well/unwell *o* ill; **~rsi di fare qc** (*essere disposto*) to feel like doing sth

sen'tito, a *ag* (*sincero*) sincere, warm; **per ~ dire** by hearsay

'**senza** ['sɛntsa] *prep, cong* without; **~ dir**

nulla without saying a word; **fare ~ qc** to do without sth; **~ di me** without me; **~ che io lo sapessi** without me *o* my knowing; **senz'altro** of course, certainly; **~ dubbio** no doubt; **~ scrupoli** unscrupulous; **~ amici** friendless

sepa'rare *vt* to separate; (*dividere*) to divide; (*tenere distinto*) to distinguish; **~rsi** *vr* (*coniugi*) to separate, part; (*amici*) to part, leave each other; **~rsi da** (*coniuge*) to separate *o* part from; (*amico, socio*) to part company with; (*oggetto*) to part with; **sepa'rato, a** *ag* (*letti, conto etc*) separate; (*coniugi*) separated; **separazi'one** *sf* separation

se'polcro *sm* sepulchre

se'polto, a *pp di* **seppellire**

seppel'lire *vt* to bury

'**seppia** *sf* cuttlefish ♦ *ag inv* sepia

se'quenza [se'kwentsa] *sf* sequence

seques'trare *vt* (DIR) to impound; (*rapire*) to kidnap; **se'questro** *sm* (DIR) impoundment; **sequestro di persona** kidnapping

'**sera** *sf* evening; **di ~** in the evening; **domani ~** tomorrow evening, tomorrow night; **se'rale** *ag* evening *cpd*; **se'rata** *sf* evening; (*ricevimento*) party

ser'bare *vt* to keep; (*mettere da parte*) to put aside; **~ rancore/odio verso qn** to bear sb a grudge/hate sb

serba'toio *sm* tank; (*cisterna*) cistern

'**serbo** *sm*: **mettere/tenere** *o* **avere in ~ qc** to put/keep sth aside

se'reno, a *ag* (*tempo, cielo*) clear; (*fig*) serene, calm

ser'gente [ser'dʒɛnte] *sm* (MIL) sergeant

'**serie** *sf inv* (*successione*) series *inv*; (*gruppo, collezione*) set; (SPORT) division; league; (COMM): **modello di ~/fuori ~** standard/custom-built model; **in ~** in quick succession; (COMM) mass *cpd*

serietà *sf* seriousness; reliability

'**serio, a** *ag* serious; (*impiegato*) responsible, reliable; (*ditta, cliente*) reliable, dependable; **sul ~** (*davvero*) really, truly; (*seriamente*) seriously, in earnest

ser'mone *sm* sermon

serpeggi'are [serped'dʒare] *vi* to wind; *(fig)* to spread

ser'pente *sm* snake; ~ **a sonagli** rattlesnake

'serra *sf* greenhouse; hothouse

ser'randa *sf* roller shutter

ser'rare *vt* to close, shut; *(a chiave)* to lock; *(stringere)* to tighten; ~ **i pugni/i denti** to clench one's fists/teeth; ~ **le file** to close ranks

serra'tura *sf* lock

'serva *sf vedi* servo

ser'vire *vt* to serve; *(clienti: al ristorante)* to wait on; *(: al negozio)* to serve, attend to; *(fig: giovare)* to aid, help; *(CARTE)* to deal ♦ *vi (TENNIS)* to serve; *(essere utile)*: ~ **a qn** to be of use to sb; ~ **a qc/a fare** *(utensile etc)* to be used for sth/for doing; ~ **(a qn) da** to serve as (for sb); ~**rsi** *vr (usare)*: ~**rsi di** to use; *(prendere: cibo)*: ~**rsi (di)** to help o.s. (to); *(essere cliente abituale)*: ~**rsi da** to be a regular customer at, go to

servitù *sf* servitude; slavery; *(personale di servizio)* servants *pl*, domestic staff

servizi'evole [servit'tsjevole] *ag* obliging, willing to help

ser'vizio [ser'vittsjo] *sm* service; *(al ristorante: sul conto)* service (charge); *(STAMPA, TV, RADIO)* report; *(da tè, caffè etc)* set, service; ~**i** *smpl (di casa)* kitchen and bathroom; *(ECON)* services; **essere di** ~ to be on duty; **fuori** ~ *(telefono etc)* out of order; ~ **compreso** service included; ~ **militare** military service; ~**i segreti** secret service *sg*

'servo, a *sm/f* servant

ses'santa *num* sixty; sessan'tesimo, a *num* sixtieth

sessan'tina *sf*: **una ~ (di)** about sixty

ⓘ **Sessantotto**, '68, refers to 1968 when the student protest movement intensified and influenced other parts of society, leading to major political and social change. Left-wing groups flourished, schools and universities became more democratic and the referendum on divorce was held.

sessi'one *sf* session

'sesso *sm* sex; sessu'ale *ag* sexual, sex *cpd*

ses'tante *sm* sextant

'sesto, a *ag, sm* sixth

'seta *sf* silk

'sete *sf* thirst; **avere** ~ to be thirsty

'setola *sf* bristle

'setta *sf* sect

set'tanta *num* seventy; settan'tesimo, a *num* seventieth

settan'tina *sf*: **una ~ (di)** about seventy

'sette *num* seven

sette'cento [sette'tʃento] *num* seven hundred ♦ *sm*: **il S~** the eighteenth century

set'tembre *sm* September

settentrio'nale *ag* northern

settentri'one *sm* north

setti'mana *sf* week; settima'nale *ag, sm* weekly

ⓘ The **settimana bianca** is a winter-sports holiday taken by many Italians.

'settimo, a *ag, sm* seventh

set'tore *sm* sector

severità *sf* severity

se'vero, a *ag* severe

sevizi'are [sevit'tsjare] *vt* to torture

se'vizie [se'vittsje] *sfpl* torture *sg*

sezio'nare [settsjo'nare] *vt* to divide into sections; *(MED)* to dissect

sezi'one [set'tsjone] *sf* section

sfaccen'dato, a [sfattʃen'dato] *ag* idle

sfacci'ato, a [sfat'tʃato] *ag (maleducato)* cheeky, impudent; *(vistoso)* gaudy

sfa'celo [sfa'tʃelo] *sm (fig)* ruin, collapse

sfal'darsi *vr* to flake (off)

sfa'mare *vt* to feed; *(sog: cibo)* to fill

'sfarzo ['sfartso] *sm* pomp, splendour

sfasci'are [sfaʃ'ʃare] *vt (ferita)* to unbandage; *(distruggere)* to smash, shatter;

~**rsi** vr (rompersi) to smash, shatter
sfa'tare vt (leggenda) to explode
sfavil'lare vi (risplendere) to spark, send out sparks; (risplendere) to sparkle
sfavo'revole ag unfavourable
'**sfera** sf sphere; '**sferico, a, ci, che** ag spherical
sfer'rare vt (fig: colpo) to land, deal; (: attacco) to launch
sfer'zare [sfer'tsare] vt (fig) to whip, (fig) to lash out at
sfi'brare vt (indebolire) to exhaust, enervate
'**sfida** sf challenge
sfi'dare vt to challenge; (fig) to defy, brave
sfi'ducia [sfi'dutʃa] sf distrust, mistrust
sfigu'rare vt (persona) to disfigure; (quadro, statua) to deface ♦ vi (far cattiva figura) to make a bad impression
sfi'lare vt (ago) to unthread; (abito, scarpe) to slip off ♦ vi (truppe) to march past; (atleti) to parade; ~**rsi** vr (perle etc) to come unstrung; (orlo, tessuto) to fray; (calza) to run, ladder; **sfi'lata** sf march past; parade; **sfilata di moda** fashion show
'**sfinge** ['sfindʒe] sf sphinx
sfi'nito, a ag exhausted
sfio'rare vt to brush (against); (argomento) to touch upon
sfio'rire vi to wither, fade
sfo'cato, a ag (FOT) out of focus
sfoci'are [sfo'tʃare] vi: ~ **in** to flow into; (fig: malcontento) to develop into
sfode'rato, a ag (vestito) unlined
sfo'gare vt to vent, pour up; ~**rsi** vr (sfogare la propria rabbia) to give vent to one's anger; (confidarsi): ~**rsi (con)** to pour out one's feelings (to); **non sfogarti su di me!** don't take your bad temper out on me!
sfoggi'are [sfod'dʒare] vt, vi to show off
'**sfoglia** ['sfoʎʎa] sf sheet of pasta dough; **pasta ~** (CUC) puff pastry
sfogli'are [sfoʎ'ʎare] vt (libro) to leaf through
'**sfogo, ghi** sm (eruzione cutanea) rash; (fig) outburst; **dare ~ a** (fig) to give vent to

sfolgo'rante ag (luce) blazing; (fig: vittoria) brilliant
sfol'lare vt to empty, clear ♦ vi to disperse; ~ **da** (città) to evacuate
sfon'dare vt (porta) to break down; (scarpe) to wear a hole in; (cesto, scatola) to burst, knock the bottom out of; (MIL) to break through ♦ vi (riuscire) to make a name for o.s.
'**sfondo** sm background
sfor'mato sm (CUC) type of soufflé
sfor'nare vt (pane etc) to take out of the oven; (fig) to churn out
sfor'nito, a ag: ~ **di** lacking in, without; (negozio) out of
sfor'tuna sf misfortune, ill luck no pl; **avere ~** to be unlucky; **sfortu'nato, a** ag unlucky; (impresa, film) unsuccessful
sfor'zare [sfor'tsare] vt to force; (voce, occhi) to strain; ~**rsi** vr: ~**rsi di** o a o **per fare** to try hard to do
'**sforzo** ['sfɔrtso] sm effort; (tensione eccessiva, TECN) strain; **fare uno ~** to make an effort
sfrat'tare vt to evict; '**sfratto** sm eviction
sfrecci'are [sfret'tʃare] vi to shoot o flash past
sfregi'are [sfre'dʒare] vt to slash, gash; (persona) to disfigure; (quadro) to deface; '**sfregio** sm gash; scar; (fig) insult
sfre'nato, a ag (fig) unrestrained, unbridled
sfron'tato, a ag shameless
sfrutta'mento sm exploitation
sfrut'tare vt (terreno) to overwork, exhaust; (miniera) to exploit, work; (fig: operai, occasione, potere) to exploit
sfug'gire [sfud'dʒire] vi to escape; ~ **a** (custode) to escape (from); (morte) to escape; ~ **a qn** (dettaglio, nome) to escape sb; ~ **di mano a qn** to slip out of sb's hand (o hands); **sfug'gita: di sfuggita** ad (rapidamente, in fretta) in passing
sfu'mare vt (colori, contorni) to soften, shade off ♦ vi to shade (off), fade; (fig: svanire) to vanish, disappear; (: speranze) to come to nothing

sfuma'tura sf shading off no pl; (tonalità) shade, tone; (fig) touch, hint

sfuri'ata sf (scatto di collera) fit of anger; (rimprovero) sharp rebuke

sga'bello sm stool

sgabuz'zino [zgabud'dzino] sm lumber room

sgambet'tare vi to kick one's legs about

sgam'betto sm: **far lo ~ a qn** to trip sb up; (fig) to oust sb

sganasci'arsi [zganaʃ'ʃarsi] vr: **~ dalle risa** to roar with laughter

sganci'are [zgan'tʃare] vt to unhook; (FERR) to uncouple; (bombe: da aereo) to release, drop; (fig: fam: soldi) to fork out; **~rsi** vr (fig): **~rsi (da)** to get away (from)

sganghe'rato, a [zgange'rato] ag (porta) off its hinges; (auto) ramshackle; (risata) wild, boisterous

sgar'bato, a ag rude, impolite

'sgarbo sm: **fare uno ~ a qn** to be rude to sb

sgattaio'lare vi to sneak away o off

sge'lare [zdʒe'lare] vi, vt to thaw

'sghembo, a ['zgembo] ag (obliquo) slanting; (storto) crooked

sghignaz'zare [zgiɲɲat'tsare] vi to laugh scornfully

sgob'bare (fam) vi (scolaro) to swot; (operaio) to slog

sgoccio'lare [zgottʃo'lare] vt (vuotare) to drain (to the last drop) ♦ vi (acqua) to drip; (recipiente) to drain; **'sgoccioli** smpl: **essere agli ~** (provviste) to be nearly finished; (periodo) to be nearly over

sgo'larsi vr to talk (o shout o sing) o.s. hoarse

sgomb(e)'rare vt to clear; (andarsene da: stanza) to vacate; (evacuare) to evacuate

'sgombro, a ag: **~ (di)** clear (of), free (from) ♦ sm (ZOOL) mackerel; (anche: **sgombero**) clearing; vacating; (evacuazione; (: trasloco) removal

sgomen'tare vt to dismay; **sgo'mento, a** ag dismayed ♦ sm dismay, consternation

sgonfi'are vt to let down, deflate; **~rsi** vr to go down

'sgorbio sm blot; scribble

sgor'gare vi to gush (out)

sgoz'zare [zgot'tsare] vt to cut the throat of

sgra'devole ag unpleasant, disagreeable

sgra'dito, a ag unpleasant, unwelcome

sgra'nare vt (piselli) to shell; **~ gli occhi** to open one's eyes wide

sgran'chirsi [zgran'kirsi] vr to stretch; **~ le gambe** to stretch one's legs

sgranocchi'are [zgranok'kjare] vt to munch

'sgravio sm: **~ fiscale** tax relief

sgrazi'ato, a [zgrat'tsjato] ag clumsy, ungainly

sgreto'lare vt to cause to crumble; **~rsi** vr to crumble

sgri'dare vt to scold; **sgri'data** sf scolding

sguai'ato, a ag coarse, vulgar

sgual'cire [zgwal'tʃire] vt to crumple (up), crease

sgual'drina (peg) sf slut

sgu'ardo sm (occhiata) look, glance; (espressione) look (in one's eye)

'sguattero, a sm/f dishwasher (person)

sguaz'zare [zgwat'tsare] vi (nell'acqua) to splash about; (nella melma) to wallow; **~ nell'oro** to be rolling in money

sguinzagli'are [zgwintsaʎ'ʎare] vt to let off the leash; (fig: persona): **~ qn dietro a qn** to set sb on sb

sgusci'are [zguʃ'ʃare] vt to shell ♦ vi (sfuggire di mano) to slip; **~ via** to slip o slink away

'shampoo ['ʃampo] sm inv shampoo

shock [ʃɔk] sm inv shock

PAROLA CHIAVE

---

si¹ (dav lo, la, li, le, ne diventa **se**) pron
1 (riflessivo: maschile) himself; (: femminile) herself; (: neutro) itself; (: impersonale) oneself; (: pl) themselves; **lavarsi** to wash (oneself); **~ è tagliato** he has cut himself; **~ credono importanti** they think a lot of themselves
2 (riflessivo: con complemento oggetto): **lavarsi le mani** to wash one's hands; **~ sta**

lavando i capelli he (*o* she) is washing his (*o* her) hair

3 (*reciproco*) one another, each other; **si amano** they love one another *o* each other

4 (*passivo*): **~ ripara facilmente** it is easily repaired

5 (*impersonale*): **~ dice che ...** they *o* people say that ...; **~ vede che è vecchio** one *o* you can see that it's old

6 (*noi*) we; **tra poco ~ parte** we're leaving soon

si² *sm* (*MUS*) B; (*solfeggiando la scala*) ti

sì *av* yes; **un giorno ~ e uno no** every other day

'sia *cong*: **~ ... ~** (*o ... o*): **~ che lavori, ~ che non lavori** whether he works or not; (*tanto ... quanto*): **verranno ~ Luigi ~ suo fratello** both Luigi and his brother will be coming

si'amo *vb vedi* **essere**

sibi'lare *vi* to hiss; (*fischiare*) to whistle; **'sibilo** *sm* hiss; whistle

si'cario *sm* hired killer

sicché [sik'ke] *cong* (*perciò*) so (that), therefore; (*e quindi*) (and) so

siccità [sittʃi'ta] *sf* drought

sic'come *cong* since, as

Si'cilia [si'tʃilja] *sf*: **la ~** Sicily; **sicili'ano, a** *ag*, *sm/f* Sicilian

si'cura *sf* safety catch; (*AUT*) safety lock

sicu'rezza [siku'rettsa] *sf* safety; security; (*fiducia*) confidence; (*certezza*) certainty; **di ~** safety *cpd*; **la ~ stradale** road safety

si'curo, a *ag* safe; (*ben difeso*) secure; (*fiducioso*) confident; (*certo*) sure, certain; (*notizia, amico*) reliable; (*esperto*) skilled ♦ *av* (*anche*: **di ~**) certainly; **essere/mettere al ~** to be safe/put in a safe place; **~ di sé** self-confident, sure of o.s.; **sentirsi ~** to feel safe *o* secure

siderur'gia [siderur'dʒia] *sf* iron and steel industry

'sidro *sm* cider

si'epe *sf* hedge

si'ero *sm* (*MED*) serum; **sieronega'tivo, a** *ag* HIV-negative; **sieroposi'tivo, a** *ag* HIV-positive

si'esta *sf* siesta, (afternoon) nap

si'ete *vb vedi* **essere**

si'filide *sf* syphilis

si'fone *sm* siphon

Sig. *abbr* (= *signore*) Mr

siga'retta *sf* cigarette

'sigaro *sm* cigar

Sigg. *abbr* (= *signori*) Messrs

sigil'lare [sidʒil'lare] *vt* to seal

si'gillo [si'dʒillo] *sm* seal

'sigla *sf* initials *pl*; acronym, abbreviation; **~ automobilistica** *abbreviation of province on vehicle number plate*; **~ musicale** signature tune

si'glare *vt* to initial

Sig.na *abbr* (= *signorina*) Miss

signifi'care [siɲɲifi'kare] *vt* to mean; **significa'tivo, a** *ag* significant; **signifi'cato** *sm* meaning

si'gnora [siɲ'ɲora] *sf* lady; **la ~ X** Mrs X; **buon giorno S~/Signore/Signorina** good morning; (*deferente*) good morning Madam/Sir/Madam; (*quando si conosce il nome*) good morning Mrs/Mr/Miss X; **Gentile S~/Signore/Signorina** (*in una lettera*) Dear Madam/Sir/Madam; **il signor Rossi e ~** Mr Rossi and his wife; **~e e signori** ladies and gentlemen

si'gnore [siɲ'ɲore] *sm* gentleman; (*padrone*) lord, master; (*REL*): **il S~** the Lord; **il signor X** Mr X; **i ~i Bianchi** (*coniugi*) Mr and Mrs Bianchi; *vedi anche* **signora**

signo'rile [siɲɲo'rile] *ag* refined

signo'rina [siɲɲo'rina] *sf* young lady; **la ~ X** Miss X; *vedi anche* **signora**

Sig.ra *abbr* (= *signora*) Mrs

silenzia'tore [silentsja'tore] *sm* silencer

si'lenzio [si'lentsjo] *sm* silence; **fare ~** to be quiet, stop talking; **silenzi'oso, a** *ag* silent, quiet

si'licio [si'litʃo] *sm* silicon

'sillaba *sf* syllable

silu'rare *vt* to torpedo; (*fig: privare del comando*) to oust

si'luro *sm* torpedo

simboleggi'are [simboled'dʒare] *vt* to

symbolize

'**simbolo** *sm* symbol

'**simile** *ag* (*analogo*) similar; (*di questo tipo*): **un uomo ~** such a man, a man like this; **libri ~i** such books; **~ a** similar to; **i suoi ~i** one's fellow men; one's peers

simme'tria *sf* symmetry

simpa'tia *sf* (*qualità*) pleasantness; (*inclinazione*) liking; **avere ~ per qn** to like sb, have a liking for sb; **sim'patico, a, ci, che** *ag* (*persona*) nice, pleasant, likeable; (*casa, albergo etc*) nice, pleasant

simpatiz'zare [simpatid'dzare] *vi*: **~ con** to take a liking to

sim'posio *sm* symposium

simu'lare *vt* to sham, simulate; (*TECN*) to simulate; **simulazi'one** *sf* shamming; simulation

simul'taneo, a *ag* simultaneous

sina'goga, ghe *sf* synagogue

sincerità [sintʃeri'ta] *sf* sincerity

sin'cero, a [sin'tʃero] *ag* sincere; genuine; heartfelt

'sincope *sf* syncopation; (*MED*) blackout

sinda'cale *ag* (trade-)union *cpd*; **sindaca'lista, i, e** *sm/f* trade unionist

sinda'cato *sm* (*di lavoratori*) (trade) union; (*AMM, ECON, DIR*) syndicate, trust, pool

'sindaco, ci *sm* mayor

sinfo'nia *sf* (*MUS*) symphony

singhioz'zare [singjot'tsare] *vi* to sob; to hiccup

singhi'ozzo [sin'gjottso] *sm* sob; (*MED*) hiccup; **avere il ~** to have the hiccups; **a ~** (*fig*) by fits and starts

singo'lare *ag* (*insolito*) remarkable, singular; (*LING*) singular ♦ *sm* (*LING*) singular; (*TENNIS*) = **maschile/femminile** men's/women's singles

'singolo, a *ag* single, individual ♦ *sm* (*persona*) individual; (*TENNIS*) = **singolare**

si'nistra *sf* (*POL*) left (wing); **a ~** on the left; (*direzione*) to the left

si'nistro, a *ag* left, left-hand; (*fig*) sinister ♦ *sm* (*incidente*) accident

'sino *prep* = **fino**

si'nonimo *sm* synonym; **~ di** synonymous with

sin'tassi *sf* syntax

'sintesi *sf* synthesis; (*riassunto*) summary, résumé

sin'tetico, a, ci, che *ag* synthetic

sintetiz'zare [sintetid'dzare] *vt* to synthesize; (*riassumere*) to summarize

sinto'matico, a, ci, che *ag* symptomatic

'sintomo *sm* symptom

sinu'oso, a *ag* (*strada*) winding

si'pario *sm* (*TEATRO*) curtain

si'rena *sf* (*apparecchio*) siren; (*nella mitologia, fig*) siren, mermaid

'Siria *sf*: **la ~** Syria

si'ringa, ghe *sf* syringe

'sismico, a, ci, che *ag* seismic

sis'mografo *sm* seismograph

sis'tema, i *sm* system; method, way

siste'mare *vt* (*mettere a posto*) to tidy, put in order; (*risolvere: questione*) to sort out, settle; (*procurare un lavoro a*) to find a job for; (*dare un alloggio a*) to settle, find accommodation for; **~rsi** *vr* (*problema*) to be settled; (*persona: trovare alloggio*) to find accommodation (*BRIT*) *o* accommodations (*US*); (: *trovarsi un lavoro*) to get fixed up with a job; **ti sistemo io!** I'll soon sort you out!

siste'matico, a, ci, che *ag* systematic

sistemazi'one [sistemat'tsjone] *sf* arrangement; order; settlement; employment; accommodation (*BRIT*); accommodations (*US*)

'sito *sm* (*Internet*) Website

situ'are *vt* to site, situate; **situ'ato, a** *ag*: **situato a/su** situated at/on

situazi'one [situat'tsjone] *sf* situation

ski-lift ['ski:lift] *sm inv* ski tow

slacci'are [zlat'tʃare] *vt* to undo, unfasten

slanci'ato, a [zlan'tʃato] *ag* slender

'slancio *sm* dash, leap; (*fig*) surge; **di ~** impetuously

sla'vato, a *ag* faded, washed out; (*fig: viso, occhi*) pale, colourless

'slavo, a *ag* Slav(onic), Slavic

sle'ale *ag* disloyal; (*concorrenza etc*) unfair

sle'gare *vt* to untie

slip [zlip] *sm inv* briefs *pl*

'slitta *sf* sledge; (*trainata*) sleigh

slit'tare *vi* to slip, slide; (*AUT*) to skid

slo'gare (*MED*) to dislocate

sloggi'are [zlod'dʒare] *vt* (*inquilino*) to turn out ♦ *vi* to move out

slo'vacco, a, chi, che *ag, sm/f* Slovak

Slovenia [zlo'vɛnja] *sf* Slovenia

slo'veno, a [zlo'vɛnja] *sf* Slovenia

smacchi'are [zmak'kjare] *vt* to remove stains from; smacchia'tore *sm* stain remover

'smacco, chi *sm* humiliating defeat

smagli'ante [zmaʎ'ʎante] *ag* brilliant, dazzling

smaglia'tura [zmaʎʎa'tura] *sf* (*su maglia, calza*) ladder; (*della pelle*) stretch mark

smalizi'ato, a [zmalit'tsjato] *ag* shrewd, cunning

smal'tare *vt* to enamel; (*ceramica*) to glaze; (*unghie*) to varnish

smal'tire *vt* (*merce*) to sell off; (*rifiuti*) to dispose of; (*cibo*) to digest; (*peso*) to lose; (*rabbia*) to get over; ~ **la sbornia** to sober up

'smalto *sm* (*anche: di denti*) enamel; (*per ceramica*) glaze; ~ **per unghie** nail varnish

'smania *sf* agitation, restlessness; (*fig*): ~ **di** thirst for, craving for; **avere la ~ addosso** to have the fidgets; **avere la ~ di fare** to be desperate to do

smantel'lare *vt* to dismantle

smarri'mento *sm* loss; (*fig*) bewilderment; dismay

smar'rire *vt* to lose; (*non riuscire a trovare*) to mislay; ~**rsi** *vr* (*perdersi*) to lose one's way, get lost; (*: oggetto*) to go astray;
smar'rito, a *ag* (*sbigottito*) bewildered

smasche'rare [zmaske'rare] *vt* to unmask

smemo'rato, a *ag* forgetful

smen'tire *vt* (*negare*) to deny; (*testimonianza*) to refute; smen'tita *sf* denial; retraction

sme'raldo *sm* emerald

smerci'are [zmer'tʃare] *vt* (*COMM*) to sell; (*: svendere*) to sell off

'smesso, a *pp di* **smettere**

'smettere *vt* to stop; (*vestiti*) to stop wearing ♦ *vi* to stop, cease; ~ **di fare** to stop doing

'smilzo, a ['zmiltso] *ag* thin, lean

sminu'ire *vt* to diminish, lessen; (*fig*) to belittle

sminuz'zare [zminut'tsare] *vt* to break into small pieces; to crumble

smis'tare *vt* (*pacchi etc*) to sort; (*FERR*) to shunt

smisu'rato, a *ag* boundless, immeasurable; (*grandissimo*) immense, enormous

smobili'tare *vt* to demobilize

smo'dato, a *ag* immoderate

smoking ['zmoukɪŋ] *sm inv* dinner jacket

smon'tare *vt* (*mobile, macchina etc*) to take to pieces, dismantle; (*fig: scoraggiare*) to dishearten ♦ *vi* (*scendere: da cavallo*) to dismount; (*: da treno*) to get off; (*terminare il lavoro*) to stop (work); ~**rsi** *vr* to lose heart; to lose one's enthusiasm

'smorfia *sf* grimace; (*atteggiamento lezioso*) simpering; **fare ~e** to make faces; to simper; smorfi'oso, a *ag* simpering

'smorto, a *ag* (*viso*) pale, wan; (*colore*) dull

smor'zare [zmor'tsare] *vt* (*suoni*) to deaden; (*colori*) to tone down; (*luce*) to dim; (*sete*) to quench; (*entusiasmo*) to dampen; ~**rsi** *vr* (*suono, luce*) to fade; (*entusiasmo*) to dampen

'smosso, a *pp di* **smuovere**

smotta'mento *sm* landslide

SMS *sigla m* (= *short message system*) SMS

s'munto, a *ag* haggard, pinched

smu'overe *vt* to move, shift; (*fig: commuovere*) to move; (*: dall'inerzia*) to rouse, stir; ~**rsi** *vr* to move, shift

smus'sare *vt* (*angolo*) to round off, smooth; (*lama etc*) to blunt; ~**rsi** *vr* to become blunt

snatu'rato, a *ag* inhuman, heartless

'snello, a *ag* (*agile*) agile; (*svelto*) slender, slim

sner'vare *vt* to enervate, wear out

sni'dare *vt* to drive out, flush out

snob'bare *vt* to snub

sno'bismo *sm* snobbery

snoccio'lare [znottʃo'lare] *vt* (*frutta*) to stone; (*fig: orazioni*) to rattle off

sno'dare *vt* (*rendere agile, mobile*) to loosen; (*articolarsi*) to come loose; (*articolarsi*) to bend; (*strada, fiume*) to wind

so *vb vedi* **sapere**

so'ave *ag* sweet, gentle, soft

sobbal'zare [sobbal'tsare] *vi* to jolt, jerk; (*trasalire*) to jump, start; **sob'balzo** *sm* jerk, jolt; jump, start

sobbar'carsi *vr*: ~ **a** to take on, undertake

sob'borgo, ghi *sm* suburb

sobil'lare *vt* to stir up, incite

'sobrio, a *ag* sober

socchi'udere [sok'kjudere] *vt* (*porta*) to leave ajar; (*occhi*) to half-close; **socchi'uso, a** *pp di* **socchiudere**

soc'correre *vt* to help, assist; **soc'corso, a** *pp di* **soccorrere** ♦ *sm* help, aid, assistance; **soccorsi** *smpl* relief *sg*, aid *sg*; **soccorso stradale** breakdown service

soci'ale [so'tʃale] *ag* social; (*di associazione*) club *cpd*, association *cpd*

socia'lismo [sotʃa'lizmo] *sm* socialism; **socia'lista, i, e** *ag, sm/f* socialist

socie'tà [sotʃe'ta] *sf inv* society; (*sportiva*) club; (*COMM*) company; ~ **per azioni** limited (*BRIT*) *o* incorporated (*US*) company; ~ **a responsabilità limitata** type of limited liability company

soci'evole [so'tʃevole] *ag* sociable

'socio [ˈsɔtʃo] *sm* (*DIR, COMM*) partner; (*membro di associazione*) member

'soda *sf* (*CHIM*) soda; (*bibita*) soda (water)

soda'lizio [soda'littsjo] *sm* association, society

soddisfa'cente [soddisfa'tʃente] *ag* satisfactory

soddis'fare *vt, vi*: ~ **a** to satisfy; (*impegno*) to fulfil; (*debito*) to pay off; (*richiesta*) to meet, comply with; **soddis'fatto, a** *pp di* **soddisfare** ♦ *ag* satisfied; **soddisfatto di** happy *o* satisfied with; pleased with; **soddisfazi'one** *sf* satisfaction

'sodo, a *ag* firm, hard; (*uovo*) hard-boiled ♦ *av* (*picchiare, lavorare*) hard; (*dormire*) soundly

so'fà *sm inv* sofa

soffe'renza [soffe'rentsa] *sf* suffering

sof'ferto, a *pp di* **soffrire**

soffi'are *vt* to blow; (*notizia, segreto*) to whisper ♦ *vi* to blow; (*sbuffare*) to puff (and blow); **~rsi il naso** to blow one's nose; ~ **qc/qn a qn** (*fig*) to pinch *o* steal sth/sb from sb; ~ **via qc** to blow sth away

'soffice [ˈsɔffitʃe] *ag* soft

'soffio *sm* (*di vento*) breath; ~ **al cuore** heart murmur

sof'fitta *sf* attic

sof'fitto *sm* ceiling

soffo'care *vi* (*anche:* **~rsi**) to suffocate, choke ♦ *vt* to suffocate, choke; (*fig*) to stifle, suppress

sof'friggere [sof'friddʒere] *vt* to fry lightly

sof'frire *vt* to suffer, endure; (*sopportare*) to bear, stand ♦ *vi* to suffer; to be in pain; ~ **(di) qc** (*MED*) to suffer from sth

sof'fritto, a *pp di* **soffriggere** ♦ *sm* (*CUC*) fried mixture of herbs, bacon and onions

sofisti'cato, a *ag* sophisticated; (*vino*) adulterated

sogget'tivo, a [soddʒet'tivo] *ag* subjective

sog'getto, a [sod'dʒetto] *ag*: ~ **a** (*sottomesso*) subject to; (*esposto: a variazioni, danni etc*) subject *o* liable to ♦ *sm* subject

soggezi'one [soddʒet'tsjone] *sf* subjection; (*timidezza*) awe; **avere ~ di qn** to stand in awe of sb; to be ill at ease in sb's presence

sogghi'gnare [soggin'nare] *vi* to sneer

soggior'nare [soddʒor'nare] *vi* to stay; **soggi'orno** *sm* (*invernale, marino*) stay; (*stanza*) living room

sog'giungere [sod'dʒundʒere] *vt* to add

'soglia [ˈsɔʎʎa] *sf* doorstep; (*anche fig*) threshold

sogli'ola [ˈsɔʎʎola] *sf* (*ZOOL*) sole

so'gnare [son'nare] *vt, vi* to dream; ~ **a occhi aperti** to daydream; **sogna'tore, 'trice** *sm/f* dreamer

'sogno [ˈsonno] *sm* dream

'soia *sf* (*BOT*) soya

sol *sm* (*MUS*) G; (*: solfeggiando*) so(h)

so'laio sm (soffitta) attic
sola'mente av only, just
so'lare ag solar, sun cpd
'solco, chi sm (scavo, fig: ruga) furrow;
  (incavo) rut, track; (di disco) groove
sol'dato sm soldier; ~ semplice private
'soldo sm (fig): non avere un ~ to be
  penniless; non vale un ~ it's not worth a
  penny; ~i smpl (denaro) money sg
'sole sm sun; (luce) sun(light); (tempo
  assolato) sun(shine); prendere il ~ to
  sunbathe
soleggi'ato, a [soled'dʒato] ag sunny
so'lenne ag solemn; solennità sf
  solemnity; (festività) holiday, feast day
sol'fato sm (CHIM) sulphate
soli'dale ag: essere ~ (con) to be in
  agreement (with)
solidarietà sf solidarity
'solido, a ag solid; (forte, robusto) sturdy,
  solid; (fig: ditta) sound, solid ♦ sm (MAT)
  solid
soli'loquio sm soliloquy
so'lista, i, e ag solo ♦ sm/f soloist
solita'mente av usually, as a rule
soli'tario, a ag (senza compagnia) solitary,
  lonely; (solo, isolato) solitary, lone; (deserto)
  lonely ♦ sm (gioiello, gioco) solitaire
'solito, a ag usual; essere ~ fare to be in
  the habit of doing; di ~ usually; più tardi
  del ~ later than usual; come al ~ as usual
soli'tudine sf solitude
solleci'tare [solletʃi'tare] vt (lavoro) to
  speed up; (persona) to urge on; (chiedere
  con insistenza) to press for, request
  urgently; (stimolare): ~ qn a fare to urge sb
  to do; sollecitazi'one sf entreaty,
  request; (fig) incentive; (TECN) stress
sol'lecito, a [sol'letʃito] ag prompt, quick
  ♦ sm (lettera) reminder; solleci'tudine sf
  promptness, speed
solleti'care vt to tickle
sol'letico sm tickling; soffrire il ~ to be
  ticklish
solleva'mento sm raising; lifting; revolt; ~
  pesi (SPORT) weight-lifting
solle'vare vt to lift, raise; (fig: persona:

alleggerire): ~ (da) to relieve (of); (: dar
  conforto) to comfort, relieve; (: questione)
  to raise; (: far insorgere) to stir (to revolt);
  ~rsi vr to rise; (fig: riprendersi) to recover;
  (: ribellarsi) to rise up
solli'evo sm relief; (conforto) comfort
'solo, a ag alone; (in senso spirituale:
  isolato) lonely; (unico): un ~ libro only one
  book, a single book; (con pl numerale):
  veniamo noi tre ~i just o only the three of
  us are coming ♦ av (soltanto) only, just;
  non ~ ... ma anche not only ... but also;
  fare qc da ~ to do sth (all) by oneself
sol'tanto av only
so'lubile ag (sostanza) soluble
soluzi'one [solut'tsjone] sf solution
sol'vente ag, sm solvent
'soma sf: bestia da ~ beast of burden
so'maro sm ass, donkey
somigli'anza [somiʎ'ʎantsa] sf resemblance
somigli'are [somiʎ'ʎare] vi: ~ a to be like,
  resemble; (nell'aspetto fisico) to look like;
  ~rsi vr to be (o look) alike
'somma sf (MAT) sum; (di denaro) sum (of
  money)
som'mare vt to add up; (aggiungere) to
  add; tutto sommato all things considered
som'mario, a ag (racconto, indagine)
  brief; (giustizia) summary ♦ sm summary
som'mergere [som'merdʒere] vt to
  submerge
sommer'gibile [sommer'dʒibile] sm
  submarine
som'merso, a pp di sommergere
som'messo, a ag (voce) soft, subdued
somminis'trare vt to give, administer
sommità sf inv summit, top; (fig) height
'sommo, a ag highest; (rispetto etc)
  highest, greatest; (poeta, artista) great,
  outstanding; per ~i capi briefly, covering
  the main points
som'mossa sf uprising
so'nare etc = suonare etc
son'daggio [son'daddʒo] sm sounding;
  probe; boring, drilling; (indagine) survey; ~
  d'opinioni opinion poll
son'dare vt (NAUT) to sound; (atmosfera,

piaga) to probe; (*MINERALOGIA*) to bore, drill; (*fig: opinione etc*) to survey, poll

so'netto *sm* sonnet

son'nambulo, a *sm/f* sleepwalker

sonnecchi'are [sonnek'kjare] *vi* to doze, nod

son'nifero *sm* sleeping drug (*o* pill)

'sonno *sm* sleep; **prendere ~** to fall asleep; **aver ~** to be sleepy

'sono *vb vedi* **essere**

so'noro, a *ag* (*ambiente*) resonant; (*voce*) sonorous, ringing; (*onde, film*) sound *cpd*

sontu'oso, a *ag* sumptuous; lavish

sopo'rifero, a *ag* soporific

soppe'sare *vt* to weigh in one's hand(s), feel the weight of; (*fig*) to weigh up

soppi'atto: **di ~** *av* secretly; furtively

soppor'tare *vt* (*reggere*) to support; (*subire: perdita, spese*) to bear, sustain; (*soffrire: dolore*) to bear, endure; (*sog: cosa: freddo*) to withstand; (*sog: persona: freddo, vino*) to take; (*tollerare*) to put up with, tolerate

sop'presso, a *pp di* **sopprimere**

sop'primere *vt* (*carica, privilegi, testimone*) to do away with; (*pubblicazione*) to suppress; (*parola, frase*) to delete

'sopra *prep* (*gen*) on; (*al di sopra di, più in alto di*) above; over; (*riguardo a*) on, about ♦ *av* on top; (*attaccato, scritto*) on it; (*al di sopra*) above; (*al piano superiore*) upstairs; **donne ~ i 30 anni** women over 30 (years of age); **abito di ~** I live upstairs; **dormirci ~** (*fig*) to sleep on it

so'prabito *sm* overcoat

soprac'ciglio [soprat'tʃiʎʎo] (*pl(f)* **soprac'ciglia**) *sm* eyebrow

sopracco'perta *sf* (*di letto*) bedspread; (*di libro*) jacket

sopraf'fare *vt* to overcome, overwhelm; sopraf'fatto, a *pp di* **sopraffare**

sopraf'fino, a *ag* (*pranzo, vino*) excellent

sopraggi'ungere [soprad'dʒundʒere] *vi* (*giungere all'improvviso*) to arrive (unexpectedly); (*accadere*) to occur (unexpectedly)

sopral'luogo, ghi *sm* (*di esperti*) inspection; (*di polizia*) on-the-spot investigation

sopram'mobile *sm* ornament

soprannatu'rale *ag* supernatural

sopran'nome *sm* nickname

so'prano, a *sm/f* (*persona*) soprano ♦ *sm* (*voce*) soprano

soprappensi'ero *av* lost in thought

sopras'salto *sm*: **di ~** with a start; suddenly

soprasse'dere *vi*: **~ a** to delay, put off

soprat'tutto *av* (*anzitutto*) above all; (*specialmente*) especially

sopravvalu'tare *vt* to overestimate

soprav'vento *sm*: **avere/prendere il ~ su** to have/get the upper hand over

sopravvis'suto, a *pp di* **sopravvivere**

soprav'vivere *vi* to survive; (*continuare a vivere*): **~ (in)** to live on (in); **~ a** (*incidente etc*) to survive; (*persona*) to outlive

soprele'vata *sf* (*strada*) flyover; (*ferrovia*) elevated railway

soprinten'dente *sm/f* supervisor; (*statale: di belle arti etc*) keeper; soprinten'denza *sf* supervision; (*ente*): **soprintendenza alle Belle Arti** *government department responsible for monuments and artistic treasures*

so'pruso *sm* abuse of power; **subire un ~** to be abused

soq'quadro *sm*: **mettere a ~** to turn upside-down

sor'betto *sm* sorbet, water ice

sor'bire *vt* to sip; (*fig*) to put up with

'sorcio, ci ['sortʃo] *sm* mouse

'sordido, a *ag* sordid; (*fig: gretto*) stingy

sor'dina *sf*: **in ~** softly; (*fig*) on the sly

sordità *sf* deafness

'sordo, a *ag* deaf; (*rumore*) muffled; (*dolore*) dull; (*odio, rancore*) veiled ♦ *sm/f* deaf person; sordo'muto, a *ag* deaf-and-dumb ♦ *sm/f* deaf-mute

so'rella *sf* sister; sorel'lastra *sf* stepsister

sor'gente [sor'dʒɛnte] *sf* (*d'acqua*) spring; (*di fiume, FISICA, fig*) source

'sorgere ['sordʒere] *vi* to rise; (*scaturire*) to spring, rise; (*fig: difficoltà*) to arise

sormon'tare vt (fig) to overcome, surmount

sorni'one, a ag sly

sorpas'sare vt (AUT) to overtake; (fig) to surpass; (: eccedere) to exceed, go beyond; ~ **in altezza** to be higher than; (persona) to be taller than; **sor'passo** sm (AUT) overtaking

sorpren'dente ag surprising

sor'prendere vt (cogliere: in flagrante etc) to catch; (stupire) to surprise; **~rsi** vr: **~rsi (di)** to be surprised (at); **sor'presa** sf surprise; **fare una sorpresa a qn** to give sb a surprise; **sor'preso, a** pp di **sorprendere**

sor'reggere [sor'reddʒere] vt to support, hold up; (fig) to sustain; **sor'retto, a** pp di **sorreggere**

sor'ridere vi to smile; **sor'riso, a** pp di **sorridere** ♦ sm smile

'sorso sm sip

'sorta sf sort, kind; **di ~** whatever, of any kind, at all

'sorte sf (fato) fate, destiny; (evento fortuito) chance; **tirare a ~** to draw lots

sor'teggio [sor'teddʒo] sm draw

sorti'legio [sorti'ledʒo] sm witchcraft no pl; (incantesimo) spell; **fare un ~ a qn** to cast a spell on sb

sor'tita sf (MIL) sortie

'sorto, a pp di **sorgere**

sorveg'lianza [sorveʎ'ʎantsa] sf watch; supervision; (POLIZIA, MIL) surveillance

sorvegli'are [sorveʎ'ʎare] vt (bambino, bagagli, prigioniero) to watch, keep an eye on; (malato) to watch over; (territorio, casa) to watch o keep watch over; (lavori) to supervise

sorvo'lare vt (territorio) to fly over ♦ vi: **~ su** (fig) to skim over

'sosia sm inv double

sos'pendere vt (appendere) to hang (up); (interrompere, privare di una carica) to suspend; (rimandare) to defer; (appendere) to hang; **sospensi'one** sf (anche CHIM, AUT) suspension; deferment; **sos'peso, a** pp di **sospendere** ♦ ag (appeso): **sospeso**

a hanging on (o from); (treno, autobus) cancelled; **in sospeso** in abeyance; (conto) outstanding; **tenere in sospeso** (fig) to keep in suspense

sospet'tare vt to suspect ♦ vi: **~ di** to suspect; (diffidare) to be suspicious of

sos'petto, a ag suspicious ♦ sm suspicion; **sospet'toso, a** ag suspicious

sos'pingere [sos'pindʒere] vt to drive, push; **sos'pinto, a** pp di **sospingere**

sospi'rare vi to sigh ♦ vt to long for, yearn for; **sos'piro** sm sigh

'sosta sf (fermata) stop, halt; (pausa) pause, break; **senza ~** non-stop, without a break

sostan'tivo sm noun, substantive

sos'tanza [sos'tantsa] sf substance; **~e** sfpl (ricchezze) wealth sg, possessions; **in ~** in short, to sum up; **sostanzi'oso, a** ag (cibo) nourishing, substantial

sos'tare vi (fermarsi) to stop (for a while), stay; (fare una pausa) to take a break

sos'tegno [sos'teɲɲo] sm support

soste'nere vt to support; (prendere su di sé) to take on, bear; (resistere) to withstand, stand up to; (affermare): **~ che** to maintain that; **~rsi** vr to hold o.s. up, support o.s.; (fig) to keep up one's strength; **~ gli esami** to sit exams; **sosteni'tore, 'trice** sm/f supporter

sostenta'mento sm maintenance, support

soste'nuto, a ag (stile) elevated; (velocità, ritmo) sustained; (prezzo) high ♦ sm/f: **fare il(la) ~(a)** to be standoffish, keep one's distance

sostitu'ire vt (mettere al posto di): **~ qn/qc a** to substitute sb/sth for; (prendere il posto di: persona) to substitute for; (: cosa) to take the place of

sosti'tuto, a sm/f substitute

sostituzi'one [sostitut'tsjone] sf substitution; **in ~ di** as a substitute for, in place of

sotta'ceti [sotta'tʃeti] smpl pickles

sot'tana sf (sottoveste) underskirt; (gonna) skirt; (REL) soutane, cassock

sotter'fugio [sotter'fudʒo] *sm* subterfuge
sotter'raneo, a *ag* underground ♦ *sm* cellar
sotter'rare *vt* to bury
sottigli'ezza [sottiʎ'ʎettsa] *sf* thinness; slimness; (*fig: acutezza*) subtlety; shrewdness; **~e** *sfpl* (*pedanteria*) quibbles
sot'tile *ag* thin; (*figura, caviglia*) thin, slim, slender; (*fine: polvere, capelli*) fine; (*fig: leggero*) light; (*: vista*) sharp, keen; (*: olfatto*) fine, discriminating; (*: mente*) subtle; shrewd ♦ *sm*: **non andare per il ~** not to mince matters
sottin'tendere *vt* (*intendere qc non espresso*) to understand; (*implicare*) to imply; **sottin'teso, a** *pp di* **sottintendere** ♦ *sm* allusion; **parlare senza sottintesi** to speak plainly
'**sotto** *prep* (*gen*) under; (*più in basso di*) below ♦ *av* underneath, beneath; below; (**al piano di**) **~** downstairs; **~ forma di** in the form of; **~ il monte** at the foot of the mountain; **siamo ~ Natale** it's nearly Christmas; **~ la pioggia/il sole** in the rain/sun(shine); **~ terra** underground; **chiuso ~ vuoto** vacuum-packed
sottoline'are *vt* to underline; (*fig*) to emphasize, stress
sottoma'rino, a *ag* (*flora*) submarine; (*cavo, navigazione*) underwater ♦ *sm* (*NAUT*) submarine
sotto'messo, a *pp di* **sottomettere**
sotto'mettere *vt* to subdue, subjugate; **~rsi** *vr* to submit
sottopas'saggio [sottopas'saddʒo] *sm* (*AUT*) underpass; (*pedonale*) subway, underpass
sotto'porre *vt* (*costringere*) to subject; (*fig: presentare*) to submit; **sottoporsi** *vr* to submit; **sottoporsi a** (*subire*) to undergo; **sotto'posto, a** *pp di* **sottoporre**
sottos'critto, a *pp di* **sottoscrivere**
sottos'crivere *vt* to sign ♦ *vi*: **~ a** to subscribe to; **sottoscrizi'one** *sf* signing; subscription
sottosegre'tario *sm*: **~ di Stato** Under-Secretary of State (*BRIT*), Assistant Secretary

of State (*US*)
sotto'sopra *av* upside-down
sotto'terra *av* underground
sotto'titolo *sm* subtitle
sottovalu'tare *vt* to underestimate
sotto'veste *sf* underskirt
sotto'voce [sotto'votʃe] *av* in a low voice
sot'trarre *vt* (*MAT*) to subtract, take away; **~ qn/qc a** (*togliere*) to remove sb/sth from; (*salvare*) to rescue sb/sth from; **~ qc a qn** (*rubare*) to steal sth from sb; **sottrarsi** *vr*: **sottrarsi a** (*sfuggire*) to escape; (*evitare*) to avoid; **sot'tratto, a** *pp di* **sottrarre**; **sottrazi'one** *sf* subtraction; removal
sovi'etico, a, ci, che *ag* Soviet ♦ *sm/f* Soviet citizen
sovraccari'care *vt* to overload
sovrannatu'rale *ag* = **soprannaturale**
so'vrano, a *ag* sovereign; (*fig: sommo*) supreme ♦ *sm/f* sovereign, monarch
sovrap'porre *vt* to place on top of, put on top of
sovras'tare *vi*: **~ a** (*vallata, fiume*) to overhang; (*fig*) to overhang, threaten ♦ *vt* to overhang; to hang over, threaten
sovrinten'dente *etc* = **soprintendente** *etc*
sovru'mano, a *ag* superhuman
sovvenzi'one [sovven'tsjone] *sf* subsidy, grant
sovver'sivo, a *ag* subversive
'**sozzo, a** ['sottso] *ag* filthy, dirty
S.p.A. *abbr* = **società per azioni**
spac'care *vt* to split, break; (*legna*) to chop; **~rsi** *vr* to split, break; **spacca'tura** *sf* split
spacci'are [spat'tʃare] *vt* (*vendere*) to sell (off); (*mettere in circolazione*) to circulate; (*droga*) to peddle, push; **~rsi** *vr*: **spacciarsi per** (*farsi credere*) to pass o.s. off as, pretend to be; **spaccia'tore, 'trice** *sm/f* (*di droga*) pusher; (*di denaro falso*) dealer; '**spaccio** *sm* (*di merce rubata, droga*): **spaccio (di)** trafficking (in); (*in denaro falso*): **spaccio (di)** passing (of); (*vendita*) sale; (*bottega*) shop
'**spacco, chi** *sm* (*fenditura*) split, crack;

(*strappo*) tear; (*di gonna*) slit

spac'cone *sm/f* boaster, braggart

'spada *sf* sword

spae'sato, a *ag* disorientated, lost

spa'ghetti [spa'getti] *smpl* (*CUC*) spaghetti *sg*

'Spagna ['spaɲɲa] *sf*: la ~ Spain; spa'gnolo, a *ag* Spanish ♦ *sm/f* Spaniard ♦ *sm* (*LING*) Spanish; gli Spagnoli the Spanish

'spago, ghi *sm* string, twine

spai'ato, a *ag* (*calza, guanto*) odd

spalan'care *vt* to open wide; ~rsi *vr* to open wide

spa'lare *vt* to shovel

'spalla *sf* shoulder; (*fig: TEATRO*) stooge; ~e *sfpl* (*dorso*) back; spalleggi'are *vt* to back up, support

spalli'era *sf* (*di sedia etc*) back; (*di letto: da capo*) head(board); (: *da piedi*) foot(board); (*GINNASTICA*) wall bars *pl*

spal'lina *sf* (*bretella*) strap; (*imbottita*) shoulder pad

spal'mare *vt* to spread

'spalti *smpl* (*di stadio*) terracing

span'dere *vt* to spread; (*versare*) to pour (out); ~rsi *vr* to spread; 'spanto, a *pp di* spandere

spa'rare *vt* to fire ♦ *vi* (*far fuoco*) to fire; (*tirare*) to shoot; spara'toria *sf* exchange of shots

sparecchi'are [sparek'kjare] *vt*: ~ (la tavola) to clear the table

spa'reggio [spa'reddʒo] *sm* (*SPORT*) play-off

'spargere ['spardʒere] *vt* (*sparpagliare*) to scatter; (*versare: vino*) to spill; (: *lacrime, sangue*) to shed; (*diffondere*) to spread; (*emanare*) to give off (*o* out); ~rsi *vr* to spread; spargi'mento *sm* scattering, strewing; spilling; shedding; spargimento di sangue bloodshed

spa'rire *vi* to disappear, vanish

spar'lare *vi*: ~ di to run down, speak ill of

'sparo *sm* shot

sparpagli'are [sparpaʎ'ʎare] *vt* to scatter; ~rsi *vr* to scatter

'sparso, a *pp di* spargere ♦ *ag* scattered;

(*sciolto*) loose

spar'tire *vt* (*eredità, bottino*) to share out; (*avversari*) to separate

spar'tito *sm* (*MUS*) score

sparti'traffico *sm inv* (*AUT*) central reservation (*BRIT*), median (strip) (*US*)

spa'ruto, a *ag* (*viso etc*) haggard

sparvi'ero *sm* (*ZOOL*) sparrowhawk

spasi'mante *sm* suitor

'spasimo *sm* pang; 'spasmo *sm* (*MED*) spasm; spas'modico, a, ci, che *ag* (*angoscioso*) agonizing; (*MED*) spasmodic

spassio'nato, a *ag* dispassionate, impartial

'spasso *sm* (*divertimento*) amusement, enjoyment; andare a ~ to go out for a walk; essere a ~ (*fig*) to be out of work; mandare qn a ~ (*fig*) to give sb the sack

'spatola *sf* spatula; (*di muratore*) trowel

spau'racchio [spau'rakkjo] *sm* scarecrow

spau'rire *vt* to frighten, terrify

spa'valdo, a *ag* arrogant, bold

spaventa'passeri *sm inv* scarecrow

spaven'tare *vt* to frighten, scare; ~rsi *vr* to be frightened, be scared; to get a fright; spa'vento *sm* fear, fright; far spavento a qn to give sb a fright; spaven'toso, a *ag* frightening, terrible; (*fig: fam*) tremendous, fantastic

spazien'tire [spattsjen'tire] *vi* (*anche*: ~rsi) to lose one's patience

'spazio ['spattsjo] *sm* space; ~ aereo airspace; spazi'oso, a *ag* spacious

spazzaca'mino [spattsaka'mino] *sm* chimney sweep

spazza'neve [spattsa'neve] *sm inv* snowplough

spaz'zare [spat'tsare] *vt* to sweep; (*foglie etc*) to sweep up; (*cacciare*) to sweep away; spazza'tura *sf* sweepings *pl*; (*immondizia*) rubbish; spaz'zino *sm* street sweeper

'spazzola ['spattsola] *sf* brush; ~ per abiti clothesbrush; ~ da capelli hairbrush; spazzo'lare *vt* to brush; spazzo'lino *sm* (small) brush; spazzolino da denti toothbrush

specchi'arsi [spek'kjarsi] *vr* to look at o.s. in a mirror; (*riflettersi*) to be mirrored, be reflected

'specchio ['spekkjo] *sm* mirror

speci'ale [spe'tʃale] *ag* special; **specia'lista, i, e** *sm/f* specialist; **specialità** *sf inv* speciality; (*branca di studio*) special field, speciality; **specializ'zarsi** *vr:* **specializzarsi (in)** to specialize (in); **special'mente** *av* especially, particularly

'specie ['spetʃe] *sf inv* (BIOL, BOT, ZOOL) species *inv*; (*tipo*) kind, sort ♦ *av* especially, particularly; **una ~ di** a kind of; **fare ~ a qn** to surprise sb; **la ~ umana** mankind

specifi'care [spetʃifi'kare] *vt* to specify, state

spe'cifico, a, ci, che [spe'tʃifiko] *ag* specific

specu'lare *vi:* **~ su** (COMM) to speculate in; (*sfruttare*) to exploit; (*meditare*) to speculate on; **speculazi'one** *sf* speculation

spe'dire *vt* to send; **spedizi'one** *sf* sending; (*collo*) consignment; (*scientifica etc*) expedition

'spegnere ['speɲɲere] *vt* (*fuoco, sigaretta*) to put out, extinguish; (*apparecchio elettrico*) to turn *o* switch off; (*gas*) to turn off; (*fig: suoni, passioni*) to stifle; (*debito*) to extinguish; **~rsi** *vr* to go out; to go off; (*morire*) to pass away

spel'lare *vt* (*scuoiare*) to skin; (*scorticare*) to graze; **~rsi** *vr* to peel

'spendere *vt* to spend

spen'nare *vt* to pluck

spensie'rato, a *ag* carefree

'spento, a *pp di* **spegnere** ♦ *ag* (*suono*) muffled; (*colore*) dull; (*sigaretta*) out; (*civiltà, vulcano*) extinct

spe'ranza [spe'rantsa] *sf* hope

spe'rare *vt* to hope for ♦ *vi:* **~ in** to trust in; **~ che/di fare** to hope that/to do; **lo spero, spero di sì** I hope so

sper'duto, a *ag* (*isolato*) out-of-the-way; (*persona: smarrita, a disagio*) lost

spergi'uro, a [sper'dʒuro] *sm/f* perjurer

♦ *sm* perjury

sperimen'tale *ag* experimental

sperimen'tare *vt* to experiment with, test; (*fig*) to test, put to the test

'sperma, i *sm* sperm

spe'rone *sm* spur

sperpe'rare *vt* to squander

'spesa *sf* (*somma di denaro*) expense; (*costo*) cost; (*acquisto*) purchase; (*fam: acquisto del cibo quotidiano*) shopping; **~e** *sfpl* (*soldi spesi*) expenses; (COMM) costs; charges; **fare la ~** to do the shopping; **a ~e di** (*a carico di*) at the expense of; **~e generali** overheads; **~e postali** postage *sg*; **~e di viaggio** travelling expenses

'speso, a *pp di* **spendere**

'spesso, a *ag* (*fitto*) thick; (*frequente*) frequent ♦ *av* often; **~e volte** frequently, often

spes'sore *sm* thickness

spet'tabile (*abbr:* **Spett.**: *in lettere*) *ag:* **~ ditta X** Messrs X and Co.

spet'tacolo *sm* (*rappresentazione*) performance, show; (*vista, scena*) sight; **dare ~ di sé** to make an exhibition *o* a spectacle of o.s.; **spettaco'loso, a** *ag* spectacular

spet'tare *vi:* **~ a** (*decisione*) to be up to; (*stipendio*) to be due to; **spetta a te decidere** it's up to you to decide

spetta'tore, 'trice *sm/f* (CINEMA, TEATRO) member of the audience; (*di avvenimento*) onlooker, witness

spetti'nare *vt:* **~ qn** to ruffle sb's hair; **~rsi** *vr* to get one's hair in a mess

'spettro *sm* (*fantasma*) spectre; (FISICA) spectrum

'spezie ['spettsje] *sfpl* (CUC) spices

spez'zare [spet'tsare] *vt* (*rompere*) to break; (*fig: interrompere*) to break up; **~rsi** *vr* to break

spezza'tino [spettsa'tino] *sm* (CUC) stew

spezzet'tare [spettset'tare] *vt* to break up (*o* chop) into small pieces

'spia *sf* spy; (*confidente della polizia*) informer; (ELETTR) indicating light; warning light; (*fessura*) peep-hole; (*fig: sintomo*) sign, indication

spia'cente [spja'tʃɛnte] *ag* sorry; **essere ~ di qc/di fare qc** to be sorry about sth/for doing sth

spia'cevole [spja'tʃevole] *ag* unpleasant

spi'aggia, ge ['spjaddʒa] *sf* beach; **~ libera** public beach

spia'nare *vt* (*terreno*) to level, make level; (*edificio*) to raze to the ground; (*pasta*) to roll out; (*rendere liscio*) to smooth (out)

spi'ano *sm*: **a tutto ~** (*lavorare*) non-stop, without a break; (*spendere*) lavishly

spian'tato, a *ag* penniless, ruined

spi'are *vt* to spy on

spi'azzo ['spjattso] *sm* open space; (*radura*) clearing

spic'care *vt* (*assegno, mandato di cattura*) to issue ♦ *vi* (*risaltare*) to stand out; **~ il volo** to fly off; (*fig*) to spread one's wings; **~ un balzo** to leap; **spic'cato, a** *ag* (*marcato*) marked, strong; (*notevole*) remarkable

spicchio ['spikkjo] *sm* (*di agrumi*) segment; (*di aglio*) clove; (*parte*) piece, slice

spicci'are [spit'tʃare] *vt* to finish off quickly; **~rsi** *vr* to hurry up

spicciolo, a ['spittʃolo] *ag*: **moneta ~a, ~i** *smpl* (small) change

spicco, chi *sm*: **di ~** outstanding; (*tema*) main, principal; **fare ~** to stand out

spie'dino *sm* (*utensile*) skewer; (*pietanza*) kebab

spi'edo *sm* (*CUC*) spit

spie'gare *vt* (*far capire*) to explain; (*tovaglia*) to unfold; (*vele*) to unfurl; **~rsi** *vr* to explain o.s., make o.s. clear; **~ qc a qn** to explain sth to sb; **spiegazi'one** *sf* explanation

spiegaz'zare [spjegat'tsare] *vt* to crease, crumple

spie'tato, a *ag* ruthless, pitiless

spiffe'rare (*fam*) *vt* to blurt out, blab

spiga, ghe *sf* (*BOT*) ear

spigli'ato, a *ag* [spiʎ'ʎato] *ag* self-possessed, self-confident

spigolo *sm* corner; (*MAT*) edge

spilla *sf* brooch; (*da cravatta, cappello*) pin; **~ di sicurezza** *o* **da balia** safety pin

spil'lare *vt* (*vino, fig*) to tap; **~ denaro/ notizie a qn** to tap sb for money/ information

spillo *sm* pin

spi'lorcio, a, ci, ce [spi'lortʃo] *ag* mean, stingy

spina *sf* (*BOT*) thorn; (*ZOOL*) spine, prickle; (*di pesce*) bone; (*ELETTR*) plug; (*di botte*) bunghole; **birra alla ~** draught beer; **~ dorsale** (*ANAT*) backbone

spi'nacio [spi'natʃo] *sm* spinach; (*CUC*): **~i** spinach *sg*

spingere ['spindʒere] *vt* to push; (*condurre: anche fig*) to drive; (*stimolare*): **~ qn a fare** to urge *o* press sb to do; **~rsi** *vr* (*inoltrarsi*) to push on, carry on; **~rsi troppo lontano** (*anche fig*) to go too far

spi'noso, a *ag* thorny, prickly

spinta *sf* (*urto*) push; (*FISICA*) thrust; (*fig: stimolo*) incentive, spur; (: *appoggio*) string-pulling *no pl*; **dare una ~a a qn** (*fig*) to pull strings for sb

spinto, a *pp di* **spingere**

spio'naggio [spio'naddʒo] *sm* espionage, spying

spi'overe *vi* to stop raining

spira *sf* coil

spi'raglio [spi'raʎʎo] *sm* (*fessura*) chink, narrow opening; (*raggio di luce, fig*) glimmer, gleam

spi'rale *sf* spiral; (*contraccettivo*) coil; **a ~** spiral(-shaped)

spi'rare *vi* (*vento*) to blow; (*morire*) to expire, pass away

spiri'tato, a *ag* possessed; (*fig: persona, espressione*) wild

spiri'tismo *sm* spiritualism

spirito *sm* (*REL, CHIM, disposizione d'animo, di legge etc, fantasma*) spirit; (*pensieri, intelletto*) mind; (*arguzia*) wit; (*umorismo*) humour, wit; **lo S~ Santo** the Holy Spirit *o* Ghost

spirito'saggine [spirito'saddʒine] *sf* witticism; (*peg*) wisecrack

spiri'toso, a *ag* witty

spiritu'ale *ag* spiritual

'splendere *vi* to shine

'splendido, a *ag* splendid; (*splendente*) shining; (*sfarzoso*) magnificent, splendid

splen'dore *sm* splendour; (*luce intensa*) brilliance, brightness

spodes'tare *vt* to deprive of power; (*sovrano*) to depose

spogli'are [spoʎ'ʎare] *vt* (*svestire*) to undress; (*privare, fig: depredare*): **~ qn di qc** to deprive sb of sth; (*togliere ornamenti: anche fig*): **~ qn/qc di** to strip sb/sth of; **~rsi** *vr* to undress, strip; **~rsi di** (*ricchezze etc*) to deprive o.s. of, give up; (*pregiudizi*) to rid o.s. of; **spoglia'toio** *sm* dressing room; (*di scuola etc*) cloakroom; (*SPORT*) changing room; **'spoglie** ['spɔʎʎe] *sfpl* (*salma*) remains; (*preda*) spoils, booty *sg*; *vedi anche* **spoglio**; **'spoglio, a** *ag* (*pianta, terreno*) bare; (*privo*): **spoglio di** stripped of; lacking in, without ♦ *sm* (*di voti*) counting

'spola *sf* (*bobina di filo*) cop; **fare la ~ (fra)** to go to and fro *o* shuttle (between)

spol'pare *vt* to strip the flesh off

spolve'rare *vt* (*anche CUC*) to dust; (*con spazzola*) to brush; (*con battipanni*) to beat; (*fig*) to polish off ♦ *vi* to dust

'sponda *sf* (*di fiume*) bank; (*di mare, lago*) shore; (*bordo*) edge

spon'taneo, a *ag* spontaneous; (*persona*) unaffected, natural

spopo'lare *vt* to depopulate ♦ *vi* (*attirare folla*) to draw the crowds; **~rsi** *vr* to become depopulated

spor'care *vt* to dirty, make dirty; (*fig*) to sully, soil; **~rsi** *vr* to get dirty

spor'cizia [spor'tʃittsja] *sf* (*stato*) dirtiness; (*sudiciume*) dirt, filth; (*cosa sporca*) dirt *no pl*, something dirty

'sporco, a, chi, che *ag* dirty, filthy

spor'genza [spor'dʒentsa] *sf* projection

'sporgere ['spɔrdʒere] *vt* to put out, stretch out ♦ *vi* (*venire in fuori*) to stick out; **~rsi** *vr* to lean out; **~ querela contro qn** (*DIR*) to take legal action against sb

sport *sm inv* sport

'sporta *sf* shopping bag

spor'tello *sm* (*di treno, auto etc*) door; (*di banca, ufficio*) window, counter; **~ automatico** (*BANCA*) cash dispenser, automated telling machine

spor'tivo, a *ag* (*gara, giornale, centro*) sports *cpd*; (*persona*) sporty; (*abito*) casual; (*spirito, atteggiamento*) sporting

'sporto, a *pp di* **sporgere**

'sposa *sf* bride; (*moglie*) wife

sposa'lizio [spoza'littsjo] *sm* wedding

spo'sare *vt* to marry; (*fig: idea, fede*) to espouse; **~rsi** *vr* to get married, marry; **~rsi con qn** to marry sb, get married to sb; **spo'sato, a** *ag* married

'sposo *sm* (*bride*)groom; (*marito*) husband; **gli ~i** *smpl* the newlyweds

spos'sato, a *ag* exhausted, weary

spos'tare *vt* to move, shift; (*cambiare: orario*) to change; **~rsi** *vr* to move

'spranga, ghe *sf* (*sbarra*) bar

'sprazzo ['sprattso] *sm* (*di sole etc*) flash; (*fig: di gioia etc*) burst

spre'care *vt* to waste; **~rsi** *vr* (*persona*) to waste one's energy; **'spreco** *sm* waste

spre'gevole [spre'dʒevole] *ag* contemptible, despicable

spregiudi'cato, a [spredʒudi'kato] *ag* unprejudiced, unbiased; (*peg*) unscrupulous

'spremere *vt* to squeeze

spre'muta *sf* fresh juice; **~ d'arancia** fresh orange juice

sprez'zante [spret'tsante] *ag* scornful, contemptuous

sprigio'nare [spridʒo'nare] *vt* to give off, emit; **~rsi** *vr* to emanate; (*uscire con impeto*) to burst out

spriz'zare [sprit'tsare] *vt, vi* to spurt; **~ gioia/salute** to be bursting with joy/health

sprofon'dare *vi* to sink; (*casa*) to collapse; (*suolo*) to give way, subside; **~rsi** *vr*: **~rsi in** (*poltrona*) to sink into; (*fig*) to become immersed *o* absorbed in

spro'nare *vt* to spur (on)

'sprone *sm* (*sperone, fig*) spur

sproporzio'nato, a [sproportsjo'nato] *ag* disproportionate, out of all proportion

sproporzi'one [spropor'tsjone] *sf* disproportion

sproposi'tato, a *ag* (*lettera, discorso*) full of mistakes; (*fig: costo*) excessive, enormous

spro'posito *sm* blunder; **a ~** at the wrong time; (*rispondere, parlare*) irrelevantly

sprovve'duto, a *ag* inexperienced, naïve

sprov'visto, a *ag* (*mancante*): **~ di** lacking in, without; **alla ~a** unawares

spruz'zare [sprut'tsare] *vt* (*a nebulizzazione*) to spray; (*aspergere*) to sprinkle; (*inzaccherare*) to splash; **spruzzo** *sm* spray; splash

'spugna ['spuɲɲa] *sf* (*ZOOL*) sponge; (*tessuto*) towelling; **spu'gnoso, a** *ag* spongy

'spuma *sf* (*schiuma*) foam; (*bibita*) fizzy drink

spu'mante *sm* sparkling wine

spumeggi'ante [spumed'dʒante] *ag* (*birra*) foaming; (*vino, fig*) sparkling

spu'mone *sm* (*CUC*) mousse

spun'tare *vt* (*coltello*) to break the point of; (*capelli*) to trim ♦ *vi* (*uscire: germogli*) to sprout; (*: capelli*) to begin to grow; (*: denti*) to come through; (*apparire*) to appear (suddenly); **~rsi** *vr* to become blunt, lose its point; **spuntarla** (*fig*) to make it, win through

spun'tino *sm* snack

'spunto *sm* (*TEATRO, MUS*) cue; (*fig*) starting point; **dare lo ~ a** (*fig*) to give rise to

spur'gare *vt* (*fogna*) to clean, clear

spu'tare *vt* to spit out; (*fig*) to belch (out) ♦ *vi* to spit; **'sputo** *sm* spittle *no pl*, spit *no pl*

'squadra *sf* (*strumento*) (set) square; (*gruppo*) team, squad; (*di operai*) gang, squad; (*MIL*) squad; (*: AER, NAUT*) squadron; (*SPORT*) team; **lavoro a ~e** teamwork

squa'drare *vt* to square, make square; (*osservare*) to look at closely

squa'driglia [skwa'driʎʎa] *sf* (*AER*) flight; (*NAUT*) squadron

squa'drone *sm* squadron

squagli'arsi [skwaʎ'ʎarsi] *vr* to melt; (*fig*) to sneak off

squa'lifica *sf* disqualification

squalifi'care *vt* to disqualify

'squallido, a *ag* wretched, bleak

squal'lore *sm* wretchedness, bleakness

'squalo *sm* shark

'squama *sf* scale; **squa'mare** *vt* to scale; **squamarsi** *vr* to flake *o* peel (off)

squarcia'gola [skwartʃa'gola]: **a ~** *av* at the top of one's voice

squarci'are [skwar'tʃare] *vt* to rip (open); (*fig*) to pierce

squar'tare *vt* to quarter, cut up

squattri'nato, a *ag* penniless

squili'brato, a *ag* (*PSIC*) unbalanced; **squi'librio** *sm* (*differenza, sbilancio*) imbalance; (*PSIC*) unbalance

squil'lante *ag* shrill, sharp

squil'lare *vi* (*campanello, telefono*) to ring (out); (*tromba*) to blare; **'squillo** *sm* ring, ringing *no pl*; blare; **ragazza f squillo** *inv* call girl

squi'sito, a *ag* exquisite; (*cibo*) delicious; (*persona*) delightful

squit'tire *vi* (*uccello*) to squawk; (*topo*) to squeak

sradi'care *vt* to uproot; (*fig*) to eradicate

sragio'nare [zradʒo'nare] *vi* to talk nonsense, rave

srego'lato, a *ag* (*senza ordine: vita*) disorderly; (*smodato*) immoderate; (*dissoluto*) dissolute

S.r.l. *abbr* = **società a responsabilità limitata**

'stabile *ag* stable, steady; (*tempo: non variabile*) settled; (*TEATRO: compagnia*) resident ♦ *sm* (*edificio*) building

stabili'mento *sm* (*edificio*) establishment; (*fabbrica*) plant, factory

stabi'lire *vt* to establish; (*fissare: prezzi, data*) to fix; (*decidere*) to decide; **~rsi** *vr* (*prendere dimora*) to settle

stac'care *vt* (*levare*) to detach, remove; (*separare: anche fig*) to separate, divide; (*strappare*) to tear off (*o* out); (*scandire: parole*) to pronounce clearly; (*SPORT*) to leave behind; **~rsi** *vr* (*bottone etc*) to come off; (*scostarsi*): **~rsi (da)** to move away (from); (*fig: separarsi*): **~rsi da** to leave; **non ~ gli occhi da qn** not to take one's eyes off sb

'**stadio** *sm* (*SPORT*) stadium; (*periodo, fase*) phase, stage

'**staffa** *sf* (*di sella, TECN*) stirrup; **perdere le ~e** (*fig*) to fly off the handle

staf'**fetta** *sf* (*messo*) dispatch rider; (*SPORT*) relay race

stagio'**nale** [stadʒo'nale] *ag* seasonal

stagio'**nare** [stadʒo'nare] *vt* (*legno*) to season; (*formaggi, vino*) to mature

stagi'**one** [sta'dʒone] *sf* season; **alta/bassa ~** high/low season

stagli'**arsi** [staʎ'ʎarsi] *vr* to stand out, be silhouetted

'**stagno, a** ['stanno] *ag* watertight; (*a tenuta d'aria*) airtight ♦ *sm* (*acquitrino*) pond; (*CHIM*) tin

sta'**gnola** [stan'ɲɔla] *sf* tinfoil

'**stalla** *sf* (*per bovini*) cowshed; (*per cavalli*) stable

stal'**lone** *sm* stallion

sta'**mani** *av* = **stamattina**

stamat'**tina** *av* this morning

stam'**becco, chi** *sm* ibex

'**stampa** *sf* (*TIP, FOT: tecnica*) printing; (*impressione, copia fotografica*) print; (*insieme di quotidiani, giornalisti etc*) press; **"~e"** *sfpl* "printed matter"

stam'**pante** *sf* (*INFORM*) printer

stam'**pare** *vt* to print; (*pubblicare*) to publish; (*coniare*) to strike, coin; (*imprimere: anche fig*) to impress

stampa'**tello** *sm* block letters *pl*

stam'**pella** *sf* crutch

'**stampo** *sm* mould; (*fig: indole*) type, kind, sort

sta'**nare** *vt* to drive out

stan'**care** *vt* to tire, make tired; (*annoiare*) to bore; (*infastidire*) to annoy; **~rsi** *vr* to get tired, tire o.s. out; **~rsi (di)** to grow weary (of), grow tired (of)

stan'**chezza** [stan'kettsa] *sf* tiredness, fatigue

'**stanco, a, chi, che** *ag* tired; **~ di** tired of, fed up with

'**stanga, ghe** *sf* bar; (*di carro*) shaft

stan'**gata** *sf* (*colpo: anche fig*) blow; (*cattivo risultato*) poor result; (*CALCIO*) shot

sta'**notte** *av* tonight; (*notte passata*) last night

'**stante** *prep*: **a sé ~** (*appartamento, casa*) independent, separate

stan'**tio, a, 'tii, 'tie** *ag* stale; (*burro*) rancid; (*fig*) old

stan'**tuffo** *sm* piston

'**stanza** ['stantsa] *sf* room; (*POESIA*) stanza; **~ da letto** bedroom

stanzi'**are** [stan'tsjare] *vt* to allocate

stap'**pare** *vt* to uncork; to uncap

'**stare** *vi* (*restare in un luogo*) to stay, remain; (*abitare*) to stay, live; (*essere situato*) to be, be situated; (*anche*: **~ in piedi**) to be, stand; (*essere, trovarsi*) to be; (*dipendere*): **se stesse in me** if it were up to me, if it depended on me; (*seguito da gerundio*): **sta studiando** he's studying; **starci** (*esserci spazio*): **nel baule non ci sta più niente** there's no more room in the boot; (*accettare*) to accept; **ci stai?** is that okay with you?; **~ a** (*attenersi a*) to follow, stick to; (*seguito dall'infinito*): **stiamo a discutere** we're talking; (*toccare a*): **sta a te giocare** it's your turn to play; **~ per fare qc** to be about to do sth; **come stai?** how are you?; **io sto bene/male** I'm very well/not very well; **~ a qn** (*abiti etc*) to fit sb; **queste scarpe mi stanno strette** these shoes are tight for me; **il rosso ti sta bene** red suits you

starnu'**tire** *vi* to sneeze; star'**nuto** *sm* sneeze

sta'**sera** *av* this evening, tonight

sta'**tale** *ag* state *cpd*; government *cpd* ♦ *sm/f* state employee, local authority employee; (*nell'amministrazione*) ≈ civil servant

sta'**tista, i** *sm* statesman

sta'**tistica** *sf* statistics *sg*

'**stato, a** *pp di* **essere**; **stare** ♦ *sm* (*condizione*) state, condition; (*POL*) state; (*DIR*) status; **essere in ~ d'accusa** (*DIR*) to be committed for trial; **~ d'assedio/**

d'emergenza state of siege/emergency; **~ civile** (*AMM*) marital status; **~ maggiore** (*MIL*) staff; **gli S~i Uniti (d'America)** the United States (of America)

'**statua** *sf* statue

statuni'tense *ag* United States *cpd,* of the United States

sta'tura *sf* (*ANAT*) height, stature; (*fig*) stature

sta'tuto *sm* (*DIR*) statute; constitution

sta'volta *av* this time

stazio'nario, a [stattsjo'narjo] *ag* stationary; (*fig*) unchanged

stazi'one [stat'tsjone] *sf* station; (*balneare, termale*) resort; **~ degli autobus** bus station; **~ balneare** seaside resort; **~ ferroviaria** railway (*BRIT*) *o* railroad (*US*) station; **~ invernale** winter sports resort; **~ di polizia** police station (*in small town*); **~ di servizio** service *o* petrol (*BRIT*) *o* filling station

'**stecca, che** *sf* stick; (*di ombrello*) rib; (*di sigarette*) carton; (*MED*) splint; (*stonatura*): **fare una ~** to sing (*o* play) a wrong note

stec'cato *sm* fence

stec'chito, a [stek'kito] *ag*: **lasciar ~ qn** (*fig*) to leave sb flabbergasted; **morto ~** stone dead

'**stella** *sf* star; **~ alpina** (*BOT*) edelweiss; **~ di mare** (*ZOOL*) starfish

'**stelo** *sm* stem; (*asta*) rod; **lampada a ~** standard lamp

'**stemma, i** *sm* coat of arms

stempe'rare *vt* to dilute; to dissolve; (*colori*) to mix

sten'dardo *sm* standard

'**stendere** *vt* (*braccia, gambe*) to stretch (out); (*tovaglia*) to spread (out); (*bucato*) to hang out; (*mettere a giacere*) to lay (down); (*spalmare: colore*) to spread; (*mettere per iscritto*) to draw up; **~rsi** *vr* (*coricarsi*) to stretch out, lie down; (*estendersi*) to extend, stretch

stenodattilo'grafo, a *sm/f* shorthand typist (*BRIT*), stenographer (*US*)

stenogra'fare *vt* to take down in shorthand; **stenogra'fia** *sf* shorthand

sten'tare *vi*: **~ a fare** to find it hard to do, have difficulty doing

'**stento** *sm* (*fatica*) difficulty; **~i** *smpl* (*privazioni*) hardship *sg,* privation *sg*; **a ~** with difficulty, barely

'**sterco** *sm* dung

stereo('fonico, a, ci, che) *ag* stereo(phonic)

'**sterile** *ag* sterile; (*terra*) barren; (*fig*) futile, fruitless; **sterilità** *sf* sterility

steriliz'zare [sterilid'dzare] *vt* to sterilize; **sterilizzazi'one** *sf* sterilization

ster'lina *sf* pound (sterling)

stermi'nare *vt* to exterminate, wipe out

stermi'nato, a *ag* immense; endless

ster'minio *sm* extermination, destruction

'**sterno** *sm* (*ANAT*) breastbone

'**sterpo** *sm* dry twig; **~i** *smpl* brushwood *sg*

ster'zare [ster'tsare] *vt, vi* (*AUT*) to steer; '**sterzo** *sm* steering; (*volante*) steering wheel

'**steso, a** *pp di* **stendere**

'**stesso, a** *ag* same; (*rafforzativo: in persona, proprio*): **il re ~** the king himself *o* in person ♦ *pron*: **lo(la) ~(a** the same (one); **i suoi ~i avversari lo ammirano** even his enemies admire him; **fa lo ~** it doesn't matter; **per me è lo ~** it's all the same to me, it doesn't matter to me; *vedi* **io; tu** *etc*

ste'sura *sf* drafting *no pl,* drawing up *no pl*; draft

'**stigmate** *sfpl* (*REL*) stigmata

sti'lare *vt* to draw up, draft

'**stile** *sm* style; **sti'lista, i** *sm* designer

stil'lare *vi* (*trasudare*) to ooze; (*gocciolare*) to drip; **stilli'cidio** *sm* (*fig*) continual pestering (*o* moaning *etc*)

stilo'grafica, che *sf* (*anche:* **penna ~**) fountain pen

'**stima** *sf* esteem; valuation; assessment, estimate

sti'mare *vt* (*persona*) to esteem, hold in high regard; (*terreno, casa etc*) to value; (*stabilire in misura approssimativa*) to estimate, assess; (*ritenere*): **~ che** to consider that; **~rsi fortunato** to consider o.s. (to be) lucky

stimo'lare *vt* to stimulate; *(incitare):* ~ **qn (a fare)** to spur sb on (to do)

'stimolo *sm (anche fig)* stimulus

'stinco, chi *sm* shin; shinbone

'stingere ['stindʒere] *vt, vi (anche:* **~rsi)** to fade; **'stinto, a** *pp di* **stingere**

sti'pare *vt* to cram, pack; **~rsi** *vr (accalcarsi)* to crowd, throng

sti'pendio *sm* salary

'stipite *sm (di porta, finestra)* jamb

stipu'lare *vt (redigere)* to draw up

sti'rare *vt (abito)* to iron; *(distendere)* to stretch; *(strappare: muscolo)* to strain; **~rsi** *vr* to stretch (o.s.); **stira'tura** *sf* ironing

'stirpe *sf* birth, stock; descendants *pl*

stiti'chezza [stiti'kettsa] *sf* constipation

'stitico, a, ci, che *ag* constipated

'stiva *sf (di nave)* hold

sti'vale *sm* boot

'stizza ['stittsa] *sf* anger, vexation; **stiz'zirsi** *vr* to lose one's temper; **stiz'zoso, a** *ag (persona)* quick-tempered, irascible; *(risposta)* angry

stocca'fisso *sm* stockfish, dried cod

stoc'cata *sf (colpo)* stab, thrust; *(fig)* gibe, cutting remark

'stoffa *sf* material, fabric; *(fig):* **aver la ~ di** to have the makings of

'stola *sf* stole

'stolto, a *ag* stupid, foolish

'stomaco, chi *sm* stomach; **dare di ~** to vomit, be sick

sto'nare *vt* to sing *(o* play) out of tune ♦ *vi* to be out of tune, sing *(o* play) out of tune; *(fig)* to be out of place, jar; *(: colori)* to clash; **stona'tura** *sf (suono)* false note

stop *sm inv (TEL)* stop; *(AUT: cartello)* stop sign; *(: fanalino d'arresto)* brake-light

'stoppa *sf* tow

stop'pino *sm* wick; *(miccia)* fuse

'storcere ['stɔrtʃere] *vt* to twist; **~rsi** *vr* to writhe, twist; **~ il naso** *(fig)* to turn up one's nose; **~rsi la caviglia** to twist one's ankle

stor'dire *vt (intontire)* to stun, daze; **~rsi** *vr:* **~rsi col bere** to dull one's senses with

drink; **stor'dito, a** *ag* stunned

'storia *sf (scienza, avvenimenti)* history; *(racconto, bugia)* story; *(faccenda, questione)* business *no pl; (pretesto)* excuse, pretext; **~e** *sfpl (smancerie)* fuss *sg;* **'storico, a, ci, che** *ag* historic(al) ♦ *sm* historian

stori'one *sm (ZOOL)* sturgeon

stor'mire *vi* to rustle

'stormo *sm (di uccelli)* flock

stor'nare *vt (COMM)* to transfer

'storno *sm (ZOOL)* starling

storpi'are *vt* to cripple, maim; *(fig: parole)* to mangle; *(: significato)* to twist

'storpio, a *ag* crippled, maimed

'storta *sf (distorsione)* sprain, twist

'storto, a *pp di* **storcere** ♦ *ag (chiodo)* twisted, bent; *(gamba, quadro)* crooked

sto'viglie [sto'viʎʎe] *sfpl* dishes *pl,* crockery

'strabico, a, ci, che *ag* squint-eyed; *(occhi)* squint

stra'bismo *sm* squinting

stra'carico, a, chi, che *ag* overloaded

strac'chino [strak'kino] *sm* type of soft cheese

stracci'are [strat'tʃare] *vt* to tear

'straccio, a, ci, ce ['strattʃo] *ag:* **carta ~a** waste paper ♦ *sm* rag; *(per pulire)* cloth, duster

stra'cotto, a *ag* overcooked ♦ *sm (CUC)* beef stew

'strada *sf* road; *(di città)* street; *(cammino, via, fig)* way; **farsi ~** *(fig)* to do well for o.s.; **essere fuori ~** *(fig)* to be on the wrong track; **~ facendo** on the way; **~ senza uscita** dead end; **stra'dale** *ag* road *cpd*

strafalci'one [strafal'tʃone] *sm* blunder, howler

stra'fare *vi* to overdo it; **stra'fatto, a** *pp di* **strafare**

strafot'tente *ag:* **è ~** he doesn't give a damn, he couldn't care less

'strage ['stradʒe] *sf* massacre, slaughter

stralu'nato, a *ag (occhi)* rolling; *(persona)* beside o.s., very upset

stramaz'zare [stramat'tsare] *vi* to fall heavily

'**strambo, a** *ag* strange, queer

strampa'lato, a *ag* odd, eccentric

stra'nezza [stra'nettsa] *sf* strangeness

strango'lare *vt* to strangle; **~rsi** *vr* to choke

strani'ero, a *ag* foreign ♦ *sm/f* foreigner

'**strano, a** *ag* strange, odd

straordi'nario, a *ag* extraordinary; (*treno etc*) special ♦ *sm* (*lavoro*) overtime

strapaz'zare [strapat'tsare] *vt* to ill-treat; **~rsi** *vr* to tire o.s. out, overdo things; **stra'pazzo** *sm* strain, fatigue; **da strapazzo** (*fig*) third-rate

strapi'ombo *sm* overhanging rock; **a ~** overhanging

strapo'tere *sm* excessive power

strap'pare *vt* (*gen*) to tear, rip; (*pagina etc*) to tear off, tear out; (*sradicare*) to pull up; (*togliere*): **~ qc a qn** to snatch sth from sb; (*fig*) to wrest sth from sb; **~rsi** *vr* (*lacerarsi*) to rip, tear; (*rompersi*) to break; **~rsi un muscolo** to tear a muscle; '**strappo** *sm* pull, tug; tear, rip; **fare uno strappo alla regola** to make an exception to the rule; **strappo muscolare** torn muscle

strari'pare *vi* to overflow

strasci'care [straʃʃi'kare] *vt* to trail; (*piedi*) to drag; **~ le parole** to drawl

'**strascico, chi** ['straʃʃiko] *sm* (*di abito*) train; (*conseguenza*) after-effect

strata'gemma, i [strata'dʒɛmma] *sm* stratagem

strate'gia, 'gie [strate'dʒia] *sf* strategy; **stra'tegico, a, ci, che** *ag* strategic

'**strato** *sm* layer; (*rivestimento*) coat, coating; (*GEO, fig*) stratum; (*METEOR*) stratus; **~ di ozono** ozone layer

strava'gante *ag* odd, eccentric; **strava'ganza** *sf* eccentricity

stra'vecchio, a [stra'vɛkkjo] *ag* very old

stra'vizio [stra'vittsjo] *sm* excess

stra'volgere [stra'vɔldʒere] *vt* (*volto*) to contort; (*fig: animo*) to trouble deeply; (: *verità*) to twist, distort; **stra'volto, a** *pp di* **stravolgere**

strazi'are [strat'tsjare] *vt* to torture, torment; '**strazio** *sm* torture; (*fig: cosa fatta male*) **essere uno ~** to be appalling

'**strega, ghe** *sf* witch

stre'gare *vt* to bewitch

stre'gone *sm* (*mago*) wizard; (*di tribù*) witch doctor

stregua *sf*: **alla ~ di** by the same standard as

stre'mare *vt* to exhaust

'**stremo** *sm* very end; **essere allo ~** to be at the end of one's tether

'**strenna** *sf* Christmas present

strepi'toso, a *ag* clamorous, deafening; (*fig: successo*) resounding

stres'sante *ag* stressful

'**stretta** *sf* (*di mano*) grasp; (*finanziaria*) squeeze; (*fig: dolore, turbamento*) pang; **una ~a di mano** a handshake; **essere alle ~e** to have one's back to the wall; *vedi anche* **stretto**

stretta'mente *av* tightly; (*rigorosamente*) strictly

stret'tezza [stret'tettsa] *sf* narrowness

'**stretto, a** *pp di* **stringere** ♦ *ag* (*corridoio, limiti*) narrow; (*gonna, scarpe, nodo, curva*) tight; (*intimo: parente, amico*) close; (*rigoroso: osservanza*) strict; (*preciso: significato*) precise, exact ♦ *sm* (*braccio di mare*) strait; **a denti ~i** with clenched teeth; **lo ~ necessario** the bare minimum; **stret'toia** *sf* bottleneck; (*fig*) tricky situation

stri'ato, a *ag* streaked

'**stridere** *vi* (*porta*) to squeak; (*animale*) to screech, shriek; (*colori*) to clash; '**stridulo, a** *ag* shrill

stril'lare *vt, vi* to scream, shriek; '**strillo** *sm* scream, shriek

stril'lone *sm* newspaper seller

strimin'zito, a [strimin'tsito] *ag* (*misero*) shabby; (*molto magro*) skinny

strimpel'lare *vt* (*MUS*) to strum

'**stringa, ghe** *sf* lace

strin'gato, a *ag* (*fig*) concise

'**stringere** ['strindʒere] *vt* (*avvicinare due cose*) to press (together), squeeze (together); (*tenere stretto*) to hold tight, clasp, clutch; (*pugno, mascella, denti*) to clench; (*labbra*) to compress; (*avvitare*) to tighten; (*abito*) to take in; (*sog: scarpe*) to pinch, be tight for; (*fig: concludere: patto*) to make; (: *accelerare: passo, tempo*) to quicken ♦ *vi* (*essere stretto*) to be tight; (*tempo: incalzare*) to be pressing; **~rsi** *vr* (*accostarsi*): **~rsi a** to press o.s. up against; **~ la mano a qn** to shake sb's hand; **~ gli occhi** to screw up one's eyes

'**striscia, sce** ['striʃʃa] *sf* (*di carta, tessuto etc*) strip; (*riga*) stripe; **~sce (pedonali)** zebra crossing *sg*

strisci'**are** [striʃ'ʃare] *vt* (*piedi*) to drag; (*muro, macchina*) to graze ♦ *vi* to crawl, creep

'**striscio** ['striʃʃo] *sm* graze; (MED) smear; **colpire di ~** to graze

strito'**lare** *vt* to grind

striz'**zare** [strit'tsare] *vt* (*panni*) to wring (out); **~ l'occhio** to wink

'**strofa** *sf* strophe

strofi'**naccio** [strofi'nattʃo] *sm* duster, cloth; (*per piatti*) dishcloth; (*per pavimenti*) floorcloth

strofi'**nare** *vt* to rub

stron'**care** *vt* to break off; (*fig: ribellione*) to suppress, put down; (: *film, libro*) to tear to pieces

stropicci'**are** [stropit'tʃare] *vt* to rub

stroz'**zare** [strot'tsare] *vt* (*soffocare*) to choke, strangle; **~rsi** *vr* to choke; strozza'**tura** *sf* (*restringimento*) narrowing; (*di strada etc*) bottleneck

'**struggersi** ['struddʒersi] *vr* (*fig*): **~ di** to be consumed with

strumen'**tale** *ag* (MUS) instrumental

strumentaliz'**zare** [strumentalid'dzare] *vt* to exploit, use to one's own ends

stru'**mento** *sm* (*arnese, fig*) instrument, tool; (MUS) instrument; **~ a corda** *o* **ad arco/a fiato** stringed/wind instrument

'**strutto** *sm* lard

strut'**tura** *sf* structure; struttu'**rare** *vt* to structure

'**struzzo** ['struttso] *sm* ostrich

stuc'**care** *vt* (*muro*) to plaster; (*vetro*) to

putty; (*decorare con stucchi*) to stucco

stuc'**chevole** [stuk'kevole] *ag* nauseating; (*fig*) tedious, boring

'**stucco, chi** *sm* plaster; (*da vetri*) putty; (*ornamentale*) stucco; **rimanere di ~** (*fig*) to be dumbfounded

stu'**dente, essa** *sm/f* student; (*scolaro*) pupil, schoolboy/girl; **studen'tesco, a, schi, sche** *ag* student *cpd*; school *cpd*

studi'**are** *vt* to study

'**studio** *sm* studying; (*ricerca, saggio, stanza*) study; (*di professionista*) office; (*di artista*, CINEMA, TV, RADIO) studio; **~i** *smpl* (INS) studies; **~ medico** doctor's surgery (BRIT) *o* office (US)

studi'**oso, a** *ag* studious, hard-working ♦ *sm/f* scholar

'**stufa** *sf* stove; **~ elettrica** electric fire *o* heater

stu'**fare** *vt* (CUC) to stew; (*fig: fam*) to bore; stu'**fato, a** (CUC) stew; '**stufo, a** (*fam*) *ag*: **essere stufo di** to be fed up with, be sick and tired of

stu'**oia** *sf* mat

stupefa'**cente** [stupefa'tʃɛnte] *ag* stunning, astounding ♦ *sm* drug, narcotic

stu'**pendo, a** *ag* marvellous, wonderful

stupi'**daggine** [stupi'daddʒine] *sf* stupid thing (to do *o* say)

stupidità *sf* stupidity

'**stupido, a** *ag* stupid

stu'**pire** *vt* to amaze, stun ♦ *vi* (*anche:* **~rsi**): **~ (di)** to be amazed (at), be stunned (by)

stu'**pore** *sm* amazement, astonishment

'**stupro** *sm* rape

stu'**rare** *vt* (*lavandino*) to clear

stuzzica'**denti** [stuttsika'dɛnti] *sm* toothpick

stuzzi'**care** [stuttsi'kare] *vt* (*ferita etc*) to poke (at), prod (at); (*fig*) to tease; (: *appetito*) to whet; (: *curiosità*) to stimulate; **~ i denti** to pick one's teeth

---

PAROLA CHIAVE

---

su (*su +il = sul, su +lo = sullo, su +l' = sull', su +la = sulla, su +i = sui, su +gli*

= **sugli,** *su* +*le* = **sulle**) *prep* 1 (*gen*) on; (*moto*) on(to); (*in cima a*) on (top of); **mettilo sul tavolo** put it on the table; **un paesino sul mare** a village by the sea 2 (*argomento*) about, on; **un libro ~ Cesare** a book on *o* about Caesar 3 (*circa*) about; **costerà sui 3 milioni** it will cost about 3 million; **una ragazza sui 17 anni** a girl of about 17 (years of age) 4: **~ misura** made to measure; **~ richiesta** on request; **3 casi ~ dieci** 3 cases out of 10

♦ *av* 1 (*in alto, verso l'alto*) up; **vieni ~** come on up; **guarda ~** look up; **~ le mani!** hands up!; **in ~** (*verso l'alto*) up(wards); (*in poi*) onwards; **dai 20 anni in ~** from the age of 20 onwards

2 (*addosso*) on; **cos'hai ~?** what have you got on?

♦ *escl* come on!; **~ coraggio!** come on, cheer up!

'**sua** *vedi* **suo**

su'**bacqueo, a** *ag* underwater ♦ *sm* skindiver

sub'**buglio** [sub'buʎʎo] *sm* confusion, turmoil

subcosci'**ente** [subkoʃ'ʃɛnte] *ag, sm* subconscious

'**subdolo, a** *ag* underhand, sneaky

suben'**trare** *vi*: **~ a qn in qc** to take over sth from sb

su'**bire** *vt* to suffer, endure

subis'**sare** *vt* (*fig*): **~ di** to overwhelm with, load with

subi'**taneo, a** *ag* sudden

'**subito** *av* immediately, at once, straight away

subodo'**rare** *vt* (*insidia etc*) to smell, suspect

subordi'**nato, a** *ag* subordinate; (*dipendente*): **~ a** dependent on, subject to

subur'**bano, a** *ag* suburban

suc'**cedere** [sut'tʃedere] *vi* (*prendere il posto di qn*): **~ a** to succeed; (*venire dopo*): **~ a** to follow; (*accadere*) to happen; **~rsi** *vr* to follow each other; **~ al trono** to succeed to the throne; **successi'one** *sf* succession; **succes'sivo, a** *ag* successive; **suc'cesso, a** *pp di* **succedere** ♦ *sm* (*esito*) outcome; (*buona riuscita*) success; **di successo** (*libro, personaggio*) successful

succhi'**are** [suk'kjare] *vt* to suck (up); **succhi'otto** *sm* (*per bambino*) dummy

suc'**cinto, a** [sut'tʃinto] *ag* (*discorso*) succinct; (*abito*) brief

'**succo, chi** *sm* juice; (*fig*) essence, gist; **~ di frutta** fruit juice; **suc'coso, a** *ag* juicy; (*fig*) pithy

succur'**sale** *sf* branch (office)

sud *sm* south ♦ *ag inv* south; (*lato*) south, southern

Su'**dafrica** *sm*: **il ~** South Africa; **sudafri'cano, a** *ag, sm/f* South African

Suda'**merica** *sm*: **il ~** South America; **sudameri'cano, a** *ag, sm/f* South American

su'**dare** *vi* to perspire, sweat; **~ freddo** to come out in a cold sweat; **su'data** *sf* sweat; **ho fatto una bella sudata per finirlo in tempo** it was a real sweat to get it finished in time

sud'**detto, a** *ag* above-mentioned

sud'**dito, a** *sm/f* subject

suddi'**videre** *vt* to subdivide

su'**dest** *sm* south-east

'**sudicio, a, ci, ce** ['sudit'ʃo] *ag* dirty, filthy; **sudici'ume** *sm* dirt, filth

su'**dore** *sm* perspiration, sweat

su'**dovest** *sm* south-west

'**sue** *vedi* **suo**

suffici'**ente** [suffi'tʃɛnte] *ag* enough, sufficient; (*borioso*) self-important; (*INS*) satisfactory; **suffici'enza** *sf* self-importance; pass mark; **a sufficienza** enough; **ne ho avuto a sufficienza!** I've had enough of this!

suf'**fisso** *sm* (*LING*) suffix

suf'**fragio** [suf'fradʒo] *sm* (*voto*) vote; **~ universale** universal suffrage

suggel'**lare** [suddʒel'lare] *vt* (*fig*) to seal

suggeri'**mento** [suddʒeri'mento] *sm* suggestion; (*consiglio*) piece of advice, advice *no pl*

sugge'rire [suddʒe'rire] *vt* (*risposta*) to tell; (*consigliare*) to advise; (*proporre*) to suggest; (*TEATRO*) to prompt; **suggeri'tore**, **'trice** *sm/f* (*TEATRO*) prompter

suggestio'nare [suddʒestjo'nare] *vt* to influence

suggesti'one [suddʒes'tjone] *sf* (*PSIC*) suggestion

sugges'tivo, a [suddʒes'tivo] *ag* (*paesaggio*) evocative; (*teoria*) interesting, attractive

'sughero ['sugero] *sm* cork

'sugli ['suλλi] *prep +det vedi* **su**

'sugo, ghi *sm* (*succo*) juice; (*di carne*) gravy; (*condimento*) sauce; (*fig*) gist, essence

'sui *prep +det vedi* **su**

sui'cida, i, e [sui'tʃida] *ag* suicidal ♦ *sm/f* suicide

suici'darsi [suitʃi'darsi] *vr* to commit suicide

sui'cidio [sui'tʃidjo] *sm* suicide

su'ino, a *ag*: **carne ~a** pork ♦ *sm* pig; **~i** *smpl* swine *pl*

sul *prep + det vedi* **su**

sull' *prep + det vedi* **su**

'sulla *prep + det vedi* **su**

'sulle *prep + det vedi* **su**

'sullo *prep + det vedi* **su**

sulta'nina *ag f*: (*uva*) ~ sultana

sul'tano, a *sm/f* sultan/sultana

'sunto *sm* summary

'suo (*f* **'sua**, *pl* **'sue**, **su'oi**) *det*: **il ~, la sua** *etc* (*di lui*) his; (*di lei*) her; (*di esso*) its; (*con valore indefinito*) one's, his/her; (*forma di cortesia: anche*: **S~**) your ♦ *pron*: **il ~, la sua** *etc* his; hers; yours; **i suoi** his (*o* her *o* one's *o* your) family

su'ocero, a ['swɔtʃero] *sm/f* father/mother-in-law; **i ~i** *smpl* father-and-mother-in-law

su'oi *vedi* **suo**

su'ola *sf* (*di scarpa*) sole

su'olo *sm* (*terreno*) ground; (*terra*) soil

suo'nare *vt* (*MUS*) to play; (*campana*) to ring; (*ore*) to strike; (*clacson, allarme*) to sound ♦ *vi* to play; (*telefono, campana*) to ring; (*ore*) to strike; (*clacson, fig: parole*) to sound

suone'ria *sf* alarm

su'ono *sm* sound

su'ora *sf* (*REL*) sister

'super *sf* (*anche*: **benzina ~**) ≈ four-star (petrol) (*BRIT*), premium (*US*)

supe'rare *vt* (*oltrepassare: limite*) to exceed, surpass; (*percorrere*) to cover; (*attraversare: fiume*) to cross; (*sorpassare: veicolo*) to overtake; (*fig: essere più bravo di*) to surpass, outdo; (*: difficoltà*) to overcome; (*: esame*) to get through; **~ qn in altezza/peso** to be taller/heavier than sb; **ha superato la cinquantina** he's over fifty (years of age)

su'perbia *sf* pride; **su'perbo, a** *ag* proud; (*fig*) magnificent, superb

superfici'ale [superfi'tʃale] *ag* superficial

super'ficie, ci [super'fitʃe] *sf* surface

su'perfluo, a *ag* superfluous

superi'ore *ag* (*piano, arto, classi*) upper; (*più elevato: temperatura, livello*): **~ (a)** higher (than); (*migliore*): **~ (a)** superior (to); **~, a** *sm/f* (*anche REL*) superior; **superiorità** *sf* superiority

superla'tivo, a *ag, sm* superlative

supermer'cato *sm* supermarket

su'perstite *ag* surviving ♦ *sm/f* survivor

superstizi'one [superstit'tsjone] *sf* superstition; **superstizi'oso, a** *ag* superstitious

super'strada *sf* ≈ (toll-free) motorway

su'pino, a *ag* supine

suppel'lettile *sf* furnishings *pl*

suppergiù [supper'dʒu] *av* more or less, roughly

supplemen'tare *ag* extra; (*treno*) relief *cpd*; (*entrate*) additional

supple'mento *sm* supplement

sup'plente *sm/f* temporary member of staff; supply (*o* substitute) teacher

'supplica, che *sf* (*preghiera*) plea; (*domanda scritta*) petition, request

suppli'care *vt* to implore, beseech

sup'plire *vi*: **~ a** to make up for,

compensate for

sup'plizio [sup'plittsjo] *sm* torture

sup'porre *vt* to suppose

sup'porto *sm* (*sostegno*) support

sup'posta *sf* (MED) suppository

sup'posto, a *pp di* **supporre**

su'premo, a *ag* supreme

surge'lare [surdʒe'lare] *vt* (deep-) freeze; surge'lati *smpl* frozen food *sg*

sur'plus *sm inv* (ECON) surplus

surriscal'dare *vt* to overheat

surro'gato *sm* substitute

suscet'tibile [suʃʃet'tibile] *ag* (*sensibile*) touchy, sensitive

susci'tare [suʃʃi'tare] *vt* to provoke, arouse

su'sina *sf* plum; su'sino *sm* plum (tree)

sussegu'ire *vt* to follow; ~rsi *vr* to follow one another

sus'sidio *sm* subsidy

sus'sistere *vi* to exist; (*essere fondato*) to be valid *o* sound

sussul'tare *vi* to shudder

sussur'rare *vt, vi* to whisper, murmur; sus'surro *sm* whisper, murmur

sutu'rare *vt* (MED) to stitch up, suture

sva'gare *vt* (*distrarre*) to distract; (*divertire*) to amuse; ~rsi *vr* to amuse o.s.; to enjoy o.s.

'svago, ghi *sm* (*riposo*) relaxation; (*ricreazione*) amusement; (*passatempo*) pastime

svaligi'are [zvali'dʒare] *vt* to rob, burgle (BRIT), burglarize (US)

svalu'tare *vt* (ECON) to devalue; (*fig*) to belittle; ~rsi *vr* (ECON) to be devalued; svalutazi'one *sf* devaluation

sva'nire *vi* to disappear, vanish

svan'taggio [zvan'taddʒo] *sm* disadvantage; (*inconveniente*) drawback, disadvantage

svapo'rare *vi* to evaporate

svari'ato, a *ag* varied; various

'svastica *sf* swastika

sve'dese *ag* Swedish ♦ *sm/f* Swede ♦ *sm* (LING) Swedish

'sveglia [zve'ʎʎa] *sf* waking up; (*orologio*) alarm (clock); ~ **telefonica** alarm call

svegli'are [zveʎ'ʎare] *vt* to wake up; (*fig*) to awaken, arouse; ~rsi *vr* to wake up; (*fig*) to be revived, reawaken

'sveglio, a ['zveʎʎo] *ag* awake; (*fig*) quick-witted

sve'lare *vt* to reveal

'svelto, a *ag* (*passo*) quick; (*mente*) quick, alert; **alla ~a** quickly

'svendita *sf* (COMM) (clearance) sale

sveni'mento *sm* fainting fit, faint

sve'nire *vi* to faint

sven'tare *vt* to foil, thwart

sven'tato, a *ag* (*distratto*) scatterbrained; (*imprudente*) rash

svento'lare *vt, vi* to wave, flutter

sven'trare *vt* to disembowel

sven'tura *sf* misfortune; sventu'rato, a *ag* unlucky, unfortunate

sve'nuto, a *pp di* **svenire**

svergo'gnato, a [zvergoɲ'ɲato] *ag* shameless

sver'nare *vi* to spend the winter

sves'tire *vt* to undress; ~rsi *vr* to get undressed

'Svezia ['zvɛttsja] *sf*: **la ~** Sweden

svez'zare [zvet'tsare] *vt* to wean

svi'are *vt* to divert; (*fig*) to lead astray; ~rsi *vr* to go astray

svi'gnarsela [zviɲ'ɲarsela] *vr* to slip away, sneak off

svilup'pare *vt* to develop; ~rsi *vr* to develop

svi'luppo *sm* development

'svincolo *sm* (*stradale*) motorway (BRIT) *o* expressway (US) intersection

svisce'rare [zviʃʃe'rare] *vt* (*fig: argomento*) to examine in depth; svisce'rato, a *ag* (*amore*) passionate; (*lodi*) obsequious

'svista *sf* oversight

svi'tare *vt* to unscrew

'Svizzera ['zvittsera] *sf*: **la ~** Switzerland

'svizzero, a ['zvittsero] *ag, sm/f* Swiss

svogli'ato, a [zvoʎ'ʎato] *ag* listless; (*pigro*) lazy

svolaz'zare [zvolat'tsare] *vi* to flutter

'svolgere ['zvɔldʒere] *vt* to unwind; (*srotolare*) to unroll; (*fig: argomento*) to develop; (: *piano, programma*) to carry out; **~rsi** *vr* to unwind; to unroll; (*fig: aver luogo*) to take place; (: *procedere*) to go on; **svolgi'mento** *sm* development; carrying out; (*andamento*) course

'**svolta** *sf* (*atto*) turning *no pl*; (*curva*) turn, bend; (*fig*) turning-point

svol'tare *vi* to turn

'**svolto, a** *pp di* **svolgere**

svuo'tare *vt* to empty (out)

T, t

tabac'caio, a *sm/f* tobacconist

tabacche'ria [tabakke'ria] *sf* tobacconist's (shop)

ta'bacco, chi *sm* tobacco

ta'bella *sf* (*tavola*) table; (*elenco*) list

tabel'lone *sm* (*pubblicitario*) billboard; (*con orario*) timetable board

taber'nacolo *sm* tabernacle

tabu'lato *sm* (INFORM) printout

'**tacca, che** [ta'kanno] *ag* mean, stingy

tac'cagno, a [tak'kanno] *ag* mean, stingy

tac'chino [tak'kino] *sm* turkey

tacci'are [tat'tʃare] *vt*: **~ qn di** to accuse sb of

'**tacco, chi** *sm* heel; **~chi a spillo** stiletto heels

taccu'ino *sm* notebook

ta'cere [ta'tʃere] *vi* to be silent *o* quiet; (*smettere di parlare*) to fall silent ♦ *vt* to keep to oneself, say nothing about; **far ~ qn** to make sb be quiet; (*fig*) to silence sb

ta'chimetro [ta'kimetro] *sm* speedometer

'**tacito, a** ['tatʃito] *ag* silent; (*sottinteso*) tacit, unspoken

ta'fano *sm* horsefly

taffe'ruglio [taffe'ruʎʎo] *sm* brawl, scuffle

taffettà *sm* taffeta

'**taglia** ['taʎʎa] *sf* (*statura*) height; (*misura*) size; (*riscatto*) ransom; (*ricompensa*) reward; **~ forte** (*di abito*) large size

taglia'carte [taʎʎa'karte] *sm inv* paperknife

tagli'ando [taʎ'ʎando] *sm* coupon

tagli'are [taʎ'ʎare] *vt* to cut; (*recidere,*

interrompere) to cut off; (*intersecare*) to cut across, intersect; (*carne*) to carve; (*vini*) to blend ♦ *vi* to cut; (*prendere una scorciatoia*) to take a short-cut; **~ corto** (*fig*) to cut short

taglia'telle [taʎʎa'telle] *sfpl* tagliatelle *pl*

taglia'unghie [taʎʎa'ungje] *sm inv* nail clippers *pl*

tagli'ente [taʎ'ʎente] *ag* sharp

'**taglio** ['taʎʎo] *sm* cutting *no pl*; cut; (*parte tagliente*) cutting edge; (*di abito*) cut, style; (*di stoffa: lunghezza*) length; (*di vini*) blending; **di ~** on edge, edgeways; **banconote di piccolo/grosso ~** notes of small/large denomination

tagli'ola [taʎ'ʎola] *sf* trap, snare

tai'lleur [ta'jœr] *sm inv* suit (*for women*)

'**talco** *sm* talcum powder

PAROLA CHIAVE

'**tale** *det* 1 (*simile, così grande*) such; **un(a) ~ ...** such (a) ...; **non accetto ~i discorsi** I won't allow such talk; **è di una ~ arroganza** he is so arrogant; **fa una ~ confusione!** he makes such a mess!

2 (*persona o cosa indeterminata*) such-and-such; **il giorno ~ all'ora ~** on such-and-such a day at such-and-such a time; **la tal persona** that person; **ha telefonato una ~ Giovanna** somebody called Giovanna phoned

3 (*nelle similitudini*): **~ ... ~** like ... like; **~ padre ~ figlio** like father, like son; **hai il vestito ~ quale il mio** your dress is just *o* exactly like mine

♦ *pron* (*indefinito: persona*): **un(a) ~** someone; **quel** (*o* **quella**) **~** that person, that man (*o* woman); **il tal dei ~i** what's-his-name

---

ta'lento *sm* talent

talis'mano *sm* talisman

tallon'cino [tallon'tʃino] *sm* counterfoil

tal'lone *sm* heel

tal'mente *av* so

ta'lora *av* = **talvolta**

'**talpa** *sf* (ZOOL) mole

tal'volta *av* sometimes, at times

tambu'rello *sm* tambourine

tam'buro *sm* drum

Ta'migi [ta'midʒi] *sm*: **il ~** the Thames

tampona'mento *sm* (AUT) collision; **~ a catena** pile-up

tampo'nare *vt* (*otturare*) to plug; (*urtare: macchina*) to crash *o* ram into

tam'pone *sm* (MED) wad, pad; (*per timbri*) ink-pad; (*respingente*) buffer; **~ assorbente** tampon

'tana *sf* lair, den

'tanfo *sm* stench; musty smell

tan'gente [tan'dʒɛnte] *ag* (MAT): **~ a** tangential to ♦ *sf* tangent; (*quota*) share

---
Tangentopoli

> *i* **Tangentopoli** *describes the corruption scandal involving a large number of politicians, industrialists and businessmen. Investigations exposed a complex system of bribes, some paid from public funds, to gain benefits for private individuals and political parties. The scandal began in Milan which was subsequently called Tangentopoli or "Bribesville".*
---

tangenzi'ale [tandʒen'tsjale] *sf* (AUT) bypass

'tanica *sf* (*contenitore*) jerry can

tan'tino: un ~ *av* a little, a bit

PAROLA CHIAVE

'tanto, a *det* 1 (*molto: quantità*) a lot of, much; (: *numero*) a lot of, many; (*così ~: quantità*) so much, such a lot of; (: *numero*) so many, such a lot of; **~e volte** so many times, so often; **~i auguri!** all the best!; **~e grazie** many thanks; **~ tempo** so long, such a long time; **ogni ~i chilometri** every so many kilometres

2: **~ ... quanto** (*quantità*) as much ... as; (*numero*) as many ... as; **ho ~a pazienza quanta ne hai tu** I have as much patience as you have *o* as you; **ha ~i amici quanti nemici** he has as many friends as he has enemies

3 (*rafforzativo*) such; **ho aspettato per ~ tempo** I waited so long *o* for such a long time

♦ *pron* 1 (*molto*) much, a lot; (*così ~*) so much, such a lot; **~i, e** many, a lot; so many, such a lot; **credevo ce ne fosse ~** I thought there was (such) a lot, I thought there was plenty

2: **~ quanto** (*denaro*) as much as; (*cioccolatini*) as many as; **ne ho ~ quanto basta** I have as much as I need; **due volte ~** twice as much

3 (*indeterminato*) so much; **~ per l'affitto, ~ per il gas** so much for the rent, so much for the gas; **costa un ~ al metro** it costs so much per metre; **di ~ in ~, ogni ~** every so often; **~ vale che ...** I (*o* we *etc*) may as well ...; **~ meglio!** so much the better!; **~ peggio per lui!** so much the worse for him!

♦ *av* 1 (*molto*) very; **vengo ~ volentieri** I'd be very glad to come; **non ci vuole ~ a capirlo** it doesn't take much to understand it

2 (*così ~: con ag, av*) so; (: *con vb*) so much, such a lot; **è ~ bella!** she's so beautiful!; **non urlare ~** don't shout so much; **sto ~ meglio adesso** I'm so much better now; **~ ... che** so ... (that); **~ ... da** so ... as

3: **~ ... quanto** as ... as; **conosco ~ Carlo quanto suo padre** I know both Carlo and his father; **non è poi ~ complicato quanto sembri** it's not as difficult as it seems; **~ più insisti, ~ più non mollerà** the more you insist, the more stubborn he'll be; **quanto più ... ~ meno** the more ... the less

4 (*solamente*) just; **~ per cambiare/ scherzare** just for a change/a joke; **una volta ~** for once

5 (*a lungo*) (for) long

♦ *cong* after all

'tappa *sf* (*luogo di sosta, fermata*) stop, halt; (*parte di un percorso*) stage, leg; (SPORT) lap; **a ~e** in stages

tap'pare *vt* to plug, stop up; (*bottiglia*) to cork

tap'peto *sm* carpet; (*anche*: **tappetino**) rug; (*SPORT*): **andare al ~** to go down for the count; **mettere sul ~** (*fig*) to bring up for discussion

tappez'zare [tappet'tsare] *vt* (*con carta*) to paper; (*rivestire*): **~ qc (di)** to cover sth (with); **tappezze'ria** *sf* (*tessuto*) tapestry; (*carta da parati*) wallpaper; (*arte*) upholstery; **far da tappezzeria** (*fig*) to be a wallflower; **tappezzi'ere** *sm* upholsterer

'tappo *sm* stopper; (*in sughero*) cork

tarchi'ato, a [tar'kjato] *ag* stocky, thickset

tar'dare *vi* to be late ♦ *vt* to delay; **~ a fare** to delay doing

'tardi *av* late; **più ~** later (on); **al più ~** at the latest; **sul ~** (*verso sera*) late in the day; **far ~** to be late; (*restare alzato*) to stay up late

tar'divo, a *ag* (*primavera*) late; (*rimedio*) belated, tardy; (*fig*) retarded

'tardo, a *ag* (*lento, fig: ottuso*) slow; (*tempo: avanzato*) late

'targa, ghe *sf* plate; (*AUT*) number (*BRIT*) o license (*US*) plate; **tar'ghetta** *sf* (*su bagaglio*) name tag; (*su porta*) nameplate

ta'riffa *sf* (*gen*) rate, tariff; (*di trasporti*) fare; (*elenco*) price list; tariff

'tarlo *sm* woodworm

'tarma *sf* moth

ta'rocco, chi *sm* tarot card; **~chi** *smpl* (*gioco*) tarot *sg*

tartagli'are [tartaʎ'ʎare] *vi* to stutter, stammer

'tartaro, a *ag, sm* (*in tutti i sensi*) tartar

tarta'ruga, ghe *sf* tortoise; (*di mare*) turtle; (*materiale*) tortoiseshell

tar'tina *sf* canapé

tar'tufo *sm* (*BOT*) truffle

'tasca, sche *sf* pocket; **tas'cabile** *ag* (*libro*) pocket *cpd*; **tasca'pane** *sm* haversack; **tas'chino** *sm* breast pocket

'tassa *sf* (*imposta*) tax; (*doganale*) duty; (*per iscrizione: a scuola etc*) fee; **~ di circolazione/di soggiorno** road/tourist tax

tas'sametro *sm* taximeter

tas'sare *vt* to tax; to levy a duty on

tassa'tivo, a *ag* peremptory

tassazi'one [tassat'tsjone] *sf* taxation

tas'sello *sm* plug; wedge

tassì *sm inv* = **taxi**; **tas'sista, i, e** *sm/f* taxi driver

'tasso *sm* (*di natalità, d'interesse etc*) rate; (*BOT*) yew; (*ZOOL*) badger; **~ di cambio/d'interesse** rate of exchange/interest

tas'tare *vt* to feel; **~ il terreno** (*fig*) to see how the land lies

tasti'era *sf* keyboard

'tasto *sm* key; (*tatto*) touch, feel

tas'toni *av*: **procedere (a) ~** to grope one's way forward

'tattica *sf* tactics *pl*

'tattico, a, ci, che *ag* tactical

'tatto *sm* (*senso*) touch; (*fig*) tact; **duro al ~** hard to the touch; **aver ~** to be tactful, have tact

tatu'aggio [tatu'addʒo] *sm* tattooing; (*disegno*) tattoo

tatu'are *vt* to tattoo

'tavola *sf* table; (*asse*) plank, board; (*lastra*) tablet; (*quadro*) panel (*painting*); (*illustrazione*) plate; **~ calda** snack bar; **~ vela** windsurfer

tavo'lato *sm* boarding; (*pavimento*) wooden floor

tavo'letta *sf* tablet, bar; **a ~** (*AUT*) flat out

tavo'lino *sm* small table; (*scrivania*) desk

'tavolo *sm* table

tavo'lozza [tavo'lɔttsa] *sf* (*ARTE*) palette

'taxi *sm inv* taxi

'tazza ['tattsa] *sf* cup; **~ da caffè/tè** coffee/tea cup; **una ~ di caffè/tè** a cup of coffee/tea

te *pron* (*soggetto: in forme comparative, oggetto*) you

tè *sm inv* tea; (*trattenimento*) tea party

tea'trale *ag* theatrical

te'atro *sm* theatre

'tecnica, che *sf* technique; (*tecnologia*) technology

'tecnico, a, ci, che *ag* technical ♦ *sm/f* technician

tecnolo'gia [teknolo'dʒia] *sf* technology

te'desco, a, schi, sche *ag, sm/f, sm* German

'tedio *sm* tedium, boredom

te'game *sm* (CUC) pan

'teglia ['teʎʎa] *sf* (per dolci) (baking) tin; (per arrosti) (roasting) tin

'tegola *sf* tile

tei'era *sf* teapot

'tela *sf* (tessuto) cloth; (per vele, quadri) canvas; (dipinto) canvas, painting; **di ~** (calzoni) (heavy) cotton *cpd*; (scarpe, borsa) canvas *cpd*; **~ cerata** oilcloth

te'laio *sm* (apparecchio) loom; (struttura) frame

tele'camera *sf* television camera

teleco'mando *sm* remote control

telecopia'trice *sf* fax (machine)

tele'cronaca *sf* television report

tele'ferica, che *sf* cableway

telefo'nare *vi* to telephone, ring; to make a phone call ♦ *vt* to telephone; **~ a** to phone up, ring up, call up

telefo'nata *sf* (telephone) call; **~ a carico del destinatario** reverse-charge (BRIT) *o* collect (US) call

tele'fonico, a, ci, che *ag* (tele)phone *cpd*

telefon'ino *sm* mobile phone

telefo'nista, i, e *sm/f* telephonist; (d'impresa) switchboard operator

te'lefono *sm* telephone; **~ a gettoni** ≈ pay phone

telegior'nale [teledʒor'nale] *sm* television news (programme)

te'legrafo *sm* telegraph

tele'gramma, i *sm* telegram

telela'voro *sm* teleworking

tele'matica *sf* data transmission; telematics *sg*

teleobiet'tivo *sm* telephoto lens *sg*

telepa'tia *sf* telepathy

teles'copio *sm* telescope

teleselezi'one [teleselet'tsjone] *sf* direct dialling

telespetta'tore, 'trice *sm/f* (television) viewer

televisi'one *sf* television

televi'sore *sm* television set

'telex *sm inv* telex

'telo *sm* cloth; **~ da bagno** bath towel; **~ da spiaggia** beach towel

'tema, i *sm* theme; (INS) essay, composition

teme'rario, a *ag* rash, reckless

te'mere *vt* to fear, be afraid of; (essere sensibile a: freddo, calore) to be sensitive to ♦ *vi* to be afraid; (essere preoccupato): **~ per** to worry about, fear for; **~ di/che** to be afraid of/that

temperama'tite *sm inv* pencil sharpener

tempera'mento *sm* temperament

tempe'rato, a *ag* moderate, temperate

tempera'tura *sf* temperature

tempe'rino *sm* penknife

tem'pesta *sf* storm; **~ di sabbia/neve** sand/snowstorm

tempes'tare *vt*: **~ qn di domande** to bombard sb with questions; **~ qn di colpi** to rain blows on sb

tempes'tivo, a *ag* timely

tempes'toso, a *ag* stormy

'tempia *sf* (ANAT) temple

'tempio *sm* (edificio) temple

'tempo *sm* (METEOR) weather; (cronologico) time; (epoca) time, times *pl*; (di film, gioco: parte) part; (MUS) time; (: battuta) beat; (LING) tense; **un ~** once; **~ fa** some time ago; **al ~ stesso** *o* **a un ~** at the same time; **per ~** early; **ha fatto il suo ~** it has had its day; **~ libero** free time; **primo/secondo ~** (TEATRO) first/second part; (SPORT) first/second half; **in ~ utile** in due time *o* course; **a ~ pieno** full-time

tempo'rale *ag* temporal ♦ *sm* (METEOR) (thunder)storm

tempo'raneo, a *ag* temporary

temporeggi'are [tempored'dʒare] *vi* to play for time, temporize

tem'prare *vt* to temper

te'nace [te'natʃe] *ag* strong, tough; (fig) tenacious; (tenace) *sf* tenacity

te'nacia *sf* tenacity

te'naglie [te'naʎʎe] *sfpl* pincers *pl*

'tenda *sf* (riparo) awning; (di finestra) curtain; (per campeggio etc) tent

ten'denza [ten'dɛntsa] *sf* tendency;
(*orientamento*) trend; **avere ~ a** *o* **per qc**
to have a bent for sth

'tendere *vt* (*allungare al massimo*) to
stretch, draw tight; (*porgere: mano*) to hold
out; (*fig: trappola*) to lay, set ♦ *vi*: **~ a qc/a
fare** to tend towards sth/to do; **~
l'orecchio** to prick up one's ears; **il tempo
tende al caldo** the weather is getting hot;
un blu che tende al verde a greenish blue

ten'dina *sf* curtain

'tendine *sm* tendon, sinew

ten'done *sm* (*da circo*) tent

'tenebre *sfpl* darkness *sg*; **tene'broso, a**
ag dark, gloomy

te'nente *sm* lieutenant

te'nere *vt* to hold; (*conservare, mantenere*)
to keep; (*ritenere, considerare*) to consider;
(*spazio: occupare*) to take up, occupy;
(*seguire: strada*) to keep to ♦ *vi* to hold;
(*colori*) to be fast; (*dare importanza*): **~ a** to
care about; **~ a fare** to want to do, be
keen to do; **~rsi** *vr* (*stare in una
determinata posizione*) to stand; (*stimarsi*)
to consider o.s.; (*aggrapparsi*): **~rsi a** to
hold on to; (*attenersi*): **~rsi a** to stick to; **~
una conferenza** to give a lecture; **~ conto
di qc** to take sth into consideration; **~
presente qc** to bear sth in mind

'tenero, a *ag* tender; (*pietra, cera, colore*)
soft; (*fig*) tender, loving

'tenia *sf* tapeworm

'tennis *sm* tennis

te'nore *sm* (*tono*) tone; (*MUS*) tenor; **~ di
vita** (*livello*) standard of living

tensi'one *sf* tension

ten'tare *vt* (*indurre*) to tempt; (*provare*): **~
qc/di fare** to attempt *o* try sth/to do;
tenta'tivo *sm* attempt; **tentazi'one** *sf*
temptation

tenten'nare *vi* to shake, be unsteady; (*fig*)
to hesitate, waver

ten'toni *av*: **andare a ~** (*anche fig*) to
grope one's way

'tenue *ag* (*sottile*) fine; (*colore*) soft; (*fig*)
slender, slight

te'nuta *sf* (*capacità*) capacity; (*divisa*)

uniform; (*abito*) dress; (*AGR*) estate; **a ~
d'aria** airtight; **~ di strada** roadholding
power

teolo'gia [teolo'dʒia] *sf* theology;
te'ologo, gi *sm* theologian

teo'rema, i *sm* theorem

teo'ria *sf* theory; **te'orico, a, ci, che** *ag*
theoretic(al)

te'pore *sm* warmth

'teppa *sf* mob, hooligans *pl*; **tep'pismo**
sm hooliganism; **tep'pista, i** *sm* hooligan

tera'pia *sf* therapy

tergicris'tallo [terdʒikris'tallo] *sm*
windscreen (*BRIT*) *o* windshield (*US*) wiper

tergiver'sare [terdʒiver'sare] *vi* to shilly-
shally

'tergo *sm*: **a ~** behind; **vedi a ~** please turn
over

ter'male *ag* thermal; **stazione** *sf* **~** spa

'terme *sfpl* thermal baths

'termico, a, ci, che *ag* thermic; (*unità*)
thermal

termi'nale *ag, sm* terminal

termi'nare *vt* to end; (*lavoro*) to finish ♦ *vi*
to end

'termine *sm* term; (*fine, estremità*) end; (*di
territorio*) boundary, limit; **contratto a ~**
(*COMM*) forward contract; **a breve/lungo ~**
short-/long-term; **parlare senza mezzi ~i**
to talk frankly, not to mince one's words

ter'mometro *sm* thermometer

termonucle'are *ag* thermonuclear

termosi'fone *sm* radiator

ter'mostato *sm* thermostat

'terra *sf* (*gen, ELETTR*) earth; (*sostanza*) soil,
earth; (*opposto al mare*) land *no pl*;
(*regione, paese*) land; (*argilla*) clay; **~e** *sfpl*
(*possedimento*) lands, land *sg*; **a** *o* **per ~**
(*stato*) on the ground (*o floor*); (*moto*) to
the ground, down; **mettere a ~** (*ELETTR*) to
earth

terra'cotta *sf* terracotta; **vasellame** *sm* **di
~** earthenware

terra'ferma *sf* dry land, terra firma;
(*continente*) mainland

terrapi'eno *sm* embankment, bank

ter'razza [ter'rattsa] *sf* terrace

ter'razzo [ter'rattso] sm = terrazza

terre'moto sm earthquake

ter'reno, a ag (vita, beni) earthly ♦ sm (suolo, fig) ground; (COMM) land no pl, plot (of land); site; (SPORT, MIL) field

ter'restre ag (superficie) of the earth, earth's; (di terra: battaglia, animale) land cpd; (REL) earthly, worldly

ter'ribile ag terrible, dreadful

terrifi'cante ag terrifying

ter'rina sf tureen

territori'ale ag territorial

terri'torio sm territory

ter'rore sm terror; terro'rismo sm terrorism; terro'rista, i, e sm/f terrorist

'terso, a ag clear

'terzo, a ['tɛrtso] ag third ♦ sm (frazione) third; (DIR) third party; la ~a pagina (STAMPA) the Arts page

'tesa sf brim

'teschio ['teskjo] sm skull

'tesi sf thesis

'teso, a pp di tendere ♦ ag (tirato) taut, tight; (fig) tense

tesore'ria sf treasury

tesori'ere sm treasurer

te'soro sm treasure; il Ministero del T~ the Treasury

'tessera sf (documento) card

'tessere vt to weave; 'tessile ag, sm textile; tessi'tore, 'trice sm/f weaver; tessi'tura sf weaving

tes'suto sm fabric, material; (BIOL) tissue

'testa sf head; (di cose: estremità, parte anteriore) head, front; di ~ (vettura etc) front; tenere ~ a qn (nemico etc) to stand up to sb; fare di ~ propria to go one's own way; in ~ (SPORT) in the lead; ~ o croce? heads or tails?; avere la ~ dura to be stubborn; ~ di serie (TENNIS) seed, seeded player

testa'mento sm (atto) will; l'Antico/il Nuovo T~ (REL) the Old/New Testament

tes'tardo, a ag stubborn, pig-headed

tes'tata sf (parte anteriore) head; (intestazione) heading

'teste sm/f witness

tes'ticolo sm testicle

testi'mone sm/f (DIR) witness

testimoni'anza [testimo'njantsa] sf testimony

testimoni'are vt to testify; (fig) to bear witness to, testify to ♦ vi to give evidence, testify

tes'tina sf (TECN) head

'testo sm text; fare ~ (opera, autore) to be authoritative; questo libro non fa ~ this book is not essential reading; testu'ale ag textual; literal, word for word

tes'tuggine [tes'tuddʒine] sf tortoise; (di mare) turtle

'tetano sm (MED) tetanus

'tetro, a ag gloomy

'tetto sm roof; tet'toia sf roofing; canopy

'Tevere sm: il ~ the Tiber

Tg abbr = telegiornale

'thermos ® ['tɛrmos] sm inv vacuum o Thermos ® flask

ti pron (dav lo, la, li, le, ne diventa te) pron (oggetto) you; (complemento di termine) (to) you; (riflessivo) yourself

'tibia sf tibia, shinbone

tic sm inv tic, (nervous) twitch; (fig) mannerism

ticchet'tio [tikket'tio] sm (di macchina da scrivere) clatter; (di orologio) ticking; (della pioggia) patter

'ticchio ['tikkjo] sm (ghiribizzo) whim; (tic) tic, (nervous) twitch

'ticket sm inv (su farmaci) prescription charge

ti'epido, a ag lukewarm, tepid

ti'fare vi: ~ per to be a fan of; (parteggiare) to side with

'tifo sm (MED) typhus; (fig): fare il ~ per to be a fan of

tifoi'dea sf typhoid

ti'fone sm typhoon

ti'foso, a sm/f (SPORT etc) fan

'tiglio ['tiʎʎo] sm lime (tree), linden (tree)

'tigre sf tiger

tim'ballo sm (strumento) kettledrum; (CUC) timbale

'timbro sm stamp; (MUS) timbre, tone

'**timido, a** *ag* shy; timid

'**timo** *sm* thyme

ti'**mone** *sm* (*NAUT*) rudder; **timoni'ere** *sm* helmsman

ti'**more** *sm* (*paura*) fear; (*rispetto*) awe; **timo'roso, a** *ag* timid, timorous

'**timpano** *sm* (*ANAT*) eardrum; (*MUS*): **~i** *smpl* kettledrums, timpani

ti'**nello** *sm* small dining room

'**tingere** ['tindʒere] *vt* to dye

'**tino** *sm* vat

ti'**nozza** [ti'nɔttsa] *sf* tub

'**tinta** *sf* (*materia colorante*) dye; (*colore*) colour, shade; **tinta'rella** (*fam*) *sf* (sun)tan

tintin'**nare** *vi* to tinkle

'**tinto, a** *pp di* **tingere**

tinto'**ria** *sf* (*lavasecco*) dry cleaner's (shop)

tin'**tura** *sf* (*operazione*) dyeing; (*colorante*) dye; **~ di iodio** tincture of iodine

'**tipico, a, ci, che** *ag* typical

'**tipo** *sm* type; (*genere*) kind, type; (*fam*) chap, fellow

tipogra'**fia** *sf* typography; (*procedimento*) letterpress (printing); (*officina*) printing house; **tipo'grafico, a, ci, che** *ag* typographic(al); letterpress *cpd*; ti'**pografo** *sm* typographer

ti'**ranno, a** *ag* tyrannical ♦ *sm* tyrant

ti'**rante** *sm* (*per tenda*) guy

ti'**rare** *vt* (*gen*) to pull; (*estrarre*): **~ qc da** to take *o* pull sth out of; to get sth out of; to extract sth from; (*chiudere: tenda etc*) to draw, pull; (*tracciare, disegnare*) to draw, trace; (*lanciare: sasso, palla*) to throw; (*stampare*) to print; (*pistola, freccia*) to fire ♦ *vi* (*pipa, camino*) to draw; (*vento*) to blow; (*abito*) to be tight; (*fare fuoco*) to fire; (*fare del tiro, CALCIO*) to shoot; **~ avanti** *vi* to struggle on ♦ *vt* to keep going; **~ fuori** (*estrarre*) to take out, pull out; **~ giù** (*abbassare*) to bring down; **~ su** to pull up; (*capelli*) to put up; (*fig: bambino*) to bring up; **~rsi indietro** to move back

tira'**tore** *sm* gunman; **un buon ~** a good shot; **~ scelto** marksman

tira'**tura** *sf* (*azione*) printing; (*di libro*) (print) run; (*di giornale*) circulation

'**tirchio, a** ['tirkjo] *ag* mean, stingy

'**tiro** *sm* shooting *no pl*, firing *no pl*; (*colpo, sparo*) shot; (*di palla: lancio*) throwing *no pl*; throw; (*fig*) trick; **cavallo da ~** draught (*BRIT*) *o* draft (*US*) horse; **~ a segno** target shooting; (*luogo*) shooting range

tiro'**cinio** [tiro'tʃinjo] *sm* apprenticeship; (*professionale*) training

ti'**roide** *sf* thyroid (gland)

Tir'**reno** *sm*: **il** (**mar**) **~** the Tyrrhenian Sea

ti'**sana** *sf* herb tea

tito'**lare** *sm/f* incumbent; (*proprietario*) owner; (*CALCIO*) regular player

'**titolo** *sm* title; (*di giornale*) headline; (*diploma*) qualification; (*COMM*) security; (*: azione*) share; **a che ~?** for what reason?; **a ~ di amicizia** out of friendship; **a ~ di premio** as a prize; **~ di credito** share

titu'**bante** *ag* hesitant, irresolute

'**tizio, a** ['tittsjo] *sm/f* fellow, chap

tiz'**zone** [tit'tsone] *sm* brand

toast [toust] *sm inv* toasted sandwich (*generally with ham and cheese*)

toc'**cante** *ag* touching

toc'**care** *vt* to touch; (*tastare*) to feel; (*fig: riguardare*) to concern; (*: commuovere*) to touch, move; (*: pungere*) to hurt, wound; (*: far cenno a: argomento*) to touch on, mention ♦ *vi*: **~ a** (*accadere*) to happen to; (*spettare*) to be up to; **~ (il fondo)** (*in acqua*) to touch the bottom; **tocca a te difenderci** it's up to you to defend us; **a chi tocca?** whose turn is it?; **mi toccò pagare** I had to pay

'**tocco, chi** *sm* touch; (*ARTE*) stroke, touch

'**toga, ghe** *sf* toga; (*di magistrato, professore*) gown

'**togliere** ['tɔʎʎere] *vt* (*rimuovere*) to take away (*o* off), remove; (*riprendere, non concedere più*) to take away, remove; (*MAT*) to take away, subtract; **~ qc a qn** to take sth (away) from sb; **ciò non toglie che** nevertheless, be that as it may; **~rsi il cappello** to take off one's hat

toi'**lette** [twa'lɛt] *sf inv* toilet; (*mobile*) dressing table

to'**letta** *sf* = **toilette**

tolle'ranza [tolle'rantsa] *sf* tolerance

tolle'rare *vt* to tolerate

'tolto, a *pp di* **togliere**

to'maia *sf (di scarpa)* upper

'tomba *sf* tomb

tom'bino *sm* manhole cover

'tombola *sf (gioco)* tombola; *(ruzzolone)* tumble

'tomo *sm* volume

'tonaca, che *sf (REL)* habit

'tondo, a *ag* round

'tonfo *sm* splash; *(rumore sordo)* thud; *(: caduta)*: **fare un ~** to take a tumble

'tonico, a, ci, che *ag, sm* tonic

tonifi'care *vt (muscoli, pelle)* to tone up; *(irrobustire)* to invigorate, brace

tonnel'laggio [tonnel'laddʒo] *sm (NAUT)* tonnage

tonnel'lata *sf* ton

'tonno *sm* tuna (fish)

'tono *sm (gen)* tone; *(MUS: di pezzo)* key; *(di colore)* shade, tone

ton'silla *sf* tonsil; **tonsil'lite** *sf* tonsillitis

'tonto, a *ag* dull, stupid

to'pazio [to'pattsjo] *sm* topaz

'topo *sm* mouse

topogra'fia *sf* topography

'toppa *sf (serratura)* keyhole; *(pezza)* patch

to'race [to'ratʃe] *sm* chest

'torba *sf* peat

'torbido, a *ag (liquido)* cloudy; *(: fiume)* muddy; *(fig)* dark; troubled ♦ *sm*: **pescare nel ~** *(fig)* to fish in troubled water

'torcere ['tɔrtʃere] *vt* to twist; **~rsi** *vr* to twist, writhe

torchi'are [tor'kjare] *vt* to press; **'torchio** *sm* press

'torcia, ce ['tɔrtʃa] *sf* torch; **~ elettrica** torch *(BRIT)*, flashlight *(US)*

torci'collo [tortʃi'kɔllo] *sm* stiff neck

'tordo *sm* thrush

To'rino *sf* Turin

tor'menta *sf* snowstorm

tormen'tare *vt* to torment; **~rsi** *vr* to fret, worry o.s.; **tor'mento** *sm* torment

torna'conto *sm* advantage, benefit

tor'nado *sm* tornado

tor'nante *sm* hairpin bend

tor'nare *vi* to return, go *(o come)* back; *(ridiventare: anche fig)* to become (again); *(riuscire giusto, esatto: conto)* to work out; *(risultare)* to turn out (to be), prove (to be); **~ utile** to prove *o* turn out (to be) useful; **~ a casa** to go *(o come)* home

torna'sole *sm inv* litmus

tor'neo *sm* tournament

'tornio *sm* lathe

'toro *sm* bull; *(dello zodiaco)*: **T~** Taurus

tor'pedine *sf* torpedo; **torpedini'era** *sf* torpedo boat

'torre *sf* tower; *(SCACCHI)* rook, castle; **~ di controllo** *(AER)* control tower

torrefazi'one [torrefat'tsjone] *sf* roasting

tor'rente *sm* torrent

tor'retta *sf* turret

torri'one *sm* keep

tor'rone *sm* nougat

torsi'one *sf* twisting; torsion

'torso *sm* torso, trunk; *(ARTE)* torso

'torsolo *sm (di cavolo etc)* stump; *(di frutta)* core

'torta *sf* cake

'torto, a *pp di* **torcere** ♦ *ag (ritorto)* twisted; *(storto)* twisted, crooked ♦ *sm (ingiustizia)* wrong; *(colpa)* fault; **a ~** wrongly; **aver ~** to be wrong

'tortora *sf* turtle dove

tortu'oso, a *ag (strada)* twisting; *(fig)* tortuous

tor'tura *sf* torture; **tortu'rare** *vt* to torture

'torvo, a *ag* menacing, grim

tosa'erba *sm o f inv* (lawn)mower

to'sare *vt (pecora)* to shear; *(siepe)* to clip

Tos'cana *sf*: **la ~** Tuscany; **tos'cano, a** *ag, sm/f* Tuscan ♦ *sm (sigaro)* strong Italian cigar

'tosse *sf* cough

'tossico, a, ci, che *ag* toxic

tossicodipen'dente *sm/f* drug addict

tossi'comane *sm/f* drug addict

tos'sire *vi* to cough

tosta'pane *sm inv* toaster

tos'tare *vt* to toast; *(caffè)* to roast

'tosto, a *ag*: **faccia ~a** cheek

to'tale *ag, sm* total; totalità *sf*: la totalità di all of, the total amount (*o* number) of; the whole +*sg*; totaliz'zare *vt* to total; (*SPORT: punti*) to score

toto'calcio [toto'kaltʃo] *sm gambling pool betting on football results*, ≈ (football) pools *pl* (*BRIT*)

to'vaglia [to'vaʎʎa] *sf* tablecloth; tovagli'olo *sm* napkin

'tozzo, a ['tɔttso] *ag* squat ♦ *sm*: ~ di pane crust of bread

tra *prep* (*di due persone, cose*) between; (*di più persone, cose*) among(st); (*tempo: entro*) within, in; ~ 5 giorni in 5 days' time; sia detto ~ noi ... between you and me ...; litigano ~ (di) loro they're fighting amongst themselves; ~ breve soon; ~ sé e sé (*parlare etc*) to oneself

trabal'lare *vi* to stagger, totter

traboc'care *vi* to overflow

traboc'chetto [trabok'ketto] *sm* (*fig*) trap

tracan'nare *vt* to gulp down

'traccia, ce ['trattʃa] *sf* (*segno, striscia*) trail, track; (*orma*) tracks *pl*; (*residuo, testimonianza*) trace, sign; (*abbozzo*) outline

tracci'are [trat'tʃare] *vt* to trace, mark (out); (*disegnare*) to draw; (*fig: abbozzare*) to outline; tracci'ato *sm* (*grafico*) layout, plan

tra'chea [tra'kɛa] *sf* windpipe, trachea

tra'colla *sf* shoulder strap; borsa a ~ shoulder bag

tra'collo *sm* (*fig*) collapse, crash

tradi'mento *sm* betrayal; (*DIR, MIL*) treason

tra'dire *vt* to betray; (*coniuge*) to be unfaithful to; (*doveri: mancare*) to fail in; (*rivelare*) to give away, reveal; tradi'tore, 'trice *sm/f* traitor

tradizio'nale [traditttsjo'nale] *ag* traditional

tradizi'one [tradit'tsjone] *sf* tradition

tra'dotto, a *pp di* tradurre

tra'durre *vt* to translate; (*spiegare*) to render, convey; tradut'tore, 'trice *sm/f* translator; traduzi'one *sf* translation

trafe'lato, a *ag* out of breath

traffi'cante *sm/f* dealer; (*peg*) trafficker

traffi'care *vi* (*commerciare*): ~ (in) to trade (in), deal (in); (*affaccendarsi*) to busy o.s. ♦ *vt* (*peg*) to traffic in

'traffico, ci *sm* traffic; (*commercio*) trade, traffic

tra'figgere [tra'fiddʒere] *vt* to run through, stab; (*fig*) to pierce

tra'fitto, a *pp di* trafiggere

trafo'rare *vt* to bore, drill; tra'foro *sm* (*azione*) boring, drilling; (*galleria*) tunnel

tra'gedia [tra'dʒedja] *sf* tragedy

tra'ghetto [tra'getto] *sm* ferry(boat)

'tragico, a, ci, che ['tradʒiko] *ag* tragic

tra'gitto [tra'dʒitto] *sm* (*passaggio*) crossing; (*viaggio*) journey

tragu'ardo *sm* (*SPORT*) finishing line; (*fig*) goal, aim

traiet'toria *sf* trajectory

trai'nare *vt* to drag, haul; (*rimorchiare*) to tow; 'traino *sm* (*carro*) wagon; (*slitta*) sledge; (*carico*) load

tralasci'are [tralaʃ'ʃare] *vt* (*studi*) to neglect; (*dettagli*) to leave out, omit

'tralcio ['traltʃo] *sm* (*BOT*) shoot

tra'liccio [tra'littʃo] *sm* (*ELETTR*) pylon

tram *sm inv* tram

'trama *sf* (*filo*) weft, woof; (*fig: argomento, maneggio*) plot

traman'dare *vt* to pass on, hand down

tra'mare *vt* (*fig*) to scheme, plot

tram'busto *sm* turmoil

trames'tio *sm* bustle

tramez'zino [tramed'dzino] *sm* sandwich

tra'mezzo [tra'meddzo] *sm* (*EDIL*) partition

'tramite *prep* through

tramon'tare *vi* to set, go down; tra'monto *sm* setting; (*del sole*) sunset

tramor'tire *vi* to faint ♦ *vt* to stun

trampo'lino *sm* (*per tuffi*) springboard, diving board; (*per sci*) ski-jump

'trampolo *sm* stilt

tramu'tare *vt*: ~ in to change into, turn into

tra'nello *sm* trap

trangugi'are [trangu'dʒare] *vt* to gulp down

'tranne *prep* except (for), but (for); ~ che

unless

tranquil'lante *sm* (*MED*) tranquillizer

tranquilli'tà *sf* calm, stillness; quietness; peace of mind

tranquilliz'zare [trankwillid'dzare] *vt* to reassure

tran'quillo, a *ag* calm, quiet; (*bambino, scolaro*) quiet; (*sereno*) with one's mind at rest; **sta' ~** don't worry

transat'lantico, ci *sm* transatlantic liner

---

transatlantico

🛈 The **transatlantico** *is a room in the* Palazzo di Montecitorio. *The* deputati *relax in it between parliamentary sessions and give media interviews and press conferences there.*

---

transazi'one [transat'tsjone] *sf* compromise; (*DIR*) settlement; (*COMM*) transaction, deal

tran'senna *sf* barrier

tran'sigere [tran'sidʒere] *vi* (*venire a patti*) to compromise, come to an agreement

tran'sistor *sm inv* transistor

transi'tabile *ag* passable

transi'tare *vi* to pass

transi'tivo, a *ag* transitive

'transito *sm* transit; **di ~** (*merci*) in transit; (*stazione*) transit *cpd*; **"divieto di ~"** "no entry"

transi'torio, a *ag* transitory, transient; (*provvisorio*) provisional

'trapano *sm* (*utensile*) drill; (: *MED*) trepan

trapas'sare *vt* to pierce

tra'passo *sm* passage

trape'lare *vi* to leak, drip; (*fig*) to leak out

tra'pezio [tra'pɛttsjo] *sm* (*MAT*) trapezium; (*attrezzo ginnico*) trapeze

trapian'tare *vt* to transplant; **trapi'anto** *sm* transplanting; (*MED*) transplant

'trappola *sf* trap

tra'punta *sf* quilt

'trarre *vt* to draw, pull; (*portare*) to take; (*prendere, tirare fuori*) to take (out), draw; (*derivare*) to obtain; **~ origine da qc** to have its origins *o* originate in sth

trasa'lire *vi* to start, jump

trasan'dato, a *ag* shabby

tras'bordo *sm* transfer

trasci'nare [traʃʃi'nare] *vt* to drag; **~rsi** *vr* to drag o.s. along; (*fig*) to drag on

tras'correre *vt* (*tempo*) to spend, pass ♦ *vi* to pass; **tras'corso, a** *pp di* **trascorrere**

tras'critto, a *pp di* **trascrivere**

tras'crivere *vt* to transcribe

trascu'rare *vt* to neglect; (*non considerare*) to disregard; **trascura'tezza** *sf* carelessness, negligence; **trascu'rato, a** *ag* (*casa*) neglected; (*persona*) careless, negligent

trasfe'ribile *ag* transferable; **"non ~"** (*su assegno*) "account payee only"

trasferi'mento *sm* transfer; (*trasloco*) removal, move

trasfe'rire *vt* to transfer; **~rsi** *vr* to move; **tras'ferta** *sf* transfer; (*indennità*) travelling expenses *pl*; (*SPORT*) away game

trasfigu'rare *vt* to transfigure

trasfor'mare *vt* to transform, change; **trasforma'tore** *sm* (*ELEC*) transformer

trasfusi'one *sf* (*MED*) transfusion

trasgre'dire *vt* to disobey, contravene

tras'lato, a *ag* metaphorical, figurative

traslo'care *vt* to move, transfer; **~rsi** *vr* to move; **tras'loco, chi** *sm* removal

tras'messo, a *pp di* **trasmettere**

tras'mettere *vt* (*passare*): **~ qc a qn** to pass sth on to sb; (*mandare*) to send; (*TECN, TEL, MED*) to transmit; (*TV, RADIO*) to broadcast; **trasmetti'tore** *sm* transmitter; **trasmissi'one** *sf* (*gen, FISICA, TECN*) transmission; (*passaggio*) transmission, passing on; (*TV, RADIO*) broadcast; **trasmit'tente** *sf* transmitting *o* broadcasting station

traso'gnato, a [trasoɲ'ɲato] *ag* dreamy

traspa'rente *ag* transparent

traspa'rire *vi* to show (through)

traspi'rare *vi* to perspire; (*fig*) to come to light, leak out; **traspirazi'one** *sf* perspiration

traspor'tare *vt* to carry, move; (*merce*) to

transport, convey; **lasciarsi ~ (da qc)** *(fig)* to let o.s. be carried away (by sth); **tras'porto** *sm* transport

trastul'lare *vt* to amuse; **~rsi** *vr* to amuse o.s.

trasu'dare *vi (filtrare)* to ooze; *(sudare)* to sweat ♦ *vt* to ooze with

trasver'sale *ag* transverse, cross(-); running at right angles

trasvo'lare *vt* to fly over

'tratta *sf (ECON)* draft; *(di persone)*: **la ~ delle bianche** the white slave trade

tratta'mento *sm* treatment; *(servizio)* service

trat'tare *vt (gen)* to treat; *(commerciare)* to deal in; *(svolgere: argomento)* to discuss, deal with; *(negoziare)* to negotiate ♦ *vi*: **~ di** to deal with; **~ con** *(persona)* to deal with; **si tratta di ...** it's about ...; **tratta'tive** *sfpl* negotiations; **trat'tato** *sm (testo)* treatise; *(accordo)* treaty; **trattazi'one** *sf* treatment

tratteggi'are [tratted'dʒare] *vt (disegnare: a tratti)* to sketch, outline; *(: col tratteggio)* to hatch

tratte'nere *vt (far rimanere: persona)* to detain; *(intrattenere: ospiti)* to entertain; *(tenere, frenare, reprimere)* to hold back, keep back; *(astenersi dal consegnare)* to hold, keep; *(detrarre: somma)* to deduct; **~rsi** *vr (astenersi)* to restrain o.s., stop o.s.; *(soffermarsi)* to stay, remain

tratteni'mento *sm* entertainment; *(festa)* party

tratte'nuta *sf* deduction

trat'tino *sm* dash; *(in parole composte)* hyphen

'tratto, a *pp di* **trarre** ♦ *sm (di penna, matita)* stroke; *(parte)* part, piece; *(di strada)* stretch; *(di mare, cielo)* expanse; *(di tempo)* period (of time); **~i** *smpl (caratteristiche)* features; *(modo di fare)* ways, manners; **a un ~, d'un ~** suddenly

trat'tore *sm* tractor

tratto'ria *sf* restaurant

'trauma, i *sm* trauma; **trau'matico, a, ci, che** *ag* traumatic

tra'vaglio [tra'vaʎʎo] *sm (angoscia)* pain, suffering; *(MED)* pains *pl*

trava'sare *vt* to decant

'trave *sf* beam

tra'versa *sf (trave)* crosspiece; *(via)* sidestreet; *(FERR)* sleeper *(BRIT)*, (railroad) tie *(US)*; *(CALCIO)* crossbar

traver'sare *vt* to cross; **traver'sata** *sf* crossing; *(AER)* flight, trip

traver'sie *sfpl* mishaps, misfortunes

traver'sina *sf (FERR)* sleeper *(BRIT)*, (railroad) tie *(US)*

tra'verso, a *ag* oblique; **di ~** *ag* askew ♦ *av* sideways; **andare di ~** *(cibo)* to go down the wrong way; **guardare di ~** to look askance at

travesti'mento *sm* disguise

traves'tire *vt* to disguise; **~rsi** *vr* to disguise o.s.

travi'are *vt (fig)* to lead astray

travi'sare *vt (fig)* to distort, misrepresent

tra'volgere [tra'vɔldʒere] *vt* to sweep away, carry away; *(fig)* to overwhelm; **tra'volto, a** *pp di* **travolgere**

tre *num* three

trebbi'are *vt* to thresh

'treccia, ce ['trettʃa] *sf* plait, braid

tre'cento [tre'tʃɛnto] *num* three hundred ♦ *sm*: **il T~** the fourteenth century

'tredici ['treditʃi] *num* thirteen

'tregua *sf* truce; *(fig)* respite

tre'mare *vi*: **~ di** *(freddo etc)* to shiver *o* tremble with; *(paura, rabbia)* to shake *o* tremble with

tre'mendo, a *ag* terrible, awful

tre'mila *num* three thousand

'tremito *sm* trembling *no pl*; shaking *no pl*; shivering *no pl*

tremo'lare *vi* to tremble; *(luce)* to flicker; *(foglie)* to quiver

tre'more *sm* tremor

'treno *sm* train; **~ di gomme** set of tyres *(BRIT)* o tires *(US)*; **~ merci** goods *(BRIT)* o freight train; **~ viaggiatori** passenger train

'trenta *num* thirty; **tren'tesimo, a** *num* thirtieth; **tren'tina** *sf*: **una trentina (di)** thirty or so, about thirty

'**trepidante** *ag* anxious

'**treppi'ede** *sm* tripod; (*CUC*) trivet

'**tresca, sche** *sf* (*fig*) intrigue; (*: relazione amorosa*) affair

'**trespolo** *sm* trestle

tri'angolo *sm* triangle

tribù *sf inv* tribe

tri'buna *sf* (*podio*) platform; (*in aule etc*) gallery; (*di stadio*) stand

tribu'nale *sm* court

tribu'tare *vt* to bestow

tri'buto *sm* tax; (*fig*) tribute

tri'checo, chi [tri'keko] *sm* (*ZOOL*) walrus

tri'ciclo [tri'tʃiklo] *sm* tricycle

trico'lore *ag* three-coloured ♦ *sm* tricolour; (*bandiera italiana*) Italian flag

tri'dente *sm* trident

tri'foglio [tri'fɔʎʎo] *sm* clover

'**triglia** ['triʎʎa] *sf* red mullet

tril'lare *vi* (*MUS*) to trill

tri'mestre *sm* period of three months; (*INS*) term, quarter (*US*); (*COMM*) quarter

'**trina** *sf* lace

trin'cea [trin'tʃea] *sf* trench; **trince'rare** *vt* to entrench

trinci'are [trin'tʃare] *vt* to cut up

trion'fare *vi* to triumph, win; **~ su** to triumph over, overcome; **tri'onfo** *sm* triumph

tripli'care *vt* to triple

'**triplice** ['triplitʃe] *ag* triple; **in ~ copia** in triplicate

'**triplo, a** *ag* triple; treble ♦ *sm*: **il ~ (di)** three times as much (as); **la spesa è ~a it** costs three times as much

'**trippa** *sf* (*CUC*) tripe

'**triste** *ag* sad; (*luogo*) dreary, gloomy; **tris'tezza** *sf* sadness; gloominess

trita'carne *sm inv* mincer, grinder (*US*)

tri'tare *vt* to mince, grind (*US*)

'**trito, a** *ag* (*tritato*) minced, ground (*US*); **~ e ritrito** (*fig*) trite, hackneyed

'**trittico, ci** *sm* (*ARTE*) triptych

trivel'lare *vt* to drill

trivi'ale *ag* vulgar, low

tro'feo *sm* trophy

'**tromba** *sf* (*MUS*) trumpet; (*AUT*) horn; **~**

d'aria whirlwind; **~ delle scale** stairwell

trom'bone *sm* trombone

trom'bosi *sf* thrombosis

tron'care *vt* to cut off; (*spezzare*) to break off

'**tronco, a, chi, che** *ag* cut off; broken off; (*LING*) truncated; (*fig*) cut short ♦ *sm* (*BOT, ANAT*) trunk; (*fig: tratto*) section; **licenziare qn in ~** to fire sb on the spot

troneggi'are [troned'dʒare] *vi*: **~ (su)** to tower (over)

'**tronfio, a** *ag* conceited

'**trono** *sm* throne

tropi'cale *ag* tropical

'**tropico, ci** *sm* tropic; **~ci** *smpl* (*GEO*) tropics

PAROLA CHIAVE

'**troppo, a** *det* (*in eccesso: quantità*) too much; (*: numero*) too many; **c'era ~a gente** there were too many people; **fa ~ caldo** it's too hot

♦ *pron* (*in eccesso: quantità*) too much; (*: numero*) too many; **ne hai messo ~** you've put in too much; **meglio ~i che pochi** better too many than too few

♦ *av* (*eccessivamente: con ag, av*) too; (*: con vb*) too much; **~ amaro/tardi** too bitter/late; **lavora ~** he works too much; **di ~** too much; too many; **qualche tazza di ~** a few cups too many; **3000 lire di ~** 3000 lire too much; **essere di ~** to be in the way

---

'**trota** *sf* trout

trot'tare *vi* to trot; **trotterel'lare** *vi* to trot along; (*bambino*) to toddle; '**trotto** *sm* trot

'**trottola** *sf* spinning top

tro'vare *vt* to find; (*giudicare*): **trovo che** I find *o* think that; **~rsi** *vr* (*reciproco: incontrarsi*) to meet; (*essere, stare*) to be; (*arrivare, capitare*) to find o.s.; **andare a ~ qn** to go and see sb; **~ qn colpevole** to find sb guilty; **~rsi bene** (*in un luogo, con qn*) to get on well; **tro'vata** *sf* good idea

truc'care *vt* (*falsare*) to fake; (*attore etc*) to

make up; (*travestire*) to disguise; (*SPORT*) to fix; (*AUT*) to soup up; **~rsi** *vr* to make up (one's face); **trucca'tore, 'trice** *sm/f* (*CINEMA, TEATRO*) make-up artist

'trucco, chi *sm* trick; (*cosmesi*) make-up

'truce ['trutʃe] *ag* fierce

truci'dare [trutʃi'dare] *vt* to slaughter

'truciolo ['trutʃolo] *sm* shaving

'truffa *sf* fraud, swindle; **truf'fare** *vt* to swindle, cheat

'truppa *sf* troop

tu *pron* you; **~ stesso(a)** you yourself; **dare del ~ a qn** to address sb as "tu"

'tua *vedi* **tuo**

'tuba *sf* (*MUS*) tuba; (*cappello*) top hat

tu'bare *vi* to coo

tuba'tura *sf* piping *no pl*, pipes *pl*

tu'betto *sm* tube

'tubo *sm* tube; pipe; **~ digerente** (*ANAT*) alimentary canal, digestive tract; **~ di scappamento** (*AUT*) exhaust pipe

'tue *vedi* **tuo**

tuf'fare *vt* to plunge, dip; **~rsi** *vr* to plunge, dive; **'tuffo** *sm* dive; (*breve bagno*) dip

tu'gurio *sm* hovel

tuli'pano *sm* tulip

tume'farsi *vr* (*MED*) to swell

'tumido, a *ag* swollen

tu'more *sm* (*MED*) tumour

tu'multo *sm* uproar, commotion; (*sommossa*) riot; (*fig*) turmoil; **tumultu'oso, a** *ag* rowdy, unruly; (*fig*) turbulent, stormy

'tunica, che *sf* tunic

Tuni'sia *sf*: **la ~** Tunisia

'tuo (*f* **'tua**, *pl* **tu'oi, 'tue**) *det*: **il ~, la tua** *etc* your ♦ *pron*: **il ~, la tua** *etc* yours

tuo'nare *vi* to thunder; **tuona** it is thundering, there's some thunder

tu'ono *sm* thunder

tu'orlo *sm* yolk

tu'racciolo [tu'rattʃolo] *sm* cap, top; (*di sughero*) cork

tu'rare *vt* to stop, plug; (*con sughero*) to cork; **~rsi il naso** to hold one's nose

turba'mento *sm* disturbance; (*di animo*) anxiety, agitation

tur'bante *sm* turban

tur'bare *vt* to disturb, trouble

'turbine *sm* whirlwind

turbo'lento, a *ag* turbulent; (*ragazzo*) boisterous, unruly

turbo'lenza [turbo'lentsa] *sf* turbulence

tur'chese [tur'kese] *sf* turquoise

Tur'chia [tur'kia] *sf*: **la ~** Turkey

tur'chino, a [tur'kino] *ag* deep blue

'turco, a, chi, che *ag* Turkish ♦ *sm/f* Turk/Turkish woman ♦ *sm* (*LING*) Turkish; **parlare ~** (*fig*) to talk double-dutch

tu'rismo *sm* tourism; tourist industry; **tu'rista, i, e** *sm/f* tourist; **tu'ristico, a, ci, che** *ag* tourist *cpd*

'turno *sm* turn; (*di lavoro*) shift; **di ~** (*soldato, medico, custode*) on duty; **a ~** (*rispondere*) in turn; (*lavorare*) in shifts; **fare a ~ a fare qc** to take turns to do sth; **è il suo ~** it's your (*o* his *etc*) turn

'turpe *ag* filthy, vile; **turpi'loquio** *sm* obscene language

'tuta *sf* overalls *pl*; (*SPORT*) tracksuit

tu'tela *sf* (*DIR: di minore*) guardianship; (*: protezione*) protection; (*difesa*) defence; **tute'lare** *vt* to protect, defend

tu'tore, 'trice *sm/f* (*DIR*) guardian

tutta'via *cong* nevertheless, yet

PAROLA CHIAVE

'tutto, a *det* **1** (*intero*) all; **~ il latte** all the milk; **~a la notte** all night, the whole night; **~ il libro** the whole book; **~a una bottiglia** a whole bottle

2 (*pl, collettivo*) all; every; **~i i libri** all the books; **~e le notti** every night; **~i i venerdì** every Friday; **~i gli uomini** all the men; (*collettivo*) all men; **~ l'anno** all year long; **~i e due** both *o* each of us (*o* them *o* you); **~i e cinque** all five of us (*o* them *o* you)

3 (*completamente*): **era ~a sporca** she was all dirty; **tremava ~** he was trembling all over; **è ~a sua madre** she's just *o* exactly like her mother

4: **a tutt'oggi** so far, up till now; **a ~a velocità** at full *o* top speed

♦ *pron* 1 *(ogni cosa)* everything, all; *(qualsiasi cosa)* anything; **ha mangiato ~** he's eaten everything; **~ considerato** all things considered; **in ~: 10,000 lire in ~** 10.000 lire in all; **in ~ eravamo 50** there were 50 of us in all

2: **~i, e** *(ognuno)* all, everybody; **vengono ~i** they are all coming, everybody's coming; **~i quanti** all and sundry

♦ *av (completamente)* entirely, quite; **è ~ il contrario** it's quite *o* exactly the opposite; **tutt'al più: saranno stati tutt'al più una cinquantina** there were about fifty of them at (the very) most; **tutt'al più possiamo prendere un treno** if the worst comes to the worst we can take a train; **tutt'altro** on the contrary; **è tutt'altro che felice** he's anything but happy; **tutt'a un tratto** suddenly

♦ *sm*: **il ~** the whole lot, all of it

tutto'fare *ag inv*: **domestica ~** general maid; **ragazzo ~** office boy ♦ *sm/f inv* handyman/woman

tut'tora *av* still

U, u

ubbidi'ente *ag* obedient; **ubbidi'enza** *sf* obedience

ubbi'dire *vi* to obey; **~ a** to obey; *(sog: veicolo, macchina)* to respond to

ubria'care *vt*: **~ qn** to get sb drunk; *(sog: alcool)* to make sb drunk; *(fig)* to make sb's head spin *o* reel; **~rsi** *vr* to get drunk; **~rsi di** *(fig)* to become intoxicated with

ubri'aco, a, chi, che *ag*, *sm/f* drunk

uccelli'era [uttʃel'ljɛra] *sf* aviary

uccel'lino [uttʃel'lino] *sm* baby bird, chick

uc'cello [ut'tʃɛllo] *sm* bird

uc'cidere [ut'tʃidere] *vt* to kill; **~rsi** *vr* *(suicidarsi)* to kill o.s.; *(perdere la vita)* to be killed; **uccisi'one** *sf* killing; **uc'ciso, a** *pp di* **uccidere**; **ucci'sore** *sm* killer

udi'enza [u'djɛntsa] *sf* audience; *(DIR)* hearing

u'dire *vt* to hear; **udi'tivo, a** *ag* auditory; **u'dito** *sm* (sense of) hearing; **udi'torio** *sm (persone)* audience

UE *sigla f (= Unione Europea)* EU

UEM *sigla f (= Unione economica e monetaria)* EMU

'uffa *escl* tut!

uffici'ale [uffi'tʃale] *ag* official ♦ *sm (AMM)* official, officer; *(MIL)* officer; **~ di stato civile** registrar

uf'ficio [uf'fitʃo] *sm (gen)* office; *(dovere)* duty; *(mansione)* task, function, job; *(agenzia)* agency, bureau; *(REL)* service; **d'~** *ag* office *cpd*; official ♦ *av* officially; **~ di collocamento** employment office; **~ informazioni** information bureau; **~ oggetti smarriti** lost property office *(BRIT)*, lost and found *(US)*; **~ postale** post office

uffici'oso, a [uffi'tʃoso] *ag* unofficial

'UFO *sm inv* UFO

'ufo: a ~ *av* free, for nothing

uguagli'anza [ugwaʎ'ʎantsa] *sf* equality

uguagli'are [ugwaʎ'ʎare] *vt* to make equal; *(essere uguale)* to equal, be equal to; *(livellare)* to level; **~rsi a** *o* **con qn** *(paragonarsi)* to compare o.s. to sb

ugu'ale *ag* equal; *(identico)* identical, the same; *(uniforme)* level, even ♦ *av*: **costano ~** they cost the same; **sono bravi ~** they're equally good; **ugual'mente** *av* equally; *(lo stesso)* all the same

'ulcera ['ultʃera] *sf* ulcer

u'livo = **olivo**

ulteri'ore *ag* further

ulti'mare *vt* to finish, complete

'ultimo, a *ag (finale)* last; *(estremo)* farthest, utmost; *(recente: notizia, moda)* latest; *(fig)* ultimate ♦ *sm/f* last (one); **fino all'~** to the last, until the end; **da ~, in ~** in the end; **abitare all'~ piano** to live on the top floor; **per ~** *(entrare, arrivare)* last

ulu'lare *vi* to howl; **ulu'lato** *sm* howling *no pl*; howl

umani'tà *sf* humanity; **umani'tario, a** *ag* humanitarian

u'mano, a *ag* human; *(comprensivo)* humane

umet'tare vt to dampen, moisten

umidità sf dampness; humidity

'umido, a ag damp; (mano, occhi) moist; (clima) humid ♦ sm dampness, damp; carne in ~ stew

'umile ag humble

umili'are vt to humiliate; ~rsi vr to humble o.s.; umiliazi'one sf humiliation

umiltà sf humility, humbleness

u'more sm (disposizione d'animo) mood; (carattere) temper; di buon/cattivo ~ in a good/bad mood

umo'rismo sm humour; avere il senso dell'~ to have a sense of humour; umo'ristico, a, ci, che ag humorous, funny

un vedi uno

un' vedi uno

'una vedi uno

u'nanime ag unanimous; unanimità sf unanimity; all'unanimità unanimously

unci'netto [untʃiˈnetto] sm crochet hook

un'cino [unˈtʃino] sm hook

'undici [ˈunditʃi] num eleven

'ungere [ˈundʒere] vt to grease, oil; (REL) to anoint; (fig) to flatter, butter up; ~rsi vr (sporcarsi) to get covered in grease; ~rsi con la crema to put on cream

unghe'rese [ungeˈrese] ag, sm/f, sm Hungarian

Unghe'ria [ungeˈria] sf: l'~ Hungary

'unghia [ˈungja] sf (ANAT) nail; (di animale) claw; (di rapace) talon; (di cavallo) hoof; unghi'ata sf (graffio) scratch

ungu'ento sm ointment

'unico, a, ci, che ag (solo) only; (ineguagliabile) unique; (singolo: binario) single; figlio(a) ~(a) only son/daughter, only child

unifamili'are ag one-family cpd

unifi'care vt to unite, unify; (sistemi) to standardize; unificazi'one sf uniting; unification; standardization

uni'forme ag uniform; (superficie) even ♦ sf (divisa) uniform

unilate'rale ag one-sided; (DIR) unilateral

uni'one sf union; (fig: concordia) unity, harmony

u'nire vt to unite; (congiungere) to join, connect; (: ingredienti, colori) to combine; (in matrimonio) to unite, join together; ~rsi vr to unite; (in matrimonio) to be joined together; ~ qc a to unite sth with; to join o connect sth with; to combine sth with; ~rsi a (gruppo, società) to join

unità sf inv (unione, concordia) unity; (MAT, MIL, COMM, di misura) unit; uni'tario, a ag unitary; prezzo unitario price per unit

u'nito, a ag (paese) united; (amici, famiglia) close; in tinta ~a plain, self-coloured

univer'sale ag universal; general

università sf inv university; universi'tario, a ag university cpd ♦ sm/f (studente) university student; (insegnante) academic, university lecturer

uni'verso sm universe

PAROLA CHIAVE

'uno, a (dav sm un +C, V, uno +s impura, gn, pn, ps, x, z; dav sf un' +V, una +C) art indet 1 a; (dav vocale) an; un bambino a child; ~a strada a street; ~ zingaro a gypsy

2 (intensivo): ho avuto ~a paura! I got such a fright!

♦ pron 1 one; prendine ~ take one (of them); l'~ o l'altro either (of them); l'~ e l'altro both (of them); aiutarsi l'un l'altro to help one another o each other; sono entrati l'~ dopo l'altro they came in one after the other

2 (un tale) someone, somebody

3 (con valore impersonale) one, you; se ~ vuole if one wants, if you want

♦ num one; ~a mela e due pere one apple and two pears; ~ più ~ fa due one plus one equals two, one and one are two

♦ sf: è l'~a it's one (o'clock)

'unto, a pp di ungere ♦ ag greasy, oily ♦ sm grease; untu'oso, a ag greasy, oily

u'omo (pl u'omini) sm man; da ~ (abito, scarpe) men's, for men; ~ d'affari businessman; ~ di paglia stooge; ~ rana frogman

u'ovo (*pl(f)* u'ova) *sm* egg; ~ affogato poached egg; ~ al tegame fried egg; ~ alla coque boiled egg; ~ bazzotto/sodo soft-/hard-boiled egg; ~ di Pasqua Easter egg; ~ in camicia poached egg; ~a strapazzate scrambled eggs

ura'gano *sm* hurricane

urba'nistica *sf* town planning

ur'bano, a *ag* urban, city *cpd*, town *cpd*; (TEL: *chiamata*) local; (*fig*) urbane

ur'gente [ur'dʒɛnte] *ag* urgent; ur'genza *sf* urgency; in caso d'urgenza in (case of) an emergency; d'urgenza *ag* emergency ♦ *av* urgently, as a matter of urgency

u'rina *sf* = orina

ur'lare *vi* (*persona*) to scream, yell; (*animale, vento*) to howl ♦ *vt* to scream, yell

'urlo (*pl(m)* 'urli, *pl(f)* 'urla) *sm* scream, yell; howl

'urna *sf* urn; (*elettorale*) ballot-box; andare alle ~e to go to the polls

urrà *escl* hurrah!

U.R.S.S. *abbr f*: l'~ the USSR

ur'tare *vt* to bump into, knock against; (*fig: irritare*) to annoy ♦ *vi*: ~ contro *o* in to bump into, knock against, crash into; (*fig: imbattersi*) to come up against; ~rsi *vr* (*reciproco: scontrarsi*) to collide; (: *fig*) to clash; (*irritarsi*) to get annoyed; 'urto *sm* (*colpo*) knock, bump; (*scontro*) crash, collision; (*fig*) clash

'U.S.A. ['uza] *smpl*: gli ~ the USA

u'sanza [u'zantsa] *sf* custom; (*moda*) fashion

u'sare *vt* to use, employ ♦ *vi* (*servirsi*): ~ di to use; (: *diritto*) to exercise; (*essere di moda*) to be fashionable; (*essere solito*): ~ fare to be in the habit of doing, be accustomed to doing ♦ *vb impers*: qui usa così it's the custom round here; u'sato, a *ag* used; (*consumato*) worn; (*di seconda mano*) used, second-hand ♦ *sm* second-hand goods *pl*

usci'ere [uʃ'ʃɛre] *sm* usher

'uscio ['uʃʃo] *sm* door

u'scire [uʃ'ʃire] *vi* (*gen*) to come out; (*partire, andare a passeggio, a uno spettacolo etc*) to go out; (*essere sorteggiato: numero*) to come up; ~ da (*gen*) to leave; (*posto*) to go (*o* come) out of, leave; (*solco, vasca etc*) to come out of; (*muro*) to stick out of; (*competenza etc*) to be outside; (*infanzia, adolescenza*) to leave behind; (*famiglia nobile etc*) to come from; ~ da *o* di casa to go out; (*fig*) to leave home; ~ in automobile to go out in the car, go for a drive; ~ di strada (AUT) to go off *o* leave the road

u'scita [uʃ'ʃita] *sf* (*passaggio, varco*) exit, way out; (*per divertimento*) outing; (ECON: *somma*) expenditure; (TEATRO) entrance; (*fig: battuta*) witty remark; ~ di sicurezza emergency exit

usi'gnolo [uziɲ'ɲɔlo] *sm* nightingale

U.S.L. [uzl] *sigla f* (= unità sanitaria locale) local health centre

'uso *sm* (*utilizzazione*) use; (*esercizio*) practice; (*abitudine*) custom; a ~ di for (the use of); d'~ (*corrente*) in use; fuori ~ out of use

usti'one *sf* burn

usu'ale *ag* common, everyday

u'sura *sf* usury; (*logoramento*) wear (and tear)

uten'sile *sm* tool, implement; ~i da cucina kitchen utensils

u'tente *sm/f* user

'utero *sm* uterus

'utile *ag* useful ♦ *sm* (*vantaggio*) advantage, benefit; (ECON: *profitto*) profit; utilità *sf* usefulness *no pl*; use; (*vantaggio*) benefit; utili'taria *sf* (AUT) economy car

utiliz'zare [utilid'dzare] *vt* to use, make use of, utilize

'uva *sf* grapes *pl*; ~ passa raisins *pl*; ~ spina gooseberry

V, v

v. *abbr* (= *vedi*) v

va *vb vedi* **andare**

va'cante *ag* vacant

va'canza [va'kantsa] *sf* (*l'essere vacante*) vacancy; (*riposo, ferie*) holiday(s *pl*) (*BRIT*), vacation (*US*); (*giorno di permesso*) day off, holiday; **~e** *sfpl* (*periodo di ferie*) holidays (*BRIT*), vacation *sg* (*US*); **essere/andare in ~** to be/go on holiday *o* vacation; **~e estive** summer holiday(s) *o* vacation

'vacca, che *sf* cow

vacci'nare [vattʃi'nare] *vt* to vaccinate

vac'cino [vat'tʃino] *sm* (*MED*) vaccine

vacil'lare [vatʃil'lare] *vi* to sway, wobble; (*luce*) to flicker; (*fig: memoria, coraggio*) to be failing, falter

'vacuo, a *ag* (*fig*) empty, vacuous

'vado *vb vedi* **andare**

vaga'bondo, a *sm/f* tramp, vagrant

va'gare *vi* to wander

va'gina [va'dʒina] *sf* vagina

va'gire [va'dʒire] *vi* to whimper

va'gito [va'dʒito] *sm* cry

'vaglia [ˈvaʎʎa] *sm inv* money order; **~ postale** postal order

vagli'are [vaʎ'ʎare] *vt* to sift; (*fig*) to weigh up; **'vaglio** *sm* sieve

'vago, a, ghi, ghe *ag* vague

va'gone *sm* (*FERR: per passeggeri*) coach; (*: per merci*) truck, wagon; **~ letto** sleeper, sleeping car; **~ ristorante** dining *o* restaurant car

'vai *vb vedi* **andare**

vai'olo *sm* smallpox

va'langa, ghe *sf* avalanche

va'lente *ag* able, talented

va'lere *vi* (*avere forza, potenza*) to have influence; (*essere valido*) to be valid; (*avere vigore, autorità*) to hold, apply; (*essere capace: poeta, studente*) to be good, be able ♦ *vt* (*prezzo, sforzo*) to be worth; (*corrispondere*) to correspond to; (*procurare*): **~ qc a qn** to earn sb sth; **~rsi**

di to make use of, take advantage of; **far ~** (*autorità etc*) to assert; **vale a dire** that is to say; **~ la pena** to be worth the effort *o* worth it

va'levole *ag* valid

vali'care *vt* to cross

'valico, chi *sm* (*passo*) pass

'valido, a *ag* valid; (*rimedio*) effective; (*aiuto*) real; (*persona*) worthwhile

valige'ria [validʒe'ria] *sf* leather goods *pl*; leather goods factory; leather goods shop

vali'getta [vali'dʒetta] *sf* briefcase

va'ligia, gie *o ge* [va'lidʒa] *sf* (*suit*)case; **fare le ~gie** to pack (up)

val'lata *sf* valley

'valle *sf* valley; **a ~** (*di fiume*) downstream; **scendere a ~** to go downhill

va'lore *sm* (*gen*) value; (*merito*) merit, worth; (*coraggio*) valour, courage; (*COMM: titolo*) security; **~i** *smpl* (*oggetti preziosi*) valuables

valoriz'zare [valorid'dzare] *vt* (*terreno*) to develop; (*fig*) to make the most of

'valso, a *pp di* **valere**

va'luta *sf* currency, money; (*BANCA*): **~ 15 gennaio** interest to run from January 15th

valu'tare *vt* (*casa, gioiello, fig*) to value; (*stabilire: peso, entrate, fig*) to estimate; **valutazi'one** *sf* valuation; estimate

'valvola *sf* (*TECN, ANAT*) valve; (*ELETTR*) fuse

'valzer [ˈvaltser] *sm inv* waltz

vam'pata *sf* (*di fiamma*) blaze; (*di calore*) blast; (*: al viso*) flush

vam'piro *sm* vampire

vanda'lismo *sm* vandalism

'vandalo *sm* vandal

vaneggi'are [vaned'dʒare] *vi* to rave

'vanga, ghe *sf* spade; **van'gare** *vt* to dig

van'gelo [van'dʒɛlo] *sm* gospel

va'niglia [va'niʎʎa] *sf* vanilla

vanità *sf* vanity; (*di promessa*) emptiness; (*di sforzo*) futility; **vani'toso, a** *ag* vain, conceited

'vanno *vb vedi* **andare**

'vano, a *ag* vain ♦ *sm* (*spazio*) space; (*apertura*) opening; (*stanza*) room

van'taggio [van'taddʒo] *sm* advantage;

essere/portarsi in ~ (*SPORT*) to be in/take the lead; **vantaggi'oso, a** *ag* advantageous; favourable

van'tare *vt* to praise, speak highly of; **~rsi** *vr*: **~rsi (di/di aver fatto)** to boast *o* brag (about/about having done); **vante'ria** *sf* boasting; **'vanto** *sm* boasting; (*merito*) virtue, merit; (*gloria*) pride

'vanvera *sf*: **a ~** haphazardly; **parlare a ~** to talk nonsense

va'pore *sm* vapour; (*anche:* **~ acqueo**) steam; (*nave:* **~** steamer; **a ~** (*turbina etc*) steam *cpd*; **a ~** (*CUC*) steamed; **vapo'retto** *sm* steamer; **vaporiz'zare** *vt* to vaporize; **vapo'roso, a** *ag* (*tessuto*) filmy; (*capelli*) soft and full

va'rare *vt* (*NAUT, fig*) to launch; (*DIR*) to pass

var'care *vt* to cross

'varco, chi *sm* passage; **aprirsi un ~ tra la folla** to push one's way through the crowd

vari'abile *ag* variable; (*tempo, umore*) changeable, variable ♦ *sf* (*MAT*) variable

vari'are *vt, vi* to vary; **~ di opinione** to change one's mind; **variazi'one** *sf* variation; change

va'rice [va'ritʃe] *sf* varicose vein

vari'cella [vari'tʃɛlla] *sf* chickenpox

vari'coso, a *ag* varicose

varie'gato, a *ag* variegated

varietà *sf inv* variety ♦ *sm inv* variety show

'vario, a *ag* varied; (*parecchi: col sostantivo al pl*) various; (*mutevole: umore*) changeable; **vario'pinto, a** *ag* multicoloured

'varo *sm* (*NAUT, fig*) launch; (*di leggi*) passing

va'saio *sm* potter

'vasca, sche *sf* basin; (*anche:* **~ da bagno**) bathtub, bath

va'scello [vaʃ'ʃɛllo] *sm* vessel, ship

vase'lina *sf* vaseline

vasel'lame *sm* (*stoviglie*) crockery; (: *di porcellana*) china; **~ d'oro/d'argento** gold/silver plate

'vaso *sm* (*recipiente*) pot; (: *barattolo*) jar; (: *decorativo*) vase; (*ANAT*) vessel; **~ da fiori**

vase; (*per piante*) flowerpot

vas'soio *sm* tray

'vasto, a *ag* vast, immense

Vati'cano *sm*: **il ~** the Vatican

ve *pron, av vedi* **vi**

vecchi'aia [vek'kjaja] *sf* old age

'vecchio, a ['vɛkkjo] *ag* old ♦ *sm/f* old man/woman; **i ~i** the old

'vece ['vetʃe] *sf*: **in ~ di** in the place of, for; **fare le ~i di qn** to take sb's place

ve'dere *vt, vi* to see; **~rsi** *vr* to meet, see one another; **avere a che ~ con** to have something to do with; **far ~ qc a qn** to show sb sth; **farsi ~** to show o.s.; (*farsi vivo*) to show one's face; **vedi di non farlo** make sure *o* see you don't do it; **non (ci) si vede** (*è buio etc*) you can't see a thing; **non lo posso ~** (*fig*) I can't stand him

ve'detta *sf* (*sentinella, posto*) look-out; (*NAUT*) patrol boat

'vedovo, a *sm/f* widower/widow

ve'duta *sf* view

vee'mente *ag* vehement; violent

vege'tale [vedʒe'tale] *ag, sm* vegetable

vegetari'ano, a [vedʒeta'rjano] *ag, sm/f* vegetarian

'vegeto, a ['vɛdʒeto] *ag* (*pianta*) thriving; (*persona*) strong, vigorous

'veglia ['veʎʎa] *sf* wakefulness; (*sorveglianza*) watch; (*trattenimento*) evening gathering; **fare la ~ a un malato** to watch over a sick person

vegli'are [veʎ'ʎare] *vi* to be awake; to stay *o* sit up; (*stare vigile*) to watch; to keep watch ♦ *vt* (*malato, morto*) to watch over, sit up with

ve'icolo *sm* vehicle

'vela *sf* (*NAUT: tela*) sail; (*sport*) sailing

ve'lare *vt* to veil; **~rsi** *vr* (*occhi, luna*) to mist over; (*voce*) to become husky; **~rsi il viso** to cover one's face (with a veil); **ve'lato, a** *ag* veiled

veleggi'are [veled'dʒare] *vi* to sail; (*AER*) to glide

ve'leno *sm* poison; **vele'noso, a** *ag* poisonous

veli'ero *sm* sailing ship

ve'lina *sf* (*anche:* **carta ~**: *per imballare*) tissue paper

ve'livolo *sm* aircraft

velleità *sf inv* vain ambition, vain desire

vel'luto *sm* velvet; **~ a coste** cord

'velo *sm* veil; (*tessuto*) voile

ve'loce [ve'lotʃe] *ag* fast, quick ♦ *av* fast, quickly; velo'cista, i, e *sm/f* (*SPORT*) sprinter; velocità *sf* speed; **a forte velocità** at high speed; **velocità di crociera** cruising speed

'vena *sf* (*gen*) vein; (*filone*) vein, seam; (*fig: ispirazione*) inspiration; (*: umore*) mood; **essere in ~ di qc** to be in the mood for sth

ve'nale *ag* (*prezzo, valore*) market *cpd*; (*fig*) venal; mercenary

ven'demmia *sf* (*raccolta*) grape harvest; (*quantità d'uva*) grape crop, grapes *pl*; (*vino ottenuto*) vintage; vendemmi'are *vt* to harvest ♦ *vi* to harvest the grapes

'vendere *vt* to sell; **"vendesi"** "for sale"

ven'detta *sf* revenge

vendi'care *vt* to avenge; **~rsi** *vr*: **~rsi (di)** to avenge o.s. (for); (*per rancore*) to take one's revenge (for); **~rsi su qn** to revenge o.s. on sb; vendica'tivo, a *ag* vindictive

'vendita *sf* sale; **la ~** (*attività*) selling; (*smercio*) sales *pl*; **in ~** on sale; **~ all'asta** sale by auction; vendi'tore *sm* seller, vendor; (*gestore di negozio*) trader, dealer

vene'rabile *ag* venerable

venerando, a *ag* = venerabile

vene'rare *vt* to venerate

venerdì *sm inv* Friday; **di** *o* **il ~** on Fridays; **V~ Santo** Good Friday

ve'nereo, a *ag* venereal

'veneto, a *ag, sm/f* Venetian

Ve'nezia [ve'nɛttsja] *sf* Venice; venezi'ana *sf* Venetian blind; venezi'ano, a *ag, sm/f* Venetian

veni'ale *ag* venial

ve'nire *vi* to come; (*riuscire: dolce, fotografia*) to turn out; (*come ausiliare: essere*): **viene ammirato da tutti** he is admired by everyone; **~ da** to come from; **quanto viene?** how much does it cost?;

far ~ (*mandare a chiamare*) to send for; **~ giù** to come down; **~ meno** (*svenire*) to faint; **~ meno a qc** not to fulfil sth; **~ su** to come up; **~ a trovare qn** to come and see sb; **~ via** to come away

ven'taglio [ven'taʎʎo] *sm* fan

ven'tata *sf* gust (of wind)

ven'tenne *ag*: **una ragazza ~** a twenty-year-old girl, a girl of twenty

ven'tesimo, a *num* twentieth

'venti *num* twenty

venti'lare *vt* (*stanza*) to air, ventilate; (*fig: idea, proposta*) to air; ventila'tore *sm* ventilator, fan

ven'tina *sf*: **una ~ (di)** around twenty, twenty or so

venti'sette *num* twenty-seven

'vento *sm* wind

'ventola *sf* (*AUT, TECN*) fan

ven'tosa *sf* (*ZOOL*) sucker; (*di gomma*) suction pad

ven'toso, a *ag* windy ♦

'ventre *sm* stomach

ven'tura *sf*: **soldato di ~** mercenary

ven'turo, a *ag* next, coming

ve'nuta *sf* coming, arrival

ve'nuto, a *pp di* venire

vera'mente *av* really

ver'bale *ag* verbal ♦ *sm* (*di riunione*) minutes *pl*

'verbo *sm* (*LING*) verb; (*parola*) word; (*REL*): **il V~** the Word

'verde *ag, sm* green; **essere al ~** to be broke; **~ bottiglia/oliva** bottle/olive green

verde'rame *sm* verdigris

ver'detto *sm* verdict

ver'dura *sf* vegetables *pl*

'verga, ghe *sf* rod

'vergine ['vɛrdʒine] *sf* virgin; (*dello zodiaco*): **V~** Virgo ♦ *ag* virgin; (*ragazza*): **essere ~** to be a virgin

ver'gogna [ver'goɲɲa] *sf* shame; (*timidezza*) shyness, embarrassment; vergo'gnarsi *vr*: **vergognarsi (di)** to be *o* feel ashamed (of); to be shy (about), be embarrassed (about); vergo'gnoso, a *ag* ashamed; (*timido*) shy, embarrassed; (*causa* *di vergogna: azione)* shameful

ve'rifica, che *sf* checking *no pl*, check

verifi'care *vt (controllare)* to check; *(confermare)* to confirm, bear out

veri'tà *sf inv* truth

veriti'ero, a *ag (che dice la verità)* truthful; *(conforme a verità)* true

'verme *sm* worm

vermi'celli [vermi'tʃelli] *smpl* vermicelli *sg*

ver'miglio [ver'miʎʎo] *sm* vermilion, scarlet

'vermut *sm inv* vermouth

ver'nice [ver'nitʃe] *sf (colorazione)* paint; *(trasparente)* varnish; *(pelle)* patent leather; **"~ fresca"** "wet paint"; **vernici'are** *vt* to paint; to varnish

'vero, a *ag (veridico: fatti, testimonianza)* true; *(autentico)* real ♦ *sm (verità)* truth; *(realtà)* real life; **un ~ e proprio delinquente** a real criminal, an out-and-out criminal

vero'simile *ag* likely, probable

ver'ruca, che *sf* wart

versa'mento *sm (pagamento)* payment; *(deposito di denaro)* deposit

ver'sante *sm* slopes *pl*, side

ver'sare *vt (fare uscire: vino, farina)* to pour (out); *(spargere: lacrime, sangue)* to shed; *(rovesciare)* to spill; *(ECON)* to pay; *(: depositare)* to deposit, pay in; **~rsi** *vr (rovesciarsi)* to spill; *(fiume, folla)*: **~rsi (in)** to pour (into)

ver'satile *ag* versatile

ver'setto *sm (REL)* verse

versi'one *sf* version; *(traduzione)* translation

'verso *sm (di poesia)* verse, line; *(di animale, uccello)* cry; *(direzione)* direction; *(modo)* way; *(di foglio di carta)* verso; *(di moneta)* reverse; **~i** *smpl (poesia)* verse *sg*; **non c'è ~ di persuaderlo** there's no way of persuading him, he can't be persuaded ♦ *prep (in direzione di)* toward(s); *(nei pressi di)* near, around (about); *(in senso temporale)* about; around; *(nei confronti di)* for; **~ di me** towards me; **~ sera** towards evening

'vertebra *sf* vertebra

verti'cale *ag, sf* vertical

'vertice ['vertitʃe] *sm* summit, top; *(MAT)* vertex; **conferenza al ~** *(POL)* summit conference

ver'tigine [ver'tidʒine] *sf* dizziness *no pl*; dizzy spell; *(MED)* vertigo; **avere le ~i** to feel dizzy; **vertigi'noso, a** *ag (altezza)* dizzy; *(fig)* breathtakingly high *(o deep etc)*

ve'scica, che [veʃ'ʃika] *sf (ANAT)* bladder; *(MED)* blister

'vescovo *sm* bishop

'vespa *sf* wasp

'vespro *sm (REL)* vespers *pl*

ves'sillo *sm* standard; *(bandiera)* flag

ves'taglia [ves'taʎʎa] *sf* dressing gown

'veste *sf* garment; *(rivestimento)* covering; *(qualità, facoltà)* capacity; **in ~ ufficiale** *(fig)* in an official capacity; **in ~ di** in the guise of, as; **vesti'ario** *sm* wardrobe, clothes *pl*

ves'tire *vt (bambino, malato)* to dress; *(avere indosso)* to have on, wear; **~rsi** *vr* to dress, get dressed; **ves'tito, a** *ag* dressed ♦ *sm* garment; *(da donna)* dress; *(da uomo)* suit; **vestiti** *smpl (indumenti)* clothes; **vestito di bianco** dressed in white

Ve'suvio *sm*: **il ~** Vesuvius

vete'rano, a *ag, sm/f* veteran

veteri'naria *sf* veterinary medicine

veteri'nario, a *ag* veterinary ♦ *sm* veterinary surgeon *(BRIT)*, veterinarian *(US)*, vet

'veto *sm inv* veto

ve'traio *sm* glassmaker; glazier

ve'trata *sf* glass door *(o window)*; *(di chiesa)* stained glass window

ve'treria *sf (stabilimento)* glassworks *sg*; *(oggetti di vetro)* glassware

ve'trina *sf (di negozio)* (shop) window; *(armadio)* display cabinet; **vetri'nista, i, e** *sm/f* window dresser

vetri'olo *sm* vitriol

'vetro *sm* glass; *(per finestra, porta)* pane (of glass)

'vetta *sf* peak, summit, top

vet'tore *sm (MAT, FISICA)* vector; *(chi trasporta)* carrier

vetto'vaglie [vetto'vaʎʎe] *sfpl* supplies

vet'tura *sf* (*carrozza*) carriage; (*FERR*) carriage (*BRIT*), car (*US*); (*auto*) car (*BRIT*), automobile (*US*)

vezzeggia'tivo [vettseddʒa'tivo] *sm* (*LING*) term of endearment

'vezzo ['vettso] *sm* habit; **~i** *smpl* (*smancerie*) affected ways; (*leggiadria*) charms; **vez'zoso, a** *ag* (*grazioso*) charming, pretty; (*lezioso*) affected

vi (*dav lo, la, li, le, ne diventa* **ve**) *pron* (*oggetto*) you; (*complemento di termine*) (to) you; (*riflessivo*) yourselves; (*reciproco*) each other ♦ *av* (*lì*) there; (*qui*) here; (*per questo/quel luogo*) through here/there; **~ è/sono** there is/are

'via *sf* (*gen*) way; (*strada*) street; (*sentiero, pista*) path, track; (*AMM: procedimento*) channels *pl* ♦ *prep* (*passando per*) via, by way of ♦ *av* away ♦ *escl* go away!; (*suvvia*) come on!; (*SPORT*) go! ♦ *sm* (*SPORT*) starting signal; **in ~ di guarigione** on the road to recovery; **per ~ di** (*a causa di*) because of, on account of; **in** *o* **per ~** on the way; **per ~ aerea** by air; (*lettere*) by airmail; **andare/essere ~** to go/be away; **~ ~ che** (*a mano a mano*) as; **dare il ~** (*SPORT*) to give the starting signal; **dare il ~ a** (*fig*) to start; **V~ lattea** (*ASTR*) Milky Way; **~ di mezzo** middle course; **in ~ provvisoria** provisionally

viabilità *sf* (*di strada*) practicability; (*rete stradale*) roads *pl*, road network

via'dotto *sm* viaduct

viaggi'are [viad'dʒare] *vi* to travel; **viaggia'tore, 'trice** *ag* travelling ♦ *sm* traveller; (*passeggero*) passenger

vi'aggio ['vjaddʒo] *sm* travel(ling); (*tragitto*) journey, trip; **buon ~!** have a good trip!; **~ di nozze** honeymoon

vi'ale *sm* avenue

via'vai *sm* coming and going, bustle

vi'brare *vi* to vibrate

vi'cario *sm* (*apostolico etc*) vicar

'vice ['vitʃe] *sm/f* deputy ♦ *prefisso:* **~'console** *sm* vice-consul; **~diret'tore** *sm* assistant manager

vi'cenda [vi'tʃenda] *sf* event; **a ~** in turn; **vicen'devole** *ag* mutual, reciprocal

vice'versa [vitʃe'vɛrsa] *av* vice versa; **da Roma a Pisa e ~** from Rome to Pisa and back

vici'nanza [vitʃi'nantsa] *sf* nearness, closeness; **~e** *sfpl* (*paraggi*) neighbourhood, vicinity

vici'nato [vitʃi'nato] *sm* neighbourhood; (*vicini*) neighbours *pl*

vi'cino, a [vi'tʃino] *ag* (*gen*) near; (*nello spazio*) near, nearby; (*accanto*) next; (*nel tempo*) near, close at hand ♦ *sm/f* neighbour ♦ *av* near, close by; **da ~** (*guardare*) close up; (*esaminare, seguire*) closely; (*conoscere*) well, intimately; **~ a** near (to), close to; (*accanto a*) beside; **~ di casa** neighbour

'vicolo *sm* alley; **~ cieco** blind alley

'video *sm inv* (*TV: schermo*) screen; **~'camera** *sf* camcorder; **~cas'setta** *sf* videocassette; **~registra'tore** *sm* video (recorder)

vie'tare *vt* to forbid; (*AMM*) to prohibit; **~ a qn di fare** to forbid sb to do; to prohibit sb from doing; **"vietato fumare/l'ingresso"** "no smoking/admittance"

Viet'nam *sm:* **il ~** Vietnam; **vietna'mita, i, e** *ag, sm/f, sm* Vietnamese *inv*

vi'gente [vi'dʒɛnte] *ag* in force

vigi'lare [vidʒi'lare] *vt* to watch over, keep an eye on; **~ che** to make sure that, see to it that

'vigile ['vidʒile] *ag* watchful ♦ *sm* (*anche:* **~ urbano**) policeman (*in towns*); **~ del fuoco** fireman

vi'gilia [vi'dʒilja] *sf* (*giorno antecedente*) eve; **la ~ di Natale** Christmas Eve

vigli'acco, a, chi, che [viʎ'ʎakko] *ag* cowardly ♦ *sm/f* coward

'vigna ['viɲɲa] *sf* = **vi'gneto**

vi'gneto [viɲ'ɲeto] *sm* vineyard

vi'gnetta [viɲ'ɲetta] *sf* cartoon

vi'gore *sm* vigour; (*DIR*): **essere/entrare in ~** to be in/come into force; **vigo'roso, a** *ag* vigorous

'vile *ag* (*spregevole*) low, mean, base;

(*codardo*) cowardly

vili'pendio *sm* contempt, scorn; public insult

'villa *sf* villa

vil'laggio [vil'laddʒo] *sm* village

villa'nia *sf* rudeness, lack of manners; **fare** (*o* **dire**) **una ~ a qn** to be rude to sb

vil'lano, a *ag* rude, ill-mannered

villeggia'tura [villeddʒa'tura] *sf* holiday(s *pl*) (*BRIT*), vacation (*US*)

vil'lino *sm* small house (with a garden), cottage

vil'loso, a *ag* hairy

viltà *sf* cowardice *no pl*; cowardly act

Viminale

i The **Viminale**, which takes its name from the hill in Rome on which it stands, is the home of the Ministry of the Interior.

'vimine *sm* wicker; **mobili di ~i** wicker furniture *sg*

'vincere ['vintʃere] *vt* (*in guerra, al gioco, a una gara*) to defeat, beat; (*premio, guerra, partita*) to win; (*fig*) to overcome, conquer ♦ *vi* to win; **~ qn in bellezza** to be better-looking than sb; **'vincita** *sf* win; (*denaro vinto*) winnings *pl*; **vinci'tore** *sm* winner; (*MIL*) victor

vinco'lare *vt* to bind; (*COMM: denaro*) to tie up; **'vincolo** *sm* (*fig*) bond, tie; (*DIR: servitù*) obligation

vi'nicolo, a *ag* wine *cpd*

'vino *sm* wine; **~ bianco/rosso** white/red wine; **~ da pasto** table wine

'vinto, a *pp di* **vincere**

vi'ola *sf* (*BOT*) violet; (*MUS*) viola ♦ *ag, sm inv* (*colore*) purple

vio'lare *vt* (*chiesa*) to desecrate, violate; (*giuramento, legge*) to violate

violen'tare *vt* to use violence on; (*donna*) to rape

vio'lento, a *ag* violent; **vio'lenza** *sf* violence; **violenza carnale** rape

vio'letta *sf* (*BOT*) violet

vio'letto, a *ag, sm* (*colore*) violet

violi'nista, i, e *sm/f* violinist

vio'lino *sm* violin

violon'cello [violon'tʃello] *sm* cello

vi'ottolo *sm* path, track

'vipera *sf* viper, adder

vi'rare *vi* (*NAUT, AER*) to turn; (*FOT*) to tone; **~ di bordo** (*NAUT*) to tack

'virgola *sf* (*LING*) comma; (*MAT*) point; **virgo'lette** *sfpl* inverted commas, quotation marks

vi'rile *ag* (*proprio dell'uomo*) masculine; (*non puerile, da uomo*) manly, virile

virtù *sf inv* virtue; **in** *o* **per ~ di** by virtue of, by

virtu'ale *ag* virtual

virtu'oso, a *ag* virtuous ♦ *sm/f* (*MUS etc*) virtuoso

'virus *sm inv* (*anche COMPUT*) virus

'viscere ['viʃʃere] *sfpl* (*di animale*) entrails *pl*; (*fig*) bowels *pl*

'vischio ['viskjo] *sm* (*BOT*) mistletoe; (*pania*) birdlime; **vischi'oso, a** *ag* sticky

'viscido, a ['viʃʃido] *ag* slimy

vi'sibile *ag* visible

visi'bilio *sm*: **andare in ~** to go into raptures

visibilità *sf* visibility

visi'era *sf* (*di elmo*) visor; (*di berretto*) peak

visi'one *sf* vision; **prendere ~ di qc** to examine sth, look sth over; **prima/seconda ~** (*CINEMA*) first/second showing

'visita *sf* visit; (*MED*) visit, call; (*: esame*) examination; **visi'tare** *vt* to visit; (*MED*) to visit, call on; (*: esaminare*) to examine; **visita'tore, 'trice** *sm/f* visitor

vi'sivo, a *ag* visual

'viso *sm* face

vi'sone *sm* mink

'vispo, a *ag* quick, lively

vis'suto, a *pp di* **vivere** ♦ *ag* (*aria, modo di fare*) experienced

'vista *sf* (*facoltà*) (eye)sight; (*fatto di vedere*): **la ~ di** the sight of; (*veduta*) view; **sparare a ~** to shoot on sight; **in ~** in sight; **perdere qn di ~** to lose sight of sb; (*fig*) to lose touch with sb; **a ~ d'occhio** as far as the eye can see; (*fig*) before one's

very eyes; **far ~ di fare** to pretend to do
'**visto, a** *pp di* **vedere** ♦ *sm* visa; **~ che** seeing (that)
vis'**toso, a** *ag* gaudy, garish; (*ingente*) considerable
visu'**ale** *ag* visual; **visualizza'tore** *sm* (INFORM) visual display unit, VDU
'**vita** *sf* life; (ANAT) waist; **a ~ for** life
vi'**tale** *ag* vital; **vita'lizio, a** *ag* life *cpd* ♦ *sm* life annuity
vita'**mina** *sf* vitamin
'**vite** *sf* (BOT) vine; (TECN) screw
vi'**tello** *sm* (ZOOL) calf; (*carne*) veal; (*pelle*) calfskin
vi'**ticcio** [vi'tittʃo] *sm* (BOT) tendril
viticol'**tore** *sm* wine grower; **viticol'tura** *sf* wine growing
'**vitreo, a** *ag* vitreous; (*occhio, sguardo*) glassy
'**vittima** *sf* victim
'**vitto** *sm* food; (*in un albergo etc*) board; **~ e alloggio** board and lodging
vit'**toria** *sf* victory
'**viva** *escl*: **~ il re!** long live the king!
vi'**vace** [vi'vatʃe] *ag* (*vivo, animato*) lively; (: *mente*) lively, sharp; (*colore*) bright; **vivacità** *sf* vivacity; liveliness; brightness
vi'**vaio** *sm* (*di pesci*) hatchery; (AGR) nursery
vi'**vanda** *sf* (*cibo*); (*piatto*) dish
vi'**vente** *ag* living, alive; **i ~i** the living
'**vivere** *vi* to live ♦ *vt* to live; (*passare: brutto momento*) to live through, go through; (*sentire: gioie, pene di qn*) to share ♦ *sm* life; (*anche*: **modo di ~**) way of life; **~i** *smpl* (*cibo*) food *sg*, provisions; **~ di** to live on
'**vivido, a** *ag* (*colore*) vivid, bright
'**vivo, a** *ag* (*vivente*) alive, living; (: *animale*) live; (*fig*) lively; (: *colore*) bright, brilliant; **i ~i** the living; **~ e vegeto** hale and hearty; **farsi ~** to show one's face; to be heard from; **ritrarre dal ~** to paint from life; **pungere qn nel ~** (*fig*) to cut sb to the quick
vizi'**are** [vit'tsjare] *vt* (*bambino*) to spoil; (*corrompere moralmente*) to corrupt; **vizi'ato, a** *ag* spoilt; (*aria, acqua*) polluted

'**vizio** ['vittsjo] *sm* (*morale*) vice; (*cattiva abitudine*) bad habit; (*imperfezione*) flaw, defect; (*errore*) fault, mistake; **vizi'oso, a** *ag* depraved; defective; (*inesatto*) incorrect, wrong
vocabo'**lario** *sm* (*dizionario*) dictionary; (*lessico*) vocabulary
vo'**cabolo** *sm* word
vo'**cale** *ag* vocal ♦ *sf* vowel
vocazi'**one** [vokat'tsjone] *sf* vocation; (*fig*) natural bent
'**voce** ['votʃe] *sf* voice; (*diceria*) rumour; (*di un elenco, in bilancio*) item; **aver ~ in capitolo** (*fig*) to have a say in the matter
voci'**are** [vo'tʃare] *vi* to shout, yell
'**voga** *sf* (NAUT) rowing; (*usanza*): **essere in ~** to be in fashion *o* in vogue
vo'**gare** *vi* to row
'**voglia** ['vɔʎʎa] *sf* desire, wish; (*macchia*) birthmark; **aver ~ di qc/di fare** to feel like sth/like doing; (*più forte*) to want sth/to do
'**voi** *pron* you; **voi'altri** *pron* you
vo'**lano** *sm* (SPORT) shuttlecock; (TECN) flywheel
vo'**lante** *ag* flying ♦ *sm* (steering) wheel
volan'**tino** *sm* leaflet
vo'**lare** *vi* (*uccello, aereo, fig*) to fly; (*cappello*) to blow away *o* off, fly away *o* off; **~ via** to fly away *o* off
vo'**latile** *ag* (CHIM) volatile ♦ *sm* (ZOOL) bird
volente'**roso, a** *ag* willing
volenti'**eri** *av* willingly; **"~"** "with pleasure", "I'd be glad to"

PAROLA CHIAVE

vo'**lere** *sm* will, wish(es); **contro il ~ di** against the wishes of; **per ~ di qn** in obedience to sb's will *o* wishes
♦ *vt* **1** (*esigere, desiderare*) to want; **voler fare/che qn faccia** to want to do/sb to do; **volete del caffè?** would you like *o* do you want some coffee?; **vorrei questo/ fare** I would *o* I'd like this/to do; **come vuoi** as you like; **senza ~** (*inavvertitamente*) without meaning to, unintentionally
2 (*consentire*): **vogliate attendere, per piacere** please wait; **vogliamo andare?**

shall we go?; **vuole essere così gentile da ...?** would you be so kind as to ...?; **non ha voluto ricevermi** he wouldn't see me **3: volerci** (essere necessario: materiale, attenzione) to need; (: tempo) to take; **quanta farina ci vuole per questa torta?** how much flour do you need for this cake?; **ci vuole un'ora per arrivare a Venezia** it takes an hour to get to Venice **4: voler bene a qn** (amore) to love sb; (affetto) to be fond of sb, like sb very much; **voler male a qn** to dislike sb; **volerne a qn** to bear sb a grudge; **voler dire** to mean

vol'gare ag vulgar; volgariz'zare vt to popularize

'volgere ['vɔldʒere] vt to turn ♦ vi to turn; (tendere): **~ a: il tempo volge al brutto** the weather is breaking; **un rosso che volge al viola** a red verging on purple; **~rsi** vr to turn; **~ al peggio** to take a turn for the worse; **~ al termine** to draw to an end

'volgo sm common people

voli'era sf aviary

voli'tivo, a ag strong-willed

'volo sm flight; **al ~: colpire qc al ~** to hit sth as it flies past; **capire al ~** to understand straight away

volontà sf will; **a ~** (mangiare, bere) as much as one likes; **buona / cattiva ~** goodwill/lack of goodwill

volon'tario, a ag voluntary ♦ sm (MIL) volunteer

'volpe sf fox

'volta sf (momento, circostanza) time; (turno, giro) turn; (curva) turn, bend; (ARCHIT) vault; (direzione): **partire alla ~ di** to set off for; **a mia** (o tua etc) **~** in turn; **una ~** once; **una ~ sola** only once; **due ~e** twice; **una cosa per ~** one thing at a time; **una ~ per tutte** once and for all; **a ~e** at times, sometimes; **una ~ che** (temporale) once; (causale) since; **3 ~e 4** 3 times 4

volta'faccia [volta'fattʃa] sm inv (fig) volte-face

vol'taggio [vol'taddʒo] sm (ELETTR) voltage

vol'tare vt to turn; (girare: moneta) to turn over; (rigirare) to turn round ♦ vi to turn; **~rsi** vr to turn; to turn over; to turn round

volteggi'are [volted'dʒare] vi (volare) to circle; (in equitazione) to do trick riding; (in ginnastica) to vault; to perform acrobatics

'volto, a pp di volgere ♦ sm face

vo'lubile ag changeable, fickle

vo'lume sm volume; volumi'noso, a ag voluminous, bulky

voluttà sf sensual pleasure o delight; voluttu'oso, a ag voluptuous

vomi'tare vt, vi to vomit; 'vomito sm vomiting no pl; vomit

'vongola sf clam

vo'race [vo'ratʃe] ag voracious, greedy

vo'ragine [vo'radʒine] sf abyss, chasm

'vortice ['vortitʃe] sm whirlwind; whirlpool; (fig) whirl

'vostro, a det: **il(la) ~(a)** etc your ♦ pron: **il(la) ~(a)** etc yours

vo'tante sm/f voter

vo'tare vi to vote ♦ vt (sottoporre a votazione) to take a vote on; (approvare) to vote for; (REL): **~ qc a** to dedicate sth to; votazi'one sf vote, voting; votazi'oni sfpl (POL) votes; (INS) marks

'voto sm (POL) vote; (INS) mark; (REL) vow; (: offerta) votive offering; **aver ~i belli / brutti** (INS) to get good/bad marks

vs. abbr (COMM) = **vostro**

vul'cano sm volcano

vulne'rabile ag vulnerable

vuo'tare vt to empty; **~rsi** vr to empty

vu'oto, a ag empty; (fig: privo): **~ di** (senso etc) devoid of ♦ sm empty space, gap; (spazio in bianco) blank; (FISICA) vacuum; (fig: mancanza) gap, void; **a mani ~e** empty-handed; **~ d'aria** air pocket; **~ a rendere** returnable bottle

W, X, Y

'water ['wɔːtə*] sm inv toilet
watt [vat] sm inv watt
'weekend ['wiːkend] sm inv weekend
'whisky ['wiski] sm inv whisky
'windsurf ['windsəːf] sm inv (tavola) windsurfer; (sport) windsurfing
'würstel ['vyrstəl] sm inv frankfurter
xi'lofono [ksi'lɔfono] sm xylophone
yacht [jɔt] sm inv yacht
'yoghurt ['jɔgurt] sm inv yoghourt

Z, z

zabai'one [dzaba'jone] sm dessert made of egg yolks, sugar and marsala
zaf'fata [tsaf'fata] sf (tanfo) stench
zaffe'rano [dzaffe'rano] sm saffron
zaf'firo [dzaf'firo] sm sapphire
'zaino ['dzaino] sm rucksack
'zampa ['tsampa] sf (di animale: gamba) leg; (: piede) paw; a quattro ~e on all fours
zampil'lare [tsampil'lare] vi to gush, spurt; zam'pillo sm gush, spurt
zam'pogna [tsam'poɲɲa] sf instrument similar to bagpipes
'zanna ['tsanna] sf (di elefante) tusk; (di carnivori) fang
zan'zara [dzan'dzara] sf mosquito; zanzari'era sf mosquito net
'zappa ['tsappa] sf hoe; zap'pare vt to hoe
'zapping ['tsapiŋ] sm (TV) channel-hopping
zar, za'rina [tsar, tsa'rina] sm/f tsar/tsarina
'zattera ['dzattera] sf raft
za'vorra [dza'vɔrra] sf ballast
'zazzera ['tsattsera] sf shock of hair
'zebra ['dzɛbra] sf zebra; ~e sfpl (AUT) zebra crossing sg (BRIT), crosswalk sg (US)
'zecca, che ['tsekka] sf (ZOOL) tick; (officina di monete) mint
'zelo ['dzɛlo] sm zeal
'zenit ['dzɛnit] sm zenith
'zenzero ['dzendzero] sm ginger

'zeppa ['tseppa] sf wedge
'zeppo, a ['tseppo] ag: ~ di crammed o packed with
zer'bino [dzer'bino] sm doormat
'zero ['dzero] sm zero, nought; vincere per tre a ~ (SPORT) to win three-nil
'zeta ['dzeta] sm o f zed, (the letter) z
'zia ['tsia] sf aunt
zibel'lino [dzibel'lino] sm sable
'zigomo ['dzigomo] sm cheekbone
zig'zag [dzig'dzag] sm inv zigzag; andare a ~ to zigzag
zim'bello [dzim'bɛllo] sm (oggetto di burle) laughing-stock
'zinco ['dzinko] sm zinc
'zingaro, a ['dzingaro] sm/f gipsy
'zio ['tsio] (pl 'zii) sm uncle; zii smpl (zio e zia) uncle and aunt
zip'pare vt, vi (INFORM) to zip
zi'tella [dzi'tella] sf spinster; (peg) old maid
'zitto, a ['tsitto] ag quiet; sta' ~! be quiet!
ziz'zania [dzid'dzanja] sf (fig): gettare o seminare ~ to sow discord
'zoccolo ['tsɔkkolo] sm (calzatura) clog; (di cavallo etc) hoof; (basamento) base; plinth
zo'diaco [dzo'diako] sm zodiac
'zolfo ['tsolfo] sm sulphur
'zolla ['dzɔlla] sf clod (of earth)
zol'letta [dzol'letta] sf sugar lump
'zona ['dzɔna] sf zone, area; ~ di depressione (METEOR) trough of low pressure; ~ disco (AUT) ≈ meter zone; ~ pedonale pedestrian precinct; ~ verde (di abitato) green area
'zonzo ['dzondzo]: a ~ av: andare a ~ to wander about, stroll about
zoo ['dzɔo] sm inv zoo
zoolo'gia [dzoolo'dʒia] sf zoology
zoppi'care [tsoppi'kare] vi to limp; to be shaky, rickety
'zoppo, a ['tsoppo] ag lame; (fig: mobile) shaky, rickety
zoti'cone [dzoti'kone] sm lout
'zucca, che ['tsukka] sf (BOT) marrow; pumpkin
zucche'rare [tsukke'rare] vt to put sugar in; zucche'rato, a ag sweet, sweetened

zuccheri'era [tsukke'rjera] *sf* sugar bowl

zuccheri'ficio [tsukkeri'fitʃo] *sm* sugar refinery

zucche'rino, a [tsukke'rino] *ag* sugary, sweet

'zucchero ['tsukkero] *sm* sugar

zuc'china [tsuk'kina] *sf* courgette (*BRIT*), zucchini (*US*)

zuc'chino [tsuk'kino] *sm* = **zucchina**

'zuffa ['tsuffa] *sf* brawl

'zuppa ['tsuppa] *sf* soup; (*fig*) mixture, muddle; ~ **inglese** (*CUC*) *dessert made with sponge cake, custard and chocolate*, ≈ trifle (*BRIT*); **zuppi'era** *sf* soup tureen

'zuppo, a ['tsuppo] *ag:* ~ **(di)** drenched (with), soaked (with)

PUZZLES AND WORDGAMES

Introduction

We are delighted that you have decided to invest in this Collins Italian Dictionary! Whether you intend to use it in school, at home, on holiday or at work, we are sure that you will find it very useful.

The purpose of this supplement is to help you become aware of the wealth of vocabulary and grammatical information your dictionary contains, to explain how this information is presented and also to point out some of the traps one can fall into when using an Italian-English English-Italian dictionary.

In the pages which follow you will find explanations and wordgames (not too difficult!) designed to give you practice in exploring the dictionary's contents and in retrieving information for a variety of purposes. Answers are provided at the end. If you spend a little time on these pages you should be able to use your dictionary more efficiently and effectively. Have fun!

Supplement by
Roy Simon
reproduced by kind permission of
Tayside Region Education Department

PUZZLES AND WORDGAMES

Contents

HOW INFORMATION IS PRESENTED IN YOUR DICTIONARY

A great deal of information is packed into your Collins Italian Dictionary using colour, various typefaces, sizes of type, symbols, abbreviations and brackets. The purpose of this section is to acquaint you with the conventions used in presenting information.

Headwords

A headword is the word you look up in a dictionary. Headwords are listed in alphabetical order throughout the dictionary. They are printed in colour so that they stand out clearly from all the other words on the dictionary page.

Note that at the top of each page two headwords appear. These tell you which is the first and last word dealt with on the page in question. They are there to help you scan through the dictionary more quickly.

The Italian alphabet consists in practice of the same 26 letters as the English alphabet but j, k, w, x and y are found only in words of foreign origin. Where words are distinguised only by an accent, the unaccented form precedes the accented – e.g. te, tè.

A dictionary entry

An entry is made up of a headword and all the information about that headword. Entries will be short or long depending on how frequently a word is used in either English or Italian and how many meanings it has. Inevitably, the fuller the dictionary entry the more care is needed in sifting through it to find the information you require.

Meanings

The translations of a headword are given in ordinary type. Where there is more than one meaning or usage, a semi-colon separates one from the other.

cannocchi'ale [kannok'kjale] *sm* telescope

can'none *sm* (MIL) gun; (: STORIA) cannon; (*tubo*) pipe, tube; (*piega*) box pleat; (*fig*) ace

can'nuccia, ce [kan'nuttʃa] *sf* (drinking) straw

ca'noa *sf* canoe

'prua *sf* (NAUT) = **prora**

pru'dente *ag* cautious, prudent;

te *pron* (*soggetto: in forme comparative, oggetto*) you

tè *sm inv* tea; (*trattenimento*) tea party

'fragola *sf* strawberry ────────────

'grande (*qualche volta* **gran** +C, **grand'** +V) *ag* (*grosso, largo, vasto*) big, large; (*alto*) tall; (*lungo*) long; (*in sensi astratti*) great ♦ *sm/f* (*persona adulta*) adult, grown-up; (*chi ha ingegno e potenza*) great man/woman; **fare le cose in ~** to do things in style; **una gran bella donna** a very beautiful woman; **non è una gran cosa** *o* **un gran che** it's nothing special; **non ne so gran che** I don't know very much about it

pueri'cul'tura *sf* paediatric nursing; infant care

fu'ori *av* outside; (*all'aperto*) outdoors, outside; (*fuori di casa,* SPORT) out; (*esclamativo*) get out! ♦ *prep*: **~ (di)** out of, outside ♦ *sm* outside; **lasciar ~ qc/qn** to leave sth/sb out; **far ~ qn** (*fam*) to kill sb, do sb in; **essere ~ di sé** to be beside o.s.; **~ luogo** (*inopportuno*) out of place, uncalled for; **~ mano** out of the way, remote; **~ pericolo** out of danger; **~ uso** old-fashioned; obsolete

289

In addition, you will often find other words appearing in *italics* in brackets before the translations. These either give some notion of the contexts in which the headword might appear (as with 'alto' opposite – 'una persona alta', 'un suono alto', etc.) or else they provide synonyms (as with 'reggere' opposite – 'tenere', 'sostenere', etc.).

Phonetic spellings

Where an Italian word contains a sound which is difficult for the English speaker, the phonetic spelling of the word – i.e. its pronunciation – is given in square brackets immediately after it. The phonetic transcription of Italian and English vowels and consonants is given on pages xiv to xv at the front of your dictionary.

Additional information about headwords

Information about the form or usage of certain headwords is given in brackets between the headword and the translation or translations. Have a look at the entries for 'A.C.I.', 'camerino', 'materia' and 'leccapiedi' opposite. This information is usually given in abbreviated form. A helpful list of abbreviations is given on pages xi to xiii at the front of your dictionary.

You should be particularly careful with colloquial words or phrases. Words labelled (*fam*) would not normally be used in formal speech, while those labelled (*fam!*) would be considered offensive. Careful consideration of such style labels will help you avoid many an embarrassing situation when using Italian!

Expressions in which the headword appears

An entry will often feature certain common expressions in which the headword appears. These expressions are in **bold** type, but in black as opposed to colour. A swung dash (~) is used instead of repeating a headword in an entry. 'Freno' and 'idea' opposite illustrate this point. Sometimes the swung dash is used with the appropriate ending shown after it; e.g. 'mano', where '~i' is used to indicate the plural form, 'mani'.

Related words

In the Italian Dictionary words related to certain headwords are sometimes given at the end of an entry, as with 'finestra' and 'accept' opposite. These are easily picked out as they are also in colour. These words are placed in alphabetical order after the headword to which they belong: cf. 'acceptable', 'acceptance' opposite.

alto, a *ag* high; (*persona*) tall; (*tessuto*) wide, broad; (*sonno, acque*) deep; (*suono*) high(-pitched); (GEO) upper; (: *settentrionale*) northern ♦ *sm* top (part) ♦ *av* high; (*parlare*) aloud, loudly; **il palazzo è ~ 20 metri** the building is 20 metres high;

pron'tezza [pron'tettsa] *sf* readiness; quickness, promptness

A.C.I. ['atʃi] *sigla m = Automobile Club d'Italia*

came'rino *sm* (TEATRO) dressing room

scocci'are [skot'tʃare] (*fam*) *vt* to bother, annoy; **~rsi** *vr* to be bothered *o* annoyed

fre'gare *vt* to rub; (*fam: truffare*) to take in, cheat; (: *rubare*) to swipe, pinch; **fregarsene** (*fam!*): **chi se ne frega?** who gives a damn (about it)?

freno *sm* brake; (*morso*) bit; **~ a disco** disc brake; **~ a mano** handbrake; **tenere a ~ to** restrain

i'dea *sf* idea; (*opinione*) opinion, view; (*ideale*) ideal; **dare l'~ di** to seem, look like; **~ fissa** obsession; **neanche** *o* **neppure per ~!** certainly not!

fi'nestra *sf* window; **fines'trino** *sm* (*di treno, auto*) window

accept [ək'sept] *vt* accettare; **~able** *adj* accettabile; **~ance** *n* accettazione *f*

'reggere ['reddʒere] *vt* (*tenere*) to hold; (*sostenere*) to support, bear, hold up; (*portare*) to carry, bear; (*resistere*) to withstand; (*dirigere: impresa*) to manage, run; (*governare*) to rule, govern;

reci'tare [retʃi'tare] *vt* (*poesia, lezione*) to recite; (*dramma*) to perform; (*ruolo*) to play *o* act (the part of); **recitazi'one** *sf* recitation; (*di attore*) acting

ma'teria *sf* (FISICA) matter; (TECN, COMM) material, matter *no pl*; (*disciplina*) subject; (*argomento*) subject matter, material;

leccapi'edi (*peg*) *sm/f inv* toady, bootlicker

'rompere *vt* to break; (*fidanzamento*) to break off ♦ *vi* to break; **~rsi** *vr* to break; **mi rompe le scatole** (*fam*) he (*o* she) is a pain in the neck; **~rsi un braccio** to break an arm;

'mano, i *sf* hand; (*strato: di vernice etc*) coat; (*notizia*) first-hand; **di prima ~** (*notizia*) first-hand; **di seconda ~** second-hand; **man ~** little by little, gradually; **man ~ che** as; **darsi** *o* **stringersi la ~** to shake hands; **mettere le ~i avanti** (*fig*) to safeguard o.s.; **restare a ~i vuote** to be left empty-handed; **venire alle ~i** to come to blows; **a ~** by hand; **~i in alto!** hands up!

291

'Key' words

Your Collins Italian Dictionary gives special status to certain Italian and English words which can be looked on as 'key' words in each language. These are words which have many different usages. 'Molto', 'volere' and 'così' opposite are typical examples in Italian. You are likely to become familiar with them in your day-to-day language studies.

There will be occasions, however, when you want to check on a particular usage. Your dictionary can be very helpful here. Note how with 'volere', for example, different parts of speech and different usages are clearly indicated by a combination of lozenges – ♦ – and numbers. Additionally, further guides to usage are given in the language of the user who needs them. These are bracketed and in italics.

vo'lere *sm* will, wish(es); **contro il ~ di** against the wishes of; **per ~ di qn** in obedience to sb's will *o* wishes

♦ *vt* **1** (*esigere, desiderare*) to want; **voler fare/che qn faccia** to want to do/sb to do; **volete del caffè?** would you like *o* do you want some coffee?; **vorrei questo/fare** I would *o* I'd like this/to do; **come vuoi** as you like; **senza ~** (*inavvertitamente*) without meaning to, unintentionally **2** (*consentire*): **vogliate attendere, per piacere** please wait; **vogliamo andare?** shall we go?; **vuole essere così gentile da ...?** would you be so kind as to ...?; **non ha voluto ricevermi** he wouldn't see me **3**: **volerci** (*essere necessario: materiale, attenzione*) to need; (: *tempo*) to take; **quanta farina ci vuole per questa torta?** how much flour do you need for this cake?; **ci vuole un'ora per arrivare a Venezia** it takes an hour to get to Venice **4**: **voler bene a qn** (*amore*) to love sb; (*affetto*) to be fond of sb, like sb very much; **voler male a qn** to dislike sb; **volerne a qn** to bear sb a grudge; **voler dire** to mean

'molto, a *det* (*quantità*) a lot of, much; (*numero*) a lot of, many; **~ pane/carbone** a lot of bread/coal; **~a gente** a lot of people, many people; **~i libri** a lot of books, many books; **non ho ~ tempo** I haven't got much time; **per ~ (tempo)** for a long time

♦ *av* **1** a lot, (very) much; **viaggia ~** he travels a lot; **non viaggia ~** he doesn't travel much *o* a lot **2** (*intensivo: con aggettivi, avverbi*) very; (: *con participio passato*) (very) much; **~ buono** very good; **~ migliore, ~ meglio** much *o* a lot better

♦ *pron* much, a lot; **~i, e** *pron pl* many, a lot; **~i pensano che ...** many (people) think ...

così *av* **1** (*in questo modo*) like this, (in) this way; (*in tal modo*) so; **le cose stanno ~!** this is the way things stand; **non ho detto ~!** I didn't say that!; **come stai? – (e) ~** how are you? — so-so; **e ~ via** and so on; **per ~ dire** so to speak **2** (*tanto*) so; **~ lontano** so far away; **un ragazzo ~ intelligente** such an intelligent boy

♦ *ag inv* (*tale*): **non ho mai visto un film ~** I've never seen such a film

♦ *cong* **1** (*perciò*) so, therefore **2**: **~ ... come** as ... as; **non è ~ bravo come te** he's not as good as you; **~ ... che** so ... that

WORDGAME 1

HEADWORDS

Study the following sentences. In each sentence a wrong word spelt very similarly to the correct word has deliberately been put in and the sentence doesn't make sense. This word is shaded each time. Write out each sentence again, putting in the correct word which you will find in your dictionary near the wrong word.

Example: Vietato l'ingrosso agli estranei

['ingrosso' ('all'ingrosso' = 'wholesale') is the wrong word and should be replaced by 'ingresso' (= 'entry')]

1. Ha agito contro il volare della maggioranza.
2. Inserire la moneta e pigliare il pulsante.
3. Non dobbiamo molare proprio adesso.
4. Ho dovuto impanare la lezione a memoria.
5. Il prato era circondato da uno stecchito.
6. Vorrei sentire il tuo parare.
7. Vorrei un po' di panno sulle fragole.
8. Qual è l'oratorio d'apertura dell'ufficio?
9. Quel negoziante mi ha imbrigliato!
10. Sedevano fiasco a fiasco.

294

WORDGAME 2

DICTIONARY ENTRIES

Complete the crossword below by looking up the English words in the list and finding the correct Italian translations. There is a slight catch, however! All the English words can be translated several ways into Italian, but only one translation will fit correctly into each part of the crossword.

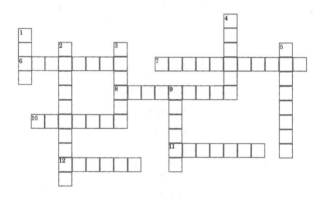

1. THREAD	7. COLD
2. PERMIT	8. WAIT
3. PRESENT	9. NOTICE
4. WANT	10. RETURN
5. JOURNEY	11. CUT
6. FREE	12. REST

WORDGAME 3

FINDING MEANINGS

In this list there are eight pairs of words that have some sort of connection with each other. For example, **'laurea'** (= 'degree') and **'studente'** (= 'student') are linked. Find the other pairs.

1. vestaglia
2. nido
3. pelletteria
4. pantofola
5. campanile
6. studente
7. libro
8. borsetta
9. passerella
10. pinna
11. laurea
12. scaffale
13. gazza
14. nave
15. campana
16. squalo

WORDGAME 4

SYNONYMS

Complete the crossword by supplying SYNONYMS of the words below. You will sometimes find the synonym you are looking for in italics and bracketed at the entries for the words listed below. Sometimes you will have to turn to the English-Italian section for help.

1. RIGUARDO
2. GALA
3. GALLERIA
4. CANCELLARE
5. GALERA

6. BUFFO
7. GIOCARE
8. RAPIDO
9. PAURA
10. MARRONE

WORDGAME 5

SPELLING

You will often use your dictionary to check spellings. The person who has compiled this list of ten Italian words has made <u>three</u> spelling mistakes. Find the three words which have been misspelt and write them out correctly.

1. uccello
2. docia
3. unghia
4. opportuno
5. temporale
6. ortica
7. ovest
8. arabiato
9. folio
10. ossigeno

WORDGAME 6

ANTONYMS

Complete the crossword by supplying ANTONYMS (i.e. opposites) in Italian of the words below. Use your dictionary to help you.

1. ricchezza
2. accettare
3. coraggioso
4. ridere
5. difendere
6. liscio
7. colpevole
8. chiaro
9. bello
10. aperto

WORDGAME 7

PHONETIC SPELLINGS

The phonetic transcriptions of ten Italian words are given below. If you study pages xiv to xv at the front of your dictionary you should be able to work out what the words are.

1. 'ridʒido

2. pit'tʃone

3. 'dʒɛlo

4. 'mattso

5. de'tʃennjo

6. 'kjave

7. 'fɔʎʎa

8. 'soɲɲo

9. 'aʃʃa

10. 'gjanda

WORDGAME 8

EXPRESSIONS IN WHICH THE HEADWORD APPEARS

If you look up the headword 'colpo' in the Italian-English section of your dictionary you will find that the word can have many meanings. Study the entry carefully and translate the following sentences into English.

1. La sua sconfitta è stata un duro colpo per tutti.

2. Ha preso un brutto colpo in testa.

3. Dammi un colpo di telefono domani mattina.

4. Sparò quattro colpi di pistola.

5. Il rumore cessò di colpo.

6. La sua fuga è stata un colpo di testa.

7. Un colpo di vento fece sbattere le persiane.

8. Gli è preso un colpo ed è morto.

9. Hai fatto colpo col tuo discorso, ieri.

10. Gli ho dato un colpo senza volere ed è caduto.

11. Con questo caldo è facile prendere un colpo di sole.

12. Hanno arrestato gli autori del fallito colpo di Stato.

WORDGAME 9

RELATED WORDS

Fill in the blanks in the pairs of sentences below. The missing words are related to the words on the left. Choose the correct 'relative' each time. You will find it in your dictionary near the headword provided.

HEADWORD	RELATED WORDS
impiegare	1. Fa l' _____ di banca. 2. Ha appena lasciato il suo _____ .
studiare	3. Ha vissuto a Firenze quand'era _____ . 4. Ha uno _____ in centro.
usare	5. Si raccomanda l' _____ delle cinture di sicurezza. 6. La tua macchina è nuova o _____ ?
unità	7. È una famiglia molto _____ . 8. Vi potete _____ a noi, se volete.
rifiuto	9. È un'offerta che non potrete _____ . 10. Dov'è il bidone dei _____ ?
festeggiare	11. Il negozio è chiuso nei giorni _____ . 12. Ha organizzato una _____ di compleanno.

WORDGAME 10

'KEY' WORDS

Study carefully the entry **'fare'** in your dictionary and find translations for the following:

1. the weather is fine

2. to do psychology

3. go ahead!

4. let me see

5. to get one's hair cut

6. this is the way it's done

7. to do the shopping

8. to be quick

9. to start up the engine

10. he made as if to leave

THE DICTIONARY AND GRAMMAR

While it is true that a dictionary can never be a substitute for a detailed grammar reference book, it nevertheless provides a great deal of grammatical information. If you know how to extract this information you will be able to use Italian more accurately both in speech and in writing.

The Collins Italian Dictionary presents grammatical information as follows.

Parts of speech

Parts of speech are given in italics immediately after the phonetic spellings of headwords. Abbreviated forms are used. Abbreviations can be checked on pages xi to xiii.

Changes in parts of speech within an entry – for example, from adjective to adverb to noun – are indicated by means of lozenges - ♦ - as with the Italian 'forte' and the English 'act' opposite.

Genders of Italian nouns

The gender of each noun in the Italian-English section of the dictionary is indicated in the following way:

> *sm* = sostantivo maschile
>
> *sf* = sostantivo femminile

You will occasionally see *'sm/f'* beside an entry. This indicates that a noun – 'insegnante', for example – can be either masculine or feminine.

Feminine and *irregular* plural forms of nouns are shown, as with 'bambino', 'autore' and 'bruco' opposite.

So many things depend on your knowing the correct gender of an Italian noun – whether you use 'il' or 'la' etc. to translate 'the'; the way you spell and pronounce certain adjectives; the changes you make to past participles, etc. If you are in any doubt as to the gender of a noun, it is always best to check it in your dictionary.

no'rare *vt* to honour; (*far onore a*) to do credit to; **~rsi** *vr*: **~rsi di** to feel honoured at, be proud of

quassù *av* up here

perciò [per'tʃɔ] *cong* so, for this (*o* that) reason

pranzo ['prandzo] *sm* dinner; (*a mezzogiorno*) lunch

cena ['tʃena] *sf* dinner; (*leggera*) supper

bam'bino, a *sm/f* child

au'tore, 'trice *sm/f* author

bruco, chi *sm* caterpillar; grub

'forte *ag* strong; (*suono*) loud; (*spesa*) considerable, great; (*passione, dolore*) great, deep ♦ *av* strongly; (*velocemente*) fast; (*a voce alta*) loud(ly); (*violentemente*) hard ♦ *sm* (*edificio*) fort; (*specialità*) forte, strong point; **essere ~ in qc** to be good at sth

act [ækt] *n* atto; (*in music-hall etc*) numero; (*LAW*) decreto ♦ *vi* agire; (*THEATRE*) recitare; (*pretend*) fingere ♦ *vt* (*part*) recitare; **to ~ as** agire da; **~ing** *adj* che fa le funzioni di ♦ *n* (*of actor*) recitazione *f*; (*activity*): **to do some ~ing** fare del teatro (*or* del cinema)

inse'gnante [insen'nante] *ag* teaching ♦ *sm/f* teacher

Adjectives

Adjectives are given in both their masculine and feminine forms, where these are different. The usual rule is to drop the 'o' of the masculine form and add an 'a' to make an adjective feminine, as with 'nero' opposite.

Some adjectives have identical masculine and feminine forms, as with 'verde' opposite.

Many Italian adjectives, however, do not follow the regular pattern. Where an adjective has irregular plural forms, this information is clearly provided in your dictionary, usually with the irregular endings, being given. Consider the entries for 'bianco' and 'lungo' opposite.

Adverbs

Advebs are not always listed in your dictionary. The normal rule for forming adverbs in Italian is to add '-mente' to the feminine form of the adjective. Thus:

vero > vera > veramente

The '-mente' ending is often the equivalent of the English '-ly':

veramente – really
certamente – certainly

Adjectives ending in '-e' and '-le' are slightly different:

recente > recentemente
reale > realmente

Where an adverb is very common in Italian, or where its translation(s) cannot be derived from translations for the adjective, it will be listed in alphabetical order, either as a headword or as a subentry. Compare 'solamente' and 'attualmente' opposite.

In many cases, however, Italian adverbs are not given, since the English translation can easily be derived from the relevant translation of the adjective headword: e.g. 'cortese' opposite.

Information about verbs

A major problem facing language learners is that the form of a verb will change according to the subject and/or the tense being used. A typical Italian verb can take on many different forms – too many to list in a dictionary entry.

'nero, a *ag* black; (*scuro*) dark ♦ *sm* black; **il Mar N~** the Black Sea

'verde *ag, sm* green; **essere al ~** to be broke; **~ bottiglia/oliva** bottle/olive green

bi'anco, a, chi, che *ag* white; (*non scritto*) blank ♦ *sm* white; (*intonaco*) whitewash ♦ *sm/f* white, white man/woman; **in ~** (*foglio, assegno*) blank; (*notte*) sleepless; **in ~ e nero** (*TV, FOT*) black and white; **mangiare in ~** to follow a bland diet; **pesce in ~** boiled fish; **andare in ~** (*non riuscire*) to fail; **~ dell'uovo** egg-white

'lungo, a, ghi, ghe *ag* long; (*lento: persona*) slow; (*diluito: caffè, brodo*) weak, watery, thin ♦ *sm* length ♦ *prep* along; **~ 3 metri** 3 metres long; **a ~** for a long time; **a ~ andare** in the long run; **di gran ~a** (*molto*) by far; **andare in ~** *o* **per le lunghe** to drag on; **saperla ~a** to know what's what; **in ~ e in largo** far and wide, all over; **~ il corso dei secoli** throughout the centuries

vera'mente *av* really

certa'mente [tʃerta'mente] *av* certainly

re'cente [re'tʃente] *ag* recent; **di ~** recently; **recente'mente** *av* recently

sola'mente *av* only, just

'solo, a *ag* alone; (*in senso spirituale: isolato*) lonely; (*unico*): **un ~ libro** only one book, a single book; (*con ag numerale*): **veniamo noi tre ~i** just *o* only the three of us are coming ♦ *av* (*soltanto*) only, just; **non ~ ... ma anche** not only ... but also; **fare qc da ~** to do sth (all) by oneself

cor'tese *ag* courteous; **corte'sia** *sf* courtesy; **per cortesia ...** excuse me, please ...

attu'ale *ag* (*presente*) present; (*di attualità*) topical; (*che è in atto*) actual; **attualità** *sf inv* topicality; (*avvenimento*) current event; **attual'mente** *av* at the moment, at present

Yet, although verbs are listed in your dictionary in their infinitive forms only, this does not mean that the dictionary is of limited value when it comes to handling the verb system of the Italian language. On the contrary, it contains much valuable information.

First of all, your dictionary will help you with the meanings of unfamiliar verbs. If you came across the word 'riempie' in a text and looked it up in your dictionary you wouldn't find it. You must deduce that it is part of a verb and look for the infinitive form. Thus you will see that 'riempie' is a form of the verb 'riempire'. You now have the basic meaning of the word you are concerned with – something to do with the English verb 'fill' – and this should be enough to help you understand the text you are reading.

It is usually an easy task to make the connection between the form of a verb and the infinitive. For example, 'riempiono', 'riempirò', 'riempissero' and 'reimpii' are all recognisable as parts of the infinitive 'riempire'. However, sometimes it is less obvious – for example, 'vengo', 'vieni' and 'verrò are all parts of 'venire'. The only real solution to this problem is to learn the various forms of the main Italian regular and irregular verbs.

And this is the second source of help offered by your dictionary. The verb tables on page 616 to 617 at the back of the Collins Italian Dictionary provide a summary of some of the main forms of the main tenses of regular and irregular verbs. Consider the verb 'venire' below where the following information is given:

2	venuto	– Past Participle
3	vengo, vieni, viene, vengono	– Present Tense forms
5	venni, venisti	– Past Tense forms
6	verrò *etc.*	– 1st Person Singular of the Future Tense
8	venga	– 1st, 2nd, 3rd Person of Present Subjunctive

The regular '-are' verb 'parlare' is presented in greater detail, as are the regular '-ire' and '-ere' verbs. The main tenses and the different endings are given in full. This information can be transferred and applied to all verbs in the list. In addition, the main parts of the most common irregular verbs are listed in the body of the dictionary.

PARLARE

1 parlando
2 parlato
3 parlo, parli, parla, parliamo, parlate, parlano
4 parlavo, parlavi, parlava, parlavamo, parlavate, parlavano
5 parlai, parlasti, parlò, parlammo, parlaste, parlarono
6 parlerò, parlerai, parlerà, parleremo, parlerete, parleranno
7 parlerei, parleresti, parlerebbe, parleremmo, parlereste, parlerebbero
8 parli, parli, parli, parliamo, parliate, parlino
9 parlassi, parlassi, parlasse, parlassimo, parlaste, parlassero
10 parla!, parli!, parlate!, parlino!

In order to make maximum use of the information contained in these pages, a good working knowledge of the various rules affecting Italian verbs is required. You will acquire this in the course of your Italian studies and your Collins dictionary will serve as a useful reminder. If you happen to forget how to form the second person singular form of the Future Tense of 'venire' there will be no need to panic – your dictionary contains the information!

WORDGAME 11

PARTS OF SPEECH

In each sentence below a word has been shaded. Put a tick in the
appropriate box to indicate the underlined part of speech each time. Remember,
different parts of speech are indicated by lozenges within entries.

SENTENCE	Noun	Adj	Adv	Verb
1. Studia diritto a Roma.				
2. Parla più piano! Il bambino dorme.				
3. Ho già versato la minestra nel piatto.				
4. Ho spento il televisore prima della fine del film.				
5. Ha finto di andarsene ed è rimasto ad ascoltare.				
6. Non gli ho permesso di venire.				
7. Vuoi una fetta di dolce?				
8. Abbassi il volume, per favore? Così è troppo forte.				
9. Dopo la notizia sembrava molto scossa.				
10. Hanno assunto un capo del personale per la nostra sezione.				

NOUNS

his list contains the feminine form of some Italian nouns. Use your
ictionary to find the **masculine** form.

MASCULINE	FEMININE
	amica
	cantante
	direttrice
	straniera
	regista
	studentessa
	cugina
	lettrice
	professoressa
	collaboratrice

WORDGAME 13

MEANING CHANGES WITH GENDER

There are some pairs of Italian nouns which are distinguished only by
their ending and gender, e.g. 'il partito' and 'la partita'. Fill in the blanks
below with the appropriate member of each pair and the correct article –
'il, la, un' etc – where an article is required.

1. L'ho scritto su _____ da qualche parte   foglio *or*
   Guarda! Sulla pianta è spuntata _____   foglia?

2. Non è questo _____ di fare le cose!   moda *or*
   È un colore che non va più di _____   modo?

3. È arrivato di _____   corso *or*
   Credo che mi iscriverò ad _____   corsa?
   di spagnolo

4. In questa zona ci sono tanti _____   castagne *or*
   Ho comprato un sacchetto di _____   castagni?

5. Fammi vedere _____ della mano!   palma *or*
   Sedevano sulla spiaggia all'ombra di _____   palmo?

6. Ti va di fare _____ a tennis?   partito *or*
   _____ si sta preparando alle elezioni   partita?

7. Devo mettere _____ su questi pantaloni   pezzo *or*
   Vuoi _____ di torta?   pezza?

8. Per oggi basta lavorare! Vado a _____   caso *or*
   Ci siamo conosciuti per _____   casa?

WORDGAME 14

NOUN AND ADJECTIVE FORMS

Use your dictionary to find the following forms of these words.

MASCULINE	FEMININE
1. bianco	
2. fresco	
3. largo	
4. verde	
5. grave	

SINGULAR	PLURAL
6. poca	
7. giovane	
8. grande	
9. veloce	
10. poeta	
11. diadema	
12. triste	
13. tronco	
14. tromba	
15. dialogo	

WORDGAME 15

ADVERBS

Translate the following Italian adverbs into English. Put an asterisk next to those that don't appear in the Italian-English section of the Collins dictionary.

1. recentemente
2. redditiziamente
3. costantemente
4. gentilmente
5. mensilmente
6. naturalmente
7. aggressivamente
8. semplicemente
9. tenacemente
10. esattamente

WORDGAME 16

VERB TENSES

Use your dictionary to help you fill in the blanks in the table below. (Remember the important pages at the back of your dictionary.)

INFINITIVE	PRESENT TENSE	PAST PARTICIPLE	FUTURE
venire			io
rimanere			
vedere			io
avere	io		
offrire			
muovere			io
finire	io		
uscire	io		
dovere			io
dormire			io
vivere			
potere	io		

315

WORDGAME 17

PAST PARTICIPLES

Use the verb tables at the back of your dictionary to work out the past participle of these verbs. Check that you have found the correct form by looking in the main text.

INFINITIVE	PAST PARTICIPLE
venire	
contrarre	
coprire	
vivere	
offrire	
sorridere	
prendere	
mettere	
sorprendere	
percorrere	
accogliere	
dipingere	
condurre	
scendere	

WORDGAME 18

IDENTIFYING INFINITIVES

In the sentences below you will see various Italian verbs shaded.
Use your dictionary to help you find the **infinitive** form of each verb.

1. Quand'ero a Londra dividevo
   un appartamento con degli amici.

2. I miei amici mi raggiunsero in discoteca.

3. Sua madre lo accompagnava a scuola in macchina.

4. Domani mi alzerò alle nove.

5. Questo fine settimana andremo tutti in campagna.

6. Hanno già venduto la casa.

7. Entrò e si mise a sedere.

8. È nato in Germania.

9. Gli piacerebbe vivere negli Stati Uniti.

10. Faranno una partita a tennis.

11. Ha ricominciato a piovere.

12. Non so cosa gli sia successo.

13. Vorremmo visitare il castello.

14. I bambini avevano freddo.

15. Non so cosa sia meglio fare.

MORE ABOUT MEANING

In this section we will consider some of the problems associated with using a bilingual dictionary.

Overdependence on your dictionary

That the dictionary is an invaluable tool for the language learner is beyond dispute. Nevertheless, it is possible to become overdependent on your dictionary, turning to it in an almost automatic fashion every time you come up against a new Italian word or phrase. Tackling an unfamiliar text in this way will turn reading in Italian into an extremely tedious activity. If you stop to look up every new word you may actually be *hindering* your ability to read in Italian – you are so concerned with the individual words that you pay no attention to the text as a whole and to the context which gives them meaning. It is therefore important to develop appropriate reading skills – using clues such as titles, headlines, illustrations, etc., understanding relations within a sentence, etc. to predict or infer what a text is about.

A detailed study of the development of reading skills is not within the scope of this supplement; we are concerned with knowing how to use a dictionary, which is only one of several important skills involved in reading. Nevertheless, it may be instructive to look at one example. You see the following text in an Italian newspaper and are interested in working out what it is about.

Contextual clues here include the words in large type which you would probably recognise as an Italian name, something that looks like a date in the middle, and the name and address in the bottom right hand corner. The Italian words 'annunciare' and 'clinica' resemble closely the words 'announce' and

> Siamo lieti di annunciare
> la nascito di
>
> # Mario, Francesco
>
> il 29 marzo 1999
>
> Monica e Fraco ROSSI
> Clinca   corso Italia n° 18
> del Sole   34142 Padova

'clinic' in English, so you would not have to look them up in your dictionary. Other 'form' words such as 'siamo', 'la', 'il', and 'di' will be familiar to you from your general studies in Italian. Given that we are dealing with a newspaper, you will probably have worked out by now that this could be an announcement placed in the 'Personal Column'.

So you have used a series of cultural, contextual and word-formation clues to get you to the point where you have understood that Monica and Franco Rossi have placed this notice in the 'Personal Column' of the newspaper and that something happened to Francesco on 29 March 1999, something connected with a hospital. And you have reached this point *without* opening your dictionary once. Common sense and your knowledge of newspaper contents in this country might suggest that this must be an announcement of someone's birth or death. Thus 'lieti' ('happy') and 'nascita' ('birth') become the only words that you need to look up in order to confirm that this is indeed a birth announcement.

When learning Italian we are helped considerably by the fact that many Italian and English words look and sound alike and have exactly the same meaning. Such words are called 'COGNATES'. Many words which look similar in Italian and English come from a common Latin root. Other words are the same or nearly the same in both languages because Italian language has borrowed a word from English or vice versa. The dictionary will often not be necessary where cognates are concerned – provided you know the English word that the Italian word resembles!

Words with more than one meaning

The need to examine with care *all* the information contained in a dictionary entry must be stressed. This is particularly important with the many Italian words which have more than one meaning. For example, the Italian 'giornale' can mean 'diary' as well as 'newspaper'. How you translated the word would depend on the context in which you found it.

Similarly, if you were trying to translate a phrase such as 'era in corso ...', you would have to look through the whole entry for 'corso' to get the right translation. If you restricted your search to the first lines of the entry and saw that the meanings given are 'course' and 'main street', you might be tempted to assume that the phrase meant 'it was in the main street'. But if you examined the entry closely you would see that 'in corso' means 'in progress, under way'. So 'era in corso' means 'it was in progress', as in the phrase 'lavori in corso'.

The same need for care applies when you are using the English-Italian section of your dictionary to translate a word from English into Italian. Watch out in particular for the lozenges indicating changes in parts of speech.

319

The noun 'sink' is 'lavandino, aquaio', while the verb is 'affondare'. If you don't watch what you are doing, you could end up with ridiculous non-Italian e.g. 'Ha messo i piatti sporchi nell'affondare.'

Phrasal verbs

Another potential source of difficulty is English phrasal verbs. These consist of a common verb ('go', 'make', etc.) plus an adverb and/or a preposition to give English expressions such as 'to make out', 'to take after', etc. Entries for such verbs tend to be fairly full, so close examination of the contents is required. Note how these verbs appear in colour within the entry.

False friends

Many Italian and English words have similar forms *and* meanings. Many Italian words, however, *look* like English words but have a

make [meɪk] (*pt, pp* **made**) *vt* fare; (*manufacture*) fare, fabbricare; (*cause to be*): **to ~ sb sad** *etc* rendere qn triste *etc*; (*force*): **to ~ sb do sth** costringere qn a fare qc, far fare qc a qn; (*equal*): **2 and 2 ~ 4** 2 più 2 fa 4 ♦ *n* fabbricazione *f*; (*brand*) marca; **to ~ a fool of sb** far fare a qn la figura dello scemo; **to ~ a profit** realizzare un profitto; **to ~ a loss** subire una perdita; **to ~ it** (*arrive*) arrivare; (*achieve sth*) farcela; **what time do you ~ it?** che ora fai?; **to ~ do with** arrangiarsi con; **~ for** *vt fus* (*place*) avviarsi verso; **~ out** *vt* (*write out*) scrivere; (: *cheque*) emettere; (*understand*) capire; (*see*) distinguere; (: *numbers*) decifrare; **~ up** *vt* (*constitute*) formare; (*invent*) inventare; (*parcel*) fare ♦ *vi* conciliarsi; (*with cosmetics*) truccarsi; **~ up for** *vt fus* compensare; ricuperare; **~-believe** *n*: **a world of ~-believe** un mondo di favole;

completely *different* meaning. For example, 'attualmente' means 'at the moment, at present'; 'eventuale' means 'possible'. This can easily lead to serious mistranslations.

Sometimes the meaning of the Italian word is *close* to the English. For example, 'la moneta' means 'small change' rather than 'money'; 'il soprannome' means 'nickname' not 'surname'. But some Italian words have two meanings, one the same as the English, the other completely different! 'L'editore' can mean 'publisher' as well as 'editor'; 'la marcia' can mean 'march/running/walking', but also 'the gear (of a car)'.

Such words are often referred to as 'false friends'. You will have to look at the context in which they appear to arrive at the correct meaning. If they seem to fit in with the sense of the passage as a whole, you will probably not need to look them up. If they don't make sense, however, you may well be dealing with 'false friends'.

WORDGAME 19

WORDS IN CONTEXT

Study the sentences below. Translations of the shaded words are given at the bottom. Match the number of the sentence and the letter of the translation correctly each time.

1. In questa zona è proibito cacciare.
2. L'ho visto cacciare i soldi in tasca.
3. È il ritratto di una dama del Settecento.
4. Facciamo una partita a dama?
5. Ha versato il vino nei bicchieri.
6. Hanno versato tutti i soldi sul loro conto.
7. Ti presento il mio fratello maggiore.
8. Aveva il grado di maggiore nell'esercito.
9. Ho finito i dadi per brodo.
10. In un angolo due uomini giocavano a dadi.
11. Sua madre è già partita per il mare.
12. Ti va di fare una partita a carte?
13. Il ladro è stato visto da un passante.
14. Devi infilare la cintura nel passante.
15. È corso verso di me.
16. Leggete ad alta voce il primo verso della poesia.

a. poured	e. loop	i. dice	m. passer-by
b. hunt	f. towards	j. major	n. draughts
c. left	g. paid	k. stock cubes	o. older
d. game	h. line	l. stick	p. lady

321

WORDGAME 20

WORDS WITH MORE THAN ONE MEANING

Look at the advertisements below. The words which are shaded can have more than one meaning. Use your dictionary to help you work out the correct translation in the context.

1

> Desidero ricevere maggiori informazioni
> per un soggiorno al Lago di Garda
>
> Nome e cognome: _____
>
> Indirizzo:_____

2

Con il patrocinio della

REGIONE TOSCANA e CAMERA DI

COMMERCIO DELLA TOSCANA

3

TRILLO
LA SVEGLIA ELETTRONICA
CHE NON TI TRADISCE
4 funzioni: ore, minuti, secondi,
sveglia
Funzionamento a pile

4

**ECONOMIA E
FINANZA
BORSA E FONDI**

5

Albergo Ristorante
"La Cantina"
cucina casalinga
a 500 metri dalla piazza

SI PREGA DI RITIRARE LO SCONTRINO ALLA CASSA

6

7

Visite guidate al paese
di Alassio

8

CASSA
rurale ed artigiana
Via Basovizza 2
Trieste

9

Una casa in riva al mare
"CALA DEI TEMPLARI"
Soggiorno, una camera da letto,
bagno, balcone

10

PRATOLINI
la cucina su misura per te
Pratolini S.p.A. – 57480 Frascati – Roma
Tel (0733) 5581 (10 linee) –
Fax (0733) 5585

WORDGAME 21

FALSE FRIENDS

Look at the advertisements below. The words which are shaded resemble English words but have different meanings here. Find a correct translation for each word in the context.

1

Boutique "La Moda"
Liquidazione di tutti gli articoli

2

Pensione Miramonti

camere con bagno/doccia

parcheggio privato

bar, ristorante

3

ACCENDERE LE
LUCI IN
GALLERIA

4

LIBRERIA
Il Gabbiano
  Libri – Giornali – Articoli
  spiaggia – Guide turistiche
  – Cartoline

  SASSARI
  Via Mazzini 46

5

ITALMODA
CRAVATTE
LE GRANDI FIRME
Divisione della BST,
Bergamo S.p.A

6

La direzione di questo albergo declina ogni responsabilità per lo smarrimento di oggetti lasciati incustoditi

7

Questo esercizio resterà chiuso nei giorni festivi e il lunedì

8

"Le bollicine"
Locale notturno
    – pianobar
        – discoteca

9

**Lago di Garda
campeggi, sport acquatici,
gite in battello**

10

Attenzione: per l'uso leggere attentamente l'istruzione interna.
Da vendersi dietro presentazione di ricetta medica.

HAVE FUN WITH YOUR DICTIONARY

Here are some word games for you to try. You will find your dictionary helpful as you attempt the activities.

WORDGAME 22

CODED WORDS

In the boxes below, the letters of eight Italian words have been replaced by numbers. A number represents the same letter each time.

Try to crack the code and find the eight words. If you need help, use your dictionary.

Here is a clue: all the words you are looking for have something to do with TRANSPORT.

1 | T¹ | R² | E³ | 4 | 5 |

2 | 6 | 7 | 8 | 9 | 5 | 4 |

3 | 4 | 7 | 10 | 3 |

4 | 7 | 11 | 1 | 5 | 12 | 11 | 16 |

5 | 1 | 2 | 7 | 13 | 14 | 3 | 1 | 1 | 5 |

6 | 8 | 5 | 1 | 5 | 6 | 9 | 6 | 15 | 3 | 1 | 1 | 7 |

7 | 12 | 7 | 2 | 6 | 7 |

8 | 7 | 11 | 1 | 5 | 8 | 5 | 12 | 9 | 15 | 3 |

WORDGAME 23

HEADLESS WORDS

If you 'behead' certain Italian words, i.e. take away their first letter, you are left with another Italian word. For example, if you behead **'maglio'** (= 'mallet'), you get **'aglio'** (= 'garlic').

The following words have their heads chopped off, i.e. the first letter has been removed. Use your dictionary to help you form a new Italian word by adding one letter to the start of each word below. Write down the new Italian word and its meaning. There may be more than one new word you can form.

1. arto (= limb)
2. alto (= high)
3. esca (= bait)
4. unto (= greasy)
5. ora (= hour)
6. acca (= letter H)
7. orale (= oral)
8. otto (= eight)
9. orda (= horde)
10. alone (= halo)
11. oca (= goose)
12. anca (= hip)
13. ascia (= axe)
14. anno (= year)
15. rete (= net)

WORDGAME 24

CROSSWORD

Complete this crossword by looking up the words listed below in the English-Italian section of your dictionary. Remember to read through the entry carefully to find the word that will fit.

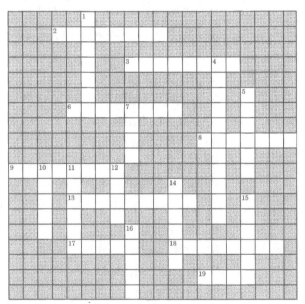

ACROSS

2. to dirty
3. to admire
6. relationship
8. deposit
9. strip
13. employ
17. ebony
18. to take off
19. night

DOWN

1. (a piece of) news
4. to reassure
5. story
7. porthole
10. rough
11. swarm
12. air
14. sad
15. adder
16. harbour

WORDGAME 25

SPLIT WORDS

There are twelve Italian words hidden in the grid below. Each word is made up of five letters but has been split into two parts. Find the Italian words. Each group of letters can only be used once. Use your dictionary to help you.

fer	ba	por	sce	za	che
an	mo	to	gam	se	duo
pri	ta	co	ro	fuo	na
fal	sen	men	so	for	mo

WORDGAME 26

KITCHEN WORDS

Here is a list of Italian words for things you will find in the kitchen.
Unfortunately, the letters have all been jumbled up. Try to work out what
each word is and put the word in the boxes on the right. You will see that
there are six shaded boxes below. With the six letters in the shaded boxes
make up <u>another</u> Italian word for an object you can find in the kitchen.

1. zazta   Vuoi una _____ di caffé?

2. grifo   Metti il burro nel _____!

3. vatloa   A _____! È pronto!

4. norfo   Cuocere in _____ per 20 minuti.

5. chiocciau   Assaggia la minestra col _____.

6. polacasta   Usa il _____ per gli spaghetti.

The word you are looking for is:

WORDGAME 27

GRID WORDS

Take the four letters given each time and put them in the four empty boxes in the centre of each grid. Arrange them in such a way that you form four six-letter words. Use your dictionary to check the words.

ANSWERS

WORDGAME 1

1	volere	6	parere
2	pigiare	7	panna
3	mollare	8	orario
4	imparare	9	imbrogliato
5	steccato	10	fianco

WORDGAME 2

1	filo	7	raffreddore
2	permettere	8	attendere
3	regalo	9	notare
4	volere	10	ritorno
5	tragitto	11	ridurre
6	liberare	12	riposo

WORDGAME 3

vestaglia + pantofola
nido + gazza
pelletteria + borsetta
campanile + campana
studente + laurea
libro + scaffale
passerella + nave
pinna + squalo

WORDGAME 4

1	attenzione	6	divertente
2	sfarzo	7	ingannare
3	traforo	8	veloce
4	annullare	9	timore
5	prigione	10	bruno

WORDGAME 5

1 doccia 2 arrabbiato 3 foglio

WORDGAME 6

1	povertà	6	ruvido
2	rifiutare	7	innocente
3	vigliacco	8	scuro
4	piangere	9	brutto
5	attaccare	10	chiuso

WORDGAME 7

1	rigido	6	chiave
2	piccione	7	foglia
3	gelo	8	sogno
4	mazzo	9	ascia
5	decennio	10	ghianda

WORDGAME 8

1 shock
2 blow
3 phone call
4 shot
5 suddenly
6 impulse *or* whim
7 gust of wind
8 stroke
9 strong impression
10 knock
11 sunstroke
12 coup d'état

WORDGAME 9

1	impiegato	7	unita
2	impiego	8	unire
3	studente	9	rifiutare
4	studio	10	rifiuti
5	uso	11	festivi
6	usata	12	festa

WORDGAME 10

1 fa bel tempo
2 fare psicologia
3 faccia pure
4 fammi vedere
5 farsi tagliare i capelli
6 si fa così
7 fare la spesa
8 fare presto
9 far partire il motore
10 fece per andarsene

WORDGAME 11

1	n	5	v	8	adj
2	adv	6	v	9	adj
3	n	7	n	10	n
4	n				

WORDGAME 12

1	amico	6	studente
2	cantante	7	cugino
3	direttore	8	lettore
4	straniero	9	professore
5	regista	10	collaboratore

WORDGAME 13

1	un foglio	5	il palmo
	una foglia		una palma
2	il modo	6	una partita
	moda		il partito
3	corsa	7	una pezza
	un corso		un pezzo
4	castagni	8	casa
	castagne		caso

WORDGAME 14

1	bianca	9	veloci
2	fresca	10	poeti
3	larga	11	diademi
4	verde	12	tristi
5	grave	13	tronchi
6	poche	14	trombe
7	giovani	15	dialoghi
8	grandi		

WORDGAME 16

1	io verrò	7	io finisco
2	rimasto	8	io esco
3	io vedrò	9	io dovrò
4	io ho	10	io dormirò
5	offerto	11	vissuto
6	mosso	12	io posso

WORDGAME 17

1	venuto	8	messo
2	contratto	9	sorpreso
3	coperto	10	percorso
4	vissuto	11	accolto
5	offerto	12	dipinto
6	sorriso	13	condotto
7	preso	14	sceso

WORDGAME 18

1	essere	9	piacere
2	raggiungere	10	fare
3	accompagnare	11	ricominciare
4	alzarsi	12	succedere
5	andare	13	volere
6	vendere	14	avere
7	mettersi	15	essere
8	nascere		

WORDGAME 19

1	b	5	a	9	k	13	m
2	l	6	g	10	i	14	e
3	p	7	o	11	c	15	f
4	n	8	j	12	d	16	h

WORDGAME 20

1	stay	7	village (here; town)
2	chamber	8	bank
3	alarm clock	9	living room
4	stock exchange; funds	10	kitchen
5	cooking		
6	checkout (here; till)		

WORDGAME 21

1	clearance sale	6	management
2	boarding house	7	business
3	tunnel	8	nightclub
4	newspapers	9	camp site
5	ties	10	prescription

WORDGAME 22

1	treno	5	traghetto
2	camion	6	motocicletta
3	nave	7	barca
4	autobus	8	automobile

WORDGAME 23

1 sarto (= tailor)
2 salto (= jump)
3 pesca (= peach)
4 punto (= dot)
5 mora (= blackberry)
6 vacca (= cow)
7 morale (= moral)
8 rotto (= broken)
9 corda (= cord)
10 salone (= sitting room)
11 foca (= seal)
12 panca (= bench)
13 fascia (= band)
14 danno (= damage)
15 prete (= priest)

WORDGAME 24

ACROSS	DOWN
2 sporcare	1 notizia
3 ammirare	4 rassicurare
6 rapporto	5 favola
8 acconto	7 oblò
9 striscia	10 rozzo
13 impiegare	11 sciame
17 ebano	12 aria
18 togliere	14 triste
19 sera	15 vipera
	16 porto

WORDGAME 25

ferro	senza	duomo
gamba	anche	fuoco
porta	primo	falso
scena	mento	forse

WORDGAME 26

1	tazza	4	forno
2	frigo	5	cucchiaio
3	tavola	6	colapasta

Missing word – FRUSTA

WORDGAME 27

1 parere	1 podere	1 volere
2 triste	2 crosta	2 stagno
3 morire	3 pedone	3 volare
4 presto	4 cresta	4 fregio

ENGLISH – ITALIAN
INGLESE – ITALIANO

A, a

A [eɪ] n (MUS) la m; (letter) A, a f or m inv; **~-road** n strada statale

a [ə] (before vowel or silent h: **an**) indef art
1 un (uno +s impure, gn, pn, ps, x, z), f una (un' +vowel); ~ **book** un libro; ~ **mirror** uno specchio; **an apple** una mela; **she's ~ doctor** è medico
2 (instead of the number "one") un(o), f una; ~ **year ago** un anno fa; ~ **hundred/ thousand** etc **pounds** cento/mille etc sterline
3 (in expressing ratios, prices etc) a, per; **3 ~ day/week** 3 al giorno/alla settimana; **10 km an hour** 10 km all'ora; **£5 ~ person** 5 sterline a persona or per persona

A.A. n abbr (= Alcoholics Anonymous) AA; (BRIT: = Automobile Association) ≈ A.C.I. m
A.A.A. (US) n abbr (= American Automobile Association) ≈ A.C.I. m
aback [ə'bæk] adv: **to be taken** ~ essere sbalordito(a)
abandon [ə'bændən] vt abbandonare ♦ n: **with** ~ sfrenatamente, spensieratamente
abate [ə'beɪt] vi calmarsi
abattoir ['æbətwɑ:ʳ] (BRIT) n mattatoio
abbey ['æbɪ] n abbazia, badia
abbot ['æbət] n abate m
abbreviation [əbri:vɪ'eɪʃən] n abbreviazione f
abdicate ['æbdɪkeɪt] vt abdicare a ♦ vi abdicare
abdomen ['æbdəmən] n addome m
abduct [æb'dʌkt] vt rapire
abide [ə'baɪd] vt: **I can't** ~ **it/him** non lo posso soffrire or sopportare; ~ **by** vt fus conformarsi a
ability [ə'bɪlɪtɪ] n abilità f inv

abject ['æbdʒɛkt] adj (poverty) abietto(a); (apology) umiliante
ablaze [ə'bleɪz] adj in fiamme
able ['eɪbl] adj capace; **to be** ~ **to do sth** essere capace di fare qc, poter fare qc; ~**-bodied** adj robusto(a); **ably** adv abilmente
abnormal [æb'nɔ:məl] adj anormale
aboard [ə'bɔ:d] adv a bordo ♦ prep a bordo di
abode [ə'bəud] n: **of no fixed** ~ senza fissa dimora
abolish [ə'bɔlɪʃ] vt abolire
abominable [ə'bɔmɪnəbl] adj abominevole
aborigine [æbə'rɪdʒɪnɪ] n aborigeno/a
abort [ə'bɔ:t] vt abortire; ~**ion** [ə'bɔ:ʃən] n aborto; **to have an** ~**ion** abortire; ~**ive** adj abortivo(a)
abound [ə'baund] vi abbondare; **to** ~ **in** or **with** abbondare di

about [ə'baut] adv **1** (approximately) circa, quasi; ~ **a hundred/thousand** etc un centinaio/migliaio etc, circa cento/mille etc; **it takes** ~ **10 hours** ci vogliono circa 10 ore; **at** ~ **2 o'clock** verso le 2; **I've just** ~ **finished** ho quasi finito
2 (referring to place) qua e là, in giro; **to leave things lying** ~ lasciare delle cose in giro; **to run** ~ correre qua e là; **to walk** ~ camminare
3: to be ~ **to do sth** stare per fare qc
♦ prep **1** (relating to) su, di; **a book** ~ **London** un libro su Londra; **what is it** ~? di che si tratta?; (book, film etc) di cosa tratta?; **we talked** ~ **it** ne abbiamo parlato; **what** or **how** ~ **doing this?** che ne dici di fare questo?
2 (referring to place): **to walk** ~ **the town**

camminare per la città; **her clothes were scattered ~ the room** i suoi vestiti erano sparsi *or* in giro per tutta la stanza

about-face *n* dietro front *m inv*
about-turn *n* dietro front *m inv*
above [ə'bʌv] *adv, prep* sopra; **mentioned ~** suddetto; **~ all** soprattutto; **~board** *adj* aperto(a); onesto(a)
abrasive [ə'breɪzɪv] *adj* abrasivo(a); *(fig)* caustico(a)
abreast [ə'brɛst] *adv* di fianco; **to keep ~** tenersi aggiornato su
abroad [ə'brɔːd] *adv* all'estero
abrupt [ə'brʌpt] *adj (sudden)* improvviso(a); *(gruff, blunt)* brusco(a)
abscess ['æbsɪs] *n* ascesso
absence ['æbsəns] *n* assenza
absent ['æbsənt] *adj* assente; **~ee** [-'tiː] *n* assente *m/f*; **~-minded** *adj* distratto(a)
absolute ['æbsəluːt] *adj* assoluto(a); **~ly** [-'luːtlɪ] *adv* assolutamente
absolve [əb'zɔlv] *vt*: **to ~ sb (from)** *(sin)* assolvere qn (da); *(oath)* sciogliere qn (da)
absorb [əb'zɔːb] *vt* assorbire; **to be ~ed in a book** essere immerso in un libro; **~ent cotton** *(US) n* cotone *m* idrofilo
absorption [əb'sɔːpʃən] *n* assorbimento
abstain [əb'steɪn] *vi*: **to ~ (from)** astenersi (da)
abstract ['æbstrækt] *adj* astratto(a)
absurd [əb'sɜːd] *adj* assurdo(a)
abuse [*n* ə'bjuːs, *vb* ə'bjuːz] *n* abuso; *(insults)* ingiurie *fpl* ♦ *vt* abusare di; **abusive** *adj* ingiurioso(a)
abysmal [ə'bɪzməl] *adj* spaventoso(a)
abyss [ə'bɪs] *n* abisso
AC *abbr* (= *alternating current*) c.a.
academic [ækə'dɛmɪk] *adj* accademico(a); *(pej: issue)* puramente formale ♦ *n* universitario/a
academy [ə'kædəmɪ] *n (learned body)* accademia; *(school)* scuola privata; **~ of music** conservatorio
accelerate [æk'sɛləreɪt] *vt, vi* accelerare; **acceleration** *n* accelerazione *f*; **accelerator** *n* acceleratore *m*

accent ['æksənt] *n* accento
accept [ək'sɛpt] *vt* accettare; **~able** *adj* accettabile; **~ance** *n* accettazione *f*
access ['æksɛs] *n* accesso; **~ible** [æk'sɛsəbl] *adj* accessibile
accessory [æk'sɛsərɪ] *n* accessorio; *(LAW)*: **~ to** complice *m/f* di
accident ['æksɪdənt] *n* incidente *m*; *(chance)* caso; **by ~** per caso; **~al** [-'dɛntl] *adj* accidentale; **~ally** [-'dɛntəlɪ] *adv* per caso; **~ insurance** *n* assicurazione *f* contro gli infortuni; **~-prone** *adj*: **he's very ~-prone** è un vero passaguai
acclaim [ə'kleɪm] *n* acclamazione *f*
accommodate [ə'kɔmədeɪt] *vt* alloggiare; *(oblige, help)* favorire
accommodating [ə'kɔmədeɪtɪŋ] *adj* compiacente
accommodation [əkɔmə'deɪʃən] *n* alloggio; **~s** *(US)* npl alloggio
accompany [ə'kʌmpənɪ] *vt* accompagnare
accomplice [ə'kʌmplɪs] *n* complice *m/f*
accomplish [ə'kʌmplɪʃ] *vt* compiere; *(goal)* raggiungere; **~ed** *adj* esperto(a); **~ment** *n* compimento; realizzazione *f*
accord [ə'kɔːd] *n* accordo ♦ *vt* accordare; **of his own ~** di propria iniziativa; **~ance** *n*: **in ~ance with** in conformità con; **~ing**: **~ing to** *prep* secondo; **~ingly** *adv* in conformità
accordion [ə'kɔːdɪən] *n* fisarmonica
account [ə'kaunt] *n (COMM)* conto; *(report)* descrizione *f*; **~s** npl *(COMM)* conti mpl; **of no ~** di nessuna importanza; **on ~** in acconto; **on no ~** per nessun motivo; **on ~ of** a causa di; **to take into ~, take ~ of** tener conto di; **~ for** *vt fus* spiegare; giustificare; **~able** *adj*: **~able (to)** responsabile (verso)
accountancy [ə'kauntənsɪ] *n* ragioneria
accountant [ə'kauntənt] *n* ragioniere/a
account number *n* numero di conto
accrued interest [ə'kruːd-] *n* interesse *m* maturato
accumulate [ə'kjuːmjuleɪt] *vt* accumulare ♦ *vi* accumularsi
accuracy ['ækjurəsɪ] *n* precisione *f*

accurate ['ækjurɪt] adj preciso(a); ~ly adv precisamente

accusation [ækju'zeɪʃən] n accusa

accuse [ə'kjuːz] vt accusare; ~d n accusato/a

accustom [ə'kʌstəm] vt abituare; ~ed adj: ~ed to abituato(a) a

ace [eɪs] n asso

ache [eɪk] n male m, dolore m ♦ vi (be sore) far male, dolere; my head ~s mi fa male la testa

achieve [ə'tʃiːv] vt (aim) raggiungere; (victory, success) ottenere; ~ment n compimento; successo

acid ['æsɪd] adj acido(a) ♦ n acido; ~ rain n pioggia acida

acknowledge [ək'nɔlɪdʒ] vt (letter: also: ~ receipt of) confermare la ricevuta di; (fact) riconoscere; ~ment n conferma; riconoscimento

acne ['æknɪ] n acne f

acorn ['eɪkɔːn] n ghianda

acoustic [ə'kuːstɪk] adj acustico(a); ~s n, npl acustica

acquaint [ə'kweɪnt] vt: to ~ sb with sth far sapere qc a qn; to be ~ed with (person) conoscere; ~ance n conoscenza; (person) conoscente m/f

acquire [ə'kwaɪə*] vt acquistare

acquit [ə'kwɪt] vt assolvere; to ~ o.s. well comportarsi bene; ~tal n assoluzione f

acre ['eɪkə*] n acro (= 4047 m²)

acrid ['ækrɪd] adj acre; pungente

acrobat ['ækrəbæt] n acrobata m/f

across [ə'krɔs] prep (on the other side) dall'altra parte di; (crosswise) attraverso ♦ adv dall'altra parte; in larghezza; to run/swim ~ attraversare di corsa/a nuoto; ~ from di fronte a

acrylic [ə'krɪlɪk] adj acrilico(a)

act [ækt] n atto; (in music-hall etc) numero; (LAW) decreto ♦ vi agire; (THEATRE) recitare; (pretend) fingere ♦ vt (part) recitare; to ~ as agire da; ~ing adj che fa le funzioni di ♦ n (of actor) recitazione f; (activity): to do some ~ing fare del teatro (or del cinema)

action ['ækʃən] n azione f; (MIL) com-

battimento; (LAW) processo; out of ~ fuori combattimento; fuori servizio; to take ~ agire; ~ replay n (TV) replay m inv

activate ['æktɪveɪt] vt (mechanism) attivare

active ['æktɪv] adj attivo(a); ~ly adv (participate) attivamente; (discourage, dislike) vivamente

activity [æk'tɪvɪtɪ] n attività f inv; ~ holiday n vacanza organizzata con attività ricreative per ragazzi

actor ['æktə*] n attore m

actress ['æktrɪs] n attrice f

actual ['æktjuəl] adj reale, vero(a); ~ly adv veramente; (even) addirittura

acute [ə'kjuːt] adj acuto(a); (mind, person) perspicace

ad [æd] n abbr = advertisement

A.D. adv abbr (= Anno Domini) d.C.

adamant ['ædəmənt] adj irremovibile

adapt [ə'dæpt] vt adattare ♦ vi: to ~ (to) adattarsi (a); ~able adj (device) adattabile; (person) che sa adattarsi; ~er or ~or n (ELEC) adattatore m

add [æd] vt aggiungere; (figures: also: ~ up) addizionare ♦ vi: to ~ to (increase) aumentare; it doesn't ~ up (fig) non quadra, non ha senso

adder ['ædə*] n vipera

addict ['ædɪkt] n tossicomane m/f; (fig) fanatico/a; ~ed [ə'dɪktɪd] adj: to be ~ed to (drink etc) essere dedito(a) a; (fig: football etc) essere tifoso(a) di; ~ion [ə'dɪkʃən] n (MED) tossicodipendenza; ~ive [ə'dɪktɪv] adj che dà assuefazione

addition [ə'dɪʃən] n addizione f; (thing added) aggiunta; in ~ inoltre; in ~ to oltre; ~al adj supplementare

additive ['ædɪtɪv] n additivo

address [ə'drɛs] n indirizzo; (talk) discorso ♦ vt indirizzare; (speak to) fare un discorso a; (issue) affrontare

adept ['ædɛpt] adj: ~ at esperto(a) in

adequate ['ædɪkwɪt] adj adeguato(a); sufficiente

adhere [əd'hɪə*] vi: to ~ to aderire a; (fig: rule, decision) seguire

adhesive [əd'hiːzɪv] n adesivo; ~ tape n

(BRIT: *for parcels etc*) nastro adesivo; (US: MED) cerotto adesivo

adjective ['ædʒɛktɪv] *n* aggettivo

adjoining [ə'dʒɔɪnɪŋ] *adj* accanto *inv*, adiacente

adjourn [ə'dʒəːn] *vt* rimandare ♦ *vi* essere aggiornato(a)

adjust [ə'dʒʌst] *vt* aggiustare; (*change*) rettificare ♦ *vi*: **to ~ (to)** adattarsi (a); **~able** *adj* regolabile; **~ment** *n* (PSYCH) adattamento; (*of machine*) regolazione *f*; (*of prices, wages*) modifica

ad-lib [æd'lɪb] *vi* improvvisare ♦ *adv*: **ad lib** a piacere, a volontà

administer [əd'mɪnɪstə*] *vt* amministrare; (*justice, drug*) somministrare

administration [ədmɪnɪs'treɪʃən] *n* amministrazione *f*

administrative [əd'mɪnɪstrətɪv] *adj* amministrativo(a)

admiral ['ædmərəl] *n* ammiraglio; **A~ty** (BRIT) *n* Ministero della Marina

admiration [ædmə'reɪʃən] *n* ammirazione *f*

admire [əd'maɪə*] *vt* ammirare

admission [əd'mɪʃən] *n* ammissione *f*; (*to exhibition, night club etc*) ingresso; (*confession*) confessione *f*

admit [əd'mɪt] *vt* ammettere; far entrare; (*agree*) riconoscere; **to ~ to** riconoscere; **~tance** *n* ingresso; **~tedly** *adv* bisogna pur riconoscere (che)

ad nauseam [æd'nɔːsɪæm] *adv* fino alla nausea, a non finire

ado [ə'duː] *n*: **without (any) more ~** senza più indugi

adolescence [ædəu'lɛsns] *n* adolescenza

adolescent [ædəu'lɛsnt] *adj*, *n* adolescente *m/f*

adopt [ə'dɔpt] *vt* adottare; **~ed** *adj* adottivo(a); **~ion** [ə'dɔpʃən] *n* adozione *f*

adore [ə'dɔː*] *vt* adorare

Adriatic [eɪdrɪ'ætɪk] *n*: **the ~ (Sea)** il mare Adriatico, l'Adriatico

adrift [ə'drɪft] *adv* alla deriva

adult ['ædʌlt] *adj* adulto(a); (*work, education*) per adulti ♦ *n* adulto/a

adultery [ə'dʌltərɪ] *n* adulterio

advance [əd'vɑːns] *n* avanzamento; (*money*) anticipo ♦ *adj* (*booking etc*) in anticipo ♦ *vt* (*money*) anticipare ♦ *vi* avanzare; **in ~** in anticipo; **~d** *adj* avanzato(a); (SCOL: *studies*) superiore

advantage [əd'vɑːntɪdʒ] *n* (*also: TENNIS*) vantaggio; **to take ~ of** approfittarsi di

advent ['ædvənt] *n* avvento; (REL): **A~** Avvento

adventure [əd'vɛntʃə*] *n* avventura

adverb ['ædvəːb] *n* avverbio

adverse ['ædvəːs] *adj* avverso(a)

advert ['ædvəːt] (BRIT) *n abbr* = **advertisement**

advertise ['ædvətaɪz] *vi* (*vt*) fare pubblicità *or* réclame (a); fare un'inserzione (per vendere); **to ~ for** (*staff*) mettere un annuncio sul giornale per trovare

advertisement [əd'vəːtɪsmənt] *n* (COMM) réclame *f inv*, pubblicità *f inv*; (*in classified ads*) inserzione *f*

advertising ['ædvətaɪzɪŋ] *n* pubblicità

advice [əd'vaɪs] *n* consigli *mpl*; (*notification*) avviso; **piece of ~** consiglio; **to take legal ~** consultare un avvocato

advisable [əd'vaɪzəbl] *adj* consigliabile

advise [əd'vaɪz] *vt* consigliare; **to ~ sb of sth** informare qn di qc; **to ~ sb against sth/doing sth** sconsigliare qc a qn/a qn di fare qc; **~r** *or* **advisor** *n* consigliere/a; **advisory** [-ərɪ] *adj* consultivo(a)

advocate [*n* 'ædvəkɪt, *vb* 'ædvəkeɪt] *n* (*upholder*) sostenitore/trice; (LAW) avvocato (difensore) ♦ *vt* propugnare

Aegean [ɪ'dʒiːən] *n*: **the ~ (Sea)** il mar Egeo, l'Egeo

aerial ['ɛərɪəl] *n* antenna ♦ *adj* aereo(a)

aerobics [ɛə'rəubɪks] *n* aerobica

aeroplane ['ɛərəpleɪn] (BRIT) *n* aeroplano

aerosol ['ɛərəsɔl] (BRIT) *n* aerosol *m inv*

aesthetic [ɪs'θɛtɪk] *adj* estetico(a)

afar [ə'fɑː*] *adv*: **from ~** da lontano

affair [ə'fɛə*] *n* affare *m*; (*also: love ~*) relazione *f* amorosa; **~s** (*business*) affari

affect [ə'fɛkt] *vt* toccare; (*influence*) influire su, incidere su; (*feign*) fingere; **~ed** *adj* affettato(a)

affection [ə'fɛkʃən] *n* affezione *f*; ~ate *adj* affettuoso(a)

afflict [ə'flɪkt] *vt* affliggere

affluence ['æfluəns] *n* abbondanza; opulenza

affluent ['æfluənt] *adj* ricco(a); **the ~ society** la società del benessere

afford [ə'fɔːd] *vt* permettersi; (*provide*) fornire

afloat [ə'fləut] *adv* a galla

afoot [ə'fut] *adv*: **there is something ~** si sta preparando qualcosa

afraid [ə'freɪd] *adj* impaurito(a); **to be ~ of** *or* **to/that** aver paura di/che; **I am ~ so/not** ho paura di sì/no

Africa ['æfrɪkə] *n* Africa; ~**n** *adj, n* africano(a)

after ['ɑːftə*] *prep, adv* dopo ♦ *conj* dopo che; **what/who are you ~?** che/chi cerca?; **~ he left/having done** dopo che se ne fu andato/dopo aver fatto; **to name sb ~ sb** dare a qn il nome di qn; **it's twenty ~ eight** (*US*) sono le otto e venti; **to ask ~ sb** chiedere di qn; **~ all** dopo tutto; **~ you!** dopo di Lei!; ~**effects** *npl* conseguenze *fpl*; (*of illness*) postumi *mpl*; ~**math** *n* conseguenze *fpl*; **in the ~math of** nel periodo dopo; ~**noon** *n* pomeriggio; ~**s** *n* (*inf: dessert*) dessert *m inv*; ~**-shave (lotion)** *n* dopobarba *m inv*; ~**sun (lotion/cream)** *n* doposole *m inv*; ~**thought** *n*: **as an ~thought** come aggiunta; ~**wards** (*US* ~**ward**) *adv* dopo

again [ə'gɛn] *adv* di nuovo; **to begin/see ~** ricominciare/rivedere; **not ... ~** non ... più; **~ and ~** ripetutamente

against [ə'gɛnst] *prep* contro

age [eɪdʒ] *n* età *f inv* ♦ *vt, vi* invecchiare; **it's been ~s since** sono secoli che; **he is 20 years of ~** ha 20 anni; **to come of ~** diventare maggiorenne; ~**d** [*adj* eɪdʒd, *npl* 'eɪdʒɪd] *adj*: ~**d 10** di 10 anni ♦ *npl* **the ~d** gli anziani; **~ group** *n* generazione *f*; **~ limit** *n* limite *m* d'età

agency ['eɪdʒənsɪ] *n* agenzia

agenda [ə'dʒɛndə] *n* ordine *m* del giorno

agent ['eɪdʒənt] *n* agente *m*

aggravate ['ægrəveɪt] *vt* aggravare; (*person*) irritare

aggregate ['ægrɪgeɪt] *n* aggregato

aggressive [ə'grɛsɪv] *adj* aggressivo(a)

agitate ['ædʒɪteɪt] *vt* turbare; agitare ♦ *vi*: **to ~ for** agitarsi per

AGM *n abbr* = **annual general meeting**

ago [ə'gəu] *adv*: **2 days ~** 2 giorni fa; **not long ~** poco tempo fa; **how long ~?** quanto tempo fa?

agonizing ['ægənaɪzɪŋ] *adj* straziante

agony ['ægənɪ] *n* dolore *m* atroce; **to be in ~** avere dolori atroci

agree [ə'griː] *vt* (*price*) pattuire ♦ *vi*: **to ~ (with)** essere d'accordo (con); (*LING*) concordare (con); **to ~ to sth/to do sth** accettare qc/di fare qc; **to ~ that** (*admit*) ammettere che; **to ~ on sth** accordarsi su qc; **garlic doesn't ~ with me** l'aglio non mi va; ~**able** *adj* gradevole; (*willing*) disposto(a); ~**d** *adj* (*time, place*) stabilito(a); ~**ment** *n* accordo; **in ~ment** d'accordo

agricultural [ægrɪ'kʌltʃərəl] *adj* agricolo(a)

agriculture ['ægrɪkʌltʃə*] *n* agricoltura

aground [ə'graund] *adv*: **to run ~** arenarsi

ahead [ə'hɛd] *adv* avanti; davanti; **~ of** davanti a; (*fig: schedule etc*) in anticipo su; **~ of time** in anticipo; **go right** *or* **straight ~** tiri dritto

aid [eɪd] *n* aiuto ♦ *vt* aiutare; **in ~ of** a favore di

aide [eɪd] *n* (*person*) aiutante *m*

AIDS [eɪdz] *n abbr* (= *acquired immune deficiency syndrome*) AIDS *f*; ~**-related** *adj* (*symptoms, illness*) legato(a) all'AIDS; (*research*) sull'AIDS

aim [eɪm] *vt*: **to ~ sth at** (*such as gun*) mirare qc a, puntare qc a; (*camera*) rivolgere qc a; (*missile*) lanciare qc contro ♦ *vi* (*also:* **to take ~**) prendere la mira ♦ *n* mira; **to ~ at** mirare; **to ~ to do** aver l'intenzione di fare; ~**less** *adj* senza scopo

ain't [eɪnt] (*inf*) = **am not**; **aren't**; **isn't**

air [ɛə*] *n* aria ♦ *vt* (*room*) arieggiare; (*clothes*) far prendere aria a; (*grievances, ideas*) esprimere pubblicamente ♦ *cpd* (*currents*) d'aria; (*attack*) aereo(a); **to throw sth into the ~** lanciare qc in aria; **by ~** (*travel*) in aereo; **on the ~** (*RADIO, TV*) in onda; **~bed** (*BRIT*) *n* materassino; **~ conditioning** *n* condizionamento d'aria; **~craft** *n inv* apparecchio; **~craft carrier** *n* portaerei *f inv*; **~field** *n* campo d'aviazione; **A~ Force** *n* aviazione *f* militare; **~ freshener** *n* deodorante *m* per ambienti; **~gun** *n* fucile *m* ad aria compressa; **~ hostess** (*BRIT*) *n* hostess *f inv*; **~ letter** (*BRIT*) *n* aerogramma *m*; **~lift** *n* ponte *m* aereo; **~line** *n* linea aerea; **~liner** *n* aereo di linea; **~mail** *n*: **by ~mail** per via aerea; **~ mattress** *n* materassino gonfiabile; **~plane** (*US*) *n* aeroplano; **~port** *n* aeroporto; **~ raid** *n* incursione *f* aerea; **~sick** *adj*: **to be ~sick** soffrire di mal d'aria; **~tight** *adj* ermetico(a); **~ traffic controller** *n* controllore *m* del traffico aereo; **~y** *adj* arioso(a); (*manners*) noncurante

aisle [aɪl] *n* (*of church*) navata laterale; navata centrale; (*of plane*) corridoio; **~ seat** *n* (*on plane*) posto sul corridoio

ajar [ə'dʒɑː*] *adj* socchiuso(a)

alarm [ə'lɑːm] *n* allarme *m ♦ vt* allarmare; **~ call** *n* (*in hotel etc*) sveglia; **~ clock** *n* sveglia

alas [ə'læs] *excl* ohimè!, ahimè!

albeit [ɔːl'biːɪt] *conj* sebbene +*sub*, benché +*sub*

album ['ælbəm] *n* album *m inv*

alcohol ['ælkəhɔl] *n* alcool *m*; **~ic** [-'hɔlɪk] *adj* alcolico(a) *♦ n* alcolizzato/a

ale [eɪl] *n* birra

alert [ə'lɜːt] *adj* vigile *♦ n* allarme *m ♦ vt* avvertire; mettere in guardia; **on the ~** all'erta

algebra ['ældʒɪbrə] *n* algebra

alias ['eɪlɪəs] *adv* alias *♦ n* pseudonimo, falso nome *m*

alibi ['ælɪbaɪ] *n* alibi *m inv*

alien ['eɪlɪən] *n* straniero/a; (*extraterrestrial*) alieno/a *♦ adj*: **~ (to)** estraneo(a) (a); **~ate** *vt* alienare

alight [ə'laɪt] *adj* acceso(a) *♦ vi* scendere;

(*bird*) posarsi

alike [ə'laɪk] *adj* simile *♦ adv* sia ... sia; **to look ~** assomigliarsi

alimony ['ælɪmənɪ] *n* (*payment*) alimenti *mpl*

alive [ə'laɪv] *adj* vivo(a); (*lively*) vivace

KEYWORD
---

all [ɔːl] *adj* tutto(a); **~ day** tutto il giorno; **~ night** tutta la notte; **~ men** tutti gli uomini; **~ five came** sono venuti tutti e cinque; **~ the books** tutti i libri; **~ the food** tutto il cibo; **~ the time** sempre; tutto il tempo; **~ his life** tutta la vita
♦ pron **1** tutto(a); **I ate it ~**, **I ate ~ of it** l'ho mangiato tutto; **~ of us went** tutti noi siamo andati; **~ of the boys went** tutti i ragazzi sono andati
2 (*in phrases*): **above ~** soprattutto; **after ~** dopotutto; **at ~: not at ~** (*in answer to question*) niente affatto; (*in answer to thanks*) prego!, di niente!, s'immagini!; **I'm not at ~ tired** non sono affatto stanco(a); **anything at ~ will do** andrà bene qualsiasi cosa; **~ in ~** tutto sommato
♦ adv: **~ alone** tutto(a) solo(a); **it's not as hard as ~ that** non è poi così difficile; **~ the more/the better** tanto più/meglio; **~ but** quasi; **the score is two ~** il punteggio è di due a due

---

allay [ə'leɪ] *vt* (*fears*) dissipare

all clear *n* (*also fig*) segnale *m* di cessato allarme

allegation [ælɪ'geɪʃən] *n* asserzione *f*

allege [ə'ledʒ] *vt* asserire; **~dly** [ə'ledʒɪdlɪ] *adv* secondo quanto si asserisce

allegiance [ə'liːdʒəns] *n* fedeltà

allergic [ə'lɜːdʒɪk] *adj*: **~ to** allergico(a) a

allergy ['ælədʒɪ] *n* allergia

alleviate [ə'liːvɪeɪt] *vt* sollevare

alley ['ælɪ] *n* vicolo

alliance [ə'laɪəns] *n* alleanza

allied ['ælaɪd] *adj* alleato(a)

all-in *adj* (*BRIT*: *also adv*: *charge*) tutto compreso

all-night *adj* aperto(a) (*or* che dura) tutta

la notte

allocate ['æləkeɪt] *vt* assegnare

allot [ə'lɒt] *vt* assegnare; **~ment** *n* assegnazione *f*; (*garden*) lotto di terra

all-out *adj* (*effort etc*) totale ♦ *adv*: **to go all out for** mettercela tutta per

allow [ə'lau] *vt* (*practice, behaviour*) permettere; (*allot*) accordare; (*sum, time estimated*) dare; (*concede*): **to ~ that** ammettere che; **to ~ sb to do** permettere a qn di fare; **he is ~ed to** lo può fare; **~ for** *vt fus* tener conto di; **~ance** *n* (*money received*) assegno; (*indennità f inv*); (*TAX*) detrazione *f* di imposta; **to make ~ances for** tener conto di

alloy ['ælɔɪ] *n* lega

all right *adv* (*feel, work*) bene; (*as answer*) va bene

all-round *adj* completo(a)

all-time *adj* (*record*) assoluto(a)

alluring [ə'ljuərɪŋ] *adj* seducente

ally ['ælaɪ] *n* alleato

almighty [ɔːl'maɪtɪ] *adj* onnipotente; (*row etc*) colossale

almond ['ɑːmənd] *n* mandorla

almost ['ɔːlməust] *adv* quasi

alone [ə'ləun] *adj, adv* solo(a); **to leave sb ~** lasciare qn in pace; **to leave sth ~** lasciare stare qc; **let ~ ...** figuriamoci poi ..., tanto meno ....

along [ə'lɒŋ] *prep* lungo ♦ *adv*: **is he coming ~?** viene con noi?; **he was limping ~** veniva zoppicando; **~ with** insieme con; **all ~** (*all the time*) sempre, fin dall'inizio; **~side** *prep* accanto a; lungo ♦ *adv* accanto

aloof [ə'luːf] *adj* distaccato(a) ♦ *adv*: **to stand ~** tenersi a distanza *or* in disparte

aloud [ə'laud] *adv* ad alta voce

alphabet ['ælfəbɛt] *n* alfabeto

alpine ['ælpaɪn] *adj* alpino(a)

Alps [ælps] *npl*: **the ~** le Alpi

already [ɔːl'redɪ] *adv* già

alright ['ɔːl'raɪt] (*BRIT*) *adv* = **all right**

Alsatian [æl'seɪʃən] (*BRIT*) *n* (*dog*) pastore *m* tedesco, (*cane m*) lupo

also ['ɔːlsəu] *adv* anche

altar ['ɒltə*] *n* altare *m*

alter ['ɒltə*] *vt, vi* alterare

alternate [*adj* ɒl'tɜːnɪt, *vb* 'ɒltəneɪt] *adj* alterno(a); (*US: plan etc*) alternativo(a) ♦ *vi*: **to ~ (with)** alternarsi (a); **on ~ days** ogni due giorni; **alternating** ['ɒltəneɪtɪŋ] *adj* (*current*) alternato(a)

alternative [ɒl'tɜːnətɪv] *adj* alternativo(a) ♦ *n* (*choice*) alternativa; **~ly** *adv*: **~ly one could ...** come alternativa si potrebbe ...; **~ medicine** *n* medicina alternativa

alternator ['ɒltəneɪtə*] *n* (*AUT*) alternatore *m*

although [ɔːl'ðəu] *conj* benché +*sub*, sebbene +*sub*

altitude ['æltɪtjuːd] *n* altitudine *f*

alto ['æltəu] *n* contralto; (*male*) contraltino

altogether [ɔːltə'geðə*] *adv* del tutto, completamente; (*on the whole*) tutto considerato; (*in all*) in tutto

aluminium [ælju'mɪnɪəm] *n* alluminio

aluminum [ə'luːmɪnəm] (*US*) *n* = **aluminium**

always ['ɔːlweɪz] *adv* sempre

Alzheimer's (disease) ['æltshaɪməz-] *n* (malattia di) Alzheimer

AM *n abbr* (= (*Welsh*) *Assembly Member*) deputato/a del Parlamento gallese

am [æm] *vb see* **be**

a.m. *adv abbr* (= *ante meridiem*) della mattina

amalgamate [ə'mælgəmeɪt] *vt* amalgamare ♦ *vi* amalgamarsi

amateur ['æmətə*] *n* dilettante *m/f* ♦ *adj* (*SPORT*) dilettante; **~ish** (*pej*) *adj* da dilettante

amaze [ə'meɪz] *vt* stupire; **to be ~d (at)** essere sbalordito (da); **~ment** *n* stupore *m*; **amazing** *adj* sorprendente, sbalorditivo(a)

ambassador [æm'bæsədə*] *n* ambasciatore/trice

amber ['æmbə*] *n* ambra; **at ~** (*BRIT: AUT*) giallo

ambiguous [æm'bɪgjuəs] *adj* ambiguo(a)

ambition [æm'bɪʃən] *n* ambizione *f*

ambitious [æm'bɪʃəs] *adj* ambizioso(a)

ambulance ['æmbjuləns] *n* ambulanza

ambush ['æmbuʃ] *n* imboscata ♦ *vt* fare un'imboscata a

amenable [ə'mi:nəbl] *adj*: ~ **to** (*advice etc*) ben disposto(a) a

amend [ə'mɛnd] *vt* (*law*) emendare; (*text*) correggere; **to make ~s** fare ammenda

amenities [ə'mi:nɪtɪz] *npl* attrezzature *fpl* ricreative e culturali

America [ə'mɛrɪkə] *n* America; **~n** *adj, n* americano(a)

amiable ['eɪmɪəbl] *adj* amabile, gentile

amicable ['æmɪkəbl] *adj* amichevole

amid(st) [ə'mɪd(st)] *prep* fra, tra, in mezzo a

amiss [ə'mɪs] *adj, adv*: **there's something ~** c'è qualcosa che non va bene; **don't take it ~** non prendertela (a male)

ammonia [ə'məunɪə] *n* ammoniaca

ammunition [æmju'nɪʃən] *n* munizioni *fpl*

amok [ə'mɔk] *adv*: **to run ~** diventare pazzo(a) furioso(a)

among(st) [ə'mʌŋ(st)] *prep* fra, tra, in mezzo a

amorous ['æmərəs] *adj* amoroso(a)

amount [ə'maunt] *n* somma; ammontare *m*; quantità *f inv* ♦ *vi*: **to ~ to** (*total*) ammontare a; (*be same as*) essere come

amp(ère) ['æmp(ɛə*)] *n* ampère *m inv*

ample ['æmpl] *adj* ampio(a); spazioso(a); (*enough*): **this is ~** questo è più che sufficiente

amplifier ['æmplɪfaɪə*] *n* amplificatore *m*

amuse [ə'mju:z] *vt* divertire; **~ment** *n* divertimento; **~ment arcade** *n* sala giochi; **~ment park** *n* luna park *m inv*

an [æn] *indef art see* **a**

anaemic [ə'ni:mɪk] *adj* anemico(a)

anaesthetic [ænɪs'θɛtɪk] *adj* anestetico(a) ♦ *n* anestetico

analog(ue) ['ænələg] *adj* (*watch, computer*) analogico(a)

analyse ['ænəlaɪz] (*BRIT*) *vt* analizzare

analysis [ə'næləsɪs] (*pl* **analyses**) *n* analisi *f inv*

analyst ['ænəlɪst] *n* (*POL etc*) analista *m/f*; (*US*) (*psic*)analista *m/f*

analyze ['ænəlaɪz] (*US*) *vt* = **analyse**

anarchy ['ænəkɪ] *n* anarchia

anatomy [ə'nætəmɪ] *n* anatomia

ancestor ['ænsɪstə*] *n* antenato/a

anchor ['æŋkə*] *n* ancora ♦ *vi* (*also*: **to drop ~**) gettare l'ancora ♦ *vt* ancorare; **to weigh ~** salpare *or* levare l'ancora

anchovy ['æntʃəvɪ] *n* acciuga

ancient ['eɪnʃənt] *adj* antico(a); (*person, car*) vecchissimo(a)

ancillary [æn'sɪlərɪ] *adj* ausiliario(a)

and [ænd] *conj* e (*often before vowel*); **~ so on** e così via; **try ~ come** cerca di venire; **he talked ~ talked** non la finiva di parlare; **better ~ better** sempre meglio

anemic [ə'ni:mɪk] (*US*) *adj* = **anaemic**

anesthetic [ænɪs'θɛtɪk] (*US*) *adj, n* = **anaesthetic**

anew [ə'nju:] *adv* di nuovo

angel ['eɪndʒəl] *n* angelo

anger ['æŋgə*] *n* rabbia

angina [æn'dʒaɪnə] *n* angina pectoris

angle ['æŋgl] *n* angolo; **from their ~** dal loro punto di vista

Anglican ['æŋglɪkən] *adj, n* anglicano(a)

angling ['æŋglɪŋ] *n* pesca con la lenza

Anglo- ['æŋgləu] *prefix* anglo-...

angrily ['æŋgrɪlɪ] *adv* con rabbia

angry ['æŋgrɪ] *adj* arrabbiato(a), furioso(a); (*wound*) infiammato(a); **to be ~ with sb/at sth** essere in collera con qn/per qc; **to get ~** arrabbiarsi; **to make sb ~** fare arrabbiare qn

anguish ['æŋgwɪʃ] *n* angoscia

animal ['ænɪməl] *adj* animale ♦ *n* animale *m*

animate ['ænɪmɪt] *adj* animato(a)

animated ['ænɪmeɪtɪd] *adj* animato(a)

aniseed ['ænɪsi:d] *n* semi *mpl* di anice

ankle ['æŋkl] *n* caviglia; **~ sock** *n* calzino

annex [*n* 'ænɛks, *vb* ə'nɛks] *n* (*also*: *BRIT*: **annexe**) (edificio) annesso ♦ *vt* annettere

anniversary [ænɪ'və:sərɪ] *n* anniversario

announce [ə'nauns] *vt* annunciare; **~ment** *n* annuncio; (*letter, card*) partecipazione *f*; **~r** *n* (*RADIO, TV: between programmes*) annunciatore/ trice; (: *in a programme*) presentatore/trice

annoy [ə'nɔɪ] *vt* dare fastidio a; **don't get**

~ed! non irritarti!; ~ance n fastidio; (cause of ~ance) noia; ~ing adj noioso(a)

annual ['ænjʊəl] adj annuale ♦ n (BOT) pianta annua; (book) annuario

annul [ə'nʌl] vt annullare

annum ['ænəm] n see **per**

anonymous [ə'nɔnɪməs] adj anonimo(a)

anorak ['ænəræk] n giacca a vento

anorexia [ænə'rɛksɪə] n (MED) anoressia

another [ə'nʌðə*] adj: ~ **book** (one more) un altro libro, ancora un libro; (a different one) un altro libro ♦ pron un altro(un'altra), ancora uno(a); see also **one**

answer ['ɑːnsə*] n risposta; soluzione f ♦ vi rispondere ♦ vt (reply to) rispondere a; (problem) risolvere; (prayer) esaudire; **in ~ to your letter** in risposta alla sua lettera; **to ~ the phone** rispondere (al telefono); **to ~ the bell** rispondere al campanello; **to ~ the door** aprire la porta; ~ **back** vi ribattere; ~ **for** vt fus essere responsabile di; ~ **to** vt fus (description) corrispondere a; ~**able** adj: ~**able (to sb/for sth)** responsabile (verso qn/di qc); ~**ing machine** n segreteria (telefonica) automatica

ant [ænt] n formica

antagonism [æn'tægənɪzəm] n antagonismo

antagonize [æn'tægənaɪz] vt provocare l'ostilità di

Antarctic [ænt'ɑːktɪk] n: **the ~** l'Antartide f

antenatal ['æntɪ'neɪtl] adj prenatale; ~ **clinic** n assistenza medica preparto

anthem ['ænθəm] n: **national ~** inno nazionale

antibiotic ['æntɪbaɪ'ɔtɪk] n antibiotico

antibody ['æntɪbɔdɪ] n anticorpo

anticipate [æn'tɪsɪpeɪt] vt prevedere; pregustare; (wishes, request) prevenire

anticipation [æntɪsɪ'peɪʃən] n anticipazione f; (expectation) aspettative fpl

anticlimax ['æntɪ'klaɪmæks] n: **it was an ~** fu una completa delusione

anticlockwise ['æntɪ'klɔkwaɪz] adj, adv in senso antiorario

antics ['æntɪks] npl buffonerie fpl

antidepressant ['æntɪdɪ'prɛsnt] n antide-

pressivo

antifreeze ['æntɪ'friːz] n anticongelante m

antihistamine [æntɪ'hɪstəmɪn] n antistaminico

antiquated ['æntɪkweɪtɪd] adj antiquato(a)

antique [æn'tiːk] n antichità f inv ♦ adj antico(a); ~ **dealer** n antiquario/a; ~ **shop** n negozio d'antichità

anti-Semitism ['æntɪ'sɛmɪtɪzəm] n antisemitismo

antiseptic [æntɪ'sɛptɪk] n antisettico

antisocial ['æntɪ'səʊʃəl] adj asociale

antlers ['æntləz] npl palchi mpl

anvil ['ænvɪl] n incudine f

anxiety [æŋ'zaɪətɪ] n ansia

anxious ['æŋkʃəs] adj ansioso(a), inquieto(a); (worrying) angosciante; (keen): ~ **to do/that** impaziente di fare/che +sub

KEYWORD

any ['ɛnɪ] adj 1 (in questions etc): **have you ~ butter?** hai del burro?, hai un po' di burro?; **have you ~ children?** hai bambini?; **if there are ~ tickets left** se ci sono ancora (dei) biglietti, se c'è ancora qualche biglietto

2 (with negative): **I haven't ~ money/ books** non ho soldi/libri

3 (no matter which): **choose ~ book you like** scegli un libro qualsiasi

4 (in phrases): **in ~ case** in ogni caso; ~ **day now** da un giorno all'altro; **at ~ moment** in qualsiasi momento, da un momento all'altro; **at ~ rate** ad ogni modo

♦ pron 1 (in questions, with negative): **have you got ~?** ne hai?; **can ~ of you sing?** qualcuno di voi sa cantare?; **I haven't ~ (of them)** non ne ho

2 (no matter which one(s)): **take ~ of those books (you like)** prendi uno qualsiasi di quei libri

♦ adv 1 (in questions etc): **do you want ~ more soup/sandwiches?** vuoi ancora un po' di minestra/degli altri panini?; **are you feeling ~ better?** ti senti meglio?

2 (with negative): **I can't hear him ~ more**

non lo sento più; **don't wait ~ longer** non aspettare più

anybody ['ɛnɪbɔdɪ] *pron (in questions etc)* qualcuno, nessuno; *(with negative)* nessuno; *(no matter who)* chiunque; **can you see ~?** vedi qualcuno *or* nessuno?; **if ~ should phone ...** se telefona qualcuno ...; **I can't see ~** non vedo nessuno; **~ could do it** chiunque potrebbe farlo

anyhow ['ɛnɪhau] *adv (at any rate)* ad ogni modo, comunque; *(haphazard)*: **do it ~ you like** fallo come ti pare; **I shall go ~** ci andrò lo stesso *or* comunque; **she leaves things just ~** lascia tutto come capita

anyone ['ɛnɪwʌn] *pron* = **anybody**

anything ['ɛnɪθɪŋ] *pron (in question etc)* qualcosa, niente; *(with negative)* niente; *(no matter what)*: **you can say ~ you like** puoi dire quello che ti pare; **can you see ~?** vedi niente *or* qualcosa?; **if ~ happens to me ...** se mi dovesse succedere qualcosa ...; **I can't see ~** non vedo niente; **~ will do** va bene qualsiasi cosa *or* tutto

anyway ['ɛnɪweɪ] *adv (at any rate)* ad ogni modo, comunque; *(besides)* ad ogni modo

anywhere ['ɛnɪwɛə*] *adv (in questions etc)* da qualche parte; *(with negative)* da nessuna parte; *(no matter where)* da qualsiasi *or* qualunque parte, dovunque; **can you see him ~?** lo vedi da qualche parte?; **I can't see him ~** non lo vedo da nessuna parte; **~ in the world** dovunque nel mondo

apart [ə'pɑːt] *adv (to one side)* a parte; *(separately)* separatamente; **with one's legs ~** con le gambe divaricate; **10 miles ~** a 10 miglia di distanza (l'uno dall'altro); **to take ~** smontare; **~ from** a parte, eccetto

apartheid [ə'pɑːteɪt] *n* apartheid *f*

apartment [ə'pɑːtmənt] *n (US)* appartamento; *(room)* locale *m*; **~ building** *(US)* edificio *m*, caseggiato

ape [eɪp] *n* scimmia ♦ *vt* scimmiottare

apéritif [ə'perɪtɪv] *n* aperitivo

aperture ['æpətʃjuə*] *n* apertura

APEX *n abbr (= advance purchase*

excursion) APEX *m inv*

apologetic [əpɔlə'dʒetɪk] *adj (tone, letter)* di scusa

apologize [ə'pɔlədʒaɪz] *vi*: **to ~ (for sth to sb)** scusarsi (di qc a qn), chiedere scusa (a qn per qc)

apology [ə'pɔlədʒɪ] *n* scuse *fpl*

apostle [ə'pɔsl] *n* apostolo

apostrophe [ə'pɔstrəfɪ] *n (sign)* apostrofo

appal [ə'pɔːl] *vt* scioccare; **~ling** *adj* spaventoso(a)

apparatus [æpə'reɪtəs] *n* apparato; *(in gymnasium)* attrezzatura

apparel [ə'pærl] *(US) n* abbigliamento, confezioni *fpl*

apparent [ə'pærənt] *adj* evidente; **~ly** *adv* evidentemente

appeal [ə'piːl] *vi (LAW)* appellarsi alla legge ♦ *n (LAW)* appello; *(request)* richiesta; *(charm)* attrattiva; **to ~ for** chiedere con insistenza; **to ~ to** *(subj: person)* appellarsi a; *(subj: thing)* piacere a; **it doesn't ~ to me** mi dice poco; **~ing** *adj (nice)* attraente

appear [ə'pɪə*] *vi* apparire; *(LAW)* comparire; *(publication)* essere pubblicato(a); *(seem)* sembrare; **it would ~ that** sembra che; **~ance** *n* apparizione *f*; apparenza; *(look, aspect)* aspetto

appease [ə'piːz] *vt* calmare, appagare

appendicitis [əpendɪ'saɪtɪs] *n* appendicite *f*

appendix [ə'pendɪks] *(pl* **appendices)** *n* appendice *f*

appetite ['æpɪtaɪt] *n* appetito

appetizer ['æpɪtaɪzə*] *n* stuzzichino

applaud [ə'plɔːd] *vt, vi* applaudire

applause [ə'plɔːz] *n* applauso

apple ['æpl] *n* mela; **~ tree** *n* melo

appliance [ə'plaɪəns] *n* apparecchio

applicant ['æplɪkənt] *n* candidato/a

application [æplɪ'keɪʃən] *n* applicazione *f*; *(for a job, a grant etc)* domanda; **~ form** *n* modulo per la domanda

applied [ə'plaɪd] *adj* applicato(a)

apply [ə'plaɪ] *vt*: **to ~ (to)** *(paint, ointment)* dare (a); *(theory, technique)* applicare (a) ♦ *vi*: **to ~ to** *(ask)* rivolgersi a; *(be suitable for, relevant to)* riguardare, riferirsi a; **to ~**

(for) (permit, grant, job) fare domanda (per); **to ~ o.s. to** dedicarsi a

appoint [ə'pɔɪnt] vt nominare; **~ed** adj: **at the ~ed time** all'ora stabilita; **~ment** n nomina; (arrangement to meet) appuntamento; **to make an ~ment (with)** prendere un appuntamento (con)

appraisal [ə'preɪzl] n valutazione f

appreciate [ə'priːʃɪeɪt] vt (like) apprezzare; (be grateful for) essere riconoscente di; (be aware of) rendersi conto di ♦ vi (FINANCE) aumentare; **I'd ~ your help** ti sono grato per l'aiuto

appreciation [əpriːʃɪ'eɪʃən] n apprezzamento; (FINANCE) aumento del valore

appreciative [ə'priːʃɪətɪv] adj (person) sensibile; (comment) elogiativo(a)

apprehend [æprɪ'hɛnd] vt (arrest) arrestare

apprehension [æprɪ'hɛnʃən] n (fear) inquietudine f

apprehensive [æprɪ'hɛnsɪv] adj apprensivo(a)

apprentice [ə'prɛntɪs] n apprendista m/f; **~ship** n apprendistato

approach [ə'prəutʃ] vi avvicinarsi ♦ vt (come near) avvicinarsi a; (ask, apply to) rivolgersi a; (subject, passer-by) avvicinare ♦ n approccio; accesso; (to problem) modo di affrontare; **~able** adj accessibile

appropriate [adj ə'prəuprɪɪt, vb ə'prəuprɪeɪt] adj appropriato(a); adatto(a) ♦ vt (take) appropriarsi

approval [ə'pruːvəl] n approvazione f; **on ~** (COMM) in prova, in esame

approve [ə'pruːv] vt, vi approvare; **~ of** vt fus approvare

approximate [ə'prɔksɪmɪt] adj approssimativo(a); **~ly** adv circa

apricot ['eɪprɪkɔt] n albicocca

April ['eɪprəl] n aprile m; **~ fool!** pesce d'aprile!

April Fool's Day

🛈 **April Fool's Day** è il primo aprile, il giorno degli scherzi e delle burle. Il nome deriva dal fatto che, se una persona cade nella trappola che gli è stata tesa, fa la figura del **fool**, cioè dello sciocco.

apron ['eɪprən] n grembiule m

apt [æpt] adj (suitable) adatto(a); (able) capace; (likely): **to be ~ to do** avere tendenza a fare

aquarium [ə'kwɛərɪəm] n acquario

Aquarius [ə'kwɛərɪəs] n Acquario

Arab ['ærəb] adj, n arabo(a)

Arabian [ə'reɪbɪən] adj arabo(a)

Arabic ['ærəbɪk] adj arabico(a), arabo(a) ♦ n arabo; **~ numerals** numeri mpl arabi

arbitrary ['ɑːbɪtrərɪ] adj arbitrario(a)

arbitration [ɑːbɪ'treɪʃən] n (LAW) arbitrato; (INDUSTRY) arbitraggio

arcade [ɑː'keɪd] n portico; (passage with shops) galleria

arch [ɑːtʃ] n arco; (of foot) arco plantare ♦ vt inarcare

archaeologist [ɑːkɪ'ɔlədʒɪst] n archeologo/a

archaeology [ɑːkɪ'ɔlədʒɪ] n archeologia

archbishop [ɑːtʃ'bɪʃəp] n arcivescovo

archeology [ɑːkɪ'ɔlədʒɪ] etc (US) = **archaeology** etc

archery ['ɑːtʃərɪ] n tiro all'arco

architect ['ɑːkɪtɛkt] n architetto; **~ure** ['ɑːkɪtɛktʃə*] n architettura

archives ['ɑːkaɪvz] npl archivi mpl

Arctic ['ɑːktɪk] adj artico(a) ♦ n: **the ~** l'Artico

ardent ['ɑːdənt] adj ardente

are [ɑː*] vb see **be**; **~n't** [ɑːnt] = **~ not**

area ['ɛərɪə] n (GEOM) area; (zone) zona; (: smaller) settore m

Argentina [ɑːdʒən'tiːnə] n Argentina; **Argentinian** [-'tɪnɪən] adj, n argentino(a)

arguably ['ɑːgjuəblɪ] adv: **it is ~ ...** si può sostenere che sia ....

argue ['ɑːgjuː] vi (quarrel) litigare; (reason) ragionare; **to ~ that** sostenere che

argument ['ɑːgjumənt] n (reasons) argomento; (quarrel) lite f; **~ative** [ɑːgju'mɛntətɪv] adj litigioso(a)

Aries ['ɛərɪz] n Ariete m

arise [ə'raɪz] (pt **arose**, pp **arisen**) vi (opportunity, problem) presentarsi

aristocrat [ˈærɪstəkræt] *n* aristocratico/a
arithmetic [əˈrɪθmətɪk] *n* aritmetica
ark [ɑːk] *n*: **Noah's A~** l'arca di Noè
arm [ɑːm] *n* braccio ♦ *vt* armare; **~s** *npl* (*weapons*) armi *fpl*; **~ in ~** a braccetto
armaments [ˈɑːməmənts] *npl* armamenti *mpl*
arm: ~chair *n* poltrona; **~ed** *adj* armato(a); **~ed robbery** *n* rapina a mano armata
armour [ˈɑːmə*] (*US* **armor**) *n* armatura; (*MIL: tanks*) mezzi *mpl* blindati; **~ed car** *n* autoblinda *f inv*
armpit [ˈɑːmpɪt] *n* ascella
armrest [ˈɑːmrest] *n* bracciolo
army [ˈɑːmɪ] *n* esercito
aroma [əˈrəumə] *n* aroma; **~therapy** *n* aromaterapia
arose [əˈrəuz] *pt of* **arise**
around [əˈraund] *adv* attorno, intorno ♦ *prep* intorno a; (*fig: about*): ~ **£5/ 3 o'clock** circa 5 sterline/le 3; **is he ~?** è in giro?
arouse [əˈrauz] *vt* (*sleeper*) svegliare; (*curiosity, passions*) suscitare
arrange [əˈreɪndʒ] *vt* sistemare; (*programme*) preparare; **to ~ to do sth** mettersi d'accordo per fare qc; **~ment** *n* sistemazione *f*; (*agreement*) accordo; **~ments** *npl* (*plans*) progetti *mpl*, piani *mpl*
array [əˈreɪ] *n*: ~ **of** fila di
arrears [əˈrɪəz] *npl* arretrati *mpl*; **to be in ~ with one's rent** essere in arretrato con l'affitto
arrest [əˈrest] *vt* arrestare; (*sb's attention*) attirare ♦ *n* arresto; **under ~** in arresto
arrival [əˈraɪvəl] *n* arrivo; (*person*) arrivato/a; **a new ~** un nuovo venuto; (*baby*) un neonato
arrive [əˈraɪv] *vi* arrivare
arrogant [ˈærəgənt] *adj* arrogante
arrow [ˈærəu] *n* freccia
arse [ɑːs] (*infl*) *n* culo (!)
arson [ˈɑːsn] *n* incendio doloso
art [ɑːt] *n* arte *f*; (*craft*) mestiere *m*; **A~s** *npl* (*SCOL*) Lettere *fpl*
artery [ˈɑːtərɪ] *n* arteria

art gallery *n* galleria d'arte
arthritis [ɑːˈθraɪtɪs] *n* artrite *f*
artichoke [ˈɑːtɪtʃəuk] *n* carciofo; **Jerusalem ~** topinambur *m inv*
article [ˈɑːtɪkl] *n* articolo; **~s** *npl* (*BRIT: LAW: training*) contratto di tirocinio; ~ **of clothing** capo di vestiario
articulate [*adj* ɑːˈtɪkjulɪt, *vb* ɑːˈtɪkjuleɪt] *adj* (*person*) che si esprime forbitamente; (*speech*) articolato(a) ♦ *vi* articolare; **~d lorry** (*BRIT*) *n* autotreno
artificial [ɑːtɪˈfɪʃəl] *adj* artificiale; ~ **respiration** *n* respirazione *f* artificiale
artist [ˈɑːtɪst] *n* artista *m/f*; **~ic** [ɑːˈtɪstɪk] *adj* artistico(a); **~ry** *n* arte *f*
art school *n* scuola d'arte

KEYWORD

---

as [æz] *conj* **1** (*referring to time*) mentre; ~ **the years went by** col passare degli anni; **he came in ~ I was leaving** arrivò mentre stavo uscendo; ~ **from tomorrow** da domani
2 (*in comparisons*): ~ **big ~** grande come; **twice ~ big ~** due volte più grande di; ~ **much/many ~** tanto quanto/tanti quanti; ~ **soon ~ possible** prima possibile
3 (*since, because*) dal momento che, siccome
4 (*referring to manner, way*) come; **do ~ you wish** fa' come vuoi; ~ **she said** come ha detto lei
5 (*concerning*): ~ **for** *or* **to that** per quanto riguarda *or* quanto a quello
6: ~ **if** *or* **though** come se; **he looked ~ if he was ill** sembrava stare male; *see also* **long; such; well**
♦ *prep*: **he works ~ a driver** fa l'autista; ~ **chairman of the company, he ...** come presidente della compagnia, lui ...; **he gave me it ~ a present** me lo ha regalato

---

a.s.a.p. *abbr* = **as soon as possible**
ascend [əˈsend] *vt* salire
ascertain [æsəˈteɪn] *vt* accertare
ash [æʃ] *n* (*dust*) cenere *f*; (*wood, tree*) frassino

ashamed [ə'ʃeɪmd] *adj* vergognoso(a); **to be ~ of** vergognarsi di

ashore [ə'ʃɔː*] *adv* a terra

ashtray ['æʃtreɪ] *n* portacenere *m*

Ash Wednesday *n* mercoledì *m inv* delle Ceneri

Asia ['eɪʃə] *n* Asia; **~n** *adj*, *n* asiatico(a)

aside [ə'saɪd] *adv* da parte ♦ *n* a parte *m*

ask [ɑːsk] *vt* (*question*) domandare; (*invite*) invitare; **to ~ sb sth/sb to do sth** chiedere qc a qn/a qn di fare qc; **to ~ sb about sth** chiedere a qn di qc; **to ~ (sb) a question** fare una domanda (a qn); **to ~ sb out to dinner** invitare qn a mangiare fuori; **~ after** *vt fus* chiedere di; **~ for** *vt fus* chiedere; (*trouble etc*) cercare

asleep [ə'sliːp] *adj* addormentato(a); **to be ~** dormire; **to fall ~** addormentarsi

asparagus [əs'pærəgəs] *n* asparagi *mpl*

aspect ['æspekt] *n* aspetto

aspersions [əs'pəːʃənz] *npl*: **to cast ~ on** diffamare

asphyxiation [æsfɪksɪ'eɪʃən] *n* asfissia

aspire [əs'paɪə*] *vi*: **to ~ to** aspirare a

aspirin ['æsprɪn] *n* aspirina

ass [æs] *n* asino; (*inf*) scemo/a; (*US: inf!*) culo (!)

assailant [ə'seɪlənt] *n* assalitore *m*

assassinate [ə'sæsɪneɪt] *vt* assassinare; **assassination** [əsæsɪ'neɪʃən] *n* assassinio

assault [ə'sɔːlt] *n* (*MIL*) assalto; (*gen: attack*) aggressione *f* ♦ *vt* assaltare; aggredire; (*sexually*) violentare

assemble [ə'sembl] *vt* riunire; (*TECH*) montare ♦ *vi* riunirsi

assembly [ə'semblɪ] *n* (*meeting*) assemblea; (*construction*) montaggio; **~ line** *n* catena di montaggio

assent [ə'sent] *n* assenso, consenso

assert [ə'səːt] *vt* asserire; (*insist on*) far valere

assess [ə'ses] *vt* valutare; **~ment** *n* valutazione *f*

asset ['æset] *n* vantaggio; **~s** *npl* (*FINANCE: of individual*) beni *mpl*; (*: of company*) attivo

assign [ə'saɪn] *vt*: **to ~ (to)** (*task*) assegnare

(a); (*resources*) riservare (a); (*cause, meaning*) attribuire (a); **to ~ a date to sth** fissare la data di qc; **~ment** *n* compito

assist [ə'sɪst] *vt* assistere, aiutare; **~ance** *n* assistenza, aiuto; **~ant** *n* assistente *m/f*; (*BRIT: also:* **shop ~ant**) commesso/a

associate [*adj, n* ə'səuʃɪɪt, *vb* ə'səuʃɪeɪt] *adj* associato(a); (*member*) aggiunto(a) ♦ *n* collega *m/f* ♦ *vt* associare ♦ *vi*: **to ~ with sb** frequentare qn

association [əsəusɪ'eɪʃən] *n* associazione *f*

assorted [ə'sɔːtɪd] *adj* assortito(a)

assortment [ə'sɔːtmənt] *n* assortimento

assume [ə'sjuːm] *vt* supporre; (*responsibilities etc*) assumere; (*attitude, name*) prendere

assumption [ə'sʌmpʃən] *n* supposizione *f*, ipotesi *f inv*; (*of power*) assunzione *f*

assurance [ə'ʃuərəns] *n* assicurazione *f*; (*self-confidence*) fiducia in se stesso

assure [ə'ʃuə*] *vt* assicurare

asthma ['æsmə] *n* asma

astonish [ə'stɒnɪʃ] *vt* stupire; **~ment** *n* stupore *m*

astound [ə'staund] *vt* sbalordire

astray [ə'streɪ] *adv*: **to go ~** smarrirsi; **to lead ~** portare sulla cattiva strada

astride [ə'straɪd] *prep* a cavalcioni di

astrology [əs'trɒlədʒɪ] *n* astrologia

astronaut ['æstrənɔːt] *n* astronauta *m/f*

astronomy [əs'trɒnəmɪ] *n* astronomia

asylum [ə'saɪləm] *n* asilo; (*building*) manicomio

KEYWORD

at [æt] *prep* **1** (*referring to position, direction*) a; **~ the top** in cima; **~ the desk** al banco, alla scrivania; **~ home/school** a casa/scuola; **~ the baker's** dal panettiere; **to look ~ sth** guardare qc; **to throw sth ~ sb** lanciare qc a qn

2 (*referring to time*) a; **~ 4 o'clock** alle 4; **~ night** di notte; **~ Christmas** a Natale; **~ times** a volte

3 (*referring to rates, speed etc*) a; **~ £1 a kilo** a 1 sterlina al chilo; **two ~ a time** due alla volta, due per volta; **~ 50 km/h** a

50 km/h
4 (*referring to manner*): ~ **a stroke** d'un solo colpo; ~ **peace** in pace
5 (*referring to activity*): **to be ~ work** essere al lavoro; **to play ~ cowboys** giocare ai cowboy; **to be good ~ sth/doing sth** essere bravo in qc/a fare qc
6 (*referring to cause*): **shocked/surprised/annoyed ~ sth** colpito da/sorpreso da/arrabbiato per qc; **I went ~ his suggestion** ci sono andato dietro suo consiglio

---

ate [eɪt] *pt of* eat
atheist ['eɪθɪɪst] *n* ateo/a
Athens ['æθɪnz] *n* Atene *f*
athlete ['æθliːt] *n* atleta *m/f*
athletic [æθ'lɛtɪk] *adj* atletico(a); **~s** *n* atletica
Atlantic [ət'læntɪk] *adj* atlantico(a) ♦ *n*: **the ~ (Ocean)** l'Atlantico, l'Oceano Atlantico
atlas ['ætləs] *n* atlante *m*
ATM *n abbr* (= *automated telling machine*) cassa automatica prelievi, sportello automatico
atmosphere ['ætməsfɪə*] *n* atmosfera
atom ['ætəm] *n* atomo; **~ic** [ə'tɔmɪk] *adj* atomico(a); **~(ic) bomb** *n* bomba atomica; **~izer** ['ætəmaɪzə*] *n* atomizzatore *m*
atone [ə'təun] *vi*: **to ~ for** espiare
atrocious [ə'trəuʃəs] *adj* pessimo(a), atroce
attach [ə'tætʃ] *vt* attaccare; (*document, letter*) allegare; (*importance etc*) attribuire; **to be ~ed to sb/sth** (*to like*) essere affezionato(a) a qn/qc
attaché case [ə'tæʃeɪ-] *n* valigetta per documenti
attachment [ə'tætʃmənt] *n* (*tool*) accessorio; (*love*): ~ **(to)** affetto (per)
attack [ə'tæk] *vt* attaccare; (*person*) aggredire; (*task etc*) iniziare; (*problem*) affrontare ♦ *n* attacco; **heart ~** infarto; **~er** *n* aggressore *m*
attain [ə'teɪn] *vt* (*also*: **to ~ to**) arrivare a, raggiungere
attempt [ə'tempt] *n* tentativo ♦ *vt* tentare;

to make an ~ on sb's life attentare alla vita di qn
attend [ə'tend] *vt* frequentare; (*meeting, talk*) andare a; (*patient*) assistere; ~ **to** *vt fus* (*needs, affairs etc*) prendersi cura di; (*customer*) occuparsi di; **~ance** *n* (*being present*) presenza; (*people present*) gente *f* presente; **~ant** *n* custode *m/f*; persona di servizio ♦ *adj* concomitante
attention [ə'tenʃən] *n* attenzione *f* ♦ *excl* (*MIL*) attenti!; **for the ~ of** (*ADMIN*) per l'attenzione di
attentive [ə'tentɪv] *adj* attento(a); (*kind*) premuroso(a)
attic ['ætɪk] *n* soffitta
attitude ['ætɪtjuːd] *n* atteggiamento; posa
attorney [ə'tɜːnɪ] *n* (*lawyer*) avvocato; (*having proxy*) mandatario; **A~ General** *n* (*BRIT*) Procuratore *m* Generale; (*US*) Ministro della Giustizia
attract [ə'trækt] *vt* attirare; **~ion** [ə'trækʃən] *n* (*gen pl: pleasant things*) attrattiva; (*PHYSICS, fig: towards sth*) attrazione *f*; **~ive** *adj* attraente
attribute [*n* 'ætrɪbjuːt, *vb* ə'trɪbjuːt] *n* attributo ♦ *vt*: **to ~ sth to** attribuire qc a
attrition [ə'trɪʃən] *n*: **war of ~** guerra di logoramento
aubergine ['əubəʒiːn] *n* melanzana
auburn ['ɔːbən] *adj* tizianesco(a)
auction ['ɔːkʃən] *n* (*also*: **sale by ~**) asta ♦ *vt* (*also*: **to sell by ~**) vendere all'asta; (*also*: **to put up for ~**) mettere all'asta; **~eer** [-'nɪə*] *n* banditore *m*
audible ['ɔːdɪbl] *adj* udibile
audience ['ɔːdɪəns] *n* (*people*) pubblico; spettatori *mpl*; ascoltatori *mpl*; (*interview*) udienza
audio-typist ['ɔːdɪəu'taɪpɪst] *n* dattilografo/a che trascrive da nastro
audio-visual [ɔːdɪəu'vɪzjuəl] *adj* audiovisivo(a); ~ **aid** *n* sussidio audiovisivo
audit ['ɔːdɪt] *vt* rivedere, verificare
audition [ɔː'dɪʃən] *n* audizione *f*
auditor ['ɔːdɪtə*] *n* revisore *m*
augment [ɔːg'ment] *vt*, *vi* aumentare
augur ['ɔːgə*] *vi*: **it ~s well** promette bene

August ['ɔːɡəst] n agosto

aunt [ɑːnt] n zia; **~ie** or **~y** n zietta

au pair ['əu'pɛə*] n (also: **~ girl**) (ragazza f) alla pari inv

auspicious [ɔːs'pɪʃəs] adj propizio(a)

Australia [ɔs'treɪlɪə] n Australia; **~n** adj, n australiano(a)

Austria ['ɔstrɪə] n Austria; **~n** adj, n austriaco(a)

authentic [ɔː'θɛntɪk] adj autentico(a)

author ['ɔːθə*] n autore/trice

authoritarian [ɔːθɔrɪ'tɛərɪən] adj autoritario(a)

authoritative [ɔː'θɔrɪtətɪv] adj (account etc) autorevole; (manner) autoritario(a)

authority [ɔː'θɔrɪtɪ] n autorità f inv; (permission) autorizzazione f; **the authorities** npl (government etc) le autorità

authorize ['ɔːθəraɪz] vt autorizzare

auto ['ɔːtəu] (US) n auto f inv

autobiography [ɔːtəbaɪ'ɔɡrəfɪ] n autobiografia

autograph ['ɔːtəɡrɑːf] n autografo ♦ vt firmare

automatic [ɔːtə'mætɪk] adj automatico(a) ♦ n (gun) arma automatica; (washing machine) lavatrice f automatica; (car) automobile f con cambio automatico; **~ally** adv automaticamente

automation [ɔːtə'meɪʃən] n automazione f

automobile ['ɔːtəməbiːl] (US) n automobile f

autonomy [ɔː'tɔnəmɪ] n autonomia

autumn ['ɔːtəm] n autunno

auxiliary [ɔːɡ'zɪlɪərɪ] adj ausiliario(a) ♦ n ausiliare m/f

Av. abbr = **avenue**

avail [ə'veɪl] vt: **to ~ o.s. of** servirsi di; approfittarsi di ♦ n: **to no ~** inutilmente

available [ə'veɪləbl] adj disponibile

avalanche ['ævəlɑːnʃ] n valanga

avant-garde ['ævɑ̃n'ɡɑːd] adj d'avanguardia

Ave. abbr = **avenue**

avenge [ə'vɛndʒ] vt vendicare

avenue ['ævənjuː] n viale m; (fig) strada, via

average ['ævərɪdʒ] n media ♦ adj medio(a)

♦ vt (a certain figure) fare di or in media; **on ~** in media; **~ out** vi: **to ~ out at** aggirarsi in media su, essere in media di

averse [ə'vɜːs] adj: **to be ~ to sth/doing** essere contrario(a) a qc/a fare

avert [ə'vɜːt] vt evitare, prevenire; (one's eyes) distogliere

aviary ['eɪvɪərɪ] n voliera, uccelliera

avid ['ævɪd] adj (supporter etc) accanito(a)

avocado [ævə'kɑːdəu] n (also: BRIT: **~ pear**) avocado m inv

avoid [ə'vɔɪd] vt evitare

await [ə'weɪt] vt aspettare

awake [ə'weɪk] (pt **awoke**, pp **awoken**, **awaked**) adj sveglio(a) ♦ vt svegliare ♦ vi svegliarsi; **~ning** [ə'weɪknɪŋ] n risveglio

award [ə'wɔːd] n premio; (LAW) risarcimento ♦ vt assegnare; (LAW: damages) accordare

aware [ə'wɛə*] adj: **~ of** (conscious) conscio(a) di; (informed) informato(a) di; **to become ~ of** accorgersi di; **~ness** n consapevolezza

away [ə'weɪ] adj, adv via; lontano(a); **two kilometres ~** a due chilometri di distanza; **two hours ~ by car** a due ore di distanza in macchina; **the holiday was two weeks ~** mancavano due settimane alle vacanze; **he's ~ for a week** è andato via per una settimana; **to take ~** togliere; **he was working/pedalling** etc **~** la particella indica la continuità e l'energia dell'azione: lavorava/pedalava etc più che poteva; **to fade/wither** etc **~** la particella rinforza l'idea della diminuzione; **~ game** n (SPORT) partita fuori casa

awe [ɔː] n timore m; **~-inspiring** imponente; **~some** adj imponente

awful ['ɔːfəl] adj terribile; **an ~ lot of** un mucchio di; **~ly** adv (very) terribilmente

awkward ['ɔːkwəd] adj (clumsy) goffo(a); (inconvenient) scomodo(a); (embarrassing) imbarazzante

awning ['ɔːnɪŋ] n (of shop, hotel etc) tenda

awoke [ə'wəuk] pt of **awake**

awoken [ə'wəukn] pp of **awake**

awry [ə'raɪ] adv di traverso

axe [æks] (US **ax**) n scure f ♦ vt (project etc)

abolire; (*jobs*) sopprimere
axes ['æksi:z] *npl of* **axis**
axis ['æksɪs] (*pl* **axes**) *n* asse *m*
axle ['æksl] *n* (*also:* **~-tree**) asse *m*
ay(e) [aɪ] *excl* (*yes*) sì

B, b

B [bi:] *n* (*MUS*) si *m*; (*letter*) B, b *f or m inv*;
~-road *n* (*BRIT: AUT*) strada secondaria
B.A. *n abbr* = **Bachelor of Arts**
baby ['beɪbɪ] *n* bambino/a; (*US*)
carrozzina; **~ food** *n* omogeneizzati
mpl; **~-sit** *vi* fare il (*or* la) baby-sitter; **~-
sitter** *n* baby-sitter *m/f inv*; **~-sitting** *n*:
to go ~-sitting fare il (*or* la) baby-sitter; **~
wipe** *n* salvietta umidificata
bachelor ['bætʃələˣ] *n* scapolo; **B~ of Arts/
Science** ≈ laureato/a in lettere/scienze
back [bæk] *n* (*of person, horse*) dorso,
schiena; (*as opposed to front*) dietro; (*of
hand*) dorso; (*of train*) coda; (*of chair*)
schienale *m*; (*of page*) rovescio; (*of book*)
retro; (*FOOTBALL*) difensore *m* ♦ *vt*
(*candidate: also:* **~ up**) appoggiare; (*horse:
at races*) puntare su; (*car*) guidare a marcia
indietro ♦ *vi* indietreggiare; (*car etc*) fare
marcia indietro ♦ *cpd* posteriore, di dietro;
(*AUT: seat, wheels*) posteriore ♦ *adv* (*not
forward*) indietro; (*returned*): **he's ~** è
tornato; **he ran ~** tornò indietro di corsa;
(*restitution*): **throw the ball ~** ritira la palla;
can I have it ~? posso riaverlo?; (*again*):
he called ~ ha richiamato; **~ down** *vi* fare
marcia indietro; **~ out** *vi* (*of promise*) tirarsi
indietro; **~ up** *vt* (*support*) appoggiare,
sostenere; (*COMPUT*) fare una copia di
riserva di; **~bencher** (*BRIT*) *n* membro del
Parlamento senza potere amministrativo;
~bone *n* spina dorsale; **~date** *vt* (*letter*)
retrodatare; **~dated pay rise** aumento
retroattivo; **~fire** *vi* (*AUT*) dar ritorni di
fiamma; (*plans*) fallire; **~ground** *n* sfondo;
(*of events*) background *m inv*; (*basic
knowledge*) base *f*; (*experience*) esperienza;
family ~ground ambiente *m* familiare;

~hand *n* (*TENNIS: also:* **~hand stroke**)
rovescio; **~handed** *adj* (*fig*) ambiguo(a);
~hander (*BRIT*) *n* (*bribe*) bustarella; **~ing**
n (*fig*) appoggio; **~lash** *n* contraccolpo,
ripercussione *f*; **~log** *n*: **~log of work**
lavoro arretrato; **~ number** *n* (*of
magazine etc*) numero arretrato; **~pack** *n*
zaino; **~packer** *n* chi viaggia con zaino e
sacco a pelo; **~ pay** *n* arretrato di paga; **~
payments** *npl* arretrati *mpl*; **~side** (*inf*) *n*
sedere *m*; **~stage** *adv* nel retroscena;
~stroke *n* nuoto sul dorso; **~up** *adj*
(*train, plane*) supplementare; (*COMPUT*) di
riserva ♦ *n* (*support*) appoggio, sostegno;
(*also:* **~up file**) file *m inv* di riserva; **~ward**
adj (*movement*) indietro *inv*; (*person*)
tardivo(a); (*country*) arretrato(a); **~wards**
adv indietro; (*fall, walk*) all'indietro; **~yard**
n cortile *m* dietro la casa
bacon ['beɪkən] *n* pancetta
bad [bæd] *adj* cattivo(a); (*accident, injury*)
brutto(a); (*meat, food*) andato(a) a male;
his ~ leg la sua gamba malata; **to go ~**
andare a male
badge [bædʒ] *n* insegna; (*of policeman*)
stemma *m*
badger ['bædʒəˣ] *n* tasso
badly ['bædlɪ] *adv* (*work, dress etc*) male; **~
wounded** gravemente ferito; **he needs it ~**
ne ha un gran bisogno; **~ off** *adj*
povero(a)
badminton ['bædmɪntən] *n* badminton *m*
bad-tempered ['bæd'tɛmpəd] *adj* irritabile;
di malumore
baffle ['bæfl] *vt* (*puzzle*) confondere
bag [bæg] *n* sacco; (*handbag etc*) borsa; **~s
of** (*inf: lots of*) un sacco di; **~gage** *n*
bagagli *mpl*; **~gage allowance** *n*
franchigia *f* bagaglio *inv*; **~gage reclaim**
n ritiro *m* bagaglio *inv*; **~gy** *adj* largo(a),
sformato(a); **~pipes** *npl* cornamusa
bail [beɪl] *n* cauzione *f* ♦ *vt* (*prisoner: also:*
grant ~ to) concedere la libertà provvisoria
su cauzione a; (*boat: also:* **~ out**) aggot-
tare; **on ~** in libertà provvisoria su cauzione;
~ out *vt* (*prisoner*) ottenere la libertà
provvisoria su cauzione di; *see also* **bale**

bailiff ['beɪlɪf] *n* (LAW: BRIT) ufficiale *m* giudiziario; (: US) usciere *m*

bait [beɪt] *n* esca ♦ *vt* (hook) innescare; (trap) munire di esca; (fig) tormentare

bake [beɪk] *vt* cuocere al forno ♦ *vi* cuocersi al forno; ~d **beans** *npl* fagioli *mpl* in salsa di pomodoro; ~d **potato** *npl* patata cotta al forno con la buccia; ~r *n* fornaio/a, panettiere/a; ~ry *n* panetteria; **baking** *n* cottura (al forno); **baking powder** *n* lievito in polvere

balance ['bæləns] *n* equilibrio; (COMM: sum) bilancio; (remainder) resto; (scales) bilancia ♦ *vt* tenere in equilibrio; (budget) far quadrare; (account) pareggiare; (compensate) contrappesare; ~ **of trade/ payments** bilancia commerciale/dei pagamenti; ~d *adj* (personality, diet) equilibrato(a); ~ **sheet** *n* bilancio

balcony ['bælkənɪ] *n* balcone *m*; (in theatre) balconata

bald [bɔːld] *adj* calvo(a); (tyre) liscio(a)

bale [beɪl] *n* balla; ~ **out** *vi* (of a plane) gettarsi col paracadute

ball [bɔːl] *n* palla; (football) pallone *m*; (for golf) pallina; (of wool, string) gomitolo; (dance) ballo; **to play** ~ (fig) stare al gioco

ballast ['bæləst] *n* zavorra

ball bearings *npl* cuscinetti a sfere

ballerina [bælə'riːnə] *n* ballerina

ballet ['bæleɪ] *n* balletto; ~ **dancer** *n* ballerino/a classico/a

balloon [bə'luːn] *n* pallone *m*

ballot paper ['bælət-] *n* scheda

ball-point pen *n* penna a sfera

ballroom ['bɔːlrum] *n* sala da ballo

balm [bɑːm] *n* balsamo

ban [bæn] *n* interdizione *f* ♦ *vt* interdire

banana [bə'nɑːnə] *n* banana

band [bænd] *n* banda; (at a dance) orchestra; (MIL) fanfara; ~ **together** *vi* collegarsi

bandage ['bændɪdʒ] *n* benda, fascia

Bandaid ® ['bændeɪd] (US) *n* cerotto

bandy-legged [-'legɪd] *adj* dalle gambe storte

bang [bæŋ] *n* (of door) lo sbattere; (of gun, blow) colpo ♦ *vt* battere (violentemente); (door) sbattere ♦ *vi* scoppiare; sbattere

Bangladesh [bæŋglə'deʃ] *n* Bangladesh *m*

bangle ['bæŋgl] *n* braccialetto

bangs [bæŋz] (US) *npl* (fringe) frangia, frangetta

banish ['bænɪʃ] *vt* bandire

banister(s) ['bænɪstə(z)] *n(pl)* ringhiera

bank [bæŋk] *n* banca, banco; (of river, lake) riva, sponda; (of earth) banco ♦ *vi* (AVIAT) inclinarsi in virata; ~ **on** *vt fus* contare su; ~ **account** *n* conto in banca; ~ **card** *n* carta *f* assegni *inv*; ~er *n* banchiere *m*; ~er's **card** (BRIT) *n* = **bank card**; **B~ holiday** (BRIT) *n* giorno di festa; ~ing *n* attività bancaria; professione *f* di banchiere; ~note *n* banconota; ~ **rate** *n* tasso bancario

---

bank holiday

ⓘ *Una* **bank holiday***, in Gran Bretagna, è una giornata in cui banche e negozi sono chiusi. Generalmente le* **bank holiday** *cadono di lunedì e molti ne approfittano per fare una breve vacanza fuori città.*

---

bankrupt ['bæŋkrʌpt] *adj* fallito(a); **to go** ~ fallire; ~cy *n* fallimento

bank statement *n* estratto conto

banner ['bænə*] *n* striscione *m*

baptism ['bæptɪzəm] *n* battesimo

bar [bɑː*] *n* (place) bar *m inv*; (counter) banco; (rod) barra; (of window etc) sbarra; (of chocolate) tavoletta; (fig) ostacolo; restrizione *f*; (MUS) battuta ♦ *vt* (road, window) sbarrare; (person) escludere; (activity) interdire; ~ **of soap** saponetta; **the B~** (LAW) l'Ordine *m* degli avvocati; **behind** ~s (prisoner) dietro le sbarre; ~ **none** senza eccezione

barbaric [bɑː'bærɪk] *adj* barbarico(a)

barbecue ['bɑːbɪkjuː] *n* barbecue *m inv*

barbed wire ['bɑːbd-] *n* filo spinato

barber ['bɑːbə*] *n* barbiere *m*

bar code *n* (on goods) codice *m* a barre

bare [bɛə*] *adj* nudo(a) ♦ *vt* scoprire,

denudare; (*teeth*) mostrare; **the ~ necessities** lo stretto necessario; **~back** *adv* senza sella; **~faced** *adj* sfacciato(a); **~foot** *adj, adv* scalzo(a); **~ly** *adv* appena

bargain ['bɑ:gɪn] *n* (*transaction*) contratto; (*good buy*) affare *m* ♦ *vi* trattare; **into the ~** per giunta; **~ for** *vt fus*: **he got more than he ~ed for** gli è andata peggio di quel che si aspettasse

barge [bɑ:dʒ] *n* chiatta; **~ in** *vi* (*walk in*) piombare dentro; (*interrupt talk*) intromettersi a sproposito

bark [bɑ:k] *n* (*of tree*) corteccia; (*of dog*) abbaio ♦ *vi* abbaiare

barley ['bɑ:lɪ] *n* orzo

barmaid ['bɑ:meɪd] *n* cameriera al banco

barman ['bɑ:mən] *n* barista *m*

bar meal *n* spuntino servito al bar

barn [bɑ:n] *n* granaio

barometer [bə'rɔmɪtə*] *n* barometro

baron ['bærən] *n* barone *m*; **~ess** *n* baronessa

barracks ['bærəks] *npl* caserma

barrage ['bærɑ:ʒ] *n* (*MIL, dam*) sbarramento; (*fig*) fiume *m*

barrel ['bærəl] *n* barile *m*; (*of gun*) canna

barren ['bærən] *adj* sterile; (*soil*) arido(a)

barricade [bærɪ'keɪd] *n* barricata

barrier ['bærɪə*] *n* barriera

barring ['bɑ:rɪŋ] *prep* salvo

barrister ['bærɪstə*] (*BRIT*) *n* avvocato/essa (*con diritto di parlare davanti a tutte le corti*)

barrow ['bærəʊ] *n* (*cart*) carriola

bartender ['bɑ:tendə*] (*US*) *n* barista *m*

barter ['bɑ:tə*] *vt*: **to ~ sth for** barattare qc con

base [beɪs] *n* base *f* ♦ *vt*: **to ~ sth on** basare qc su ♦ *adj* vile

baseball ['beɪsbɔ:l] *n* baseball *m*

basement ['beɪsmənt] *n* seminterrato; (*of shop*) interrato

bases[1] ['beɪsi:z] *npl of* **basis**

bases[2] ['beɪsɪz] *npl of* **base**

bash [bæʃ] (*inf*) *vt* picchiare

bashful ['bæʃful] *adj* timido(a)

basic ['beɪsɪk] *adj* rudimentale; essenziale; **~ally** [-lɪ] *adv* fondamentalmente;

sostanzialmente; **~s** *npl*: **the ~s** l'essenziale *m*

basil ['bæzl] *n* basilico

basin ['beɪsn] *n* (*vessel, also GEO*) bacino; (*also:* **wash~**) lavabo

basis ['beɪsɪs] (*pl* **bases**) *n* base *f*; **on a part-time** ~ part-time; **on a trial** ~ in prova

bask [bɑ:sk] *vi*: **to ~ in the sun** crogiolarsi al sole

basket ['bɑ:skɪt] *n* cesta; (*smaller*) cestino; (*with handle*) paniere *m*; **~ball** *n* pallacanestro *f*

bass [beɪs] *n* (*MUS*) basso

bassoon [bə'su:n] *n* fagotto

bastard ['bɑ:stəd] *n* bastardo/a; (*inf!*) stronzo (*!*)

bat [bæt] *n* pipistrello; (*for baseball etc*) mazza; (*BRIT: for table tennis*) racchetta ♦ *vt*: **he didn't ~ an eyelid** non batté ciglio

batch [bætʃ] *n* (*of bread*) infornata; (*of papers*) cumulo

bated ['beɪtɪd] *adj*: **with ~ breath** col fiato sospeso

bath [bɑ:θ] *n* bagno; (*bathtub*) vasca da bagno ♦ *vt* far fare il bagno a; **to have a** ~ fare un bagno; *see also* **baths**

bathe [beɪð] *vi* fare il bagno ♦ *vt* (*wound*) lavare; **~r** *n* bagnante *m/f*

bathing ['beɪðɪŋ] *n* bagni *mpl*; ~ **costume** (*US* ~ **suit**) *n* costume *m* da bagno

bathrobe ['bɑ:θrəʊb] *n* accappatoio

bathroom ['bɑ:θrʊm] *n* stanza da bagno

baths [bɑ:ðz] *npl* bagni *mpl* pubblici

bath towel *n* asciugamano da bagno

baton ['bætən] *n* (*MUS*) bacchetta; (*ATHLETICS*) testimone *m*; (*club*) manganello

batter ['bætə*] *vt* battere ♦ *n* pastetta; **~ed** *adj* (*hat*) sformato(a); (*pan*) ammaccato(a)

battery ['bætərɪ] *n* batteria; (*of torch*) pila; ~ **farming** *n* allevamento in batteria

battle ['bætl] *n* battaglia ♦ *vi* battagliare, lottare; **~field** *n* campo di battaglia; **~ship** *n* nave *f* da guerra

bawl [bɔ:l] *vi* urlare

bay [beɪ] *n* (*of sea*) baia; **to hold sb at** ~ tenere qn a bada; ~ **leaf** *n* foglia d'alloro;

~ **window** n bovindo
bazaar [bə'zɑː:*] n bazar m inv; vendita di beneficenza
B. & B. abbr = **bed and breakfast**
BBC n abbr (= British Broadcasting Corporation) rete nazionale di radiotelevisione in Gran Bretagna
B.C. adv abbr (= before Christ) a.C.

KEYWORD

be [biː] (pt **was, were**, pp **been**) aux vb
1 (with present participle: forming continuous tenses): **what are you doing?** che fa?, che fai facendo?; **they're coming tomorrow** vengono domani; **I've been waiting for her for hours** sono ore che l'aspetto
2 (with pp: forming passives) essere; **to ~ killed** essere or venire ucciso(a); **the box had been opened** la scatola era stata aperta; **the thief was nowhere to ~ seen** il ladro non si trovava da nessuna parte
3 (in tag questions): **it was fun, wasn't it?** è stato divertente, no?; **he's good-looking, isn't he?** è un bell'uomo, vero?; **she's back, is she?** così è tornata, eh?
4 (+to +infinitive): **the house is to ~ sold** abbiamo (or hanno etc) intenzione di vendere casa; **you're to ~ congratulated for all your work** dovremo farvi i complimenti per tutto il vostro lavoro; **he's not to open it** non deve aprirlo

♦ vb +complement **1** (gen) essere; **I'm English** sono inglese; **I'm tired** sono stanco(a); **I'm hot/cold** ho caldo/freddo; **he's a doctor** è medico; **2 and 2 are 4** 2 più 2 fa 4; **~ careful!** sta attento(a)!; **~ good** sii buono(a)
2 (of health) stare; **how are you?** come sta?; **he's very ill** sta molto male
3 (of age): **how old are you?** quanti anni hai?; **I'm sixteen (years old)** ho sedici anni
4 (cost) costare; **how much was the meal?** quant'era or quanto costava il pranzo?; **that'll ~ £5, please** (fa) 5 sterline, per favore

♦ vi **1** (exist, occur etc) essere, esistere; **the**

best singer that ever was il migliore cantante mai esistito or di tutti tempi; **~ that as it may** comunque sia, sia come sia; **so ~ it** sia pure, e sia
2 (referring to place) essere, trovarsi; **I won't ~ here tomorrow** non ci sarò domani; **Edinburgh is in Scotland** Edimburgo si trova in Scozia
3 (referring to movement): **where have you been?** dov'è stato?; **I've been to China** sono stato in Cina

♦ impers vb **1** (referring to time, distance) essere; **it's 5 o'clock** sono le 5; **it's the 28th of April** è il 28 aprile; **it's 10 km to the village** di qui al paese sono 10 km
2 (referring to the weather) fare; **it's too hot/cold** fa troppo caldo/freddo; **it's windy** c'è vento
3 (emphatic): **it's me** sono io; **it was Maria who paid the bill** è stata Maria che ha pagato il conto

beach [biːtʃ] n spiaggia ♦ vt tirare in secco
beacon ['biːkən] n (lighthouse) faro; (marker) segnale m
bead [biːd] n perlina
beak [biːk] n becco
beaker ['biːkə*] n coppa
beam [biːm] n trave f; (of light) raggio ♦ vi brillare
bean [biːn] n fagiolo; (of coffee) chicco; **runner ~** fagiolino; **broad ~** fava; **~sprouts** npl germogli mpl di soia
bear [bɛə*] (pt **bore**, pp **borne**) n orso ♦ vt portare; (endure) sopportare; (produce) generare ♦ vi: **to ~ right/left** piegare a destra/sinistra; **~ out** vt (suspicions) confermare, convalidare; (person) dare il proprio appoggio a; **~ up** vi (person) fare buon viso a cattiva sorte
beard [bɪəd] n barba
bearer ['bɛərə*] n portatore m
bearing ['bɛərɪŋ] n portamento; (connection) rapporto; **~s** npl (also: **ball ~s**) cuscinetti mpl a sfere; **to take a ~** fare un rilevamento; **to find one's ~s** orientarsi
beast [biːst] n bestia; **~ly** adj meschino(a);

(*weather*) da cani

beat [biːt] (*pt* **beat**, *pp* **beaten**) *n* colpo; (*of heart*) battito; (*MUS*) tempo; battuta; (*of policeman*) giro ♦ *vt* battere; (*eggs, cream*) sbattere ♦ *vi* battere; **off the ~en track** fuori mano; **~ it!** (*inf*) fila!, fuori dai piedi!; **~ off** *vt* respingere; **~ up** *vt* (*person*) picchiare; (*eggs*) sbattere; **beaten** *pp of* **beat**; **~ing** *n* bastonata

beautiful [ˈbjuːtɪful] *adj* bello(a); **~ly** *adv* splendidamente

beauty [ˈbjuːtɪ] *n* bellezza; **~ salon** *n* istituto di bellezza; **~ spot** (*BRIT*) *n* (*TOURISM*) luogo pittoresco

beaver [ˈbiːvə*] *n* castoro

became [bɪˈkeɪm] *pt of* **become**

because [bɪˈkɔz] *conj* perché; **~ of** a causa di

beckon [ˈbɛkən] *vt* (*also*: **~ to**) chiamare con un cenno

become [bɪˈkʌm] (*irreg: like* **come**) *vt* diventare; **to ~ fat/thin** ingrassarsi/dimagrire

becoming [bɪˈkʌmɪn] *adj* (*behaviour*) che si conviene; (*clothes*) grazioso(a)

bed [bɛd] *n* letto; (*of flowers*) aiuola; (*of coal, clay*) strato; **single/double ~** letto a una piazza/a due piazze *or* matrimoniale; **~ and breakfast** *n* (*place*) ≈ pensione *f* familiare; (*terms*) camera con colazione; **~clothes** [ˈbɛdkləʊðz] *npl* biancheria e coperte *fpl* da letto; **~ding** *n* coperte e lenzuola *fpl*

---
bed and breakfast

I bed and breakfast, *anche* B & B, sono piccole pensioni a conduzione familiare, più economiche rispetto agli alberghi, dove al mattino viene servita la tradizionale colazione all'inglese.

---

bed linen *n* biancheria da letto

bedraggled [bɪˈdræɡld] *adj* fradicio(a)

bed: **~ridden** *adj* costretto(a) a letto; **~room** *n* camera da letto; **~side** *n*: **at sb's ~side** al capezzale di qn; **~sit(ter)** (*BRIT*) *n* monolocale *m*; **~spread** *n*

copriletto; **~time** *n*: **it's ~time** è ora di andare a letto

bee [biː] *n* ape *f*

beech [biːtʃ] *n* faggio

beef [biːf] *n* manzo; **roast ~** arrosto di manzo; **~burger** *n* hamburger *m inv*; **B~eater** *n* guardia della Torre di Londra

beehive [ˈbiːhaɪv] *n* alveare *m*

beeline [ˈbiːlaɪn] *n*: **to make a ~ for** buttarsi a capo fitto verso

been [biːn] *pp of* **be**

beer [bɪə*] *n* birra

beetle [ˈbiːtl] *n* scarafaggio; coleottero

beetroot [ˈbiːtruːt] (*BRIT*) *n* barbabietola

before [bɪˈfɔː*] *prep* (*in time*) prima di; (*in space*) davanti a ♦ *conj* prima che +*sub*; prima di ♦ *adv* prima; **~ going** prima di andare; **~ she goes** prima che vada; **the week ~** la settimana prima; **I've seen it ~** l'ho già visto; **I've never seen it ~** è la prima volta che lo vedo; **~hand** *adv* in anticipo

beg [bɛɡ] *vi* chiedere l'elemosina ♦ *vt* (*also*: **~ for**) chiedere in elemosina; (*: favour*) chiedere; **to ~ sb to do** pregare qn di fare

began [bɪˈɡæn] *pt of* **begin**

beggar [ˈbɛɡə*] *n* mendicante *m/f*

begin [bɪˈɡɪn] (*pt* **began**, *pp* **begun**) *vt*, *vi* cominciare; **to ~ doing** *or* **to do sth** incominciare *or* iniziare a fare qc; **~ner** *n* principiante *m/f*; **~ning** *n* inizio, principio

begun [bɪˈɡʌn] *pp of* **begin**

behalf [bɪˈhɑːf] *n*: **on ~ of** per conto di; a nome di

behave [bɪˈheɪv] *vi* comportarsi; (*well*: *also*: **~ o.s.**) comportarsi bene

behaviour [bɪˈheɪvjə*] (*US* **behavior**) *n* comportamento, condotta

behind [bɪˈhaɪnd] *prep* dietro; (*followed by pronoun*) dietro di; (*time*) in ritardo con ♦ *adv* dietro, indietro ♦ *n* didietro; **to be ~ (schedule)** essere in ritardo rispetto al programma; **~ the scenes** (*fig*) dietro le quinte

behold [bɪˈhəʊld] (*irreg: like* **hold**) *vt* vedere, scorgere

beige [beɪʒ] *adj* beige *inv*

Beijing ['beɪ'dʒɪŋ] *n* Pechino *f*

being ['biːɪŋ] *n* essere *m*

Beirut [beɪ'ruːt] *n* Beirut *f*

Belarus [belə'rus] *n* Bielorussia *f*

belated [bɪ'leɪtɪd] *adj* tardo(a)

belch [beltʃ] *vi* ruttare ♦ *vt* (*gen*: ~ **out**: *smoke etc*) eruttare

Belgian ['beldʒən] *adj*, *n* belga *m/f*

Belgium ['beldʒəm] *n* Belgio *m*

belie [bɪ'laɪ] *vt* smentire

belief [bɪ'liːf] *n* (*opinion*) opinione *f*, convinzione *f*; (*trust, faith*) fede *f*

believe [bɪ'liːv] *vt*, *vi* credere; **to ~ in** (*God*) credere in; (*ghosts*) credere a; (*method*) avere fiducia in; **~r** *n* (*REL*) credente *m/f*; (*in idea, activity*): **to be a ~r in** credere in

belittle [bɪ'lɪtl] *vt* sminuire

bell [bel] *n* campana; (*small, on door, electric*) campanello

belligerent [bɪ'lɪdʒərənt] *adj* bellicoso(a)

bellow ['beləʊ] *vi* muggire

bellows ['beləʊz] *npl* soffietto

belly ['belɪ] *n* pancia

belong [bɪ'lɔŋ] *vi*: **to ~ to** appartenere a; (*club etc*) essere socio di; **this book ~s here** questo libro va qui; **~ings** *npl* cose *fpl*, roba

beloved [bɪ'lʌvɪd] *adj* adorato(a)

below [bɪ'ləʊ] *prep* sotto, al di sotto di ♦ *adv* sotto, di sotto; giù; **see ~** vedi sotto *or* oltre

belt [belt] *n* cintura; (*TECH*) cinghia ♦ *vt* (*thrash*) picchiare ♦ *vi* (*inf*) filarsela; **~way** (*US*) *n* (*AUT*: *ring road*) circonvallazione *f*; (: *motorway*) autostrada

bemused [bɪ'mjuːzd] *adj* perplesso(a), stupito(a)

bench [bentʃ] *n* panca; (*in workshop, POL*) banco; **the B~** (*LAW*) la Corte

bend [bend] (*pt, pp* **bent**) *vt* curvare; (*leg, arm*) piegare ♦ *vi* curvarsi; piegarsi ♦ *n* (*BRIT*: *in road*) curva; (*in pipe, river*) gomito; **~ down** *vi* chinarsi; **~ over** *vi* piegarsi

beneath [bɪ'niːθ] *prep* sotto, al di sotto di; (*unworthy of*) indegno(a) di ♦ *adv* sotto, di sotto

benefactor ['benɪfæktə*] *n* benefattore *m*

beneficial [benɪ'fɪʃəl] *adj* che fa bene; vantaggioso(a)

benefit ['benɪfɪt] *n* beneficio, vantaggio; (*allowance of money*) indennità *f inv* ♦ *vt* far bene a ♦ *vi*: **he'll ~ from it** ne trarrà beneficio *or* profitto

benevolent [bɪ'nevələnt] *adj* benevolo(a)

benign [bɪ'naɪn] *adj* (*person, smile*) benevolo(a); (*MED*) benigno(a)

bent [bent] *pt, pp of* **bend** ♦ *n* inclinazione *f* ♦ *adj* (*inf*: *dishonest*) losco(a); **to be ~ on** essere deciso(a) a

bequest [bɪ'kwest] *n* lascito

bereaved [bɪ'riːvd] *n*: **the ~** i familiari in lutto

beret ['bereɪ] *n* berretto

Berlin [bəː'lɪn] *n* Berlino *f*

berm [bəːm] (*US*) *n* (*AUT*) corsia d'emergenza

berry ['berɪ] *n* bacca

berserk [bə'səːk] *adj*: **to go ~** montare su tutte le furie

berth [bəːθ] *n* (*bed*) cuccetta; (*for ship*) ormeggio ♦ *vi* (*in harbour*) entrare in porto; (*at anchor*) gettare l'ancora

beseech [bɪ'siːtʃ] (*pt, pp* **besought**) *vt* implorare

beset [bɪ'set] (*pt, pp* **beset**) *vt* assalire

beside [bɪ'saɪd] *prep* accanto a; **to be ~ o.s. (with anger)** essere fuori di sé (dalla rabbia); **that's ~ the point** non c'entra

besides [bɪ'saɪdz] *adv* inoltre, per di più ♦ *prep* oltre a; a parte

besiege [bɪ'siːdʒ] *vt* (*town*) assediare; (*fig*) tempestare

best [best] *adj* migliore ♦ *adv* meglio; **the ~ part of** (*quantity*) la maggior parte di; **at ~** tutt'al più; **to make the ~ of sth** cavare il meglio possibile da qc; **to do one's ~** fare del proprio meglio; **to the ~ of my knowledge** per quel che ne so; **to the ~ of my ability** al massimo delle mie capacità; **~-before date** *n* scadenza; **~ man** *n* testimone *m* dello sposo

bestow [bɪ'stəʊ] *vt* accordare; (*title*) conferire

bet [bet] (*pt, pp* **bet** *or* **betted**) *n* scommessa ♦ *vt*, *vi* scommettere; **to ~ sb sth**

scommettere qc con qn

betray [bɪˈtreɪ] *vt* tradire; **~al** *n* tradimento
better [ˈbetə*] *adj* migliore ♦ *adv* meglio ♦ *vt* migliorare ♦ *n*: **to get the ~ of** avere la meglio su; **you had ~ do it** è meglio che lo faccia; **he thought ~ of it** cambiò idea; **to get ~** migliorare; **~ off** *adj* più ricco(a); *(fig)*: **you'd be ~ off this way** starebbe meglio così
betting [ˈbetɪŋ] *n* scommesse *fpl*; **~ shop** *(BRIT)* *n* ufficio dell'allibratore
between [bɪˈtwiːn] *prep* tra ♦ *adv* in mezzo, nel mezzo
beverage [ˈbevərɪdʒ] *n* bevanda
beware [bɪˈweə*] *vt, vi*: **to ~ (of)** stare attento(a) (a); **"~ of the dog"** "attenti al cane"
bewildered [bɪˈwɪldəd] *adj* sconcertato(a), confuso(a)
beyond [bɪˈjɒnd] *prep (in space)* oltre; *(exceeding)* al di sopra di ♦ *adv* di là; **~ doubt** senza dubbio; **~ repair** irreparabile
bias [ˈbaɪəs] *n (prejudice)* pregiudizio; *(preference)* preferenza; **~(s)ed** *adj* parziale
bib [bɪb] *n* bavaglino
Bible [ˈbaɪbl] *n* Bibbia
bicarbonate of soda [baɪˈkɑːbənɪt-] *n* bicarbonato (di sodio)
bicker [ˈbɪkə*] *vi* bisticciare
bicycle [ˈbaɪsɪkl] *n* bicicletta
bid [bɪd] *(pt* **bade** *or* **bid**, *pp* **bidden** *or* **bid)** *n* offerta; *(attempt)* tentativo ♦ *vi* fare un'offerta ♦ *vt* fare un'offerta di; **to ~ sb good day** dire buon giorno a qn; **bidden** *pp of* **bid**; **~der** *n*: **the highest ~der** il maggior offerente; **~ding** *n* offerte *fpl*
bide [baɪd] *vt*: **to ~ one's time** aspettare il momento giusto
bifocals [baɪˈfəuklz] *npl* occhiali *mpl* bifocali
big [bɪg] *adj* grande; grosso(a)
big dipper [-ˈdɪpə*] *n* montagne *fpl* russe, otto *m inv* volante
bigheaded [ˈbɪgˈhedɪd] *adj* presuntuoso(a)
bigot [ˈbɪgət] *n* persona gretta; **~ed** *adj* gretto(a); **~ry** *n* grettezza
big top *n* tendone *m* del circo
bike [baɪk] *n* bici *f inv*

bikini [bɪˈkiːnɪ] *n* bikini *m inv*
bilingual [baɪˈlɪŋgwəl] *adj* bilingue
bill [bɪl] *n* conto; *(POL)* atto; *(US: banknote)* banconota; *(of bird)* becco; *(of show)* locandina; **"post no ~s"** "divieto di affissione"; **to fit** *or* **fill the ~** *(fig)* fare al caso; **~board** *n* tabellone *m*
billet [ˈbɪlɪt] *n* alloggio
billfold [ˈbɪlfəuld] *(US)* *n* portafoglio
billiards [ˈbɪljədz] *n* biliardo
billion [ˈbɪljən] *n (BRIT)* bilione *m*; *(US)* miliardo
bimbo [ˈbɪmbəu] *n (pej, col)* pollastrella, svampitella
bin [bɪn] *n (for coal, rubbish)* bidone *m*; *(for bread)* cassetta; *(dust~)* pattumiera; *(litter ~)* cestino
bind [baɪnd] *(pt, pp* **bound)** *vt* legare; *(oblige)* obbligare ♦ *n (inf)* scocciatura; **~ing** *adj (contract)* vincolante
binge [bɪndʒ] *(inf)* *n*: **to go on a ~** fare baldoria
bingo [ˈbɪŋgəu] *n* gioco simile alla tombola
binoculars [bɪˈnɔkjuləz] *npl* binocolo
bio... [baɪə*...] *prefix*: **~chemistry** *n* biochimica; **~degradable** *adj* biodegradabile; **~graphy** [baɪˈɔgrəfɪ] *n* biografia; **~logical** *adj* biologico(a); **~logy** [baɪˈɔlədʒɪ] *n* biologia
birch [bəːtʃ] *n* betulla
bird [bəːd] *n* uccello; *(BRIT: inf: girl)* bambola; **~'s eye view** *n* vista panoramica; **~ watcher** *n* ornitologo/a dilettante
Biro ® [ˈbaɪrəu] *n* biro ® *f inv*
birth [bəːθ] *n* nascita; **to give ~ to** partorire; **~ certificate** *n* certificato di nascita; **~ control** *n* controllo delle nascite; contraccezione *f*; **~day** *n* compleanno ♦ *cpd* di compleanno; **~ rate** *n* indice *m* di natalità
biscuit [ˈbɪskɪt] *(BRIT)* *n* biscotto
bisect [baɪˈsekt] *vt* tagliare in due (parti)
bishop [ˈbɪʃəp] *n* vescovo
bit [bɪt] *pt of* **bite** ♦ *n* pezzo; *(COMPUT)* bit *m inv*; *(of horse)* morso; **a ~ of** un po' di; **a ~ mad** un po' matto; **~ by ~** a poco a poco
bitch [bɪtʃ] *n (dog)* cagna; *(inf!)* vacca

bite [baɪt] (*pt* **bit**, *pp* **bitten**) *vt, vi* mordere; (*subj: insect*) pungere ♦ *n* morso; (*insect ~*) puntura; (*mouthful*) boccone *m*; **let's have a ~ (to eat)** mangiamo un boccone; **to ~ one's nails** mangiarsi le unghie; **bitten** [ˈbɪtn] *pp of* **bite**

bitter [ˈbɪtə*] *adj* amaro(a); (*wind, criticism*) pungente ♦ *n* (*BRIT: beer*) birra amara; **~ness** *n* amarezza; gusto amaro

black [blæk] *adj* nero(a) ♦ *n* nero; (*person*): **B~** negro/a ♦ *vt* (*BRIT: INDUSTRY*) boicottare; **to give sb a ~ eye** fare un occhio nero a qn; **in the ~** (*bank account*) in attivo; **~ and blue** *adj* tutto(a) pesto(a); **~berry** *n* mora; **~bird** *n* merlo; **~board** *n* lavagna; **~ coffee** *n* caffè *m inv* nero; **~currant** *n* ribes *m inv*; **~en** *vt* annerire; **~ ice** *n* strato trasparente di ghiaccio; **~leg** (*BRIT*) *n* crumiro; **~list** *n* lista nera; **~mail** *n* ricatto ♦ *vt* ricattare; **~ market** *n* mercato nero; **~out** *n* oscuramento; (*TV, RADIO*) interruzione *f* delle trasmissioni; (*fainting*) svenimento; **B~ Sea** *n*: **the B~ Sea** il Mar Nero; **~ sheep** *n* pecora nera; **~smith** *n* fabbro ferraio; **~ spot** *n* (*AUT*) luogo famigerato per gli incidenti; (*for unemployment etc*) zona critica

bladder [ˈblædə*] *n* vescica

blade [bleɪd] *n* lama; (*of oar*) pala; **~ of grass** filo d'erba

blame [bleɪm] *n* colpa ♦ *vt*: **to ~ sb/sth for sth** dare la colpa di qc a qn/qc; **who's to ~?** chi è colpevole?

bland [blænd] *adj* mite; (*taste*) blando(a)

blank [blæŋk] *adj* bianco(a); (*look*) distratto(a) ♦ *n* spazio vuoto; (*cartridge*) cartuccia a salve; **~ cheque** *n* assegno in bianco

blanket [ˈblæŋkɪt] *n* coperta

blare [blɛə*] *vi* strombettare

blasphemy [ˈblæsfɪmɪ] *n* bestemmia

blast [blɑːst] *n* (*of wind*) raffica; (*of bomb etc*) esplosione *f* ♦ *vt* far saltare; **~-off** *n* (*SPACE*) lancio

blatant [ˈbleɪtənt] *adj* flagrante

blaze [bleɪz] *n* (*fire*) incendio; (*fig*) vampata; splendore *m* ♦ *vi* (*fire*) ardere, fiammeggiare; (*guns*) sparare senza sosta; (*fig: eyes*) ardere ♦ *vt*: **to ~ a trail** (*fig*) tracciare una via nuova; **in a ~ of publicity** circondato da grande pubblicità

blazer [ˈbleɪzə*] *n* blazer *m inv*

bleach [bliːtʃ] *n* (*also:* **household ~**) varechina ♦ *vt* (*material*) candeggiare; **~ed** *adj* (*hair*) decolorato(a); **~ers** (*US*) *npl* (*SPORT*) posti *mpl* di gradinata

bleak [bliːk] *adj* tetro(a)

bleat [bliːt] *vi* belare

bled [bled] *pt, pp of* **bleed**

bleed [bliːd] (*pt, pp* **bled**) *vi* sanguinare; **my nose is ~ing** mi viene fuori sangue dal naso

bleeper [ˈbliːpə*] *n* (*device*) cicalino

blemish [ˈblemɪʃ] *n* macchia

blend [blend] *n* miscela ♦ *vt* mescolare ♦ *vi* (*colours etc: also:* **~ in**) armonizzare

bless [bles] (*pt, pp* **blessed** *or* **blest**) *vt* benedire; **~ you!** (*after sneeze*) salute!; **~ing** *n* benedizione *f*; fortuna; **blest** [blest] *pt, pp of* **bless**

blew [bluː] *pt of* **blow**

blight [blaɪt] *vt* (*hopes etc*) deludere; (*life*) rovinare

blimey [ˈblaɪmɪ] (*BRIT: inf*) *excl* accidenti!

blind [blaɪnd] *adj* cieco(a) ♦ *n* (*for window*) avvolgibile *m*; (*Venetian ~*) veneziana ♦ *vt* accecare; **the ~** *npl* i ciechi; **~ alley** *n* vicolo cieco; **~ corner** (*BRIT*) *n* svolta cieca; **~fold** *n* benda ♦ *adj, adv* bendato(a) ♦ *vt* bendare gli occhi a; **~ly** *adv* ciecamente; **~ness** *n* cecità; **~ spot** *n* (*AUT etc*) punto cieco; (*fig*) punto debole

blink [blɪŋk] *vi* battere gli occhi; (*light*) lampeggiare; **~ers** *npl* paraocchi *mpl*

bliss [blɪs] *n* estasi *f*

blister [ˈblɪstə*] *n* (*on skin*) vescica; (*on paintwork*) bolla ♦ *vi* (*paint*) coprirsi di bolle

blizzard [ˈblɪzəd] *n* bufera di neve

bloated [ˈbləʊtɪd] *adj* gonfio(a)

blob [blɒb] *n* (*drop*) goccia; (*stain, spot*) macchia

bloc [blɒk] *n* (*POL*) blocco

block [blɔk] *n* blocco; (*in pipes*) ingombro; (*toy*) cubo; (*of buildings*) isolato ♦ *vt* bloccare; ~**ade** [-'keɪd] *n* blocco; ~**age** *n* ostacolo; ~**buster** *n* (*film, book*) grande successo; ~ **letters** *npl* stampatello; ~ **of flats** (*BRIT*) *n* caseggiato.

bloke [bləuk] (*BRIT: inf*) *n* tizio

blond(e) [blɔnd] *adj, n* biondo(a)

blood [blʌd] *n* sangue *m*; ~ **donor** *n* donatore/trice di sangue; ~ **group** *n* gruppo sanguigno; ~**hound** *n* segugio; ~ **poisoning** *n* setticemia; ~ **pressure** *n* pressione *f* sanguigna; ~**shed** *n* spargimento di sangue; ~**shot** *adj*: ~**shot eyes** occhi iniettati di sangue; ~**stream** *n* flusso del sangue; ~ **test** *n* analisi *f inv* del sangue; ~**thirsty** *adj* assetato(a) di sangue; ~**y** *adj* (*fight*) sanguinoso(a); (*nose*) sanguinante; (*BRIT: inf!*): **this ~y ...** questo maledetto ...; ~**y awful/good** (*inf!*) veramente terribile/forte; ~**y-minded** (*BRIT: inf*) *adj* indisponente

bloom [blu:m] *n* fiore *m* ♦ *vi* (*tree*) essere in fiore; (*flower*) aprirsi

blossom ['blɔsəm] *n* fiore *m*; (*with pl sense*) fiori *mpl* ♦ *vi* essere in fiore

blot [blɔt] *n* macchia ♦ *vt* macchiare; ~ **out** *vt* (*memories*) cancellare; (*view*) nascondere

blotchy ['blɔtʃi] *adj* (*complexion*) coperto(a) di macchie

blotting paper ['blɔtɪŋ-] *n* carta assorbente

blouse [blauz] *n* (*feminine garment*) camicetta

blow [bləu] (*pt* **blew**, *pp* **blown**) *n* colpo ♦ *vi* soffiare ♦ *vt* (*fuse*) far saltare; (*subj: wind*) spingere; (*instrument*) suonare; **to ~ one's nose** soffiarsi il naso; **to ~ a whistle** fischiare; ~ **away** *vt* portare via; ~ **down** *vt* abbattere; ~ **off** *vt* far volare via; ~ **out** *vi* scoppiare; ~ **over** *vi* calmarsi; ~ **up** *vi* saltare in aria ♦ *vt* far saltare in aria; (*tyre*) gonfiare; (*PHOT*) ingrandire; ~-**dry** *n* messa in piega a föhn; ~**lamp** (*BRIT*) *n* lampada a benzina per saldare; **blown** *pp of* **blow**; ~-**out** *n* (*of tyre*) scoppio; ~**torch** *n* = ~**lamp**

blue [blu:] *adj* azzurro(a); (*depressed*) giù *inv*; ~ **film/joke** film/ barzelletta pornografico(a); **out of the ~** (*fig*) all'improvviso; ~**bell** *n* giacinto dei boschi; ~**bottle** *n* moscone *m*; ~**print** *n* (*fig*): ~**print (for)** formula (di)

bluff [blʌf] *vi* bluffare ♦ *n* bluff *m inv* ♦ *adj* (*person*) brusco(a); **to call sb's ~** mettere alla prova il bluff di qn

blunder ['blʌndə*] *n* abbaglio ♦ *vi* prendere un abbaglio

blunt [blʌnt] *adj* smussato(a); spuntato(a); (*person*) brusco(a)

blur [blə:*] *n* forma indistinta ♦ *vt* offuscare

blush [blʌʃ] *vi* arrossire ♦ *n* rossore *m*

blustering ['blʌstərɪŋ] *adj* infuriato(a)

blustery ['blʌstəri] *adj* (*weather*) burrascoso(a)

boar [bɔ:*] *n* cinghiale *m*

board [bɔ:d] *n* tavola; (*on wall*) tabellone *m*; (*committee*) consiglio, comitato; (*in firm*) consiglio d'amministrazione; (*NAUT, AVIAT*): **on ~** a bordo ♦ *vt* (*ship*) salire a bordo di; (*train*) salire su; **full ~** (*BRIT*) pensione completa; **half ~** (*BRIT*) mezza pensione; ~ **and lodging** vitto e alloggio; **which goes by the ~** (*fig*) che viene abbandonato; ~ **up** *vt* (*door*) chiudere con assi; ~**er** *n* (*SCOL*) convittore/trice; ~**ing card** *n* = ~**ing pass**; ~**ing house** *n* pensione *f*; ~**ing pass** *n* (*AVIAT, NAUT*) carta d'imbarco; ~**ing school** *n* collegio; ~ **room** *n* sala del consiglio

boast [bəust] *vi*: **to ~ (about or of)** vantarsi (di)

boat [bəut] *n* nave *f*; (*small*) barca; ~**swain** ['bəusn] *n* nostromo

bob [bɔb] *vi* (*boat, cork on water: also:* ~ **up and down**) andare su e giù; ~ **up** *vi* saltare fuori

bobby ['bɔbi] (*BRIT: inf*) *n* poliziotto

bobsleigh ['bɔbsleɪ] *n* bob *m inv*

bode [bəud] *vi*: **to ~ well/ill (for)** essere di buon/cattivo auspicio (per)

bodily ['bɔdɪli] *adj* fisico(a), corporale ♦ *adv* corporalmente; interamente; in persona

body ['bɔdi] *n* corpo; (*of car*) carrozzeria; (*of*

plane) fusoliera; (fig: group) gruppo;
(: organization) organizzazione f;
(: quantity) quantità f inv; ~-building n
culturismo; ~guard n guardia del corpo;
~work n carrozzeria

bog [bɔg] n palude f ♦ vt: to get ~ged
down (fig) impantanarsi

bogus ['bəʊgəs] adj falso(a); finto(a)

boil [bɔɪl] vt, vi bollire ♦ n (MED) foruncolo;
to come to the (BRIT) or a (US) ~
raggiungere l'ebollizione; ~ down to vt
fus (fig) ridursi a; ~ over vi traboccare
(bollendo); ~ed egg n uovo alla coque;
~ed potatoes npl patate fpl bollite or
lesse; ~er n caldaia; ~er suit (BRIT) n tuta;
~ing point n punto di ebollizione

boisterous ['bɔɪstərəs] adj chiassoso(a)

bold [bəʊld] adj audace; (child) impudente;
(colour) deciso(a)

bollard ['bɔləd] (BRIT) n (AUT) colonnina
luminosa

bolt [bəʊlt] n chiavistello; (with nut) bullone
m ♦ adv: ~ upright diritto(a) come un fuso
♦ vt serrare; (also: ~ together) imbullonare;
(food) mangiare in fretta ♦ vi scappare via

bomb [bɔm] n bomba ♦ vt bombardare

bombastic [bɔm'bæstɪk] adj magniloquente

bomb: ~ disposal unit n corpo degli
artificieri; ~er n (AVIAT) bombardiere m;
~shell n (fig) notizia bomba

bond [bɔnd] n legame m; (binding promise,
FINANCE) obbligazione f; (COMM): in ~ in
attesa di sdoganamento

bondage ['bɔndɪdʒ] n schiavitù f

bone [bəʊn] n osso; (of fish) spina, lisca ♦ vt
disossare; togliere le spine a; ~ idle adj
pigrissimo(a); ~ marrow n midollo osseo

bonfire ['bɔnfaɪə*] n falò m inv

bonnet ['bɔnɪt] n cuffia; (BRIT: of car) cofano

bonus ['bəʊnəs] n premio; (fig) sovrappiù m
inv

bony ['bəʊnɪ] adj (MED: tissue) osseo(a);
(arm, face) ossuto(a); (meat) pieno(a) di
ossi; (fish) pieno(a) di spine

boo [bu:] excl ba! ♦ vt fischiare

booby trap ['bu:bɪ-] n trappola

book [buk] n libro; (of stamps etc)
blocchetto ♦ vt (ticket, seat, room)
prenotare; (driver) multare; (football player)
ammonire; ~s npl (COMM) conti mpl;
~case n scaffale m; ~ing office (BRIT) n
(RAIL) biglietteria; (THEATRE) botteghino; ~-
keeping n contabilità; ~let n libricino; ~-
maker n allibratore m; ~seller n
libraio; ~shop, ~store n libreria

boom [bu:m] n (noise) rimbombo; (in prices
etc) boom m inv ♦ vi rimbombare; andare
a gonfie vele

boon [bu:n] n vantaggio

boost [bu:st] n spinta ♦ vt spingere; ~er n
(MED) richiamo

boot [bu:t] n stivale m; (for hiking) scarpone
m da montagna; (for football etc) scarpa;
(BRIT: of car) portabagagli m inv ♦ vt
(COMPUT) inizializzare; to ~ (in addition) per
giunta, in più

booth [bu:ð] n cabina; (at fair) baraccone m

booty ['bu:tɪ] n bottino

booze [bu:z] (inf) n alcool m

border ['bɔːdə*] n orlo; margine m; (of a
country) frontiera; (for flowers) aiuola
(laterale) ♦ vt (road) costeggiare; (another
country: also: ~ on) confinare con; the B~s
la zona di confine tra l'Inghilterra e la
Scozia; ~ on vt fus (fig: insanity etc)
sfiorare; ~line n frontiera; (fig): on the ~line
incerto(a); ~line case n caso incerto

bore [bɔː*] pt of bear ♦ vt (hole etc) scavare;
(person) annoiare ♦ n (person) seccatore/
trice; (of gun) calibro; to be ~d annoiarsi;
~dom n noia; boring adj noioso(a)

born [bɔːn] adj: to be ~ nascere; I was ~ in
1960 sono nato nel 1960

borne [bɔːn] pp of bear

borough ['bʌrə] n comune m

borrow ['bɔrəʊ] vt: to ~ sth (from sb)
prendere in prestito qc (da qn)

Bosnia(-Herzegovina) ['bɔznɪə-
(hɜːzə'gəʊvɪːnə)] n Bosnia-Erzegovina

Bosnian ['bɔznɪən] n, adj bosniaco(a) m/f

boss [bɔs] n capo ♦ vt comandare; ~y adj
prepotente

bosun ['bəʊsn] n nostromo

botany ['bɔtənɪ] n botanica

botch [bɔtʃ] vt (also: ~ **up**) fare un pasticcio di

both [bəuθ] adj entrambi(e), tutt'e due ♦ pron: ~ (**of them**) entrambi(e); ~ **of us went, we ~ went** ci siamo andati tutt'e due ♦ adv: **they sell ~ meat and poultry** vendono insieme la carne ed il pollame

bother ['bɔðə*] vt (worry) preoccupare; (annoy) infastidire ♦ vi (also: ~ **o.s.**) preoccuparsi ♦ n: **it is a ~ to have to do** è una seccatura dover fare; **it was no ~** non c'era problema; **to ~ doing sth** darsi la pena di fare qc

bottle ['bɔtl] n bottiglia; (baby's) biberon m inv ♦ vt imbottigliare; ~ **up** vt contenere; ~ **bank** n contenitore m per la raccolta del vetro; ~**neck** n imbottigliamento; ~-**opener** n apribottiglie m inv

bottom ['bɔtəm] n fondo; (buttocks) sedere m ♦ adj più basso(a); ultimo(a); **at the ~ of** in fondo a

bough [bau] n ramo

bought [bɔːt] pt, pp of **buy**

boulder ['bəuldə*] n masso (tondeggiante)

bounce [bauns] vi (ball) rimbalzare; (cheque) essere restituito(a) ♦ vt far rimbalzare ♦ n (rebound) rimbalzo; ~**r** (inf) n buttafuori m inv

bound [baund] pt, pp of **bind** ♦ n (gen pl) limite m; (leap) salto ♦ vi saltare ♦ vt (limit) delimitare ♦ adj: ~ **by law** obbligato(a) per legge; **to be ~ to do sth** (obliged) essere costretto(a) a fare qc; **he's ~ to fail** (likely) fallirà di certo; ~ **for** diretto(a) a; **out of ~s** il cui accesso è vietato

boundary ['baundri] n confine m

boundless ['baundlis] adj senza limiti

bourgeois ['buəʒwaː] adj borghese

bout [baut] n periodo; (of malaria etc) attacco; (BOXING etc) incontro

bow[1] [bəu] n nodo; (weapon) arco; (MUS) archetto

bow[2] [bau] n (with body) inchino; (NAUT: also: ~**s**) prua ♦ vi inchinarsi; (yield): **to ~ to** or **before** sottomettersi a

bowels ['bauəlz] npl intestini mpl; (fig) viscere fpl

bowl [bəul] n (for eating) scodella; (for washing) bacino; (ball) boccia ♦ vi (CRICKET) servire (la palla)

bow-legged ['bəu'legid] adj dalle gambe storte

bowler ['bəulə*] n (CRICKET, BASEBALL) lanciatore m; (BRIT: also: ~ **hat**) bombetta

bowling ['bəulɪŋ] n (game) gioco delle bocce; ~ **alley** n pista da bowling; ~ **green** n campo di bocce

bowls [bəulz] n gioco delle bocce

bow tie n cravatta a farfalla

box [bɔks] n scatola; (also: **cardboard ~**) cartone m; (THEATRE) palco ♦ vt inscatolare ♦ vi fare il pugilato; ~**er** n (person) pugile m; ~**ing** n (SPORT) pugilato; **B~ing Day** (BRIT) n ≈ Santo Stefano; ~**ing gloves** npl guantoni mpl da pugile; ~**ing ring** n ring m inv; ~ **office** n biglietteria; ~ **room** n ripostiglio

---

Boxing Day

ⓘ Il **Boxing Day** è il primo giorno infrasettimanale dopo Natale. Prende il nome dalla tradizionale usanza di donare pacchi regalo natalizi, un tempo chiamati "Christmas boxes", a fornitori e dipendenti.

---

boy [bɔɪ] n ragazzo

boycott ['bɔɪkɔt] n boicottaggio ♦ vt boicottare

boyfriend ['bɔɪfrend] n ragazzo

boyish ['bɔɪʃ] adj da ragazzo

B.R. abbr (formerly) = **British Rail**

bra [braː] n reggipetto, reggiseno

brace [breis] n (on teeth) apparecchio correttore; (tool) trapano ♦ vt rinforzare, sostenere; ~**s** (BRIT) npl (DRESS) bretelle fpl; **to ~ o.s.** (also fig) tenersi forte

bracelet ['breislit] n braccialetto

bracing ['breisiŋ] adj invigorante

bracken ['brækən] n felce f

bracket ['brækit] n (TECH) mensola; (group) gruppo; (TYP) parentesi f inv ♦ vt mettere fra parentesi

brag [bræg] vi vantarsi

braid [breid] n (trimming) passamano; (of

hair) treccia

brain [breɪn] *n* cervello; **~s** *npl* (*intelligence*) cervella *fpl*; **he's got ~s** è intelligente; **~wash** *vt* fare un lavaggio di cervello a; **~wave** *n* lampo di genio; **~y** *adj* intelligente

braise [breɪz] *vt* brasare

brake [breɪk] *n* (*on vehicle*) freno ♦ *vi* frenare; **~ fluid** *n* liquido dei freni; **~ light** *n* (fanalino dello) stop *m inv*

bramble ['bræmbl] *n* rovo

bran [bræn] *n* crusca

branch [brɑːntʃ] *n* ramo; (*COMM*) succursale *f*; **~ out** *vi* (*fig*) intraprendere una nuova attività

brand [brænd] *n* (*also:* **~ name**) marca; (*fig*) tipo ♦ *vt* (*cattle*) marcare (a ferro rovente)

brand-new *adj* nuovo(a) di zecca

brandy ['brændɪ] *n* brandy *m inv*

brash [bræʃ] *adj* sfacciato(a)

brass [brɑːs] *n* ottone *m*; **the ~** (*MUS*) gli ottoni; **~ band** *n* fanfara

brat [bræt] (*pej*) *n* marmocchio, monello/a

bravado [brə'vɑːdəu] *n* spavalderia

brave [breɪv] *adj* coraggioso(a) ♦ *vt* affrontare; **~ry** *n* coraggio

brawl [brɔːl] *n* rissa

brawny ['brɔːnɪ] *adj* muscoloso(a)

bray [breɪ] *vi* ragliare

brazen ['breɪzn] *adj* sfacciato(a) ♦ *vt*: **to ~ it out** fare lo sfacciato

brazier ['breɪzɪə*] *n* braciere *m*

Brazil [brə'zɪl] *n* Brasile *m*

breach [briːtʃ] *vt* aprire una breccia in ♦ *n* (*gap*) breccia, varco; (*breaking*): **~ of contract** rottura di contratto; **~ of the peace** violazione *f* dell'ordine pubblico

bread [bred] *n* pane *m*; **~ and butter** *n* pane e burro; (*fig*) mezzi *mpl* di sussistenza; **~bin** *n* cassetta *f* portapane *inv*; **~crumbs** *npl* briciole *fpl*; (*CULIN*) pangrattato; **~line** *n*: **to be on the ~line** avere appena il denaro per vivere

breadth [bretθ] *n* larghezza; (*fig: of knowledge etc*) ampiezza

breadwinner ['bredwɪnə*] *n* chi guadagna il pane per tutta la famiglia

break [breɪk] (*pt* **broke**, *pp* **broken**) *vt* rompere; (*law*) violare; (*record*) battere ♦ *vi* rompersi; (*storm*) scoppiare; (*weather*) cambiare; (*dawn*) spuntare; (*news*) saltare fuori ♦ *n* (*gap*) breccia; (*fracture*) rottura; (*rest, also SCOL*) intervallo; (: *short*) pausa; (*chance*) possibilità *f inv*; **to ~ one's leg** *etc* rompersi la gamba *etc*; **to ~ the news to sb** comunicare per primo la notizia a qn; **to ~ even** coprire le spese; **to ~ free** *or* **loose** spezzare i legami; **to ~ open** (*door etc*) sfondare; **~ down** *vt* (*figures, data*) analizzare ♦ *vi* (*person*) avere un esaurimento (nervoso); (*AUT*) guastarsi; **~ in** *vt* (*horse etc*) domare ♦ *vi* (*burglar*) fare irruzione; (*interrupt*) interrompere; **~ into** *vt fus* (*house*) fare irruzione in; **~ off** *vi* (*speaker*) interrompersi; (*branch*) troncarsi; **~ out** *vi* evadere; (*war, fight*) scoppiare; **to ~ out in spots** coprirsi di macchie; **~ up** *vi* (*ship*) sfondarsi; (*meeting*) sciogliersi; (*crowd*) disperdersi; (*marriage*) andare a pezzi; (*SCOL*) chiudere ♦ *vt* fare a pezzi, spaccare; (*fight etc*) interrompere, far cessare; **~age** *n* rottura; (*object broken*) cosa rotta; **~down** *n* (*AUT*) guasto; (*in communications*) interruzione *f*; (*of marriage*) rottura; (*MED: also:* **nervous ~down**) esaurimento nervoso; (*of statistics*) resoconto; **~down van** (*BRIT*) *n* carro *m* attrezzi *inv*; **~er** *n* frangente *m*

breakfast ['brekfəst] *n* colazione *f*

break: **~-in** *n* irruzione *f*; **~ing and entering** *n* (*LAW*) violazione *f* di domicilio con scasso; **~through** *n* (*fig*) passo avanti; **~water** *n* frangiflutti *m inv*

breast [brest] *n* (*of woman*) seno; (*chest, CULIN*) petto; **~-feed** (*irreg: like* **feed**) *vt, vi* allattare (al seno); **~-stroke** *n* nuoto a rana

breath [breθ] *n* respiro; **out of ~** senza fiato

Breathalyser ® ['breθəlaɪzə*] (*BRIT*) *n* alcoltest *m inv*

breathe [briːð] *vt, vi* respirare; **~ in** *vt* respirare ♦ *vi* inspirare; **~ out** *vt, vi* espirare; **~r** *n* attimo di respiro; **breathing** *n* respiro, respirazione *f*

breathless ['breθlɪs] *adj* senza fiato
breathtaking ['breθteɪkɪŋ] *adj* mozzafiato *inv*
bred [brɛd] *pt, pp of* **breed**
breed [briːd] (*pt, pp* **bred**) *vt* allevare ♦ *vi* riprodursi ♦ *n* razza; (*type, class*) varietà *f inv*; ~**ing** *n* riproduzione *f*; allevamento; (*upbringing*) educazione *f*
breeze [briːz] *n* brezza
breezy ['briːzɪ] *adj* allegro(a); ventilato(a)
brew [bruː] *vt* (*tea*) fare un infuso di; (*beer*) fare ♦ *vi* (*storm, fig: trouble etc*) prepararsi; ~**ery** *n* fabbrica di birra
bribe [braɪb] *n* bustarella ♦ *vt* comprare; ~**ry** *n* corruzione *f*
brick [brɪk] *n* mattone *m*; ~**layer** *n* muratore *m*
bridal ['braɪdl] *adj* nuziale
bride [braɪd] *n* sposa; ~**groom** *n* sposo; ~**smaid** *n* damigella d'onore
bridge [brɪdʒ] *n* ponte *m*; (*NAUT*) ponte di comando; (*of nose*) dorso; (*CARDS*) bridge *m inv* ♦ *vt* (*fig: gap*) colmare
bridle ['braɪdl] *n* briglia; ~ **path** *n* sentiero (per cavalli)
brief [briːf] *adj* breve ♦ *n* (*LAW*) comparsa; (*gen*) istruzioni *fpl* ♦ *vt* mettere al corrente; ~**s** *npl* (*underwear*) mutande *fpl*; ~**case** *n* cartella; ~**ing** *n* briefing *m inv*; ~**ly** *adv* (*glance*) di sfuggita; (*explain, say*) brevemente
bright [braɪt] *adj* luminoso(a); (*clever*) sveglio(a); (*lively*) vivace; ~**en** (*also*: ~**en up**) *vt* (*room*) rendere luminoso(a) ♦ *vi* schiarirsi; (*person*) rallegrarsi
brilliance ['brɪljəns] *n* splendore *m*
brilliant ['brɪljənt] *adj* brillante; (*light, smile*) radioso(a); (*inf*) splendido(a)
brim [brɪm] *n* orlo
brine [braɪn] *n* (*CULIN*) salamoia
bring [brɪŋ] (*pt, pp* **brought**) *vt* portare; ~ **about** *vt* causare; ~ **back** *vt* riportare; ~ **down** *vt* portare giù; abbattere; ~ **forward** *vt* (*proposal*) avanzare; (*meeting*) anticipare; ~ **off** *vt* (*task, plan*) portare a compimento; ~ **out** *vt* tirar fuori; (*meaning*) mettere in evidenza; (*book,*

album) far uscire; ~ **round** *vt* (*unconscious person*) far rinvenire; ~ **up** *vt* (*carry up*) portare su; (*child*) allevare; (*question*) introdurre; (*food: vomit*) rimettere, rigurgitare
brink [brɪŋk] *n* orlo
brisk [brɪsk] *adj* (*manner*) spiccio(a); (*trade*) vivace; (*pace*) svelto(a)
bristle ['brɪsl] *n* setola ♦ *vi* rizzarsi; **bristling with** irto(a) di
Britain ['brɪtən] *n* (*also*: **Great ~**) Gran Bretagna
British ['brɪtɪʃ] *adj* britannico(a); **the ~** *npl* i Britannici; **the ~ Isles** *npl* le Isole Britanniche; **~ Rail** *n* compagnia ferroviaria britannica, ≈ Ferrovie *fpl* dello Stato
Briton ['brɪtən] *n* britannico/a
brittle ['brɪtl] *adj* fragile
broach [brəutʃ] *vt* (*subject*) affrontare
broad [brɔːd] *adj* largo(a); (*distinction*) generale; (*accent*) spiccato(a); **in ~ daylight** in pieno giorno; ~**cast** (*pt, pp* ~**cast**) *n* trasmissione *f* ♦ *vt* trasmettere per radio (*or* per televisione) ♦ *vi* fare una trasmissione; ~**en** *vt* allargare ♦ *vi* allargarsi; ~**ly** *adv* (*fig*) in generale; ~**-minded** *adj* di mente aperta
broccoli ['brɔkəlɪ] *n* broccoli *mpl*
brochure ['brəuʃjuə*] *n* dépliant *m inv*
broil [brɔɪl] *vt* cuocere a fuoco vivo
broke [brəuk] *pt of* **break** ♦ *adj* (*inf*) squattrinato(a)
broken ['brəukn] *pp of* **break** ♦ *adj* rotto(a); **a ~ leg** una gamba rotta; **in ~ English** in un inglese stentato; ~**-hearted** *adj*: **to be ~-hearted** avere il cuore spezzato
broker ['brəukə*] *n* agente *m*
brolly ['brɔlɪ] (*BRIT: inf*) *n* ombrello
bronchitis [brɔŋ'kaɪtɪs] *n* bronchite *f*
bronze [brɔnz] *n* bronzo
brooch [brəutʃ] *n* spilla
brood [bruːd] *n* covata ♦ *vi* (*person*) rimuginare
brook [bruk] *n* ruscello
broom [brum] *n* scopa; (*BOT*) ginestra
Bros. *abbr* (= *Brothers*) F.lli

broth [brɔθ] n brodo
brothel ['brɔθl] n bordello
brother ['brʌðə*] n fratello; **~-in-law** n
cognato
brought [brɔːt] pt, pp of **bring**
brow [brau] n fronte f; (rare, gen: eye~)
sopracciglio; (of hill) cima
brown [braun] adj bruno(a), marrone;
(tanned) abbronzato(a) ♦ n (colour) color m
bruno or marrone ♦ vt (CULIN) rosolare; ~
bread n pane m integrale, pane nero
Brownie ['brauni] n giovane esploratrice f;
b~ (US: cake) dolce al cioccolato e nocciole
brown paper n carta da pacchi or da
imballaggio
brown sugar n zucchero greggio
browse [brauz] vi (among books) curiosare
fra i libri; **to ~ through a book** sfogliare un
libro; **~r** n (COMPUT) browser m inv
bruise [bruːz] n (on person) livido ♦ vt farsi
un livido a
brunette [bruː'nɛt] n bruna
brunt [brʌnt] n: **the ~ of** (attack, criticism
etc) il peso maggiore di
brush [brʌʃ] n spazzola; (for painting,
shaving) pennello; (quarrel) schermaglia
♦ vt spazzolare; (also: ~ **against**) sfiorare; ~
aside vt scostare; ~ **up** vt (knowledge)
rinfrescare; **~wood** n macchia
Brussels ['brʌslz] n Bruxelles f; ~ **sprout** n
cavolo di Bruxelles
brutal ['bruːtl] adj brutale
brute [bruːt] n bestia ♦ adj: **by ~ force** con
la forza, a viva forza
B.Sc. n abbr (UNIV) = **Bachelor of Science**
BSE n abbr (= bovine spongiform
encephalopathy) encefalite f bovina
spongiforme
BTW abbr a proposito
bubble ['bʌbl] n bolla ♦ vi ribollire; (sparkle,
fig) essere effervescente; ~ **bath** n
bagnoschiuma m inv; ~ **gum** n gomma
americana
buck [bʌk] n maschio (di camoscio, caprone,
coniglio etc); (US: inf) dollaro ♦ vi
sgroppare; **to pass the ~ (to sb)** scaricare
(su di qn) la propria responsabilità; ~ **up** vi

(cheer up) rianimarsi
bucket ['bʌkɪt] n secchio

Buckingham Palace

ⓘ **Buckingham Palace** è la residenza
ufficiale a Londra del sovrano
britannico. Fu costruita nel 1703 per il duca
di Buckingham.

---

buckle ['bʌkl] n fibbia ♦ vt allacciare ♦ vi
(wheel etc) piegarsi
bud [bʌd] n gemma; (of flower) bocciolo
♦ vi germogliare; (flower) sbocciare
Buddhism ['budɪzəm] n buddismo
budding ['bʌdɪŋ] adj (poet etc) in erba
buddy ['bʌdɪ] (US) n compagno
budge [bʌdʒ] vt scostare; (fig) smuovere
♦ vi spostarsi; smuoversi
budgerigar ['bʌdʒərɪgɑː*] n pappagallino
budget ['bʌdʒɪt] n bilancio preventivo ♦ vi:
to ~ for sth fare il bilancio per qc
budgie ['bʌdʒɪ] n = **budgerigar**
buff [bʌf] adj color camoscio ♦ n (inf:
enthusiast) appassionato/a
buffalo ['bʌfələu] (pl ~ or ~es) n bufalo;
(US) bisonte m
buffer ['bʌfə*] n respingente m; (COMPUT)
memoria tampone, buffer m inv
buffet[1] ['bufeɪ] n (food, BRIT: bar) buffet m
inv; ~ **car** (BRIT) (RAIL) ≈ servizio ristoro
buffet[2] ['bʌfɪt] vt sferzare
bug [bʌg] n (esp US: insect) insetto; (COMPUT,
fig: germ) virus m inv; (spy device)
microfono spia ♦ vt mettere sotto
controllo; (inf: annoy) scocciare
buggy ['bʌgɪ] n (baby ~) passeggino
bugle ['bjuːgl] n tromba
build [bɪld] (pt, pp **built**) n (of person) corporatura ♦ vt costruire; ~ **up** vt accumulare;
aumentare; **~er** n costruttore m; **~ing** n
costruzione f; edificio; (industry) edilizia; **~ing
society** (BRIT) n società f inv immobiliare
built [bɪlt] pt, pp of **build** ♦ adj: **~-in**
(cupboard) a muro; (device) incorporato(a);
~-up area n abitato
bulb [bʌlb] n (BOT) bulbo; (ELEC) lampadina
bulge [bʌldʒ] n rigonfiamento ♦ vi essere

protuberante *or* rigonfio(a); **to be bulging with** essere pieno(a) *or* zeppo(a) di

bulk [bʌlk] *n* massa, volume *m*; **in ~** a pacchi *or* cassette *etc*); (*COMM*) all'ingrosso; **the ~ of** il grosso di; ~**y** *adj* grosso(a); voluminoso(a)

bull [bul] *n* toro; (*male elephant, whale*) maschio; ~**dog** *n* bulldog *m inv*

bulldozer ['buldəuzə*] *n* bulldozer *m inv*

bullet ['bulɪt] *n* pallottola

bulletin ['bulɪtɪn] *n* bollettino

bulletproof ['bulɪtpru:f] *adj* (*car*) blindato(a); (*vest etc*) antiproiettile *inv*

bullfight ['bulfaɪt] *n* corrida; ~**er** *n* torero; ~**ing** *n* tauromachia

bullion ['buljən] *n* oro *or* argento in lingotti

bullock ['bulək] *n* manzo

bullring ['bulrɪŋ] *n* arena (per corride)

bull's-eye ['bulzaɪ] *n* centro del bersaglio

bully ['bulɪ] *n* prepotente *m* ♦ *vt* angariare; (*frighten*) intimidire

bum [bʌm] (*inf*) *n* (*backside*) culo; (*tramp*) vagabondo/a

bumblebee ['bʌmblbi:] *n* bombo

bump [bʌmp] *n* (*in car*) piccolo tamponamento; (*jolt*) scossa; (*on road etc*) protuberanza; (*on head*) bernoccolo ♦ *vt* battere; ~ **into** *vt fus* scontrarsi con; (*person*) imbattersi in; ~**er** *n* paraurti *m inv* ♦ *adj*: ~**er harvest** raccolto eccezionale; ~**er cars** *npl* autoscontri *mpl*

bumpy ['bʌmpɪ] *adj* (*road*) dissestato(a)

bun [bʌn] *n* focaccia; (*of hair*) crocchia

bunch [bʌntʃ] *n* (*of flowers, keys*) mazzo; (*of bananas*) casco; (*of people*) gruppo; ~ **of grapes** grappolo d'uva; ~**es** *npl* (*in hair*) codine *fpl*

bundle ['bʌndl] *n* fascio ♦ *vt* (*also*: ~ **up**) legare in un fascio; (*put*): **to ~ sth/sb into** spingere qc/qn in

bungalow ['bʌŋgələu] *n* bungalow *m inv*

bungle ['bʌŋgl] *vt* fare un pasticcio di

bunion ['bʌnjən] *n* callo (al piede)

bunk [bʌŋk] *n* cuccetta; ~ **beds** *npl* letti *mpl* a castello

bunker ['bʌŋkə*] *n* (*coal store*) ripostiglio per il carbone; (*MIL, GOLF*) bunker *m inv*

bunny ['bʌnɪ] *n* (*also*: ~ **rabbit**) coniglietto

bunting ['bʌntɪŋ] *n* pavesi *mpl*, bandierine *fpl*

buoy [bɔɪ] *n* boa; ~**ant** *adj* galleggiante; (*fig*) vivace

burden ['bə:dn] *n* carico, fardello ♦ *vt*: **to ~ sb with** caricare qn di

bureau [bjuə'rəu] (*pl* **bureaux**) *n* (*BRIT: writing desk*) scrivania; (*US: chest of drawers*) cassettone *m*; (*office*) ufficio, agenzia

bureaucracy [bjuə'rɔkrəsɪ] *n* burocrazia

bureaux [bjuə'rəuz] *npl of* **bureau**

burglar ['bə:glə*] *n* scassinatore *m*; ~ **alarm** *n* campanello antifurto; ~**y** *n* furto con scasso

burial ['berɪəl] *n* sepoltura

burly ['bə:lɪ] *adj* robusto(a)

Burma ['bə:mə] *n* Birmania

burn [bə:n] (*pt, pp* **burned** *or* **burnt**) *vt, vi* bruciare ♦ *n* bruciatura, scottatura; ~ **down** *vt* distruggere col fuoco; ~**er** *n* (*on cooker*) fornello; (*TECH*) bruciatore *m*, becco (a gas); ~**ing** *adj* in fiamme; (*sand*) che scotta; (*ambition*) bruciante; **burnt** *pt, pp of* **burn**

burrow ['bʌrəu] *n* tana ♦ *vt* scavare

bursary ['bə:sərɪ] (*BRIT*) *n* (*SCOL*) borsa di studio

burst [bə:st] (*pt, pp* **burst**) *vt* far scoppiare ♦ *vi* esplodere; (*tyre*) scoppiare ♦ *n* scoppio; (*also*: ~ **pipe**) rottura nel tubo, perdita; **a ~ of speed** uno scatto di velocità; **to ~ into flames/tears** scoppiare in fiamme/lacrime; **to ~ out laughing** scoppiare a ridere; **to be ~ing with** scoppiare di; ~ **into** *vt fus* (*room etc*) irrompere in

bury ['berɪ] *vt* seppellire

bus [bʌs] (*pl* ~**es**) *n* autobus *m inv*

bush [buʃ] *n* cespuglio; (*scrub land*) macchia; **to beat about the ~** menare il cane per l'aia

bushy ['buʃɪ] *adj* cespuglioso(a)

busily ['bɪzɪlɪ] *adv* con impegno, alacremente

business ['bɪznɪs] *n* (*matter*) affare *m*; (*trading*) affari *mpl*; (*firm*) azienda; (*job,* duty) lavoro; **to be away on ~** essere andato via per affari; **it's none of my ~** questo non mi riguarda; **he means ~** non scherza; **~like** adj serio(a); efficiente; **~man/woman** (irreg) n uomo/donna d'affari; **~ trip** n viaggio d'affari

busker ['bʌskə*] (BRIT) n suonatore/trice ambulante

bus: **~ shelter** n pensilina (alla fermata dell'autobus); **~ station** n stazione f delle corriere, autostazione f; **~-stop** n fermata d'autobus

bust [bʌst] n busto; (ANAT) seno ♦ adj (inf: broken) rotto(a); **to go ~** fallire

bustle ['bʌsl] n movimento, attività ♦ vi darsi da fare; **bustling** adj movimentato(a)

busy ['bɪzɪ] adj occupato(a); (shop, street) molto frequentato(a) ♦ vt: **to ~ o.s.** darsi da fare; **~body** n ficcanaso m/f inv; **~ signal** (US) n (TEL) segnale m di occupato

KEYWORD

but [bʌt] conj ma; **I'd love to come, ~ I'm busy** vorrei tanto venire, ma ho da fare ♦ prep (apart from, except) eccetto, tranne, meno; **he was nothing ~ trouble** non dava altro che guai; **no-one ~ him can do it** nessuno può farlo tranne lui; **~ for you/ your help** se non fosse per te/per il tuo aiuto; **anything ~ that** tutto ma non questo ♦ adv (just, only) solo, soltanto; **she's ~ a child** è solo una bambina; **had I ~ known** se solo avessi saputo; **I can ~ try** tentar non nuoce; **all ~ finished** quasi finito

butcher ['butʃə*] n macellaio ♦ vt macellare; **~'s (shop)** n macelleria

butler ['bʌtlə*] n maggiordomo

butt [bʌt] n (cask) grossa botte f; (of gun) calcio; (of cigarette) mozzicone m; (BRIT: fig: target) oggetto ♦ vt cozzare; **~ in** vi (interrupt) interrompere

butter ['bʌtə*] n burro ♦ vt imburrare; **~cup** n ranuncolo

butterfly ['bʌtəflaɪ] n farfalla; (SWIMMING:

also: **~ stroke**) (nuoto a) farfalla

buttocks ['bʌtəks] npl natiche fpl

button ['bʌtn] n bottone m; (US: badge) distintivo ♦ vt (also: **~ up**) abbottonare ♦ vi abbottonarsi

buttress ['bʌtrɪs] n contrafforte f

buy [baɪ] (pt, pp **bought**) vt comprare ♦ n acquisto; **to ~ sb sth/sth from sb** comprare qc per qn/qc da qn; **to ~ sb a drink** offrire da bere a qn; **~er** n compratore/trice

buzz [bʌz] n ronzio; (inf: phone call) colpo di telefono ♦ vi ronzare

buzzer ['bʌzə*] n cicalino

buzz word (inf) n termine m di gran moda

KEYWORD

by [baɪ] prep 1 (referring to cause, agent) da; **killed ~ lightning** ucciso da un fulmine; **surrounded ~ a fence** circondato da uno steccato; **a painting ~ Picasso** un quadro di Picasso

2 (referring to method, manner, means): **~ bus/car/train** in autobus/macchina/treno, con l'autobus/la macchina/il treno; **to pay ~ cheque** pagare con (un) assegno; **~ moonlight** al chiaro di luna; **~ saving hard, he ...** risparmiando molto, lui ...

3 (via, through) per; **we came ~ Dover** siamo venuti via Dover

4 (close to, past) accanto a; **the house ~ the river** la casa sul fiume; **a holiday ~ the sea** una vacanza al mare; **she sat ~ his bed** si sedette accanto al suo letto; **she rushed ~ me** mi è passata accanto correndo; **I go ~ the post office every day** passo davanti all'ufficio postale ogni giorno

5 (not later than) per, entro; **~ 4 o'clock** per or entro le 4; **~ this time tomorrow** domani a quest'ora; **~ the time I got here it was too late** quando sono arrivato era ormai troppo tardi

6 (during): **~ day/night** di giorno/notte

7 (amount) a; **~ the kilo/metre** a chili/ metri; **paid ~ the hour** pagato all'ora; **one ~ one** uno per uno; **little ~ little** a poco a poco

8 (MATH, measure): **to divide/multiply ~ 3** dividere/moltiplicare per 3; **it's broader ~ a metre** è un metro più largo, è più largo di un metro

9 (according to) per; **to play ~ the rules** attenersi alle regole; **it's all right ~ me** per me va bene

10: **(all) ~ oneself** etc (tutto(a)) solo(a); **he did it (all) ~ himself** lo ha fatto (tutto) da solo

11: **~ the way** a proposito; **this wasn't my idea ~ the way** tra l'altro l'idea non è stata mia

♦ adv 1 see **go**; **pass** etc

2: **~ and ~** (in past) poco dopo; (in future) fra breve; **~ and large** nel complesso

bye(-bye) ['baɪ'baɪ] excl ciao!, arrivederci!
by(e)-law n legge f locale
by-election (BRIT) n elezione f straordinaria
bygone ['baɪɡɔn] adj passato(a) ♦ n: **let ~s be ~s** mettiamoci una pietra sopra
bypass ['baɪpɑːs] n circonvallazione f; (MED) by-pass m inv ♦ vt fare una deviazione intorno a
by-product n sottoprodotto; (fig) conseguenza secondaria
bystander ['baɪstændə*] n spettatore/trice
byte [baɪt] n (COMPUT) byte m inv, bicarattere m
byword ['baɪwəːd] n: **to be a ~ for** essere sinonimo di

C, c

C [siː] n (MUS) do
C. abbr (= centigrade) C.
C.A. n abbr = **chartered accountant**
cab [kæb] n taxi m inv; (of truck) cabina
cabaret ['kæbəreɪ] n cabaret m inv
cabbage ['kæbɪdʒ] n cavolo
cabin ['kæbɪn] n capanna; (on ship) cabina; **~ crew** n equipaggio; **~ cruiser** n cabinato
cabinet ['kæbɪnɪt] n (POL) consiglio dei ministri; (furniture) armadietto; (also:

display ~) vetrinetta
cable ['keɪbl] n cavo; fune f; (TEL) cablogramma m ♦ vt telegrafare; **~-car** n funivia; **~ television** n televisione f via cavo
cache [kæʃ] n deposito segreto
cackle ['kækl] vi schiamazzare
cactus ['kæktəs] (pl **cacti**) n cactus m inv
cadet [kə'dɛt] n (MIL) cadetto
cadge [kædʒ] (inf) vt scroccare
café ['kæfeɪ] n caffè m inv
cafeteria [kæfɪ'tɪərɪə] n self-service m inv
cage [keɪdʒ] n gabbia
cagey ['keɪdʒɪ] (inf) adj chiuso(a); guardingo(a)
cagoule [kə'ɡuːl] n K-way ® m inv
cajole [kə'dʒəul] vt allettare
cake [keɪk] n (large) torta; (small) pasticcino; **~ of soap** saponetta; **~d** adj: **~d with** incrostato(a) di
calculate ['kælkjuleɪt] vt calcolare; **calculation** [-'leɪʃən] n calcolo; **calculator** n calcolatrice f
calendar ['kæləndə*] n calendario; **~ year** n anno civile
calf [kɑːf] (pl **calves**) n (of cow) vitello; (of other animals) piccolo; (also: **~skin**) (pelle f di) vitello; (ANAT) polpaccio
calibre ['kælɪbə*] (US **caliber**) n calibro
call [kɔːl] vt (gen, also TEL) chiamare; (meeting) indire ♦ vi chiamare; (visit: also: **~ in, ~ round**) passare ♦ n (shout) grido, urlo; (TEL) telefonata; **to be ~ed** (person, object) chiamarsi; **to be on ~** essere a disposizione; **~ back** vi (return) ritornare; (TEL) ritelefonare, richiamare; **~ for** vt fus richiedere; (fetch) passare a prendere; **~ off** vt disdire; **~ on** vt fus (visit) passare da; (appeal to) chiedere a; **~ out** vi (in pain) urlare; (to person) chiamare; **~ up** vt (MIL) richiamare; (TEL) telefonare a; **~box** (BRIT) n cabina telefonica; **~ centre** n centro informazioni telefoniche; **~er** n persona che chiama; visitatore/trice; **~ girl** n ragazza f squillo inv; **~-in** (US) n (phone-in) trasmissione f a filo diretto con gli ascoltatori; **~ing** n vocazione f; **~ing card**

(US) n biglietto da visita

callous ['kæləs] adj indurito(a), insensibile

calm [kɑːm] adj calmo(a) ♦ n calma ♦ vt calmare; ~ **down** vi calmarsi ♦ vt calmare

Calor gas ® ['kælə*-] n butano

calorie ['kælərɪ] n caloria

calves [kɑːvz] npl of **calf**

Cambodia [kæm'bəʊdjə] n Cambogia

camcorder ['kæmkɔːdə*] n camcorder f inv

came [keɪm] pt of **come**

camel ['kæməl] n cammello

camera ['kæmərə] n macchina fotografica; (CINEMA, TV) cinepresa; **in ~** a porte chiuse; **~man** (irreg) n cameraman m inv

camouflage ['kæməflɑːʒ] n (MIL, ZOOL) mimetizzazione f ♦ vt mimetizzare

camp [kæmp] n campeggio; (MIL) campo ♦ vi accamparsi ♦ adj effeminato(a)

campaign [kæm'peɪn] n (MIL, POL etc) campagna ♦ vi (also fig) fare una campagna

camp bed (BRIT) n brandina

camper ['kæmpə*] n campeggiatore/trice; (vehicle) camper m inv

camping ['kæmpɪŋ] n campeggio; **to go ~** andare in campeggio

campsite ['kæmpsaɪt] n campeggio

campus ['kæmpəs] n campus m inv

can[1] [kæn] n (of milk) scatola; (of oil) bidone m; (of water) tanica; (tin) scatola ♦ vt mettere in scatola

---

KEYWORD

can[2] [kæn] (negative **cannot, can't**; conditional and pt **could**) aux vb 1 (be able to) potere; **I ~'t go any further** non posso andare oltre; **you ~ do it if you try** sei in grado di farlo — basta provarci; **I'll help you all I ~** ti aiuterò come potrò; **I ~'t see you** non ti vedo

2 (know how to) sapere, essere capace di; **I ~ swim** so nuotare; **~ you speak French?** parla francese?

3 (may) potere; **could I have a word with you?** posso parlarle un momento?

4 (expressing disbelief, puzzlement etc): **it ~'t be true!** non può essere vero!; **what**

CAN he want? cosa può mai volere?

5 (expressing possibility, suggestion etc): **he could be in the library** può darsi che sia in biblioteca; **she could have been delayed** può avere avuto un contrattempo

---

Canada ['kænədə] n Canada m

Canadian [kə'neɪdɪən] adj, n canadese m/f

canal [kə'næl] n canale m

canary [kə'nɛərɪ] n canarino

cancel ['kænsəl] vt annullare; (train) sopprimere; (cross out) cancellare; **~lation** [-'leɪʃən] n annullamento; soppressione f; cancellazione f; (TOURISM) prenotazione f annullata

cancer ['kænsə*] n cancro; **C~** (sign) Cancro

candid ['kændɪd] adj onesto(a)

candidate ['kændɪdeɪt] n candidato/a

candle ['kændl] n candela; (in church) cero; **~light** n: **by ~light** a lume di candela; **~stick** n bugia; (bigger, ornate) candeliere m

candour ['kændə*] (US **candor**) n sincerità

candy ['kændɪ] n zucchero candito; (US) caramella; caramelle fpl; **~-floss** (BRIT) n zucchero filato

cane [keɪn] n canna; (for furniture) bambù m; (stick) verga ♦ vt (BRIT: SCOL) punire a colpi di verga

canister ['kænɪstə*] n scatola metallica

cannabis ['kænəbɪs] n canapa indiana

canned [kænd] adj (food) in scatola

cannon ['kænən] (pl ~ or ~s) n (gun) cannone m

cannot ['kænɔt] = **can not**

canny ['kænɪ] adj furbo(a)

canoe [kə'nuː] n canoa; **~ing** n canottaggio

canon ['kænən] n (clergyman) canonico; (standard) canone m

can opener [-'əʊpnə*] n apriscatole m inv

canopy ['kænəpɪ] n baldacchino

cant [kænt] n gergo ♦ vt inclinare ♦ vi inclinarsi

can't [kænt] = **can not**

canteen [kæn'tiːn] n mensa; (BRIT: of cutlery) portaposate m inv

canter ['kæntə*] vi andare al piccolo

galoppo

canvas ['kænvəs] *n* tela

canvass ['kænvəs] *vi (POL)*: **to ~ for** raccogliere voti per ♦ *vt* fare un sondaggio di

cap [kæp] *n (hat)* berretto; *(of pen)* coperchio; *(of bottle, toy gun)* tappo; *(contraceptive)* diaframma *m* ♦ *vt (outdo)* superare; *(limit)* fissare un tetto (a)

capability [keɪpə'bɪlɪtɪ] *n* capacità *f inv*, abilità *f inv*

capable ['keɪpəbl] *adj* capace

capacity [kə'pæsɪtɪ] *n* capacità *f inv*; *(of lift etc)* capienza

cape [keɪp] *n (garment)* cappa; *(GEO)* capo

caper ['keɪpə*] *n (CULIN)* cappero; *(prank)* scherzetto

capital ['kæpɪtl] *n (also: ~ city)* capitale *f*; *(money)* capitale *m*; *(also: ~ letter)* (lettera) maiuscola; **~ gains tax** *n* imposta sulla plusvalenza; **~ism** *n* capitalismo; **~ist** *adj*, *n* capitalista *(m/f)*; **~ize**: **to ~ize on** *vt fus* trarre vantaggio da; **~ punishment** *n* pena capitale

Capitol ['kæpɪtl] *n*: **the ~** il Campidoglio

Capitol

> *Il* **Capitol** *è l'edificio dove si svolgono le riunioni del Congresso degli Stati Uniti. È situato sull'omonimo colle, Capitol Hill, a Washington D.C.*

Capricorn ['kæprɪkɔːn] *n* Capricorno

capsize [kæp'saɪz] *vt* capovolgere ♦ *vi* capovolgersi

capsule ['kæpsjuːl] *n* capsula

captain ['kæptɪn] *n* capitano

caption ['kæpʃən] *n* leggenda

captivate ['kæptɪveɪt] *vt* avvincere

captive ['kæptɪv] *adj*, *n* prigioniero(a)

captivity [kæp'tɪvɪtɪ] *n* cattività

capture ['kæptʃə*] *vt* catturare; *(COMPUT)* registrare ♦ *n* cattura; *(data ~)* registrazione *f or* rilevazione *f* di dati

car [kɑ:*] *n (AUT)* macchina, automobile *f*; *(RAIL)* vagone *m*

carafe [kə'ræf] *n* caraffa

caramel ['kærəməl] *n* caramello

caravan ['kærəvæn] *n (BRIT)* roulotte *f inv*; *(of camels)* carovana; **~ning** *n* vacanze *fpl* in roulotte; **~ site** *(BRIT)* *n* campeggio per roulotte

carbohydrates [kɑ:bəu'haɪdreɪts] *npl (foods)* carboidrati *mpl*

carbon ['kɑ:bən] *n* carbonio; **~ paper** *n* carta carbone

car boot sale *n* mercatino dell'usato dove la merce viene esposta nei bagagliai delle macchine

carburettor [kɑ:bju'retə*] *(US* **carburetor***) n* carburatore *m*

card [kɑ:d] *n* carta; *(visiting ~ etc)* biglietto; *(Christmas ~ etc)* cartolina; **~board** *n* cartone *m*; **~ game** *n* gioco di carte

cardiac ['kɑ:dɪæk] *adj* cardiaco(a)

cardigan ['kɑ:dɪgən] *n* cardigan *m inv*

cardinal ['kɑ:dɪnl] *adj* cardinale ♦ *n* cardinale *m*

card index *n* schedario

cardphone ['kɑ:dfəun] *n* telefono a scheda

care [keə*] *n* cura, attenzione *f*; *(worry)* preoccupazione *f* ♦ *vi*: **to ~ about** curarsi di; *(thing, idea)* interessarsi di; **~ of** presso; **in sb's ~** alle cure di qn; **to take ~ (to do)** fare attenzione (a fare); **to take ~ of** curarsi di; *(bill, problem)* occuparsi di; **I don't ~** non me ne importa; **I couldn't ~ less** non m'interessa affatto; **~ for** *vt fus* aver cura di; *(like)* volere bene a

career [kə'rɪə*] *n* carriera ♦ *vi (also: ~ along)* andare di (gran) carriera

carefree ['keəfri:] *adj* sgombro(a) di preoccupazioni

careful ['keəful] *adj* attento(a); *(cautious)* cauto(a); **(be) ~!** attenzione!; **~ly** *adv* con cura; cautamente

careless ['keəlɪs] *adj* negligente; *(heedless)* spensierato(a)

carer ['keərə*] *n* assistente *m/f (di persone malata o handicappata)*

caress [kə'res] *n* carezza ♦ *vt* accarezzare

caretaker ['keəteɪkə*] *n* custode *m*

car-ferry *n* traghetto

cargo ['kɑ:gəu] *(pl* **~es***) n* carico

car hire n autonoleggio
Caribbean [kærɪˈbiːən] adj: **the ~ (Sea)** il Mar dei Caraibi
caring [ˈkɛərɪŋ] adj (person) premuroso(a); (society, organization) umanitario(a)
carnage [ˈkɑːnɪdʒ] n carneficina
carnation [kɑːˈneɪʃən] n garofano
carnival [ˈkɑːnɪvəl] n (public celebration) carnevale m; (US: funfair) luna park m inv
carol [ˈkærəl] n: **(Christmas) ~** canto di Natale
carp [kɑːp] n (fish) carpa
car park (BRIT) n parcheggio
carpenter [ˈkɑːpɪntə*] n carpentiere m
carpentry [ˈkɑːpɪntrɪ] n carpenteria
carpet [ˈkɑːpɪt] n tappeto ♦ vt coprire con tappeto
car phone n telefonino per auto, cellulare m per auto
car rental (US) n autonoleggio
carriage [ˈkærɪdʒ] n vettura; (of goods) trasporto; **~way** (BRIT) n (part of road) carreggiata
carrier [ˈkærɪə*] n (of disease) portatore/trice; (COMM) impresa di trasporti; **~ bag** (BRIT) n sacchetto
carrot [ˈkærət] n carota
carry [ˈkærɪ] vt (subj: person) portare; (: vehicle) trasportare; (involve: responsibilities etc) comportare; (MED) essere portatore/trice di ♦ vi (sound) farsi sentire; **to be** or **get carried away** (fig) entusiasmarsi; **~ on** vi: **to ~ on with sth/doing** continuare qc/a fare ♦ vt mandare avanti; **~ out** vt (orders) eseguire; (investigation) svolgere; **~cot** (BRIT) n culla portabile; **~-on** (inf) n (fuss) casino, confusione f
cart [kɑːt] n carro ♦ vt (inf) trascinare
carton [ˈkɑːtən] n (box) scatola di cartone; (of yogurt) cartone m; (of cigarettes) stecca
cartoon [kɑːˈtuːn] n (PRESS) disegno umoristico; (comic strip) fumetto; (CINEMA) disegno animato
cartridge [ˈkɑːtrɪdʒ] n (for gun, pen) cartuccia; (music tape) cassetta
carve [kɑːv] vt (meat) trinciare; (wood,

stone) intagliare; **~ up** vt (fig: country) suddividere; **carving** n (in wood etc) scultura; **carving knife** n trinciante m
car wash n lavaggio auto
cascade [kæsˈkeɪd] n cascata
case [keɪs] n caso; (LAW) causa, processo; (box) scatola; (BRIT: also: **suit~**) valigia; **in ~ of** in caso di; **in ~ he** caso mai lui; **in any ~** in ogni caso; **just in ~** in caso di bisogno
cash [kæʃ] n denaro; (coins, notes) denaro liquido ♦ vt incassare; **to pay (in) ~** pagare in contanti; **~ on delivery** pagamento alla consegna; **~-book** n giornale m di cassa; **~ card** (BRIT) n tesserino di prelievo; **~ desk** (BRIT) n cassa; **~ dispenser** (BRIT) n sportello automatico
cashew [kæˈʃuː] n (also: **~ nut**) anacardio
cashier [kæˈʃɪə*] n cassiere/a
cashmere [ˈkæʃmɪə*] n cachemire m
cash register n registratore m di cassa
casing [ˈkeɪsɪŋ] n rivestimento
casino [kəˈsiːnəu] n casinò m inv
cask [kɑːsk] n botte f
casket [ˈkɑːskɪt] n cofanetto; (US: coffin) bara
casserole [ˈkæsərəul] n casseruola; (food): **chicken ~** pollo in casseruola
cassette [kæˈset] n cassetta; **~ player** n riproduttore m a cassette; **~ recorder** n registratore m a cassette
cast [kɑːst] (pt, pp cast) vt (throw) gettare; (metal) gettare, fondere; (THEATRE): **to ~ sb as Hamlet** scegliere qn per la parte di Amleto ♦ n (THEATRE) cast m inv; (also: **plaster ~**) ingessatura; **to ~ one's vote** votare, dare il voto; **~ off** vi (NAUT) salpare; (KNITTING) calare; **~ on** vi (KNITTING) avviare le maglie
castaway [ˈkɑːstəweɪ] n naufrago/a
caster sugar [ˈkɑːstə*-] (BRIT) n zucchero semolato
casting vote [ˈkɑːstɪŋ-] (BRIT) n voto decisivo
cast iron n ghisa
castle [ˈkɑːsl] n castello
castor oil [ˈkɑːstə*-] n olio di ricino
casual [ˈkæʒjul] adj (by chance) casuale,

fortuito(a); (*irregular: work etc*)
avventizio(a); (*unconcerned*) noncurante,
indifferente; **~ wear** casual *m*; **~ly** *adv* (*in
a relaxed way*) con noncuranza; (*dress*)
casual

casualty ['kæʒjultɪ] *n* ferito/a; (*dead*)
morto/a, vittima; (*MED: department*) pronto
soccorso

cat [kæt] *n* gatto

catalogue ['kætəlɔg] (*US* **catalog**) *n*
catalogo ♦ *vt* catalogare

catalyst ['kætəlɪst] *n* catalizzatore *m*

catalytic convertor [kætəlɪtɪk-] *n*
marmitta catalitica, catalizzatore *m*

catapult ['kætəpʌlt] *n* catapulta; fionda

cataract ['kætərækt] *n* (*also MED*) cateratta

catarrh [kə'tɑː*] *n* catarro

catastrophe [kə'tæstrəfi] *n* catastrofe *f*

catch [kætʃ] (*pt, pp* **caught**) *vt* prendere;
(*ball*) afferrare; (*surprise: person*)
sorprendere; (*attention*) attirare; (*comment,
whisper*) cogliere; (*person: also:* **~ up**)
raggiungere ♦ *vi* (*fire*) prendere ♦ *n* (*fish
etc caught*) retata; (*of ball*) presa; (*trick*)
inganno; (*TECH*) gancio; (*game*) catch *m
inv*; **to ~ fire** prendere fuoco; **to ~ sight of**
scorgere; **~ on** *vi* capire; (*become popular*)
affermarsi, far presa; **~ up** *vi* mettersi in
pari ♦ *vt* (*also:* **~ up with**) raggiungere

catching ['kætʃɪŋ] *adj* (*MED*) contagioso(a)

catchment area ['kætʃmənt-] (*BRIT*) *n*
(*SCOL*) circoscrizione *f* scolare

catch phrase *n* slogan *m inv*; frase *f* fatta

catchy ['kætʃɪ] *adj* orecchiabile

category ['kætɪgərɪ] *n* categoria

cater ['keɪtə*] *vi*: **~ for** (*BRIT: needs*)
provvedere a; (*: readers, consumers*)
incontrare i gusti di; (*COMM: provide food*)
provvedere alla ristorazione di; **~er** *n*
fornitore *m*; **~ing** *n* approvvigionamento

caterpillar ['kætəpɪlə*] *n* bruco

cathedral [kə'θiːdrəl] *n* cattedrale *f*, duomo

catholic ['kæθəlɪk] *adj* universale; aperto(a);
eclettico(a); **C~** *adj, n* (*REL*) cattolico(a)

CAT scan *n* (= *computerized axial
tomography*) TAC *f inv*

Catseye ® [kæts'aɪ] (*BRIT*) *n* (*AUT*) cata-

rifrangente *m*

cattle ['kætl] *npl* bestiame *m*, bestie *fpl*

catty ['kætɪ] *adj* maligno(a), dispettoso(a)

caucus ['kɔːkəs] *n* (*POL: group*) comitato di
dirigenti; (: *US*) (riunione *f* del) comitato
elettorale

caught [kɔːt] *pt, pp of* **catch**

cauliflower ['kɔlɪflauə*] *n* cavolfiore *m*

cause [kɔːz] *n* causa ♦ *vt* causare

caution ['kɔːʃən] *n* prudenza; (*warning*)
avvertimento ♦ *vt* avvertire; ammonire

cautious ['kɔːʃəs] *adj* cauto(a), prudente

cavalry ['kævəlrɪ] *n* cavalleria

cave [keɪv] *n* caverna, grotta; **~ in** *vi* (*roof
etc*) crollare; **~man** (*irreg*) *n* uomo delle
caverne

caviar(e) ['kævɪɑː*] *n* caviale *m*

CB *n abbr* (= *Citizens' Band (Radio)*): **~
radio (set)** baracchino

CBI *n abbr* (= *Confederation of British
Industries*) ≈ Confindustria

cc *abbr* = **cubic centimetres; carbon copy**

CCTV *n abbr* (= *closed-circuit television*)
televisione *f* a circuito chiuso

CD *n abbr* (*disc*) CD *m inv*

CDI *n abbr* (= *compact disk interactive*) CD-I
m inv, compact disc *m inv* interattivo

CD player *n* lettore *m* CD

CD-ROM [-rɔm] *n abbr* CD-ROM *m inv*

cease [siːs] *vt, vi* cessare; **~fire** *n* cessate il
fuoco *m inv*; **~less** *adj* incessante,
continuo(a)

cedar ['siːdə*] *n* cedro

ceiling ['siːlɪŋ] *n* soffitto; (*on wages etc*)
tetto

celebrate ['selɪbreɪt] *vt, vi* celebrare; **~d** *adj*
celebre; **celebration** [-'breɪʃən] *n*
celebrazione *f*

celery ['selərɪ] *n* sedano

cell [sel] *n* cella; (*of revolutionaries, BIOL*)
cellula; (*ELEC*) elemento (di batteria)

cellar ['selə*] *n* sottosuolo; cantina

'cello ['tʃeləu] *n* violoncello

cellphone ['selfəun] *n* cellulare *m*

Celt [kelt, selt] *n* celta *m/f*

cement [sə'ment] *n* cemento; **~ mixer** *n*
betoniera

cemetery ['sɛmɪtrɪ] n cimitero

censor ['sɛnsə*] n censore m ♦ vt censurare; **~ship** n censura

censure ['sɛnʃə*] vt riprovare, censurare

census ['sɛnsəs] n censimento

cent [sɛnt] n (US: coin) centesimo (= 1:100 di un dollaro); (unit of euro) centesimo; see also **per**

centenary [sɛn'tiːnərɪ] n centenario

center ['sɛntə*] (US) n, vt = **centre**

centigrade ['sɛntɪgreɪd] adj centigrado(a)

centimetre ['sɛntɪmiːtə*] (US **centimeter**) n centimetro

centipede ['sɛntɪpiːd] n centopiedi m inv

central ['sɛntrəl] adj centrale; **C~ America** n America centrale; **~ heating** n riscaldamento centrale; **~ize** vt accentrare

centre ['sɛntə*] (US **center**) n centro ♦ vt centrare; **~-forward** n (SPORT) centroavanti m inv; **~-half** n (SPORT) centromediano

century ['sɛntjʊrɪ] n secolo; **20th ~** ventesimo secolo

ceramic [sɪ'ræmɪk] adj ceramico(a); **~s** npl ceramica

cereal ['siːrɪəl] n cereale m

ceremony ['sɛrɪmənɪ] n cerimonia; **to stand on ~** fare complimenti

certain ['sɜːtən] adj certo(a); **to make ~ of** assicurarsi di; **for ~** per certo, di sicuro; **~ly** adv certamente, certo; **~ty** n certezza

certificate [sə'tɪfɪkɪt] n certificato; diploma m

certified ['sɜːtɪfaɪd]: **~ mail** (US) n posta raccomandata con ricevuta di ritorno; **~ public accountant** (US) n ≈ commercialista m/f

certify ['sɜːtɪfaɪ] vt certificare; (award diploma to) conferire un diploma a; (declare insane) dichiarare pazzo(a)

cervical ['sɜːvɪkl] adj: **~ cancer** cancro della cervice; **~ smear** Pap-test m inv

cervix ['sɜːvɪks] n cervice f

cf. abbr (= compare) cfr

CFC n (= chlorofluorocarbon) CFC m inv

ch. abbr (= chapter) cap

chafe [tʃeɪf] vt fregare, irritare

chain [tʃeɪn] n catena ♦ vt (also: **~ up**) incatenare; **~ reaction** n reazione f a catena; **~-smoke** vi fumare una sigaretta dopo l'altra; **~ store** n negozio a catena

chair [tʃɛə*] n sedia; (armchair) poltrona; (of university) cattedra; (of meeting) presidenza ♦ vt (meeting) presiedere; **~lift** n seggiovia; **~man** (irreg) n presidente m

chalet ['ʃæleɪ] n chalet m inv

chalk [tʃɔːk] n gesso

challenge ['tʃælɪndʒ] n sfida ♦ vt sfidare; (statement, right) mettere in dubbio; **to ~ sb to do** sfidare qn a fare; **challenging** adj (task) impegnativo(a); (look) di sfida

chamber ['tʃeɪmbə*] n camera; **~ of commerce** n camera di commercio; **~maid** n cameriera; **~ music** n musica da camera

chamois ['ʃæmwɑː] n camoscio; (also: **~ leather**) panno in pelle di camoscio

champagne [ʃæm'peɪn] n champagne m inv

champion ['tʃæmpɪən] n campione/essa; **~ship** n campionato

chance [tʃɑːns] n caso; (opportunity) occasione f; (likelihood) possibilità f inv ♦ vt: **to ~ it** rischiare, provarci ♦ adj fortuito(a); **to take a ~** rischiare; **by ~** per caso

chancellor ['tʃɑːnsələ*] n cancelliere m; **C~ of the Exchequer** (BRIT) n Cancelliere dello Scacchiere

chandelier [ʃændə'lɪə*] n lampadario

change [tʃeɪndʒ] vt cambiare; (transform): **to ~ sb into** trasformare qn in ♦ vi cambiare; (~ one's clothes) cambiarsi; (be transformed): **to ~ into** trasformarsi in ♦ n cambiamento; (of clothes) cambio; (money) resto; **to ~ one's mind** cambiare idea; **for a ~** tanto per cambiare; **~able** adj (weather) variabile; **~ machine** n distributore automatico di monete; **~over** n cambiamento, passaggio

changing ['tʃeɪndʒɪŋ] adj che cambia; (colours) cangiante; **~ room** n (BRIT: in shop) camerino; (: SPORT) spogliatoio

channel ['tʃænl] n canale m; (of river, sea) alveo ♦ vt canalizzare; **the (English) C~**

n la Manica; ~-**hopping** n (TV) zapping m
inv; the C~ **Islands** npl le Isole
Normanne; the C~ **Tunnel** n il tunnel
sotto la Manica

chant [tʃɑ:nt] n canto; salmodia ♦ vt
cantare; salmodiare

chaos ['keɪɒs] n caos m

chap [tʃæp] (BRIT: inf) n (man) tipo

chapel ['tʃæpəl] n cappella

chaperone ['ʃæpərəun] n accompagnatrice
f ♦ vt accompagnare

chaplain ['tʃæplɪn] n cappellano

chapped [tʃæpt] adj (skin, lips)
screpolato(a)

chapter ['tʃæptə*] n capitolo

char [tʃɑ:*] vt (burn) carbonizzare

character ['kærɪktə*] n carattere m; (in
novel, film) personaggio; ~**istic** [-'rɪstɪk] adj
caratteristico(a) ♦ n caratteristica

charcoal ['tʃɑ:kəul] n carbone m di legna

charge [tʃɑ:dʒ] n accusa; (cost) prezzo;
(responsibility) responsabilità ♦ vt (gun,
battery, MIL: enemy) caricare; (customer)
fare pagare a; (sum) fare pagare; (LAW): to
~ **sb (with)** accusare qn (di) ♦ vi (gen with:
up, along) lanciarsi; ~**s** npl (bank ~s etc)
tariffe fpl; **to reverse the ~s** (TEL) fare una
telefonata a carico del destinatario; **to take
~ of** incaricarsi di; **to be in ~ of** essere
responsabile per; **how much do you ~?**
quanto addebitate?; **to ~ an expense (up) to
sb** addebitare una spesa a qn; ~ **card** n
carta f clienti inv

charitable ['tʃærɪtəbl] adj caritatevole

charity ['tʃærɪti] n carità; (organization)
opera pia

charm [tʃɑ:m] n fascino; (on bracelet)
ciondolo ♦ vt affascinare, incantare; ~**ing**
adj affascinante

chart [tʃɑ:t] n tabella; grafico; (map) carta
nautica ♦ vt fare una carta nautica di; ~**s**
npl (MUS) hit parade f

charter ['tʃɑ:tə*] vt (plane) noleggiare ♦ n
(document) statuto; ~**ed accountant** (BRIT)
n ragioniere/a professionista; ~ **flight** n
volo m charter inv

charwoman ['tʃɑ:wumən] n = **charlady**

chase [tʃeɪs] vt inseguire; (also: ~ **away**)
cacciare ♦ n caccia

chasm ['kæzəm] n abisso

chassis ['ʃæsɪ] n telaio

chat [tʃæt] vi (also: **have a ~**) chiacchierare
♦ n chiacchierata; ~ **show** (BRIT) n talk
show m inv

chatter ['tʃætə*] vi (person) ciarlare; (bird)
cinguettare; (teeth) battere ♦ n ciarle fpl;
cinguettio; ~**box** (inf) n chiacchierone/a

chatty ['tʃætɪ] adj (style) familiare; (person)
chiacchierino(a)

chauffeur ['ʃəufə*] n autista m

chauvinist ['ʃəuvɪnɪst] n (male ~)
maschilista m; (nationalist) sciovinista m/f

cheap [tʃi:p] adj a buon mercato; (joke)
grossolano(a); (poor quality) di cattiva
qualità ♦ adv a buon mercato; ~ **day
return** n biglietto ridotto di andata e
ritorno valido in giornata; ~**er** adj meno
caro(a); ~**ly** adv a buon prezzo, a buon
mercato

cheat [tʃi:t] vi imbrogliare; (at school)
copiare ♦ vt ingannare ♦ n imbroglione m;
to ~ sb out of sth defraudare qn di qc

check [tʃek] vt verificare; (passport, ticket)
controllare; (halt) fermare; (restrain)
contenere ♦ n verifica; controllo; (curb)
freno; (US: bill) conto; (pattern: gen pl)
quadretti mpl; (US) = **cheque** ♦ adj
(pattern, cloth) a quadretti; ~ **in** vi (in
hotel) registrare; (at airport) presentarsi
all'accettazione ♦ vt (luggage) depositare; ~
out vi (in hotel) saldare il conto; ~ **up** vi:
to ~ up (on sth) investigare (qc); **to ~ up
on sb** informarsi sul conto di qn; ~**ered**
(US) adj = **chequered**; ~**ers** (US) n dama;
~**-in (desk)** n check-in m inv,
accettazione f (bagagli inv); ~**ing
account** (US) n conto corrente; ~**mate** n
scaccomatto; ~**out** n (in supermarket)
cassa; ~**point** n posto di blocco; ~**room**
(US) n deposito m bagagli inv; ~**up** n
(MED) controllo medico

cheek [tʃi:k] n guancia; (impudence) faccia
tosta; ~**bone** n zigomo; ~**y** adj
sfacciato(a)

cheep [tʃiːp] vi pigolare

cheer [tʃɪə*] vt applaudire; (gladden) rallegrare ♦ vi applaudire ♦ n grido (di incoraggiamento); **~s** npl (of approval, encouragement) applausi mpl; evviva mpl; **~s!** salute!; **~** vt rallegrarsi, farsi animo ♦ vt rallegrare; **~ful** adj allegro(a)

cheerio ['tʃɪərɪəʊ] (BRIT) excl ciao!

cheese [tʃiːz] n formaggio; **~board** n piatto del (or per il) formaggio

cheetah ['tʃiːtə] n ghepardo

chef [ʃef] n capocuoco

chemical ['kemɪkəl] adj chimico(a) ♦ n prodotto chimico

chemist ['kemɪst] n (BRIT: pharmacist) farmacista m/f; (scientist) chimico/a; **~ry** n chimica; **~'s (shop)** (BRIT) n farmacia

cheque [tʃek] (BRIT) n assegno; **~book** n libretto degli assegni; **~ card** n carta f assegni inv

chequered ['tʃekəd] (US **checkered**) adj (fig) movimentato(a)

cherish ['tʃerɪʃ] vt aver caro

cherry ['tʃerɪ] n ciliegia; (also: **~ tree**) ciliegio

chess [tʃes] n scacchi mpl; **~board** n scacchiera

chest [tʃest] n petto; (box) cassa; **~ of drawers** n cassettone m

chestnut ['tʃesnʌt] n castagna; (also: **~ tree**) castagno

chew [tʃuː] vt masticare; **~ing gum** n chewing gum m

chic [ʃiːk] adj elegante

chick [tʃɪk] n pulcino; (inf) pollastrella

chicken ['tʃɪkɪn] n pollo; (inf: coward) coniglio; **~ out** (inf) vi avere fifa; **~pox** n varicella

chicory ['tʃɪkərɪ] n cicoria

chief [tʃiːf] n capo ♦ adj principale; **~ executive** n direttore m generale; **~ly** adv per lo più, soprattutto

chilblain ['tʃɪlbleɪn] n gelone m

child [tʃaɪld] (pl **~ren**) n bambino/a; **~birth** n parto; **~hood** n infanzia; **~ish** adj puerile; **~like** adj fanciullesco(a); **~ minder** (BRIT) n bambinaia

children ['tʃɪldrən] npl of **child**

child seat n seggiolino per bambini (in auto)

Chile ['tʃɪlɪ] n Cile m

chill [tʃɪl] n freddo; (MED) infreddatura ♦ vt raffreddare

chilli ['tʃɪlɪ] n peperoncino

chilly ['tʃɪlɪ] adj freddo(a), fresco(a); **to feel ~** sentirsi infreddolito(a)

chime [tʃaɪm] n carillon m inv ♦ vi suonare, scampanare

chimney ['tʃɪmnɪ] n camino; **~ sweep** n spazzacamino

chimpanzee [tʃɪmpæn'ziː] n scimpanzé m inv

chin [tʃɪn] n mento

China ['tʃaɪnə] n Cina

china ['tʃaɪnə] n porcellana

Chinese [tʃaɪ'niːz] adj cinese ♦ n inv cinese m/f; (LING) cinese m

chink [tʃɪŋk] n (opening) fessura; (noise) tintinnio

chip [tʃɪp] n (gen pl: CULIN) patatina fritta; (: US: also: **potato ~**) patatina; (of wood, glass, stone) scheggia; (also: **micro~**) chip m inv ♦ vt (cup, plate) scheggiare

chip shop

i I **chip shops**, anche chiamati *"fish and chip shops"*, sono friggitorie che vendono principalmente filetti di pesce impanati e patatine fritte.

chiropodist [kɪ'rɔpədɪst] (BRIT) n pedicure m/f inv

chirp [tʃəːp] vi cinguettare; fare cri cri

chisel ['tʃɪzl] n cesello

chit [tʃɪt] n biglietto

chitchat ['tʃɪttʃæt] n chiacchiere fpl

chivalry ['ʃɪvəlrɪ] n cavalleria; cortesia

chives [tʃaɪvz] npl erba cipollina

chock-a-block ['tʃɔk-] adj pieno(a) zeppo(a)

chock-full ['tʃɔk-] adj = **chock-a-block**

chocolate ['tʃɔklɪt] n (substance) cioccolato, cioccolata; (drink) cioccolata; (a sweet) cioccolatino

choice [tʃɔɪs] n scelta ♦ adj scelto(a)

choir ['kwaɪə*] n coro; **~boy** n corista m fanciullo

choke [tʃəuk] vi soffocare ♦ vt soffocare; (block): **to be ~d with** essere intasato(a) di ♦ n (AUT) valvola dell'aria

cholera ['kɔlərə] n colera m

cholesterol [kə'lestərɔl] n colesterolo

choose [tʃuːz] (pt **chose**, pp **chosen**) vt scegliere; **to ~ to do** decidere di fare; preferire fare

choosy ['tʃuːzɪ] adj schizzinoso(a)

chop [tʃɔp] vt (wood) spaccare; (CULIN: also: **~ up**) tritare ♦ n (CULIN) costoletta; **~s** npl (jaws) mascelle fpl

chopper ['tʃɔpə*] n (helicopter) elicottero

choppy ['tʃɔpɪ] adj (sea) mosso(a)

chopsticks ['tʃɔpstɪks] npl bastoncini mpl cinesi

choral ['kɔːrəl] adj corale

chord [kɔːd] n (MUS) accordo

chore [tʃɔː*] n faccenda; **household ~s** faccende fpl domestiche

chortle ['tʃɔːtl] vi ridacchiare

chorus ['kɔːrəs] n coro; (repeated part of song, also fig) ritornello

chose [tʃəuz] pt of **choose**

chosen ['tʃəuzn] pp of **choose**

chowder ['tʃaudə*] n (esp US) zuppa di pesce

Christ [kraɪst] n Cristo

christen ['krɪsn] vt battezzare

Christian ['krɪstɪən] adj, n cristiano(a); **~ity** [-'ænɪtɪ] n cristianesimo; **~ name** n nome m (di battesimo)

Christmas ['krɪsməs] n Natale m; **Merry ~!** Buon Natale!; **~ card** n cartolina di Natale; **~ Day** n il giorno di Natale; **~ Eve** n la vigilia di Natale; **~ tree** n albero di Natale

chrome [krəum] n cromo

chromium ['krəumɪəm] n cromo

chronic ['krɔnɪk] adj cronico(a)

chronological [krɔnə'lɔdʒɪkəl] adj cronologico(a)

chrysanthemum [krɪ'sænθəməm] n crisantemo

chubby ['tʃʌbɪ] adj paffuto(a)

chuck [tʃʌk] (inf) vt buttare, gettare; (BRIT: also: **~ up**) piantare; **~ out** vt buttar fuori

chuckle ['tʃʌkl] vi ridere sommessamente

chug [tʃʌg] vi fare ciuf ciuf

chum [tʃʌm] n compagno/a

chunk [tʃʌŋk] n pezzo

church [tʃəːtʃ] n chiesa; **~yard** n sagrato

churn [tʃəːn] n (for butter) zangola; (for milk) bidone m; **~ out** vt sfornare

chute [ʃuːt] n (also: **rubbish ~**) canale m di scarico; (BRIT: children's slide) scivolo

chutney ['tʃʌtnɪ] n salsa piccante (di frutta, zucchero e spezie)

CIA (US) n abbr (= Central Intelligence Agency) CIA f

CID (BRIT) n abbr (= Criminal Investigation Department) ≈ polizia giudiziaria

cider ['saɪdə*] n sidro

cigar [sɪ'gɑː*] n sigaro

cigarette [sɪgə'ret] n sigaretta; **~ case** n portasigarette m inv; **~ end** n mozzicone m

Cinderella [sɪndə'relə] n Cenerentola

cinders ['sɪndəz] npl ceneri fpl

cine camera ['sɪnɪ-] (BRIT) n cinepresa

cine film ['sɪnɪ-] (BRIT) n pellicola

cinema ['sɪnəmə] n cinema m inv

cinnamon ['sɪnəmən] n cannella

cipher ['saɪfə*] n cifra

circle ['səːkl] n cerchio; (of friends etc) circolo; (in cinema) galleria ♦ vi girare in circolo ♦ vt (surround) circondare; (move round) girare intorno a

circuit ['səːkɪt] n circuito; **~ous** [səː'kjuɪtəs] adj indiretto(a)

circular ['səːkjulə*] adj circolare ♦ n circolare f

circulate ['səːkjuleɪt] vi circolare ♦ vt far circolare; **circulation** [-'leɪʃən] n circolazione f; (of newspaper) tiratura

circumstances ['səːkəmstənsɪz] npl circostanze fpl; (financial condition) condizioni fpl finanziarie

circus ['səːkəs] n circo

CIS n abbr (= Commonwealth of Independent States) CSI f

cistern ['sɪstən] n cisterna; (in toilet)

serbatoio d'acqua

citizen ['sɪtɪzn] *n* (*of country*) cittadino/a; (*of town*) abitante *m/f*; **~ship** *n* cittadinanza

citrus fruit ['sɪtrəs-] *n* agrume *m*

city ['sɪtɪ] *n* città *f inv*; **the C~** la Città di Londra (*centro commerciale*)

civic ['sɪvɪk] *adj* civico(a); **~ centre** (*BRIT*) *n* centro civico

civil ['sɪvɪl] *adj* civile; **~ engineer** *n* ingegnere *m* civile; **~ian** [sɪ'vɪlɪən] *adj, n* borghese *m/f*

civilization [sɪvɪlaɪ'zeɪʃən] *n* civiltà *f inv*

civilized ['sɪvɪlaɪzd] *adj* civilizzato(a); (*fig*) cortese

civil: ~ law *n* codice *m* civile; (*study*) diritto civile; **~ servant** *n* impiegato/a statale; **C~ Service** *n* amministrazione *f* statale; **~ war** *n* guerra civile

clad [klæd] *adj:* **~ (in)** vestito(a) (di)

claim [kleɪm] *vt* (*assert*): **to ~ (that)/to be** sostenere (che)/di essere; (*credit, rights etc*) rivendicare; (*damages*) richiedere ♦ *vt* (*for insurance*) fare una domanda d'indennizzo ♦ *n* pretesa; rivendicazione *f*; richiesta; **~ant** *n* (*ADMIN, LAW*) richiedente *m/f*

clairvoyant [kleə'vɔɪənt] *n* chiaroveggente *m/f*

clam [klæm] *n* vongola

clamber ['klæmbə*] *vi* arrampicarsi

clammy ['klæmɪ] *adj* (*weather*) caldo(a) umido(a); (*hands*) viscido(a)

clamour ['klæmə*] (*US* **clamor**) *vi:* **to ~ for** chiedere a gran voce

clamp [klæmp] *n* pinza; morsa ♦ *vt* stringere con una morsa; (*AUT: wheel*) applicare i ceppi bloccaruote a; **~ down on** *vt fus* dare un giro di vite a

clan [klæn] *n* clan *m inv*

clang [klæŋ] *vi* emettere un suono metallico

clap [klæp] *vi* applaudire; **~ping** *n* applausi *mpl*

claret ['klærət] *n* vino di Bordeaux

clarify ['klærɪfaɪ] *vt* chiarificare, chiarire

clarinet [klærɪ'nɛt] *n* clarinetto

clarity ['klærɪtɪ] *n* chiarità

clash [klæʃ] *n* frastuono; (*fig*) scontro ♦ *vi* scontrarsi; cozzare

clasp [klɑːsp] *n* (*hold*) stretta; (*of necklace, bag*) fermaglio, fibbia ♦ *vt* stringere

class [klɑːs] *n* classe *f* ♦ *vt* classificare

classic ['klæsɪk] *adj* classico(a) ♦ *n* classico; **~al** *adj* classico(a)

classified ['klæsɪfaɪd] *adj* (*information*) segreto(a), riservato(a); **~ advertisement** *n* annuncio economico

classmate ['klɑːsmeɪt] *n* compagno/a di classe

classroom ['klɑːsrum] *n* aula

clatter ['klætə*] *n* tintinnio; scalpitio ♦ *vi* tintinnare; scalpitare

clause [klɔːz] *n* clausola; (*LING*) proposizione *f*

claw [klɔː] *n* (*of bird of prey*) artiglio; (*of lobster*) pinza

clay [kleɪ] *n* argilla

clean [kliːn] *adj* pulito(a); (*clear, smooth*) liscio(a) ♦ *vt* pulire; **~ out** *vt* ripulire; **~ up** *vt* (*also fig*) ripulire; **~-cut** *adj* (*man*) curato(a); **~er** *n* (*person*) donna delle pulizie; **~er's** *n* (*also: **dry ~er's***) tintoria; **~ing** *n* pulizia; **~liness** ['klɛnlɪnɪs] *n* pulizia

cleanse [klɛnz] *vt* pulire; purificare; **~r** *n* detergente *m*

clean-shaven [-'ʃeɪvn] *adj* sbarbato(a)

cleansing department ['klɛnzɪŋ-] (*BRIT*) *n* nettezza urbana

clear [klɪə*] *adj* chiaro(a); (*glass etc*) trasparente; (*road, way*) libero(a); (*conscience*) pulito(a) ♦ *vt* sgombrare; liberare; (*table*) sparecchiare; (*cheque*) fare la compensazione di; (*LAW: suspect*) discolpare; (*obstacle*) superare ♦ *vi* (*weather*) rasserenarsi; (*fog*) andarsene ♦ *adv:* **~ of** distante da; **~ up** *vt* mettere in ordine; (*mystery*) risolvere; **~ance** *n* (*removal*) sgombro; (*permission*) autorizzazione *f*, permesso; **~-cut** *adj* ben delineato(a), distinto(a); **~ing** *n* radura; **~ing bank** (*BRIT*) *n* banca (che fa uso della camera di compensazione); **~ly** *adv* chiaramente; **~way** (*BRIT*) *n* strada con divieto di sosta

cleaver ['kliːvə*] *n* mannaia

clef [klɛf] n (MUS) chiave f

cleft [klɛft] n (in rock) crepa, fenditura

clench [klɛntʃ] vt stringere

clergy [ˈkləːdʒɪ] n clero; **~man** (irreg) n ecclesiastico

clerical [ˈklɛrɪkəl] adj d'impiegato; (REL) clericale

clerk [klɑːk, (US) kləːrk] n (BRIT) impiegato/a; (US) commesso/a

clever [ˈklɛvə*] adj (mentally) intelligente; (deft, skilful) abile; (device) ingegnoso(a)

click [klɪk] vi scattare ♦ vt (heels etc) battere; (tongue) far schioccare ♦ **~on** vt (COMPUT) cliccare su

client [ˈklaɪənt] n cliente m/f

cliff [klɪf] n scogliera scoscesa, rupe f

climate [ˈklaɪmɪt] n clima m

climax [ˈklaɪmæks] n culmine m; (sexual) orgasmo

climb [klaɪm] vi salire; (clamber) arrampicarsi ♦ vt salire; (CLIMBING) scalare ♦ n salita; arrampicata; scalata; **~-down** n marcia indietro; **~er** n rocciatore/trice; alpinista m/f; **~ing** n alpinismo

clinch [klɪntʃ] vt (deal) concludere

cling [klɪŋ] (pt, pp **clung**) vi: **to ~ (to)** aggrapparsi (a); (of clothes) aderire strettamente (a)

clinic [ˈklɪnɪk] n clinica; **~al** adj clinico(a); (fig) distaccato(a); (: room) freddo(a)

clink [klɪŋk] vi tintinnare

clip [klɪp] n (for hair) forcina; (also: **paper ~**) graffetta; (TV, CINEMA) sequenza ♦ vt attaccare insieme; (hair, nails) tagliare; (hedge) tosare; **~pers** npl (for gardening) cesoie fpl; (also: **nail ~pers**) forbicine fpl per le unghie; **~ping** n (from newspaper) ritaglio

clique [kliːk] n cricca

cloak [kləuk] n mantello ♦ vt avvolgere; **~room** n (for coats etc) guardaroba m inv; (BRIT: W.C.) gabinetti mpl

clock [klɔk] n orologio; **~ in** or **on** vi timbrare il cartellino (all'entrata); **~ off** or **out** vi timbrare il cartellino (all'uscita); **~wise** adv in senso orario; **~work** n movimento or meccanismo a orologeria

♦ adj a molla

clog [klɔg] n zoccolo ♦ vt intasare ♦ vi (also: **~ up**) intasarsi, bloccarsi

cloister [ˈklɔɪstə*] n chiostro

clone [kləun] n clone m

close[^1] [kləus] adj: **~ (to)** vicino(a) (a); (watch, link, relative) stretto(a); (examination) attento(a); (contest) combattuto(a); (weather) afoso(a) ♦ adv vicino, dappresso; **~ to** vicino a; **~ by**, **~ at hand** a portata di mano; **a ~ friend** un amico intimo; **to have a ~ shave** (fig) scamparla bella

close[^2] [kləuz] vt chiudere ♦ vi (shop etc) chiudere; (lid, door etc) chiudersi; (end) finire ♦ n (end) fine f; **~ down** vi cessare (definitivamente); **~d** adj chiuso(a); **~d shop** n azienda o fabbrica che impiega solo aderenti ai sindacati

close-knit [ˈkləusˈnɪt] adj (family, community) molto unito(a)

closely [ˈkləuslɪ] adv (examine, watch) da vicino; (related) strettamente

closet [ˈklɔzɪt] n (cupboard) armadio

close-up [ˈkləusʌp] n primo piano

closure [ˈkləuʒə*] n chiusura

clot [klɔt] n (also: **blood ~**) coagulo; (inf: idiot) scemo/a ♦ vi coagularsi

cloth [klɔθ] n (material) tessuto, stoffa; (rag) strofinaccio

clothe [kləuð] vt vestire; **~s** npl abiti mpl, vestiti mpl; **~s brush** n spazzola per abiti; **~s line** n corda (per stendere il bucato); **~s peg** (US **~s pin**) n molletta

clothing [ˈkləuðɪŋ] n = **clothes**

cloud [klaud] n nuvola; **~burst** n acquazzone m; **~y** adj nuvoloso(a); (liquid) torbido(a)

clout [klaut] vt dare un colpo a

clove [kləuv] n chiodo di garofano; **~ of garlic** spicchio d'aglio

clover [ˈkləuvə*] n trifoglio

clown [klaun] n pagliaccio ♦ vi (also: **~ about**, **~ around**) fare il pagliaccio

cloying [ˈklɔɪɪŋ] adj (taste, smell) nauseabondo(a)

club [klʌb] n (society) club m inv, circolo;

(*weapon, GOLF*) mazza ♦ *vt* bastonare ♦ *vi*: **to ~ together** associarsi; **~s** *npl* (*CARDS*) fiori *mpl*; **~ class** *n* (*AVIAT*) classe *f* club *inv*; **~house** *n* sede *f* del circolo

cluck [klʌk] *vi* chiocciare

clue [kluː] *n* indizio; (*in crosswords*) definizione *f*; **I haven't a ~** non ho la minima idea

clump [klʌmp] *n* (*of flowers, trees*) gruppo; (*of grass*) ciuffo

clumsy ['klʌmzi] *adj* goffo(a)

clung [klʌŋ] *pt, pp of* **cling**

cluster ['klʌstə*] *n* gruppo ♦ *vi* raggrupparsi

clutch [klʌtʃ] *n* (*grip, grasp*) presa, stretta; (*AUT*) frizione *f* ♦ *vt* afferrare, stringere forte

clutter ['klʌtə*] *vt* ingombrare

CND *n abbr* = **Campaign for Nuclear Disarmament**

Co. *abbr* = **county; company**

c/o *abbr* (= *care of*) presso

coach [kəʊtʃ] *n* (*bus*) pullman *m inv*; (*horse-drawn, of train*) carrozza; (*SPORT*) allenatore/trice; (*tutor*) chi dà ripetizioni ♦ *vt* allenare; dare ripetizioni a; **~ trip** *n* viaggio in pullman

coal [kəʊl] *n* carbone *m*; **~ face** *n* fronte *f*; **~field** *n* bacino carbonifero

coalition [kəʊə'lɪʃən] *n* coalizione *f*

coalman ['kəʊlmən] (*irreg*) *n* negoziante *m* di carbone

coalmine ['kəʊlmaɪn] *n* miniera di carbone

coarse [kɔːs] *adj* (*salt, sand etc*) grosso(a); (*cloth, person*) rozzo(a)

coast [kəʊst] *n* costa ♦ *vi* (*with cycle etc*) scendere a ruota libera; **~al** *adj* costiero(a); **~guard** *n* guardia costiera; **~line** *n* linea costiera

coat [kəʊt] *n* cappotto; (*of animal*) pelo; (*of paint*) mano *f* ♦ *vt* coprire; **~ hanger** *n* attaccapanni *m inv*; **~ing** *n* rivestimento; **~ of arms** *n* stemma *m*

coax [kəʊks] *vt* indurre (con moine)

cobbler ['kɔblə*] *n* calzolaio

cobbles ['kɔblz] *npl* ciottoli *mpl*

cobblestones ['kɔblstəʊnz] *npl* ciottoli *mpl*

cobweb ['kɔbwɛb] *n* ragnatela

cocaine [kə'keɪn] *n* cocaina

cock [kɔk] *n* (*rooster*) gallo; (*male bird*) maschio ♦ *vt* (*gun*) armare; **~erel** *n* galletto

cockle ['kɔkl] *n* cardio

cockney ['kɔkni] *n* cockney *m/f inv* (*abitante dei quartieri popolari dell'East End di Londra*)

cockpit ['kɔkpɪt] *n* abitacolo

cockroach ['kɔkrəʊtʃ] *n* blatta

cocktail ['kɔkteɪl] *n* cocktail *m inv*; **~ cabinet** *n* mobile *m* bar *inv*; **~ party** *n* cocktail *m inv*

cocoa ['kəʊkəʊ] *n* cacao

coconut ['kəʊkənʌt] *n* noce *f* di cocco

cocoon [kə'kuːn] *n* bozzolo

cod [kɔd] *n* merluzzo

C.O.D. *abbr* = **cash on delivery**

code [kəʊd] *n* codice *m*

cod-liver oil *n* olio di fegato di merluzzo

coercion [kəʊ'əːʃən] *n* coercizione *f*

coffee ['kɔfi] *n* caffè *m inv*; **~ bar** (*BRIT*) *n* caffè *m inv*; **~ break** *n* pausa per il caffè; **~pot** *n* caffettiera; **~ table** *n* tavolino

coffin ['kɔfɪn] *n* bara

cog [kɔg] *n* dente *m*

cogent ['kəʊdʒənt] *adj* convincente

coherent [kəʊ'hɪərənt] *adj* coerente

coil [kɔɪl] *n* rotolo; (*ELEC*) bobina; (*contraceptive*) spirale *f* ♦ *vt* avvolgere

coin [kɔɪn] *n* moneta ♦ *vt* (*word*) coniare; **~age** *n* sistema *m* monetario; **~-box** (*BRIT*) *n* telefono a gettoni

coincide [kəʊɪn'saɪd] *vi* coincidere; **coincidence** [kəʊ'ɪnsɪdəns] *n* combinazione *f*

Coke ® [kəʊk] *n* coca

coke [kəʊk] *n* coke *m*

colander ['kɔləndə*] *n* colino

cold [kəʊld] *adj* freddo(a) ♦ *n* freddo; (*MED*) raffreddore *m*; **it's ~** fa freddo; **to be ~** (*person*) aver freddo; (*object*) essere freddo(a); **to catch ~** prendere freddo; **to catch a ~** prendere un raffreddore; **in ~ blood** a sangue freddo; **~-shoulder** *vt* trattare con freddezza; **~ sore** *n* erpete *m*

coleslaw ['kəʊlslɔ:] n insalata di cavolo bianco

colic ['kɒlɪk] n colica

collapse [kə'læps] vi crollare ♦ n crollo; (MED) collasso

collapsible [kə'læpsəbl] adj pieghevole

collar ['kɒlə*] n (of coat, shirt) colletto; (of dog, cat) collare m; ~bone n clavicola

collateral [kə'lætərl] n garanzia

colleague ['kɒli:g] n collega m/f

collect [kə'lekt] vt (gen) raccogliere; (as a hobby) fare collezione di; (BRIT: call and pick up) prendere; (money owed, pension) riscuotere; (donations, subscriptions) fare una colletta di ♦ vi adunarsi, riunirsi; ammucchiarsi; **to call ~** (US: TEL) fare una chiamata a carico del destinatario; ~**ion** [kə'lekʃən] n raccolta; collezione f; (for money) colletta

collector [kə'lektə*] n collezionista m/f

college ['kɒlɪdʒ] n college m inv; (of technology etc) istituto superiore

collide [kə'laɪd] vi: **to ~ (with)** scontrarsi (con)

colliery ['kɒlɪərɪ] (BRIT) n miniera di carbone

collision [kə'lɪʒən] n collisione f, scontro

colloquial [kə'ləʊkwɪəl] adj familiare

colon ['kəʊlən] n (sign) due punti mpl; (MED) colon m inv

colonel ['kə:nl] n colonnello

colonial [kə'ləʊnɪəl] adj coloniale

colony ['kɒlənɪ] n colonia

colour ['kʌlə*] (US **color**) n colore m ♦ vt colorare; (tint, dye) tingere; (fig: affect) influenzare ♦ vi (blush) arrossire; **~s** npl (of party, club) colori mpl; **in ~** a colori; **~ in** vt colorare; **~ bar** n discriminazione f razziale (in locali etc); **~-blind** adj daltonico(a); **~ed** adj (photo) a colori; (person) di colore; **~ film** n (for camera) pellicola a colori; **~ful** adj pieno(a) di colore, a vivaci colori; (personality) colorato(a); **~ing** n (substance) colorante m; (complexion) colorito; **~ scheme** n combinazione f di colori; **~ television** n televisione f a colori

colt [kəʊlt] n puledro

column ['kɒləm] n colonna; **~ist** ['kɒləmnɪst]

n articolista m/f

coma ['kəʊmə] n coma m inv

comb [kəʊm] n pettine m ♦ vt (hair) pettinare; (area) battere a tappeto

combat ['kɒmbæt] n combattimento ♦ vt combattere, lottare contro

combination [kɒmbɪ'neɪʃən] n combinazione f

combine [vb kəm'baɪn, n 'kɒmbaɪn] vt: **to ~ (with)** combinare (con); (one quality with another) unire (a) ♦ vi unirsi; (CHEM) combinarsi ♦ n (ECON) associazione f; **~ (harvester)** n mietitrebbia

come [kʌm] (pt **came**, pp **come**) vi venire; arrivare; **to ~ to** (decision etc) raggiungere; **I've ~ to like him** ha cominciato a piacermi; **to ~ undone** slacciarsi; **to ~ loose** allentarsi; **~ about** vi succedere; **~ across** vt fus trovare per caso; **~ away** vi venire via; staccarsi; **~ back** vi ritornare; **~ by** vt fus (acquire) ottenere; procurarsi; **~ down** vi scendere; (prices) calare; (buildings) essere demolito(a); **~ forward** vi farsi avanti; presentarsi; **~ from** vt fus venire da; provenire da; **~ in** vi entrare; **~ in for** vt fus (criticism etc) ricevere; **~ into** vt fus (money) ereditare; **~ off** vi (button) staccarsi; (stain) andar via; (attempt) riuscire; **~ on** vi (pupil, work, project) fare progressi; (lights) accendersi; (electricity) entrare in funzione; **~ on!** avanti!, andiamo!, forza!; **~ out** vi uscire; (stain) andare via; **~ round** vi (after faint, operation) riprendere conoscenza, rinvenire; **~ to** vi rinvenire; **~ up** vi (sun) salire; (problem) sorgere; (event) essere in arrivo; (in conversation) saltar fuori; **~ up against** vt fus (resistance, difficulties) urtare contro; **~ up with** vt fus: **he came up with an idea** venne fuori con un'idea; **~ upon** vt fus trovare per caso; **~back** n (THEATRE etc) ritorno

comedian [kə'mi:dɪən] n comico

comedienne [kəmi:dɪ'en] n attrice f comica

comedy ['kɒmɪdɪ] n commedia

comeuppance [kʌm'ʌpəns] n: **to get**

one's ~ ricevere ciò che si merita
comfort ['kʌmfət] n comodità f inv,
benessere m; (relief) consolazione f,
conforto ♦ vt consolare, confortare; ~s npl
comodità fpl; ~able adj comodo(a);
(financially) agiato(a); ~ably adv (sit etc)
comodamente; (live) bene; ~ station (US)
n gabinetti mpl
comic ['kɔmɪk] adj (also: ~al) comico(a) ♦ n
comico; (BRIT: magazine) giornaletto; ~
strip n fumetto
coming ['kʌmɪŋ] n arrivo ♦ adj (next)
prossimo(a); (future) futuro(a); ~(s) and
going(s) n(pl) andirivieni m inv
comma ['kɔmə] n virgola
command [kə'mɑːnd] n ordine m,
comando; (MIL: authority) comando;
(mastery) padronanza ♦ vt comandare; to ~
sb to do ordinare a qn di fare; ~eer
[kɔmən'dɪə*] vt requisire; ~er n capo; (MIL)
comandante m
commando [kə'mɑːndəu] n commando m
inv; membro di un commando
commence [kə'mɛns] vt, vi cominciare
commend [kə'mɛnd] vt lodare;
raccomandare
commensurate [kə'mɛnsərɪt] adj: ~ with
proporzionato(a) a
comment ['kɔmɛnt] n commento ♦ vi: to ~
(on) fare commenti (su); ~ary ['kɔmən tərɪ]
n commentario; (SPORT) radiocronaca;
telecronaca; ~ator ['kɔmən teɪtə*] n
commentatore/trice; radiocronista m/f,
telecronista m/f
commerce ['kɔmə:s] n commercio
commercial [kə'mə:ʃəl] adj commerciale
♦ n (TV, RADIO: advertisement) pubblicità f
inv; ~ radio/television n radio f inv/
televisione f privata
commiserate [kə'mɪzəreɪt] vi: to ~ with
partecipare al dolore di
commission [kə'mɪʃən] n commissione f
♦ vt (work of art) commissionare; out of ~
(NAUT) in disarmo; ~aire [kəmɪʃə'nɛə*] (BRIT)
n (at shop, cinema etc) portiere m in livrea;
~er n (POLICE) questore m
commit [kə'mɪt] vt (act) commettere; (to

sb's care) affidare; to ~ o.s. (to do)
impegnarsi (a fare); to ~ suicide suicidarsi;
~ment n impegno; promessa
committee [kə'mɪtɪ] n comitato
commodity [kə'mɔdɪtɪ] n prodotto, articolo
common ['kɔmən] adj comune; (pej)
volgare; (usual) normale ♦ n terreno
comune; the C~s (BRIT) npl la Camera dei
Comuni; in ~ in comune; ~er n cittadino/a
(non nobile); ~ law n diritto
consuetudinario; ~ly adv comunemente,
usualmente; C~ Market n Mercato
Comune; ~place adj banale, ordinario(a);
~room n sala di riunione; (SCOL) sala dei
professori; ~ sense n buon senso; the
C~wealth n il Commonwealth
commotion [kə'məuʃən] n confusione f,
tumulto
communal ['kɔmju:nl] adj (for common
use) pubblico(a)
commune [n 'kɔmju:n, vb kə'mju:n] n
(group) comune f ♦ vi: to ~ with mettersi
in comunione con
communicate [kə'mju:nɪkeɪt] vt
comunicare, trasmettere ♦ vi: to ~ (with)
comunicare (con)
communication [kəmju:nɪ'keɪʃən] n
comunicazione f; ~ cord (BRIT) n segnale
m d'allarme
communion [kə'mju:nɪən] n (also: Holy
C~) comunione f
communiqué [kə'mju:nɪkeɪ] n comunicato
communism ['kɔmjunɪzəm] n comunismo;
communist adj, n comunista m/f
community [kə'mju:nɪtɪ] n comunità f inv;
~ centre n circolo ricreativo; ~ chest
(US) n fondo di beneficenza
commutation ticket [kɔmju'teɪʃən-] (US) n
biglietto di abbonamento
commute [kə'mju:t] vi fare il pendolare
♦ vt (LAW) commutare; ~r n pendolare m/f
compact [adj kəm'pækt, n 'kɔmpækt] adj
compatto(a) ♦ n (also: powder ~)
portacipria m inv; ~ disc n compact disc
m inv; ~ disc player n lettore m CD inv
companion [kəm'pænɪən] n compagno/a;
~ship n compagnia

company ['kʌmpənɪ] *n* (also COMM, MIL, THEATRE) compagnia; **to keep sb ~** tenere compagnia a qn; **~ secretary** (BRIT) *n* segretario/a generale

comparable ['kɔmpərəbl] *adj* simile

comparative [kəm'pærətɪv] *adj* relativo(a); (*adjective etc*) comparativo(a); **~ly** *adv* relativamente

compare [kəm'pɛə*] *vt*: **to ~ sth/sb with/ to** confrontare qc/qn con/a ♦ *vi*: **to ~ (with)** reggere il confronto (con); **comparison** [-'pærɪsn] *n* confronto; **in comparison (with)** in confronto (a)

compartment [kəm'pɑːtmənt] *n* compartimento; (RAIL) scompartimento

compass ['kʌmpəs] *n* bussola; **~es** *npl* (MATH) compasso

compassion [kəm'pæʃən] *n* compassione *f*

compatible [kəm'pætɪbl] *adj* compatibile

compel [kəm'pɛl] *vt* costringere, obbligare

compensate ['kɔmpənseɪt] *vt* risarcire ♦ *vi*: **to ~ for** compensare; **compensation** [-'seɪʃən] *n* compensazione *f*; (*money*) risarcimento

compère ['kɔmpɛə*] *n* presentatore/trice

compete [kəm'piːt] *vi* (*take part*) concorrere; (*vie*): **to ~ (with)** fare concorrenza (a)

competent ['kɔmpɪtənt] *adj* competente

competition [kɔmpɪ'tɪʃən] *n* gara; concorso; (ECON) concorrenza

competitive [kəm'petɪtɪv] *adj* (ECON) concorrenziale; (*sport*) agonistico(a); (*person*) che ha spirito di competizione; che ha spirito agonistico

competitor [kəm'petɪtə*] *n* concorrente *m/f*

complacency [kəm'pleɪsnsɪ] *n* compiacenza di sé

complain [kəm'pleɪn] *vi* lagnarsi, lamentarsi; **~t** *n* lamento; (*in shop etc*) reclamo; (MED) malattia

complement [*n* 'kɔmplɪmənt, *vb* 'kɔmplɪment] *n* complemento; (*especially of ship's crew etc*) effettivo *m* ♦ *vt* (*enhance*) accompagnarsi bene a; **~ary** [kɔmplɪ'mentərɪ] *adj* complementare

complete [kəm'pliːt] *adj* completo(a) ♦ *vt*

completare; (*a form*) riempire; **~ly** *adv* completamente; **completion** [-'pliːʃən] *n* completamento

complex ['kɔmpleks] *adj* complesso(a) ♦ *n* (PSYCH, *buildings etc*) complesso

complexion [kəm'plekʃən] *n* (*of face*) carnagione *f*

compliance [kəm'plaɪəns] *n* acquiescenza; **in ~ with** (*orders, wishes etc*) in conformità con

complicate ['kɔmplɪkeɪt] *vt* complicare; **~d** *adj* complicato(a); **complication** [-'keɪʃən] *n* complicazione *f*

compliment [*n* 'kɔmplɪmənt, *vb* 'kɔmplɪment] *n* complimento ♦ *vt* fare un complimento a; **~s** *npl* (*greetings*) complimenti *mpl*; rispetti *mpl*; **to pay sb a ~** fare un complimento a qn; **~ary** [-'mentərɪ] *adj* complimentoso(a), elogiativo(a); (*free*) in omaggio; **~ary ticket** *n* biglietto omaggio

comply [kəm'plaɪ] *vi*: **to ~ with** assentire a; conformarsi a

component [kəm'pəunənt] *adj* componente ♦ *n* componente *m*

compose [kəm'pəuz] *vt* (*form*): **to be ~d of** essere composto di; (*music, poem etc*) comporre; **to ~ o.s.** ricomporsi; **~d** *adj* calmo(a); **~r** *n* (MUS) compositore/trice

composition [kɔmpə'zɪʃən] *n* composizione *f*

composure [kəm'pəuʒə*] *n* calma

compound ['kɔmpaund] *n* (CHEM, LING) composto; (*enclosure*) recinto ♦ *adj* composto(a); **~ fracture** *n* frattura esposta

comprehend [kɔmprɪ'hend] *vt* comprendere, capire; **comprehension** [-'henʃən] *n* comprensione *f*

comprehensive [kɔmprɪ'hensɪv] *adj* comprensivo(a); **~ policy** *n* (INSURANCE) polizza che copre tutti i rischi; **~ (school)** (BRIT) *n* scuola secondaria aperta a tutti

compress [*vb* kəm'pres, *n* 'kɔmpres] *vt* comprimere ♦ *n* (MED) compressa

comprise [kəm'praɪz] *vt* (also: **be ~d of**) comprendere

compromise ['kɔmprəmaɪz] n compromesso ♦ vt compromettere ♦ vi venire a un compromesso

compulsion [kəm'pʌlʃən] n costrizione f

compulsive [kəm'pʌlsɪv] adj (liar, gambler) che non riesce a controllarsi; (viewing, reading) cui non si può fare a meno

compulsory [kəm'pʌlsərɪ] adj obbligatorio(a)

computer [kəm'pju:tə*] n computer m inv, elaboratore m elettronico; ~ **game** n gioco per computer; **~-generated** adj realizzato(a) al computer; **~ize** vt computerizzare; ~ **programmer** n programmatore/trice; ~ **programming** n programmazione f di computer; ~ **science** n informatica; **computing** n informatica

comrade ['kɔmrɪd] n compagno/a; **~ship** n cameratismo

con [kɔn] (inf) vt truffare ♦ n truffa

conceal [kən'si:l] vt nascondere

concede [kən'si:d] vt ammettere

conceit [kən'si:t] n presunzione f, vanità; **~ed** adj presuntuoso(a), vanitoso(a)

conceive [kən'si:v] vt concepire ♦ vi concepire un bambino

concentrate ['kɔnsəntreɪt] vi concentrarsi ♦ vt concentrare

concentration [kɔnsən'treɪʃən] n concentrazione f; ~ **camp** n campo di concentramento

concept ['kɔnsept] n concetto

concern [kən'sə:n] n affare m; (COMM) azienda, ditta; (anxiety) preoccupazione f ♦ vt riguardare; **to be ~ed (about)** preoccuparsi (di); **~ing** prep riguardo a, circa

concert ['kɔnsət] n concerto; **~ed** [kən'sə:tɪd] adj concertato(a); ~ **hall** n sala da concerti

concertina [kɔnsə'ti:nə] n piccola fisarmonica

conclude [kən'klu:d] vt concludere; **conclusion** [-'klu:ʒən] n conclusione f; **conclusive** [-'klu:sɪv] adj conclusivo(a)

concoct [kən'kɔkt] vt inventare; **~ion**

[-'kɔkʃən] n miscuglio

concourse ['kɔŋkɔ:s] n (hall) atrio

concrete ['kɔŋkri:t] n calcestruzzo ♦ adj concreto(a); di calcestruzzo

concur [kən'kə:*] vi concordare

concurrently [kən'kʌrntlɪ] adv simultaneamente

concussion [kən'kʌʃən] n commozione f cerebrale

condemn [kən'dem] vt condannare; (building) dichiarare pericoloso(a)

condensation [kɔnden'seɪʃən] n condensazione f

condense [kən'dens] vi condensarsi ♦ vt condensare; **~d milk** n latte m condensato

condescending [kɔndɪ'sendɪŋ] adj (person) che ha un'aria di superiorità

condition [kən'dɪʃən] n condizione f; (MED) malattia ♦ vt condizionare; **on ~ that** a condizione che +sub, a condizione di; **~er** n (for hair) balsamo; (for fabrics) ammorbidente m

condolences [kən'dəʊlənsɪz] npl condoglianze fpl

condom ['kɔndəm] n preservativo

condominium [kɔndə'mɪnɪəm] (US) n condominio

conducive [kən'dju:sɪv] adj: ~ **to** favorevole a

conduct [n 'kɔndʌkt, vb kən'dʌkt] n condotta ♦ vt condurre; (manage) dirigere; amministrare; (MUS) dirigere; **to ~ o.s.** comportarsi; **~ed tour** n gita accompagnata; **~or** n (of orchestra) direttore m d'orchestra; (on bus) bigliettaio; (US: on train) controllore m; (ELEC) conduttore m; **~ress** n (on bus) bigliettaia

cone [kəʊn] n cono; (BOT) pigna; (traffic ~) birillo

confectioner [kən'fekʃənə*] n pasticciere m; **~'s (shop)** n ≈ pasticceria; **~y** n dolciumi mpl

confer [kən'fə:*] vt: **to ~ sth on** conferire qc a ♦ vi conferire

conference ['kɔnfərns] n congresso

confess [kən'fes] vt confessare, ammettere

♦ *vi* confessare; **~ion** [-'fɛʃən] *n* confessione *f*

confetti [kən'fɛtɪ] *n* coriandoli *mpl*

confide [kən'faɪd] *vi*: **to ~ in** confidarsi con

confidence ['kɒnfɪdns] *n* confidenza; (*trust*) fiducia; (*self-assurance*) sicurezza di sé; **in ~** (*speak, write*) in confidenza, confidenzialmente; **~ trick** *n* truffa; **confident** *adj* sicuro(a); sicuro(a) di sé; **confidential** [kɒnfɪ'dɛnʃəl] *adj* riservato(a), confidenziale

confine [kən'faɪn] *vt* limitare; (*shut up*) rinchiudere; **~d** *adj* (*space*) ristretto(a); **~ment** *n* prigionia; **~s** ['kɒnfaɪnz] *npl* confini *mpl*

confirm [kən'fə:m] *vt* confermare; **~ation** [kɒnfə'meɪʃən] *n* conferma; (*REL*) cresima; **~ed** *adj* inveterato(a)

confiscate ['kɒnfɪskeɪt] *vt* confiscare

conflict [*n* 'kɒnflɪkt, *vb* kən'flɪkt] *n* conflitto ♦ *vi* essere in conflitto; **~ing** *adj* contrastante

conform [kən'fɔ:m] *vi*: **to ~ (to)** conformarsi (a)

confound [kən'faʊnd] *vt* confondere

confront [kən'frʌnt] *vt* (*enemy, danger*) affrontare; **~ation** [kɒnfrən'teɪʃən] *n* scontro

confuse [kən'fju:z] *vt* (*one thing with another*) confondere; **~d** *adj* confuso(a); **confusing** *adj* che fa confondere; **confusion** [-'fju:ʒən] *n* confusione *f*

congeal [kən'dʒi:l] *vi* (*blood*) congelarsi

congenial [kən'dʒi:nɪəl] *adj* (*person*) simpatico(a); (*thing*) congeniale

congested [kən'dʒɛstɪd] *adj* congestionato(a)

congestion [kən'dʒɛstʃən] *n* congestione *f*

congratulate [kən'grætjuleɪt] *vt*: **to ~ sb (on)** congratularsi con qn (per *or* di); **congratulations** [-'leɪʃənz] *npl* auguri *mpl*; (*on success*) complimenti *mpl*, congratulazioni *fpl*

congregate ['kɒŋɡrɪɡeɪt] *vi* congregarsi, riunirsi

congress ['kɒŋɡrɛs] *n* congresso; **C~man** (*US*) *n* membro del Congresso

conjunction [kən'dʒʌŋkʃən] *n* congiunzione *f*

conjunctivitis [kəndʒʌŋktɪ'vaɪtɪs] *n* congiuntivite *f*

conjure ['kʌndʒə*] *vi* fare giochi di prestigio; **~ up** *vt* (*ghost, spirit*) evocare; (*memories*) rievocare; **~r** *n* prestidigitatore/trice, prestigiatore/trice

conk out [kɒŋk-] (*inf*) *vi* andare in panne

con man *n* truffatore *m*

connect [kə'nɛkt] *vt* connettere, collegare; (*ELEC, TEL*) collegare; (*fig*) associare ♦ *vi* (*train*): **to ~ with** essere in coincidenza con; **to be ~ed with** (*associated*) aver rapporti con; **~ion** [-ʃən] *n* relazione *f*, rapporto; (*ELEC*) connessione *f*; (*train, plane*) coincidenza; (*TEL*) collegamento

connive [kə'naɪv] *vi*: **to ~ at** essere connivente in

connoisseur [kɒnɪ'sə*] *n* conoscitore/trice

conquer ['kɒŋkə*] *vt* conquistare; (*feelings*) vincere

conquest ['kɒŋkwɛst] *n* conquista

cons [kɒnz] *npl see* **convenience**; **pro**

conscience ['kɒnʃəns] *n* coscienza

conscientious [kɒnʃɪ'ɛnʃəs] *adj* coscienzioso(a)

conscious ['kɒnʃəs] *adj* consapevole; (*MED*) cosciente; **~ness** *n* consapevolezza; coscienza

conscript ['kɒnskrɪpt] *n* coscritto; **~ion** [-'skrɪpʃən] *n* arruolamento (obbligatorio)

consent [kən'sɛnt] *n* consenso ♦ *vi*: **to ~ (to)** acconsentire (a)

consequence ['kɒnsɪkwəns] *n* conseguenza, risultato; importanza

consequently ['kɒnsɪkwəntlɪ] *adv* di conseguenza, dunque

conservation [kɒnsə'veɪʃən] *n* conservazione *f*

conservative [kən'sə:vətɪv] *adj* conservatore(trice); (*cautious*) cauto(a); **C~** (*BRIT*) *adj, n* (*POL*) conservatore(trice)

conservatory [kən'sə:vətrɪ] *n* (*greenhouse*) serra; (*MUS*) conservatorio

conserve [kən'sə:v] *vt* conservare ♦ *n* conserva

consider [kən'sɪdə*] *vt* considerare; (*take*

into account) tener conto di; **to ~ doing sth** considerare la possibilità di fare qc

considerable [kən'sɪdərəbl] *adj* considerevole, notevole; **considerably** *adv* notevolmente, decisamente

considerate [kən'sɪdərt] *adj* premuroso(a)

consideration [kənsɪdə'reɪʃən] *n* considerazione *f*

considering [kən'sɪdərɪŋ] *prep* in considerazione di

consign [kən'saɪn] *vt*: **to ~ to** (*sth unwanted*) relegare in; (*person: to sb's care*) consegnare a; (*: to poverty*) condannare a; **~ment** *n* (*of goods*) consegna; spedizione *f*

consist [kən'sɪst] *vi*: **to ~ of** constare di, essere composto(a) di

consistency [kən'sɪstənsɪ] *n* consistenza; (*fig*) coerenza

consistent [kən'sɪstənt] *adj* coerente

consolation [kɔnsə'leɪʃən] *n* consolazione *f*

console¹ [kən'səul] *vt* consolare

console² ['kɔnsəul] *n* quadro di comando

consonant ['kɔnsənənt] *n* consonante *f*

consortium [kən'sɔːtɪəm] *n* consorzio

conspicuous [kən'spɪkjuəs] *adj* cospicuo(a)

conspiracy [kən'spɪrəsɪ] *n* congiura, cospirazione *f*

constable ['kʌnstəbl] (*BRIT*) *n* ≈ poliziotto, agente *m* di polizia; **chief ~** ≈ questore *m*

constabulary [kən'stæbjulərɪ] *n* forze *fpl* dell'ordine

constant ['kɔnstənt] *adj* costante; continuo(a); **~ly** *adv* costantemente; continuamente

constipated ['kɔnstɪpeɪtɪd] *adj* stitico(a)

constipation [kɔnstɪ'peɪʃən] *n* stitichezza

constituency [kən'stɪtjuənsɪ] *n* collegio elettorale

constituent [kən'stɪtjuənt] *n* elettore/trice; (*part*) elemento componente

constitution [kɔnstɪ'tjuːʃən] *n* costituzione *f*; **~al** *adj* costituzionale

constraint [kən'streɪnt] *n* costrizione *f*

construct [kən'strʌkt] *vt* costruire; **~ion** [-ʃən] *n* costruzione *f*; **~ive** *adj* costruttivo(a)

consul ['kɔnsl] *n* console *m*; **~ate**

['kɔnsjulɪt] *n* consolato

consult [kən'sʌlt] *vt* consultare; **~ant** *n* (*MED*) consulente *m* medico; (*other specialist*) consulente; **~ation** [-'teɪʃən] *n* (*MED*) consulto; (*discussion*) consultazione *f*; **~ing room** (*BRIT*) *n* ambulatorio

consume [kən'sjuːm] *vt* consumare; **~r** *n* consumatore/trice; **~r goods** *npl* beni *mpl* di consumo; **~r society** *n* società dei consumi

consumption [kən'sʌmpʃən] *n* consumo

cont. *abbr* = **continued**

contact ['kɔntækt] *n* contatto; (*person*) conoscenza ♦ *vt* mettersi in contatto con; **~ lenses** *npl* lenti *fpl* a contatto

contagious [kən'teɪdʒəs] *adj* (*also fig*) contagioso(a)

contain [kən'teɪn] *vt* contenere; **to ~ o.s.** contenersi; **~er** *n* recipiente *m*; (*for shipping etc*) container *m inv*

contaminate [kən'tæmɪneɪt] *vt* contaminare

cont'd *abbr* = **continued**

contemplate ['kɔntəmpleɪt] *vt* contemplare; (*consider*) pensare a (*or* di)

contemporary [kən'tempərərɪ] *adj*, *n* contemporaneo(a)

contempt [kən'tempt] *n* disprezzo; **~ of court** (*LAW*) oltraggio alla Corte; **~ible** *adj* deprecabile

contend [kən'tend] *vt*: **to ~ that** sostenere che ♦ *vi*: **to ~ with** lottare contro; **~er** *n* contendente *m/f*; concorrente *m/f*

content¹ ['kɔntent] *n* contenuto; **~s** *npl* (*of box, case etc*) contenuto; (**table of**) **~s** indice *m*

content² [kən'tent] *adj* contento(a), soddisfatto(a) ♦ *vt* contentare, soddisfare; **~ed** *adj* contento(a), soddisfatto(a)

contention [kən'tenʃən] *n* contesa; (*assertion*) tesi *f inv*

contentment [kən'tentmənt] *n* contentezza

contest [*n* 'kɔntest, *vb* kən'test] *n* lotta; (*competition*) gara, concorso ♦ *vt* contestare; impugnare; (*compete for*) essere in lizza per; **~ant** [kən'testənt] *n* concorrente *m/f*; (*in fight*) avversario/a

context ['kɔntɛkst] *n* contesto

continent ['kɔntɪnənt] *n* continente *m*; **the C~** (*BRIT*) l'Europa continentale; **~al** [-'nɛntl] *adj* continentale; **~-al breakfast** *n* colazione *f* all'europea (*senza piatti caldi*); **~al quilt** (*BRIT*) *n* piumino

contingency [kən'tɪndʒənsɪ] *n* eventualità *f inv*

continual [kən'tɪnjuəl] *adj* continuo(a)

continuation [kəntɪnju'eɪʃən] *n* continuazione *f*; (*after interruption*) ripresa; (*of story*) seguito

continue [kən'tɪnjuː] *vi* continuare ♦ *vt* continuare; (*start again*) riprendere

continuity [kɔntɪ'njuːɪtɪ] *n* continuità *f*; (*TV, CINEMA*) (ordine *m* della) sceneggiatura

continuous [kən'tɪnjuəs] *adj* continuo(a); ininterrotto(a)

contort [kən'tɔːt] *vt* contorcere

contour ['kɔntuə] *n* contorno, profilo; (*also:* **~ line**) curva di livello

contraband ['kɔntrəbænd] *n* contrabbando

contraceptive [kɔntrə'sɛptɪv] *adj* contraccettivo(a) ♦ *n* contraccettivo

contract [*n* 'kɔntrækt, *vb* kən'trækt] *n* contratto ♦ *vi* (*become smaller*) contrarsi; (*COMM*): **to ~ to do sth** fare un contratto per fare qc ♦ *vt* (*illness*) contrarre; **~ion** [-ʃən] *n* contrazione *f*; **~or** *n* imprenditore *m*

contradict [kɔntrə'dɪkt] *vt* contraddire

contraflow ['kɔntrəfləu] *n* (*AUT*) senso unico alternato

contraption [kən'træpʃən] (*pej*) *n* aggeggio

contrary[1] ['kɔntrərɪ] *adj* contrario(a); (*unfavourable*) avverso(a), contrario(a) ♦ *n* contrario; **on the ~** al contrario; **unless you hear to the ~** salvo contrordine

contrary[2] [kən'trɛərɪ] *adj* (*perverse*) bisbetico(a)

contrast [*n* 'kɔntrɑːst, *vb* kən'trɑːst] *n* contrasto ♦ *vt* mettere in contrasto; **in ~ to** contrariamente a

contribute [kən'trɪbjuːt] *vi* contribuire ♦ *vt*: **to ~ £10/an article** to dare 10 sterline/un articolo a; **to ~ to** contribuire a; (*newspaper*) scrivere per; **contribution** [kɔntrɪ'bjuːʃən] *n* contributo; **contributor**

n (*to newspaper*) collaboratore/trice

contrivance [kən'traɪvəns] *n* congegno; espediente *m*

contrive [kən'traɪv] *vi*: **to ~ to do** fare in modo di fare

control [kən'trəul] *vt* controllare; (*firm, operation etc*) dirigere ♦ *n* controllo; **~s** *npl* (*of vehicle etc*) comandi *mpl*; (*governmental*) controlli *mpl*; **under ~** sotto controllo; **to be in ~ of** avere il controllo di; **to go out of ~** (*car*) non rispondere ai comandi; (*situation*) sfuggire di mano; **~led substance** *n* sostanza stupefacente; **~ panel** *n* quadro dei comandi; **~ room** *n* (*NAUT, MIL*) sala di comando; (*RADIO, TV*) sala di regia; **~ tower** *n* (*AVIAT*) torre *f* di controllo

controversial [kɔntrə'vəːʃl] *adj* controverso(a), polemico(a)

controversy ['kɔntrəvəːsɪ] *n* controversia, polemica

convalesce [kɔnvə'lɛs] *vi* rimettersi in salute

convene [kən'viːn] *vt* convocare ♦ *vi* convenire, adunarsi

convenience [kən'viːnɪəns] *n* comodità *f inv*; **at your ~** a suo comodo; **all modern ~s**, (*BRIT*) **all mod cons** tutte le comodità moderne

convenient [kən'viːnɪənt] *adj* conveniente, comodo(a)

convent ['kɔnvənt] *n* convento

convention [kən'vɛnʃən] *n* convenzione *f*; (*meeting*) convegno; **~al** *adj* convenzionale

conversant [kən'vəːsnt] *adj*: **to be ~ with** essere al corrente di; essere pratico(a) di

conversation [kɔnvə'seɪʃən] *n* conversazione *f*; **~al** *adj* non formale

converse[1] [kən'vəːs] *vi* conversare

converse[2] ['kɔnvəːs] *n* contrario, opposto; **~ly** [-'vəːslɪ] *adv* al contrario, per contro

convert [*vb* kən'vəːt, *n* 'kɔnvəːt] *vt* (*COMM, REL*) convertire; (*alter*) trasformare ♦ *n* convertito(a); **~ible** *n* macchina decappottabile

convex ['kɔnvɛks] *adj* convesso(a)

convey [kən'veɪ] *vt* trasportare; (*thanks*)

comunicare; (*idea*) dare; ~**or belt** *n* nastro trasportatore

convict [*vb* kən'vɪkt, *n* 'kɔnvɪkt] *vt* dichiarare colpevole ♦ *n* carcerato/a; ~**ion** [-ʃən] *n* condanna; (*belief*) convinzione *f*

convince [kən'vɪns] *vt* convincere, persuadere; **convincing** *adj* convincente

convoluted [kɔnvə'luːtɪd] *adj* (*argument etc*) involuto(a)

convoy ['kɔnvɔɪ] *n* convoglio

convulse [kən'vʌls] *vt*: **to be ~d with laughter** contorcersi dalle risa

cook [kuk] *vt* cucinare, cuocere ♦ *vi* cuocere; (*person*) cuoco/a; ~**book** *n* libro di cucina; ~**er** *n* fornello, cucina; ~**ery** *n* cucina; ~**ery book** (*BRIT*) *n* = ~**book**; ~**ie** (*US*) *n* biscotto; ~**ing** *n* cucina

cool [kuːl] *adj* fresco(a); (*not afraid, calm*) calmo(a); (*unfriendly*) freddo(a) ♦ *vt* raffreddare; (*room*) rinfrescare ♦ *vi* (*water*) raffreddarsi; (*air*) rinfrescarsi

coop [kuːp] *n* stia ♦ *vt*: **to ~ up** (*fig*) rinchiudere

cooperate [kəu'ɔpəreɪt] *vi* cooperare, collaborare; **cooperation** [-'reɪʃən] *n* cooperazione *f*, collaborazione *f*

cooperative [kəu'ɔpərətɪv] *adj* cooperativo(a) ♦ *n* cooperativa

coordinate [*vb* kəu'ɔːdɪneɪt, *n* kəu'ɔːdɪnət] *vt* coordinare ♦ *n* (*MATH*) coordinata; ~**s** *npl* (*clothes*) coordinati *mpl*

co-ownership [kəu'əunəʃɪp] *n* comproprietà

cop [kɔp] (*inf*) *n* sbirro

cope [kəup] *vi*: **to ~ with** (*problems*) far fronte a

copper ['kɔpə*] *n* rame *m*; (*inf: policeman*) sbirro; ~**s** *npl* (*coins*) spiccioli *mpl*

copse [kɔps] *n* bosco ceduo

copy ['kɔpɪ] *n* copia ♦ *vt* copiare; ~**right** *n* diritto d'autore

coral ['kɔrəl] *n* corallo

cord [kɔːd] *n* corda; (*ELEC*) filo

cordial ['kɔːdɪəl] *adj* cordiale ♦ *n* (*BRIT*) cordiale *m*

cordon ['kɔːdn] *n* cordone *m*; ~ **off** *vt* fare

cordone a

corduroy ['kɔːdərɔɪ] *n* fustagno

core [kɔː*] *n* (*of fruit*) torsolo; (*of organization etc*) cuore *m* ♦ *vt* estrarre il torsolo da

cork [kɔːk] *n* sughero; (*of bottle*) tappo; ~**screw** *n* cavatappi *m inv*

corn [kɔːn] *n* (*BRIT: wheat*) grano; (*US: maize*) granturco; (*on foot*) callo; ~ **on the cob** (*CULIN*) pannocchia cotta

corned beef ['kɔːnd-] *n* carne *f* di manzo in scatola

corner ['kɔːnə*] *n* angolo; (*AUT*) curva ♦ *vt* intrappolare; mettere con le spalle al muro; (*COMM: market*) accaparrare ♦ *vi* prendere una curva; ~**stone** *n* pietra angolare

cornet ['kɔːnɪt] *n* (*MUS*) cornetta; (*BRIT: of ice-cream*) cono

cornflakes ['kɔːnfleɪks] *npl* fiocchi *mpl* di granturco

cornflour ['kɔːnflauə*] (*BRIT*) *n* farina finissima di granturco

cornstarch ['kɔːnstɑːtʃ] (*US*) *n* = **cornflour**

Cornwall ['kɔːnwəl] *n* Cornovaglia

corny ['kɔːnɪ] (*inf*) *adj* trito(a)

coronary ['kɔrənərɪ] *n*: ~ **(thrombosis)** trombosi *f* coronaria

coronation [kɔrə'neɪʃən] *n* incoronazione *f*

coroner ['kɔrənə*] *n* magistrato incaricato di indagare la causa di morte in circostanze sospette

coronet ['kɔrənɪt] *n* diadema *m*

corporal ['kɔːpərl] *n* caporalmaggiore *m* ♦ *adj*: ~ **punishment** pena corporale

corporate ['kɔːpərɪt] *adj* costituito(a) (in corporazione); comune

corporation [kɔːpə'reɪʃən] *n* (*of town*) consiglio comunale; (*COMM*) ente *m*

corps [kɔː*, *pl* kɔːz] *n inv* corpo

corpse [kɔːps] *n* cadavere *m*

correct [kə'rɛkt] *adj* (*accurate*) corretto(a), esatto(a); (*proper*) corretto(a) ♦ *vt* correggere; ~**ion** [-ʃən] *n* correzione *f*

correspond [kɔrɪs'pɔnd] *vi* corrispondere; ~**ence** *n* corrispondenza; ~**ence course** *n* corso per corrispondenza; ~**ent** *n* corrispondente *m/f*

corridor ['kɒrɪdɔː*] n corridoio

corrode [kə'rəud] vt corrodere ♦ vi corrodersi

corrugated ['kɒrəgeɪtɪd] adj increspato(a); ondulato(a); ~ **iron** n lamiera di ferro ondulata

corrupt [kə'rʌpt] adj corrotto(a); (COMPUT) alterato(a) ♦ vt corrompere

corset ['kɔːsɪt] n busto

Corsica ['kɔːsɪkə] n Corsica

cosh [kɒʃ] (BRIT) n randello (corto)

cosmetic [kɒz'metɪk] n cosmetico ♦ adj (fig: measure etc) superficiale

cost [kɒst] (pt, pp **cost**) n costo ♦ vt costare; (find out the ~ of) stabilire il prezzo di; ~**s** npl (COMM, LAW) spese fpl; **how much does it ~?** quanto costa?; **at all ~s** a ogni costo

co-star ['kəu-] n attore/trice della stessa importanza del protagonista

cost-effective adj conveniente

costly ['kɒstlɪ] adj costoso(a), caro(a)

cost-of-living adj: ~ **allowance** indennità f inv di contingenza

cost price (BRIT) n prezzo all'ingrosso

costume ['kɒstjuːm] n costume m; (lady's suit) tailleur m inv; (BRIT: also: **swimming** ~) costume da bagno; ~ **jewellery** n bigiotteria

cosy ['kəuzɪ] (US **cozy**) adj intimo(a); **I'm very ~ here** sto proprio bene qui

cot [kɒt] n (BRIT: child's) lettino; (US: campbed) brandina

cottage ['kɒtɪdʒ] n cottage m inv; ~ **cheese** n fiocchi mpl di latte magro

cotton ['kɒtn] n cotone m; ~ **on to** (inf) fus afferrare; ~ **candy** (US) n zucchero filato; ~ **wool** (BRIT) n cotone idrofilo

couch [kautʃ] n sofà m inv

couchette [kuː'ʃet] n (on train, boat) cuccetta

cough [kɒf] vi tossire ♦ n tosse f; ~ **drop** n pasticca per la tosse

could [kud] pt of **can²**; ~**n't** = **could not**

council ['kaunsl] n consiglio; **city** or **town** ~ consiglio comunale; ~ **estate** (BRIT) n quartiere m di case popolari; ~ **house**

(BRIT) n casa popolare; ~**lor** n consigliere/a

counsel ['kaunsl] n avvocato; consultazione f ♦ vt consigliare; ~**lor** n (US: ~**or**) consigliere/a; (US) avvocato

count [kaunt] vt, vi contare ♦ n (of votes etc) conteggio; (of pollen etc) livello; (nobleman) conte m; ~ **on** vt fus contare su; ~**down** n conto alla rovescia

countenance ['kauntɪnəns] n volto, aspetto ♦ vt approvare

counter ['kauntə*] n banco ♦ vt opporsi a ♦ adv: ~ **to** contro; in opposizione a; ~**act** vt agire in opposizione a; (poison etc) annullare gli effetti di; ~**-espionage** n controspionaggio

counterfeit ['kauntəfɪt] n contraffazione f, falso ♦ vt contraffare, falsificare ♦ adj falso(a)

counterfoil ['kauntəfɔɪl] n matrice f

counterpart ['kauntəpɑːt] n (of document etc) copia; (of person) corrispondente m/f

counter-productive [-prə'dʌktɪv] adj controproducente

countersign ['kauntəsaɪn] vt controfirmare

countess ['kauntɪs] n contessa

countless ['kauntlɪs] adj innumerevole

country ['kʌntrɪ] n paese m; (native land) patria; (as opposed to town) campagna; (region) regione f; ~ **dancing** (BRIT) n danza popolare; ~ **house** n villa in campagna; ~**man** (irreg) n (national) compatriota m; (rural) contadino; ~**side** n campagna

county ['kauntɪ] n contea

coup [kuː] n (pl **coups**) n colpo; (also: ~ **d'état**) colpo di Stato

couple ['kʌpl] n coppia; **a ~ of** un paio di

coupon ['kuːpɒn] n buono; (detachable form) coupon m inv

courage ['kʌrɪdʒ] n coraggio

courgette [kuə'ʒet] (BRIT) n zucchina

courier ['kurɪə*] n corriere m; (for tourists) guida

course [kɔːs] n corso; (of ship) rotta; (for golf) campo; (part of meal) piatto; **of ~** senz'altro, naturalmente; ~ **of action** modo d'agire; **a ~ of treatment** (MED) una cura

court [kɔːt] *n* corte *f*; (TENNIS) campo ♦ *vt* (woman) fare la corte a; **to take to ~** citare in tribunale

courteous ['kəːtɪəs] *adj* cortese

courtesy ['kəːtəsɪ] *n* cortesia; **(by) ~ of** per gentile concessione di; **~ bus**, **~ coach** *n* autobus *m inv* gratuito (di hotel, aeroporto)

court-house (US) *n* palazzo di giustizia

courtier ['kɔːtɪə*] *n* cortigiano/a

court-martial [-'mɑːʃəl] (*pl* **courts-martial**) *n* corte *f* marziale

courtroom ['kɔːtrum] *n* tribunale *m*

courtyard ['kɔːtjɑːd] *n* cortile *m*

cousin ['kʌzn] *n* cugino/a; **first ~** cugino di primo grado

cove [kəuv] *n* piccola baia

covenant ['kʌvənənt] *n* accordo

cover ['kʌvə*] *vt* coprire; (book, table) rivestire; (include) comprendere; (PRESS) fare un servizio su ♦ *n* (of pan) coperchio; (over furniture) fodera; (of bed) copriletto; (of book) copertina; (shelter) riparo; (COMM, INSURANCE, of spy) copertura; **to take ~** (shelter) ripararsi; **under ~** al riparo; **under ~ of darkness** protetto dall'oscurità; **under separate ~** (COMM) a parte, in plico separato; **~ up** *vi*: **to ~ up for sb** coprire qn; **~age** *n* (PRESS, RADIO, TV): **to give full ~age to sth** fare un ampio servizio su qc; **~ charge** *n* coperto; **~ing** *n* copertura; **~ing letter** (US **~ letter**) *n* lettera d'accompagnamento; **~ note** *n* (INSURANCE) polizza (di assicurazione) provvisoria

covert ['kʌvət] *adj* (hidden) nascosto(a); (glance) furtivo(a)

cover-up *n* occultamento (di informazioni)

cow [kau] *n* vacca ♦ *vt* (person) intimidire

coward ['kauəd] *n* vigliacco/a; **~ice** [-ɪs] *n* vigliaccheria; **~ly** *adj* vigliacco(a)

cowboy ['kaubɔɪ] *n* cow-boy *m inv*

cower ['kauə*] *vi* acquattarsi

coxswain ['kɔksn] (abbr: **cox**) *n* timoniere *m*

coy [kɔɪ] *adj* falsamente timido(a)

cozy ['kəuzɪ] (US) *adj* = **cosy**

CPA (US) *n abbr* = **certified public accountant**

crab [kræb] *n* granchio; **~ apple** *n* mela selvatica

crack [kræk] *n* fessura, crepa; incrinatura; (noise) schiocco; (: of gun) scoppio; (drug) crack *m inv* ♦ *vt* spaccare; incrinare; (whip) schioccare; (nut) schiacciare; (problem) risolvere; (code) decifrare ♦ *adj* (troops) fuori classe; **to ~ a joke** fare una battuta; **~ down on** *vt fus* porre freno a; **~ up** *vi* crollare; **~er** *n* cracker *m inv*; petardo

crackle ['krækl] *vi* crepitare

cradle ['kreɪdl] *n* culla

craft [krɑːft] *n* mestiere *m*; (cunning) astuzia; (boat) naviglio; **~sman** (irreg) *n* artigiano; **~smanship** *n* abilità; **~y** *adj* furbo(a), astuto(a)

crag [kræg] *n* roccia

cram [kræm] *vt* (fill): **to ~ sth with** riempire qc di; (put): **to ~ sth into** stipare qc in ♦ *vi* (for exams) prepararsi (in gran fretta)

cramp [kræmp] *n* crampo; **~ed** *adj* ristretto(a)

crampon ['kræmpən] *n* (CLIMBING) rampone *m*

cranberry ['krænbərɪ] *n* mirtillo

crane [kreɪn] *n* gru *f inv*

crank [kræŋk] *n* manovella; (person) persona stramba

cranny ['krænɪ] *n* see **nook**

crash [kræʃ] *n* fragore *m*; (of car) incidente *m*; (of plane) caduta; (of business etc) crollo ♦ *vt* fracassare ♦ *vi* (plane) fracassarsi; (car) avere un incidente; (two cars) scontrarsi; (business etc) fallire, andare in rovina; **~ course** *n* corso intensivo; **~ helmet** *n* casco; **~ landing** *n* atterraggio di fortuna

crate [kreɪt] *n* cassa

cravat(e) [krə'væt] *n* fazzoletto da collo

crave [kreɪv] *vt*, *vi*: **to ~ (for)** desiderare ardentemente

crawl [krɔːl] *vi* strisciare carponi; (vehicle) avanzare lentamente ♦ *n* (SWIMMING) crawl *m*

crayfish ['kreɪfɪʃ] *n inv* (freshwater) gambero (d'acqua dolce); (saltwater) gambero

crayon ['kreɪən] n matita colorata

craze [kreɪz] n mania

crazy ['kreɪzɪ] adj matto(a); (*inf: keen*): ~ **about sb** pazzo(a) di qn; ~ **about sth** matto(a) per qc

creak [kriːk] vi cigolare, scricchiolare

cream [kriːm] n crema; (*fresh*) panna ♦ adj (*colour*) color crema inv; ~ **cake** n torta alla panna; ~ **cheese** n formaggio fresco; ~**y** adj cremoso(a)

crease [kriːs] n grinza; (*deliberate*) piega ♦ vt sgualcire ♦ vi sgualcirsi

create [kriː'eɪt] vt creare; **creation** [-ʃən] n creazione f; **creative** adj creativo(a)

creature ['kriːtʃə*] n creatura

crèche [krɛʃ] n asilo infantile

credence ['kriːdns] n: **to lend** or **give ~ to** prestar fede a

credentials [krɪ'dɛnʃlz] npl credenziali fpl

credit ['krɛdɪt] n credito; onore m ♦ vt (*COMM*) accreditare; (*believe: also*: **give ~ to**) credere, prestar fede a; ~**s** npl (*CINEMA*) titoli mpl; **to ~ sb with** (*fig*) attribuire a qn; **to be in ~** (*person*) essere creditore (trice); (*bank account*) essere coperto(a); ~ **card** n carta di credito; ~**or** n creditore/trice

creed [kriːd] n credo; dottrina

creek [kriːk] n insenatura; (*US*) piccolo fiume m

creep [kriːp] (*pt, pp* **crept**) vi avanzare furtivamente (*or* pian piano); ~**er** n pianta rampicante; ~**y** adj (*frightening*) che fa accapponare la pelle

crematorium [krɛmə'tɔːrɪəm] (*pl* **crematoria**) n forno crematorio

crêpe [kreɪp] n crespo; ~ **bandage** (*BRIT*) n fascia elastica

crept [krɛpt] *pt, pp of* **creep**

crescent ['krɛsnt] n (*shape*) mezzaluna; (*street*) strada semicircolare

cress [krɛs] n crescione m

crest [krɛst] n cresta; (*of coat of arms*) cimiero; ~**fallen** adj mortificato(a)

Crete [kriːt] n Creta

crevasse [krɪ'væs] n crepaccio

crevice ['krɛvɪs] n fessura, crepa

crew [kruː] n equipaggio; ~**-cut** n: **to have a ~-cut** avere i capelli a spazzola; ~**-neck** n girocollo

crib [krɪb] n culla ♦ vt (*inf*) copiare

crick [krɪk] n crampo

cricket ['krɪkɪt] n (*insect*) grillo; (*game*) cricket m

crime [kraɪm] n crimine m; **criminal** ['krɪmɪnl] adj, n criminale m/f

crimson ['krɪmzn] adj color cremisi inv

cringe [krɪndʒ] vi acquattarsi; (*in embarrassment*) sentirsi sprofondare

crinkle ['krɪŋkl] vt arricciare, increspare

cripple ['krɪpl] n zoppo/a ♦ vt azzoppare

crises ['kraɪsiːz] npl of **crisis**

crisis ['kraɪsɪs] (*pl* **crises**) n crisi f inv

crisp [krɪsp] adj croccante; (*fig*) frizzante; vivace; deciso(a); ~**s** (*BRIT*) npl patatine fpl

criss-cross ['krɪs-] adj incrociato(a)

criteria [kraɪ'tɪərɪə] npl of **criterion**

criterion [kraɪ'tɪərɪən] (*pl* **criteria**) n criterio

critic ['krɪtɪk] n critico; ~**al** adj critico(a); ~**ally** adv (*speak etc*) criticamente; ~**ally ill** gravemente malato; ~**ism** ['krɪtɪsɪzm] n critica; ~**ize** ['krɪtɪsaɪz] vt criticare

croak [krəʊk] vi gracchiare; (*frog*) gracidare

Croatia [krəʊ'eɪʃə] n Croazia

crochet ['krəʊʃeɪ] n lavoro all'uncinetto

crockery ['krɔkərɪ] n vasellame m

crocodile ['krɔkədaɪl] n coccodrillo

crocus ['krəʊkəs] n croco

croft [krɔft] (*BRIT*) n piccolo podere m

crony ['krəʊnɪ] (*inf: pej*) n compare m

crook [krʊk] n truffatore m; (*of shepherd*) bastone m; ~**ed** ['krʊkɪd] adj curvo(a), storto(a); (*action*) disonesto(a)

crop [krɔp] n (*produce*) coltivazione f; (*amount produced*) raccolto; (*riding* ~) frustino ♦ vt (*hair*) rapare; ~ **up** vi presentarsi

croquette [krə'kɛt] n crocchetta

cross [krɔs] n croce f; (*BIOL*) incrocio ♦ vt (*street etc*) attraversare; (*arms, legs, BIOL*) incrociare; (*cheque*) sbarrare ♦ adj di cattivo umore; ~ **out** vt cancellare; ~ **over** vi attraversare; ~**bar** n traversa; ~**country** (*race*) n cross-country m inv; ~**-examine**

vt (*LAW*) interrogare in contraddittorio; ~-
eyed *adj* strabico(a); ~**ing** *n* incrocio;
incrociato; ~**ing** *n* incrocio; (*sea passage*)
traversata; (*also:* **pedestrian ~ing**) passaggio pedonale; ~**ing guard** (*US*) *n* dipendente comunale che aiuta i bambini ad
attraversare la strada; ~ **purposes** *npl*:
to be at ~ purposes non parlare della
stessa cosa; ~-**reference** *n* rinvio,
rimando; ~**roads** *n* incrocio; ~ **section** *n*
sezione *f* trasversale; (*in population*) settore
m rappresentativo; ~**walk** (*US*) *n* strisce *fpl*
pedonali, passaggio pedonale; ~**wind** *n*
vento di traverso; ~**word** *n* cruciverba *m*
inv

crotch [krɔtʃ] *n* (*ANAT*) inforcatura; (*of
garment*) pattina

crotchet ['krɔtʃit] *n* (*MUS*) semiminima

crouch [krautʃ] *vi* acquattarsi; rannicchiarsi

crow [krəu] *n* (*bird*) cornacchia; (*of cock*)
canto del gallo ♦ *vi* (*cock*) cantare

crowbar ['krəubɑ:*] *n* piede *m* di porco

crowd [kraud] *n* folla ♦ *vt* affollare, stipare
♦ *vi*: **to ~ round/in** affollarsi intorno a/in;
~**ed** *adj* affollato(a); ~**ed with** stipato(a) di

crown [kraun] *n* corona; (*of head*) calotta
cranica; (*of hat*) cocuzzolo; (*of hill*) cima
♦ *vt* incoronare; (*fig: career*) coronare; ~
jewels *npl* gioielli *mpl* della Corona; ~
prince *n* principe *m* ereditario

crow's feet *npl* zampe *fpl* di gallina

crucial ['kru:ʃl] *adj* cruciale, decisivo(a)

crucifix ['kru:sifiks] *n* crocifisso; ~**ion**
[-'fikʃən] *n* crocifissione *f*

crude [kru:d] *adj* (*materials*) greggio(a); non
raffinato(a); (*fig: basic*) crudo(a), primi-
tivo(a); (*: vulgar*) rozzo(a), grossolano(a);
~ **(oil)** *n* (*petrolio*) greggio

cruel ['kruəl] *adj* crudele; ~**ty** *n* crudeltà *f*
inv

cruise [kru:z] *n* crociera ♦ *vi* andare a
velocità di crociera; (*taxi*) circolare; ~**r** *n*
incrociatore *m*

crumb [krʌm] *n* briciola

crumble ['krʌmbl] *vt* sbriciolare ♦ *vi*
sbriciolarsi; (*plaster etc*) sgretolarsi; (*land,
earth*) franare; (*building, fig*) crollare;

crumbly *adj* friabile

crumpet ['krʌmpit] *n specie di frittella*

crumple ['krʌmpl] *vt* raggrinzare,
spiegazzare

crunch [krʌntʃ] *vt* sgranocchiare; (*underfoot*)
scricchiolare ♦ *n* (*fig*) punto *or* momento
cruciale; ~**y** *adj* croccante

crusade [kru:'seid] *n* crociata

crush [krʌʃ] *n* folla; (*love*): **to have a ~ on
sb** avere una cotta per qn; (*drink*): **lemon
~** spremuta di limone ♦ *vt* schiacciare;
(*crumple*) sgualcire

crust [krʌst] *n* crosta

crutch [krʌtʃ] *n* gruccia

crux [krʌks] *n* nodo

cry [krai] *vi* piangere; (*shout: also:* ~ **out**)
urlare ♦ *n* urlo, grido; ~ **off** *vi* ritirarsi

cryptic ['kriptik] *adj* ermetico(a)

crystal ['kristl] *n* cristallo; ~-**clear** *adj*
cristallino(a)

cub [kʌb] *n* cucciolo; (*also:* ~ **scout**) lupetto

Cuba ['kju:bə] *n* Cuba

cube [kju:b] *n* cubo ♦ *vt* (*MATH*) elevare al
cubo; **cubic** *adj* cubico(a); (*metre, foot*)
cubo(a); **cubic capacity** *n* cilindrata

cubicle ['kju:bikl] *n* scompartimento
separato; cabina

cuckoo ['kuku:] *n* cucù *m inv*; ~ **clock** *n*
orologio a cucù

cucumber ['kju:kʌmbə*] *n* cetriolo

cuddle ['kʌdl] *vt* abbracciare, coccolare ♦ *vi*
abbracciarsi

cue [kju:] *n* (*snooker ~*) stecca; (*THEATRE etc*)
segnale *m*

cuff [kʌf] *n* (*BRIT: of shirt, coat etc*) polsino;
(*US: of trousers*) risvolto; **off the ~**
improvvisando; ~**link** *n* gemello

cuisine [kwi'zi:n] *n* cucina

cul-de-sac ['kʌldəsæk] *n* vicolo cieco

cull [kʌl] *vt* (*ideas etc*) scegliere ♦ *n* (*of
animals*) abbattimento selettivo

culminate ['kʌlmineit] *vi*: **to ~ in**
culminare con; **culmination** [-'neiʃən] *n*
culmine *m*

culottes [kju:'lɔts] *npl* gonna *f* pantalone
inv

culpable ['kʌlpəbl] *adj* colpevole

culprit ['kʌlprɪt] *n* colpevole *m/f*

cult [kʌlt] *n* culto

cultivate ['kʌltɪveɪt] *vt* (*also fig*) coltivare; **cultivation** [-'veɪʃən] *n* coltivazione *f*

cultural ['kʌltʃərəl] *adj* culturale

culture ['kʌltʃə*] *n* (*also fig*) cultura; **~d** *adj* colto(a)

cumbersome ['kʌmbəsəm] *adj* ingombrante

cunning ['kʌnɪŋ] *n* astuzia, furberia ♦ *adj* astuto(a), furbo(a)

cup [kʌp] *n* tazza; (*prize, of bra*) coppa

cupboard ['kʌbəd] *n* armadio

cup-tie (*BRIT*) *n* partita di coppa

curate ['kjuərɪt] *n* cappellano

curator [kjuə'reɪtə*] *n* direttore *m* (*di museo etc*)

curb [kəːb] *vt* tenere a freno ♦ *n* freno; (*US*) bordo del marciapiede

curdle ['kəːdl] *vi* cagliare

cure [kjuə*] *vt* guarire; (*CULIN*) trattare; affumicare; essiccare ♦ *n* rimedio

curfew ['kəːfjuː] *n* coprifuoco

curiosity [kjuərɪ'ɔsɪtɪ] *n* curiosità

curious ['kjuərɪəs] *adj* curioso(a)

curl [kəːl] *n* riccio ♦ *vt* ondulare; (*tightly*) arricciare ♦ *vi* arricciarsi; **~ up** *vi* rannicchiarsi; **~er** *n* bigodino

curly ['kəːlɪ] *adj* ricciuto(a)

currant ['kʌrnt] *n* (*dried*) sultanina; (*bush, fruit*) ribes *m inv*

currency ['kʌrnsɪ] *n* moneta; **to gain ~** (*fig*) acquistare larga diffusione

current ['kʌrnt] *adj* corrente ♦ *n* corrente *f*; **~ account** (*BRIT*) *n* conto corrente; **~ affairs** *npl* attualità *fpl*; **~ly** *adv* attualmente

curricula [kə'rɪkjulə] *npl* of **curriculum**

curriculum [kə'rɪkjuləm] (*pl* **~s** or **curricula**) *n* curriculum *m inv*; **~ vitae** *n* curriculum vitae *m inv*

curry ['kʌrɪ] *n* curry *m inv* ♦ *vt*: **to ~ favour with** cercare di attirarsi i favori di; **~ powder** *n* curry *m*

curse [kəːs] *vt* maledire ♦ *vi* bestemmiare ♦ *n* maledizione *f*; bestemmia

cursor ['kəːsə*] *n* (*COMPUT*) cursore *m*

cursory ['kəːsərɪ] *adj* superficiale

curt [kəːt] *adj* secco(a)

curtail [kəː'teɪl] *vt* (*visit etc*) accorciare; (*expenses etc*) ridurre

curtain ['kəːtn] *n* tenda; (*THEATRE*) sipario

curts(e)y ['kəːtsɪ] *vi* fare un inchino *or* una riverenza

curve [kəːv] *n* curva ♦ *vi* curvarsi

cushion ['kuʃən] *n* cuscino ♦ *vt* (*shock*) fare da cuscinetto a

custard ['kʌstəd] *n* (*for pouring*) crema

custodian [kʌs'təudɪən] *n* custode *m/f*

custody ['kʌstədɪ] *n* (*of child*) tutela; **to take into ~** (*suspect*) mettere in detenzione preventiva

custom ['kʌstəm] *n* costume *m*, consuetudine *f*; (*COMM*) clientela; **~ary** *adj* consueto(a)

customer ['kʌstəmə*] *n* cliente *m/f*

customized ['kʌstəmaɪzd] *adj* (*car etc*) fuoriserie *inv*

custom-made *adj* (*clothes*) fatto(a) su misura; (*other goods*) fatto(a) su ordinazione

customs ['kʌstəmz] *npl* dogana; **~ duty** *n* tassa doganale; **~ officer** *n* doganiere *m*

cut [kʌt] (*pt, pp* **cut**) *vt* tagliare; (*shape, make*) intagliare; (*reduce*) ridurre ♦ *vi* tagliare ♦ *n* taglio; (*in salary etc*) riduzione *f*; **to ~ a tooth** mettere un dente; **~ down** *vt* (*tree etc*) abbattere ♦ *vt fus* (*also:* **~ down on**) ridurre; **~ off** *vt* tagliare; (*fig*) isolare; **~ out** *vt* tagliare fuori; eliminare; ritagliare; **~ up** *vt* tagliare a pezzi; **~back** *n* riduzione *f*

cute [kjuːt] *adj* (*sweet*) carino(a)

cuticle ['kjuːtɪkl] *n* (*on nail*) pellicina, cuticola

cutlery ['kʌtlərɪ] *n* posate *fpl*

cutlet ['kʌtlɪt] *n* costoletta; (*nut etc* **~**) cotoletta vegetariana

cut: **~out** *n* interruttore *m*; (*cardboard ~out*) ritaglio; **~-price** (*US* **~-rate**) *adj* a prezzo ridotto; **~throat** *n* assassino ♦ *adj* (*competition*) spietato(a)

cutting ['kʌtɪŋ] *adj* tagliente ♦ *n* (*from newspaper*) ritaglio (di giornale); (*from plant*) talea

CV n abbr = **curriculum vitae**
cwt abbr = **hundredweight(s)**
cyanide ['saɪənaɪd] n cianuro
cybercafé ['saɪbəkæfeɪ] n cybercaffè m inv
cycle ['saɪkl] n ciclo; (bicycle) bicicletta ♦ vi andare in bicicletta; **~ hire** n noleggio m biciclette inv; **~ lane, ~ path** n pista ciclabile
cycling ['saɪklɪŋ] n ciclismo
cyclist ['saɪklɪst] n ciclista m/f
cygnet ['sɪgnɪt] n cigno giovane
cylinder ['sɪlɪndə*] n cilindro; **~-head gasket** n guarnizione f della testata del cilindro
cymbals ['sɪmblz] npl cembali mpl
cynic ['sɪnɪk] n cinico/a; **~al** adj cinico(a); **~ism** ['sɪnɪsɪzəm] n cinismo
Cyprus ['saɪprəs] n Cipro
cyst [sɪst] n cisti f inv
cystitis [sɪs'taɪtɪs] n cistite f
czar [zɑ:*] n zar m inv
Czech [tʃɛk] adj ceco(a) ♦ n ceco/a; (LING) ceco
Czech Republic n: **the ~** la Repubblica Ceca

D, d

D [di:] n (MUS) re m
dab [dæb] vt (eyes, wound) tamponare; (paint, cream) applicare (con leggeri colpetti)
dabble ['dæbl] vi: **to ~ in** occuparsi (da dilettante) di
dad(dy) [dæd(ɪ)] (inf) n babbo, papà m inv
daffodil ['dæfədɪl] n trombone m, giunchiglia
daft [dɑ:ft] adj sciocco(a)
dagger ['dægə*] n pugnale m
daily ['deɪlɪ] adj quotidiano(a), giornaliero(a) ♦ n quotidiano ♦ adv tutti i giorni
dainty ['deɪntɪ] adj delicato(a), grazioso(a)
dairy ['deərɪ] n (BRIT: shop) latteria; (on farm) caseificio ♦ adj caseario(a); **~ farm** n caseificio; **~ products** npl latticini mpl; **~**

store (US) n latteria
daisy ['deɪzɪ] n margherita
dale [deɪl] (BRIT) n valle f
dam [dæm] n diga ♦ vt sbarrare; costruire dighe su
damage ['dæmɪdʒ] n danno, danni mpl; (fig) danno ♦ vt danneggiare; **~s** npl (LAW) danni
damn [dæm] vt condannare; (curse) maledire ♦ n (inf): **I don't give a ~** non me ne frega niente ♦ adj (inf: also: **~ed**): **this ~ ...** questo maledetto ...; **~ (it)!** accidenti!; **~ing** adj (evidence) schiacciante
damp [dæmp] adj umido(a) ♦ n umidità, umido ♦ vt (also: **~en**: cloth, rag) inumidire, bagnare; (: enthusiasm etc) spegnere
damson ['dæmzən] n susina damaschina
dance [dɑ:ns] n danza, ballo; (ball) ballo ♦ vi ballare; **~ hall** n dancing m inv, sala da ballo; **~r** n danzatore/trice; (professional) ballerino/a
dancing ['dɑ:nsɪŋ] n danza, ballo
dandelion ['dændɪlaɪən] n dente m di leone
dandruff ['dændrəf] n forfora
Dane [deɪn] n danese m/f
danger ['deɪndʒə*] n pericolo; **there is a ~ of fire** c'è pericolo di incendio; **in ~** in pericolo; **he was in ~ of falling** rischiava di cadere; **~ous** adj pericoloso(a)
dangle ['dæŋgl] vt dondolare; (fig) far balenare ♦ vi pendolare
Danish ['deɪnɪʃ] adj danese ♦ n (LING) danese m
dare [deə*] vt: **to ~ sb to do** sfidare qn a fare ♦ vi: **to ~ (to) do sth** osare fare qc; **I ~ say** (I suppose) immagino (che); **daring** adj audace, ardito(a) ♦ n audacia
dark [dɑ:k] adj (night, room) buio(a), scuro(a); (colour, complexion) scuro(a); (fig) cupo(a), tetro(a), nero(a) ♦ n: **in the ~** al buio; **in the ~ about** (fig) all'oscuro di; **after ~** a notte fatta; **~en** vt (colour) scurire ♦ vi (sky, room) oscurarsi; **~ glasses** npl occhiali mpl scuri; **~ness** n oscurità, buio; **~room** n camera oscura
darling ['dɑ:lɪŋ] adj caro(a) ♦ n tesoro
darn [dɑ:n] vt rammendare

dart [dɑːt] *n* freccetta; (SEWING) pince *f inv* ♦ *vi*: **to ~ towards** precipitarsi verso; **to ~ away/along** sfrecciare via/lungo; **~board** *n* bersaglio (per freccette); **~s** *n* tiro al bersaglio (con freccette)

dash [dæʃ] *n* (sign) lineetta; (small quantity) punta ♦ *vt* (missile) gettare; (hopes) infrangere ♦ *vi*: **to ~ towards** precipitarsi verso; **~ away** or **off** *vi* scappare via

dashboard [ˈdæʃbɔːd] *n* (AUT) cruscotto

dashing [ˈdæʃɪŋ] *adj* ardito(a)

data [ˈdeɪtə] *npl* dati *mpl*; **~base** *n* base *f* di dati, data base *m inv*; **~ processing** *n* elaborazione *f* (elettronica) dei dati

date [deɪt] *n* data; appuntamento; (fruit) dattero ♦ *vt* datare; (person) uscire con; **~ of birth** data di nascita; **to ~** (until now) fino a oggi; **~d** *adj* passato(a) di moda; **~ rape** *n* stupro perpetrato da persona conosciuta

daub [dɔːb] *vt* imbrattare

daughter [ˈdɔːtə*] *n* figlia; **~-in-law** *n* nuora

daunting [ˈdɔːntɪŋ] *adj* non invidiabile

dawdle [ˈdɔːdl] *vi* bighellonare

dawn [dɔːn] *n* alba ♦ *vi* (day) spuntare; (fig): **it ~ed on him that ...** gli è venuto in mente che ....

day [deɪ] *n* giorno; (as duration) giornata; (period of time, age) tempo, epoca; **the ~ before** il giorno avanti or prima; **the ~ after, the following** il giorno dopo or seguente; **the ~ after tomorrow** dopodomani; **the ~ before yesterday** l'altroieri; **by ~** di giorno; **~break** *n* spuntar *m* del giorno; **~dream** *vi* sognare a occhi aperti; **~light** *n* luce *f* del giorno; **~ return** (BRIT) *n* biglietto giornaliero di andata e ritorno; **~time** *n* giorno; **~-to-~** *adj* (life, organization) quotidiano(a)

daze [deɪz] *vt* (subj: drug) inebetire; (: blow) stordire ♦ *n*: **in a ~** inebetito(a); stordito(a)

dazzle [ˈdæzl] *vt* abbagliare

DC *abbr* (= direct current) c.c.

D-day *n* giorno dello sbarco alleato in Normandia

dead [dɛd] *adj* morto(a); (numb) intirizzito(a); (telephone) muto(a); (battery) scarico(a) ♦ *adv* assolutamente, perfettamente ♦ *npl*: **the ~** i morti; **he was shot ~** fu colpito a morte; **~ tired** stanco(a) morto(a); **to stop ~** fermarsi di colpo; **~en** *vt* (blow, sound) ammortire; **~ end** *n* vicolo cieco; **~ heat** *n* (SPORT): **to finish in a ~ heat** finire alla pari; **~line** *n* scadenza; **~lock** *n* punto morto; **~ loss** *n*: **to be a ~ loss** (inf: person, thing) non valere niente; **~ly** *adj* mortale; (weapon, poison) micidiale; **~pan** *adj* a faccia impassibile

deaf [dɛf] *adj* sordo(a); **~en** *vt* assordare; **~ness** *n* sordità

deal [diːl] (pt, pp **dealt**) *n* accordo; (business ~) affare *m* ♦ *vt* (blow, cards) dare; **a great ~ (of)** molto(a); **~ in** *vt fus* occuparsi di; **~ with** *vt fus* (COMM) fare affari con, trattare con; (handle) occuparsi di; (be about: book etc) trattare di; **~er** *n* commerciante *m/f*; **~ings** *npl* (COMM) relazioni *fpl*; (relations) rapporti *mpl*; **dealt** [dɛlt] *pt, pp of* **deal**

dean [diːn] *n* (REL) decano; (SCOL) preside *m* di facoltà (or di collegio)

dear [dɪə*] *adj* caro(a) ♦ *n*: **my ~** caro mio/cara mia ♦ *excl*: **~ me!** Dio mio!; **D~ Sir/Madam** (in letter) Egregio Signore/Egregia Signora; **D~ Mr/Mrs X** Gentile Signor/Signora X; **~ly** *adv* (love) moltissimo; (pay) a caro prezzo

death [dɛθ] *n* morte *f*; (ADMIN) decesso; **~ certificate** *n* atto di decesso; **~ly** *adj* di morte; **~ penalty** *n* pena di morte; **~ rate** *n* indice *m* di mortalità; **~ toll** *n* vittime *fpl*

debacle [dɪˈbækl] *n* fiasco

debase [dɪˈbeɪs] *vt* (currency) adulterare; (person) degradare

debatable [dɪˈbeɪtəbl] *adj* discutibile

debate [dɪˈbeɪt] *n* dibattito ♦ *vt* dibattere; discutere

debit [ˈdɛbɪt] *n* debito ♦ *vt*: **to ~ a sum to sb** or **to sb's account** addebitare una somma a qn

debris [ˈdɛbriː] *n* detriti *mpl*

debt [dɛt] *n* debito; **to be in ~** essere

indebitato(a); ~or n debitore/trice

début ['deɪbjuː] n debutto

decade ['dɛkeɪd] n decennio

decadence ['dɛkədəns] n decadenza

decaff ['diːkæf] (inf) n decaffeinato

decaffeinated [dɪ'kæfɪneɪtɪd] adj
decaffeinato(a)

decanter [dɪ'kæntə*] n caraffa

decay [dɪ'keɪ] n decadimento; (also: **tooth**
~) carie f ♦ vi (rot) imputridire

deceased [dɪ'siːst] n defunto/a

deceit [dɪ'siːt] n inganno; ~**ful** adj
ingannevole, perfido(a)

deceive [dɪ'siːv] vt ingannare

December [dɪ'sɛmbə*] n dicembre m

decent ['diːsənt] adj decente; (respectable)
per bene; (kind) gentile

deception [dɪ'sɛpʃən] n inganno

deceptive [dɪ'sɛptɪv] adj ingannevole

decide [dɪ'saɪd] vt (person) far prendere una
decisione a; (question, argument) risolvere,
decidere ♦ vi decidere, decidersi; **to ~ to
do/that** decidere di fare/che; **to ~ on**
decidere per; ~**d** adj (resolute) deciso(a);
(clear, definite) netto(a), chiaro(a); ~**dly**
[-dɪdlɪ] adv indubbiamente; decisamente

decimal ['dɛsɪməl] adj decimale ♦ n
decimale m; ~ **point** n ≈ virgola

decipher [dɪ'saɪfə*] vt decifrare

decision [dɪ'sɪʒən] n decisione f

decisive [dɪ'saɪsɪv] adj decisivo(a); (person)
deciso(a)

deck [dɛk] n (NAUT) ponte m; (of bus): **top ~**
imperiale m; (record ~) piatto; (of cards)
mazzo; ~**chair** n sedia a sdraio

declaration [dɛklə'reɪʃən] n dichiarazione f

declare [dɪ'klɛə*] vt dichiarare

decline [dɪ'klaɪn] n (decay) declino;
(lessening) ribasso ♦ vt declinare; rifiutare
♦ vi declinare; diminuire

decode [diː'kəʊd] vt decifrare

decoder [diː'kəʊdə*] n (TV) decodificatore
m

decompose [diːkəm'pəʊz] vi decomporre

décor ['deɪkɔː*] n decorazione f

decorate ['dɛkəreɪt] vt (adorn, give a medal
to) decorare; (paint and paper) tinteggiare

e tappezzare; **decoration** [-'reɪʃən] n
(medal etc, adornment) decorazione f;
decorator n decoratore m

decorum [dɪ'kɔːrəm] n decoro

decoy ['diːkɔɪ] n zimbello

decrease [n 'diːkriːs, vb diː'kriːs] n
diminuzione f ♦ vt, vi diminuire

decree [dɪ'kriː] n decreto; ~ **nisi** [-'naɪsaɪ] n
sentenza provvisoria di divorzio

dedicate ['dɛdɪkeɪt] vt consacrare; (book
etc) dedicare

dedication [dɛdɪ'keɪʃən] n (devotion)
dedizione f; (in book etc) dedica

deduce [dɪ'djuːs] vt dedurre

deduct [dɪ'dʌkt] vt: **to ~ sth (from)** dedurre
qc (da); ~**ion** [dɪ'dʌkʃən] n deduzione f

deed [diːd] n azione f, atto; (LAW) atto

deep [diːp] adj profondo(a); **4 metres ~**
profondo(a) 4 metri ♦ adv: **spectators
stood 20 ~** c'erano 20 file di spettatori;
~**en** vt (hole) approfondire ♦ vi
approfondirsi; (darkness) farsi più buio; ~
end n: **the ~ end** (of swimming pool) la
parte più profonda; ~**-freeze** n
congelatore m; ~**-fry** vt friggere in olio
abbondante; ~**ly** adv profondamente; ~**-
sea diving** n immersione f in alto mare;
~**-seated** adj radicato(a)

deer [dɪə*] n inv: **the ~** i cervidi; **(red) ~**
cervo; **(fallow) ~** daino; **(roe) ~** capriolo;
~**skin** n pelle f di daino

deface [dɪ'feɪs] vt imbrattare

default [dɪ'fɔːlt] n (COMPUT: also: ~ **value**)
default m inv; **by ~** (SPORT) per abbandono

defeat [dɪ'fiːt] n sconfitta ♦ vt (team,
opponents) sconfiggere; ~**ist** adj, n
disfattista m/f

defect [n 'diːfɛkt, vb dɪ'fɛkt] n difetto ♦ vi: **to
~ to the enemy** passare al nemico; ~**ive**
[dɪ'fɛktɪv] adj difettoso(a)

defence [dɪ'fɛns] (US **defense**) n difesa;
~**less** adj senza difesa

defend [dɪ'fɛnd] vt difendere; ~**ant** n
imputato/a; ~**er** n difensore/a

defense [dɪ'fɛns] (US) n = **defence**

defensive [dɪ'fɛnsɪv] adj difensivo(a) ♦ n:
on the ~ sulla difensiva

defer [dɪ'fəː*] vt (*postpone*) differire, rinviare
defiance [dɪ'faɪəns] n sfida; **in ~ of** a dispetto di
defiant [dɪ'faɪənt] adj (*attitude*) di sfida; (*person*) ribelle
deficiency [dɪ'fɪʃənsɪ] n deficienza; carenza
deficit ['dɛfɪsɪt] n deficit m inv
define [dɪ'faɪn] vt definire
definite ['dɛfɪnɪt] adj (*fixed*) definito(a), preciso(a); (*clear, obvious*) ben definito(a), esatto(a); (*LING*) determinativo(a); **he was ~ about it** ne era sicuro; **~ly** adv indubbiamente
definition [dɛfɪ'nɪʃən] n definizione f
deflate [diː'fleɪt] vt sgonfiare
deflect [dɪ'flɛkt] vt deflettere, deviare
deformed [dɪ'fɔːmd] adj deforme
defraud [dɪ'frɔːd] vt defraudare
defrost [diː'frɔst] vt (*fridge*) disgelare; **~er** (*US*) n (*demister*) sbrinatore m
deft [dɛft] adj svelto(a), destro(a)
defunct [dɪ'fʌŋkt] adj che non esiste più
defuse [diː'fjuːz] vt disinnescare; (*fig*) distendere
defy [dɪ'faɪ] vt sfidare; (*efforts etc*) resistere a; **it defies description** supera ogni descrizione
degenerate [vb dɪ'dʒɛnəreɪt, adj dɪ'dʒɛnərɪt] vi degenerare ♦ adj degenere
degree [dɪ'griː] n grado; (*SCOL*) laurea (universitaria); **a (first) ~ in maths** una laurea in matematica; **by ~s** (*gradually*) gradualmente, a poco a poco; **to some ~** fino a un certo punto, in certa misura
dehydrated [diːhaɪ'dreɪtɪd] adj disidratato(a); (*milk, eggs*) in polvere
de-ice [diː'aɪs] vt (*windscreen*) disgelare
deign [deɪn] vi: **to ~ to do** degnarsi di fare
deity ['diːɪtɪ] n divinità f inv
dejected [dɪ'dʒɛktɪd] adj abbattuto(a), avvilito(a)
delay [dɪ'leɪ] vt ritardare ♦ vi: **to ~ (in doing sth)** ritardare (a fare qc) ♦ n ritardo; **to be ~ed** subire un ritardo; (*person*) essere trattenuto(a)
delectable [dɪ'lɛktəbl] adj (*person, food*) delizioso(a)

delegate [n 'dɛlɪgɪt, vb 'dɛlɪgeɪt] n delegato/a ♦ vt delegare; **delegation** [-'geɪʃən] n (*group*) delegazione f; (*by manager*) delega
delete [dɪ'liːt] vt cancellare
deliberate [adj dɪ'lɪbərɪt, vb dɪ'lɪbəreɪt] adj (*intentional*) intenzionale; (*slow*) misurato(a) ♦ vi deliberare, riflettere; **~ly** adv (*on purpose*) deliberatamente
delicacy ['dɛlɪkəsɪ] n delicatezza
delicate ['dɛlɪkɪt] adj delicato(a)
delicatessen [dɛlɪkə'tɛsn] n ≈ salumeria
delicious [dɪ'lɪʃəs] adj delizioso(a), squisito(a)
delight [dɪ'laɪt] n delizia, gran piacere m ♦ vt dilettare; **to take (a) ~ in** dilettarsi in; **~ed** adj: **~ed (at or with)** contentissimo(a) (di), felice (di); **~ed to do** felice di fare; **~ful** adj delizioso(a); incantevole
delinquent [dɪ'lɪŋkwənt] adj, n delinquente m/f
delirious [dɪ'lɪrɪəs] adj: **to be ~** delirare
deliver [dɪ'lɪvə*] vt (*mail*) distribuire; (*goods*) consegnare; (*speech*) pronunciare; (*MED*) far partorire; **~y** n distribuzione f; consegna; (*of speaker*) dizione f; (*MED*) parto
delude [dɪ'luːd] vt illudere
deluge ['dɛljuːdʒ] n diluvio
delusion [dɪ'luːʒən] n illusione f
demand [dɪ'mɑːnd] vt richiedere; (*rights*) rivendicare ♦ n domanda; (*claim*) rivendicazione f; in ~ ricercato(a), richiesto(a); **on ~** a richiesta; **~ing** adj (*boss*) esigente; (*work*) impegnativo(a)
demean [dɪ'miːn] vt: **to ~ o.s.** umiliarsi
demeanour [dɪ'miːnə*] (*US* **demeanor**) n comportamento; contegno
demented [dɪ'mɛntɪd] adj demente, impazzito(a)
demise [dɪ'maɪz] n decesso
demister [diː'mɪstə*] (*BRIT*) n (*AUT*) sbrinatore m
demo ['dɛməʊ] (*inf*) n abbr (= *demonstration*) manifestazione f
democracy [dɪ'mɔkrəsɪ] n democrazia
democrat ['dɛməkræt] n democratico/a; **~ic** [dɛmə'krætɪk] adj democratico(a)

demolish [dɪ'mɔlɪʃ] vt demolire
demonstrate ['demənstreɪt] vt dimostrare, provare ♦ vi dimostrare, manifestare; **demonstration** [-'streɪʃən] n dimostrazione f; (POL) dimostrazione, manifestazione f; **demonstrator** n (POL) dimostrante m/f; (COMM) dimostratore/trice
demote [dɪ'məut] vt far retrocedere
demure [dɪ'mjuə*] adj contegnoso(a)
den [dɛn] n tana, covo; (room) buco
denial [dɪ'naɪəl] n diniego; rifiuto
denim ['denɪm] n tessuto di cotone ritorto; **~s** npl (jeans) blue jeans mpl
Denmark ['dɛnmɑːk] n Danimarca
denomination [dɪnɔmɪ'neɪʃən] n (money) valore m; (REL) confessione f
denounce [dɪ'nauns] vt denunciare
dense [dɛns] adj fitto(a); (smoke) denso(a); (inf: person) ottuso(a), duro(a)
density ['densɪtɪ] n densità f inv
dent [dɛnt] n ammaccatura ♦ vt (also: **make a ~ in**) ammaccare
dental ['dɛntl] adj dentale; **~ surgeon** n medico/a dentista
dentist ['dɛntɪst] n dentista m/f
dentures ['dɛntʃəz] npl dentiera
deny [dɪ'naɪ] vt negare; (refuse) rifiutare
deodorant [diː'əudərənt] n deodorante m
depart [dɪ'pɑːt] vi partire; **to ~ from** (fig) deviare da
department [dɪ'pɑːtmənt] n (COMM) reparto; (SCOL) sezione f, dipartimento; (POL) ministero; **~ store** n grande magazzino
departure [dɪ'pɑːtʃə*] n partenza; (fig): **~ from** deviazione f da; **a new ~** una svolta (decisiva); **~ lounge** n (at airport) sala d'attesa
depend [dɪ'pɛnd] vi: **to ~ on** dipendere da; (rely on) contare su; **it ~s** dipende; **~ing on the result ...** a seconda del risultato ...; **~able** adj fidato(a); (car etc) affidabile; **~ant** n persona a carico; **~ent** adj: **to be ~ent on** dipendere da; (child, relative) essere a carico di ♦ n = **~ant**
depict [dɪ'pɪkt] vt (in picture) dipingere; (in words) descrivere

depleted [dɪ'pliːtɪd] adj diminuito(a)
deploy [dɪ'plɔɪ] vt dispiegare
depopulation ['diːpɔpju'leɪʃən] n spopolamento
deport [dɪ'pɔːt] vt deportare; espellere
deportment [dɪ'pɔːtmənt] n portamento
deposit [dɪ'pɔzɪt] n (COMM, GEO) deposito; (of ore, oil) giacimento; (CHEM) sedimento; (part payment) acconto; (for hired goods etc) cauzione f ♦ vt depositare; dare in acconto; mettere or lasciare in deposito; **~ account** n conto vincolato
depot ['depəu] n deposito; (US) stazione f ferroviaria
depreciate [dɪ'priːʃieɪt] vi svalutarsi
depress [dɪ'prɛs] vt deprimere; (price, wages) abbassare; (press down) premere; **~ed** adj (person) depresso(a), abbattuto(a); (price) in ribasso; (industry) in crisi; **~ing** adj deprimente; **~ion** [dɪ'prɛʃən] n depressione f
deprivation [dɛprɪ'veɪʃən] n privazione f
deprive [dɪ'praɪv] vt: **to ~ sb of** privare qn di; **~d** adj disgraziato(a)
depth [depθ] n profondità f inv; **in the ~s of** nel profondo di; nel cuore di; **out of one's ~** (in water) dove non si tocca; (fig) a disagio
deputize ['depjutaɪz] vi: **to ~ for** svolgere le funzioni di
deputy ['depjutɪ] adj: **~ head** (BRIT: SCOL) vicepreside m/f ♦ n (assistant) vice m/f inv; (US: also: **~ sheriff**) vice-sceriffo
derail [dɪ'reɪl] vt: **to be ~ed** deragliare
deranged [dɪ'reɪndʒd] adj: **to be (mentally) ~** essere pazzo(a)
derby ['dɑːbɪ] (US) n (bowler hat) bombetta
derelict ['derɪlɪkt] adj abbandonato(a)
derisory [dɪ'raɪsərɪ] adj (sum) irrisorio(a); (laughter, person) beffardo(a)
derive [dɪ'raɪv] vt: **to ~ sth from** derivare qc da; trarre qc da ♦ vi: **to ~ from** derivare da
derogatory [dɪ'rɔgətərɪ] adj denigratorio(a)
derv [dɑːv] (BRIT) n gasolio
descend [dɪ'sɛnd] vt, vi discendere, scendere; **to ~ from** discendere da; **to ~ to** (lying, begging) abbassarsi a; **~ant** n

discendente *m/f*

descent [dɪ'sɛnt] *n* discesa; (*origin*) discendenza, famiglia

describe [dɪs'kraɪb] *vt* descrivere; **description** [-'krɪpʃən] *n* descrizione *f*; (*sort*) genere *m*, specie *f*

desecrate ['dɛsɪkreɪt] *vt* profanare

desert [*n* 'dɛzət, *vb* dɪ'zə:t] *n* deserto ♦ *vt* lasciare, abbandonare ♦ *vi* (MIL) disertare; ~**er** *n* disertore *m*; ~**ion** [dɪ'zə:ʃən] *n* (MIL) diserzione *f*; (LAW) abbandono del tetto coniugale; ~ **island** *n* isola deserta; ~**s** [dɪ'zə:ts] *npl*: **to get one's just** ~**s** avere ciò che si merita

deserve [dɪ'zə:v] *vt* meritare; **deserving** *adj* (*person*) meritevole, degno(a); (*cause*) meritorio(a)

design [dɪ'zaɪn] *n* (*art, sketch*) disegno; (*layout, shape*) linea; (*pattern*) fantasia; (*intention*) intenzione *f* ♦ *vt* disegnare; progettare

designer [dɪ'zaɪnə*] *n* (ART, TECH) disegnatore/trice; (*of fashion*) modellista *m/f*

desire [dɪ'zaɪə*] *n* desiderio, voglia ♦ *vt* desiderare, volere

desk [dɛsk] *n* (*in office*) scrivania; (*for pupil*) banco; (BRIT: *in shop, restaurant*) cassa; (*in hotel*) ricevimento; (*at airport*) accettazione *f*

desolate ['dɛsəlɪt] *adj* desolato(a)

despair [dɪs'pɛə*] *n* disperazione *f* ♦ *vi*: **to ~ of** disperare di

despatch [dɪs'pætʃ] *n*, *vt* = **dispatch**

desperate ['dɛspərɪt] *adj* disperato(a); (*fugitive*) capace di tutto; **to be ~ for sth/to do** volere disperatamente qc/fare; ~**ly** *adv* disperatamente; (*very*) terribilmente, estremamente

desperation [dɛspə'reɪʃən] *n* disperazione *f*

despicable [dɪs'pɪkəbl] *adj* disprezzabile

despise [dɪs'paɪz] *vt* disprezzare, sdegnare

despite [dɪs'paɪt] *prep* malgrado, a dispetto di, nonostante

despondent [dɪs'pɔndənt] *adj* abbattuto(a), scoraggiato(a)

dessert [dɪ'zə:t] *n* dolce *m*; frutta; ~**spoon** *n* cucchiaio da dolci

destination [dɛstɪ'neɪʃən] *n* destinazione *f*

destined ['dɛstɪnd] *adj*: **to be ~ to do/for** essere destinato(a) a fare/per

destiny ['dɛstɪnɪ] *n* destino

destitute ['dɛstɪtjuːt] *adj* indigente, bisognoso(a)

destroy [dɪs'trɔɪ] *vt* distruggere; ~**er** *n* (NAUT) cacciatorpediniere *m*

destruction [dɪs'trʌkʃən] *n* distruzione *f*

detach [dɪ'tætʃ] *vt* staccare, distaccare; ~**ed** *adj* (*attitude*) distante; ~**ed house** *n* villa; ~**ment** *n* (MIL) distaccamento; (*fig*) distacco

detail ['diːteɪl] *n* particolare *m*, dettaglio ♦ *vt* dettagliare, particolareggiare; **in ~** nei particolari; ~**ed** *adj* particolareggiato(a)

detain [dɪ'teɪn] *vt* trattenere; (*in captivity*) detenere

detect [dɪ'tɛkt] *vt* scoprire, scorgere; (MED, POLICE, RADAR *etc*) individuare; ~**ion** [dɪ'tɛkʃən] *n* scoperta; individuazione *f*; ~**ive** *n* investigatore/trice; ~**ive story** *n* giallo

détente [deɪ'tɑːnt] *n* (POL) distensione *f*

detention [dɪ'tɛnʃən] *n* detenzione *f*; (SCOL) *permanenza forzata per punizione*

deter [dɪ'tə:*] *vt* dissuadere

detergent [dɪ'tə:dʒənt] *n* detersivo

deteriorate [dɪ'tɪərɪəreɪt] *vi* deteriorarsi

determine [dɪ'tə:mɪn] *vt* determinare; ~**d** *adj* (*person*) risoluto(a), deciso(a); ~**d to do** deciso(a) a fare

detour ['diːtuə*] *n* deviazione *f*

detract [dɪ'trækt] *vi*: **to ~ from** detrarre da

detriment ['dɛtrɪmənt] *n*: **to the ~ of** a detrimento di, a danno di; ~**al** [dɛtrɪ'mɛntl] *adj*: ~**al to** dannoso(a) a, nocivo(a) a

devaluation [dɪvælju'eɪʃən] *n* svalutazione *f*

devastate ['dɛvəsteɪt] *vt* devastare; (*fig*): ~**d by** sconvolto(a) da; **devastating** *adj* devastatore(trice); sconvolgente

develop [dɪ'vɛləp] *vt* sviluppare; (*habit*) prendere (gradualmente) ♦ *vi* svilupparsi; (*facts, symptoms: appear*) manifestarsi, rivelarsi; ~**er** *n* (*also*: **property ~er**) costruttore *m* edile; ~**ing country** *n* paese *m* in via di sviluppo; ~ment *n* sviluppo

device [dɪ'vaɪs] *n* (*apparatus*) congegno

devil ['dɛvl] *n* diavolo; demonio

devious ['diːvɪəs] *adj* (*person*) subdolo(a)

devise [dɪ'vaɪz] *vt* escogitare, concepire

devoid [dɪ'vɔɪd] *adj*: ~ **of** privo(a) di

devolution [diːvə'luːʃən] *n* (*POL*) decentramento

devote [dɪ'vəut] *vt*: **to** ~ **sth to** dedicare qc a; ~**d** *adj* devoto(a); **to be** ~**d to sb** essere molto affezionato(a) a qn; ~**e** [dɛvəu'tiː] *n* (*MUS, SPORT*) appassionato/a

devotion [dɪ'vəuʃən] *n* devozione *f*, attaccamento; (*REL*) atto di devozione, preghiera

devour [dɪ'vauə*] *vt* divorare

devout [dɪ'vaut] *adj* pio(a), devoto(a)

dew [djuː] *n* rugiada

dexterity [dɛks'tɛrɪtɪ] *n* destrezza

diabetes [daɪə'biːtiːz] *n* diabete *m*; **diabetic** [-'bɛtɪk] *adj*, *n* diabetico(a)

diabolical [daɪə'bɔlɪkl] (*inf*) *adj* orribile

diagnosis [daɪəg'nəusɪs] (*pl* **diagnoses**) *n* diagnosi *f inv*

diagonal [daɪ'ægənl] *adj* diagonale ♦ *n* diagonale *f*

diagram ['daɪəgræm] *n* diagramma *m*

dial ['daɪəl] *n* quadrante *m*; (*on radio*) lancetta; (*on telephone*) disco combinatore ♦ *vt* (*number*) fare

dialect ['daɪəlɛkt] *n* dialetto

dialling code ['daɪəlɪŋ-] (*US* **area code**) *n* prefisso

dialling tone ['daɪəlɪŋ-] (*US* **dial tone**) *n* segnale *m* di linea libera

dialogue ['daɪəlɔg] (*US* **dialog**) *n* dialogo

diameter [daɪ'æmɪtə*] *n* diametro

diamond ['daɪəmənd] *n* diamante *m*; (*shape*) rombo; ~**s** *npl* (*CARDS*) quadri *mpl*

diaper ['daɪəpə*] (*US*) *n* pannolino

diaphragm ['daɪəfræm] *n* diaframma *m*

diarrhoea [daɪə'riːə] (*US* **diarrhea**) *n* diarrea

diary ['daɪərɪ] *n* (*daily account*) diario; (*book*) agenda

dice [daɪs] *n inv* dado ♦ *vt* (*CULIN*) tagliare a dadini

Dictaphone ® ['dɪktəfəun] *n* dittafono ®

dictate [dɪk'teɪt] *vt* dettare

dictation [dɪk'teɪʃən] *n* dettatura; (*SCOL*) dettato

dictator [dɪk'teɪtə*] *n* dittatore *m*; ~**ship** *n* dittatura

dictionary ['dɪkʃənrɪ] *n* dizionario

did [dɪd] *pt of* **do**

didn't = **did not**

die [daɪ] *vi* morire; **to be dying for sth/to do sth** morire dalla voglia di qc/di fare qc; ~ **away** *vi* spegnersi a poco a poco; ~ **down** *vi* abbassarsi; ~ **out** *vi* estinguersi

diesel ['diːzl] *n* (*vehicle*) diesel *m inv*; ~ **engine** *n* motore *m* diesel *inv*; ~ (**oil**) *n* gasolio (per motori diesel), diesel *m inv*

diet ['daɪət] *n* alimentazione *f*; (*restricted food*) dieta ♦ *vi* (*also*: **be on a** ~) stare a dieta

differ ['dɪfə*] *vi*: **to** ~ **from sth** differire da qc; essere diverso(a) da qc; **to** ~ **from sb over sth** essere in disaccordo con qn su qc; ~**ence** *n* differenza; (*disagreement*) screzio; ~**ent** *adj* diverso(a); ~**entiate** [-'rɛnʃɪeɪt] *vi*: **to** ~**entiate between** discriminare *or* fare differenza fra

difficult ['dɪfɪkəlt] *adj* difficile; ~**y** *n* difficoltà *f inv*

diffident ['dɪfɪdənt] *adj* sfiduciato(a)

diffuse [*adj* dɪ'fjuːs, *vb* dɪ'fjuːz] *adj* diffuso(a) ♦ *vt* diffondere

dig [dɪg] (*pt, pp* **dug**) *vt* (*hole*) scavare; (*garden*) vangare ♦ *n* (*prod*) gomitata; (*archaeological*) scavo; ~ **into** *vt fus* (*savings*) scavare in; **to** ~ **one's nails into** conficcare le unghie in; ~ **up** *vt* (*tree etc*) sradicare; (*information*) scavare fuori

digest [*vb* daɪ'dʒɛst, *n* 'daɪdʒɛst] *vt* digerire ♦ *n* compendio; ~**ion** [dɪ'dʒɛstʃən] *n* digestione *f*; ~**ive** *adj* (*juices, system*) digerente

digit ['dɪdʒɪt] *n* cifra; (*finger*) dito; ~**al** *adj* digitale; ~**al camera** *n* macchina fotografica digitale; ~**al TV** *n* televisione *f* digitale

dignified ['dɪgnɪfaɪd] *adj* dignitoso(a)

dignity ['dɪgnɪtɪ] *n* dignità

digress [daɪˈgrɛs] *vi*: **to ~ from** divagare da

digs [dɪgz] (*BRIT: inf*) *npl* camera ammobiliata

dike [daɪk] *n* = **dyke**

dilapidated [dɪˈlæpɪdeɪtɪd] *adj* cadente

dilemma [daɪˈlɛmə] *n* dilemma *m*

diligent [ˈdɪlɪdʒənt] *adj* diligente

dilute [daɪˈluːt] *vt* diluire; (*with water*) annacquare

dim [dɪm] *adj* (*light*) debole; (*outline, figure*) vago(a); (*room*) in penombra; (*inf: person*) tonto(a) ♦ *vt* (*light*) abbassare

dime [daɪm] (*US*) *n* = 10 cents

dimension [daɪˈmɛnʃən] *n* dimensione *f*

diminish [dɪˈmɪnɪʃ] *vt, vi* diminuire

diminutive [dɪˈmɪnjʊtɪv] *adj* minuscolo(a) ♦ *n* (*LING*) diminutivo

dimmers [ˈdɪməz] (*US*) *npl* (*AUT*) anabbaglianti *mpl*; luci *fpl* di posizione

dimple [ˈdɪmpl] *n* fossetta

din [dɪn] *n* chiasso, fracasso

dine [daɪn] *vi* pranzare; **~r** *n* (*person*) cliente *m/f*; (*US: place*) tavola calda

dinghy [ˈdɪŋgɪ] *n* battello pneumatico; (*also:* **rubber ~**) gommone *m*

dingy [ˈdɪndʒɪ] *adj* grigio(a)

dining car [ˈdaɪnɪŋ-] (*BRIT*) *n* vagone *m* ristorante

dining room [ˈdaɪnɪŋ-] *n* sala da pranzo

dinner [ˈdɪnə*] *n* (*lunch*) pranzo; (*evening meal*) cena; (*public*) banchetto; **~ jacket** *n* smoking *m inv*; **~ party** *n* cena; **~ time** *n* ora di pranzo (*or* cena)

dip [dɪp] *n* discesa; (*in sea*) bagno; (*CULIN*) salsetta ♦ *vt* immergere; bagnare; (*BRIT: AUT: lights*) abbassare ♦ *vi* abbassarsi

diploma [dɪˈpləʊmə] *n* diploma *m*

diplomacy [dɪˈpləʊməsɪ] *n* diplomazia

diplomat [ˈdɪpləmæt] *n* diplomatico; **~ic** [dɪpləˈmætɪk] *adj* diplomatico(a)

diprod [ˈdɪprɒd] (*US*) *n* = **dipstick**

dipstick [ˈdɪpstɪk] *n* (*AUT*) indicatore *m* di livello dell'olio

dipswitch [ˈdɪpswɪtʃ] (*BRIT*) *n* (*AUT*) levetta dei fari

dire [daɪə*] *adj* terribile; estremo(a)

direct [daɪˈrɛkt] *adj* diretto(a) ♦ *vt* dirigere; (*order*): **to ~ sb to do sth** dare direttive a qn di fare qc ♦ *adv* direttamente; **can you ~ me to ...?** mi può indicare la strada per ...?

direction [dɪˈrɛkʃən] *n* direzione *f*; **~s** *npl* (*advice*) chiarimenti *mpl*; **sense of ~** senso dell'orientamento; **~s for use** istruzioni *fpl*

directly [dɪˈrɛktlɪ] *adv* (*in straight line*) direttamente; (*at once*) subito

director [dɪˈrɛktə*] *n* direttore/trice; amministratore/trice; (*THEATRE, CINEMA*) regista *m/f*

directory [dɪˈrɛktərɪ] *n* elenco; **~ enquiries**, **~ assistance** (*US*) *n* informazioni *fpl* elenco abbonati *inv*

dirt [dɜːt] *n* sporcizia; immondizia; (*earth*) terra; **~-cheap** *adj* da due soldi; **~y** *adj* sporco(a) ♦ *vt* sporcare; **~y trick** *n* brutto scherzo

disability [dɪsəˈbɪlɪtɪ] *n* invalidità *f inv*; (*LAW*) incapacità *f inv*

disabled [dɪsˈeɪbld] *adj* invalido(a); (*mentally*) ritardato(a) ♦ *npl*: **the ~** gli invalidi

disadvantage [dɪsədˈvɑːntɪdʒ] *n* svantaggio

disagree [dɪsəˈgriː] *vi* (*differ*) discordare; (*be against, think otherwise*): **to ~ (with)** essere in disaccordo (con), dissentire (da); **~able** *adj* sgradevole; (*person*) antipatico(a); **~ment** *n* disaccordo; (*argument*) dissapore *m*

disallow [dɪsəˈlaʊ] *vt* (*appeal*) respingere

disappear [dɪsəˈpɪə*] *vi* scomparire; **~ance** *n* scomparsa

disappoint [dɪsəˈpɔɪnt] *vt* deludere; **~ed** *adj* deluso(a); **~ing** *adj* deludente; **~ment** *n* delusione *f*

disapproval [dɪsəˈpruːvəl] *n* disapprovazione *f*

disapprove [dɪsəˈpruːv] *vi*: **to ~ of** disapprovare

disarm [dɪsˈɑːm] *vt* disarmare; **~ament** *n* disarmo

disarray [dɪsəˈreɪ] *n*: **in ~** (*army*) in rotta; (*organization*) in uno stato di confusione; (*clothes, hair*) in disordine

disaster [dɪ'zɑ:stə*] n disastro
disband [dɪs'bænd] vt sbandare; (MIL)
congedare ♦ vi sciogliersi
disbelief ['dɪsbə'li:f] n incredulità
disc [dɪsk] n disco; (COMPUT) = **disk**
discard [dɪs'kɑ:d] vt (old things) scartare;
(fig) abbandonare
discern [dɪ'sə:n] vt discernere, distinguere;
~ing adj perspicace
discharge [vb dɪs'tʃɑ:dʒ, n 'dɪstʃɑ:dʒ] vt
(duties) compiere; (ELEC, waste etc)
scaricare; (MED) emettere; (patient)
dimettere; (employee) licenziare; (soldier)
congedare; (defendant) liberare ♦ n (ELEC)
scarica; (MED) emissione f; (dismissal)
licenziamento; congedo; liberazione f
disciple [dɪ'saɪpl] n discepolo
discipline ['dɪsɪplɪn] n disciplina ♦ vt
disciplinare; (punish) punire
disc jockey n disc jockey m inv
disclaim [dɪs'kleɪm] vt negare, smentire
disclose [dɪs'kləʊz] vt rivelare, svelare;
disclosure [-'kləʊʒə*] n rivelazione f
disco ['dɪskəʊ] n abbr = **discotheque**
discoloured [dɪs'kʌləd] (US **discolored**) adj
scolorito(a); ingiallito(a)
discomfort [dɪs'kʌmfət] n disagio; (lack of
comfort) scomodità f inv
disconcert [dɪskən'sə:t] vt sconcertare
disconnect [dɪskə'nekt] vt sconnettere,
staccare; (ELEC, RADIO) staccare; (gas, water)
chiudere
discontent [dɪskən'tent] n scontentezza;
~ed adj scontento(a)
discontinue [dɪskən'tɪnju:] vt smettere,
cessare; **"~d"** (COMM) "fuori produzione"
discord ['dɪskɔ:d] n disaccordo; (MUS)
dissonanza
discotheque ['dɪskəʊtek] n discoteca
discount [n 'dɪskaʊnt, vb dɪs'kaʊnt] n sconto
♦ vt scontare; (idea) non badare a
discourage [dɪs'kʌrɪdʒ] vt scoraggiare
discourteous [dɪs'kə:tɪəs] adj scortese
discover [dɪs'kʌvə*] vt scoprire; **~y** n
scoperta
discredit [dɪs'kredɪt] vt screditare; mettere
in dubbio

discreet [dɪ'skri:t] adj discreto(a)
discrepancy [dɪ'skrepənsɪ] n discrepanza
discriminate [dɪ'skrɪmɪneɪt] vi: **to ~
between** distinguere tra; **to ~ against**
discriminare contro; **discriminating** adj
fine, giudizioso(a); **discrimination**
[-'neɪʃən] n discriminazione f; (judgment)
discernimento
discuss [dɪ'skʌs] vt discutere; (debate)
dibattere; **~ion** [dɪ'skʌʃən] n discussione f
disdain [dɪs'deɪn] n disdegno
disease [dɪ'zi:z] n malattia
disembark [dɪsɪm'bɑ:k] vt, vi sbarcare
disentangle [dɪsɪn'tæŋgl] vt liberare; (wool
etc) sbrogliare
disfigure [dɪs'fɪgə*] vt sfigurare
disgrace [dɪs'greɪs] n vergogna; (disfavour)
disgrazia ♦ vt disonorare, far cadere in
disgrazia; **~ful** adj scandaloso(a),
vergognoso(a)
disgruntled [dɪs'grʌntld] adj scontento(a),
di cattivo umore
disguise [dɪs'gaɪz] n travestimento ♦ vt: **to
~ (as)** travestire (da); **in ~** travestito(a)
disgust [dɪs'gʌst] n disgusto, nausea ♦ vt
disgustare, far schifo a; **~ing** adj
disgustoso(a); ripugnante
dish [dɪʃ] n piatto; **to do** or **wash the ~es**
fare i piatti; **~ out** vt distribuire; **~ up** vt
servire; **~cloth** n strofinaccio
dishearten [dɪs'hɑ:tn] vt scoraggiare
dishevelled [dɪ'ʃevəld] (US **disheveled**) adj
arruffato(a); scapigliato(a)
dishonest [dɪs'ɒnɪst] adj disonesto(a)
dishonour [dɪs'ɒnə*] (US **dishonor**) n
disonore m; **~able** adj disonorevole
dishtowel ['dɪʃtaʊəl] (US) n strofinaccio dei
piatti
dishwasher ['dɪʃwɒʃə*] n lavastoviglie f inv
disillusion [dɪsɪ'lu:ʒən] vt disilludere,
disingannare
disinfect [dɪsɪn'fekt] vt disinfettare; **~ant** n
disinfettante m
disintegrate [dɪs'ɪntɪgreɪt] vi disintegrarsi
disinterested [dɪs'ɪntrəstɪd] adj
disinteressato(a)
disjointed [dɪs'dʒɔɪntɪd] adj sconnesso(a)

disk [dɪsk] *n* (COMPUT) disco; **single-/
double-sided ~** disco a facciata singola/
doppia; **~ drive** *n* lettore *m*; **~ette** (US) *n*
= **disk**

dislike [dɪsˈlaɪk] *n* antipatia, avversione *f*;
(*gen pl*) cosa che non piace ♦ *vt*: **he ~s it**
non gli piace

dislocate [ˈdɪsləkeɪt] *vt* slogare

dislodge [dɪsˈlɒdʒ] *vt* rimuovere

disloyal [dɪsˈlɔɪəl] *adj* sleale

dismal [ˈdɪzml] *adj* triste, cupo(a)

dismantle [dɪsˈmæntl] *vt* (*machine*)
smontare

dismay [dɪsˈmeɪ] *n* costernazione *f* ♦ *vt*
sgomentare

dismiss [dɪsˈmɪs] *vt* congedare; (*employee*)
licenziare; (*idea*) scacciare; (*LAW*)
respingere; **~al** *n* congedo; licenziamento

dismount [dɪsˈmaunt] *vi* scendere

disobedience [dɪsəˈbiːdɪəns] *n*
disubbidienza

disobedient [dɪsəˈbiːdɪənt] *adj*
disubbidiente

disobey [dɪsəˈbeɪ] *vt* disubbidire a

disorder [dɪsˈɔːdə*] *n* disordine *m*; (*rioting*)
tumulto; (*MED*) disturbo; **~ly** *adj*
disordinato(a); tumultuoso(a)

disorientated [dɪsˈɔːrɪenteɪtɪd] *adj*
disorientato(a)

disown [dɪsˈəun] *vt* rinnegare

disparaging [dɪsˈpærɪdʒɪŋ] *adj*
spregiativo(a), sprezzante

dispassionate [dɪsˈpæʃənət] *adj* calmo(a),
freddo(a); imparziale

dispatch [dɪsˈpætʃ] *vt* spedire, inviare ♦ *n*
spedizione *f*, invio; (*MIL*, *PRESS*) dispaccio

dispel [dɪsˈpel] *vt* dissipare, scacciare

dispense [dɪsˈpens] *vt* distribuire,
amministrare; **~ with** *vt fus* fare a meno
di; **~r** *n* (*container*) distributore *m*;
dispensing chemist (*BRIT*) *n* farmacista
m/f

disperse [dɪsˈpəːs] *vt* disperdere;
(*knowledge*) disseminare ♦ *vi* disperdersi

dispirited [dɪsˈpɪrɪtɪd] *adj* scoraggiato(a),
abbattuto(a)

displace [dɪsˈpleɪs] *vt* spostare; **~d person**

n (POL) profugo/a

display [dɪsˈpleɪ] *n* esposizione *f*; (*of feeling
etc*) manifestazione *f*; (*screen*) schermo ♦ *vt*
mostrare; (*goods*) esporre; (*pej*) ostentare

displease [dɪsˈpliːz] *vt* dispiacere a,
scontentare; **~d with** scontento di;
displeasure [-ˈpleʒə*] *n* dispiacere *m*

disposable [dɪsˈpəuzəbl] *adj* (*pack etc*) a
perdere; (*income*) disponibile; **~ nappy** *n*
pannolino di carta

disposal [dɪsˈpəuzl] *n* eliminazione *f*; (*of
property*) cessione *f*; **at one's ~** alla sua
disposizione

dispose [dɪsˈpəuz] *vi*: **~ of** sbarazzarsi di;
~d *adj*: **~d to do** disposto(a) a fare;
disposition [-ˈzɪʃən] *n* disposizione *f*;
(*temperament*) carattere *m*

disproportionate [dɪsprəˈpɔːʃənət] *adj*
sproporzionato(a)

disprove [dɪsˈpruːv] *vt* confutare

dispute [dɪsˈpjuːt] *n* disputa; (*also*: **industrial ~**) controversia (sindacale) ♦ *vt* contestare; (*matter*) discutere; (*victory*) disputare

disqualify [dɪsˈkwɒlɪfaɪ] *vt* (SPORT)
squalificare; **to ~ sb from sth/from doing**
rendere qn incapace a qc/a fare;
squalificare qn da qc/da fare; **to ~ sb from
driving** ritirare la patente a qn

disquiet [dɪsˈkwaɪət] *n* inquietudine *f*

disregard [dɪsrɪˈgɑːd] *vt* non far caso a, non
badare a

disrepair [dɪsrɪˈpeə*] *n*: **to fall into ~**
(*building*) andare in rovina; (*machine*)
deteriorarsi

disreputable [dɪsˈrepjutəbl] *adj* poco
raccomandabile; indecente

disrupt [dɪsˈrʌpt] *vt* disturbare; creare
scompiglio in

dissatisfaction [dɪssætɪsˈfækʃən] *n*
scontentezza, insoddisfazione *f*

dissect [dɪˈsekt] *vt* sezionare

dissent [dɪˈsent] *n* dissenso

dissertation [dɪsəˈteɪʃən] *n* tesi *f inv*,
dissertazione *f*

disservice [dɪsˈsəːvɪs] *n*: **to do sb a ~** fare
un cattivo servizio a qn

dissimilar [dɪˈsɪmɪlə*] *adj*: **~ (to)** dissimile

or diverso(a) (da)

dissipate ['dɪsɪpeɪt] vt dissipare

dissolve [dɪ'zɔlv] vt dissolvere, sciogliere; (POL, marriage etc) sciogliere ♦ vi dissolversi, sciogliersi

distance ['dɪstns] n distanza; **in the ~** in lontananza

distant ['dɪstnt] adj lontano(a), distante; (manner) riservato(a), freddo(a)

distaste [dɪs'teɪst] n ripugnanza; **~ful** adj ripugnante, sgradevole

distended [dɪs'tendɪd] adj (stomach) dilatato(a)

distil [dɪs'tɪl] (US **distill**) vt distillare; **~lery** n distilleria

distinct [dɪs'tɪŋkt] adj distinto(a); **as ~ from** a differenza di; **~ion** [dɪs'tɪŋkʃən] n distinzione f; (in exam) lode f; **~ive** adj distintivo(a)

distinguish [dɪs'tɪŋgwɪʃ] vt distinguere; discernere; **~ed** adj (eminent) eminente; **~ing** adj (feature) distinto(a), caratteristico(a)

distort [dɪs'tɔːt] vt distorcere; (TECH) deformare

distract [dɪs'trækt] vt distrarre; **~ed** adj distratto(a); **~ion** [dɪs'trækʃən] n distrazione f

distraught [dɪs'trɔːt] adj stravolto(a)

distress [dɪs'tres] n angoscia ♦ vt affliggere; **~ing** adj doloroso(a); **~ signal** n segnale m di soccorso

distribute [dɪs'trɪbjuːt] vt distribuire; **distribution** [-'bjuːʃən] n distribuzione f; **distributor** n distributore m

district ['dɪstrɪkt] n (of country) regione f; (of town) quartiere m; (ADMIN) distretto; **~ attorney** (US) n ≈ sostituto procuratore m della Repubblica; **~ nurse** (BRIT) n infermiera di quartiere

distrust [dɪs'trʌst] n diffidenza, sfiducia ♦ vt non aver fiducia in

disturb [dɪs'təːb] vt disturbare; **~ance** n disturbo; (political etc) disordini mpl; **~ed** adj (worried, upset) turbato(a); **emotionally ~ed** con turbe emotive; **~ing** adj sconvolgente

disuse [dɪs'juːs] n: **to fall into ~** cadere in disuso

disused [dɪs'juːzd] adj abbandonato(a)

ditch [dɪtʃ] n fossa ♦ vt (inf) piantare in asso

dither ['dɪðə*] (pej) vi vacillare

ditto ['dɪtəu] adv idem

dive [daɪv] n tuffo; (of submarine) immersione f ♦ vi tuffarsi; immergersi; **~r** n tuffatore/trice; palombaro

diverse [daɪ'vəːs] adj vario(a)

diversion [daɪ'vəːʃən] n (BRIT: AUT) deviazione f; (distraction) divertimento

divert [daɪ'vəːt] vt deviare

divide [dɪ'vaɪd] vt dividere; (separate) separare ♦ vi dividersi; **~d highway** (US) n strada a doppia carreggiata

dividend ['dɪvɪdɛnd] n dividendo; (fig): **to pay ~s** dare dei frutti

divine [dɪ'vaɪn] adj divino(a)

diving ['daɪvɪŋ] n tuffo; **~ board** n trampolino

divinity [dɪ'vɪnɪtɪ] n divinità f inv; teologia

division [dɪ'vɪʒən] n divisione f; separazione f; (esp FOOTBALL) serie f

divorce [dɪ'vɔːs] n divorzio ♦ vt divorziare da; (dissociate) separare; **~d** adj divorziato(a); **~e** [-'siː] n divorziato/a

D.I.Y. (BRIT) n abbr = **do-it-yourself**

dizzy ['dɪzɪ] adj: **to feel ~** avere il capogiro

DJ n abbr = **disc jockey**

KEYWORD

do [duː] (pt **did**, pp **done**) n (inf: party etc) festa; **it was rather a grand ~** è stato un ricevimento piuttosto importante

♦ vb 1 (in negative constructions) non tradotto; **I don't understand** non capisco

2 (to form questions) non tradotto; **didn't you know?** non lo sapevi?; **why didn't you come?** perché non sei venuto?

3 (for emphasis, in polite expressions): **she does seem rather late** sembra essere piuttosto in ritardo; **~ sit down** si accomodi la prego, prego si sieda; **~ take care!** mi raccomando, sta attento!

4 (used to avoid repeating vb): **she swims better than I** lei nuota meglio di me; **~**

you agree? – yes, I ~/no, I don't sei d'accordo? — sì/no; **she lives in Glasgow – so ~ I** lei vive a Glasgow — anch'io; **he asked me to help him and I did** mi ha chiesto di aiutarlo ed io l'ho fatto
5 (*in question tags*): **you like him, don't you?** ti piace, vero?; **I don't know him, ~ I?** non lo conosco, vero?
♦ *vt* (*gen, carry out, perform etc*) fare; **what are you ~ing tonight?** che fa stasera?; **to ~ the cooking** cucinare; **to ~ the washing-up** fare i piatti; **to ~ one's teeth** lavarsi i denti; **to ~ one's hair/nails** farsi i capelli/le unghie; **the car was ~ing 100** la macchina faceva i 100 all'ora
♦ *vi* 1 (*act, behave*) fare; **~ as I ~** faccia come me, faccia come faccio io
2 (*get on, fare*) andare; **he's ~ing well/badly at school** va bene/male a scuola; **how ~ you ~?** piacere!
3 (*suit*) andare bene; **this room will ~** questa stanza va bene
4 (*be sufficient*) bastare; **will £10 ~?** basteranno 10 sterline?; **that'll ~** basta così; **that'll ~!** (*in annoyance*) ora basta!; **to make ~ (with)** arrangiarsi (con)

do away with *vt fus* (*kill*) far fuori; (*abolish*) abolire
do up *vt* (*laces*) allacciare; (*dress, buttons*) abbottonare; (*renovate: room, house*) rimettere a nuovo, rifare
do with *vt fus* (*need*) aver bisogno di; (*be connected*): **what has it got to ~ with you?** e tu che c'entri?; **I won't have anything to ~ with it** non voglio avere niente a che farci; **it has to ~ with money** si tratta di soldi
do without *vi* fare senza ♦ *vt fus* fare a meno di

dock [dɔk] *n* (*NAUT*) bacino; (*LAW*) banco degli imputati ♦ *vi* entrare in bacino; (*SPACE*) agganciarsi; **~s** *npl* (*NAUT*) dock *m inv*; **~er** *n* scaricatore *m*; **~yard** *n* cantiere *m* (navale)
doctor ['dɔktə*] *n* medico/a; (*Ph.D. etc*) dottore/essa ♦ *vt* (*drink etc*) adulterare; **D~**

of Philosophy *n* dottorato di ricerca; (*person*) titolare *m/f* di un dottorato di ricerca
doctrine ['dɔktrɪn] *n* dottrina
document ['dɔkjumənt] *n* documento; **~ary** [-'mɛntərɪ] *adj* (*evidence*) documentato(a) ♦ *n* documentario
dodge [dɔdʒ] *n* trucco; schivata ♦ *vt* schivare, eludere
dodgems ['dɔdʒəmz] (*BRIT*) *npl* autoscontri *mpl*
doe [dəu] *n* (*deer*) femmina di daino; (*rabbit*) coniglia
does [dʌz] *vb see* **do**; **doesn't = does not**
dog [dɔg] *n* cane *m* ♦ *vt* (*follow closely*) pedinare; (*fig: memory etc*) perseguitare; **~ collar** *n* collare *m* di cane; (*fig*) collarino; **~-eared** *adj* (*book*) con orecchie
dogged ['dɔgɪd] *adj* ostinato(a), tenace
dogsbody ['dɔgzbɔdɪ] (*BRIT*: *inf*) *n* factotum *m inv*
doing ['du:ɪŋ] *n*: **this is your ~** è opera tua, sei stato tu
do-it-yourself *n* il far da sé
doldrums ['dɔldrəmz] *npl* (*fig*): **to be in the ~** avere un brutto periodo
dole [dəul] (*BRIT*) *n* sussidio di disoccupazione; **to be on the ~** vivere del sussidio; **~ out** *vt* distribuire
doll [dɔl] *n* bambola; **~ed up** (*inf*) *adj* in ghingheri
dollar ['dɔlə*] *n* dollaro
dolly ['dɔlɪ] *n* bambola
dolphin ['dɔlfɪn] *n* delfino
domain [də'meɪn] *n* dominio
dome [dəum] *n* cupola
domestic [də'mɛstɪk] *adj* (*duty, happiness, animal*) domestico(a); (*policy, affairs, flights*) nazionale; **~ated** *adj* addomesticato(a)
dominant ['dɔmɪnənt] *adj* dominante
dominate ['dɔmɪneɪt] *vt* dominare
domineering [dɔmɪ'nɪərɪŋ] *adj* dispotico(a), autoritario(a)
dominion [də'mɪnɪən] *n* dominio; sovranità; dominion *m inv*
domino ['dɔmɪnəu] (*pl* **~es**) *n* domino; **~es** *n* (*game*) gioco del domino

don [dɔn] (BRIT) n docente m/f universitario(a)

donate [dəˈneɪt] vt donare

done [dʌn] pp of **do**

donkey [ˈdɔŋkɪ] n asino

donor [ˈdəʊnə*] n donatore/trice; ~ **card** n tessera di donatore di organi

don't [dəʊnt] = **do not**

doodle [ˈduːdl] vi scarabocchiare

doom [duːm] n destino; rovina ♦ vt: **to be ~ed (to failure)** essere predestinato(a) (a fallire)

door [dɔː*] n porta; ~**bell** n campanello; ~ **handle** n maniglia; ~**man** (irreg) n (in hotel) portiere m in livrea; ~**mat** n stuoia della porta; ~**step** n gradino della porta; ~**way** n porta

dope [dəʊp] n (inf: drugs) roba ♦ vt drogare

dormant [ˈdɔːmənt] adj inattivo(a)

dormitory [ˈdɔːmɪtrɪ] n dormitorio; (US) casa dello studente

dormouse [ˈdɔːmaus] (pl **dormice**) n ghiro

dosage [ˈdəʊsɪdʒ] n posologia

dose [dəus] n dose f; (bout) attacco

doss house [ˈdɔs-] (BRIT) n asilo notturno

dot [dɔt] n punto; macchiolina ♦ vt: ~**ted with** punteggiato(a) di; **on the ~** in punto; ~**ted line** [ˈdɔtɪd-] n linea punteggiata

double [ˈdʌbl] adj doppio(a) ♦ adv (twice): **to cost ~ (sth)** costare il doppio (di qc) ♦ n sosia m inv ♦ vt raddoppiare; (fold) piegare doppio or in due ♦ vi raddoppiarsi; **at the ~** (BRIT), **on the ~** a passo di corsa; ~ **bass** n contrabbasso; ~ **bed** n letto matrimoniale; ~**-breasted** adj a doppio petto; ~**cross** vt fare il doppio gioco con; ~**decker** n autobus m inv a due piani; ~ **glazing** (BRIT) n doppi vetri mpl; ~ **room** n camera per due; ~**s** n (TENNIS) doppio; **doubly** adv doppiamente

doubt [daut] n dubbio ♦ vt dubitare di; **to ~ that** dubitare che +sub; ~**ful** adj dubbioso(a), incerto(a); (person) equivoco(a); ~**less** adv indubbiamente

dough [dəʊ] n pasta, impasto; ~**nut** n bombolone m

dove [dʌv] n colombo/a

Dover [ˈdəʊvə*] n Dover f

dovetail [ˈdʌvteɪl] vi (fig) combaciare

dowdy [ˈdaudɪ] adj trasandato(a); malvestito(a)

down [daun] n piume fpl ♦ adv giù, di sotto ♦ prep giù per ♦ vt (inf: drink) scolarsi; ~ **with X!** abbasso X!; ~**-and-out** n barbone m; ~**-at-heel** adj scalcagnato(a); ~**cast** adj abbattuto(a); ~**fall** n caduta; rovina; ~**hearted** adj scoraggiato(a); ~**hill** adv: **to go ~hill** andare in discesa; (fig) lasciarsi andare; andare a rotoli; ~**load** vt (COMPUT) scaricare; ~ **payment** n acconto; ~**pour** n scroscio di pioggia; ~**right** adj franco(a), (refusal) assoluto(a); ~**size** vi (ECON: company) ridurre il personale; ~**stairs** adv di sotto; al piano inferiore; ~**stream** adv a valle; ~**-to-earth** adj pratico(a); ~**town** adv in città; ~ **under** adv (Australia etc) agli antipodi; ~**ward** [ˈdaunwəd] adj, adv in giù, in discesa; ~**wards** [ˈdaunwədz] adv = ~**ward**

Downing Street

ⓘ Al numero 10 di **Downing Street**, nel quartiere di Westminster a Londra, si trova la residenza del primo ministro inglese, al numero 11 quella del **Chancellor of the Exchequer**.

dowry [ˈdaurɪ] n dote f

doz. abbr = **dozen**

doze [dəuz] vi sonnecchiare; ~ **off** vi appisolarsi

dozen [ˈdʌzn] n dozzina; **a ~ books** una dozzina di libri; ~**s of** decine fpl di

Dr. abbr (= doctor) dott.; (in street names) = **drive**

drab [dræb] adj tetro(a), grigio(a)

draft [drɑːft] n abbozzo; (POL) bozza; (COMM) tratta; (US: call-up) leva ♦ vt abbozzare; see also **draught**

draftsman [ˈdrɑːftsmən] (US) n = **draughtsman**

drag [dræg] vt trascinare; (river) dragare ♦ vi trascinarsi ♦ n (inf) noioso/a; noia, fatica; (women's clothing): **in ~** travestito (da donna); **~ on** *vi* tirar avanti lentamente

dragon ['drægən] *n* drago

dragonfly ['drægənflaɪ] *n* libellula

drain [dreɪn] *n* (*for sewage*) fogna; (*on resources*) salasso ♦ *vt* (*land, marshes*) prosciugare; (*vegetables*) scolare ♦ *vi* (*water*) defluire (via); **~age** *n* prosciugamento; fognatura; **~ing board** (*US* **~board**) *n* piano del lavello; **~pipe** *n* tubo di scarico

drama ['drɑːmə] *n* (*art*) dramma *m*, teatro; (*play*) commedia; (*event*) dramma; **~tic** [drə'mætɪk] *adj* drammatico(a); **~tist** ['dræmətɪst] *n* drammaturgo/a; **~tize** ['dræmətaɪz] *vt* (*events*) drammatizzare

drank [dræŋk] *pt of* **drink**

drape [dreɪp] *vt* drappeggiare; **~r** (*BRIT*) *n* negoziante *m/f* di stoffe; **~s** (*US*) *npl* (*curtains*) tende *fpl*

drastic ['dræstɪk] *adj* drastico(a)

draught [drɑːft] (*US* **draft**) *n* corrente *f* d'aria; (*NAUT*) pescaggio; **on ~** (*beer*) alla spina; **~ beer** *n* birra alla spina; **~board** (*BRIT*) *n* scacchiera; **~s** (*BRIT*) *n* (*gioco della*) dama

draughtsman ['drɑːftsmən] (*US* **draftsman**) (*irreg*) *n* disegnatore *m*

draw [drɔː] (*pt* **drew**, *pp* **drawn**) *vt* tirare; (*take out*) estrarre; (*attract*) attirare; (*picture*) disegnare; (*line, circle*) tracciare; (*money*) ritirare ♦ *vi* (*SPORT*) pareggiare ♦ *n* pareggio; (*in lottery*) estrazione *f*; **to ~ near** avvicinarsi; **~ out** *vi* (*lengthen*) allungarsi ♦ *vt* (*money*) ritirare; **~ up** *vi* (*stop*) arrestarsi, fermarsi ♦ *vt* (*chair*) avvicinare; (*document*) compilare; **~back** *n* svantaggio, inconveniente *m*; **~bridge** *n* ponte *m* levatoio

drawer [drɔː*] *n* cassetto

drawing ['drɔːɪŋ] *n* disegno; **~ board** *n* tavola da disegno; **~ pin** (*BRIT*) *n* puntina da disegno; **~ room** *n* salotto

drawl [drɔːl] *n* pronuncia strascicata

drawn [drɔːn] *pp of* **draw**

dread [dred] *n* terrore *m* ♦ *vt* tremare all'idea di; **~ful** *adj* terribile

dream [driːm] (*pt, pp* **dreamed** *or* **dreamt**)

n sogno ♦ *vt, vi* sognare; **~y** *adj* sognante

dreary ['drɪərɪ] *adj* tetro(a); monotono(a)

dredge [dredʒ] *vt* dragare

dregs [dregz] *npl* feccia

drench [drentʃ] *vt* inzuppare

dress [dres] *n* vestito; (*no pl: clothing*) abbigliamento ♦ *vt* vestire; (*wound*) fasciare ♦ *vi* vestirsi; **to get ~ed** vestirsi; **~ up** *vi* vestirsi a festa; (*in fancy dress*) vestirsi in costume; **~ circle** (*BRIT*) *n* prima galleria; **~er** *n* (*BRIT: cupboard*) credenza; (*US*) cassettone *m*; **~ing** *n* (*MED*) benda; (*CULIN*) condimento; **~ing gown** (*BRIT*) *n* vestaglia; **~ing room** *n* (*THEATRE*) camerino; (*SPORT*) spogliatoio; **~ing table** *n* toilette *f inv*; **~maker** *n* sarta; **~ rehearsal** *n* prova generale; **~y** (*inf*) *adj* elegante

drew [druː] *pt of* **draw**

dribble ['drɪbl] *vi* (*baby*) sbavare ♦ *vt* (*ball*) dribblare

dried [draɪd] *adj* (*fruit, beans*) secco(a); (*eggs, milk*) in polvere

drier ['draɪə*] *n* = **dryer**

drift [drɪft] *n* (*of current etc*) direzione *f*; forza; (*of snow*) cumulo; turbine *m*; (*general meaning*) senso ♦ *vi* (*boat*) essere trasportato(a) dalla corrente; (*sand, snow*) ammucchiarsi; **~wood** *n* resti *mpl* della mareggiata

drill [drɪl] *n* trapano; (*MIL*) esercitazione *f* ♦ *vt* trapanare; (*troops*) addestrare ♦ *vi* (*for oil*) fare trivellazioni

drink [drɪŋk] (*pt* **drank**, *pp* **drunk**) *n* bevanda, bibita; (*alcoholic ~*) bicchierino; (*sip*) sorso ♦ *vt, vi* bere; **to have a ~** bere qualcosa; **a ~ of water** un po' d'acqua; **~er** *n* bevitore/trice; **~ing water** *n* acqua potabile

drip [drɪp] *n* goccia; gocciolamento; (*MED*) fleboclisi *f inv* ♦ *vi* gocciolare; (*tap*) sgocciolare; **~-dry** *adj* (*shirt*) che non si stira; **~ping** *n* grasso d'arrosto

drive [draɪv] (*pt* **drove**, *pp* **driven**) *n* passeggiata *or* giro in macchina; (*also:* **~way**) viale *m* d'accesso; (*energy*) energia; (*campaign*) campagna; (*also:* **disk ~**) lettore _m ♦ vt_ guidare; (_nail_) piantare; (_push_) cacciare, spingere; (TECH: _motor_) azionare; far funzionare ♦ _vi_ (AUT: _at controls_) guidare; (: _travel_) andare in macchina; **left-/right-hand ~** guida a sinistra/destra; **to ~ sb mad** far impazzire qn

drivel ['drɪvl] (_inf_) _n_ idiozie _fpl_

driven ['drɪvn] _pp of_ **drive**

driver ['draɪvə*] _n_ conducente _m/f_; (_of taxi_) tassista _m_; (_chauffeur, of bus_) autista _m/f_; **~'s license** (US) _n_ patente _f_ di guida

driveway ['draɪvweɪ] _n_ viale _m_ d'accesso

driving ['draɪvɪŋ] _n_ guida; **~ instructor** _n_ istruttore/trice di scuola guida; **~ lesson** _n_ lezione _f_ di guida; **~ licence** (BRIT) _n_ patente _f_ di guida; **~ mirror** _n_ specchietto retrovisore; **~ school** _n_ scuola _f_ guida _inv_; **~ test** _n_ esame _m_ di guida

drizzle ['drɪzl] _n_ pioggerella

drool [druːl] _vi_ sbavare

droop [druːp] _vi_ (_flower_) appassire; (_head, shoulders_) chinarsi

drop [drɒp] _n_ (_of water_) goccia; (_lessening_) diminuzione _f_; (_fall_) caduta ♦ _vt_ lasciare cadere; (_voice, eyes, price_) abbassare; (_set down from car_) far scendere; (_name from list_) lasciare fuori ♦ _vi_ cascare; (_wind_) abbassarsi; **~s** _npl_ (MED) gocce _fpl_; **~ off** _vi_ (_sleep_) addormentarsi ♦ _vt_ (_passenger_) far scendere; **~ out** _vi_ (_withdraw_) ritirarsi; (_student etc_) smettere di studiare; **~-out** _n_ (_from society/from university_) chi ha abbandonato (la società/gli studi); **~per** _n_ contagocce _m inv_; **~pings** _npl_ sterco

drought [draut] _n_ siccità _f inv_

drove [drəuv] _pt of_ **drive**

drown [draun] _vt_ affogare; (_fig: noise_) soffocare ♦ _vi_ affogare

drowsy ['drauzɪ] _adj_ sonnolento(a), assonnato(a)

drug [drʌg] _n_ farmaco; (_narcotic_) droga ♦ _vt_ drogare; **to be on ~s** drogarsi; (MED) prendere medicinali; **hard/soft ~s** droghe pesanti/leggere; **~ addict** _n_ tossicomane _m/f_; **~gist** (US) _n_ persona che gestisce un _drugstore_; **~store** (US) _n_ drugstore _m inv_

drum [drʌm] _n_ tamburo; (_for oil, petrol_)

fusto ♦ _vi_ tamburellare; **~s** _npl_ (_set of ~s_) batteria; **~mer** _n_ batterista _m/f_

drunk [drʌŋk] _pp of_ **drink** ♦ _adj_ ubriaco(a); ebbro(a) ♦ _n_ (_also:_ **~ard**) ubriacone/a; **~en** _adj_ ubriaco(a); da ubriaco

dry [draɪ] _adj_ secco(a); (_day, clothes_) asciutto(a) ♦ _vt_ seccare; (_clothes, hair, hands_) asciugare ♦ _vi_ asciugarsi; **~ up** _vi_ seccarsi; **~-cleaner's** _n_ lavasecco _m inv_; **~-cleaning** _n_ pulitura a secco; **~er** _n_ (_for hair_) föhn _m inv_, asciugacapelli _m inv_; (_for clothes_) asciugabiancheria; (US: _spin-dryer_) centrifuga; **~ goods store** (US) _n_ negozio di stoffe; **~ rot** _n_ fungo del legno

DSS _n abbr_ (= _Department of Social Security_) ministero della Previdenza sociale

DTP _n abbr_ (= _desk-top publishing_) desktop publishing _m inv_

dual ['djuːəl] _adj_ doppio(a); **~ carriageway** (BRIT) _n_ strada a doppia carreggiata; **~-purpose** _adj_ a doppio uso

dubbed [dʌbd] _adj_ (CINEMA) doppiato(a)

dubious ['djuːbɪəs] _adj_ dubbio(a)

Dublin ['dʌblɪn] _n_ Dublino _f_

duchess ['dʌtʃɪs] _n_ duchessa

duck [dʌk] _n_ anatra ♦ _vi_ abbassare la testa; **~ling** _n_ anatroccolo

duct [dʌkt] _n_ condotto; (ANAT) canale _m_

dud [dʌd] _n_ (_object, tool_): **it's a ~** è inutile, non funziona ♦ _adj_: **~ cheque** (BRIT) assegno a vuoto

due [djuː] _adj_ dovuto(a); (_expected_) atteso(a); (_fitting_) giusto(a) ♦ _n_ dovuto ♦ _adv_: **~ north** diritto verso nord; **~s** _npl_ (_for club, union_) quota; (_in harbour_) diritti _mpl_ di porto; **in ~ course** a tempo debito; finalmente; **~ to** dovuto a; a causa di; **to be ~ to do** dover fare

duet [djuːˈet] _n_ duetto

duffel bag ['dʌfl-] _n_ sacca da viaggio di tela

duffel coat ['dʌfl-] _n_ montgomery _m inv_

dug [dʌg] _pt, pp of_ **dig**

duke [djuːk] _n_ duca _m_

dull [dʌl] _adj_ (_light_) debole; (_boring_) noioso(a); (_slow-witted_) ottuso(a); (_sound, pain_) sordo(a); (_weather, day_) fosco(a), scuro(a) ♦ *vt* (*pain, grief*) attutire; (*mind, senses*) intorpidire

duly ['dju:lɪ] *adv* (*on time*) a tempo debito; (*as expected*) debitamente

dumb [dʌm] *adj* muto(a); (*pej*) stupido(a); **~founded** [dʌm'faundɪd] *adj* stupito(a), stordito(a)

dummy ['dʌmɪ] *n* (*tailor's model*) manichino; (*TECH, COMM*) riproduzione *f*; (*BRIT: for baby*) tettarella ♦ *adj* falso(a), finto(a)

dump [dʌmp] *n* (*also:* **rubbish ~**) discarica di rifiuti; (*inf: place*) buco ♦ *vt* (*put down*) scaricare; mettere giù; (*get rid of*) buttar via

dumpling ['dʌmplɪŋ] *n* specie di gnocco

dumpy ['dʌmpɪ] *adj* tracagnotto(a)

dunce [dʌns] *n* (*SCOL*) somaro/a

dung [dʌŋ] *n* concime *m*

dungarees [dʌŋgə'ri:z] *npl* tuta

dungeon ['dʌndʒən] *n* prigione *f* sotterranea

dupe [dju:p] *n* zimbello ♦ *vt* gabbare, ingannare

duplex ['dju:plɛks] (*US*) *n* (*house*) casa con muro divisorio in comune con un'altra; (*apartment*) appartamento su due piani

duplicate [*n* 'dju:plɪkət, *vb* 'dju:plɪkeɪt] *n* doppio ♦ *vt* duplicare; **in ~** in doppia copia

durable ['djuərəbl] *adj* durevole; (*clothes, metal*) resistente

duration [djuə'reɪʃən] *n* durata

during ['djuərɪŋ] *prep* durante, nel corso di

dusk [dʌsk] *n* crepuscolo

dust [dʌst] *n* polvere *f* ♦ *vt* (*furniture*) spolverare; (*cake etc*) **to ~ with** cospargere con; **~bin** (*BRIT*) *n* pattumiera; **~er** *n* straccio per la polvere; **~man** (*BRIT: irreg*) *n* netturbino; **~y** *adj* polveroso(a)

Dutch [dʌtʃ] *adj* olandese ♦ *n* (*LING*) olandese *m*; **the ~** *npl* gli Olandesi; **to go ~** (*inf*) fare alla romana; **~man/woman** (*irreg*) *n* olandese *m/f*

duty ['dju:tɪ] *n* dovere *m*; (*tax*) dazio, tassa; **on ~** di servizio; **off ~** libero(a), fuori servizio; **~ chemist's** *n* farmacia di turno; **~-free** *adj* esente da dazio

duvet ['du:veɪ] (*BRIT*) *n* piumino, piumone *m*

DVD *n abbr* (= *digital versatile* (*or*) *video*

disk) DVD *m inv*

dwarf [dwɔ:f] *n* nano/a ♦ *vt* far apparire piccolo

dwell [dwɛl] (*pt, pp* **dwelt**) *vi* dimorare; **~ on** *vt fus* indugiare su

dwindle ['dwɪndl] *vi* diminuire, decrescere

dye [daɪ] *n* tinta ♦ *vt* tingere

dying ['daɪɪŋ] *adj* morente, moribondo(a)

dyke [daɪk] (*BRIT*) *n* diga

dynamic [daɪ'næmɪk] *adj* dinamico(a)

dynamite ['daɪnəmaɪt] *n* dinamite *f*

dynamo ['daɪnəməu] *n* dinamo *f inv*

dyslexia [dɪs'lɛksɪə] *n* dislessia

E, e

E [i:] *n* (*MUS*) mi *m*

each [i:tʃ] *adj* ogni, ciascuno(a) ♦ *pron* ciascuno(a), ognuno(a); **~ one** ognuno(a); **~ other** si (*or ci etc*); **they hate ~ other** si odiano (l'un l'altro); **you are jealous of ~ other** siete gelosi l'uno dell'altro; **they have 2 books ~** hanno 2 libri ciascuno

eager ['i:gə*] *adj* impaziente; desideroso(a); ardente; **to be ~ for** essere desideroso di, aver gran voglia di

eagle ['i:gl] *n* aquila

ear [ɪə*] *n* orecchio; (*of corn*) pannocchia; **~ache** *n* mal *m* d'orecchi; **~drum** *n* timpano

earl [ə:l] (*BRIT*) *n* conte *m*

earlier ['ə:lɪə*] *adj* precedente ♦ *adv* prima

early ['ə:lɪ] *adv* presto, di buon'ora; (*ahead of time*) in anticipo ♦ *adj* (*near the start*) primo(a); (*sooner than expected*) prematuro(a); (*quick: reply*) veloce; **at an ~ hour** di buon'ora; **to have an ~ night** andare a letto presto; **in the ~ or ~ in the spring** all'inizio della primavera; **~ retirement** *n* ritiro anticipato

earmark ['ɪəmɑ:k] *vt*: **to ~ sth for** destinare qc a

earn [ə:n] *vt* guadagnare; (*rest, reward*) meritare

earnest ['ə:nɪst] *adj* serio(a); **in ~** sul serio

earnings ['ə:nɪŋz] *npl* guadagni *mpl*;

(*salary*) stipendio

earphones ['ɪəfəʊnz] *npl* cuffia

earring ['ɪərɪŋ] *n* orecchino

earshot ['ɪəʃɒt] *n*: **within ~** a portata d'orecchio

earth [ə:θ] *n* terra ♦ *vt* (*BRIT: ELEC*) mettere a terra; **~enware** *n* terracotta; stoviglie *fpl* di terracotta; **~quake** *n* terremoto; **~y** *adj* (*fig*) grossolano(a)

ease [i:z] *n* agio, comodo ♦ *vt* (*soothe*) calmare; (*loosen*) allentare; **to ~ sth out/in** tirare fuori/infilare qc con delicatezza; facilitare l'uscita/l'entrata di qc; **at ~** a proprio agio; (*MIL*) a riposo; **~ off** *or* **up** *vi* diminuire; (*slow down*) rallentare

easel ['i:zl] *n* cavalletto

easily ['i:zɪlɪ] *adv* facilmente

east [i:st] *n* est *m* ♦ *adj* dell'est ♦ *adv* a oriente; **the E~** l'Oriente *m*; (*POL*) l'Est

Easter ['i:stə*] *n* Pasqua; **~ egg** *n* uovo di Pasqua

easterly ['i:stəlɪ] *adj* dall'est, d'oriente

eastern ['i:stən] *adj* orientale, d'oriente; dell'est

East Germany *n* Germania dell'Est

eastward(s) ['i:stwəd(z)] *adv* verso est, verso levante

easy ['i:zɪ] *adj* facile; (*manner*) disinvolto(a) ♦ *adv*: **to take it** *or* **things ~** prendersela con calma; **~ chair** *n* poltrona; **~-going** *adj* accomodante

eat [i:t] (*pt* **ate**, *pp* **eaten**) *vt*, *vi* mangiare; **~ away at** *vt fus* rodere; **~ into** *vt fus* rodere

eaves [i:vz] *npl* gronda

eavesdrop ['i:vzdrɒp] *vi*: **to ~ (on a conversation)** origliare (una conversazione)

ebb [ɛb] *n* riflusso ♦ *vi* rifluire; (*fig: also*: **~ away**) declinare

ebony ['ɛbənɪ] *n* ebano

EC *n abbr* (= *European Community*) CEE *f*

ECB *n abbr* (= *European Central Bank*) BCE *f*

eccentric [ɪk'sɛntrɪk] *adj*, *n* eccentrico(a)

echo ['ɛkəʊ] (*pl* **~es**) *n* eco *m or f* ♦ *vt* ripetere; fare eco a ♦ *vi* echeggiare; dare un eco

éclair [eɪ'klɛə*] *n* ≈ bignè *m inv*

eclipse [ɪ'klɪps] *n* eclissi *f inv*

ecology [ɪ'kɒlədʒɪ] *n* ecologia

e-commerce *n* commercio elettronico

economic [i:kə'nɒmɪk] *adj* economico(a); **~al** *adj* economico(a); (*person*) economo(a); **~s** *n* economia ♦ *npl* lato finanziario

economize [ɪ'kɒnəmaɪz] *vi* risparmiare, fare economia

economy [ɪ'kɒnəmɪ] *n* economia; **~ class** *n* (*AVIAT*) classe *f* turistica; **~ size** *n* (*COMM*) confezione *f* economica

ecstasy ['ɛkstəsɪ] *n* estasi *f inv*

ECU ['eɪkju:] *n abbr* (= *European Currency Unit*) ECU *m inv*

edge [ɛdʒ] *n* margine *m*; (*of table, plate, cup*) orlo; (*of knife etc*) taglio ♦ *vt* bordare; **on ~** (*fig*) = **edgy**; **to ~ away from** sgattaiolare da; **~ways** *adv*: **he couldn't get a word in ~ways** non riuscì a dire una parola; **edgy** *adj* nervoso(a)

edible ['ɛdɪbl] *adj* commestibile; (*meal*) mangiabile

edict ['i:dɪkt] *n* editto

Edinburgh ['ɛdɪnbərə] *n* Edimburgo *f*

edit ['ɛdɪt] *vt* curare; **~ion** [ɪ'dɪʃən] *n* edizione *f*; **~or** *n* (*in newspaper*) redattore/trice; redattore/trice capo; (*of sb's work*) curatore/trice; **~orial** [-'tɔ:rɪəl] *adj* redazionale, editoriale ♦ *n* editoriale *m*

educate ['ɛdjukeɪt] *vt* istruire; educare

education [ɛdju'keɪʃən] *n* educazione *f*; (*schooling*) istruzione *f*; **~al** *adj* pedagogico(a); scolastico(a); istruttivo(a)

EEC *n abbr* = **EC**

eel [i:l] *n* anguilla

eerie ['ɪərɪ] *adj* che fa accapponare la pelle

effect [ɪ'fɛkt] *n* effetto ♦ *vt* effettuare; **to take ~** (*law*) entrare in vigore; (*drug*) fare effetto; **in ~** effettivamente; **~ive** *adj* efficace; (*actual*) effettivo(a); **~ively** *adv* efficacemente; effettivamente; **~iveness** *n* efficacia

effeminate [ɪ'fɛmɪnɪt] *adj* effeminato(a)

efficiency [ɪ'fɪʃənsɪ] *n* efficienza

efficient [ɪ'fɪʃənt] *adj* efficiente

effort [ˈɛfət] *n* sforzo

effusive [ɪˈfjuːsɪv] *adj (handshake, welcome)* caloroso(a)

e.g. *adv abbr* (= *exempli gratia*) per esempio, p.es.

egg [ɛg] *n* uovo; **hard-boiled/soft-boiled ~** uovo sodo/alla coque; **~ on** *vt* incitare; **~cup** *n* portauovo *m inv*; **~plant** *n (esp US)* melanzana; **~shell** *n* guscio d'uovo

ego [ˈiːgəu] *n* ego *m inv*

egotism [ˈɛgəutɪzəm] *n* egotismo

Egypt [ˈiːdʒɪpt] *n* Egitto; **~ian** [ɪˈdʒɪpʃən] *adj, n* egiziano(a)

eiderdown [ˈaɪdədaun] *n* piumino

eight [eɪt] *num* otto; **~een** *num* diciotto; **eighth** [eɪtθ] *num* ottavo(a); **~y** *num* ottanta

Eire [ˈɛərə] *n* Repubblica d'Irlanda

either [ˈaɪðə*] *adj* l'uno o l'altro(a); *(both, each)* ciascuno(a) ♦ *pron*: **~ (of them)** (o) l'uno(a) o l'altro(a) ♦ *adv* neanche ♦ *conj*: **~ good or bad** o buono o cattivo; **on ~ side** su ciascun lato; **I don't like ~** non mi piace né l'uno né l'altro; **no, I don't ~** no, neanch'io

eject [ɪˈdʒɛkt] *vt* espellere; lanciare

elaborate [*adj* ɪˈlæbərɪt, *vb* ɪˈlæbəreɪt] *adj* elaborato(a), minuzioso(a) ♦ *vt* elaborare ♦ *vi* fornire i particolari

elastic [ɪˈlæstɪk] *adj* elastico(a) ♦ *n* elastico; **~ band** *(BRIT)* *n* elastico

elated [ɪˈleɪtɪd] *adj* pieno(a) di gioia

elbow [ˈɛlbəu] *n* gomito

elder [ˈɛldə*] *adj* maggiore, più vecchio(a) ♦ *n (tree)* sambuco; **one's ~s** i più anziani; **~ly** *adj* anziano(a) ♦ *npl*: **the ~ly** gli anziani

eldest [ˈɛldɪst] *adj, n*: **the ~ (child)** il(la) maggiore (dei bambini)

elect [ɪˈlɛkt] *vt* eleggere ♦ *adj*: **the president ~** il presidente designato; **to ~ to do** decidere di fare; **~ion** [ɪˈlɛkʃən] *n* elezione *f*; **~ioneering** [ɪlɛkʃəˈnɪərɪŋ] *n* propaganda elettorale; **~or** *n* elettore/trice; **~orate** *n* elettorato

electric [ɪˈlɛktrɪk] *adj* elettrico(a); **~al** *adj* elettrico(a); **~ blanket** *n* coperta elettrica;

~ fire *n* stufa elettrica

electrician [ɪlɛkˈtrɪʃən] *n* elettricista *m*

electricity [ɪlɛkˈtrɪsɪtɪ] *n* elettricità

electrify [ɪˈlɛktrɪfaɪ] *vt (RAIL)* elettrificare; *(audience)* elettrizzare

electrocute [ɪˈlɛktrəukjuːt] *vt* fulminare

electronic [ɪlɛkˈtrɔnɪk] *adj* elettronico(a); **~ mail** *n* posta elettronica; **~s** *n* elettronica

elegant [ˈɛlɪgənt] *adj* elegante

element [ˈɛlɪmənt] *n* elemento; *(of heater, kettle etc)* resistenza; **~ary** [-ˈmɛntərɪ] *adj* elementare

elephant [ˈɛlɪfənt] *n* elefante/essa

elevation [ɛlɪˈveɪʃən] *n* elevazione *f*

elevator [ˈɛlɪveɪtə*] *n* elevatore *m*; *(US: lift)* ascensore *m*

eleven [ɪˈlɛvn] *num* undici; **~ses** *(BRIT)* *n* caffè *m* a metà mattina; **~th** *adj* undicesimo(a)

elicit [ɪˈlɪsɪt] *vt*: **to ~ (from)** trarre (da), cavare fuori (da)

eligible [ˈɛlɪdʒəbl] *adj* eleggibile; *(for membership)* che ha i requisiti

elm [ɛlm] *n* olmo

elocution [ɛləˈkjuːʃən] *n* dizione *f*

elongated [ˈiːlɔŋgeɪtɪd] *adj* allungato(a)

elope [ɪˈləup] *vi (lovers)* scappare; **~ment** *n* fuga

eloquent [ˈɛləkwənt] *adj* eloquente

else [ɛls] *adv* altro; **something ~** qualcos'altro; **somewhere ~** altrove; **everywhere ~** in qualsiasi altro luogo; **nobody ~** nessun altro; **where ~?** in quale altro luogo?; **little ~** poco altro; **~where** *adv* altrove

elude [ɪˈluːd] *vt* eludere

elusive [ɪˈluːsɪv] *adj* elusivo(a)

emaciated [ɪˈmeɪsɪeɪtɪd] *adj* emaciato(a)

E-mail, e-mail *n abbr* (= *electronic mail*) posta elettronica ♦ *vt*, *vi* mandare un messaggio di posta elettronica a

emanate [ˈɛməneɪt] *vi*: **to ~ from** provenire da

emancipate [ɪˈmænsɪpeɪt] *vt* emancipare

embankment [ɪmˈbæŋkmənt] *n (of road, railway)* terrapieno

embark [ɪmˈbɑːk] *vi*: **to ~ (on)** imbarcarsi

(su) ♦ *vt* imbarcare; **to ~ on** (*fig*) imbarcarsi in; **~ation** [embaːˈkeɪʃən] *n* imbarco

embarrass [ɪmˈbærəs] *vt* imbarazzare; **~ed** *adj* imbarazzato(a); **~ing** *adj* imbarazzante; **~ment** *n* imbarazzo

embassy [ˈembəsɪ] *n* ambasciata

embedded [ɪmˈbedɪd] *adj* incastrato(a)

embellish [ɪmˈbelɪʃ] *vt* abbellire

embers [ˈembəz] *npl* braci *fpl*

embezzle [ɪmˈbezl] *vt* appropriarsi indebitamente di

embitter [ɪmˈbɪtə*] *vt* amareggiare; inasprire

embody [ɪmˈbɔdɪ] *vt* (*features*) racchiudere, comprendere; (*ideas*) dar forma concreta a, esprimere

embossed [ɪmˈbɔst] *adj* in rilievo; goffrato(a)

embrace [ɪmˈbreɪs] *vt* abbracciare ♦ *vi* abbracciarsi ♦ *n* abbraccio

embroider [ɪmˈbrɔɪdə*] *vt* ricamare; **~y** *n* ricamo

embryo [ˈembrɪəu] *n* embrione *m*

emerald [ˈemərəld] *n* smeraldo

emerge [ɪˈməːdʒ] *vi* emergere

emergency [ɪˈməːdʒənsɪ] *n* emergenza; **in an ~** in caso di emergenza; **~ cord** (*US*) *n* segnale *m* d'allarme; **~ exit** *n* uscita di sicurezza; **~ landing** *n* atterraggio forzato; **~ services** *npl* (*fire, police, ambulance*) servizi *mpl* di pronto intervento

emery board [ˈemərɪ-] *n* limetta di carta smerigliata

emigrate [ˈemɪgreɪt] *vi* emigrare

eminent [ˈemɪnənt] *adj* eminente

emissions [ɪˈmɪʃənz] *npl* emissioni *fpl*

emit [ɪˈmɪt] *vt* emettere

emotion [ɪˈməuʃən] *n* emozione *f*; **~al** *adj* (*person*) emotivo(a); (*scene*) commovente; (*tone, speech*) carico(a) d'emozione

emperor [ˈempərə*] *n* imperatore *m*

emphasis [ˈemfəsɪs] (*pl* **-ases**) *n* enfasi *f inv*; importanza

emphasize [ˈemfəsaɪz] *vt* (*word, point*) sottolineare; (*feature*) mettere in evidenza

emphatic [emˈfætɪk] *adj* (*strong*) vigoroso(a); (*unambiguous, clear*) netto(a)

empire [ˈempaɪə*] *n* impero

employ [ɪmˈplɔɪ] *vt* impiegare; **~ee** [-ˈiː] *n* impiegato/a; **~er** *n* principale *m/f*, datore *m* di lavoro; **~ment** *n* impiego; **~ment agency** *n* agenzia di collocamento

empower [ɪmˈpauə*] *vt*: **to ~ sb to do** concedere autorità a qn di fare

empress [ˈemprɪs] *n* imperatrice *f*

emptiness [ˈemptɪnɪs] *n* vuoto

empty [ˈemptɪ] *adj* vuoto(a); (*threat, promise*) vano(a) ♦ *vt* vuotare ♦ *vi* vuotarsi; (*liquid*) scaricarsi; **~-handed** *adj* a mani vuote

EMU *n abbr* (= *economic and monetary union*) unione *f* economica e monetaria

emulate [ˈemjuleɪt] *vt* emulare

emulsion [ɪˈmʌlʃən] *n* emulsione *f*; **~ (paint)** *n* colore *m* a tempera

enable [ɪˈneɪbl] *vt*: **to ~ sb to do** permettere a qn di fare

enamel [ɪˈnæməl] *n* smalto; (*also*: **~ paint**) vernice *f* a smalto

enchant [ɪnˈtʃɑːnt] *vt* incantare; (*subj: magic spell*) catturare; **~ing** *adj* incantevole, affascinante

encircle [ɪnˈsəːkl] *vt* accerchiare

encl. *abbr* (= *enclosed*) all

enclave [ˈenkleɪv] *n* enclave *f*

enclose [ɪnˈkləuz] *vt* (*land*) circondare, recingere; (*letter etc*): **to ~ (with)** allegare (con); **please find ~d** trovi qui accluso

enclosure [ɪnˈkləuʒə*] *n* recinto

encompass [ɪnˈkʌmpəs] *vt* comprendere

encore [ɔŋˈkɔː*] *excl* bis ♦ *n* bis *m inv*

encounter [ɪnˈkauntə*] *n* incontro ♦ *vt* incontrare

encourage [ɪnˈkʌrɪdʒ] *vt* incoraggiare; **~ment** *n* incoraggiamento

encroach [ɪnˈkrəutʃ] *vi*: **to ~ (up)on** (*rights*) usurpare; (*time*) abusare di; (*land*) oltrepassare i limiti di

encyclop(a)edia [ensaɪkləuˈpiːdɪə] *n* enciclopedia

end [end] *n* fine *f*; (*aim*) fine *m*; (*of table*) bordo estremo; (*of pointed object*) punta ♦ *vt* finire; (*also*: **bring to an ~, put an ~ to**) mettere fine a ♦ *vi* finire; **in the ~** alla fine; **on ~** (*object*) ritto(a); **to stand on ~** (*hair*) rizzarsi; **for hours on ~** per ore ed ore; **~ up** *vi*: **to ~ up in** finire in

endanger [ɪnˈdeɪndʒə*] *vt* mettere in pericolo

endearing [ɪnˈdɪərɪŋ] *adj* accattivante

endeavour [ɪnˈdevə*] (*US* **endeavor**) *n* sforzo, tentativo ♦ *vi*: **to ~ to do** cercare *or* sforzarsi di fare

ending [ˈendɪŋ] *n* fine *f*, conclusione *f*; (*LING*) desinenza

endive [ˈendaɪv] *n* (*curly*) indivia (riccia); (*smooth, flat*) indivia belga

endless [ˈendlɪs] *adj* senza fine

endorse [ɪnˈdɔːs] *vt* (*cheque*) girare; (*approve*) approvare, appoggiare; **~ment** *n* approvazione *f*; (*on driving licence*) *contravvenzione registrata sulla patente*

endurance [ɪnˈdjuərəns] *n* resistenza; pazienza

endure [ɪnˈdjuə*] *vt* sopportare, resistere a ♦ *vi* durare

enemy [ˈenəmɪ] *adj, n* nemico(a)

energetic [ɛnəˈdʒetɪk] *adj* energico(a); attivo(a)

energy [ˈenədʒɪ] *n* energia

enforce [ɪnˈfɔːs] *vt* (*LAW*) applicare, far osservare

engage [ɪnˈgeɪdʒ] *vt* (*hire*) assumere; (*lawyer*) incaricare; (*attention, interest*) assorbire; (*TECH*): **to ~ the clutch** innestare la marcia/la frizione ♦ *vi* (*TECH*) ingranare; **to ~ in** impegnarsi in; **~d** *adj* (*BRIT: busy, in use*) occupato(a); (*betrothed*) fidanzato(a); **to get ~d** fidanzarsi; **~d tone** (*BRIT*) *n* (*TEL*) segnale *m* di occupato; **~ment** *n* impegno, obbligo; appuntamento; (*to marry*) fidanzamento; **~ment ring** *n* anello di fidanzamento

engaging [ɪnˈgeɪdʒɪŋ] *adj* attraente

engine [ˈendʒɪn] *n* (*AUT*) motore *m*; (*RAIL*) locomotiva; **~ driver** *n* (*of train*) macchinista *m*

engineer [endʒɪˈnɪə*] *n* ingegnere *m*; (*BRIT: for repairs*) tecnico; (*on ship, US: RAIL*) macchinista *m*; **~ing** *n* ingegneria

England [ˈɪŋglənd] *n* Inghilterra

English [ˈɪŋglɪʃ] *adj* inglese ♦ *n* (*LING*) inglese *m*; **the ~** *npl* gli Inglesi; **the ~ Channel** *n* la Manica; **~man/woman** (*irreg*) *n* inglese *m/f*

engraving [ɪnˈgreɪvɪŋ] *n* incisione *f*

engrossed [ɪnˈgrəust] *adj*: **~ in** assorbito(a) da, preso(a) da

engulf [ɪnˈgʌlf] *vt* inghiottire

enhance [ɪnˈhɑːns] *vt* accrescere

enjoy [ɪnˈdʒɔɪ] *vt* godere; (*have: success, fortune*) avere; **to ~ o.s.** godersela, divertirsi; **~able** *adj* piacevole; **~ment** *n* piacere *m*, godimento

enlarge [ɪnˈlɑːdʒ] *vt* ingrandire ♦ *vi*: **to ~ on** (*subject*) dilungarsi su

enlighten [ɪnˈlaɪtn] *vt* illuminare; dare schiarimenti a; **~ed** *adj* illuminato(a); **~ment** *n*: **the E~ment** (*HISTORY*) l'Illuminismo

enlist [ɪnˈlɪst] *vt* arruolare; (*support*) procurare ♦ *vi* arruolarsi

enmity [ˈenmɪtɪ] *n* inimicizia

enormous [ɪˈnɔːməs] *adj* enorme

enough [ɪˈnʌf] *adj, n*: **~ time/books** assai tempo/libri; **have you got ~?** ne ha abbastanza *or* a sufficienza? ♦ *adv*: **big ~** abbastanza grande; **he has not worked ~** non ha lavorato abbastanza; **~!** basta!; **that's ~, thanks** basta così, grazie; **I've had ~ of him** ne ho abbastanza di lui; **... which, funnily** *or* **oddly ~** ... che, strano a dirsi

enquire [ɪnˈkwaɪə*] *vt, vi* = **inquire**

enrage [ɪnˈreɪdʒ] *vt* fare arrabbiare

enrich [ɪnˈrɪtʃ] *vt* arricchire

enrol [ɪnˈrəul] (*US* **enroll**) *vt* iscrivere ♦ *vi* iscriversi; **~ment** (*US* **enrollment**) *n* iscrizione *f*

en suite [ɒnˈswiːt] *adj*: **room with ~ bathroom** camera con bagno

ensure [ɪnˈʃuə*] *vt* assicurare; garantire

entail [ɪnˈteɪl] *vt* comportare

entangled [ɪnˈtæŋgld] *adj*: **to become ~ (in)** impigliarsi in

enter [ˈentə*] *vt* entrare in; (*army*) arruolarsi in; (*competition*) partecipare a; (*sb for a competition*) iscrivere; (*write down*) registrare; (*COMPUT*) inserire ♦ *vi* entrare; ~ **for** *vt fus* iscriversi a; ~ **into** *vt fus* (*explanation*) cominciare a dare; (*debate*) partecipare a; (*agreement*) concludere

enterprise ['ɛntəpraɪz] *n* (*undertaking, company*) impresa; (*spirit*) iniziativa; **free ~** liberalismo economico; **private ~** iniziativa privata

enterprising ['ɛntəpraɪzɪŋ] *adj* intraprendente

entertain [ɛntə'teɪn] *vt* divertire; (*invite*) ricevere; (*idea, plan*) nutrire; **~er** *n* comico/a; **~ing** *adj* divertente; **~ment** *n* (*amusement*) divertimento; (*show*) spettacolo

enthralled [ɪn'θrɔːld] *adj* affascinato(a)

enthusiasm [ɪn'θuːzɪæzəm] *n* entusiasmo

enthusiast [ɪn'θuːzɪæst] *n* entusiasta *m/f*; **~ic** [-'æstɪk] *adj* entusiasta, entusiastico(a); **to be ~ic about sth/sb** essere appassionato(a) di qc/entusiasta di qn

entire [ɪn'taɪə*] *adj* intero(a); **~ly** *adv* completamente, interamente; **~ty** [ɪn'taɪərətɪ] *n*: **in its ~ty** nel suo complesso

entitle [ɪn'taɪtl] *vt* (*give right*): **to ~ sb to sth/to do** dare diritto a qn a qc/a fare; **~d** *adj* (*book*) che si intitola; **to be ~d to do** avere il diritto di fare

entrails ['ɛntreɪlz] *npl* interiora *fpl*

entrance [*n* 'ɛntrns, *vb* ɪn'trɑːns] *n* entrata, ingresso; (*of person*) entrata ♦ *vt* incantare, rapire; **to gain ~ to** (*university etc*) essere ammesso a; **~ examination** *n* esame *m* di ammissione; **~ fee** *n* tassa d'iscrizione; (*to museum etc*) prezzo d'ingresso; **~ ramp** (*US*) *n* (*AUT*) rampa di accesso

entrant ['ɛntrnt] *n* partecipante *m/f*; concorrente *m/f*

entreat [ɛn'triːt] *vt* supplicare

entrenched [ɛn'trɛntʃt] *adj* radicato(a)

entrepreneur [ɔntrəprə'nəː*] *n* imprenditore *m*

entrust [ɪn'trʌst] *vt*: **to ~ sth to** affidare qc a

entry ['ɛntrɪ] *n* entrata; (*way in*) entrata, ingresso; (*item: on list*) iscrizione *f*; (*in dictionary*) voce *f*; **no ~** vietato l'ingresso; (*AUT*) divieto di accesso; **~ form** *n* modulo

d'iscrizione; **~ phone** *n* citofono

envelop [ɪn'vɛləp] *vt* avvolgere, avviluppare

envelope ['ɛnvələup] *n* busta

envious ['ɛnvɪəs] *adj* invidioso(a)

environment [ɪn'vaɪərnmənt] *n* ambiente *m*; **~al** [-'mɛntl] *adj* ecologico(a); ambientale; **~-friendly** *adj* che rispetta l'ambiente

envisage [ɪn'vɪzɪdʒ] *vt* immaginare; prevedere

envoy ['ɛnvɔɪ] *n* inviato/a

envy ['ɛnvɪ] *n* invidia ♦ *vt* invidiare; **to ~ sb sth** invidiare qn per qc

epic ['ɛpɪk] *n* poema *m* epico ♦ *adj* epico(a)

epidemic [ɛpɪ'dɛmɪk] *n* epidemia

epilepsy ['ɛpɪlɛpsɪ] *n* epilessia

episode ['ɛpɪsəud] *n* episodio

epistle [ɪ'pɪsl] *n* epistola

epitome [ɪ'pɪtəmɪ] *n* epitome *f*; quintessenza; **epitomize** *vt* (*fig*) incarnare

equal ['iːkwl] *adj* uguale ♦ *n* pari *m/f inv* ♦ *vt* uguagliare; ~ **to** (*task*) all'altezza di; **~ity** [iː'kwɔlɪtɪ] *n* uguaglianza; **~ize** *vi* pareggiare; **~ly** *adv* ugualmente

equanimity [ɛkwə'nɪmɪtɪ] *n* serenità

equate [ɪ'kweɪt] *vt*: **to ~ sth with** considerare qc uguale a; (*compare*) paragonare qc con; **equation** [ɪ'kweɪʃən] *n* (*MATH*) equazione *f*

equator [ɪ'kweɪtə*] *n* equatore *m*

equilibrium [iːkwɪ'lɪbrɪəm] *n* equilibrio

equip [ɪ'kwɪp] *vt* equipaggiare, attrezzare; **to ~ sb/sth with** fornire qn/qc di; **to be well ~ped** (*office etc*) essere ben attrezzato(a); **he is well ~ped for the job** ha i requisiti necessari per quel lavoro; **~ment** *n* attrezzatura; (*electrical etc*) apparecchiatura

equitable ['ɛkwɪtəbl] *adj* equo(a), giusto(a)

equities ['ɛkwɪtɪz] (*BRIT*) *npl* (*COMM*) azioni *fpl* ordinarie

equivalent [ɪ'kwɪvəlnt] *adj* equivalente ♦ *n* equivalente *m*; **to be ~ to** equivalere a

era ['ɪərə] *n* era, età *f inv*

eradicate [ɪ'rædɪkeɪt] *vt* sradicare

erase [ɪ'reɪz] *vt* cancellare; **~r** *n* gomma

erect [ɪ'rɛkt] *adj* eretto(a) ♦ *vt* costruire; (*assemble*) montare; **~ion** [ɪ'rɛkʃən] *n* costruzione f; montaggio; (PHYSIOL) erezione f

ERM n (= Exchange Rate Mechanism) ERM m

ermine ['əːmɪn] n ermellino

erode [ɪ'rəʊd] vt erodere; (metal) corrodere

erotic [ɪ'rɔtɪk] adj erotico(a)

errand ['ɛrənd] n commissione f

erratic [ɪ'rætɪk] adj imprevedibile; (person, mood) incostante

error ['ɛrə*] n errore m

erupt [ɪ'rʌpt] vi (volcano) mettersi (or essere) in eruzione; (war, crisis) scoppiare; ~ion [ɪ'rʌpʃən] n eruzione f; scoppio

escalate ['ɛskəleɪt] vi intensificarsi

escalator ['ɛskəleɪtə*] n scala mobile

escapade [ɛskə'peɪd] n scappatella; avventura

escape [ɪ'skeɪp] n evasione f; fuga; (of gas etc) fuga, fuoriuscita ♦ vi fuggire; (from jail) evadere, scappare; (leak) uscire ♦ vt sfuggire a; to ~ from (place) fuggire da; (person) sfuggire a; escapism n evasione f (dalla realtà)

escort [n 'ɛskɔːt, vb ɪ'skɔːt] n scorta; (male companion) cavaliere m ♦ vt scortare; accompagnare

Eskimo ['ɛskɪməʊ] n eschimese m/f

especially [ɪ'spɛʃlɪ] adv specialmente; soprattutto; espressamente

espionage ['ɛspɪɑːnɑːʒ] n spionaggio

esplanade [ɛsplə'neɪd] n lungomare m inv

Esq. abbr = Esquire

Esquire [ɪ'skwaɪə*] n: J. Brown, ~ Signor J. Brown

essay ['ɛseɪ] n (SCOL) composizione f; (LITERATURE) saggio

essence ['ɛsns] n essenza

essential [ɪ'sɛnʃl] adj essenziale ♦ n elemento essenziale; ~ly adv essenzialmente

establish [ɪ'stæblɪʃ] vt stabilire; (business) mettere su; (one's power etc) affermare; ~ed adj (business etc) affermato(a); ~ment n stabilimento; the E~ment la classe dirigente, l'establishment m

estate [ɪ'steɪt] n proprietà f inv; beni mpl, patrimonio; (BRIT: also: housing ~) complesso

edilizio; ~ agent (BRIT) n agente m immobiliare; ~ car (BRIT) n giardiniera

esteem [ɪ'stiːm] n stima ♦ vt (think highly of) stimare; (consider) considerare

esthetic [ɪs'θɛtɪk] (US) adj = aesthetic

estimate [n 'ɛstɪmət, vb 'ɛstɪmeɪt] n stima; (COMM) preventivo ♦ vt stimare, valutare; estimation [-'meɪʃən] n stima; opinione f

estranged [ɪ'streɪndʒd] adj separato(a)

etc abbr (= et cetera) etc, ecc

eternal [ɪ'təːnl] adj eterno(a)

eternity [ɪ'təːnɪtɪ] n eternità

ether ['iːθə*] n etere m

ethical ['ɛθɪkl] adj etico(a), morale

ethics ['ɛθɪks] n etica ♦ npl morale f

Ethiopia [iːθɪ'əʊpɪə] n Etiopia

ethnic ['ɛθnɪk] adj etnico(a); ~ minority n minoranza etnica

ethos ['iːθɔs] n norma di vita

etiquette ['ɛtɪkɛt] n etichetta

EU n abbr (= European Union) UE

euro ['jʊərəʊ] n (currency) euro m inv

Euroland ['jʊərəʊlænd] n Eurolandia

Eurocheque ['jʊərəʊtʃɛk] n eurochèque m inv

Europe ['jʊərəp] n Europa; European [-'piːən] adj, n europeo(a); European Community n Comunità Europea

evacuate [ɪ'vækjʊeɪt] vt evacuare

evade [ɪ'veɪd] vt (tax) evadere; (duties etc) sottrarsi a; (person) schivare

evaluate [ɪ'væljʊeɪt] vt valutare

evaporate [ɪ'væpəreɪt] vi evaporare; ~d milk n latte m concentrato

evasion [ɪ'veɪʒən] n evasione f

evasive [ɪ'veɪsɪv] adj evasivo(a)

eve [iːv] n: on the ~ of alla vigilia di

even ['iːvn] adj regolare; (number) pari inv ♦ adv anche, perfino; ~ if, ~ though anche se; ~ more ancora di più; ~ so ciò nonostante; not ~ nemmeno; to get ~ with sb dare la pari a qn

evening ['iːvnɪŋ] n sera; (as duration, event) serata; in the ~ la sera; ~ class n corso serale; ~ dress n (woman's) abito da sera; in ~ dress (man) in abito scuro; (woman) in abito lungo

event [ɪ'vɛnt] *n* avvenimento; (*SPORT*) gara; **in the ~ of** in caso di; **~ful** *adj* denso(a) di eventi

eventual [ɪ'vɛntʃuəl] *adj* finale; **~ity** [-'ælɪtɪ] *n* possibilità *f inv*, eventualità *f inv*; **~ly** *adv* alla fine

ever ['ɛvə*] *adv* mai; (*at all times*) sempre; **the best ~** il migliore che ci sia mai stato; **have you ~ seen it?** l'ha mai visto?; **~ since** *adv* da allora ♦ *conj* sin da quando; **~ so pretty** così bello(a); **~green** *n* sempreverde *m*; **~lasting** *adj* eterno(a)

every ['ɛvrɪ] *adj* ogni; **~ day** tutti i giorni, ogni giorno; **~ other/third day** ogni due/ tre giorni; **~ other car** una macchina su due; **~ now and then** ogni tanto, di quando in quando; **~body** *pron* = **~one**; **~day** *adj* quotidiano(a); di ogni giorno; **~one** *pron* ognuno, tutti *pl*; **~thing** *pron* tutto, ogni cosa; **~where** *adv* (*gen*) dappertutto; (*wherever*) ovunque

evict [ɪ'vɪkt] *vt* sfrattare

evidence ['ɛvɪdns] *n* (*proof*) prova; (*of witness*) testimonianza; (*sign*): **to show ~ of** dare segni di; **to give ~** deporre

evident ['ɛvɪdnt] *adj* evidente; **~ly** *adv* evidentemente

evil ['iːvl] *adj* cattivo(a), maligno(a) ♦ *n* male *m*

evoke [ɪ'vəuk] *vt* evocare

evolution [iːvə'luːʃən] *n* evoluzione *f*

evolve [ɪ'vɔlv] *vt* elaborare ♦ *vi* sviluparsi, evolversi

ewe [juː] *n* pecora

ex- [ɛks] *prefix* ex

exacerbate [ɛks'æsəbeɪt] *vt* aggravare

exact [ɪg'zækt] *adj* esatto(a) ♦ *vt*: **to ~ sth (from)** estorcere qc (da); esigere qc (da); **~ing** *adj* esigente; (*work*) faticoso(a); **~ly** *adv* esattamente

exaggerate [ɪg'zædʒəreɪt] *vt, vi* esagerare; **exaggeration** [-'reɪʃən] *n* esagerazione *f*

exalted [ɪg'zɔːltɪd] *adj* esaltato(a); elevato(a)

exam [ɪg'zæm] *n abbr* (*SCOL*) = **examination**

examination [ɪgzæmɪ'neɪʃən] *n* (*SCOL*) esame *m*; (*MED*) controllo

examine [ɪg'zæmɪn] *vt* esaminare; **~r** *n* esaminatore/trice

example [ɪg'zɑːmpl] *n* esempio; **for ~** ad *or* per esempio

exasperate [ɪg'zɑːspəreɪt] *vt* esasperare; **exasperating** *adj* esasperante; **exasperation** [-'reɪʃən] *n* esasperazione *f*

excavate ['ɛkskəveɪt] *vt* scavare

exceed [ɪk'siːd] *vt* superare; (*one's powers, time limit*) oltrepassare; **~ingly** *adv* eccessivamente

excellent ['ɛksələnt] *adj* eccellente

except [ɪk'sɛpt] *prep* (*also*: **~ for, ~ing**) salvo, all'infuori di, eccetto ♦ *vt* escludere; **~ if/when** salvo se/quando; **~ that** salvo che; **~ion** [ɪk'sɛpʃən] *n* eccezione *f*; **to take ~ion to** trovare a ridire su; **~ional** [ɪk'sɛpʃənl] *adj* eccezionale

excerpt ['ɛksəːpt] *n* estratto

excess [ɪk'sɛs] *n* eccesso; **~ baggage** *n* bagaglio in eccedenza; **~ fare** *n* supplemento; **~ive** *adj* eccessivo(a)

exchange [ɪks'tʃeɪndʒ] *n* scambio; (*also*: **telephone ~**) centralino ♦ *vt*: **to ~ (for)** scambiare (con); **~ rate** *n* tasso di cambio

Exchequer [ɪks'tʃɛkə*] *n*: **the ~** (*BRIT*) lo Scacchiere, ≈ il ministero delle Finanze

excise ['ɛksaɪz] *n* imposta, dazio

excite [ɪk'saɪt] *vt* eccitare; **to get ~d** eccitarsi; **~ment** *n* eccitazione *f*; agitazione *f*; **exciting** *adj* avventuroso(a); (*film, book*) appassionante

exclaim [ɪk'skleɪm] *vi* esclamare; **exclamation** [ɛksklə'meɪʃən] *n* esclamazione *f*; **exclamation mark** *n* punto esclamativo

exclude [ɪk'skluːd] *vt* escludere

exclusive [ɪk'skluːsɪv] *adj* esclusivo(a); **~ of VAT** I.V.A. esclusa

excommunicate [ɛkskə'mjuːnɪkeɪt] *vt* scomunicare

excruciating [ɪk'skruːʃɪeɪtɪŋ] *adj* straziante, atroce

excursion [ɪk'skəːʃən] *n* escursione *f*, gita

excuse [*n* ɪk'skjuːs, *vb* ɪk'skjuːz] *n* scusa ♦ *vt* scusare; **to ~ sb from** (*activity*) dispensare qn da; **~ me!** mi scusi!; **now, if you will ~**

me ... ora, mi scusi ma ....

ex-directory (BRIT) adj (TEL): **to be ~** non essere sull'elenco

execute ['ɛksɪkjuːt] vt (prisoner) giustiziare; (plan etc) eseguire

execution [ɛksɪ'kjuːʃən] n esecuzione f; **~er** n boia m inv

executive [ɪɡ'zɛkjʊtɪv] n (COMM) dirigente m; (POL) esecutivo ♦ adj esecutivo(a)

exemplify [ɪɡ'zɛmplɪfaɪ] vt esemplificare

exempt [ɪɡ'zɛmpt] adj esentato(a) ♦ vt: **to ~ sb from** esentare qn da; **~ion** [ɪɡ'zɛmpʃən] n esenzione f

exercise ['ɛksəsaɪz] n (keep fit) moto; (SCOL, MIL etc) esercizio ♦ vt esercitare; (patience) usare; (dog) portar fuori ♦ vi (also: **take ~**) fare del moto; **~bike** n cyclette f inv; **~ book** n quaderno

exert [ɪɡ'zəːt] vt esercitare; **to ~ o.s.** sforzarsi; **~ion** [-ʃən] n sforzo

exhale [ɛks'heɪl] vt, vi espirare

exhaust [ɪɡ'zɔːst] n (also: **~ fumes**) scappamento; (also: **~ pipe**) tubo di scappamento ♦ vt esaurire; **~ed** adj esaurito(a); **~ion** [ɪɡ'zɔːstʃən] n esaurimento; **nervous ~ion** sovraffaticamento mentale; **~ive** adj esauriente

exhibit [ɪɡ'zɪbɪt] n (ART) oggetto esposto; (LAW) documento or oggetto esibito ♦ vt esporre; (courage, skill) dimostrare; **~ion** [ɛksɪ'bɪʃən] n mostra, esposizione f

exhilarating [ɪɡ'zɪləreɪtɪŋ] adj esilarante; stimolante

exhort [ɪɡ'zɔːt] vt esortare

exile ['ɛksaɪl] n esilio; (person) esiliato/a ♦ vt esiliare

exist [ɪɡ'zɪst] vi esistere; **~ence** n esistenza; **~ing** adj esistente

exit ['ɛksɪt] n uscita ♦ vi (THEATRE, COMPUT) uscire; **~ poll** n exit poll m inv; **~ ramp** (US) n (AUT) rampa di uscita

exodus ['ɛksədəs] n esodo

exonerate [ɪɡ'zɔnəreɪt] vt: **to ~ from** discolpare da

exotic [ɪɡ'zɔtɪk] adj esotico(a)

expand [ɪk'spænd] vt espandere; estendere; allargare ♦ vi (business, gas) espandersi; (metal) dilatarsi

expanse [ɪk'spæns] n distesa, estensione f

expansion [ɪk'spænʃən] n (gen) espansione f; (of town, economy) sviluppo; (of metal) dilatazione f

expect [ɪk'spɛkt] vt (anticipate) prevedere, aspettarsi, prevedere or aspettarsi che +sub; (require) richiedere, esigere; (suppose) supporre; (await, also baby) aspettare ♦ vi: **to be ~ing** essere in stato interessante; **to ~ sb to do** aspettarsi che qn faccia; **~ancy** n (anticipation) attesa; **life ~ancy** probabilità fpl di vita; **~ant mother** n gestante f; **~ation** [ɛkspɛk'teɪʃən] n aspettativa; speranza

expediency [ɪk'spiːdɪənsɪ] n convenienza

expedient [ɪk'spiːdɪənt] adj conveniente; vantaggioso(a) ♦ n espediente m

expedition [ɛkspə'dɪʃən] n spedizione f

expel [ɪk'spɛl] vt espellere

expend [ɪk'spɛnd] vt spendere; (use up) consumare; **~iture** [ɪk'spɛndɪtʃə*] n spesa

expense [ɪk'spɛns] n spesa; (high cost) costo; **~s** npl (COMM) spese fpl, indennità fpl; **at the ~ of** a spese di; **~ account** n conto m spese inv

expensive [ɪk'spɛnsɪv] adj caro(a), costoso(a)

experience [ɪk'spɪərɪəns] n esperienza ♦ vt (pleasure) provare; (hardship) soffrire; **~d** adj esperto(a)

experiment [n ɪk'spɛrɪmənt, vb ɪk'spɛrɪmɛnt] n esperimento, esperienza ♦ vi: **to ~ (with/on)** fare esperimenti (con/su)

expert ['ɛkspəːt] adj, n esperto(a); **~ise** [-'tiːz] n competenza

expire [ɪk'spaɪə*] vi (period of time, licence) scadere; **expiry** n scadenza

explain [ɪk'spleɪn] vt spiegare; **explanation** [ɛksplə'neɪʃən] n spiegazione f; **explanatory** [ɪk'splænətrɪ] adj esplicativo(a)

explicit [ɪk'splɪsɪt] adj esplicito(a)

explode [ɪk'spləʊd] vi esplodere

exploit [n 'ɛksplɔɪt, vb ɪk'splɔɪt] n impresa ♦ vt sfruttare; **~ation** [-'teɪʃən] n sfruttamento

exploratory [ɪkˈsplɔrətrɪ] *adj* esplorativo(a)

explore [ɪkˈsplɔ:*] *vt* esplorare; (*possibilities*) esaminare; **~r** *n* esploratore/trice

explosion [ɪkˈspləuʒən] *n* esplosione *f*

explosive [ɪkˈspləusɪv] *adj* esplosivo(a) ♦ *n* esplosivo

exponent [ɪkˈspəunənt] *n* esponente *m/f*

export [*vb* εkˈspɔːt, *n* ˈεkspɔːt] *vt* esportare ♦ *n* esportazione *f*; articolo di esportazione ♦ *cpd* d'esportazione; **~er** *n* esportatore *m*

expose [ɪkˈspəuz] *vt* esporre; (*unmask*) smascherare; **~d** *adj* (*position*) esposto(a)

exposure [ɪkˈspəuʒə*] *n* esposizione *f*; (*PHOT*) posa; (*MED*) assideramento; **~ meter** *n* esposimetro

express [ɪkˈsprɛs] *adj* (*definite*) chiaro(a), espresso(a); (*BRIT: letter etc*) espresso *inv* ♦ *n* (*train*) espresso ♦ *vt* esprimere; **~ion** [ɪkˈsprɛʃən] *n* espressione *f*; **~ive** *adj* espressivo(a); **~ly** *adv* espressamente; **~way** (*US*) *n* (*urban motorway*) autostrada che attraversa la città

exquisite [εkˈskwɪzɪt] *adj* squisito(a)

extend [ɪkˈstɛnd] *vt* (*visit*) protrarre; (*road, deadline*) prolungare; (*building*) ampliare; (*offer*) offrire, porgere ♦ *vi* (*land, period*) estendersi

extension [ɪkˈstɛnʃən] *n* (*of road, term*) prolungamento; (*of contract, deadline*) proroga; (*building*) annesso; (*to wire, table*) prolunga; (*telephone*) interno; (*: in private house*) apparecchio supplementare

extensive [ɪkˈstɛnsɪv] *adj* esteso(a), ampio(a); (*damage*) su larga scala; (*coverage, discussion*) esauriente; (*use*) grande; **~ly** *adv*: **he's travelled ~ly** ha viaggiato molto

extent [ɪkˈstɛnt] *n* estensione *f*; **to some ~** fino a un certo punto; **to such an ~ that ...** a un tal punto che ...; **to what ~?** fino a che punto?; **to the ~ of ...** fino al punto di ...

extenuating [ɪksˈtɛnjueɪtɪŋ] *adj*: **~ circumstances** attenuanti *fpl*

exterior [εkˈstɪərɪə*] *adj* esteriore, esterno(a) ♦ *n* esteriore *m*, esterno; aspetto (esteriore)

exterminate [ɪkˈstəːmɪneɪt] *vt* sterminare

external [εkˈstəːnl] *adj* esterno(a), esteriore

extinct [ɪkˈstɪŋkt] *adj* estinto(a)

extinguish [ɪkˈstɪŋgwɪʃ] *vt* estinguere; **~er** *n* estintore *m*

extort [ɪkˈstɔːt] *vt*: **to ~ sth (from)** estorcere qc (da); **~ionate** [ɪkˈstɔːʃənɪt] *adj* esorbitante

extra [ˈεkstrə] *adj* extra *inv*, supplementare ♦ *adv* (*in addition*) di più ♦ *n* extra *m inv*; (*surcharge*) supplemento; (*CINEMA, THEATRE*) comparsa

extra... [ˈεkstrə] *prefix* extra...

extract [*vb* ɪkˈstrækt, *n* ˈεkstrækt] *vt* estrarre; (*money, promise*) strappare ♦ *n* estratto; (*passage*) brano

extracurricular [ˈεkstrəkəˈrɪkjulə*] *adj* extrascolastico(a)

extradite [ˈεkstrədaɪt] *vt* estradare

extramarital [εkstrəˈmærɪtl] *adj* extraconiugale

extramural [εkstrəˈmjuərl] *adj* fuori dell'università

extraordinary [ɪkˈstrɔːdnrɪ] *adj* straordinario(a)

extravagance [ɪkˈstrævəgəns] *n* sperpero; stravaganza

extravagant [ɪkˈstrævəgənt] *adj* (*lavish*) prodigo(a); (*wasteful*) dispendioso(a)

extreme [ɪkˈstriːm] *adj* estremo(a) ♦ *n* estremo; **~ly** *adv* estremamente

extricate [ˈεkstrɪkeɪt] *vt*: **to ~ sth (from)** districare qc (da)

extrovert [ˈεkstrəvɜːt] *n* estroverso/a

exude [ɪgˈzjuːd] *vt* trasudare; (*fig*) emanare

eye [aɪ] *n* occhio; (*of needle*) cruna ♦ *vt* osservare; **to keep an ~ on** tenere d'occhio; **~brow** *n* sopracciglio; **~drops** *npl* gocce *fpl* oculari, collirio; **~lash** *n* ciglio; **~lid** *n* palpebra; **~liner** *n* eye-liner *m inv*; **~-opener** *n* rivelazione *f*; **~shadow** *n* ombretto; **~sight** *n* vista; **~sore** *n* pugno nell'occhio; **~ witness** *n* testimone *m/f* oculare

F, f

F [ɛf] n (MUS) fa m

fable ['feɪbl] n favola

fabric ['fæbrɪk] n stoffa, tessuto

fabulous ['fæbjuləs] adj favoloso(a); (super) favoloso(a), fantastico(a)

façade [fə'sɑːd] n (also fig) facciata

face [feɪs] n faccia, viso, volto; (expression) faccia; (of clock) quadrante m; (of building) facciata ♦ vt essere di fronte a; (facts, situation) affrontare; ~ **down** a faccia in giù; **to make** or **pull a** ~ fare una smorfia; **in the** ~ **of** (difficulties etc) di fronte a; **on the** ~ **of it** a prima vista; ~ **to** ~ faccia a faccia; ~ **up to** vt fus affrontare, far fronte a; ~ **cloth** (BRIT) n guanto di spugna; ~ **cream** n crema per il viso; ~ **lift** n lifting m inv; (of façade etc) ripulita; ~ **powder** n cipria; ~-**saving** adj per salvare la faccia

facet ['fæsɪt] n sfaccettatura

facetious [fə'siːʃəs] adj faceto(a)

face value n (of coin) valore m facciale or nominale; **to take sth at** ~ (fig) giudicare qc dalle apparenze

facial ['feɪʃəl] adj del viso

facile ['fæsaɪl] adj superficiale

facilities [fə'sɪlɪtɪz] npl attrezzature fpl; **credit** ~ facilitazioni fpl di credito

facing ['feɪsɪŋ] prep di fronte a

facsimile [fæk'sɪmɪlɪ] n facsimile m inv; ~ **machine** n telecopiatrice f

fact [fækt] n fatto; **in** ~ infatti

factor ['fæktə*] n fattore m

factory ['fæktərɪ] n fabbrica, stabilimento

factual ['fæktjuəl] adj che si attiene ai fatti

faculty ['fækəltɪ] n facoltà f inv; (US) corpo insegnante

fad [fæd] n mania; capriccio

fade [feɪd] vi sbiadire, sbiadirsi; (light, sound, hope) attenuarsi, affievolirsi; (flower) appassire

fag [fæg] (BRIT: inf) n (cigarette) cicca

fail [feɪl] vt (exam) non superare; (candidate) bocciare; (subj: courage, memory) mancare a ♦ vi fallire; (student) essere respinto(a); (eyesight, health, light) venire a mancare; **to** ~ **to do sth** (neglect) mancare di fare qc; (be unable) non riuscire a fare qc; **without** ~ senza fallo; certamente; ~**ing** n difetto ♦ prep in mancanza di; ~**ure** ['feɪljə*] n fallimento; (person) fallito/a; (mechanical etc) guasto

faint [feɪnt] adj debole; (recollection) vago(a); (mark) indistinto(a) ♦ n (MED) svenimento ♦ vi svenire; **to feel** ~ sentirsi svenire

fair [feə*] adj (person, decision) giusto(a), equo(a); (quite large, quite good) discreto(a); (hair etc) biondo(a); (skin, complexion) chiaro(a); (weather) bello(a), clemente ♦ adv (play) lealmente ♦ n fiera; (BRIT: funfair) luna park m inv; ~**ly** adv equamente; (quite) abbastanza; ~**ness** n equità, giustizia; ~ **play** n correttezza

fairy ['feərɪ] n fata; ~ **tale** n fiaba

faith [feɪθ] n fede f; (trust) fiducia; (sect) religione f, fede f; ~**ful** adj fedele; ~**fully** adv fedelmente; **yours** ~**fully** (BRIT: in letters) distinti saluti

fake [feɪk] n imitazione f; (picture) falso; (person) impostore/a ♦ adj falso(a) ♦ vt (accounts) falsificare; (illness) fingere; (painting) contraffare

fall [fɔːl] (pt fell, pp fallen) n caduta; (in temperature) abbassamento; (in price) ribasso; (US: autumn) autunno ♦ vi cadere; (temperature, price, night) scendere; ~**s** npl (waterfall) cascate fpl; **to** ~ **flat** (on one's face) cadere bocconi; (joke) fare cilecca; (plan) fallire; ~ **back** vi (retreat) indietreggiare; (MIL) ritirarsi; ~ **back on** vt fus (remedy etc) ripiegare su; ~ **behind** vi rimanere indietro; ~ **down** vi (person) cadere; (building) crollare; ~ **for** vt fus (person) prendere una cotta per; **to** ~ **for a trick** (or a story etc) cascarci; ~ **in** vi crollare; (MIL) mettersi in riga; ~ **off** vi cadere; (diminish) diminuire, abbassarsi; ~ **out** vi (hair, teeth) cadere; (friends etc) litigare; ~ **through** vi (plan, project) fallire

fallacy ['fæləsɪ] n errore m

fallen ['fɔːlən] *pp of* fall

fallout ['fɔːlaut] *n* fall-out *m*

fallow ['fæləu] *adj* incolto(a), a maggese

false [fɔːls] *adj* falso(a); **under ~ pretences** con l'inganno; **~ teeth** (*BRIT*) *npl* denti *mpl* finti

falter ['fɔːltə*] *vi* esitare, vacillare

fame [feɪm] *n* fama, celebrità

familiar [fə'mɪlɪə*] *adj* familiare; (*close*) intimo(a); **to be ~ with** (*subject*) conoscere; **~ize** [fə'mɪlɪəraɪz] *vt*: **to ~ize o.s. with** familiarizzare con

family ['fæmɪlɪ] *n* famiglia; **~ business** *n* ditta a conduzione familiare

famine ['fæmɪn] *n* carestia

famished ['fæmɪʃt] *adj* affamato(a)

famous ['feɪməs] *adj* famoso(a); **~ly** *adv* (*get on*) a meraviglia

fan [fæn] *n* (*folding*) ventaglio; (*ELEC*) ventilatore *m*; (*person*) ammiratore/trice; tifoso/a ♦ *vt* far vento a; (*fire, quarrel*) alimentare

fanatic [fə'nætɪk] *n* fanatico/a

fan belt *n* cinghia del ventilatore

fanciful ['fænsɪful] *adj* fantasioso(a)

fancy ['fænsɪ] *n* immaginazione *f*, fantasia; (*whim*) capriccio ♦ *adj* (*hat*) stravagante; (*hotel, food*) speciale ♦ *vt* (*feel like, want*) aver voglia di; (*imagine, think*) immaginare; **to take a ~ to** incapricciarsi di; **he fancies her** (*inf*) gli piace; **~ dress** *n* costume *m* (per maschera); **~-dress ball** *n* ballo in maschera

fang [fæŋ] *n* zanna; (*of snake*) dente *m*

fantastic [fæn'tæstɪk] *adj* fantastico(a)

fantasy ['fæntəsɪ] *n* fantasia, immaginazione *f*; fantasticheria; chimera

far [faː*] *adj* lontano(a) ♦ *adv* lontano; (*much, greatly*) molto; **~ away, ~ off** lontano, distante; **~ better** assai migliore; **~ from** lontano da; **by ~** di gran lunga; **go as ~ as the farm** vada fino alla fattoria; **as ~ as I know** per quel che so; **how ~?** quanto lontano?; (*referring to activity etc*) fino a dove?; **~away** *adj* lontano(a)

farce [faːs] *n* farsa

fare [feə*] *n* (*on trains, buses*) tariffa; (*in taxi*)

prezzo della corsa; (*food*) vitto, cibo; **half ~** metà tariffa; **full ~** tariffa intera

Far East *n*: **the ~** l'Estremo Oriente *m*

farewell [feə'wel] *excl, n* addio

farm [faːm] *n* fattoria, podere *m* ♦ *vt* coltivare; **~er** *n* coltivatore/trice; agricoltore/trice; **~hand** *n* bracciante *m* agricolo; **~house** *n* fattoria; **~ing** *n* (*gen*) agricoltura; (*of crops*) coltivazione *f*; (*of animals*) allevamento; **~land** *n* terreno coltivabile; **~ worker** *n* = **~hand**; **~yard** *n* aia

far-reaching [-'riːtʃɪŋ] *adj* di vasta portata

fart [faːt] (*inf!*) *vi* scoreggiare (!)

farther ['faːðə*] *adv* più lontano ♦ *adj* più lontano(a)

farthest ['faːðɪst] *superl of* far

fascinate ['fæsɪneɪt] *vt* affascinare; **fascinating** *adj* affascinante; **fascination** [-'neɪʃən] *n* fascino

fascism ['fæʃɪzəm] *n* fascismo

fashion ['fæʃən] *n* moda; (*manner*) maniera, modo ♦ *vt* foggiare, formare; **in ~** alla moda; **out of ~** passato(a) di moda; **~able** *adj* alla moda, di moda; **~ show** *n* sfilata di moda

fast [faːst] *adj* rapido(a), svelto(a), veloce; (*clock*): **to be ~** andare avanti; (*dye, colour*) solido(a) ♦ *adv* rapidamente; (*stuck, held*) saldamente ♦ *n* digiuno ♦ *vi* digiunare; **~ asleep** profondamente addormentato

fasten ['faːsn] *vt* chiudere, fissare; (*coat*) abbottonare, allacciare ♦ *vi* chiudersi, fissarsi; abbottonarsi, allacciarsi; **~er** *n* fermaglio, chiusura; **~ing** *n* = **~er**

fast food *n* fast food *m*

fastidious [fæs'tɪdɪəs] *adj* esigente, difficile

fat [fæt] *adj* grasso(a); (*book, profit etc*) grosso(a) ♦ *n* grasso

fatal ['feɪtl] *adj* fatale; mortale; disastroso(a); **~ity** [fə'tælɪtɪ] *n* (*road death etc*) morto/a, vittima; **~ly** *adv* a morte

fate [feɪt] *n* destino; (*of person*) sorte *f*; **~ful** *adj* fatidico(a)

father ['faːðə*] *n* padre *m*; **~-in-law** *n* suocero; **~ly** *adj* paterno(a)

fathom ['fæðəm] *n* braccio (= *1828 mm*)

♦ *vt* (*mystery*) penetrare, sondare

fatigue [fə'tiːg] *n* stanchezza

fatten ['fætn] *vt, vi* ingrassare

fatty ['fætɪ] *adj* (*food*) grasso(a) ♦ *n* (*inf*) ciccione/a

fatuous ['fætjuəs] *adj* fatuo(a)

faucet ['fɔːsɪt] (*US*) *n* rubinetto

fault [fɔːlt] *n* colpa; (*TENNIS*) fallo; (*defect*) difetto; (*GEO*) faglia ♦ *vt* criticare; **it's my ~** è colpa mia; **to find ~ with** trovare da ridire su; **at ~** in fallo; **~y** *adj* difettoso(a)

fauna ['fɔːnə] *n* fauna

favour ['feɪvə*] (*US* **favor**) *n* favore *m* ♦ *vt* (*proposition*) favorire, essere favorevole a; (*pupil etc*) favorire; (*team, horse*) dare per vincente; **to do sb a ~** fare un favore *or* una cortesia a qn; **to find ~ with** (*subj: person*) entrare nelle buone grazie di; (: *suggestion*) avere l'approvazione di; **in ~ of** in favore di; **~able** *adj* favorevole; **~ite** [-rɪt] *adj, n* favorito(a)

fawn [fɔːn] *n* daino ♦ *adj* (*also*: **~-coloured**) marrone chiaro *inv* ♦ *vi*: **to ~ (up)on** adulare servilmente

fax [fæks] *n* (*document*) facsimile *m inv*, telecopia; (*machine*) telecopiatrice *f* ♦ *vt* telecopiare, trasmettere in facsimile

FBI (*US*) *n abbr* (= *Federal Bureau of Investigation*) F.B.I. *f*

fear [fɪə*] *n* paura, timore *m* ♦ *vt* aver paura di, temere; **for ~ of** per paura di; **~ful** *adj* pauroso(a); (*sight, noise*) terribile, spaventoso(a)

feasible ['fiːzəbl] *adj* possibile, realizzabile

feast [fiːst] *n* festa, banchetto; (*REL: also*: **~ day**) festa ♦ *vi* banchettare

feat [fiːt] *n* impresa, fatto insigne

feather ['feðə*] *n* penna

feature ['fiːtʃə*] *n* caratteristica; (*PRESS, TV*) articolo ♦ *vt* (*subj: film*) avere come protagonista ♦ *vi* figurare; **~s** *npl* (*of face*) fisionomia; **~ film** *n* film *m inv* principale

February ['februərɪ] *n* febbraio

fed [fed] *pt, pp of* **feed**

federal ['fedərəl] *adj* federale

fed-up *adj*: **to be ~** essere stufo(a)

fee [fiː] *n* pagamento; (*of doctor, lawyer*) onorario; (*for examination*) tassa d'esame; **school ~s** tasse *fpl* scolastiche

feeble ['fiːbl] *adj* debole

feed [fiːd] (*pt, pp* **fed**) *n* (*of baby*) pappa; (*of animal*) mangime *m*; (*on printer*) meccanismo di alimentazione ♦ *vt* nutrire; (*baby*) allattare; (*horse etc*) dare da mangiare a; (*fire, machine*) alimentare; (*data, information*): **to ~ into** inserire in; **~ on** *vt fus* nutrirsi di; **~back** *n* feed-back *m*

feel [fiːl] (*pt, pp* **felt**) *n* consistenza; (*sense of touch*) tatto ♦ *vt* toccare; palpare; tastare; (*cold, pain, anger*) sentire; (*think, believe*): **to ~ (that)** pensare che; **to ~ hungry/cold** aver fame/freddo; **to ~ lonely/better** sentirsi solo/meglio; **I don't ~ well** non mi sento bene; **it ~s soft** è morbido al tatto; **to ~ like** (*want*) aver voglia di; **to ~ about** *or* **around for** cercare a tastoni; **~er** *n* (*of insect*) antenna; **~ing** *n* sensazione *f*; (*emotion*) sentimento

feet [fiːt] *npl of* **foot**

feign [feɪn] *vt* fingere, simulare

fell [fel] *pt of* **fall** ♦ *vt* (*tree*) abbattere

fellow ['feləu] *n* individuo, tipo; compagno; (*of learned society*) membro ♦ *cpd*: **~ citizen** *n* concittadino/a; **~ countryman** (*irreg*) *n* compatriota *m*; **~ men** *npl* simili *mpl*; **~ship** *n* associazione *f*; compagnia; specie di borsa di studio universitaria

felony ['felənɪ] *n* reato, crimine *m*

felt [felt] *pt, pp of* **feel** ♦ *n* feltro; **~-tip pen** *n* pennarello

female ['fiːmeɪl] *n* (*ZOOL*) femmina; (*pej: woman*) donna, femmina ♦ *adj* (*BIOL, ELEC*) femmina *inv*; (*sex, character*) femminile; (*vote etc*) di donne

feminine ['femɪnɪn] *adj* femminile

feminist ['femɪnɪst] *n* femminista *m/f*

fence [fens] *n* recinto ♦ *vt* (*also*: **~ in**) recingere ♦ *vi* (*SPORT*) tirare di scherma; **fencing** (*SPORT*) *n* scherma

fend [fend] *vi*: **to ~ for o.s.** arrangiarsi; **~ off** *vt* (*attack, questions*) respingere, difendersi da

fender ['fendə*] *n* parafuoco; (*on boat*) parabordo; (*US*) parafango; paraurti *m inv*

ferment [vb fəˈment, n ˈfɜːment] vi fermentare ♦ n (fig) agitazione f, eccitazione f

fern [fɜːn] n felce f

ferocious [fəˈrəʊʃəs] adj feroce

ferret [ˈferɪt] n furetto; ~ **out** vt (information) scovare

ferry [ˈferɪ] n (small) traghetto; (large: also: ~**boat**) nave f traghetto inv ♦ vt traghettare

fertile [ˈfɜːtaɪl] adj fertile; (BIOL) fecondo(a); **fertilizer** [ˈfɜːtɪlaɪzə*] n fertilizzante m

fester [ˈfestə*] vi suppurare

festival [ˈfestɪvəl] n (REL) festa; (ART, MUS) festival m inv

festive [ˈfestɪv] adj di festa; **the ~ season** (BRIT: Christmas) il periodo delle feste

festivities [fesˈtɪvɪtɪz] npl festeggiamenti mpl

festoon [fesˈtuːn] vt: **to ~ with** ornare di

fetch [fetʃ] vt andare a prendere; (sell for) essere venduto(a) per

fête [feɪt] n festa

fetus [ˈfiːtəs] (US) n = **foetus**

feud [fjuːd] n contesa, lotta

feudal [ˈfjuːdl] adj feudale

fever [ˈfiːvə*] n febbre f; ~**ish** adj febbrile

few [fjuː] adj pochi(e); **a ~** adj qualche inv ♦ pron alcuni(e); ~**er** adj meno inv; meno numerosi(e); ~**est** adj il minor numero di

fiancé [fɪˈɑːnseɪ] n fidanzato; ~**e** n fidanzata

fib [fɪb] n piccola bugia

fibre [ˈfaɪbə*] (US **fiber**) n fibra; **F~glass** ® n fibra di vetro

fickle [ˈfɪkl] adj incostante, capriccioso(a)

fiction [ˈfɪkʃən] n narrativa, romanzi mpl; (sth made up) finzione f; ~**al** adj immaginario(a)

fictitious [fɪkˈtɪʃəs] adj fittizio(a)

fiddle [ˈfɪdl] n (MUS) violino; (cheating) imbroglio, truffa ♦ vt (BRIT: accounts) falsificare, falsare; ~ **with** vt fus gingillarsi con

fidelity [fɪˈdelɪtɪ] n fedeltà; (accuracy) esattezza

fidget [ˈfɪdʒɪt] vi agitarsi

field [fiːld] n campo; ~ **marshal** n feldmaresciallo; ~**work** n ricerche fpl esterne

fiend [fiːnd] n demonio

fierce [fɪəs] adj (animal, person, fighting) feroce; (loyalty) assoluto(a); (wind) furioso(a); (heat) intenso(a)

fiery [ˈfaɪərɪ] adj ardente; infocato(a)

fifteen [fɪfˈtiːn] num quindici

fifth [fɪfθ] num quinto(a)

fifty [ˈfɪftɪ] num cinquanta; ~**-**~ adj: **a ~-~ chance** una possibilità su due ♦ adv fifty-fifty, metà per ciascuno

fig [fɪg] n fico

fight [faɪt] (pt, pp **fought**) n zuffa, rissa; (MIL) battaglia, combattimento; (against cancer etc) lotta ♦ vt (person) azzuffarsi con; (enemy: also: MIL) combattere; (cancer, alcoholism, emotion) lottare contro, combattere; (election) partecipare a ♦ vi combattere; ~**er** n combattente m; (plane) aeroplano da caccia; ~**ing** n combattimento

figment [ˈfɪgmənt] n: **a ~ of the imagination** un parto della fantasia

figurative [ˈfɪgjʊrətɪv] adj figurato(a)

figure [ˈfɪgə*] n figura; (number, cipher) cifra ♦ vt (think: esp US) pensare ♦ vi (appear) figurare; ~ **out** vt riuscire a capire; calcolare; ~**head** n (NAUT) polena; (pej) prestanome m/f inv; ~ **of speech** n figura retorica

file [faɪl] n (tool) lima; (dossier) incartamento; (folder) cartellina; (COMPUT) archivio; (row) fila ♦ vt (nails, wood) limare; (papers) archiviare; (LAW: claim) presentare; passare agli atti; ~ **in/out** vi entrare/uscire in fila

filing cabinet [ˈfaɪlɪŋ-] n casellario

fill [fɪl] vt riempire; (job) coprire ♦ n: **to eat one's** ~ mangiare a sazietà; ~ **in** vt (hole) riempire; (form) compilare; ~ **up** vt riempire ♦ vi (AUT) fare il pieno

fillet [ˈfɪlɪt] n filetto; ~ **steak** n bistecca di filetto

filling [ˈfɪlɪŋ] n (CULIN) impasto, ripieno; (for tooth) otturazione f; ~ **station** n stazione f di rifornimento

film [fɪlm] n (CINEMA) film m inv; (PHOT) pellicola; (of powder, liquid) sottile strato ♦ vt, vi girare; ~ **star** n divo/a dello schermo

filter ['fɪltə*] n filtro ♦ vt filtrare; ~ **lane** (BRIT) n (AUT) corsia di svincolo; ~**tipped** adj con filtro

filth [fɪlθ] n sporcizia; ~**y** adj lordo(a), sozzo(a); (language) osceno(a)

fin [fɪn] n (of fish) pinna

final ['faɪnl] adj finale, ultimo(a); definitivo(a) ♦ n (SPORT) finale f; ~**s** npl (SCOL) esami mpl finali

finale [fɪ'nɑːlɪ] n finale m

finalize ['faɪnəlaɪz] vt mettere a punto

finally ['faɪnəlɪ] adv (lastly) alla fine; (eventually) finalmente

finance [faɪ'næns] n finanza; (capital) capitale m ♦ vt finanziare; ~**s** npl (funds) finanze fpl

financial [faɪ'nænʃəl] adj finanziario(a)

financier [faɪ'nænsɪə*] n finanziatore m

find [faɪnd] (pt, pp found) vt trovare; (lost object) ritrovare ♦ n trovata, scoperta; to ~ sb guilty (LAW) giudicare qn colpevole; ~ out vt (truth, secret) scoprire; (person) cogliere in fallo; to ~ out about informarsi su; (by chance) scoprire; ~**ings** npl (LAW) sentenza, conclusioni fpl; (of report) conclusioni

fine [faɪn] adj bello(a); ottimo(a); (thin, subtle) fine ♦ adv (well) molto bene ♦ n (LAW) multa ♦ vt (LAW) multare; to be ~ (person) stare bene; (weather) far bello; ~ **arts** npl belle arti fpl

finery ['faɪnərɪ] n abiti mpl eleganti

finger ['fɪŋgə*] n dito ♦ vt toccare, tastare; **little/index** ~ mignolo/(dito) indice m; ~**nail** n unghia; ~**print** n impronta digitale; ~**tip** n punta del dito

finish ['fɪnɪʃ] n fine f; (polish etc) finitura ♦ vt, vi finire; to ~ **doing sth** finire di fare qc; to ~ **third** arrivare terzo(a); ~ **off** vt compiere; (kill) uccidere; ~ **up** vi, vt finire; ~**ing line** n linea d'arrivo

finite ['faɪnaɪt] adj limitato(a); (verb) finito(a)

Finland ['fɪnlənd] n Finlandia

Finn [fɪn] n finlandese m/f; ~**ish** adj finlandese ♦ n (LING) finlandese m

fir [fə:*] n abete m

fire [faɪə*] n fuoco; (destructive) incendio; (gas ~, electric ~) stufa ♦ vt (gun) far fuoco con; (arrow) sparare; (fig) infiammare; (inf: dismiss) licenziare ♦ vi sparare, far fuoco; **on** ~ in fiamme; ~ **alarm** n allarme m d'incendio; ~**arm** n arma da fuoco; ~ **brigade** (US ~ **department**) n (corpo dei) pompieri mpl; ~ **engine** n autopompa; ~ **escape** n scala di sicurezza; ~ **extinguisher** n estintore m; ~**guard** n parafuoco; ~**man** (irreg) n pompiere m; ~**place** n focolare m; ~**side** n angolo del focolare; ~ **station** n caserma dei pompieri; ~**wood** n legna; ~**works** npl fuochi mpl d'artificio

firing squad ['faɪərɪŋ-] n plotone m d'esecuzione

firm [fə:m] adj fermo(a) ♦ n ditta, azienda; ~**ly** adv fermamente

first [fə:st] adj primo(a) ♦ adv (before others) il primo, la prima; (before other things) per primo; (when listing reasons etc) per prima cosa ♦ n (person: in race) primo/a; (BRIT: SCOL) laurea con lode; (AUT) prima; **at** ~ dapprima, all'inizio; ~ **of all** prima di tutto; ~ **aid** n pronto soccorso; ~**aid kit** n cassetta pronto soccorso; ~**class** adj di prima classe; ~ **floor** n il primo piano (BRIT); il pianterreno (US); ~**hand** adj di prima mano; ~ **lady** (US) n moglie f del presidente; ~**ly** adv in primo luogo; ~ **name** n prenome m; ~**rate** adj di prima qualità, ottimo(a)

fish [fɪʃ] n inv pesce m ♦ vt (river, area) pescare in ♦ vi pescare; **to go ~ing** andare a pesca; ~**erman** n pescatore m; ~ **farm** n vivaio; ~ **fingers** (BRIT) npl bastoncini mpl di pesce (surgelati); ~**ing boat** n barca da pesca; ~**ing line** n lenza; ~**ing rod** n canna da pesca; ~**monger** n pescivendolo; ~**monger's (shop)** n pescheria; ~ **sticks** (US) npl = ~ **fingers**; ~**y** (inf) adj (tale, story) sospetto(a)

fist [fɪst] n pugno

fit [fɪt] *adj* (MED, SPORT) in forma; (*proper*) adatto(a), appropriato(a); conveniente ♦ *vt* (*subj: clothes*) stare bene a; (*put in, attach*) mettere; installare; (*equip*) fornire, equipaggiare ♦ *vi* (*clothes*) stare bene; (*parts*) andare bene, adattarsi; (*in space, gap*) entrare ♦ *n* (MED) accesso, attacco; **~ to** in grado di; **~ for** adatto(a) a; degno(a) di; **a ~ of anger** un accesso d'ira; **this dress is a good ~** questo vestito sta bene; **by ~s and starts** a sbalzi; **~ in** *vi* accordarsi; adattarsi; **~ful** *adj* saltuario(a); **~ness** *n* (MED) forma fisica; **~ted carpet** *n* moquette *f*; **~ted kitchen** *n* cucina componibile; **~ter** *n* aggiustatore *m or* montatore *m* meccanico; **~ting** *adj* appropriato(a) ♦ *n* (*of dress*) prova; (*of piece of equipment*) montaggio, aggiustaggio; **~tings** *npl* (*in building*) impianti *mpl*; **~ting room** *n* camerino

five [faɪv] *num* cinque; **~r** (*inf*) *n* (BRIT) biglietto da cinque sterline; (US) biglietto da cinque dollari

fix [fɪks] *vt* fissare; (*mend*) riparare; (*meal, drink*) preparare ♦ *n*: **to be in a ~** essere nei guai; **~ up** *vt* (*meeting*) fissare; **to ~ sb up with sth** procurare qc a qn; **~ation** *n* fissazione *f*; **~ed** [fɪkst] *adj* (*prices etc*) fisso(a); **~ture** ['fɪkstʃə*] *n* impianto (fisso); (SPORT) incontro (del calendario sportivo)

fizzy ['fɪzɪ] *adj* frizzante; gassato(a)

flabbergasted ['flæbəgɑːstɪd] *adj* sbalordito(a)

flabby ['flæbɪ] *adj* flaccido(a)

flag [flæg] *n* bandiera; (*also:* **~stone**) pietra da lastricare ♦ *vi* stancarsi; affievolirsi; **~ down** *vt* fare segno (di fermarsi) a

flagpole ['flæɡpəʊl] *n* albero

flagship ['flæɡʃɪp] *n* nave *f* ammiraglia

flair [flɛə*] *n* (*for business etc*) fiuto; (*for languages etc*) facilità; (*style*) stile *m*

flak [flæk] *n* (MIL) fuoco d'artiglieria; (*inf: criticism*) critiche *fpl*

flake [fleɪk] *n* (*of rust, paint*) scaglia; (*of snow, soap powder*) fiocco ♦ *vi* (*also:* **~ off**) sfaldarsi

flamboyant [flæm'bɔɪənt] *adj* sgargiante

flame [fleɪm] *n* fiamma

flamingo [flə'mɪŋɡəʊ] *n* fenicottero, fiammingo

flammable ['flæməbl] *adj* infiammabile

flan [flæn] (BRIT) *n* flan *m inv*

flank [flæŋk] *n* fianco ♦ *vt* fiancheggiare

flannel ['flænl] *n* (BRIT: *also:* **face ~**) guanto di spugna; (*fabric*) flanella

flap [flæp] *n* (*of pocket*) patta; (*of envelope*) lembo ♦ *vt* (*wings*) battere ♦ *vi* (*sail, flag*) sbattere; (*inf: also:* **be in a ~**) essere in agitazione

flare [flɛə*] *n* razzo; (*in skirt etc*) svasatura; **~ up** *vi* andare in fiamme; (*fig: person*) infiammarsi di rabbia; (*: revolt*) scoppiare

flash [flæʃ] *n* vampata; (*also:* **news ~**) notizia *f* lampo *inv*; (PHOT) flash *m inv* ♦ *vt* accendere e spegnere; (*send: message*) trasmettere; (*: look, smile*) lanciare ♦ *vi* brillare; (*light on ambulance, eyes etc*) lampeggiare; **in a ~** in un lampo; **to ~ one's headlights** lampeggiare; **he ~ed by** *or* **past** ci passò davanti come un lampo; **~bulb** *n* cubo *m* flash *inv*; **~cube** *n* flash *m inv*; **~light** *n* lampadina tascabile

flashy ['flæʃɪ] (*pej*) *adj* vistoso(a)

flask [flɑːsk] *n* fiasco; (*also:* **vacuum ~**) thermos ® *m inv*

flat [flæt] *adj* piatto(a); (*tyre*) sgonfio(a), a terra; (*battery*) scarico(a); (*beer*) svampito(a); (*denial*) netto(a); (MUS) bemolle *inv*; (*: voice*) stonato(a); (*rate, fee*) unico(a) ♦ *n* (BRIT: *rooms*) appartamento; (AUT) pneumatico sgonfio; (MUS) bemolle *m*; **to work ~ out** lavorare a più non posso; **~ly** *adv* categoricamente; **~ten** *vt* (*also:* **~ten out**) appiattire; (*building, city*) spianare

flatter ['flætə*] *vt* lusingare; **~ing** *adj* lusinghiero(a); (*dress*) che dona; **~y** *n* adulazione *f*

flaunt [flɔːnt] *vt* fare mostra di

flavour ['fleɪvə*] (US **flavor**) *n* gusto ♦ *vt* insaporire, aggiungere sapore a; **strawberry-~ed** al gusto di fragola; **~ing** *n* essenza (artificiale)

flaw [flɔː] *n* difetto

flax [flæks] *n* lino

flea [fliː] n pulce f

fleck [flɛk] n (mark) macchiolina; (pattern) screziatura

fled [flɛd] pt, pp of **flee**

flee [fliː] (pt, pp **fled**) vt fuggire da ♦ vi fuggire, scappare

fleece [fliːs] n vello ♦ vt (inf) pelare

fleet [fliːt] n flotta; (of lorries etc) convoglio; parco

fleeting ['fliːtɪŋ] adj fugace, fuggitivo(a); (visit) volante

Flemish ['flɛmɪʃ] adj fiammingo(a)

flesh [flɛʃ] n carne f; (of fruit) polpa; ~ wound n ferita superficiale

flew [fluː] pt of **fly**

flex [flɛks] n filo (flessibile) ♦ vt flettere; (muscles) contrarre; ~**ible** adj flessibile

flick [flɪk] n colpetto; scarto ♦ vt dare un colpetto a; ~ **through** vt fus sfogliare

flicker ['flɪkə*] vi tremolare

flier ['flaɪə*] n aviatore m

flight [flaɪt] n volo; (escape) fuga; (also: ~ **of steps**) scalinata; ~ **attendant** (US) n steward m inv, hostess f inv; ~ **deck** n (AVIAT) cabina di controllo; (NAUT) ponte m di comando

flimsy ['flɪmzɪ] adj (shoes, clothes) leggero(a); (building) poco solido(a); (excuse) che non regge

flinch [flɪntʃ] vi ritirarsi; **to ~ from** tirarsi indietro di fronte a

fling [flɪŋ] (pt, pp **flung**) vt lanciare, gettare

flint [flɪnt] n selce f; (in lighter) pietrina

flip [flɪp] vt (switch) far scattare; (coin) lanciare in aria

flippant ['flɪpənt] adj senza rispetto, irriverente

flipper ['flɪpə*] n pinna

flirt [fləːt] vi flirtare ♦ n civetta

float [fləut] n galleggiante m; (in procession) carro; (money) somma ♦ vi galleggiare

flock [flɔk] n (of sheep, REL) gregge m; (of birds) stormo ♦ vi: **to ~ to** accorrere in massa a

flog [flɔg] vt flagellare

flood [flʌd] n alluvione m; (of letters etc) marea ♦ vt allagare; (subj: people) invadere

♦ vi (place) allagarsi; (people): **to ~ into** riversarsi in; ~**ing** n inondazione f; ~**light** n riflettore m ♦ vt illuminare a giorno

floor [flɔː*] n pavimento; (storey) piano; (of sea, valley) fondo ♦ vt (subj: blow) atterrare; (: question) ridurre al silenzio; **ground ~**, (US) **first ~**, primo piano; **first ~**, (US) **second ~** primo piano; ~**board** n tavellone m di legno; ~ **show** n spettacolo di varietà

flop [flɔp] n fiasco ♦ vi far fiasco; (fall) lasciarsi cadere

floppy ['flɔpɪ] adj floscio(a), molle; ~ **(disk)** n (COMPUT) floppy disk m inv

Florence ['flɔrəns] n Firenze f; **Florentine** ['flɔrəntaɪn] adj fiorentino(a)

florid ['flɔrɪd] adj (complexion) florido(a); (style) fiorito(a)

florist ['flɔrɪst] n fioraio/a

flounder ['flaundə*] vi annaspare ♦ n (ZOOL) passera di mare

flour ['flauə*] n farina

flourish ['flʌrɪʃ] vi fiorire ♦ n (bold gesture): **with a ~** con ostentazione; ~**ing** adj florido(a)

flout [flaut] vt (order) contravvenire a

flow [fləu] n flusso; circolazione f ♦ vi fluire; (traffic, blood in veins) circolare; (hair) scendere; ~ **chart** n schema m di flusso

flower ['flauə*] n fiore m ♦ vi fiorire; ~ **bed** n aiuola; ~**pot** n vaso da fiori; ~**y** adj (perfume) di fiori; (pattern) a fiori; (speech) fiorito(a)

flown [fləun] pp of **fly**

flu [fluː] n influenza

fluctuate ['flʌktjueɪt] vi fluttuare, oscillare

fluent ['fluːənt] adj (speech) facile, sciolto(a); corrente; **he speaks ~ Italian, he's ~ in Italian** parla l'italiano correntemente

fluff [flʌf] n lanugine f; ~**y** adj lanuginoso(a); (toy) di peluche

fluid ['fluːɪd] adj fluido(a) ♦ n fluido

fluke [fluːk] (inf) n colpo di fortuna

flung [flʌŋ] pt, pp of **fling**

fluoride ['fluəraɪd] n fluoruro; ~ **toothpaste** dentifricio al fluoro

flurry ['flʌrɪ] n (of snow) tempesta; **a ~ of**

activity uno scoppio di attività

flush [flʌʃ] n rossore m; (fig: of youth, beauty etc) rigoglio, pieno vigore ♦ vt ripulire con un getto d'acqua ♦ vi arrossire ♦ adj: ~ **with** a livello di, pari a; **to ~ the toilet** tirare l'acqua; **~ed** adj tutto(a) rosso(a)

flustered ['flʌstəd] adj sconvolto(a)

flute [fluːt] n flauto

flutter ['flʌtə*] n agitazione f; (of wings) battito ♦ vi (bird) battere le ali

flux [flʌks] n: **in a state of ~** in continuo mutamento

fly [flaɪ] (pt **flew**, pp **flown**) n (insect) mosca; (on trousers: also: **flies**) chiusura ♦ vt pilotare; (passengers, cargo) trasportare (in aereo); (distances) percorrere ♦ vi volare; (passengers) andare in aereo; (escape) fuggire; (flag) sventolare; **~ away** or **off** vi volare via; **~ing** n (activity) aviazione f; (action) volo ♦ adj: **~ing visit** visita volante; **with ~ing colours** con risultati brillanti; **~ing saucer** n disco volante; **~ing start** n: **to get off to a ~ing start** partire come un razzo; **~over** (BRIT) n (bridge) cavalcavia m inv; **~sheet** n (for tent) sopratetto

foal [fəʊl] n puledro

foam [fəʊm] n schiuma; (also: **~ rubber**) gommapiuma ® ♦ vi schiumare; (soapy water) fare la schiuma

fob [fɒb] vt: **to ~ sb off with** rifilare a qn

focus ['fəʊkəs] (pl **~es**) n fuoco; (of interest) centro ♦ vt (field glasses etc) mettere a fuoco ♦ vi: **to ~ on** (with camera) mettere a fuoco; (person) fissare lo sguardo su; **in ~** a fuoco; **out of ~** sfocato(a)

fodder ['fɒdə*] n foraggio

foe [fəʊ] n nemico

foetus ['fiːtəs] (US **fetus**) n feto

fog [fɒg] n nebbia; **~gy** adj: **it's ~gy** c'è nebbia; **~ lamp** (US **~ light**) n (AUT) faro m antinebbia inv

foil [fɔɪl] vt confondere, frustrare ♦ n lamina di metallo; (kitchen ~) foglio di alluminio; (FENCING) fioretto; **to act as a ~ to** (fig) far risaltare

fold [fəʊld] n (bend, crease) piega; (AGR) ovile m; (fig) gregge m ♦ vt piegare; (arms)

incrociare; **~ up** vi (map, bed, table) piegarsi; (business) crollare ♦ vt (map etc) piegare, ripiegare; **~er** n (for papers) cartella; cartellina; **~ing** adj (chair, bed) pieghevole

foliage ['fəʊlɪdʒ] n fogliame m

folk [fəʊk] npl gente f ♦ adj popolare; **~s** npl (family) famiglia; **~lore** ['fəʊklɔː*] n folclore m; **~ song** n canto popolare

follow ['fɒləʊ] vt seguire ♦ vi seguire; (result) conseguire, risultare; **to ~ suit** fare lo stesso; **~ up** vt (letter, offer) fare seguito a; (case) seguire; **~er** n seguace m/f, discepolo/a; **~ing** adj seguente ♦ n seguito, discepoli mpl; **~-on call** n chiamata successiva

folly ['fɒlɪ] n pazzia, follia

fond [fɒnd] adj (memory, look) tenero(a), affettuoso(a); **to be ~ of sb** volere bene a qn; **he's ~ of walking** gli piace fare camminate

fondle ['fɒndl] vt accarezzare

font [fɒnt] n (in church) fonte m battesimale; (TYP) caratteri mpl

food [fuːd] n cibo; **~ mixer** n frullatore m; **~ poisoning** n intossicazione f; **~ processor** n tritatutto m inv elettrico; **~stuffs** npl generi fpl alimentari

fool [fuːl] n sciocco/a; (CULIN) frullato ♦ vt ingannare ♦ vi (gen: **~ around**) fare lo sciocco; **~hardy** adj avventato(a); **~ish** adj scemo(a), stupido(a); imprudente; **~proof** adj (plan etc) sicurissimo(a)

foot [fʊt] (pl **feet**) n piede m; (measure) piede (= 304 mm; 12 inches); (of animal) zampa ♦ vt (bill) pagare; **on ~** a piedi; **~age** n (CINEMA: length) ≈ metraggio; **~ball** n pallone m; (sport: BRIT) calcio m; (: US) football m americano; **~ball player** n (BRIT: also: **~baller**) calciatore m; (US) giocatore m di football americano; **~brake** n freno a pedale; **~bridge** n passerella; **~hills** npl contrafforti fpl, primi pendii; **~hold** n punto d'appoggio; **~ing** n (fig) posizione f; **to lose one's ~ing** mettere un piede in fallo; **~note** n nota (a piè di pagina); **~path** n sentiero; (in street) marciapiede m; ~print n orma, impronta; ~step n passo; (~print) orma, impronta; ~wear n calzatura

---

KEYWORD

---

for [fɔ:*] prep 1 (indicating destination, intention, purpose) per; **the train ~ London** il treno per Londra; **he went ~ the paper** è andato a prendere il giornale; **it's time ~ lunch** è ora di pranzo; **what's it ~?** a che serve?; **what ~?** (why) perché?

2 (on behalf of, representing) per; **to work ~ sb/sth** lavorare per qn/qc; **I'll ask him ~ you** glielo chiederò a nome tuo; **G ~ George** G come George

3 (because of) per, a causa di; **~ this reason** per questo motivo

4 (with regard to) per; **it's cold ~ July** è freddo per luglio; **~ everyone who voted yes, 50 voted no** per ogni voto a favore ce n'erano 50 contro

5 (in exchange for) per; **I sold it ~ £5** l'ho venduto per 5 sterline

6 (in favour of) per, a favore di; **are you ~ or against us?** è con noi o contro di noi?; **I'm all ~ it** sono completamente a favore

7 (referring to distance, time) per; **there are roadworks ~ 5 km** ci sono lavori in corso per 5 km; **he was away ~ 2 years** è stato via per 2 anni; **she will be away ~ a month** starà via un mese; **it hasn't rained ~ 3 weeks** non piove da 3 settimane; **can you do it ~ tomorrow?** può farlo per domani?

8 (with infinitive clauses): **it is not ~ me to decide** non sta a me decidere; **it would be best ~ you to leave** sarebbe meglio che lei se ne andasse; **there is still time ~ you to do it** ha ancora tempo per farlo; **~ this to be possible ...** perché ciò sia possibile ...

9 (in spite of) nonostante; **~ all his complaints, he's very fond of her** nonostante tutte le sue lamentele, le vuole molto bene

♦ conj (since, as: rather formal) dal momento che, poiché

forage ['fɔrɪdʒ] vi: **to ~ (for)** andare in cerca (di)

foray ['fɔreɪ] n incursione f

forbid [fə'bɪd] (pt **forbad(e)**, pp **forbidden**) vt vietare, interdire; **to ~ sb to do sth** proibire a qn di fare qc; **~ding** adj minaccioso(a)

force [fɔ:s] n forza ♦ vt forzare; **the F~s** (BRIT) npl le forze armate; **to ~ o.s. to do** costringersi a fare; **in ~** (in large numbers) in gran numero; (law) in vigore; **~d** adj forzato(a); **~-feed** vt (animal, prisoner) sottoporre ad alimentazione forzata; **~ful** adj forte, vigoroso(a)

forceps ['fɔ:sɛps] npl forcipe m

forcibly ['fɔ:səblɪ] adv con la forza; (vigorously) vigorosamente

ford [fɔ:d] n guado

fore [fɔ:*] n: **to come to the ~** mettersi in evidenza

forearm ['fɔ:rɑ:m] n avambraccio

foreboding [fɔ:'bəudɪŋ] n cattivo presagio

forecast ['fɔ:kɑ:st] (irreg: like cast) n previsione f ♦ vt prevedere

forecourt ['fɔ:kɔ:t] n (of garage) corte f esterna

forefinger ['fɔ:fɪŋgə*] n (dito) indice m

forefront ['fɔ:frʌnt] n: **in the ~ of** all'avanguardia in

forego [fɔ:'gəu] (irreg: like go) vt rinunciare a

foregone [fɔ:'gɔn] pp of forego ♦ adj: **it's a ~ conclusion** è una conclusione scontata

foreground ['fɔ:graund] n primo piano

forehead ['fɔrɪd] n fronte f

foreign ['fɔrɪn] adj straniero(a); (trade) estero(a); (object, matter) estraneo(a); **~er** n straniero/a; **~ exchange** n cambio con l'estero; (currency) valuta estera; **F~ Office** (BRIT) n Ministero degli Esteri; **F~ Secretary** (BRIT) n ministro degli Affari esteri

foreleg ['fɔ:lɛg] n zampa anteriore

foreman ['fɔ:mən] (irreg) n caposquadra m

foremost ['fɔ:məust] adj principale; più in vista ♦ adv: **first and ~** innanzitutto

forensic [fə'rɛnsɪk] *adj*: **~ medicine** medicina legale

forerunner ['fɔːrʌnə*] *n* precursore *m*

foresaw [fɔː'sɔː] *pt of* **foresee**

foresee [fɔː'siː] *(irreg: like* **see)** *vt* prevedere; **~able** *adj* prevedibile; **foreseen** *pp of* **foresee**

foreshadow [fɔː'ʃædəu] *vt* presagire, far prevedere

foresight ['fɔːsaɪt] *n* previdenza

forest ['fɒrɪst] *n* foresta

forestry ['fɒrɪstrɪ] *n* silvicoltura

foretaste ['fɔːteɪst] *n* pregustazione *f*

foretell [fɔː'tɛl] *(irreg: like* **tell)** *vt* predire; **foretold** [fɔː'təuld] *pt, pp of* **foretell**

forever [fə'rɛvə*] *adv* per sempre; (*endlessly*) sempre, di continuo

foreword ['fɔːwəːd] *n* prefazione *f*

forfeit ['fɔːfɪt] *vt* perdere; (*one's happiness, health*) giocarsi

forgave [fə'geɪv] *pt of* **forgive**

forge [fɔːdʒ] *n* fucina ♦ *vt* (*signature, money*) contraffare, falsificare; (*wrought iron*) fucinare, foggiare; **~ ahead** *vi* tirare avanti; **~ry** *n* falso; (*activity*) contraffazione *f*

forget [fə'gɛt] *(pt* **forgot,** *pp* **forgotten)** *vt, vi* dimenticare; **~ful** *adj* di corta memoria; **~ful of** dimentico(a) di; **~-me-not** *n* nontiscordardimé *m inv*

forgive [fə'gɪv] *(pt* **forgave,** *pp* **forgiven)** *vt* perdonare; **to ~ sb for sth** perdonare qc a qn; **~ness** *n* perdono

forgo [fɔː'gəu] = **forego**

forgot [fə'gɒt] *pt of* **forget**

forgotten [fə'gɒtn] *pp of* **forget**

fork [fɔːk] *n* (*for eating*) forchetta; (*for gardening*) forca; (*of roads, rivers, railways*) biforcazione *f* ♦ *vi* (*road etc*) biforcarsi; **~ out** (*inf*) *vt* (*pay*) sborsare; **~-lift truck** *n* carrello elevatore

forlorn [fə'lɔːn] *adj* (*person*) sconsolato(a); (*place*) abbandonato(a); (*attempt*) disperato(a); (*hope*) vano(a)

form [fɔːm] *n* forma; (*SCOL*) classe *f*; (*questionnaire*) scheda ♦ *vt* formare; **in top ~** in gran forma

formal ['fɔːməl] *adj* formale; (*gardens*) simmetrico(a), regolare; **~ly** *adv* formalmente

format ['fɔːmæt] *n* formato ♦ *vt* (*COMPUT*) formattare

formation [fɔː'meɪʃən] *n* formazione *f*

formative ['fɔːmətɪv] *adj*: **~ years** anni *mpl* formativi

former ['fɔːmə*] *adj* vecchio(a) (*before n*), ex *inv* (*before n*); **the ~ ... the latter** quello ... questo; **~ly** *adv* in passato

formula ['fɔːmjulə] *n* formula

forsake [fə'seɪk] *(pt* **forsook,** *pp* **forsaken)** *vt* abbandonare

fort [fɔːt] *n* forte *m*

forth [fɔːθ] *adv* in avanti; **back and ~** avanti e indietro; **and so ~** e così via; **~coming** *adj* (*event*) prossimo(a); (*help*) disponibile; (*character*) aperto(a), comunicativo(a); **~right** *adj* franco(a), schietto(a); **~with** *adv* immediatamente, subito

fortify ['fɔːtɪfaɪ] *vt* (*city*) fortificare; (*person*) armare

fortitude ['fɔːtɪtjuːd] *n* forza d'animo

fortnight ['fɔːtnaɪt] (*BRIT*) *n* quindici giorni *mpl*, due settimane *fpl*; **~ly** *adj* bimensile ♦ *adv* ogni quindici giorni

fortress ['fɔːtrɪs] *n* fortezza, rocca

fortunate ['fɔːtʃənɪt] *adj* fortunato(a); **it is ~ that** è una fortuna che; **~ly** *adv* fortunatamente

fortune ['fɔːtʃən] *n* fortuna; **~-teller** *n* indovino/a

forty ['fɔːtɪ] *num* quaranta

forum ['fɔːrəm] *n* foro

forward ['fɔːwəd] *adj* (*ahead of schedule*) in anticipo; (*movement, position*) in avanti; (*not shy*) aperto(a); diretto(a) ♦ *n* (*SPORT*) avanti *m inv* ♦ *vt* (*letter*) inoltrare; (*parcel, goods*) spedire; (*career, plans*) promuovere, appoggiare; **to move ~** avanzare; **~(s)** *adv* avanti

fossil ['fɒsl] *adj* fossile ♦ *n* fossile *m*

foster ['fɒstə*] *vt* incoraggiare, nutrire; (*child*) avere in affidamento; **~ child** *n* bambino(a) preso(a) in affidamento

fought [fɔːt] *pt, pp of* **fight**

foul [faul] adj (smell, food, temper etc) cattivo(a); (weather) brutto(a); (language) osceno(a) ♦ n (SPORT) fallo ♦ vt sporcare; ~ **play** n (LAW): **the police suspect ~ play** la polizia sospetta un atto criminale

found [faund] pt, pp of **find** ♦ vt (establish) fondare; **~ation** [-'deɪʃən] n (act) fondazione f; (base) base f; (also: **~ation cream**) fondo tinta; **~ations** npl (of building) fondamenta fpl

founder ['faundə*] n fondatore/trice ♦ vi affondare

foundry ['faundrɪ] n fonderia

fountain ['fauntɪn] n fontana; ~ **pen** n penna stilografica

four [fɔ:*] num quattro; **on all ~s** a carponi; **~-poster** n (also: **~-poster bed**) letto a quattro colonne; **~teen** num quattordici; **~th** num quarto(a)

fowl [faul] n pollame m; volatile m

fox [fɔks] n volpe f ♦ vt confondere

foyer ['fɔɪeɪ] n atrio; (THEATRE) ridotto

fraction ['frækʃən] n frazione f

fracture ['fræktʃə*] n frattura

fragile ['frædʒaɪl] adj fragile

fragment ['frægmənt] n frammento

fragrant ['freɪgrənt] adj fragrante, profumato(a)

frail [freɪl] adj debole, delicato(a)

frame [freɪm] n (of building) armatura; (of human, animal) ossatura, corpo; (of picture) cornice f; (of door, window) telaio; (of spectacles: also: **~s**) montatura ♦ vt (picture) incorniciare; ~ **of mind** n stato d'animo; **~work** n struttura

France [frɑːns] n Francia

franchise ['fræntʃaɪz] n (POL) diritto di voto; (COMM) concessione f

frank [fræŋk] adj franco(a), aperto(a) ♦ vt (letter) affrancare; **~ly** adv francamente, sinceramente

frantic ['fræntɪk] adj frenetico(a)

fraternity [frə'tɜːnɪtɪ] n (club) associazione f; (spirit) fratellanza

fraud [frɔːd] n truffa; (LAW) frode f; (person) impostore/a

fraught [frɔːt] adj: ~ **with** pieno(a) di, intriso(a) da

fray [freɪ] vt logorare ♦ vi logorarsi

freak [friːk] n fenomeno, mostro

freckle ['frɛkl] n lentiggine f

free [friː] adj libero(a); (gratis) gratuito(a) ♦ vt (prisoner, jammed person) liberare; (jammed object) districare; ~ **(of charge)**, **for ~** gratuitamente; **~dom** ['friːdəm] n libertà; **F~fone** ® n numero verde; **~-for-all** n parapiglia m generale; ~ **gift** n regalo, omaggio; **~hold** n proprietà assoluta; ~ **kick** n calcio libero; **~lance** adj indipendente; **~ly** adv liberamente; (liberally) liberalmente; **F~mason** n massone m; **F~post** ® n affrancatura a carico del destinatario; **~-range** adj (hen) ruspante; (eggs) di gallina ruspante; **~style** n (SPORT) stile m libero; ~ **trade** n libero scambio; **~way** (US) n superstrada; ~ **will** n libero arbitrio; **of one's own ~ will** di spontanea volontà

freeze [friːz] (pt **froze**, pp **frozen**) vi gelare ♦ vt gelare; (food) congelare; (prices, salaries) bloccare ♦ n gelo; blocco; **~-dried** adj liofilizzato(a); **~r** n congelatore m

freezing ['friːzɪŋ] adj (wind, weather) gelido(a); ~ **point** n punto di congelamento; **3 degrees below ~ point** 3 gradi sotto zero

freight [freɪt] n (goods) merce f, merci fpl; (money charged) spese fpl di trasporto; ~ **train** (US) n treno m merci inv

French [frɛntʃ] adj francese ♦ n (LING) francese m; **the ~** npl i Francesi; ~ **bean** n fagiolino; ~ **fried potatoes** (US ~ **fries**) npl patate fpl fritte; **~man** (irreg) n francese m; ~ **window** n portafinestra; **~woman** (irreg) n francese f

frenzy ['frenzɪ] n frenesia

frequency ['friːkwənsɪ] n frequenza

frequent [adj 'friːkwənt, vb frɪ'kwent] adj frequente ♦ vt frequentare; **~ly** adv frequentemente, spesso

fresco ['freskəu] n affresco

fresh [freʃ] adj fresco(a); (new) nuovo(a); (cheeky) sfacciato(a); **~en** vi (wind, air)

rinfrescare; ~**en up** vi rinfrescarsi; ~**er**
(*BRIT: inf*) n (*SCOL*) matricola; ~**ly** adv di
recente, di fresco; ~**man** (*irreg*) (*US*) n
= ~**er**; ~**ness** n freschezza; ~**water** adj
(*fish*) d'acqua dolce

fret [frɛt] vi agitarsi, affliggersi

friar ['fraɪə*] n frate m

friction ['frɪkʃən] n frizione f, attrito

Friday ['fraɪdɪ] n venerdì m inv

fridge [frɪdʒ] (*BRIT*) n frigo, frigorifero

fried [fraɪd] pt, pp of **fry** ♦ adj fritto(a)

friend [frɛnd] n amico/a; ~**ly** adj
amichevole; ~**ly fire** n (*MIL*) fuoco amico;
~**ship** n amicizia

frieze [fri:z] n fregio

fright [fraɪt] n paura, spavento; **to take** ~
spaventarsi; ~**en** vt spaventare, far paura
a; ~**ened** adj spaventato(a); ~**ening** adj
spaventoso(a), pauroso(a); ~**ful** adj orribile

frill [frɪl] n balza

fringe [frɪndʒ] n (*decoration, BRIT: of hair*)
frangia; (*edge: of forest etc*) margine m; ~
benefits npl vantaggi mpl

frisk [frɪsk] vt perquisire

frisky ['frɪskɪ] adj vivace, vispo(a)

fritter ['frɪtə*] n frittella; ~ **away** vt sprecare

frivolous ['frɪvələs] adj frivolo(a)

frizzy ['frɪzɪ] adj crespo(a)

fro [frəʊ] *see* **to**

frock [frɒk] n vestito

frog [frɒg] n rana; ~**man** (*irreg*) n uomo m
rana inv

frolic ['frɒlɪk] vi sgambettare

KEYWORD

from [frɒm] prep **1** (*indicating starting place,
origin etc*) da; **where do you come** ~?,
where are you ~? da dove viene?, di
dov'è?; ~ **London to Glasgow** da Londra a
Glasgow; **a letter** ~ **my sister** una lettera
da mia sorella; **tell him** ~ **me that ...** gli
dica da parte mia che ...

2 (*indicating time*) da; ~ **one o'clock to** or
until or **till two** dall'una alle due; ~
January (on) da gennaio, a partire da
gennaio

3 (*indicating distance*) da; **the hotel is**

1 km ~ **the beach** l'albergo è a 1 km dalla
spiaggia

4 (*indicating price, number etc*) da; **prices
range** ~ **£10 to £50** i prezzi vanno dalle 10
alle 50 sterline

5 (*indicating difference*) da; **he can't tell
red** ~ **green** non sa distinguere il rosso dal
verde

6 (*because of, on the basis of*): ~ **what he
says** da quanto dice lui; **weak** ~ **hunger**
debole per la fame

---

front [frʌnt] n (*of house, dress*) davanti m
inv; (*of train*) testa; (*of book*) copertina;
(*promenade: also:* **sea** ~) lungomare m;
(*MIL, POL, METEOR*) fronte m; (*fig:
appearances*) fronte f ♦ adj primo(a);
anteriore, davanti inv; **in** ~ **of** davanti a; ~
door n porta d'entrata; (*of car*) sportello
anteriore; ~**ier** ['frʌntɪə*] n frontiera; ~
page n prima pagina; ~ **room** (*BRIT*) n
salotto; ~-**wheel drive** n trasmissione f
anteriore

frost [frɒst] n gelo; (*also:* **hoar**~) brina;
~**bite** n congelamento; ~**ed** adj (*glass*)
smerigliato(a); ~**y** adj (*weather, look*)
gelido(a)

froth ['frɒθ] n spuma; schiuma

frown [fraʊn] vi acci gliarsi

froze [frəʊz] pt of **freeze**; **frozen** pp of
freeze

fruit [fru:t] n inv (*also fig*) frutto; (*collectively*)
frutta; ~**erer** n fruttivendolo; ~**erer's
(shop)** n: **at the** ~**erer's (shop)** dal
fruttivendolo; ~**ful** adj fruttuoso(a); ~**ion**
[fru:'ɪʃən] n: **to come to** ~**ion** realizzarsi; ~
juice n succo di frutta; ~ **machine** (*BRIT*)
n macchina f mangiasoldi inv; ~ **salad** n
macedonia

frustrate [frʌs'treɪt] vt frustrare

fry [fraɪ] (*pt, pp* **fried**) vt friggere; *see also*
small; ~**ing pan** n padella

ft. abbr = **foot**; **feet**

fudge [fʌdʒ] n (*CULIN*) specie di caramella a
base di latte, burro e zucchero

fuel [fjʊəl] n (*for heating*) combustibile m;
(*for propelling*) carburante m; ~ **tank** n

deposito *m* nafta *inv*; (*on vehicle*) serbatoio (della benzina)

fugitive ['fjuːdʒɪtɪv] *n* fuggitivo/a, profugo/a

fulfil [ful'fɪl] *vt* (*function*) compiere; (*order*) eseguire; (*wish, desire*) soddisfare, appagare; **~ment** (*US* **fulfillment**) *n* (*of wishes*) soddisfazione *f*, appagamento; **sense of ~ment** soddisfazione *f*

full [ful] *adj* pieno(a); (*details, skirt*) ampio(a) ♦ *adv*: **to know ~ well that** sapere benissimo che; **I'm ~ (up)** sono pieno; **a ~ two hours** due ore intere; **at ~ speed** a tutta velocità; **in ~** per intero; **~ board** (*BRIT*) *n* pensione *f* completa; **~ employment** *n* piena occupazione; **~-length** *adj* (*film*) a lungometraggio; (*coat, novel*) lungo(a); (*portrait*) in piedi; **~ moon** *n* luna piena; **~-scale** *adj* (*attack, war*) su larga scala; (*model*) in grandezza naturale; **~ stop** *n* punto; **~-time** *adj, adv* (*work*) a tempo pieno; **~y** *adv* interamente, pienamente, completamente; (*at least*) almeno; **~y-fledged** *adj* (*teacher, member etc*) a tutti gli effetti; **~y licensed** *adj* (*hotel, restaurant*) autorizzato(a) alla vendita di alcolici

fumble ['fʌmbl] *vi*: **to ~ with sth** armeggiare con qc

fume [fjuːm] *vi* essere furioso(a); **~s** *npl* esalazioni *fpl*, vapori *mpl*

fun [fʌn] *n* divertimento, spasso; **to have ~** divertirsi; **for ~** per scherzo; **to make ~ of** prendersi gioco di

function ['fʌŋkʃən] *n* funzione *f*; cerimonia, ricevimento ♦ *vi* funzionare; **~al** *adj* funzionale

fund [fʌnd] *n* fondo, cassa; (*source*) fondo; (*store*) riserva; **~s** *npl* (*money*) fondi *mpl*

fundamental [fʌndə'mɛntl] *adj* fondamentale

funeral ['fjuːnərəl] *n* funerale *m*; **~ parlour** *n* impresa di pompe funebri; **~ service** *n* ufficio funebre

fun fair (*BRIT*) *n* luna park *m inv*

fungus ['fʌŋgəs] (*pl* **fungi**) *n* fungo; (*mould*) muffa

funnel ['fʌnl] *n* imbuto; (*of ship*) ciminiera

funny ['fʌnɪ] *adj* divertente, buffo(a); (*strange*) strano(a), bizzarro(a)

fur [fɜː*] *n* pelo; pelliccia; (*BRIT: in kettle etc*) deposito calcare; **~ coat** *n* pelliccia

furious ['fjuərɪəs] *adj* furioso(a); (*effort*) accanito(a)

furlong ['fɜːlɔŋ] *n* = 201.17 m (*termine ippico*)

furnace ['fɜːnɪs] *n* fornace *f*

furnish ['fɜːnɪʃ] *vt* ammobiliare; (*supply*) fornire; **~ings** *npl* mobili *mpl*, mobilia

furniture ['fɜːnɪtʃə*] *n* mobili *mpl*; **piece of ~** mobile *m*

furrow ['fʌrəu] *n* solco

furry ['fɜːrɪ] *adj* (*animal*) peloso(a)

further ['fɜːðə*] *adj* supplementare, altro(a); nuovo(a); più lontano(a) ♦ *adv* più lontano; (*more*) di più; (*moreover*) inoltre ♦ *vt* favorire, promuovere; **college of ~ education** *n* istituto statale con corsi specializzati (di formazione professionale, aggiornamento professionale etc); **~more** [fɜːðə'mɔː*] *adv* inoltre, per di più

furthest ['fɜːðɪst] *superl of* **far**

fury ['fjuərɪ] *n* furore *m*

fuse [fjuːz] *n* fusibile *m*; (*for bomb etc*) miccia, spoletta ♦ *vt* fondere ♦ *vi* fondersi; **to ~ the lights** (*BRIT: ELEC*) far saltare i fusibili; **~ box** *n* cassetta dei fusibili

fuselage ['fjuːzəlɑːʒ] *n* fusoliera

fuss [fʌs] *n* agitazione *f*; (*complaining*) storie *fpl*; **to make a ~** fare delle storie; **~y** *adj* (*person*) puntiglioso(a), esigente; che fa le storie; (*dress*) carico(a) di fronzoli; (*style*) elaborato(a)

future ['fjuːtʃə*] *adj* futuro(a) ♦ *n* futuro, avvenire *m*; (*LING*) futuro; **in ~** in futuro

fuze [fjuːz] (*US*) = **fuse**

fuzzy ['fʌzɪ] *adj* (*PHOT*) indistinto(a), sfocato(a); (*hair*) crespo(a)

G, g

G [dʒiː] n (MUS) sol m

G7 abbr (= Group of Seven) G7

gabble ['gæbl] vi borbottare; farfugliare

gable ['geɪbl] n frontone m

gadget ['gædʒɪt] n aggeggio

Gaelic ['geɪlɪk] adj gaelico(a) ♦ n (LING) gaelico

gag [gæg] n bavaglio; (joke) facezia, scherzo ♦ vt imbavagliare

gaiety ['geɪtɪ] n gaiezza

gaily ['geɪlɪ] adv allegramente

gain [geɪn] n guadagno, profitto ♦ vt guadagnare ♦ vi (clock, watch) andare avanti; (benefit): **to ~ (from)** trarre beneficio (da); **to ~ 3lbs (in weight)** aumentare di 3 libbre; **to ~ on sb** (in race etc) guadagnare su qn

gal. abbr = **gallon**

galaxy ['gæləksɪ] n galassia

gale [geɪl] n vento forte; burrasca

gallant ['gælənt] adj valoroso(a); (towards ladies) galante, cortese

gall bladder ['gɔːl-] n cistifellea

gallery ['gælərɪ] n galleria

gallon ['gælən] n gallone m (= 8 pints; BRIT = 4.543l; US = 3.785l)

gallop ['gæləp] n galoppo ♦ vi galoppare

gallows ['gæləuz] n forca

gallstone ['gɔːlstəun] n calcolo biliare

galore [gə'lɔː*] adv a iosa, a profusione

galvanize ['gælvənaɪz] vt galvanizzare

gambit ['gæmbɪt] n (fig): **(opening) ~** prima mossa

gamble ['gæmbl] n azzardo, rischio calcolato ♦ vt, vi giocare; **to ~ on** (fig) giocare su; **~r** n giocatore/trice d'azzardo; **gambling** n gioco d'azzardo

game [geɪm] n gioco; (event) partita; (TENNIS) game m inv; (CULIN, HUNTING) selvaggina ♦ adj (ready): **to be ~ (for sth/ to do)** essere pronto(a) (a qc/a fare); **big ~** selvaggina grossa; **~keeper** n guardacaccia m inv

gammon ['gæmən] n (bacon) quarto di maiale; (ham) prosciutto affumicato

gamut ['gæmət] n gamma

gang [gæŋ] n banda, squadra ♦ vi: **to ~ up on sb** far combutta contro qn

gangrene ['gæŋgriːn] n cancrena

gangster ['gæŋstə*] n gangster m inv

gangway ['gæŋweɪ] n passerella; (BRIT: of bus) corridoio

gaol [dʒeɪl] (BRIT) n, vt = **jail**

gap [gæp] n (space) spazio; (in time) intervallo; (difference): **~ (between)** divario (tra)

gape [geɪp] vi (person) restare a bocca aperta; (shirt, hole) essere spalancato(a); **gaping** adj spalancato(a)

gap year (SCOL) n anno di pausa durante il quale gli studenti viaggiano o lavorano

garage ['gærɑːʒ] n garage m inv

garbage ['gɑːbɪdʒ] n (US) immondizie fpl, rifiuti mpl; (inf) sciocchezze fpl; **~ can** (US) n bidone m della spazzatura

garbled ['gɑːbld] adj deformato(a); ingarbugliato(a)

garden ['gɑːdn] n giardino; **~s** npl (public park) giardini pubblici; **~er** n giardiniere/a; **~ing** n giardinaggio

gargle ['gɑːgl] vi fare gargarismi

garish ['gɛərɪʃ] adj vistoso(a)

garland ['gɑːlənd] n ghirlanda; corona

garlic ['gɑːlɪk] n aglio

garment ['gɑːmənt] n indumento

garnish ['gɑːnɪʃ] vt (food) guarnire

garrison ['gærɪsn] n guarnigione f

garter ['gɑːtə*] n giarrettiera

gas [gæs] n gas m inv; (US: gasoline) benzina ♦ vt asfissiare con il gas; **~ cooker** (BRIT) n cucina a gas; **~ cylinder** n bombola del gas; **~ fire** (BRIT) n radiatore m a gas

gash [gæʃ] n sfregio ♦ vt sfregiare

gasket ['gæskɪt] n (AUT) guarnizione f

gas mask n maschera f antigas inv

gas meter n contatore m del gas

gasoline ['gæsəliːn] (US) n benzina

gasp [gɑːsp] n respiro affannoso, ansito ♦ vi ansare, ansimare; (in surprise) restare senza fiato

gas station (US) n distributore m di benzina

gassy ['gæsɪ] *adj* gassoso(a)

gate [geɪt] *n* cancello; (*at airport*) uscita; **~crash** (*BRIT*) *vt* partecipare senza invito a; **~way** *n* porta

gather ['gæðə*] *vt* (*flowers, fruit*) cogliere; (*pick up*) raccogliere; (*assemble*) radunare; raccogliere; (*understand*) capire; (*SEWING*) increspare ♦ *vi* (*assemble*) radunarsi; **to ~ speed** acquistare velocità; **~ing** *n* adunanza

gauche [gəʊʃ] *adj* goffo(a), maldestro(a)

gaudy ['gɔːdɪ] *adj* vistoso(a)

gauge [geɪdʒ] *n* (*instrument*) indicatore *m* ♦ *vt* misurare; (*fig*) valutare

gaunt [gɔːnt] *adj* scarno(a); (*grim, desolate*) desolato(a)

gauntlet ['gɔːntlɪt] *n* guanto; (*fig*): **to run the ~ through an angry crowd** passare sotto il fuoco di una folla ostile; **to throw down the ~** gettare il guanto

gauze [gɔːz] *n* garza

gave [geɪv] *pt of* **give**

gay [geɪ] *adj* (*homosexual*) omosessuale; (*cheerful*) gaio(a), allegro(a); (*colour*) vivace, vivo(a)

gaze [geɪz] *n* sguardo fisso ♦ *vi*: **to ~ at** guardare fisso

GB *abbr* = **Great Britain**

GCE (*BRIT*) *n abbr* (= *General Certificate of Education*) ≈ maturità

GCSE (*BRIT*) *n abbr* = *General Certificate of Secondary Education*

gear [gɪə*] *n* attrezzi *mpl*, equipaggiamento; (*TECH*) ingranaggio; (*AUT*) marcia ♦ *vt* (*fig: adapt*): **to ~ sth to** adattare qc a; **in top** *or* (*US*) **high/low ~** in quarta (*or* quinta)/ seconda; **in ~** in marcia; **~ box** *n* scatola del cambio; **~ lever** (*US* **~ shift**) *n* leva del cambio

geese [giːs] *npl of* **goose**

gel [dʒɛl] *n* gel *m inv*

gem [dʒɛm] *n* gemma

Gemini ['dʒɛmɪnaɪ] *n* Gemelli *mpl*

gender ['dʒɛndə*] *n* genere *m*

general ['dʒɛnərl] *n* generale *m* ♦ *adj* generale; **in ~** in genere; **~ delivery** (*US*) *n* fermo posta *m*; **~ election** *n* elezioni

fpl generali; **~ly** *adv* generalmente; **~ practitioner** *n* medico generico

generate ['dʒɛnəreɪt] *vt* generare

generation [dʒɛnə'reɪʃən] *n* generazione *f*

generator ['dʒɛnəreɪtə*] *n* generatore *m*

generosity [dʒɛnə'rɔsɪtɪ] *n* generosità

generous ['dʒɛnərəs] *adj* generoso(a); (*copious*) abbondante

genetic engineering [dʒɪ'nɛtɪk-] *n* ingegneria genetica

genetic fingerprinting [dʒɪ'nɛtɪk-] *n* rilevamento delle impronte genetiche

Geneva [dʒɪ'niːvə] *n* Ginevra

genial ['dʒiːnɪəl] *adj* geniale, cordiale

genitals ['dʒɛnɪtlz] *npl* genitali *mpl*

genius ['dʒiːnɪəs] *n* genio

Genoa ['dʒɛnəʊə] *n* Genova

gent [dʒɛnt] *n abbr* = **gentleman**

genteel [dʒɛn'tiːl] *adj* raffinato(a), distinto(a)

gentle ['dʒɛntl] *adj* delicato(a); (*person*) dolce

gentleman ['dʒɛntlmən] *n* signore *m*; (*well-bred man*) gentiluomo

gently ['dʒɛntlɪ] *adv* delicatamente

gentry ['dʒɛntrɪ] *n* nobiltà minore

gents [dʒɛnts] *n* W.C. *m* (per signori)

genuine ['dʒɛnjuɪn] *adj* autentico(a); sincero(a)

geography [dʒɪ'ɔgrəfɪ] *n* geografia

geology [dʒɪ'ɔlədʒɪ] *n* geologia

geometric(al) [dʒɪə'mɛtrɪk(l)] *adj* geometrico(a)

geometry [dʒɪ'ɔmɪtrɪ] *n* geometria

geranium [dʒɪ'reɪnjəm] *n* geranio

geriatric [dʒɛrɪ'ætrɪk] *adj* geriatrico(a)

germ [dʒɜːm] *n* (*MED*) microbo; (*BIOL, fig*) germe *m*

German ['dʒɜːmən] *adj* tedesco(a) ♦ *n* tedesco/a; (*LING*) tedesco; **~ measles** (*BRIT*) *n* rosolia

Germany ['dʒɜːmənɪ] *n* Germania

gesture ['dʒɛstjə*] *n* gesto

KEYWORD

get [gɛt] (*pt, pp* **got**, (*US*) *pp* **gotten**) *vi*
1 (*become, be*) diventare, farsi; **to ~ old**

invecchiare; **to ~ tired** stancarsi; **to ~ drunk** ubriacarsi; **to ~ killed** venire or rimanere ucciso(a); **when do I ~ paid?** quando mi pagate?; **it's ~ting late** si sta facendo tardi
2 (go): **to ~ to/from** andare a/da; **to ~ home** arrivare or tornare a casa; **how did you ~ here?** come sei venuto?
3 (begin) mettersi a, cominciare a; **to ~ to know sb** incominciare a conoscere qn; **let's ~ going** or **started** muoviamoci
4 (modal aux vb): **you've got to do it** devi farlo
♦ vt **1**: **to ~ sth done** (do) fare qc; (have done) far fare qc; **to ~ one's hair cut** tagliarsi i capelli; **to ~ sb to do sth** far fare qc a qn
2 (obtain: money, permission, results) ottenere; (find: job, flat) trovare; (fetch: person, doctor) chiamare; (: object) prendere; **to ~ sth for sb** prendere or procurare qc a qn; **~ me Mr Jones, please** (TEL) mi passi il signor Jones, per favore; **can I ~ you a drink?** le posso offrire da bere?
3 (receive: present, letter, prize) ricevere; (acquire: reputation) farsi; **how much did you ~ for the painting?** quanto le hanno dato per il quadro?
4 (catch) prendere; (hit: target etc) colpire; **to ~ sb by the arm/throat** afferrare qn per un braccio/alla gola; **~ him!** prendetelo!
5 (take, move) portare; **to ~ sth to sb** far avere qc a qn; **do you think we'll ~ it through the door?** pensi che riusciremo a farlo passare per la porta?
6 (catch, take: plane, bus etc) prendere
7 (understand) afferrare; (hear) sentire; **I've got it!** ci sono arrivato!, ci sono!; **I'm sorry, I didn't ~ your name** scusi, non ho capito (or sentito) il suo nome
8 (have, possess): **to have got** avere; **how many have you got?** quanti ne ha?
get about vi muoversi; (news) diffondersi
get along vi (agree) andare d'accordo; (depart) andarsene; (manage) = **get by**
get at vt fus (attack) prendersela con; (reach) raggiungere, arrivare a

get away vi partire, andarsene; (escape) scappare
get away with vt fus cavarsela; farla franca
get back vi (return) ritornare, tornare ♦ vt riottenere, riavere
get by vi (pass) passare; (manage) farcela
get down vi, vt fus scendere ♦ vt far scendere; (depress) buttare giù
get down to vt fus (work) mettersi a (fare)
get in vi entrare; (train) arrivare; (arrive home) ritornare, tornare
get into vt fus entrare in; **to ~ into a rage** incavolarsi
get off vi (from train etc) scendere; (depart: person, car) andare via; (escape) cavarsela ♦ vt (remove: clothes, stain) levare ♦ vt fus (train, bus) scendere da
get on vi (at exam etc) andare; (agree): **to ~ on (with)** andare d'accordo (con) ♦ vt fus montare in; (horse) montare su
get out vi uscire; (of vehicle) scendere ♦ vt tirar fuori, far uscire
get out of vt fus uscire da; (duty etc) evitare
get over vt fus (illness) riaversi da
get round vt fus aggirare; (fig: person) rigirare
get through vi (TEL) avere la linea
get through to vt fus (TEL) parlare a
get together vi riunirsi ♦ vt raccogliere; (people) adunare
get up vi (rise) alzarsi ♦ vt fus salire su per
get up to vt fus (reach) raggiungere; (prank etc) fare

getaway ['gɛtəweɪ] n fuga
geyser ['giːzə*] n (BRIT) scaldabagno; (GEO) geyser m inv
Ghana ['gɑːnə] n Ghana m
ghastly ['gɑːstlɪ] adj orribile, orrendo(a); (pale) spettrale
gherkin ['gəːkɪn] n cetriolino
ghetto blaster ['gɛtəublɑːstə*] n maxistereo m inv portatile
ghost [gəʊst] n fantasma m, spettro

giant ['dʒaɪənt] *n* gigante *m* ♦ *adj* gigantesco(a), enorme

gibberish ['dʒɪbərɪʃ] *n* parole *fpl* senza senso

gibe [dʒaɪb] *n* = **jibe**

giblets ['dʒɪblɪts] *npl* frattaglie *fpl*

Gibraltar [dʒɪ'brɔːltə*] *n* Gibilterra

giddy ['gɪdɪ] *adj* (*dizzy*): **to be ~** aver le vertigini

gift [gɪft] *n* regalo; (*donation, ability*) dono; **~ed** *adj* dotato(a); **~ token** *n* buono *m* in omaggio *inv*; **~ voucher** *n* = **~ token**

gigantic [dʒaɪ'gæntɪk] *adj* gigantesco(a)

giggle ['gɪgl] *vi* ridere scioccamente

gill [dʒɪl] *n* (*measure*) = 0.25 pints (*BRIT* = 0.148*l*, *US* = 0.118*l*)

gills [gɪlz] *npl* (*of fish*) branchie *fpl*

gilt [gɪlt] *n* doratura ♦ *adj* dorato(a); **~-edged** *adj* (*COMM*) della massima sicurezza

gimmick ['gɪmɪk] *n* trucco

gin [dʒɪn] *n* (*liquor*) gin *m inv*

ginger ['dʒɪndʒə*] *n* zenzero; **~ ale**, **~ beer** *n* bibita gassosa allo zenzero; **~bread** *n* pan *m* di zenzero

gingerly ['dʒɪndʒəlɪ] *adv* cautamente

gipsy ['dʒɪpsɪ] *n* zingaro(a)

giraffe [dʒɪ'rɑːf] *n* giraffa

girder ['gɜːdə*] *n* trave *f*

girl [gɜːl] *n* ragazza; (*young unmarried woman*) signorina; (*daughter*) figlia, figliola; **~friend** *n* (*of girl*) amica; (*of boy*) ragazza; **~ish** *adj* da ragazza

giro ['dʒaɪrəu] *n* (*bank ~*) versamento bancario; (*post office ~*) postagiro; (*BRIT: welfare cheque*) assegno del sussidio di assistenza sociale

gist [dʒɪst] *n* succo

give [gɪv] (*pt* **gave**, *pp* **given**) *vt* dare ♦ *vi* cedere; **to ~ sb sth**, **~ sth to sb** dare qc a qn; **I'll ~ you £5 for it** te lo pago 5 sterline; **to ~ a cry/sigh** emettere un grido/sospiro; **to ~ a speech** fare un discorso; **~ away** *vt* dare via; (*disclose*) rivelare; (*bride*) condurre all'altare; **~ back** *vt* rendere; **~ in** *vi* cedere ♦ *vt* consegnare; **~ off** *vt* emettere; **~ out** *vt* distribuire;

~ up *vi* rinunciare ♦ *vt* rinunciare a; **to ~ up smoking** smettere di fumare; **to ~ o.s. up** arrendersi; **~ way** *vi* cedere; (*BRIT: AUT*) dare la precedenza

glacier ['glæsɪə*] *n* ghiacciaio

glad [glæd] *adj* lieto(a), contento(a)

gladly ['glædlɪ] *adv* volentieri

glamorous ['glæmərəs] *adj* affascinante, seducente

glamour ['glæmə*] *n* fascino

glance [glɑːns] *n* occhiata, sguardo ♦ *vi*: **to ~ at** dare un'occhiata a; **to ~ off** (*bullet*) rimbalzare su; **glancing** *adj* (*blow*) che colpisce di striscio

gland [glænd] *n* ghiandola

glare [glɛə*] *n* (*of anger*) sguardo furioso; (*of light*) riverbero, luce *f* abbagliante; (*of publicity*) chiasso ♦ *vi* abbagliare; **to ~ at** guardare male; **glaring** *adj* (*mistake*) madornale

glass [glɑːs] *n* (*substance*) vetro; (*tumbler*) bicchiere *m*; **~es** *npl* (*spectacles*) occhiali *mpl*; **~ware** *n* vetrame *m*; **~y** *adj* (*eyes*) vitreo(a)

glaze [gleɪz] *vt* (*door*) fornire di vetri; (*pottery*) smaltare ♦ *n* smalto; **~d** *adj* (*eyes*) vitreo(a); (*pottery*) smaltato(a)

glazier ['gleɪzɪə*] *n* vetraio

gleam [gliːm] *vi* luccicare

glean [gliːn] *vt* (*information*) racimolare

glee [gliː] *n* allegrezza, gioia

glen [glɛn] *n* valletta

glib [glɪb] *adj* dalla parola facile; facile

glide [glaɪd] *vi* scivolare; (*AVIAT, birds*) planare; **~r** *n* (*AVIAT*) aliante *m*; **gliding** *n* (*AVIAT*) volo a vela

glimmer ['glɪmə*] *n* barlume *m*

glimpse [glɪmps] *n* impressione *f* fugace ♦ *vt* vedere al volo

glint [glɪnt] *vi* luccicare

glisten ['glɪsn] *vi* luccicare

glitter ['glɪtə*] *vi* scintillare

gloat [gləut] *vi*: **to ~ (over)** gongolare di piacere (per)

global ['gləubl] *adj* globale; **~ warming** *n* effetto *m* serra *inv*

globe [gləub] *n* globo, sfera

gloom [glu:m] n oscurità, buio; (sadness) tristezza, malinconia; **~y** adj scuro(a); fosco(a), triste

glorious ['glɔːrɪəs] adj glorioso(a); magnifico(a)

glory ['glɔːrɪ] n gloria; splendore m

gloss [glɒs] n (shine) lucentezza; (paint) vernice f a olio; **~ over** vt fus scivolare su

glossary ['glɒsərɪ] n glossario

glossy ['glɒsɪ] adj lucente

glove [glʌv] n guanto; **~ compartment** n (AUT) vano portaoggetti

glow [gləu] vi ardere; (face) essere luminoso(a)

glower ['glauə*] vi: **to ~ (at sb)** guardare (qn) in cagnesco

glucose ['glu:kəus] n glucosio

glue [glu:] n colla ♦ vt incollare

glum [glʌm] adj abbattuto(a)

glut [glʌt] n eccesso

glutton ['glʌtn] n ghiottone/a; **a ~ for work** un(a) patito(a) del lavoro

GM adj abbr (= genetically modified) geneticamente modificato(a)

gnat [næt] n moscerino

gnaw [nɔː] vt rodere

go [gəu] (pt went, pp gone; pl **~es**) vi andare; (depart) partire, andarsene; (work) funzionare; (time) passare; (break etc) rompersi; (be sold): **to ~ for £10** essere venduto per 10 sterline; (fit, suit): **to ~ with** andare bene a; (become): **to ~ pale** diventare pallido(a); (be about to, intend to): **to be going to do** sta per fare; **to be on the ~** essere in moto; **whose ~ is it?** a chi tocca?; **he's going to do** sta per fare; **to ~ for a walk** andare a fare una passeggiata; **to ~ dancing/shopping** andare a ballare/fare la spesa; **just then the bell went** proprio allora suonò il campanello; **how did it ~?** com'è andato?; **to ~ round the back/by the shop** passare da dietro/davanti al negozio; **~ about** vi (also: **~ round**: rumour) circolare ♦ vt fus: **how do I ~ about this?** qual'è la prassi per questo?; **~ ahead** vi andare avanti; **~ along** vi andare, avanzare ♦ vt

fus percorrere; **to ~ along with** (plan, idea) appoggiare; **~ away** vi partire, andarsene; **~ back** vi tornare, ritornare; **~ back on** vt fus (promise) non mantenere; **~ by** vi (time) scorrere ♦ vt fus attenersi a, seguire (alla lettera); prestar fede a; **~ down** vi scendere; (ship) affondare; (sun) tramontare ♦ vt fus scendere; **~ for** vt fus (fetch) andare a prendere; (like) andar matto/a per; (attack) attaccare; saltare addosso a; **~ in** vi entrare; **~ in for** vt fus (competition) iscriversi a; (be interested in) interessarsi di; **~ into** vt fus entrare in; (investigate) indagare, esaminare; (embark on) lanciarsi in; **~ off** vi partire, andar via; (food) guastarsi; (explode) esplodere, scoppiare; (event) passare ♦ vt fus: **I've gone off chocolate** la cioccolata non mi piace più; **the gun went off** il fucile si scaricò; **~ on** vi continuare; (happen) succedere; **to ~ on doing** continuare a fare; **~ out** vi uscire; (couple): **they went out for 3 years** sono stati insieme per 3 anni; (fire, light) spegnersi; **~ over** vt fus (check) esaminare; **~ through** vt fus (town etc) attraversare; (files, papers) leggere da cima a fondo; (examine: list etc) leggere da cima a fondo; **~ up** vi salire; **~ without** vt fus fare a meno di

goad [gəud] vt spronare

go-ahead adj intraprendente ♦ n via m

goal [gəul] n (SPORT) gol m, rete f; (: place) porta; (fig: aim) fine m, scopo; **~keeper** n portiere m; **~-post** n palo (della porta)

goat [gəut] n capra

gobble ['gɒbl] vt (also: **~ down**, **~ up**) ingoiare

go-between n intermediario/a

god [gɒd] n dio; **G~** n Dio; **~child** n figlioccio/a; **~daughter** n figlioccia; **~dess** n dea; **~father** n padrino; **~-forsaken** adj desolato(a), sperduto(a); **~mother** n madrina; **~send** n dono del cielo; **~son** n figlioccio

goggles ['gɒglz] npl occhiali mpl (di protezione)

going ['gəuɪŋ] n (conditions) andare m, stato del terreno ♦ adj: **the ~ rate** la tariffa in vigore

gold [gəʊld] n oro ♦ adj d'oro; **~en** adj (made of ~) d'oro; (~ in colour) dorato(a); **~fish** n pesce m dorato or rosso; **~mine** n (also fig) miniera d'oro; **~-plated** adj placcato(a) oro inv; **~smith** n orefice m, orafo

golf [gɔlf] n golf m; **~ ball** n (for game) pallina da golf; (on typewriter) pallina; **~ club** n circolo di golf; (stick) bastone m or mazza da golf; **~ course** n campo di golf; **~er** n giocatore/trice di golf

gondola ['gɔndələ] n gondola

gone [gɔn] pp of **go** ♦ adj partito(a)

gong [gɔŋ] n gong m inv

good [gʊd] adj buono(a); (kind) buono(a), gentile; (child) bravo(a) ♦ n bene m; **~s** npl (COMM etc) beni mpl; merci fpl; **~! bene!**, ottimo!; **to be ~ at** essere bravo(a) in; **to be ~ for** andare bene per; **it's ~ for you** fa bene; **would you be ~ enough to ...?** avrebbe la gentilezza di ...?; **a ~ deal (of)** molto(a), una buona quantità (di); **a ~ many** molti(e); **to make ~** (loss, damage) compensare; **it's no ~ complaining** brontolare non serve a niente; **for ~** per sempre, definitivamente; **~ morning!** buon giorno!; **~ afternoon/evening!** buona sera!; **~ night!** buona notte!; **~bye** excl arrivederci!; **G~ Friday** n Venerdì Santo; **~-looking** adj bello(a); **~-natured** adj affabile; **~ness** n (of person) bontà; **for ~ness sake!** per amor di Dio!; **~ness gracious!** santo cielo!, mamma mia!; **~s train** (BRIT) n treno m merci inv; **~will** n amicizia, benevolenza

goose [gu:s] (pl **geese**) n oca

gooseberry ['gʊzbərɪ] n uva spina; **to play ~** (BRIT) tenere la candela

gooseflesh ['gu:sfleʃ] n pelle f d'oca

goose pimples npl pelle f d'oca

gore [gɔː*] vt incornare ♦ n sangue m (coagulato)

gorge [gɔːdʒ] n gola ♦ vt: **to ~ o.s. (on)** ingozzarsi (di)

gorgeous ['gɔːdʒəs] adj magnifico(a)

gorilla [gə'rɪlə] n gorilla m inv

gorse [gɔːs] n ginestrone m

gory ['gɔːrɪ] adj sanguinoso(a)

go-slow (BRIT) n rallentamento dei lavori (per agitazione sindacale)

gospel ['gɔspl] n vangelo

gossip ['gɔsɪp] n chiacchiere fpl; pettegolezzi mpl; (person) pettegolo/a ♦ vi chiacchierare

got [gɔt] pt, pp of **get**; **~ten** (US) pp of **get**

gout [gaʊt] n gotta

govern ['gʌvən] vt governare

governess ['gʌvənɪs] n governante f

government ['gʌvnmənt] n governo

governor ['gʌvənə*] n (of state, bank) governatore m; (of school, hospital) amministratore m; (BRIT: of prison) direttore/trice

gown [gaʊn] n vestito lungo; (of teacher, BRIT: of judge) toga

G.P. n abbr = **general practitioner**

grab [græb] vt afferrare, arraffare; (property, power) impadronirsi di ♦ vi: **to ~ at** cercare di afferrare

grace [greɪs] n grazia ♦ vt onorare; **5 days' ~** dilazione f di 5 giorni; **~ful** adj elegante, aggraziato(a); **~ious** ['greɪʃəs] adj grazioso(a); misericordioso(a)

grade [greɪd] n (COMM) qualità f inv; classe f; categoria; (in hierarchy) grado; (SCOL: mark) voto; (US: school class) classe ♦ vt classificare; ordinare; graduare; **~ crossing** (US) n passaggio a livello; **~ school** (US) n scuola elementare

gradient ['greɪdɪənt] n pendenza, inclinazione f

gradual ['grædjʊəl] adj graduale; **~ly** adv man mano, a poco a poco

graduate [n 'grædjʊɪt, vb 'grædjʊeɪt] n (of university) laureato/a; (US: of high school) diplomato/a ♦ vi laurearsi; diplomarsi; **graduation** [-'eɪʃən] n (ceremony) consegna delle lauree (or dei diplomi)

graffiti [grə'fi:tɪ] npl graffiti mpl

graft [grɑːft] n (AGR, MED) innesto; (bribery) corruzione f; (BRIT: hard work): **it's hard ~** è un lavoraccio ♦ vt innestare

grain [greɪn] n grano; (of sand) granello; (of

wood) venatura

gram [græm] n grammo

grammar ['græmə*] n grammatica; ~ **school** (BRIT) n ≈ liceo

grammatical [grə'mætɪkl] adj grammaticale

gramme [græm] n = **gram**

grand [grænd] adj grande, magnifico(a); grandioso(a); ~**children** npl nipoti mpl; ~**dad** (inf) n nonno; ~**daughter** n nipote f; ~**eur** ['grændjə*] n grandiosità; ~**father** n nonno; ~**ma** (inf) n nonna; ~**mother** n nonna; ~**pa** (inf) n = ~**dad**; ~**parents** npl nonni mpl; ~ **piano** n pianoforte m a coda; ~**son** n nipote m; ~**stand** n (SPORT) tribuna

granite ['grænɪt] n granito

granny ['grænɪ] (inf) n nonna

grant [grɑːnt] vt accordare; (a request) accogliere; (admit) ammettere, concedere ♦ n (SCOL) borsa; (ADMIN) sussidio, sovvenzione f; **to take sth for** ~**ed** dare qc per scontato; **to take sb for** ~**ed** dare per scontata la presenza di qn

granulated ['grænjuleɪtɪd] adj: ~ **sugar** zucchero cristallizzato

granule ['grænjuːl] n granello

grape [greɪp] n chicco d'uva, acino

grapefruit ['greɪpfruːt] n pompelmo

graph [grɑːf] n grafico; ~**ic** adj grafico(a); (vivid) vivido(a); ~**ics** n grafica ♦ npl illustrazioni fpl

grapple ['græpl] vi: **to** ~ **with** essere alle prese con

grasp [grɑːsp] vt afferrare ♦ n (grip) presa; (fig) potere m; comprensione f; ~**ing** adj avido(a)

grass [grɑːs] n erba; ~**hopper** n cavalletta; ~**-roots** adj di base

grate [greɪt] n graticola (del focolare) ♦ vi cigolare, stridere ♦ vt (CULIN) grattugiare

grateful ['greɪtful] adj grato(a), riconoscente

grater ['greɪtə*] n grattugia

grating ['greɪtɪŋ] n (iron bars) grata ♦ adj (noise) stridente, stridulo(a)

gratitude ['grætɪtjuːd] n gratitudine f

gratuity [grə'tjuːɪtɪ] n mancia

grave [greɪv] n tomba ♦ adj grave, serio(a)

gravel ['grævl] n ghiaia

gravestone ['greɪvstəun] n pietra tombale

graveyard ['greɪvjɑːd] n cimitero

gravity ['grævɪtɪ] n (PHYSICS) gravità; pesantezza; (seriousness) gravità, serietà

gravy ['greɪvɪ] n intingolo della carne; salsa

gray [greɪ] adj = **grey**

graze [greɪz] vi pascolare, pascere ♦ vt (touch lightly) sfiorare; (scrape) escoriare ♦ n (MED) escoriazione f

grease [griːs] n (fat) grasso; (lubricant) lubrificante m ♦ vt ingrassare; lubrificare; ~**proof paper** (BRIT) n carta oleata; **greasy** adj grasso(a), untuoso(a)

great [greɪt] adj grande; (inf) magnifico(a), meraviglioso(a); **G~ Britain** n Gran Bretagna; ~**-grandfather** n bisnonno; ~-**grandmother** n bisnonna; ~**ly** adv molto; ~**ness** n grandezza

Greece [griːs] n Grecia

greed [griːd] n (also: ~**iness**) avarizia; (for food) golosità, ghiottoneria; ~**y** adj avido(a); goloso(a), ghiotto(a)

Greek [griːk] adj greco(a) ♦ n greco/a; (LING) greco

green [griːn] adj verde; (inexperienced) inesperto(a), ingenuo(a) ♦ n verde m; (stretch of grass) prato; (on golf course) green m inv; ~**s** npl (vegetables) verdura; ~ **belt** n (round town) cintura di verde; ~ **card** n (BRIT: AUT) carta verde; (US: ADMIN) permesso di soggiorno e di lavoro; ~**ery** n verde m; ~**grocer** (BRIT) n fruttivendolo/a, erbivendolo/a; ~**house** n serra; ~**house effect** n effetto serra; ~**house gas** n gas responsabile dell'effetto serra; ~**ish** adj verdastro(a)

Greenland ['griːnlənd] n Groenlandia

greet [griːt] vt salutare; ~**ing** n saluto; ~**ing(s) card** n cartolina d'auguri

gregarious [grə'geəriəs] adj (person) socievole

grenade [grə'neɪd] n (also: **hand ~**) granata

grew [gruː] pt of **grow**

grey [greɪ] adj grigio(a); ~**haired** adj dai

capelli grigi; **~hound** *n* levriere *m*

grid [grɪd] *n* grata; (ELEC) rete *f*

gridlock ['grɪdlɒk] *n* (*traffic jam*) paralisi *f inv* del traffico; **~ed** *adj* paralizzato(a) dal traffico; (*talks etc*) in fase di stallo

grief [griːf] *n* dolore *m*

grievance ['griːvəns] *n* lagnanza

grieve [griːv] *vi* addolorarsi; rattristarsi ♦ *vt* addolorare; **to ~ for sb** (*dead person*) piangere qn

grievous ['griːvəs] *adj*: **~ bodily harm** (LAW) aggressione *f*

grill [grɪl] *n* (*on cooker*) griglia; (*also*: **mixed ~**) grigliata mista ♦ *vt* (BRIT) cuocere ai ferri; (*inf*: *question*) interrogare senza sosta

grille [grɪl] *n* grata; (AUT) griglia

grim [grɪm] *adj* sinistro(a), brutto(a)

grimace [grɪ'meɪs] *n* smorfia ♦ *vi* fare smorfie; fare boccacce

grime [graɪm] *n* sudiciume *m*

grin [grɪn] *n* sorriso smagliante ♦ *vi* fare un gran sorriso

grind [graɪnd] (*pt, pp* **ground**) *vt* macinare; (*make sharp*) arrotare ♦ *n* (*work*) sgobbata

grip [grɪp] *n* impugnatura; presa; (*holdall*) borsa da viaggio ♦ *vt* (*object*) afferrare; (*attention*) catturare; **to come to ~s with** affrontare; cercare di risolvere

gripping ['grɪpɪŋ] *adj* avvincente

grisly ['grɪzlɪ] *adj* macabro(a), orrido(a)

gristle ['grɪsl] *n* cartilagine *f*

grit [grɪt] *n* ghiaia; (*courage*) fegato ♦ *vt* (*road*) coprire di sabbia; **to ~ one's teeth** stringere i denti

groan [grəun] *n* gemito ♦ *vi* gemere

grocer ['grəusə*] *n* negoziante *m* di generi alimentari; **~ies** *npl* provviste *fpl*; **~'s (shop)** *n* negozio di (generi) alimentari

groggy ['grɒgɪ] *adj* barcollante

groin [grɔɪn] *n* inguine *m*

groom [gruːm] *n* palafreniere *m*; (*also*: **bride~**) sposo ♦ *vt* (*horse*) strigliare; (*fig*): **to ~ sb for** avviare qn a; **well-~ed** (*person*) curato(a)

groove [gruːv] *n* scanalatura, solco

grope [grəup] *vi*: **to ~ for** cercare a tastoni

gross [grəus] *adj* grossolano(a); (COMM)

lordo(a); **~ly** *adv* (*greatly*) molto

grotesque [grəu'tɛsk] *adj* grottesco(a)

grotto ['grɒtəu] *n* grotta

grotty ['grɒtɪ] (*inf*) *adj* terribile

ground [graund] *pt, pp* of **grind** ♦ *n* suolo, terra; (*land*) terreno; (SPORT) campo; (*reason*: *gen pl*) ragione *f*; (US: *also*: **~ wire**) terra ♦ *vt* (*plane*) tenere a terra; (US: ELEC) mettere la presa di terra a; **~s** *npl* (*of coffee etc*) fondi *mpl*; (*gardens etc*) terreno, giardini *mpl*; **on/to the ~** per/a terra; **to gain/lose ~** guadagnare/perdere terreno; **~ cloth** (US) *n* = **~sheet**; **~ing** *n* (*in education*) basi *fpl*; **~less** *adj* infondato(a); **~sheet** (BRIT) *n* telone *m* impermeabile; **~ staff** *n* personale *m* di terra; **~work** *n* preparazione *f*

group [gruːp] *n* gruppo ♦ *vt* (*also*: **~ together**) raggruppare ♦ *vi* (*also*: **~ together**) raggrupparsi

grouse [graus] *n inv* (*bird*) tetraone *m* ♦ *vi* (*complain*) brontolare

grove [grəuv] *n* boschetto

grovel ['grɒvl] *vi* (*fig*): **to ~ (before)** strisciare (di fronte a)

grow [grəu] (*pt* **grew**, *pp* **grown**) *vi* crescere; (*increase*) aumentare; (*develop*) svilupparsi; (*become*): **to ~ rich/weak** arricchirsi/indebolirsi ♦ *vt* coltivare, far crescere; **~ up** *vi* farsi grande, crescere; **~er** *n* coltivatore/trice; **~ing** *adj* (*fear, amount*) crescente

growl [graul] *vi* ringhiare

grown [grəun] *pp* of **grow**; **~-up** *n* adulto/a, grande *m/f*

growth [grəuθ] *n* crescita, sviluppo; (*what has grown*) crescita; (MED) escrescenza, tumore *m*

grub [grʌb] *n* larva; (*inf*: *food*) roba (da mangiare)

grubby ['grʌbɪ] *adj* sporco(a)

grudge [grʌdʒ] *n* rancore *m* ♦ *vt*: **to ~ sb sth** dare qc a qn di malavoglia; invidiare qc a qn; **to bear sb a ~ (for)** serbar rancore a qn (per)

gruelling ['gruəlɪŋ] (US **grueling**) *adj* estenuante

gruesome ['gru:səm] *adj* orribile

gruff [grʌf] *adj* rozzo(a)

grumble ['grʌmbl] *vi* brontolare, lagnarsi

grumpy ['grʌmpɪ] *adj* scorbutico(a)

grunt [grʌnt] *vi* grugnire

G-string *n* tanga *m inv*

guarantee [gærən'ti:] *n* garanzia ♦ *vt* garantire

guard [gɑ:d] *n* guardia; (*one man*) guardia, sentinella; (*BRIT: RAIL*) capotreno; (*on machine*) schermo protettivo; (*also:* **fire~**) parafuoco ♦ *vt* fare la guardia a; (*protect*): **to ~ (against)** proteggere (da); **to be on one's ~** stare in guardia; **~ against** *vt fus* guardarsi da; **~ed** *adj* (*fig*) cauto(a), guardingo(a); **~ian** *n* custode *m*; (*of minor*) tutore/trice; **~'s van** (*BRIT*) *n* (*RAIL*) vagone *m* di servizio

guerrilla [gə'rɪlə] *n* guerrigliero

guess [ges] *vi* indovinare ♦ *vt* indovinare; (*US*) credere, pensare ♦ *n*: **to make** or **have a ~** provare a indovinare; **~work** *n*: **I got the answer by ~work** ho azzeccato la risposta

guest [gest] *n* ospite *m/f*; (*in hotel*) cliente *m/f*; **~-house** *n* pensione *f*; **~ room** *n* camera degli ospiti

guffaw [gʌ'fɔ:] *vi* scoppiare in una risata sonora

guidance ['gaɪdəns] *n* guida, direzione *f*

guide [gaɪd] *n* (*person, book etc*) guida; (*BRIT: also:* **girl ~**) giovane esploratrice *f* ♦ *vt* guidare; **~book** *n* guida; **~ dog** *n* cane *m* guida *inv*; **~lines** *npl* (*fig*) indicazioni *fpl*, linee *fpl* direttive

guild [gɪld] *n* arte *f*, corporazione *f*; associazione *f*

guillotine ['gɪləti:n] *n* ghigliottina; (*for paper*) taglierina

guilt [gɪlt] *n* colpevolezza; **~y** *adj* colpevole

guinea pig ['gɪnɪ-] *n* cavia

guise [gaɪz] *n* maschera

guitar [gɪ'tɑ:*] *n* chitarra

gulf [gʌlf] *n* golfo; (*abyss*) abisso

gull [gʌl] *n* gabbiano

gullible ['gʌlɪbl] *adj* credulo(a)

gully ['gʌlɪ] *n* burrone *m*; gola; canale *m*

gulp [gʌlp] *vi* deglutire; (*from emotion*) avere il nodo in gola ♦ *vt* (*also:* **~ down**) tracannare, inghiottire

gum [gʌm] *n* (*ANAT*) gengiva; (*glue*) colla; (*also:* **~drop**) caramella gommosa; (*also:* **chewing ~**) chewing-gum *m* ♦ *vt*: **to ~ (together)** incollare; **~boots** (*BRIT*) *npl* stivali *mpl* di gomma

gumption ['gʌmpʃən] *n* spirito d'iniziativa, buonsenso

gun [gʌn] *n* fucile *m*; (*small*) pistola, rivoltella; (*rifle*) carabina; (*shotgun*) fucile da caccia; (*cannon*) cannone *m*; **~boat** *n* cannoniera; **~fire** *n* spari *mpl*; **~man** *n* bandito armato; **~point** *n*: **at ~point** sotto minaccia di fucile; **~powder** *n* polvere *f* da sparo; **~shot** *n* sparo

gurgle ['gə:gl] *vi* gorgogliare

gush [gʌʃ] *vi* sgorgare; (*fig*) abbandonarsi ad effusioni

gusset ['gʌsɪt] *n* gherone *m*

gust [gʌst] *n* (*of wind*) raffica; (*of smoke*) buffata

gusto ['gʌstəu] *n* entusiasmo

gut [gʌt] *n* intestino, budello; **~s** *npl* (*ANAT*) interiora *fpl*; (*courage*) fegato

gutter ['gʌtə*] *n* (*of roof*) grondaia; (*in street*) cunetta

guy [gaɪ] *n* (*inf: man*) tipo, elemento; (*also:* **~rope**) cavo or corda di fissaggio; (*figure*) effigie di Guy Fawkes

---

Guy Fawkes' Night

i Il 5 novembre si festeggia con falò e fuochi d'artificio la **Guy Fawkes' Night**, *la notte in cui, nel 1605, fallì la Congiura delle Polveri contro Giacomo I;* **Guy Fawkes** *era il nome di uno dei cospiratori.*

---

guzzle ['gʌzl] *vt* tranguiare

gym [dʒɪm] *n* (*also:* **gymnasium**) palestra; (*also:* **gymnastics**) ginnastica

gymnast ['dʒɪmnæst] *n* ginnasta *m/f*; **~ics** [-'næstɪks] *n, npl* ginnastica

gym shoes *npl* scarpe *fpl* da ginnastica

gym slip (*BRIT*) *n* grembiule *m* da scuola

(*per ragazze*)
gynaecologist [gaɪnɪ'kɔlədʒɪst] (*US*
gynecologist) *n* ginecologo/a
gypsy ['dʒɪpsɪ] *n* = **gipsy**
gyrate [dʒaɪ'reɪt] *vi* girare

H, h

haberdashery ['hæbə'dæʃərɪ] (*BRIT*) *n*
merceria
habit ['hæbɪt] *n* abitudine *f*; (*costume*) abito;
(*REL*) tonaca
habitual [hə'bɪtjuəl] *adj* abituale; (*drinker,
liar*) inveterato(a)
hack [hæk] *vt* tagliare, fare a pezzi ♦ *n* (*pej:
writer*) scribacchino/a
hacker ['hækə*] *n* (*COMPUT*) pirata *m*
informatico
hackney cab ['hæknɪ-] *n* carrozza a nolo
hackneyed ['hæknɪd] *adj* comune, trito(a)
had [hæd] *pt, pp of* **have**
haddock ['hædək] (*pl ~ or ~s*) *n* eglefino
hadn't ['hædnt] = **had not**
haemorrhage ['hemərɪdʒ] (*US*
hemorrhage) *n* emorragia
haemorrhoids ['hemərɔɪdz] (*US
hemorrhoids*) *npl* emorroidi *fpl*
haggard ['hægəd] *adj* smunto(a)
haggle ['hægl] *vi* mercanteggiare
Hague [heɪg] *n*: **The ~** L'Aia
hail [heɪl] *n* grandine *f*; (*of criticism etc*)
pioggia ♦ *vt* (*call*) chiamare; (*flag down:
taxi*) fermare; (*greet*) salutare ♦ *vi*
grandinare; **~stone** *n* chicco di grandine
hair [heə*] *n* capelli *mpl*; (*single hair: on
head*) capello; (*: on body*) pelo; **to do
one's ~** pettinarsi; **~brush** *n* spazzola per
capelli; **~cut** *n* taglio di capelli; **~do**
['heədu:] *n* acconciatura, pettinatura;
~dresser *n* parrucchiere/a; **~-dryer** *n*
asciugacapelli *m inv*; **~ grip** *n* forcina;
~net *n* retina per capelli; **~pin** *n* forcina;
~pin bend (*US* **~pin curve**) *n* tornante *m*;
~raising *adj* orripilante; **~ removing
cream** *n* crema depilatoria; **~ spray** *n*
lacca per capelli; **~style** *n* pettinatura,

acconciatura; **~y** *adj* irsuto(a); peloso(a);
(*inf: frightening*) spaventoso(a)
hake [heɪk] (*pl ~ or ~s*) *n* nasello
half [hɑ:f] (*pl* **halves**) *n* mezzo, metà *f inv*
♦ *adj* mezzo(a) ♦ *adv* a mezzo, a metà; **~
an hour** mezz'ora; **~ a dozen** mezza
dozzina; **~ a pound** mezza libbra; **two and
a ~** due e mezzo; **a week and a ~** una
settimana e mezza; **~ (of it)** la metà; **~ (of)**
la metà di; **to cut sth in ~** tagliare qc in
due; **~ asleep** mezzo(a) addormentato(a);
~-baked *adj* (*scheme*) che non sta in
piedi; **~ board** (*BRIT*) *n* mezza pensione;
~-caste ['hɑ:kɑ:st] *n* meticcio/a; **~ fare** *n*
tariffa a metà prezzo; **~-hearted** *adj*
tiepido(a); **~-hour** *n* mezz'ora; **~-mast**:
at ~-mast *adv* (*flag*) a mezz'asta; **~penny**
['heɪpnɪ] (*BRIT*) *n* mezzo penny *m inv*; **~-
price** *adj, adv* a metà prezzo; **~ term**
(*BRIT*) *n* (*SCOL*) vacanza a *or* di metà
trimestre; **~-time** *n* (*SPORT*) intervallo;
~way *adv* a metà strada
halibut ['hælɪbət] *n inv* ippoglosso
hall [hɔ:l] *n* sala, salone *m*; (*entrance way*)
entrata; **~ of residence** (*BRIT*) *n* casa
dello studente
hallmark ['hɔ:lmɑ:k] *n* marchio di garanzia;
(*fig*) caratteristica
hallo [hə'ləu] *excl* = **hello**
Hallowe'en [hæləu'i:n] *n* vigilia
d'Ognissanti

Hallowe'en
---

i *Negli Stati Uniti e in Scozia il 31 ottobre
si festeggia* **Hallowe'en**, *la notte delle
streghe e dei fantasmi; i bambini, travestiti
da fantasmi e con lanterne ricavate da
zucche, bussano alle porte e raccolgono dolci
e piccoli doni.*

---

hallucination [həlu:sɪ'neɪʃən] *n*
allucinazione *f*
hallway ['hɔ:lweɪ] *n* corridoio; (*entrance*)
ingresso
halo ['heɪləu] *n* (*of saint etc*) aureola
halt [hɔ:lt] *n* fermata ♦ *vt* fermare ♦ *vi*
fermarsi

halve [hɑːv] vt (apple etc) dividere a metà; (expense) ridurre di metà

halves [hɑːvz] npl of half

ham [hæm] n prosciutto

Hamburg ['hæmbəːg] n Amburgo f

hamburger ['hæmbəːgə*] n hamburger m inv

hamlet ['hæmlɪt] n paesetto

hammer ['hæmə*] n martello ♦ vt martellare ♦ vi: **to ~ on** or **at the door** picchiare alla porta

hammock ['hæmək] n amaca

hamper ['hæmpə*] vt impedire ♦ n cesta

hamster ['hæmstə*] n criceto

hand [hænd] n mano f; (of clock) lancetta; (handwriting) scrittura; (at cards) mano; (: game) partita; (worker) operaio/a ♦ vt dare, passare; **to give sb a ~** dare una mano a qn; **at ~** a portata di mano; **in ~** a disposizione; (work) in corso; **on ~** (person) disponibile; (services) pronto(a) a intervenire; **to ~** (information etc) a portata di mano; **on the one ~ ..., on the other ~** da un lato ..., dall'altro; **~ in** vt consegnare; **~ out** vt distribuire; **~ over** vt passare; cedere; **~bag** n borsetta; **~book** n manuale m; **~brake** n freno a mano; **~cuffs** npl manette fpl; **~ful** n manciata, pugno

handicap ['hændɪkæp] n handicap m inv ♦ vt handicappare; **to be physically ~ped** essere handicappato(a); **to be mentally ~ped** essere un(a) handicappato(a) mentale

handicraft ['hændɪkrɑːft] n lavoro d'artigiano

handiwork ['hændɪwəːk] n opera

handkerchief ['hæŋkətʃɪf] n fazzoletto

handle ['hændl] n (of door etc) maniglia; (of cup etc) ansa; (of knife etc) impugnatura; (of saucepan) manico; (for winding) manovella ♦ vt toccare, maneggiare; (deal with) occuparsi di; (treat: people) trattare; **"~ with care"** "fragile"; **to fly off the ~** (fig) perdere le staffe, uscire dai gangheri; **~bar(s)** n(pl) manubrio

hand: **~ luggage** n bagagli mpl a mano;

~made adj fatto(a) a mano; **~out** n (money, food) elemosina; (leaflet) volantino; (at lecture) prospetto; **~rail** n corrimano; **~set** n (TEL) ricevitore m; **please replace the ~set** riagganciare il ricevitore; **~shake** n stretta di mano

handsome ['hænsəm] adj bello(a); (profit, fortune) considerevole

handwriting ['hændraɪtɪŋ] n scrittura

handy ['hændɪ] adj (person) bravo(a); (close at hand) a portata di mano; (convenient) comodo(a)

hang [hæŋ] (pt, pp hung) vt appendere; (criminal: pt, pp hanged) impiccare ♦ vi (painting) essere appeso(a); (hair) scendere; (drapery) cadere; **to get the ~ of sth** (inf) capire come qc funziona; **~ about** or **around** vi bighellonare, ciondolare; **~ on** vi (wait) aspettare; **~ up** vi (TEL) riattaccare ♦ vt appendere

hangar ['hæŋə*] n hangar m inv

hanger ['hæŋə*] n gruccia

hanger-on n parassita m

hang-gliding ['-glaɪdɪŋ] n volo col deltaplano

hangover ['hæŋəuvə*] n (after drinking) postumi mpl di sbornia

hang-up n complesso

hanker ['hæŋkə*] vi: **to ~ after** bramare

hankie ['hæŋkɪ] n abbr = **handkerchief**

hanky ['hæŋkɪ] n abbr = **handkerchief**

haphazard [hæp'hæzəd] adj a casaccio, alla carlona

happen ['hæpən] vi accadere, succedere; (chance): **to ~ to do sth** fare qc per caso; **as it ~s** guarda caso; **~ing** n avvenimento

happily ['hæpɪlɪ] adv felicemente; fortunatamente

happiness ['hæpɪnɪs] n felicità, contentezza

happy ['hæpɪ] adj felice, contento(a); **~ with** (arrangements etc) soddisfatto di; **to be ~ to do** (willing) fare volentieri; **~ birthday!** buon compleanno!; **~-go-lucky** adj spensierato(a); **~ hour** n orario in cui i bar hanno prezzi ridotti

harangue [hə'ræŋ] vt arringare

harass ['hærəs] vt molestare; **~ment** n

molestia

harbour ['hɑːbə*] (*US* **harbor**) *n* porto ♦ *vt* (*hope, fear*) nutrire; (*criminal*) dare rifugio a

hard [hɑːd] *adj* duro(a) ♦ *adv* (*work*) sodo; (*think, try*) bene; **to look ~ at** guardare fissamente; esaminare attentamente; **no ~ feelings!** senza rancore!; **to be ~ of hearing** essere duro(a) d'orecchio; **to be ~ done by** essere trattato(a) ingiustamente; **~back** *n* libro rilegato; **~ cash** *n* denaro in contanti; **~ disk** *n* (*COMPUT*) disco rigido; **~en** *vt, vi* indurire; **~-headed** *adj* pratico(a); **~ labour** *n* lavori forzati *mpl*

hardly ['hɑːdlɪ] *adv* (*scarcely*) appena; **it's ~ the case** non è proprio il caso; **~ anyone/anywhere** quasi nessuno/da nessuna parte; **~ ever** quasi mai

hardship ['hɑːdʃɪp] *n* avversità *f inv*; privazioni *fpl*

hard shoulder (*BRIT*) *n* (*AUT*) corsia d'emergenza

hard-up (*inf*) *adj* al verde

hardware ['hɑːdwɛə*] *n* ferramenta *fpl*; (*COMPUT*) hardware *m*; (*MIL*) armamenti *mpl*; **~ shop** *n* (negozio di) ferramenta *fpl*

hard-wearing [-'wɛərɪŋ] *adj* resistente; (*shoes*) robusto(a)

hard-working [-'wəːkɪŋ] *adj* lavoratore(trice)

hardy ['hɑːdɪ] *adj* robusto(a); (*plant*) resistente al gelo

hare [hɛə*] *n* lepre *f*; **~-brained** *adj* folle; scervellato(a)

harm [hɑːm] *n* male *m*; (*wrong*) danno ♦ *vt* (*person*) fare male a; (*thing*) danneggiare; **out of ~'s way** al sicuro; **~ful** *adj* dannoso(a); **~less** *adj* innocuo(a); inoffensivo(a)

harmonica [hɑː'mɔnɪkə] *n* armonica *f*

harmonious [hɑː'məʊnɪəs] *adj* armonioso(a)

harmony ['hɑːmənɪ] *n* armonia

harness ['hɑːnɪs] *n* (*for horse*) bardatura, finimenti *mpl*; (*for child*) briglie *fpl*; (*safety ~*) imbracatura ♦ *vt* (*horse*) bardare; (*resources*) sfruttare

harp [hɑːp] *n* arpa ♦ *vi*: **to ~ on about** insistere tediosamente su

harpoon [hɑː'puːn] *n* arpione *m*

harrowing ['hærəʊɪŋ] *adj* straziante

harsh [hɑːʃ] *adj* (*life, winter*) duro(a); (*judge, criticism*) severo(a); (*sound*) rauco(a); (*light*) violento(a)

harvest ['hɑːvɪst] *n* raccolto; (*of grapes*) vendemmia ♦ *vt* fare il raccolto di, raccogliere; vendemmiare

has [hæz] *vb see* **have**

hash [hæʃ] *n* (*CULIN*) specie di spezzatino fatto con carne già cotta; (*fig: mess*) pasticcio

hasn't ['hæznt] = **has not**

hassle ['hæsl] (*inf*) *n* sacco di problemi

haste [heɪst] *n* fretta; precipitazione *f*; **~n** ['heɪsn] *vt* affrettare ♦ *vi*: **to ~n (to)** affrettarsi (a); **hastily** *adv* in fretta, precipitosamente; **hasty** *adj* affrettato(a); precipitoso(a)

hat [hæt] *n* cappello

hatch [hætʃ] *n* (*NAUT: also:* **~way**) boccaporto; (*also:* **service ~**) portello di servizio ♦ *vi* (*bird*) uscire dal guscio; (*egg*) schiudersi

hatchback ['hætʃbæk] *n* (*AUT*) tre (*or* cinque) porte *f inv*

hatchet ['hætʃɪt] *n* accetta

hate [heɪt] *vt* odiare, detestare ♦ *n* odio; **~ful** *adj* odioso(a), detestabile

hatred ['heɪtrɪd] *n* odio

haughty ['hɔːtɪ] *adj* altero(a), arrogante

haul [hɔːl] *vt* trascinare, tirare ♦ *n* (*of fish*) pescata; (*of stolen goods etc*) bottino; **~age** *n* trasporto; autotrasporto; **~ier** (*US* **~er**) *n* trasportatore *m*

haunch [hɔːntʃ] *n* anca; (*of meat*) coscia

haunt [hɔːnt] *vt* (*subj: fear*) pervadere; (*: person*) frequentare ♦ *n* rifugio; **this house is ~ed** questa casa è abitata da un fantasma

─────────────
│ KEYWORD │
─────────────

have [hæv] (*pt, pp* **had**) *aux vb* **1** (*gen*) avere; essere; **to ~ arrived/gone** essere arrivato(a)/andato(a); **to ~ eaten/slept** avere mangiato/dormito; **he has been**

kind/promoted è stato gentile/promosso; **having finished** or **when he had finished, he left** dopo aver finito, se n'è andato 2 (in tag questions): **you've done it, ~n't you?** l'ha fatto, (non è) vero?; **he hasn't done it, has he?** non l'ha fatto, vero? 3 (in short answers and questions): **you've made a mistake – no I ~n't/so I ~** ha fatto un errore — ma no, niente affatto/sì, è vero; **we ~n't paid – yes we ~!** non abbiamo pagato — ma sì che abbiamo pagato!; **I've been there before, ~ you?** ci sono già stato, e lei?
♦ modal aux vb (be obliged): **to ~ (got) to do sth** dover fare qc; **I ~n't got** or **I don't ~ to wear glasses** non ho bisogno di portare gli occhiali
♦ vt 1 (possess, obtain) avere; **he has (got) blue eyes/dark hair** ha gli occhi azzurri/i capelli scuri; **do you ~ or** or **you got a car/ phone?** ha la macchina/il telefono?; **may I ~ your address?** potrebbe darmi il suo indirizzo?; **you can ~ it for £5** te lo lascio per 5 sterline
2 (+noun: take, hold etc): **to ~ breakfast/a swim/a bath** fare colazione/una nuotata/ un bagno; **to ~ lunch** pranzare; **to ~ dinner** cenare; **to ~ a drink** bere qualcosa; **to ~ a cigarette** fumare una sigaretta
3: **to ~ sth done** far fare qc; **to ~ one's hair cut** farsi tagliare i capelli; **to ~ sb do sth** far fare qc a qn
4 (experience, suffer) avere; **to ~ a cold/flu** avere il raffreddore/l'influenza; **she had her bag stolen** le hanno rubato la borsa
5 (inf: dupe): **you've been had!** ci sei cascato!
have out vt: **to ~ it out with sb** (settle a problem etc) mettere le cose in chiaro con qn

haven ['heɪvn] n porto; (fig) rifugio
haven't ['hævnt] = **have not**
havoc ['hævək] n caos m
hawk [hɔːk] n falco
hay [heɪ] n fieno; **~ fever** n febbre f da fieno; **~stack** n pagliaio

haywire ['heɪwaɪə*] (inf) adj: **to go ~** impazzire
hazard ['hæzəd] n azzardo, ventura; pericolo, rischio ♦ vt (guess etc) azzardare; **~ous** adj pericoloso(a); **~ (warning) lights** npl (AUT) luci fpl di emergenza
haze [heɪz] n foschia
hazelnut ['heɪzlnʌt] n nocciola
hazy ['heɪzɪ] adj fosco(a); (idea) vago(a)
he [hiː] pronoun lui, egli; **it is ~ who ...** è lui che ....
head [hɛd] n testa; (leader) capo; (of school) preside m/f ♦ vt (list) essere in testa a; (group) essere a capo di; **~s (or tails)** testa (o croce), pari (o dispari); **~ first** a capofitto, di testa; **~ over heels in love** pazzamente innamorato(a); **to ~ the ball** colpire una palla di testa; **~ for** vt fus dirigersi verso; **~ache** n mal m di testa; **~dress** (BRIT) n (of bride) acconciatura; **~ing** n titolo; intestazione f; **~lamp** (BRIT) n = **~light**; **~land** n promontorio; **~light** n fanale m; **~line** n titolo; **~long** adv (fall) a capofitto; (rush) precipitosamente; **~master/mistress** n preside m/f; **~ office** n sede f (centrale); **~-on** adj (collision) frontale; **~phones** npl cuffia; **~quarters** npl ufficio centrale; (MIL) quartiere m generale; **~rest** n poggiacapo; **~room** n (in car) altezza dell'abitacolo; (under bridge) altezza limite; **~scarf** n foulard m inv; **~strong** adj testardo(a); **~ waiter** n capocameriere m; **~way** n: **to make ~way** fare progressi; **~wind** n controvento; **~y** adj (experience, period) inebriante
heal [hiːl] vt, vi guarire
health [hɛlθ] n salute f; **~ centre** (BRIT) n poliambulatorio; **~ food(s)** n(pl) cibo macrobiotico; **~ food store** n negozio di alimenti dietetici e macrobiotici; **the H~ Service** (BRIT) n ≈ il Servizio Sanitario Statale; **~y** adj (person) sano(a), in buona salute; (climate) salubre; (appetite, economy etc) sano(a)
heap [hiːp] n mucchio ♦ vt (stones, sand): **to ~ (up)** ammucchiare; (plate, sink): **to ~**

sth with riempire qc di; **~s of** (*inf*) un mucchio di

hear [hɪə*] (*pt, pp* **heard**) *vt* sentire; (*news*) ascoltare ♦ *vi* sentire; **to ~ about** avere notizie di; sentire parlare di; **to ~ from sb** ricevere notizie da qn; **~ing** *n* (*sense*) udito; (*of witnesses*) audizione *f*; (*of a case*) udienza; **~ing aid** *n* apparecchio acustico; **~say** *n* dicerie *fpl*, chiacchiere *fpl*

hearse [hɜːs] *n* carro funebre

heart [hɑːt] *n* cuore *m*; **~s** *npl* (*CARDS*) cuori *mpl*; **to lose ~** scoraggiarsi; **to take ~** farsi coraggio; **at ~** in fondo; **by ~** (*learn, know*) a memoria; **~ attack** *n* attacco di cuore; **~beat** *n* battito del cuore; **~breaking** *adj* straziante; **~broken** *adj*: **to be ~broken** avere il cuore spezzato; **~burn** *n* bruciore *m* di stomaco; **~ failure** *n* arresto cardiaco; **~felt** *adj* sincero(a)

hearth [hɑːθ] *n* focolare *m*

heartland ['hɑːtlænd] *n* regione *f* centrale

heartless ['hɑːtlɪs] *adj* senza cuore

hearty ['hɑːtɪ] *adj* caloroso(a); robusto(a), sano(a); vigoroso(a)

heat [hiːt] *n* calore *m*; (*fig*) ardore *m*; fuoco; (*SPORT: also*: **qualifying ~**) prova eliminatoria ♦ *vt* scaldare; **~ up** *vi* (*liquids*) scaldarsi; (*room*) riscaldarsi ♦ *vt* riscaldare; **~ed** *adj* riscaldato(a); (*argument*) acceso(a); **~er** *n* radiatore *m*; (*stove*) stufa

heath [hiːθ] (*BRIT*) *n* landa

heathen ['hiːðən] *n* pagano/a

heather ['hɛðə*] *n* erica

heating ['hiːtɪŋ] *n* riscaldamento

heatstroke ['hiːtstrəuk] *n* colpo di sole

heatwave ['hiːtweɪv] *n* ondata di caldo

heave [hiːv] *vt* (*pull*) tirare (con forza); (*push*) spingere (con forza); (*lift*) sollevare (con forza) ♦ *vi* sollevarsi; (*retch*) aver conati di vomito ♦ *n* (*push*) grande spinta; **to ~ a sigh** emettere un sospiro

heaven ['hɛvn] *n* paradiso, cielo; **~ly** *adj* divino(a), celeste

heavily ['hɛvɪlɪ] *adv* pesantemente; (*drink, smoke*) molto

heavy ['hɛvɪ] *adj* pesante; (*sea*) grosso(a); (*rain, blow*) forte; (*weather*) afoso(a);

(*drinker, smoker*) gran (*before noun*); **~ goods vehicle** *n* veicolo per trasporti pesanti; **~weight** *n* (*SPORT*) peso massimo

Hebrew ['hiːbruː] *adj* ebreo(a) ♦ *n* (*LING*) ebraico

Hebrides ['hɛbrɪdiːz] *npl*: **the ~** le Ebridi

heckle ['hɛkl] *vt* interpellare e dare noia a (*un oratore*)

hectic ['hɛktɪk] *adj* movimentato(a)

he'd [hiːd] = **he would**; **he had**

hedge [hɛdʒ] *n* siepe *f* ♦ *vi* essere elusivo(a); **to ~ one's bets** (*fig*) coprirsi dai rischi

hedgehog ['hɛdʒhɔg] *n* riccio

heed [hiːd] *vt* (*also*: **take ~ of**) badare a, far conto di; **~less (of)** *adj*: **~less (of)** sordo(a) (a)

heel [hiːl] *n* (*ANAT*) calcagno; (*of shoe*) tacco ♦ *vt* (*shoe*) rifare i tacchi a

hefty ['hɛftɪ] *adj* (*person*) robusto(a); (*parcel*) pesante; (*profit*) grosso(a)

heifer ['hɛfə*] *n* giovenca

height [haɪt] *n* altezza; (*high ground*) altura; (*fig: of glory*) apice *m*; (: *of stupidity*) colmo; **~en** *vt* (*fig*) accrescere

heir [ɛə*] *n* erede *m*; **~ess** *n* erede *f*; **~loom** *n* mobile *m* (*or* gioiello *or* quadro) di famiglia

held [hɛld] *pt, pp of* **hold**

helicopter ['hɛlɪkɔptə*] *n* elicottero

heliport ['hɛlɪpɔːt] *n* eliporto

helium ['hiːlɪəm] *n* elio

hell [hɛl] *n* inferno; **~!** (*inf*) porca miseria!, accidenti!

he'll [hiːl] = **he will**; **he shall**

hellish ['hɛlɪʃ] (*inf*) *adj* infernale

hello [hə'ləu] *excl* buon giorno!; ciao! (*to sb one addresses as "tu"*); (*surprise*) ma guarda!

helm [hɛlm] *n* (*NAUT*) timone *m*

helmet ['hɛlmɪt] *n* casco

help [hɛlp] *n* aiuto; (*charwoman*) donna di servizio ♦ *vt* aiutare; **~!** aiuto!; **~ yourself (to bread)** si serva (del pane); **he can't ~ it** non ci può far niente; **~er** *n* aiutante *m/f*, assistente *m/f*; **~ful** *adj* di grande aiuto; (*useful*) utile; **~ing** *n* porzione *f*; **~less** *adj* impotente; debole

hem [hɛm] *n* orlo ♦ *vt* fare l'orlo a; **~ in** *vt* cingere

hemisphere ['hɛmɪsfɪə*] *n* emisfero

hemorrhage ['hɛmərɪdʒ] (*US*) *n* = **haemorrhage**

hemorrhoids ['hɛmərɔɪdz] (*US*) *npl* = **haemorroids**

hen [hɛn] *n* gallina; (*female bird*) femmina

hence [hɛns] *adv* (*therefore*) dunque; **2 years ~** di qui a 2 anni; **~forth** *adv* d'ora in poi

henpecked ['hɛnpɛkt] *adj* dominato dalla moglie

hepatitis [hɛpə'taɪtɪs] *n* epatite *f*

her [həː*] *pron* (*direct*) la, l' +*vowel*; (*indirect*) le; (*stressed, after prep*) lei ♦ *adj* il(la) suo(a), i(le) suoi(sue); *see also* **me**; **my**

herald ['hɛrəld] *n* araldo ♦ *vt* annunciare

heraldry ['hɛrəldrɪ] *n* araldica

herb [həːb] *n* erba

herd [həːd] *n* mandria

here [hɪə*] *adv* qui, qua ♦ *excl* ehi!; **~!** (*at roll call*) presente!; **~ is/are** ecco, **~ he/she is** eccolo/eccola; **~after** *adv* in futuro; dopo questo; **~by** *adv* (*in letter*) con la presente

hereditary [hɪ'rɛdɪtrɪ] *adj* ereditario(a)

heresy ['hɛrəsɪ] *n* eresia

heretic ['hɛrətɪk] *n* eretico/a

heritage ['hɛrɪtɪdʒ] *n* eredità; (*fig*) retaggio

hermetically [həː'mɛtɪklɪ] *adv*: **~ sealed** ermeticamente chiuso(a)

hermit ['həːmɪt] *n* eremita *m*

hernia ['həːnɪə] *n* ernia

hero ['hɪərəu] (*pl* **~es**) *n* eroe *m*

heroin ['hɛrəuɪn] *n* eroina

heroine ['hɛrəuɪn] *n* eroina

heron ['hɛrən] *n* airone *m*

herring ['hɛrɪŋ] *n* aringa

hers [həːz] *pron* il(la) suo(a), i(le) suoi(sue); *see also* **mine**[1]

herself [həː'sɛlf] *pron* (*reflexive*) si; (*emphatic*) lei stessa; (*after prep*) se stessa, sé; *see also* **oneself**

he's [hiːz] = **he is**; **he has**

hesitant ['hɛzɪtənt] *adj* esitante, indeciso(a)

hesitate ['hɛzɪteɪt] *vi*: **to ~ (about/to do)** esitare (su/a fare); **hesitation** [-'teɪʃən] *n* esitazione *f*

heterosexual ['hɛtərəu'sɛksjuəl] *adj*, *n* eterosessuale *m/f*

hexagonal [hɛk'sægənəl] *adj* esagonale

heyday ['heɪdeɪ] *n*: **the ~ of** i bei giorni di, l'età d'oro di

HGV *n abbr* = **heavy goods vehicle**

hi [haɪ] *excl* ciao!

hiatus [haɪ'eɪtəs] *n* vuoto; (*LING*) iato

hibernate ['haɪbəneɪt] *vi* ibernare

hiccough ['hɪkʌp] *vi* singhiozzare; **~s** *npl*: **to have ~s** avere il singhiozzo

hiccup ['hɪkʌp] = **hiccough**

hid [hɪd] *pt of* **hide**; **~den** ['hɪdn] *pp of* **hide**

hide [haɪd] (*pt* **hid**, *pp* **hidden**) *n* (*skin*) pelle *f* ♦ *vt*: **to ~ sth (from sb)** nascondere qc (a qn) ♦ *vi*: **to ~ (from sb)** nascondersi (da qn); **~-and-seek** *n* rimpiattino

hideous ['hɪdɪəs] *adj* laido(a); orribile

hiding ['haɪdɪŋ] *n* (*beating*) bastonata; **to be in ~** (*concealed*) tenersi nascosto(a)

hierarchy ['haɪərɑːkɪ] *n* gerarchia

hi-fi ['haɪfaɪ] *n* stereo ♦ *adj* ad alta fedeltà, hi-fi *inv*

high [haɪ] *adj* alto(a); (*speed, respect, number*) grande; (*wind*) forte; (*voice*) acuto(a) ♦ *adv* alto, in alto; **20m ~** alto(a) 20m; **~brow** *adj*, *n* intellettuale *m/f*; **~chair** *n* seggiolone *m*; **~er education** *n* studi *mpl* superiori; **~-handed** *adj* prepotente; **~-heeled** *adj* con i tacchi alti; **~ jump** *n* (*SPORT*) salto in alto; **the H~lands** *npl* le Highlands scozzesi; **~light** *n* (*fig: of event*) momento culminante; (*in hair*) colpo di sole ♦ *vt* mettere in evidenza; **~ly** *adv* molto; **to speak ~ly of** parlare molto bene di; **~ly strung** *adj* teso(a) di nervi, eccitabile; **~ness** *n*: **Her H~ness** Sua Altezza; **~-pitched** *adj* acuto(a); **~-rise block** *n* palazzone *m*; **~ school** *n* scuola secondaria; (*US*) istituto superiore d'istruzione; **~ season** (*BRIT*) *n* alta stagione; **~ street** (*BRIT*) *n* strada principale

highway ['haɪweɪ] *n* strada maestra; **H~ Code** (*BRIT*) *n* codice *m* della strada

hijack [ˈhaɪdʒæk] *vt* dirottare; **~er** *n* dirottatore/trice

hike [haɪk] *vi* fare un'escursione a piedi ♦ *n* escursione *f* a piedi; **~r** *n* escursionista *m/f*; **hiking** *n* escursioni *fpl* a piedi

hilarious [hɪˈlɛərɪəs] *adj* (*behaviour, event*) spassosissimo(a)

hill [hɪl] *n* collina, colle *m*; (*fairly high*) montagna; (*on road*) salita; **~side** *n* fianco della collina; **~ walking** *n* escursioni *fpl* in collina; **~y** *adj* collinoso(a); montagnoso(a)

hilt [hɪlt] *n* (*of sword*) elsa; **to the ~** (*fig: support*) fino in fondo

him [hɪm] *pron* (*direct*) lo, l' +*vowel*; (*indirect*) gli; (*stressed, after prep*) lui; *see also* **me**; **~self** *pron* (*reflexive*) si; (*emphatic*) lui stesso; (*after prep*) se stesso, sé; *see also* **oneself**

hinder [ˈhɪndə*] *vt* ostacolare; **hindrance** [ˈhɪndrəns] *n* ostacolo, impedimento

hindsight [ˈhaɪndsaɪt] *n*: **with ~** con il senno di poi

Hindu [ˈhɪnduː] *n* indù *m/f inv*

hinge [hɪndʒ] *n* cardine *m* ♦ *vi* (*fig*): **to ~ on** dipendere da

hint [hɪnt] *n* (*suggestion*) allusione *f*; (*advice*) consiglio; (*sign*) accenno ♦ *vt*: **to ~ that** lasciar capire che ♦ *vi*: **to ~ at** alludere a

hip [hɪp] *n* anca, fianco

hippopotamus [hɪpəˈpɔtəməs] (*pl* **~es** *or* **hippopotami**) *n* ippopotamo

hire [ˈhaɪə*] *vt* (*BRIT: car, equipment*) noleggiare; (*worker*) assumere, dare lavoro a ♦ *n* nolo, noleggio; **for ~** da nolo; (*taxi*) libero(a); **~(d) car** (*BRIT*) *n* macchina a nolo; **~ purchase** (*BRIT*) *n* acquisto (*or* vendita) rateale

his [hɪz] *adj, pron* il(la) suo(sua), i(le) suoi(sue); *see also* **my; mine**[1]

hiss [hɪs] *vi* fischiare; (*cat, snake*) sibilare

historic(al) [hɪˈstɔrɪk(l)] *adj* storico(a)

history [ˈhɪstərɪ] *n* storia

hit [hɪt] (*pt, pp* **hit**) *vt* colpire, picchiare; (*knock against*) battere; (*reach: target*) raggiungere; (*collide with: car*) urtare contro; (*fig: affect*) colpire; (*find: problem etc*) incontrare ♦ *n* colpo; (*success, song*) successo; **to ~ it off with sb** andare molto d'accordo con qn; **~-and-run driver** *n* pirata *m* della strada

hitch [hɪtʃ] *vt* (*fasten*) attaccare; (*also:* **~ up**) tirare su ♦ *n* (*difficulty*) intoppo, difficoltà *f inv*; **to ~ a lift** fare l'autostop

hitch-hike *vi* fare l'autostop; **~r** *n* autostoppista *m/f*; **hitch-hiking** *n* autostop *m*

hi-tech [ˈhaɪˈtek] *adj* di alta tecnologia ♦ *n* alta tecnologia

hitherto [hɪðəˈtuː] *adv* in precedenza

HIV *abbr*: **HIV-negative/-positive** *adj* sieronegativo(a)/sieropositivo(a)

hive [haɪv] *n* alveare *m*

H.M.S. *abbr* = **His(Her) Majesty's Ship**

hoard [hɔːd] *n* (*of food*) provviste *fpl*; (*of money*) gruzzolo ♦ *vt* ammassare

hoarding [ˈhɔːdɪŋ] (*BRIT*) *n* (*for posters*) tabellone *m* per affissioni

hoarse [hɔːs] *adj* rauco(a)

hoax [həʊks] *n* scherzo; falso allarme

hob [hɔb] *n* piastra (con fornelli)

hobble [ˈhɔbl] *vi* zoppicare

hobby [ˈhɔbɪ] *n* hobby *m inv*, passatempo

hobo [ˈhəʊbəʊ] (*US*) *n* vagabondo

hockey [ˈhɔkɪ] *n* hockey *m*

hoe [həʊ] *n* zappa

hog [hɔg] *n* maiale *m* ♦ *vt* (*fig*) arraffare; **to go the whole ~** farlo fino in fondo

hoist [hɔɪst] *n* paranco ♦ *vt* issare

hold [həʊld] (*pt, pp* **held**) *vt* tenere; (*contain*) contenere; (*keep back*) trattenere; (*believe*) mantenere; considerare; (*possess*) avere, possedere; detenere ♦ *vi* (*withstand pressure*) tenere; (*be valid*) essere valido(a) ♦ *n* presa; (*control*): **to have a ~ over** avere controllo su; (*NAUT*) stiva; **~ the line!** (*TEL*) resti in linea!; **to ~ one's own** (*fig*) difendersi bene; **~ it!** o get (a) **~ of** afferrare; **~ back** *vt* trattenere; (*secret*) tenere celato(a); **~ down** *vt* (*person*) tenere a terra; (*job*) tenere; **~ off** *vt* tener lontano; **~ on** *vi* tener fermo; (*wait*) aspettare; **~ on!** (*TEL*) resti in linea!; **~ on to** *vt fus* tenersi stretto(a) a; (*keep*) conservare; **~ out** *vt* offrire ♦ *vi* (*resist*) resistere; **~ up** vt (raise) alzare; (support) sostenere; (delay) ritardare; (rob) assaltare; **~all** (BRIT) n borsone m; **~er** n (container) contenitore m; (of ticket, title) possessore/posseditrice; (of office etc) incaricato/a; (of record) detentore/trice; **~ing** n (share) azioni fpl, titoli mpl; (farm) podere m, tenuta f; **~up** n (robbery) rapina a mano armata; (delay) ritardo; (BRIT: in traffic) blocco

hole [haul] n buco, buca

holiday ['hɔlədɪ] n vacanza; (day off) giorno di vacanza; (public) giorno festivo; **on ~** in vacanza; **~ camp** (BRIT) n (also: **~ centre**) ≈ villaggio (di vacanze); **~-maker** (BRIT) n villeggiante m/f; **~ resort** n luogo di villeggiatura

holiness ['haulɪnɪs] n santità

Holland ['hɔlənd] n Olanda

hollow ['hɔləu] adj cavo(a); (container, claim) vuoto(a); (laugh, sound) cupo(a) ♦ n cavità f inv; (in land) valletta, depressione f ♦ vt: **to ~ out** scavare

holly ['hɔlɪ] n agrifoglio

holocaust ['hɔləkɔːst] n olocausto

holster ['həulstə*] n fondina (di pistola)

holy ['həulɪ] adj santo(a); (bread) benedetto(a), consacrato(a); (ground) consacrato(a)

homage ['hɔmɪdʒ] n omaggio; **to pay ~ to** rendere omaggio a

home [həum] n casa; (country) patria; (institution) casa, ricovero ♦ cpd familiare; (ECON, POL) nazionale, interno(a); (SPORT) di casa ♦ adv a casa; in patria; (right in: nail etc) fino in fondo; **at ~** a casa (in situation) a proprio agio; **to go** (or **come**) **~** tornare a casa (or in patria); **make yourself at ~** si metta a suo agio; **~ address** n indirizzo di casa; **~land** n patria; **~less** adj senza tetto; **~ly** adj semplice, alla buona; accogliente; **~-made** adj casalingo(a); **H~ Office** (BRIT) n ministero degli Interni; **~ page** n (COMPUT) home page f inv; **~ rule** n autogoverno; **H~ Secretary** (BRIT) n ministro degli Interni; **~sick** adj: **to be ~sick** avere la nostalgia; **~ town** n città f

inv natale; **~ward** ['həumwəd] adj (journey) di ritorno; **~work** n compiti mpl (per casa)

homicide ['hɔmɪsaɪd] (US) n omicidio

homoeopathic [həumɪə'pæθɪk] (US **homeopathic**) adj omeopatico(a)

homosexual [hɔməu'sɛksjuəl] adj, n omosessuale m/f

honest ['ɔnɪst] adj onesto(a); sincero(a); **~ly** adv onestamente; sinceramente; **~y** n onestà

honey ['hʌnɪ] n miele m; **~comb** n favo; **~moon** n luna di miele, viaggio di nozze; **~suckle** n (BOT) caprifoglio

honk [hɔŋk] vi suonare il clacson

honorary ['ɔnərərɪ] adj onorario(a); (duty, title) onorifico(a)

honour ['ɔnə*] (US **honor**) vt onorare ♦ n onore m; **~able** adj onorevole; **~s degree** n (SCOL) laurea specializzata

hood [hud] n cappuccio; (on cooker) cappa; (BRIT: AUT) capote f; (US: AUT) cofano

hoodlum ['huːdləm] n teppista m/f

hoof [huːf] (pl **hooves**) n zoccolo

hook [huk] n gancio; (for fishing) amo ♦ vt uncinare; (dress) agganciare

hooligan ['huːlɪgən] n giovinastro, teppista m

hoop [huːp] n cerchio

hooray [huː'reɪ] excl = **hurray**

hoot [huːt] vi (AUT) suonare il clacson; (siren) ululare; (owl) gufare; **~er** n (BRIT: AUT) clacson m inv; (NAUT) sirena

Hoover ® ['huːvə*] (BRIT) n aspirapolvere m inv ♦ vt: **h~** pulire con l'aspirapolvere

hooves [huːvz] npl of **hoof**

hop [hɔp] vi saltellare, saltare; (on one foot) saltare su una gamba

hope [həup] vt: **to ~ that/to do** sperare che/di fare ♦ vi sperare ♦ n speranza; **I ~ so/not** spero di sì/no; **~ful** adj (person) pieno(a) di speranza; (situation) promettente; **~fully** adv con speranza; **~fully he will recover** speriamo che si riprenda; **~less** adj senza speranza, disperato(a); (useless) inutile

hops [hɔps] npl luppoli mpl

horde [hɔːd] n orda

horizon [həˈraɪzn] n orizzonte m; ~**tal** [hɒrɪˈzɒntl] adj orizzontale

hormone [ˈhɔːməʊn] n ormone m

horn [hɔːn] n (ZOOL, MUS) corno; (AUT) clacson m inv

hornet [ˈhɔːnɪt] n calabrone m

horoscope [ˈhɒrəskəʊp] n oroscopo

horrendous [həˈrendəs] adj orrendo(a)

horrible [ˈhɒrɪbl] adj orribile, tremendo(a)

horrid [ˈhɒrɪd] adj orrido(a); (person) odioso(a)

horrify [ˈhɒrɪfaɪ] vt scandalizzare

horror [ˈhɒrə*] n orrore m; ~ **film** n film m inv dell'orrore

hors d'œuvre [ɔːˈdəːvrə] n antipasto

horse [hɔːs] n cavallo; ~**back**: **on ~back** adj, adv a cavallo; ~ **chestnut** n ippocastano; ~**man** (irreg) n cavaliere m; ~**power** n cavallo (vapore); ~-**racing** n ippica; ~**radish** n rafano; ~**shoe** n ferro di cavallo; ~**woman** (irreg) n amazzone f

horticulture [ˈhɔːtɪkʌltʃə*] n orticoltura

hose [həʊz] n (also: ~**pipe**) tubo; (also: **garden** ~) tubo per annaffiare

hosiery [ˈhəʊʒərɪ] n maglieria

hospice [ˈhɒspɪs] n ricovero, ospizio

hospitable [hɒsˈpɪtəbl] adj ospitale

hospital [ˈhɒspɪtl] n ospedale m

hospitality [hɒspɪˈtælɪtɪ] n ospitalità

host [həʊst] n ospite m; (REL) ostia; (large number): **a ~ of** una schiera di

hostage [ˈhɒstɪdʒ] n ostaggio/a

hostel [ˈhɒstl] n ostello; (also: **youth** ~) ostello della gioventù

hostess [ˈhəʊstɪs] n ospite f; (BRIT: **air** ~) hostess f inv

hostile [ˈhɒstaɪl] adj ostile

hostility [hɒsˈtɪlɪtɪ] n ostilità f inv

hot [hɒt] adj caldo(a); (as opposed to only **warm**) molto caldo(a); (spicy) piccante; (fig) accanito(a); ardente; violento(a), focoso(a); **to be ~** (person) aver caldo; (object) essere caldo(a); (weather) far caldo; ~**bed** n (fig) focolaio; ~ **dog** n hot dog m inv

hotel [həʊˈtel] n albergo; ~**ier** n albergatore/trice

hot: ~**house** n serra; ~ **line** n (POL)

telefono rosso; ~**ly** adv violentemente; ~**plate** n piastra riscaldante; ~**pot** (BRIT) n stufato coperto da uno strato di patate; ~-**water bottle** n borsa dell'acqua calda

hound [haʊnd] vt perseguitare ♦ n segugio

hour [ˈaʊə*] n ora; ~**ly** adj all'ora

house [n haus, pl ˈhaʊzɪz, vb haʊz] n (also firm) casa; (POL) camera; (THEATRE) sala; pubblico; spettacolo ♦ vt (person) ospitare, alloggiare; **on the ~** (fig) offerto(a) dalla casa; ~ **arrest** n arresti mpl domiciliari; ~**boat** n house boat f inv; ~**bound** adj confinato(a) in casa; ~**breaking** n furto con scasso; ~**hold** n famiglia; casa; ~**keeper** n governante f; ~**keeping** n (work) governo della casa; (money) soldi mpl per le spese di casa; ~**warming party** n festa per inaugurare la casa nuova; ~**wife** (irreg) n massaia, casalinga; ~**work** n faccende fpl domestiche

housing [ˈhaʊzɪŋ] n alloggio; ~ **development** (BRIT ~ **estate**) n zona residenziale con case popolari e/o private

hovel [ˈhɒvl] n casupola

hover [ˈhɒvə*] vi (bird) librarsi; ~**craft** n hovercraft m inv

how [haʊ] adv come; ~ **are you?** come sta?; ~ **do you do?** piacere!; ~ **far is it to the river?** quanto è lontano il fiume?; ~ **long have you been here?** da quando è qui?; ~ **lovely!/awful!** che bello!/orrore!; ~ **many?** quanti(e)?; ~ **much?** quanto?; ~ **much milk?** quanto latte?; ~ **many people?** quante persone?; ~ **old are you?** quanti anni ha?; ~**ever** adv in qualsiasi modo or maniera che; (+adjective) per quanto +sub; (in questions) come ♦ conj comunque, però

howl [haʊl] vi ululare; (baby, person) urlare

H.P. abbr = **hire purchase**; **horsepower**

h.p. n abbr = **H.P.**

HQ n abbr = **headquarters**

HTML abbr (= hypertext markup language) HTML m inv

hub [hʌb] n (of wheel) mozzo; (fig) fulcro

hubcap [ˈhʌbkæp] n coprimozzo

huddle [ˈhʌdl] vi: **to ~ together** rannicchiarsi l'uno contro l'altro

hue [hju:] *n* tinta

huff [hʌf] *n*: **in a ~** stizzito(a)

hug [hʌg] *vt* abbracciare; (*shore, kerb*) stringere

huge [hju:dʒ] *adj* enorme, immenso(a)

hulk [hʌlk] *n* (*ship*) nave *f* in disarmo; (*car*) carcassa; (*person*) mastodonte *m*

hull [hʌl] *n* (*of ship*) scafo

hullo [hə'ləu] *excl* = **hello**

hum [hʌm] *vt* (*tune*) canticchiare ♦ *vi* canticchiare; (*insect, plane, tool*) ronzare

human ['hju:mən] *adj* umano(a) ♦ *n* essere *m* umano

humane [hju:'mein] *adj* umanitario(a)

humanitarian [hju:mænɪ'tɛəriən] *adj* umanitario(a)

humanity [hju:'mænɪtɪ] *n* umanità

humble ['hʌmbl] *adj* umile, modesto(a) ♦ *vt* umiliare

humdrum ['hʌmdrʌm] *adj* monotono(a), tedioso(a)

humid ['hju:mɪd] *adj* umido(a)

humiliate [hju:'mɪlɪeɪt] *vt* umiliare; **humiliation** [-'eɪʃən] *n* umiliazione *f*

humility [hju:'mɪlɪtɪ] *n* umiltà

humorous ['hju:mərəs] *adj* umoristico(a); (*person*) buffo(a)

humour ['hju:mə*] (*US* **humor**) *n* umore *m* ♦ *vt* accontentare

hump [hʌmp] *n* gobba

hunch [hʌntʃ] *n* (*premonition*) intuizione *f*; **~ed** *adj* incurvato(a)

hundred ['hʌndrəd] *num* cento; **~s of** centinaia *fpl* di; **~weight** *n* (*BRIT*) = *50.8 kg*; *112 lb*; (*US*) = *45.3 kg*; *100 lb*

hung [hʌŋ] *pt, pp of* **hang**

Hungary ['hʌŋgərɪ] *n* Ungheria

hunger ['hʌŋgə*] *n* fame *f* ♦ *vi*: **to ~ for** desiderare ardentemente; **~ strike** *n* sciopero della fame

hungry ['hʌŋgrɪ] *adj* affamato(a); (*avid*): **~ for** avido(a) di; **to be ~** aver fame

hunk [hʌŋk] *n* (*of bread etc*) bel pezzo

hunt [hʌnt] *vt* (*seek*) cercare; (*SPORT*) cacciare ♦ *vi*: **to ~ (for)** andare a caccia (di) ♦ *n* caccia; **~er** *n* cacciatore *m*; **~ing** *n* caccia

hurdle ['hə:dl] *n* (*SPORT, fig*) ostacolo

hurl [hə:l] *vt* lanciare con violenza

hurrah [hu'rɑ:] *excl* = **hurray**

hurray [hu'reɪ] *excl* urra!, evviva!

hurricane ['hʌrɪkən] *n* uragano

hurried ['hʌrɪd] *adj* affrettato(a); (*work*) fatto(a) in fretta; **~ly** *adv* in fretta

hurry ['hʌrɪ] *n* fretta ♦ *vi* (*also*: **~ up**) affrettarsi ♦ *vt* (*also*: **~ person**) affrettare; (*: work*) far in fretta; **to be in a ~** aver fretta

hurt [hə:t] (*pt, pp* **hurt**) *vt* (*cause pain to*) far male a; (*injure, fig*) ferire ♦ *vi* far male; **~ful** *adj* (*remark*) che ferisce

hurtle ['hə:tl] *vi*: **to ~ past/down** passare/scendere a razzo

husband ['hʌzbənd] *n* marito

hush [hʌʃ] *n* silenzio, calma ♦ *vt* zittire; **~!** zitto(a)!; **~ up** *vt* (*scandal*) mettere a tacere

husk [hʌsk] *n* (*of wheat*) cartoccio; (*of rice, maize*) buccia

husky ['hʌskɪ] *adj* roco(a) ♦ *n* cane *m* eschimese

hustle ['hʌsl] *vt* spingere, incalzare ♦ *n*: **~ and bustle** trambusto

hut [hʌt] *n* rifugio; (*shed*) ripostiglio

hutch [hʌtʃ] *n* gabbia

hyacinth ['haɪəsɪnθ] *n* giacinto

hybrid ['haɪbrɪd] *n* ibrido

hydrant ['haɪdrənt] *n* (*also*: **fire ~**) idrante *m*

hydraulic [haɪ'drɔ:lɪk] *adj* idraulico(a)

hydroelectric [haɪdrəu'lektrɪk] *adj* idroelettrico(a)

hydrofoil ['haɪdrəufɔɪl] *n* aliscafo

hydrogen ['haɪdrədʒən] *n* idrogeno

hyena [haɪ'i:nə] *n* iena

hygiene ['haɪdʒi:n] *n* igiene *f*

hymn [hɪm] *n* inno; cantica

hype [haɪp] (*inf*) *n* campagna pubblicitaria

hypermarket ['haɪpəmɑ:kɪt] (*BRIT*) *n* ipermercato

hypertext ['haɪpətekst] *n* (*COMPUT*) ipertesto

hyphen ['haɪfn] *n* trattino

hypnotize ['hɪpnətaɪz] *vt* ipnotizzare

hypocrisy [hɪ'pɔkrɪsɪ] *n* ipocrisia

hypocrite ['hɪpəkrɪt] *n* ipocrita *m/f*; **hypocritical** [-'krɪtɪkl] *adj* ipocrita

hypothesis [haɪ'pɔθɪsɪs] (*pl* **hypotheses**) *n* ipotesi *f inv*

hypothetical [haɪpəʊ'θetɪkl] *adj* ipotetico(a)

hysterical [hɪ'sterɪkl] *adj* isterico(a)

hysterics [hɪ'sterɪks] *npl* accesso di isteria; (*laughter*) attacco di riso

I, i

I [aɪ] *pron* io

ice [aɪs] *n* ghiaccio; (*on road*) gelo; (*~ cream*) gelato ♦ *vt* (*cake*) glassare ♦ *vi* (*also*: **~ over**) ghiacciare; (*also*: **~ up**) gelare; **~berg** *n* iceberg *m inv*; **~box** *n* (*US*) frigorifero; (*BRIT*) reparto ghiaccio; (*insulated box*) frigo portatile; **~ cream** *n* gelato; **~ hockey** *n* hockey *m* su ghiaccio

Iceland ['aɪslənd] *n* Islanda

ice: **~ lolly** (*BRIT*) *n* ghiacciolo; **~ rink** *n* pista di pattinaggio; **~ skating** *n* pattinaggio sul ghiaccio

icicle ['aɪsɪkl] *n* ghiacciolo

icing ['aɪsɪŋ] *n* (*CULIN*) glassa; **~ sugar** (*BRIT*) *n* zucchero a velo

icon ['aɪkɔn] *n* icona

icy ['aɪsɪ] *adj* ghiacciato(a); (*weather, temperature*) gelido(a)

I'd [aɪd] = **I would**; **I had**

idea [aɪ'dɪə] *n* idea

ideal [aɪ'dɪəl] *adj* ideale ♦ *n* ideale *m*

identical [aɪ'dentɪkl] *adj* identico(a)

identification [aɪdentɪfɪ'keɪʃən] *n* identificazione *f*; (**means of**) **~** carta d'identità

identify [aɪ'dentɪfaɪ] *vt* identificare

Identikit picture ® [aɪ'dentɪkɪt-] *n* identikit *m inv*

identity [aɪ'dentɪtɪ] *n* identità *f inv*; **~ card** *n* carta d'identità

ideology [aɪdɪ'ɔlədʒɪ] *n* ideologia

idiom ['ɪdɪəm] *n* idioma *m*; (*phrase*) espressione *f* idiomatica

idiot ['ɪdɪət] *n* idiota *m/f*; **~ic** [-'ɔtɪk] *adj* idiota

idle ['aɪdl] *adj* inattivo(a); (*lazy*) pigro(a),

ozioso(a); (*unemployed*) disoccupato(a); (*question, pleasures*) ozioso(a) ♦ *vi* (*engine*) girare al minimo

idol ['aɪdl] *n* idolo; **~ize** *vt* idoleggiare

i.e. *adv abbr* (= *that is*) cioè

if [ɪf] *conj* se; **~ I were you ...** se fossi in te ..., io al tuo posto ...; **~ so** se è così; **~ not** se no; **~ only** se solo *or* soltanto

ignite [ɪg'naɪt] *vt* accendere ♦ *vi* accendersi

ignition [ɪg'nɪʃən] *n* (*AUT*) accensione *f*; **to switch on/off the ~** accendere/spegnere il motore; **~ key** *n* (*AUT*) chiave *f* dell'accensione

ignorant ['ɪgnərənt] *adj* ignorante; **to be ~ of** (*subject*) essere ignorante in; (*events*) essere ignaro(a) di

ignore [ɪg'nɔː*] *vt* non tener conto di; (*person, fact*) ignorare

I'll [aɪl] = **I will**; **I shall**

ill [ɪl] *adj* (*sick*) malato(a); (*bad*) cattivo(a) ♦ *n* male *m* ♦ *adv*: **to speak** *etc* **~ of sb** parlare *etc* male di qn; **to take** *or* **be taken ~** ammalarsi; **~-advised** *adj* (*decision*) poco giudizioso(a); (*person*) mal consigliato(a); **~-at-ease** *adj* a disagio

illegal [ɪ'liːgl] *adj* illegale

illegible [ɪ'ledʒɪbl] *adj* illeggibile

illegitimate [ɪlɪ'dʒɪtɪmət] *adj* illegittimo(a)

ill-fated [ɪl'feɪtɪd] *adj* nefasto(a)

ill feeling *n* rancore *m*

illiterate [ɪ'lɪtərət] *adj* analfabeta, illetterato(a); (*letter*) scorretto(a)

ill-mannered [ɪl'mænəd] *adj* maleducato(a)

illness ['ɪlnɪs] *n* malattia

ill-treat *vt* maltrattare

illuminate [ɪ'luːmɪneɪt] *vt* illuminare;

illumination [-'neɪʃən] *n* illuminazione *f*; **illuminations** *npl* (*decorative*) luminarie *fpl*

illusion [ɪ'luːʒən] *n* illusione *f*

illustrate ['ɪləstreɪt] *vt* illustrare

illustration [ɪlə'streɪʃən] *n* illustrazione *f*

I'm [aɪm] = **I am**

image ['ɪmɪdʒ] *n* immagine *f*; (*public face*) immagine (pubblica); **~ry** *n* immagini *fpl*

imaginary [ɪ'mædʒɪnərɪ] *adj* immaginario(a)

imagination [ɪmædʒɪ'neɪʃən] *n* immaginazione *f*, fantasia

imaginative [ɪ'mædʒɪnətɪv] *adj*
immaginoso(a)

imagine [ɪ'mædʒɪn] *vt* immaginare

imbalance [ɪm'bæləns] *n* squilibrio

imbue [ɪm'bjuː] *vt*: **to ~ sb/sth with**
permeare qn/qc di

imitate ['ɪmɪteɪt] *vt* imitare; **imitation**
[-'teɪʃən] *n* imitazione *f*

immaculate [ɪ'mækjulət] *adj*
immacolato(a); (*dress, appearance*)
impeccabile

immaterial [ɪmə'tɪərɪəl] *adj* immateriale,
indifferente

immature [ɪmə'tjuə*] *adj* immaturo(a)

immediate [ɪ'miːdɪət] *adj* immediato(a);
~ly *adv* (*at once*) subito, immediatamente;
~ly next to proprio accanto a

immense [ɪ'mɛns] *adj* immenso(a); enorme

immerse [ɪ'mɜːs] *vt* immergere

immersion heater [ɪ'mɜːʃən-] (*BRIT*) *n*
scaldaacqua *m inv* a immersione

immigrant ['ɪmɪgrənt] *n* immigrante *m/f*;
immigrato/a

immigration [ɪmɪ'greɪʃən] *n* immigrazione *f*

imminent ['ɪmɪnənt] *adj* imminente

immoral [ɪ'mɔrəl] *adj* immorale

immortal [ɪ'mɔːtl] *adj*, *n* immortale *m/f*

immune [ɪ'mjuːn] *adj*: **~ (to)** immune (da);
immunity *n* immunità

impact ['ɪmpækt] *n* impatto

impair [ɪm'pɛə*] *vt* danneggiare

impart [ɪm'pɑːt] *vt* (*make known*)
comunicare; (*bestow*) impartire

impartial [ɪm'pɑːʃl] *adj* imparziale

impassable [ɪm'pɑːsəbl] *adj* insuperabile;
(*road*) impraticabile

impassive [ɪm'pæsɪv] *adj* impassibile

impatience [ɪm'peɪʃəns] *n* impazienza

impatient [ɪm'peɪʃənt] *adj* impaziente; **to
get** *or* **grow ~** perdere la pazienza

impeccable [ɪm'pɛkəbl] *adj* impeccabile

impede [ɪm'piːd] *vt* impedire

impediment [ɪm'pɛdɪmənt] *n*
impedimento; (*also:* **speech ~**) difetto di
pronuncia

impending [ɪm'pɛndɪŋ] *adj* imminente

imperative [ɪm'pɛrətɪv] *adj* imperativo(a);

necessario(a), urgente; (*voice*) imperioso(a)

imperfect [ɪm'pɜːfɪkt] *adj* imperfetto(a);
(*goods etc*) difettoso(a) ♦ *n* (*LING: also:* **~
tense**) imperfetto

imperial [ɪm'pɪərɪəl] *adj* imperiale;
(*measure*) legale

impersonal [ɪm'pɜːsənl] *adj* impersonale

impersonate [ɪm'pɜːsəneɪt] *vt* impersonare;
(*THEATRE*) fare la mimica di

impertinent [ɪm'pɜːtɪnənt] *adj* insolente,
impertinente

impervious [ɪm'pɜːvɪəs] *adj* (*fig*): **~ to**
insensibile a; impassibile di fronte a

impetuous [ɪm'pɛtjuəs] *adj* impetuoso(a),
precipitoso(a)

impetus ['ɪmpətəs] *n* impeto

impinge on [ɪm'pɪndʒ-] *vt fus* (*person*)
colpire; (*rights*) ledere

implement [*n* 'ɪmplɪmənt, *vb* 'ɪmplɪmɛnt] *n*
attrezzo; (*for cooking*) utensile *m* ♦ *vt*
effettuare

implicit [ɪm'plɪsɪt] *adj* implicito(a);
(*complete*) completo(a)

imply [ɪm'plaɪ] *vt* insinuare; suggerire

impolite [ɪmpə'laɪt] *adj* scortese

import [*vb* ɪm'pɔːt, *n* 'ɪmpɔːt] *vt* importare
♦ *n* (*COMM*) importazione *f*

importance [ɪm'pɔːtns] *n* importanza

important [ɪm'pɔːtnt] *adj* importante; **it's
not ~** non ha importanza

importer [ɪm'pɔːtə*] *n* importatore/trice

impose [ɪm'pəuz] *vt* imporre ♦ *vi*: **to ~ on
sb** sfruttare la bontà di qn

imposing [ɪm'pəuzɪŋ] *adj* imponente

imposition [ɪmpə'zɪʃən] *n* (*of tax etc*)
imposizione *f*; **to be an ~ on** (*person*)
abusare della gentilezza di

impossibility [ɪmpɔsə'bɪlɪtɪ] *n* impossibilità

impossible [ɪm'pɔsɪbl] *adj* impossibile

impotent ['ɪmpətnt] *adj* impotente

impound [ɪm'paund] *vt* confiscare

impoverished [ɪm'pɔvərɪʃt] *adj*
impoverito(a)

impracticable [ɪm'præktɪkəbl] *adj*
inattuabile

impractical [ɪm'præktɪkl] *adj* non pratico(a)

impress [ɪm'prɛs] *vt* impressionare; (*mark*)

imprimere, stampare; **to ~ sth on sb** far capire qc a qn

impression [ɪmˈprɛʃən] *n* impressione *f*; **to be under the ~ that** avere l'impressione che

impressive [ɪmˈprɛsɪv] *adj* notevole

imprint [ˈɪmprɪnt] *n* (*of hand etc*) impronta; (*PUBLISHING*) sigla editoriale

imprison [ɪmˈprɪzn] *vt* imprigionare; **~ment** *n* imprigionamento

improbable [ɪmˈprɒbəbl] *adj* improbabile; (*excuse*) inverosimile

impromptu [ɪmˈprɒmptjuː] *adj* improvvisato(a)

improper [ɪmˈprɒpə*] *adj* scorretto(a); (*unsuitable*) inadatto(a), improprio(a); sconveniente, indecente

improve [ɪmˈpruːv] *vt* migliorare ♦ *vi* migliorare; (*pupil etc*) fare progressi; **~ment** *n* miglioramento; progresso

improvise [ˈɪmprəvaɪz] *vt, vi* improvvisare

impudent [ˈɪmpjudnt] *adj* impudente, sfacciato(a)

impulse [ˈɪmpʌls] *n* impulso; **on ~** d'impulso, impulsivamente

impulsive [ɪmˈpʌlsɪv] *adj* impulsivo(a)

KEYWORD

in [ɪn] *prep* **1** (*indicating place, position*) in; **~ the house/garden** in casa/giardino; **~ the box** nella scatola; **~ the fridge** nel frigorifero; **I have it ~ my hand** ce l'ho in mano; **~ town/the country** in città/campagna; **~ school** a scuola; **~ here/there** qui/lì dentro

2 (*with place names: of town, region, country*): **~ London** a Londra; **~ England** in Inghilterra; **~ the United States** negli Stati Uniti; **~ Yorkshire** nello Yorkshire

3 (*indicating time: during, in the space of*) in; **~ spring/summer** in primavera/estate; **~ 1999** nel 1999; **~ May** in *or* a maggio; **I'll see you ~ July** ci vediamo a luglio; **~ the afternoon** nel pomeriggio; **at 4 o'clock ~ the afternoon** alle 4 del pomeriggio; **I did it ~ 3 hours/days** l'ho fatto in 3 ore/giorni; **I'll see you ~ 2**

weeks *or* **~ 2 weeks' time** ci vediamo tra 2 settimane

4 (*indicating manner etc*) a; **~ a loud/soft voice** a voce alta/bassa; **~ pencil** a matita; **~ English/French** in inglese/francese; **the boy ~ the blue shirt** il ragazzo con la camicia blu

5 (*indicating circumstances*): **~ the sun** al sole; **~ the shade** all'ombra; **~ the rain** sotto la pioggia; **a rise ~ prices** un aumento dei prezzi

6 (*indicating mood, state*): **~ tears** in lacrime; **~ anger** per la rabbia; **~ despair** disperato(a); **~ good condition** in buono stato, in buone condizioni; **to live ~ luxury** vivere nel lusso

7 (*with ratios, numbers*): **1 ~ 10** 1 su 10; **20 pence ~ the pound** 20 pence per sterlina; **they lined up ~ twos** si misero in fila a due a due

8 (*referring to people, works*) in; **the disease is common ~ children** la malattia è comune nei bambini; **~ (the works of) Dickens** in Dickens

9 (*indicating profession etc*) in; **to be ~ teaching** fare l'insegnante, insegnare; **to be ~ publishing** essere nell'editoria

10 (*after superlative*) di; **the best ~ the class** il migliore della classe

11 (*with present participle*): **~ saying this** dicendo questo, nel dire questo

♦ *adv*: **to be ~** (*person: at home, work*) esserci; (*train, ship, plane*) essere arrivato(a); (*in fashion*) essere di moda; **to ask sb ~** invitare qn ad entrare; **to run/limp** *etc* **~** entrare di corsa/zoppicando *etc*

♦ *n*: **the ~s and outs of the problem** tutti i particolari del problema

in. *abbr* = **inch**

inability [ɪnəˈbɪlɪtɪ] *n*: **~ (to do)** incapacità (di fare)

inaccurate [ɪnˈækjurət] *adj* inesatto(a), impreciso(a)

inadequate [ɪnˈædɪkwət] *adj* insufficiente

inadvertently [ɪnədˈvəːtntlɪ] *adv* senza volerlo

inadvisable [ɪnəd'vaɪzəbl] *adj* consigliabile

inane [ɪ'neɪn] *adj* vacuo(a), stupido(a)

inanimate [ɪn'ænɪmət] *adj* inanimato(a)

inappropriate [ɪnə'prəʊprɪət] *adj* non adatto(a); (*word, expression*) improprio(a)

inarticulate [ɪnɑː'tɪkjʊlət] *adj* (*person*) che si esprime male; (*speech*) inarticolato(a)

inasmuch as [ɪnəz'mʌtʃæz] *adv* in quanto che; (*insofar as*) poiché

inaudible [ɪn'ɔːdɪbl] *adj* che non si riesce a sentire

inauguration [ɪnɔːgju'reɪʃən] *n* inaugurazione *f*; insediamento in carica

in-between *adj* fra i (*or* le) due

inborn [ɪn'bɔːn] *adj* innato(a)

inbred [ɪn'bred] *adj* innato(a); (*family*) connaturato(a)

Inc. (*US*) *abbr* (= incorporated) S.A

incapable [ɪn'keɪpəbl] *adj* incapace

incapacitate [ɪnkə'pæsɪteɪt] *vt*: **to ~ sb from doing** rendere qn incapace di fare

incense [*n* 'ɪnsens, *vb* ɪn'sens] *n* incenso ♦ *vt* (*anger*) infuriare

incentive [ɪn'sentɪv] *n* incentivo

incessant [ɪn'sesnt] *adj* incessante; **~ly** *adv* di continuo, senza sosta

inch [ɪntʃ] *n* pollice *m* (= 25 mm; 12 in a foot); **within an ~ of** a un pelo da; **he didn't give an ~** non ha ceduto di un millimetro

incidence ['ɪnsɪdns] *n* (*of crime, disease*) incidenza

incident ['ɪnsɪdnt] *n* incidente *m*; (*in book*) episodio

incidental [ɪnsɪ'dentl] *adj* accessorio(a), d'accompagnamento; (*unplanned*) incidentale; **~ to** marginale a; **~ly** [-'dentəlɪ] *adv* (*by the way*) a proposito

inclination [ɪnklɪ'neɪʃən] *n* inclinazione *f*

incline [*n* 'ɪnklaɪn, *vb* ɪn'klaɪn] *n* pendenza, pendio ♦ *vt* inclinare ♦ *vi* (*surface*) essere inclinato(a); **to be ~d to do** tendere a fare; essere propenso(a) a fare

include [ɪn'kluːd] *vt* includere, comprendere; **including** *prep* compreso(a), incluso(a)

inclusive [ɪn'kluːsɪv] *adj* incluso(a), compreso(a); **~ of tax** *etc* tasse *etc* comprese

incoherent [ɪnkəʊ'hɪərənt] *adj* incoerente

income ['ɪnkʌm] *n* reddito; **~ tax** *n* imposta sul reddito

incoming ['ɪnkʌmɪŋ] *adj* (*flight, mail*) in arrivo; (*government*) subentrante; (*tide*) montante

incompetent [ɪn'kɒmpɪtnt] *adj* incompetente, incapace

incomplete [ɪnkəm'pliːt] *adj* incompleto(a)

incongruous [ɪn'kɒŋgruəs] *adj* poco appropriato(a); (*remark, act*) incongruo(a)

inconsiderate [ɪnkən'sɪdərət] *adj* sconsiderato(a)

inconsistency [ɪnkən'sɪstənsɪ] *n* incoerenza

inconsistent [ɪnkən'sɪstənt] *adj* incoerente; **~ with** non coerente con

inconspicuous [ɪnkən'spɪkjuəs] *adj* incospicuo(a); (*colour*) poco appariscente; (*dress*) dimesso(a)

inconvenience [ɪnkən'viːnjəns] *n* inconveniente *m*; (*trouble*) disturbo ♦ *vt* disturbare

inconvenient [ɪnkən'viːnjənt] *adj* scomodo(a)

incorporate [ɪn'kɔːpəreɪt] *vt* incorporare; (*contain*) contenere; **~d company** (*US*) società *f inv* anonima

incorrect [ɪnkə'rekt] *adj* scorretto(a); (*statement*) inesatto(a)

increase [*n* 'ɪnkriːs, *vb* ɪn'kriːs] *n* aumento ♦ *vi, vt* aumentare

increasing [ɪn'kriːsɪŋ] *adj* (*number*) crescente; **~ly** *adv* sempre più

incredible [ɪn'kredɪbl] *adj* incredibile

increment ['ɪnkrɪmənt] *n* aumento, incremento

incriminate [ɪn'krɪmɪneɪt] *vt* compromettere

incubator ['ɪnkjubeɪtə*] *n* incubatrice *f*

incumbent [ɪn'kʌmbənt] *adj*: **to be ~ on sb** spettare a qn

incur [ɪn'kə:*] *vt* (*expenses*) incorrere; (*anger, risk*) esporsi a; (*debt*) contrarre; (*loss*) subire

indebted [ɪn'detɪd] *adj*: **to be ~ to sb (for)** essere obbligato(a) verso qn (per)

indecent [ɪn'diːsnt] *adj* indecente; ~ **assault** (*BRIT*) *n* aggressione *f* a scopo di violenza sessuale; ~ **exposure** *n* atti *mpl* osceni in luogo pubblico

indecisive [ɪndɪ'saɪsɪv] *adj* indeciso(a)

indeed [ɪn'diːd] *adv* infatti; veramente; **yes ~!** certamente!

indefinite [ɪn'defɪnɪt] *adj* indefinito(a); (*answer*) vago(a); (*period, number*) indeterminato(a); **~ly** *adv* (*wait*) indefinitamente

indemnity [ɪn'demnɪtɪ] *n* (*insurance*) assicurazione *f*; (*compensation*) indennità, indennizzo

independence [ɪndɪ'pendns] *n* indipendenza

Independence Day

i Negli Stati Uniti il 4 luglio si festeggia l'**Independence Day**, *giorno in cui, nel 1776, 13 colonie britanniche proclamarono la propria indipendenza dalla Gran Bretagna ed entrarono ufficialmente a far parte degli Stati Uniti d'America.*

---

independent [ɪndɪ'pendnt] *adj* indipendente

index ['ɪndeks] (*pl* **~es**) *n* (*in book*) indice *m*; (: *in library etc*) catalogo; (*pl* **indices**: *ratio, sign*) indice *m*; ~ **card** *n* scheda; ~ **finger** *n* (dito) indice *m*; **~-linked** (*US* **~ed**) *adj* legato(a) al costo della vita

India ['ɪndɪə] *n* India; **~n** *adj, n* indiano(a)

indicate ['ɪndɪkeɪt] *vt* indicare; **indication** [-'keɪʃən] *n* indicazione *f*, segno

indicative [ɪn'dɪkətɪv] *adj*: ~ **of** indicativo(a) di

indicator ['ɪndɪkeɪtə*] *n* indicatore *m*; (*AUT*) freccia

indices ['ɪndɪsiːz] *npl of* **index**

indictment [ɪn'daɪtmənt] *n* accusa

indifference [ɪn'dɪfrəns] *n* indifferenza

indifferent [ɪn'dɪfrənt] *adj* indifferente; (*poor*) mediocre

indigenous [ɪn'dɪdʒɪnəs] *adj* indigeno(a)

indigestion [ɪndɪ'dʒestʃən] *n* indigestione *f*

indignant [ɪn'dɪgnənt] *adj*: ~ **(at sth/with**

sb) indignato(a) (per qc/contro qn)

indignity [ɪn'dɪgnɪtɪ] *n* umiliazione *f*

indigo ['ɪndɪgəʊ] *n* indaco

indirect [ɪndɪ'rekt] *adj* indiretto(a)

indiscreet [ɪndɪ'skriːt] *adj* indiscreto(a); (*rash*) imprudente

indiscriminate [ɪndɪ'skrɪmɪnət] *adj* indiscriminato(a)

indisputable [ɪndɪ'spjuːtəbl] *adj* incontestabile, indiscutibile

individual [ɪndɪ'vɪdjuəl] *n* individuo ♦ *adj* individuale; (*characteristic*) particolare, originale

indoctrination [ɪndɒktrɪ'neɪʃən] *n* indottrinamento

Indonesia [ɪndə'niːzɪə] *n* Indonesia

indoor ['ɪndɔː*] *adj* da interno; (*plant*) d'appartamento; (*swimming pool*) coperto(a); (*sport, games*) fatto(a) al coperto; **~s** [ɪn'dɔːz] *adv* all'interno

induce [ɪn'djuːs] *vt* persuadere; (*bring about, MED*) provocare

indulge [ɪn'dʌldʒ] *vt* (*whim*) compiacere, soddisfare; (*child*) viziare ♦ *vi*: **to ~ in sth** concedersi qc; abbandonarsi a qc; **~nce** *n* lusso (che uno si permette); (*leniency*) indulgenza; **~nt** *adj* indulgente

industrial [ɪn'dʌstrɪəl] *adj* industriale; (*injury*) sul lavoro; ~ **action** *n* azione *f* rivendicativa; ~ **estate** (*BRIT*) *n* zona industriale; ~ **park** (*US*) *n* = ~ **estate**

industrious [ɪn'dʌstrɪəs] *adj* industrioso(a), assiduo(a)

industry ['ɪndəstrɪ] *n* industria; (*diligence*) operosità

inedible [ɪn'edɪbl] *adj* immangiabile; (*poisonous*) non commestibile

ineffective [ɪnɪ'fektɪv] *adj* inefficace; incompetente

ineffectual [ɪnɪ'fektʃuəl] *adj* inefficace; incompetente

inefficient [ɪnɪ'fɪʃənt] *adj* inefficiente

inept [ɪ'nept] *adj* inetto(a)

inequality [ɪnɪ'kwɒlɪtɪ] *n* ineguaglianza

inescapable [ɪnɪ'skeɪpəbl] *adj* inevitabile

inevitable [ɪn'evɪtəbl] *adj* inevitabile; **inevitably** *adv* inevitabilmente

inexact [ɪnɪg'zækt] *adj* inesatto(a)
inexcusable [ɪnɪks'kju:zəbl] *adj* ingiustificabile
inexpensive [ɪnɪk'spɛnsɪv] *adj* poco costoso(a)
inexperienced [ɪnɪks'pɪərɪənst] *adj* inesperto(a), senza esperienza
infallible [ɪn'fælɪbl] *adj* infallibile
infamous ['ɪnfəməs] *adj* infame
infancy ['ɪnfənsɪ] *n* infanzia
infant ['ɪnfənt] *n* bambino/a; **~ school** (BRIT) scuola elementare (*per bambini dall'età di 5 a 7 anni*)
infantry ['ɪnfəntrɪ] *n* fanteria
infatuated [ɪn'fætjueɪtɪd] *adj*: **~ with** infatuato(a) di
infatuation [ɪnfætju'eɪʃən] *n* infatuazione *f*
infect [ɪn'fɛkt] *vt* infettare; **~ion** [ɪn'fɛkʃən] *n* infezione *f*; **~ious** [ɪn'fɛkʃəs] *adj* (*disease*) infettivo(a), contagioso(a); (*person, fig: enthusiasm*) contagioso(a)
infer [ɪn'fɜː*] *vt* inferire, dedurre
inferior [ɪn'fɪərɪə*] *adj* inferiore; (*goods*) di qualità scadente ♦ *n* inferiore *m/f*; (*in rank*) subalterno/a; **~ity** [ɪnfɪərɪ'ɔrətɪ] *n* inferiorità; **~ity complex** *n* complesso di inferiorità
infertile [ɪn'fɜːtaɪl] *adj* sterile
in-fighting ['ɪnfaɪtɪŋ] *n* lotte *fpl* intestine
infiltrate ['ɪnfɪltreɪt] *vt* infiltrarsi in
infinite ['ɪnfɪnɪt] *adj* infinito(a)
infinitive [ɪn'fɪnɪtɪv] *n* infinito
infinity [ɪn'fɪnɪtɪ] *n* infinità; (*also* MATH) infinito
infirmary [ɪn'fɜːmərɪ] *n* ospedale *m*; (*in school, factory*) infermeria
inflamed [ɪn'fleɪmd] *adj* infiammato(a)
inflammable [ɪn'flæməbl] *adj* infiammabile
inflammation [ɪnflə'meɪʃən] *n* infiammazione *f*
inflatable [ɪn'fleɪtəbl] *adj* gonfiabile
inflate [ɪn'fleɪt] *vt* (*tyre, balloon*) gonfiare; (*fig*) esagerare; gonfiare; **inflation** [ɪn'fleɪʃən] *n* (ECON) inflazione *f*; **inflationary** [ɪn'fleɪʃnərɪ] *adj* inflazionistico(a)
inflict [ɪn'flɪkt] *vt*: **to ~ on** infliggere a
influence ['ɪnfluəns] *n* influenza ♦ *vt*

influenzare; **under the ~ of alcohol** sotto l'effetto dell'alcool
influential [ɪnflu'ɛnʃl] *adj* influente
influenza [ɪnflu'ɛnzə] *n* (MED) influenza
influx ['ɪnflʌks] *n* afflusso
inform [ɪn'fɔːm] *vt*: **to ~ sb (of)** informare qn (di) ♦ *vi*: **to ~ on sb** denunciare qn
informal [ɪn'fɔːml] *adj* informale; (*announcement, invitation*) non ufficiale; **~ity** [-'mælɪtɪ] *n* informalità; carattere *m* non ufficiale
informant [ɪn'fɔːmənt] *n* informatore/trice
information [ɪnfə'meɪʃən] *n* informazioni *fpl*; particolari *mpl*; **a piece of ~** un'informazione; **~ desk** *n* banco *m* informazioni *inv*; **~ office** *n* ufficio *m* informazioni *inv*
informative [ɪn'fɔːmətɪv] *adj* istruttivo(a)
informer [ɪn'fɔːmə*] *n* (*also*: **police ~**) informatore/trice
infringe [ɪn'frɪndʒ] *vt* infrangere ♦ *vi*: **to ~ on** calpestare; **~ment** *n* infrazione *f*
infuriating [ɪn'fjuərieɪtɪŋ] *adj* molto irritante
ingenious [ɪn'dʒiːnjəs] *adj* ingegnoso(a)
ingenuity [ɪndʒɪ'nju:ɪtɪ] *n* ingegnosità
ingenuous [ɪn'dʒɛnjuəs] *adj* ingenuo(a)
ingot ['ɪŋgət] *n* lingotto
ingrained [ɪn'greɪnd] *adj* radicato(a)
ingratiate [ɪn'greɪʃɪeɪt] *vt*: **to ~ o.s. with sb** ingraziarsi qn
ingredient [ɪn'griːdɪənt] *n* ingrediente *m*; elemento
inhabit [ɪn'hæbɪt] *vt* abitare
inhabitant [ɪn'hæbɪtnt] *n* abitante *m/f*
inhale [ɪn'heɪl] *vt* inalare ♦ *vi* (*in smoking*) aspirare
inherent [ɪn'hɪərənt] *adj*: **~ (in or to)** inerente (a)
inherit [ɪn'hɛrɪt] *vt* ereditare; **~ance** *n* eredità
inhibit [ɪn'hɪbɪt] *vt* (PSYCH) inibire; **~ion** [-'bɪʃən] *n* inibizione *f*
inhospitable [ɪnhɔs'pɪtəbl] *adj* inospitale
inhuman [ɪn'hju:mən] *adj* inumano(a)
initial [ɪ'nɪʃl] *adj* iniziale ♦ *n* iniziale *f* ♦ *vt* siglare; **~s** *npl* (*of name*) iniziali *fpl*; (*as signature*) sigla; **~ly** *adv* inizialmente,

all'inizio

initiate [ɪ'nɪʃɪeɪt] *vt* (*start*) avviare;
intraprendere; iniziare; (*person*) iniziare; **to
~ sb into a secret** mettere qn a parte di
un segreto; **to ~ proceedings against sb**
(*LAW*) intentare causa contro qn

initiative [ɪ'nɪʃətɪv] *n* iniziativa

inject [ɪn'dʒekt] *vt* (*liquid*) iniettare; (*patient*):
to ~ sb with sth fare a qn un'iniezione di
qc; (*funds*) immettere; **~ion** [ɪn'dʒekʃən] *n*
iniezione *f*, puntura

injure ['ɪndʒə*] *vt* ferire; (*damage: reputation
etc*) nuocere a; **~d** *adj* ferito(a)

injury ['ɪndʒərɪ] *n* ferita; **~ time** (*SPORT*)
tempo di ricupero

injustice [ɪn'dʒʌstɪs] *n* ingiustizia

ink [ɪŋk] *n* inchiostro

inkling ['ɪŋklɪŋ] *n* sentore *m*, vaga idea

inlaid ['ɪnleɪd] *adj* incrostato(a); (*table etc*)
intarsiato(a)

inland [*adj* 'ɪnlənd, *adv* ɪn'lænd] *adj*
interno(a) ♦ *adv* all'interno; **I~ Revenue**
(*BRIT*) *n* Fisco

in-laws ['ɪnlɔːz] *npl* suoceri *mpl*; famiglia
del marito (*or* della moglie)

inlet ['ɪnlet] *n* (*GEO*) insenatura, baia

inmate ['ɪnmeɪt] *n* (*in prison*) carcerato/a;
(*in asylum*) ricoverato/a

inn [ɪn] *n* locanda

innate [ɪ'neɪt] *adj* innato(a)

inner ['ɪnə*] *adj* interno(a), interiore; **~ city**
n centro di una zona urbana; **~ tube** *n*
camera d'aria

innings ['ɪnɪŋz] *n* (*CRICKET*) turno di battuta

innocence ['ɪnəsns] *n* innocenza

innocent ['ɪnəsnt] *adj* innocente

innocuous [ɪ'nɔkjuəs] *adj* innocuo(a)

innuendo [ɪnju'endəu] (*pl* **~es**) *n*
insinuazione *f*

innumerable [ɪ'njuːmrəbl] *adj*
innumerevole

in-patient *n* ricoverato/a

input ['ɪnput] *n* input *m*

inquest ['ɪnkwest] *n* inchiesta

inquire [ɪn'kwaɪə*] *vi* informarsi ♦ *vt*
domandare, informarsi su; **~ about** *vt fus*

informarsi di *or* su; **~ into** *vt fus* fare
indagini su; **inquiry** *n* domanda; (*LAW*)
indagine *f*, investigazione *f*; **"inquiries"**
"informazioni"; **inquiry office** (*BRIT*) *n*
ufficio *m* informazioni *inv*

inquisitive [ɪn'kwɪzɪtɪv] *adj* curioso(a)

ins. *abbr* = **inches**

insane [ɪn'seɪn] *adj* matto(a), pazzo(a);
(*MED*) alienato(a)

insanity [ɪn'sænɪtɪ] *n* follia; (*MED*)
alienazione *f* mentale

inscription [ɪn'skrɪpʃən] *n* iscrizione *f*;
dedica

insect ['ɪnsekt] *n* insetto; **~icide**
[ɪn'sektɪsaɪd] *n* insetticida *m*; **~ repellent** *n*
insettifugo

insecure [ɪnsɪ'kjuə*] *adj* malsicuro(a);
(*person*) insicuro(a)

insemination [ɪnsemɪ'neɪʃən] *n*: **artificial ~**
fecondazione *f* artificiale

insensible [ɪn'sensɪbl] *adj* (*unconscious*)
privo(a) di sensi

insensitive [ɪn'sensɪtɪv] *adj* insensibile

insert [ɪn'sɜːt] *vt* inserire, introdurre; **~ion**
[ɪn'sɜːʃən] *n* inserzione *f*

in-service *adj* (*training, course*) durante
l'orario di lavoro

inshore [ɪn'ʃɔː*] *adj* costiero(a) ♦ *adv*
presso la riva; verso la riva

inside ['ɪn'saɪd] *n* interno, parte *f* interiore
♦ *adj* interno(a), interiore ♦ *adv* dentro,
all'interno ♦ *prep* dentro, all'interno di; (*of
time*): **~ 10 minutes** entro 10 minuti; **~s**
npl (*inf: stomach*) ventre *m*; **~ forward** *n*
(*SPORT*) mezzala, interno; **~ lane** *n* (*AUT*)
corsia di marcia; **~ out** *adv* (*turn*) a
rovescio; (*know*) in fondo; **~r dealing** *n*
insider dealing *m inv*; **~r trading** *n* insider
trading *m inv*

insight ['ɪnsaɪt] *n* acume *m*, perspicacia;
(*glimpse, idea*) percezione *f*

insignia [ɪn'sɪgnɪə] *npl* insegne *fpl*

insignificant [ɪnsɪg'nɪfɪknt] *adj*
insignificante

insincere [ɪnsɪn'sɪə*] *adj* insince-
ro(a)

insinuate [ɪn'sɪnjueɪt] *vt* insinuare

insist [ɪn'sɪst] *vi* insistere; **to ~ on doing** insistere per fare; **to ~ that** insistere perché +*sub*; (*claim*) sostenere che; **~ent** *adj* insistente

insole ['ɪnsəul] *n* soletta

insolent ['ɪnsələnt] *adj* insolente

insomnia [ɪn'sɒmnɪə] *n* insonnia

inspect [ɪn'spɛkt] *vt* ispezionare; (*BRIT: ticket*) controllare; **~ion** [ɪn'spɛkʃən] *n* ispezione *f*; controllo; **~or** *n* ispettore/trice; (*BRIT: on buses, trains*) controllore *m*

inspire [ɪn'spaɪə*] *vt* ispirare

install [ɪn'stɔ:l] *vt* installare; **~ation** [ɪnstə'leɪʃən] *n* installazione *f*

instalment [ɪn'stɔ:lmənt] (*US* **installment**) *n* rata; (*of TV serial etc*) puntata; **in ~s** (*pay*) a rate; (*receive*) una parte per volta; (: *publication*) a fascicoli

instance ['ɪnstəns] *n* esempio, caso; **for ~** per *or* ad esempio; **in the first ~** in primo luogo

instant ['ɪnstənt] *n* istante *m*, attimo ♦ *adj* immediato(a); urgente; (*coffee, food*) in polvere; **~ly** *adv* immediatamente, subito

instead [ɪn'stɛd] *adv* invece; **~ of** invece di

instep ['ɪnstɛp] *n* collo del piede; (*of shoe*) collo della scarpa

instil [ɪn'stɪl] *vt*: **to ~ (into)** inculcare (in)

instinct ['ɪnstɪŋkt] *n* istinto

institute ['ɪnstɪtju:t] *n* istituto ♦ *vt* istituire, stabilire; (*inquiry*) avviare; (*proceedings*) iniziare

institution [ɪnstɪ'tju:ʃən] *n* istituzione *f*; (*educational ~, mental ~*) istituto

instruct [ɪn'strʌkt] *vt*: **to ~ sb in sth** insegnare qc a qn; **to ~ sb to do** dare ordini a qn di fare; **~ion** [ɪn'strʌkʃən] *n* istruzione *f*; **~ions (for use)** istruzioni per l'uso; **~or** *n* istruttore/trice; (*for skiing*) maestro/a

instrument ['ɪnstrəmənt] *n* strumento; **~al** [-'mɛntl] *adj* (*MUS*) strumentale; **to be ~al in** essere d'aiuto in; **~ panel** *n* quadro *m* portastrumenti *inv*

insufferable [ɪn'sʌfərəbl] *adj* insopportabile

insufficient [ɪnsə'fɪʃənt] *adj* insufficiente

insular ['ɪnsjulə*] *adj* insulare; (*person*) di

mente ristretta

insulate ['ɪnsjuleɪt] *vt* isolare; **insulation** [-'leɪʃən] *n* isolamento

insulin ['ɪnsjulɪn] *n* insulina

insult [*n* 'ɪnsʌlt, *vb* ɪn'sʌlt] *n* insulto, affronto ♦ *vt* insultare; **~ing** *adj* offensivo(a), ingiurioso(a)

insuperable [ɪn'sju:prəbl] *adj* insormontabile, insuperabile

insurance [ɪn'ʃuərəns] *n* assicurazione *f*; **fire/life ~** assicurazione contro gli incendi/ sulla vita; **~ policy** *n* polizza d'assicurazione

insure [ɪn'ʃuə*] *vt* assicurare

intact [ɪn'tækt] *adj* intatto(a)

intake ['ɪnteɪk] *n* (*TECH*) immissione *f*; (*of food*) consumo; (*BRIT: of pupils etc*) afflusso

integral ['ɪntɪgrəl] *adj* integrale; (*part*) integrante

integrate ['ɪntɪgreɪt] *vt* integrare ♦ *vi* integrarsi

integrity [ɪn'tɛgrɪtɪ] *n* integrità

intellect ['ɪntəlɛkt] *n* intelletto; **~ual** [-'lɛktjuəl] *adj*, *n* intellettuale *m/f*

intelligence [ɪn'tɛlɪdʒəns] *n* intelligenza; (*MIL etc*) informazioni *fpl*; **~ service** *n* servizio segreto

intelligent [ɪn'tɛlɪdʒənt] *adj* intelligente

intend [ɪn'tɛnd] *vt* (*gift etc*): **to ~ sth for** destinare qc a; **to ~ to do** aver l'intenzione di fare; **~ed** *adj* (*effect*) voluto(a)

intense [ɪn'tɛns] *adj* intenso(a); (*person*) di forti sentimenti; **~ly** *adv* intensamente; profondamente

intensive [ɪn'tɛnsɪv] *adj* intensivo(a); **~ care unit** *n* reparto terapia intensiva

intent [ɪn'tɛnt] *n* intenzione *f* ♦ *adj*: **~ (on)** intento(a) (a), immerso(a) (in); **to all ~s and purposes** a tutti gli effetti; **to be ~ on doing sth** essere deciso a fare qc

intention [ɪn'tɛnʃən] *n* intenzione *f*; **~al** *adj* intenzionale, deliberato(a); **~ally** *adv* apposta

intently [ɪn'tɛntlɪ] *adv* attentamente

interact [ɪntər'ækt] *vi* interagire

interactive *adj* (*COMPUT*) interattivo(a)

interchange ['ɪntətʃeɪndʒ] *n* (*exchange*)

scambio; (*on motorway*) incrocio pluridirezionale; **~able** [-'tʃeɪndʒəbl] *adj* intercambiabile

intercom ['ɪntəkɔm] *n* interfono

intercourse ['ɪntəkɔːs] *n* rapporti *mpl*

interest ['ɪntrɪst] *n* interesse *m*; (*COMM: stake, share*) interessi *mpl* ♦ *vt* interessare; **~ed** *adj* interessato(a); **to be ~ed in** interessarsi di; **~ing** *adj* interessante; **~ rate** *n* tasso di interesse

interface ['ɪntəfeɪs] *n* (*COMPUT*) interfaccia

interfere [ɪntə'fɪə*] *vi*: **to ~ in** (*quarrel, other people's business*) immischiarsi in; **to ~ with** (*object*) toccare; (*plans, duty*) interferire con

interference [ɪntə'fɪərəns] *n* interferenza

interim ['ɪntərɪm] *adj* provvisorio(a) ♦ *n*: **in the ~** nel frattempo

interior [ɪn'tɪərɪə*] *n* interno; (*of country*) entroterra ♦ *adj* interno(a); (*minister*) degli Interni; **~ designer** *n* arredatore/trice

interlock [ɪntə'lɔk] *vi* ingranarsi

interlude ['ɪntəluːd] *n* intervallo; (*THEATRE*) intermezzo

intermediate [ɪntə'miːdɪət] *adj* intermedio(a)

intermission [ɪntə'mɪʃən] *n* pausa; (*THEATRE, CINEMA*) intermissione *f*, intervallo

intern [*vb* ɪn'təːn, *n* 'ɪntəːn] *vt* internare ♦ *n* (*US*) medico interno

internal [ɪn'təːnl] *adj* interno(a); **~ly** *adv*: **"not to be taken ~ly"** "per uso esterno"; **I~ Revenue Service** (*US*) *n* Fisco

international [ɪntə'næʃənl] *adj* internazionale ♦ *n* (*BRIT: SPORT*) incontro internazionale

Internet ['ɪntənet] *n*: **the ~** Internet *f*; **~ café** *n* cybercaffè *m inv*

interplay ['ɪntəpleɪ] *n* azione e reazione *f*

interpret [ɪn'təːprɪt] *vt* interpretare ♦ *vi* fare da interprete; **~er** *n* interprete *m/f*

interrogate [ɪn'terəugeɪt] *vt* interrogare; **interrogation** [-'geɪʃən] *n* interrogazione *f*; (*of suspect etc*) interrogatorio

interrupt [ɪntə'rʌpt] *vt, vi* interrompere; **~ion** [-'rʌpʃən] *n* interruzione *f*

intersect [ɪntə'sekt] *vi* (*roads*) incrociarsi; **~ion** [-'sekʃən] *n* intersezione *f*; (*of roads*)

incrocio

intersperse [ɪntə'spəːs] *vt*: **to ~ with** costellare di

intertwine [ɪntə'twaɪn] *vi* intrecciarsi

interval ['ɪntəvl] *n* intervallo; **at ~s** a intervalli

intervene [ɪntə'viːn] *vi* (*time*) intercorrere; (*event, person*) intervenire; **intervention** [-'venʃən] *n* intervento

interview ['ɪntəvjuː] *n* (*RADIO, TV etc*) intervista; (*for job*) colloquio ♦ *vt* intervistare; avere un colloquio con; **~er** *n* intervistatore/trice

intestine [ɪn'testɪn] *n* intestino

intimacy ['ɪntɪməsɪ] *n* intimità

intimate [*adj* 'ɪntɪmət, *vb* 'ɪntɪmeɪt] *adj* intimo(a); (*knowledge*) profondo(a) ♦ *vt* lasciar capire

into ['ɪntuː] *prep* dentro, in; **come ~ the house** entra in casa; **he worked late ~ the night** lavorò fino a tarda notte; **~ Italian** in italiano

intolerable [ɪn'tɔlərəbl] *adj* intollerabile

intolerance [ɪn'tɔlərns] *n* intolleranza

intolerant [ɪn'tɔlərnt] *adj*: **~ of** intollerante di

intoxicated [ɪn'tɔksɪkeɪtɪd] *adj* inebriato(a)

intractable [ɪn'træktəbl] *adj* intrattabile

intranet ['ɪntrənet] *n* intranet *f*

intransitive [ɪn'trænsɪtɪv] *adj* intransitivo(a)

intravenous [ɪntrə'viːnəs] *adj* endovenoso(a)

in-tray *n* contenitore *m* per la corrispondenza in arrivo

intricate ['ɪntrɪkət] *adj* intricato(a), complicato(a)

intrigue [ɪn'triːg] *n* intrigo ♦ *vt* affascinare; **intriguing** *adj* affascinante

intrinsic [ɪn'trɪnsɪk] *adj* intrinseco(a)

introduce [ɪntrə'djuːs] *vt* introdurre; **to ~ sb (to sb)** presentare qn (a qn); **to ~ sb to** (*pastime, technique*) iniziare qn a; **introduction** [-'dʌkʃən] *n* introduzione *f*; (*of person*) presentazione *f*; (*to new experience*) iniziazione *f*; **introductory** *adj* introduttivo(a)

intrude [ɪn'truːd] *vi* (*person*): **to ~ (on)** intromettersi (in); **~r** *n* intruso/a

intuition [ɪntjuː'ɪʃən] *n* intuizione *f*

inundate ['ɪnʌndeɪt] vt: **to ~ with** inondare di

invade [ɪn'veɪd] vt invadere

invalid [n 'ɪnvəlɪd, adj ɪn'vælɪd] n malato/a; (with disability) invalido/a ♦ adj (not valid) invalido(a), non valido(a)

invaluable [ɪn'væljuəbl] adj prezioso(a); inestimabile

invariably [ɪn'veərɪəblɪ] adv invariabilmente; sempre

invasion [ɪn'veɪʒən] n invasione f

invent [ɪn'vent] vt inventare; **~ion** [ɪn'venʃən] n invenzione f; **~ive** adj inventivo(a); **~or** n inventore m

inventory ['ɪnvəntrɪ] n inventario

invert [ɪn'vɜːt] vt invertire; (cup, object) rovesciare; **~ed commas** (BRIT) npl virgolette fpl

invest [ɪn'vest] vt investire ♦ vi: **to ~ (in)** investire (in)

investigate [ɪn'vestɪgeɪt] vt investigare, indagare; (crime) fare indagini su; **investigation** [-'geɪʃən] n investigazione f; (of crime) indagine f

investment [ɪn'vestmənt] n investimento

investor [ɪn'vestə*] n investitore/trice; azionista m/f

invidious [ɪn'vɪdɪəs] adj odioso(a); (task) spiacevole

invigilator [ɪn'vɪdʒɪleɪtə*] n (in exam) sorvegliante m/f

invigorating [ɪn'vɪgəreɪtɪŋ] adj stimolante; vivificante

invisible [ɪn'vɪzɪbl] adj invisibile

invitation [ɪnvɪ'teɪʃən] n invito

invite [ɪn'vaɪt] vt invitare; (opinions etc) sollecitare; **inviting** adj invitante, attraente

invoice ['ɪnvɔɪs] n fattura ♦ vt fatturare

involuntary [ɪn'vɔləntrɪ] adj involontario(a)

involve [ɪn'vɔlv] vt (entail) richiedere, comportare; (associate): **to ~ sb (in)** implicare qn (in); coinvolgere qn (in); **~d** adj involuto(a), complesso(a); **to be ~d in** essere coinvolto(a) in; **~ment** n implicazione f; coinvolgimento

inward ['ɪnwəd] adj (movement) verso l'interno; (thought, feeling) interiore,

intimo(a); **~(s)** adv verso l'interno

I/O abbr (COMPUT: = input/output) I/O

iodine ['aɪəudiːn] n iodio

ioniser ['aɪənaɪzə*] n ionizzatore m

iota [aɪ'əutə] n (fig) briciolo

IOU n abbr (= I owe you) pagherò m inv

IQ n abbr (= intelligence quotient) quoziente m d'intelligenza

IRA n abbr (= Irish Republican Army) IRA f

Iran [ɪ'rɑːn] n Iran m; **~ian** adj, n iraniano(a)

Iraq [ɪ'rɑːk] n Iraq m; **~i** adj, n iracheno(a)

irate [aɪ'reɪt] adj adirato(a)

Ireland ['aɪələnd] n Irlanda

iris ['aɪrɪs] (pl **~es**) n iride f; (BOT) giaggiolo, iride

Irish ['aɪrɪʃ] adj irlandese ♦ npl: **the ~** gli Irlandesi; **~man** (irreg) n irlandese m; **~ Sea** n Mar m d'Irlanda; **~woman** (irreg) n irlandese f

irksome ['ɜːksəm] adj seccante

iron ['aɪən] n ferro; (for clothes) ferro da stiro ♦ adj di or in ferro ♦ vt (clothes) stirare; **~ out** vt (crease) appianare; (fig) spianare; far sparire

ironic(al) [aɪ'rɔnɪk(l)] adj ironico(a)

ironing ['aɪənɪŋ] n (act) stirare m; (clothes) roba da stirare; **~ board** n asse f da stiro

ironmonger's (shop) ['aɪənmʌŋgəz-] (BRIT) n negozio di ferramenta

irony ['aɪrənɪ] n ironia

irrational [ɪ'ræʃənl] adj irrazionale

irregular [ɪ'regjulə*] adj irregolare

irrelevant [ɪ'reləvənt] adj non pertinente

irreplaceable [ɪrɪ'pleɪsəbl] adj insostituibile

irrepressible [ɪrɪ'presəbl] adj irrefrenabile

irresistible [ɪrɪ'zɪstɪbl] adj irresistibile

irrespective [ɪrɪ'spektɪv]: **~ of** prep senza riguardo a

irresponsible [ɪrɪ'spɔnsɪbl] adj irresponsabile

irrigate ['ɪrɪgeɪt] vt irrigare; **irrigation** [-'geɪʃən] n irrigazione f

irritable ['ɪrɪtəbl] adj irritabile

irritate ['ɪrɪteɪt] vt irritare; **irritating** adj (person, sound etc) irritante; **irritation** [-'teɪʃən] n irritazione f

IRS (*US*) *n abbr* = **Internal Revenue Service**

is [ɪz] *vb see* **be**

Islam [ˈɪzlɑːm] *n* Islam *m*

island [ˈaɪlənd] *n* isola; **~er** *n* isolano/a

isle [aɪl] *n* isola

isn't [ˈɪznt] = **is not**

isolate [ˈaɪsəleɪt] *vt* isolare; **~d** *adj* isolato(a); **isolation** [-ˈleɪʃən] *n* isolamento

ISP *n abbr* (= *Internet Service Provider*) provider *m inv*

Israel [ˈɪzreɪl] *n* Israele *m*; **~i** [ɪzˈreɪlɪ] *adj, n* israeliano(a)

issue [ˈɪʃuː] *n* questione *f*, problema *m*; (*of banknotes etc*) emissione *f*; (*of newspaper etc*) numero ♦ *vt* (*statement*) rilasciare; (*rations, equipment*) distribuire; (*book*) pubblicare; (*banknotes, cheques, stamps*) emettere; **at ~** in gioco, in discussione; **to take ~ with sb (over sth)** prendere posizione contro qn (riguardo a qc); **to make an ~ of sth** fare un problema di qc

KEYWORD

it [ɪt] *pron* **1** (*specific: subject*) esso(a); (: *direct object*) lo(la), l'; (: *indirect object*) gli(le); **where's my book? — ~'s on the table** dov'è il mio libro? — è sulla tavola; **I can't find ~** non lo (*or* la) trovo; **give ~ to me** dammelo (*or* dammela); **about/from/of ~** ne; **I spoke to him about ~** gliene ho parlato; **what did you learn from ~?** quale insegnamento ne hai tratto?; **I'm proud of ~** ne sono fiero; **did you go to ~?** ci sei andato?; **put the book in ~** mettici il libro

2 (*impers*): **~'s raining** piove; **~'s Friday tomorrow** domani è venerdì; **~'s 6 o'clock** sono le 6; **who is ~? — ~'s me** chi è? — sono io

Italian [ɪˈtæljən] *adj* italiano(a) ♦ *n* italiano/a; (*LING*) italiano; **the ~s** gli Italiani

italics [ɪˈtælɪks] *npl* corsivo

Italy [ˈɪtəlɪ] *n* Italia

itch [ɪtʃ] *n* prurito ♦ *vi* (*person*) avere il prurito; (*part of body*) prudere; **to ~ to do sth** aver una gran voglia di fare qc; **~y** *adj*

che prude; **to be ~y = to ~**

it'd [ˈɪtd] = **it would**; **it had**

item [ˈaɪtəm] *n* articolo; (*on agenda*) punto; (*also*: **news ~**) notizia; **~ize** *vt* specificare, dettagliare

itinerant [ɪˈtɪnərənt] *adj* ambulante

itinerary [aɪˈtɪnərərɪ] *n* itinerario

it'll [ˈɪtl] = **it will**; **it shall**

its [ɪts] *adj* il(la) suo(a), i(le) suoi(sue)

it's [ɪts] = **it is**; **it has**

itself [ɪtˈsɛlf] *pron* (*emphatic*) esso(a) stesso(a); (*reflexive*) si

ITV (*BRIT*) *n abbr* (= *Independent Television*) rete televisiva in concorrenza con la BBC

I.U.D. *n abbr* (= *intra-uterine device*) spirale *f*

I've [aɪv] = **I have**

ivory [ˈaɪvərɪ] *n* avorio

ivy [ˈaɪvɪ] *n* edera

J, j

jab [dʒæb] *vt* dare colpetti a ♦ *n* (*MED*: *inf*) puntura; **to ~ sth into** affondare *or* piantare qc dentro

jack [dʒæk] *n* (*AUT*) cricco; (*CARDS*) fante *m*; **~ up** *vt* sollevare col cricco

jackal [ˈdʒækl] *n* sciacallo

jackdaw [ˈdʒækdɔː] *n* taccola

jacket [ˈdʒækɪt] *n* giacca; (*of book*) copertura

jack-knife *vi*: **the lorry ~d** l'autotreno si è piegato su stesso

jack plug *n* (*ELEC*) jack *m inv*

jackpot [ˈdʒækpɔt] *n* primo premio (in denaro)

jade [dʒeɪd] *n* (*stone*) giada

jaded [ˈdʒeɪdɪd] *adj* sfinito(a), spossato(a)

jagged [ˈdʒægɪd] *adj* seghettato(a); (*cliffs etc*) frastagliato(a)

jail [dʒeɪl] *n* prigione *f* ♦ *vt* mandare in prigione

jam [dʒæm] *n* marmellata; (*also*: **traffic ~**) ingorgo; (*inf*) pasticcio ♦ *vt* (*passage etc*) ingombrare, ostacolare; (*mechanism, drawer etc*) bloccare; (*RADIO*) disturbare con interferenze ♦ *vi* incepparsi; **to ~ sth into** forzare qc dentro; infilare qc a forza dentro

Jamaica [dʒə'meɪkə] n Giamaica

jangle ['dʒæŋgl] vi risuonare; (bracelet) tintinnare

janitor ['dʒænɪtə*] n (caretaker) portiere m; (: SCOL) bidello

January ['dʒænjuərɪ] n gennaio

Japan [dʒə'pæn] n Giappone m; ~ese [dʒæpə'niːz] adj giapponese ♦ n inv giapponese m/f; (LING) giapponese m

jar [dʒɑː*] n (glass) barattolo, vasetto ♦ vi (sound) stridere; (colours etc) stonare

jargon ['dʒɑːgən] n gergo

jasmin(e) ['dʒæzmɪn] n gelsomino

jaundice ['dʒɔːndɪs] n itterizia

jaunt [dʒɔːnt] n gita

javelin ['dʒævlɪn] n giavellotto

jaw [dʒɔː] n mascella

jay [dʒeɪ] n ghiandaia

jaywalker ['dʒeɪwɔːkə*] n pedone(a) indisciplinato(a)

jazz [dʒæz] n jazz m; ~ up vt rendere vivace

jealous ['dʒeləs] adj geloso(a); ~y n gelosia

jeans [dʒiːnz] npl (blue-)jeans mpl

jeer [dʒɪə*] vi: to ~ (at) fischiare; beffeggiare

jelly ['dʒelɪ] n gelatina; ~fish n medusa

jeopardy ['dʒepədɪ] n: in ~ in pericolo

jerk [dʒɜːk] n sobbalzo, scossa; sussulto; (inf: idiot) tonto/a ♦ vt dare una scossa a ♦ vi (vehicles) sobbalzare

jersey ['dʒɜːzɪ] n maglia; (fabric) jersey m

jest [dʒest] n scherzo

Jesus ['dʒiːzəs] n Gesù m

jet [dʒet] n (of gas, liquid) getto; (AVIAT) aviogetto; ~-black adj nero(a) come l'ebano, corvino(a); ~ engine n motore m a reazione; ~ lag n (problemi mpl dovuti allo) sbalzo dei fusi orari

jettison ['dʒetɪsn] vt gettare in mare

jetty ['dʒetɪ] n molo

Jew [dʒuː] n ebreo

jewel ['dʒuːəl] n gioiello; ~ler (US ~er) n orefice m, gioielliere/a; ~(l)er's (shop) n oreficeria, gioielleria; ~lery (US ~ery) n gioielli mpl

Jewess ['dʒuːɪs] n ebrea

Jewish ['dʒuːɪʃ] adj ebreo(a), ebraico(a)

jibe [dʒaɪb] n beffa

jiffy ['dʒɪfɪ] (inf) n: in a ~ in un batter d'occhio

jig [dʒɪg] n giga

jigsaw ['dʒɪgsɔː] n (also: ~ puzzle) puzzle m inv

jilt [dʒɪlt] vt piantare in asso

jingle ['dʒɪŋgl] n (for advert) sigla pubblicitaria ♦ vi tintinnare, scampanellare

jinx [dʒɪŋks] n iettatura; (person) iettatore/trice

jitters ['dʒɪtəz] (inf) npl: to get the ~ aver fifa

job [dʒɔb] n lavoro; (employment) impiego, posto; it's not my ~ (duty) non è compito mio; it's a good ~ that ... meno male che ...; just the ~! proprio quello che ci vuole; ~ centre n (BRIT) ufficio di collocamento; ~less adj senza lavoro, disoccupato(a)

jockey ['dʒɔkɪ] n fantino, jockey m inv ♦ vi: to ~ for position manovrare per una posizione di vantaggio

jog [dʒɔg] vt urtare ♦ vi (SPORT) fare footing, fare jogging; to ~ sb's memory rinfrescare la memoria a qn; to ~ along trottare; (fig) andare avanti piano piano; ~ging n footing m, jogging m

join [dʒɔɪn] vt unire, congiungere; (become member of) iscriversi a; (meet) raggiungere; riunirsi a ♦ vi (roads, rivers) confluire ♦ n giuntura; ~ in vi partecipare ♦ vt fus unirsi a; ~ up vi incontrarsi; (MIL) arruolarsi

joiner ['dʒɔɪnə*] (BRIT) n falegname m

joint [dʒɔɪnt] n (TECH) giuntura; giunto; (ANAT) articolazione f, giuntura; (BRIT: CULIN) arrosto; (inf: place) locale m; (: of cannabis) spinello ♦ adj comune; ~ account n (at bank etc) conto in partecipazione, conto comune

joist [dʒɔɪst] n trave f

joke [dʒəuk] n scherzo; (funny story) barzelletta; (also: practical ~) beffa ♦ vi scherzare; to play a ~ on sb fare uno scherzo a qn; ~r n (CARDS) matta, jolly m inv

jolly ['dʒɔlɪ] adj allegro(a), gioioso(a) ♦ adv (BRIT: inf) veramente, proprio

jolt [dʒəult] n scossa, sobbalzo ♦ vt urtare

Jordan ['dʒɔːdən] n (country) Giordania; (river) Giordano

jostle ['dʒɔsl] vt spingere coi gomiti

jot [dʒɔt] n: **not one ~** nemmeno un po'; **~ down** vt annotare in fretta, buttare giù; **~ter** (BRIT) n blocco

journal ['dʒɔːnl] n giornale m; rivista; diario; **~ism** n giornalismo; **~ist** n giornalista m/f

journey ['dʒɔːni] n viaggio; (distance covered) tragitto

joy [dʒɔi] n gioia; **~ful** adj gioioso(a), allegro(a); **~rider** n chi ruba un'auto per farvi un giro; **~stick** n (AVIAT) barra di comando; (COMPUT) joystick m inv

JP n abbr = **Justice of the Peace**

Jr abbr = **junior**

jubilant ['dʒuːbɪlnt] adj giubilante; trionfante

jubilee ['dʒuːbɪliː] n giubileo; **silver ~** venticinquesimo anniversario

judge [dʒʌdʒ] n giudice m/f ♦ vt giudicare; **judg(e)ment** n giudizio

judiciary [dʒuːˈdɪʃɪəri] n magistratura

judo ['dʒuːdəu] n judo

jug [dʒʌg] n brocca, bricco

juggernaut ['dʒʌgənɔːt] (BRIT) n (huge truck) bestione m

juggle ['dʒʌgl] vi fare giochi di destrezza; **~r** n giocoliere/a

juice [dʒuːs] n succo

juicy ['dʒuːsi] adj succoso(a)

jukebox ['dʒuːkbɔks] n juke-box m inv

July [dʒuːˈlai] n luglio

jumble ['dʒʌmbl] n miscuglio ♦ vt (also: **~ up**) mischiare; **~ sale** (BRIT) n vendita di beneficenza

---
jumble sale

ⓘ Una **jumble sale** è un mercatino di oggetti di seconda mano organizzato in chiese, scuole o in circoli ricreativi, i cui proventi vengono devoluti in beneficenza.

---

jumbo (jet) ['dʒʌmbəu-] n jumbo-jet m inv

jump [dʒʌmp] vi saltare, balzare; (start) sobbalzare; (increase) rincarare ♦ vt saltare ♦ n salto, balzo; sobbalzo

jumper ['dʒʌmpə*] n (BRIT: pullover) maglione m, pullover m inv; (US: dress) scamiciato; **~ cables** (US) npl = **jump leads**

jump leads (BRIT) npl cavi mpl per batteria

jumpy ['dʒʌmpi] adj nervoso(a), agitato(a)

Jun. abbr = **junior**

junction ['dʒʌŋkʃən] n (BRIT: of roads) incrocio; (of rails) nodo ferroviario

juncture ['dʒʌŋktʃə*] n: **at this ~** in questa congiuntura

June [dʒuːn] n giugno

jungle ['dʒʌŋgl] n giungla

junior ['dʒuːniə*] adj, n: **he's ~ to me (by 2 years), he's my ~ (by 2 years)** è più giovane di me (di 2 anni); **he's ~ to me** (seniority) è al di sotto di me, ho più anzianità di lui; **~ school** (BRIT) n scuola elementare (da 8 a 11 anni)

junk [dʒʌŋk] n cianfrusaglie fpl; (cheap goods) robaccia; **~ food** n porcherie fpl

junkie ['dʒʌŋki] (inf) n drogato/a

junk mail n stampe fpl pubblicitarie

junk shop n chincaglieria

Junr abbr = **junior**

juror ['dʒuərə*] n giurato/a

jury ['dʒuəri] n giuria

just [dʒʌst] adj giusto(a) ♦ adv: **he's ~ done it/left** lo ha appena fatto/è appena partito; **~ right** proprio giusto; **~ 2 o'clock** le 2 precise; **she's ~ as clever as you** è in gamba proprio quanto te; **it's ~ as well that ...** meno male che ...; **~ as I arrived** proprio mentre arrivavo; **it was ~ before/ enough/here** era poco prima/appena assai/proprio qui; **it's ~ me** sono solo io; **~ missed/caught** appena perso/preso; **~ listen to this!** senta un po' questo!

justice ['dʒʌstis] n giustizia; **J~ of the Peace** n giudice m conciliatore

justify ['dʒʌstɪfai] vt giustificare

jut [dʒʌt] vi (also: **~ out**) sporgersi

juvenile ['dʒuːvənail] adj giovane, giovanile; (court) dei minorenni; (books) per ragazzi ♦ n giovane m/f, minorenne m/f

juxtapose ['dʒʌkstəpəuz] vt giustapporre

K, k

K *abbr* (= *one thousand*) mille; (= *kilobyte*) K
Kampuchea [kæmpuˈtʃɪə] *n* Cambogia
kangaroo [kæŋgəˈruː] *n* canguro
karate [kəˈrɑːtɪ] *n* karatè *m*
kebab [kəˈbæb] *n* spiedino
keel [kiːl] *n* chiglia; **on an even ~** (*fig*) in uno stato normale
keen [kiːn] *adj* (*interest, desire*) vivo(a); (*eye, intelligence*) acuto(a); (*competition*) serrato(a); (*edge*) affilato(a); (*eager*) entusiasta; **to be ~ to do** *or* **doing sth** avere una gran voglia di fare qc; **to be ~ on sth** essere appassionato(a) di qc; **to be ~ on sb** avere un debole per qn
keep [kiːp] (*pt, pp* **kept**) *vt* tenere; (*hold back*) trattenere; (*feed: one's family etc*) mantenere, sostentare; (*a promise*) mantenere; (*chickens, bees, pigs etc*) allevare ♦ *vi* (*food*) mantenersi; (*remain: in a certain state or place*) restare ♦ *n* (*of castle*) maschio; (*food etc*): **enough for his ~** abbastanza per vitto e alloggio; (*inf*): **for ~s** per sempre; **to ~ doing sth** continuare a fare qc; fare qc di continuo; **to ~ sb from doing** impedire a qn di fare; **to ~ sb busy/a place tidy** tenere qn occupato(a)/un luogo in ordine; **to ~ sth to o.s.** tenere qc per sé; **to ~ sth (back) from sb** celare qc a qn; **to ~ time** (*clock*) andar bene; **~ on** *vi*: **to ~ on doing** continuare a fare; **to ~ on (about sth)** continuare a insistere (su qc); **~ out** *vt* tener fuori; **"~ out"** "vietato l'accesso"; **~ up** *vt* continuare, mantenere ♦ *vi*: **to ~ up with** tener dietro a, andare di pari passo con; (*work etc*) farcela a seguire; **~er** *n* custode *m/f*, guardiano/a; **~-fit** *n* ginnastica; **~ing** *n* (*care*) custodia; **in ~ing with** in armonia con; in accordo con; **~sake** *n* ricordo
kennel [ˈkɛnl] *n* canile *m*; **to put a dog in ~s** mettere un cane al canile
kept [kɛpt] *pt, pp of* **keep**
kerb [kəːb] (*BRIT*) *n* orlo del marciapiede

kernel [ˈkəːnl] *n* nocciolo
kettle [ˈkɛtl] *n* bollitore *m*
kettle drum *n* timpano
key [kiː] *n* (*gen, MUS*) chiave *f*; (*of piano, typewriter*) tasto ♦ *adj* chiave *inv* ♦ *vt* (*also*: **~ in**) digitare; **~board** *n* tastiera; **~ed up** *adj* (*person*) agitato(a); **~hole** *n* buco della serratura; **~hole surgery** *n* chirurgia non invasiva; **~note** *n* (*MUS*) tonica; (*fig*) nota dominante; **~ring** *n* portachiavi *m inv*
khaki [ˈkɑːkɪ] *adj* cachi ♦ *n* cachi *m*
kick [kɪk] *vt* calciare, dare calci a; (*inf: habit etc*) liberarsi di ♦ *vi* (*horse*) tirar calci ♦ *n* calcio; (*thrill*): **he does it for ~s** lo fa giusto per il piacere di farlo; **~ off** *vi* (*SPORT*) dare il primo calcio
kid [kɪd] *n* (*inf: child*) ragazzino/a; (*animal, leather*) capretto ♦ *vi* (*inf*) scherzare
kidnap [ˈkɪdnæp] *vt* rapire, sequestrare; **~per** *n* rapitore/trice; **~ping** *n* sequestro (di persona)
kidney [ˈkɪdnɪ] *n* (*ANAT*) rene *m*; (*CULIN*) rognone *m*
kill [kɪl] *vt* uccidere, ammazzare ♦ *n* uccisione *f*; **~er** *n* uccisore *m*, killer *m inv*; assassino/a; **~ing** *n* assassinio; **to make a ~ing** (*inf*) fare un bel colpo; **~joy** *n* guastafeste *m/f inv*
kiln [kɪln] *n* forno
kilo [ˈkiːləʊ] *n* chilo; **~byte** *n* (*COMPUT*) kilobyte *m inv*; **~gram(me)** [ˈkɪləʊgræm] *n* chilogrammo; **~metre** [ˈkɪləmiːtə*] (*US* **~meter**) *n* chilometro; **~watt** [ˈkɪləʊwɔt] *n* chilowatt *m inv*
kilt [kɪlt] *n* gonnellino scozzese
kin [kɪn] *n see* **next**; **kith**
kind [kaɪnd] *adj* gentile, buono(a) ♦ *n* sorta, specie *f*; (*species*) genere *m*; **to be two of a ~** essere molto simili; **in ~** (*COMM*) in natura
kindergarten [ˈkɪndəgɑːtn] *n* giardino d'infanzia
kind-hearted [-ˈhɑːtɪd] *adj* di buon cuore
kindle [ˈkɪndl] *vt* accendere, infiammare
kindly [ˈkaɪndlɪ] *adj* pieno(a) di bontà, benevolo(a) ♦ *adv* con bontà, gentilmente; **will you ~ ...** vuole ... per favore
kindness [ˈkaɪndnɪs] *n* bontà, gentilezza

king [kɪŋ] n re m inv; **~dom** n regno, reame m; **~fisher** n martin m inv pescatore; **~-size** adj super inv; gigante

kiosk ['kiːɔsk] n edicola, chiosco; (BRIT: TEL) cabina (telefonica)

kipper ['kɪpə*] n aringa affumicata

kiss [kɪs] n bacio ♦ vt baciare; **to ~ (each other)** baciarsi; **~ of life** n respirazione f bocca a bocca

kit [kɪt] n equipaggiamento, corredo; (set of tools etc) attrezzi mpl; (for assembly) scatola di montaggio

kitchen ['kɪtʃɪn] n cucina; **~ sink** n acquaio

kite [kaɪt] n (toy) aquilone m

kitten ['kɪtn] n gattino/a, micino/a

kitty ['kɪtɪ] n (money) fondo comune

knack [næk] n: **to have the ~ of** avere l'abilità di

knapsack ['næpsæk] n zaino, sacco da montagna

knead [niːd] vt impastare

knee [niː] n ginocchio; **~cap** n rotula

kneel [niːl] (pt, pp knelt) vi (also: **~ down**) inginocchiarsi

knew [njuː] pt of **know**

knickers ['nɪkəz] (BRIT) npl mutandine fpl

knife [naɪf] (pl knives) n coltello ♦ vt accoltellare, dare una coltellata a

knight [naɪt] n cavaliere m; (CHESS) cavallo; **~hood** (BRIT) n (title): **to get a ~hood** essere fatto cavaliere

knit [nɪt] vt fare a maglia ♦ vi lavorare a maglia; (broken bones) saldarsi; **to ~ one's brows** aggrottare le sopracciglia; **~ting** n lavoro a maglia; **~ting machine** n macchina per maglieria; **~ting needle** n ferro (da calza); **~wear** n maglieria

knives [naɪvz] npl of **knife**

knob [nɔb] n bottone m; manopola

knock [nɔk] vt colpire; urtare; (fig: inf) criticare ♦ vi (at door etc): **to ~ at/on** bussare a ♦ n bussata; colpo, botta; **~ down** vt abbattere; **~ off** vi (inf: finish) smettere (di lavorare) ♦ vt (from price) far abbassare; (inf: steal) sgraffignare; **~ out** vt stendere; (BOXING) mettere K.O.; (defeat) battere; **~ over** vt (person) investire;

(object) far cadere; **~er** n (on door) battente m; **~out** n (BOXING) knock out m inv ♦ cpd a eliminazione

knot [nɔt] n nodo ♦ vt annodare

know [nəu] (pt knew, pp known) vt sapere; (person, author, place) conoscere; **to ~ how to do** sapere fare; **to ~ about** or **of sth/sb** conoscere qc/qn; **~-all** n sapientone/a; **~-how** n tecnica; pratica; **~ing** adj (look etc) d'intesa; **~ingly** adv (purposely) consapevolmente; (smile, look) con aria d'intesa

knowledge ['nɔlɪdʒ] n consapevolezza; (learning) conoscenza, sapere m; **~able** adj ben informato(a)

known [nəun] pp of **know**

knuckle ['nʌkl] n nocca

Koran [kɔ'rɑːn] n Corano

Korea [kə'rɪə] n Corea

kosher ['kəuʃə*] adj kasher inv

L, l

L (BRIT) abbr = **learner driver**

lab [læb] n abbr (= laboratory) laboratorio

label ['leɪbl] n etichetta, cartellino; (brand: of record) casa ♦ vt etichettare

labor etc ['leɪbə*] (US) = **labour** etc

laboratory [lə'bɔrətərɪ] n laboratorio

labour ['leɪbə*] (US labor) n (task) lavoro; (workmen) manodopera; (MED): **to be in ~** avere le doglie ♦ vi: **to ~ (at)** lavorare duro (a); **L~, the L~ party** (BRIT) il partito laburista, i laburisti; **hard ~** lavori mpl forzati; **~ed** adj (breathing) affannoso(a); **~er** n manovale m; **farm ~er** lavoratore m agricolo

lace [leɪs] n merletto, pizzo; (of shoe etc) laccio ♦ vt (shoe: also: **~ up**) allacciare

lack [læk] n mancanza ♦ vt mancare di; **through** or **for ~ of** per mancanza di; **to be ~ing** mancare; **to be ~ing in** mancare di

lackadaisical [lækə'deɪzɪkl] adj disinteressato(a), noncurante

lacquer ['lækə*] n lacca

lad [læd] n ragazzo, giovanotto

ladder ['lædə*] n scala; (BRIT: in tights) smagliatura

laden ['leɪdn] adj: ~ (**with**) carico(a) or caricato(a) (di)

ladle ['leɪdl] n mestolo

lady ['leɪdɪ] n signora; dama; **L~ Smith** lady Smith; **the ladies' (room)** i gabinetti per signore; ~**bird** (US ~**bug**) n coccinella; ~**like** adj da signora, distinto(a); ~**ship** n: **your ~ship** signora contessa (or baronessa etc)

lag [læg] n (of time) lasso, intervallo ♦ vi (also: ~ **behind**) trascinarsi ♦ vt (pipes) rivestire di materiale isolante

lager ['lɑːgə*] n lager m inv

lagoon [lə'guːn] n laguna

laid [leɪd] pt, pp of **lay**; ~ **back** (inf) adj rilassato(a), tranquillo(a); ~ **up** adj: ~ **up (with)** costretto(a) a letto (da)

lain [leɪn] pp of **lie**

lair [leə*] n covo, tana

lake [leɪk] n lago

lamb [læm] n agnello

lame [leɪm] adj zoppo(a); (excuse etc) zoppicante

lament [lə'ment] n lamento ♦ vt lamentare, piangere

laminated ['læmɪneɪtɪd] adj laminato(a)

lamp [læmp] n lampada

lamppost ['læmppəust] (BRIT) n lampione m

lampshade ['læmpʃeɪd] n paralume m

lance [lɑːns] vt (MED) incidere

land [lænd] n (as opposed to sea) terra (ferma); (country) paese m; (soil) terreno; suolo; (estate) terreni mpl, terre fpl ♦ vi (from ship) sbarcare; (AVIAT) atterrare; (fig: fall) cadere ♦ vt (passengers) sbarcare; (goods) scaricare; **to ~ sb with sth** affibbiare qc a qn; ~ **up** vi andare a finire; ~**fill site** n discarica; ~**ing** n atterraggio; (of staircase) pianerottolo; ~**ing gear** n carrello di atterraggio; ~**lady** n padrona or proprietaria di casa; ~**locked** adj senza sbocco sul mare; ~**lord** n padrone m or proprietario di casa; (of pub etc) padrone m; ~**mark** n punto di riferimento; (fig) pietra miliare; ~**owner** n proprietario(a)

terriero(a); ~**scape** n paesaggio; ~**slide** n (GEO) frana; (fig: POL) valanga

lane [leɪn] n stradina; (AUT, in race) corsia; **"get in lane"** "immettersi in corsia"

language ['læŋgwɪdʒ] n lingua; (way one speaks) linguaggio; **bad ~** linguaggio volgare; ~ **laboratory** n laboratorio linguistico

languid ['læŋgwɪd] adj languido(a)

lank [læŋk] adj (hair) liscio(a) e opaco(a)

lanky ['læŋkɪ] adj allampanato(a)

lantern ['læntn] n lanterna

lap [læp] n (of track) giro; (of body): **in** or **on one's ~** in grembo ♦ vt (also: ~ **up**) papparsi, leccare ♦ vi (waves) sciabordare; ~ **up** vt (fig) bearsi di

lapel [lə'pel] n risvolto

Lapland ['læplænd] n Lapponia

lapse [læps] n lapsus m inv; (longer) caduta ♦ vi (law) cadere; (membership, contract) scadere; **to ~ into bad habits** pigliare cattive abitudini; ~ **of time** spazio di tempo

laptop (computer) ['læp,tɒp-] n laptop m inv

larch [lɑːtʃ] n larice m

lard [lɑːd] n lardo

larder ['lɑːdə*] n dispensa

large [lɑːdʒ] adj grande; (person, animal) grosso(a); **at ~** (free) in libertà; (generally) in generale; nell'insieme; ~**ly** adv in gran parte

largesse [lɑː'ʒes] n generosità

lark [lɑːk] n (bird) allodola; (joke) scherzo, gioco

laryngitis [lærɪn'dʒaɪtɪs] n laringite f

laser ['leɪzə*] n laser m; ~ **printer** n stampante f laser inv

lash [læʃ] n frustata; (also: **eye~**) ciglio ♦ vt frustare; (tie): **to ~ to/together** legare a/insieme; ~ **out** vi: **to ~ out (at** or **against sb)** attaccare violentemente (qn)

lass [læs] n ragazza

lasso [læ'suː] n laccio

last [lɑːst] adj ultimo(a); (week, month, year) scorso(a), passato(a) ♦ adv per ultimo ♦ vi durare; ~ **week** la settimana scorsa; ~ **night** ieri sera, la notte scorsa; **at ~** finalmente, alla fine; **~ but one** penultimo(a); **~-ditch** *adj* (*attempt*) estremo(a); **~ing** *adj* durevole; **~ly** *adv* infine, per finire; **~-minute** *adj* fatto(a) (*or* preso(a) *etc*) all'ultimo momento

latch [lætʃ] *n* chiavistello

late [leɪt] *adj* (*not on time*) in ritardo; (*far on in day etc*) tardi *inv*; tardo(a); (*former*) ex; (*dead*) defunto(a) ♦ *adv* tardi; (*behind time, schedule*) in ritardo; **of ~** di recente; **in the ~ afternoon** nel tardo pomeriggio; **in ~ May** verso la fine di maggio; **~comer** *n* ritardatario/a; **~ly** *adv* recentemente

later [ˈleɪtə*] *adj* (*date etc*) posteriore; (*version etc*) successivo(a) ♦ *adv* più tardi; **~ on** più avanti

lateral [ˈlætərl] *adj* laterale

latest [ˈleɪtɪst] *adj* ultimo(a), più recente; **at the ~** al più tardi

lathe [leɪð] *n* tornio

lather [ˈlɑːðə*] *n* schiuma di sapone ♦ *vt* insaponare

Latin [ˈlætɪn] *n* latino ♦ *adj* latino(a); **~ America** *n* America Latina; **~-American** *adj, n* sudamericano(a)

latitude [ˈlætɪtjuːd] *n* latitudine *f*; (*fig*) libertà d'azione

latter [ˈlætə*] *adj* secondo(a); più recente ♦ *n*: **the ~** quest'ultimo, il secondo; **~ly** *adv* recentemente, negli ultimi tempi

lattice [ˈlætɪs] *n* traliccio; graticolato

laudable [ˈlɔːdəbl] *adj* lodevole

laugh [lɑːf] *n* risata ♦ *vi* ridere; **~ at** *vt fus* (*misfortune etc*) ridere di; **~ off** *vt* prendere alla leggera; **~able** *adj* ridicolo(a); **~ing stock** *n*: **the ~ing stock of** lo zimbello di; **~ter** *n* riso; risate *fpl*

launch [lɔːntʃ] *n* (*of rocket, COMM*) lancio; (*of new ship*) varo; (*also*: **motor ~**) lancia ♦ *vt* (*rocket, COMM*) lanciare; (*ship, plan*) varare; **~ into** *vt fus* lanciarsi in; **~(ing) pad** *n* rampa di lancio

launder [ˈlɔːndə*] *vt* lavare e stirare

launderette [lɔːnˈdrɛt] (*BRIT*) *n* lavanderia (automatica)

Laundromat ® [ˈlɔːndrəmæt] (*US*) *n* lavanderia automatica

laundry [ˈlɔːndrɪ] *n* lavanderia; (*clothes*) biancheria; (: *dirty*) panni *mpl* da lavare

laurel [ˈlɔrl] *n* lauro

lava [ˈlɑːvə] *n* lava

lavatory [ˈlævətərɪ] *n* gabinetto

lavender [ˈlævəndə*] *n* lavanda

lavish [ˈlævɪʃ] *adj* copioso(a); abbondante; (*giving freely*): **~ with** prodigo(a) di, largo(a) in ♦ *vt*: **to ~ sth on sb** colmare qn di qc

law [lɔː] *n* legge *f*; **civil / criminal ~** diritto civile/penale; **~-abiding** *adj* ubbidiente alla legge; **~ and order** *n* l'ordine *m* pubblico; **~ court** *n* tribunale *m*, corte *f* di giustizia; **~ful** *adj* legale; lecito(a); **~less** *adj* che non conosce nessuna legge

lawn [lɔːn] *n* tappeto erboso; **~ mower** *n* tosaerba *m or f inv*; **~ tennis** *n* tennis *m* su prato

law school *n* facoltà *f inv* di legge

lawsuit [ˈlɔːsuːt] *n* processo, causa

lawyer [ˈlɔːjə*] *n* (*for sales, wills etc*) ≈ notaio; (*partner, in court*) ≈ avvocato/ essa

lax [læks] *adj* rilassato(a); negligente

laxative [ˈlæksətɪv] *n* lassativo

lay [leɪ] (*pt, pp* **laid**) *pt of* **lie** ♦ *adj* laico(a); (*not expert*) profano(a) ♦ *vt* posare, mettere; (*eggs*) fare; (*trap*) tendere; (*plans*) fare, elaborare; **to ~ the table** apparecchiare la tavola; **~ aside** *or* **by** *vt* mettere da parte; **~ down** *vt* mettere giù; (*rules etc*) formulare, fissare; **to ~ down the law** dettar legge; **to ~ down one's life** dare la propria vita; **~ off** *vt* (*workers*) licenziare; **~ on** *vt* (*provide*) fornire; **~ out** *vt* (*display*) presentare, disporre; **~about** *n* sfaccendato/a, fannullone/a; **~-by** (*BRIT*) *n* piazzola (di sosta)

layer [ˈleɪə*] *n* strato

layman [ˈleɪmən] *n* laico; profano

layout [ˈleɪaut] *n* lay-out *m inv*, disposizione *f*; (*PRESS*) impaginazione *f*

laze [leɪz] *vi* oziare

lazy [ˈleɪzɪ] *adj* pigro(a)

lb. *abbr* = **pound** (*weight*)

lead[1] [liːd] (*pt, pp* **led**) *n* (*front position*) posizione f di testa; (distance, time ahead) vantaggio; (clue) indizio; (ELEC) filo (elettrico); (for dog) guinzaglio; (THEATRE) parte f principale ♦ vt guidare, condurre; (induce) indurre; (be leader of) essere a capo di ♦ vi condurre; (SPORT) essere in testa; **in the ~** in testa; **to ~ the way** fare strada; **~ away** vt condurre via; **~ back** vt: **to ~ back to** ricondurre a; **~ on** vt (tease) tenere sulla corda; **~ to** vt fus condurre a; portare a; **~ up to** vt fus portare a

lead² [lɛd] n (metal) piombo; (in pencil) mina; **~ed petrol** n benzina con piombo

leaden ['lɛdn] adj (sky, sea) plumbeo(a)

leader ['liːdə*] n capo; leader m inv; (in newspaper) articolo di fondo; (SPORT) chi è in testa; **~ship** n direzione f; capacità di comando

leading ['liːdɪŋ] adj primo(a); principale; **~ light** n (person) personaggio di primo piano; **~ man/lady** n (THEATRE) primo attore/prima attrice

lead singer n cantante alla testa di un gruppo

leaf [liːf] (pl **leaves**) n foglia ♦ vi: **to ~ through sth** sfogliare qc; **to turn over a new ~** cambiar vita

leaflet ['liːflɪt] n dépliant m inv; (POL, REL) volantino

league [liːg] n lega; (FOOTBALL) campionato; **to be in ~ with** essere in lega con

leak [liːk] n (out) fuga; (in) infiltrazione f; (security ~) fuga d'informazioni ♦ vi (roof, bucket) perdere; (liquid) uscire; (shoes) lasciar passare l'acqua ♦ vt (information) divulgare; **~ out** vi uscire; (information) trapelare

lean [liːn] (pt, pp **leaned** or **leant**) adj magro(a) ♦ vt: **to ~ sth on sth** appoggiare qc su qc ♦ vi (slope) pendere; (rest): **to ~ against** appoggiarsi contro; essere appoggiato(a) a; **to ~ on** appoggiarsi a; **~ back/forward** vi sporgersi indietro/in avanti; **~ out** vi sporgersi; **~ over** vi inclinarsi; **~ing** n: **~ing (towards)** propensione f (per)

leap [liːp] (pt, pp **leaped** or **leapt**) n salto, balzo ♦ vi saltare, balzare; **~frog** n gioco della cavallina; **~ year** n anno bisestile

learn [ləːn] (pt, pp **learned** or **learnt**) vt, vi imparare; **to ~ about sth** (hear, read) apprendere qc; **to ~ to do sth** imparare a fare qc; **~ed** ['ləːnɪd] adj erudito(a), dotto(a); **~er** n principiante m/f; apprendista m/f; (BRIT: also: **~er driver**) guidatore/trice principiante; **~ing** n erudizione f, sapienza

lease [liːs] n contratto d'affitto ♦ vt affittare

leash [liːʃ] n guinzaglio

least [liːst] adj: **the ~** (+noun) il(la) più piccolo(a), il(la) minimo(a); (smallest amount of) il(la) meno ♦ adv (+verb) meno; **the ~** (+adjective): **the ~ beautiful girl** la ragazza meno bella; **the ~ possible effort** il minimo sforzo possibile; **I have the ~ money** ho meno denaro di tutti; **at ~** almeno; **not in the ~** affatto, per nulla

leather ['lɛðə*] n cuoio

leave [liːv] (pt, pp **left**) vt lasciare; (go away from) partire da ♦ vi partire, andarsene; (bus, train) partire ♦ n (time off) congedo; (MIL, also: consent) licenza; **to be left** rimanere; **there's some milk left over** c'è rimasto del latte; **on ~** in congedo; **~ behind** vt (person, object) lasciare; (: forget) dimenticare; **~ out** vt omettere, tralasciare; **~ of absence** n congedo

leaves [liːvz] npl of **leaf**

Lebanon ['lɛbənən] n Libano

lecherous ['lɛtʃərəs] adj lascivo(a), lubrico(a)

lecture ['lɛktʃə*] n conferenza; (SCOL) lezione f ♦ vi fare conferenze; fare lezioni ♦ vt (scold): **to ~ sb on** or **about sth** rimproverare qn or fare una ramanzina a qn per qc; **to give a ~ on** tenere una conferenza su

lecturer ['lɛktʃərə*] (BRIT) n (at university) professore/essa, docente m/f

led [lɛd] pt, pp of **lead**

ledge [lɛdʒ] n (of window) davanzale m; (on wall etc) sporgenza; (of mountain) cornice f, cengia

ledger ['lɛdʒə*] *n* libro maestro, registro

lee [li:] *n* lato sottovento

leech [li:tʃ] *n* sanguisuga

leek [li:k] *n* porro

leer [lɪə*] *vi*: **to ~ at sb** gettare uno sguardo voglioso (*or* maligno) su qn

leeway ['li:weɪ] *n* (*fig*): **to have some ~** avere una certa libertà di azione

left [lɛft] *pt, pp of* **leave** ♦ *adj* sinistro(a) ♦ *adv* a sinistra ♦ *n* sinistra; **on the ~, to the ~** a sinistra; **the L~** (*POL*) la sinistra; **~-hand drive** *n* guida a sinistra; **~-handed** *adj* mancino(a); **~-hand side** *n* lato *or* fianco sinistro; **~-luggage locker** *n* armadietto per deposito bagagli; **~ luggage (office)** (*BRIT*) *n* deposito *m* bagagli *inv*; **~overs** *npl* avanzi *mpl*, resti *mpl*; **~-wing** *adj* (*POL*) di sinistra

leg [lɛg] *n* gamba; (*of animal*) zampa; (*of furniture*) piede *m*; (*CULIN: of chicken*) coscia; (*of journey*) tappa; **1st/2nd ~** (*SPORT*) partita di andata/ritorno

legacy ['lɛgəsɪ] *n* eredità *f inv*

legal ['li:gl] *adj* legale; **~ holiday** (*US*) *n* giorno festivo, festa nazionale; **~ tender** *n* moneta legale

legend ['lɛdʒənd] *n* leggenda

legislation [lɛdʒɪs'leɪʃən] *n* legislazione *f*; **legislature** ['lɛdʒɪslətʃə*] *n* corpo legislativo

legitimate [lɪ'dʒɪtɪmət] *adj* legittimo(a)

leg-room *n* spazio per le gambe

leisure ['lɛʒə*] *n* agio, tempo libero; ricreazioni *fpl*; **at ~** a comodo; **~ centre** *n* centro di ricreazione; **~ly** *adj* tranquillo(a); fatto(a) con comodo *or* senza fretta

lemon ['lɛmən] *n* limone *m*; **~ade** [-'neɪd] *n* limonata; **~ tea** *n* tè *m inv* al limone

lend [lɛnd] (*pt, pp* **lent**) *vt*: **to ~ sth (to sb)** prestare qc (a qn); **~ing library** *n* biblioteca che consente prestiti di libri

length [lɛŋθ] *n* lunghezza; (*distance*) distanza; (*section: of road, pipe etc*) pezzo, tratto; (*of time*) periodo; **at ~** (*at last*) finalmente, alla fine; (*lengthily*) a lungo; **~en** *vt* allungare, prolungare ♦ *vi*

allungarsi; **~ways** *adv* per il lungo; **~y** *adj* molto lungo(a)

lenient ['li:nɪənt] *adj* indulgente, clemente

lens [lɛnz] *n* lente *f*; (*of camera*) obiettivo

Lent [lɛnt] *n* Quaresima

lent [lɛnt] *pt, pp of* **lend**

lentil ['lɛntl] *n* lenticchia

Leo ['li:əu] *n* Leone *m*

leotard ['li:ətɑ:d] *n* calzamaglia

leprosy ['lɛprəsɪ] *n* lebbra

lesbian ['lɛzbɪən] *n* lesbica

less [lɛs] *adj, pron, adv* meno ♦ *prep*: **~ tax/10% discount** meno tasse/il 10% di sconto; **~ than ever** meno che mai; **~ than half** meno della metà; **~ and ~** sempre meno; **the ~ he works ...** meno lavora ....

lessen ['lɛsn] *vi* diminuire, attenuarsi ♦ *vt* diminuire, ridurre

lesser ['lɛsə*] *adj* minore, più piccolo(a); **to a ~ extent** in grado *or* misura minore

lesson ['lɛsn] *n* lezione *f*; **to teach sb a ~** dare una lezione a qn

let [lɛt] (*pt, pp* **let**) *vt* lasciare; (*BRIT: lease*) dare in affitto; **to ~ sb do sth** lasciar fare qc a qn, lasciare che qn faccia qc; **to ~ sb know sth** far sapere qc a qn; **~'s go** andiamo; **~ him come** lo lasci venire; **"to ~"** "affittasi"; **~ down** *vt* (*lower*) abbassare; (*dress*) allungare; (*hair*) sciogliere; (*tyre*) sgonfiare; (*disappoint*) deludere; **~ go** *vt, vi* mollare; **~ in** *vt* lasciare entrare; (*visitor etc*) far entrare; **~ off** *vt* (*allow to go*) lasciare andare; (*firework etc*) far partire; **~ on** (*inf*) *vi* dire; **~ out** *vt* lasciare uscire; (*scream*) emettere; **~ up** *vi* diminuire

lethal ['li:θl] *adj* letale, mortale

lethargic [lɛ'θɑ:dʒɪk] *adj* letargico(a)

letter ['lɛtə*] *n* lettera; **~ bomb** *n* lettera esplosiva; **~box** (*BRIT*) *n* buca delle lettere; **~ing** *n* iscrizione *f*; caratteri *mpl*

lettuce ['lɛtɪs] *n* lattuga, insalata

let-up *n* pausa

leukaemia [lu:'ki:mɪə] (*US* **leukemia**) *n* leucemia

level ['lɛvl] *adj* piatto(a), piano(a); orizzontale ♦ *adv*: **to draw ~ with** mettersi alla pari di ♦ n livello ♦ vt livellare, spianare; **to be ~ with** essere alla pari di; **A ~s** (BRIT) npl ≈ esami mpl di maturità; **O ~s** (BRIT) npl esami fatti in Inghilterra all'età di 16 anni; **on the ~** piatto(a); (fig) onesto(a); **~ off** or **out** vi (prices etc) stabilizzarsi; **~ crossing** (BRIT) n passaggio a livello; **~-headed** adj equilibrato(a)

lever ['liːvə*] n leva ♦ **~age** n: **~age (on** or **with)** forza (su); (fig) ascendente m (su)

levy ['lɛvɪ] n tassa, imposta ♦ vt imporre

lewd [luːd] adj osceno(a), lascivo(a)

liability [laɪə'bɪlətɪ] n responsabilità f inv; (handicap) peso; **liabilities** npl debiti mpl; (on balance sheet) passivo

liable ['laɪəbl] adj (subject): **~ to** soggetto(a) a; passibile di; (responsible): **~ (for)** responsabile (di); (likely): **~ to do** propenso(a) a fare

liaise [liː'eɪz] vi: **to ~ (with)** mantenere i contatti (con)

liaison [liː'eɪzɔn] n relazione f; (MIL) collegamento

liar ['laɪə*] n bugiardo/a

libel ['laɪbl] n libello, diffamazione f ♦ vt diffamare

liberal ['lɪbərl] adj liberale; (generous): **to be ~ with** distribuire liberalmente

liberation [lɪbə'reɪʃən] n liberazione f

liberty ['lɪbətɪ] n libertà f inv; **at ~** (criminal) in libertà; **at ~ to do** libero(a) di fare

Libra ['liːbrə] n Bilancia

librarian [laɪ'brɛərɪən] n bibliotecario/a

library ['laɪbrərɪ] n biblioteca

Libya ['lɪbɪə] n Libia; **~n** adj, n libico(a)

lice [laɪs] npl of **louse**

licence ['laɪsns] (US **license**) n autorizzazione f, permesso; (COMM) licenza; (RADIO, TV) canone m, abbonamento; (also: **driving ~**, (US) **driver's ~**) patente f di guida; (excessive freedom) licenza; **~ number** n numero di targa; **~ plate** n targa

license ['laɪsns] n (US) = **licence** ♦ vt dare una licenza a; **~d** adj (for alcohol) che ha la licenza di vendere bibite alcoliche

lick [lɪk] vt leccare; (inf: defeat) stracciare; **to**

~ one's lips (fig) leccarsi i baffi

licorice ['lɪkərɪs] (US) n = **liquorice**

lid [lɪd] n coperchio; (eye~) palpebra

lie [laɪ] (pt **lay**, pp **lain**) vi (rest) giacere; star disteso(a); (of object: be situated) trovarsi, essere; (tell lies: pt, pp **lied**) mentire, dire bugie ♦ n bugia, menzogna; **to ~ low** (fig) latitare; **~ about** or **around** vi (things) essere in giro; (person) bighellonare; **~-down** (BRIT) n: **to have a ~-down** sdraiarsi, riposarsi; **~-in** (BRIT) n: **to have a ~-in** rimanere a letto

lieu [luː]: **in ~ of** prep invece di, al posto di

lieutenant [lɛf'tɛnənt, (US) luː'tɛnənt] n tenente m

life [laɪf] (pl **lives**) n vita ♦ cpd di vita; della vita; a vita; **to come to ~** rianimarsi; **~ assurance** (BRIT) n = **~ insurance**; **~belt** (BRIT) n salvagente m; **~boat** n scialuppa di salvataggio; **~guard** n bagnino; **~ imprisonment** n carcere m a vita; **~ insurance** n assicurazione f sulla vita; **~ jacket** n giubbotto di salvataggio; **~less** adj senza vita; **~like** adj verosimile; rassomigliante; **~long** adj per tutta la vita; **~ preserver** (US) n salvagente m; giubbotto di salvataggio; **~ sentence** n ergastolo; **~-size(d)** adj a grandezza naturale; **~ span** n (durata della) vita; **~style** n stile m di vita; **~ support system** n respiratore m automatico; **~time** n: **in his ~time** durante la sua vita; **once in a ~time** una volta nella vita

lift [lɪft] vt sollevare; (ban, rule) levare ♦ vi (fog) alzarsi ♦ n (BRIT: elevator) ascensore m; **to give sb a ~** (BRIT) dare un passaggio a qn; **~-off** n decollo

light [laɪt] (pt, pp **lighted** or **lit**) n luce f, lume m; (daylight) luce f, giorno; (lamp) lampada; (AUT: rear ~) luce f di posizione; (: headlamp) fanale m; (for cigarette etc): **have you got a ~?** ha da accendere?; **~s** npl (AUT: traffic ~s) semaforo ♦ vt (candle, cigarette, fire) accendere; (room) illuminare; **to be lit by** essere illuminato(a) da ♦ adj (room, colour) chiaro(a); (not heavy, also fig) leggero(a); **to come to ~** venire alla luce, emergere; ~ **up** *vi* illuminarsi ♦ *vt* illuminare; ~ **bulb** *n* lampadina; ~**en** *vt* (*make less heavy*) alleggerire; ~**er** *n* (*also:* **cigarette ~er**) accendino; ~**-headed** *adj* stordito(a); ~**-hearted** *adj* gioioso(a), gaio(a); ~**house** *n* faro; ~**ing** *n* illuminazione *f*; ~**ly** *adv* leggermente; **to get off ~ly** cavarsela a buon mercato; ~ **meter** *n* (*PHOT*) esposimetro; ~**ness** *n* chiarezza; (*in weight*) leggerezza

lightning ['laɪtnɪŋ] *n* lampo, fulmine *m*; ~ **conductor** (*US* ~ **rod**) *n* parafulmine *m*

light pen *n* penna ottica

lightweight ['laɪtweɪt] *adj* (*suit*) leggero(a) ♦ *n* (*BOXING*) peso leggero

light year *n* anno *m* luce *inv*

like [laɪk] *vt* (*person*) volere bene a; (*activity, object, food*): **I ~ swimming/that book/ chocolate** mi piace nuotare/quel libro/il cioccolato ♦ *prep* come ♦ *adj* simile, uguale ♦ *n*: **the ~** uno(a) uguale; **his ~s and dislikes** i suoi gusti; **I would ~, I'd ~** mi piacerebbe, vorrei; **would you ~ a coffee?** gradirebbe un caffè?; **to be/look ~ sb/sth** somigliare a qn/qc; **what does it look/taste ~?** che aspetto/gusto ha?; **what does it sound ~?** come fa?; **that's just ~ him** è proprio da lui; **do it ~ this** fallo così; **it is nothing ~ ...** non è affatto come ...; ~**able** *adj* simpatico(a)

likelihood ['laɪklɪhud] *n* probabilità

likely ['laɪklɪ] *adj* probabile; plausibile; **he's ~ to leave** probabilmente partirà, è probabile che parta; **not ~!** neanche per sogno!

likeness ['laɪknɪs] *n* somiglianza

likewise ['laɪkwaɪz] *adv* similmente, nello stesso modo

liking ['laɪkɪŋ] *n*: ~ (**for**) debole *m* (per); **to be to sb's ~** piacere a qn

lilac ['laɪlək] *n* lilla *m inv*

lily ['lɪlɪ] *n* giglio; ~ **of the valley** *n* mughetto

limb [lɪm] *n* arto

limber up ['lɪmbə*-*] *vi* riscaldarsi i muscoli

limbo ['lɪmbəu] *n*: **to be in ~** (*fig*) essere lasciato(a) nel dimenticatoio

lime [laɪm] *n* (*tree*) tiglio; (*fruit*) limetta; (*GEO*) calce *f*

limelight ['laɪmlaɪt] *n*: **in the ~** (*fig*) alla ribalta, in vista

limerick ['lɪmərɪk] *n* poesiola umoristica di 5 versi

limestone ['laɪmstəun] *n* pietra calcarea; (*GEO*) calcare *m*

limit ['lɪmɪt] *n* limite *m* ♦ *vt* limitare; ~**ed** *adj* limitato(a), ristretto(a); **to be ~ed to** limitarsi a; ~**ed (liability) company** (*BRIT*) *n* ≈ società *f inv* a responsabilità limitata

limp [lɪmp] *n*: **to have a ~** zoppicare ♦ *vi* zoppicare ♦ *adj* floscio(a), flaccido(a)

limpet ['lɪmpɪt] *n* patella

line [laɪn] *n* linea; (*rope*) corda; (*for fishing*) lenza; (*wire*) filo; (*of poem*) verso; (*row, series*) fila, riga; coda; (*on face*) ruga ♦ *vt* (*clothes*): **to ~ (with)** foderare (di); (*box*): **to ~ (with)** rivestire or foderare (di); (*subj: trees, crowd*) fiancheggiare; ~ **of business** settore *m* or ramo d'attività; **in ~ with** in linea con; ~ **up** *vi* allinearsi, mettersi in fila ♦ *vt* mettere in fila; (*event, celebration*) preparare

lined [laɪnd] *adj* (*face*) rugoso(a); (*paper*) a righe, rigato(a)

linen ['lɪnɪn] *n* biancheria, panni *mpl*; (*cloth*) tela di lino

liner ['laɪnə*] *n* nave *f* di linea; (*for bin*) sacchetto

linesman ['laɪnzmən] *n* guardalinee *m inv*

line-up *n* allineamento, fila; (*SPORT*) formazione *f* di gioco

linger ['lɪŋgə*] *vi* attardarsi; indugiare; (*smell, tradition*) persistere

lingerie ['lænʒəri:] *n* biancheria intima femminile

linguistics [lɪŋ'gwɪstɪks] *n* linguistica

lining ['laɪnɪŋ] *n* fodera

link [lɪŋk] *n* (*of a chain*) anello; (*relationship*) legame *m*; (*connection*) collegamento ♦ *vt* collegare, unire, congiungere; (*associate*): **to ~ with** or **to** collegare a; ~**s** *npl* (*GOLF*) pista or terreno da golf; ~ **up** *vt* collegare, unire ♦ *vi* riunirsi; associarsi

lino ['laɪnəu] *n* = **linoleum**

linoleum [lɪ'nəuliəm] *n* linoleum *m inv*

lion ['laɪən] *n* leone *m*; **~ess** *n* leonessa

lip [lɪp] *n* labbro; (*of cup etc*) orlo

liposuction ['lɪpəusʌkʃən] *n* liposuzione *f*

lip: **~read** *vi* leggere sulle labbra; **~ salve** *n* burro di cacao; **~ service** *n*: **to pay ~ service to sth** essere favorevole a qc solo a parole; **~stick** *n* rossetto

liqueur [lɪ'kjuə*] *n* liquore *m*

liquid ['lɪkwɪd] *n* liquido ♦ *adj* liquido(a)

liquidize ['lɪkwɪdaɪz] *vt* (*CULIN*) passare al frullatore; **~r** *n* frullatore *m* (a brocca)

liquor ['lɪkə*] *n* alcool *m*

liquorice ['lɪkərɪs] (*BRIT*) *n* liquirizia

liquor store (*US*) *n* negozio di liquori

lisp [lɪsp] *n* pronuncia blesa della "*s*"

list [lɪst] *n* lista, elenco ♦ *vt* (*write down*) mettere in lista; fare una lista di; (*enumerate*) elencare; **~ed building** (*BRIT*) *n* edificio sotto la protezione delle Belle Arti

listen ['lɪsn] *vi* ascoltare; **to ~ to** ascoltare; **~er** *n* ascoltatore/trice

listless ['lɪstlɪs] *adj* apatico(a)

lit [lɪt] *pt, pp of* **light**

liter ['li:tə*] (*US*) *n* = **litre**

literacy ['lɪtərəsɪ] *n* il sapere leggere e scrivere

literal ['lɪtərl] *adj* letterale; **~ly** *adv* alla lettera, letteralmente

literary ['lɪtərərɪ] *adj* letterario(a)

literate ['lɪtərət] *adj* che sa leggere e scrivere

literature ['lɪtərɪtʃə*] *n* letteratura; (*brochures etc*) materiale *m*

lithe [laɪð] *adj* agile, snello(a)

litigation [lɪtɪ'geɪʃən] *n* causa

litre ['li:tə*] (*US* **liter**) *n* litro

litter ['lɪtə*] *n* (*rubbish*) rifiuti *mpl*; (*young animals*) figliata; **~ bin** (*BRIT*) *n* cestino per rifiuti; **~ed** *adj*: **~ed with** coperto(a) di

little ['lɪtl] *adj* (*small*) piccolo(a); (*not much*) poco(a) ♦ *adv* poco; **a ~** un po' (di); **a ~ bit** un pochino; **~ by ~** a poco a poco; **~ finger** *n* mignolo

live¹ [lɪv] *vi* vivere; (*reside*) vivere, abitare;

~ down *vt* far dimenticare (alla gente); **~ on** *vt fus* (*food*) vivere di; **~ together** *vi* vivere insieme, convivere; **~ up to** *vt fus* tener fede a, non venir meno a

live² [laɪv] *adj* (*animal*) vivo(a); (*wire*) sotto tensione; (*bullet, missile*) inesploso(a); (*broadcast*) diretto(a); (*performance*) dal vivo

livelihood ['laɪvlɪhud] *n* mezzi *mpl* di sostentamento

lively ['laɪvlɪ] *adj* vivace, vivo(a)

liven up ['laɪvn'ʌp] *vt* (*discussion, evening*) animare ♦ *vi* ravvivarsi

liver ['lɪvə*] *n* fegato

lives [laɪvz] *npl of* **life**

livestock ['laɪvstɔk] *n* bestiame *m*

livid ['lɪvɪd] *adj* livido(a); (*furious*) livido(a) di rabbia, furibondo(a)

living ['lɪvɪŋ] *adj* vivo(a), vivente ♦ *n*: **to earn** *or* **make a ~** guadagnarsi la vita; **~ conditions** *npl* condizioni *fpl* di vita; **~ room** *n* soggiorno; **~ standards** *npl* tenore *m* di vita; **~ wage** *n* salario sufficiente per vivere

lizard ['lɪzəd] *n* lucertola

load [ləud] *n* (*weight*) peso; (*thing carried*) carico ♦ *vt* (*also*: **~ up**): **to ~ (with)** (*lorry, ship*) caricare (di); (*gun, camera, COMPUT*) caricare (con); **a ~ of**, **~s of** (*fig*) un sacco di; **~ed** *adj* (*vehicle*): **~ed (with)** carico(a) (di); (*question*) capzioso(a); (*inf: rich*) carico(a) di soldi

loaf [ləuf] (*pl* **loaves**) *n* pane *m*, pagnotta

loan [ləun] *n* prestito ♦ *vt* dare in prestito; **on ~** in prestito

loath [ləuθ] *adj*: **to be ~ to do** essere restio(a) a fare

loathe [ləuð] *vt* detestare, aborrire

loaves [ləuvz] *npl of* **loaf**

lobby ['lɔbɪ] *n* atrio, vestibolo; (*POL: pressure group*) gruppo di pressione ♦ *vt* fare pressione su

lobster ['lɔbstə*] *n* aragosta

local ['ləukl] *adj* locale ♦ *n* (*BRIT: pub*) ≈ bar *m inv* all'angolo; **the ~s** *npl* (*local inhabitants*) la gente della zona; **~ anaesthetic** *n* anestesia locale; **~**

authority n ente m locale; ~ **call** n (TEL) telefonata urbana; ~ **government** n amministrazione f locale

locality [ləʊˈkælɪtɪ] n località f inv; (position) posto, luogo

locally [ˈləʊkəlɪ] adv da queste parti; nel vicinato

locate [ləʊˈkeɪt] vt (find) trovare; (situate) collocare; situare

location [ləʊˈkeɪʃən] n posizione f; **on ~** (CINEMA) all'esterno

loch [lɔx] n lago

lock [lɔk] n (of door, box) serratura; (of canal) chiusa; (of hair) ciocca, riccio ♦ vt (with key) chiudere a chiave ♦ vi (door etc) chiudersi; (wheels) bloccarsi, incepparsi; ~ **in** vt chiudere dentro (a chiave); ~ **out** vt chiudere fuori; ~ **up** vt (criminal, mental patient) rinchiudere; (house) chiudere (a chiave) ♦ vi chiudere tutto (a chiave)

locker [ˈlɔkə*] n armadietto

locket [ˈlɔkɪt] n medaglione m

locksmith [ˈlɔksmɪθ] n magnano

lockup [ˈlɔkʌp] (US) n prigione f; guardina

locum [ˈləʊkəm] n (MED) medico sostituto

lodge [lɔdʒ] n casetta, portineria; (hunting ~) casino di caccia ♦ vi (person): **to ~ (with)** essere a pensione (presso o da); (bullet etc) conficcarsi ♦ vt (appeal etc) presentare, fare; **to ~ a complaint** presentare un reclamo; ~**r** n affittuario/a; (with room and meals) pensionante m/f

lodgings [ˈlɔdʒɪŋz] npl camera d'affitto; camera ammobiliata

loft [lɔft] n solaio, soffitta

lofty [ˈlɔftɪ] adj alto(a); (haughty) altezzoso(a)

log [lɔg] n (of wood) ceppo; (book) = **logbook** ♦ vt registrare; ~ **in** or **on** vi (COMPUT) collegarsi; ~ **off** or **out** vi (COMPUT) scollegarsi

logbook [ˈlɔgbʊk] n (NAUT, AVIAT) diario di bordo; (AUT) libretto di circolazione

loggerheads [ˈlɔgəhedz] npl: **at ~ (with)** ai ferri corti (con)

logic [ˈlɔdʒɪk] n logica; ~**al** adj logico(a)

loin [lɔɪn] n (CULIN) lombata

loiter [ˈlɔɪtə*] vi attardarsi

loll [lɔl] vi (also: ~ **about**) essere stravaccato(a)

lollipop [ˈlɔlɪpɔp] n lecca lecca m inv; ~ **man/lady** (BRIT: irreg) n see box

---
lollipop man/lady
---

i In Gran Bretagna il **lollipop man** e la **lollipop lady** sono persone incaricate di aiutare i bambini ad attraversare la strada in prossimità delle scuole; usano una paletta la cui forma ricorda quella di un lecca lecca, in inglese **lollipop**.

London [ˈlʌndən] n Londra; ~**er** n londinese m/f

lone [ləʊn] adj solitario(a)

loneliness [ˈləʊnlɪnɪs] n solitudine f, isolamento

lonely [ˈləʊnlɪ] adj solo(a); solitario(a), isolato(a)

long [lɔŋ] adj lungo(a) ♦ adv a lungo, per molto tempo ♦ vi: **to ~ for sth/to do** desiderare qc/di fare; non veder l'ora di aver qc/di fare; **so** or **as ~ as** (while) finché; (provided that) sempre che +sub; **don't be ~!** fai presto!; **how ~ is this river/course?** quanto è lungo questo fiume/corso?; **6 metres ~** lungo 6 metri; **6 months ~** che dura 6 mesi, di 6 mesi; **all night ~** tutta la notte; **he no ~er comes** non viene più; ~ **before** molto prima; ~ **after** molto tempo dopo; **at ~ last** finalmente; ~**-distance** adj (race) di fondo; (call) interurbano(a); ~**-haired** adj dai capelli lunghi; ~**hand** n scrittura normale; ~**ing** n desiderio, voglia, brama

longitude [ˈlɔŋgɪtjuːd] n longitudine f

long: ~ **jump** n salto in lungo; ~**-life** (milk) a lunga conservazione; (batteries) di lunga durata; ~**-lost** adj perduto(a) da tempo; ~**-range** adj a lunga portata; ~**-sighted** adj presbite; ~**-standing** adj di vecchia data; ~**-suffering** adj estremamente paziente; infinitamente tollerante; ~**-term** adj a lungo termine; ~

wave n onde fpl lunghe; **~-winded** adj prolisso(a), interminabile
loo [luː] (BRIT: inf) n W.C. m inv, cesso
look [luk] vi guardare; (seem) sembrare, parere; (building etc): **to ~ south/on to the sea** dare a sud/sul mare ♦ n sguardo; (appearance) aspetto, aria; **~s** npl (good ~s) bellezza; **~ after** vt fus occuparsi di, prendere cura di; (keep an eye on) guardare, badare a; **~ at** vt fus guardare; **~ back** vi: **to ~ back on** (event etc) ripensare a; **~ down on** vt fus (fig) guardare dall'alto, disprezzare; **~ for** vt fus cercare; **~ forward to** vt fus non veder l'ora di; (in letters): **we ~ forward to hearing from you** in attesa di una vostra gentile risposta; **~ into** vt fus esaminare; **~ on** vi fare da spettatore; **~ out** vi (beware): **to ~ out (for)** stare in guardia (per); **~ out for** vt fus cercare; **~ round** vi (turn) girarsi, voltarsi; (in shop) dare un'occhiata; **~ to** vt fus (rely on) contare su; **~ up** vi alzare gli occhi; (improve) migliorare ♦ vt (word) cercare; (friend) andare a trovare; **~ up to** vt fus avere rispetto per; **~-out** n posto d'osservazione; guardia; **to be on the ~-out (for)** stare in guardia (per)
loom [luːm] n telaio ♦ vi (also: **~ up**) apparire minaccioso(a); (event) essere imminente
loony ['luːnɪ] (inf) n pazzo/a
loop [luːp] n cappio ♦ vt: **to ~ sth round sth** passare qc intorno a qc; **~hole** n via d'uscita; scappatoia
loose [luːs] adj (knot) sciolto(a); (screw) allentato(a); (stone) cadente; (clothes) ampio(a), largo(a); (animal) in libertà, scappato(a); (life, morals) dissoluto(a) ♦ n: **to be on the ~** essere in libertà; **~ change** n spiccioli mpl, moneta; **~ chippings** npl (on road) ghiaino; **~ end** n: **to be at a ~ end** (BRIT) or **at ~ ends** (US) non saper che fare; **~ly** adv senza stringere; approssimativamente; **~n** vt sciogliere; (belt etc) allentare
loot [luːt] n bottino ♦ vt saccheggiare

lop [lɔp] vt (also: **~ off**) tagliare via, recidere
lop-sided ['lɔp'saɪdɪd] adj non equilibrato(a), asimmetrico(a)
lord [lɔːd] n signore m; **L~ Smith** lord Smith; **the L~** il Signore; **good L~!** buon Dio!; **the (House of) L~s** (BRIT) la Camera dei Lord; **~ship** n: **your L~ship** Sua Eccellenza
lore [lɔː*] n tradizioni fpl
lorry ['lɔrɪ] (BRIT) n camion m inv; **~ driver** (BRIT) n camionista m
lose [luːz] (pt, pp **lost**) vt perdere ♦ vi perdere; **to ~ (time)** (clock) ritardare; **~r** n perdente m/f
loss [lɔs] n perdita; **to be at a ~** essere perplesso(a)
lost [lɔst] pt, pp of **lose** ♦ adj perduto(a); **~ property** (US **~ and found**) n oggetti mpl smarriti
lot [lɔt] n (at auctions) lotto; (destiny) destino, sorte f; **the ~** tutto(a) quanto(a); tutti(e) quanti(e); **a ~** molto; **a ~ of** una gran quantità di, un sacco di; **~s of** molto(a); **to draw ~s (for sth)** tirare a sorte (per qc)
lotion ['ləʊʃən] n lozione f
lottery ['lɔtərɪ] n lotteria
loud [laud] adj forte, alto(a); (gaudy) vistoso(a), sgargiante ♦ adv (speak etc) forte; **out ~** (read etc) ad alta voce; **~hailer** (BRIT) n portavoce m inv; **~ly** adv fortemente, ad alta voce; **~speaker** n altoparlante m
lounge [laundʒ] n salotto, soggiorno; (at airport, station) sala d'attesa; (BRIT: also: **~ bar**) bar m inv con servizio a tavolino ♦ vi oziare; **~ about** or **around** vi starsene colle mani in mano
louse [laus] (pl **lice**) n pidocchio
lousy ['lauzɪ] (inf) adj orrendo(a), schifoso(a); **to feel ~** stare da cani
lout [laut] n zoticone m
lovable ['lʌvəbl] adj simpatico(a), carino(a); amabile
love [lʌv] n amore m ♦ vt amare; voler bene a; **to ~ to do: I ~ to do** mi piace fare; **to be/fall in ~ with** essere innamorato(a)/

innamorarsi di; **to make ~** fare l'amore; **"15 ~"** (TENNIS) "15 a zero"; **~ affair** n relazione f; **~ life** n vita sentimentale

lovely ['lʌvlɪ] adj bello(a); (delicious: smell, meal) buono(a)

lover ['lʌvə*] n amante m/f; (person in love) innamorato/a; (amateur): **a ~ of** un(un')amante di; un(un')appassionato(a) di

loving ['lʌvɪŋ] adj affettuoso(a)

low [ləu] adj basso(a) ♦ adv in basso ♦ n (METEOR) depressione f; **to be ~ on** (supplies etc) avere scarsità di; **to feel ~** sentirsi giù; **~-alcohol** adj a basso contenuto alcolico; **~-calorie** adj a basso contenuto calorico; **~-cut** adj (dress) scollato(a); **~er** adj (bottom: of 2 things) più basso; (less important) meno importante ♦ vt calare; (prices, eyes, voice) abbassare; **~-fat** adj magro(a); **~lands** npl (GEO) pianura f; **~ly** adj umile, modesto(a)

loyal ['lɔɪəl] adj fedele, leale; **~ty** n fedeltà, lealtà; **~ card** n carta che offre sconti a clienti abituali

lozenge ['lɔzɪndʒ] n (MED) pastiglia

L.P. n abbr = **long-playing record**

L-plates (BRIT) npl contrassegno P principiante

> *i* Le **L-plates** sono delle tabelle bianche con una L rossa che in Gran Bretagna i guidatori principianti, **learner drivers**, devono applicare alla propria autovettura finché non ottengono la patente.

Ltd abbr (= limited) ≈ S.r.l.

lubricate ['lu:brɪkeɪt] vt lubrificare

luck [lʌk] n fortuna, sorte f; **bad ~** sfortuna, mala sorte; **good ~!** buona fortuna!; **~ily** adv fortunatamente, per fortuna; **~y** adj fortunato(a); (number etc) che porta fortuna

ludicrous ['lu:dɪkrəs] adj ridicolo(a)

lug [lʌg] (inf) vt trascinare

luggage ['lʌgɪdʒ] n bagagli mpl; **~ rack** n portabagagli m inv

lukewarm ['lu:kwɔ:m] adj tiepido(a)

lull [lʌl] n intervallo di calma ♦ vt: **to ~ sb to sleep** cullare qn finché si addormenta

lullaby ['lʌləbaɪ] n ninnananna

lumbago [lʌm'beɪgəu] n (MED) lombaggine f

lumber ['lʌmbə*] n (wood) legname m; (junk) roba vecchia; **~ with** vt: **to be ~ed with sth** doversi sorbire qc; **~jack** n boscaiolo

luminous ['lu:mɪnəs] adj luminoso(a)

lump [lʌmp] n pezzo; (in sauce) grumo; (swelling) gonfiore m; (also: **sugar ~**) zolletta ♦ vt (also: **~ together**) riunire, mettere insieme; **a ~ sum** una somma globale; **~y** adj (sauce) pieno(a) di grumi; (bed) bitorzoluto(a)

lunatic ['lu:nətɪk] adj pazzo(a), matto(a)

lunch [lʌntʃ] n pranzo, colazione f

luncheon ['lʌntʃən] n pranzo; **~ voucher** (BRIT) n buono m pasto inv

lunch time n ora di pranzo

lung [lʌŋ] n polmone m

lunge [lʌndʒ] vi (also: **~ forward**) fare un balzo in avanti; **to ~ at** balzare su

lurch [lə:tʃ] vi vacillare, barcollare ♦ n scatto improvviso; **to leave sb in the ~** piantare in asso qn

lure [luə*] n richiamo; lusinga ♦ vt attirare (con l'inganno)

lurid ['luərɪd] adj sgargiante; (details etc) impressionante

lurk [lə:k] vi stare in agguato

luscious ['lʌʃəs] adj succulento(a); delizioso(a)

lush [lʌʃ] adj lussureggiante

lust [lʌst] n lussuria; cupidigia; desiderio; (fig): **~ for** sete f di

lusty ['lʌstɪ] adj vigoroso(a), robusto(a)

Luxembourg ['lʌksəmbə:g] n (state) Lussemburgo m; (city) Lussemburgo f

luxuriant [lʌg'zjuərɪənt] adj lussureggiante; (hair) folto(a)

luxurious [lʌg'zjuərɪəs] adj sontuoso(a), di lusso

luxury ['lʌkʃərɪ] n lusso ♦ cpd di lusso

lying ['laɪɪŋ] n bugie fpl, menzogne fpl

♦ *adj* bugiardo(a)

lynch [lɪntʃ] *vt* linciare

lyrical ['lɪrɪkl] *adj* lirico(a); *(fig)* entusiasta

lyrics ['lɪrɪks] *npl (of song)* parole *fpl*

M, m

m. *abbr* = **metre; mile; million**

M.A. *abbr* = **Master of Arts**

mac [mæk] *(BRIT) n* impermeabile *m*

macaroni [mækəˈrəʊnɪ] *n* maccheroni *mpl*

machine [məˈʃiːn] *n* macchina ♦ *vt (TECH)* lavorare a macchina; *(dress etc)* cucire a macchina; ~ **gun** *n* mitragliatrice *f*; ~**ry** *n* macchinario, macchine *fpl*; *(fig)* macchina

mackerel ['mækrl] *n inv* sgombro

mackintosh ['mækɪntɒʃ] *(BRIT) n* impermeabile *m*

mad [mæd] *adj* matto(a), pazzo(a); *(foolish)* sciocco(a); *(angry)* furioso(a); **to be ~ about** *(keen)* andare pazzo(a) per

madam ['mædəm] *n* signora

madden ['mædn] *vt* fare infuriare

made [meɪd] *pt, pp* **of make**

Madeira [məˈdɪərə] *n (GEO)* Madera; *(wine)* madera

made-to-measure *(BRIT) adj* fatto(a) su misura

madly ['mædlɪ] *adv* follemente

madman ['mædmən] *(irreg) n* pazzo, alienato

madness ['mædnɪs] *n* pazzia

magazine [mægəˈziːn] *n (PRESS)* rivista; *(RADIO, TV)* rubrica

maggot ['mægət] *n* baco, verme *m*

magic ['mædʒɪk] *n* magia ♦ *adj* magico(a); ~**al** *adj* magico(a); ~**ian** [məˈdʒɪʃən] *n* mago/a

magistrate ['mædʒɪstreɪt] *n* magistrato; giudice *m/f*

magnet ['mægnɪt] *n* magnete *m*, calamita; ~**ic** [-'netɪk] *adj* magnetico(a)

magnificent [mægˈnɪfɪsnt] *adj* magnifico(a)

magnify ['mægnɪfaɪ] *vt* ingrandire; ~**ing glass** *n* lente *f* d'ingrandimento

magnitude ['mægnɪtjuːd] *n* grandezza;

importanza

magpie ['mægpaɪ] *n* gazza

mahogany [məˈhɒgənɪ] *n* mogano

maid [meɪd] *n* domestica; *(in hotel)* cameriera

maiden ['meɪdn] *n* fanciulla ♦ *adj (aunt etc)* nubile; *(speech, voyage)* inaugurale; ~ **name** *n* nome *m* da nubile *or* da ragazza

mail [meɪl] *n* posta ♦ *vt* spedire (per posta); ~**box** *(US) n* cassetta delle lettere; ~**ing list** *n* elenco d'indirizzi; ~**-order** *n* vendita *(or* acquisto) per corrispondenza

maim [meɪm] *vt* mutilare

main [meɪn] *adj* principale ♦ *n (pipe)* conduttura principale; **the ~s** *npl (ELEC)* la linea principale; **in the ~** nel complesso, nell'insieme; ~**frame** *n (COMPUT)* mainframe *m inv*; ~**land** *n* continente *m*; ~**ly** *adv* principalmente, soprattutto; ~ **road** *n* strada principale; ~**stay** *n (fig)* sostegno principale; ~**stream** *n (fig)* corrente *f* principale

maintain [meɪnˈteɪn] *vt* mantenere; *(affirm)* sostenere; **maintenance** ['meɪntənəns] *n* manutenzione *f*; *(alimony)* alimenti *mpl*

maize [meɪz] *n* granturco, mais *m*

majestic [məˈdʒestɪk] *adj* maestoso(a)

majesty ['mædʒɪstɪ] *n* maestà *f inv*

major ['meɪdʒə*] *n (MIL)* maggiore *m* ♦ *adj (greater, MUS)* maggiore; *(in importance)* principale, importante

Majorca [məˈjɔːkə] *n* Maiorca

majority [məˈdʒɒrɪtɪ] *n* maggioranza

make [meɪk] *(pt, pp* **made**) *vt* fare; *(manufacture)* fare, fabbricare; *(cause to be):* **to ~ sb sad** *etc* rendere qn triste *etc*; *(force):* **to ~ sb do sth** costringere qn a fare qc, far fare qc a qn; *(equal):* **2 and 2 ~ 4** 2 più 2 fa 4 ♦ *n* fabbricazione *f*; *(brand)* marca; **to ~ a fool of sb** far fare a qn la figura dello scemo; **to ~ a profit** realizzare un profitto; **to ~ a loss** subire una perdita; **to ~ it** *(arrive)* arrivare; *(achieve sth)* farcela; **what time do you ~ it?** che ora fai?; **to ~ do with** arrangiarsi con; ~ **for** *vt fus (place)* avviarsi verso; ~ **out** *vt (write out)* scrivere; *(: cheque)* emettere; *(understand)* capire; (see) distinguere; (: numbers) decifrare; ~ **up** vt (constitute) formare; (invent) inventare; (parcel) fare ♦ vi conciliarsi; (with cosmetics) truccarsi; ~ up for vt fus compensare; ricuperare; **~-believe** n: **a world of ~-believe** un mondo di favole; **it's just ~-believe** è tutta un'invenzione; **~r** n (of programme etc) creatore/trice; (manufacturer) fabbricante m; **~shift** adj improvvisato(a); **~-up** n trucco; **~-up remover** n struccatore m

making ['meɪkɪŋ] n (fig): **in the ~** in formazione; **to have the ~s of** (actor, athlete etc) avere la stoffa di

maladjusted [mælə'dʒʌstɪd] adj disadattato(a)

malaria [mə'lɛərɪə] n malaria

Malaysia [mə'leɪzɪə] n Malaysia

male [meɪl] n (BIOL) maschio ♦ adj maschile; maschio(a)

malfunction [mæl'fʌŋkʃən] n funzione f difettosa

malice ['mælɪs] n malevolenza; **malicious** [mə'lɪʃəs] adj malevolo(a); (LAW) doloso(a)

malignant [mə'lɪgnənt] adj (MED) maligno(a)

mall [mɔːl] n (also: **shopping ~**) centro commerciale

mallet ['mælɪt] n maglio

malnutrition [mælnjuː'trɪʃən] n denutrizione f

malpractice [mæl'præktɪs] n prevaricazione f; negligenza

malt [mɔːlt] n malto

Malta ['mɔːltə] n Malta

mammal ['mæml] n mammifero

mammoth ['mæməθ] adj enorme, gigantesco(a)

man [mæn] (pl **men**) n uomo ♦ vt fornire d'uomini; stare a; **an old ~** un vecchio; **~ and wife** marito e moglie

manage ['mænɪdʒ] vi farcela ♦ vt (be in charge of) occuparsi di; gestire; **to ~ to do sth** riuscire a far qc; **~able** adj maneggevole; fattibile; **~ment** n amministrazione f, direzione f; **~r** n direttore m; (of shop, restaurant) gerente

m; (of artist, SPORT) manager m inv; **~ress** [-ə'rɛs] n direttrice f; gerente f; **~rial** [-ə'dʒɪərɪəl] adj dirigenziale; **managing director** n amministratore m delegato

mandarin ['mændərɪn] n (person, fruit) mandarino

mandatory ['mændətərɪ] adj obbligatorio(a); ingiuntivo(a)

mane [meɪn] n criniera

maneuver etc [mə'nuːvə*] (US) = **manoeuvre** etc

manfully ['mænfəlɪ] adv valorosamente

mangle ['mæŋgl] vt straziare; mutilare

mango ['mæŋgəu] (pl **~es**) n mango

mangy ['meɪndʒɪ] adj rognoso(a)

manhandle ['mænhændl] vt malmenare

manhole ['mænhəul] n botola stradale

manhood ['mænhud] n età virile; virilità

man-hour n ora di lavoro

manhunt ['mænhʌnt] n caccia all'uomo

mania ['meɪnɪə] n mania; **~c** ['meɪnɪæk] n maniaco/a

manic ['mænɪk] adj (behaviour, activity) maniacale

manicure ['mænɪkjuə*] n manicure f inv; **~ set** n trousse f inv della manicure

manifest ['mænɪfɛst] vt manifestare ♦ adj manifesto(a), palese

manifesto [mænɪ'fɛstəu] n manifesto

manipulate [mə'nɪpjuleɪt] vt manipolare

mankind [mæn'kaɪnd] n umanità, genere m umano

manly ['mænlɪ] adj virile; coraggioso(a)

man-made adj sintetico(a); artificiale

manner ['mænə*] n maniera, modo; (behaviour) modo di fare; (type, sort): **all ~ of things** ogni genere di cosa; **~s** npl (conduct) maniere fpl; **bad ~s** maleducazione f; **~ism** n vezzo, tic m inv

manoeuvre [mə'nuːvə*] (US **maneuver**) vt manovrare ♦ vi far manovre ♦ n manovra

manor ['mænə*] n (also: **~ house**) maniero

manpower ['mænpauə*] n manodopera

mansion ['mænʃən] n casa signorile

manslaughter ['mænslɔːtə*] n omicidio preterintenzionale

mantelpiece ['mæntlpiːs] n mensola del

caminetto

manual ['mænjuəl] *adj* manuale ♦ *n* manuale *m*

manufacture [mænju'fæktʃə*] *vt* fabbricare ♦ *n* fabbricazione *f*, manifattura; ~**r** *n* fabbricante *m*

manure [mə'njuə*] *n* concime *m*

manuscript ['mænjuskrɪpt] *n* manoscritto

many ['mɛnɪ] *adj* molti(e) ♦ *pron* molti(e); **a great** ~ moltissimi(e), un gran numero (di); ~ **a time** molte volte

map [mæp] *n* carta (geografica); ~ **out** *vt* tracciare un piano di

maple ['meɪpl] *n* acero

mar [mɑ:*] *vt* sciupare

marathon ['mærəθən] *n* maratona

marauder [mə'rɔ:də*] *n* saccheggiatore *m*

marble ['mɑ:bl] *n* marmo; (*toy*) pallina, bilia

March [mɑ:tʃ] *n* marzo

march [mɑ:tʃ] *vi* marciare; sfilare ♦ *n* marcia

mare [mɛə*] *n* giumenta

margarine [mɑ:dʒə'ri:n] *n* margarina

margin ['mɑ:dʒɪn] *n* margine *m*; ~**al** (**seat**) *n* (POL) seggio elettorale ottenuto con una stretta maggioranza

marigold ['mærɪgəuld] *n* calendola

marina [mə'ri:nə] *n* marina

marine [mə'ri:n] *adj* (*animal, plant*) marino(a); (*forces, engineering*) marittimo(a) ♦ *n* (BRIT) fante *m* di marina; (US) marine *m inv*

marital ['mærɪtl] *adj* maritale, coniugale; ~ **status** stato coniugale

mark [mɑ:k] *n* segno; (*stain*) macchia; (*of skid etc*) traccia; (BRIT: SCOL) voto; (SPORT) bersaglio; (*currency*) marco ♦ *vt* segnare; (*stain*) macchiare; (*indicate*) indicare; (BRIT: SCOL) dare un voto a; correggere; **to ~ time** segnare il passo; ~**ed** *adj* spiccato(a), chiaro(a); ~**er** *n* (*sign*) segno; (*bookmark*) segnalibro

market ['mɑ:kɪt] *n* mercato ♦ *vt* (COMM) mettere in vendita; ~ **garden** (BRIT) *n* orto industriale; ~**ing** *n* marketing *m*; ~ **place** *n* piazza del mercato; (COMM) piazza, mercato; ~ **research** *n* indagine *f or* ricerca di mercato

marksman ['mɑ:ksmən] *n* tiratore *m* scelto

marmalade ['mɑ:məleɪd] *n* marmellata d'arance

maroon [mə'ru:n] *vt* (*also fig*): **to ~ed (in or at)** essere abbandonato(a) (in) ♦ *adj* bordeaux *inv*

marquee [mɑ:'ki:] *n* padiglione *m*

marquess ['mɑ:kwɪs] *n* = **marquis**

marquis ['mɑ:kwɪs] *n* marchese *m*

marriage ['mærɪdʒ] *n* matrimonio; ~ **certificate** *n* certificato di matrimonio

married ['mærɪd] *adj* sposato(a); (*life, love*) coniugale, matrimoniale

marrow ['mærəu] *n* midollo; (*vegetable*) zucca

marry ['mærɪ] *vt* sposare, sposarsi con; (*subj: vicar, priest etc*) dare in matrimonio ♦ *vi* (*also: **get married***) sposarsi

Mars [mɑ:z] *n* (*planet*) Marte *m*

marsh [mɑ:ʃ] *n* palude *f*

marshal ['mɑ:ʃl] *n* maresciallo; (US: *fire*) capo; (: *police*) capitano ♦ *vt* (*thoughts, support*) ordinare; (*soldiers*) adunare

martyr ['mɑ:tə*] *n* martire *m/f*; ~**dom** *n* martirio

marvel ['mɑ:vl] *n* meraviglia ♦ *vi*: **to ~ (at)** meravigliarsi (di); ~**lous** (US ~**ous**) *adj* meraviglioso(a)

Marxist ['mɑ:ksɪst] *adj, n* marxista *m/f*

marzipan ['mɑ:zɪpæn] *n* marzapane *m*

mascara [mæs'kɑ:rə] *n* mascara *m*

masculine ['mæskjulɪn] *adj* maschile; (*woman*) mascolino(a)

mash [mæʃ] *vt* passare, schiacciare; ~**ed potatoes** *npl* purè *m* di patate

mask [mɑ:sk] *n* maschera ♦ *vt* mascherare

mason ['meɪsn] *n* (*also*: **stone~**) scalpellino; (*also*: **free~**) massone *m*; ~**ry** *n* muratura

masquerade [mæskə'reɪd] *vi*: **to ~ as** farsi passare per

mass [mæs] *n* moltitudine *f*, massa; (PHYSICS) massa; (REL) messa ♦ *cpd* di massa ♦ *vi* ammassarsi; **the ~es** *npl* (*ordinary people*) le masse; ~**es of** (*inf*) una montagna di

massacre ['mæsəkə*] *n* massacro

massage ['mæsɑ:ʒ] *n* massaggio

masseur [mæˈsəː*] n massaggiatore m; **masseuse** [-ˈsəːz] n massaggiatrice f
massive [ˈmæsɪv] adj enorme, massiccio(a)
mass media npl mass media mpl
mass-production n produzione f in serie
mast [mɑːst] n albero
master [ˈmɑːstə*] n padrone m; (ART etc, teacher: in primary school) maestro; (: in secondary school) professore m; (title for boys): **M~ X** Signorino X ♦ vt domare; (learn) imparare a fondo; (understand) conoscere a fondo; ~ **key** n chiave f maestra; ~**ly** adj magistrale; ~**mind** n mente f superiore ♦ vt essere il cervello di; **M~ of Arts/Science** n Master m inv in lettere/scienze; ~**piece** n capolavoro; ~**y** n dominio; padronanza
mat [mæt] n stuoia; (also: **door~**) stoino, zerbino; (also: **table ~**) sottopiatto ♦ adj = **matt**
match [mætʃ] n fiammifero; (game) partita, incontro; (fig) uguale m/f; matrimonio; partito ♦ vt intonare; (go well with) andare benissimo con; (equal) uguagliare; (correspond to) corrispondere a; (pair: also: ~ **up**) accoppiare ♦ vi combaciare; **to be a good** ~ andare bene; ~**box** n scatola per fiammiferi; ~**ing** adj ben assortito(a)
mate [meɪt] n compagno/a di lavoro; (inf: friend) amico/a; (animal) compagno/a; (in merchant navy) secondo ♦ vi accoppiarsi
material [məˈtɪərɪəl] n (substance) materiale m, materia; (cloth) stoffa ♦ adj materiale; ~**s** npl (equipment) materiali mpl
maternal [məˈtəːnl] adj materno(a)
maternity [məˈtəːnɪtɪ] n maternità; ~ **dress** n vestito m pre-maman inv; ~ **hospital** n ≈ clinica ostetrica
math [mæθ] (US) n = **maths**
mathematical [mæθəˈmætɪkl] adj matematico(a)
mathematics [mæθəˈmætɪks] n matematica
maths [mæθs] (US **math**) n matematica
matinée [ˈmætɪneɪ] n matinée f inv
mating call [ˈmeɪtɪŋ-] n richiamo sessuale
matriculation [mətrɪkjuˈleɪʃən] n immatricolazione f

matrimonial [mætrɪˈməunɪəl] adj matrimoniale, coniugale
matrimony [ˈmætrɪmənɪ] n matrimonio
matron [ˈmeɪtrən] n (in hospital) capoinfermiera; (in school) infermiera
mat(t) [mæt] adj opaco(a)
matted [ˈmætɪd] adj ingarbugliato(a)
matter [ˈmætə*] n questione f; (PHYSICS) materia, sostanza; (content) contenuto; (MED: pus) pus m ♦ vi importare; **it doesn't** ~ non importa; (I don't mind) non fa niente; **what's the ~?** che cosa c'è?; **no ~ what** qualsiasi cosa accada; **as a ~ of course** come cosa naturale; **as a ~ of fact** in verità; ~-**of-fact** adj prosaico(a)
mattress [ˈmætrɪs] n materasso
mature [məˈtjuə*] adj maturo(a); (cheese) stagionato(a) ♦ vi maturare; stagionare
maul [mɔːl] vt lacerare
mauve [məuv] adj malva inv
maxim [ˈmæksɪm] n massima
maximum [ˈmæksɪməm] (pl **maxima**) adj massimo(a) ♦ n massimo
May [meɪ] n maggio
may [meɪ] (conditional: **might**) vi (indicating possibility): **he** ~ **come** può darsi che venga; (be allowed to): ~ **I smoke?** posso fumare?; (wishes): ~ **God bless you!** Dio la benedica!; **you** ~ **as well go** tanto vale che tu te ne vada
maybe [ˈmeɪbiː] adv forse, può darsi; ~ **he'll ...** può darsi che lui ... +sub, forse lui ....
May Day n il primo maggio
mayhem [ˈmeɪhem] n cagnara
mayonnaise [meɪəˈneɪz] n maionese f
mayor [mɛə*] n sindaco; ~**ess** n sindaco (donna); moglie f del sindaco
maze [meɪz] n labirinto, dedalo
M.D. abbr = **Doctor of Medicine**
me [miː] pron mi, m' +vowel or silent "h"; (stressed, after prep) me; **he heard** ~ mi ha or m'ha sentito; **give** ~ **a book** dammi (or mi dia) un libro; **it's** ~ sono io; **with** ~ con me; **without** ~ senza di me
meadow [ˈmedəu] n prato
meagre [ˈmiːgə*] (US **meager**) adj magro(a)

meal [miːl] *n* pasto; *(flour)* farina; **~time** *n* l'ora di mangiare

mean [miːn] *(pt, pp meant) adj (with money)* avaro(a), gretto(a); *(unkind)* meschino(a), maligno(a); *(shabby)* misero(a); *(average)* medio(a) ♦ *vt (signify)* significare, voler dire; *(intend)*: **to ~ to do** aver l'intenzione di fare ♦ *n* mezzo; *(MATH)* media; **~s** *npl (way, money)* mezzi *mpl*; **by ~s of** per mezzo di; **by all ~s** ma certo, prego; **to be meant for** essere destinato(a) a; **do you ~ it?** dice sul serio?; **what do you ~?** che cosa vuol dire?

meander [mɪˈændə*] *vi* far meandri

meaning [ˈmiːnɪŋ] *n* significato, senso; **~ful** *adj* significativo(a); **~less** *adj* senza senso

means [miːnz] *npl* mezzi *mpl*; **by ~ of** per mezzo di; *(person)* a mezzo di; **by all ~** ma certo, prego

meant [ment] *pt, pp of* **mean**

meantime [ˈmiːntaɪm] *adv (also: in the ~)* nel frattempo

meanwhile [ˈmiːnwaɪl] *adv* nel frattempo

measles [ˈmiːzlz] *n* morbillo

measure [ˈmɛʒə*] *vt, vi* misurare ♦ *n* misura; *(also: tape ~)* metro; **~ments** *npl (size)* misure *fpl*

meat [miːt] *n* carne *f*; **cold ~** affettato; **~ball** *n* polpetta di carne; **~ pie** *n* pasticcio di carne in crosta

Mecca [ˈmɛkə] *n (also fig)* la Mecca

mechanic [mɪˈkænɪk] *n* meccanico; **~al** *adj* meccanico(a); **~s** *n* meccanica ♦ *npl* meccanismo

mechanism [ˈmɛkənɪzəm] *n* meccanismo

medal [ˈmɛdl] *n* medaglia; **~lion** [mɪˈdælɪən] *n* medaglione *m*; **~list** *(US* **~ist)** *n (SPORT)*: **to be a gold ~list** essere medaglia d'oro

meddle [ˈmɛdl] *vi*: **to ~ in** immischiarsi in, mettere le mani in; **to ~ with** toccare

media [ˈmiːdɪə] *npl* media *mpl*

mediaeval [mɛdɪˈiːvl] *adj* = **medieval**

median [ˈmiːdɪən] *(US) n (also: ~ strip)* banchina *f* spartitraffico

mediate [ˈmiːdɪeɪt] *vi* fare da mediatore/trice

Medicaid ® [ˈmɛdɪkeɪd] *(US) n* assistenza medica ai poveri

medical [ˈmɛdɪkl] *adj* medico(a) ♦ *n* visita medica

Medicare ® [ˈmɛdɪkeə*] *(US) n* assistenza medica agli anziani

medication [mɛdɪˈkeɪʃən] *n* medicinali *mpl*, farmaci *mpl*

medicine [ˈmɛdsɪn] *n* medicina

medieval [mɛdɪˈiːvl] *adj* medievale

mediocre [miːdɪˈəukə*] *adj* mediocre

meditate [ˈmɛdɪteɪt] *vi*: **to ~ (on)** meditare (su)

Mediterranean [mɛdɪtəˈreɪnɪən] *adj* mediterraneo(a); **the ~ (Sea)** il (mare) Mediterraneo

medium [ˈmiːdɪəm] *(pl media) adj* medio(a) ♦ *n (means)* mezzo; *(pl mediums: person)* medium *m inv*; **~ wave** *n* onde *fpl* medie

meek [miːk] *adj* dolce, umile

meet [miːt] *(pt, pp met) vt* incontrare; *(for the first time)* fare la conoscenza di; *(go and fetch)* andare a prendere; *(fig)* affrontare; soddisfare; raggiungere ♦ *vi* incontrarsi; *(in session)* riunirsi; *(join: objects)* unirsi; **~ with** *vt fus* incontrare; **~ing** *n* incontro; *(session: of club etc)* riunione *f*; *(interview)* intervista; **she's at a ~ing** *(COMM)* è in riunione

megabyte [ˈmɛgəbaɪt] *n (COMPUT)* megabyte *m inv*

megaphone [ˈmɛgəfəun] *n* megafono

melancholy [ˈmɛlənkəlɪ] *n* malinconia ♦ *adj* malinconico(a)

mellow [ˈmɛləu] *adj (wine, sound)* ricco(a); *(light)* dolce; *(colour)* caldo(a) ♦ *vi (person)* addolcirsi

melody [ˈmɛlədɪ] *n* melodia

melon [ˈmɛlən] *n* melone *m*

melt [mɛlt] *vi (gen)* sciogliersi, struggersi; *(metals)* fondersi ♦ *vt* sciogliere, struggere; fondere; **~ down** *vt* fondere; **~down** *n (in nuclear reactor)* fusione *f* (dovuta a surriscaldamento); **~ing pot** *n (fig)* crogiolo

member [ˈmɛmbə*] *n* membro; **M~ of the European Parliament** *(BRIT) n* euro-deputato; **M~ of Parliament** *(BRIT) n* deputato/a; **M~ of the Scottish Parliament** (*BRIT*) n deputato/a del Parlamento scozzese; **~ship** n iscrizione f; (numero d')iscritti mpl, membri mpl; **~ship card** n tessera (di iscrizione)

memento [mə'mɛntəu] n ricordo, souvenir m inv

memo ['mɛməu] n appunto; (*COMM etc*) comunicazione f di servizio

memoirs ['mɛmwɑːz] npl memorie fpl, ricordi mpl

memorandum [mɛmə'rændəm] (pl **memoranda**) n appunto; (*COMM etc*) comunicazione f di servizio

memorial [mɪ'mɔːrɪəl] n monumento commemorativo ♦ adj commemorativo(a)

memorize ['mɛməraɪz] vt memorizzare

memory ['mɛmərɪ] n (*also COMPUT*) memoria; (*recollection*) ricordo

men [mɛn] npl of **man**

menace ['mɛnəs] n minaccia ♦ vt minacciare

mend [mɛnd] vt aggiustare, riparare; (*darn*) rammendare ♦ n: **on the ~** in via di guarigione; **to ~ one's ways** correggersi

menial ['miːnɪəl] adj da servo, domestico(a); umile

meningitis [mɛnɪn'dʒaɪtɪs] n meningite f

menopause ['mɛnəupɔːz] n menopausa

menstruation [mɛnstru'eɪʃən] n mestruazione f

mental ['mɛntl] adj mentale

mentality [mɛn'tælɪtɪ] n mentalità f inv

menthol ['mɛnθɒl] n mentolo

mention ['mɛnʃən] n menzione f ♦ vt menzionare, far menzione di; **don't ~ it!** non c'è di che!, prego!

menu ['mɛnjuː] n (*set ~*, *COMPUT*) menù m inv; (*printed*) carta

MEP n abbr = **Member of the European Parliament**

merchandise ['mɜːtʃəndaɪz] n merci fpl

merchant ['mɜːtʃənt] n mercante m, commerciante m; **~ bank** (*BRIT*) n banca d'affari; **~ navy** (*US* **~ marine**) n marina mercantile

merciful ['mɜːsɪful] adj pietoso(a), clemente

merciless ['mɜːsɪlɪs] adj spietato(a)

mercury ['mɜːkjurɪ] n mercurio

mercy ['mɜːsɪ] n pietà f; (*REL*) misericordia; **at the ~ of** alla mercè di

mere [mɪə*] adj semplice; **by a ~ chance** per mero caso; **~ly** adv semplicemente, non ... che

merge [mɜːdʒ] vt unire ♦ vi fondersi, unirsi; (*COMM*) fondersi; **~r** n (*COMM*) fusione f

meringue [mə'ræŋ] n meringa

merit ['mɛrɪt] n merito, valore m ♦ vt meritare

mermaid ['mɜːmeɪd] n sirena

merry ['mɛrɪ] adj gaio(a), allegro(a); **M~ Christmas!** Buon Natale!; **~-go-round** n carosello

mesh [mɛʃ] n maglia; rete f

mesmerize ['mɛzməraɪz] vt ipnotizzare; affascinare

mess [mɛs] n confusione f, disordine m; (*fig*) pasticcio; (*dirt*) sporcizia; (*MIL*) mensa; **~ about** (*inf*) vi (*also:* **~ around**) trastullarsi; **~ about with** (*inf*) vt fus (*also:* **~ around with**) gingillarsi con; (*plans*) fare un pasticcio di; **~ up** vt sporcare; fare un pasticcio di; rovinare

message ['mɛsɪdʒ] n messaggio

messenger ['mɛsɪndʒə*] n messaggero/a

Messrs ['mɛsəz] abbr (*on letters*) Spett

messy ['mɛsɪ] adj sporco(a); disordinato(a)

met [mɛt] pt, pp of **meet**

metal ['mɛtl] n metallo; **~lic** [-'tælɪk] adj metallico(a)

metaphor ['mɛtəfə*] n metafora

meteorology [miːtɪə'rɒlədʒɪ] n meteorologia

meter ['miːtə*] n (*instrument*) contatore m; (*parking ~*) parchimetro; (*US: unit*) = **metre**

method ['mɛθəd] n metodo; **~ical** [mɪ'θɒdɪkl] adj metodico(a)

Methodist ['mɛθədɪst] n metodista m/f

meths [mɛθs] (*BRIT*) n = **methylated spirit**

methylated spirit ['mɛθɪleɪtɪd-] (*BRIT*) n alcool m denaturato

metre ['miːtə*] (*US* **meter**) n metro

metric ['mɛtrɪk] adj metrico(a)

metropolitan [mɛtrə'pɒlɪtən] adj

metropolitano(a); **the M~ Police** (BRIT) n la polizia di Londra

mettle ['mɛtl] n: **to be on one's ~** essere pronto(a) a dare il meglio di se stesso(a)

mew [mjuː] vi (cat) miagolare

mews [mjuːz] (BRIT) n: **~ flat** appartamento ricavato da un'antica scuderia

Mexico ['mɛksɪkəʊ] n Messico

miaow [miːˈaʊ] vi miagolare

mice [maɪs] npl of **mouse**

micro... ['maɪkrəʊ] prefix micro...; **~chip** n microcircuito integrato; **~(computer)** n microcomputer m inv; **~phone** n microfono; **~scope** n microscopio; **~wave** n (also: **~wave oven**) forno a microonde

mid [mɪd] adj: **~ May** metà maggio; **~ afternoon** metà pomeriggio; **in ~ air** a mezz'aria; **~day** n mezzogiorno

middle ['mɪdl] n mezzo; centro; (waist) vita ♦ adj di mezzo; **in the ~ of the night** nel bel mezzo della notte; **~-aged** adj di mezza età; **the M~ Ages** npl il Medioevo; **~-class** adj ≈ borghese; **the ~ class(es)** n(pl) ≈ la borghesia; **M~ East** n Medio Oriente m; **~man** (irreg) n intermediario; agente m rivenditore; **~ name** n secondo nome m; **~-of-the-road** adj moderato(a); **~weight** n (BOXING) peso medio

middling ['mɪdlɪŋ] adj medio(a)

midge [mɪdʒ] n moscerino

midget ['mɪdʒɪt] n nano/a

Midlands ['mɪdləndz] npl contee del centro dell'Inghilterra

midnight ['mɪdnaɪt] n mezzanotte f

midriff ['mɪdrɪf] n diaframma m

midst [mɪdst] n: **in the ~ of** in mezzo a

midsummer [mɪdˈsʌmə*] n mezza or piena estate f

midway [mɪdˈweɪ] adj, adv: **~ (between)** a mezza strada (fra); **~ (through)** a metà (di)

midweek [mɪdˈwiːk] adv a metà settimana

midwife ['mɪdwaɪf] (pl **midwives**) n levatrice f

might [maɪt] vb see **may** ♦ n potere m, forza; **~y** adj forte, potente

migraine ['miːgreɪn] n emicrania

migrant ['maɪgrənt] adj (bird) migratore(trice); (worker) emigrato(a)

migrate [maɪˈgreɪt] vi (bird) migrare; (person) emigrare

mike [maɪk] n abbr (= microphone) microfono

Milan [mɪˈlæn] n Milano f

mild [maɪld] adj mite; (person, voice) dolce; (flavour) delicato(a); (illness) leggero(a); (interest) blando(a) ♦ n (beer) birra leggera

mildew ['mɪldjuː] n muffa

mildly ['maɪldlɪ] adv mitemente; dolcemente; delicatamente; leggermente; blandamente; **to put it ~** a dire poco

mile [maɪl] n miglio; **~age** n distanza in miglia, ≈ chilometraggio

mileometer [maɪˈlɒmɪtə*] n ≈ conta-chilometri m inv

milestone ['maɪlstəʊn] n pietra miliare

milieu ['miːljɜː] n ambiente m

militant ['mɪlɪtnt] adj militante

military ['mɪlɪtərɪ] adj militare

milk [mɪlk] n latte m ♦ vt (cow) mungere; (fig) sfruttare; **~ chocolate** n cioccolato al latte; **~man** (irreg) n lattaio; **~ shake** n frappé m inv; **~y** adj lattiginoso(a); (colour) latteo(a); **M~y Way** n Via Lattea

mill [mɪl] n mulino; (small: for coffee, pepper etc) macinino; (factory) fabbrica; (spinning ~) filatura ♦ vt macinare ♦ vi (also: **~ about**) brulicare

millennia [mɪˈlɛnɪə] npl of **millennium**

millennium [mɪˈlɛnɪəm] (pl **~s** or **millennia**) n millennio; **~ bug** n baco di fine millennio

miller ['mɪlə*] n mugnaio

milli... ['mɪlɪ] prefix: **~gram(me)** n milligrammo; **~metre** (US **~meter**) n millimetro

million ['mɪljən] n milione m; **~aire** n milionario, ≈ miliardario

milometer [maɪˈlɒmɪtə*] n = **mileometer**

mime [maɪm] n mimo ♦ vt, vi mimare

mimic ['mɪmɪk] n imitatore/trice ♦ vt fare la mimica di

min. abbr = **minute(s)**; **minimum**

mince [mɪns] vt tritare, macinare ♦ n (BRIT:

CULIN) carne f tritata or macinata; **~meat** n frutta secca tritata per uso in pasticceria; (US) carne f tritata or macinata; **~ pie** n specie di torta con frutta secca; **~r** n tritacarne m inv

mind [maɪnd] n mente f ♦ vt (attend to, look after) badare a, occuparsi di; (be careful) fare attenzione a, stare attento(a) a; (object to): **I don't ~ the noise** il rumore non mi dà alcun fastidio; **I don't ~** non m'importa; **it is on my ~** mi preoccupa; **to my ~** secondo me, a mio parere; **to be out of one's ~** essere uscito(a) di mente; **to keep** or **bear sth in ~** non dimenticare qc; **to make up one's ~** decidersi; **~ you, ...** sì, però va detto che ...; **never ~** non importa, non fa niente; (don't worry) non preoccuparti; **"~ the step"** "attenzione allo scalino"; **~er** n (child~er) bambinaia; (bodyguard) guardia del corpo; **~less** adj idiota

mine1 [maɪn] pron il(la) mio(a), pl i(le) miei(mie); **that book is ~** quel libro è mio; **yours is red, ~ is green** il tuo è rosso, il mio è verde; **a friend of ~** un mio amico

mine2 [maɪn] n miniera; (explosive) mina ♦ vt (coal) estrarre; (ship, beach) minare; **~field** n (also fig) campo minato

miner ['maɪnə*] n minatore m

mineral ['mɪnərəl] adj minerale ♦ n minerale m; **~s** npl (BRIT: soft drinks) bevande fpl gasate; **~ water** n acqua minerale

mingle ['mɪŋgl] vi: **to ~ with** mescolarsi a, mischiarsi con

miniature ['mɪnətʃə*] adj in miniatura

minibus ['mɪnɪbʌs] n minibus m inv

Minidisc® ['mɪnɪdɪsk] n minidisc m inv

minim ['mɪnɪm] n (MUS) minima

minimum ['mɪnɪməm] (pl **minima**) n minimo ♦ adj minimo(a)

mining ['maɪnɪŋ] n industria mineraria

miniskirt ['mɪnɪskə:t] n minigonna

minister ['mɪnɪstə*] n (BRIT: POL) ministro; (REL) pastore m; **to ~ to sb's needs** provvedere ai bisogni di qn

ministry ['mɪnɪstrɪ] n (BRIT: POL) ministero; (REL): **to go into the ~** diventare pastore

mink [mɪŋk] n visone m

minnow ['mɪnəu] n pesciolino d'acqua dolce

minor ['maɪnə*] adj minore, di poca importanza; (MUS) minore ♦ n (LAW) minorenne m/f

minority [maɪ'nɔrɪtɪ] n minoranza

mint [mɪnt] n (plant) menta; (sweet) pasticca di menta ♦ vt (coins) battere; **the (Royal) M~** (BRIT), **the (US) M~** (US) la Zecca; **in ~ condition** come nuovo(a) di zecca

minus ['maɪnəs] n (also: **~ sign**) segno meno ♦ prep meno

minute [adj maɪ'nju:t, n 'mɪnɪt] adj minuscolo(a); (detail) minuzioso(a) ♦ n minuto; **~s** npl (of meeting) verbale m

miracle ['mɪrəkl] n miracolo

mirage ['mɪrɑ:ʒ] n miraggio

mirror ['mɪrə*] n specchio; (in car) specchietto

mirth [mə:θ] n ilarità

misadventure [mɪsəd'ventʃə*] n disavventura; **death by ~** morte f accidentale

misapprehension ['mɪsæprɪ'henʃən] n malinteso

misappropriate [mɪsə'prəuprɪeɪt] vt appropriarsi indebitamente di

misbehave [mɪsbɪ'heɪv] vi comportarsi male

miscarriage ['mɪskærɪdʒ] n (MED) aborto spontaneo; **~ of justice** errore m giudiziario

miscellaneous [mɪsɪ'leɪnɪəs] adj (items) vario(a); (selection) misto(a)

mischance [mɪs'tʃɑ:ns] n sfortuna

mischief ['mɪstʃɪf] n (naughtiness) birichineria; (maliciousness) malizia; **mischievous** adj birichino(a)

misconception ['mɪskən'sepʃən] n idea sbagliata

misconduct [mɪs'kɔndʌkt] n cattiva condotta; **professional ~** reato professionale

misdemeanour [mɪsdɪ'mi:nə*] (US **misdemeanor**) n misfatto; infrazione f

miser ['maɪzə*] n avaro

miserable ['mɪzərəbl] *adj* infelice; (*wretched*) miserabile; (*weather*) deprimente; (*offer, failure*) misero(a)

miserly ['maɪzəlɪ] *adj* avaro(a)

misery ['mɪzərɪ] *n* (*unhappiness*) tristezza; (*wretchedness*) miseria

misfire [mɪs'faɪə*] *vi* far cilecca; (*car engine*) perdere colpi

misfit ['mɪsfɪt] *n* (*person*) spostato/a

misfortune [mɪs'fɔ:tʃən] *n* sfortuna

misgiving [mɪs'gɪvɪŋ] *n* apprensione *f*; **to have ~s about** avere dei dubbi per quanto riguarda

misguided [mɪs'gaɪdɪd] *adj* sbagliato(a); poco giudizioso(a)

mishandle [mɪs'hændl] *vt* (*mismanage*) trattare male

mishap ['mɪshæp] *n* disgrazia

misinterpret [mɪsɪn'tə:prɪt] *vt* interpretare male

misjudge [mɪs'dʒʌdʒ] *vt* giudicare male

mislay [mɪs'leɪ] (*irreg*) *vt* smarrire

mislead [mɪs'li:d] (*irreg*) *vt* sviare; **~ing** *adj* ingannevole

mismanage [mɪs'mænɪdʒ] *vt* gestire male

misplace [mɪs'pleɪs] *vt* smarrire

misprint ['mɪsprɪnt] *n* errore *m* di stampa

Miss [mɪs] *n* Signorina

miss [mɪs] *vt* (*fail to get*) perdere; (*fail to hit*) mancare; (*fail to see*): **you can't ~ it** non puoi non vederlo; (*regret the absence of*): **I ~ him** sento la sua mancanza ♦ *vi* mancare ♦ *n* (*shot*) colpo mancato; **~ out** (*BRIT*) *vt* omettere

misshapen [mɪs'ʃeɪpən] *adj* deforme

missile ['mɪsaɪl] *n* (*MIL*) missile *m*; (*object thrown*) proiettile *m*

missing ['mɪsɪŋ] *adj* perso(a), smarrito(a); (*person*) scomparso(a); (: *after disaster, MIL*) disperso(a); (*removed*) mancante; **to be ~** mancare

mission ['mɪʃən] *n* missione *f*; **~ary** *n* missionario/a

mist [mɪst] *n* nebbia, foschia ♦ *vi* (*also*: **~ over, ~ up**) annebbiarsi; (: *BRIT: windows*) appannarsi

mistake [mɪs'teɪk] (*irreg: like* **take**) *n* sbaglio, errore *m* ♦ *vt* sbagliarsi di; fraintendere; **to make a ~** fare uno sbaglio, sbagliare; **by ~** per sbaglio; **to ~ for** prendere per; **mistaken** *pp of* **mistake** ♦ *adj* (*idea etc*) sbagliato(a); **to be mistaken** sbagliarsi

mister ['mɪstə*] (*inf*) *n* signore *m*; *see* **Mr**

mistletoe ['mɪsltəu] *n* vischio

mistook [mɪs'tuk] *pt of* **mistake**

mistress ['mɪstrɪs] *n* padrona; (*lover*) amante *f*; (*BRIT: SCOL*) insegnante *f*

mistrust [mɪs'trʌst] *vt* diffidare di

misty ['mɪstɪ] *adj* nebbioso(a), brumoso(a)

misunderstand [mɪsʌndə'stænd] (*irreg*) *vt, vi* capire male, fraintendere; **~ing** *n* malinteso, equivoco

misuse [*n* mɪs'ju:s, *vb* mɪs'ju:z] *n* cattivo uso; (*of power*) abuso ♦ *vt* far cattivo uso di; abusare di

mitigate ['mɪtɪgeɪt] *vt* mitigare

mitt(en) ['mɪt(n)] *n* mezzo guanto; manopola

mix [mɪks] *vt* mescolare ♦ *vi* (*people*): **to ~ with** avere a che fare con ♦ *n* mescolanza; preparato; **~ up** *vt* mescolare; (*confuse*) confondere; **~ed** *adj* misto(a); **~ed-up** *adj* (*confused*) confuso(a); **~er** *n* (*for food: electric*) frullatore *m*; (: *hand*) frullino; (*person*): **he is a good ~er** è molto socievole; **~ture** *n* mescolanza; (*blend: of tobacco etc*) miscela; (*MED*) sciroppo; **~-up** *n* confusione *f*

moan [məun] *n* gemito ♦ *vi* (*inf: complain*): **to ~ (about)** lamentarsi (di)

moat [məut] *n* fossato

mob [mɔb] *n* calca ♦ *vt* accalcarsi intorno a

mobile ['məubaɪl] *adj* mobile ♦ *n* (*decoration*) mobile *m*; **~ home** *n* grande roulotte *f inv* (utilizzata come domicilio); **~ phone** telefono portatile, telefonino

mock [mɔk] *vt* deridere, burlarsi di ♦ *adj* falso(a); **~ery** *n* derisione *f*; **to make a ~ery of** burlarsi di; (*exam*) rendere una farsa; **~-up** *n* modello

mod [mɔd] *adj see* **convenience**

mode [məud] *n* modo

model ['mɔdl] *n* modello; (*person: for*

fashion) indossatore/trice; (: *for artist*) modello/a ♦ *adj* (*small-scale: railway etc*) in miniatura; (*child, factory*) modello *inv* ♦ *vt* modellare ♦ *vi* fare l'indossatore (*or* l'indossatrice); **to ~ clothes** presentare degli abiti

modem ['məʊdɛm] *n* modem *m inv*

moderate [*adj* 'mɒdərət, *vb* 'mɒdəreɪt] *adj* moderato(a) ♦ *vi* moderarsi, placarsi ♦ *vt* moderare

modern ['mɒdən] *adj* moderno(a); **~ize** *vt* modernizzare

modest ['mɒdɪst] *adj* modesto(a); **~y** *n* modestia

modify ['mɒdɪfaɪ] *vt* modificare

mogul ['məʊgl] *n* (*fig*) magnate *m*, pezzo grosso

mohair ['məʊhɛə*] *n* mohair *m*

moist [mɔɪst] *adj* umido(a); **~en** ['mɔɪsn] *vt* inumidire; **~ure** ['mɔɪstʃə*] *n* umidità; (*on glass*) goccioline *fpl* di vapore; **~urizer** ['mɔɪstʃəraɪzə*] *n* idratante *f*

molar ['məʊlə*] *n* molare *m*

mold [məʊld] (*US*) *n, vt* = **mould**

mole [məʊl] *n* (*animal, fig*) talpa; (*spot*) neo

molest [məʊ'lɛst] *vt* molestare

mollycoddle ['mɒlɪkɒdl] *vt* coccolare, vezzeggiare

molt [məʊlt] (*US*) *vi* = **moult**

molten ['məʊltən] *adj* fuso(a)

mom [mɒm] (*US*) *n* = **mum**

moment ['məʊmənt] *n* momento, istante *m*; **at that ~** in quel momento; **at the ~** al momento, in questo momento; **~ary** *adj* momentaneo(a), passeggero(a); **~ous** [-'mɛntəs] *adj* di grande importanza

momentum [məʊ'mɛntəm] *n* (*PHYSICS*) momento; (*fig*) impeto; **to gather ~** aumentare di velocità

mommy ['mɒmɪ] (*US*) *n* = **mummy**

Monaco ['mɒnəkəʊ] *n* Principato di Monaco

monarch ['mɒnək] *n* monarca *m*; **~y** *n* monarchia

monastery ['mɒnəstərɪ] *n* monastero

Monday ['mʌndɪ] *n* lunedì *m inv*

monetary ['mʌnɪtərɪ] *adj* monetario(a)

money ['mʌnɪ] *n* denaro, soldi *mpl*; **~ belt**

n marsupio (*per soldi*); **~ order** *n* vaglia *m inv*; **~-spinner** (*inf*) *n* miniera d'oro (*fig*)

mongol ['mɒŋgəl] *adj*, *n* (*MED*) mongoloide *m/f*

mongrel ['mʌŋgrəl] *n* (*dog*) cane *m* bastardo

monitor ['mɒnɪtə*] *n* (*TV, COMPUT*) monitor *m inv* ♦ *vt* controllare

monk [mʌŋk] *n* monaco

monkey ['mʌŋkɪ] *n* scimmia; **~ nut** (*BRIT*) *n* nocciolina americana; **~ wrench** *n* chiave *f* a rullino

mono ['mɒnəʊ] *adj* (*recording*) (in) mono *inv*

monopoly [mə'nɒpəlɪ] *n* monopolio

monotone ['mɒnətəʊn] *n* pronunzia (*or* voce *f*) monotona

monotonous [mə'nɒtənəs] *adj* monotono(a)

monsoon [mɒn'su:n] *n* monsone *m*

monster ['mɒnstə*] *n* mostro

monstrous ['mɒnstrəs] *adj* mostruoso(a); (*huge*) gigantesco(a)

month [mʌnθ] *n* mese *m*; **~ly** *adj* mensile ♦ *adv* al mese; ogni mese

monument ['mɒnjumənt] *n* monumento

moo [mu:] *vi* muggire, mugghiare

mood [mu:d] *n* umore *m*; **to be in a good/bad ~** essere di buon/cattivo umore; **~y** *adj* (*variable*) capriccioso(a), lunatico(a); (*sullen*) imbronciato(a)

moon [mu:n] *n* luna; **~light** *n* chiaro di luna; **~lighting** *n* lavoro nero; **~lit** *adj*: **a ~lit night** una notte rischiarata dalla luna

Moor [mʊə*] *n* moro/a

moor [mʊə*] *n* brughiera ♦ *vt* (*ship*) ormeggiare ♦ *vi* ormeggiarsi

moorland ['mʊələnd] *n* brughiera

moose [mu:s] *n inv* alce *m*

mop [mɒp] *n* lavapavimenti *m inv*; (*also*: **~ of hair**) zazzera ♦ *vt* lavare con lo straccio; (*face*) asciugare; **~ up** *vt* asciugare con uno straccio

mope [məʊp] *vi* fare il broncio

moped ['məʊpɛd] *n* (*BRIT*) ciclomotore *m*

moral ['mɒrl] *adj* morale ♦ *n* morale *f*; **~s** *npl* (*principles*) moralità

morality [mə'ræltɪ] *n* moralità
morass [mə'ræs] *n* palude *f*, pantano
morbid ['mɔːbɪd] *adj* morboso(a)

KEYWORD
---

more [mɔː*] *adj* **1** (*greater in number etc*)
più; **~ people/letters than we expected**
più persone/lettere di quante ne
aspettavamo; **I have ~ wine/money than
you** ho più vino/soldi di te; **I have ~ wine
than beer** ho più vino che birra
2 (*additional*) altro(a), ancora; **do you
want (some) ~ tea?** vuole dell'altro tè?,
vuole ancora del tè?; **I have no** *or* **I don't
have any ~ money** non ho più soldi
♦ *pron* **1** (*greater amount*) più; **~ than 10**
più di 10; **it cost ~ than we expected** ha
costato più di quanto ci aspettavamo
2 (*further or additional amount*) ancora; **is
there any ~?** ce n'è ancora?; **there's no ~**
non ce n'è più; **a little ~** ancora un po';
many/much ~ molti(e)/molto(a) di più
♦ *adv*: **~ dangerous/easily (than)** più
pericoloso/facilmente (di); **~ and ~** sempre
di più; **~ and ~ difficult** sempre più
difficile; **~ or less** più o meno; **~ than ever**
più che mai

moreover [mɔː'rəuvə*] *adv* inoltre, di più
morgue [mɔːg] *n* obitorio
morning ['mɔːnɪŋ] *n* mattina, mattino;
(*duration*) mattinata ♦ *cpd* del mattino; **in
the ~** la mattina; **7 o'clock in the ~** le 7 di
or della mattina; **~ sickness** *n* nausee *fpl*
mattutine
Morocco [mə'rɔkəu] *n* Marocco
moron ['mɔːrɔn] (*inf*) *n* deficiente *m/f*
morose [mə'rəus] *adj* cupo(a), tetro(a)
Morse [mɔːs] *n* (*also*: **~ code**) alfabeto
Morse
morsel ['mɔːsl] *n* boccone *m*
mortal ['mɔːtl] *adj* mortale ♦ *n* mortale *m*
mortgage ['mɔːgɪdʒ] *n* ipoteca; (*loan*)
prestito ipotecario ♦ *vt* ipotecare; **~
company** (*US*) *n* società *f inv* di credito
immobiliare
mortuary ['mɔːtjuərɪ] *n* camera mortuaria;

obitorio
mosaic [məu'zeɪɪk] *n* mosaico
Moscow ['mɔskəu] *n* Mosca
Moslem ['mɔzləm] *adj*, *n* = **Muslim**
mosque [mɔsk] *n* moschea
mosquito [mɔs'kiːtəu] (*pl* **~es**) *n* zanzara
moss [mɔs] *n* muschio
most [məust] *adj* (*almost all*) la maggior
parte di; (*largest, greatest*): **who has (the)
~ money?** chi ha più soldi di tutti? ♦ *pron*
la maggior parte ♦ *adv* più; (*work, sleep
etc*) di più; (*very*) molto, estremamente;
the ~ (*also*: +*adjective*) il(la) più; **~ of** la
maggior parte di; **~ of them** quasi tutti; **I
saw (the) ~** ho visto più io; **at the (very) ~**
al massimo; **to make the ~ of** trarre il
massimo vantaggio da; **a ~ interesting
book** un libro estremamente interessante;
~ly *adv* per lo più
MOT (*BRIT*) *n abbr* (= *Ministry of Transport*):
the ~ (test) revisione annuale obbligatoria
degli autoveicoli
motel [məu'tel] *n* motel *m inv*
moth [mɔθ] *n* farfalla notturna; tarma
mother ['mʌðə*] *n* madre ♦ *vt* (*care for*)
fare da madre a; **~hood** *n* maternità; **~-
in-law** *n* suocera; **~ly** *adj* materno(a); **~-
of-pearl** [mʌðərəv'pəːl] *n* madreperla; **~-
to-be** [mʌðətə'biː] *n* futura mamma; **~
tongue** *n* madrelingua
motion ['məuʃən] *n* movimento, moto;
(*gesture*) gesto; (*at meeting*) mozione *f*
♦ *vt*, *vi*: **to ~ (to) sb to do** fare cenno a qn
di fare; **~less** *adj* immobile; **~ picture** *n*
film *m inv*
motivated ['məutɪveɪtɪd] *adj* motivato(a)
motive ['məutɪv] *n* motivo
motley ['mɔtlɪ] *adj* eterogeneo(a), molto
vario(a)
motor ['məutə*] *n* motore *m*; (*BRIT: inf:
vehicle*) macchina ♦ *cpd* automobilistico(a);
~bike *n* moto *f inv*; **~boat** *n* motoscafo;
~car (*BRIT*) *n* automobile *f*; **~cycle** *n*
motocicletta; **~cyclist** *n* motociclista *m/f*;
~ing (*BRIT*) *n* turismo automobilistico; **~ist**
n automobilista *m/f*; **~ racing** (*BRIT*) *n*
corse *fpl* automobilistiche; **~way** (*BRIT*) *n*

autostrada

mottled ['mɔtld] *adj* chiazzato(a), marezzato(a)

motto ['mɔtəu] (*pl* **~es**) *n* motto

mould [məuld] (*US* **mold**) *n* forma, stampo; (*mildew*) muffa ♦ *vt* formare; (*fig*) foggiare; **~y** *adj* ammuffito(a); (*smell*) di muffa

moult [məult] (*US* **molt**) *vi* far la muta

mound [maund] *n* rialzo, collinetta; (*heap*) mucchio

mount [maunt] *n* (*GEO*) monte *m* ♦ *vt* montare; (*horse*) montare a ♦ *vi* (*increase*) aumentare; **~ up** *vi* (*build up*) accumularsi

mountain ['mauntin] *n* montagna ♦ *cpd* di montagna; **~ bike** *n* mountain bike *f inv*; **~eer** [-'niə*] *n* alpinista *m/f*; **~eering** [-'niəriŋ] *n* alpinismo; **~ous** *adj* montagnoso(a); **~ rescue team** *n* squadra di soccorso alpino; **~side** *n* fianco della montagna

mourn [mɔ:n] *vt* piangere, lamentare ♦ *vi*: **to ~ (for sb)** piangere (la morte di qn); **~er** *n* parente *m/f or* amico/a del defunto; **~ing** *n* lutto; **in ~ing** in lutto

mouse [maus] (*pl* **mice**) *n* topo; (*COMPUT*) mouse *m inv*; **~ mat**, **~ pad** *n* (*COMPUT*) tappetino del mouse; **~trap** *n* trappola per i topi

mousse [mu:s] *n* mousse *f inv*

moustache [məs'tɑ:ʃ] (*US* **mustache**) *n* baffi *mpl*

mousy ['mausi] *adj* (*hair*) né chiaro(a) né scuro(a)

mouth [mauθ, *pl* mauðz] *n* bocca; (*of river*) bocca, foce *f*; (*opening*) orifizio; **~ful** *n* boccata; **~ organ** *n* armonica; **~piece** *n* (*MUS*) imboccatura, bocchino; (*spokesman*) portavoce *m/f inv*; **~wash** *n* collutorio; **~-watering** *adj* che fa venire l'acquolina in bocca

movable ['mu:vəbl] *adj* mobile

move [mu:v] *n* (*movement*) movimento; (*in game*) mossa; (: *turn to play*) turno; (*change: of house*) trasloco; (: *of job*) cambiamento ♦ *vt* muovere, spostare; (*emotionally*) commuovere; (*POL: resolution etc*) proporre ♦ *vi* (*gen*) muoversi, spostarsi; (*also:* ~ *house*) cambiar casa, traslocare; **to get a ~ on**

affrettarsi, sbrigarsi; **to ~ sb to do sth** indurre *or* spingere qn a fare qc; **to ~ towards** andare verso; **~ about *or* around** *vi* spostarsi; **~ along** *vi* muoversi avanti; **~ away** *vi* allontanarsi, andarsene; **~ back** *vi* (*return*) ritornare; **~ forward** *vi* avanzare; **~ in** *vi* (*to a house*) entrare (in una nuova casa); (*police etc*) intervenire; **~ on** *vi* riprendere la strada; **~ out** *vi* (*of house*) sgombrare; **~ over** *vi* spostarsi; **~ up** *vi* avanzare

moveable ['mu:vəbl] *adj* = **movable**

movement ['mu:vmənt] *n* (*gen*) movimento; (*gesture*) gesto; (*of stars, water, physical*) moto

movie ['mu:vi] *n* film *m inv*; **the ~s** il cinema

moviecamera *n* cinepresa

moving ['mu:viŋ] *adj* mobile; (*causing emotion*) commovente

mow [məu] (*pt* **mowed**, *pp* **mowed** *or* **mown**) *vt* (*grass*) falciare; (*corn*) mietere; **~ down** *vt* falciare; **~er** *n* (*also:* **lawnmower**) tagliaerba *m inv*

MP *n abbr* = **Member of Parliament**

MP3 *n abbr* M3

m.p.h. *n abbr* = **miles per hour** (60 m.p.h. = 96 km/h)

Mr ['mistə*] (*US* **Mr.**) *n*: **~ X** Signor X, Sig. X

Mrs ['misiz] (*US* **Mrs.**) *n*: **~ X** Signora X, Sig.ra X

Ms [miz] (*US* **Ms.**) *n* (= *Miss or Mrs*): **~ X** ≈ Signora X, Sig.ra X

M.Sc. *abbr* = **Master of Science**

MSP *n abbr* = **Member of the Scottish Parliament**

KEYWORD

much [mʌtʃ] *adj, pron* molto(a); **he's done so ~ work** ha lavorato così tanto; **I have as ~ money as you** ho tanti soldi quanti ne hai tu; **how ~ is it?** quant'è?; **it costs too ~** costa troppo; **as ~ as you want** quanto vuoi ♦ *adv* 1 (*greatly*) molto, tanto; **thank you very ~** molte grazie; **he's very ~ the gentleman** è il vero gentiluomo; **I read as ~ as I can** leggo quanto posso; **as ~ as you** tanto quanto te

2 (*by far*) molto; **it's ~ the biggest**

company in Europe è di gran lunga la più grossa società in Europa
3 (*almost*) grossomodo, praticamente; **they're ~ the same** sono praticamente uguali

muck [mʌk] *n* (*dirt*) sporcizia; **~ about** *or* **around** (*inf*) *vi* fare lo stupido; (*waste time*) gingillarsi; **~ up** (*inf*) *vt* (*ruin*) rovinare

mud [mʌd] *n* fango

muddle ['mʌdl] *n* confusione *f*, disordine *m*; pasticcio ♦ *vt* (*also:* **~ up**) confondere; **~ through** *vi* cavarsela alla meno peggio

muddy ['mʌdɪ] *adj* fangoso(a)

mudguard ['mʌdgɑːd] *n* parafango

muesli ['mjuːzlɪ] *n* muesli *m*

muffin ['mʌfɪn] *n specie di pasticcino soffice da tè*

muffle ['mʌfl] *vt* (*sound*) smorzare, attutire; (*against cold*) imbacuccare

muffler ['mʌflə*] (*US*) *n* (*AUT*) marmitta; (*: on motorbike*) silenziatore *m*

mug [mʌg] *n* (*cup*) tazzone *m*; (*for beer*) boccale *m*; (*inf: face*) muso; (*: fool*) scemo/a ♦ *vt* (*assault*) assalire; **~ging** *n* assalto

muggy ['mʌgɪ] *adj* afoso(a)

mule [mjuːl] *n* mulo

multi-level [mʌltɪ-] (*US*) *adj* = **multistorey**

multiple ['mʌltɪpl] *adj* multiplo(a); molteplice ♦ *n* multiplo; **~ sclerosis** *n* sclerosi *f* a placche

multiplex cinema ['mʌltɪpleks-] *n* cinema *m inv* multisala *inv*

multiplication [mʌltɪplɪ'keɪʃən] *n* moltiplicazione *f*

multiply ['mʌltɪplaɪ] *vt* moltiplicare ♦ *vi* moltiplicarsi

multistorey ['mʌltɪ'stɔːrɪ] (*BRIT*) *adj* (*building, car park*) a più piani

mum [mʌm] (*BRIT: inf*) *n* mamma ♦ *adj*: **to keep ~** non aprire bocca

mumble ['mʌmbl] *vt, vi* borbottare

mummy ['mʌmɪ] *n* (*BRIT: mother*) mamma; (*embalmed*) mummia

mumps [mʌmps] *n* orecchioni *mpl*

munch [mʌntʃ] *vt, vi* sgranocchiare

mundane [mʌn'deɪn] *adj* terra a terra *inv*

municipal [mjuː'nɪsɪpl] *adj* municipale

mural ['mjuərl] *n* dipinto murale

murder ['mɜːdə*] *n* assassinio, omicidio ♦ *vt* assassinare; **~er** *n* omicida *m*, assassino; **~ous** *adj* omicida

murky ['mɜːkɪ] *adj* tenebroso(a)

murmur ['mɜːmə*] *n* mormorio ♦ *vt, vi* mormorare

muscle ['mʌsl] *n* muscolo; (*fig*) forza; **~ in** *vi* immischiarsi

muscular ['mʌskjulə*] *adj* muscolare; (*person, arm*) muscoloso(a)

muse [mjuːz] *vi* meditare, sognare ♦ *n* musa

museum [mjuː'zɪəm] *n* museo

mushroom ['mʌʃrum] *n* fungo ♦ *vi* crescere in fretta

music ['mjuːzɪk] *n* musica; **~al** *adj* musicale; (*person*) portato(a) per la musica ♦ *n* (*show*) commedia musicale; **~al instrument** *n* strumento musicale; **~ hall** *n* teatro di varietà; **~ian** [-'zɪʃən] *n* musicista *m/f*

Muslim ['mʌzlɪm] *adj*, *n* = **musulmano(a)**

muslin ['mʌzlɪn] *n* mussola

mussel ['mʌsl] *n* cozza

must [mʌst] *aux vb* (*obligation*): **I ~ do it** devo farlo; (*probability*): **he ~ be there by now** dovrebbe essere arrivato ormai; **I ~ have made a mistake** devo essermi sbagliato ♦ *n*: **it's a ~** è d'obbligo

mustache ['mʌstæʃ] (*US*) *n* = **moustache**

mustard ['mʌstəd] *n* senape *f*, mostarda

muster ['mʌstə*] *vt* radunare

mustn't ['mʌsnt] = **must not**

musty ['mʌstɪ] *adj* che sa di muffa *or* di rinchiuso

mute [mjuːt] *adj*, *n* muto(a)

muted ['mjuːtɪd] *adj* smorzato(a)

mutiny ['mjuːtɪnɪ] *n* ammutinamento

mutter ['mʌtə*] *vt, vi* borbottare, brontolare

mutton ['mʌtn] *n* carne *f* di montone

mutual ['mjuːtʃuəl] *adj* mutuo(a), reciproco(a); **~ly** *adv* reciprocamente

muzzle ['mʌzl] *n* muso; (*protective device*) museruola; (*of gun*) bocca ♦ *vt* mettere la museruola a

my [maɪ] *adj* il(la) mio(a), *pl* i(le) miei(mie); **~ house** la mia casa; **~ books** i miei libri; **~ brother** mio fratello; **I've washed ~ hair/cut ~ finger** mi sono lavato i capelli/tagliato il dito

myself [maɪ'self] *pron* (*reflexive*) mi; (*emphatic*) io stesso(a); (*after prep*) me; *see also* **oneself**

mysterious [mɪs'tɪərɪəs] *adj* misterioso(a)

mystery ['mɪstərɪ] *n* mistero

mystify ['mɪstɪfaɪ] *vt* mistificare; (*puzzle*) confondere

mystique [mɪs'tiːk] *n* fascino

myth [mɪθ] *n* mito

mythology [mɪ'θɒlədʒɪ] *n* mitologia

N, n

n / a *abbr* = **not applicable**

nag [næg] *vt* tormentare ♦ *vi* brontolare in continuazione; **~ging** *adj* (*doubt, pain*) persistente

nail [neɪl] *n* (*human*) unghia; (*metal*) chiodo ♦ *vt* inchiodare; **to ~ sb down to (doing) sth** costringere qn a (fare) qc; **~brush** *n* spazzolino da *or* per unghie; **~file** *n* lima da *or* per unghie; **~ polish** *n* smalto da *or* per unghie; **~ polish remover** *n* acetone *m*, solvente *m*; **~ scissors** *npl* forbici *fpl* da *or* per unghie; **~ varnish** (*BRIT*) *n* = **~ polish**

naïve [naɪ'iːv] *adj* ingenuo(a)

naked ['neɪkɪd] *adj* nudo(a)

name [neɪm] *n* nome *m*; (*reputation*) nome, reputazione *f* ♦ *vt* (*baby etc*) chiamare; (*plant, illness*) nominare; (*person, object*) identificare; (*price, date*) fissare; **what's your ~?** come si chiama?; **by ~** di nome; **she knows them all by ~** li conosce tutti per nome; **~ly** *adv* cioè; **~sake** *n* omonimo

nanny ['nænɪ] *n* bambinaia

nap [næp] *n* (*sleep*) pisolino; (*of cloth*) peluria; **to be caught ~ping** essere preso alla sprovvista

nape [neɪp] *n*: **~ of the neck** nuca

napkin ['næpkɪn] *n* (*also*: **table ~**) tovagliolo

nappy ['næpɪ] (*BRIT*) *n* pannolino; **~ rash** *n* arrossamento (causato dal pannolino)

narcissus [naː'sɪsəs] (*pl* **narcissi**) *n* narciso

narcotic [naː'kɒtɪk] *n* narcotico ♦ *adj* narcotico(a)

narrative ['nærətɪv] *n* narrativa

narrow ['nærəu] *adj* stretto(a); (*fig*) limitato(a), ristretto(a) ♦ *vi* restringersi; **to have a ~ escape** farcela per un pelo; **to ~ sth down to** ridurre qc a; **~ly** *adv* per un pelo; (*time*) per poco; **~-minded** *adj* meschino(a)

nasty ['naːstɪ] *adj* (*person, remark: unpleasant*) cattivo(a); (: *rude*) villano(a); (*smell, wound, situation*) brutto(a)

nation ['neɪʃən] *n* nazione *f*

national ['næʃənl] *adj* nazionale ♦ *n* cittadino/a; **~ dress** *n* costume *m* nazionale; **N~ Health Service** (*BRIT*) *n* servizio nazionale di assistenza sanitaria, ≈ S.S.N. *m*; **N~ Insurance** (*BRIT*) *n* ≈ Previdenza Sociale; **~ism** *n* nazionalismo; **~ity** [-'nælɪtɪ] *n* nazionalità *f inv*; **~ize** *vt* nazionalizzare; **~ly** *adv* a livello nazionale; **~ park** *n* parco nazionale

---

National Trust

ⓘ Fondato nel 1895, il **National Trust** *è un'organizzazione che si occupa della tutela e della salvaguardia di luoghi di interesse storico o ambientale*

---

nationwide ['neɪʃənwaɪd] *adj* diffuso(a) in tutto il paese ♦ *adv* in tutto il paese

native ['neɪtɪv] *n* abitante *m/f* del paese ♦ *adj* indigeno(a); (*country*) natio(a); (*ability*) innato(a); **a ~ of Russia** un nativo della Russia; **a ~ speaker of French** una persona di madrelingua francese; **N~ American** *n* discendente *m* di tribù dell'America settentrionale; **~ language** *n* madrelingua

Nativity [nə'tɪvɪtɪ] *n*: **the ~** la Natività

NATO ['neɪtəu] *n abbr* (= *North Atlantic Treaty Organization*) N.A.T.O. *f*

natural ['nætʃrəl] *adj* naturale; (*ability*)

innato(a); (*manner*) semplice; ~ **gas** *n* gas *m* metano; ~**ly** *adv* naturalmente; (*by nature*: gifted) di natura

nature ['neɪtʃəʳ] *n* natura; (*character*) natura, indole *f*; **by** ~ di natura

naught [nɔːt] *n* = **nought**

naughty ['nɔːtɪ] *adj* (*child*) birichino(a), cattivello(a); (*story, film*) spinto(a)

nausea ['nɔːsɪə] *n* (*MED*) nausea; (*fig: disgust*) schifo

nautical ['nɔːtɪkl] *adj* nautico(a)

naval ['neɪvl] *adj* navale; ~ **officer** *n* ufficiale *m* di marina

nave [neɪv] *n* navata centrale

navel ['neɪvl] *n* ombelico

navigate ['nævɪgeɪt] *vt* percorrere navigando ♦ *vi* navigare; (*AUT*) fare da navigatore; **navigation** [-'geɪʃən] *n* navigazione *f*; **navigator** *n* (*NAUT, AVIAT*) ufficiale *m* di rotta; (*explorer*) navigatore *m*; (*AUT*) copilota *m/f*

navvy ['nævɪ] (*BRIT*) *n* manovale *m*

navy ['neɪvɪ] *n* marina; ~**(-blue)** *adj* blu scuro *inv*

Nazi ['nɑːtsɪ] *n* nazista *m/f*

NB *abbr* (= *nota bene*) N.B.

near [nɪəʳ] *adj* vicino(a); (*relation*) prossimo(a) ♦ *adv* vicino ♦ *prep* (*also*: ~ **to**) vicino a, presso; (: *time*) verso ♦ *vt* avvicinarsi a; ~**by** [nɪə'baɪ] *adj* vicino(a) ♦ *adv* vicino; ~**ly** *adv* quasi; **I ~ly fell** per poco non sono caduto; ~ **miss** *n*: **that was a ~ miss** c'è mancato poco; ~**side** *n* (*AUT: in Britain*) lato sinistro; (: *in US, Europe etc*) lato destro; ~**-sighted** [nɪə'saɪtɪd] *adj* miope

neat [niːt] *adj* (*person, room*) ordinato(a); (*work*) pulito(a); (*solution, plan*) ben indovinato(a), azzeccato(a); (*spirits*) liscio(a); ~**ly** *adv* con ordine; (*skilfully*) abilmente

necessarily ['nɛsɪsrɪlɪ] *adv* necessariamente

necessary ['nɛsɪsrɪ] *adj* necessario(a)

necessity [nɪ'sɛsɪtɪ] *n* necessità *f inv*

neck [nɛk] *n* collo; (*of garment*) colletto ♦ *vi* (*inf*) pomiciare, sbaciucchiarsi; ~ **and** ~ testa a testa

necklace ['nɛklɪs] *n* collana

neckline ['nɛklaɪn] *n* scollatura

necktie ['nɛktaɪ] *n* cravatta

née [neɪ] *adj*: ~ **Scott** nata Scott

need [niːd] *n* bisogno ♦ *vt* aver bisogno di; **to ~ to do** dover fare; aver bisogno di fare; **you don't ~ to go** non devi andare, non c'è bisogno che tu vada

needle ['niːdl] *n* ago; (*on record player*) puntina ♦ *vt* punzecchiare

needless ['niːdlɪs] *adj* inutile

needlework ['niːdlwəːk] *n* cucito

needn't ['niːdnt] = **need not**

needy ['niːdɪ] *adj* bisognoso(a)

negative ['nɛgətɪv] *n* (*LING*) negazione *f*; (*PHOT*) negativo ♦ *adj* negativo(a); ~ **equity** *n* situazione in cui l'ammontare del mutuo su un immobile supera il suo valore sul mercato

neglect [nɪ'glɛkt] *vt* trascurare ♦ *n* (*of person, duty*) negligenza; (*of child, house etc*) scarsa cura; **state of ~** stato di abbandono

negligence ['nɛglɪdʒəns] *n* negligenza

negligible ['nɛglɪdʒɪbl] *adj* insignificante, trascurabile

negotiable [nɪ'gəʊʃɪəbl] *adj* (*cheque*) trasferibile

negotiate [nɪ'gəʊʃɪeɪt] *vi*: **to ~ (with)** negoziare (con) ♦ *vt* (*COMM*) negoziare; (*obstacle*) superare; **negotiation** [-'eɪʃən] *n* negoziato, trattativa

Negro ['niːgrəʊ] (*pl* ~**es**) *n* negro(a)

neigh [neɪ] *vi* nitrire

neighbour ['neɪbəʳ] (*US* **neighbor**) *n* vicino/a; ~**hood** *n* vicinato; ~**ing** *adj* vicino(a); ~**ly** *adj*: **he is a ~ly person** è un buon vicino

neither ['naɪðəʳ] *adj, pron* né l'uno(a) né l'altro(a), nessuno(a) dei(delle) due ♦ *conj* neanche, nemmeno, neppure ♦ *adv*: ~ **good nor bad** né buono né cattivo; **I didn't move and ~ did Claude** io non mi mossi e nemmeno Claude; **..., ~ did I refuse ...**, ma non ho nemmeno rifiutato

neon light ['niːɔn-] *n* luce *f* al neon

nephew ['nɛvjuː] *n* nipote *m*

nerve [nə:v] *n* nervo; (*fig*) coraggio; (*impudence*) faccia tosta; **a fit of ~s** una crisi di nervi; **~-racking** *adj* che spezza i nervi

nervous ['nə:vəs] *adj* nervoso(a); (*anxious*) agitato(a), in apprensione; **~ breakdown** *n* esaurimento nervoso

nest [nɛst] *n* nido ♦ *vi* fare il nido, nidificare; **~ egg** *n* (*fig*) gruzzolo

nestle ['nɛsl] *vi* accoccolarsi

net [nɛt] *n* rete *f* ♦ *adj* netto(a) ♦ *vt* (*fish etc*) prendere con la rete; (*profit*) ricavare un utile netto di; **the N~** (*Internet*) Internet *f*; **~ball** *n* specie di pallacanestro

Netherlands ['nɛðələndz] *npl*: **the ~** i Paesi Bassi

nett [nɛt] *adj* = **net**

netting ['nɛtɪŋ] *n* (*for fence etc*) reticolato

nettle ['nɛtl] *n* ortica

network ['nɛtwə:k] *n* rete *f*

neurotic [njuə'rɔtɪk] *adj*, *n* nevrotico(a)

neuter ['nju:tə*] *adj* neutro(a) ♦ *vt* (*cat etc*) castrare

neutral ['nju:trəl] *adj* neutro(a); (*person, nation*) neutrale ♦ *n* (*AUT*): **in ~** in folle; **~ize** *vt* neutralizzare

never ['nɛvə*] *adv* (non...) mai; **~ again** mai più; **I'll ~ go there again** non ci vado più; **~ in my life** mai in vita mia; *see also* **mind**; **~-ending** *adj* interminabile; **~theless** [nɛvəðə'lɛs] *adv* tuttavia, ciò nonostante, ciò nondimeno

new [nju:] *adj* nuovo(a); (*brand new*) nuovo(a) di zecca; **N~ Age** *n* New Age *f* *inv*; **~born** *adj* neonato(a); **~comer** ['nju:kʌmə*] *n* nuovo(a) venuto(a); **~-fangled** ['nju:fæŋgld] (*pej*) *adj* stramoderno(a); **~-found** *adj* nuovo(a); **~ly** *adv* di recente; **~ly-weds** *npl* sposini *mpl*, sposi *mpl* novelli

news [nju:z] *n* notizie *fpl*; (*RADIO*) giornale *m* radio; (*TV*) telegiornale *m*; **a piece of ~** una notizia; **~ agency** *n* agenzia di stampa; **~agent** (*BRIT*) *n* giornalaio; **~caster** *n* (*RADIO, TV*) annunciatore/trice; **~ flash** *n* notizia *f* lampo *inv*; **~letter** *n* bollettino; **~paper** *n* giornale *m*; **~print** *n* carta da giornale; **~reader** *n* = **~caster**; **~reel** *n* cinegiornale *m*; **~ stand** *n* edicola

newt [nju:t] *n* tritone *m*

New Year *n* Anno Nuovo; **~'s Day** *n* il Capodanno; **~'s Eve** *n* la vigilia di Capodanno

New York [-'jɔ:k] *n* New York *f*

New Zealand [-'zi:lənd] *n* Nuova Zelanda; **~er** *n* neozelandese *m/f*

next [nɛkst] *adj* prossimo(a) ♦ *adv* accanto; (*in time*) dopo; **the ~ day** il giorno dopo, l'indomani; **~ time** la prossima volta; **~ year** l'anno prossimo; **when do we meet ~?** quando ci rincontriamo?; **~ to** accanto a; **~ to nothing** quasi niente; **~ please!** (*avanti*) il prossimo!; **~ door** *adv*, *adj* accanto *inv*; **~-of-kin** *n* parente *m/f* prossimo(a)

NHS *n abbr* = **National Health Service**

nib [nɪb] *n* (*of pen*) pennino

nibble ['nɪbl] *vt* mordicchiare

Nicaragua [nɪkə'ræɡjuə] *n* Nicaragua *m*

nice [naɪs] *adj* (*holiday, trip*) piacevole; (*flat, picture*) bello(a); (*person*) simpatico(a), gentile; **~ly** *adv* bene

niceties ['naɪsɪtɪz] *npl* finezze *fpl*

nick [nɪk] *n* taglietto; tacca ♦ *vt* (*inf*) rubare; **in the ~ of time** appena in tempo

nickel ['nɪkl] *n* nichel *m*; (*US*) moneta da cinque centesimi di dollaro

nickname ['nɪkneɪm] *n* soprannome *m*

niece [ni:s] *n* nipote *f*

Nigeria [naɪ'dʒɪərɪə] *n* Nigeria

niggling ['nɪɡlɪŋ] *adj* insignificante; (*annoying*) irritante

night [naɪt] *n* notte *f*; (*evening*) sera; **at ~** la sera; **by ~** di notte; **the ~ before last** l'altro ieri notte (*or* sera); **~cap** *n* bicchierino *prima di andare a letto*; **~ club** *n* locale *m* notturno; **~dress** *n* camicia da notte; **~fall** *n* crepuscolo; **~gown** *n* = **~dress**; **~ie** ['naɪtɪ] *n* = **~dress**

nightingale ['naɪtɪŋgeɪl] *n* usignolo

nightlife ['naɪtlaɪf] *n* vita notturna

nightly ['naɪtlɪ] *adj* di ogni notte *or* sera; (*by night*) notturno(a) ♦ *adv* ogni notte *or* sera

nightmare ['naɪtmeə*] *n* incubo

night: ~ **porter** *n* portiere *m* di notte; ~ **school** *n* scuola serale; ~ **shift** *n* turno di notte; ~**-time** *n* notte *f*

nil [nɪl] *n* nulla *m*; (*BRIT: SPORT*) zero

Nile [naɪl] *n*: **the** ~ il Nilo

nimble ['nɪmbl] *adj* agile

nine [naɪn] *num* nove; ~**teen** *num* diciannove; ~**ty** *num* novanta

ninth [naɪnθ] *adj* nono(a)

nip [nɪp] *vt* pizzicare; (*bite*) mordere

nipple ['nɪpl] *n* (*ANAT*) capezzolo

nitrogen ['naɪtrədʒən] *n* azoto

KEYWORD
---

no [nəu] (*pl* ~**es**) *adv* (*opposite of "yes"*) no; **are you coming? – ~ (I'm not)** viene? — no (non vengo); **would you like some more? – ~ thank you** ne vuole ancora un po'? — no, grazie

♦ *adj* (*not any*) nessuno(a); **I have ~ money/time/books** non ho soldi/tempo/libri; ~ **student would have done it** nessuno studente lo avrebbe fatto; "**~ parking**" "divieto di sosta"; "**~ smoking**" "vietato fumare"

♦ *n* no *m inv*

nobility [nəu'bɪlɪtɪ] *n* nobiltà

noble ['nəubl] *adj* nobile

nobody ['nəubədɪ] *pron* nessuno

nod [nɒd] *vi* accennare col capo, fare un cenno; (*in agreement*) annuire con un cenno del capo; (*sleep*) sonnecchiare ♦ *vt*: **to ~ one's head** fare di sì col capo ♦ *n* cenno; ~ **off** *vi* assopirsi

noise [nɔɪz] *n* rumore *m*; (*din, racket*) chiasso; **noisy** *adj* (*street, car*) rumoroso(a); (*person*) chiassoso(a)

nominal ['nɒmɪnl] *adj* nominale; (*rent*) simbolico(a)

nominate ['nɒmɪneɪt] *vt* (*propose*) proporre come candidato; (*elect*) nominare

nominee [nɒmɪ'niː] *n* persona nominata; candidato/a

non... [nɒn] *prefix* non...; ~**-alcoholic** *adj* analcolico(a)

nonchalant ['nɒnʃələnt] *adj* disinvolto(a), noncurante

non-committal ['nɒnkə'mɪtl] *adj* evasivo(a)

nondescript ['nɒndɪskrɪpt] *adj* qualunque *inv*

none [nʌn] *pron* (*not one thing*) niente; (*not one person*) nessuno(a); ~ **of you** nessuno(a) di voi; **I've ~ left** non ne ho più; **he's ~ the worse for it** non ne ha risentito

nonentity [nɒ'nentɪtɪ] *n* persona insignificante

nonetheless [nʌnðə'les] *adv* nondimeno

non-existent [-ɪg'zɪstənt] *adj* inesistente

non-fiction *n* saggistica

nonplussed [nɒn'plʌst] *adj* sconcertato(a)

nonsense ['nɒnsəns] *n* sciocchezze *fpl*

non: ~**-smoker** *n* non fumatore/trice; ~**-smoking** *adj* (*person*) che non fuma; (*area, section*) per non fumatori; ~**-stick** *adj* antiaderente, antiadesivo(a); ~**-stop** *adj* continuo(a); (*train, bus*) direttissimo(a) ♦ *adv* senza sosta

noodles ['nuːdlz] *npl* taglierini *mpl*

nook [nuk] *n*: ~**s and crannies** angoli *mpl*

noon [nuːn] *n* mezzogiorno

no one ['nəuwʌn] *pron* = **nobody**

noose [nuːs] *n* nodo scorsoio; (*hangman's*) cappio

nor [nɔː*] *conj* = **neither** ♦ *adv see* **neither**

norm [nɔːm] *n* norma

normal ['nɔːml] *adj* normale; ~**ly** *adv* normalmente

north [nɔːθ] *n* nord *m*, settentrione *m* ♦ *adj* nord *inv*, del nord, settentrionale ♦ *adv* verso nord; **N~ America** *n* America del Nord; ~**-east** *n* nord-est *m*; ~**erly** ['nɔːðəlɪ] *adj* (*point, direction*) verso nord; ~**ern** ['nɔːðən] *adj* del nord, settentrionale; **N~ern Ireland** *n* Irlanda del Nord; **N~ Pole** *n* Polo Nord; **N~ Sea** *n* Mare *m* del Nord; ~**ward(s)** ['nɔːθwəd(z)] *adv* verso nord; ~**-west** *n* nord-ovest *m*

Norway ['nɔːweɪ] *n* Norvegia

Norwegian [nɔː'wiːdʒən] *adj* norvegese ♦ *n* norvegese *m/f*; (*LING*) norvegese *m*

nose [nəuz] *n* naso; (*of animal*) muso ♦ *vi*:

to ~ about aggirarsi; **~bleed** n emorragia
nasale; **~-dive** n picchiata; **~y** (inf) adj
= **nosy**
nostalgia [nɔs'tældʒɪə] n nostalgia
nostril ['nɔstrɪl] n narice f; (of horse) frogia
nosy ['nəʊzɪ] (inf) adj curioso(a)
not [nɔt] adv non; **he is ~ or isn't here** non
è qui, non c'è; **you must ~ or you mustn't
do that** non devi fare quello; **it's too late,
isn't it or is it ~?** è troppo tardi, vero?; **~
that I don't like him** non che (lui) non mi
piaccia; **~ yet/now** non ancora/ora; see
also **all**; **only**
notably ['nəʊtəblɪ] adv (markedly)
notevolmente; (particularly) in particolare
notary ['nəʊtərɪ] n notaio
notch [nɔtʃ] n tacca; (in saw) dente m
note [nəʊt] n nota; (letter, banknote)
biglietto ♦ vt (also: **~ down**) prendere nota
di; **to take ~s** prendere appunti; **~book** n
taccuino; **~d** ['nəʊtɪd] adj celebre; **~pad** n
bloc-notes m inv; **~paper** n carta da
lettere
nothing ['nʌθɪŋ] n nulla m, niente m; (zero)
zero; **he does ~** non fa niente; **~ new/
much** etc niente di nuovo/speciale etc; **for
~** per niente
notice ['nəʊtɪs] n avviso; (of leaving)
preavviso ♦ vt notare, accorgersi di; **to
take ~ of** fare attenzione a; **to bring sth to
sb's ~** far notare qc a qn; **at short ~** con
un breve preavviso; **until further ~** fino a
nuovo avviso; **to hand in one's ~**
licenziarsi; **~able** adj evidente; **~ board**
(BRIT) n tabellone m per affissi
notify ['nəʊtɪfaɪ] vt: **to ~ sth to sb** far sapere
qc a qn; **to ~ sb of sth** avvisare qn di qc
notion ['nəʊʃən] n idea; (concept) nozione f
notorious [nəʊ'tɔːrɪəs] adj famigerato(a)
nougat ['nuːgɑː] n torrone m
nought [nɔːt] n zero
noun [naʊn] n nome m, sostantivo
nourish ['nʌrɪʃ] vt nutrire
novel ['nɔvl] n romanzo ♦ adj nuovo(a);
~ist n romanziere/a; **~ty** n novità f inv
November [nəʊ'vɛmbə*] n novembre m
novice ['nɔvɪs] n principiante m/f; (REL)

novizio/a
now [naʊ] adv ora, adesso ♦ conj: **~ (that)**
adesso che, ora che; **by ~** ormai; **just ~**
proprio ora; **right ~** subito, immediatamente; **~ and then, ~ and again** ogni
tanto; **from ~ on** da ora in poi; **~adays**
['naʊədeɪz] adv oggidì
nowhere ['nəʊwɛə*] adv in nessun luogo,
da nessuna parte
nozzle ['nɔzl] n (of hose etc) boccaglio; (of
fire extinguisher) lancia
nuance ['njuːɑːns] n sfumatura
nuclear ['njuːklɪə*] adj nucleare
nucleus ['njuːklɪəs] (pl nuclei) n nucleo
nude [njuːd] adj nudo(a) ♦ n (ART) nudo; **in
the ~** tutto(a) nudo(a)
nudge [nʌdʒ] vt dare una gomitata a
nudist ['njuːdɪst] n nudista m/f
nuisance ['njuːsns] n: **it's a ~** è una
seccatura; **he's a ~** è uno scocciatore
null [nʌl] adj: **~ and void** nullo(a)
numb [nʌm] adj: **~ (with)** intorpidito(a)
(da); (with fear) impietrito(a) (da); **~ with
cold** intirizzito(a) (dal freddo)
number ['nʌmbə*] n numero ♦ vt
numerare; (include) contare; **a ~ of** un
certo numero di; **to be ~ed among** venire
annoverato(a) tra; **they were 10 in ~** erano
in tutto 10; **~ plate** (BRIT) n (AUT) targa
numeral ['njuːmərəl] n numero, cifra
numerate ['njuːmərɪt] adj: **to be ~** avere
nozioni di aritmetica
numerical [njuː'mɛrɪkl] adj numerico(a)
numerous ['njuːmərəs] adj numeroso(a)
nun [nʌn] n suora, monaca
nurse [nɜːs] n infermiere/a; (also: **~maid**)
bambinaia ♦ vt (patient, cold) curare;
(baby: BRIT) cullare; (: US) allattare, dare il
latte a
nursery ['nɜːsərɪ] n (room) camera dei
bambini; (institution) asilo; (for plants)
vivaio; **~ rhyme** n filastrocca; **~ school** n
scuola materna; **~ slope** (BRIT) n (SKI) pista
per principianti
nursing ['nɜːsɪŋ] n (profession) professione f
di infermiere (or di infermiera); (care) cura;
~ home n casa di cura

nurture ['nə:tʃə*] vt allevare; nutrire
nut [nʌt] n (of metal) dado; (fruit) noce f;
~**crackers** npl schiaccianoci m inv
nutmeg ['nʌtmɛg] n noce f moscata
nutritious [nju:'trɪʃəs] adj nutriente
nuts [nʌts] (inf) adj matto(a)
nutshell ['nʌtʃɛl] n: **in a ~** in poche parole
nylon ['naɪlɔn] n nailon m ♦ adj di nailon

O, o

oak [əuk] n quercia ♦ adj di quercia
O.A.P. (BRIT) n abbr = **old age pensioner**
oar [ɔ:*] n remo
oasis [əu'eɪsɪs] (pl **oases**) n oasi f inv
oath [əuθ] n giuramento; (swear word)
bestemmia
oatmeal ['əutmi:l] n farina d'avena
oats [əuts] npl avena
obedience [ə'bi:dɪəns] n ubbidienza
obedient [ə'bi:dɪənt] adj ubbidiente
obey [ə'beɪ] vt ubbidire a; (instructions,
regulations) osservare
obituary [ə'bɪtjuərɪ] n necrologia
object [n 'ɔbdʒɪkt, vb əb'dʒɛkt] n oggetto m;
(purpose) scopo, intento; (LING)
complemento oggetto ♦ vi: **to ~ to**
(attitude) disapprovare; (proposal)
protestare contro, sollevare delle obiezioni
contro; **expense is no ~** non si bada a
spese; **to ~** that obiettare che; **I ~!** mi
oppongo!; ~**ion** [əb'dʒɛkʃən] n obiezione f;
~**ionable** [əb'dʒɛkʃənəbl] adj antipatico(a);
(language) scostumato(a); ~**ive** n obiettivo
obligation [ɔblɪ'geɪʃən] n obbligo, dovere
m; **without ~** senza impegno
oblige [ə'blaɪdʒ] vt (force): **to ~ sb to do**
costringere qn a fare; (do a favour) fare una
cortesia a; **to be ~d to sb for sth** essere
grato a qn per qc; **obliging** adj
servizievole, compiacente
oblique [ə'bli:k] adj obliquo(a); (allusion)
indiretto(a)
obliterate [ə'blɪtəreɪt] vt cancellare
oblivion [ə'blɪvɪən] n oblio
oblivious [ə'blɪvɪəs] adj: **~ of** incurante di;
inconscio(a) di
oblong ['ɔblɔŋ] adj oblungo(a) ♦ n
rettangolo
obnoxious [əb'nɔkʃəs] adj odioso(a); (smell)
disgustoso(a), ripugnante
oboe ['əubəu] n oboe m
obscene [əb'si:n] adj osceno(a)
obscure [əb'skjuə*] adj oscuro(a) ♦ vt
oscurare; (hide: sun) nascondere
observant [əb'zə:vnt] adj attento(a)
observation [ɔbzə'veɪʃən] n osservazione f;
(by police etc) sorveglianza
observatory [əb'zə:vətrɪ] n osservatorio
observe [əb'zə:v] vt osservare; (remark) fare
osservare; ~**r** n osservatore/trice
obsess [əb'sɛs] vt ossessionare; ~**ive** adj
ossessivo(a)
obsolescence [ɔbsə'lɛsns] n obsolescenza
obsolete ['ɔbsəli:t] adj obsoleto(a)
obstacle ['ɔbstəkl] n ostacolo
obstinate ['ɔbstɪnɪt] adj ostinato(a)
obstruct [əb'strʌkt] vt (block) ostruire,
ostacolare; (halt) fermare; (hinder) impedire
obtain [əb'teɪn] vt ottenere; ~**able** adj
ottenibile
obvious ['ɔbvɪəs] adj ovvio(a), evidente; ~**ly**
adv ovviamente; certo
occasion [ə'keɪʒən] n occasione f; (event)
avvenimento; ~**al** adj occasionale; ~**ally**
adv ogni tanto
occupation [ɔkju'peɪʃən] n occupazione f;
(job) mestiere m, professione f; ~**al**
hazard n rischio del mestiere
occupier ['ɔkjupaɪə*] n occupante m/f
occupy ['ɔkjupaɪ] vt occupare; **to ~ o.s. in**
doing occuparsi a fare
occur [ə'kə:*] vi accadere, capitare; **to ~ to**
sb venire in mente a qn; ~**rence** n caso,
fatto; presenza
ocean ['əuʃən] n oceano
o'clock [ə'klɔk] adv: **it is 5 ~** sono le 5
OCR n abbr (= optical character recognition)
lettura ottica; (= optical character reader)
lettore m ottico
octave ['ɔktɪv] n ottavo
October [ɔk'təubə*] n ottobre m
octopus ['ɔktəpəs] n polpo, piovra

odd [ɔd] *adj* (*strange*) strano(a), bizzarro(a); (*number*) dispari *inv*; (*not of a set*) spaiato(a); **60-~** 60 e oltre; **at ~ times** di tanto in tanto; **the ~ one out** l'eccezione *f*; **~ity** *n* bizzarria; (*person*) originale *m*; **~-job man** *n* tuttofare *m inv*; **~ jobs** *npl* lavori *mpl* occasionali; **~ly** *adv* stranamente; **~ments** *npl* (COMM) rimanenze *fpl*; **~s** *npl* (*in betting*) quota; **~s and ends** *npl* avanzi *mpl*; **it makes no ~s** non importa; **at ~s** in contesa

odometer [ɔ'dɔmitə*] *n* odometro

odour ['əudə*] (*US* **odor**) *n* odore *m*; (*unpleasant*) cattivo odore

---

KEYWORD

of [ɔv, əv] *prep* 1 (*gen*) di; **a boy ~ 10** un ragazzo di 10 anni; **a friend ~ ours** un nostro amico; **that was kind ~ you** è stato molto gentile da parte sua

2 (*expressing quantity, amount, dates etc*) di; **a kilo ~ flour** un chilo di farina; **how much ~ this do you need?** quanto gliene serve?; **there were 3 ~ them** (*people*) erano in 3; (*objects*) ce n'erano 3; **3 ~ us went** 3 di noi sono andati; **the 5th ~ July** il 5 luglio

3 (*from, out of*) di, in; **made ~ wood** (*fatto*) di *or* in legno

---

KEYWORD

off [ɔf] *adv* 1 (*distance, time*): **it's a long way ~** è lontano; **the game is 3 days ~** la partita è tra 3 giorni

2 (*departure, removal*) via; **to go ~ to Paris** andarsene a Parigi; **I must be ~** devo andare via; **to take ~ one's coat** togliersi il cappotto; **the button came ~** il bottone è venuto via *or* si è staccato; **10% ~** con lo sconto del 10%

3 (*not at work*): **to have a day ~** avere un giorno libero; **to be ~ sick** essere assente per malattia

♦ *adj* (*engine*) spento(a); (*tap*) chiuso(a); (*cancelled*) sospeso(a); (BRIT: *food*) andato(a) a male; **on the ~ chance** nel caso; **to have**

an ~ day non essere in forma

♦ *prep* 1 (*motion, removal etc*) da; (*distant from*) a poca distanza da; **a street ~ the square** una strada che parte dalla piazza

2: **to be ~ meat** non mangiare più la carne

---

offal ['ɔfl] *n* (CULIN) frattaglie *fpl*

off-colour (BRIT) *adj* (*ill*) malato(a), indisposto(a)

offence [ə'fens] (*US* **offense**) *n* (LAW) contravvenzione *f*; (: *more serious*) reato; **to take ~ at** offendersi per

offend [ə'fend] *vt* (*person*) offendere; **~er** *n* delinquente *m/f*; (*against regulations*) contravventore/trice

offense [ə'fens] (*US*) *n* = **offence**

offensive [ə'fensɪv] *adj* offensivo(a); (*smell etc*) sgradevole, ripugnante ♦ *n* (MIL) offensiva

offer ['ɔfə*] *n* offerta, proposta ♦ *vt* offrire; **"on ~"** (COMM) "in offerta speciale"; **~ing** *n* offerta

offhand [ɔf'hænd] *adj* disinvolto(a), noncurante ♦ *adv* su due piedi

office ['ɔfis] *n* (*place*) ufficio *m*; (*position*) carica; **doctor's ~** (*US*) studio; **to take ~** entrare in carica; **~ automation** *n* automazione *f* d'ufficio; burotica; **~ block** (*US* **~ building**) *n* complesso di uffici; **~ hours** *npl* orario d'ufficio; (*US: MED*) orario di visite

officer ['ɔfisə*] *n* (MIL etc) ufficiale *m*; (*also*: **police ~**) agente *m* di polizia; (*of organization*) funzionario

office worker *n* impiegato/a d'ufficio

official [ə'fiʃl] *adj* (*authorized*) ufficiale ♦ *n* ufficiale *m*; (*civil servant*) impiegato/a statale; funzionario

officiate [ə'fiʃieit] *vi* presenziare

officious [ə'fiʃəs] *adj* invadente

offing ['ɔfiŋ] *n*: **in the ~** (*fig*) in vista

off: ~-licence (BRIT) *n* (*shop*) spaccio di bevande alcoliche; **~-line** *adj, adv* (COMPUT) off-line *inv*, fuori linea; (: *switched off*) spento(a); **~-peak** *adj* (*ticket, heating etc*) a tariffa ridotta; (*time*) non di punta; **~-putting** (BRIT) *adj* sgradevole,

antipatico(a); **~-road vehicle** *n*
fuoristrada *m inv*; **~-season** *adj, adv*
fuori stagione

off-licence

In Gran Bretagna e in Irlanda, gli **off-licence** *sono rivendite di vini, liquori e superalcolici, spesso aperti fino a tarda ora.*

offset ['ɔfset] (*irreg*) *vt* (*counteract*)
controbilanciare, compensare
offshoot ['ɔfʃuːt] *n* (*fig*) diramazione *f*
offshore [ɔf'ʃɔː*] *adj* (*breeze*) di terra;
(*island*) vicino alla costa; (*fishing*)
costiero(a)
offside ['ɔf'saɪd] *adj* (*SPORT*) fuori gioco;
(*AUT: in Britain*) destro(a); (: *in Italy etc*)
sinistro(a)
offspring ['ɔfsprɪŋ] *n inv* prole *f*,
discendenza
off: **~stage** *adv* dietro le quinte; **~-the-
peg** (*US* **~-the-rack**) *adv* prêt-à-porter; **~-
white** *adj* bianco sporco *inv*
often ['ɔfn] *adv* spesso; **how ~ do you go?**
quanto spesso ci vai?
oh [əu] *excl* oh!
oil [ɔɪl] *n* olio; (*petroleum*) petrolio; (*for
central heating*) nafta ♦ *vt* (*machine*)
lubrificare; **~can** *n* oliatore *m* a mano; (*for
storing*) latta da olio; **~field** *n* giacimento
petrolifero; **~ filter** *n* (*AUT*) filtro dell'olio;
~ painting *n* quadro a olio; **~ refinery**
[-rɪ'faɪnərɪ] *n* raffineria di petrolio; **~ rig** *n*
derrick *m inv*; (*at sea*) piattaforma per
trivellazioni subacquee; **~ tanker** *n* (*ship*)
petroliera; (*truck*) autocisterna per petrolio;
~ well *n* pozzo petrolifero; **~y** *adj*
unto(a), oleoso(a); (*food*) grasso(a)
ointment ['ɔɪntmənt] *n* unguento
O.K. ['əu'keɪ] *excl* d'accordo! ♦ *adj* non
male ♦ *vt* approvare; **is it ~?, are you
~?** tutto bene?
okay ['əu'keɪ] *excl*, *adj*, *vt* = **O.K.**
old [əuld] *adj* vecchio(a); (*ancient*) antico(a),
vecchio(a); (*person*) anziano(a);
how ~ are you? quanti anni ha?; **he's 10
years ~** ha 10 anni; **~er brother** fratello

maggiore; **~ age** *n* vecchiaia; **~ age
pensioner** (*BRIT*) *n* pensionato/a; **~-
fashioned** *adj* antiquato(a), fuori moda;
(*person*) all'antica
olive ['ɔlɪv] *n* (*fruit*) oliva; (*tree*) olivo ♦ *adj*
(*also*: **~-green**) verde oliva *inv*; **~ oil** *n* olio
d'oliva
Olympic [əu'lɪmpɪk] *adj* olimpico(a); **the ~
Games, the ~s** i giochi olimpici, le
Olimpiadi
omelet(te) ['ɔmlɪt] *n* omelette *f inv*
omen ['əumen] *n* presagio, augurio
ominous ['ɔmɪnəs] *adj* minaccioso(a);
(*event*) di malaugurio
omit [əu'mɪt] *vt* omettere

KEYWORD

on [ɔn] *prep* **1** (*indicating position*) su; **~ the
wall** sulla parete; **~ the left** a *or* sulla
sinistra
2 (*indicating means, method, condition etc*):
~ foot a piedi; **~ the train/plane** in treno/
aereo; **~ the telephone** al telefono; **~ the
radio/television** alla radio/televisione; **to
be ~ drugs** drogarsi; **~ holiday** in vacanza
3 (*of time*): **~ Friday** venerdì; **~ Fridays** il
or di venerdì; **~ June 20th** il 20 giugno; **a
week ~ Friday** venerdì a otto; **~ his
arrival** al suo arrivo; **~ seeing this**
vedendo ciò
4 (*about, concerning*) su, di; **information ~
train services** informazioni sui
collegamenti ferroviari; **a book ~
Goldoni/physics** un libro su Goldoni/di *or*
sulla fisica
♦ *adv* **1** (*referring to dress, covering*): **to
have one's coat ~** avere indosso il
cappotto; **to put one's coat ~** mettersi il
cappotto; **what's she got ~?** cosa
indossa?; **she put her boots/gloves/hat ~**
si mise gli stivali/i guanti/il cappello; **screw
the lid ~ tightly** avvita bene il coperchio
2 (*further, continuously*): **to walk ~, go ~**
etc continuare, proseguire *etc*; **to read ~**
continuare a leggere; **~ and off** ogni tanto
♦ *adj* **1** (*in operation: machine, TV, light*)

acceso(a); (: *tap*) aperto(a); (: *brake*) inserito(a); **is the meeting still ~?** (*in progress*) la riunione è ancora in corso?; (*not cancelled*) è confermato l'incontro?; **there's a good film ~ at the cinema** danno un buon film al cinema 2 (*inf*): **that's not ~!** (*not acceptable*) non si fa così!; (*not possible*) non se ne parla neanche!

once [wʌns] *adv* una volta ♦ *conj* non appena, quando; **~ he had left/it was done** dopo che se n'era andato/fu fatto; **at ~** subito; (*simultaneously*) a un tempo; **~ a week** una volta per settimana; **~ more** ancora una volta; **~ and for all** una volta per sempre; **~ upon a time** c'era una volta

oncoming [ˈɔnkʌmɪŋ] *adj* (*traffic*) che viene in senso opposto

---

KEYWORD

one [wʌn] *num* uno(a); **~ hundred and fifty** centocinquanta; **~ day** un giorno
♦ *adj* 1 (*sole*) unico(a); **the ~ book which** l'unico libro che; **the ~ man who** l'unico che 2 (*same*) stesso(a); **they came in the ~ car** sono venuti nella stessa macchina
♦ *pron* 1: **this ~** questo/a; **that ~** quello/a; **I've already got ~/a red ~** ne ho già uno/uno rosso; **~ by ~** uno per uno
2: **~ another** l'un l'altro; **to look at ~ another** guardarsi; **to help ~ another** aiutarsi l'un l'altro *or* a vicenda
3 (*impersonal*) si; **~ never knows** non si sa mai; **to cut ~'s finger** tagliarsi un dito; **~ needs to eat** bisogna mangiare

---

one: **~-day excursion** (*US*) *n* biglietto giornaliero di andata e ritorno; **~-man** *adj* (*business*) diretto(a) *etc* da un solo uomo; **~-man band** *n* suonatore ambulante con vari strumenti; **~-off** (*BRIT: inf*) *n* fatto eccezionale

oneself [wʌnˈsɛlf] *pron* (*reflexive*) si; (*after prep*) se stesso(a), sé; **to do sth (by) ~** fare qc da sé; **to hurt ~** farsi male; **to keep sth for ~** tenere qc per sé; **to talk to ~** parlare

da solo

one: **~-sided** *adj* (*argument*) unilaterale; **~-to-~** *adj* (*relationship*) univoco(a); **~-way** *adj* (*street, traffic*) a senso unico

ongoing [ˈɔngəuɪŋ] *adj* in corso; in attuazione

onion [ˈʌnjən] *n* cipolla

on-line *adj, adv* (*COMPUT*) on-line *inv*

onlooker [ˈɔnlukə*] *n* spettatore/trice

only [ˈəunlɪ] *adv* solo, soltanto ♦ *adj* solo(a), unico(a) ♦ *conj* solo che, ma; **an ~ child** un figlio unico; **not ~ ... but also** non solo ... ma anche

onset [ˈɔnsɛt] *n* inizio

onshore [ˈɔnʃɔː*] *adj* (*wind*) di mare

onslaught [ˈɔnslɔːt] *n* attacco, assalto

onto [ˈɔntu] *prep* = **on to**

onus [ˈəunəs] *n* onere *m*, peso

onward(s) [ˈɔnwəd(z)] *adv* (*move*) in avanti; **from that time ~** da quella volta in poi

ooze [uːz] *vi* stillare

open [ˈəupn] *adj* aperto(a); (*road*) libero(a); (*meeting*) pubblico(a) ♦ *vt* aprire ♦ *vi* (*eyes, door, debate*) aprirsi; (*flower*) sbocciare; (*shop, bank, museum*) aprire; (*book etc: commence*) cominciare; **in the ~** (*air*) all'aperto; **~ on to** *vt fus* (*subj: room, door*) dare su; **~ up** *vt* aprire; (*blocked road*) sgombrare ♦ *vi* (*shop, business*) aprire; **~ing** *adj* (*speech*) di apertura ♦ *n* apertura; (*opportunity*) occasione *f*, opportunità *f inv*; sbocco; **~ing hours** *npl* orario d'apertura; **~ learning centre** *n* sistema educativo nel quale lo studente ha maggiore controllo e gestione delle modalità di apprendimento; **~ly** *adv* apertamente; **~-minded** *adj* che ha la mente aperta; **~-necked** *adj* col collo slacciato; **~-plan** *adj* senza pareti divisorie

---

Open University

La **Open University**, *fondata in Gran Bretagna nel 1969, organizza corsi universitari per corrispondenza, basati anche su lezioni trasmesse per radio e per televisione e su corsi estivi.*

opera ['ɔpərə] *n* opera

operate ['ɔpəreɪt] *vt* (*machine*) azionare, far funzionare; (*system*) usare ♦ *vi* funzionare; (*drug*) essere efficace; **to ~ on sb (for)** (*MED*) operare qn (di)

operatic [ɔpə'rætɪk] *adj* dell'opera, lirico(a)

operating ['ɔpəreɪtɪŋ] *adj*: **~ table** tavolo operatorio; **~ theatre** sala operatoria

operation [ɔpə'reɪʃən] *n* operazione *f*; **to be in ~** (*machine*) essere in azione *or* funzionamento; (*system*) essere in vigore; **to have an ~** (*MED*) subire un'operazione; **~al** *adj* in funzione; d'esercizio

operative ['ɔpərətɪv] *adj* (*measure*) operativo(a)

operator ['ɔpəreɪtə*] *n* (*of machine*) operatore/trice; (*TEL*) centralinista *m/f*

opinion [ə'pɪnɪən] *n* opinione *f*, parere *m*; **in my ~** secondo me, a mio avviso; **~ated** *adj* dogmatico(a); **~ poll** *n* sondaggio di opinioni

opium ['əupɪəm] *n* oppio

opponent [ə'pəunənt] *n* avversario/a

opportunist [ɔpə'tjuːnɪst] *n* opportunista *m/f*

opportunity [ɔpə'tjuːnɪtɪ] *n* opportunità *f inv*, occasione *f*; **to take the ~ of doing** cogliere l'occasione per fare

oppose [ə'pəuz] *vt* opporsi a; **~d to** contrario(a) a; **as ~d to** in contrasto con; **opposing** *adj* opposto(a); (*team*) avversario(a)

opposite ['ɔpəzɪt] *adj* opposto(a); (*house etc*) di fronte ♦ *adv* di fronte, dirimpetto ♦ *prep* di fronte a ♦ *n*: **the ~** il contrario, l'opposto; **the ~ sex** l'altro sesso

opposition [ɔpə'zɪʃən] *n* opposizione *f*

opt [ɔpt] *vi*: **to ~ for** optare per; **to ~ to do** scegliere di fare; **~ out** *vi*: **to ~ out of** ritirarsi da

optical ['ɔptɪkl] *adj* ottico(a)

optician [ɔp'tɪʃən] *n* ottico

optimist ['ɔptɪmɪst] *n* ottimista *m/f*; **~ic** [-'mɪstɪk] *adj* ottimistico(a)

optimum ['ɔptɪməm] *adj* ottimale

option ['ɔpʃən] *n* scelta; (*SCOL*) materia facoltativa; (*COMM*) opzione *f*; **~al** *adj*

facoltativo(a); (*COMM*) a scelta

or [ɔː*] *conj* o, oppure; (*with negative*): **he hasn't seen ~ heard anything** non ha visto né sentito niente; **~ else** se no, altrimenti; oppure

oral ['ɔːrəl] *adj* orale ♦ *n* esame *m* orale

orange ['ɔrɪndʒ] *n* (*fruit*) arancia ♦ *adj* arancione

orbit ['ɔːbɪt] *n* orbita ♦ *vt* orbitare intorno a

orbital (motorway) ['ɔːbɪtl-] *n* raccordo anulare

orchard ['ɔːtʃəd] *n* frutteto

orchestra ['ɔːkɪstrə] *n* orchestra; (*US: seating*) platea

orchid ['ɔːkɪd] *n* orchidea

ordain [ɔː'deɪn] *vt* (*REL*) ordinare; (*decide*) decretare

ordeal [ɔː'diːl] *n* prova, travaglio

order ['ɔːdə*] *n* ordine *m*; (*COMM*) ordinazione *f* ♦ *vt* ordinare; **in ~** in ordine; (*of document*) in regola; **in (working) ~** funzionante; **in ~ to do** per fare; **in ~ that** affinché +*sub*; **on ~** (*COMM*) in ordinazione; **out of ~** non in ordine; (*not working*) guasto; **to ~ sb to do** ordinare a qn di fare; **~ form** *n* modulo d'ordinazione; **~ly** *n* (*MIL*) attendente *m*; (*MED*) inserviente *m* ♦ *adj* (*room*) in ordine; (*mind*) metodico(a); (*person*) ordinato(a), metodico(a)

ordinary ['ɔːdnrɪ] *adj* normale, comune; (*pej*) mediocre; **out of the ~** diverso dal solito, fuori dell'ordinario

Ordnance Survey ['ɔːdnəns-] (*BRIT*) *n* istituto cartografico britannico

ore [ɔː*] *n* minerale *m* grezzo

organ ['ɔːgən] *n* organo; **~ic** [ɔː'gænɪk] *adj* organico(a); (*of food*) biologico(a)

organization [ɔːgənaɪ'zeɪʃən] *n* organizzazione *f*

organize ['ɔːgənaɪz] *vt* organizzare; **to get ~d** organizzarsi; **~r** *n* organizzatore/trice

orgasm ['ɔːgæzəm] *n* orgasmo

orgy ['ɔːdʒɪ] *n* orgia

Orient ['ɔːrɪənt] *n*: **the ~** l'Oriente *m*; **oriental** [-'ɛntl] *adj*, *n* orientale *m/f*

origin ['ɔrɪdʒɪn] *n* origine *f*

original [ə'rɪdʒɪnl] *adj* originale; (*earliest*)

originario(a) ♦ *n* originale *m*; ~ly *adv* (*at first*) all'inizio

originate [ə'rɪdʒɪneɪt] *vi*: to ~ from essere originario(a) di; (*suggestion*) provenire da; to ~ in avere origine in

Orkneys ['ɔːknɪz] *npl*: the ~ (*also*: the Orkney Islands) le Orcadi

ornament ['ɔːnəmənt] *n* ornamento; (*trinket*) ninnolo; ~al [-'mentl] *adj* ornamentale

ornate [ɔː'neɪt] *adj* molto ornato(a)

orphan ['ɔːfn] *n* orfano/a

orthodox ['ɔːθədɔks] *adj* ortodosso(a)

orthopaedic [ɔːθə'piːdɪk] (*US* orthopedic) *adj* ortopedico(a)

ostensibly [ɔs'tensɪblɪ] *adv* all'apparenza

ostentatious [ɔsten'teɪʃəs] *adj* pretenzioso(a); ostentato(a)

ostrich ['ɔstrɪtʃ] *n* struzzo

other ['ʌðə*] *adj* altro(a) ♦ *pron*: the ~ (one) l'altro(a); ~s (= *people*) altri *mpl*; ~ than altro che; a parte; ~wise *adv, conj* altrimenti

otter ['ɔtə*] *n* lontra

ouch [autʃ] *excl* ohi!, ahi!

ought [ɔːt] (*pt* ought) *aux vb*: I ~ to do it dovrei farlo; this ~ to have been corrected questo avrebbe dovuto essere corretto; he ~ to win dovrebbe vincere

ounce [auns] *n* oncia (= 28.35 *g*; 16 *in a pound*)

our ['auə*] *adj* il(la) nostro(a), *pl* i(le) nostri(e); *see also* my; ~s *pron* il(la) nostro(a), *pl* i(le) nostri(e); *see also* mine; ~selves *pron pl* (*reflexive*) ci; (*after preposition*) noi; (*emphatic*) noi stessi(e); *see also* oneself

oust [aust] *vt* cacciare, espellere

KEYWORD

out [aut] *adv* (*gen*) fuori; ~ here/there qui/là fuori; to speak ~ loud parlare forte; to have a night ~ uscire una sera; the boat was 10 km ~ la barca era a 10 km dalla costa; 3 days ~ from Plymouth a 3 giorni da Plymouth

♦ *adj*: to be ~ (*gen*) essere fuori;

(*unconscious*) aver perso i sensi; (*style, singer*) essere fuori moda; before the week was ~ prima che la settimana fosse finita; to be ~ to do sth avere intenzione di fare qc; to be ~ in one's calculations aver sbagliato i calcoli

♦ out of *prep* 1 (*outside, beyond*) fuori di; to go ~ of the house uscire di casa; to look ~ of the window guardare fuori dalla finestra

2 (*because of*) per

3 (*origin*) da; to drink ~ of a cup bere da una tazza

4 (*from among*): ~ of 10 su 10

5 (*without*) senza; ~ of petrol senza benzina

out-and-out *adj* (*liar, thief etc*) vero(a) e proprio(a)

outback ['autbæk] *n* (*in Australia*) interno, entroterra

outboard ['autbɔːd] *n*: ~ (motor) (motore *m*) fuoribordo

outbreak ['autbreɪk] *n* scoppio; epidemia

outburst ['autbɜːst] *n* scoppio

outcast ['autkɑːst] *n* esule *m/f*; (*socially*) paria *m inv*

outcome ['autkʌm] *n* esito, risultato

outcrop ['autkrɔp] *n* (*of rock*) affioramento

outcry ['autkraɪ] *n* protesta, clamore *m*

outdated [aut'deɪtɪd] *adj* (*custom, clothes*) fuori moda; (*idea*) sorpassato(a)

outdo [aut'duː] (*irreg*) *vt* sorpassare

outdoor [aut'dɔː*] *adj* all'aperto; ~s *adv* fuori; all'aria aperta

outer ['autə*] *adj* esteriore; ~ space *n* spazio cosmico

outfit ['autfɪt] *n* (*clothes*) completo; (: *for sport*) tenuta

outgoing ['autgəuɪŋ] *adj* (*character*) socievole; ~s (*BRIT*) *npl* (*expenses*) spese *fpl*, uscite *fpl*

outgrow [aut'grəu] (*irreg*) *vt*: he has ~n his clothes tutti i vestiti gli sono diventati piccoli

outhouse ['authaus] *n* costruzione *f* annessa

outing ['autɪŋ] n gita; escursione f

outlaw ['autlɔ:] n fuorilegge m/f ♦ vt bandire

outlay ['autleɪ] n spese fpl; (investment) sborsa, spesa

outlet ['autlet] n (for liquid etc) sbocco, scarico; (US: ELEC) presa di corrente; (also: **retail ~**) punto di vendita

outline ['autlaɪn] n contorno, profilo; (summary) abbozzo, grandi linee fpl ♦ vt (fig) descrivere a grandi linee

outlive [aut'lɪv] vt sopravvivere a

outlook ['autluk] n prospettiva, vista

outlying ['autlaɪɪŋ] adj periferico(a)

outmoded [aut'məudɪd] adj passato(a) di moda; antiquato(a)

outnumber [aut'nʌmbə*] vt superare in numero

out-of-date adj (passport) scaduto(a); (clothes) fuori moda inv

out-of-the-way adj (place) fuori mano inv

outpatient ['autpeɪʃənt] n paziente m/f esterno(a)

outpost ['autpəust] n avamposto

output ['autput] n produzione f; (COMPUT) output m inv

outrage ['autreɪdʒ] n oltraggio; scandalo ♦ vt oltraggiare; **~ous** [-'reɪdʒəs] adj oltraggioso(a); scandaloso(a)

outreach worker ['autri:tʃ-] n assistente sociale che opera direttamente nei luoghi di aggregazione di emarginati, tossicodipendenti ecc

outright [adv aut'raɪt, adj 'autraɪt] adv completamente; schiettamente; apertamente; sul colpo ♦ adj completo(a); schietto(a) e netto(a)

outset ['autset] n inizio

outside [aut'saɪd] n esterno, esteriore m ♦ adj esterno(a), esteriore ♦ adv fuori, all'esterno ♦ prep fuori di, all'esterno di; **at the ~** (fig) al massimo; **~ lane** n (AUT) corsia di sorpasso; **~ line** n (TEL) linea esterna; **~r** n (in race etc) outsider m inv; (stranger) estraneo/a

outsize ['autsaɪz] adj (clothes) per taglie forti

outskirts ['autskə:ts] npl sobborghi mpl

outspoken [aut'spəukən] adj molto franco(a)

outstanding [aut'stændɪŋ] adj eccezionale, di rilievo; (unfinished) non completo(a); non evaso(a); non regolato(a)

outstay [aut'steɪ] vt: **to ~ one's welcome** diventare un ospite sgradito

outstretched [aut'stretʃt] adj (hand) teso(a); (body) disteso(a)

outstrip [aut'strɪp] vt (competitors, demand) superare

out-tray n contenitore m per la corrispondenza in partenza

outward ['autwəd] adj (sign, appearances) esteriore; (journey) d'andata

outweigh [aut'weɪ] vt avere maggior peso di

outwit [aut'wɪt] vt superare in astuzia

oval ['əuvl] adj ovale ♦ n ovale m

Oval Office

i L'**Oval Office** è *una grande sala di forma ovale nella* **White House**, *la Casa Bianca, dove ha sede l'ufficio del Presidente degli Stati Uniti*

---

ovary ['əuvərɪ] n ovaia

oven ['ʌvn] n forno; **~proof** adj da forno

over ['əuvə*] adv al di sopra ♦ adj (or adv) (finished) finito(a), terminato(a); (too) troppo; (remaining) che avanza ♦ prep su; sopra; (above) al di sopra di; (on the other side of) di là di; (more than) più di; (during) durante; **~ here** qui; **~ there** là; **all ~** (everywhere) dappertutto; (finished) tutto(a) finito(a); **~ and ~ (again)** più e più volte; **~ and above** oltre (a); **to ask sb ~** invitare qn (a passare)

overall [adj, n 'əuvərɔ:l, adv əuvər'ɔ:l] adj totale ♦ n (BRIT) grembiule m ♦ adv nell'insieme, complessivamente; **~s** npl (worker's ~s) tuta (da lavoro)

overawe [əuvər'ɔ:] vt intimidire

overbalance [əuvə'bæləns] vi perdere l'equilibrio

overboard ['əuvəbɔ:d] adv (NAUT) fuori bordo, in mare

overbook [əuvəˈbuk] *vt*: **the hotel was ~ed** le prenotazioni all'albergo superavano i posti disponibili

overcast [ˈəuvəkɑːst] *adj* (*sky*) coperto(a)

overcharge [əuvəˈtʃɑːdʒ] *vt*: **to ~ sb for sth** far pagare troppo caro a qn per qc

overcoat [ˈəuvəkəut] *n* soprabito, cappotto

overcome [əuvəˈkʌm] (*irreg*) *vt* superare; sopraffare

overcrowded [əuvəˈkraudɪd] *adj* sovraffollato(a)

overdo [əuvəˈduː] (*irreg*) *vt* esagerare; (*overcook*) cuocere troppo

overdose [ˈəuvədəus] *n* dose *f* eccessiva

overdraft [ˈəuvədrɑːft] *n* scoperto (di conto)

overdrawn [əuvəˈdrɔːn] *adj* (*account*) scoperto(a)

overdue [əuvəˈdjuː] *adj* in ritardo

overestimate [əuvərˈɛstɪmeɪt] *vt* sopravvalutare

overflow [*vb* əuvəˈfləu, *n* ˈəuvəfləu] *vi* traboccare ♦ *n* (*also*: **~ pipe**) troppopieno

overgrown [əuvəˈgrəun] *adj* (*garden*) ricoperto(a) di vegetazione

overhaul [*vb* əuvəˈhɔːl, *n* ˈəuvəhɔːl] *vt* revisionare ♦ *n* revisione *f*

overhead [*adv* əuvəˈhɛd, *adj*, *n* ˈəuvəhɛd] *adv* di sopra ♦ *adj* aereo(a); (*lighting*) verticale ♦ *n* (*US*) = **~s**; **~s** *npl* spese *fpl* generali

overhear [əuvəˈhɪə*] (*irreg*) *vt* sentire (per caso)

overheat [əuvəˈhiːt] *vi* (*engine*) surriscaldare

overjoyed [əuvəˈdʒɔɪd] *adj* pazzo(a) di gioia

overlap [əuvəˈlæp] *vi* sovrapporsi

overleaf [əuvəˈliːf] *adv* a tergo

overload [əuvəˈləud] *vt* sovraccaricare

overlook [əuvəˈluk] *vt* (*have view of*) dare su; (*miss*) trascurare; (*forgive*) passare sopra a

overnight [əuvəˈnaɪt] *adv* (*happen*) durante la notte; (*fig*) tutto ad un tratto ♦ *adj* di notte; **he stayed there ~** ci ha passato la notte

overpass [ˈəuvəpɑːs] *n* cavalcavia *m inv*

overpower [əuvəˈpauə*] *vt* sopraffare; **~ing** *adj* irresistibile; (*heat, stench*) soffocante

overrate [əuvəˈreɪt] *vt* sopravvalutare

override [əuvəˈraɪd] (*irreg: like* **ride**) *vt* (*order, objection*) passar sopra a; (*decision*) annullare; **overriding** *adj* preponderante

overrule [əuvəˈruːl] *vt* (*decision*) annullare; (*claim*) respingere

overrun [əuvəˈrʌn] (*irreg: like* **run**) *vt* (*country*) invadere; (*time limit*) superare

overseas [əuvəˈsiːz] *adv* oltremare; (*abroad*) all'estero ♦ *adj* (*trade*) estero(a); (*visitor*) straniero(a)

overshadow [əuvəˈʃædəu] *vt* far ombra su; (*fig*) eclissare

overshoot [əuvəˈʃuːt] (*irreg*) *vt* superare

oversight [ˈəuvəsaɪt] *n* omissione *f*, svista

oversleep [əuvəˈsliːp] (*irreg*) *vt* dormire troppo a lungo

overstep [əuvəˈstɛp] *vt*: **to ~ the mark** superare ogni limite

overt [əuˈvəːt] *adj* palese

overtake [əuvəˈteɪk] (*irreg*) *vt* sorpassare

overthrow [əuvəˈθrəu] (*irreg*) *vt* (*government*) rovesciare

overtime [ˈəuvətaɪm] *n* (lavoro) straordinario

overtone [ˈəuvətəun] *n* sfumatura

overture [ˈəuvətʃuə*] *n* (*MUS*) ouverture *f inv*; (*fig*) approccio

overturn [əuvəˈtəːn] *vt* rovesciare ♦ *vi* rovesciarsi

overweight [əuvəˈweɪt] *adj* (*person*) troppo grasso(a)

overwhelm [əuvəˈwɛlm] *vt* sopraffare; sommergere; schiacciare; **~ing** *adj* (*victory, defeat*) schiacciante; (*heat, desire*) intenso(a)

overwrought [əuvəˈrɔːt] *adj* molto agitato(a)

owe [əu] *vt*: **to ~ sb sth, to ~ sth to sb** dovere qc a qn; **owing to** *prep* a causa di

owl [aul] *n* gufo

own [əun] *vt* possedere ♦ *adj* proprio(a); **a room of my ~** la mia propria camera; **to get one's ~ back** vendicarsi; **on one's ~** tutto(a) solo(a); **~ up** *vi* confessare; **~er** *n* proprietario/a; **~ership** *n* possesso

ox [ɔks] (*pl* **oxen**) *n* bue *m*

oxen ['ɔksn] *npl of* **ox**

oxtail ['ɔksteɪl] *n*: ~ **soup** minestra di coda di bue

oxygen ['ɔksɪdʒən] *n* ossigeno; ~ **mask/tent** *n* maschera/tenda ad ossigeno

oyster ['ɔɪstə*] *n* ostrica

oz. *abbr* = **ounce(s)**

ozone ['əuzəun] *n* ozono; ~**-friendly** *adj* che non danneggia l'ozono; ~ **hole** *n* buco nell'ozono

P, p

p [piː] *abbr* = **penny; pence**

P.A. *n abbr* = **personal assistant; public address system**

p.a. *abbr* = **per annum**

pa [pɑː] (*inf*) *n* papà *m inv*, babbo

pace [peɪs] *n* passo; (*speed*) passo; velocità ♦ *vi*: **to ~ up and down** camminare su e giù; **to keep ~ with** camminare di pari passo a; (*events*) tenersi al corrente di; ~**maker** *n* (*MED*) segnapasso; (*SPORT: also*: ~ **setter**) battistrada *m inv*

pacific [pə'sɪfɪk] *n*: **the P~ (Ocean)** il Pacifico, l'Oceano Pacifico

pacify ['pæsɪfaɪ] *vt* calmare, placare

pack [pæk] *n* pacco; (*US: of cigarettes*) pacchetto; (*back~*) zaino; (*of hounds*) muta; (*of thieves etc*) banda; (*of cards*) mazzo ♦ *vt* (*in suitcase etc*) mettere; (*box*) riempire; (*cram*) stipare, pigiare; **to ~ (one's bags)** fare la valigia; **to ~ sb off** spedire via qn; ~ **it in!** (*inf*) dacci un taglio!

package ['pækɪdʒ] *n* pacco; (*US: also*: ~ **deal**) pacchetto; forfait *m inv*; ~ **holiday** *n* vacanza organizzata; ~ **tour** *n* viaggio organizzato

packed lunch *n* pranzo al sacco

packet ['pækɪt] *n* pacchetto

packing ['pækɪŋ] *n* imballaggio; ~ **case** *n* cassa da imballaggio

pact [pækt] *n* patto, accordo; trattato

pad [pæd] *n* blocco; (*to prevent friction*) cuscinetto; (*inf: flat*) appartamentino ♦ *vt* imbottire; ~**ding** *n* imbottitura

paddle ['pædl] *n* (*oar*) pagaia; (*US: for table tennis*) racchetta da ping-pong ♦ *vi* sguazzare ♦ *vt*: **to ~ a canoe** *etc* vogare con la pagaia; **paddling pool** (*BRIT*) *n* piscina per bambini

paddock ['pædək] *n* prato recintato; (*at racecourse*) paddock *m inv*

padlock ['pædlɔk] *n* lucchetto

paediatrics [piːdɪ'ætrɪks] (*US* **pediatrics**) *n* pediatria

pagan ['peɪgən] *adj, n* pagano(a)

page [peɪdʒ] *n* pagina; (*also*: ~ **boy**) paggio ♦ *vt* (*in hotel etc*) (far) chiamare

pageant ['pædʒənt] *n* spettacolo storico; grande cerimonia; ~**ry** *n* pompa

pager ['peɪdʒə*] *n* (*TEL*) cercapersone *m inv*

paging device ['peɪdʒɪŋ-] *n* (*TEL*) cercapersone *m inv*

paid [peɪd] *pt, pp of* **pay** ♦ *adj* (*work, official*) rimunerato(a); **to put ~ to** (*BRIT*) mettere fine a

pail [peɪl] *n* secchio

pain [peɪn] *n* dolore *m*; **to be in ~** soffrire, aver male; **to take ~s to do** mettercela tutta per fare; ~**ed** *adj* addolorato(a), afflitto(a); ~**ful** *adj* doloroso(a), che fa male; difficile, penoso(a); ~**fully** *adv* (*fig: very*) fin troppo; ~**killer** *n* antalgico, antidolorifico; ~**less** *adj* indolore

painstaking ['peɪnzteɪkɪŋ] *adj* (*person*) sollecito(a); (*work*) accurato(a)

paint [peɪnt] *n* vernice *f*, colore *m* ♦ *vt* dipingere; (*walls, door etc*) verniciare; **to ~ the door blue** verniciare la porta di azzurro; ~**brush** *n* pennello; ~**er** *n* (*artist*) pittore *m*; (*decorator*) imbianchino; ~**ing** *n* pittura; verniciatura; (*picture*) dipinto, quadro; ~**work** *n* tinta; (*of car*) vernice *f*

pair [peə*] *n* (*of shoes, gloves etc*) paio; (*of people*) coppia; duo *m inv*; **a ~ of scissors/trousers** un paio di forbici/pantaloni

pajamas [pɪ'dʒɑːməz] (*US*) *npl* pigiama *m*

Pakistan [pɑːkɪ'stɑːn] *n* Pakistan *m*; ~**i** *adj, n* pakistano(a)

pal [pæl] (*inf*) *n* amico/a, compagno/a

palace ['pæləs] *n* palazzo

palatable ['pælɪtəbl] *adj* gustoso(a)

palate ['pælɪt] *n* palato

palatial [pə'leɪʃəl] *adj* sontuoso(a), sfarzoso(a)

pale [peɪl] *adj* pallido(a) ♦ *n*: **to be beyond the ~** aver oltrepassato ogni limite

Palestine ['pælɪstaɪn] *n* Palestina; **Palestinian** [-'tɪnɪən] *adj*, *n* palestinese *m/f*

palette ['pælɪt] *n* tavolozza

palings ['peɪlɪŋz] *npl* (*fence*) palizzata

pallet ['pælɪt] *n* (*for goods*) paletta

pallid ['pælɪd] *adj* pallido(a), smorto(a)

pallor ['pælə*] *n* pallore *m*

palm [pɑːm] *n* (ANAT) palma, palmo; (*also:* ~ **tree**) palma ♦ *vt*: **to ~ sth off on sb** (*inf*) rifilare qc a qn; **P~ Sunday** *n* Domenica delle Palme

paltry ['pɔːltrɪ] *adj* irrisorio(a); insignificante

pamper ['pæmpə*] *vt* viziare, coccolare

pamphlet ['pæmflət] *n* dépliant *m inv*

pan [pæn] *n* (*also:* **sauce~**) casseruola; (*also:* **frying ~**) padella

panache [pə'næʃ] *n* stile *m*

pancake ['pænkeɪk] *n* frittella

pancreas ['pæŋkrɪəs] *n* pancreas *m inv*

panda ['pændə] *n* panda *m inv*; ~ **car** (BRIT) *n* auto *f* della polizia

pandemonium [pændɪ'məʊnɪəm] *n* pandemonio

pander ['pændə*] *vi*: **to ~ to** lusingare; concedere tutto a

pane [peɪn] *n* vetro

panel ['pænl] *n* (*of wood, cloth etc*) pannello; (RADIO, TV) giuria; ~**ling** (US ~**ing**) *n* rivestimento a pannelli

pang [pæŋ] *n*: **a ~ of regret** un senso di rammarico; **hunger ~s** morsi *mpl* della fame

panic ['pænɪk] *n* panico ♦ *vi* perdere il sangue freddo; ~**ky** *adj* (*person*) pauroso(a); ~**-stricken** *adj* (*person*) preso(a) dal panico, in preda al panico; (*look*) terrorizzato(a)

pansy ['pænzɪ] *n* (BOT) viola del pensiero, pensée *f inv*; (*inf*: *pej*) femminuccia

pant [pænt] *vi* ansare

panther ['pænθə*] *n* pantera

panties ['pæntɪz] *npl* slip *m*, mutandine *fpl*

pantihose ['pæntɪhəʊz] (US) *n* collant *m inv*

pantomime ['pæntəmaɪm] (BRIT) *n* pantomima

---
pantomime
---

i In Gran Bretagna la **pantomime** è una sorta di libera interpretazione delle favole più conosciute, che vengono messe in scena a teatro durante il periodo natalizio. È uno spettacolo per tutta la famiglia che prevede la partecipazione del pubblico.

---

pantry ['pæntrɪ] *n* dispensa

pants [pænts] *npl* mutande *fpl*, slip *m*; (US: *trousers*) pantaloni *mpl*

papal ['peɪpəl] *adj* papale, pontificio(a)

paper ['peɪpə*] *n* carta; (*also:* **wall~**) carta da parati, tappezzeria; (*also:* **news~**) giornale *m*; (*study, article*) saggio; (*exam*) prova scritta ♦ *adj* di carta ♦ *vt* tappezzare; ~**s** *npl* (*also:* **identity ~s**) carte *fpl*, documenti *mpl*; ~**back** *n* tascabile *m*; edizione *f* economica; ~ **bag** *n* sacchetto di carta; ~ **clip** *n* graffetta, clip *f inv*; ~ **hankie** *n* fazzolettino di carta; ~**weight** *n* fermacarte *m inv*; ~**work** *n* lavoro amministrativo

papier-mâché ['pæpɪer'mæʃeɪ] *n* cartapesta

par [pɑː*] *n* parità, pari *f*; (GOLF) norma; **on a ~ with** alla pari con

parachute ['pærəʃuːt] *n* paracadute *m inv*

parade [pə'reɪd] *n* parata ♦ *vt* (*fig*) fare sfoggio di ♦ *vi* sfilare in parata

paradise ['pærədaɪs] *n* paradiso

paradox ['pærədɒks] *n* paradosso; ~**ically** [-'dɒksɪklɪ] *adv* paradossalmente

paraffin ['pærəfɪn] (BRIT) *n*: ~ **(oil)** paraffina

paragon ['pærəgən] *n* modello di perfezione *or* di virtù

paragraph ['pærəgrɑːf] *n* paragrafo

parallel ['pærəlɛl] *adj* parallelo(a); (*fig*) analogo(a) ♦ *n* (*line*) parallela; (*fig, GEO*) parallelo

paralyse ['pærəlaɪz] (US **paralyze**) *vt* paralizzare

paralysis [pəˈrælisis] *n* paralisi *f inv*
paralyze [ˈpærəlaiz] (*US*) *vt* = **paralyse**
paramount [ˈpærəmaunt] *adj*: **of ~ importance** di capitale importanza
paranoid [ˈpærənɔid] *adj* paranoico(a)
paraphernalia [pærəfəˈneiliə] *n* attrezzi *mpl*, roba
parasol [ˈpærəsɔl] *n* parasole *m*
paratrooper [ˈpærətruːpə*] *n* paracadutista *m* (*soldato*)
parcel [ˈpɑːsl] *n* pacco, pacchetto ♦ *vt* (*also:* **~ up**) impaccare
parched [pɑːtʃt] *adj* (*person*) assetato(a)
parchment [ˈpɑːtʃmənt] *n* pergamena
pardon [ˈpɑːdn] *n* perdono; grazia ♦ *vt* perdonare; (*LAW*) graziare; **~ me!** mi scusi!; **I beg your ~!** scusi!; **I beg your ~?** (*BRIT*), **~ me?** (*US*) prego?
parent [ˈpɛərənt] *n* genitore *m*; **~s** *npl* (*mother and father*) genitori *mpl*; **~al** [pəˈrentl] *adj* dei genitori
parentheses [pəˈrenθisiːz] *npl of* **parenthesis**
parenthesis [pəˈrenθisis] (*pl* **parentheses**) *n* parentesi *f inv*
Paris [ˈpæris] *n* Parigi *f*
parish [ˈpæriʃ] *n* parrocchia; (*BRIT: civil*) ≈ municipio
park [pɑːk] *n* parco ♦ *vt, vi* parcheggiare
parka [ˈpɑːkə] *n* eskimo
parking [ˈpɑːkiŋ] *n* parcheggio; "**no ~**" "sosta vietata"; **~ lot** (*US*) *n* posteggio, parcheggio; **~ meter** *n* parchimetro; **~ ticket** *n* multa per sosta vietata
parliament [ˈpɑːləmənt] *n* parlamento
parliamentary [pɑːləˈmentəri] *adj* parlamentare
parlour [ˈpɑːlə*] (*US* **parlor**) *n* salotto
parochial [pəˈrəukiəl] (*pej*) *adj* provinciale
parole [pəˈrəul] *n*: **on ~** in libertà per buona condotta
parrot [ˈpærət] *n* pappagallo
parry [ˈpæri] *vt* parare
parsley [ˈpɑːsli] *n* prezzemolo
parsnip [ˈpɑːsnip] *n* pastinaca
parson [ˈpɑːsn] *n* prete *m*; (*Church of England*) parroco

part [pɑːt] *n* parte *f*; (*of machine*) pezzo; (*US: in hair*) scriminatura ♦ *adj* in parte ♦ *adv* = **partly** ♦ *vt* separare ♦ *vi* (*people*) separarsi; **to take ~** prendere parte a; **for my ~** per parte mia; **to take sth in good ~** prendere bene qc; **to take sb's ~** parteggiare per *or* prendere le parti di qn; **for the most ~** in generale; nella maggior parte dei casi; **~ with** *vt fus* separarsi da; rinunciare a; **~ exchange** (*BRIT*) *n*: **in ~ exchange** in pagamento parziale
partial [ˈpɑːʃl] *adj* parziale; **to be ~ to** avere un debole per
participate [pɑːˈtisipeit] *vi*: **to ~ (in)** prendere parte (a), partecipare (a); **participation** [-ˈpeiʃən] *n* partecipazione *f*
participle [ˈpɑːtisipl] *n* participio
particle [ˈpɑːtikl] *n* particella
particular [pəˈtikjulə*] *adj* particolare; speciale; (*fussy*) difficile; meticoloso(a); **in ~** in particolare, particolarmente; **~ly** *adv* particolarmente; in particolare; **~s** *npl* particolari *mpl*, dettagli *mpl*; (*information*) informazioni *fpl*
parting [ˈpɑːtiŋ] *n* separazione *f*; (*BRIT: in hair*) scriminatura ♦ *adj* d'addio
partisan [pɑːtiˈzæn] *n* partigiano/a ♦ *adj* partigiano(a); di parte
partition [pɑːˈtiʃən] *n* (*POL*) partizione *f*; (*wall*) tramezzo
partly [ˈpɑːtli] *adv* parzialmente; in parte
partner [ˈpɑːtnə*] *n* (*COMM*) socio/a; (*wife, husband etc, SPORT*) compagno/a; (*at dance*) cavaliere/dama; **~ship** *n* associazione *f*; (*COMM*) società *f inv*
partridge [ˈpɑːtridʒ] *n* pernice *f*
part-time *adj, adv* a orario ridotto
party [ˈpɑːti] *n* (*POL*) partito; (*group*) gruppo; (*LAW*) parte *f*; (*celebration*) ricevimento; serata; festa ♦ *cpd* (*POL*) del partito, di partito; **~ dress** *n* vestito della festa
pass [pɑːs] *vt* (*gen*) passare; (*place*) passare davanti a; (*exam*) passare, superare; (*candidate*) promuovere; (*overtake, surpass*) sorpassare, superare; (*approve*) approvare ♦ *vi* passare ♦ *n* (*permit*) lasciapassare *m inv*; permesso; (*in mountains*) passo, gola;

(SPORT) passaggio; (SCOL): **to get a ~** prendere la sufficienza; **to ~ sth through a hole** etc far passare qc attraverso un buco etc; **to make a ~ at sb** (inf) fare delle proposte or delle avances a qn; **~ away** vi morire; **~ by** vi passare ♦ vt trascurare; **~ on** vt passare; **~ out** vi svenire; **~ up** vt (opportunity) lasciarsi sfuggire, perdere; **~able** adj (road) praticabile; (work) accettabile

passage ['pæsɪdʒ] n (gen) passaggio; (also: **~way**) corridoio; (in book) brano, passo; (by boat) traversata

passbook ['pɑːsbuk] n libretto di risparmio

passenger ['pæsɪndʒə*] n passeggero/a

passer-by [pɑːsə'baɪ] n passante m/f

passing ['pɑːsɪŋ] adj (fig) fuggevole; **to mention sth in ~** accennare a qc di sfuggita; **~ place** n (AUT) piazzola di sosta

passion ['pæʃən] n passione f; amore m; **~ate** adj appassionato(a)

passive ['pæsɪv] adj (also LING) passivo(a); **~ smoking** n fumo passivo

Passover ['pɑːsəuvə*] n Pasqua ebraica

passport ['pɑːspɔːt] n passaporto; **~ control** n controllo m passaporti inv; **~ office** n ufficio m passaporti inv

password ['pɑːswəːd] n parola d'ordine

past [pɑːst] prep (further than) oltre, di là di; dopo; (later than) dopo ♦ adj passato(a); (president etc) ex inv ♦ n passato; **he's ~ forty** ha più di quarant'anni; **ten ~ eight** le otto e dieci; **for the ~ few days** da qualche giorno; in questi ultimi giorni; **to run ~** passare di corsa

pasta ['pæstə] n pasta

paste [peɪst] n (glue) colla; (CULIN) pâté m inv; pasta ♦ vt collare

pastel ['pæstl] adj pastello inv

pasteurized ['pæstəraɪzd] adj pastorizzato(a)

pastille ['pæstl] n pastiglia

pastime ['pɑːstaɪm] n passatempo

pastry ['peɪstrɪ] n pasta

pasture ['pɑːstʃə*] n pascolo

pasty¹ ['pæstɪ] n pasticcio di carne

pasty² ['peɪstɪ] adj (face etc) smorto(a)

pat [pæt] vt accarezzare, dare un colpetto (affettuoso) a

patch [pætʃ] n (of material, on tyre) toppa; (eye ~) benda; (spot) macchia ♦ vt (clothes) rattoppare; **(to go through) a bad ~** (attraversare) un brutto periodo; **~ up** vt rappezzare; (quarrel) appianare; **~y** adj irregolare

pâté ['pæteɪ] n pâté m inv

patent ['peɪtnt] n brevetto ♦ vt brevettare ♦ adj patente, manifesto(a); **~ leather** n cuoio verniciato

paternal [pə'təːnl] adj paterno(a)

path [pɑːθ] n sentiero, viottolo; viale m; (fig) via, strada; (of planet, missile) traiettoria

pathetic [pə'θetɪk] adj (pitiful) patetico(a); (very bad) penoso(a)

pathological [pæθə'lɔdʒɪkl] adj patologico(a)

pathway ['pɑːθweɪ] n sentiero

patience ['peɪʃns] n pazienza; (BRIT: CARDS) solitario

patient ['peɪʃnt] n paziente m/f; malato/a ♦ adj paziente

patio ['pætɪəu] n terrazza

patriot ['peɪtrɪət] n patriota m/f; **~ic** [pætrɪ'ɔtɪk] adj patriottico(a); **~ism** n patriottismo

patrol [pə'trəul] n pattuglia ♦ vt pattugliare; **~ car** n autoradio f inv (della polizia); **~man** (US: irreg) n poliziotto

patron ['peɪtrən] n (in shop) cliente m/f; (of charity) benefattore/trice; **~ of the arts** mecenate m/f; **~ize** ['pætrənaɪz] vt essere cliente abituale di; (fig) trattare dall'alto in basso

patter ['pætə*] n picchiettio; (sales talk) propaganda di vendita ♦ vi picchiettare; **a ~ of footsteps** un rumore di passi

pattern ['pætən] n modello; (design) disegno, motivo

pauper ['pɔːpə*] n indigente m/f

pause [pɔːz] n pausa ♦ vi fare una pausa, arrestarsi

pave [peɪv] vt pavimentare; **to ~ the way for** aprire la via a

pavement ['peɪvmənt] (BRIT) n marciapiede

m

pavilion [pə'vɪlɪən] *n* (SPORT) edificio *annesso a campo sportivo*

paving ['peɪvɪŋ] *n* pavimentazione *f;* ~ **stone** *n* lastra di pietra

paw [pɔ:] *n* zampa

pawn [pɔ:n] *n* (CHESS) pedone *m;* (fig) pedina ♦ *vt* dare in pegno; ~**broker** *n* prestatore *m* su pegno; ~**shop** *n* monte *m* di pietà

pay [peɪ] (*pt, pp* **paid**) *n* stipendio; paga ♦ *vt* pagare ♦ *vi* (be profitable) rendere; **to ~ attention (to)** fare attenzione (a); **to ~ sb a visit** far visita a qn; **to ~ one's respects to sb** porgere i propri rispetti a qn; ~ **back** *vt* rimborsare; ~ **for** *vt fus* pagare; ~ **in** *vt* versare; ~ **off** *vt* (debt) saldare; (person) pagare; (employee) pagare e licenziare ♦ *vi* (scheme, decision) dare dei frutti; ~ **up** *vt* saldare; ~**able** *adj* pagabile; ~**ee** *n* beneficiario/a; ~ **envelope** (US) *n* = ~ **packet**; ~**ing** *adj:* ~**ing guest** ospite *m/f* pagante, pensionante *m/f;* ~**ment** *n* pagamento; versamento; saldo; ~ **packet** (BRIT) *n* busta *f* paga *inv;* ~ **phone** *n* cabina telefonica; ~**roll** *n* ruolo (organico); ~ **slip** *n* foglio *m* paga *inv;* ~ **television** *n* televisione *f* a pagamento, pay-tv *f inv*

PC *n abbr* = **personal computer**; *adv abbr* = **politically correct**

p.c. *abbr* = **per cent**

pea [pi:] *n* pisello

peace [pi:s] *n* pace *f;* ~**ful** *adj* pacifico(a), calmo(a)

peach [pi:tʃ] *n* pesca

peacock ['pi:kɔk] *n* pavone *m*

peak [pi:k] *n* (of mountain) cima, vetta; (mountain itself) picco; (of cap) visiera; (fig) apice *m,* culmine *m;* ~ **hours** *npl* ore *fpl* di punta; ~ **period** *n* = ~ **hours**

peal [pi:l] *n* (of bells) scampanio, carillon *m inv;* ~**s of laughter** scoppi *mpl* di risa

peanut ['pi:nʌt] *n* arachide *f,* nocciolina americana; ~ **butter** *n* burro di arachidi

pear [pɛə*] *n* pera

pearl [pə:l] *n* perla

peasant ['pɛznt] *n* contadino/a

peat [pi:t] *n* torba

pebble ['pɛbl] *n* ciottolo

peck [pɛk] *vt* (also: ~ **at**) beccare ♦ *n* colpo di becco; (kiss) bacetto; ~**ing order** *n* ordine *m* gerarchico; ~**ish** (BRIT: inf) adj: **I feel ~ish** ho un languorino

peculiar [pɪ'kju:lɪə*] *adj* strano(a), bizzarro(a); peculiare; ~ **to** peculiare di

pedal ['pɛdl] *n* pedale *m* ♦ *vi* pedalare

pedantic [pɪ'dæntɪk] *adj* pedantesco(a)

peddler ['pɛdlə*] *n* (also: **drug ~**) spacciatore/trice

pedestal ['pɛdəstl] *n* piedestallo

pedestrian [pɪ'dɛstrɪən] *n* pedone/a ♦ *adj* pedonale; (fig) prosaico(a), pedestre; ~ **crossing** (BRIT) *n* passaggio pedonale; ~ **precinct** (BRIT), ~ **zone** (US) *n* zona pedonale

pediatrics [pi:dɪ'ætrɪks] (US) *n* = **paediatrics**

pedigree ['pɛdɪgri:] *n* (of animal) pedigree *m inv;* (fig) background *m inv* ♦ *cpd* (animal) di razza

pee [pi:] (inf) *vi* pisciare

peek [pi:k] *vi* guardare furtivamente

peel [pi:l] *n* buccia; (of orange, lemon) scorza ♦ *vt* sbucciare ♦ *vi* (paint etc) staccarsi

peep [pi:p] *n* (BRIT: look) sguardo furtivo, sbirciata; (sound) pigolio ♦ *vi* (BRIT) guardare furtivamente; ~ **out** *vi* mostrarsi furtivamente; ~**hole** *n* spioncino

peer [pɪə*] *vi:* **to ~ at** scrutare ♦ *n* (noble) pari *m inv;* (equal) pari *m/f inv,* uguale *m/f;* (contemporary) contemporaneo/a; ~**age** *n* dignità di pari; pari *mpl*

peeved [pi:vd] *adj* stizzito(a)

peevish ['pi:vɪʃ] *adj* stizzoso(a)

peg [pɛg] *n* caviglia; (for coat etc) attaccapanni *m inv;* (BRIT: also: **clothes ~**) molletta

Peking [pi:'kɪŋ] *n* Pechino *f*

pelican ['pɛlɪkən] *n* pellicano; ~ **crossing** (BRIT) *n* (AUT) attraversamento pedonale con semaforo a controllo manuale

pellet ['pɛlɪt] *n* pallottola, pallina

pelt [pɛlt] *vt:* **to ~ sb (with)** bombardare qn

(con) ♦ *vi* (*rain*) piovere a dirotto; (*inf: run*) filare ♦ *n* pelle *f*

pelvis ['pelvɪs] *n* pelvi *f inv*, bacino

pen [pɛn] *n* penna; (*for sheep*) recinto

penal ['piːnl] *adj* penale; **~ize** *vt* punire; (*SPORT, fig*) penalizzare

penalty ['pɛnltɪ] *n* penalità *f inv*; sanzione *f* penale; (*fine*) ammenda; (*SPORT*) penalizzazione *f*; **~ (kick)** *n* (*SPORT*) calcio di rigore

penance ['pɛnəns] *n* penitenza

pence [pɛns] (*BRIT*) *npl of* **penny**

pencil ['pɛnsl] *n* matita; **~ case** *n* astuccio per matite; **~ sharpener** *n* temperamatite *m inv*

pendant ['pɛndnt] *n* pendaglio

pending ['pɛndɪŋ] *prep* in attesa di ♦ *adj* in sospeso

pendulum ['pɛndjuləm] *n* pendolo

penetrate ['pɛnɪtreɪt] *vt* penetrare

penfriend ['pɛnfrɛnd] (*BRIT*) *n* corrispondente *m/f*

penguin ['pɛŋgwɪn] *n* pinguino

penicillin [pɛnɪ'sɪlɪn] *n* penicillina

peninsula [pə'nɪnsjulə] *n* penisola

penis ['piːnɪs] *n* pene *m*

penitentiary [pɛnɪ'tɛnʃərɪ] (*US*) *n* carcere *m*

penknife ['pɛnnaɪf] *n* temperino

pen name *n* pseudonimo

penniless ['pɛnɪlɪs] *adj* senza un soldo

penny ['pɛnɪ] (*pl* **pennies** *or* **pence** (*BRIT*)) *n* penny *m*; (*US*) centesimo

penpal ['pɛnpæl] *n* corrispondente *m/f*

pension ['pɛnʃən] *n* pensione *f*; **~er** (*BRIT*) *n* pensionato/a

pensive ['pɛnsɪv] *adj* pensoso(a)

penthouse ['pɛnthaus] *n* appartamento (di lusso) nell'attico

pent-up ['pɛntʌp] *adj* (*feelings*) represso(a)

people ['piːpl] *npl* gente *f*; persone *fpl*; (*citizens*) popolo ♦ *n* (*nation, race*) popolo; **4/several ~ came** 4/parecchie persone sono venute; **~ say that ...** si dice che ....

pep [pɛp] (*inf*): **~ up** *vt* vivacizzare; (*food*) rendere più gustoso(a)

pepper ['pɛpə*] *n* pepe *m*; (*vegetable*) peperone *m* ♦ *vt* (*fig*): **to ~ with** spruzzare

di; **~mint** *n* (*sweet*) pasticca di menta

peptalk ['pɛptɔːk] (*inf*) *n* discorso di incoraggiamento

per [pə:*] *prep* per; a; **~ hour** all'ora; **~ kilo** *etc* il chilo *etc*; **~ day** al giorno; **~ annum** *adv* all'anno; **~ capita** *adj, adv* pro capite *inv*

perceive [pə'siːv] *vt* percepire; (*notice*) accorgersi di

per cent [pə'sɛnt] *adv* per cento

percentage [pə'sɛntɪdʒ] *n* percentuale *f*

perception [pə'sɛpʃən] *n* percezione *f*; sensibilità; perspicacia

perceptive [pə'sɛptɪv] *adj* percettivo(a); perspicace

perch [pə:tʃ] *n* (*fish*) pesce *m* persico; (*for bird*) sostegno, ramo ♦ *vi* appollaiarsi

percolator ['pə:kəleɪtə*] *n* (*also*: **coffee ~**) caffettiera a pressione; caffettiera elettrica

percussion [pə'kʌʃən] *n* percussione *f*; (*MUS*) strumenti *mpl* a percussione

perennial [pə'rɛnɪəl] *adj* perenne

perfect [*adj, n* 'pə:fɪkt, *vb* pə'fɛkt] *adj* perfetto(a) ♦ *n* (*also*: **~ tense**) perfetto, passato prossimo ♦ *vt* perfezionare; mettere a punto; **~ly** *adv* perfettamente, alla perfezione

perforate ['pə:fəreɪt] *vt* perforare; **perforation** [-'reɪʃən] *n* perforazione *f*

perform [pə'fɔːm] *vt* (*carry out*) eseguire, fare; (*symphony etc*) suonare; (*play, ballet*) dare; (*opera*) fare ♦ *vi* suonare; recitare; **~ance** *n* esecuzione *f*; (*at theatre etc*) rappresentazione *f*, spettacolo; (*of an artist*) interpretazione *f*; (*of player etc*) performance *f*; (*of car, engine*) prestazione *f*; **~er** *n* artista *m/f*

perfume ['pə:fjuːm] *n* profumo

perhaps [pə'hæps] *adv* forse

peril ['pɛrɪl] *n* pericolo

perimeter [pə'rɪmɪtə*] *n* perimetro

period ['pɪərɪəd] *n* periodo; (*HISTORY*) epoca; (*SCOL*) lezione *f*; (*full stop*) punto; (*MED*) mestruazioni *fpl* ♦ *adj* (*costume, furniture*) d'epoca; **~ic(al)** [-'ɔdɪk(l)] *adj* periodico(a); **~ical** [-'ɔdɪkl] *n* periodico

peripheral [pə'rɪfərəl] *adj* periferico(a) ♦ *n*

(COMPUT) unità f inv periferica

perish ['perɪʃ] vi perire, morire; (decay) deteriorarsi; ~**able** adj deperibile

perjury ['pə:dʒərɪ] n spergiuro

perk [pə:k] (inf) n vantaggio; ~ **up** vi (cheer up) rianimarsi

perm [pə:m] n (for hair) permanente f

permanent ['pə:mənənt] adj permanente

permeate ['pə:mɪeɪt] vi penetrare ♦ vt permeare

permissible [pə'mɪsɪbl] adj permissibile, ammissibile

permission [pə'mɪʃən] n permesso

permissive [pə'mɪsɪv] adj permissivo(a)

permit [n 'pə:mɪt, vb pə'mɪt] n permesso ♦ vt permettere; **to ~ sb to do** permettere a qn di fare

perpendicular [pə:pən'dɪkjulə*] adj perpendicolare ♦ n perpendicolare f

perplex [pə'plɛks] vt lasciare perplesso(a)

persecute ['pə:sɪkju:t] vt perseguitare

persevere [pə:sɪ'vɪə*] vi perseverare

Persian ['pə:ʃən] adj persiano(a) ♦ n (LING) persiano; **the (~) Gulf** n il Golfo Persico

persist [pə'sɪst] vi: **to ~ (in doing)** persistere (nel fare); ostinarsi (a fare); ~**ent** adj persistente; ostinato(a)

person ['pə:sn] n persona; **in ~** di or in persona, personalmente; ~**al** adj personale; individuale; ~**al assistant** n segretaria personale; ~**al column** n ≈ messaggi mpl personali; ~**al computer** n personal computer m inv; ~**ality** [-'nælɪtɪ] n personalità f inv; ~**ally** adv personalmente; **to take sth ~ally** prendere qc come una critica personale; ~**al organizer** n (Filofax ®) Fulltime ®; (electronic) agenda elettronica; ~**al stereo** n Walkman ® m inv

personnel [pə:sə'nɛl] n personale m

perspective [pə'spɛktɪv] n prospettiva

Perspex ® ['pə:spɛks] (BRIT) n tipo di resina termoplastica

perspiration [pə:spɪ'reɪʃən] n traspirazione f, sudore m

persuade [pə'sweɪd] vt: **to ~ sb to do sth** persuadere qn a fare qc

perturb [pə'tə:b] vt turbare

pervert [n 'pə:və:t, vb pə'və:t] n pervertito/a ♦ vt pervertire

pessimism ['pesɪmɪzəm] n pessimismo

pessimist ['pesɪmɪst] n pessimista m/f; ~**ic** [-'mɪstɪk] adj pessimistico(a)

pest [pest] n animale m (or insetto) pestifero; (fig) peste f

pester ['pestə*] vt tormentare, molestare

pet [pet] n animale m domestico ♦ cpd favorito(a) ♦ vt accarezzare; **teacher's ~** favorito/a del maestro

petal ['petl] n petalo

peter ['pi:tə*]: **to ~ out** vi esaurirsi; estinguersi

petite [pə'ti:t] adj piccolo(a) e aggraziato(a)

petition [pə'tɪʃən] n petizione f

petrified ['petrɪfaɪd] adj (fig) morto(a) di paura

petrol ['petrəl] (BRIT) n benzina; **two/four-star ~** ≈ benzina normale/super; ~ **can** n tanica per benzina

petroleum [pə'trəulɪəm] n petrolio

petrol: ~ **pump** (BRIT) n (in car, at garage) pompa di benzina; ~ **station** (BRIT) n stazione f di rifornimento; ~ **tank** (BRIT) n serbatoio della benzina

petticoat ['petɪkəut] n sottana

petty ['petɪ] adj (mean) meschino(a); (unimportant) insignificante; ~ **cash** n piccola cassa; ~ **officer** n sottufficiale m di marina

petulant ['petjulənt] adj irritabile

pew [pju:] n panca (di chiesa)

pewter ['pju:tə*] n peltro

phallic ['fælɪk] adj fallico(a)

phantom ['fæntəm] n fantasma m

pharmaceutical [fɑ:mə'sju:tɪkl] adj farmaceutico(a)

pharmacy ['fɑ:məsɪ] n farmacia

phase [feɪz] n fase f, periodo ♦ vt: **to ~ sth in/out** introdurre/eliminare qc progressivamente

Ph.D. n abbr = **Doctor of Philosophy**

pheasant ['feznt] n fagiano

phenomena [fə'nɔmɪnə] npl of **phenomenon**

phenomenon [fə'nɔmɪnən] (*pl* **phenomena**) *n* fenomeno

Philippines ['fɪlɪpiːnz] *npl*: **the ~** le Filippine

philosophical [fɪlə'sɔfɪkl] *adj* filosofico(a)

philosophy [fɪ'lɔsəfɪ] *n* filosofia

phobia ['fəubjə] *n* fobia

phone [fəun] *n* telefono ♦ *vt* telefonare; **to be on the ~** avere il telefono; (*be calling*) essere al telefono; **~ back** *vt*, *vi* richiamare; **~ up** *vt* telefonare a ♦ *vi* telefonare; **~ book** *n* guida del telefono, elenco telefonico; **~ booth** *n* = **~ box**; **~ box** *n* cabina telefonica; **~ call** *n* telefonata; **~card** *n* scheda telefonica; **~-in** *n* (*BRIT: RADIO, TV*) trasmissione *f* a filo diretto con gli ascoltatori

phonetics [fə'nɛtɪks] *n* fonetica

phoney ['fəunɪ] *adj* falso(a), fasullo(a)

phosphorus ['fɔsfərəs] *n* fosforo

photo ['fəutəu] *n* foto *f inv*

photo... ['fəutəu] *prefix*: **~copier** *n* fotocopiatrice *f*; **~copy** *n* fotocopia ♦ *vt* fotocopiare; **~graph** *n* fotografia ♦ *vt* fotografare; **~grapher** [fə'tɔgrəfə*] *n* fotografo; **~graphy** [fə'tɔgrəfɪ] *n* fotografia

phrase [freɪz] *n* espressione *f*; (*LING*) locuzione *f*; (*MUS*) frase *f* ♦ *vt* esprimere; **~ book** *n* vocabolarietto

physical ['fɪzɪkl] *adj* fisico(a); **~ education** *n* educazione *f* fisica; **~ly** *adv* fisicamente

physician [fɪ'zɪʃən] *n* medico

physicist ['fɪzɪsɪst] *n* fisico

physics ['fɪzɪks] *n* fisica

physiology [fɪzɪ'ɔlədʒɪ] *n* fisiologia

physique [fɪ'ziːk] *n* fisico; costituzione *f*

pianist ['piːənɪst] *n* pianista *m/f*

piano [pɪ'ænəu] *n* pianoforte *m*

piccolo ['pɪkələu] *n* ottavino

pick [pɪk] *n* (*tool: also*: **~-axe**) piccone *m* ♦ *vt* scegliere; (*gather*) cogliere; (*remove*) togliere; (*lock*) far scattare; **take your ~** scelga; **the ~ of** il fior fiore di; **to ~ one's nose** mettersi le dita nel naso; **to ~ one's teeth** pulirsi i denti con lo stuzzicadenti; **to ~ a quarrel** attaccar briga; **~ at** *vt fus*: **to ~ at one's food** piluccare; **~ on** *vt fus*

(*person*) avercela con; **~ out** *vt* scegliere; (*distinguish*) distinguere; **~ up** *vi* (*improve*) migliorarsi ♦ *vt* raccogliere; (*POLICE, RADIO*) prendere; (*collect*) passare a prendere; (*AUT: give lift to*) far salire; (*person: for sexual encounter*) rimorchiare; (*learn*) imparare; **to ~ up speed** acquistare velocità; **to ~ o.s. up** rialzarsi

picket ['pɪkɪt] *n* (*in strike*) scioperante *m/f* che fa parte di un picchetto; picchetto ♦ *vt* picchettare

pickle ['pɪkl] *n* (*also*: **~s**: *as condiment*) sottaceti *mpl*; (*fig: mess*) pasticcio ♦ *vt* mettere sottaceto; mettere in salamoia

pickpocket ['pɪkpɔkɪt] *n* borsaiolo

pickup ['pɪkʌp] *n* (*small truck*) camioncino

picnic ['pɪknɪk] *n* picnic *m inv*

picture ['pɪktʃə*] *n* quadro; (*painting*) pittura; (*photograph*) foto(grafia); (*drawing*) disegno; (*film*) film *m inv* ♦ *vt* raffigurarsi; **~s** (*BRIT*) *npl* (*cinema*): **the ~s** il cinema; **~ book** *n* libro illustrato

picturesque [pɪktʃə'rɛsk] *adj* pittoresco(a)

pie [paɪ] *n* torta; (*of meat*) pasticcio

piece [piːs] *n* pezzo; (*of land*) appezzamento; (*item*): **a ~ of furniture/ advice** un mobile/consiglio ♦ *vt*: **to ~ together** mettere insieme; **to take to ~s** smontare; **~meal** *adv* pezzo a pezzo, a spizzico; **~work** *n* (*lavoro a*) cottimo

pie chart *n* grafico a torta

pier [pɪə*] *n* molo; (*of bridge etc*) pila

pierce [pɪəs] *vt* forare; (*with arrow etc*) trafiggere

piercing ['pɪəsɪŋ] *adj* (*cry*) acuto(a); (*eyes*) penetrante; (*wind*) pungente

pig [pɪg] *n* maiale *m*, porco

pigeon ['pɪdʒən] *n* piccione *m*; **~hole** *n* casella

piggy bank ['pɪgɪ-] *n* salvadanaro

pigheaded ['pɪg'hɛdɪd] *adj* caparbio(a), cocciuto(a)

piglet ['pɪglɪt] *n* porcellino

pigskin ['pɪgskɪn] *n* cinghiale *m*

pigsty ['pɪgstaɪ] *n* porcile *m*

pigtail ['pɪgteɪl] *n* treccina

pike [paɪk] *n* (*fish*) luccio

pilchard ['pɪltʃəd] *n* specie di sardina

pile [paɪl] *n* (*pillar, of books*) pila; (*heap*) mucchio; (*of carpet*) pelo ♦ *vt* (*also:* ~ **up**) ammucchiare ♦ *vi* (*also:* ~ **up**) ammucchiarsi; **to** ~ **into** (*car*) stiparsi *or* ammucchiarsi in

piles [paɪlz] *npl* emorroidi *fpl*

pile-up ['paɪlʌp] *n* (*AUT*) tamponamento a catena

pilfering ['pɪlfərɪŋ] *n* rubacchiare *m*

pilgrim ['pɪlgrɪm] *n* pellegrino/a; ~**age** *n* pellegrinaggio

pill [pɪl] *n* pillola; **the** ~ la pillola

pillage ['pɪlɪdʒ] *vt* saccheggiare

pillar ['pɪlə*] *n* colonna; ~ **box** (*BRIT*) *n* cassetta postale

pillion ['pɪljən] *n*: **to ride** ~ (*on motor cycle*) viaggiare dietro

pillow ['pɪləu] *n* guanciale *m*; ~**case** *n* federa

pilot ['paɪlət] *n* pilota *m/f* ♦ *cpd* (*scheme etc*) pilota *inv* ♦ *vt* pilotare; ~ **light** *n* fiamma pilota

pimp [pɪmp] *n* mezzano

pimple ['pɪmpl] *n* foruncolo

pin [pɪn] *n* spillo; (*TECH*) perno ♦ *vt* attaccare con uno spillo; ~**s and needles** formicolio; **to** ~ **sb down** (*fig*) obbligare qn a pronunziarsi; **to** ~ **sth on sb** (*fig*) addossare la colpa di qc a qn

pinafore ['pɪnəfɔ:*] *n* (*also:* ~ **dress**) grembiule *m* (senza maniche)

pinball ['pɪnbɔ:l] *n* flipper *m inv*

pincers ['pɪnsəz] *npl* pinzette *fpl*

pinch [pɪntʃ] *n* pizzicotto, pizzico ♦ *vt* pizzicare; (*inf: steal*) grattare; **at a** ~ in caso di bisogno

pincushion ['pɪnkuʃən] *n* puntaspilli *m inv*

pine [paɪn] *n* (*also:* ~ **tree**) pino ♦ *vi*: **to** ~ **for** struggersi dal desiderio di; ~ **away** *vi* languire

pineapple ['paɪnæpl] *n* ananas *m inv*

ping [pɪŋ] *n* (*noise*) tintinnio; ~**-pong** ® *n* ping-pong ® *m*

pink [pɪŋk] *adj* rosa *inv* ♦ *n* (*colour*) rosa *inv*; (*BOT*) garofano

PIN (number) [pɪn-] *n abbr* codice *m* segreto

pinpoint ['pɪnpɔɪnt] *vt* indicare con precisione

pint [paɪnt] *n* pinta (*BRIT* = 0.57l; *US* = 0.47l); (*BRIT: inf*) ≈ birra da mezzo

pioneer [paɪə'nɪə*] *n* pioniere/a

pious ['paɪəs] *adj* pio(a)

pip [pɪp] *n* (*seed*) seme *m*; (*BRIT: time signal on radio*) segnale *m* orario

pipe [paɪp] *n* tubo; (*for smoking*) pipa ♦ *vt* portare per mezzo di tubazione; ~**s** *npl* (*also:* **bag**~**s**) cornamusa (scozzese); ~ **cleaner** *n* scovolino; ~ **dream** *n* vana speranza; ~**line** *n* conduttura; (*for oil*) oleodotto; ~**r** *n* piffero; suonatore/trice di cornamusa

piping ['paɪpɪŋ] *adv*: ~ **hot** caldo bollente

pique [pi:k] *n* picca

pirate ['paɪərət] *n* pirata *m* ♦ *vt* riprodurre abusivamente

Pisces ['paɪsi:z] *n* Pesci *mpl*

piss [pɪs] (*inf*) *vi* pisciare; ~**ed** (*inf*) *adj* (*drunk*) ubriaco(a) fradicio(a)

pistol ['pɪstl] *n* pistola

piston ['pɪstən] *n* pistone *m*

pit [pɪt] *n* buca, fossa; (*also:* **coal** ~) miniera; (*quarry*) cava ♦ *vt*: **to** ~ **sb against sb** opporre qn a qn; ~**s** *npl* (*AUT*) box *m*

pitch [pɪtʃ] *n* (*BRIT: SPORT*) campo; (*MUS*) tono; (*tar*) pece *f*; (*fig*) grado, punto ♦ *vt* (*throw*) lanciare ♦ *vi* (*fall*) cascare; **to** ~ **a tent** piantare una tenda; ~**ed battle** *n* battaglia campale

pitfall ['pɪtfɔ:l] *n* trappola

pith [pɪθ] *n* (*of plant*) midollo; (*of orange*) parte *f* interna della scorza; (*fig*) essenza, succo; vigore *m*

pithy ['pɪθɪ] *adj* conciso(a); vigoroso(a)

pitiful ['pɪtɪful] *adj* (*touching*) pietoso(a)

pitiless ['pɪtɪlɪs] *adj* spietato(a)

pittance ['pɪtns] *n* miseria, magro salario

pity ['pɪtɪ] *n* pietà ♦ *vt* aver pietà di; **what a** ~**!** che peccato!

pivot ['pɪvət] *n* perno

pizza ['pi:tsə] *n* pizza

placard ['plækɑ:d] *n* affisso

placate [plə'keɪt] *vt* placare, calmare

place [pleɪs] n posto, luogo; (proper position, rank, seat) posto; (house) casa, alloggio; (home): **at/to his ~** a casa sua ♦ vt (object) posare, mettere; (identify) riconoscere; individuare; **to take ~** aver luogo; succedere; **to change ~s with sb** scambiare il posto con qn; **out of ~** (not suitable) inopportuno(a); **in the first ~** in primo luogo; **to ~ an order** dare un'ordinazione; **to be ~d** (in race, exam) classificarsi

placid ['plæsɪd] adj placido(a), calmo(a)

plagiarism ['pleɪdʒərɪzəm] n plagio

plague [pleɪg] n peste f ♦ vt tormentare

plaice [pleɪs] n inv pianuzza

plaid [plæd] n plaid m inv

plain [pleɪn] adj (clear) chiaro(a), palese; (simple) semplice; (frank) franco(a), aperto(a); (not handsome) bruttino(a); (without seasoning etc) scondito(a); naturale; (in one colour) tinta unita inv ♦ adv francamente, chiaramente ♦ n pianura; **~ chocolate** npl cioccolato fondente; **~ clothes** npl: **in ~ clothes** (police) in borghese; **~ly** adv chiaramente; (frankly) francamente

plaintiff ['pleɪntɪf] n attore/trice

plaintive ['pleɪntɪv] adj (cry, voice) dolente, lamentoso(a)

plait [plæt] n treccia

plan [plæn] n pianta; (scheme) progetto, piano ♦ vt (think in advance) progettare; (prepare) organizzare ♦ vi far piani or progetti; **to ~ to do** progettare di fare

plane [pleɪn] n (AVIAT) aereo; (tree) platano; (tool) pialla; (ART, MATH etc) piano ♦ adj piano(a), piatto(a) ♦ vt (with tool) piallare

planet ['plænɪt] n pianeta m

plank [plæŋk] n tavola, asse f

planner ['plænə*] n pianificatore/trice

planning ['plænɪŋ] n progettazione f; **family ~** pianificazione f delle nascite; **~ permission** n permesso di costruzione

plant [plɑːnt] n pianta; (machinery) impianto; (factory) fabbrica ♦ vt piantare; (bomb) mettere

plantation [plæn'teɪʃən] n piantagione f

plaque [plæk] n placca

plaster ['plɑːstə*] n intonaco; (also: ~ of Paris) gesso; (BRIT: also: sticking ~) cerotto ♦ vt intonacare; ingessare; (cover): **to ~ with** coprire di; **~ed** (inf) adj ubriaco(a) fradicio(a)

plastic ['plæstɪk] n plastica ♦ adj (made of ~) di or in plastica; **~ bag** n sacchetto di plastica

Plasticine ® ['plæstɪsiːn] n plastilina ®

plastic surgery n chirurgia plastica

plate [pleɪt] n (dish) piatto; (in book) tavola; (dental ~) dentiera; **gold/silver ~** vasellame m d'oro/d'argento

plateau ['plætəu] (pl ~s or ~x) n altipiano

plateaux ['plætəuz] npl of **plateau**

plate glass n vetro piano

platform ['plætfɔːm] n (stage, at meeting) palco; (RAIL) marciapiede m; (BRIT: of bus) piattaforma

platinum ['plætɪnəm] n platino

platitude ['plætɪtjuːd] n luogo comune

platoon [plə'tuːn] n plotone m

platter ['plætə*] n piatto

plausible ['plɔːzɪbl] adj plausibile, credibile; (person) convincente

play [pleɪ] n gioco; (THEATRE) commedia ♦ vt (game) giocare a; (team, opponent) giocare contro; (instrument, piece of music) suonare; (record, tape) ascoltare; (role, part) interpretare ♦ vi giocare; suonare; recitare; **to ~ safe** giocare sul sicuro; **~ down** vt minimizzare; **~ up** vi (cause trouble) fare i capricci; **~boy** n playboy m inv; **~er** n giocatore/trice; (THEATRE) attore/trice; (MUS) musicista m/f; **~ful** adj gioioso(a); **~ground** n (in school) cortile m per la ricreazione; (in park) parco m giochi inv; **~group** n giardino d'infanzia; **~ing card** n carta da gioco; **~ing field** n campo sportivo; **~mate** n compagno/a di gioco; **~-off** n (SPORT) bella; **~pen** n box m inv; **~thing** n giocattolo; **~time** n (SCOL) ricreazione f; **~wright** n drammaturgo/a

plc abbr (= public limited company) società per azioni a responsabilità limitata quotata in borsa

plea [pli:] n (*request*) preghiera, domanda; (*LAW*) (argomento di difesa); ~ **bargaining** n (*LAW*) patteggiamento (della pena)

plead [pli:d] vt patrocinare; (*give as excuse*) addurre a pretesto ♦ vi (*LAW*) perorare la causa; (*beg*): **to ~ with sb** implorare qn

pleasant ['plɛznt] adj piacevole, gradevole; **~ries** npl (*polite remarks*): **to exchange ~ries** scambiarsi i convenevoli

please [pli:z] excl per piacere!, per favore!; (*acceptance*): **yes, ~** sì, grazie ♦ vt piacere a ♦ vi piacere; (*think fit*): **do as you ~** faccia come le pare; **~ yourself!** come ti (*or* le) pare!; ~**d** adj: ~**d (with)** contento(a) (di); ~**d to meet you!** piacere!; **pleasing** adj piacevole, che fa piacere

pleasure ['plɛʒə*] n piacere m; **"it's a ~"** "prego"

pleat [pli:t] n piega

pledge [plɛdʒ] n pegno; (*promise*) promessa ♦ vt impegnare; promettere

plentiful ['plɛntɪful] adj abbondante, copioso(a)

plenty ['plɛntɪ] n: ~ **of** tanto(a), molto(a); un'abbondanza di

pleurisy ['pluərɪsɪ] n pleurite f

pliable ['plaɪəbl] adj flessibile; (*fig: person*) malleabile

pliant ['plaɪənt] adj = **pliable**

pliers ['plaɪəz] npl pinza

plight [plaɪt] n situazione f critica

plimsolls ['plɪmsəlz] (*BRIT*) npl scarpe fpl da tennis

plinth [plɪnθ] n plinto; piedistallo

plod [plɔd] vi camminare a stento; (*fig*) sgobbare

plonk [plɔŋk] (*inf*) n (*BRIT: wine*) vino da poco ♦ vt: **to ~ sth down** buttare giù qc bruscamente

plot [plɔt] n congiura, cospirazione f; (*of story, play*) trama; (*of land*) lotto ♦ vt (*mark out*) fare la pianta di; rilevare; (*: diagram etc*) tracciare; (*conspire*) congiurare, cospirare ♦ vi congiurare

plough [plau] (*US* **plow**) n aratro ♦ vt (*earth*) arare; **to ~ money into** (*company etc*) investire danaro in; ~ **through** vt fus (*snow etc*) procedere a fatica in; ~**man's lunch** (*BRIT*) n pasto a base di pane, formaggio e birra

ploy [plɔɪ] n stratagemma m

pluck [plʌk] vt (*fruit*) cogliere; (*musical instrument*) pizzicare; (*bird*) spennare; (*hairs*) togliere ♦ n coraggio, fegato; **to ~ up courage** farsi coraggio

plug [plʌg] n tappo; (*ELEC*) spina; (*AUT: also:* **spark(ing) ~**) candela ♦ vt (*hole*) tappare; (*inf: advertise*) spingere; ~ **in** vt (*ELEC*) attaccare a una presa

plum [plʌm] n (*fruit*) susina

plumb [plʌm] vt: **to ~ the depths** (*fig*) toccare il fondo

plumber ['plʌmə*] n idraulico

plumbing ['plʌmɪŋ] n (*trade*) lavoro di idraulico; (*piping*) tubature fpl

plummet ['plʌmɪt] vi: **to ~ (down)** cadere a piombo

plump [plʌmp] adj grassoccio(a) ♦ vi: **to ~ for** (*inf: choose*) decidersi per; ~ **up** vt (*cushion etc*) sprimacciare

plunder ['plʌndə*] n saccheggio ♦ vt saccheggiare

plunge [plʌndʒ] n tuffo; (*fig*) caduta ♦ vt immergere ♦ vi (*fall*) cadere, precipitare; (*dive*) tuffarsi; **to take the ~** saltare il fosso; **plunging** adj (*neckline*) profondo(a)

pluperfect [plu:'pə:fɪkt] n piuccheperfetto

plural ['pluərl] adj plurale ♦ n plurale m

plus [plʌs] n (*also:* ~ **sign**) segno più ♦ prep più; **ten/twenty ~** piu di dieci/venti

plush [plʌʃ] adj lussuoso(a)

ply [plaɪ] vt (*a trade*) esercitare ♦ vi (*ship*) fare il servizio ♦ n (*of wool, rope*) capo; **to ~ sb with drink** dare di bere continuamente a qn; ~**wood** n legno compensato

P.M. n abbr = **prime minister**

p.m. adv abbr (= *post meridiem*) del pomeriggio

pneumatic drill [nju:'mætɪk-] n martello pneumatico

pneumonia [nju:'məunɪə] n polmonite f

poach [pəutʃ] vt (*cook: egg*) affogare; (*: fish*) cuocere in bianco; (*steal*) cacciare (*or* pescare) di frodo ♦ *vi* fare il bracconiere; **~er** *n* bracconiere *m*

P.O. Box *n abbr* = **Post Office Box**

pocket ['pɔkɪt] *n* tasca ♦ *vt* intascare; **to be out of ~** (*BRIT*) rimetterci; **~book** (*US*) *n* (*wallet*) portafoglie; **~ knife** *n* temperino; **~ money** *n* paghetta, settimana

pod [pɔd] *n* guscio

podgy ['pɔdʒɪ] *adj* grassoccio(a)

podiatrist [pɔ'diːətrɪst] (*US*) *n* callista *m/f*, pedicure *m/f*

poem ['pəuɪm] *n* poesia

poet ['pəuɪt] *n* poeta/essa; **~ic** [-'ɛtɪk] *adj* poetico(a); **~ry** *n* poesia

poignant ['pɔɪnjənt] *adj* struggente

point [pɔɪnt] *n* (*gen*) punto; (*tip: of needle etc*) punta; (*in time*) punto, momento; (*SCOL*) voto; (*main idea, important part*) nocciolo; (*ELEC*) presa (di corrente); (*also*: **decimal ~**): **2 ~ 3 (2.3)** 2 virgola 3 (2,3) ♦ *vt* (*show*) indicare; (*gun etc*): **to ~ sth at** puntare qc contro ♦ *vi*: **to ~ at** mostrare a dito; **~s** *npl* (*AUT*) puntine *fpl*; (*RAIL*) scambio; **to be on the ~ of doing sth** essere sul punto di *or* stare per fare qc; **to make a ~** fare un'osservazione; **to get/miss the ~** capire/non capire; **to come to the ~** venire al fatto; **there's no ~ (in doing)** è inutile (fare); **~ out** *vt* far notare; **~ to** *vt fus* indicare; (*fig*) dimostrare; **~-blank** *adv* (*also*: **at ~-blank range**) a bruciapelo; (*fig*) categoricamente; **~ed** *adj* (*shape*) aguzzo(a), appuntito(a); (*remark*) specifico(a); **~edly** *adv* in maniera inequivocabile; **~er** *n* (*needle*) lancetta; (*fig*) indicazione *f*, consiglio; **~less** *adj* inutile, vano(a); **~ of view** *n* punto di vista

poise [pɔɪz] *n* (*composure*) portamento; **~d** *adj*: **to be ~d to do** tenersi pronto(a) a fare

poison ['pɔɪzn] *n* veleno ♦ *vt* avvelenare; **~ing** *n* avvelenamento; **~ous** *adj* velenoso(a)

poke [pəuk] *vt* (*fire*) attizzare; (*jab with finger, stick etc*) punzecchiare; (*put*): **to ~ sth in(to)** spingere qc dentro; **~ about** *vi* frugare

poker ['pəukə*] *n* attizzatoio; (*CARDS*) poker *m*

poky ['pəukɪ] *adj* piccolo(a) e stretto(a)

Poland ['pəulənd] *n* Polonia

polar ['pəulə*] *adj* polare; **~ bear** *n* orso bianco

Pole [pəul] *n* polacco/a

pole [pəul] *n* (*of wood*) palo; (*ELEC, GEO*) polo; **~ bean** (*US*) *n* (*runner bean*) fagiolino; **~ vault** *n* salto con l'asta

police [pə'liːs] *n* polizia ♦ *vt* mantenere l'ordine in; **~ car** *n* macchina della polizia; **~man** (*irreg*) *n* poliziotto, agente *m* di polizia; **~ station** *n* posto di polizia; **~woman** (*irreg*) *n* donna *f* poliziotto *inv*

policy ['pɔlɪsɪ] *n* politica; (*also*: **insurance ~**) polizza (d'assicurazione)

polio ['pəulɪəu] *n* polio *f*

Polish ['pəulɪʃ] *adj* polacco(a) ♦ *n* (*LING*) polacco

polish ['pɔlɪʃ] *n* (*for shoes*) lucido; (*for floor*) cera; (*for nails*) smalto; (*shine*) lucentezza, lustro; (*fig: refinement*) raffinatezza ♦ *vt* lucidare; (*fig: improve*) raffinare; **~ off** *vt* (*food*) mangiarsi; **~ed** *adj* (*fig*) raffinato(a)

polite [pə'laɪt] *adj* cortese; **~ness** *n* cortesia

political [pə'lɪtɪkl] *adj* politico(a); **~ly** *adv* politicamente; **~ly correct** politicamente corretto(a)

politician [pɔlɪ'tɪʃən] *n* politico

politics ['pɔlɪtɪks] *n* politica ♦ *npl* (*views, policies*) idee *fpl* politiche

poll [pəul] *n* scrutinio; (*votes cast*) voti *mpl*; (*also*: **opinion ~**) sondaggio (d'opinioni) ♦ *vt* ottenere

pollen ['pɔlən] *n* polline *m*

polling day ['pəulɪŋ-] (*BRIT*) *n* giorno delle elezioni

polling station ['pəulɪŋ-] (*BRIT*) *n* sezione *f* elettorale

pollute [pə'luːt] *vt* inquinare

pollution [pə'luːʃən] *n* inquinamento

polo ['pəuləu] *n* polo; **~-necked** *adj* a collo alto risvoltato; **~ shirt** *n* polo *f inv*

polyester [pɔlɪ'ɛstə*] *n* poliestere *m*

polystyrene [pɔlɪ'staɪriːn] *n* polistirolo

polytechnic [pɔlɪ'tɛknɪk] *n* (*college*) istituto

superiore ad indirizzo tecnologico

polythene ['pɔlɪθiːn] n politene m; ~ **bag** n sacco di plastica

pomegranate ['pɔmɪgrænɪt] n melagrana

pomp [pɔmp] n pompa, fasto

pompom ['pɔmpɔm] n pompon m inv

pompon ['pɔmpɔn] n = **pompom**

pompous ['pɔmpəs] adj pomposo(a)

pond [pɔnd] n pozza; stagno

ponder ['pɔndə*] vt ponderare, riflettere su; **~ous** adj ponderoso(a), pesante

pong [pɔŋ] (BRIT: inf) n puzzo

pony ['pəʊnɪ] n pony m inv; **~tail** n coda di cavallo; ~ **trekking** (BRIT) n escursione f a cavallo

poodle ['puːdl] n barboncino, barbone m

pool [puːl] n (puddle) pozza; (pond) stagno; (also: **swimming** ~) piscina; (fig: of light) cerchio; (billiards) specie di biliardo a buca ♦ vt mettere in comune; **~s** npl (football ~s) ≈ totocalcio; **typing** ~ servizio comune di dattilografia

poor [pʊə*] adj povero(a); (mediocre) mediocre, cattivo(a) ♦ npl: **the** ~ i poveri; ~ **in** povero(a) di; **~ly** adv poveramente, male ♦ adj indisposto(a), malato(a)

pop [pɔp] n (noise) schiocco; (MUS) musica pop; (drink) bibita gasata; (US: inf: father) babbo ♦ vt (put) mettere (in fretta) ♦ vi scoppiare; (cork) schioccare; ~ **in** vi passare; ~ **out** vi fare un salto fuori; ~ **up** vi apparire, sorgere; **~corn** n pop-corn m

pope [pəʊp] n papa m

poplar ['pɔplə*] n pioppo

popper ['pɔpə*] n bottone m a pressione

poppy ['pɔpɪ] n papavero

Popsicle ® ['pɔpsɪkl] (US) n (ice lolly) ghiacciolo

populace ['pɔpjʊlɪs] n popolino

popular ['pɔpjʊlə*] adj popolare; (fashionable) in voga; **~ity** [-'lærɪtɪ] n popolarità

population [pɔpjʊ'leɪʃən] n popolazione f

porcelain ['pɔːslɪn] n porcellana

porch [pɔːtʃ] n veranda

porcupine ['pɔːkjʊpaɪn] n porcospino

pore [pɔː*] n poro ♦ vi: **to** ~ **over** essere immerso(a) in

pork [pɔːk] n carne f di maiale

pornographic [pɔːnə'græfɪk] adj pornografico(a)

pornography [pɔː'nɔgrəfɪ] n pornografia

porpoise ['pɔːpəs] n focena

porridge ['pɔrɪdʒ] n porridge m

port [pɔːt] n (gen, wine) porto; (NAUT: left side) babordo; ~ **of call** (porto di) scalo

portable ['pɔːtəbl] adj portatile

porter ['pɔːtə*] n (for luggage) facchino, portabagagli m inv; (doorkeeper) portiere m, portinaio

portfolio [pɔːt'fəʊlɪəʊ] n (case) cartella; (POL, FINANCE) portafoglio; (of artist) raccolta dei propri lavori

porthole ['pɔːthəʊl] n oblò m inv

portion ['pɔːʃən] n porzione f

portrait ['pɔːtreɪt] n ritratto

portray [pɔː'treɪ] vt fare il ritratto di; (character on stage) rappresentare; (in writing) ritrarre

Portugal ['pɔːtjʊgl] n Portogallo

Portuguese [pɔːtjʊ'giːz] adj portoghese ♦ n inv portoghese m/f; (LING) portoghese m

pose [pəʊz] n posa ♦ vi posare; (pretend): **to** ~ **as** atteggiarsi a, posare a ♦ vt porre

posh [pɔʃ] (inf) adj elegante; (family) per bene

position [pə'zɪʃən] n posizione f; (job) posto ♦ vt sistemare

positive ['pɔzɪtɪv] adj positivo(a); (certain) sicuro(a), certo(a); (definite) preciso(a); definitivo(a)

posse ['pɔsɪ] (US) n drappello

possess [pə'zes] vt possedere; **~ion** [pə'zeʃən] n possesso; **~ions** npl (belongings) beni mpl; **~ive** adj possessivo(a)

possibility [pɔsɪ'bɪlɪtɪ] n possibilità f inv

possible ['pɔsɪbl] adj possibile; **as big as** ~ il più grande possibile

possibly ['pɔsɪblɪ] adv (perhaps) forse; **if you** ~ **can** se te lo è possibile; **I cannot** ~ **come** proprio non posso venire

post [pəʊst] n (BRIT) posta; (: collection) levata; (job, situation) posto; (MIL) postazione f; (*pole*) palo ♦ vt (*BRIT: send by post*) impostare; (: *appoint*): **to ~ to** assegnare a; **~age** n affrancatura; **~age stamp** n francobollo; **~al order** n vaglia m inv postale; **~box** (*BRIT*) n cassetta postale; **~card** n cartolina; **~ code** (*BRIT*) n codice m (di avviamento) postale

poster ['pəustə*] n manifesto, affisso

poste restante [pəust'restã:nt] (*BRIT*) n fermo posta m

postgraduate ['pəust'grædjuət] n laureato/a che continua gli studi

posthumous ['pɔstjuməs] adj postumo(a)

postman ['pəustmən] (*irreg*) n postino

postmark ['pəustmɑ:k] n bollo or timbro postale

post-mortem [-'mɔ:təm] n autopsia

post office n (*building*) ufficio postale; (*organization*): **the Post Office** ≈ le Poste e Telecomunicazioni; **Post Office Box** n casella postale

postpone [pəs'pəun] vt rinviare

postscript ['pəustskrɪpt] n poscritto

posture ['pɔstʃə*] n portamento; (*pose*) posa, atteggiamento

postwar ['pəust'wɔ:*] adj del dopoguerra

posy ['pəuzɪ] n mazzetto di fiori

pot [pɔt] n (*for cooking*) pentola, casseruola; (*tea~*) teiera; (*coffee~*) caffettiera; (*for plants, jam*) vaso; (*inf: marijuana*) erba ♦ vt (*plant*) piantare in vaso; **a ~ of tea for two** tè per due; **to go to ~** (*inf: work, performance*) andare in malora

potato [pə'teɪtəu] (*pl ~es*) n patata; **~ peeler** n sbucciapatate m inv

potent ['pəutnt] adj potente, forte

potential [pə'tenʃl] adj potenziale ♦ n possibilità fpl

pothole ['pɔthəul] n (*in road*) buca; (*BRIT: underground*) caverna; **potholing** (*BRIT*) n: **to go potholing** fare speleologia

potluck [pɔt'lʌk] n: **to take ~** tentare la sorte

potted ['pɔtɪd] adj (*food*) in conserva; (*plant*) in vaso; (*account etc*) condensato(a)

potter ['pɔtə*] n vasaio ♦ vi: **to ~ around, ~ about** (*BRIT*) lavoracchiare; **~y** n ceramiche

fpl; (*factory*) fabbrica di ceramiche

potty ['pɔtɪ] adj (*inf: mad*) tocco(a) ♦ n (*child's*) vasino

pouch [pautʃ] n borsa; (*ZOOL*) marsupio

poultry ['pəultrɪ] n pollame m

pounce [pauns] vi: **to ~ (on)** piombare (su)

pound [paund] n (*weight*) libbra; (*money*) (*lira*) sterlina ♦ vt (*beat*) battere; (*crush*) pestare, polverizzare ♦ vi (*beat*) battere, martellare; **~ sterling** n sterlina (inglese)

pour [pɔ:*] vt versare ♦ vi riversarsi; (*rain*) piovere a dirotto; **~ away** vt vuotare; **~ in** vi affluire in gran quantità; **~ off** vt vuotare; **~ out** vi (*people*) uscire a fiumi ♦ vt vuotare; versare; (*fig*) sfogare; **~ing** adj: **~ing rain** pioggia torrenziale

pout [paut] vi sporgere le labbra; fare il broncio

poverty ['pɔvətɪ] n povertà, miseria; **~-stricken** adj molto povero(a), misero(a)

powder ['paudə*] n polvere f ♦ vt: **to ~ one's face** incipriarsi il viso; **~ compact** n portacipria m inv; **~ed milk** n latte m in polvere; **~ room** n toilette f inv (per signore)

power ['pauə*] n (*strength*) potenza, forza; (*ability, POL: of party, leader*) potere m; (*ELEC*) corrente f; **to be in ~** (*POL etc*) essere al potere; **~ cut** (*BRIT*) n interruzione f or mancanza di corrente; **~ed** adj: **~ed by** azionato(a) da; **~ failure** n interruzione f della corrente elettrica; **~ful** adj potente, forte; **~less** adj impotente; **~less to do** impossibilitato(a) a fare; **~ point** (*BRIT*) n presa di corrente; **~ station** n centrale f elettrica

p.p. abbr (= *per procurationem*): **~ J. Smith** per J. Smith; (= *pages*) p.p.

PR abbr = **public relations**

practicable ['præktɪkəbl] adj (*scheme*) praticabile

practical ['præktɪkl] adj pratico(a); **~ity** [-'kælɪtɪ] (*no pl*) n (*of situation etc*) lato pratico; **~ joke** n beffa; **~ly** adv praticamente

practice ['præktɪs] n pratica; (*of profession*) esercizio; (*at football etc*) allenamento;

(*business*) gabinetto; clientela ♦ *vt, vi* (*US*)
= **practise; in ~** (*in reality*) in pratica; **out
of ~** fuori esercizio

practise ['præktıs] (*US* **practice**) *vt* (*work at*:
piano, one's backhand etc) esercitarsi a;
(*train for*: *skiing, running etc*) allenarsi a; (*a
sport, religion*) praticare; (*method*) usare;
(*profession*) esercitare ♦ *vi* esercitarsi; (*train*)
allenarsi; (*lawyer, doctor*) esercitare

practising *adj* (*Christian etc*) praticante;
(*lawyer*) che esercita la professione

practitioner [præk'tıʃənə*] *n* professionista
m/f

pragmatic [præg'mætık] *adj* pragmatico(a)

prairie ['prɛərı] *n* prateria

praise [preız] *n* elogio, lode *f* ♦ *vt* elogiare,
lodare; **~worthy** *adj* lodevole

pram [præm] (*BRIT*) *n* carrozzina

prank [præŋk] *n* burla

prawn [prɔːn] *n* gamberetto

pray [preı] *vi* pregare

prayer [prɛə*] *n* preghiera

preach [priːtʃ] *vt, vi* predicare

precarious [prı'kɛərıəs] *adj* precario(a)

precaution [prı'kɔːʃən] *n* precauzione *f*

precede [prı'siːd] *vt* precedere

precedent ['presıdənt] *n* precedente *m*

precept ['priːsept] *n* precetto

precinct ['priːsıŋkt] *n* (*US*) circoscrizione *f*;
~s *npl* (*of building*) zona recintata;
pedestrian ~ (*BRIT*) zona pedonale;
shopping ~ (*BRIT*) centro commerciale
(chiuso al traffico)

precious ['preʃəs] *adj* prezioso(a)

precipitate [prı'sıpıteıt] *vt* precipitare

precise [prı'saıs] *adj* preciso(a); **~ly** *adv*
precisamente

precocious [prı'kəuʃəs] *adj* precoce

precondition [priːkən'dıʃən] *n* condizione *f*
necessaria

predecessor ['priːdısesə*] *n* predecessore/a

predicament [prı'dıkəmənt] *n* situazione *f*
difficile

predict [prı'dıkt] *vt* predire; **~able** *adj*
prevedibile

predominantly [prı'dɔmınəntlı] *adv* in
maggior parte; soprattutto

predominate [prı'dɔmıneıt] *vi*
predominare

pre-empt [priː'empt] *vt* pregiudicare

preen [priːn] *vt*: **to ~ itself** (*bird*) lisciarsi le
penne; **to ~ o.s.** agghindarsi

prefab ['priːfæb] *n* casa prefabbricata

preface ['prefəs] *n* prefazione *f*

prefect ['priːfekt] *n* (*BRIT*: *in school*)
studente/essa con funzioni disciplinari;
(*French etc, Admin*) prefetto

prefer [prı'fəː*] *vt* preferire; **to ~ doing** *or* **to
do** preferire fare; **~ably** ['prefrəblı] *adv*
preferibilmente; **~ence** ['prefrəns] *n*
preferenza; **~ential** [prefə'renʃəl] *adj*
preferenziale

prefix ['priːfıks] *n* prefisso

pregnancy ['pregnənsı] *n* gravidanza

pregnant ['pregnənt] *adj* incinta *af*

prehistoric ['priːhıs'tɔrık] *adj* preistorico(a)

prejudice ['predʒudıs] *n* pregiudizio; (*harm*)
torto, danno; **~d** *adj*: **~d (against)**
prevenuto(a) (contro); **~d (in favour of)**
ben disposto(a) (verso)

preliminary [prı'lımınərı] *adj* preliminare

premarital ['priː'mærıtl] *adj*
prematrimoniale

premature ['premətʃuə*] *adj* prematuro(a)

premenstrual syndrome
[priː'menstruəl-] *n* (*MED*) sindrome *f*
premestruale

premier ['premıə*] *adj* primo(a) ♦ *n* (*POL*)
primo ministro

première ['premıɛə*] *n* prima

premise ['premıs] *n* premessa; **~s** *npl* (*of
business, institution*) locale *m*; **on the ~s** sul
posto

premium ['priːmıəm] *n* premio; **to be at a
~** essere ricercatissimo; **~ bond** (*BRIT*) *n*
obbligazione *f* a premio

premonition [premə'nıʃən] *n* premonizione
f

preoccupied [priː'ɔkjupaıd] *adj*
preoccupato(a)

prep [prep] *n* (*SCOL*: *study*) studio

prepaid [priː'peıd] *adj* pagato(a) in anticipo

preparation [prepə'reıʃən] *n* preparazione *f*;
~s *npl* (*for trip, war*) preparativi *mpl*

preparatory [prɪ'pærətərɪ] *adj*
preparatorio(a); **~ school** *n* scuola
elementare privata
prepare [prɪ'peə*] *vt* preparare ♦ *vi*: **to ~
for** prepararsi a; **~d to** pronto(a) a
preposition [prepə'zɪʃən] *n* preposizione *f*
preposterous [prɪ'pɒstərəs] *adj* assurdo(a)
prep school *n* = **preparatory school**
prerequisite [priː'rekwɪzɪt] *n* requisito
indispensabile
prescribe [prɪ'skraɪb] *vt* (MED) prescrivere
prescription [prɪ'skrɪpʃən] *n* prescrizione *f*;
(MED) ricetta
presence ['prezns] *n* presenza; **~ of mind**
presenza di spirito
present [*adj, n* 'preznt, *vb* prɪ'zent] *adj*
presente; (*wife, residence, job*) attuale ♦ *n*
(*actuality*): **the ~** il presente; (*gift*) regalo
♦ *vt* presentare; (*give*): **to ~ sb with sth**
offrire qc a qn; **to give sb a ~** fare un
regalo a qn; **at ~** al momento; **~ation**
[-'teɪʃən] *n* presentazione *f*; (*ceremony*)
consegna ufficiale; **~-day** *adj* attuale,
d'oggiorno; **~er** *n* (RADIO, TV)
presentatore/trice; **~ly** *adv* (*soon*) fra poco,
presto; (*at present*) al momento
preservative [prɪ'zɜːvətɪv] *n* conservante *m*
preserve [prɪ'zɜːv] *vt* (*keep safe*) preservare,
proteggere; (*maintain*) conservare; (*food*)
mettere in conserva ♦ *n* (*often pl: jam*)
marmellata; (: *fruit*) frutta sciroppata
preside [prɪ'zaɪd] *vi*: **to ~ (over)** presiedere
(a)
president ['prezɪdənt] *n* presidente *m*; **~ial**
[-'denʃl] *adj* presidenziale
press [pres] *n* (*newspapers etc*): **the P~** la
stampa; (*tool, machine*) pressa; (*for wine*)
torchio ♦ *vt* (*push*) premere, pigiare;
(*squeeze*) spremere; (: *hand*) stringere;
(*clothes: iron*) stirare; (*pursue*) incalzare;
(*insist*): **to ~ sth on sb** far accettare qc da
qn ♦ *vi* premere; accalcare; **we are ~ed
for time** ci manca il tempo; **to ~ for sth**
insistere per avere qc; **to ~ on** *vi* continuare;
~ conference *n* conferenza *f* stampa *inv*;
~ing *adj* urgente; **~ stud** (BRIT) *n* bottone
m a pressione; **~-up** (BRIT) *n* flessione *f*

sulle braccia
pressure ['preʃə*] *n* pressione *f*; **to put ~
on sb (to do)** mettere qn sotto pressione
(affinché faccia); **~ cooker** *n* pentola a
pressione; **~ gauge** *n* manometro; **~
group** *n* gruppo di pressione
prestige [pres'tiːʒ] *n* prestigio
presumably [prɪ'zjuːməblɪ] *adv*
presumibilmente
presume [prɪ'zjuːm] *vt* supporre
presumption [prɪ'zʌmpʃən] *n* presunzione
f
presumptuous [prɪ'zʌmpʃəs] *adj*
presuntuoso(a)
pretence [prɪ'tens] (US **pretense**) *n* (*claim*)
pretesa; **to make a ~ of doing** far finta di
fare; **under false ~s** con l'inganno
pretend [prɪ'tend] *vt* (*feign*) fingere ♦ *vi* far
finta; **to ~ to do** far finta di fare
pretense [prɪ'tens] (US) *n* = **pretence**
pretentious [prɪ'tenʃəs] *adj* pretenzioso(a)
pretext ['priːtekst] *n* pretesto
pretty ['prɪtɪ] *adj* grazioso(a), carino(a)
♦ *adv* abbastanza, assai
prevail [prɪ'veɪl] *vi* (*win, be usual*) prevalere;
(*persuade*): **to ~ (up)on sb to do**
persuadere qn a fare; **~ing** *adj* dominante
prevalent ['prevələnt] *adj* (*belief*)
predominante; (*customs*) diffuso(a);
(*fashion*) corrente; (*disease*) comune
prevent [prɪ'vent] *vt*: **to ~ sb from doing**
impedire a qn di fare; **to ~ sth from
happening** impedire che qc succeda;
~ative *adj* = **~ive**; **~ion** [-'venʃən] *n*
prevenzione *f*; **~ive** *adj* preventivo(a)
preview ['priːvjuː] *n* (*of film*) anteprima
previous ['priːvɪəs] *adj* precedente;
anteriore; **~ly** *adv* prima
prewar ['priː'wɔː*] *adj* anteguerra *inv*
prey [preɪ] *n* preda ♦ *vi*: **to ~ on** far preda
di; **it was ~ing on his mind** lo stava
ossessionando
price [praɪs] *n* prezzo ♦ *vt* (*goods*) fissare il
prezzo di; valutare; **~less** *adj*
inapprezzabile; **~ list** *n* listino (dei) prezzi
prick [prɪk] *n* puntura ♦ *vt* pungere; **to ~ up
one's ears** drizzare gli orecchi

prickle ['prɪkl] n (of plant) spina; (sensation) pizzicore m

prickly ['prɪklɪ] adj spinoso(a); ~ **heat** n sudamina

pride [praɪd] n orgoglio; superbia ♦ vt: **to ~ o.s. on** essere orgoglioso(a) di; vantarsi di

priest [priːst] n prete m, sacerdote m; ~**hood** n sacerdozio

prim [prɪm] adj pudico(a); contegnoso(a)

primarily ['praɪmərɪlɪ] adv principalmente, essenzialmente

primary ['praɪmərɪ] adj primario(a); (first in importance) primo(a) ♦ n (US: election) primarie fpl; ~ **school** (BRIT) n scuola elementare

prime [praɪm] adj primario(a), fondamentale; (excellent) di prima qualità ♦ vt (wood) preparare; (fig) mettere al corrente ♦ n: **in the ~ of life** nel fiore della vita; **P~ Minister** n primo ministro

primeval [praɪ'miːvl] adj primitivo(a)

primitive ['prɪmɪtɪv] adj primitivo(a)

primrose ['prɪmrəʊz] n primavera

primus (stove) ® ['praɪməs(-)] (BRIT) n fornello a petrolio

prince [prɪns] n principe m

princess [prɪn'ses] n principessa

principal ['prɪnsɪpl] adj principale ♦ n (headmaster) preside m

principle ['prɪnsɪpl] n principio; **in ~** in linea di principio; **on ~** per principio

print [prɪnt] n (mark) impronta; (letters) caratteri mpl; (fabric) tessuto stampato; (ART, PHOT) stampa ♦ vt imprimere; (publish) stampare, pubblicare; (write in capitals) scrivere in stampatello; **out of ~** esaurito(a); ~**ed matter** n stampe fpl; ~**er** n tipografo; (machine) stampante f; ~**ing** n stampa; ~**-out** n (COMPUT) tabulato

prior ['praɪə*] adj precedente; (claim etc) più importante; ~ **to doing** prima di fare

priority [praɪ'ɒrɪtɪ] n priorità f inv; precedenza

prise [praɪz] vt: **to ~ open** forzare

prison ['prɪzn] n prigione f ♦ cpd (system) carcerario(a); (conditions, food) nelle or delle prigioni; ~**er** n prigioniero/a

pristine ['prɪstiːn] adj immacolato(a)

privacy ['prɪvəsɪ] n solitudine f, intimità

private ['praɪvɪt] adj privato(a); personale ♦ n soldato semplice; "**~**" (on envelope) "riservata"; (on door) "privato"; **in ~** in privato; ~ **enterprise** n iniziativa privata; ~ **eye** n investigatore m privato; ~**ly** adv in privato; (within oneself) dentro di sé; ~ **property** n proprietà privata; **privatize** vt privatizzare

privet ['prɪvɪt] n ligustro

privilege ['prɪvɪlɪdʒ] n privilegio

privy ['prɪvɪ] adj: **to be ~ to** essere al corrente di

prize [praɪz] n premio ♦ adj (example, idiot) perfetto(a); (bull, novel) premiato(a) ♦ vt apprezzare, pregiare; ~**-giving** n premiazione f; ~**winner** n premiato/a

pro [prəʊ] n (SPORT) professionista m/f ♦ prep pro; **the ~s and cons** il pro e il contro

probability [prɒbə'bɪlɪtɪ] n probabilità f inv; **in all ~** con tutta probabilità

probable ['prɒbəbl] adj probabile; **probably** adv probabilmente

probation [prə'beɪʃən] n: **on ~** (employee) in prova; (LAW) in libertà vigilata

probe [prəʊb] n (MED, SPACE) sonda; (enquiry) indagine f, investigazione f ♦ vt sondare, esplorare; indagare

problem ['prɒbləm] n problema m

procedure [prə'siːdʒə*] n (ADMIN, LAW) procedura; (method) metodo, procedimento

proceed [prə'siːd] vi (go forward) avanzare, andare avanti; (go about it) procedere; (continue): **to ~ (with)** continuare; **to ~ to** andare a; passare a; **to ~ to do** mettersi a fare; ~**ings** npl misure fpl; (LAW) procedimento; (meeting) riunione f; (records) rendiconti mpl; atti mpl; ~**s** ['prəʊsiːdʒ] npl profitto, incasso

process ['prəʊses] n processo; (method) metodo, sistema m ♦ vt trattare; (information) elaborare; ~**ing** n trattamento; elaborazione f

procession [prə'seʃən] n processione f,

corteto; **funeral ~** corteo funebre

pro-choice [prəʊ'tʃɔɪs] *adj* per la libertà di scelta di gravidanza

proclaim [prə'kleɪm] *vt* proclamare, dichiarare

procrastinate [prəʊ'kræstɪneɪt] *vi* procrastinare

prod [prɒd] *vt* dare un colpetto a; pungolare ♦ *n* colpetto

prodigal ['prɒdɪgl] *adj* prodigo(a)

prodigy ['prɒdɪdʒɪ] *n* prodigio

produce [*n* 'prɒdjuːs, *vb* prə'djuːs] *n* (AGR) prodotto, prodotti *mpl* ♦ *vt* produrre; (*to show*) esibire, mostrare; (*cause*) cagionare, causare; **~r** *n* (THEATRE) regista *m/f*, (AGR, CINEMA) produttore *m*

product ['prɒdʌkt] *n* prodotto

production [prə'dʌkʃən] *n* produzione *f*; **~ line** *n* catena di lavorazione

productivity [prɒdʌk'tɪvɪtɪ] *n* produttività

profane [prə'feɪn] *adj* profano(a); (*language*) empio(a)

profess [prə'fes] *vt* (*claim*) dichiarare; (*opinion etc*) professare

profession [prə'feʃən] *n* professione *f*; **~al** *n* professionista *m/f* ♦ *adj* professionale; (*work*) da professionista

professor [prə'fesə*] *n* professore *m* (*titolare di una cattedra*); (US) professore/essa

proficiency [prə'fɪʃənsɪ] *n* competenza, abilità

profile ['prəʊfaɪl] *n* profilo

profit ['prɒfɪt] *n* profitto; beneficio ♦ *vi*: **to ~ (by or from)** approfittare (di); **~ability** [-'bɪlɪtɪ] *n* redditività; **~able** *adj* redditizio(a)

profound [prə'faʊnd] *adj* profondo(a)

profusely [prə'fjuːslɪ] *adv* con grande effusione

programme ['prəʊgræm] (US **program**) *n* programma *m* ♦ *vt* programmare; **~r** (US **programer**) *n* programmatore/trice

progress [*n* 'prəʊgres, *vb* prə'gres] *n* progresso ♦ *vi* avanzare, procedere; **in ~** in corso; **to make ~** far progressi; **~ive** [-'gresɪv] *adj* progressivo(a); (*person*) progressista

prohibit [prə'hɪbɪt] *vt* proibire, vietare; **~ion** [prəʊɪ'bɪʃən] *n* proibizione *f*, divieto; (US): **P~ion** proibizionismo; **~ive** *adj* (*price etc*) proibitivo(a)

project [*n* 'prɒdʒekt, *vb* prə'dʒekt] *n* (*plan*) piano; (*venture*) progetto; (SCOL) studio ♦ *vt* proiettare ♦ *vi* (*stick out*) sporgere

projectile [prə'dʒektaɪl] *n* proiettile *m*

projector [prə'dʒektə*] *n* proiettore *m*

pro-life [prəʊ'laɪf] *adj* per il diritto alla vita

prolific [prə'lɪfɪk] *adj* (*artist etc*) fecondo(a)

prolong [prə'lɒŋ] *vt* prolungare

Prom

*ⓘ In Gran Bretagna i **Prom** (promenade concert) sono concerti di musica classica, i più noti dei quali sono quelli eseguiti nella Royal Albert Hall a Londra. Un tempo il pubblico seguiva i concerti in piedi, passeggiando. Negli Stati Uniti, invece, con **prom** si intende il ballo studentesco di un'università o di un college.*

---

prom [prɒm] *n abbr* = **promenade**; (US: *ball*) ballo studentesco

promenade [prɒmə'nɑːd] *n* (*by sea*) lungomare *m*; **~ concert** *n* concerto (*con posti in piedi*)

prominent ['prɒmɪnənt] *adj* (*standing out*) prominente; (*important*) importante

promiscuous [prə'mɪskjuəs] *adj* (*sexually*) di facili costumi

promise ['prɒmɪs] *n* promessa ♦ *vt, vi* promettere; **to ~ sb sth, ~ sth to sb** promettere qc a qn; **to ~ (sb) that/to do sth** promettere (a qn) che/di fare qc; **promising** *adj* promettente

promote [prə'məʊt] *vt* promuovere; (*venture, event*) organizzare; **~r** *n* promotore/trice; (*of sporting event*) organizzatore/trice; **promotion** [-'məʊʃən] *n* promozione *f*

prompt [prɒmpt] *adj* rapido(a), svelto(a); puntuale; (*reply*) sollecito(a) ♦ *adv* (*punctually*) in punto ♦ *n* (COMPUT) prompt *m* ♦ *vt* incitare; provocare; (THEATRE) suggerire a; **to ~ sb to do** incitare qn a fare; **~ly** adv prontamente; puntualmente

prone [prəun] adj (lying) prono(a); **~ to** propenso(a) a, incline a

prong [prɒŋ] n rebbio, punta

pronoun ['prəunaun] n pronome m

pronounce [prə'nauns] vt pronunciare

pronunciation [prənʌnsɪ'eɪʃən] n pronuncia

proof [pru:f] n prova; (of book) bozza; (PHOT) provino ♦ adj: **~ against** a prova di

prop [prɒp] n sostegno, appoggio ♦ vt (also: **~ up**) sostenere, appoggiare; (lean): **to ~ sth against** appoggiare qc contro or a

propaganda [prɒpə'gændə] n propaganda

propel [prə'pɛl] vt spingere (in avanti), muovere; **~ler** n elica

propensity [prə'pɛnsɪtɪ] n tendenza

proper ['prɒpə*] adj (suited, right) adatto(a), appropriato(a); (seemly) decente; (authentic) vero(a); (inf: real) noun +vero(a) e proprio(a); **~ly** ['prɒpəlɪ] adv (eat, study) bene; (behave) come si deve; **~ noun** n nome m proprio

property ['prɒpətɪ] n (things owned) beni mpl; (land, building) proprietà f inv; (CHEM etc: quality) proprietà; **~ owner** n proprietario/a

prophecy ['prɒfɪsɪ] n profezia

prophesy ['prɒfɪsaɪ] vt predire

prophet ['prɒfɪt] n profeta m

proportion [prə'pɔ:ʃən] n proporzione f; (share) parte f; **~al** adj proporzionale; **~ate** adj proporzionato(a)

proposal [prə'pəuzl] n proposta; (plan) progetto; (of marriage) proposta di matrimonio

propose [prə'pəuz] vt proporre, suggerire ♦ vi fare una proposta di matrimonio; **to ~ to do** proporsi di fare, aver l'intenzione di fare

proposition [prɒpə'zɪʃən] n proposizione f; (offer) proposta

proprietor [prə'praɪətə*] n proprietario/a

propriety [prə'praɪətɪ] n (seemliness) decoro, rispetto delle convenienze sociali

pro rata ['prəu'rɑ:tə] adv in proporzione

prose [prəuz] n prosa

prosecute ['prɒsɪkju:t] vt processare;

prosecution [-'kju:ʃən] n processo; (accusing side) accusa; **prosecutor** n (also: public prosecutor) ≈ procuratore m della Repubblica

prospect [n 'prɒspɛkt, vb prə'spɛkt] n prospettiva; (hope) speranza ♦ vi: **to ~ for** cercare; **~s** npl (for work etc) prospettive fpl; **~ive** [-'spɛktɪv] adj possibile; futuro(a)

prospectus [prə'spɛktəs] n prospetto, programma m

prosperity [prɒ'spɛrɪtɪ] n prosperità

prostitute ['prɒstɪtju:t] n prostituta; **male ~** uomo che si prostituisce

protect [prə'tɛkt] vt proteggere, salvaguardare; **~ed species** n specie f protetta; **~ion** n protezione f; **~ive** adj protettivo(a)

protégé ['prəutəʒeɪ] n protetto

protein ['prəuti:n] n proteina

protest [n 'prəutɛst, vb prə'tɛst] n protesta ♦ vt, vi protestare

Protestant ['prɒtɪstənt] adj, n protestante m/f

protester [prə'tɛstə*] n dimostrante m/f

prototype ['prəutətaɪp] n prototipo

protracted [prə'træktɪd] adj tirato(a) per le lunghe

protrude [prə'tru:d] vi sporgere

proud [praud] adj fiero(a), orgoglioso(a); (pej) superbo(a)

prove [pru:v] vt provare, dimostrare ♦ vi: **to ~ (to be) correct** etc risultare vero(a) etc; **to ~ o.s.** mostrare le proprie capacità

proverb ['prɒvə:b] n proverbio

provide [prə'vaɪd] vt fornire, provvedere; **to ~ sb with sth** fornire or provvedere qn di qc; **~ for** vt fus provvedere a; (future event) prevedere; **~d (that)** conj purché +sub, a condizione che +sub

providing [prə'vaɪdɪŋ] conj purché +sub, a condizione che +sub

province ['prɒvɪns] n provincia; **provincial** [prə'vɪnʃəl] adj provinciale

provision [prə'vɪʒən] n (supply) riserva; (supplying) provvista; rifornimento; (stipulation) condizione f; **~s** npl (food) provviste fpl; **~al** adj provvisorio(a)

proviso [prə'vaɪzəʊ] n condizione f

provocative [prə'vɒkətɪv] adj (aggressive) provocatorio(a); (thought-provoking) stimolante; (seductive) provocante

provoke [prə'vəʊk] vt provocare; incitare

prowess ['praʊɪs] n prodezza

prowl [praʊl] vi (also: ~ about, ~ around) aggirarsi ♦ n: to be on the ~ aggirarsi; ~er n tipo sospetto (che s'aggira con l'intenzione di rubare, aggredire etc)

proximity [prɒk'sɪmɪtɪ] n prossimità

proxy ['prɒksɪ] n: by ~ per procura

prude [pruːd] n puritano/a

prudent ['pruːdnt] adj prudente

prudish ['pruːdɪʃ] adj puritano(a)

prune [pruːn] n prugna secca ♦ vt potare

pry [praɪ] vi: to ~ into ficcare il naso in

PS abbr (= postscript) P.S.

psalm [sɑːm] n salmo

pseudonym ['sjuːdənɪm] n pseudonimo

psyche ['saɪkɪ] n psiche f

psychiatric [saɪkɪ'ætrɪk] adj psichiatrico(a)

psychiatrist [saɪ'kaɪətrɪst] n psichiatra m/f

psychic ['saɪkɪk] adj (also: ~al) psichico(a); (person) dotato(a) di qualità telepatiche

psychoanalyst [saɪkəʊ'ænəlɪst] n psicanalista m/f

psychological [saɪkə'lɒdʒɪkl] adj psicologico(a)

psychologist [saɪ'kɒlədʒɪst] n psicologo/a

psychology [saɪ'kɒlədʒɪ] n psicologia

psychopath ['saɪkəʊpæθ] n psicopatico/a

P.T.O. abbr (= please turn over) v.r.

pub [pʌb] n abbr (= public house) pub m inv

ℹ️ In Gran Bretagna e in Irlanda i **pub** sono locali dove vengono servite bevande alcoliche ed analcoliche e dove spesso è possibile anche mangiare, giocare a biliardo o a freccette e guardare la televisione.

pubic ['pjuːbɪk] adj pubico(a), del pube

public ['pʌblɪk] adj pubblico(a) ♦ n pubblico; **in ~** in pubblico; **~ address system** n impianto di amplificazione

publican ['pʌblɪkən] n proprietario di un pub

publication [pʌblɪ'keɪʃən] n pubblicazione f

public: ~ company n società f inv per azioni (costituita tramite pubblica sottoscrizione); **~ convenience** (BRIT) n gabinetti mpl; **~ holiday** n giorno festivo, festa nazionale; **~ house** (BRIT) n pub m inv

publicity [pʌb'lɪsɪtɪ] n pubblicità

publicize ['pʌblɪsaɪz] vt rendere pubblico(a)

publicly ['pʌblɪklɪ] adv pubblicamente

public: ~ opinion n opinione f pubblica; **~ relations** n pubbliche relazioni fpl; **~ school** n (BRIT) scuola privata; (US) scuola statale; **~-spirited** adj che ha senso civico; **~ transport** n mezzi mpl pubblici

publish ['pʌblɪʃ] vt pubblicare; **~er** n editore m; **~ing** n (industry) editoria; (of a book) pubblicazione f

pub lunch n pranzo semplice ed economico servito nei pub

puce [pjuːs] adj marroncino rosato inv

pucker ['pʌkə*] vt corrugare

pudding ['pʊdɪŋ] n budino; (BRIT: dessert) dolce m; **black ~**, (US) **blood ~** sanguinaccio

puddle ['pʌdl] n pozza, pozzanghera

puff [pʌf] n sbuffo ♦ vt: **to ~ one's pipe** tirare sboccate di fumo ♦ vi (pant) ansare; **~ out** vt (cheeks etc) gonfiare; **~ pastry** n pasta sfoglia; **~y** adj gonfio(a)

pull [pʊl] n (tug): **to give sth a ~** tirare su qc ♦ vt tirare; (muscle) strappare; (trigger) premere ♦ vi tirare; **to ~ to pieces** fare a pezzi; **to ~ one's punches** (BOXING) risparmiare l'avversario; **to ~ one's weight** dare il proprio contributo; **to ~ o.s. together** ricomporsi, riprendersi; **to ~ sb's leg** prendere in giro qn; **~ apart** vt (break) fare a pezzi; **~ down** vt (house) demolire; (tree) abbattere; **~ in** vi (AUT: at the kerb) accostarsi; (RAIL) entrare in stazione; **~ off** vt (clothes) togliere; (deal etc) portare a compimento; **~ out** vi partire; (AUT: come out of line) spostarsi sulla mezzeria ♦ vt staccare; far uscire; (withdraw) ritirare; **~**

over *vi* (*AUT*) accostare; ~ **through** *vi* farcela; ~ **up** *vi* (*stop*) fermarsi ♦ *vt* (*raise*) sollevare; (*uproot*) sradicare

pulley ['pulɪ] *n* puleggia, carrucola

pullover ['puləuvə*] *n* pullover *m inv*

pulp [pʌlp] *n* (*of fruit*) polpa

pulpit ['pulpɪt] *n* pulpito

pulsate [pʌl'seɪt] *vi* battere, palpitare

pulse [pʌls] *n* polso; (*BOT*) legume *m*

pummel ['pʌml] *vt* dare pugni a

pump [pʌmp] *n* pompa; (*shoe*) scarpetta ♦ *vt* pompare; ~ **up** *vt* gonfiare

pumpkin ['pʌmpkɪn] *n* zucca

pun [pʌn] *n* gioco di parole

punch [pʌntʃ] *n* (*blow*) pugno; (*tool*) punzone *m*; (*drink*) ponce *m* ♦ *vt* (*hit*): **to ~ sb/sth** dare un pugno a qn/qc; ~ **line** *n* (*of joke*) battuta finale; ~-**up** (*BRIT*: *inf*) *n* rissa

punctual ['pʌŋktjuəl] *adj* puntuale

punctuation [pʌŋktju'eɪʃən] *n* interpunzione *f*, punteggiatura

puncture ['pʌŋktʃə*] *n* foratura ♦ *vt* forare

pundit ['pʌndɪt] *n* sapientone/a

pungent ['pʌndʒənt] *adj* pungente

punish ['pʌnɪʃ] *vt* punire; ~**ment** *n* punizione *f*

punk [pʌŋk] *n* (*also*: ~ **rocker**) punk *m/f inv*; (*also*: ~ **rock**) musica punk, punk rock *m*; (*US*: *inf*: *hoodlum*) teppista *m*

punt [pʌnt] *n* (*boat*) barchino

punter ['pʌntə*] (*BRIT*) *n* (*gambler*) scommettitore/trice; (: *inf*) cliente *m/f*

puny ['pju:nɪ] *adj* gracile

pup [pʌp] *n* cucciolo/a

pupil ['pju:pl] *n* allievo/a; (*ANAT*) pupilla

puppet ['pʌpɪt] *n* burattino

puppy ['pʌpɪ] *n* cucciolo/a, cagnolino/a

purchase ['pə:tʃɪs] *n* acquisto, compera ♦ *vt* comprare; ~**r** *n* compratore/trice

pure [pjuə*] *adj* puro(a)

purée ['pjuəreɪ] *n* (*of potatoes*) purè *m*; (*of tomatoes*) passato; (*of apples*) crema

purely ['pjuəlɪ] *adv* puramente

purge [pə:dʒ] *n* (*MED*) purga; (*POL*) epurazione *f* ♦ *vt* purgare

puritan ['pjuərɪtən] *adj*, *n* puritano(a)

purity ['pjuərɪtɪ] *n* purezza

purple ['pə:pl] *adj* di porpora; viola *inv*

purpose ['pə:pəs] *n* intenzione *f*, scopo; **on ~** apposta; ~**ful** *adj* deciso(a), risoluto(a)

purr [pə:*] *vi* fare le fusa

purse [pə:s] *n* (*BRIT*) borsellino; (*US*) borsetta ♦ *vt* contrarre

purser ['pə:sə*] *n* (*NAUT*) commissario di bordo

pursue [pə'sju:] *vt* inseguire; (*fig*: *activity etc*) continuare con; (: *aim etc*) perseguire

pursuit [pə'sju:t] *n* inseguimento; (*fig*) ricerca; (*pastime*) passatempo

push [puʃ] *n* spinta; (*effort*) grande sforzo; (*drive*) energia ♦ *vt* spingere; (*button*) premere; (*thrust*): **to ~ sth (into)** ficcare qc (in); (*fig*) fare pubblicità a ♦ *vi* spingere; premere; **to ~ for** (*fig*) insistere per; ~ **aside** *vt* scostare; ~ **off** (*inf*) *vi* filare; ~ **on** *vi* (*continue*) continuare; ~ **through** *vi* farsi largo spingendo ♦ *vt* (*measure*) far approvare; ~ **up** *vt* (*total, prices*) far salire; ~**chair** (*BRIT*) *n* passeggino; ~**er** *n* (*drug ~er*) spacciatore/trice; ~**over** (*inf*) *n*: **it's a ~over** è un lavoro da bambini; ~-**up** (*US*) *n* (*press-up*) flessione *f* sulle braccia; ~**y** (*pej*) *adj* opportunista

puss [pus] (*inf*) *n* = **pussy(-cat)**

pussy(-cat) ['pusɪ(-)] *n* micio

put [put] (*pt, pp* **put**) *vt* mettere, porre; (*say*) dire, esprimere; (*a question*) fare; (*estimate*) stimare; ~ **about** *or* **around** *vt* (*rumour*) diffondere; ~ **across** *vt* (*ideas etc*) comunicare; far capire; ~ **away** *vt* (*return*) mettere a posto; ~ **back** *vt* (*replace*) rimettere a posto); (*postpone*) rinviare; (*delay*) ritardare; ~ **by** *vt* (*money*) mettere da parte; ~ **down** *vt* (*parcel etc*) posare, mettere giù; (*pay*) versare; (*in writing*) mettere per iscritto; (*revolt, animal*) sopprimere; (*attribute*) attribuire; ~ **forward** *vt* (*ideas*) avanzare, proporre; ~ **in** *vt* (*application, complaint*) presentare; (*time, effort*) mettere; ~ **off** *vt* (*postpone*) rimandare, rinviare; (*discourage*) dissuadere; ~ **on** *vt* (*clothes, lipstick etc*) mettere; (*light etc*) accendere; (*play etc*) mettere in scena;

(*food, meal*) mettere su; (*brake*) mettere; **to ~ on weight** ingrassare; **to ~ on airs** darsi delle arie; **~ out** *vt* mettere fuori; (*one's hand*) porgere; (*light etc*) spegnere; (*person: inconvenience*) scomodare; **~ through** *vt* (*TEL: call*) passare; (*: person*) mettere in comunicazione; (*plan*) far approvare; **~ up** *vt* (*raise*) sollevare, alzare; (*: umbrella*) aprire; (*: tent*) montare; (*pin up*) affiggere; (*hang*) appendere; (*build*) costruire, erigere; (*increase*) aumentare; (*accommodate*) alloggiare; **~ up with** *vt fus* sopportare

putt [pʌt] *n* colpo leggero; **~ing green** *n* green *m inv*; campo da putting

putty ['pʌtɪ] *n* stucco

puzzle ['pʌzl] *n* enigma *m*, mistero; (*jigsaw*) puzzle *m*; (*also:* **crossword ~**) parole *fpl* incrociate, cruciverba *m inv* ♦ *vt* confondere, rendere perplesso(a) ♦ *vi* scervellarsi

pyjamas [pɪ'dʒɑːməz] (*BRIT*) *npl* pigiama *m*

pylon ['paɪlən] *n* pilone *m*

pyramid ['pɪrəmɪd] *n* piramide *f*

Pyrenees [pɪrɪ'niːz] *npl*: **the ~** i Pirenei

Q, q

quack [kwæk] *n* (*of duck*) qua qua *m inv*; (*pej: doctor*) dottoruccio/a

quad [kwɔd] *n abbr* = **quadrangle**; **quadruplet**

quadrangle ['kwɔdræŋgl] *n* (*courtyard*) cortile *m*

quadruple [kwɔ'druːpl] *vt* quadruplicare ♦ *vi* quadruplicarsi

quadruplets [kwɔ'druːplɪts] *npl* quattro gemelli *mpl*

quail [kweɪl] *n* (*ZOOL*) quaglia ♦ *vi* (*person*): **to ~ at** *or* **before** perdersi d'animo davanti a

quaint [kweɪnt] *adj* bizzarro(a); (*old-fashioned*) antiquato(a); grazioso(a), pittoresco(a)

quake [kweɪk] *vi* tremare ♦ *n abbr* = **earthquake**

Quaker ['kweɪkə*] *n* quacchero/a

qualification [kwɔlɪfɪ'keɪʃən] *n* (*degree etc*) qualifica, titolo; (*ability*) competenza, qualificazione *f*; (*limitation*) riserva, restrizione *f*

qualified ['kwɔlɪfaɪd] *adj* qualificato(a); (*able*): **~ to** competente in, qualificato(a) a; (*limited*) condizionato(a)

qualify ['kwɔlɪfaɪ] *vt* abilitare; (*limit: statement*) modificare, precisare ♦ *vi*: **to ~ (as)** qualificarsi (come); **to ~ (for)** acquistare i requisiti necessari (per); (*SPORT*) qualificarsi (per *or* a)

quality ['kwɔlɪtɪ] *n* qualità *f inv*

quality press

ⓘ *Il termine* **quality press** *si riferisce ai quotidiani e ai settimanali che offrono un'informazione più seria ed approfondita rispetto ai* **tabloid**, *i giornali popolari; vedi anche* **tabloid press**.

qualm [kwɑːm] *n* dubbio; scrupolo

quandary ['kwɔndrɪ] *n*: **in a ~** in un dilemma

quantity ['kwɔntɪtɪ] *n* quantità *f inv*

quantity surveyor [-sə'veɪə*] *n* geometra *m* (*specializzato nel calcolare la quantità e il costo del materiale da costruzione*)

quarantine ['kwɔrəntiːn] *n* quarantena

quarrel ['kwɔrəl] *n* lite *f*, disputa ♦ *vi* litigare

quarry ['kwɔrɪ] *n* (*for stone*) cava; (*animal*) preda

quart [kwɔːt] *n* ≈ litro

quarter ['kwɔːtə*] *n* quarto; (*US: coin*) quarto di dollaro; (*of year*) trimestre *m*; (*district*) quartiere *m* ♦ *vt* dividere in quattro; (*MIL*) alloggiare; **~s** *npl* (*living ~s*) alloggio (*MIL*) alloggi *mpl*, quadrato; **a ~ of an hour** un quarto d'ora; **~ final** *n* quarto di finale; **~ly** *adj* trimestrale ♦ *adv* trimestralmente

quartet(te) [kwɔː'tet] *n* quartetto

quartz [kwɔːts] *n* quarzo

quash [kwɔʃ] *vt* (*verdict*) annullare

quaver ['kweɪvə*] *n* (*BRIT: MUS*) croma ♦ *vi* tremolare

quay [kiː] *n* (*also:* **~side**) banchina

queasy ['kwi:zɪ] *adj* (*stomach*) delicato(a); **to feel ~** aver la nausea

queen [kwi:n] *n* (*gen*) regina; (*CARDS etc*) regina, donna; **~ mother** *n* regina madre

queer [kwɪə*] *adj* strano(a), curioso(a) ♦ *n* (*inf*) finocchio

quell [kwel] *vt* domare

quench [kwentʃ] *vt*: **to ~ one's thirst** dissetarsi

query ['kwɪərɪ] *n* domanda, questione *f* ♦ *vt* mettere in questione

quest [kwest] *n* cerca, ricerca

question ['kwestʃən] *n* domanda, questione *f* ♦ *vt* (*person*) interrogare; (*plan, idea*) mettere in questione *or* in dubbio; **it's a ~ of doing** si tratta di fare; **beyond ~** fuori di dubbio; **out of the ~** fuori discussione, impossibile; **~able** *adj* discutibile; **~ mark** *n* punto interrogativo

questionnaire [kwestʃə'neə*] *n* questionario

queue [kju:] (*BRIT*) *n* coda, fila ♦ *vi* fare la coda

quibble ['kwɪbl] *vi* cavillare

quiche [ki:ʃ] *n* torta salata a base di uova, formaggio, prosciutto *o* altro

quick [kwɪk] *adj* rapido(a), veloce; (*reply*) pronto(a); (*mind*) pronto(a), acuto(a) ♦ *n*: **cut to the ~** (*fig*) toccato(a) sul vivo; **be ~!** fa presto!; **~en** *vt* accelerare, affrettare ♦ *vi* accelerare, affrettarsi; **~ly** *adv* rapidamente, velocemente; **~sand** *n* sabbie *fpl* mobili; **~-witted** *adj* pronto(a) d'ingegno

quid [kwɪd] (*BRIT: inf*) *n inv* sterlina

quiet ['kwaɪət] *adj* tranquillo(a), quieto(a); (*ceremony*) semplice ♦ *n* tranquillità, calma ♦ *vt, vi* (*US*) = **~en**; **keep ~!** sta zitto!; **~en** (*also*: **~en down**) *vi* calmarsi, chetarsi ♦ *vt* calmare, chetare; **~ly** *adv* tranquillamente, calmamente; sommessamente

quilt [kwɪlt] *n* trapunta; (*continental ~*) piumino

quin [kwɪn] *n abbr* = **quintuplet**

quintuplets [kwɪn'tju:plɪts] *npl* cinque gemelli *mpl*

quip [kwɪp] *n* frizzo

quirk [kwə:k] *n* ghiribizzo

quit [kwɪt] (*pt, pp* **quit** *or* **quitted**) *vt* mollare; (*premises*) lasciare, partire da ♦ *vi* (*give up*) mollare; (*resign*) dimettersi

quite [kwaɪt] *adv* (*rather*) assai; (*entirely*) completamente, del tutto; **I ~ understand** capisco perfettamente; **that's not ~ big enough** non è proprio sufficiente; **~ a few of them** non pochi di loro; **~ (so)!** esatto!

quits [kwɪts] *adj*: **~ (with)** pari (con); **let's call it ~** adesso siamo pari

quiver ['kwɪvə*] *vi* tremare, fremere

quiz [kwɪz] *n* (*game*) quiz *m inv*; indovinello ♦ *vt* interrogare; **~zical** *adj* enigmatico(a)

quota ['kwəʊtə] *n* quota

quotation [kwəʊ'teɪʃən] *n* citazione *f*; (*of shares etc*) quotazione *f*; (*estimate*) preventivo; **~ marks** *npl* virgolette *fpl*

quote [kwəʊt] *n* citazione *f* ♦ *vt* (*sentence*) citare; (*price*) dare, fissare; (*shares*) quotare ♦ *vi*: **to ~ from** citare; **~s** *npl* = **quotation marks**

R, r

rabbi ['ræbaɪ] *n* rabbino

rabbit ['ræbɪt] *n* coniglio; **~ hutch** *n* conigliera

rabble ['ræbl] (*pej*) *n* canaglia, plebaglia

rabies ['reɪbi:z] *n* rabbia

RAC (*BRIT*) *n abbr* = **Royal Automobile Club**

rac(c)oon [rə'ku:n] *n* procione *m*

race [reɪs] *n* razza; (*competition, rush*) corsa ♦ *vt* (*horse*) far correre ♦ *vi* correre; (*engine*) imballarsi; **~ car** (*US*) *n* = **racing car**; **~ car driver** (*US*) *n* = **racing driver**; **~course** *n* campo di corse, ippodromo; **~horse** *n* cavallo da corsa; **~track** *n* pista

racial ['reɪʃl] *adj* razziale

racing ['reɪsɪŋ] *n* corsa; **~ car** (*BRIT*) *n* macchina da corsa; **~ driver** (*BRIT*) *n* corridore *m* automobilista

racism ['reɪsɪzəm] *n* razzismo; **racist** *adj*, *n* razzista *m/f*

rack [ræk] *n* rastrelliera; (*also*: **luggage ~**) rete *f*, portabagagli *m inv*; (*also*: **roof ~**)

portabagagli; (*dish ~*) scolapiatti *m inv* ♦ *vt*: **~ed by** torturato(a) da; **to ~ one's brains** scervellarsi

racket ['rækɪt] *n* (*for tennis*) racchetta; (*noise*) fracasso; baccano; (*swindle*) imbroglio, truffa; (*organized crime*) racket *m inv*

racoon [rə'ku:n] *n* = **raccoon**

racquet ['rækɪt] *n* racchetta

racy ['reɪsɪ] *adj* brioso(a); piccante

radar ['reɪdɑ:*] *n* radar *m*

radial ['reɪdɪəl] *adj* (*also:* **~-ply**) radiale

radiant ['reɪdɪənt] *adj* raggiante; (PHYSICS) radiante

radiate ['reɪdɪeɪt] *vt* (*heat*) irraggiare, irradiare ♦ *vi* (*lines*) irradiarsi

radiation [reɪdɪ'eɪʃən] *n* irradiamento; (*radioactive*) radiazione *f*

radiator ['reɪdɪeɪtə*] *n* radiatore *m*

radical ['rædɪkl] *adj* radicale

radii ['reɪdɪaɪ] *npl of* **radius**

radio ['reɪdɪəu] *n* radio *f inv*; **on the ~** alla radio

radioactive [reɪdɪəu'æktɪv] *adj* radioattivo(a)

radio station *n* stazione *f* radio *inv*

radish ['rædɪʃ] *n* ravanello

radius ['reɪdɪəs] (*pl* **radii**) *n* raggio

RAF *n abbr* = **Royal Air Force**

raffle ['ræfl] *n* lotteria

raft [rɑ:ft] *n* zattera; (*also:* **life ~**) zattera di salvataggio

rafter ['rɑ:ftə*] *n* trave *f*

rag [ræg] *n* straccio, cencio; (*pej: newspaper*) giornalaccio, bandiera; (*for charity*) iniziativa studentesca a scopo benefico; **~s** *npl* (*torn clothes*) stracci *mpl*, brandelli *mpl*; **~ doll** *n* bambola di pezza

rage [reɪdʒ] *n* (*fury*) collera, furia ♦ *vi* (*person*) andare su tutte le furie; (*storm*) infuriare; **it's all the ~** fa furore

ragged ['rægɪd] *adj* (*edge*) irregolare; (*clothes*) logoro(a); (*appearance*) pezzente

raid [reɪd] *n* (MIL) incursione *f*; (*criminal*) rapina; (*by police*) irruzione *f* ♦ *vt* fare un'incursione in; rapinare; fare irruzione in

rail [reɪl] *n* (*on stair*) ringhiera; (*on bridge*,

balcony) parapetto; (*of ship*) battagliola; **~s** *npl* (*for train*) binario, rotaie *fpl*; **by ~** per ferrovia; **~ing(s)** *n(pl)* ringhiere *fpl*; **~road** (US) *n* = **~way**; **~way** (BRIT) *n* ferrovia; **~way line** (BRIT) *n* linea ferroviaria; **~wayman** (BRIT: *irreg*) *n* ferroviere *m*; **~way station** (BRIT) *n* stazione *f* ferroviaria

rain [reɪn] *n* pioggia ♦ *vi* piovere; **in the ~** sotto la pioggia; **it's ~ing** piove; **~bow** *n* arcobaleno; **~coat** *n* impermeabile *m*; **~drop** *n* goccia di pioggia; **~fall** *n* pioggia, (*measurement*) piovosità; **~forest** *n* foresta pluviale; **~y** *adj* piovoso(a)

raise [reɪz] *n* aumento ♦ *vt* (*lift*) alzare; sollevare; (*increase*) aumentare; (*a protest, doubt, question*) sollevare; (*cattle, family*) allevare; (*crop*) coltivare; (*army, funds*) raccogliere; (*loan*) ottenere; **to ~ one's voice** alzare la voce

raisin ['reɪzn] *n* uva secca

rake [reɪk] *n* (*tool*) rastrello ♦ *vt* (*garden*) rastrellare

rally ['rælɪ] *n* (POL etc) riunione *f*; (AUT) rally *m inv*; (TENNIS) scambio ♦ *vt* riunire, radunare ♦ *vi* (*sick person, Stock Exchange*) riprendersi; **~ round** *vt fus* raggrupparsi intorno a; venire in aiuto di

RAM [ræm] *n abbr* (= *random access memory*) memoria ad accesso casuale

ram [ræm] *n* montone *m*, ariete *m* ♦ *vt* conficcare; (*crash into*) cozzare, sbattere contro; percuotere; speronare

ramble ['ræmbl] *n* escursione *f* ♦ *vi* (*pej: also:* **~ on**) divagare; **~r** *n* escursionista *m/f*; (BOT) rosa rampicante; **rambling** *adj* (*speech*) sconnesso(a); (*house*) tutto(a) a nicchie e corridoi; (BOT) rampicante

ramp [ræmp] *n* rampa; **on/off ~** (US: AUT) raccordo di entrata/uscita

rampage [ræm'peɪdʒ] *n*: **to go on the ~** scatenarsi in modo violento

rampant ['ræmpənt] *adj* (*disease etc*) che infierisce

rampart ['ræmpɑ:t] *n* bastione *m*

ram raiding *n* il rapinare un negozio o una banca sfondandone la vetrina con un'auto-ariete

ramshackle ['ræmʃækl] *adj* (*house*) cadente; (*car etc*) sgangherato(a)

ran [ræn] *pt of* **run**

ranch [rɑːntʃ] *n* ranch *m inv*; **~er** *n* proprietario di un ranch; cowboy *m inv*

rancid ['rænsɪd] *adj* rancido(a)

rancour ['ræŋkə*] (*US* **rancor**) *n* rancore *m*

random ['rændəm] *adj* fatto(a) *or* detto(a) per caso; (COMPUT, MATH) casuale ♦ *n*: **at ~** a casaccio; **~ access** *n* (COMPUT) accesso casuale

randy ['rændɪ] (BRIT: *inf*) *adj* arrapato(a); lascivo(a)

rang [ræŋ] *pt of* **ring**

range [reɪndʒ] *n* (*of mountains*) catena; (*of missile, voice*) portata; (*of proposals, products*) gamma; (MIL: *also*: **shooting ~**) campo di tiro; (*also*: **kitchen ~**) fornello, cucina economica ♦ *vt* disporre ♦ *vi*: **to ~ over** coprire; **to ~ from ... to** andare da ... a

ranger ['reɪndʒə*] *n* guardia forestale

rank [ræŋk] *n* fila; (*status*, MIL) grado; (BRIT: *also*: **taxi ~**) posteggio di taxi ♦ *vi*: **to ~ among** essere tra ♦ *adj* puzzolente; vero(a) e proprio(a); **the ~ and file** (*fig*) la gran massa

ransack ['rænsæk] *vt* rovistare; (*plunder*) saccheggiare

ransom ['rænsəm] *n* riscatto; **to hold sb to ~** (*fig*) esercitare pressione su qn

rant [rænt] *vi* vociare

rap [ræp] *vt* bussare a; picchiare su ♦ *n* (*music*) rap *m inv*

rape [reɪp] *n* violenza carnale, stupro; (BOT) ravizzone *m* ♦ *vt* violentare; **~(seed) oil** *n* olio di ravizzone

rapid ['ræpɪd] *adj* rapido(a); **~s** *npl* (GEO) rapida; **~ly** *adv* rapidamente

rapist ['reɪpɪst] *n* violentatore *m*

rapport [ræ'pɔː*] *n* rapporto

rare [rɛə*] *adj* raro(a); (CULIN: *steak*) al sangue

rarely ['rɛəlɪ] *adv* raramente

raring ['rɛərɪŋ] *adj*: **to be ~ to go** (*inf*) non veder l'ora di cominciare

rascal ['rɑːskl] *n* mascalzone *m*

rash [ræʃ] *adj* imprudente, sconsiderato(a) ♦ *n* (MED) eruzione *f*; (*of events etc*) scoppio

rasher ['ræʃə*] *n* fetta sottile (di lardo *or* prosciutto)

raspberry ['rɑːzbərɪ] *n* lampone *m*

rasping ['rɑːspɪŋ] *adj* stridulo(a)

rat [ræt] *n* ratto

rate [reɪt] *n* (*proportion*) tasso, percentuale *f*; (*speed*) velocità *f inv*; (*price*) tariffa ♦ *vt* giudicare; stimare; **~s** *npl* (BRIT: *property tax*) imposte *fpl* comunali; (*fees*) tariffe *fpl*; **to ~ sb/sth as** valutare qn/qc come; **~able value** (BRIT) *n* valore *m* imponibile *or* locativo (di una proprietà); **~payer** (BRIT) *n* contribuente *m/f* (che paga le imposte comunali)

rather ['rɑːðə*] *adv* piuttosto; **it's ~ expensive** è piuttosto caro; (*too*) è un po' caro; **there's ~ a lot** ce n'è parecchio; **I would** *or* **I'd ~ go** preferirei andare

rating ['reɪtɪŋ] *n* (*assessment*) valutazione *f*; (*score*) punteggio di merito

ratio ['reɪʃɪəʊ] *n* proporzione *f*, rapporto

ration ['ræʃən] *n* (*gen pl*) razioni *fpl* ♦ *vt* razionare

rational ['ræʃənl] *adj* razionale, ragionevole; (*solution, reasoning*) logico(a); **~e** [-'nɑːl] *n* fondamento logico; giustificazione *f*; **~ize** *vt* razionalizzare

rat race *n* carrierismo, corsa al successo

rattle ['rætl] *n* tintinnio; (*louder*) strepito; (*for baby*) sonaglino ♦ *vi* risuonare, tintinnare; fare un rumore di ferraglia ♦ *vt* scuotere (con strepito); **~snake** *n* serpente *m* a sonagli

raucous ['rɔːkəs] *adj* rumoroso(a), fragoroso(a)

ravage ['rævɪdʒ] *vt* devastare; **~s** *npl* danni *mpl*

rave [reɪv] *vi* (*in anger*) infuriarsi; (*with enthusiasm*) andare in estasi; (MED) delirare ♦ (BRIT: *inf*) *n* (*party*) rave *m inv*

raven ['reɪvən] *n* corvo

ravenous ['rævənəs] *adj* affamato(a)

ravine [rə'viːn] *n* burrone *m*

raving ['reɪvɪŋ] *adj*: **~ lunatic** pazzo(a)

furioso(a)

ravishing ['rævɪʃɪŋ] *adj* incantevole

raw [rɔ:] *adj* (*uncooked*) crudo(a); (*not processed*) greggio(a); (*sore*) vivo(a); (*inexperienced*) inesperto(a); (*weather, day*) gelido(a); ~ **deal** (*inf*) *n* bidonata; ~ **material** *n* materia prima

ray [reɪ] *n* raggio; **a ~ of hope** un barlume di speranza

rayon ['reɪɔn] *n* raion *m*

raze [reɪz] *vt* radere, distruggere

razor ['reɪzə*] *n* rasoio; ~ **blade** *n* lama di rasoio

Rd *abbr* = **road**

re [ri:] *prep* con riferimento a

reach [ri:tʃ] *n* portata; (*of river etc*) tratto ♦ *vt* raggiungere; arrivare a ♦ *vi* stendersi; **out of/within** ~ fuori/a portata di mano; **within ~ of the shops/station** vicino ai negozi/alla stazione; ~ **out** *vt* (*hand*) allungare ♦ *vi*: **to ~ out for** stendere la mano per prendere

react [ri:'ækt] *vi* reagire; ~**ion** [-'ækʃən] *n* reazione *f*

reactor [ri:'æktə*] *n* reattore *m*

read [ri:d, *pt, pp* red] (*pt, pp* **read**) *vi* leggere ♦ *vt* leggere; (*understand*) intendere, interpretare; (*study*) studiare; ~ **out** *vt* leggere ad alta voce; ~**able** *adj* (*writing*) leggibile; (*book etc*) che si legge volentieri; ~**er** *n* lettore/trice; (*BRIT: at university*) professore con funzioni preminenti di ricerca; ~**ership** *n* (*of paper etc*) numero di lettori

readily ['redɪlɪ] *adv* volentieri; (*easily*) facilmente; (*quickly*) prontamente

readiness ['redɪnɪs] *n* prontezza; **in ~** (*prepared*) pronto(a)

reading ['ri:dɪŋ] *n* lettura; (*understanding*) interpretazione *f*; (*on instrument*) indicazione *f*

readjust [ri:ə'dʒʌst] *vt* riaggiustare ♦ *vi* (*person*): **to ~ (to)** riadattarsi (a)

ready ['redɪ] *adj* pronto(a); (*willing*) pronto(a), disposto(a); (*available*) disponibile ♦ *n*: **at the ~** (*MIL*) pronto a sparare; **to get ~** *vi* prepararsi ♦ *vt*

preparare; ~**-made** *adj* prefabbricato(a); (*clothes*) confezionato(a); ~ **reckoner** *n* prontuario di calcolo; ~**-to-wear** *adj* prêt-à-porter *inv*

reaffirm [ri:ə'fɜ:m] *vt* riaffermare

real [rɪəl] *adj* reale; vero(a); **in ~ terms** in realtà; ~ **estate** *n* beni *mpl* immobili; ~**ism** *n* (*also ART*) realismo; ~**ist** *n* realista *m/f*; ~**istic** [-'lɪstɪk] *adj* realistico(a)

reality [ri:'ælɪtɪ] *n* realtà *f inv*

realization [rɪəlaɪ'zeɪʃən] *n* presa di coscienza; realizzazione *f*

realize ['rɪəlaɪz] *vt* (*understand*) rendersi conto di

really ['rɪəlɪ] *adv* veramente, davvero; ~**!** (*indicating annoyance*) oh, insomma!

realm [relm] *n* reame *m*, regno

Realtor ® ['rɪəltɔ:*] (*US*) *n* agente *m* immobiliare

reap [ri:p] *vt* mietere; (*fig*) raccogliere

reappear [ri:ə'pɪə*] *vi* ricomparire, riapparire

rear [rɪə*] *adj* di dietro; (*AUT: wheel etc*) posteriore ♦ *n* didietro, parte *f* posteriore ♦ *vt* (*cattle, family*) allevare ♦ *vi* (*also*: ~ **up**: *animal*) impennarsi

rearmament [ri:'ɑ:məmənt] *n* riarmo

rearrange [ri:ə'reɪndʒ] *vt* riordinare

rear-view: ~ **mirror** *n* (*AUT*) specchio retrovisore

reason ['ri:zn] *n* ragione *f*; (*cause, motive*) ragione, motivo ♦ *vi*: **to ~ with sb** far ragionare qn; **it stands to ~ that** è ovvio che; ~**able** *adj* ragionevole; (*not bad*) accettabile; ~**ably** *adv* ragionevolmente; ~**ed** *adj*: **a well-~ed argument** una forte argomentazione; ~**ing** *n* ragionamento

reassurance [ri:ə'ʃuərəns] *n* rassicurazione *f*

reassure [ri:ə'ʃuə*] *vt* rassicurare; **to ~ sb of** rassicurare qn di *or* su

rebate ['ri:beɪt] *n* (*on tax etc*) sgravio

rebel [*n* 'rebl, *vb* rɪ'bel] *n* ribelle *m/f* ♦ *vi* ribellarsi; ~**lion** *n* ribellione *f*; ~**lious** *adj* ribelle

rebound [*vb* rɪ'baund, *n* 'ri:baund] *vi* (*ball*) rimbalzare ♦ *n*: **on the ~** di rimbalzo

rebuff [rɪ'bʌf] n secco rifiuto

rebuke [rɪ'bju:k] vt rimproverare

rebut [rɪ'bʌt] vt rifiutare

recall [rɪ'kɔ:l] vt richiamare; (remember) ricordare, richiamare alla mente ♦ n richiamo

recap ['ri:kæp], **recapitulate** [ri:kə'pɪtjuleɪt] vt ricapitolare ♦ vi riassumere

rec'd abbr = **received**

recede [rɪ'si:d] vi allontanarsi; ritirarsi; calare; **receding** adj (forehead, chin) sfuggente; **he's got a receding hairline** sta stempiando

receipt [rɪ'si:t] n (document) ricevuta; (act of receiving) ricevimento; **~s** npl (COMM) introiti mpl

receive [rɪ'si:v] vt ricevere; (guest) ricevere, accogliere

receiver [rɪ'si:və*] n (TEL) ricevitore m; (RADIO, TV) apparecchio ricevente; (of stolen goods) ricettatore/trice; (COMM) curatore m fallimentare

recent ['ri:snt] adj recente; **~ly** adv recentemente

receptacle [rɪ'septɪkl] n recipiente m

reception [rɪ'sepʃən] n ricevimento; (welcome) accoglienza; (TV etc) ricezione f; **~ desk** n (in hotel) reception f inv; (in hospital, at doctor's) accettazione f; (in offices etc) portineria; **~ist** n receptionist m/f inv

receptive [rɪ'septɪv] adj ricettivo(a)

recess [rɪ'ses] n (in room, secret place) alcova; (POL etc: holiday) vacanze fpl; **~ion** [-'seʃən] n recessione f

recharge [ri:'tʃɑ:dʒ] vt (battery) ricaricare

recipe ['resɪpɪ] n ricetta

recipient [rɪ'sɪpɪənt] n beneficiario/a; (of letter) destinatario/a

recital [rɪ'saɪtl] n recital m inv

recite [rɪ'saɪt] vt (poem) recitare

reckless ['rekləs] adj (driver etc) spericolato(a); (spending) folle

reckon ['rekən] vt (count) calcolare; (think): **I ~ that ...** penso che ...; **~ on** vt fus contare su; **~ing** n conto; stima

reclaim [rɪ'kleɪm] vt (demand back) richiedere, reclamare; (land) bonificare; (materials) recuperare; **reclamation** [reklə'meɪʃən] n bonifica

recline [rɪ'klaɪn] vi stare sdraiato(a); **reclining** adj (seat) ribaltabile

recognition [rekəg'nɪʃən] n riconoscimento; **transformed beyond ~** irriconoscibile

recognize ['rekəgnaɪz] vt: **to ~ (by/as)** riconoscere (a or da/come)

recoil [rɪ'kɔɪl] vi (person): **to ~ from doing sth** rifuggire dal fare qc ♦ n (of gun) rinculo

recollect [rekə'lekt] vt ricordare; **~ion** [-'lekʃən] n ricordo

recommend [rekə'mend] vt raccomandare; (advise) consigliare

reconcile ['rekənsaɪl] vt (two people) riconciliare; (two facts) conciliare, quadrare; **to ~ o.s. to** rassegnarsi a

recondition [ri:kən'dɪʃən] vt rimettere a nuovo

reconnoitre [rekə'nɔɪtə*] (US **reconnoiter**) vt (MIL) fare una ricognizione di

reconstruct [ri:kən'strʌkt] vt ricostruire

record [n 'rekɔ:d, vb rɪ'kɔ:d] n ricordo, documento; (of meeting etc) nota, verbale m; (register) registro; (file) pratica, dossier m inv; (COMPUT) record m inv; (also: **criminal ~**) fedina penale sporca; (MUS: disc) disco; (SPORT) record m inv, primato ♦ vt (set down) prendere nota di, registrare; (MUS: song etc) registrare; **in ~ time** a tempo di record; **off the ~** adj ufficioso(a) ♦ adv ufficiosamente; **~ card** n (in file) scheda; **~ed delivery** (BRIT) n (POST): **~ed delivery letter** etc lettera etc raccomandata; **~er** n (MUS) flauto diritto; **~ holder** n (SPORT) primatista m/f; **~ing** n (MUS) registrazione f; **~ player** n giradischi m inv

recount [rɪ'kaunt] vt raccontare, narrare

re-count ['ri:kaunt] n (POL: of votes) nuovo computo

recoup [rɪ'ku:p] vt ricuperare

recourse [rɪ'kɔ:s] n: **to have ~ to** ricorrere a, far ricorso a

recover [rɪ'kʌvə*] vt ricuperare ♦ vi: **to ~**

(from) riprendersi (da)

recovery [rɪˈkʌvərɪ] n ricupero;
ristabilimento; ripresa

recreation [rekrɪˈeɪʃən] n ricreazione f;
svago; **~al** adj ricreativo(a); **~al drug** n
sostanza stupefacente usata a scopo
ricreativo

recrimination [rɪkrɪmɪˈneɪʃən] n
recriminazione f

recruit [rɪˈkruːt] n recluta; (in company)
nuovo(a) assunto(a) ♦ vt reclutare

rectangle [ˈrektæŋgl] n rettangolo;
rectangular [-ˈtæŋgjulə*] adj rettangolare

rectify [ˈrektɪfaɪ] vt (error) rettificare;
(omission) riparare

rector [ˈrektə*] n (REL) parroco (anglicano);
~y n presbiterio

recuperate [rɪˈkjuːpəreɪt] vi ristabilirsi

recur [rɪˈkəː*] vi riaccadere; (symptoms)
ripresentarsi; **~rent** adj ricorrente,
periodico(a)

recycle [riːˈsaɪkl] vt riciclare

red [red] n rosso; (POL: pej) rosso/a ♦ adj
rosso(a); **in the ~** (account) scoperto;
(business) in deficit; **~ carpet treatment**
n cerimonia col gran pavese; **R~ Cross** n
Croce f Rossa; **~currant** n ribes m inv;
~den vt arrossare ♦ vi arrossire

redeem [rɪˈdiːm] vt (debt) riscattare; (sth in
pawn) ritirare; (fig, also REL) redimere; **~ing**
adj: **~ing feature** unico aspetto positivo

redeploy [riːdɪˈplɔɪ] vt (resources)
riorganizzare

red-haired [-ˈhɛəd] adj dai capelli rossi

red-handed [-ˈhændɪd] adj: **to be caught
~** essere preso(a) in flagrante or con le
mani nel sacco

redhead [ˈredhed] n rosso/a

red herring n (fig) falsa pista

red-hot adj arroventato(a)

redirect [riːdaɪˈrekt] vt (mail) far seguire

red light n: **to go through a ~** (AUT)
passare col rosso; **red-light district** n
quartiere m a luci rosse

redo [riːˈduː] (irreg) vt rifare

redouble [riːˈdʌbl] vt: **to ~ one's efforts**
raddoppiare gli sforzi

redress [rɪˈdres] vt riparare

Red Sea n: **the ~** il Mar Rosso

redskin [ˈredskɪn] n pellerossa m/f

red tape n (fig) burocrazia

reduce [rɪˈdjuːs] vt ridurre; (lower) ridurre,
abbassare; **"~ speed now"** (AUT)
"rallentare"; **at a ~d price** scontato(a);
reduction [rɪˈdʌkʃən] n riduzione f; (of
price) ribasso; (discount) sconto

redundancy [rɪˈdʌndənsɪ] n licenziamento

redundant [rɪˈdʌndnt] adj (worker)
licenziato(a); (detail, object) superfluo(a); **to
be made ~** essere licenziato (per eccesso di
personale)

reed [riːd] n (BOT) canna; (MUS: of clarinet
etc) ancia

reef [riːf] n (at sea) scogliera

reek [riːk] vi: **to ~ (of)** puzzare (di)

reel [riːl] n bobina, rocchetto; (FISHING)
mulinello; (CINEMA) rotolo; (dance) danza
veloce scozzese ♦ vi (sway) barcollare; **~ in**
vt tirare su

ref [ref] (inf) n abbr (= referee) arbitro

refectory [rɪˈfektərɪ] n refettorio

refer [rɪˈfəː*] vt: **to ~ sth to** (dispute,
decision) deferire qc a; **to ~ sb to** (inquirer,
MED: patient) indirizzare qn a; (reader: to
text) rimandare qn a ♦ vi: **~ to** (allude to)
accennare a; (consult) rivolgersi a

referee [refəˈriː] n arbitro; (BRIT: for job
application) referenza ♦ vt arbitrare

reference [ˈrefrəns] n riferimento; (mention)
menzione f, allusione f; (for job application)
referenza; **with ~ to** (COMM: in letter) in or
con riferimento a; **~ book** n libro di
consultazione; **~ number** n numero di
riferimento

referenda [refəˈrendə] npl of **referendum**

referendum [refəˈrendəm] (pl **referenda**) n
referendum m inv

refill [vb riːˈfɪl, n ˈriːfɪl] vt riempire di nuovo;
(pen, lighter etc) ricaricare ♦ n (for pen etc)
ricambio

refine [rɪˈfaɪn] vt raffinare; **~d** adj (person,
taste) raffinato(a)

reflect [rɪˈflekt] vt (light, image) riflettere;
(fig) rispecchiare ♦ vi (think) riflettere,

considerare; **it ~s badly/well on him** si ripercuote su di lui in senso negativo/positivo; **~ion** [-'flekʃən] n riflessione f; (image) riflesso; (criticism): **~ion on** giudizio su; attacco a; **on ~ion** pensandoci sopra

reflex ['ri:fleks] adj riflesso(a) ♦ n riflesso; **~ive** [rɪ'fleksɪv] adj (LING) riflessivo(a)

reform [rɪ'fɔːm] n (of sinner etc) correzione f; (of law etc) riforma ♦ vt correggere; riformare; **~atory** (US) n riformatorio

refrain [rɪ'freɪn] vi: **to ~ from doing** trattenersi dal fare ♦ n ritornello

refresh [rɪ'freʃ] vt rinfrescare; (subj: food, sleep) ristorare; **~er course** (BRIT) n corso di aggiornamento; **~ing** adj (drink) rinfrescante; (sleep) riposante, ristoratore(trice); **~ments** npl rinfreschi mpl

refrigerator [rɪ'frɪdʒəreɪtə*] n frigorifero

refuel [ri:'fjuəl] vi far rifornimento (di carburante)

refuge ['refjuːdʒ] n rifugio; **to take ~ in** rifugiarsi in

refugee [refjuˈdʒiː] n rifugiato/a, profugo/a

refund [n 'riːfʌnd, vb rɪ'fʌnd] n rimborso ♦ vt rimborsare

refurbish [riː'fɜːbɪʃ] vt rimettere a nuovo

refusal [rɪ'fjuːzəl] n rifiuto; **to have first ~ on** avere il diritto d'opzione su

refuse [n 'refjuːs, vb rɪ'fjuːz] n rifiuti mpl ♦ vt, vi rifiutare; **to ~ to do** rifiutare di fare; **~ collection** n raccolta di rifiuti

refute [rɪ'fjuːt] vt confutare

regain [rɪ'geɪn] vt riguadagnare; riacquistare, ricuperare

regal ['riːgl] adj regale; **~ia** [rɪ'geɪlɪə] n insegne fpl regie

regard [rɪ'gɑːd] n riguardo, stima ♦ vt considerare, stimare; **to give one's ~s to** porgere i suoi saluti a; **"with kindest ~s"** "cordiali saluti"; **~ing, as ~s, with ~ to** riguardo a; **~less** adv lo stesso; **~less of** a dispetto di, nonostante

regenerate [rɪ'dʒenəreɪt] vt rigenerare

régime [reɪ'ʒiːm] n regime m

regiment ['redʒɪmənt] n reggimento; **~al** [-'mentl] adj reggimentale

region ['riːdʒən] n regione f; **in the ~ of** (fig) all'incirca di; **~al** adj regionale

register ['redʒɪstə*] n registro; (also: **electoral ~**) lista elettorale ♦ vt registrare; (vehicle) immatricolare; (letter) assicurare; (subj: instrument) segnare ♦ vi iscriversi; (at hotel) firmare il registro; (make impression) entrare in testa; **~ed** (BRIT) adj (letter) assicurato(a); **~ed trademark** n marchio depositato

registrar ['redʒɪstrɑː*] n ufficiale m di stato civile; segretario

registration [redʒɪs'treɪʃən] n (act) registrazione f; iscrizione f; (AUT: also: **~ number**) numero di targa

registry ['redʒɪstrɪ] n ufficio del registro; **~ office** (BRIT) n anagrafe f; **to get married in a ~ office** ≈ sposarsi in municipio

regret [rɪ'gret] n rimpianto, rincrescimento ♦ vt rimpiangere; **~fully** adv con rincrescimento; **~table** adj deplorevole

regular ['regjulə*] adj regolare; (usual) abituale, normale; (soldier) dell'esercito regolare ♦ n (client etc) cliente m/f abituale; **~ly** adv regolarmente

regulate ['regjuleɪt] vt regolare; **regulation** [-'leɪʃən] n regolazione f; (rule) regola, regolamento

rehabilitation ['riːhəbɪlɪ'teɪʃən] n (of offender) riabilitazione f; (of disabled) riadattamento

rehearsal [rɪ'hɜːsəl] n prova

rehearse [rɪ'hɜːs] vt provare

reign [reɪn] n regno ♦ vi regnare

reimburse [riːɪm'bɜːs] vt rimborsare

rein [reɪn] n (for horse) briglia

reindeer ['reɪndɪə*] n inv renna

reinforce [riːɪn'fɔːs] vt rinforzare; **~d concrete** n cemento armato; **~ment** n rinforzo; **~ments** npl (MIL) rinforzi mpl

reinstate [riːɪn'steɪt] vt reintegrare

reiterate [riː'ɪtəreɪt] vt reiterare, ripetere

reject [n 'riːdʒekt, vb rɪ'dʒekt] n (COMM) scarto ♦ vt rifiutare, respingere; (COMM: goods) scartare; **~ion** [rɪ'dʒekʃən] n rifiuto

rejoice [rɪ'dʒɔɪs] vi: **to ~ (at or over)** provare diletto in

rejuvenate [rɪ'dʒuːvəneɪt] *vt* ringiovanire

relapse [rɪ'læps] *n* (MED) ricaduta

relate [rɪ'leɪt] *vt* (*tell*) raccontare; (*connect*) collegare ♦ *vi*: **to ~ to** (*connect*) riferirsi a; (*get on with*) stabilire un rapporto con; **relating to** che riguarda, rispetto a; **~d** *adj*: **~d (to)** imparentato/a (con); collegato(a) *or* connesso(a) (a)

relation [rɪ'leɪʃən] *n* (*person*) parente *m/f*; (*link*) rapporto, relazione *f*; **~ship** *n* rapporto; (*personal ties*) rapporti *mpl*, relazioni *fpl*; (*also*: **family ~ship**) legami *mpl* di parentela

relative ['rɛlətɪv] *n* parente *m/f* ♦ *adj* relativo(a); (*respective*) rispettivo(a); **~ly** *adv* relativamente; (*fairly, rather*) abbastanza

relax [rɪ'læks] *vi* rilasciarsi; (*person: unwind*) rilassarsi ♦ *vt* rilasciare; (*mind, person*) rilassare; **~ation** [riːlæk'seɪʃən] *n* rilasciamento; rilassamento; (*entertainment*) ricreazione *f*, svago; **~ed** *adj* rilassato(a); **~ing** *adj* rilassante

relay ['riːleɪ] *n* (SPORT) corsa a staffetta ♦ *vt* (*message*) trasmettere

release [rɪ'liːs] *n* (*from prison*) rilascio; (*from obligation*) liberazione *f*; (*of gas etc*) emissione *f*; (*of film etc*) distribuzione *f*; (*record*) disco; (*device*) disinnesto ♦ *vt* (*prisoner*) rilasciare; (*from obligation, wreckage etc*) liberare; (*book, film*) fare uscire; (*news*) rendere pubblico(a); (*gas etc*) emettere; (*TECH: catch, spring etc*) disinnestare

relegate ['rɛləgeɪt] *vt* relegare; (*BRIT: SPORT*): **to be ~d** essere retrocesso(a)

relent [rɪ'lɛnt] *vi* cedere; **~less** *adj* implacabile

relevant ['rɛləvənt] *adj* pertinente; (*chapter*) in questione; **~ to** pertinente a

reliability [rɪlaɪə'bɪlɪtɪ] *n* (*of person*) serietà; (*of machine*) affidabilità

reliable [rɪ'laɪəbl] *adj* (*person, firm*) fidato(a), che dà affidamento; (*method*) sicuro(a); (*machine*) affidabile; **reliably** *adv*: **to be reliably informed** sapere da fonti sicure

reliance [rɪ'laɪəns] *n*: **~ (on)** fiducia (in); bisogno (di)

relic ['rɛlɪk] *n* (REL) reliquia; (*of the past*) resto

relief [rɪ'liːf] *n* (*from pain, anxiety*) sollievo; (*help, supplies*) soccorsi *mpl*; (*ART, GEO*) rilievo

relieve [rɪ'liːv] *vt* (*pain, patient*) sollevare; (*bring help*) soccorrere; (*take over from: gen*) sostituire; (: *guard*) rilevare; **to ~ sb of sth** (*load*) alleggerire qn di qc; **to ~ o.s.** fare i propri bisogni

religion [rɪ'lɪdʒən] *n* religione *f*; **religious** *adj* religioso(a)

relinquish [rɪ'lɪŋkwɪʃ] *vt* abbandonare; (*plan, habit*) rinunciare a

relish ['rɛlɪʃ] *n* (CULIN) condimento; (*enjoyment*) gran piacere *m* ♦ *vt* (*food etc*) godere; **to ~ doing** adorare fare

relocate ['riːləʊkeɪt] *vt* trasferire ♦ *vi* trasferirsi

reluctance [rɪ'lʌktəns] *n* riluttanza

reluctant [rɪ'lʌktənt] *adj* riluttante, mal disposto(a); **~ly** *adv* di mala voglia, a malincuore

rely [rɪ'laɪ]: **to ~ on** *vt fus* contare su; (*be dependent*) dipendere da

remain [rɪ'meɪn] *vi* restare, rimanere; **~der** *n* resto; (COMM) rimanenza; **~ing** *adj* che rimane; **~s** *npl* resti *mpl*

remand [rɪ'mɑːnd] *n*: **on ~** in detenzione preventiva ♦ *vt*: **to ~ in custody** rinviare in carcere; trattenere a disposizione della legge; **~ home** (BRIT) *n* riformatorio, casa di correzione

remark [rɪ'mɑːk] *n* osservazione *f* ♦ *vt* osservare, dire; **~able** *adj* notevole; eccezionale

remedial [rɪ'miːdɪəl] *adj* (*tuition, classes*) di riparazione; (*exercise*) correttivo(a)

remedy ['rɛmədɪ] *n*: **~ (for)** rimedio (per) ♦ *vt* rimediare a

remember [rɪ'mɛmbə*] *vt* ricordare, ricordarsi di; **~ me to him** salutalo da parte mia; **remembrance** *n* memoria; ricordo; **Remembrance Day** *n* 11 *novembre, giorno della commemorazione dei caduti in* *guerra*

Remembrance Day

🛈 In Gran Bretagna, il **Remembrance Day** è un giorno di commemorazione dei caduti in guerra. Si celebra ogni anno la domenica più vicina all'11 novembre, anniversario della firma dell'armistizio con la Germania nel 1918.

remind [rɪ'maɪnd] *vt*: **to ~ sb of sth** ricordare qc a qn; **to ~ sb to do** ricordare a qn di fare; **~er** *n* richiamo; (*note etc*) promemoria *m inv*

reminisce [rɛmɪ'nɪs] *vi*: **to ~ (about)** abbandonarsi ai ricordi (di)

reminiscent [rɛmɪ'nɪsnt] *adj*: **~ of** che fa pensare a, che richiama

remiss [rɪ'mɪs] *adj* negligente

remission [rɪ'mɪʃən] *n* remissione *f*

remit [rɪ'mɪt] *vt* (*send: money*) rimettere; **~tance** *n* rimessa

remnant ['rɛmnənt] *n* resto, avanzo; **~s** *npl* (*COMM*) scampoli *mpl*; fine *f* serie

remorse [rɪ'mɔːs] *n* rimorso; **~ful** *adj* pieno(a) di rimorsi; **~less** *adj* (*fig*) spietato(a)

remote [rɪ'məut] *adj* remoto(a), lontano(a); (*person*) distaccato(a); **~ control** *n* telecomando; **~ly** *adv* remotamente, (*slightly*) vagamente

remould ['riːməuld] (*BRIT*) *n* (*tyre*) gomma rivestita

removable [rɪ'muːvəbl] *adj* (*detachable*) staccabile

removal [rɪ'muːvəl] *n* (*taking away*) rimozione *f*; soppressione *f*; (*BRIT: from house*) trasloco; (*from office: dismissal*) destituzione *f*; (*MED*) ablazione *f*; **~ van** (*BRIT*) *n* furgone *m* per traslochi

remove [rɪ'muːv] *vt* togliere, rimuovere; (*employee*) destituire; (*stain*) far sparire; (*doubt, abuse*) sopprimere, eliminare; **~rs** (*BRIT*) *npl* (*company*) ditta *or* impresa di traslochi

Renaissance [rɪ'neɪsɑ̃ːns] *n*: **the ~** il Rinascimento

render ['rɛndə*] *vt* rendere; **~ing** *n* (*MUS etc*) interpretazione *f*

rendez-vous ['rɔndɪvuː] *n* appuntamento; (*place*) luogo d'incontro; (*meeting*) incontro

renegade ['rɛnɪɡeɪd] *n* rinnegato/a

renew [rɪ'njuː] *vt* rinnovare; (*negotiations*) riprendere; **~able** *adj* rinnovabile; **~al** *n* rinnovo; ripresa

renounce [rɪ'nauns] *vt* rinunziare a

renovate ['rɛnəveɪt] *vt* rinnovare; (*art work*) restaurare; **renovation** [-'veɪʃən] *n* rinnovamento; restauro

renown [rɪ'naun] *n* rinomanza; **~ed** *adj* rinomato(a)

rent [rɛnt] *n* affitto ♦ *vt* (*take for ~*) prendere in affitto; (*also*: **~ out**) dare in affitto; **~al** *n* (*for television, car*) affitto

renunciation [rɪnʌnsɪ'eɪʃən] *n* rinunzia

rep [rɛp] *n abbr* (*COMM*: = *representative*) rappresentante *m/f*; (*THEATRE*: = *repertory*) teatro di repertorio

repair [rɪ'pɛə*] *n* riparazione *f* ♦ *vt* riparare; **in good/bad ~** in buone/cattive condizioni; **~ kit** *n* corredo per riparazioni

repatriate [riː'pætrɪeɪt] *vt* rimpatriare

repay [riː'peɪ] (*irreg*) *vt* (*money, creditor*) rimborsare, ripagare; (*sb's efforts*) ricompensare; (*favour*) ricambiare; **~ment** *n* pagamento; rimborso

repeal [rɪ'piːl] *n* (*of law*) abrogazione *f* ♦ *vt* abrogare

repeat [rɪ'piːt] *n* (*RADIO, TV*) replica ♦ *vt* ripetere; (*pattern*) riprodurre; (*promise, attack, also COMM: order*) rinnovare ♦ *vi* ripetere; **~edly** *adv* ripetutamente, spesso

repel [rɪ'pɛl] *vt* respingere; (*disgust*) ripugnare a; **~lent** *adj* repellente ♦ *n*: **insect ~lent** prodotto *m* anti-insetti *inv*

repent [rɪ'pɛnt] *vi*: **to ~ (of)** pentirsi (di); **~ance** *n* pentimento

repertoire ['rɛpətwɑː*] *n* repertorio

repertory ['rɛpətərɪ] *n* (*also*: **~ theatre**) teatro di repertorio

repetition [rɛpɪ'tɪʃən] *n* ripetizione *f*

repetitive [rɪ'pɛtɪtɪv] *adj* (*movement*) che si ripete; (*work*) monotono(a); (*speech*) pieno(a) di ripetizioni

replace [rɪ'pleɪs] *vt* (*put back*) rimettere a posto; (*take the place of*) sostituire; ~**ment** *n* rimessa; sostituzione *f*; (*person*) sostituto/a

replay ['riːpleɪ] *n* (*of match*) partita ripetuta; (*of tape, film*) replay *m inv*

replenish [rɪ'plenɪʃ] *vt* (*glass*) riempire; (*stock etc*) rifornire

replete [rɪ'pliːt] *adj* (*well-fed*) sazio(a)

replica ['replɪkə] *n* replica, copia

reply [rɪ'plaɪ] *n* risposta ♦ *vi* rispondere; ~ **coupon** *n* buono di risposta

report [rɪ'pɔːt] *n* rapporto; (*PRESS etc*) cronaca; (*BRIT: also:* **school ~**) pagella; (*of gun*) sparo ♦ *vt* riportare; (*PRESS etc*) fare una cronaca su; (*bring to notice: occurrence*) segnalare; (: *person*) denunciare ♦ *vi* (*make a report*) fare un rapporto (*or* una cronaca); (*present o.s.*): **to ~ (to sb)** presentarsi (a qn); ~ **card** (*US, SCOTTISH*) *n* pagella; ~**edly** *adv* stando a quanto si dice; **he ~edly told them to ...** avrebbe detto loro di ...; ~**er** *n* reporter *m inv*

repose [rɪ'pəʊz] *n*: **in ~** (*face, mouth*) in riposo

reprehensible [reprɪ'hensɪbl] *adj* riprovevole

represent [reprɪ'zent] *vt* rappresentare; ~**ation** [-'teɪʃən] *n* rappresentazione *f*; (*petition*) rappresentanza; ~**ations** *npl* (*protest*) protesta; ~**ative** *n* rappresentante *m/f*; (*US: POL*) deputato/a ♦ *adj* rappresentativo/a

repress [rɪ'pres] *vt* reprimere; ~**ion** [-'preʃən] *n* repressione *f*

reprieve [rɪ'priːv] *n* (*LAW*) sospensione *f* dell'esecuzione della condanna; (*fig*) dilazione *f*

reprimand ['reprɪmɑːnd] *n* rimprovero ♦ *vt* rimproverare

reprint ['riːprɪnt] *n* ristampa

reprisal [rɪ'praɪzl] *n* rappresaglia

reproach [rɪ'prəʊtʃ] *n* rimprovero ♦ *vt*: **to ~ sb for sth** rimproverare qn di qc; ~**ful** *adj* di rimprovero

reproduce [riːprə'djuːs] *vt* riprodurre ♦ *vi* riprodursi; **reproduction** [-'dʌkʃən] *n* riproduzione *f*

reproof [rɪ'pruːf] *n* riprovazione *f*

reprove [rɪ'pruːv] *vt*: **to ~ (for)** biasimare (per)

reptile ['reptaɪl] *n* rettile *m*

republic [rɪ'pʌblɪk] *n* repubblica; ~**an** *adj, n* repubblicano(a)

repudiate [rɪ'pjuːdɪeɪt] *vt* (*accusation*) respingere

repulse [rɪ'pʌls] *vt* respingere

repulsive [rɪ'pʌlsɪv] *adj* ripugnante, ripulsivo(a)

reputable ['repjʊtəbl] *adj* di buona reputazione; (*occupation*) rispettabile

reputation [repjʊ'teɪʃən] *n* reputazione *f*

reputed [rɪ'pjuːtɪd] *adj* reputato(a); ~**ly** *adv* secondo quanto si dice

request [rɪ'kwest] *n* domanda; (*formal*) richiesta ♦ *vt*: **to ~ (of or from sb)** chiedere (a qn); ~ **stop** (*BRIT*) *n* (*for bus*) fermata facoltativa *or* a richiesta

require [rɪ'kwaɪə*] *vt* (*need: subj: person*) aver bisogno di; (: *thing, situation*) richiedere; (*want*) volere; esigere; (*order*): **to ~ sb to do sth** ordinare a qn di fare qc; ~**ment** *n* esigenza; bisogno; requisito

requisition [rekwɪ'zɪʃən] *n*: ~ **(for)** richiesta (di) ♦ *vt* (*MIL*) requisire

rescue ['reskjuː] *n* salvataggio; (*help*) soccorso ♦ *vt* salvare; ~ **party** *n* squadra di salvataggio; ~**r** *n* salvatore/trice

research [rɪ'sɜːtʃ] *n* ricerca, ricerche *fpl* ♦ *vt* fare ricerche su; ~**er** *n* ricercatore/trice

resemblance [rɪ'zembləns] *n* somiglianza

resemble [rɪ'zembl] *vt* assomigliare a

resent [rɪ'zent] *vt* risentirsi di; ~**ful** *adj* pieno(a) di risentimento; ~**ment** *n* risentimento

reservation [rezə'veɪʃən] *n* (*booking*) prenotazione *f*; (*doubt*) dubbio; (*protected area*) riserva; (*BRIT: on road: also:* **central ~**) spartitraffico *m inv*

reserve [rɪ'zɜːv] *n* riserva ♦ *vt* (*seats etc*) prenotare; ~**s** *npl* (*MIL*) riserve *fpl*; **in ~** in serbo; ~**d** *adj* (*shy*) riservato(a)

reservoir ['rezəvwɑː*] *n* serbatoio

reshuffle [riːˈʃʌfl] *n*: **Cabinet ~** (*POL*) rimpasto governativo

reside [rɪˈzaɪd] *vi* risiedere

residence [ˈrezɪdəns] *n* residenza; ~ **permit** (*BRIT*) *n* permesso di soggiorno

resident [ˈrezɪdənt] *n* residente *m/f*; (*in hotel*) cliente *m/f* fisso(a) ♦ *adj* residente; (*doctor*) fisso(a); (*course, college*) a tempo pieno con pernottamento; ~**ial** [-ˈdenʃəl] *adj* di residenza; (*area*) residenziale

residue [ˈrezɪdjuː] *n* resto; (*CHEM, PHYSICS*) residuo

resign [rɪˈzaɪn] *vt* (*one's post*) dimettersi da ♦ *vi* dimettersi; **to ~ o.s. to** rassegnarsi a; ~**ation** [rezɪgˈneɪʃən] *n* dimissioni *fpl*; rassegnazione *f*; ~**ed** *adj* rassegnato(a)

resilience [rɪˈzɪlɪəns] *n* (*of material*) elasticità, resilienza; (*of person*) capacità di recupero

resilient [rɪˈzɪlɪənt] *adj* elastico(a); (*person*) che si riprende facilmente

resin [ˈrezɪn] *n* resina

resist [rɪˈzɪst] *vt* resistere a; ~**ance** *n* resistenza

resolution [rezəˈluːʃən] *n* risoluzione *f*

resolve [rɪˈzɒlv] *n* risoluzione *f* ♦ *vi* (*decide*): **to ~ to do** decidere di fare ♦ *vt* (*problem*) risolvere

resort [rɪˈzɔːt] *n* (*town*) stazione *f*; (*recourse*) ricorso ♦ *vi*: **to ~ to** aver ricorso a; **in the last ~** come ultima risorsa

resounding [rɪˈzaʊndɪŋ] *adj* risonante; (*fig*) clamoroso(a)

resource [rɪˈzɔːs] *n* risorsa; ~**s** *npl* (*coal, iron etc*) risorse *fpl*; ~**ful** *adj* pieno(a) di risorse, intraprendente

respect [rɪsˈpekt] *n* rispetto ♦ *vt* rispettare; ~**s** *npl* (*greetings*) ossequi *mpl*; **with ~ to** rispetto a, riguardo a; **in this ~** per questo riguardo; ~**able** *adj* rispettabile; ~**ful** *adj* rispettoso(a)

respective [rɪsˈpektɪv] *adj* rispettivo(a)

respite [ˈrespaɪt] *n* respiro, tregua

respond [rɪsˈpɒnd] *vi* rispondere

response [rɪsˈpɒns] *n* risposta

responsibility [rɪspɒnsɪˈbɪlɪtɪ] *n* responsabilità *f inv*

responsible [rɪsˈpɒnsɪbl] *adj* (*trustworthy*) fidato(a); (*job*) di (grande) responsabilità; ~ **(for)** responsabile (di)

responsive [rɪsˈpɒnsɪv] *adj* che reagisce

rest [rest] *n* riposo; (*stop*) sosta, pausa; (*MUS*) pausa; (*object: to support sth*) appoggio, sostegno; (*remainder*) resto, avanzi *mpl* ♦ *vi* riposarsi; (*remain*) rimanere, restare; (*be supported*): **to ~ on** appoggiarsi su ♦ *vt* (far) riposare; (*lean*): **to ~ sth on/against** appoggiare qc su/contro; **the ~ of them** gli altri; **it ~s with him to decide** sta a lui decidere

restaurant [ˈrestərɒŋ] *n* ristorante *m*; ~ **car** (*BRIT*) *n* vagone *m* ristorante

restful [ˈrestful] *adj* riposante

rest home *n* casa di riposo

restitution [restɪˈtjuːʃən] *n*: **to make ~ to sb for sth** compensare qn di qc

restive [ˈrestɪv] *adj* agitato(a), impaziente

restless [ˈrestlɪs] *adj* agitato(a), irrequieto(a)

restoration [restəˈreɪʃən] *n* restauro; restituzione *f*

restore [rɪˈstɔː*] *vt* (*building, to power*) restaurare; (*sth stolen*) restituire; (*peace, health*) ristorare

restrain [rɪsˈtreɪn] *vt* (*feeling, growth*) contenere, frenare; (*person*): **to ~ (from doing)** trattenere (dal fare); ~**ed** *adj* (*style*) contenuto(a), sobrio(a); (*person*) riservato(a); ~**t** *n* (*restriction*) limitazione *f*; (*moderation*) ritegno; (*of style*) contenutezza

restrict [rɪsˈtrɪkt] *vt* restringere, limitare; ~**ion** [-kʃən] *n*: ~**ion (on)** restrizione *f* (di), limitazione *f*

rest room (*US*) *n* toletta

restructure [riːˈstrʌktʃə*] *vt* ristrutturare

result [rɪˈzʌlt] *n* risultato ♦ *vi*: **to ~ in** avere per risultato; **as a ~ of** in or di conseguenza a, in seguito a

resume [rɪˈzjuːm] *vt, vi* (*work, journey*) riprendere

résumé [ˈreɪzjuːmeɪ] *n* riassunto; (*US*) curriculum *m inv* vitae

resumption [rɪˈzʌmpʃən] *n* ripresa

resurgence [rɪˈsəːdʒəns] n rinascita

resurrection [rezəˈrekʃən] n risurrezione f

resuscitate [rɪˈsʌsɪteɪt] vt (MED) risuscitare; **resuscitation** [-ˈteɪʃən] n rianimazione f

retail [ˈriːteɪl] adj, adv al minuto ♦ vt vendere al minuto; **~er** n commerciante m/f al minuto, dettagliante m/f; **~ price** n prezzo al minuto

retain [rɪˈteɪn] vt (keep) tenere, serbare; **~er** n (fee) onorario

retaliate [rɪˈtælɪeɪt] vi: **to ~ (against)** vendicarsi (di); **retaliation** [-ˈeɪʃən] n rappresaglie fpl

retarded [rɪˈtɑːdɪd] adj ritardato(a)

retch [retʃ] vi aver conati di vomito

retire [rɪˈtaɪə*] vi (give up work) andare in pensione; (withdraw) ritirarsi, andarsene; (go to bed) andare a letto, ritirarsi; **~d** adj (person) pensionato(a); **~ment** n pensione f; (act) pensionamento; **retiring** adj (leaving) uscente; (shy) riservato(a)

retort [rɪˈtɔːt] vi rimbeccare

retrace [riːˈtreɪs] vt: **to ~ one's steps** tornare sui passi

retract [rɪˈtrækt] vt (statement) ritrattare; (claws, undercarriage, aerial) ritrarre, ritirare

retrain [riːˈtreɪn] vt (worker) riaddestrare

retread [ˈriːtred] n (tyre) gomma rigenerata

retreat [rɪˈtriːt] n ritirata; (place) rifugio ♦ vi battere in ritirata

retribution [retrɪˈbjuːʃən] n castigo

retrieval [rɪˈtriːvəl] n (see vb) ricupero; riparazione f

retrieve [rɪˈtriːv] vt (sth lost) ricuperare, ritrovare; (situation, honour) salvare; (error, loss) rimediare a; **~r** n cane m da riporto

retrospect [ˈretrəspekt] n: **in ~** guardando indietro; **~ive** [-ˈspektɪv] adj retrospettivo(a); (law) retroattivo(a)

return [rɪˈtəːn] n (going or coming back) ritorno; (of sth stolen etc) restituzione f; (FINANCE: from land, shares) profitto, reddito ♦ cpd (journey, match) di ritorno; (BRIT: ticket) di andata e ritorno ♦ vi tornare, ritornare ♦ vt rendere, restituire; (bring back) riportare; (send back) mandare indietro; (put back) rimettere; (POL: candidate) eleggere; **~s** npl (COMM) incassi mpl; profitti mpl; **in ~ (for)** in cambio (di); **by ~ of post** a stretto giro di posta; **many happy ~s (of the day)!** cento di questi giorni!

reunion [riːˈjuːnɪən] n riunione f

reunite [riːjuːˈnaɪt] vt riunire

rev [rev] n abbr (AUT: = revolution) giro ♦ vt (also: ~ up) imballare

revamp [ˈriːvæmp] vt (firm) riorganizzare

reveal [rɪˈviːl] vt (make known) rivelare, svelare; (display) rivelare, mostrare; **~ing** adj rivelatore(trice); (dress) scollato(a)

revel [ˈrevl] vi: **to ~ in sth/in doing** dilettarsi di qc/a fare

revelation [revəˈleɪʃən] n rivelazione f

revenge [rɪˈvendʒ] n vendetta ♦ vt vendicare; **to take ~ on** vendicarsi di

revenue [ˈrevənjuː] n reddito

reverberate [rɪˈvəːbəreɪt] vi (sound) rimbombare; (light) riverberarsi; (fig) ripercuotersi

revere [rɪˈvɪə*] vt venerare

reverence [ˈrevərəns] n venerazione f, riverenza

Reverend [ˈrevərənd] adj (in titles) reverendo(a)

reverie [ˈrevərɪ] n fantasticheria

reversal [rɪˈvəːsl] n capovolgimento

reverse [rɪˈvəːs] n contrario, opposto; (back, defeat) rovescio; (AUT: also: ~ gear) marcia indietro ♦ adj (order, direction) contrario(a), opposto(a) ♦ vt (turn) invertire, rivoltare; (change) capovolgere, rovesciare; (LAW: judgment) cassare; (car) fare marcia indietro con ♦ vi (BRIT: AUT, person etc) fare marcia indietro; **~-charge call** (BRIT) n (TEL) telefonata con addebito al ricevente; **reversing lights** (BRIT) npl (AUT) luci fpl per la retromarcia

revert [rɪˈvəːt] vi: **to ~ to** tornare a

review [rɪˈvjuː] n rivista; (of book, film) recensione f; (of situation) esame m ♦ vt passare in rivista; fare la recensione di; fare il punto di; **~er** n recensore/a

revise [rɪˈvaɪz] vt (manuscript) rivedere, correggere; (opinion) emendare,

modificare; (*study: subject, notes*) ripassare;
revision [rɪ'vɪʒən] *n* revisione *f*; ripasso
revitalize [riː'vaɪtəlaɪz] *vt* ravvivare
revival [rɪ'vaɪvəl] *n* ripresa; ristabilimento *m*; (*of faith*) risveglio
revive [rɪ'vaɪv] *vt* (*person*) rianimare; (*custom*) far rivivere; (*hope, courage, economy*) ravvivare; (*play, fashion*) riesumare ♦ *vi* (*person*) rianimarsi; (*hope*) ravvivarsi; (*activity*) riprendersi
revolt [rɪ'vəʊlt] *n* rivolta, ribellione *f* ♦ *vi* rivoltarsi, ribellarsi ♦ *vt* (far) rivoltare; **~ing** *adj* ripugnante
revolution [revə'luːʃən] *n* rivoluzione *f*; (*of wheel etc*) rivoluzione, giro; **~ary** *adj, n* rivoluzionario(a)
revolve [rɪ'vɒlv] *vi* girare
revolver [rɪ'vɒlvə*] *n* rivoltella
revolving [rɪ'vɒlvɪŋ] *adj* girevole
revue [rɪ'vjuː] *n* (THEATRE) rivista
revulsion [rɪ'vʌlʃən] *n* ripugnanza
reward [rɪ'wɔːd] *n* ricompensa, premio ♦ *vt*: **to ~ (for)** ricompensare (per); **~ing** *adj* (*fig*) gratificante
rewind [riː'waɪnd] (*irreg*) *vt* (*watch*) ricaricare; (*ribbon etc*) riavvolgere
rewire [riː'waɪə*] *vt* (*house*) rifare l'impianto elettrico di
reword [riː'wɜːd] *vt* formulare *or* esprimere con altre parole
rheumatism ['ruːmətɪzəm] *n* reumatismo
Rhine [raɪn] *n*: **the ~** il Reno
rhinoceros [raɪ'nɒsərəs] *n* rinoceronte *m*
rhododendron [rəʊdə'dendrən] *n* rododendro
Rhone [rəʊn] *n*: **the ~** il Rodano
rhubarb ['ruːbɑːb] *n* rabarbaro
rhyme [raɪm] *n* rima; (*verse*) poesia
rhythm ['rɪðm] *n* ritmo
rib [rɪb] *n* (ANAT) costola ♦ *vt* (*tease*) punzecchiare
ribbon ['rɪbən] *n* nastro; **in ~s** (*torn*) a brandelli
rice [raɪs] *n* riso; **~ pudding** *n* budino di riso
rich [rɪtʃ] *adj* ricco(a); (*clothes*) sontuoso(a); (*abundant*): **~ in** ricco(a) di; **the ~** *npl*

(*wealthy people*) i ricchi; **~es** *npl* ricchezze *fpl*; **~ly** *adv* riccamente; (*dressed*) sontuosamente; (*deserved*) pienamente
rickets ['rɪkɪts] *n* rachitismo
ricochet ['rɪkəʃeɪ] *vi* rimbalzare
rid [rɪd] (*pt, pp* **rid**) *vt*: **to ~ sb of** sbarazzare *or* liberare qn di; **to get ~ of** sbarazzarsi di
ridden ['rɪdn] *pp of* **ride**
riddle ['rɪdl] *n* (*puzzle*) indovinello ♦ *vt*: **to be ~d with** (*holes*) essere crivellato(a) di; (*doubts*) essere pieno(a) di
ride [raɪd] (*pt* **rode**, *pp* **ridden**) *n* (*on horse*) cavalcata; (*outing*) passeggiata; (*distance covered*) cavalcata; corsa ♦ *vi* (*as sport*) cavalcare; (*go somewhere: on horse, bicycle*) andare (a cavallo *or* in bicicletta *etc*); (*journey: on bicycle, motorcycle, bus*) andare, viaggiare ♦ *vt* (*a horse*) montare, cavalcare; **to take sb for a ~** (*fig*) prendere in giro qn; fregare qn; **to ~ a horse/bicycle/camel** montare a cavallo/in bicicletta/in groppa a un cammello; **~r** *n* cavalcatore/trice; (*in race*) fantino; (*on bicycle*) ciclista *m/f*; (*on motorcycle*) motociclista *m/f*
ridge [rɪdʒ] *n* (*of hill*) cresta; (*of roof*) colmo; (*on object*) riga in rilievo)
ridicule ['rɪdɪkjuːl] *n* ridicolo; scherno ♦ *vt* mettere in ridicolo
ridiculous [rɪ'dɪkjʊləs] *adj* ridicolo(a)
riding ['raɪdɪŋ] *n* equitazione *f*; **~ school** *n* scuola d'equitazione
rife [raɪf] *adj* diffuso(a); **to be ~ with** abbondare di
riffraff ['rɪfræf] *n* canaglia
rifle ['raɪfl] *n* carabina ♦ *vt* vuotare; **~ through** *vt fus* frugare tra; **~ range** *n* campo di tiro; (*at fair*) tiro a segno
rift [rɪft] *n* fessura, crepatura; (*fig: disagreement*) incrinatura, disaccordo
rig [rɪg] *n* (*also*: **oil ~**: *on land*) derrick *m inv*; (*: at sea*) piattaforma di trivellazione ♦ *vt* (*election etc*) truccare; **~ out** (BRIT) *vt*: **to ~ out as/in** vestire da/in; **~ up** *vt* allestire; **~ging** *n* (NAUT) attrezzatura
right [raɪt] *adj* giusto(a); (*suitable*) appropriato(a); (*not left*) destro(a) ♦ *n* giusto; (*title, claim*) diritto; (*not left*) destra

♦ *adv* (*answer*) correttamente; (*not on the left*) a destra ♦ *vt* raddrizzare; (*fig*) riparare ♦ *excl* bene!; **to be ~** (*person*) aver ragione; (*answer*) essere giusto(a) *or* corretto(a); **by ~s** di diritto; **on the ~** a destra; **to be in the ~** aver ragione, essere nel giusto; **~ now** proprio adesso; subito; **~ away** subito; **~ angle** *n* angolo retto; **~eous** ['raɪtʃəs] *adj* retto(a), virtuoso(a); (*anger*) giusto(a), giustificato(a); **~ful** *adj* (*heir*) legittimo(a); **~-handed** *adj* (*person*) che adopera la mano destra; **~-hand man** *n* braccio destro; **~-hand side** *n* il lato destro; **~ly** *adv* bene, correttamente; (*with reason*) a ragione; **~ of way** *n* diritto di passaggio; (*AUT*) precedenza; **~-wing** *adj* (*POL*) di destra

rigid ['rɪdʒɪd] *adj* rigido(a); (*principle*) rigoroso(a)

rigmarole ['rɪgmərəul] *n* tiritera; commedia

rile [raɪl] *vt* irritare, seccare

rim [rɪm] *n* orlo; (*of spectacles*) montatura; (*of wheel*) cerchione *m*

rind [raɪnd] *n* (*of bacon*) cotenna; (*of lemon etc*) scorza

ring [rɪŋ] (*pt* **rang**, *pp* **rung**) *n* anello; (*of people, objects*) cerchio; (*of spies*) giro; (*of smoke etc*) spirale *m*; (*arena*) pista, arena; (*for boxing*) ring *m inv*; (*sound of bell*) scampanio ♦ *vi* (*person, bell, telephone*) suonare; (*also:* **~ out**: *voice, words*) risuonare; (*TEL*) telefonare; (*ears*) fischiare ♦ *vt* (*BRIT: TEL*) telefonare a; (*bell, doorbell*) suonare; **to give sb a ~** (*BRIT: TEL*) dare un colpo di telefono a qn; **~ back** *vt, vi* (*TEL*) richiamare; **~ off** (*BRIT*) *vi* (*TEL*) mettere giù, riattaccare; **~ up** (*BRIT*) *vt* (*TEL*) telefonare a; **~ing** *n* (*of bell*) scampanio; (*of telephone*) squillo; (*in ears*) ronzio; **~ing tone** (*BRIT*) *n* (*TEL*) segnale *m* di libero; **~leader** *n* (*of gang*) capobanda *m*

ringlets ['rɪŋlɪts] *npl* boccoli *mpl*

ring road (*BRIT*) *n* raccordo anulare

rink [rɪŋk] *n* (*also:* **ice ~**) pista di pattinaggio

rinse [rɪns] *n* risciacquatura; (*hair tint*) cachet *m inv* ♦ *vt* sciacquare

riot ['raɪət] *n* sommossa, tumulto; (*of colours*) orgia ♦ *vi* tumultuare; **to run ~** creare disordine; **~ous** *adj* tumultuoso(a); (*living*) sfrenato(a); (*party*) scatenato(a)

rip [rɪp] *n* strappo ♦ *vt* strappare ♦ *vi* strapparsi; **~cord** *n* cavo di sfilamento

ripe [raɪp] *adj* (*fruit, grain*) maturo(a); (*cheese*) stagionato(a); **~n** *vt* maturare ♦ *vi* maturarsi

ripple ['rɪpl] *n* increspamento, ondulazione *f*; mormorio ♦ *vi* incresparsi

rise [raɪz] (*pt* **rose**, *pp* **risen**) *n* (*slope*) salita, pendio; (*hill*) altura; (*increase: in wages*: *BRIT*) aumento; (: *in prices, temperature*) rialzo, aumento; (*fig: to power etc*) ascesa ♦ *vi* alzarsi, levarsi; (*prices*) aumentare; (*waters, river*) crescere; (*sun, wind, person: from chair, bed*) levarsi; (*also:* **~ up**: *building*) ergersi; (: *rebel*) insorgere; ribellarsi; (*in rank*) salire; **to give ~ to** provocare, dare origine a; **to ~ to the occasion** essere all'altezza; **risen** ['rɪzn] *pp of* **rise**; **rising** *adj* (*increasing: number*) sempre crescente; (: *prices*) in aumento; (*tide*) montante; (*sun, moon*) nascente, che sorge

risk [rɪsk] *n* rischio; pericolo ♦ *vt* rischiare; **to take** *or* **run the ~ of doing** correre il rischio di fare; **at ~** in pericolo; **at one's own ~** a proprio rischio e pericolo; **~y** *adj* rischioso(a)

risqué ['riːskeɪ] *adj* (*joke*) spinto(a)

rissole ['rɪsəul] *n* crocchetta

rite [raɪt] *n* rito; **last ~s** l'estrema unzione

ritual ['rɪtjuəl] *adj* rituale ♦ *n* rituale *m*

rival ['raɪvl] *n* rivale *m/f*; (*in business*) concorrente *m/f* ♦ *adj* rivale; che fa concorrenza ♦ *vt* essere in concorrenza con; **to ~ sb/sth in** competere con qn/qc in; **~ry** *n* rivalità; concorrenza

river ['rɪvə*] *n* fiume *m* ♦ *cpd* (*port, traffic*) fluviale; **up/down ~** a monte/valle; **~bank** *n* argine *m*; **~bed** *n* letto di fiume

rivet ['rɪvɪt] *n* ribattino, rivetto ♦ *vt* (*fig*) concentrare, fissare

Riviera [rɪvɪˈɛərə] *n*: **the (French) ~** la Costa Azzurra; **the Italian ~** la Riviera

road [rəud] *n* strada; (*small*) cammino; (*in town*) via ♦ *cpd* stradale; **major/minor ~**

strada con/senza diritto di precedenza; ~ **accident** n incidente m stradale; ~**block** n blocco stradale; ~**hog** n guidatore m egoista e spericolato; ~ **map** n carta stradale; ~ **rage** n comportamento aggressivo al volante; ~**safety** n sicurezza sulle strade; ~**side** n margine m della strada; ~**sign** n cartello stradale; ~ **user** n chi usa la strada; ~**way** n carreggiata; ~**works** npl lavori mpl stradali; ~**worthy** adj in buono stato di marcia

roam [rəum] vi errare, vagabondare

roar [rɔː*] n ruggito; (of crowd) tumulto; (of thunder, storm) muggito; (of laughter) scoppio ♦ vi ruggire; tumultuare; muggire; **to ~ with laughter** scoppiare dalle risa; **to do a ~ing trade** fare affari d'oro

roast [rəust] n arrosto ♦ vt arrostire; (coffee) tostare, torrefare; ~ **beef** n arrosto di manzo

rob [rɒb] vt (person) rubare; (bank) svaligiare; **to ~ sb of sth** derubare qn di qc; (fig: deprive) privare qn di qc; ~**ber** n ladro; (armed) rapinatore m; ~**bery** n furto, rapina

robe [rəub] n (for ceremony etc) abito; (also: **bath ~**) accappatoio; (US: also: **lap ~**) coperta

robin ['rɒbɪn] n pettirosso

robot ['rəubɒt] n robot m inv

robust [rəu'bʌst] adj robusto(a); (economy) solido(a)

rock [rɒk] n (substance) roccia; (boulder) masso; roccia; (in sea) scoglio; (US: pebble) ciottolo; (BRIT: sweet) zucchero candito ♦ vt (swing gently: cradle) dondolare; (: child) cullare; (shake) scrollare, far tremare ♦ vi dondolarsi; scrollarsi, tremare; **on the ~s** (drink) col ghiaccio; (marriage etc) in crisi; ~ **and roll** n rock and roll m; ~-**bottom** adj bassissimo(a); ~**ery** n giardino roccioso

rocket ['rɒkɪt] n razzo

rock fall n parete f della roccia

rocking ['rɒkɪŋ]: ~ **chair** n sedia a dondolo; ~ **horse** n cavallo a dondolo

rocky ['rɒkɪ] adj (hill) roccioso(a); (path) sassoso(a); (marriage etc) instabile

rod [rɒd] n (metallic, TECH) asta; (wooden) bacchetta; (also: **fishing ~**) canna da pesca

rode [rəud] pt of **ride**

rodent ['rəudnt] n roditore m

rodeo ['rəudɪəu] n rodeo

roe [rəu] n (species: also: ~ **deer**) capriolo; (of fish, also: **hard ~**) uova fpl di pesce; **soft ~** latte m di pesce

rogue [rəug] n mascalzone m

role [rəul] n ruolo

roll [rəul] n rotolo; (of banknotes) mazzo; (also: **bread ~**) panino; (register) lista; (sound: of drums etc) rullo ♦ vt rotolare; (also: ~ **up**: string) aggomitolare; (also: ~ **up**: sleeves) rimboccare; (cigarettes) arrotolare; (eyes) roteare; (also: ~ **out**: pastry) stendere; (lawn, road etc) spianare ♦ vi rotolare; (wheel) girare; (drum) rullare; (vehicle: also: ~ **along**) avanzare; (ship) rollare; ~ **about** or **around** vi rotolare qua e là; (person) rotolarsi; ~ **by** vi (time) passare; ~ **over** vi rivoltarsi; ~ **up** (inf) vi (arrive) arrivare ♦ vt (carpet) arrotolare; ~ **call** n appello; ~**er** n rullo; (wheel) rotella; (for hair) bigodino; ~**er blades** npl pattini mpl in linea; ~**er coaster** n montagne fpl russe; ~**er skates** npl pattini mpl a rotelle

rolling ['rəulɪŋ] adj (landscape) ondulato(a); ~ **pin** n matterello; ~ **stock** n (RAIL) materiale m rotabile

ROM [rɒm] n abbr (= read only memory) memoria di sola lettura

Roman ['rəumən] adj, n romano(a); ~ **Catholic** adj, n cattolico(a)

romance [rə'mæns] n storia (or avventura or film m inv) romantico(a); (charm) poesia; (love affair) idillio

Romania [rəu'meɪnɪə] n = **Rumania**

Roman numeral n numero romano

romantic [rə'mæntɪk] adj romantico(a); sentimentale

Rome [rəum] n Roma

romp [rɒmp] n gioco rumoroso ♦ vi (also: ~ **about**) far chiasso, giocare in un modo rumoroso

rompers ['rɒmpəz] npl pagliaccetto

roof [ruːf] n tetto; (of tunnel, cave) volta ♦ vt

coprire (con un tetto); **~ of the mouth** palato; **~ing** *n* materiale *m* per copertura; **~ rack** *n* (AUT) portabagagli *m inv*

rook [ruk] *n* (*bird*) corvo nero; (CHESS) torre *f*

room [ru:m] *n* (*in house*) stanza; (*bed~, in hotel*) camera; (*in school etc*) sala; (*space*) posto, spazio; **~s** *npl* (*lodging*) alloggio; **"~s to let"** (BRIT), **"~s for rent"** (US) "si affittano camere"; **there is ~ for improvement** si potrebbe migliorare; **~ing house** (US) *n* casa in cui si affittano camere o appartamentini ammobiliati; **~mate** *n* compagno/a di stanza; **~ service** *n* servizio da camera; **~y** *adj* spazioso(a); (*garment*) ampio(a)

roost [ru:st] *vi* appollaiarsi

rooster [ˈru:stə*] *n* gallo

root [ru:t] *n* radice *f* ♦ *vi* (*plant, belief*) attecchire; **~ about** *vi* (*fig*) frugare; **~ for** *vt fus* fare il tifo per; **~ out** *vt* estirpare

rope [rəup] *n* corda, fune *f*; (NAUT) cavo ♦ *vt* (*box*) legare; (*climbers*) legare in cordata; (*area: also*: **~ off**) isolare cingendo con cordoni; **to know the ~s** (*fig*) conoscere i trucchi del mestiere; **~ in** *vt* (*fig*) coinvolgere; **~ ladder** *n* scala a corda

rosary [ˈrəuzəri] *n* rosario; roseto

rose [rəuz] *pt of* **rise** ♦ *n* rosa; (*also*: **~ bush**) rosaio; (*on watering can*) rosetta

rosé [ˈrəuzeɪ] *n* vino rosato

rosebud [ˈrəuzbʌd] *n* bocciolo di rosa

rosebush [ˈrəuzbuʃ] *n* rosaio

rosemary [ˈrəuzməri] *n* rosmarino

rosette [rəuˈzɛt] *n* coccarda

roster [ˈrɔstə*] *n*: **duty ~** ruolino di servizio

rostrum [ˈrɔstrəm] *n* tribuna

rosy [ˈrəuzi] *adj* roseo(a)

rot [rɔt] *n* (*decay*) putrefazione *f*; (*inf: nonsense*) stupidaggini *fpl* ♦ *vt, vi* imputridire, marcire

rota [ˈrəutə] *n* tabella dei turni

rotary [ˈrəutəri] *adj* rotante

rotate [rəuˈteɪt] *vt* (*revolve*) far girare; (*change round: jobs*) fare a turno ♦ *vi* (*revolve*) girare; **rotating** *adj* (*movement*) rotante

rotten [ˈrɔtn] *adj* (*decayed*) putrido(a),

marcio(a); (*dishonest*) corrotto(a); (*inf: bad*) brutto(a); (*: action*) vigliacco(a); **to feel ~** (*ill*) sentirsi da cani

rouble [ˈru:bl] (US **ruble**) *n* rublo

rouge [ru:ʒ] *n* belletto

rough [rʌf] *adj* (*skin, surface*) ruvido(a); (*terrain, road*) accidentato(a); (*voice*) rauco(a); (*person, manner: coarse*) rozzo(a), aspro(a); (*: violent*) brutale; (*district*) malfamato(a); (*weather*) cattivo(a); (*sea*) mosso(a); (*plan*) abbozzato(a); (*guess*) approssimativo(a) ♦ *n* (GOLF) macchia; **to ~ it** far vita dura; **to sleep ~** (BRIT) dormire all'addiaccio; **~age** *n* alimenti *mpl* ricchi di cellulosa; **~-and-ready** *adj* rudimentale; **~cast** *n* intonaco grezzo; **~ copy** *n* brutta copia; **~ly** *adv* (*handle*) rudemente, brutalmente; (*make*) grossolanamente; (*speak*) bruscamente; (*approximately*) approssimativamente; **~ness** *n* ruvidità; (*of manner*) rozzezza

roulette [ru:ˈlɛt] *n* roulette *f*

Roumania [ru:ˈmeɪnɪə] *n* = **Rumania**

round [raund] *adj* rotondo(a); (*figures*) tondo(a) ♦ *n* (BRIT: of toast) fetta; (*duty: of policeman, milkman etc*) giro; (*: of doctor*) visite *fpl*; (*game: of cards, golf, in competition*) partita; (*of ammunition*) cartuccia; (BOXING) round *m inv*; (*of talks*) serie *f inv* ♦ *vt* (*corner*) girare; (*bend*) prendere ♦ *prep* intorno a ♦ *adv*: **all ~** tutt'attorno; **to go the long way ~** fare il giro più lungo; **all the year ~** tutto l'anno; **it's just ~ the corner** (*also fig*) è dietro l'angolo; **~ the clock** ininterrottamente; **to go ~ to sb's house** andare da qn; **go ~ the back** passi dietro; **enough to go ~** abbastanza per tutti; **~ of applause** applausi *mpl*; **~ of drinks** giro di bibite; **~ of sandwiches** sandwich *m inv*; **~ off** *vt* (*speech etc*) finire; **~ up** *vt* radunare; (*criminals*) fare una retata di; (*prices*) arrotondare; **~about** *n* (BRIT: AUT) rotatoria; (*: at fair*) giostra ♦ *adj* (*route, means*) indiretto(a); **~ers** *npl* (*game*) gioco simile al baseball; **~ly** *adv* (*fig*) chiaro e tondo; **~ trip** *n* (viaggio di) andata e

ritorno; **~up** n raduno; (of criminals) retata
rouse [rauz] vt (wake up) svegliare; (stir up)
destare; provocare; risvegliare; **rousing**
adj (speech, applause) entusiastico(a)
route [ru:t] n itinerario; (of bus) percorso
routine [ru:'ti:n] adj (work) corrente,
abituale; (procedure) solito(a) ♦ n (pej)
routine f, tran tran m; (THEATRE) numero
rove [rəuv] vt vagabondare per
row¹ [rəu] n (line) riga, fila; (KNITTING) ferro;
(behind one another: of cars, people) fila; (in
boat) remata ♦ vi (in boat) remare; (as
sport) vogare ♦ vt (boat) manovrare a remi;
in a ~ (fig) di fila
row² [rau] n (racket) baccano, chiasso;
(dispute) lite f; (scolding) sgridata ♦ vi
(argue) litigare
rowboat ['rəubəut] (US) n barca a remi
rowdy ['raudɪ] adj chiassoso(a);
turbolento(a) ♦ n teppista m/f
rowing ['rəuɪŋ] n canottaggio; **~ boat**
(BRIT) n barca a remi
royal ['rɔɪəl] adj reale; **R~ Air Force** n
aeronautica militare britannica
royalty ['rɔɪəltɪ] n (royal persons) (membri
mpl della) famiglia reale; (payment: to
author) diritti mpl d'autore
r.p.m. abbr (= revolutions per minute) giri/
min
R.S.V.P. abbr (= répondez s'il vous plaît)
R.S.V.P.
Rt Hon. (BRIT) abbr (= Right Honourable)
≈ Onorevole
rub [rʌb] n: **to give sth a ~** strofinare qc;
(sore place) massaggiare qc ♦ vt strofinare;
massaggiare; (hands: also: **~ together**)
sfregarsi; **to ~ sb up** (BRIT) or **~ sb the
wrong way** (US) lisciare qn contro pelo; **~
off** vi andare via; **~ off on** vt fus lasciare
una traccia su; **~ out** vt cancellare
rubber ['rʌbə*] n gomma; **~ band** n
elastico; **~ plant** n ficus m inv
rubbish ['rʌbɪʃ] n (from household)
immondizie fpl, rifiuti mpl; (fig: pej) cose
fpl senza valore; robaccia; sciocchezze fpl;
~ bin (BRIT) n pattumiera; **~ dump** n (in
town) immondezzaio

rubble ['rʌbl] n macerie fpl; (smaller)
pietrisco
ruble ['ru:bl] (US) n = **rouble**
ruby ['ru:bɪ] n rubino
rucksack ['rʌksæk] n zaino
rudder ['rʌdə*] n timone m
ruddy ['rʌdɪ] adj (face) rubicondo(a); (inf:
damned) maledetto(a)
rude [ru:d] adj (impolite: person) scortese,
rozzo(a); (: word, manners) grossolano(a),
rozzo(a); (shocking) indecente; **~ness** n
scortesia; grossolanità
ruffle ['rʌfl] vt (hair) scompigliare; (clothes,
water) increspare; (fig: person) turbare
rug [rʌg] n tappeto; (BRIT: for knees) coperta
rugby ['rʌgbɪ] n (also: **~ football**) rugby m
rugged ['rʌgɪd] adj (landscape) aspro(a);
(features, determination) duro(a); (character)
brusco(a)
ruin ['ru:ɪn] n rovina ♦ vt rovinare; **~s** npl (of
building, castle etc) rovine fpl, ruderi mpl;
~ous adj rovinoso(a); (expenditure)
inverosimile
rule [ru:l] n regola; (regulation)
regolamento, regola; (government)
governo; (~r) riga ♦ vt (country) governare;
(person) dominare ♦ vi regnare; decidere;
(LAW) dichiarare; **as a ~** normalmente; **~
out** vt escludere; **~d** adj (paper)
vergato(a); **~r** n (sovereign) sovrano/a; (for
measuring) regolo, riga; **ruling** adj (party)
al potere; (class) dirigente ♦ n (LAW)
decisione f
rum [rʌm] n rum m
Rumania [ru:'meɪnɪə] n Romania
rumble ['rʌmbl] n rimbombo; brontolio ♦ vi
rimbombare; (stomach, pipe) brontolare
rummage ['rʌmɪdʒ] vi frugare
rumour ['ru:mə*] (US **rumor**) n voce f ♦ vt:
it is ~ed that corre voce che
rump [rʌmp] n groppa; **~ steak** n bistecca
di girello
rumpus ['rʌmpəs] (inf) n baccano; (quarrel)
rissa
run [rʌn] (pt ran, pp run) n corsa; (outing)
gita (in macchina); (distance travelled)
percorso, tragitto; (SKI) pista; (CRICKET,

BASEBALL) meta; (*series*) serie f; (*THEATRE*) periodo di rappresentazione; (*in tights, stockings*) smagliatura ♦ vt (*distance*) correre; (*operate: business*) gestire, dirigere; (*: competition, course*) organizzare; (*: hotel*) gestire; (*: house*) governare; (*COMPUT*) eseguire; (*water, bath*) far scorrere; (*force through: rope, pipe*): **to ~ sth through** far passare qc attraverso; (*pass: hand, finger*): **to ~ sth over** passare qc su; (*PRESS: feature*) presentare ♦ vi correre; (*flee*) scappare; (*pass: road etc*) passare; (*work: machine, factory*) funzionare, andare; (*bus, train: operate*) far servizio; (*: travel*) circolare; (*continue: play, contract*) durare; (*slide: drawer; flow: river, bath*) scorrere; (*colours, washing*) stemperarsi; (*in election*) presentarsi candidato; (*nose*) colare; **there was a ~ on ...** c'era una corsa a ...; **in the long ~** a lungo andare; **on the ~** in fuga; **to ~ a race** partecipare ad una gara; **I'll ~ you to the station** la porto alla stazione; **to ~ a risk** correre un rischio; **~ about** or **around** vi (*children*) correre qua e là; **~ across** vt fus (*find*) trovare per caso; **~ away** vi fuggire; **~ down** vt (*production*) ridurre gradualmente; (*factory*) rallentare l'attività di; (*AUT*) investire; (*criticize*) criticare; **to be ~ down** (*person: tired*) essere esausto(a); **~ in** (*BRIT*) vt (*car*) rodare, fare il rodaggio di; **~ into** vt fus (*meet: person*) incontrare per caso; (*: trouble*) incontrare, trovare; (*collide with*) andare a sbattere contro; **~ off** vi fuggire ♦ vt (*water*) far scolare; (*copies*) fare; **~ out** vi (*person*) uscire di corsa; (*liquid*) colare; (*lease*) scadere; (*money*) esaurirsi; **~ out of** vt fus rimanere a corto di; **~ over** vt (*AUT*) investire, mettere sotto ♦ vt fus (*revise*) rivedere; **~ through** vt fus (*instructions*) dare una scorsa a; (*rehearse: play*) riprovare, ripetere; **~ up** vt (*debt*) lasciar accumulare; **to ~ up against** (*difficulties*) incontrare; **~away** adj (*person*) fuggiasco(a); (*horse*) in libertà; (*truck*) fuori controllo

rung [rʌŋ] pp of **ring** ♦ n (*of ladder*) piolo

runner [ˈrʌnə*] n (*in race*) corridore m; (*: horse*) partente m/f; (*on sledge*) pattino; (*for drawer etc*) guida; **~ bean** (*BRIT*) n fagiolo rampicante; **~-up** n secondo(a) arrivato(a)

running [ˈrʌnɪŋ] n corsa; direzione f; organizzazione f; funzionamento ♦ adj (*water*) corrente; (*commentary*) simultaneo(a); **to be in/out of the ~ for sth** essere/non essere più in lizza per qc; **6 days ~** 6 giorni di seguito; **~ costs** npl costi mpl d'esercizio; (*of car*) spese fpl di mantenimento

runny [ˈrʌnɪ] adj che cola

run-of-the-mill adj solito(a), banale

runt [rʌnt] n (*also pej*) omuncolo; (*ZOOL*) animale m più piccolo del normale

run-through n prova

run-up n: **~ to** (*election etc*) periodo che precede

runway [ˈrʌnweɪ] n (*AVIAT*) pista (di decollo)

rupture [ˈrʌptʃə*] n (*MED*) ernia

rural [ˈrʊrəl] adj rurale

ruse [ruːz] n trucco

rush [rʌʃ] n corsa precipitosa; (*hurry*) furia, fretta; (*sudden demand*): **~ for** corsa a; (*current*) flusso; (*of emotion*) impeto; (*BOT*) giunco ♦ vt mandare or spedire velocemente; (*attack: town etc*) prendere d'assalto ♦ vi precipitarsi; **~ hour** n ora di punta

rusk [rʌsk] n biscotto

Russia [ˈrʌʃə] n Russia; **~n** adj russo(a) ♦ n russo/a; (*LING*) russo

rust [rʌst] n ruggine f ♦ vi arrugginirsi

rustic [ˈrʌstɪk] adj rustico(a)

rustle [ˈrʌsl] vi frusciare ♦ vt (*paper*) far frusciare

rustproof [ˈrʌstpruːf] adj inossidabile

rusty [ˈrʌstɪ] adj arrugginito(a)

rut [rʌt] n solco; (*ZOOL*) fregola; **to get into a ~** (*fig*) adagiarsi troppo

ruthless [ˈruːθlɪs] adj spietato(a)

rye [raɪ] n segale f; **~ bread** n pane m di segale

S, s

Sabbath ['sæbəθ] *n* (*Jewish*) sabato; (*Christian*) domenica

sabotage ['sæbətɑːʒ] *n* sabotaggio ♦ *vt* sabotare

saccharin(e) ['sækərɪn] *n* saccarina

sachet ['sæʃeɪ] *n* bustina

sack [sæk] *n* (*bag*) sacco ♦ *vt* (*dismiss*) licenziare, mandare a spasso; (*plunder*) saccheggiare; **to get the ~** essere mandato a spasso; **~ing** *n* tela di sacco; (*dismissal*) licenziamento

sacrament ['sækrəmənt] *n* sacramento

sacred ['seɪkrɪd] *adj* sacro(a)

sacrifice ['sækrɪfaɪs] *n* sacrificio ♦ *vt* sacrificare

sad [sæd] *adj* triste

saddle ['sædl] *n* sella ♦ *vt* (*horse*) sellare; **to be ~d with sth** (*inf*) avere qc sulle spalle; **~bag** *n* (*on bicycle*) borsa

sadistic [sə'dɪstɪk] *adj* sadico(a)

sadness ['sædnɪs] *n* tristezza

s.a.e. *n abbr* = **stamped addressed envelope**

safe [seɪf] *adj* sicuro(a); (*out of danger*) salvo(a), al sicuro; (*cautious*) prudente ♦ *n* cassaforte *f*; **~ from** al sicuro da; **~ and sound** sano(a) e salvo(a); **(just) to be on the ~ side** per non correre rischi; **~-conduct** *n* salvacondotto; **~-deposit** *n* (*vault*) caveau *m inv*; (*box*) cassetta di sicurezza; **~guard** *n* salvaguardia ♦ *vt* salvaguardare; **~keeping** *n* custodia; **~ly** *adv* sicuramente; sano(a) e salvo(a); prudentemente; **~ sex** *n* sesso sicuro

safety ['seɪftɪ] *n* sicurezza; **~ belt** *n* cintura di sicurezza; **~ pin** *n* spilla di sicurezza; **~ valve** *n* valvola di sicurezza

saffron ['sæfrən] *n* zafferano

sag [sæg] *vi* incurvarsi; afflosciarsi

sage [seɪdʒ] *n* (*herb*) salvia; (*man*) saggio

Sagittarius [sædʒɪ'tɛərɪəs] *n* Sagittario

Sahara [sə'hɑːrə] *n*: **the ~ (Desert)** il (deserto del) Sahara

said [sɛd] *pt, pp of* **say**

sail [seɪl] *n* (*on boat*) vela; (*trip*): **to go for a ~** fare un giro in barca a vela ♦ *vt* (*boat*) condurre, governare ♦ *vi* (*travel: ship*) navigare; (*: passenger*) viaggiare per mare; (*set off*) salpare; (*sport*) fare della vela; **they ~ed into Genoa** entrarono nel porto di Genova; **~ through** *vt fus* (*fig*) superare senza difficoltà; **~boat** (*US*) *n* barca a vela; **~ing** *n* (*sport*) vela; **to go ~ing** fare della vela; **~ing boat** *n* barca a vela; **~ing ship** *n* veliero; **~or** *n* marinaio

saint [seɪnt] *n* santo/a; **~ly** *adj* santo(a)

sake [seɪk] *n*: **for the ~ of** per, per amore di

salad ['sæləd] *n* insalata; **~ bowl** *n* insalatiera; **~ cream** (*BRIT*) *n* (tipo di) maionese *f*; **~ dressing** *n* condimento per insalata

salami [sə'lɑːmɪ] *n* salame *m*

salary ['sælərɪ] *n* stipendio

sale [seɪl] *n* vendita; (*at reduced prices*) svendita, liquidazione *f*; (*auction*) vendita all'asta; **"for ~"** "in vendita"; **on ~** in vendita; **on ~ or return** da vendere o rimandare; **~room** *n* sala delle aste; **~s assistant** (*US* **~s clerk**) *n* commesso/a; **~sman/swoman** (*irreg*) *n* commesso/a; (*representative*) rappresentante *m/f*

salmon ['sæmən] *n inv* salmone *m*

saloon [sə'luːn] *n* (*US*) saloon *m inv*, bar *m inv*; (*BRIT: AUT*) berlina; (*ship's lounge*) salone *m*

salt [sɔlt] *n* sale *m* ♦ *vt* salare; **~ cellar** *n* saliera; **~water** *adj* di mare; **~y** *adj* salato(a)

salute [sə'luːt] *n* saluto ♦ *vt* salutare

salvage ['sælvɪdʒ] *n* (*saving*) salvataggio; (*things saved*) beni *mpl* salvati *or* recuperati ♦ *vt* salvare, mettere in salvo

salvation [sæl'veɪʃən] *n* salvezza; **S~ Army** *n* Esercito della Salvezza

same [seɪm] *adj* stesso(a), medesimo(a) ♦ *pron*: **the ~** lo(la) stesso(a), gli(le) stessi(e); **the ~ book as** lo stesso libro di (*o* che); **at the ~ time** allo stesso tempo; **all** *or* **just the ~** tuttavia; **to do the ~ as sb** fare come qn; **the ~ to you!** altrettanto a te!

sample ['sɑːmpl] *n* campione *m* ♦ *vt (food)* assaggiare; *(wine)* degustare

sanction ['sæŋkʃən] *n* sanzione *f* ♦ *vt* sancire, sanzionare

sanctity ['sæŋktɪtɪ] *n* santità

sanctuary ['sæŋktjuərɪ] *n (holy place)* santuario; *(refuge)* rifugio; *(for wildlife)* riserva

sand [sænd] *n* sabbia ♦ *vt (also: ~ down)* cartavetrare

sandal ['sændl] *n* sandalo

sandbox ['sændbɒks] *(US) n =* **sandpit**

sandcastle ['sændkɑːsl] *n* castello di sabbia

sandpaper ['sændpeɪpə*] *n* carta vetrata

sandpit ['sændpɪt] *n (for children)* buca di sabbia

sandstone ['sændstəun] *n* arenaria

sandwich ['sændwɪtʃ] *n* tramezzino, panino, sandwich *m inv* ♦ *vt:* **~ed between** incastrato(a) fra; **cheese/ham ~** sandwich al formaggio/prosciutto; **~ course** *(BRIT) n* corso di formazione professionale

sandy ['sændɪ] *adj* sabbioso(a); *(colour)* color sabbia *inv*, biondo(a) rossiccio(a)

sane [seɪn] *adj (person)* sano(a) di mente; *(outlook)* sensato(a)

sang [sæŋ] *pt of* **sing**

sanitary ['sænɪtərɪ] *adj (system, arrangements)* sanitario(a); *(clean)* igienico(a); **~ towel** *(US* **~ napkin**) *n* assorbente *m* (igienico)

sanitation [sænɪ'teɪʃən] *n (in house)* impianti *mpl* sanitari; *(in town)* fognature *fpl*; **~ department** *(US) n* nettezza urbana

sanity ['sænɪtɪ] *n* sanità mentale; *(common sense)* buon senso

sank [sæŋk] *pt of* **sink**

Santa Claus [sæntə'klɔːz] *n* Babbo Natale

sap [sæp] *n (of plants)* linfa ♦ *vt (strength)* fiaccare

sapling ['sæplɪŋ] *n* alberello

sapphire ['sæfaɪə*] *n* zaffiro

sarcasm ['sɑːkæzm] *n* sarcasmo

sardine [sɑː'diːn] *n* sardina

Sardinia [sɑː'dɪnɪə] *n* Sardegna

sash [sæʃ] *n* fascia

sat [sæt] *pt, pp of* **sit**

Satan ['seɪtən] *n* Satana *m*

satchel ['sætʃl] *n* cartella

satellite ['sætəlaɪt] *adj* satellite ♦ *n* satellite *m*; **~ dish** *n* antenna parabolica; **~ television** *n* televisione *f* via satellite

satin ['sætɪn] *n* raso ♦ *adj* di raso

satire ['sætaɪə*] *n* satira

satisfaction [sætɪs'fækʃən] *n* soddisfazione *f*

satisfactory [sætɪs'fæktərɪ] *adj* soddisfacente

satisfy ['sætɪsfaɪ] *vt* soddisfare; *(convince)* convincere; **~ing** *adj* soddisfacente

Saturday ['sætədɪ] *n* sabato

sauce [sɔːs] *n* salsa; *(containing meat, fish)* sugo; **~pan** *n* casseruola

saucer ['sɔːsə*] *n* sottocoppa *m*, piattino

Saudi ['saudɪ]: **~ Arabia** *n* Arabia Saudita; **~ (Arabian)** *adj, n* arabo(a) saudita

sauna ['sɔːnə] *n* sauna

saunter ['sɔːntə*] *vi* andare a zonzo, bighellonare

sausage ['sɒsɪdʒ] *n* salsiccia; **~ roll** *n* rotolo di pasta sfoglia ripieno di salsiccia

sauté ['səuteɪ] *adj:* **~ potatoes** patate *fpl* saltate in padella

savage ['sævɪdʒ] *adj (cruel, fierce)* selvaggio(a), feroce; *(primitive)* primitivo(a) ♦ *n* selvaggio/a ♦ *vt* attaccare selvaggiamente

save [seɪv] *vt (person, belongings, COMPUT)* salvare; *(money)* risparmiare, mettere da parte; *(time)* risparmiare; *(food)* conservare; *(avoid: trouble)* evitare; *(SPORT)* parare ♦ *vi (also: ~ up)* economizzare ♦ *n (SPORT)* parata ♦ *prep* salvo, a eccezione di

saving ['seɪvɪŋ] *n* risparmio ♦ *adj:* **the ~ grace of** l'unica cosa buona di; **~s** *npl (money)* risparmi *mpl*; **~s account** *n* libretto di risparmio; **~s bank** *n* cassa di risparmio

saviour ['seɪvjə*] *(US* **savior**) *n* salvatore *m*

savour ['seɪvə*] *(US* **savor**) *vt* gustare; **~y** *adj (dish: not sweet)* salato(a)

saw [sɔː] *(pt* **sawed**, *pp* **sawed** *or* **sawn**) *of* **see** ♦ *n (tool)* sega ♦ *vt* segare; **~dust** *n* segatura; **~mill** *n* segheria; **sawn** *pp of*

saw; **~n-off shotgun** n fucile m a canne mozze

saxophone ['sæksəfəʊn] n sassofono

say [seɪ] (pt, pp **said**) n: **to have one's ~** fare sentire il proprio parere; **to have a** or **some ~** avere voce in capitolo ♦ vt dire; **could you ~ that again?** potrebbe ripeterlo?; **that goes without ~ing** va da sé; **~ing** n proverbio, detto

scab [skæb] n crosta; (pej) crumiro/a

scaffold ['skæfəʊld] n (gallows) patibolo; **~ing** n impalcatura

scald [skɔ:ld] n scottatura ♦ vt scottare

scale [skeɪl] n scala; (of fish) squama ♦ vt (mountain) scalare; **~s** npl (for weighing) bilancia; **on a large ~** su vasta scala; **~ of charges** tariffa; **~ down** vt ridurre (proporzionalmente)

scallop ['skɔləp] n (ZOOL) pettine m; (SEWING) smerlo

scalp [skælp] n cuoio capelluto ♦ vt scotennare

scalpel ['skælpl] n bisturi m inv

scampi ['skæmpɪ] npl scampi mpl

scan [skæn] vt scrutare; (glance at quickly) scorrere, dare un'occhiata a; (TV) analizzare; (RADAR) esplorare ♦ n (MED) ecografia

scandal ['skændl] n scandalo; (gossip) pettegolezzi mpl

Scandinavia [skændɪ'neɪvɪə] n Scandinavia; **~n** adj, n scandinavo(a)

scant [skænt] adj scarso(a); **~y** adj insufficiente; (swimsuit) ridotto(a)

scapegoat ['skeɪpgəʊt] n capro espiatorio

scar [skɑ:] n cicatrice f ♦ vt sfregiare

scarce [skɛəs] adj scarso(a); (copy, edition) raro(a); **to make o.s. ~** (inf) squagliarsela; **~ly** adv appena; **scarcity** n scarsità, mancanza

scare [skɛə*] n spavento; panico ♦ vt spaventare, atterrire; **there was a bomb ~ at the bank** hanno evacuato la banca per paura di un attentato dinamitardo; **to ~ sb stiff** spaventare a morte qn; **~ off** or **away** vt mettere in fuga; **~crow** n spaventapasseri m inv; **~d** adj: **to be ~d** aver paura

scarf [skɑ:f] (pl **scarves** or **~s**) n (long) sciarpa; (square) fazzoletto da testa, foulard m inv

scarlet ['skɑ:lɪt] adj scarlatto(a); **~ fever** n scarlattina

scarves [skɑ:vz] npl of **scarf**

scary ['skɛərɪ] adj che spaventa

scathing ['skeɪðɪŋ] adj aspro(a)

scatter ['skætə*] vt spargere; (crowd) disperdere ♦ vi disperdersi; **~brained** adj sbadato(a)

scavenger ['skævəndʒə*] n (person) accattone/a

scenario [sɪ'nɑ:rɪəʊ] n (THEATRE, CINEMA) copione m; (fig) situazione f

scene [si:n] n (THEATRE, fig etc) scena; (of crime, accident) scena, luogo; (sight, view) vista, veduta; **~ry** n (THEATRE) scenario; (landscape) panorama m; **scenic** adj scenico(a); panoramico(a)

scent [sent] n profumo; (sense of smell) olfatto, odorato; (fig: track) pista

sceptical ['skeptɪkəl] (US **skeptical**) adj scettico(a)

sceptre ['septə*] (US **scepter**) n scettro

schedule ['ʃedju:l, (US) 'skedju:l] n programma m, piano; (of trains) orario; (of prices etc) lista, tabella ♦ vt (pension ~ etc) programma m ♦ vi fare progetti; **on ~** in orario; **to be ahead of/behind ~** essere in anticipo/ritardo sul previsto; **~d flight** n volo di linea

scheme [ski:m] n piano, progetto; (method) sistema m; (dishonest plan, plot) intrigo, trama; (arrangement) disposizione f, sistemazione f; (pension ~ etc) programma m ♦ vi fare progetti; (intrigue) complottare; **scheming** adj intrigante ♦ n intrighi mpl, macchinazioni fpl

schism ['skɪzəm] n scisma m

scholar ['skɔlə*] n erudito/a; (pupil) scolaro/a; **~ship** n erudizione f; (grant) borsa di studio

school [sku:l] n (primary, secondary) scuola; (university: US) università f inv ♦ cpd scolare, scolastico(a) ♦ vt (animal) addestrare; **~ age** n età scolare; **~bag** n cartella; ~**book** n libro scolastico; ~**boy** n scolaro; ~**children** npl scolari mpl; ~**girl** n scolara; ~**ing** n istruzione f; ~**master** n (*primary*) maestro; (*secondary*) insegnante m; ~**mistress** n maestra; insegnante f; ~**teacher** n insegnante m/f, docente m/f; (*primary*) maestro/a

sciatica [sar'ætɪkə] n sciatica

science ['saɪəns] n scienza; ~ **fiction** n fantascienza; **scientific** [-'tɪfɪk] adj scientifico(a); **scientist** n scienziato/a

scissors ['sɪzəz] npl forbici fpl

scoff [skɔf] vt (*BRIT: inf: eat*) tranguiare, ingozzare ♦ vi: **to ~ (at)** (*mock*) farsi beffe (di)

scold [skəuld] vt rimproverare

scone [skɔn] n focaccina da tè

scoop [sku:p] n mestolo; (*for ice cream*) cucchiaio dosatore; (*PRESS*) colpo giornalistico, notizia (in) esclusiva; ~ **out** vt scavare; ~ **up** vt tirare su, sollevare

scooter ['sku:tə*] n (*motor cycle*) motoretta, scooter m inv; (*toy*) monopattino

scope [skəup] n (*capacity: of plan, undertaking*) portata f; (*: of person*) capacità fpl; (*opportunity*) possibilità fpl

scorch [skɔ:tʃ] vt (*clothes*) strinare, bruciacchiare; (*earth, grass*) seccare, bruciare

score [skɔ:*] n punti mpl, punteggio; (*MUS*) partitura, spartito; (*twenty*) venti ♦ vt (*goal, point*) segnare, fare; (*success*) ottenere ♦ vi segnare; (*FOOTBALL*) fare un goal; (*keep score*) segnare i punti; ~**s of** (*very many*) un sacco di; **on that ~** a questo riguardo; **to ~ 6 out of 10** prendere 6 su 10; ~ **out** vt cancellare con un segno; ~**board** n tabellone m segnapunti

scorn [skɔ:n] n disprezzo ♦ vt disprezzare

scornful ['skɔ:nful] adj sprezzante

Scorpio ['skɔ:pɪəu] n Scorpione m

scorpion ['skɔ:pɪən] n scorpione m

Scot [skɔt] n scozzese m/f

Scotch [skɔtʃ] n whisky m scozzese, scotch m

scot-free adv: **to get off ~** farla franca

Scotland ['skɔtlənd] n Scozia

Scots [skɔts] adj scozzese; ~**man/woman** (*irreg*) n scozzese m/f

Scottish ['skɔtɪʃ] adj scozzese

scoundrel ['skaundrl] n farabutto/a; (*child*) furfantello/a

scour ['skauə*] vt (*search*) battere, perlustrare

scout [skaut] n (*MIL*) esploratore m; (*also:* **boy ~**) giovane esploratore, scout m inv; ~ **around** vi cercare in giro; **girl ~** (*US*) n giovane esploratrice f

scowl [skaul] vi accigliarsi, aggrottare le sopracciglia; **to ~ at** guardare torvo

scrabble ['skræbl] vi (*claw*): **to ~ (at)** graffiare, grattare; (*also:* **~ around:** *search*) cercare a tentoni ♦ n: **S~** ® Scarabeo ®

scraggy ['skrægɪ] adj scarno(a), molto magro(a)

scram [skræm] (*inf*) vi filare via

scramble ['skræmbl] n arrampicata ♦ vi inerpicarsi; **to ~ out** etc uscire etc in fretta; **to ~ for** azzuffarsi per; ~**d eggs** npl uova fpl strapazzate

scrap [skræp] n pezzo, pezzetto; (*fight*) zuffa; (*also:* ~ **iron**) rottami mpl di ferro, ferraglia ♦ vt demolire; (*fig*) scartare ♦ vi: **to ~ (with sb)** fare a botte (con qn); ~**s** npl (*waste*) scarti mpl; ~**book** n album m inv di ritagli; ~ **dealer** n commerciante m di ferraglia

scrape [skreɪp] vt, vi raschiare, grattare ♦ n: **to get into a** ~ cacciarsi in un guaio; ~ **through** vi farcela per un pelo; ~ **together** vt (*money*) raggranellare; ~**r** n raschietto

scrap: ~ **heap** n: **on the ~ heap** (*fig*) nel dimenticatoio; ~ **merchant** (*BRIT*) n commerciante m di ferraglia; ~ **paper** n cartaccia

scratch [skrætʃ] n graffio ♦ cpd: ~ **team** squadra raccogliticcia ♦ vt graffiare, rigare ♦ vi grattare; (*paint, car*) graffiare; **to start from ~** cominciare or partire da zero; **to be up to ~** essere all'altezza

scrawl [skrɔ:l] n scarabocchio ♦ vi scarabocchiare

scrawny ['skrɔ:nɪ] adj scarno(a)

scream [skri:m] *n* grido, urlo ♦ *vi* urlare, gridare

scree [skri:] *n* ghiaione *m*

screech [skri:tʃ] *vi* stridere

screen [skri:n] *n* schermo; (*fig*) muro, cortina, velo ♦ *vt* schermare, fare schermo a; (*from the wind etc*) riparare; (*film*) proiettare; (*book*) adattare per lo schermo; (*candidates etc*) selezionare; **~ing** *n* (MED) dépistage *m inv*; **~play** *n* sceneggiatura; **~saver** *n* (COMPUT) screen saver *m inv*

screw [skru:] *n* vite *f* ♦ *vt* avvitare; **~ up** *vt* (*paper etc*) spiegazzare; (*inf: ruin*) rovinare; **to ~ up one's eyes** strizzare gli occhi; **~driver** *n* cacciavite *m*

scribble ['skrɪbl] *n* scarabocchio ♦ *vt* scribacchiare in fretta ♦ *vi* scarabocchiare

script [skrɪpt] *n* (CINEMA etc) copione *m*; (*in exam*) elaborato *or* compito d'esame

scripture(s) ['skrɪptʃə(z)] *n(pl)* sacre Scritture *fpl*

scroll [skrəʊl] *n* rotolo di carta

scrounge [skraʊndʒ] (*inf*) *vt*: **to ~ sth (off** *or* **from sb)** scroccare qc (a qn) ♦ *n*: **on the ~** a sbafo

scrub [skrʌb] *n* (*land*) boscaglia ♦ *vt* pulire strofinando; (*reject*) annullare

scruff [skrʌf] *n*: **by the ~ of the neck** per la collottola

scruffy ['skrʌfɪ] *adj* sciatto(a)

scrum(mage) ['skrʌm(ɪdʒ)] *n* mischia

scruple ['skru:pl] *n* scrupolo

scrutiny ['skru:tɪnɪ] *n* esame *m* accurato

scuff [skʌf] *vt* (*shoes*) consumare strascicando

scuffle ['skʌfl] *n* baruffa, tafferuglio

sculptor ['skʌlptə*] *n* scultore *m*

sculpture ['skʌlptʃə*] *n* scultura

scum [skʌm] *n* schiuma; (*pej: people*) feccia

scupper ['skʌpə*] (BRIT: *inf*) *vt* far naufragare

scurry ['skʌrɪ] *vi* sgambare, affrettarsi; **~ off** *vi* andarsene a tutta velocità

scuttle ['skʌtl] *n* (*also*: **coal ~**) secchio del carbone ♦ *vt* (*ship*) autoaffondare ♦ *vi* (*scamper*): **to ~ away, ~ off** darsela a gambe, scappare

scythe [saɪð] *n* falce *f*

SDP (BRIT) *n abbr* = **Social Democratic Party**

sea [si:] *n* mare *m* ♦ *cpd* marino(a), del mare; (*bird, fish*) di mare; (*route, transport*) marittimo(a); **by ~** per mare; **on the ~** (*boat*) in mare; (*town*) di mare; **to be all at ~** (*fig*) non sapere che pesci pigliare; **out to ~** al largo; **(out) at ~** in mare; **~board** *n* costa; **~food** *n* frutti *mpl* di mare; **~ front** *n* lungomare *m*; **~gull** *n* seduta spiritica

seal [si:l] *n* (*animal*) foca; (*stamp*) sigillo; (*impression*) impronta del sigillo ♦ *vt* sigillare; **~ off** *vt* (*close*) sigillare; (*forbid entry to*) bloccare l'accesso a

sea level *n* livello del mare

seam [si:m] *n* cucitura; (*of coal*) filone *m*

seaman ['si:mən] (*irreg*) *n* marinaio

seance ['seɪɒns] *n* seduta spiritica

seaplane ['si:pleɪn] *n* idrovolante *m*

seaport ['si:pɔ:t] *n* porto di mare

search [sə:tʃ] *n* ricerca; (LAW: *at sb's home*) perquisizione *f* ♦ *vt* frugare ♦ *vi*: **to ~ for** ricercare; **in ~ of** alla ricerca di; **~ through** *vt fus* frugare; **~ engine** *n* (COMPUT) motore *m* di ricerca; **~ing** *adj* minuzioso(a); penetrante; **~light** *n* proiettore *m*; **~ party** *n* squadra di soccorso; **~ warrant** *n* mandato di perquisizione

seashore ['si:ʃɔ:*] *n* spiaggia

seasick ['si:sɪk] *adj* che soffre il mal di mare

seaside ['si:saɪd] *n* spiaggia; **~ resort** *n* stazione *f* balneare

season ['si:zn] *n* stagione *f* ♦ *vt* condire, insaporire; **~al** *adj* stagionale; **~ed** *adj* (*fig*) con esperienza; **~ing** *n* condimento; **~ ticket** *n* abbonamento

seat [si:t] *n* sedile *m*; (*in bus, train: place*) posto; (PARLIAMENT) seggio; (*buttocks*) didietro; (*of trousers*) fondo ♦ *vt* far sedere; (*have room for*) avere *or* essere fornito(a) di posti a sedere per; **to be ~ed** essere seduto(a); **~ belt** *n* cintura di sicurezza

sea water *n* acqua di mare

seaweed ['si:wi:d] *n* alghe *fpl*

seaworthy ['si:wə:ðɪ] *adj* atto(a) alla navigazione

sec. *abbr* = **second(s)**

secluded [sɪ'kluːdɪd] *adj* isolato(a), appartato(a)

seclusion [sɪ'kluːʒən] *n* isolamento

second[1] [sɪ'kɔnd] (*BRIT*) *vt* (*worker*) distaccare

second[2] ['sɛkənd] *num* secondo(a) ♦ *adv* (*in race etc*) al secondo posto ♦ *n* (*unit of time*) secondo; (*AUT: also*: ~ **gear**) seconda; (*COMM: imperfect*) scarto; (*BRIT: SCOL: degree*) *laurea con punteggio discreto* ♦ *vt* (*motion*) appoggiare; **~ary** *adj* secondario(a); **~ary school** *n* scuola secondaria; **~-class** *adj* di seconda classe ♦ *adv* in seconda classe; **~er** *n* sostenitore/trice; **~hand** *adj* di seconda mano, usato(a); ~ **hand** *n* (*on clock*) lancetta dei secondi; **~ly** *adv* in secondo luogo; **~-rate** *adj* scadente; ~ **thoughts** *npl* ripensamenti *mpl*; **on** ~ **thoughts** (*BRIT*) *or* **thought** (*US*) ripensandoci bene

secrecy ['siːkrəsɪ] *n* segretezza

secret ['siːkrɪt] *adj* segreto(a) ♦ *n* segreto; **in** ~ in segreto

secretarial [sɛkrɪ'tɛərɪəl] *adj* di segretario(a)

secretariat [sɛkrɪ'tɛərɪət] *n* segretariato

secretary ['sɛkrətrɪ] *n* segretario/a; **S~ of State (for)** (*BRIT: POL*) ministro (di)

secretive ['siːkrətɪv] *adj* riservato(a)

sect [sɛkt] *n* setta; **~arian** [-'tɛərɪən] *adj* settario(a)

section ['sɛkʃən] *n* sezione *f*

sector ['sɛktə*] *n* settore *m*

secure [sɪ'kjuə*] *adj* sicuro(a); (*firmly fixed*) assicurato(a), ben fermato(a); (*in safe place*) al sicuro ♦ *vt* (*fix*) fissare, assicurare; (*get*) ottenere, assicurarsi

security [sɪ'kjuərɪtɪ] *n* sicurezza; (*for loan*) garanzia

sedate [sɪ'deɪt] *adj* posato(a); calmo(a) ♦ *vt* calmare

sedation [sɪ'deɪʃən] *n* (*MED*) effetto dei sedativi

sedative ['sɛdɪtɪv] *n* sedativo, calmante *m*

seduce [sɪ'djuːs] *vt* sedurre; **seduction** [-'dʌkʃən] *n* seduzione *f*; **seductive** [-'dʌktɪv] *adj* seducente

see [siː] (*pt* **saw**, *pp* **seen**) *vt* vedere; (*accompany*): **to** ~ **sb to the door** accompagnare qn alla porta ♦ *vi* vedere; (*understand*) capire ♦ *n* sede *f* vescovile; **to** ~ **that** (*ensure*) badare che +*sub*, fare in modo che +*sub*; **~ you soon!** a presto!; ~ **about** *vt fus* occuparsi di; ~ **off** *vt* salutare alla partenza; ~ **through** *vt* portare a termine ♦ *vt fus* non lasciarsi ingannare da; ~ **to** *vt fus* occuparsi di

seed [siːd] *n* seme *m*; (*fig*) germe *m*; (*TENNIS etc*) testa di serie; **to go to** ~ fare seme; (*fig*) scadere; **~ling** *n* piantina di semenzaio; **~y** *adj* (*shabby: person*) sciatto(a); (: *place*) cadente

seeing ['siːɪŋ] *conj*: ~ **(that)** visto che

seek [siːk] (*pt*, *pp* **sought**) *vt* cercare

seem [siːm] *vi* sembrare, parere; **there ~s to be ...** sembra che ci sia ...; **~ingly** *adv* apparentemente

seen [siːn] *pp of* **see**

seep [siːp] *vi* filtrare, trapelare

seesaw ['siːsɔː] *n* altalena a bilico

seethe [siːð] *vi* ribollire; **to** ~ **with anger** fremere di rabbia

see-through *adj* trasparente

segregate ['sɛgrɪgeɪt] *vt* segregare, isolare

seize [siːz] *vt* (*grasp*) afferrare; (*take possession of*) impadronirsi di; (*LAW*) sequestrare; ~ **(up)on** *vt fus* ricorrere a; ~ **up** *vi* (*TECH*) grippare

seizure ['siːʒə*] *n* (*MED*) attacco; (*LAW*) confisca, sequestro

seldom ['sɛldəm] *adv* raramente

select [sɪ'lɛkt] *adj* scelto(a) ♦ *vt* scegliere, selezionare; **~ion** [-'lɛkʃən] *n* selezione *f*, scelta

self [sɛlf] *n*: **the** ~ l'io *m* ♦ *prefix* auto...; **~-assured** *adj* sicuro(a) di sé; **~-catering** (*BRIT*) *adj* in cui si fa cucina da sé; **~-centred** (*US* **~-centered**) *adj* egocentrico(a); **~-confidence** *n* sicurezza di sé; **~-conscious** *adj* timido(a); **~-contained** (*BRIT*) *adj* (*flat*) indipendente; **~-control** *n* autocontrollo; **~-defence** (*US* **~-defense**) *n* autodifesa; (*LAW*) legittima difesa; **~-discipline** *n* autodisciplina; **~-employed** *adj* che lavora in proprio; **~-evident** *adj* evidente; **~-governing** *adj* autonomo(a); **~-indulgent** *adj* indulgente verso se stesso(a); **~-interest** *n* interesse *m* personale; **~ish** *adj* egoista; **~ishness** *n* egoismo; **~less** *adj* dimentico(a) di sé, altruista; **~-pity** *n* autocommiserazione *f*; **~-portrait** *n* autoritratto; **~-possessed** *adj* controllato(a); **~-preservation** *n* istinto di conservazione; **~-respect** *n* rispetto di sé, amor proprio; **~-righteous** *adj* soddisfatto(a) di sé; **~-sacrifice** *n* abnegazione *f*; **~-satisfied** *adj* compiaciuto(a) di sé; **~-service** *n* autoservizio, self-service *m*; **~-sufficient** *adj* autosufficiente; **~-taught** *adj* autodidatta

sell [sɛl] (*pt, pp* **sold**) *vt* vendere ♦ *vi* vendersi; **to ~ at** *or* **for 1000 lire** essere in vendita a 1000 lire; **~ off** *vt* svendere, liquidare; **~ out** *vi:* **to ~ out (of sth)** esaurire (qc); **the tickets are all sold out** i biglietti sono esauriti; **~-by date** *n* data di scadenza; **~er** *n* venditore/trice; **~ing price** *n* prezzo di vendita

Sellotape ® ['sɛləuteɪp] (*BRIT*) *n* nastro adesivo, scotch ® *m*

selves [sɛlvz] *npl of* **self**

semaphore ['sɛməfɔ:*] *n* segnalazioni *fpl* con bandierine; (*RAIL*) semaforo (ferroviario)

semblance ['sɛmbləns] *n* parvenza, apparenza

semen ['si:mən] *n* sperma *m*

semester [sɪ'mɛstə*] (*US*) *n* semestre *m*

semi... ['sɛmɪ] *prefix* semi...; **~circle** *n* semicerchio; **~colon** *n* punto e virgola; **~detached (house)** (*BRIT*) *n* casa gemella; **~final** *n* semifinale *f*

seminar ['sɛmɪnɑ:*] *n* seminario

seminary ['sɛmɪnərɪ] *n* (*REL*) seminario

semiskilled ['sɛmɪ'skɪld] *adj* (*worker*) parzialmente qualificato(a); (*work*) che richiede una qualificazione parziale

semi-skimmed ['sɛmɪ'skɪmd] *adj* (*milk*) parzialmente scremato(a)

senate ['sɛnɪt] *n* senato; **senator** *n* senatore/trice

send [sɛnd] (*pt, pp* **sent**) *vt* mandare; **~ away** *vt* (*letter, goods*) spedire; (*person*) mandare via; **~ away for** *vt fus* richiedere per posta, farsi spedire; **~ back** *vt* rimandare; **~ for** *vt fus* mandare a chiamare, far venire; **~ off** *vt* (*goods*) spedire; (*BRIT: SPORT: player*) espellere; **~ out** *vt* (*invitation*) diramare; **~ up** *vt* (*person, price*) far salire; (*BRIT: parody*) mettere in ridicolo; **~er** *n* mittente *m/f*; **~-off** *n:* **to give sb a good ~-off** festeggiare la partenza di qn

senior ['si:nɪə*] *adj* (*older*) più vecchio(a); (*of higher rank*) di grado più elevato; **~ citizen** *n* persona anziana; **~ity** [-'ɔrɪtɪ] *n* anzianità

sensation [sɛn'seɪʃən] *n* sensazione *f*; **~al** *adj* sensazionale; (*marvellous*) eccezionale

sense [sɛns] *n* senso; (*feeling*) sensazione *f*, senso; (*meaning*) senso, significato; (*wisdom*) buonsenso ♦ *vt* sentire, percepire; **it makes ~** ha senso; **~less** *adj* sciocco(a); (*unconscious*) privo(a) di sensi

sensible ['sɛnsɪbl] *adj* sensato(a), ragionevole

sensitive ['sɛnsɪtɪv] *adj* sensibile; (*skin, question*) delicato(a)

sensual ['sɛnsjuəl] *adj* sensuale

sensuous ['sɛnsjuəs] *adj* sensuale

sent [sɛnt] *pt, pp of* **send**

sentence ['sɛntns] *n* (*LING*) frase *f*; (*LAW: judgment*) sentenza; (*: punishment*) condanna ♦ *vt:* **to ~ sb to death/to 5 years** condannare qn a morte/a 5 anni

sentiment ['sɛntɪmənt] *n* sentimento; (*opinion*) opinione *f*; **~al** [-'mɛntl] *adj* sentimentale

sentry ['sɛntrɪ] *n* sentinella

separate [*adj* 'sɛprɪt, *vb* 'sɛpəreɪt] *adj* separato(a) ♦ *vt* separare ♦ *vi* separarsi; **~ly** *adv* separatamente; **~s** *npl* (*clothes*) coordinati *mpl*; **separation** [-'reɪʃən] *n* separazione *f*

September [sɛp'tɛmbə*] *n* settembre *m*

septic ['sɛptɪk] *adj* settico(a); (*wound*) infettato(a); **~ tank** *n* fossa settica

sequel ['si:kwl] *n* conseguenza; (*of story*) seguito; (*of film*) sequenza

sequence ['si:kwəns] *n* (*series*) serie *f*; (*order*) ordine *m*

sequin ['si:kwɪn] *n* lustrino, paillette *f inv*

serene [sə'ri:n] *adj* sereno(a), calmo(a)

sergeant ['sa:dʒənt] *n* sergente *m*; (*POLICE*) brigadiere *m*

serial ['sɪərɪəl] *n* (*PRESS*) romanzo a puntate; (*RADIO, TV*) trasmissione *f* a puntate, serial *m inv*; ~**ize** *vt* pubblicare (*or* trasmettere) a puntate; ~ **killer** *n* serial-killer *m/f inv*; ~ **number** *n* numero di serie

series ['sɪəri:z] *n inv* serie *f inv*; (*PUBLISHING*) collana

serious ['sɪərɪəs] *adj* serio(a), grave; ~**ly** *adv* seriamente

sermon ['sə:mən] *n* sermone *m*

serrated [sɪ'reɪtɪd] *adj* seghettato(a)

serum ['sɪərəm] *n* siero

servant ['sə:vənt] *n* domestico/a

serve [sə:v] *vt* (*employer etc*) servire, essere a servizio di; (*purpose*) servire a; (*customer, food, meal*) servire; (*apprenticeship*) fare; (*prison term*) scontare ♦ *vi* (*also TENNIS*) servire; (*be useful*): **to ~ as/for/to do** servire da/per/per fare ♦ *n* (*TENNIS*) servizio; **it ~s him right** ben gli sta, se l'è meritata; ~ **out**, ~ **up** *vt* (*food*) servire

service ['sə:vɪs] *n* servizio; (*AUT: maintenance*) assistenza, revisione *f* ♦ *vt* (*car, washing machine*) revisionare; **the S~s** le forze armate; **to be of ~ to sb** essere d'aiuto a qn; ~ **included/not included** servizio compreso/escluso; ~**able** *adj* pratico(a), utile; ~ **area** *n* (*on motorway*) area di servizio; ~ **charge** (*BRIT*) *n* servizio; ~**man** (*irreg*) *n* militare *m*; ~ **station** *n* stazione *f* di servizio

serviette [sə:vɪ'ɛt] (*BRIT*) *n* tovagliolo

session ['sɛʃən] *n* (*sitting*) seduta, sessione *f*; (*SCOL*) anno scolastico (*or* accademico)

set [sɛt] (*pt, pp* **set**) *n* serie *f inv*; (*of cutlery etc*) servizio; (*RADIO, TV*) apparecchio; (*TENNIS*) set *m inv*; (*group of people*) mondo, ambiente *m*; (*CINEMA*) scenario; (*THEATRE: stage*) scene *fpl*; (: *scenery*)

scenario; (*MATH*) insieme *m*; (*HAIRDRESSING*) messa in piega ♦ *adj* (*fixed*) stabilito(a), determinato(a); (*ready*) pronto(a) ♦ *vt* (*place*) posare, mettere; (*arrange*) sistemare; (*fix*) fissare; (*adjust*) regolare; (*decide: rules etc*) stabilire, fissare ♦ *vi* (*sun*) tramontare; (*jam, jelly*) rapprendersi; (*concrete*) fare presa; **to be ~ on doing** essere deciso a fare; **to ~ to music** mettere in musica; **to ~ on fire** dare fuoco a; **to ~ free** liberare; **to ~ sth going** mettere in moto qc; **to ~ sail** prendere il mare; ~ **about** *vt fus* (*task*) intraprendere, mettersi a; ~ **aside** *vt* mettere da parte; ~ **back** *vt* (*in time*): **to ~ back (by)** mettere indietro (di); (*inf: cost*): **it ~ me back £5** mi è costato la bellezza di 5 sterline; ~ **off** *vi* partire ♦ *vt* (*bomb*) far scoppiare; (*cause to start*) mettere in moto; (*show up well*) dare risalto a; ~ **out** *vi* partire ♦ *vt* (*arrange*) disporre; (*state*) esporre, presentare; **to ~ out to do** proporsi di fare; ~ **up** *vt* (*organization*) fondare, costituire; ~**back** *n* (*hitch*) contrattempo, inconveniente *m*; ~ **menu** *n* menù *m inv* fisso

settee [sɛ'ti:] *n* divano, sofà *m inv*

setting ['sɛtɪŋ] *n* (*background*) ambiente *m*; (*of controls*) posizione *f*; (*of sun*) tramonto; (*of jewel*) montatura

settle ['sɛtl] *vt* (*argument, matter*) appianare; (*accounts*) regolare; (*MED: calm*) calmare ♦ *vi* (*bird, dust etc*) posarsi; (*sediment*) depositarsi; (*also:* ~ **down**) sistemarsi, stabilirsi; calmarsi; **to ~ for sth** accontentarsi di qc; **to ~ on sth** decidersi per qc; ~ **in** *vi* sistemarsi; ~ **up** *vi*: **to ~ up with sb** regolare i conti con qn; ~**ment** *n* (*payment*) pagamento, saldo; (*agreement*) accordo; (*colony*) colonia; (*village etc*) villaggio, comunità *f inv*; ~**r** *n* colonizzatore/trice

setup ['sɛtʌp] *n* (*arrangement*) sistemazione *f*; (*situation*) situazione *f*

seven ['sɛvn] *num* sette; ~**teen** *num* diciassette; ~**th** *num* settimo(a); ~**ty** *num* settanta

sever ['sɛvə*] *vt* recidere, tagliare; (*relations*)

troncare

several ['sevərl] *adj, pron* alcuni(e), diversi(e); **~ of us** alcuni di noi

severance ['sevərəns] *n* (*of relations*) rottura; **~ pay** *n* indennità di licenziamento

severe [sɪ'vɪə*] *adj* severo(a); (*serious*) serio(a), grave; (*hard*) duro(a); (*plain*) semplice, sobrio(a); (*weather*) rigido(a) ♦ **severity** [sɪ'vɛrɪtɪ] *n* severità; gravità; (*of weather*) rigore *m*

sew [səu] (*pt* **sewed**, *pp* **sewn**) *vt, vi* cucire; **~ up** *vt* ricucire

sewage ['su:ɪdʒ] *n* acque *fpl* di scolo

sewer ['su:ə*] *n* fogna

sewing ['səuɪŋ] *n* cucitura; cucito; **~ machine** *n* macchina da cucire

sewn [səun] *pp of* **sew**

sex [sɛks] *n* sesso; **to have ~ with** avere rapporti sessuali con; **~ist** *adj, n* sessista *m/f*

sexual ['sɛksjuəl] *adj* sessuale

sexy ['sɛksɪ] *adj* provocante, sexy *inv*

shabby ['ʃæbɪ] *adj* malandato(a); (*behaviour*) vergognoso(a)

shack [ʃæk] *n* baracca, capanna

shackles ['ʃæklz] *npl* ferri *mpl*, catene *fpl*

shade [ʃeɪd] *n* ombra; (*for lamp*) paralume *m*; (*of colour*) tonalità *f inv*; (*small quantity*): **a ~ (more/too large)** un po' (di più/troppo grande) ♦ *vt* ombreggiare, fare ombra a; **in the ~** all'ombra

shadow ['ʃædəu] *n* ombra ♦ *vt* (*follow*) pedinare; **~ cabinet** (*BRIT*) *n* (*POL*) governo *m* ombra *inv*; **~y** *adj* ombreggiato(a), ombroso(a); (*dim*) vago(a), indistinto(a)

shady ['ʃeɪdɪ] *adj* ombroso(a); (*fig: dishonest*) losco(a), equivoco(a)

shaft [ʃɑːft] *n* (*of arrow, spear*) asta; (*AUT, TECH*) albero; (*of mine*) pozzo; (*of lift*) tromba; (*of light*) raggio

shaggy ['ʃægɪ] *adj* ispido(a)

shake [ʃeɪk] (*pt* **shook**, *pp* **shaken**) *vt* scuotere; (*bottle, cocktail*) agitare ♦ *vi* tremare; **to ~ one's head** (*in refusal, dismay*) scuotere la testa; **to ~ hands with sb** stringere *or* dare la mano a qn; **~ off** *vt* scrollare (via); (*fig*) sbarazzarsi di; **~ up** *vt*

scuotere; **~n** *pp of* **shake**; **shaky** *adj* (*hand, voice*) tremante; (*building*) traballante

shall [ʃæl] *aux vb*: **I ~ go** andrò; **~ I open the door?** apro io la porta?; **I'll get some, ~ I?** ne prendo un po', va bene?

shallow ['ʃæləu] *adj* poco profondo(a); (*fig*) superficiale

sham [ʃæm] *n* finzione *f*, messinscena; (*jewellery, furniture*) imitazione *f*

shambles ['ʃæmblz] *n* confusione *f*, baraonda, scompiglio

shame [ʃeɪm] *n* vergogna ♦ *vt* far vergognare; **it is a ~ (that/to do)** è un peccato (che +*sub*/fare); **what a ~!** che peccato!; **~ful** *adj* vergognoso(a); **~less** *adj* sfrontato(a); (*immodest*) spudorato(a)

shampoo [ʃæm'pu:] *n* shampoo *m inv* ♦ *vt* fare lo shampoo a; **~ and set** *n* shampoo e messa in piega

shamrock ['ʃæmrɔk] *n* trifoglio (*simbolo nazionale dell'Irlanda*)

shandy ['ʃændɪ] *n* birra con gassosa

shan't [ʃɑːnt] = **shall not**

shanty town ['ʃæntɪ-] *n* bidonville *f inv*

shape [ʃeɪp] *n* forma ♦ *vt* formare; (*statement*) formulare; (*sb's ideas*) condizionare; **to take ~** prendere forma; **~ up** *vi* (*events*) andare, mettersi; (*person*) cavarsela; **-shaped** *suffix*: **heart-shaped** a forma di cuore; **~less** *adj* senza forma, informe; **~ly** *adj* ben proporzionato(a)

share [ʃɛə*] *n* (*thing received, contribution*) parte *f*; (*COMM*) azione *f* ♦ *vt* dividere; (*have in common*) condividere, avere in comune; **~ out** *vi* dividere; **~holder** *n* azionista *m/f*

shark [ʃɑːk] *n* squalo, pescecane *m*

sharp [ʃɑːp] *adj* (*razor, knife*) affilato(a); (*point*) acuto(a), acuminato(a); (*nose, chin*) aguzzo(a); (*outline, contrast*) netto(a); (*cold, pain*) pungente; (*voice*) stridulo(a); (*person: quick-witted*) sveglio(a); (: *unscrupulous*) disonesto(a); (*MUS*): **C ~** do diesis ♦ *n* (*MUS*) diesis *m inv* ♦ *adv*: **at 2 o'clock ~** alle due in punto; **~en** *vt* affilare; (*pencil*) fare la punta a; (*fig*) acuire; **~ener** *n* (*also*: **pencil**

~ener) temperamatite *m inv*; ~-eyed *adj* dalla vista acuta; ~ly *adv* (*turn, stop*) bruscamente; (*stand out, contrast*) nettamente; (*criticize, retort*) duramente, aspramente

shatter ['ʃætə*] *vt* mandare in frantumi, frantumare; (*fig: upset*) distruggere; (: *ruin*) rovinare ♦ *vi* frantumarsi, andare in pezzi

shave [ʃeɪv] *vt* radere, rasare ♦ *vi* radersi, farsi la barba ♦ *n*: **to have a ~** farsi la barba; ~r *n* (*also:* **electric ~r**) rasoio elettrico

shaving ['ʃeɪvɪŋ] *n* (*action*) rasatura; ~s *npl* (*of wood etc*) trucioli *mpl*; ~ **brush** *n* pennello da barba; ~ **cream** *n* crema da barba; ~ **foam** *n* = ~ **cream**

shawl [ʃɔːl] *n* scialle *m*

she [ʃiː] *pron* ella, lei; ~-**cat** gatta; ~-**elephant** elefantessa

sheaf [ʃiːf] (*pl* **sheaves**) *n* covone *m*; (*of papers*) fascio

shear [ʃɪə*] (*pt* ~**ed**, *pp* ~**ed** *or* **shorn**) *vt* (*sheep*) tosare; ~s *npl* (*for hedge*) cesoie *fpl*

sheath [ʃiːθ] *n* fodero, guaina; (*contraceptive*) preservativo

sheaves [ʃiːvz] *npl of* **sheaf**

shed [ʃed] (*pt, pp* **shed**) *n* capannone *m* ♦ *vt* (*leaves, fur etc*) perdere; (*tears, blood*) versare; (*workers*) liberarsi di

she'd [ʃiːd] = **she had; she would**

sheen [ʃiːn] *n* lucentezza

sheep [ʃiːp] *n inv* pecora; ~**dog** *n* cane *m* da pastore; ~**skin** *n* pelle *f* di pecora

sheer [ʃɪə*] *adj* (*utter*) vero(a) (e proprio(a)); (*steep*) a picco, perpendicolare; (*almost transparent*) sottile ♦ *adv* a picco

sheet [ʃiːt] *n* (*on bed*) lenzuolo; (*of paper*) foglio; (*of glass, ice*) lastra; (*of metal*) foglio, lamina; ~ **lightning** *n* lampo diffuso

sheik(h) [ʃeɪk] *n* sceicco

shelf [ʃelf] (*pl* **shelves**) *n* scaffale *m*, mensola

shell [ʃel] *n* (*on beach*) conchiglia; (*of egg, nut etc*) guscio; (*explosive*) granata; (*of building*) scheletro ♦ *vt* (*peas*) sgranare; (*MIL*) bombardare; ~ **suit** *n* (*lightweight*) tuta di acetato; (*heavier*) tuta di trilobato

she'll [ʃiːl] = **she will; she shall**

shellfish ['ʃelfɪʃ] *n inv* (*crab etc*) crostaceo; (*scallop etc*) mollusco; (*pl: as food*) crostacei; molluschi

shelter ['ʃeltə*] *n* riparo, rifugio ♦ *vt* riparare, proteggere; (*give lodging to*) dare rifugio *or* asilo a ♦ *vi* ripararsi, mettersi al riparo; ~**ed** *adj* riparato(a); ~**ed housing** (*BRIT*) *n* alloggi dotati di strutture per anziani *o* handicappati

shelve [ʃelv] *vt* (*fig*) accantonare, rimandare; ~**s** *npl of* **shelf**

shepherd ['ʃepəd] *n* pastore *m* ♦ *vt* (*guide*) guidare; ~**'s pie** (*BRIT*) *n* timballo di carne macinata *o* purè di patate

sheriff ['ʃerɪf] (*US*) *n* sceriffo

sherry ['ʃerɪ] *n* sherry *m inv*

she's [ʃiːz] = **she is; she has**

Shetland ['ʃetlənd] *n* (*also:* **the ~s, the ~ Isles**) le isole Shetland, le Shetland

shield [ʃiːld] *n* scudo; (*trophy*) scudetto; (*protection*) schermo ♦ *vt*: **to ~ (from)** riparare (da), proteggere (da *or* contro)

shift [ʃɪft] *n* (*change*) cambiamento; (*of workers*) turno ♦ *vt* spostare, muovere; (*remove*) rimuovere ♦ *vi* spostarsi, muoversi; ~ **work** *n* lavoro a squadre; ~**y** *adj* ambiguo(a); (*eyes*) sfuggente

shilling ['ʃɪlɪŋ] (*BRIT*) *n* scellino (= *12 old pence; 20 in a pound*)

shimmer ['ʃɪmə*] *vi* brillare, luccicare

shin [ʃɪn] *n* tibia

shine [ʃaɪn] (*pt, pp* **shone**) *n* splendore *m*, lucentezza ♦ *vi* (ri)splendere, brillare ♦ *vt* far brillare, far risplendere; (*torch*): **to ~ sth on** puntare qc verso

shingle ['ʃɪŋgl] *n* (*on beach*) ciottoli *mpl*; ~**s** *n* (*MED*) herpes zoster *m*

shiny ['ʃaɪnɪ] *adj* lucente, lucido(a)

ship [ʃɪp] *n* nave *f* ♦ *vt* trasportare (via mare); (*send*) spedire (via mare); ~**building** *n* costruzione *f* navale; ~**ment** *n* carico; ~**ping** *n* (*ships*) naviglio; (*traffic*) navigazione *f*; ~**shape** *adj* in perfetto ordine; ~**wreck** *n* relitto; (*event*) naufragio ♦ *vt*: **to be ~wrecked** naufragare, fare naufragio; ~**yard** *n* cantiere *m* navale

shire ['ʃaɪə*] (BRIT) n contea

shirt [ʃəːt] n camicia; **in ~ sleeves** in maniche di camicia

shit [ʃɪt] (inf!) excl merda (!)

shiver ['ʃɪvə*] n brivido ♦ vi rabbrividire, tremare

shoal [ʃəʊl] n (of fish) banco; (fig) massa

shock [ʃɒk] n (impact) urto, colpo; (ELEC) scossa; (emotional) colpo, shock m inv; (MED) shock ♦ vt colpire, scioccare; scandalizzare; ~ **absorber** n ammortizzatore m; ~**ing** adj scioccante, traumatizzante; scandaloso(a)

shoddy ['ʃɒdɪ] adj scadente

shoe [ʃuː] (pt, pp **shod**) n scarpa; (also: **horse~**) ferro di cavallo ♦ vt (horse) ferrare; ~**brush** n spazzola per scarpe; ~**lace** n stringa; ~ **polish** n lucido per scarpe; ~**shop** n calzoleria; ~**string** n (fig): **on a ~string** con quattro soldi

shone [ʃɒn] pt, pp of **shine**

shook [ʃʊk] pt of **shake**

shoot [ʃuːt] (pt, pp **shot**) n (on branch, seedling) germoglio ♦ vt (game) cacciare, andare a caccia di; (person) sparare a; (execute) fucilare; (film) girare ♦ vi (with gun): **to ~ (at)** sparare a), fare fuoco (su); (with bow): **to ~ (at)** tirare (su); (FOOTBALL) sparare, tirare (forte); ~ **down** vt (plane) abbattere; ~ **in/out** vi entrare/uscire come una freccia; ~ **up** vi (fig) salire alle stelle; ~**ing** n (shots) sparatoria; (HUNTING) caccia; ~**ing star** n stella cadente

shop [ʃɒp] n negozio; (workshop) officina ♦ vi (also: **go ~ping**) fare spese; ~ **assistant** n commesso/a; ~ **floor** n officina; (BRIT: fig) operai mpl, maestranze fpl; ~**keeper** n negoziante m/f, bottegaio/a; ~**lifting** n taccheggio; ~**per** n compratore/trice; ~**ping** n (goods) spesa, acquisti mpl; ~**ping bag** n borsa per la spesa; ~**ping centre** (US ~**ping center**) n centro commerciale; ~-**soiled** adj sciupato(a) a forza di stare in vetrina; ~ **steward** (BRIT) n (INDUSTRY) rappresentante m sindacale; ~ **window** n vetrina

shore [ʃɔː*] n (of sea) riva, spiaggia; (of lake) riva ♦ vt: **to ~ (up)** puntellare; **on ~** a riva

shorn [ʃɔːn] pp of **shear**

short [ʃɔːt] adj (not long) corto(a); (soon finished) breve; (person) basso(a); (curt) brusco(a), secco(a); (insufficient) insufficiente ♦ n (also: ~ **film**) cortometraggio; (a pair of) ~**s** (i) calzoncini; **to be ~ of sth** essere a corto di or mancare di qc; **in ~** in breve; ~ **of doing** a meno che non si faccia; **everything ~ of** tutto fuorché; **it is ~ for** è l'abbreviazione or il diminutivo di; **to cut ~** (speech, visit) accorciare, abbreviare; **to fall ~ of** venir meno a; non soddisfare; **to run ~ of** rimanere senza; **to stop ~** fermarsi di colpo; **to stop ~ of** non arrivare fino a; ~**age** n scarsezza, carenza; ~**bread** n biscotto di pasta frolla; ~-**change** vt: **to ~-change sb** imbrogliare qn sul resto; ~-**circuit** n cortocircuito; ~**coming** n difetto; ~(**crust**) **pastry** (BRIT) n pasta frolla; ~**cut** n scorciatoia; ~**en** vt accorciare, ridurre; ~**fall** n deficit m; ~**hand** (BRIT) n stenografia; ~**hand typist** (BRIT) n stenodattilografo/a; ~ **list** (BRIT) n (for job) rosa dei candidati; ~-**lived** adj di breve durata; ~**ly** adv fra poco; ~-**sighted** adj miope; ~-**staffed** adj a corto di personale; ~-**stay** adj (car park) a tempo limitato; ~ **story** n racconto, novella; ~-**tempered** adj irascibile; ~-**term** adj (effect) di or a breve durata; (borrowing) a breve scadenza; ~ **wave** n (RADIO) onde fpl corte

shot [ʃɒt] pt, pp of **shoot** ♦ n sparo, colpo; (try) prova; (FOOTBALL) tiro; (injection) iniezione f; (PHOT) foto f inv; **like a ~** come un razzo; (very readily) immediatamente; ~**gun** n fucile m da caccia

should [ʃʊd] aux vb: **I ~ go now** dovrei andare ora; **he ~ be there now** dovrebbe essere arrivato ora; **I ~ go if I were you** se fossi in te andrei; **I ~ like to** mi piacerebbe

shoulder ['ʃəʊldə*] n spalla; (BRIT: of road): **hard ~** banchina ♦ vt (fig) addossarsi, prendere sulle proprie spalle; ~ **bag** n borsa a tracolla; ~ **blade** n scapola

shouldn't [ʃʊdnt] = **should not**

shout [ʃaʊt] n urlo, grido ♦ vt gridare ♦ vi (also: ~ **out**) urlare, gridare; ~ **down** vt zittire gridando; ~**ing** n urli mpl

shove [ʃʌv] vt spingere; (inf: put): **to ~ sth in** ficcare qc in; ~ **off** (inf) vi sloggiare, smammare

shovel [ˈʃʌvl] n pala ♦ vt spalare

show [ʃəʊ] (pt ~**ed**, pp **shown**) n (of emotion) dimostrazione f, manifestazione f; (semblance) apparenza; (exhibition) mostra, esposizione f; (THEATRE, CINEMA) spettacolo ♦ vt far vedere, mostrare; (courage etc) dimostrare, dar prova di; (exhibit) esporre ♦ vi vedersi, essere visibile; **for ~** per fare scena; **on ~** (exhibits etc) esposto(a); ~ **in** vt (person) far entrare; ~ **off** vi (pej) esibirsi, mettersi in mostra ♦ vt (display) mettere in risalto; (pej) mettere in mostra; ~ **out** vt (person) accompagnare alla porta; ~ **up** vi (stand out) essere ben visibile; (inf: turn up) farsi vedere ♦ vt mettere in risalto; ~ **business** n industria dello spettacolo; ~**down** n prova di forza

shower [ˈʃaʊə*] n (rain) acquazzone m; (of stones etc) pioggia; (also: ~**bath**) doccia ♦ vi fare la doccia ♦ vt: **to ~ sb with** (gifts, abuse etc) coprire qn di; (missiles) lanciare contro qn una pioggia di; **to have a ~** fare la doccia; ~**proof** adj impermeabile

showing [ˈʃəʊɪŋ] n (of film) proiezione f

show jumping n concorso ippico (di salto ad ostacoli)

shown [ʃəʊn] pp of **show**

show-off (inf) n (person) esibizionista m/f

showpiece [ˈʃəʊpiːs] n pezzo forte

showroom [ˈʃəʊrʊm] n sala d'esposizione

shrank [ʃræŋk] pt of **shrink**

shrapnel [ˈʃræpnl] n shrapnel m

shred [ʃred] n (gen pl) brandello ♦ vt fare a brandelli; (CULIN) sminuzzare, tagliuzzare; ~**der** n (vegetable ~der) grattugia; (document ~der) distruttore m di documenti

shrewd [ʃruːd] adj astuto(a), scaltro(a)

shriek [ʃriːk] n strillo ♦ vi strillare

shrill [ʃrɪl] adj acuto(a), stridulo(a), stridente

shrimp [ʃrɪmp] n gamberetto

shrine [ʃraɪn] n reliquario; (place) santuario

shrink [ʃrɪŋk] (pt **shrank**, pp **shrunk**) vi restringersi, (fig) ridursi; (also: ~ **away**) ritrarsi ♦ vt (wool) far restringere ♦ n (inf: pej) psicanalista m/f; **to ~ from doing sth** rifuggire dal fare qc; ~**wrap** vt confezionare con pellicola di plastica

shrivel [ˈʃrɪvl] (also: ~ **up**) vt raggrinzare, avvizzire ♦ vi raggrinzirsi, avvizzire

shroud [ʃraʊd] n lenzuolo funebre ♦ vt: ~**ed in mystery** avvolto(a) nel mistero

Shrove Tuesday [ˈʃrəʊv-] n martedì m grasso

shrub [ʃrʌb] n arbusto; ~**bery** n arbusti mpl

shrug [ʃrʌg] n scrollata di spalle ♦ vt, vi: **to ~ (one's shoulders)** alzare le spalle, fare spallucce; ~ **off** vt passare sopra a

shrunk [ʃrʌŋk] pp of **shrink**

shudder [ˈʃʌdə*] n brivido ♦ vi rabbrividire

shuffle [ˈʃʌfl] vt (cards) mescolare; **to ~ (one's feet)** strascicare i piedi

shun [ʃʌn] vt sfuggire, evitare

shunt [ʃʌnt] vt (RAIL: direct) smistare; (: divert) deviare; (object) spostare

shut [ʃʌt] (pt, pp **shut**) vt chiudere ♦ vi chiudersi, chiudere; ~ **down** vt, vi chiudere definitivamente; ~ **off** vt fermare, bloccare; ~ **up** vi (inf: keep quiet) stare zitto(a), fare silenzio ♦ vt (close) chiudere; (silence) far tacere; ~**ter** n imposta; (PHOT) otturatore m

shuttle [ˈʃʌtl] n spola, navetta; (space ~) navetta (spaziale); (also: ~ **service**) servizio m navetta inv

shuttlecock [ˈʃʌtlkɔk] n volano

shuttle diplomacy n la gestione dei rapporti diplomatici caratterizzata da frequenti viaggi e incontri dei rappresentanti del governo

shy [ʃaɪ] adj timido(a)

Sicily [ˈsɪsɪlɪ] n Sicilia

sick [sɪk] adj (ill) malato(a); (vomiting): **to be ~** vomitare; (humour) macabro(a); **to feel ~** avere la nausea; **to be ~ of** (fig) averne abbastanza di; ~ **bay** n infermeria; ~**en** vt

nauseare ♦ vi: **to be ~ening for sth** (*cold etc*) covare qc
sickle ['sɪkl] n falcetto
sick: ~ **leave** n congedo per malattia; **~ly** adj malaticcio(a); (*causing nausea*) nauseante; **~ness** n malattia; (*vomiting*) vomito; ~ **pay** n sussidio per malattia
side [saɪd] n lato; (*of lake*) riva; (*team*) squadra ♦ cpd (*door, entrance*) laterale ♦ vi: **to ~ with sb** parteggiare per qn, prendere le parti di qn; **by the ~ of** a fianco di; (*road*) sul ciglio di; ~ **by** ~ fianco a fianco; **from ~ to** ~ da una parte all'altra; **to take ~s (with)** schierarsi (con); **~board** n credenza; **~burns** (BRIT **~boards**) npl (*whiskers*) basette fpl; ~ **effect** n (MED) effetto collaterale; **~light** n (AUT) luce f di posizione; **~line** n (SPORT) linea laterale; (*fig*) attività secondaria; **~long** adj obliquo(a); ~ **order** n contorno (*pietanza*); ~ **show** n attrazione f; **~step** n (*question*) eludere; (*problem*) scavalcare; ~ **street** n traversa; **~track** vt (*fig*) distrarre; **~walk** (US) n marciapiede m; **~ways** adv (*move*) di lato, di fianco
siding ['saɪdɪŋ] n (RAIL) binario di raccordo
siege [siːdʒ] n assedio
sieve [sɪv] n setaccio ♦ vt setacciare
sift [sɪft] vt passare al crivello; (*fig*) vagliare
sigh [saɪ] n sospiro ♦ vi sospirare
sight [saɪt] n (*faculty*) vista; (*spectacle*) spettacolo; (*on gun*) mira ♦ vt avvistare; **in** ~ in vista; **on** ~ a vista; **out of** ~ non visibile; **~seeing** n giro turistico; **to go ~seeing** visitare una località
sign [saɪn] n segno; (*with hand etc*) segno, gesto; (*notice*) insegna, cartello ♦ vt firmare; (*player*) ingaggiare; ~ **on** vi (MIL) arruolarsi; (*as unemployed*) iscriversi sulla lista (dell'ufficio di collocamento) vt (MIL) arruolare; (*employee*) assumere; ~ **over** vt: **to ~ sth over to sb** cedere qc con scrittura legale a qn; ~ **up** vi (MIL) arruolarsi; (*for course*) iscriversi vt (*player*) ingaggiare; (*recruits*) reclutare
signal ['sɪɡnl] n segnale m ♦ vi (AUT) segnalare, mettere la freccia ♦ vt (*person*)

fare segno a; (*message*) comunicare per mezzo di segnali; **~man** (*irreg*) n (RAIL) deviatore m
signature ['sɪɡnətʃə*] n firma; ~ **tune** n sigla musicale
signet ring ['sɪɡnət-] n anello con sigillo
significance [sɪɡ'nɪfɪkəns] n significato; importanza
significant [sɪɡ'nɪfɪkənt] adj significativo(a)
sign language n linguaggio dei muti
signpost ['saɪnpəust] n cartello indicatore
silence ['saɪlns] n silenzio ♦ vt far tacere, ridurre al silenzio; **~r** n (*on gun*, BRIT: AUT) silenziatore m
silent ['saɪlnt] adj silenzioso(a); (*film*) muto(a); **to remain** ~ tacere, stare zitto; ~ **partner** n (COMM) socio inattivo
silhouette [sɪlu:'et] n silhouette f inv
silicon chip ['sɪlɪkən-] n piastrina di silicio
silk [sɪlk] n seta ♦ adj di seta; **~y** adj di seta
silly ['sɪlɪ] adj stupido(a), sciocco(a)
silt [sɪlt] n limo
silver ['sɪlvə*] n argento; (*money*) monete da 5, 10 or 50 pence; (*also*: **~ware**) argenteria ♦ adj d'argento; ~ **paper** (BRIT) n carta argentata, (*carta*) stagnola; **~-plated** adj argentato(a); **~smith** n argentiere m; **~y** adj (*colour*) argenteo(a); (*sound*) argentino(a)
similar ['sɪmɪlə*] adj: ~ **(to)** simile (a); **~ly** adv allo stesso modo; così pure
simmer ['sɪmə*] vi cuocere a fuoco lento
simple ['sɪmpl] adj semplice; **simplicity** [-'plɪsɪtɪ] n semplicità; **simply** adv semplicemente
simultaneous [sɪməl'teɪnɪəs] adj simultaneo(a)
sin [sɪn] n peccato ♦ vi peccare
since [sɪns] adv da allora ♦ prep da ♦ conj (*time*) da quando; (*because*) poiché, dato che; ~ **then, ever** ~ da allora
sincere [sɪn'sɪə*] adj sincero(a); **~ly** adv: **yours ~ly** (*in letters*) distinti saluti; **sincerity** [-'serɪtɪ] n sincerità
sinew ['sɪnju:] n tendine m
sing [sɪŋ] (*pt* **sang**, *pp* **sung**) vt, vi cantare
singe [sɪndʒ] vt bruciacchiare

singer ['sɪŋə*] n cantante m/f

singing ['sɪŋɪŋ] n canto

single ['sɪŋgl] adj solo(a), unico(a); (unmarried: man) celibe; (: woman) nubile; (not double) semplice ♦ n (BRIT: also: ~ ticket) biglietto di (sola) andata; (record) 45 giri m; **~s** n (TENNIS) singolo; ~ **out** vt scegliere; (distinguish) distinguere; ~ **bed** n letto singolo; **~-breasted** adj a un petto; ~ **file** n: **in ~ file** in fila indiana; **~-handed** adv senza aiuto, da solo(a); **~-minded** adj tenace, risoluto(a); ~ **parent** n (mother) ragazza f madre inv; (father) ragazzo m padre inv; ~ **room** n camera singola; **~-track road** n strada a una carreggiata

singly ['sɪŋglɪ] adv separatamente

singular ['sɪŋgjulə*] adj (exceptional, LING) singolare ♦ n (LING) singolare m

sinister ['sɪnɪstə*] adj sinistro(a)

sink [sɪŋk] (pt **sank**, pp **sunk**) n lavandino, acquaio ♦ vt (ship) (fare) affondare, colare a picco; (foundations) scavare; (piles etc): **to ~ sth into** conficcare qc in ♦ vi affondare, andare a fondo; (ground etc) cedere, avvallarsi; **my heart sank** mi sentii venir meno; ~ **in** vi penetrare

sinner ['sɪnə*] n peccatore/trice

sinus ['saɪnəs] n (ANAT) seno

sip [sɪp] n sorso ♦ vt sorseggiare

siphon ['saɪfən] n sifone m; ~ **off** vt travasare; (fig) sottrarre

sir [sə*] n signore m; **S~ John Smith** Sir John Smith; **yes ~** sì, signore

sirloin ['sə:lɔɪn] n controfiletto

sissy ['sɪsɪ] (inf) n femminuccia

sister ['sɪstə*] n sorella; (nun) suora; (BRIT: nurse) infermiera f caposala inv; **~-in-law** n cognata

sit [sɪt] (pt, pp **sat**) vi sedere, sedersi; (assembly) essere in seduta; (for painter) posare ♦ vt (exam) sostenere, dare; ~ **down** vi sedersi; ~ **in on** vt fus assistere a; ~ **up** vi tirarsi su a sedere; (not go to bed) stare alzato(a) fino a tardi

sitcom ['sɪtkɔm] n abbr (= situation comedy) commedia di situazione

site [saɪt] n posto; (also: **building ~**) cantiere m ♦ vt situare

sit-in n (demonstration) sit-in m inv

sitting ['sɪtɪŋ] n (of assembly etc) seduta; (in canteen) turno; ~ **room** n soggiorno

situated ['sɪtjueɪtɪd] adj situato(a)

situation [sɪtju'eɪʃən] n situazione f; (job) lavoro; (location) posizione f; **"~s vacant"** (BRIT) "offerte fpl di impiego"

six [sɪks] num sei; **~teen** num sedici; **~th** num sesto(a); **~ty** num sessanta

size [saɪz] n dimensioni fpl; (of clothing) taglia, misura; (of shoes) numero; (glue) colla; ~ **up** vt giudicare, farsi un'idea di; **~able** adj considerevole

sizzle ['sɪzl] vi sfrigolare

skate [skeɪt] n pattino; (fish: pl inv) razza ♦ vi pattinare; **~board** n skateboard m inv; **~r** n pattinatore/trice; **skating** n pattinaggio; **skating rink** n pista di pattinaggio

skeleton ['skelɪtn] n scheletro; ~ **staff** n personale m ridotto

skeptical ['skeptɪkl] (US) adj = **sceptical**

sketch [sketʃ] n (drawing) schizzo, abbozzo; (THEATRE) scenetta comica, sketch m inv ♦ vt abbozzare, schizzare; ~ **book** n album m inv per schizzi; **~y** adj incompleto(a), lacunoso(a)

skewer ['skju:ə*] n spiedo

ski [ski:] n sci m inv ♦ vi sciare; ~ **boot** n scarpone m da sci; ~ **pass** n ski pass m inv

skid [skɪd] n slittamento ♦ vi slittare

skier ['ski:ə*] n sciatore/trice

skiing ['ski:ɪŋ] n sci m

ski jump n (ramp) trampolino; (event) salto con gli sci

skilful ['skɪlful] (US **skillful**) adj abile

ski lift n ['ski:lɪft] n sciovia

skill [skɪl] n abilità f inv, capacità f inv; **~ed** adj esperto(a); (worker) qualificato(a), specializzato(a); **~ful** (US) adj = **skilful**

skim [skɪm] vt (milk) scremare; (glide over) sfiorare ♦ vi: **to ~ through** (fig) scorrere, dare una scorsa a; **~med milk** n latte m scremato

skimp [skɪmp] vt (work: also: ~ **on**) fare alla carlona; (cloth etc) lesinare; ~y adj misero(a); striminzito(a); frugale

skin [skɪn] n pelle f ♦ vt (fruit etc) sbucciare; (animal) scuoiare, spellare; ~ **cancer** n cancro alla pelle; ~**-deep** adj superficiale; ~ **diving** n nuoto subacqueo; ~ny adj molto magro(a), pelle e ossa inv; ~**tight** adj (dress etc) aderente

skip [skɪp] n saltello, balzo; (BRIT: container) benna ♦ vi saltare; (with rope) saltare la corda ♦ vt saltare

ski pole n racchetta (da sci)

skipper ['skɪpə*] n (NAUT, SPORT) capitano

skipping rope ['skɪpɪŋ-] (BRIT) n corda per saltare

skirmish ['skə:mɪʃ] n scaramuccia

skirt [skə:t] n gonna, sottana ♦ vt fiancheggiare, costeggiare; ~**ing board** (BRIT) n zoccolo

ski slope n pista da sci

ski suit n tuta da sci

skit [skɪt] n parodia; scenetta satirica

ski tow n sciovia, ski-lift m inv

skittle ['skɪtl] n birillo; ~s n (game) (gioco dei) birilli mpl

skive [skaɪv] (BRIT: inf) vi fare il lavativo

skull [skʌl] n cranio, teschio

skunk [skʌŋk] n moffetta

sky [skaɪ] n cielo; ~**light** n lucernario; ~**scraper** n grattacielo

slab [slæb] n lastra; (of cake, cheese) fetta

slack [slæk] adj (loose) allentato(a); (slow) lento(a); (careless) negligente; ~**en** (also: ~**en off**) vi rallentare, diminuire ♦ vt allentare; (speed) diminuire; ~s npl (trousers) pantaloni mpl

slag heap [slæg-] n ammasso di scorie

slag off [slæg-] (BRIT: inf) vt sparlare di

slam [slæm] vt (door) sbattere; (throw) scaraventare; (criticize) stroncare ♦ vi sbattere

slander ['slɑ:ndə*] n calunnia; diffamazione f

slang [slæŋ] n gergo, slang m

slant [slɑ:nt] n pendenza, inclinazione f; (fig) angolazione f, punto di vista; ~**ed** adj in pendenza, inclinato(a); (eyes) obliquo(a); ~**ing** adj = ~**ed**

slap [slæp] n manata, pacca; (on face) schiaffo ♦ vt dare una manata a; schiaffeggiare ♦ adv (directly) in pieno; ~ **a coat of paint on it** dagli una mano di vernice; ~**dash** adj negligente; (work) raffazzonato(a); ~**stick** n (comedy) farsa grossolana; ~**-up** (BRIT) adj: **a ~-up meal** un pranzo (or una cena) coi fiocchi

slash [slæʃ] vt tagliare; (face) sfregiare; (fig: prices) ridurre drasticamente, tagliare

slat [slæt] n (of wood) stecca; (of plastic) lamina

slate [sleɪt] n ardesia; (piece) lastra di ardesia ♦ vt (fig: criticize) stroncare, distruggere

slaughter ['slɔ:tə*] n strage f, massacro ♦ vt (animal) macellare; (people) trucidare, massacrare

slave [sleɪv] n schiavo/a ♦ vi (also: ~ **away**) lavorare come uno schiavo; ~**ry** n schiavitù f; **slavish** adj servile; (copy) pedissequo(a)

slay [sleɪ] (pt **slew**, pp **slain**) vt (formal) uccidere

sleazy ['sli:zɪ] adj trasandato(a)

sledge [sledʒ] n slitta; ~**hammer** n mazza, martello da fabbro

sleek [sli:k] adj (hair, fur) lucido(a), lucente; (car, boat) slanciato(a), affusolato(a)

sleep [sli:p] (pt, pp **slept**) n sonno ♦ vi dormire; **to go to** ~ addormentarsi; ~ **around** vi andare a letto con tutti; ~ **in** vi (oversleep) dormire fino a tardi; ~**er** (BRIT) n (RAIL: on track) traversina; (: train) treno di vagoni letto; ~**ing bag** n sacco a pelo; ~**ing car** n vagone m letto inv, carrozza f letto inv; ~**ing partner** (BRIT) n (COMM) socio inattivo; ~**ing pill** n sonnifero; ~**less** adj: **a ~less night** una notte in bianco; ~**walker** n sonnambulo/a; ~y adj assonnato(a), sonnolento(a); (fig) addormentato(a)

sleet [sli:t] n nevischio

sleeve [sli:v] n manica; (of record) copertina

sleigh [sleɪ] n slitta

sleight [slaɪt] n: ~ **of hand** gioco di destrezza

slender ['slɛndə*] *adj* snello(a), sottile; (*not enough*) scarso(a), esiguo(a)

slept [slɛpt] *pt, pp of* **sleep**

slew [sluː] *pt of* **slay** ♦ *vi* (BRIT) girare

slice [slaɪs] *n* fetta ♦ *vt* affettare, tagliare a fette

slick [slɪk] *adj* (*skilful*) brillante; (*clever*) furbo(a) ♦ *n* (*also*: **oil ~**) chiazza di petrolio

slide [slaɪd] (*pt, pp* **slid**) *n* scivolone *m*; (*in playground*) scivolo; (PHOT) diapositiva; (BRIT: *also*: **hair ~**) fermaglio (per capelli) ♦ *vt* far scivolare ♦ *vi* scivolare; **~ rule** *n* regolo calcolatore; **sliding** *adj* (*door*) scorrevole; **sliding scale** *n* scala mobile

slight [slaɪt] *adj* (*slim*) snello(a), sottile; (*frail*) delicato(a), fragile; (*trivial*) insignificante; (*small*) piccolo(a) ♦ *n* offesa, affronto; **not in the ~est** affatto, neppure per sogno; **~ly** *adv* lievemente, un po'

slim [slɪm] *adj* magro(a), snello(a) ♦ *vi* dimagrire; fare (*or* seguire) una dieta dimagrante

slime [slaɪm] *n* limo, melma; viscidume *m*

slimming ['slɪmɪŋ] *adj* (*diet*) dimagrante; (*food*) ipocalorico(a)

sling [slɪŋ] (*pt, pp* **slung**) *n* (MED) fascia al collo; (*for baby*) marsupio ♦ *vt* lanciare, tirare

slip [slɪp] *n* scivolata, scivolone *m*; (*mistake*) errore *m*, sbaglio; (*underskirt*) sottoveste *f*; (*of paper*) striscia di carta; tagliando, scontrino ♦ *vt* (*slide*) far scivolare ♦ *vi* (*slide*) scivolare; (*move smoothly*): **to ~ into/out of** scivolare in/fuori da; (*decline*) declinare; **to ~ sth on/off** infilarsi/togliersi qc; **to give sb the ~** sfuggire qn; **a ~ of the tongue** un lapsus linguae; **~ away** *vi* svignarsela; **~ in** *vt* infilare ♦ *vi* (*error*) scivolare; **~ out** *vi* scivolare fuori; **~ up** *vi* sbagliarsi; **~ped disc** *n* spostamento delle vertebre

slipper ['slɪpə*] *n* pantofola

slippery ['slɪpərɪ] *adj* scivoloso(a)

slip road (BRIT) *n* (*to motorway*) rampa di accesso

slip-up *n* granchio (*fig*)

slipway ['slɪpweɪ] *n* scalo di costruzione

slit [slɪt] (*pt, pp* **slit**) *n* fessura, fenditura; (*cut*) taglio ♦ *vt* fendere; tagliare

slither ['slɪðə*] *vi* scivolare, sdrucciolare

sliver ['slɪvə*] *n* (*of glass, wood*) scheggia; (*of cheese etc*) fettina

slob [slɔb] (*inf*) *n* sciattone/a

slog [slɔg] (BRIT) *n* faticata ♦ *vi* lavorare con accanimento, sgobbare

slogan ['sləʊgən] *n* motto, slogan *m inv*

slope [sləʊp] *n* pendio; (*side of mountain*) versante *m*; (*ski ~*) pista; (*of roof*) pendenza; (*of floor*) inclinazione *f* ♦ *vi*: **to ~ down** declinare; **to ~ up** essere in salita; **sloping** *adj* inclinato(a)

sloppy ['slɔpɪ] *adj* (*work*) tirato(a) via; (*appearance*) sciatto(a)

slot [slɔt] *n* fessura ♦ *vt*: **to ~ sth into** infilare qc in

sloth [sləʊθ] *n* (*laziness*) pigrizia, accidia

slot machine *n* (BRIT: *vending machine*) distributore *m* automatico; (*for gambling*) slot-machine *f inv*

slouch [slaʊtʃ] *vi* (*when walking*) camminare dinoccolato(a); **she was ~ing in a chair** era sprofondata in una poltrona

Slovenia [sləʊˈviːnɪə] *n* Slovenia

slovenly ['slʌvənlɪ] *adj* sciatto(a), trasandato(a)

slow [sləʊ] *adj* lento(a); (*watch*): **to be ~** essere indietro ♦ *adv* lentamente ♦ *vt, vi* (*also*: **~ down, ~ up**) rallentare; **"~"** (*road sign*) "rallentare"; **~ly** *adv* lentamente; **~ motion** *n*: **in ~ motion** al rallentatore

sludge [slʌdʒ] *n* fanghiglia

slug [slʌg] *n* lumaca; (*bullet*) pallottola; **~gish** *adj* lento(a); (*trading*) stagnante

sluice [sluːs] *n* chiusa

slum [slʌm] *n* catapecchia

slumber ['slʌmbə*] *n* sonno

slump [slʌmp] *n* crollo, caduta; (*economic*) depressione *f*, crisi *f inv* ♦ *vi* crollare

slung [slʌŋ] *pt, pp of* **sling**

slur [sləː*] *n* (*fig*): **~ (on)** calunnia (su) ♦ *vt* pronunciare in modo indistinto

slush [slʌʃ] *n* neve *f* mista a fango; **~ fund** *n* fondi *mpl* neri

slut [slʌt] *n* donna trasandata, sciattona

sly [slaɪ] *adj* (*smile, remark*) sornione(a); (*person*) furbo(a)

smack [smæk] *n* (*slap*) pacca; (*on face*) schiaffo ♦ *vt* schiaffeggiare; (*child*) picchiare ♦ *vi*: **to ~ of** puzzare di

small [smɔːl] *adj* piccolo(a); **~ ads** (*BRIT*) *npl* piccola pubblicità; **~ change** *n* moneta, spiccioli *mpl*; **~-holder** *n* piccolo proprietario; **~ hours** *npl*: **in the ~ hours** alle ore piccole; **~pox** *n* vaiolo; **~ talk** *n* chiacchiere *fpl*

smart [smɑːt] *adj* elegante; (*fashionable*) alla moda; (*clever*) intelligente; (*quick*) sveglio(a) ♦ *vi* bruciare; **~ card** *n* carta intelligente; **~en up** *vi* farsi bello/a ♦ *vt* (*people*) fare bello(a); (*things*) abbellire

smash [smæʃ] *n* (*also*: **~-up**) scontro, collisione *f*; (*~ hit*) successore *m* ♦ *vt* frantumare, fracassare; (*SPORT: record*) battere ♦ *vi* frantumarsi, andare in pezzi; **~ing** (*inf*) *adj* favoloso(a), formidabile

smattering ['smætərɪŋ] *n*: **a ~ of** un'infarinatura di

smear [smɪə*] *n* macchia; (*MED*) striscio ♦ *vt* spalmare; (*make dirty*) sporcare; **~ campaign** *n* campagna diffamatoria

smell [smɛl] (*pt, pp* **smelt** *or* **smelled**) *n* odore *m*; (*sense*) olfatto, odorato ♦ *vt* sentire (l')odore di ♦ *vi* (*food etc*): **to ~ (of)** avere odore (di); (*pej*) puzzare, avere un cattivo odore di; **~y** *adj* puzzolente

smile [smaɪl] *n* sorriso ♦ *vi* sorridere

smirk [smɜːk] *n* sorriso furbo; sorriso compiaciuto

smog [smɔg] *n* smog *m*

smoke [sməuk] *n* fumo ♦ *vt, vi* fumare; **~d** *adj* (*bacon, glass*) affumicato(a); **~r** *n* (*person*) fumatore/trice; (*RAIL*) carrozza per fumatori; **~ screen** *n* (*MIL*) cortina fumogena *or* di fumo; (*fig*) copertura; **smoking** *n* fumo; **"no smoking"** (*sign*) "vietato fumare"; **smoking compartment** (*BRIT*), **smoking car** (*US*) *n* scompartimento (per) fumatori; **smoky** *adj* fumoso(a); (*taste*) affumicato(a)

smolder ['sməuldə*] (*US*) *vi* = **smoulder**

smooth [smuːð] *adj* liscio(a); (*sauce*) omogeneo(a); (*flavour, whisky*) amabile; (*movement*) regolare; (*person*) mellifluo(a) ♦ *vt* (*also*: **~ out**) lisciare, spianare; (: *difficulties*) appianare

smother ['smʌðə*] *vt* soffocare

smoulder ['sməuldə*] (*US* **smolder**) *vi* covare sotto la cenere

smudge [smʌdʒ] *n* macchia; sbavatura ♦ *vt* imbrattare, sporcare

smug [smʌg] *adj* soddisfatto(a), compiaciuto(a)

smuggle ['smʌgl] *vt* contrabbandare; **~r** *n* contrabbandiere/a; **smuggling** *n* contrabbando

smutty ['smʌtɪ] *adj* (*fig*) osceno(a), indecente

snack [snæk] *n* spuntino; **~ bar** *n* tavola calda, snack bar *m inv*

snag [snæg] *n* intoppo, ostacolo imprevisto

snail [sneɪl] *n* chiocciola

snake [sneɪk] *n* serpente *m*

snap [snæp] *n* (*sound*) schianto, colpo secco; (*photograph*) istantanea ♦ *adj* improvviso(a) ♦ *vt* (far) schioccare; (*break*) spezzare di netto ♦ *vi* spezzarsi con un rumore secco; (*fig: person*) parlare con tono secco; **to ~ shut** chiudersi di scatto; **~ at** *vt fus* (*subj: dog*) cercare di mordere; **~ off** *vt* (*break*) schiantare; **~ up** *vt* afferrare; **~py** (*inf*) *adj* (*answer, slogan*) d'effetto; **make it ~py!** (*hurry up*) sbrigati!, svelto!; **~shot** *n* istantanea

snare [snɛə*] *n* trappola

snarl [snɑːl] *vi* ringhiare

snatch [snætʃ] *n* (*small amount*) frammento ♦ *vt* strappare (con violenza); (*fig*) rubare

sneak [sniːk] (*pt* (*US*) **snuck**) *vi*: **to ~ in/out** entrare/uscire di nascosto ♦ *n* spione/a; **to ~ up on sb** avvicinarsi quatto quatto a qn; **~ers** *npl* scarpe *fpl* da ginnastica

sneer [snɪə*] *vi* sogghignare; **to ~ at** farsi beffe di

sneeze [sniːz] *n* starnuto ♦ *vi* starnutire

sniff [snɪf] *n* fiutata, annusata ♦ *vi* tirare su col naso ♦ *vt* fiutare, annusare

snigger ['snɪgə*] *vi* ridacchiare, ridere sotto i baffi

snip [snɪp] n pezzetto; (bargain) (buon) affare m, occasione f ♦ vt tagliare

sniper ['snaɪpə*] n (marksman) franco tiratore m, cecchino

snippet ['snɪpɪt] n frammento

snob [snɔb] n snob m/f inv; **~bery** n snobismo; **~bish** adj snob inv

snooker ['snu:kə*] n tipo di gioco del biliardo

snoop ['snu:p] vi: **to ~ about** curiosare

snooze [snu:z] n sonnellino, pisolino ♦ vi fare un sonnellino

snore [snɔ:*] vi russare

snorkel ['snɔ:kl] n (of swimmer) respiratore m a tubo

snort [snɔ:t] n sbuffo ♦ vi sbuffare

snout [snaut] n muso

snow [snəu] n neve f ♦ vi nevicare; **~ball** n palla di neve ♦ vi (fig) crescere a vista d'occhio; **~bound** adj bloccato(a) dalla neve; **~drift** n cumulo di neve (ammucchiato dal vento); **~drop** n bucaneve m inv; **~fall** n nevicata; **~flake** n fiocco di neve; **~man** (irreg) n pupazzo di neve; **~plough** (US **~plow**) n spazzaneve m inv; **~shoe** n racchetta da neve; **~storm** n tormenta

snub [snʌb] vt snobbare ♦ n offesa, affronto; **~-nosed** adj dal naso camuso

snuff [snʌf] n tabacco da fiuto

snug [snʌg] adj comodo(a); (room, house) accogliente, comodo(a)

snuggle ['snʌgl] vi: **to ~ up to sb** stringersi a qn

KEYWORD

so [səu] adv 1 (thus, likewise) così; **if ~** se è così, quand'è così; **I didn't do it – you did ~!** non l'ho fatto io — sì che l'hai fatto!; **~ do I, ~ am I** etc anch'io; **it's 5 o'clock – ~ it is!** sono le 5 — davvero!; **I hope ~** lo spero; **I think ~** penso di sì; **~ far** finora, fin qui; (in past) fino ad allora

2 (in comparisons etc: to such a degree) così; **~ big (that)** così grande (che); **she's not ~ clever as her brother** lei non è (così) intelligente come suo fratello

3: **~ much** adj tanto(a) ♦ adv tanto; **I've got ~ much work/money** ho tanto lavoro/tanti soldi; **I love you ~ much** ti amo tanto; **~ many** tanti(e)

4 (phrases): **10 or ~** circa 10; **~ long!** (inf: goodbye) ciao!, ci vediamo!

♦ conj 1 (expressing purpose): **~ as to do** in modo or così da fare; **we hurried ~ as not to be late** ci affrettammo per non fare tardi; **~ (that)** affinché +sub, perché +sub

2 (expressing result): **he didn't arrive ~ I left** non è venuto così me ne sono andata; **~ you see, I could have gone** vedi, sarei potuto andare

soak [səuk] vt inzuppare; (clothes) mettere a mollo ♦ vi (clothes etc) essere a mollo; **~ in** vi penetrare; **~ up** vt assorbire

soap [səup] n sapone m; **~flakes** npl sapone m in scaglie; **~ opera** n soap opera f inv; **~ powder** n detersivo; **~y** adj insaponato(a)

soar [sɔ:*] vi volare in alto; (price etc) salire alle stelle; (building) ergersi

sob [sɔb] n singhiozzo ♦ vi singhiozzare

sober ['səubə*] adj sobrio(a); (not drunk) non ubriaco(a); (moderate) moderato(a); **~ up** vt far passare la sbornia a ♦ vi farsi passare la sbornia

so-called ['səu'kɔ:ld] adj cosiddetto(a)

soccer ['sɔkə*] n calcio

sociable ['səuʃəbl] adj socievole

social ['səuʃl] adj sociale ♦ n festa, serata; **~ club** n club m inv sociale; **~ism** n socialismo; **~ist** adj, n socialista m/f; **~ize** vi: **to ~ize (with)** socializzare (con); **~ security** (BRIT) n previdenza sociale; **~ work** n servizio sociale; **~ worker** n assistente m/f sociale

society [sə'saɪətɪ] n società f inv; (club) società, associazione f; (also: **high ~**) alta società

sociology [səusɪ'ɔlədʒɪ] n sociologia

sock [sɔk] n calzino

socket ['sɔkɪt] n cavità f inv; (of eye) orbita; (BRIT: ELEC: also: **wall ~**) presa di corrente

sod [sɔd] n (of earth) zolla erbosa; (BRIT: inf!)

bastardo/a (*!*)

soda ['səʊdə] *n* (CHEM) soda; (*also*: **~ water**) acqua di seltz; (US: *also*: **~ pop**) gassosa

sodium ['səʊdɪəm] *n* sodio

sofa ['səʊfə] *n* sofà *m inv*

soft [sɒft] *adj* (*not rough*) morbido(a); (*not hard*) soffice; (*not loud*) sommesso(a); (*not bright*) tenue; (*kind*) gentile; **~ drink** *n* analcolico; **~en** ['sɒfn] *vt* ammorbidire; addolcire; attenuare ♦ **power** vi ammorbidirsi; addolcirsi; attenuarsi; **~ly** *adv* dolcemente; morbidamente; **~ness** *n* dolcezza; morbidezza

software ['sɒftwɛə*] *n* (COMPUT) software *m*

soggy ['sɒgɪ] *adj* inzuppato(a)

soil [sɔɪl] *n* terreno ♦ *vt* sporcare

solar ['səʊlə*] *adj* solare; **~ panel** *n* pannello solare; **~ power** *n* energie solare

sold [səʊld] *pt, pp of* **sell**; **~ out** *adj* (COMM) esaurito(a)

solder ['səʊldə*] *vt* saldare ♦ *n* saldatura

soldier ['səʊldʒə*] *n* soldato, militare *m*

sole [səʊl] *n* (*of foot*) pianta (del piede); (*of shoe*) suola; (*fish: pl inv*) sogliola ♦ *adj* solo(a), unico(a)

solemn ['sɒləm] *adj* solenne

sole trader *n* (COMM) commerciante *m* in proprio

solicit [sə'lɪsɪt] *vt* (*request*) richiedere, sollecitare ♦ *vi* (*prostitute*) adescare i passanti

solicitor [sə'lɪsɪtə*] (BRIT) *n* (*for wills etc*) ≈ notaio; (*in court*) ≈ avvocato

solid ['sɒlɪd] *adj* solido(a); (*not hollow*) pieno(a); (*meal*) sostanzioso(a) ♦ *n* solido

solidarity [sɒlɪ'dærɪtɪ] *n* solidarietà

solitaire [sɒlɪ'tɛə*] *n* (*games, gem*) solitario

solitary ['sɒlɪtərɪ] *adj* solitario(a); **~ confinement** *n* (LAW) isolamento

solo ['səʊləʊ] *n* assolo; **~ist** *n* solista *m/f*

soluble ['sɒljʊbl] *adj* solubile

solution [sə'luːʃən] *n* soluzione *f*

solve [sɒlv] *vt* risolvere

solvent ['sɒlvənt] *adj* (COMM) solvibile ♦ *n* (CHEM) solvente *m*

sombre ['sɒmbə*] (US **somber**) *adj* scuro(a); (*mood, person*) triste

---

KEYWORD

some [sʌm] *adj* **1** (*a certain amount or number of*): **~ tea/water/cream** del tè/dell'acqua/della panna; **~ children/apples** dei bambini/delle mele

2 (*certain: in contrasts*) certo(a); **~ people say that ...** alcuni dicono che ..., certa gente dice che ...

3 (*unspecified*) un(a) certo(a), qualche; **~ woman was asking for you** una tale chiedeva di lei; **~ day** un giorno; **~ day next week** un giorno della prossima settimana

♦ *pron* **1** (*a certain number*) alcuni(e), certi(e); **I've got ~** (*books etc*) ne ho alcuni; **~ (of them) have been sold** alcuni sono stati venduti

2 (*a certain amount*) un po'; **I've got ~** (*money, milk*) ne ho un po'; **I've read ~ of the book** ho letto parte del libro

♦ *adv*: **~ 10 people** circa 10 persone

---

somebody ['sʌmbədɪ] *pron* = **someone**

somehow ['sʌmhaʊ] *adv* in un modo o nell'altro, in qualche modo; (*for some reason*) per qualche ragione

someone ['sʌmwʌn] *pron* qualcuno

someplace ['sʌmpleɪs] (US) *adv* = **somewhere**

somersault ['sʌməsɔːlt] *n* capriola; salto mortale ♦ *vi* fare una capriola (*or* un salto mortale); (*car*) cappottare

something ['sʌmθɪŋ] *pron* qualcosa, qualche cosa; **~ nice** qualcosa di bello; **~ to do** qualcosa da fare

sometime ['sʌmtaɪm] *adv* (*in future*) una volta o l'altra; (*in past*): **~ last month** durante il mese scorso

sometimes ['sʌmtaɪmz] *adv* qualche volta

somewhat ['sʌmwɒt] *adv* piuttosto

somewhere ['sʌmwɛə*] *adv* in *or* da qualche parte

son [sʌn] *n* figlio

song [sɒŋ] *n* canzone *f*

sonic ['sɒnɪk] *adj* (*boom*) sonico(a)

son-in-law *n* genero

sonnet ['sɔnɪt] *n* sonetto

sonny ['sʌnɪ] (*inf*) *n* ragazzo mio

soon [suːn] *adv* presto, fra poco; (*early, a short time after*) presto; **~ afterwards** poco dopo; *see also* **as**; **~er** *adv* (*time*) prima; (*preference*): **I would ~er do** preferirei fare; **~er or later** prima o poi

soot [sʊt] *n* fuliggine *f*

soothe [suːð] *vt* calmare

sophisticated [sə'fɪstɪkeɪtɪd] *adj* sofisticato(a); raffinato(a); complesso(a)

sophomore ['sɔfəmɔː*] (*US*) *n* studente/essa del secondo anno

sopping ['sɔpɪŋ] *adj* (*also*: **~ wet**) bagnato(a) fradicio(a)

soppy ['sɔpɪ] (*pej*) *adj* sentimentale

soprano [sə'prɑːnəu] *n* (*voice*) soprano *m*; (*singer*) soprano *m/f*

sorcerer ['sɔːsərə*] *n* stregone *m*, mago

sore [sɔː*] *adj* (*painful*) dolorante ♦ *n* piaga; **~ly** *adv* (*tempted*) fortemente

sorrow ['sɔrəu] *n* dolore *m*; **~ful** *adj* doloroso(a)

sorry ['sɔrɪ] *adj* spiacente; (*condition, excuse*) misero(a); **~!** scusa! (*or* scusi! *or* scusate!); **to feel ~ for sb** rincrescersi per qn

sort [sɔːt] *n* specie *f*, genere *m* ♦ *vt* (*also*: **~ out**: *papers*) classificare; ordinare; (: *letters etc*) smistare; (: *problems*) risolvere; **~ing office** *n* ufficio *m* smistamento *inv*

SOS *n abbr* (= *save our souls*) S.O.S. *m inv*

so-so *adv* così così

sought [sɔːt] *pt, pp of* **seek**

soul [səul] *n* anima; **~ful** *adj* pieno(a) di sentimento

sound [saund] *adj* (*healthy*) sano(a); (*safe, not damaged*) solido(a), in buono stato; (*reliable, not superficial*) solido(a); (*sensible*) giudizioso(a), di buon senso ♦ *adv*: **~ asleep** profondamente addormentato ♦ *n* suono; (*noise*) rumore *m*; (*GEO*) stretto ♦ *vt* (*alarm*) suonare ♦ *vi* suonare; (*fig: seem*) sembrare; **to ~ like** rassomigliare a; **~ out** *vt* sondare; **~ barrier** *n* muro del suono; **~bite** *n* dichiarazione breve ed incisiva (*trasmessa per radio o per TV*); **~ effects** *npl* effetti sonori; **~ly** *adv* (*sleep*)

profondamente; (*beat*) duramente; **~proof** *adj* insonorizzato(a), isolato(a) acusticamente; **~track** *n* (*of film*) colonna sonora

soup [suːp] *n* minestra; brodo; zuppa; **~ plate** *n* piatto fondo; **~spoon** *n* cucchiaio da minestra

sour ['sauə*] *adj* aspro(a); (*fruit*) acerbo(a); (*milk*) acido(a); (*fig*) arcigno(a); acido(a); **it's ~ grapes** è soltanto invidia

source [sɔːs] *n* fonte *f*, sorgente *f*; (*fig*) fonte

south [sauθ] *n* sud *m*, meridione *m*, mezzogiorno ♦ *adj* del sud, sud *inv*, meridionale ♦ *adv* verso sud; **S~ Africa** *n* Sudafrica *m*; **S~ African** *adj, n* sudafricano(a); **S~ America** *n* Sudamerica *m*, America del sud; **S~ American** *adj, n* sudamericano(a); **~-east** *n* sud-est *m*; **~erly** ['sʌðəlɪ] *adj* del sud; **~ern** ['sʌðən] *adj* del sud, meridionale; esposto(a) a sud; **S~ Pole** *n* Polo Sud; **~ward(s)** *adv* verso sud; **~-west** *n* sud-ovest *m*

souvenir [suːvə'nɪə*] *n* ricordo, souvenir *m inv*

sovereign ['sɔvrɪn] *adj, n* sovrano(a)

soviet ['səuvɪət] *adj* sovietico(a); **the S~ Union** l'Unione *f* Sovietica

sow[1] [səu] (*pt* **~ed**, *pp* **sown**) *vt* seminare

sow[2] [sau] *n* scrofa

sown [səun] *pp of* **sow**

soy [sɔɪ] (*US*) *n* = **soya**

soya ['sɔɪə] (*US* **soy**) *n*: **~ bean** *n* seme *m* di soia; **~ sauce** *n* salsa di soia

spa [spɑː] *n* (*resort*) stazione *f* termale; (*US: also*: **health ~**) centro di cure estetiche

space [speɪs] *n* spazio; (*room*) posto; spazio; (*length of time*) intervallo ♦ *cpd* spaziale ♦ *vt* (*also*: **~ out**) distanziare; **~craft** *n inv* veicolo spaziale; **~man/woman** (*irreg*) *n* astronauta *m/f*, cosmonauta *m/f*; **~ship** *n* = **~craft**; **spacing** *n* spaziatura

spacious ['speɪʃəs] *adj* spazioso(a), ampio(a)

spade [speɪd] *n* (*tool*) vanga, pala; (*child's*) paletta; **~s** *npl* (*CARDS*) picche *fpl*

Spain [speɪn] n Spagna

span [spæn] n (of bird, plane) apertura alare; (of arch) campata; (in time) periodo; durata ♦ vt attraversare; (fig) abbracciare

Spaniard ['spænjəd] n spagnolo/a

spaniel ['spænjəl] n spaniel m inv

Spanish ['spænɪʃ] adj spagnolo/a ♦ n (LING) spagnolo; **the ~** npl gli Spagnoli

spank [spæŋk] vt sculacciare

spanner ['spænə*] (BRIT) n chiave f inglese

spare [spɛə*] adj di riserva, di scorta; (surplus) in più, d'avanzo ♦ n (part) pezzo di ricambio ♦ vt (do without) fare a meno di; (afford to give) concedere; (refrain from hurting, using) risparmiare; **to ~** (surplus) d'avanzo; **~ part** n pezzo di ricambio; **~ time** n tempo libero; **~ wheel** n (AUT) ruota di scorta

sparingly ['spɛərɪŋlɪ] adv moderatamente

spark [spɑ:k] n scintilla; **~(ing) plug** n candela

sparkle ['spɑ:kl] n scintillio, sfavillio ♦ vi scintillare, sfavillare; **sparkling** adj scintillante, sfavillante; (conversation, wine, water) frizzante

sparrow ['spærəu] n passero

sparse [spɑ:s] adj sparso(a), rado(a)

spartan ['spɑ:tən] adj (fig) spartano(a)

spasm ['spæzm] n (MED) spasmo; (fig) accesso, attacco; **~odic** [spæz'mɔdɪk] adj spasmodico(a); (fig) intermittente

spastic ['spæstɪk] n spastico/a

spat [spæt] pt, pp of **spit**

spate [speɪt] n (fig): **~ of** diluvio or fiume m di

spawn [spɔ:n] vi deporre le uova ♦ n uova fpl

speak [spi:k] (pt **spoke**, pp **spoken**) vt (language) parlare; (truth) dire ♦ vi parlare; **to ~ to sb/of or about sth** parlare a qn/di qc; **~ up!** parla più forte!; **~er** n (in public) oratore/trice; (also: **loud~er**) altoparlante m; (POL): **the S~er** il presidente della Camera dei Comuni (BRIT) or dei Rappresentanti (US)

spear [spɪə*] n lancia ♦ vt infilzare; **~head** vt (attack etc) condurre

spec [spɛk] (inf) n: **on ~** sperando bene

special ['spɛʃl] adj speciale; **~ist** n specialista m/f; **~ity** [spɛʃɪ'ælɪtɪ] n specialità f inv; **~ize** vi: **to ~ize (in)** specializzarsi (in); **~ly** adv specialmente, particolarmente; **~ needs** adj: **~ needs children** bambini mpl con difficoltà di apprendimento; **~ty** n = **speciality**

species ['spi:ʃi:z] n inv specie f inv

specific [spə'sɪfɪk] adj specifico(a); preciso(a); **~ally** adv esplicitamente; (especially) appositamente

specimen ['spɛsɪmən] n esemplare m, modello; (MED) campione m

speck [spɛk] n puntino, macchiolina; (particle) granello

speckled ['spɛkld] adj macchiettato(a)

specs [spɛks] npl occhiali mpl

spectacle ['spɛktəkl] n spettacolo; **~s** npl (glasses) occhiali mpl; **spectacular** [-'tækjulə*] adj spettacolare

spectator [spɛk'teɪtə*] n spettatore m

spectra ['spɛktrə] npl of **spectrum**

spectre ['spɛktə*] (US **specter**) n spettro

spectrum ['spɛktrəm] (pl **spectra**) n spettro

speculation [spɛkju'leɪʃən] n speculazione f; congetture fpl

speech [spi:tʃ] n (faculty) parola; (talk, THEATRE) discorso; (manner of speaking) parlata; **~less** adj ammutolito(a), muto(a)

speed [spi:d] n velocità f inv; (promptness) prontezza; **at full** or **top ~** a tutta velocità; **~ up** vi, vt accelerare; **~boat** n motoscafo; **~ily** adv velocemente; prontamente; **~ing** n (AUT) eccesso di velocità; **~ limit** n limite m di velocità; **~ometer** [spɪ'dɔmɪtə*] n tachimetro; **~way** n (sport) corsa motociclistica (su pista); **~y** adj veloce, rapido(a); pronto(a)

spell [spɛl] (pt, pp **spelt** (BRIT) or **~ed**) n (also: **magic ~**) incantesimo; (period of time) (breve) periodo ♦ vt (in writing) scrivere (lettera per lettera); (aloud) dire lettera per lettera; (fig) significare; **to cast a ~ on sb** fare un incantesimo a qn; **he can't ~** fa errori di ortografia; **~bound** adj incantato(a); affascinato(a); ~ing n ortografia; spelt (BRIT) pt, pp of spell

spend [spɛnd] (pt, pp spent) vt (money) spendere; (time, life) passare; ~thrift n spendaccione/a; spent pt, pp of spend

sperm [spəːm] n sperma m

sphere [sfɪə*] n sfera

spice [spaɪs] n spezia ♦ vt aromatizzare

spicy ['spaɪsɪ] adj piccante

spider ['spaɪdə*] n ragno

spike [spaɪk] n punta

spill [spɪl] (pt, pp spilt or ~ed) vt versare, rovesciare ♦ vi versarsi, rovesciarsi; ~ over vi (liquid) versarsi; (crowd) riversarsi; spilt pt, pp of spill

spin [spɪn] (pt, pp spun) n (revolution of wheel) rotazione f; (AVIAT) avvitamento; (trip in car) giretto ♦ vt (wool etc) filare; (wheel) far girare ♦ vi girare

spinach ['spɪnɪtʃ] n spinacio; (as food) spinaci mpl

spinal ['spaɪnl] adj spinale; ~ cord n midollo spinale

spin doctor (inf) n esperto di comunicazioni responsabile dell'immagine di un partito politico

spin-dryer (BRIT) n centrifuga

spine [spaɪn] n spina dorsale; (thorn) spina

spinning ['spɪnɪŋ] n filatura; ~ top n trottola

spin-off n (product) prodotto secondario

spinster ['spɪnstə*] n nubile f; zitella

spiral ['spaɪərl] n spirale f ♦ vi (fig) salire a spirale; ~ staircase n scala a chiocciola

spire ['spaɪə*] n guglia

spirit ['spɪrɪt] n spirito; (ghost) spirito, fantasma m; (mood) stato d'animo, umore m; (courage) coraggio; ~s npl (drink) alcolici mpl; in good ~s di buon umore; ~ed adj vivace, vigoroso(a); (horse) focoso(a); ~ level n livella a bolla (d'aria)

spiritual ['spɪrɪtjuəl] adj spirituale

spit [spɪt] (pt, pp spat) n (for roasting) spiedo; (saliva) sputo; saliva ♦ vi sputare; (fire, fat) scoppiettare

spite [spaɪt] n dispetto ♦ vt contrariare, far dispetto a; in ~ of nonostante, malgrado;

~ful adj dispettoso(a)

spittle ['spɪtl] n saliva; sputo

splash [splæʃ] n spruzzo; (sound) splash m inv; (of colour) schizzo ♦ vt spruzzare ♦ vi (also: ~ about) sguazzare

spleen [spliːn] n (ANAT) milza

splendid ['splɛndɪd] adj splendido(a), magnifico(a)

splint [splɪnt] n (MED) stecca

splinter ['splɪntə*] n scheggia ♦ vi scheggiarsi

split [splɪt] (pt, pp split) n spaccatura; (fig: division, quarrel) scissione f ♦ vt spaccare; (party) dividere; (work, profits) spartire, ripartire ♦ vi (divide) dividersi; ~ up vi (couple) separarsi, rompere; (meeting) sciogliersi

spoil [spɔɪl] (pt, pp spoilt or ~ed) vt (damage) rovinare, guastare; (mar) sciupare; (child) viziare; ~s npl bottino; ~sport n guastafeste m/f inv; spoilt pt, pp of spoil

spoke [spəuk] pt of speak ♦ n raggio

spoken ['spəukn] pp of speak

spokesman ['spəuksmən] (irreg) n portavoce m inv

spokeswoman ['spəukswumən] (irreg) n portavoce f inv

sponge [spʌndʒ] n spugna; (also: ~ cake) pan m di spagna ♦ vt spugnare, pulire con una spugna ♦ vi: to ~ off or on scroccare a; ~ bag (BRIT) n nécessaire m inv

sponsor ['spɒnsə*] n (RADIO, TV, SPORT etc) sponsor m inv; (POL: of bill) promotore/trice ♦ vt sponsorizzare; (bill) presentare; ~ship n sponsorizzazione f

spontaneous [spɒn'teɪnɪəs] adj spontaneo(a)

spooky ['spuːkɪ] (inf) adj che fa accapponare la pelle

spool [spuːl] n bobina

spoon [spuːn] n cucchiaio; ~-feed vt nutrire con il cucchiaio; (fig) imboccare; ~ful n cucchiaiata

sport [spɔːt] n sport m inv; (person) persona di spirito ♦ vt sfoggiare; ~ing adj sportivo(a); to give sb a ~ing chance dare a qn una possibilità (di vincere); **~ jacket** (*US*) *n* = **~s jacket**; **~s car** *n* automobile *f* sportiva; **~s jacket** (*BRIT*) *n* giacca sportiva; **~sman** (*irreg*) *n* sportivo; **~smanship** *n* spirito sportivo; **~swear** *n* abiti *mpl* sportivi; **~swoman** (*irreg*) *n* sportiva; **~y** *adj* sportivo(a)

spot [spɔt] *n* punto; (*mark*) macchia; (*dot: on pattern*) pallino; (*pimple*) foruncolo; (*place*) posto; (*RADIO, TV*) spot *m inv*; (*small amount*): **a ~ of** un po' di ♦ *vt* (*notice*) individuare, distinguere; **on the ~** sul posto; (*immediately*) su due piedi; (*in difficulty*) nei guai; **~ check** *n* controllo senza preavviso; **~less** *adj* immacolato(a); **~light** *n* proiettore *m*; (*AUT*) faro ausiliario; **~ted** *adj* macchiato(a); a puntini, a pallini; **~ty** *adj* (*face*) foruncoloso(a)

spouse [spauz] *n* sposo/a

spout [spaut] *n* (*of jug*) beccuccio; (*of pipe*) scarico ♦ *vi* zampillare

sprain [spreɪn] *n* storta, distorsione *f* ♦ *vt*: **to ~ one's ankle** storcersi una caviglia

sprang [spræŋ] *pt of* **spring**

sprawl [sprɔːl] *vi* sdraiarsi (in modo scomposto); (*place*) estendersi (disordinatamente)

spray [spreɪ] *n* spruzzo; (*container*) nebulizzatore *m*, spray *m inv*; (*of flowers*) mazzetto ♦ *vt* spruzzare; (*crops*) irrorare

spread [spred] (*pt, pp* **spread**) *n* diffusione *f*; (*distribution*) distribuzione *f*; (*CULIN*) pasta (da spalmare); (*inf: food*) banchetto ♦ *vt* (*cloth*) stendere, distendere; (*butter etc*) spalmare; (*disease, knowledge*) propagare, diffondere ♦ *vi* stendersi, distendersi; spalmarsi; propagarsi, diffondersi; **~ out** *vi* separarsi; **~-eagled** [ˈspredɪːgld] *adj* a gambe e braccia aperte; **~sheet** *n* foglio elettronico ad espansione

spree [spriː] *n*: **to go on a ~** fare baldoria

sprightly [ˈspraɪtlɪ] *adj* vivace

spring [sprɪŋ] (*pt* **sprang**, *pp* **sprung**) *n* (*leap*) salto, balzo; (*coiled metal*) molla; (*season*) primavera; (*of water*) sorgente *f* ♦ *vi* saltare, balzare; **~ up** *vi* (*problem*) presentarsi; **~board** *n* trampolino; **~-**

clean(ing) *n* grandi pulizie *fpl* di primavera; **~time** *n* primavera

sprinkle [ˈsprɪŋkl] *vt* spruzzare; spargere; **to ~ water etc on, ~ with water** *etc* spruzzare dell'acqua *etc* su; **~r** *n* (*for lawn*) irrigatore *m*; (*to put out fire*) sprinkler *m inv*

sprint [sprɪnt] *n* scatto ♦ *vi* scattare; **~er** *n* (*SPORT*) velocista *m/f*

sprout [spraut] *vi* germogliare; **~s** *npl* (*also:* **Brussels ~s**) cavolini *mpl* di Bruxelles

spruce [spruːs] *n inv* abete *m* rosso ♦ *adj* lindo(a); azzimato(a)

sprung [sprʌŋ] *pp of* **spring**

spun [spʌn] *pt, pp of* **spin**

spur [spəː*] *n* sperone *m*; (*fig*) sprone *m*, incentivo ♦ *vt* (*also:* **~ on**) spronare; **on the ~ of the moment** lì per lì

spurious [ˈspjuərɪəs] *adj* falso(a)

spurn [spəːn] *vt* rifiutare con disprezzo, sdegnare

spurt [spəːt] *n* (*of water*) getto; (*of energy*) scatto ♦ *vi* sgorgare

spy [spaɪ] *n* spia ♦ *vi*: **to ~ on** spiare ♦ *vt* (*see*) scorgere; **~ing** *n* spionaggio

sq. *abbr* = **square**

squabble [ˈskwɔbl] *vi* bisticciarsi

squad [skwɔd] *n* (*MIL*) plotone *m*; (*POLICE*) squadra

squadron [ˈskwɔdrn] *n* (*MIL*) squadrone *m*; (*AVIAT, NAUT*) squadriglia

squalid [ˈskwɔlɪd] *adj* squallido(a)

squall [skwɔːl] *n* raffica; burrasca

squalor [ˈskwɔlə*] *n* squallore *m*

squander [ˈskwɔndə*] *vt* dissipare

square [skwɛə*] *n* quadrato; (*in town*) piazza ♦ *adj* quadrato(a); (*inf: ideas, person*) di vecchio stampo ♦ *vt* (*arrange*) regolare; (*MATH*) elevare al quadrato; (*reconcile*) conciliare; **all ~** pari; **a ~ meal** un pasto abbondante; **2 metres ~** di 2 metri per 2; **1 ~ metre** 1 metro quadrato; **~ly** *adv* diritto; fermamente

squash [skwɔʃ] *n* (*SPORT*) squash *m*; (*BRIT: drink*): **lemon/orange ~** sciroppo di limone/arancia; (*US*) zucca; (*SPORT*) squash *m* ♦ *vt* schiacciare

squat [skwɔt] *adj* tarchiato(a), tozzo(a) ♦ *vi*

(*also*: ~ **down**) accovacciarsi; ~**ter** *n* occupante *m/f* abusivo(a)

squeak [skwiːk] *vi* squittire

squeal [skwiːl] *vi* strillare

squeamish ['skwiːmɪʃ] *adj* schizzinoso(a); disgustato(a)

squeeze [skwiːz] *n* pressione *f*; (*also ECON*) stretta ♦ *vt* premere; (*hand, arm*) stringere; ~ **out** *vt* spremere

squelch [skwɛltʃ] *vi* fare ciac; sguazzare

squid [skwɪd] *n* calamaro

squiggle ['skwɪgl] *n* ghirigoro

squint [skwɪnt] *vi* essere strabico(a) ♦ *n*: **he has a ~** è strabico

squirm [skwəːm] *vi* contorcersi

squirrel ['skwɪrəl] *n* scoiattolo

squirt [skwəːt] *vi* schizzare; zampillare ♦ *vt* spruzzare

Sr *abbr* = **senior**

St *abbr* = **saint**; **street**

stab [stæb] *n* (*with knife etc*) pugnalata; (*of pain*) fitta; (*inf*: *try*): **to have a ~ at (doing) sth** provare a (fare) qc ♦ *vt* pugnalare

stable ['steɪbl] *n* (*for horses*) scuderia; (*for cattle*) stalla ♦ *adj* stabile

stack [stæk] *n* catasta, pila ♦ *vt* accatastare, ammucchiare

stadium ['steɪdɪəm] *n* stadio

staff [stɑːf] *n* (*work force: gen*) personale *m*; (: *BRIT: SCOL*) personale insegnante ♦ *vt* fornire di personale

stag [stæg] *n* cervo

stage [steɪdʒ] *n* palcoscenico; (*profession*): **the ~** il teatro, la scena; (*point*) punto; (*platform*) palco ♦ *vt* (*play*) allestire, mettere in scena; (*demonstration*) organizzare; **in ~s** per gradi; a tappe; ~**coach** *n* diligenza; ~ **manager** *n* direttore *m* di scena

stagger ['stægə*] *vi* barcollare ♦ *vt* (*person*) sbalordire; (*hours, holidays*) scaglionare; ~**ing** *adj* (*amazing*) sbalorditivo(a)

stagnate [stæg'neɪt] *vi* stagnare

stag party *n* festa di addio al celibato

staid [steɪd] *adj* posato(a), serio(a)

stain [steɪn] *n* macchia; (*colouring*) colorante *m* ♦ *vt* macchiare; (*wood*) tingere; ~**ed**

glass window *n* vetrata; ~**less** *adj* (*steel*) inossidabile; ~ **remover** *n* smacchiatore *m*

stair [stɛə*] *n* (*step*) gradino; ~**s** *npl* (*flight of* ~*s*) scale *fpl*, scala; ~**case** *n* scale *fpl*, scala; ~**way** *n* = ~**case**

stake [steɪk] *n* palo, piolo; (*COMM*) interesse *m*; (*BETTING*) puntata, scommessa ♦ *vt* (*bet*) scommettere; (*risk*) rischiare; **to be at ~** essere in gioco

stale [steɪl] *adj* (*bread*) raffermo(a); (*food*) stantio(a); (*air*) viziato(a); (*beer*) svaporato(a); (*smell*) di chiuso

stalemate ['steɪlmeɪt] *n* stallo; (*fig*) punto morto

stalk [stɔːk] *n* gambo, stelo ♦ *vt* inseguire; ~ **off** *vi* andarsene impettito(a)

stall [stɔːl] *n* bancarella; (*in stable*) box *m inv* di stalla ♦ *vt* (*AUT*) far spegnere; (*fig*) bloccare ♦ *vi* (*AUT*) spegnersi, fermarsi; (*fig*) temporeggiare; ~**s** *npl* (*BRIT: in cinema, theatre*) platea

stallion ['stælɪən] *n* stallone *m*

stalwart ['stɔːlwət] *adj* fidato(a); risoluto(a)

stamina ['stæmɪnə] *n* vigore *m*, resistenza

stammer ['stæmə*] *n* balbuzie *f* ♦ *vi* balbettare

stamp [stæmp] *n* (*postage* ~) francobollo; (*implement*) timbro; (*mark, also fig*) marchio, impronta; (*on document*) bollo; timbro ♦ *vi* (*also*: ~ **one's foot**) battere il piede ♦ *vt* battere; (*letter*) affrancare; (*mark with a* ~) timbrare; ~ **album** *n* album *m inv* per francobolli; ~ **collecting** *n* filatelia

stampede [stæm'piːd] *n* fuggi fuggi *m inv*

stance [stæns] *n* posizione *f*

stand [stænd] (*pt, pp* **stood**) *n* (*position*) posizione *f*; (*for taxis*) posteggio; (*structure*) supporto, sostegno; (*at exhibition*) stand *m inv*; (*in shop*) banco; (*at market*) bancarella; (*booth*) chiosco; (*SPORT*) tribuna ♦ *vi* stare in piedi; (*rise*) alzarsi in piedi; (*be placed*) trovarsi ♦ *vt* (*place*) mettere, porre; (*tolerate, withstand*) resistere, sopportare; (*treat*) offrire; **to make a ~** prendere posizione; **to ~ for parliament** (*BRIT*) presentarsi come candidato (per il parlamento); ~ **by** *vi* (*be ready*) tenersi pronto(a) ♦ *vt fus* (*opinion*) sostenere; ~ **down** *vi* (*withdraw*) ritirarsi; ~ **for** *vt fus* (*signify*) rappresentare, significare; (*tolerate*) sopportare, tollerare; ~ **in for** *vt fus* sostituire; ~ **out** *vi* (*be prominent*) spiccare; ~ **up** *vi* (*rise*) alzarsi in piedi; ~ **up for** *vt fus* difendere; ~ **up to** *vt fus* tener testa a, resistere a

standard ['stændəd] *n* modello, standard *m inv*; (*level*) livello; (*flag*) stendardo ♦ *adj* (*size etc*) normale, standard *inv*; **~s** *npl* (*morals*) principi *mpl*, valori *mpl*; ~ **lamp** (*BRIT*) *n* lampada a stelo; ~ **of living** *n* livello di vita

stand-by *n* riserva, sostituto; **to be on ~** (*gen*) tenersi pronto(a); (*doctor*) essere di guardia; ~ **ticket** *n* (*AVIAT*) biglietto senza garanzia

stand-in *n* sostituto/a

standing ['stændɪŋ] *adj* diritto(a), in piedi; (*permanent*) permanente ♦ *n* rango, condizione *f*, posizione *f*; **of many years' ~** che data da molti anni; ~ **joke** *n* barzelletta; ~ **order** (*BRIT*) *n* (*at bank*) ordine *m* di pagamento (permanente); ~ **room** *n* posto all'impiedi

standpoint ['stændpɔɪnt] *n* punto di vista

standstill ['stændstɪl] *n*: **at a ~** fermo(a); (*fig*) a un punto morto; **to come to a ~** fermarsi; giungere a un punto morto

stank [stæŋk] *pt of* **stink**

staple ['steɪpl] *n* (*for papers*) graffetta ♦ *adj* (*food etc*) di base ♦ *vt* cucire; ~**r** *n* cucitrice *f*

star [stɑː*] *n* stella; (*celebrity*) divo/a ♦ *vi*: **to ~ (in)** essere il (*or* la) protagonista (di) ♦ *vt* (*CINEMA*) essere interpretato(a) da

starboard ['stɑːbəd] *n* dritta

starch [stɑːtʃ] *n* amido

stardom ['stɑːdəm] *n* celebrità

stare [stɛə*] *n* sguardo fisso ♦ *vi*: **to ~ at** fissare

starfish ['stɑːfɪʃ] *n* stella di mare

stark [stɑːk] *adj* (*bleak*) desolato(a) ♦ *adv*: ~ **naked** completamente nudo(a)

starling ['stɑːlɪŋ] *n* storno

starry ['stɑːrɪ] *adj* stellato(a); ~**-eyed** *adj* (*innocent*) ingenuo(a)

start [stɑːt] *n* inizio; (*of race*) partenza; (*sudden movement*) sobbalzo; (*advantage*) vantaggio ♦ *vt* cominciare, iniziare; (*car*) mettere in moto ♦ *vi* cominciare; (*on journey*) partire, mettersi in viaggio; (*jump*) sobbalzare; **to ~ doing** *or* **to do sth** (in)cominciare a fare qc; ~ **off** *vi* cominciare; (*leave*) partire; ~ **up** *vi* cominciare; (*car*) avviarsi ♦ *vt* iniziare; (*car*) avviare; ~**er** *n* (*AUT*) motorino d'avviamento; (*SPORT: official*) starter *m inv*; (*BRIT: CULIN*) primo piatto; ~**ing point** *n* punto di partenza

startle ['stɑːtl] *vt* far trasalire; **startling** *adj* sorprendente

starvation [stɑː'veɪʃən] *n* fame *f*, inedia

starve [stɑːv] *vi* morire di fame; soffrire la fame ♦ *vt* far morire di fame, affamare

state [steɪt] *n* stato ♦ *vt* dichiarare, affermare; annunciare; **the S~s** (*USA*) gli Stati Uniti; **to be in a ~** essere agitato(a); ~**ly** *adj* maestoso(a), imponente; ~**ly home** *n* residenza nobiliare (*d'interesse storico e artistico*); ~**ment** *n* dichiarazione *f*; ~**sman** (*irreg*) *n* statista *m*

static ['stætɪk] *n* (*RADIO*) scariche *fpl* ♦ *adj* statico(a)

station ['steɪʃən] *n* stazione *f* ♦ *vt* collocare, disporre

stationary ['steɪʃənərɪ] *adj* fermo(a), immobile

stationer ['steɪʃənə*] *n* cartolaio/a; ~**'s (shop)** *n* cartoleria; ~**y** *n* articoli *mpl* di cancelleria

station master *n* (*RAIL*) capostazione *m*

station wagon (*US*) *n* giardinetta

statistic [stə'tɪstɪk] *n* statistica; ~**s** *n* (*science*) statistica

statue ['stætjuː] *n* statua

status ['steɪtəs] *n* posizione *f*, condizione *f* sociale; prestigio; stato; ~ **symbol** *n* simbolo di prestigio

statute ['stætjuːt] *n* legge *f*; **statutory** *adj* stabilito(a) dalla legge, statutario(a)

staunch [stɔ:ntʃ] *adj* fidato(a), leale
stay [steɪ] *n* (*period of time*) soggiorno, permanenza ♦ *vi* rimanere; (*reside*) alloggiare, stare; (*spend some time*) trattenersi, soggiornare; **to ~ put** non muoversi; **to ~ the night** fermarsi per la notte; **~ behind** *vi* restare indietro; **~ in** *vi* (*at home*) stare in casa; **~ on** *vi* restare, rimanere; **~ out** *vi* (*of house*) rimanere fuori (di casa); **~ up** *vi* (*at night*) stare alzato(a); **~ing power** *n* capacità di resistenza
stead [stɛd] *n*: **in sb's ~** al posto di qn; **to stand sb in good ~** essere utile a qn
steadfast ['stɛdfɑ:st] *adj* fermo(a), risoluto(a)
steadily ['stɛdɪlɪ] *adv* (*firmly*) saldamente, (*constantly*) continuamente; (*fixedly*) fisso; (*walk*) con passo sicuro
steady ['stɛdɪ] *adj* (*not wobbling*) fermo(a); (*regular*) costante; (*person, character*) serio(a); (: *calm*) calmo(a), tranquillo(a) ♦ *vt* stabilizzare; calmare
steak [steɪk] *n* (*meat*) bistecca; (*fish*) trancia
steal [sti:l] (*pt* **stole**, *pp* **stolen**) *vt* rubare ♦ *vi* rubare; (*move*) muoversi furtivamente
stealth [stɛlθ] *n*: **by ~** furtivamente; **~y** *adj* furtivo(a)
steam [sti:m] *n* vapore *m* ♦ *vt* (*CULIN*) cuocere a vapore ♦ *vi* fumare; **~ engine** *n* macchina a vapore; (*RAIL*) locomotiva a vapore; **~er** *n* piroscafo, vapore *m*; **~roller** *n* rullo compressore; **~ship** *n* = **~er**; **~y** *adj* (*room*) pieno(a) di vapore; (*window*) appannato(a)
steel [sti:l] *n* acciaio ♦ *adj* di acciaio; **~works** *n* acciaieria
steep [sti:p] *adj* ripido(a), scosceso(a); (*price*) eccessivo(a) ♦ *vt* inzuppare; (*washing*) mettere a mollo
steeple ['sti:pl] *n* campanile *m*
steer [stɪə*] *vt* guidare ♦ *vi* (*NAUT*: *person*) governare; (*car*) guidarsi; **~ing** *n* (*AUT*) sterzo; **~ing wheel** *n* volante *m*
stem [stɛm] *n* (*of flower, plant*) stelo; (*of tree*) fusto; (*of glass*) gambo; (*of fruit, leaf*) picciolo ♦ *vt* contenere, arginare; **~ from**

vt fus provenire da, derivare da
stench [stɛntʃ] *n* puzzo, fetore *m*
stencil ['stɛnsl] *n* (*of metal, cardboard*) stampino, mascherina; (*in typing*) matrice *f* ♦ *vt* disegnare con stampino
stenographer [stɛ'nɔgrəfə*] (*US*) *n* stenografo/a
step [stɛp] *n* passo; (*stair*) gradino, scalino; (*action*) mossa, azione *f* ♦ *vi*: **to ~ forward/back** fare un passo avanti/indietro; **~s** *npl* (*BRIT*) = **stepladder**; **to be in/out of ~ (with)** stare/non stare al passo (con); **~ down** *vi* (*fig*) ritirarsi; **~ on** *vt fus* calpestare; **~ up** *vt* aumentare; **~brother** *n* fratellastro; **~daughter** *n* figliastra; **~father** *n* patrigno; **~ladder** *n* scala a libretto; **~mother** *n* matrigna; **~ping stone** *n* pietra di un guado; **~sister** *n* sorellastra; **~son** *n* figliastro
stereo ['stɛrɪəʊ] *n* (*system*) sistema *m* stereofonico; (*record player*) stereo *m inv* ♦ *adj* (*also*: **~phonic**) stereofonico(a)
sterile ['stɛraɪl] *adj* sterile; **sterilize** ['stɛrɪlaɪz] *vt* sterilizzare
sterling ['stɑ:lɪŋ] *adj* (*gold, silver*) di buona lega ♦ *n* (*ECON*) (lira) sterlina; **a pound ~** una lira sterlina
stern [stɜ:n] *adj* severo(a) ♦ *n* (*NAUT*) poppa
stew [stju:] *n* stufato ♦ *vt* cuocere in umido
steward ['stju:əd] *n* (*AVIAT, NAUT, RAIL*) steward *m inv*; (*in club etc*) dispensiere *m*; **~ess** *n* assistente *f* di volo, hostess *f inv*
stick [stɪk] (*pt, pp* **stuck**) *n* bastone *m*; (*of rhubarb, celery*) gambo; (*of dynamite*) candelotto ♦ *vt* (*glue*) attaccare; (*thrust*): **to ~ sth into** conficcare *or* piantare *or* infiggere qc in; (*inf*: *put*) ficcare; (*inf*: *tolerate*) sopportare ♦ *vi* attaccarsi; (*remain*) restare, rimanere; **~ out** *vi* sporgere, spuntare; **~ up** *vi* sporgere, spuntare; **~ up for** *vt fus* difendere; **~er** *n* cartellino adesivo; **~ing plaster** *n* cerotto adesivo
stick-up (*inf*) *n* rapina a mano armata
sticky ['stɪkɪ] *adj* attaccaticcio(a), vischioso(a); (*label*) adesivo(a); (*fig*: *situation*) difficile

stiff [stɪf] *adj* rigido(a), duro(a); *(muscle)* legato(a), indolenzito(a); *(difficult)* difficile, arduo(a); *(cold)* freddo(a), formale; *(strong)* forte; *(high: price)* molto alto(a) ♦ *adv*: **bored ~** annoiato(a) a morte; **~en** *vt* irrigidire; rinforzare ♦ *vi* irrigidirsi; indurirsi; **~ neck** *n* torcicollo

stifle ['staɪfl] *vt* soffocare

stigma ['stɪgmə] *n (fig)* stigma *m*

stile [staɪl] *n* cavalcasiepe *m*; cavalcasteccato

stiletto [stɪ'lɛtəu] *(BRIT) n (also:* **~ heel)** tacco a spillo

still [stɪl] *adj* fermo(a); silenzioso(a) ♦ *adv (up to this time, even)* ancora; *(nonetheless)* tuttavia, ciò nonostante; **~born** nato(a) morto(a); **~ life** *n* natura morta

stilt [stɪlt] *n* trampolo; *(pile)* palo

stilted ['stɪltɪd] *adj* freddo(a), formale; artificiale

stimulate ['stɪmjuleɪt] *vt* stimolare

stimuli ['stɪmjulaɪ] *npl of* **stimulus**

stimulus ['stɪmjuləs] *(pl* **stimuli)** *n* stimolo

sting [stɪŋ] *(pt, pp* **stung)** *n* puntura; *(organ)* pungiglione *m* ♦ *vt* pungere

stingy ['stɪndʒɪ] *adj* spilorcio(a), tirchio(a)

stink [stɪŋk] *(pt* **stank,** *pp* **stunk)** *n* fetore *m*, puzzo ♦ *vi* puzzare; **~ing** *(inf) adj (fig):* **a ~ing ...** uno schifo di ..., un(a) maledetto(a) ....

stint [stɪnt] *n* lavoro, compito ♦ *vi*: **to ~ on** lesinare su

stir [stə:*] *n* agitazione *f*, clamore *m* ♦ *vt* mescolare; *(fig)* risvegliare ♦ *vi* muoversi; **~ up** *vt* provocare, suscitare

stirrup ['stɪrəp] *n* staffa

stitch [stɪtʃ] *n (SEWING)* punto; *(KNITTING)* maglia; *(MED)* punto (di sutura); *(pain)* fitta ♦ *vt* cucire, attaccare; suturare

stoat [stəut] *n* ermellino

stock [stɔk] *n* riserva, provvista; *(COMM)* giacenza, stock *m inv*; *(AGR)* bestiame *m*; *(CULIN)* brodo; *(descent)* stirpe *f*; *(FINANCE)* titoli *mpl*, azioni *fpl* ♦ *adj (fig: reply etc)* consueto(a); classico(a) ♦ *vt (have in stock)* avere, vendere; **~s and shares** valori *mpl* di borsa; **in ~** in magazzino; **out of ~** esaurito(a); **~ up** *vi*: **to ~ up (with)** fare

provvista (di)

stockbroker ['stɔkbrəukə*] *n* agente *m* di cambio

stock cube *(BRIT) n* dado

stock exchange *n* Borsa (valori)

stocking ['stɔkɪŋ] *n* calza

stock: **~ market** *n* Borsa, mercato finanziario; **~pile** *n* riserva ♦ *vt* accumulare riserve di; **~taking** *(BRIT) n (COMM)* inventario

stocky ['stɔkɪ] *adj* tarchiato(a), tozzo(a)

stodgy ['stɔdʒɪ] *adj* pesante, indigesto(a)

stoke [stəuk] *vt* alimentare

stole [stəul] *pt of* **steal** ♦ *n* stola

stolen ['stəuln] *pp of* **steal**

stomach ['stʌmək] *n* stomaco; *(belly)* pancia ♦ *vt* sopportare, digerire; **~ache** *n* mal *m* di stomaco

stone [stəun] *n* pietra; *(pebble)* sasso, ciottolo; *(in fruit)* nocciolo; *(MED)* calcolo; *(BRIT: weight)* = 6.348 kg.; 14 libbre ♦ *adj* di pietra ♦ *vt* lapidare; *(fruit)* togliere il nocciolo a; **~-cold** *adj* gelido(a); **~-deaf** *adj* sordo(a) come una campana; **~work** *n* muratura; **stony** *adj* sassoso(a); *(fig)* di pietra

stood [stud] *pt, pp of* **stand**

stool [stu:l] *n* sgabello

stoop [stu:p] *vi (also:* **have a ~)** avere una curvatura; *(also:* **~ down)** chinarsi, curvarsi

stop [stɔp] *n* arresto; *(stopping place)* fermata; *(in punctuation)* punto ♦ *vt* arrestare, fermare; *(break off)* interrompere; *(also:* **put a ~ to)** porre fine a ♦ *vi* fermarsi; *(rain, noise etc)* cessare, finire; **to ~ doing sth** cessare *or* finire di fare qc; **to ~ dead** fermarsi di colpo; **~ off** *vi* sostare brevemente; **~ up** *vt (hole)* chiudere, turare; **~gap** *n* tappabuchi *m inv*; **~lights** *npl (AUT)* stop *mpl*; **~over** *n* breve sosta; *(AVIAT)* scalo

stoppage ['stɔpɪdʒ] *n* arresto, fermata; *(of pay)* trattenuta; *(strike)* interruzione *f* del lavoro

stopper ['stɔpə*] *n* tappo

stop press *n* ultimissime *fpl*

stopwatch ['stɔpwɔtʃ] *n* cronometro

storage ['stɔːrɪdʒ] *n* immagazzinamento; ~ **heater** *n* radiatore *m* elettrico che accumula calore

store [stɔː*] *n* provvista, riserva; *(depot)* deposito; *(BRIT: department ~)* grande magazzino; *(US: shop)* negozio ♦ *vt* immagazzinare; ~**s** *npl (provisions)* rifornimenti *mpl*, scorte *fpl*; **in ~** di riserva; in serbo; ~ **up** *vt* conservare; mettere in serbo; ~**room** *n* dispensa

storey ['stɔːrɪ] *(US* **story**) *n* piano

stork [stɔːk] *n* cicogna

storm [stɔːm] *n* tempesta, temporale *m*, burrasca; uragano ♦ *vi (fig)* infuriarsi ♦ *vt* prendere d'assalto; ~**y** *adj* tempestoso(a), burrascoso(a)

story ['stɔːrɪ] *n* storia; favola; racconto; *(US)* = **storey**; ~**book** *n* libro di racconti

stout [staut] *adj* solido(a), robusto(a); *(friend, supporter)* tenace; *(fat)* corpulento(a), grasso(a) ♦ *n* birra scura

stove [stəuv] *n (for cooking)* fornello; (: *small)* fornelletto; *(for heating)* stufa

stow [stəu] *vt (also: ~ away)* mettere via; ~**away** *n* passeggero/a clandestino/a

straddle ['strædl] *vt* stare a cavalcioni di; *(fig)* essere a cavallo di

straggle ['strægl] *vi* crescere *(or* estendersi) disordinatamente; trascinarsi; rimanere indietro ♦ **straggly** *adj (hair)* in disordine

straight [streɪt] *adj* dritto(a); *(frank)* onesto(a), franco(a); *(simple)* semplice ♦ *adv* diritto(a); *(drink)* liscio(a); **to put** *or* **get ~** mettere in ordine, mettere ordine in; ~ **away**, ~ **off** *(at once)* immediatamente; ~**en** *(also: ~en out)* raddrizzare; ~-**faced** *adj* impassibile, imperturbabile; ~**forward** *adj* semplice; onesto(a), franco(a)

strain [streɪn] *n (TECH)* sollecitazione *f*; *(physical)* sforzo; *(mental)* tensione *f*; *(MED)* strappo; distorsione *f*; *(streak, trace)* tendenza; elemento ♦ *vt* tendere; *(muscle)* sforzare; *(ankle)* storcere; *(resources)* pesare su; *(food)* colare; passare; ~**s** *npl (MUS)* note *fpl*; ~**ed** *adj (muscle)* stirato(a); *(laugh etc)* forzato(a); *(relations)* teso(a); ~**er** *n*

passino, colino

strait [streɪt] *n (GEO)* stretto(a); ~**s** *npl*: **to be in dire ~s** *(fig)* essere nei guai; ~**jacket** *n* camicia di forza; ~-**laced** *adj* bacchettone(a)

strand [strænd] *n (of thread)* filo; ~**ed** *adj* nei guai; senza mezzi di trasporto

strange [streɪndʒ] *adj (not known)* sconosciuto(a); *(odd)* strano(a), bizzarro(a); ~**ly** *adv* stranamente; ~**r** *n* sconosciuto/a; estraneo/a

strangle ['stræŋgl] *vt* strangolare; ~**hold** *n (fig)* stretta (mortale)

strap [stræp] *n* cinghia; *(of slip, dress)* spallina, bretella

strategic [strə'tiːdʒɪk] *adj* strategico(a)

strategy ['strætɪdʒɪ] *n* strategia

straw [strɔː] *n* paglia; *(drinking ~)* cannuccia; **that's the last ~!** è la goccia che fa traboccare il vaso!

strawberry ['strɔːbərɪ] *n* fragola

stray [streɪ] *adj (animal)* randagio(a); *(bullet)* vagante; *(scattered)* sparso(a) ♦ *vi* perdersi

streak [striːk] *n* striscia; *(of hair)* mèche *f inv* ♦ *vt* striare, screziare ♦ *vi*: **to ~ past** passare come un fulmine

stream [striːm] *n* ruscello; corrente *f*; *(of people, smoke etc)* fiume *m* ♦ *vt (SCOL)* dividere in livelli di rendimento ♦ *vi* scorrere; **to ~ in/out** entrare/uscire a fiotti

streamer ['striːmə*] *n (of paper)* stella filante

streamlined ['striːmlaɪnd] *adj* aerodinamico(a), affusolato(a)

street [striːt] *n* strada, via; ~**car** *(US) n* tram *m inv*; ~ **lamp** *n* lampione *m*; ~ **plan** *n* pianta (di una città); ~**wise** *(inf) adj* esperto(a) dei bassifondi

strength [streŋθ] *n* forza; ~**en** *vt* rinforzare; fortificare; consolidare

strenuous ['strenjuəs] *adj* vigoroso(a), energico(a); *(tiring)* duro(a), pesante

stress [stres] *n (force, pressure)* pressione *f*; *(mental strain)* tensione *f*; *(accent)* accento ♦ *vt* insistere su, sottolineare; accentare

stretch [stretʃ] *n (of sand etc)* distesa ♦ *vi* stirarsi; *(extend)*: **to ~ to** *or* **as far as**

estendersi fino a ♦ vt tendere, allungare; (spread) distendere; (fig) spingere (al massimo); ~ out vi allungarsi, estendersi ♦ vt (arm etc) allungare, tendere; (to spread) distendere

stretcher ['strɛtʃə*] n barella, lettiga

strewn [stru:n] adj: ~ **with** cosparso(a) di

stricken ['strɪkən] adj (person) provato(a); (city, industry etc) colpito(a); ~ **with** (disease etc) colpito(a) da

strict [strɪkt] adj (severe) rigido(a), severo(a); (precise) preciso(a), stretto(a); ~**ly** adv severamente; rigorosamente; strettamente

stridden ['strɪdn] pp of **stride**

stride [straɪd] (pt **strode**, pp **stridden**) n passo lungo ♦ vi camminare a grandi passi

strife [straɪf] n conflitto; litigi mpl

strike [straɪk] (pt, pp **struck**) n sciopero; (of oil etc) scoperta; (attack) attacco ♦ vt colpire; (oil etc) scoprire, trovare (bargain) fare; (fig): **the thought** or **it ~s me that ...** mi viene in mente che ... ♦ vi scioperare; (attack) attaccare; (clock) suonare; **on ~** (workers) in sciopero; **to ~ a match** accendere un fiammifero; ~ **down** vt (fig) atterrare; ~ **up** vt (MUS, conversation) attaccare; **to ~ up a friendship with** fare amicizia con; ~**r** n scioperante m/f; (SPORT) attaccante m; **striking** adj che colpisce

string [strɪŋ] (pt, pp **strung**) n spago, (row) fila; sequenza; catena; (MUS) corda ♦ vt: **to ~ out** disporre di fianco a; **to ~ together** (words, ideas) mettere insieme; **the ~s** npl (MUS) gli archi; **to pull ~s for sb** (fig) raccomandare qn; ~ **bean** n fagiolino; ~**(ed) instrument** n (MUS) strumento a corda

stringent ['strɪndʒənt] adj rigoroso(a)

strip [strɪp] n striscia ♦ vt spogliare; (paint) togliere; (also: ~ **down**: machine) smontare ♦ vi spogliarsi; ~ **cartoon** n fumetto

stripe [straɪp] n striscia, riga; (MIL, POLICE) gallone m; ~**d** adj a strisce or righe

strip lighting n illuminazione f al neon

stripper ['strɪpə*] n spogliarellista m/f

strip-search ['strɪpsəːtʃ] vt: **to ~ sb** perquisire qn facendolo(a) spogliare ♦ n

perquisizione (facendo spogliare il perquisto)

striptease ['strɪptiːz] n spogliarello

strive [straɪv] (pt **strove**, pp **striven**) vi: **to ~ to do** sforzarsi di fare; **striven** ['strɪvn] pp of **strive**

strode [strəud] pt of **stride**

stroke [strəuk] n colpo; (SWIMMING) bracciata; (: style) stile m; (MED) colpo apoplettico ♦ vt accarezzare; **at a ~** in un attimo

stroll [strəul] n giretto, passeggiatina ♦ vi andare a spasso; ~**er** n (US) passeggino

strong [strɔŋ] adj (gen) forte; (sturdy: table, fabric etc) robusto(a); **they are 50 ~** sono in 50; ~**box** n cassaforte f; ~**hold** n (also fig) roccaforte f; ~**ly** adv fortemente, con forza; energicamente; vivamente; ~**room** n camera di sicurezza

strove [strəuv] pt of **strive**

struck [strʌk] pt, pp of **strike**

structural ['strʌktʃərəl] adj strutturale

structure ['strʌktʃə*] n struttura; (building) costruzione f, fabbricato

struggle ['strʌgl] n lotta ♦ vi lottare

strum [strʌm] vt (guitar) strimpellare

strung [strʌŋ] pt, pp of **string**

strut [strʌt] n sostegno, supporto ♦ vi pavoneggiarsi

stub [stʌb] n mozzicone m; (of ticket etc) matrice f, talloncino ♦ vt: **to ~ one's toe** urtare or sbattere il dito del piede; ~ **out** vt schiacciare

stubble ['stʌbl] n stoppia; (on chin) barba ispida

stubborn ['stʌbən] adj testardo(a), ostinato(a)

stuck [stʌk] pt, pp of **stick** ♦ adj (jammed) bloccato(a); ~-**up** adj presuntuoso(a)

stud [stʌd] n bottoncino; borchia; (also: ~ **earring**) orecchino a pressione; (also: ~ **farm**) scuderia, allevamento di cavalli; (also: ~ **horse**) stallone m ♦ vt (fig): ~**ded with** tempestato(a) di

student ['stjuːdənt] n studente/essa ♦ cpd studentesco(a); universitario(a); degli studenti; ~ **driver** n (US) conducente m/f principiante

studio ['stju:dɪəʊ] *n* studio; ~ **flat** (*US* ~ **apartment**) *n* monolocale *m*

studious ['stju:dɪəs] *adj* studioso(a); (*studied*) studiato(a), voluto(a); ~**ly** *adv* (*carefully*) deliberatamente, di proposito

study ['stʌdɪ] *n* studio ♦ *vt* studiare; esaminare ♦ *vi* studiare

stuff [stʌf] *n* roba; (*substance*) sostanza, materiale *m* ♦ *vt* imbottire; (*CULIN*) farcire; (*dead animal*) impagliare; (*inf: push*) ficcare; ~**ing** *n* imbottitura; (*CULIN*) ripieno; ~**y** *adj* (*room*) mal ventilato(a), senz'aria; (*ideas*) antiquato(a)

stumble ['stʌmbl] *vi* inciampare; **to ~ across** (*fig*) imbattersi in; **stumbling block** *n* ostacolo, scoglio

stump [stʌmp] *n* ceppo; (*of limb*) moncone *m* ♦ *vt*: **to be ~ed** essere sconcertato(a)

stun [stʌn] *vt* stordire; (*amaze*) sbalordire

stung [stʌŋ] *pt, pp of* **sting**

stunk [stʌŋk] *pp of* **stink**

stunning ['stʌnɪŋ] *adj* sbalorditivo(a); (*girl etc*) fantastico(a)

stunt [stʌnt] *n* bravata; trucco pubblicitario; ~**man** (*irreg*) *n* cascatore *m*

stupefy ['stju:pɪfaɪ] *vt* stordire; intontire; (*fig*) stupire

stupendous [stju:'pɛndəs] *adj* stupendo(a), meraviglioso(a)

stupid ['stju:pɪd] *adj* stupido(a); ~**ity** [-'pɪdɪtɪ] *n* stupidità *f inv*, stupidaggine *f*

stupor ['stju:pə*] *n* torpore *m*

sturdy ['stɜ:dɪ] *adj* robusto(a), vigoroso(a); solido(a)

stutter ['stʌtə*] *n* balbuzie *f* ♦ *vi* balbettare

sty [staɪ] *n* (*of pigs*) porcile *m*

stye [staɪ] *n* (*MED*) orzaiolo

style [staɪl] *n* stile *m*; (*distinction*) eleganza, classe *f*; **stylish** *adj* elegante

stylus ['staɪləs] *n* (*of record player*) puntina

suave [swɑ:v] *adj* untuoso(a)

sub... [sʌb] *prefix* sub..., sotto...; ~**conscious** *adj* subcosciente ♦ *n* subcosciente *m*; ~**contract** *vt* subappaltare

subdue [səb'dju:] *vt* sottomettere, soggiogare; ~**d** *adj* pacato(a); (*light*)

attenuato(a)

subject [*n* 'sʌbdʒɪkt, *vb* səb'dʒɛkt] *n* soggetto; (*citizen etc*) cittadino/a; (*SCOL*) materia ♦ *vt*: **to ~ to** sottomettere a; esporre a; **to be ~ to** (*law*) essere sottomesso(a) a; (*disease*) essere soggetto(a) a; ~**ive** [-'dʒɛktɪv] *adj* soggettivo(a); ~ **matter** *n* argomento; contenuto

sublet [sʌb'lɛt] *vt* subaffittare

submachine gun ['sʌbmə'ʃi:n-] *n* mitra *m inv*

submarine [sʌbmə'ri:n] *n* sommergibile *m*

submerge [səb'mə:dʒ] *vt* sommergere; immergere ♦ *vi* immergersi

submission [səb'mɪʃən] *n* sottomissione *f*; (*claim*) richiesta

submissive [səb'mɪsɪv] *adj* remissivo(a)

submit [səb'mɪt] *vt* sottomettere ♦ *vi* sottomettersi

subnormal [sʌb'nɔ:məl] *adj* subnormale

subordinate [sə'bɔ:dɪnət] *adj, n* subordinato(a)

subpoena [səb'pi:nə] *n* (*LAW*) citazione *f*, mandato di comparizione

subscribe [səb'skraɪb] *vi* contribuire; **to ~ to** (*opinion*) approvare, condividere; (*fund*) sottoscrivere a; (*newspaper*) abbonarsi a; essere abbonato(a) a; ~**r** *n* (*to periodical, telephone*) abbonato/a

subscription [səb'skrɪpʃən] *n* sottoscrizione *f*; abbonamento

subsequent ['sʌbsɪkwənt] *adj* successivo(a), seguente; conseguente; ~**ly** *adv* in seguito, successivamente

subside [səb'saɪd] *vi* cedere, abbassarsi; (*flood*) decrescere; (*wind*) calmarsi; ~**nce** [-'saɪdns] *n* cedimento, abbassamento

subsidiary [səb'sɪdɪərɪ] *adj* sussidiario(a); accessorio(a) ♦ *n* filiale *f*

subsidize ['sʌbsɪdaɪz] *vt* sovvenzionare

subsidy ['sʌbsɪdɪ] *n* sovvenzione *f*

subsistence [səb'sɪstəns] *n* esistenza; mezzi *mpl* di sostentamento; ~ **allowance** *n* indennità *f inv* di trasferta

substance ['sʌbstəns] *n* sostanza

substantial [səb'stænʃl] *adj* solido(a);

substantiate → sultana

(*amount, progress etc*) notevole; (*meal*) sostanzioso/a

substantiate [səb'stænʃɪeɪt] *vt* comprovare

substitute ['sʌbstɪtjuːt] *n* (*person*) sostituto/a; (*thing*) succedaneo, surrogato ♦ *vt*: **to ~ sth/sb for** sostituire qc/qn a

subterfuge ['sʌbtəfjuːdʒ] *n* sotterfugio

subterranean [sʌbtə'reɪnɪən] *adj* sotterraneo/a

subtitle ['sʌbtaɪtl] *n* (*CINEMA*) sottotitolo; **~d** *adj* sottotitolato(a)

subtle ['sʌtl] *adj* sottile; **~ty** *n* sottigliezza

subtotal [sʌb'təʊtl] *n* somma parziale

subtract [səb'trækt] *vt* sottrarre; **~ion** [-'trækʃən] *n* sottrazione *f*

suburb ['sʌbɜːb] *n* sobborgo; **the ~s** la periferia; **~an** [sə'bɜːbən] *adj* suburbano(a); **~ia** *n* periferia, sobborghi *mpl*

subversive [səb'vɜːsɪv] *adj* sovversivo(a)

subway ['sʌbweɪ] *n* (*US: underground*) metropolitana; (*BRIT: underpass*) sottopassaggio

succeed [sək'siːd] *vi* riuscire; avere successo ♦ *vt* succedere a; **to ~ in doing** riuscire a fare; **~ing** *adj* (*following*) successivo(a)

success [sək'ses] *n* successo; **~ful** *adj* (*venture*) coronato(a) da successo, riuscito(a); **to be ~ful (in doing)** riuscire (a fare); **~fully** *adv* con successo

succession [sək'seʃən] *n* successione *f*

successive [sək'sesɪv] *adj* successivo(a); consecutivo(a)

succumb [sə'kʌm] *vi* soccombere

such [sʌtʃ] *adj* tale; (*of that kind*): **~ a book** un tale libro, un libro del genere; **~ books** tali libri, libri del genere; (*so much*): **~ courage** tanto coraggio ♦ *adv* talmente, così; **~ a long trip** un viaggio così lungo; **~ a lot of** talmente *or* così tanto(a); **~ as** (*like*) come; **as ~** come *or* in quanto tale; **~-and-~** *adj* tale (*after noun*)

suck [sʌk] *vt* succhiare; (*breast, bottle*) poppare; **~er** *n* (*ZOOL, TECH*) ventosa; (*inf*) gonzo/a, babbeo/a

suction ['sʌkʃən] *n* succhiamento; (*TECH*) aspirazione *f*

sudden ['sʌdn] *adj* improvviso(a); **all of a ~** improvvisamente, all'improvviso; **~ly** *adv* bruscamente, improvvisamente, di colpo

suds [sʌdz] *npl* schiuma (di sapone)

sue [suː] *vt* citare in giudizio

suede [sweɪd] *n* pelle *f* scamosciata

suet ['suɪt] *n* grasso di rognone

suffer ['sʌfə*] *vt* soffrire, patire; (*bear*) sopportare, tollerare ♦ *vi* soffrire; **to ~ from** soffrire di; **~er** *n* malato/a; **~ing** *n* sofferenza

suffice [sə'faɪs] *vi* essere sufficiente, bastare

sufficient [sə'fɪʃənt] *adj* sufficiente; **~ money** abbastanza soldi; **~ly** *adv* sufficientemente, abbastanza

suffocate ['sʌfəkeɪt] *vi* (*have difficulty breathing*) soffocare; (*die through lack of air*) asfissiare

sugar ['ʃʊgə*] *n* zucchero ♦ *vt* zuccherare; **~ beet** *n* barbabietola da zucchero; **~ cane** *n* canna da zucchero

suggest [sə'dʒest] *vt* proporre, suggerire; indicare; **~ion** [-'dʒestʃən] *n* suggerimento, proposta; indicazione *f*; **~ive** (*pej*) *adj* indecente

suicide ['suɪsaɪd] *n* (*person*) suicida *m/f*; (*act*) suicidio; *see also* **commit**

suit [suːt] *n* (*man's*) vestito; (*woman's*) completo, tailleur *m inv*; (*LAW*) causa; (*CARDS*) seme *m*, colore *m* ♦ *vt* andar bene a *or* per; essere adatto(a) a *or* per; (*adapt*): **to ~ sth to** adattare qc a; **well ~ed** ben assortito(a); **~able** *adj* adatto(a); appropriato(a); **~ably** *adv* (*dress*) in modo adatto; (*impressed*) favorevolmente

suitcase ['suːtkeɪs] *n* valigia

suite [swiːt] *n* (*of rooms*) appartamento; (*MUS*) suite *f inv*; (*furniture*): **bedroom/ dining room ~** arredo *or* mobilia per la camera da letto/sala da pranzo

suitor ['suːtə*] *n* corteggiatore *m*, spasimante *m*

sulfur ['sʌlfə*] (*US*) *n* = **sulphur**

sulk [sʌlk] *vi* fare il broncio; **~y** *adj* imbronciato(a)

sullen ['sʌlən] *adj* scontroso(a); cupo(a)

sulphur ['sʌlfə*] (*US* **sulfur**) *n* zolfo

sultana [sʌl'tɑːnə] *n* (*fruit*) uva (secca)

sultanina

sultry ['sʌltrɪ] *adj* afoso(a)

sum [sʌm] *n* somma; (*SCOL etc*) addizione *f*; ~ **up** *vt, vi* riassumere

summarize ['sʌməraɪz] *vt* riassumere, riepilogare

summary ['sʌmərɪ] *n* riassunto

summer ['sʌmə*] *n* estate *f* ♦ *cpd* d'estate, estivo(a); ~ **holidays** *npl* vacanze *fpl* estive; ~**house** *n* (*in garden*) padiglione *m*; ~**time** *n* (*season*) estate *f*; ~ **time** *n* (*by clock*) ora legale (estiva)

summit ['sʌmɪt] *n* cima, sommità; (*POL*) vertice *m*

summon ['sʌmən] *vt* chiamare, convocare; ~ **up** *vt* raccogliere, fare appello a; ~**s** *n* ordine *m* di comparizione ♦ *vt* citare

sump [sʌmp] (*BRIT*) *n* (*AUT*) coppa dell'olio

sumptuous ['sʌmptjuəs] *adj* sontuoso(a)

sun [sʌn] *n* sole *m*; ~**bathe** *vi* prendere un bagno di sole; ~**block** *n* protezione *f* solare totale; ~**burn** *n* (*painful*) scottatura; ~**burnt** *adj* abbronzato(a); (*painfully*) scottato(a)

Sunday ['sʌndɪ] *n* domenica; ~ **school** *n* ≈ scuola di catechismo

sundial ['sʌndaɪəl] *n* meridiana

sundown ['sʌndaun] *n* tramonto

sundry ['sʌndrɪ] *adj* vari(e), diversi(e); **all and** ~ tutti quanti; **sundries** *npl* articoli diversi, cose diverse

sunflower ['sʌnflauə*] *n* girasole *m*

sung [sʌŋ] *pp of* **sing**

sunglasses ['sʌnglɑːsɪz] *npl* occhiali *mpl* da sole

sunk [sʌŋk] *pp of* **sink**

sun: ~**light** *n* (luce *f* del) sole *m*; ~**lit** *adj* soleggiato(a); ~**ny** *adj* assolato(a), soleggiato(a), (*fig*) allegro(a), felice; ~**rise** *n* levata del sole, alba; ~ **roof** *n* (*AUT*) tetto apribile; ~**screen** *n* (*protective ingredient*) filtro solare; (*cream*) crema solare protettiva; ~**set** *n* tramonto; ~**shade** *n* parasole *m*; ~**shine** *n* (luce *f* del) sole *m*; ~**stroke** *n* insolazione *f*, colpo di sole; ~**tan** *n* abbronzatura; ~**tan lotion** *n* lozione *f* solare; ~**tan oil** *n* olio solare

super ['suːpə*] (*inf*) *adj* fantastico(a)

superannuation [suːpərænjuˈeɪʃən] *n* contributi *mpl* pensionistici; pensione *f*

superb [suːˈpəːb] *adj* magnifico(a)

supercilious [suːpəˈsɪlɪəs] *adj* sprezzante, sdegnoso(a)

superficial [suːpəˈfɪʃəl] *adj* superficiale

superhuman [suːpəˈhjuːmən] *adj* sovrumano(a)

superimpose ['suːpərɪmˈpəuz] *vt* sovrapporre

superintendent [suːpərɪnˈtɛndənt] *n* direttore/trice; (*POLICE*) ≈ commissario (capo)

superior [suˈpɪərɪə*] *adj, n* superiore *m/f*; ~**ity** [-ˈɔrɪtɪ] *n* superiorità

superlative [suˈpəːlətɪv] *adj* superlativo(a), supremo(a) ♦ *n* (*LING*) superlativo

superman ['suːpəmæn] (*irreg*) *n* superuomo

supermarket ['suːpəmɑːkɪt] *n* supermercato

supernatural [suːpəˈnætʃərəl] *adj* soprannaturale ♦ *n* soprannaturale *m*

superpower ['suːpəpauə*] *n* (*POL*) superpotenza

supersede [suːpəˈsiːd] *vt* sostituire, soppiantare

superstitious [suːpəˈstɪʃəs] *adj* superstizioso(a)

supertanker ['suːpətæŋkə*] *n* superpetroliera

supervise ['suːpəvaɪz] *vt* (*person etc*) sorvegliare; (*organization*) soprintendere a; **supervision** [-ˈvɪʒən] *n* sorveglianza; supervisione *f*; **supervisor** *n* sorvegliante *m/f*; soprintendente *m/f*; (*in shop*) capocommesso/a

supine ['suːpaɪn] *adj* supino(a)

supper ['sʌpə*] *n* cena

supplant [səˈplɑːnt] *vt* (*person, thing*) soppiantare

supple ['sʌpl] *adj* flessibile; agile

supplement [*n* 'sʌplɪmənt, *vb* sʌplɪˈmɛnt] *n* supplemento ♦ *vt* completare, integrare; ~**ary** [-ˈmɛntərɪ] *adj* supplementare

supplier [səˈplaɪə*] *n* fornitore *m*

supply [səˈplaɪ] *vt* (*provide*) fornire; (*equip*):

to ~ (with) approvvigionare (di); attrezzare (con) ♦ *n* riserva, provvista; (*supplying*) approvvigionamento; (*TECH*) alimentazione *f*; **supplies** *npl* (*food*) viveri *mpl*; (*MIL*) sussistenza; **~ teacher** (*BRIT*) *n* supplente *m/f*

support [sə'pɔːt] *n* (*moral, financial etc*) sostegno, appoggio; (*TECH*) supporto ♦ *vt* sostenere; (*financially*) mantenere; (*uphold*) sostenere, difendere; **~er** *n* (*POL etc*) sostenitore/trice, fautore/trice; (*SPORT*) tifoso/a

suppose [sə'pəuz] *vt* supporre; immaginare; **to be ~d to do** essere tenuto(a) a fare; **~dly** [sə'pəuzɪdlɪ] *adv* presumibilmente; **supposing** *conj* se, ammesso che +*sub*

suppository [sə'pɔzɪtərɪ] *n* suppositorio

suppress [sə'prɛs] *vt* reprimere; sopprimere; occultare

supreme [su'priːm] *adj* supremo(a)

surcharge ['səːtʃɑːdʒ] *n* supplemento

sure [ʃuə*] *adj* sicuro(a); (*definite, convinced*) sicuro(a), certo(a); **~!** (*of course*) senz'altro!, certo!; **~ enough** infatti; **to make ~ of sth/that** assicurarsi di qc/che; **~-footed** *adj* dal passo sicuro; **~ly** *adv* sicuramente; certamente

surf [səːf] *n* (*waves*) cavalloni *mpl*; (*foam*) spuma

surface ['səːfɪs] *n* superficie *f* ♦ *vt* (*road*) asfaltare ♦ *vi* risalire alla superficie; (*fig: news, feeling*) venire a galla; **~ mail** *n* posta ordinaria

surfboard ['səːfbɔːd] *n* tavola per surfing

surfeit ['səːfɪt] *n*: **a ~ of** un eccesso di; un'indigestione di

surfing ['səːfɪŋ] *n* surfing *m*

surge [səːdʒ] *n* (*strong movement*) ondata; (*of feeling*) impeto ♦ *vi* gonfiarsi; (*people*) riversarsi

surgeon ['səːdʒən] *n* chirurgo

surgery ['səːdʒərɪ] *n* chirurgia; (*BRIT: room*) studio *or* gabinetto medico, ambulatorio; (*: also:* **~ hours**) orario delle visite *or* di consultazione; **to undergo ~** subire un intervento chirurgico

surgical ['səːdʒɪkl] *adj* chirurgico(a); **~**

spirit (*BRIT*) *n* alcool *m* denaturato

surname ['səːneɪm] *n* cognome *m*

surpass [səː'pɑːs] *vt* superare

surplus ['səːpləs] *n* eccedenza; (*ECON*) surplus *m inv* ♦ *adj* eccedente, d'avanzo

surprise [sə'praɪz] *n* sorpresa; (*astonishment*) stupore *m* ♦ *vt* sorprendere; stupire; **surprising** *adj* sorprendente, stupefacente; **surprisingly** *adv* (*easy, helpful*) sorprendentemente

surrender [sə'rɛndə*] *n* resa, capitolazione *f* ♦ *vi* arrendersi

surreptitious [sʌrəp'tɪʃəs] *adj* furtivo(a)

surrogate ['sʌrəgɪt] *n* surrogato; **~ mother** *n* madre *f* provetta

surround [sə'raund] *vt* circondare; (*MIL etc*) accerchiare; **~ing** *adj* circostante; **~ings** *npl* dintorni *mpl*; (*fig*) ambiente *m*

surveillance [səː'veɪləns] *n* sorveglianza, controllo

survey [*n* 'səːveɪ, *vb* səː'veɪ] *n* quadro generale; (*study*) esame *m*; (*in housebuying etc*) perizia; (*of land*) rilevamento, rilievo topografico ♦ *vt* osservare; esaminare; valutare; rilevare; **~or** *n* perito; geometra *m*; (*of land*) agrimensore *m*

survival [sə'vaɪvl] *n* sopravvivenza; (*relic*) reliquia, vestigio

survive [sə'vaɪv] *vi* sopravvivere ♦ *vt* sopravvivere a; **survivor** *n* superstite *m/f*, sopravvissuto/a

susceptible [sə'sɛptəbl] *adj*: **~ (to)** sensibile (a); (*disease*) predisposto(a) (a)

suspect [*adj, n* 'sʌspɛkt, *vb* səs'pɛkt] *adj* sospetto(a) ♦ *n* persona sospetta ♦ *vt* sospettare; (*think likely*) supporre; (*doubt*) dubitare

suspend [səs'pɛnd] *vt* sospendere; **~ed sentence** *n* condanna con la condizionale; **~er belt** *n* reggicalze *m inv*; **~ers** *npl* (*BRIT*) giarrettiere *fpl*; (*US*) bretelle *fpl*

suspense [səs'pɛns] *n* apprensione *f*; (*in film etc*) suspense *m*; **to keep sb in ~** tenere qn in sospeso

suspension [səs'pɛnʃən] *n* (*gen AUT*) sospensione *f*; (*of driving licence*) ritiro temporaneo; ~ **bridge** n ponte m sospeso

suspicion [səs'pɪʃən] n sospetto

suspicious [səs'pɪʃəs] adj (*suspecting*) sospettoso(a); (*causing suspicion*) sospetto(a)

sustain [səs'teɪn] vt sostenere; sopportare; (*LAW: charge*) confermare; (*suffer*) subire; **~able** adj sostenibile; **~ed** adj (*effort*) prolungato(a)

sustenance ['sʌstɪnəns] n nutrimento; mezzi mpl di sostentamento

swab [swɔb] n (*MED*) tampone m

swagger ['swægə*] vi pavoneggiarsi

swallow ['swɔləu] n (*bird*) rondine f ♦ vt inghiottire; (*fig: story*) bere; ~ **up** vt inghiottire

swam [swæm] pt of **swim**

swamp [swɔmp] n palude f ♦ vt sommergere

swan [swɔn] n cigno

swap [swɔp] vt: **to ~ (for)** scambiare (con)

swarm [swɔ:m] n sciame m ♦ vi (*bees*) sciamare; (*people*) brulicare; (*place*): **to be ~ing with** brulicare di

swastika ['swɔstɪkə] n croce f uncinata, svastica

swat [swɔt] vt schiacciare

sway [sweɪ] vi (*tree*) ondeggiare; (*person*) barcollare ♦ vt (*influence*) influenzare, dominare

swear [sweə*] (*pt* **swore**, *pp* **sworn**) vi (*curse*) bestemmiare, imprecare ♦ vt (*promise*) giurare; **~word** n parolaccia

sweat [swet] n sudore m, traspirazione f ♦ vi sudare

sweater ['swetə*] n maglione m

sweatshirt ['swetʃə:t] n felpa

sweaty ['swetɪ] adj sudato(a); bagnato(a) di sudore

Swede [swi:d] n svedese m/f

swede [swi:d] (*BRIT*) n rapa svedese

Sweden ['swi:dn] n Svezia

Swedish ['swi:dɪʃ] adj svedese ♦ n (*LING*) svedese m

sweep [swi:p] (*pt, pp* **swept**) n spazzata; (*also:* **chimney ~**) spazzacamino ♦ vt spazzare, scopare; (*current*) spazzare ♦ vi

(*hand*) muoversi con gesto ampio; (*wind*) infuriare; ~ **away** vt spazzare via; trascinare via; ~ **past** vi sfrecciare accanto passare accanto maestosamente; ~ **up** vt, vi spazzare; **~ing** adj (*gesture*) ampio(a); circolare; **a ~ing statement** un'affermazione generica

sweet [swi:t] n (*BRIT: pudding*) dolce m; (*candy*) caramella ♦ adj dolce; (*fresh*) fresco(a); (*fig*) piacevole; delicato(a), grazioso(a); gentile; **~corn** n granturco dolce; **~en** vt addolcire; zuccherare; **~heart** n innamorato/a; **~ness** n sapore m dolce; dolcezza; ~ **pea** n pisello odoroso

swell [swel] (*pt* **~ed**, *pp* **swollen**, **~ed**) n (*of sea*) mare m lungo ♦ adj (*US: inf: excellent*) favoloso(a) ♦ vt gonfiare, ingrossare; aumentare ♦ vi gonfiarsi, ingrossarsi; (*sound*) crescere; (*also:* ~ **up**) gonfiarsi; **~ing** n (*MED*) tumefazione f, gonfiore m

sweltering ['sweltərɪŋ] adj soffocante

swept [swept] pt, pp of **sweep**

swerve [swə:v] vi deviare; (*driver*) sterzare; (*boxer*) scartare

swift [swɪft] n (*bird*) rondone m ♦ adj rapido(a), veloce

swig [swɪg] (*inf*) n (*drink*) sorsata

swill [swɪl] vt (*also:* ~ **out**, ~ **down**) risciacquare

swim [swɪm] (*pt* **swam**, *pp* **swum**) n: **to go for a ~** andare a fare una nuotata ♦ vi nuotare; (*SPORT*) fare del nuoto; (*head, room*) girare ♦ vt (*river, channel*) attraversare *or* percorrere a nuoto; (*length*) nuotare; **~mer** n nuotatore/trice; **~ming** n nuoto; **~ming cap** n cuffia; **~ming costume** (*BRIT*) n costume m da bagno; **~ming pool** n piscina; **~ming trunks** npl costume m da bagno (da uomo); **~suit** n costume m da bagno

swindle ['swɪndl] n truffa ♦ vt truffare

swine [swaɪn] (*inf!*) n inv porco (!)

swing [swɪŋ] (*pt, pp* **swung**) n altalena; (*movement*) oscillazione f; (*MUS*) ritmo; swing m ♦ vt dondolare, far oscillare; (*also:* ~ **round**) far girare ♦ vi oscillare, dondo-

lare; (also: ~ round: object) roteare;
(: person) girarsi, voltarsi; **to be in full ~**
(activity) essere in piena attività; (party etc)
essere nel pieno; ~ **door** (US ~**ing door**) n
porta battente

swingeing ['swɪndʒɪŋ] adj (BRIT: defeat)
violento(a); (: cuts) enorme

swipe [swaɪp] vt (hit) colpire con forza; dare
uno schiaffo a; (inf: steal) sgraffignare;
~**board** n tessera magnetica

swirl [swəːl] vi turbinare, far mulinello

Swiss [swɪs] adj, n inv svizzero(a)

switch [swɪtʃ] n (for light, radio etc)
interruttore m; (change) cambiamento ♦ vt
(change) cambiare; scambiare; ~ **off** vt
spegnere; ~ **on** vt accendere; (engine,
machine) mettere in moto, avviare;
~**board** n (TEL) centralino

Switzerland ['swɪtsələnd] n Svizzera

swivel ['swɪvl] vi (also: ~ round) girare

swollen ['swəulən] pp of **swell**

swoon [swuːn] vi svenire

swoop [swuːp] n incursione f ♦ vi (also: ~
down) scendere in picchiata, piombare

swop [swɔp] n, vt = **swap**

sword [sɔːd] n spada; ~**fish** n pesce m
spada inv

swore [swɔː*] pt of **swear**

sworn [swɔːn] pp of **swear** ♦ adj giurato(a)

swot [swɔt] vi sgobbare

swum [swʌm] pp of **swim**

swung [swʌŋ] pt, pp of **swing**

syllable ['sɪləbl] n sillaba

syllabus ['sɪləbəs] n programma m

symbol ['sɪmbl] n simbolo

symmetry ['sɪmɪtrɪ] n simmetria

sympathetic [sɪmpə'θetɪk] adj (showing
pity) compassionevole; (kind)
comprensivo(a); ~ **towards** ben disposto(a)
verso

sympathize ['sɪmpəθaɪz] vi: **to ~ with**
(person) compatire; partecipare al dolore
di; (cause) simpatizzare per; ~**r** n (POL)
simpatizzante m/f

sympathy ['sɪmpəθɪ] n compassione f;
sympathies npl (support, tendencies)
simpatie fpl; **in ~ with** (strike) per

solidarietà con; **with our deepest ~** con le
nostre più sincere condoglianze

symphony ['sɪmfənɪ] n sinfonia

symptom ['sɪmptəm] n sintomo; indizio

synagogue ['sɪnəgɔg] n sinagoga

syndicate ['sɪndɪkɪt] n sindacato

synopses [sɪ'nɔpsiːz] npl of **synopsis**

synopsis [sɪ'nɔpsɪs] (pl **synopses**) n
sommario, sinossi f inv

syntheses ['sɪnθəsiːz] npl of **synthesis**

synthesis ['sɪnθəsɪs] (pl **syntheses**) n
sintesi f inv

synthetic [sɪn'θetɪk] adj sintetico(a)

syphon ['saɪfən] n, vb = **siphon**

Syria ['sɪrɪə] n Siria

syringe [sɪ'rɪndʒ] n siringa

syrup ['sɪrəp] n sciroppo; (also: **golden ~**)
melassa raffinata

system ['sɪstəm] n sistema m; (order)
metodo; (ANAT) organismo; ~**atic** [-'mætɪk]
adj sistematico(a); metodico(a); ~ **disk** n
(COMPUT) disco del sistema; ~**s analyst** n
analista m di sistemi

T, t

ta [taː] (BRIT: inf) excl grazie!

tab [tæb] n (loop on coat etc) laccetto; (label)
etichetta; **to keep ~s on** (fig) tenere d'occhio

tabby ['tæbɪ] n (also: ~ **cat**) (gatto) soriano,
gatto tigrato

table ['teɪbl] n tavolo, tavola; (MATH, CHEM
etc) tavola ♦ vt (BRIT: motion etc)
presentare; **to lay** or **set the ~**
apparecchiare or preparare la tavola;
~**cloth** n tovaglia; ~ **d'hôte** [taːbl'dəut]
adj (meal) a prezzo fisso; ~ **lamp** n
lampada da tavolo; ~**mat** n sottopiatto;
~ **of contents** n indice m; ~**spoon** n
cucchiaio da tavola; (also: ~**spoonful**: as
measurement) cucchiaiata

tablet ['tæblɪt] n (MED) compressa; (of stone)
targa

table: ~ **tennis** n tennis m da tavolo,
ping-pong ® m; ~ **wine** n vino da tavola

tabloid press

*Il termine **tabloid press** si riferisce ai giornali popolari, che hanno un formato ridotto e pubblicano le notizie in modo sensazionalistico; vedi anche **quality press**.*

tacit ['tæsɪt] *adj* tacito(a)

tack [tæk] *n* (*nail*) bulletta; (*fig*) approccio ♦ *vt* imbullettare; imbastire ♦ *vi* bordeggiare

tackle ['tækl] *n* attrezzatura, equipaggiamento; (*for lifting*) paranco; (*FOOTBALL*) contrasto; (*RUGBY*) placcaggio ♦ *vt* (*difficulty*) affrontare; (*FOOTBALL*) contrastare; (*RUGBY*) placcare

tacky ['tækɪ] *adj* appiccicaticcio(a); (*pej*) scadente

tact [tækt] *n* tatto; **~ful** *adj* delicato(a), discreto(a)

tactical ['tæktɪkl] *adj* tattico(a)

tactics ['tæktɪks] *n, npl* tattica

tactless ['tæktlɪs] *adj* che manca di tatto

tadpole ['tædpəʊl] *n* girino

tag [tæg] *n* etichetta; ~ **along** *vi* seguire

tail [teɪl] *n* coda; (*of shirt*) falda ♦ *vt* (*follow*) seguire, pedinare; ~ **away** *vi* = ~ **off**; ~ **off** *vi* (*in size, quality etc*) diminuire gradatamente; **~back** (*BRIT*) *n* (*AUT*) ingorgo; ~ **end** *n* (*of train, procession etc*) coda; (*of meeting etc*) fine *f*; **~gate** *n* (*AUT*) portellone *m* posteriore

tailor ['teɪlə*] *n* sarto, **~ing** *n* (*cut*) stile *m*; (*craft*) sartoria; **~-made** *adj* (*also fig*) fatto(a) su misura

tailwind ['teɪlwɪnd] *n* vento di coda

tainted ['teɪntɪd] *adj* (*food*) guasto(a); (*water, air*) infetto(a); (*fig*) corrotto(a)

take [teɪk] (*pt* **took**, *pp* **taken**) *vt* prendere; (*gain: prize*) ottenere, vincere; (*require: effort, courage*) occorrere, volerci; (*tolerate*) accettare, sopportare; (*hold: passengers etc*) contenere; (*accompany*) accompagnare; (*bring, carry*) portare; (*exam*) sostenere, presentarsi a; **to ~ a photo/a shower** fare una fotografia/una doccia; **I ~ it that** suppongo che; ~ **after** *vt fus* assomigliare

a; ~ **apart** *vt* smontare; ~ **away** *vt* portare via; togliere; ~ **back** *vt* (*return*) restituire; riportare; (*one's words*) ritirare; ~ **down** *vt* (*building*) demolire; (*letter etc*) scrivere; ~ **in** *vt* (*deceive*) imbrogliare, abbindolare; (*understand*) comprendere; (*include*) comprendere, includere; (*lodger*) prendere, ospitare; ~ **off** *vi* (*AVIAT*) decollare; (*go away*) andarsene ♦ *vt* (*remove*) togliere; ~ **on** *vt* (*work*) accettare, intraprendere; (*employee*) assumere; (*opponent*) sfidare, affrontare; ~ **out** *vt* portare fuori; (*remove*) togliere; (*licence*) prendere, ottenere; **to ~ sth out of sth** (*drawer, pocket etc*) tirare qc fuori da qc; estrarre qc da qc; ~ **over** *vt* (*business*) rilevare ♦ *vi*: **to ~ over from sb** prendere le consegne or il controllo da qn; ~ **to** *vt fus* (*person*) prendere in simpatia; (*activity*) prendere gusto a; ~ **up** *vt* (*dress*) accorciare; (*occupy: time, space*) occupare; (*engage in: hobby etc*) mettersi a; **to ~ sb up on sth** accettare qc da qn; **~away** (*BRIT*) *n* (*shop etc*) ≈ rosticceria; (*food*) pasto per asporto; **~off** *n* (*AVIAT*) decollo; **~out** (*US*) *n* = **~away**; **~over** *n* (*COMM*) assorbimento

takings ['teɪkɪŋz] *npl* (*COMM*) incasso

talc [tælk] *n* (*also*: **~um powder**) talco

tale [teɪl] *n* racconto, storia; **to tell ~s** (*fig: to teacher, parent etc*) fare la spia

talent ['tælnt] *n* talento; **~ed** *adj* di talento

talk [tɔːk] *n* discorso; (*gossip*) chiacchiere *fpl*; (*conversation*) conversazione *f*; (*interview*) discussione *f* ♦ *vi* parlare; **~s** *npl* (*POL etc*) colloqui *mpl*; **to ~ about** parlare di; **to ~ sb out of/into doing** dissuadere qn da/convincere qn a fare; **to ~ shop** parlare di lavoro *or* di affari; ~ **over** *vt* discutere; **~ative** *adj* loquace, ciarliero(a); ~ **show** *n* conversazione *f* televisiva, talk show *m inv*

tall [tɔːl] *adj* alto(a); **to be 6 feet ~** ≈ essere alto 1 metro e 80; ~ **story** *n* panzana, frottola

tally ['tælɪ] *n* conto, conteggio ♦ *vi*: **to ~ (with)** corrispondere (a)

talon ['tælən] *n* artiglio

tambourine [tæmbə'ri:n] n tamburello
tame [teɪm] adj addomesticato(a); (fig: story, style) insipido(a), scialbo(a)
tamper ['tæmpə*] vi: **to ~ with** manomettere
tampon ['tæmpɔn] n tampone m
tan [tæn] n (also: **sun~**) abbronzatura ♦ vi abbronzarsi ♦ adj (colour) marrone rossiccio inv
tang [tæŋ] n odore m penetrante; sapore m piccante
tangent ['tændʒənt] n: **to go off at a ~** (fig) partire per la tangente
tangerine [tændʒə'ri:n] n mandarino
tangle ['tæŋgl] n groviglio; **to get into a ~** aggrovigliarsi; (fig) combinare un pasticcio
tank [tæŋk] n serbatoio; (for fish) acquario; (MIL) carro armato
tanker ['tæŋkə*] n (ship) nave f cisterna inv; (truck) autobotte f, autocisterna
tanned [tænd] adj abbronzato(a)
tantalizing ['tæntəlaɪzɪŋ] adj allettante
tantamount ['tæntəmaunt] adj: **~ to** equivalente a
tantrum ['tæntrəm] n accesso di collera
tap [tæp] n (on sink etc) rubinetto; (gentle blow) colpetto ♦ vt dare un colpetto a; (resources) sfruttare, utilizzare; (telephone) mettere sotto controllo; **on** ♦ (fig: resources) a disposizione; **~ dancing** n tip tap m
tape [teɪp] n nastro; (also: **magnetic ~**) nastro (magnetico); (sticky ~) nastro adesivo ♦ vt (record) registrare (su nastro); (stick) attaccare con nastro adesivo; **~ deck** n piastra; **~ measure** n metro a nastro
taper ['teɪpə*] n candelina ♦ vi assottigliarsi
tape recorder n registratore m (a nastro)
tapestry ['tæpɪstrɪ] n arazzo; tappezzeria
tar [tɑ:*] n catrame m
target ['tɑ:gɪt] n bersaglio; (fig: objective) obiettivo
tariff ['tærɪf] n tariffa
tarmac ['tɑ:mæk] n (BRIT: on road) macadam m al catrame; (AVIAT) pista di decollo
tarnish ['tɑ:nɪʃ] vt offuscare, annerire; (fig)

macchiare
tarpaulin [tɑ:'pɔ:lɪn] n tela incatramata
tarragon ['tærəgən] n dragoncello
tart [tɑ:t] n (CULIN) crostata; (BRIT: inf: pej: woman) sgualdrina ♦ adj (flavour) aspro(a), agro(a); **~ up** (inf) vt agghindare
tartan ['tɑ:tn] n tartan m inv
tartar ['tɑ:tə*] n (on teeth) tartaro; **~(e) sauce** n salsa tartara
task [tɑ:sk] n compito; **to take to ~** rimproverare; **~ force** n (MIL, POLICE) unità operativa
taste [teɪst] n gusto; (flavour) sapore m, gusto; (sample) assaggio; (fig: glimpse, idea) idea ♦ vt gustare; (sample) assaggiare ♦ vi: **to ~ of** or **like** (fish etc) sapere or avere sapore di; **you can ~ the garlic (in it)** (ci) si sente il sapore dell'aglio; **in good/bad ~** di buon/cattivo gusto; **~ful** adj di buon gusto; **~less** adj (food) insipido(a); (remark) di cattivo gusto; **tasty** adj saporito(a), gustoso(a)
tatters ['tætəz] npl: **in ~** a brandelli
tattoo [tə'tu:] n tatuaggio; (spectacle) parata militare ♦ vt tatuare
tatty ['tætɪ] adj malridotto(a)
taught [tɔ:t] pt, pp of **teach**
taunt [tɔ:nt] n scherno ♦ vt schernire
Taurus ['tɔ:rəs] n Toro
taut [tɔ:t] adj teso(a)
tax [tæks] n (on goods) imposta; (on services) tassa; (on income) imposte fpl, tasse fpl ♦ vt tassare; (fig: strain: patience etc) mettere alla prova; **~able** adj (income) imponibile; **~ation** [-'seɪʃən] n tassazione f; tasse fpl, imposte fpl; **~ avoidance** n elusione f fiscale; **~ disc** (BRIT) n (AUT) ≈ bollo; **~ evasion** n evasione f fiscale; **~-free** adj esente da imposte
taxi ['tæksɪ] n taxi m inv ♦ vi (AVIAT) rullare; **~ driver** n tassista m/f; **~ rank** (BRIT) n = **~ stand**; **~ stand** n posteggio dei taxi
tax: ~ payer n contribuente m/f; **~ relief** n agevolazioni fpl fiscali; **~ return** n dichiarazione f dei redditi
TB n abbr = **tuberculosis**
tea [ti:] n tè m inv; (BRIT: snack: for children)

merenda; **high ~** (BRIT) cena leggera (presa nel tardo pomeriggio); ~ **bag** n bustina di tè; ~ **break** (BRIT) n intervallo per il tè

teach [tiːtʃ] (pt, pp **taught**) vt: **to ~ sb sth, ~ sth to sb** insegnare qc a qn ♦ vi insegnare; ~**er** n insegnante m/f; (in secondary school) professore/essa; (in primary school) maestro/a; ~**ing** n insegnamento

tea cosy n copriteiera m inv

teacup ['tiːkʌp] n tazza da tè

teak [tiːk] n teak m

tea leaves npl foglie fpl di tè

team [tiːm] n squadra; (of animals) tiro; ~**work** n lavoro di squadra

teapot ['tiːpɔt] n teiera

tear¹ [tɛə*] (pt **tore**, pp **torn**) n strappo ♦ vt strappare ♦ vi strapparsi; ~ **along** vi (rush) correre all'impazzata; ~ **up** vt (sheet of paper etc) strappare

tear² [tɪə*] n lacrima; **in ~s** in lacrime; ~**ful** adj piangente, lacrimoso(a); ~ **gas** n gas m lacrimogeno

tearoom ['tiːruːm] n sala da tè

tease [tiːz] vt canzonare; (unkindly) tormentare

tea set n servizio da tè

teaspoon ['tiːspuːn] n cucchiaino da tè; (also: ~**ful**: as measurement) cucchiaino

teat [tiːt] n capezzolo

teatime ['tiːtaɪm] n ora del tè

tea towel (BRIT) n strofinaccio (per i piatti)

technical ['tɛknɪkl] adj tecnico(a); ~ **college** (BRIT) n ≈ istituto tecnico; ~**ity** [-'kælɪtɪ] n tecnicità; (detail) dettaglio tecnico; (legal) cavillo

technician [tɛk'nɪʃən] n tecnico/a

technique [tɛk'niːk] n tecnica

technological [tɛknə'lɔdʒɪkl] adj tecnologico(a)

technology [tɛk'nɔlədʒɪ] n tecnologia

teddy (bear) ['tɛdɪ-] n orsacchiotto

tedious ['tiːdɪəs] adj noioso(a), tedioso(a)

tee [tiː] n (GOLF) tee m inv

teem [tiːm] vi: **to ~ with** brulicare di; **it is ~ing (with rain)** piove a dirotto

teenage ['tiːneɪdʒ] adj (fashions etc) per giovani, per adolescenti; ~**r** n adolescente

m/f

teens [tiːnz] npl: **to be in one's ~** essere adolescente

tee-shirt ['tiːʃəːt] n = T-shirt

teeter ['tiːtə*] vi barcollare, vacillare

teeth [tiːθ] npl of **tooth**

teethe [tiːð] vi mettere i denti

teething ring ['tiːðɪŋ-] n dentaruolo

teething troubles ['tiːðɪŋ-] npl (fig) difficoltà fpl iniziali

teetotal ['tiː'təutl] adj astemio(a)

tele: ~**conferencing** n teleconferenza; ~**gram** n telegramma m; ~**graph** n telegrafo; ~**pathy** [tə'lɛpəθɪ] n telepatia

telephone ['tɛlɪfəun] n telefono ♦ vt (person) telefonare a; (message) comunicare per telefono; ~ **booth** (BRIT ~ **box**) n cabina telefonica; ~ **call** n telefonata; ~ **directory** n elenco telefonico; ~ **number** n numero di telefono; **telephonist** [tə'lɛfənɪst] (BRIT) n telefonista m/f

telescope ['tɛlɪskəup] n telescopio

telesales ['tɛlɪseɪlz] n vendita per telefono

television ['tɛlɪvɪʒən] n televisione f; **on ~** alla televisione; ~ **set** n televisore m

teleworking ['tɛlɪwəːkɪŋ] n telelavoro

telex ['tɛlɛks] n telex m inv ♦ vt trasmettere per telex

tell [tɛl] (pt, pp **told**) vt dire; (relate: story) raccontare; (distinguish): **to ~ sth from** distinguere qc da ♦ vi (talk): **to ~ (of)** parlare (di); (have effect) farsi sentire, avere effetto; **to ~ sb to do** ordinare a qn di fare; ~ **off** vt rimproverare, sgridare; ~**er** n (in bank) cassiere/a; ~**ing** adj (remark, detail) rivelatore(trice); ~**tale** adj (sign) rivelatore(trice)

telly ['tɛlɪ] (BRIT: inf) n abbr (= television) tivù f inv

temerity [tə'mɛrɪtɪ] n temerarietà

temp [tɛmp] n abbr (= temporary) segretaria temporanea

temper ['tɛmpə*] n (nature) carattere m; (mood) umore m; (fit of anger) collera ♦ vt (moderate) moderare; **to be in a ~** essere in collera; **to lose one's ~** andare in collera

temperament ['tɛmprəmənt] n (nature)

temperamento; **~al** [-'mɛntl] *adj*
capriccioso(a)

temperate ['tɛmprət] *adj* moderato(a);
(*climate*) temperato(a)

temperature ['tɛmprətʃə*] *n* temperatura;
to have *or* **run a ~** avere la febbre

tempest ['tɛmpɪst] *n* tempesta

template ['tɛmplɪt] *n* sagoma

temple ['tɛmpl] *n* (*building*) tempio; (*ANAT*)
tempia

temporary ['tɛmpərərɪ] *adj* temporaneo(a);
(*job, worker*) avventizio(a), temporaneo(a)

tempt [tɛmpt] *vt* tentare; **to ~ sb into doing**
indurre qn a fare; **~ation** [-'teɪʃən] *n*
tentazione *f*; **~ing** *adj* allettante

ten [tɛn] *num* dieci

tenacity [tə'næsɪtɪ] *n* tenacia

tenancy ['tɛnənsɪ] *n* affitto; condizione *f* di
inquilino

tenant ['tɛnənt] *n* inquilino/a

tend [tɛnd] *vt* badare a, occuparsi di ♦ *vi*: **to**
~ to do tendere a fare

tendency ['tɛndənsɪ] *n* tendenza

tender ['tɛndə*] *adj* tenero(a); (*sore*)
dolorante ♦ *n* (*COMM: offer*) offerta;
(*money*): **legal ~** moneta in corso legale
♦ *vt* offrire

tendon ['tɛndən] *n* tendine *m*

tenement ['tɛnəmənt] *n* casamento

tennis ['tɛnɪs] *n* tennis *m*; **~ ball** *n* palla da
tennis; **~ court** *n* campo da tennis; **~**
player *n* tennista *m/f*; **~ racket** *n*
racchetta da tennis; **~ shoes** *npl* scarpe
fpl da tennis

tenor ['tɛnə*] *n* (*MUS*) tenore *m*

tenpin bowling ['tɛnpɪn-] *n* bowling *m*

tense [tɛns] *adj* teso(a) ♦ *n* (*LING*) tempo

tension ['tɛnʃən] *n* tensione *f*

tent [tɛnt] *n* tenda

tentative ['tɛntətɪv] *adj* esitante, incerto(a);
(*conclusion*) provvisorio(a)

tenterhooks ['tɛntəhuks] *npl*: **on ~** sulle
spine

tenth [tɛnθ] *num* decimo(a)

tent: **~ peg** *n* picchetto da tenda; **~ pole**
n palo da tenda, montante *m*

tenuous ['tɛnjuəs] *adj* tenue

tenure ['tɛnjuə*] *n* (*of property*) possesso; (*of*
job) permanenza; titolarità

tepid ['tɛpɪd] *adj* tiepido(a)

term [tə:m] *n* termine *m*; (*SCOL*) trimestre *m*;
(*LAW*) sessione *f* ♦ *vt* chiamare, definire; **~s**
npl (*conditions*) condizioni *fpl*; (*COMM*)
prezzi *mpl*, tariffe *fpl*; **in the short/long ~**
a breve/lunga scadenza; **to be on good ~s**
with sb essere in buoni rapporti con qn; **to**
come to ~s with (*problem*) affrontare

terminal ['tə:mɪnl] *adj* finale, terminale;
(*disease*) terminale ♦ *n* (*ELEC*) morsetto;
(*COMPUT*) terminale *m*; (*AVIAT, for oil, ore*
etc) terminal *m inv*; (*BRIT: also*: **coach ~**)
capolinea *m*

terminate ['tə:mɪneɪt] *vt* mettere fine a

termini ['tə:mɪnaɪ] *npl of* **terminus**

terminus ['tə:mɪnəs] (*pl* **termini**) *n* (*for*
buses) capolinea *m*; (*for trains*) stazione *f*
terminale

terrace ['tɛrəs] *n* terrazza; (*BRIT: row of*
houses) fila di case a schiera; **the ~s** *npl*
(*BRIT: SPORT*) le gradinate; **~d** *adj* (*garden*) a
terrazze

terracotta ['tɛrə'kɔtə] *n* terracotta

terrain [tɛ'reɪn] *n* terreno

terrible ['tɛrɪbl] *adj* terribile; **terribly** *adv*
terribilmente; (*very badly*) malissimo

terrier ['tɛrɪə*] *n* terrier *m inv*

terrific [tə'rɪfɪk] *adj* incredibile, fantastico(a);
(*wonderful*) formidabile, eccezionale

terrify ['tɛrɪfaɪ] *vt* terrorizzare

territory ['tɛrɪtərɪ] *n* territorio

terror ['tɛrə*] *n* terrore *m*; **~ism** *n*
terrorismo; **~ist** *n* terrorista *m/f*

Terylene ® ['tɛrəliːn] *n* terital ® *m*,
terilene ® *m*

test [tɛst] *n* (*trial, check, of courage etc*)
prova; (*MED*) esame *m*; (*CHEM*) analisi *f inv*;
(*exam: of intelligence etc*) test *m inv*; (: *in*
school) compito in classe; (*also*: **driving ~**)
esame *m* di guida ♦ *vt* provare; esaminare;
analizzare; sottoporre ad esame; **to ~ sb in**
history esaminare qn in storia

testament ['tɛstəmənt] *n* testamento; **the**
Old/New T~ il Vecchio/Nuovo testamento

testicle ['tɛstɪkl] *n* testicolo

testify ['testifai] *vi* (*LAW*) testimoniare, deporre; **to ~ to sth** (*LAW*) testimoniare qc; (*gen*) comprovare *or* dimostrare qc

testimony ['testimǝni] *n* (*LAW*) testimonianza, deposizione *f*

test match *n* (*CRICKET, RUGBY*) partita internazionale

test tube *n* provetta

tetanus ['tɛtǝnǝs] *n* tetano

tether ['tɛðǝ*] *vt* legare ♦ *n*: **at the end of one's ~** al limite (della pazienza)

text [tɛkst] *n* testo; **~book** *n* libro di testo

textiles ['tɛkstailz] *npl* tessuti *mpl*; (*industry*) industria tessile

texting ['tɛkstin] *n* il mandare messaggi con il telefono

texture ['tɛkstʃǝ*] *n* tessitura; (*of skin, paper etc*) struttura

Thames [tɛmz] *n*: **the ~** il Tamigi

than [ðæn, ðǝn] *conj* (*in comparisons*) che; (*with numerals, pronouns, proper names*) di; **more ~ 10/once** più di 10/una volta; **I have more/less ~ you** ne ho più/meno di te; **I have more pens ~ pencils** ho più penne che matite; **she is older ~ you think** è più vecchia di quanto tu (non) pensi

thank [θæŋk] *vt* ringraziare; **~ you (very much)** grazie (tante); **~s** *npl* ringraziamenti *mpl*, grazie *fpl* ♦ *excl* grazie!; **~s to** grazie a; **~ful** *adj*: **~ful (for)** riconoscente (per); **~less** *adj* ingrato(a); **T~sgiving (Day)** *n see box*

Thanksgiving (Day)

> *Negli Stati Uniti ogni quarto giovedì di novembre ricorre il Thanksgiving (Day), festa in ricordo della celebrazione con cui i Padri Pellegrini, fondatori della colonia di Plymouth in Massachussets, ringraziarono Dio del buon raccolto del 1621.*

KEYWORD

that [ðæt] (*pl* **those**) *adj* (*demonstrative*) quel(quell', quello) *m*; quella(quell') *f*; **~ man/woman/book** quell'uomo/quella donna/quel libro; (*not "this"*) quell'uomo/

quella donna/quel libro là; **~ one** quello(a) là

♦ *pron* **1** (*demonstrative*) ciò; (*not "this one"*) quello(a); **who's ~?** chi è?; **what's ~?** cos'è quello?; **is ~ you?** sei tu?; **I prefer this to ~** preferisco questo a quello; **~'s what he said** questo è ciò che ha detto; **what happened after ~?** che è successo dopo?; **~ is (to say)** cioè

2 (*relative: direct*) che; (*: indirect*) cui; **the book (~) I read** il libro che ho letto; **the box (~) I put it in** la scatola in cui l'ho messo; **the people (~) I spoke to** le persone con cui *or* con le quali ho parlato

3 (*relative: of time*) in cui; **the day (~) he came** il giorno in cui è venuto

♦ *conj* che; **he thought ~ I was ill** pensava che io fossi malato

♦ *adv* (*demonstrative*) così; **I can't work ~ much** non posso lavorare (così) tanto; **~ high** così alto; **the wall's about ~ high and ~ thick** il muro è alto circa così e spesso circa così

thatched [θætʃt] *adj* (*roof*) di paglia; **~ cottage** *n* cottage *m inv* col tetto di paglia

thaw [θɔ:] *n* disgelo ♦ *vi* (*ice*) sciogliersi; (*food*) scongelarsi ♦ *vt* (*food: also:* **~ out**) (fare) scongelare

KEYWORD

the [ðiː, ðǝ] *def art* **1** (*gen*) il(lo, l') *m*; la(l') *f*; i(gli) *mpl*; le *fpl*; **~ boy/girl/ink** il ragazzo/la ragazza/l'inchiostro; **~ books/pencils** i libri/le matite; **~ history of ~ world** la storia del mondo; **give it to ~ postman** dallo al postino; **I haven't ~ time/money** non ho tempo/soldi; **~ rich and ~ poor** i ricchi e i poveri

2 (*in titles*): **Elizabeth ~ First** Elisabetta prima; **Peter ~ Great** Pietro il grande

3 (*in comparisons*): **~ more he works, ~ more he earns** più lavora più guadagna

theatre ['θiǝtǝ*] (*US* **theater**) *n* teatro; (*also:* **lecture ~**) aula magna; (*also:* **operating ~**)

sala operatoria; **~-goer** n frequentatore/trice di teatri

theatrical [θɪ'ætrɪkl] adj teatrale

theft [θɛft] n furto

their [ðɛə*] adj il(la) loro, pl i(le) loro; **~s** pron il(la) loro, pl i(le) loro; see also **my; mine**

them [ðɛm, ðəm] pron (direct) li(le); (indirect) gli, loro (after vb); (stressed, after prep: people) loro; (: people, things) essi(e); see also **me**

theme [θi:m] n tema m; **~ park** n parco di divertimenti (intorno a un tema centrale); **~ song** n tema musicale

themselves [ðəm'sɛlvz] pl pron (reflexive) si; (emphatic) loro stessi(e); (after prep) se stessi(e)

then [ðɛn] adv (at that time) allora; (next) poi, dopo; (and also) e poi ♦ conj (therefore) perciò, dunque, quindi ♦ adj: **the ~ president** il presidente di allora; **by ~** allora; **from ~ on** da allora in poi

theology [θɪ'ɔlədʒɪ] n teologia

theorem ['θɪərəm] n teorema m

theoretical [θɪə'rɛtɪkl] adj teorico(a)

theory ['θɪərɪ] n teoria

therapy ['θɛrəpɪ] n terapia

---KEYWORD---

there [ðɛə*] adv 1: **~ is, ~ are** c'è, ci sono; **~ are 3 of them** (people) sono in 3; (things) ce ne sono 3; **~ is no-one here** non c'è nessuno qui; **~ has been an accident** c'è stato un incidente

2 (referring to place) là, lì; **up/in/down ~** lassù/là dentro/laggiù; **he went ~ on Friday** ci è andato venerdì; **I want that book ~** voglio quel libro là or lì; **he is!** eccolo!

3: ~, ~ (esp to child) su, su

thereabouts [ðɛərə'bauts] adv (place) nei pressi, da quelle parti; (amount) giù di lì, all'incirca

thereafter [ðɛər'ɑ:ftə*] adv da allora in poi

thereby [ðɛə'baɪ] adv con ciò

therefore ['ðɛəfɔ:*] adv perciò, quindi

there's [ðɛəz] = **there is; there has**

thermal ['θə:ml] adj termico(a)

thermometer [θə'mɔmɪtə*] n termometro

Thermos ® ['θə:məs] n (also: **~ flask**) thermos ® m inv

thesaurus [θɪ'sɔ:rəs] n dizionario dei sinonimi

these [ði:z] pl pron, adj questi(e)

theses ['θi:si:z] npl of **thesis**

thesis ['θi:sɪs] (pl **theses**) n tesi f inv

they [ðeɪ] pl pron essi(esse); (people only) loro; **~ say that ...** (it is said that) si dice che ...; **~'d** = **they had; they would; ~'ll** = **they shall; they will; ~'re** = **they are; ~'ve** = **they have**

thick [θɪk] adj spesso(a); (crowd) compatto(a); (stupid) ottuso(a), lento(a) ♦ n: **in the ~ of** nel folto di; **it's 20 cm ~** ha uno spessore di 20 cm; **~en** vi ispessire ♦ vt (sauce etc) ispessire, rendere più denso(a); **~ly** adv (spread) a strati spessi; (cut) a fette grosse; (populated) densamente; **~ness** n spessore m; **~set** adj tarchiato(a), tozzo(a)

thief [θi:f] (pl **thieves**) n ladro/a

thieves [θi:vz] npl of **thief**

thigh [θaɪ] n coscia

thimble ['θɪmbl] n ditale m

thin [θɪn] adj sottile; (person) magro(a); (soup) poco denso(a) ♦ vt: **to ~ (down)** (sauce, paint) diluire

thing [θɪŋ] n cosa; (object) oggetto; (mania): **to have a ~ about** essere fissato(a) con; **~s** npl (belongings) cose fpl; **poor ~** poverino(a); **the best ~ would be to** la cosa migliore sarebbe di; **how are ~s?** come va?

think [θɪŋk] (pt, pp **thought**) vi pensare, riflettere ♦ vt pensare, credere; (imagine) immaginare; **to ~ of** pensare a; **what did you ~ of them?** cosa ne ha pensato?; **to ~ about sth/sb** pensare a qc/qn; **I'll ~ about it** ci penserò; **to ~ of doing** pensare di fare; **I ~ so/not** penso di sì/no; **to ~ well of** avere una buona opinione di; **~ out** vt (plan) elaborare; (solution) trovare; **~ over** vt riflettere su; **~ through** vt riflettere a fondo su; ~ **up** *vt* ideare; ~ **tank** *n* commissione *f* di esperti

third [θəːd] *num* terzo(a) ♦ *n* terzo/a; *(fraction)* terzo, terza parte *f*; *(AUT)* terza; *(BRIT: SCOL: degree) laurea col minimo dei voti*; ~**ly** *adv* in terzo luogo; ~ **party insurance** *(BRIT)* *n* assicurazione *f* contro terzi; ~**rate** *adj* di qualità scadente; **the T~ World** *n* il Terzo Mondo

thirst [θəːst] *n* sete *f*; ~**y** *adj (person)* assetato(a), che ha sete

thirteen [θəːˈtiːn] *num* tredici

thirty [ˈθəːtɪ] *num* trenta

KEYWORD

this [ðɪs] *(pl* **these**) *adj (demonstrative)* questo(a); ~ **man/woman/book** quest'uomo/questa donna/questo libro; *(not "that")* quest'uomo/questa donna/ questo libro qui; ~ **one** questo(a) qui ♦ *pron (demonstrative)* questo(a); *(not "that one")* questo(a) qui; **who/what is ~?** chi è/che cos'è questo?; **I prefer ~ to that** preferisco questo a quello; ~ **is where I live** è qui abito qui; ~ **is what he said** questo è ciò che ha detto; ~ **is Mr Brown** *(in introductions, photo)* questo è il signor Brown; *(on telephone)* sono il signor Brown ♦ *adv (demonstrative)*: ~ **high/long** *etc* alto/lungo *etc* così; **I didn't know things were ~ bad** non sapevo andasse così male

---

thistle [ˈθɪsl] *n* cardo

thong [θɒŋ] *n* cinghia

thorn [θɔːn] *n* spina; ~**y** *adj* spinoso(a)

thorough [ˈθʌrə] *adj (search)* minuzioso(a); *(knowledge, research)* approfondito(a), profondo(a); *(person)* coscienzioso(a); *(cleaning)* a fondo; ~**bred** *n (horse)* purosangue *m/f inv*; ~**fare** *n* strada transitabile; **"no ~fare"** "divieto di transito"; ~**ly** *adv (search)* minuziosamente; *(wash, study)* a fondo; *(very)* assolutamente

those [ðəʊz] *pl pron* quelli(e) ♦ *pl adj* quei(quegli) *mpl*; quelle *fpl*

though [ðəʊ] *conj* benché, sebbene ♦ *adv*

comunque

thought [θɔːt] *pt, pp of* **think** ♦ *n* pensiero; *(opinion)* opinione *f*; ~**ful** *adj* pensieroso(a), pensoso(a); *(considerate)* premuroso(a); ~**less** *adj* sconsiderato(a); *(behaviour)* scortese

thousand [ˈθaʊzənd] *num* mille; **one ~** mille; ~**s of** migliaia di; ~**th** *num* millesimo(a)

thrash [θræʃ] *vt* picchiare; bastonare; *(defeat)* battere; ~ **about** *vi* dibattersi; ~ **out** *vt* dibattere

thread [θred] *n* filo; *(of screw)* filetto ♦ *vt (needle)* infilare; ~**bare** *adj* consumato(a), logoro(a)

threat [θret] *n* minaccia; ~**en** *vi (storm)* minacciare ♦ *vt*: **to ~en sb with/to do** minacciare qn con/di fare

three [θriː] *num* tre; ~**dimensional** *adj* tridimensionale; *(film)* stereoscopico(a); ~**piece suit** *n* completo (con gilè); ~**piece suite** *n* salotto comprendente un divano e due poltrone; ~**ply** *adj (wool)* a tre fili

threshold [ˈθreʃhəʊld] *n* soglia

threw [θruː] *pt of* **throw**

thrifty [ˈθrɪftɪ] *adj* economico(a)

thrill [θrɪl] *n* brivido ♦ *vt (audience)* elettrizzare; **to be ~ed** *(with gift etc)* essere elettrizzato(a); ~**er** *n* thriller *m inv*; ~**ing** *adj (book)* pieno(a) di suspense; *(news, discovery)* elettrizzante

thrive [θraɪv] *(pt* **thrived**, *pp* **thrived**) *vi* crescere *or* svilupparsi bene; *(business)* prosperare; **he ~s on it** gli fa bene, ne gode; **thriving** *adj* fiorente

throat [θrəʊt] *n* gola; **to have a sore ~** avere (un *or* il) mal di gola

throb [θrɒb] *vi* palpitare; pulsare; vibrare

throes [θrəʊz] *npl*: **in the ~ of** alle prese con; in preda a

thrombosis [θrɒmˈbəʊsɪs] *n* trombosi *f*

throne [θrəʊn] *n* trono

throng [θrɒŋ] *n* moltitudine *f* ♦ *vt* affollare

throttle [ˈθrɒtl] *n (AUT)* valvola a farfalla ♦ *vt* strangolare

through [θruː] *prep* attraverso; *(time)* per,

durante; (*by means of*) per mezzo di; (*owing to*) a causa di ♦ *adj* (*ticket, train, passage*) diretto(a) ♦ *adv* attraverso; **to put sb ~ to sb** (*TEL*) passare qn a qn; **to be ~** (*TEL*) ottenere la comunicazione; (*have finished*) essere finito(a); **"no ~ road"** (*BRIT*) "strada senza sbocco"; **~out** *prep* (*place*) dappertutto in; (*time*) per *or* durante tutto(a) ♦ *adv* dappertutto; sempre

throw [θrəʊ] (*pt* **threw**, *pp* **thrown**) *n* (*SPORT*) lancio, tiro ♦ *vt* tirare, gettare; (*SPORT*) lanciare, tirare; (*rider*) disarcionare; (*fig*) confondere; **to ~ a party** dare una festa; **~ away** *vt* gettare *or* buttare via; **~ off** *vt* sbarazzarsi di; **~ out** *vt* buttare fuori; (*reject*) respingere; **~ up** *vi* vomitare; **~away** *adj* da buttare; **~-in** *n* (*SPORT*) rimessa in gioco; **thrown** *pp of* **throw**

thru [θruː] (*US*) *prep, adj, adv* = **through**

thrush [θrʌʃ] *n* tordo

thrust [θrʌst] (*pt, pp* **thrust**) *vt* spingere con forza; (*push in*) conficcare

thud [θʌd] *n* tonfo

thug [θʌg] *n* delinquente *m*

thumb [θʌm] *n* (*ANAT*) pollice *m*; **to ~ a lift** fare l'autostop; **~ through** *vt fus* (*book*) sfogliare; **~tack** (*US*) *n* puntina da disegno

thump [θʌmp] *n* colpo forte; (*sound*) tonfo ♦ *vt* (*person*) picchiare; (*object*) battere su ♦ *vi* picchiare; battere

thunder ['θʌndə*] *n* tuono ♦ *vi* tuonare; (*train etc*): **to ~ past** passare con un rombo; **~bolt** *n* fulmine *m*; **~clap** *n* rombo di tuono; **~storm** *n* temporale *m*; **~y** *adj* temporalesco(a)

Thursday ['θɜːzdɪ] *n* giovedì *m inv*

thus [ðʌs] *adv* così

thwart [θwɔːt] *vt* contrastare

thyme [taɪm] *n* timo

thyroid ['θaɪrɔɪd] *n* (*also*: **~ gland**) tiroide *f*

tiara [tɪ'ɑːrə] (*woman's*) *n* diadema *m*

Tiber ['taɪbə*] *n*: **the ~** il Tevere

tick [tɪk] *n* (*sound: of clock*) tic tac *m inv*; (*mark*) segno; spunta; (*ZOOL*) zecca; (*BRIT: inf*): **in a ~** in un attimo ♦ *vi* fare tic tac ♦ *vt* spuntare; **~ off** *vt* spuntare; (*person*) sgridare; **~ over** *vi* (*engine*) andare al

minimo; (*fig*) andare avanti come al solito

ticket ['tɪkɪt] *n* biglietto; (*in shop: on goods*) etichetta; (*parking ~*) multa; (*for library*) scheda; **~ collector** *n* bigliettaio; **~ office** *n* biglietteria

tickle ['tɪkl] *vt* fare il solletico a; (*fig*) solleticare ♦ *vi*: **it ~s** mi (*or gli etc*) fa il solletico; **ticklish** [-lɪʃ] *adj* che soffre il solletico; (*problem*) delicato(a)

tidal ['taɪdl] *adj* di marea; (*estuary*) soggetto(a) alla marea; **~ wave** *n* onda anomala

tidbit ['tɪdbɪt] (*US*) *n* (*food*) leccornia; (*news*) notizia ghiotta

tiddlywinks ['tɪdlɪwɪŋks] *n* gioco della pulce

tide [taɪd] *n* marea; (*fig: of events*) corso; **high/low ~** alta/bassa marea; **~ over** *vt* dare una mano a

tidy ['taɪdɪ] *adj* (*room*) ordinato(a), lindo(a); (*dress, work*) curato(a), in ordine; (*person*) ordinato(a) ♦ *vt* (*also*: **~ up**) riordinare, mettere in ordine

tie [taɪ] *n* (*string etc*) legaccio; (*BRIT: also*: **neck~**) cravatta; (*fig: link*) legame *m*; (*SPORT: draw*) pareggio ♦ *vt* (*parcel*) legare; (*ribbon*) annodare ♦ *vi* (*SPORT*) pareggiare; **to ~ sth in a bow** annodare qc; **to ~ a knot in sth** fare un nodo a qc; **~ down** *vt* legare; (*to price etc*) costringere ad accettare; **~ up** *vt* (*parcel, dog*) legare; (*boat*) ormeggiare; (*arrangements*) concludere; **to be ~d up** (*busy*) essere occupato(a) *or* preso(a)

tier [tɪə*] *n* fila; (*of cake*) piano, strato

tiger ['taɪgə*] *n* tigre *f*

tight [taɪt] *adj* (*rope*) teso(a), tirato(a); (*money*) poco(a); (*clothes, budget, bend etc*) stretto(a); (*control*) severo(a), fermo(a); (*inf: drunk*) sbronzo(a) ♦ *adv* (*squeeze*) fortemente; (*shut*) ermeticamente; **~s** (*BRIT*) *npl* collant *m inv*; **~en** *vt* (*rope*) tendere; (*screw*) stringere; (*control*) rinforzare ♦ *vi* tendersi; stringersi; **~-fisted** *adj* avaro(a); **~ly** *adv* (*grasp*) bene, saldamente; **~rope** *n* corda (da acrobata)

tile [taɪl] *n* (*on roof*) tegola; (*on wall or floor*) piastrella, mattonella; ~d adj di tegole; a piastrelle, a mattonelle

till [til] n registratore m di cassa ♦ vt (land) coltivare ♦ prep, conj = until

tiller ['tilə*] n (NAUT) barra del timone

tilt [tilt] vt inclinare, far pendere ♦ vi inclinarsi, pendere

timber [timbə*] n (material) legname m

time [taim] n tempo; (epoch: often pl) epoca, tempo; (by clock) ora; (moment) momento; (occasion) volta; (MUS) tempo ♦ vt (race) cronometrare; (programme) calcolare la durata di; (fix moment for) programmare; (remark etc) dire (or fare) al momento giusto; a long ~ molto tempo; for the ~ being per il momento; 4 at a ~ 4 per or alla volta; from ~ to ~ ogni tanto; at ~s a volte; in ~ (soon enough) in tempo; (after some ~) col tempo; (MUS) a tempo; in a week's ~ fra una settimana; in no ~ in un attimo; any ~ in qualsiasi momento; on ~ puntualmente; 5 ~s 5 5 volte 5, 5 per 5; what ~ is it? che ora è?, che ore sono?; to have a good ~ divertirsi; ~ bomb n bomba a orologeria; ~less adj eterno(a); ~ly adj opportuno(a); ~ off n tempo libero; ~r n (~ switch) temporizzatore m; (in kitchen) contaminuti m inv; ~ scale n periodo; ~-share adj: ~-share apartment/villa appartamento/villa in multiproprietà; ~ switch (BRIT) n temporizzatore m; ~table n orario; ~ zone n fuso orario

timid ['timid] adj timido(a); (easily scared) pauroso(a)

timing ['taimiŋ] n (SPORT) cronometraggio; (fig) scelta del momento opportuno

timpani ['timpəni] npl timpani mpl

tin [tin] n stagno; (also: ~ plate) latta; (container) scatola; (BRIT: can) barattolo (di latta), lattina; ~foil n stagnola

tinge [tindʒ] n sfumatura ♦ vt: ~d with tinto(a) di

tingle ['tiŋgl] vi pizzicare

tinker ['tiŋkə*]: ~ with vt fus armeggiare intorno a; cercare di riparare

tinned [tind] (BRIT) adj (food) in scatola

tin opener ['-əupnə*] (BRIT) n apriscatole m inv

tinsel ['tinsl] n decorazioni fpl natalizie (argentate)

tint [tint] n tinta; ~ed adj (hair) tinto(a); (spectacles, glass) colorato(a)

tiny ['taini] adj minuscolo(a)

tip [tip] n (end) punta; (gratuity) mancia; (BRIT: for rubbish) immondezzaio; (advice) suggerimento ♦ vt (waiter) dare la mancia a; (tilt) inclinare; (overturn: also: ~ over) capovolgere; (empty: also: ~ out) scaricare; ~-off n (hint) soffiata; ~ped (BRIT) adj (cigarette) col filtro

Tipp-Ex ® ['tipeks] n correttore m

tipsy ['tipsi] adj brillo(a)

tiptoe ['tiptəu] n: on ~ in punta di piedi

tiptop ['tip'top] adj: in ~ condition in ottime condizioni

tire ['taiə*] n (US) = tyre ♦ vt stancare ♦ vi stancarsi; (fig) stancarsi; ~d adj stanco(a); to be ~d of essere stanco or stufo di; ~less adj instancabile; ~some adj noioso(a); tiring adj faticoso(a)

tissue ['tiʃuː] n tessuto; (paper handkerchief) fazzoletto di carta; ~ paper n carta velina

tit [tit] n (bird) cinciallegra; to give ~ for tat rendere pan per focaccia

titbit ['titbit] (BRIT) n (food) leccornia; (news) notizia ghiotta

title ['taitl] n titolo; ~ deed n (LAW) titolo di proprietà; ~ role n ruolo or parte f principale

TM abbr = trademark

KEYWORD

to [tuː, tə] prep 1 (direction) a; to go ~ France/London/school andare in Francia/a Londra/a scuola; to go ~ Paul's/the doctor's andare da Paul/dal dottore; the road ~ Edinburgh la strada per Edimburgo; ~ the left/right a sinistra/destra

2 (as far as) (fino) a; from here ~ London da qui a Londra; to count ~ 10 contare fino a 10; from 40 ~ 50 people da 40 a 50 persone

3 (with expressions of time): **a quarter ~ 5** le 5 meno un quarto; **it's twenty ~ 3** sono le 3 meno venti

4 (for, of): **the key ~ the front door** la chiave della porta d'ingresso; **a letter ~ his wife** una lettera per la moglie

5 (expressing indirect object) a; **to give sth ~ sb** dare qc a qn; **to talk ~ sb** parlare a qn; **to be a danger ~ sb/sth** rappresentare un pericolo per qn/qc

6 (in relation to) a; **3 goals ~ 2** 3 goal a 2; **30 miles ~ the gallon** ≈ 11 chilometri con un litro

7 (purpose, result): **to come ~ sb's aid** venire in aiuto a qn; **to sentence sb ~ death** condannare a morte qn; **~ my surprise** con mia sorpresa

♦ with vb 1 (simple infinitive): **~ go/eat** etc andare/mangiare etc

2 (following another vb): **to want/try/start ~ do** volere/cercare di/cominciare a fare

3 (with vb omitted): **I don't want ~** non voglio (farlo); **you ought ~** devi (farlo)

4 (purpose, result) per; **I did it ~ help you** l'ho fatto per aiutarti

5 (equivalent to relative clause): **I have things ~ do** ho da fare; **the main thing is ~ try** la cosa più importante è provare

6 (after adjective etc): **ready ~ go** pronto a partire; **too old/young ~ ...** troppo vecchio/giovane per ...

♦ adv: **to push the door ~** accostare la porta

toad [təud] n rospo; **~stool** n fungo (velenoso)

toast [təust] n (CULIN) pane m tostato; (drink, speech) brindisi m inv ♦ vt (CULIN) tostare; (drink to) brindare a; **a piece** or **slice of ~** una fetta di pane tostato; **~er** n tostapane m inv

tobacco [tə'bækəu] n tabacco; **~nist** n tabaccaio/a; **~nist's (shop)** n tabaccheria

toboggan [tə'bɔgən] n toboga m inv

today [tə'deɪ] adv oggi ♦ n (also fig) oggi m

toddler ['tɔdlə*] n bambino/a che impara a camminare

toe [təu] n dito del piede; (of shoe) punta; **to ~ the line** (fig) stare in riga, conformarsi; **~nail** n unghia del piede

toffee ['tɔfɪ] n caramella; **~ apple** n mela caramellata

toga ['təugə] n toga

together [tə'geðə*] adv insieme; (at same time) allo stesso tempo; **~ with** insieme a

toil [tɔɪl] n travaglio, fatica ♦ vi affannarsi; sgobbare

toilet ['tɔɪlət] n (BRIT: lavatory) gabinetto ♦ cpd (bag, soap etc) da toletta; **~ paper** n carta igienica; **~ries** npl articoli mpl da toletta; **~ roll** n rotolo di carta igienica; **~ water** n acqua di colonia

token ['təukən] n (sign) segno; (substitute coin) gettone m; **book/record/gift ~** (BRIT) buono-libro/disco/regalo

told [təuld] pt, pp of **tell**

tolerable ['tɔlərəbl] adj (bearable) tollerabile; (fairly good) passabile

tolerant ['tɔlərnt] adj: **~ (of)** tollerante (nei confronti di)

tolerate ['tɔləreɪt] vt sopportare; (MED, TECH) tollerare

toll [təul] n (tax, charge) pedaggio ♦ vi (bell) suonare; **the accident ~ on the roads** il numero delle vittime della strada

tomato [tə'mɑ:təu] (pl **~es**) n pomodoro

tomb [tu:m] n tomba

tomboy ['tɔmbɔɪ] n maschiaccio

tombstone ['tu:mstəun] n pietra tombale

tomcat ['tɔmkæt] n gatto

tomorrow [tə'mɔrəu] adv domani ♦ n (also fig) domani m inv; **the day after ~** dopodomani; **~ morning** domani mattina

ton [tʌn] n tonnellata (BRIT = 1016 kg; US = 907 kg; metric = 1000 kg); **~s of** (inf) un mucchio or sacco di

tone [təun] n tono ♦ vi (also: **~ in**) intonarsi; **~ down** vt (colour, criticism, sound) attenuare; **~ up** vt (muscles) tonificare; **~-deaf** adj che non ha orecchio (musicale)

tongs [tɔŋz] npl tenaglie fpl; (for coal) molle fpl; (for hair) arricciacapelli m inv

tongue [tʌŋ] n lingua; **~ in cheek** (say, speak) ironicamente; **~-tied** adj (fig) muto(a); **~-twister** n scioglilingua m inv

tonic ['tɒnɪk] n (MED) tonico; (also: **~ water**) acqua tonica

tonight [tə'naɪt] adv stanotte; (this evening) stasera ♦ n questa notte; questa sera

tonnage ['tʌnɪdʒ] n (NAUT) tonnellaggio, stazza

tonsil ['tɒnsl] n tonsilla; **~litis** [-'laɪtɪs] n tonsillite f

too [tuː] adv (excessively) troppo; (also) anche; **~ much** adv troppo ♦ adj troppo(a); **~ many** troppi(e)

took [tuk] pt of **take**

tool [tuːl] n utensile m, attrezzo; **~ box** n cassetta f portautensili

toot [tuːt] n (of horn) colpo di clacson; (of whistle) fischio ♦ vi suonare; (with car horn) suonare il clacson

tooth [tuːθ] (pl **teeth**) n (ANAT, TECH) dente m; **~ache** n mal m di denti; **~brush** n spazzolino da denti; **~paste** n dentifricio; **~pick** n stuzzicadenti m inv

top [tɒp] n (of mountain, page, ladder) cima; (of box, cupboard, table) sopra m inv, parte f superiore; (lid: of box, jar) coperchio; (: of bottle) tappo; (blouse etc) sopra m inv; (toy) trottola ♦ adj più alto(a); (in rank) primo(a); (best) migliore ♦ vt (exceed) superare; (be first in) essere in testa a; **on ~ of** sopra, in cima a; (in addition to) oltre a; **from ~ to bottom** da cima a fondo; **~ up** (US **~ off**) vt riempire; (salary) integrare; **~ floor** n ultimo piano; **~ hat** n cilindro; **~-heavy** adj (object) con la parte superiore troppo pesante

topic ['tɒpɪk] n argomento; **~al** adj d'attualità

top: ~less adj (bather etc) col seno scoperto; **~-level** adj (talks) ad alto livello; **~most** adj il(la) più alto(a)

topple ['tɒpl] vt rovesciare, far cadere ♦ vi cadere; traballare

top-secret adj segretissimo(a)

topsy-turvy ['tɒpsɪ'tɜːvɪ] adj, adv sottosopra inv

torch [tɔːtʃ] n torcia; (BRIT: electric) lampadina tascabile

tore [tɔː*] pt of **tear**[1]

torment [n 'tɔːmɛnt, vb tɔː'mɛnt] n tormento ♦ vt tormentare

torn [tɔːn] pp of **tear**[1]

torpedo [tɔː'piːdəu] (pl **~es**) n siluro

torrent ['tɒrnt] n torrente m

torrid ['tɒrɪd] adj torrido(a); (love affair) infuocato(a)

tortoise ['tɔːtəs] n tartaruga; **~shell** ['tɔːtəʃel] adj di tartaruga

torture ['tɔːtʃə*] n tortura ♦ vt torturare

Tory ['tɔːrɪ] (BRIT: POL) adj dei tories, conservatore(trice) ♦ n tory m/f inv, conservatore/trice

toss [tɒs] vt gettare, lanciare; (one's head) scuotere; **to ~ a coin** fare a testa o croce; **to ~ up for sth** fare a testa o croce per qc; **to ~ and turn** (in bed) girarsi e rigirarsi

tot [tɒt] n (BRIT: drink) bicchierino; (child) bimbo/a

total ['təutl] adj totale ♦ n totale m ♦ vt (add up) sommare; (amount to) ammontare a

totally ['təutəlɪ] adv completamente

touch [tʌtʃ] n tocco; (sense) tatto; (contact) contatto ♦ vt toccare; **a ~ of** (fig) un tocco di; un pizzico di; **to get in ~ with** mettersi in contatto con; **to lose ~** (friends) perdersi di vista; **~ on** vt fus (topic) sfiorare, accennare a; **~ up** vt (paint) ritoccare; **~-and-go** adj incerto(a); **~down** n atterraggio; (on sea) ammaraggio; (US: FOOTBALL) meta; **~ed** adj commosso(a); **~ing** adj commovente; **~line** n (SPORT) linea laterale; **~y** adj (person) suscettibile

tough [tʌf] adj duro(a); (resistant) resistente; **~en** vt rinforzare

toupee ['tuːpeɪ] n parrucchino

tour ['tuə*] n viaggio; (also: **package ~**) viaggio organizzato or tutto compreso; (of town, museum) visita; (by artist) tournée f inv ♦ vt visitare; **~ guide** n guida turistica; **~ing** n turismo

tourism ['tuərɪzəm] n turismo

tourist ['tuərɪst] n turista m/f ♦ adv (travel) in classe turistica ♦ cpd turistico(a); **~ office** n pro loco f inv

ournament ['tʊənəmənt] n torneo
ousled ['taʊzld] adj (hair) arruffato(a)
out [taʊt] vi: **to ~ for** procacciare,
raccogliere; cercare clienti per ♦ n (also:
ticket ~) bagarino
ow [taʊ] vt rimorchiare; **"on ~"** (BRIT), **"in
~"** (US) "veicolo rimorchiato"
oward(s) [tə'wɔːd(z)] prep verso; (of
attitude) nei confronti di; (of purpose) per
owel ['taʊəl] n asciugamano; (also: **tea ~**)
strofinaccio; **~ling** n (fabric) spugna; **~ rail**
(US **~ rack**) n portasciugamano
ower ['taʊə*] n torre f; **~ block** (BRIT) n
palazzone m; **~ing** adj altissimo(a),
imponente
own [taʊn] n città f inv; **to go to ~** andare
in città; (fig) mettercela tutta; **~ centre** n
centro (città); **~ council** n consiglio
comunale; **~ hall** n ≈ municipio; **~ plan**
n pianta della città; **~ planning** n
urbanistica
owrope ['təʊrəʊp] n (cavo da) rimorchio
ow truck (US) n carro m attrezzi inv
oxic ['tɒksɪk] adj tossico(a)
oy [tɔɪ] n giocattolo; **~ with** vt fus giocare
con; (idea) accarezzare, trastullarsi con;
~ shop n negozio di giocattoli
race [treɪs] n traccia ♦ vt (draw) tracciare;
(follow) seguire; (locate) rintracciare;
tracing paper n carta da ricalco
rack [træk] n (of person, animal) traccia; (on
tape, SPORT, path: gen) pista; (: of bullet etc)
traiettoria; (: of suspect, animal) pista,
tracce fpl; (RAIL) binario, rotaie fpl ♦ vt
seguire le tracce di; **to keep ~ of** seguire; **~
down** vt (prey) scovare; snidare; (sth lost)
rintracciare; **~suit** n tuta sportiva
ract [trækt] n (GEO) tratto, estensione f
ractor ['træktə*] n trattore m
rade [treɪd] n mestiere m ♦ vi commerciare ♦ vt: **to ~ sth
(for sth)** barattare qc (con qc); **to ~ with/
in** commerciare con/in; **~ in** vt (old car etc)
dare come pagamento parziale; **~ fair** n
fiera commerciale; **~mark** n marchio di
fabbrica; **~ name** n marca, nome m
depositato; **~r** n commerciante m/f;

~sman (irreg) n fornitore m; (shopkeeper)
negoziante m; **~ union** n sindacato; **~
unionist** sindacalista m/f
tradition [trə'dɪʃən] n tradizione f; **~al** adj
tradizionale
traffic ['træfɪk] n traffico ♦ vi: **to ~ in** (pej:
liquor, drugs) trafficare in; **~ circle** (US) n
isola rotatoria; **~ jam** n ingorgo (del
traffico); **~ lights** npl semaforo; **~
warden** n addetto/a al controllo del
traffico e del parcheggio
tragedy ['trædʒədɪ] n tragedia
tragic ['trædʒɪk] adj tragico(a)
trail [treɪl] n (tracks) tracce fpl, pista; (path)
sentiero; (of smoke etc) scia ♦ vt trascinare,
strascicare; (follow) seguire ♦ vi essere al
traino; (dress etc) strusciare; (plant)
arrampicarsi; strisciare; (in game) essere in
svantaggio; **~ behind** vi essere al traino;
~er n (AUT) rimorchio; (US) roulotte f inv;
(CINEMA) prossimamente m inv; **~er truck**
(US) n (articulated lorry) autoarticolato
train [treɪn] n treno; (of dress) coda,
strascico ♦ vt (apprentice, doctor etc)
formare; (sportsman) allenare; (dog)
addestrare; (memory) esercitare; (point: gun
etc): **to ~ sth on** puntare qc contro ♦ vi
formarsi; allenarsi; **one's ~ of thought** il
filo dei propri pensieri; **~ed** adj
qualificato(a); allenato(a); addestrato(a);
~ee [treɪ'niː] n (in trade) apprendista m/f;
~er n (SPORT) allenatore/trice; (: shoe)
scarpa da ginnastica; (of dogs etc)
addestratore/trice; **~ing** n formazione f;
allenamento; addestramento; **in ~ing**
(SPORT) in allenamento; **~ing college** n
istituto professionale; (for teachers)
≈ istituto magistrale; **~ing shoes** npl
scarpe fpl da ginnastica
traipse [treɪt] n tratto
traitor ['treɪtə*] n traditore m
tram [træm] (BRIT) n (also: **~car**) tram m inv
tramp [træmp] n (person) vagabondo/a; (inf:
pej: woman) sgualdrina
trample ['træmpl] vt: **to ~ (underfoot)**
calpestare
trampoline ['træmpəliːn] n trampolino

tranquil ['træŋkwɪl] *adj* tranquillo(a); **~lizer** *n* (MED) tranquillante *m*

transact [træn'zækt] *vt* (business) trattare; **~ion** [-'zækʃən] *n* transazione *f*

transatlantic [trænzət'læntɪk] *adj* transatlantico(a)

transfer [*n* 'trænsfə*, *vb* træns'fə*] *n* (gen, also SPORT) trasferimento *m*; (POL: of power) passaggio; (picture, design) decalcomania; (: stick-on) autoadesivo ♦ *vt* trasferire; passare; **to ~ the charges** (BRIT: TEL) fare una chiamata a carico del destinatario; **~ desk** *n* (AVIAT) banco *m* transiti *inv*

transform [træns'fɔ:m] *vt* trasformare

transfusion [træns'fju:ʒən] *n* trasfusione *f*

transient ['trænzɪənt] *adj* transitorio(a), fugace

transistor [træn'zɪstə*] *n* (ELEC) transistor *m* *inv*; (also: **~ radio**) radio *f* *inv* a transistor

transit ['trænzɪt] *n*: **in ~** in transito

transitive ['trænzɪtɪv] *adj* (LING) transitivo(a)

translate [trænz'leɪt] *vt* tradurre; **translation** [-'leɪʃən] *n* traduzione *f*; **translator** *n* traduttore/trice

transmission [trænz'mɪʃən] *n* trasmissione *f*

transmit [trænz'mɪt] *vt* trasmettere; **~ter** *n* trasmettitore *m*

transparency [træns'pɛərənsɪ] *n* trasparenza; (BRIT: PHOT) diapositiva

transparent [træns'pærnt] *adj* trasparente

transpire [træn'spaɪə*] *vi* (happen) succedere; (turn out): **it ~d that** si venne a sapere che

transplant [*vb* træns'plɑ:nt, *n* 'trænsplɑ:nt] *vt* trapiantare ♦ *n* (MED) trapianto

transport [*n* 'trænspɔ:t, *vb* træns'pɔ:t] *n* trasporto ♦ *vt* trasportare; **~ation** [-'teɪʃən] *n* (mezzo di) trasporto; **~ café** (BRIT) *n* trattoria per camionisti

trap [træp] *n* (snare, trick) trappola; (carriage) calesse *m* ♦ *vt* prendere in trappola, intrappolare; **~ door** *n* botola

trapeze [trə'pi:z] *n* trapezio

trappings ['træpɪŋz] *npl* ornamenti *mpl*; indoratura, sfarzo

trash [træʃ] (pej) *n* (goods) ciarpame *m*; (nonsense) sciocchezze *fpl*; **~ can** (US) *n* secchio della spazzatura

trauma ['trɔ:mə] *n* trauma *m*; **~tic** [-'mætɪk] *adj* traumatico(a)

travel ['trævl] *n* viaggio; viaggi *mpl* ♦ *vi* viaggiare ♦ *vt* (distance) percorrere; **~ agency** *n* agenzia (di) viaggi; **~ agent** *n* agente *m* di viaggio; **~ler** (US **~er**) *n* viaggiatore/trice; **~ler's cheque** (US **~er's check**) *n* assegno turistico; **~ling** (US **~ing**) *n* viaggi *mpl*; **~ sickness** *n* mal *m* d'auto (or di mare or d'aria)

travesty ['trævəstɪ] *n* parodia

trawler ['trɔ:lə*] *n* peschereccio (a strascico)

tray [treɪ] *n* (for carrying) vassoio; (on desk) vaschetta

treacherous ['tretʃərəs] *adj* infido(a)

treachery ['tretʃərɪ] *n* tradimento

treacle ['tri:kl] *n* melassa

tread [tred] (pt **trod**, pp **trodden**) *n* passo; (sound) rumore *m* di passi; (of stairs) pedata; (of tyre) battistrada *m* *inv* ♦ *vi* camminare; **~ on** *vt* *fus* calpestare

treason ['tri:zn] *n* tradimento

treasure ['treʒə*] *n* tesoro ♦ *vt* (value) tenere in gran conto, apprezzare molto; (store) custodire gelosamente

treasurer ['treʒərə*] *n* tesoriere/a

treasury ['treʒərɪ] *n*: **the T~** (BRIT), **the T~ Department** (US) il ministero del Tesoro

treat [tri:t] *n* regalo ♦ *vt* trattare; (MED) curare; **to ~ sb to sth** offrire qc a qn

treatment ['tri:tmənt] *n* trattamento

treaty ['tri:tɪ] *n* patto, trattato

treble ['trebl] *adj* triplo(a), triplice ♦ *vt* triplicare ♦ *vi* triplicarsi; **~ clef** *n* chiave *f* di violino

tree [tri:] *n* albero; **~ trunk** *n* tronco d'albero

trek [trek] *n* escursione *f* a piedi; escursione *f* in macchina; (tiring walk) camminata sfiancante ♦ *vi* (as holiday) fare dell'escursionismo

trellis ['trelɪs] *n* graticcio

tremble ['trembl] *vi* tremare

tremendous [trɪ'mendəs] *adj* (enormous) enorme; (excellent) meraviglioso(a), formidabile

tremor ['tremə*] n tremore m, tremito; (also: **earth ~**) scossa sismica

trench [trentʃ] n trincea

trend [trend] n (tendency) tendenza; (of events) corso; (fashion) moda; **~y** adj (idea) di moda; (clothes) all'ultima moda

trespass ['trespas] vi: **to ~ on** entrare abusivamente in; **"no ~ing"** "proprietà privata", "vietato l'accesso"

trestle ['tresl] n cavalletto

trial ['traɪəl] n (LAW) processo; (test: of machine etc) collaudo; **~s** npl (unpleasant experiences) dure prove fpl; **on ~** (LAW) sotto processo; **by ~ and error** a tentoni; **~ period** periodo di prova

triangle ['traɪæŋgl] n (MATH, MUS) triangolo

tribe [traɪb] n tribù f inv; **~sman** (irreg) n membro di tribù

tribunal [traɪ'bjuːnl] n tribunale m

tributary ['trɪbjutəri] n (river) tributario, affluente m

tribute ['trɪbjuːt] n tributo, omaggio; **to pay ~ to** rendere omaggio a

trick [trɪk] n trucco; (joke) tiro; (CARDS) presa ♦ vt imbrogliare, ingannare; **to play a ~ on sb** giocare un tiro a qn; **that should do the ~** vedrai che funziona; **~ery** n inganno

trickle ['trɪkl] n (of water etc) rivolo; gocciolio ♦ vi gocciolare

tricky ['trɪkɪ] adj difficile, delicato(a)

tricycle ['traɪsɪkl] n triciclo

trifle ['traɪfl] n sciocchezza; (BRIT: CULIN) ≈ zuppa inglese ♦ adv: **a ~ long** un po' lungo; **trifling** adj insignificante

trigger ['trɪgə*] n (of gun) grilletto; **~ off** vt dare l'avvio a

trim [trɪm] adj (house, garden) ben tenuto(a); (figure) snello(a) ♦ n (haircut etc) spuntata, regolata; (embellishment) finiture fpl; (on car) guarnizioni fpl ♦ vt spuntare; (decorate): **to ~ (with)** decorare (con); (NAUT: a sail) orientare; **~mings** npl decorazioni fpl; (extras: gen CULIN) guarnizione f

trinket ['trɪŋkɪt] n gingillo; (piece of jewellery) ciondolo

trip [trɪp] n viaggio; (excursion) gita, escursione f; (stumble) passo falso ♦ vi inciampare; (go lightly) camminare con passo leggero; **on a ~** in viaggio; **~ up** vi inciampare ♦ vt fare lo sgambetto a

tripe [traɪp] n (CULIN) trippa; (pej: rubbish) sciocchezze fpl, fesserie fpl

triple ['trɪpl] adj triplo(a)

triplets ['trɪplɪts] npl bambini(e) trigemini(e)

triplicate ['trɪplɪkət] n: **in ~** in triplice copia

tripod ['traɪpɔd] n treppiede m

trite [traɪt] adj banale, trito(a)

triumph ['traɪʌmf] n trionfo ♦ vi: **to ~ (over)** trionfare (su)

trivia ['trɪvɪə] npl banalità fpl

trivial ['trɪvɪəl] adj insignificante; (commonplace) banale

trod [trɔd] pt of **tread**; **~den** pp of **tread**

trolley ['trɔlɪ] n carrello; **~ bus** n filobus m inv

trombone [trɔm'bəun] n trombone m

troop [truːp] n gruppo; (MIL) squadrone m; **~s** npl (MIL) truppe fpl; **~ in/out** vi entrare/uscire a frotte; **~ing the colour** n (ceremony) sfilata della bandiera

trophy ['trəufɪ] n trofeo

tropic ['trɔpɪk] n tropico; **~al** adj tropicale

trot [trɔt] n trotto ♦ vi trottare; **on the ~** (BRIT: fig) di fila, uno(a) dopo l'altro(a)

trouble ['trʌbl] n difficoltà f inv, problema m; difficoltà fpl, problemi; (worry) preoccupazione f; (bother, effort) sforzo; (POL) conflitti mpl, disordine m; (MED): **stomach etc ~** disturbi mpl gastrici etc ♦ vt disturbare; (worry) preoccupare ♦ vi: **to ~ to do** disturbarsi a fare; **~s** npl (POL etc) disordini mpl; **to be in ~** avere dei problemi; **it's no ~!** di niente!; **what's the ~?** cosa c'è che non va?; **~d** adj (person) preoccupato(a), inquieto(a); (epoch, life) agitato(a), difficile; **~maker** n elemento disturbatore, agitatore/trice; (child) discolo/a; **~shooter** n (in conflict) conciliatore m; **~some** adj fastidioso(a), seccante

trough [trɔf] n (also: **drinking ~**) abbeveratoio; (also: **feeding ~**) trogolo, mangiatoia; (*channel*) canale *m*

trousers ['trauzəz] *npl* pantaloni *mpl*, calzoni *mpl*; **short ~** calzoncini *mpl*

trousseau ['tru:səu] (*pl* **~x** *or* **~s**) *n* corredo da sposa

trousseaux ['tru:səuz] *npl of* **trousseau**

trout [traut] *n inv* trota

trowel ['trauəl] *n* cazzuola

truant ['truənt] (*BRIT*) *n*: **to play ~** marinare la scuola

truce [tru:s] *n* tregua

truck [trʌk] *n* autocarro, camion *m inv*; (*RAIL*) carro merci aperto; (*for luggage*) carrello *m* portabagagli *inv*; ~ **driver** *n* camionista *m/f*; ~ **farm** (*US*) *n* orto industriale

true [tru:] *adj* vero(a); (*accurate*) accurato(a), esatto(a); (*genuine*) reale; (*faithful*) fedele; **to come ~** avverarsi

truffle ['trʌfl] *n* tartufo

truly ['tru:lɪ] *adv* veramente; (*truthfully*) sinceramente; (*faithfully*): **yours ~** (*in letter*) distinti saluti

trump [trʌmp] *n* (*also*: ~ **card**) atout *m inv*

trumpet ['trʌmpɪt] *n* tromba

truncheon ['trʌntʃən] *n* sfollagente *m inv*

trundle ['trʌndl] *vt* far rotolare rumorosamente ♦ *vi*: **to ~ along** rotolare rumorosamente

trunk [trʌŋk] *n* (*of tree, person*) tronco; (*of elephant*) proboscide *f*; (*case*) baule *m*; (*US: AUT*) bagagliaio; ~**s** *npl* (*also*: **swimming ~s**) calzoncini *mpl* da bagno

truss [trʌs] *vt*: ~ (**up**) (*CULIN*) legare

trust [trʌst] *n* fiducia; (*LAW*) amministrazione *f* fiduciaria; (*COMM*) trust *m inv* ♦ *vt* (*rely on*) contare su; (*hope*) sperare; (*entrust*): **to ~ sth to sb** affidare qc a qn; ~**ed** *adj* fidato(a); ~**ee** [trʌs'ti:] *n* (*LAW*) amministratore(trice) fiduciario(a); (*of school etc*) amministratore/trice; ~**ful** *adj* fiducioso(a); ~**ing** *adj* = ~**ful**; ~**worthy** *adj* fidato(a), degno(a) di fiducia

truth [tru:θ, *pl* tru:ðz] *n* verità *f inv*; ~**ful** *adj* (*person*) sincero(a); (*description*) veritiero(a), esatto(a)

try [traɪ] *n* prova, tentativo; (*RUGBY*) meta

♦ *vt* (*LAW*) giudicare; (*test: also*: ~ **out**) provare; (*strain*) mettere alla prova ♦ *vi* provare; **to have a ~** fare un tentativo; **to ~ to do** (*seek*) cercare di fare; ~ **on** *vt* (*clothes*) provare; ~**ing** *adj* (*day, experience*) logorante, pesante; (*child*) difficile, insopportabile

tsar [zɑ:*] *n* zar *m inv*

T-shirt ['ti:-] *n* maglietta

T-square ['ti:-] *n* riga a T

tub [tʌb] *n* tinozza; mastello; (*bath*) bagno

tuba ['tju:bə] *n* tuba

tubby ['tʌbɪ] *adj* grassoccio(a)

tube [tju:b] *n* tubo; (*BRIT: underground*) metropolitana, metrò *m inv*; (*for tyre*) camera d'aria; ~ **station** (*BRIT*) *n* stazione *f* della metropolitana

tubular ['tju:bjulə*] *adj* tubolare

TUC (*BRIT*) *n abbr* (= *Trades Union Congress*) confederazione *f* dei sindacati britannici

tuck [tʌk] *vt* (*put*) mettere; ~ **away** *vt* riporre; (*building*): **to be ~ed away** essere in un luogo isolato; ~ **in** *vt* mettere dentro; (*child*) rimboccare ♦ *vi* (*eat*) mangiare di buon appetito; abbuffarsi; ~ **up** *vt* (*child*) rimboccare le coperte a; ~ **shop** *n* negozio di pasticceria (*in una scuola*)

Tuesday ['tju:zdɪ] *n* martedì *m inv*

tuft [tʌft] *n* ciuffo

tug [tʌg] *n* (*ship*) rimorchiatore *m* ♦ *vt* tirare con forza; ~-**of-war** *n* tiro alla fune

tuition [tju:'ɪʃən] *n* (*BRIT*) lezioni *fpl*; (: *private* ~) lezioni *fpl* private; (*US: school fees*) tasse *fpl* scolastiche

tulip ['tju:lɪp] *n* tulipano

tumble ['tʌmbl] *n* (*fall*) capitombolo ♦ *vi* capitombolare, ruzzolare; **to ~ to sth** (*inf*) realizzare qc; ~**down** *adj* cadente, diroccato(a); ~ **dryer** (*BRIT*) *n* asciugatrice *f*

tumbler ['tʌmblə*] *n* bicchiere *m* (senza stelo)

tummy ['tʌmɪ] (*inf*) *n* pancia; ~ **upset** *n* mal *m* di pancia

tumour ['tju:mə*] (*US* **tumor**) *n* tumore *m*

tuna ['tjuːnə] *n inv* (*also:* ~ **fish**) tonno
tune [tjuːn] *n* (*melody*) melodia, aria ♦ *vt*
(*MUS*) accordare; (*RADIO, TV, AUT*) regolare,
mettere a punto; **to be in/out of** ~
(*instrument*) essere accordato(a)/
scordato(a); (*singer*) essere intonato(a)/
stonato(a); ~ **in** *vi*: **to** ~ **in (to)** (*RADIO, TV*)
sintonizzarsi (su); ~ **up** *vi* (*musician*)
accordare lo strumento; ~**ful** *adj*
melodioso(a); ~**r** *n*: **piano** ~**r** accordatore
m
tunic ['tjuːnɪk] *n* tunica
Tunisia [tjuːˈnɪzɪə] *n* Tunisia
tunnel ['tʌnl] *n* galleria ♦ *vi* scavare una
galleria
turban ['təːbən] *n* turbante *m*
turbulence ['təːbjuləns] *n* (*AVIAT*)
turbolenza
tureen [təˈriːn] *n* zuppiera
turf [təːf] *n* terreno erboso; (*clod*) zolla ♦ *vt*
coprire di zolle erbose; ~ **out** (*inf*) *vt*
buttar fuori
Turin [tjuəˈrɪn] *n* Torino *f*
Turk [təːk] *n* turco/a
Turkey ['təːkɪ] *n* Turchia
turkey ['təːkɪ] *n* tacchino
Turkish ['təːkɪʃ] *adj* turco(a) ♦ *n* (*LING*)
turco
turmoil ['təːmɔɪl] *n* confusione *f*, tumulto
turn [təːn] *n* giro; (*change*) cambiamento;
(*in road*) curva; (*tendency: of mind, events*)
tendenza; (*performance*) numero; (*chance*)
turno; (*MED*) crisi *f* inv, attacco ♦ *vt* girare,
voltare; (*change*): **to** ~ **sth into** trasformare
qc in ♦ *vi* girare; (*person: look back*) girarsi,
voltarsi; (*reverse direction*) girare; (*change*)
cambiare; (*milk*) andare a male; (*become*)
diventare; **a good** ~ un buon servizio; **it**
gave me quite a ~ mi ha fatto prendere
un bello spavento; **"no left** ~**"** (*AUT*)
"divieto di svolta a sinistra"; **it's your** ~
tocca a lei; **in** ~ a sua volta; a turno; **to**
take ~**s (at sth)** fare (qc) a turno; ~ **away**
vi girarsi (dall'altra parte) ♦ *vt* mandare via;
~ **back** *vi* ritornare, tornare indietro ♦ *vt*
far tornare indietro; (*clock*) spostare
indietro; ~ **down** *vt* (*refuse*) rifiutare;

(*reduce*) abbassare; (*fold*) ripiegare; ~ **in** *vi*
(*inf: go to bed*) andare a letto ♦ *vt* (*fold*)
voltare in dentro; ~ **off** *vi* (*from road*)
girare, voltare ♦ *vt* (*light, radio, engine etc*)
spegnere; ~ **on** *vt* (*light, radio etc*)
accendere; ~ **out** *vt* (*light, gas*) chiudere;
spegnere ♦ *vt* (*voters*) presentarsi; **to** ~ **out**
to be ... rivelarsi ..., risultare ...; ~ **over** *vi*
(*person*) girarsi ♦ *vt* girare; ~ **round** *vi*
girare; (*person*) girarsi ♦ *vt* girare; ~ **up** *vi* (*person*)
arrivare, presentarsi; (*lost object*) saltar fuori
♦ *vt* (*collar, sound*) alzare; ~**ing** *n* (*in road*)
curva; ~**ing point** *n* (*fig*) svolta decisiva
turnip ['təːnɪp] *n* rapa
turnout ['təːnaut] *n* presenza, affluenza
turnover ['təːnəuvə*] *n* (*COMM*) turnover *m*
inv; (*CULIN*): **apple** *etc* ~ sfogliatella alle
melle ecc
turnpike ['təːnpaɪk] (*US*) *n* autostrada a
pedaggio
turnstile ['təːnstaɪl] *n* tornella
turntable ['təːnteɪbl] *n* (*on record player*)
piatto
turn-up (*BRIT*) *n* (*on trousers*) risvolto
turpentine ['təːpəntaɪn] *n* (*also:* **turps**)
acqua ragia
turquoise ['təːkwɔɪz] *n* turchese *m* ♦ *adj*
turchese
turret ['tʌrɪt] *n* torretta
turtle ['təːtl] *n* testuggine *f*; ~**neck**
(sweater) *n* maglione *m* con il collo alto
Tuscany ['tʌskənɪ] *n* Toscana
tusk [tʌsk] *n* zanna
tutor ['tjuːtə*] *n* (*in college*) docente *m/f*
(*responsabile di un gruppo di studenti*);
(*private teacher*) precettore *m*; ~**ial** [-'tɔːrɪəl]
n (*SCOL*) lezione *f* con discussione (*a un
gruppo limitato*)
tuxedo [tʌkˈsiːdəu] (*US*) *n* smoking *m inv*
TV [tiːˈviː] *n abbr* (= *television*) tivù *f inv*
twang [twæŋ] *n* (*of instrument*) suono
vibrante; (*of voice*) accento nasale
tweed [twiːd] *n* tweed *m inv*
tweezers ['twiːzəz] *npl* pinzette *fpl*
twelfth [twelfθ] *num* dodicesimo(a)
twelve [twelv] *num* dodici; **at** ~ **(o'clock)**
alle dodici, a mezzogiorno; (*midnight*) a

mezzanotte

twentieth ['twɛntɪɪθ] *num* ventesimo(a)

twenty ['twɛntɪ] *num* venti

twice [twaɪs] *adv* due volte; **~ as much** due volte tanto; **~ a week** due volte alla settimana

twiddle ['twɪdl] *vt, vi*: **to ~ (with) sth** giocherellare con qc; **to ~ one's thumbs** (*fig*) girarsi i pollici

twig [twɪg] *n* ramoscello ♦ *vt, vi* (*inf*) capire

twilight ['twaɪlaɪt] *n* crepuscolo

twin [twɪn] *adj, n* gemello(a) ♦ *vt*: **to ~ one town with another** fare il gemellaggio di una città con un'altra; **~-bedded room** *n* stanza con letti gemelli; **~ beds** *npl* letti *mpl* gemelli

twine [twaɪn] *n* spago, cordicella ♦ *vi* attorcigliarsi

twinge [twɪndʒ] *n* (*of pain*) fitta; **a ~ of conscience/regret** un rimorso/rimpianto

twinkle ['twɪŋkl] *vi* scintillare; (*eyes*) brillare

twirl [twəːl] *vt* far roteare ♦ *vi* roteare

twist [twɪst] *n* torsione *f*; (*in wire, flex*) piega; (*in road*) curva; (*in story*) colpo di scena ♦ *vt* attorcigliare; (*ankle*) slogare; (*weave*) intrecciare; (*roll around*) arrotolare; (*fig*) distorcere ♦ *vi* (*road*) serpeggiare

twit [twɪt] (*inf*) *n* cretino(a)

twitch [twɪtʃ] *n* tiratina; (*nervous*) tic *m inv* ♦ *vi* contrarsi

two [tuː] *num* due; **to put ~ and ~ together** (*fig*) fare uno più uno; **~-door** *adj* (*AUT*) a due porte; **~-faced** (*pej*) *adj* (*person*) falso(a); **~fold** *adv*: **to increase ~fold** aumentare del doppio; **~-piece (suit)** *n* due pezzi *m inv*; **~-piece (swimsuit)** *n* (costume *m* da bagno a) due pezzi *m inv*; **~some** *n* (*people*) coppia; **~-way** *adj* (*traffic*) a due sensi

tycoon [taɪ'kuːn] *n*: **(business) ~** magnate *m*

type [taɪp] *n* (*category*) genere *m*; (*model*) modello; (*example*) tipo; (*TYP*) tipo, carattere *m* ♦ *vt* (*letter etc*) battere (a macchina), dattilografare; **~-cast** *adj* (*actor*) a ruolo fisso; **~face** *n* carattere *m* tipografico; **~script** *n* dattiloscritto;

~writer *n* macchina da scrivere; **~written** *adj* dattiloscritto(a), battuto(a) a macchina

typhoid ['taɪfɔɪd] *n* tifoidea

typhoon [taɪ'fuːn] *n* tifone *m*

typical ['tɪpɪkl] *adj* tipico(a)

typify ['tɪpɪfaɪ] *vt* caratterizzare; (*person*) impersonare

typing ['taɪpɪŋ] *n* dattilografia

typist ['taɪpɪst] *n* dattilografo/a

tyrant ['taɪərnt] *n* tiranno

tyre ['taɪə*] (*US* **tire**) *n* pneumatico, gomma; **~ pressure** *n* pressione *f* (delle gomme)

tzar [zɑː*] *n* = **tsar**

U, u

U-bend ['juː'-] *n* (*in pipe*) sifone *m*

ubiquitous [juː'bɪkwɪtəs] *adj* onnipresente

udder ['ʌdə*] *n* mammella

UFO ['juːfəu] *n abbr* (= *unidentified flying object*) UFO *m inv*

ugh [əːh] *excl* puah!

ugly ['ʌglɪ] *adj* brutto(a)

UHT *abbr* (= *ultra heat treated*) UHT *inv*, a lunga conservazione

UK *n abbr* = **United Kingdom**

ulcer ['ʌlsə*] *n* ulcera; (*also*: **mouth ~**) afta

Ulster ['ʌlstə*] *n* Ulster *m*

ulterior [ʌl'tɪərɪə*] *adj* ulteriore; **~ motive** *n* secondo fine *m*

ultimate ['ʌltɪmət] *adj* ultimo(a), finale; (*authority*) massimo(a), supremo(a); **~ly** *adv* alla fine; in definitiva, in fin dei conti

ultrasound [ʌltrə'saund] *n* (*MED*) ultrasuono

umbilical cord [ʌmbɪ'laɪkl-] *n* cordone *m* ombelicale

umbrella [ʌm'brɛlə] *n* ombrello

umpire ['ʌmpaɪə*] *n* arbitro

umpteen [ʌmp'tiːn] *adj* non so quanti(e); **for the ~th time** per l'ennesima volta

UN *n abbr* (= *United Nations*) ONU *f*

unable [ʌn'eɪbl] *adj*: **to be ~ to** non potere, essere nell'impossibilità di; essere incapace di

unaccompanied [ʌnə'kʌmpənɪd] *adj* (*child, lady*) non accompagnato(a)

unaccustomed [ʌnəˈkʌstəmd] *adj*: **to be ~ to sth** non essere abituato a qc

unanimous [juːˈnænɪməs] *adj* unanime; **~ly** *adv* all'unanimità

unarmed [ʌnˈɑːmd] *adj* (*without a weapon*) disarmato(a); (*combat*) senz'armi

unattached [ʌnəˈtætʃt] *adj* senza legami, libero(a)

unattended [ʌnəˈtɛndɪd] *adj* (*car, child, luggage*) incustodito(a)

unattractive [ʌnəˈtræktɪv] *adj* poco attraente

unauthorized [ʌnˈɔːθəraɪzd] *adj* non autorizzato(a)

unavoidable [ʌnəˈvɔɪdəbl] *adj* inevitabile

unaware [ʌnəˈwɛə*] *adj*: **to be ~ of** non sapere, ignorare; **~s** *adv* di sorpresa, alla sprovvista

unbalanced [ʌnˈbælənst] *adj* squilibrato(a)

unbearable [ʌnˈbɛərəbl] *adj* insopportabile

unbeknown(st) [ʌnbɪˈnəun(st)] *adv*: **~ to** all'insaputa di

unbelievable [ʌnbɪˈliːvəbl] *adj* incredibile

unbend [ʌnˈbɛnd] (*irreg: like* **bend**) *vi* distendersi ♦ *vt* (*wire*) raddrizzare

unbias(s)ed [ʌnˈbaɪəst] *adj* (*person, report*) obiettivo(a), imparziale

unborn [ʌnˈbɔːn] *adj* non ancora nato(a)

unbreakable [ʌnˈbreɪkəbl] *adj* infrangibile

unbroken [ʌnˈbrəukən] *adj* intero(a); (*series*) continuo(a); (*record*) imbattuto(a)

unbutton [ʌnˈbʌtn] *vt* sbottonare

uncalled-for [ʌnˈkɔːld-] *adj* (*remark*) fuori luogo *inv*; (*action*) ingiustificato(a)

uncanny [ʌnˈkænɪ] *adj* misterioso(a), strano(a)

unceasing [ʌnˈsiːsɪŋ] *adj* incessante

unceremonious [ˈʌnsɛrɪˈməunɪəs] *adj* (*abrupt, rude*) senza tante cerimonie

uncertain [ʌnˈsəːtn] *adj* incerto(a); dubbio(a); **~ty** *n* incertezza

unchanged [ʌnˈtʃeɪndʒd] *adj* invariato(a)

uncivilized [ʌnˈsɪvɪlaɪzd] *adj* (*gen*) selvaggio(a); (*fig*) incivile, barbaro(a)

uncle [ˈʌŋkl] *n* zio

uncomfortable [ʌnˈkʌmfətəbl] *adj* scomodo(a); (*uneasy*) a disagio, agitato(a);

(*unpleasant*) fastidioso(a)

uncommon [ʌnˈkɔmən] *adj* raro(a), insolito(a), non comune

uncompromising [ʌnˈkɔmprəmaizɪŋ] *adj* intransigente, inflessibile

unconcerned [ʌnkənˈsəːnd] *adj*: **to be ~ (about)** non preoccuparsi (di *or* per)

unconditional [ʌnkənˈdɪʃənl] *adj* incondizionato(a), senza condizioni

unconscious [ʌnˈkɔnʃəs] *adj* privo(a) di sensi, svenuto(a); (*unaware*) inconsapevole, inconscio(a) ♦ *n*: **the ~** l'inconscio; **~ly** *adv* inconsciamente

uncontrollable [ʌnkənˈtrəuləbl] *adj* incontrollabile; indisciplinato(a)

unconventional [ʌnkənˈvɛnʃənl] *adj* poco convenzionale

uncouth [ʌnˈkuːθ] *adj* maleducato(a), grossolano(a)

uncover [ʌnˈkʌvə*] *vt* scoprire

undecided [ʌndɪˈsaɪdɪd] *adj* indeciso(a)

under [ˈʌndə*] *prep* sotto; (*less than*) meno di; al disotto di; (*according to*) secondo, in conformità a ♦ *adv* (al) disotto; **~ there** là sotto; **~ repair** in riparazione

under... [ˈʌndə*] *prefix* sotto..., sub...; **~-age** *adj* minorenne; **~carriage** (*BRIT*) *n* carrello (d'atterraggio); **~charge** *vt* far pagare di meno a; **~clothes** *npl* biancheria (intima); **~coat** *n* (*paint*) mano *f* di fondo; **~cover** *adj* segreto(a), clandestino(a); **~current** *n* corrente *f* sottomarina; **~cut** *vt irreg* vendere a prezzo minore di; **~developed** *adj* sottosviluppato(a); **~dog** *n* oppresso/a; **~done** *adj* (*CULIN*) al sangue; (*pej*) poco cotto(a); **~estimate** *vt* sottovalutare; **~fed** *adj* denutrito(a); **~foot** *adv* sotto i piedi; **~go** *vt irreg* subire; (*treatment*) sottoporsi a; **~graduate** *n* studente(essa) universitario(a); **~ground** *n* (*BRIT: railway*) metropolitana; (*POL*) movimento clandestino ♦ *adj* sotterraneo(a); (*fig*) clandestino(a) ♦ *adv* sottoterra; **to go ~ground** (*fig*) darsi alla macchia; **~growth** *n* sottobosco; **~hand(ed)** *adj* (*fig*) furtivo(a), subdolo(a); **~lie** *vt irreg* essere alla base di; **~line** *vt* sottolineare; **~mine** *vt* minare; **~neath** [ʌndə'niːθ] *adv* sotto, disotto ♦ *prep* sotto, al di sotto di; **~paid** *adj* sottopagato(a); **~pants** *npl* mutande *fpl*, slip *m inv*; **~pass** (*BRIT*) *n* sottopassaggio; **~privileged** *adj* non abbiente; meno favorito(a); **~rate** *vt* sottovalutare; **~shirt** (*US*) *n* maglietta; **~shorts** (*US*) *npl* mutande *fpl*, slip *m inv*; **~side** *n* disotto; **~skirt** (*BRIT*) *n* sottoveste *f*

understand [ʌndə'stænd] (*irreg: like* **stand**) *vt*, *vi* capire, comprendere; **I ~ that ...** sento che ...; credo di capire che ...; **~able** *adj* comprensibile; **~ing** *adj* comprensivo(a) ♦ *n* comprensione *f*; (*agreement*) accordo

understatement [ʌndə'steɪtmənt] *n*: **that's an ~!** a dire poco!

understood [ʌndə'stud] *pt*, *pp of* **understand** ♦ *adj* inteso(a); (*implied*) sottinteso(a)

understudy ['ʌndəstʌdɪ] *n* sostituto/a, attore/trice supplente

undertake [ʌndə'teɪk] (*irreg: like* **take**) *vt* intraprendere; **to ~ to do sth** impegnarsi a fare qc

undertaker ['ʌndəteɪkə*] *n* impresario di pompe funebri

undertaking [ʌndə'teɪkɪŋ] *n* impresa; (*promise*) promessa

undertone ['ʌndətəun] *n*: **in an ~** a mezza voce, a voce bassa

underwater [ʌndə'wɔːtə*] *adv* sott'acqua ♦ *adj* subacqueo(a)

underwear ['ʌndəwɛə*] *n* biancheria (intima)

underworld ['ʌndəwəːld] *n* (*of crime*) malavita

underwriter ['ʌndəraɪtə*] *n* (*INSURANCE*) sottoscrittore/trice

undesirable [ʌndɪ'zaɪərəbl] *adj* sgradevole

undies ['ʌndɪz] (*inf*) *npl* biancheria intima da donna

undo [ʌn'duː] *vt irreg* disfare; **~ing** *n* rovina, perdita

undoubted [ʌn'dautɪd] *adj* sicuro(a),

certo(a); **~ly** *adv* senza alcun dubbio

undress [ʌn'drɛs] *vi* spogliarsi

undue [ʌn'djuː] *adj* eccessivo(a)

undulating ['ʌndjuleɪtɪŋ] *adj* ondeggiante; ondulato(a)

unduly [ʌn'djuːlɪ] *adv* eccessivamente

unearth [ʌn'əːθ] *vt* dissotterrare; (*fig*) scoprire

unearthly [ʌn'əːθlɪ] *adj* (*hour*) impossibile

uneasy [ʌn'iːzɪ] *adj* a disagio; (*worried*) preoccupato(a); (*peace*) precario(a)

uneconomic(al) ['ʌniːkə'nɔmɪk(l)] *adj* antieconomico(a)

unemployed [ʌnɪm'plɔɪd] *adj* disoccupato(a) ♦ *npl*: **the ~** i disoccupati

unemployment [ʌnɪm'plɔɪmənt] *n* disoccupazione *f*

unending [ʌn'endɪŋ] *adj* senza fine

unerring [ʌn'əːrɪŋ] *adj* infallibile

uneven [ʌn'iːvn] *adj* ineguale; irregolare

unexpected [ʌnɪk'spektɪd] *adj* inatteso(a), imprevisto(a); **~ly** *adv* inaspettatamente

unfailing [ʌn'feɪlɪŋ] *adj* (*supply, energy*) inesauribile; (*remedy*) infallibile

unfair [ʌn'fɛə*] *adj*: **~ (to)** ingiusto(a) (nei confronti di)

unfaithful [ʌn'feɪθful] *adj* infedele

unfamiliar [ʌnfə'mɪlɪə*] *adj* sconosciuto(a), strano(a); **to be ~ with** non avere familiarità con

unfashionable [ʌn'fæʃnəbl] *adj* (*clothes*) fuori moda; (*district*) non alla moda

unfasten [ʌn'fɑːsn] *vt* slacciare; sciogliere

unfavourable [ʌn'feɪvərəbl] (*US* **unfavorable**) *adj* sfavorevole

unfeeling [ʌn'fiːlɪŋ] *adj* insensibile, duro(a)

unfinished [ʌn'fɪnɪʃt] *adj* incompleto(a)

unfit [ʌn'fɪt] *adj* (*ill*) malato(a), in cattiva salute; (*incompetent*): **~ (for)** incompetente (in); (*: work, MIL*) inabile (a)

unfold [ʌn'fəuld] *vt* spiegare ♦ *vi* (*story, plot*) svelarsi

unforeseen ['ʌnfɔː'siːn] *adj* imprevisto(a)

unforgettable [ʌnfə'getəbl] *adj* indimenticabile

unfortunate [ʌn'fɔːtʃnət] *adj* sfortunato(a); (*event, remark*) infelice; **~ly** *adv* sfortunatamente, purtroppo

unfounded [ʌnˈfaʊndɪd] *adj* infondato(a)

unfriendly [ʌnˈfrɛndlɪ] *adj* poco amichevole, freddo(a)

ungainly [ʌnˈgeɪnlɪ] *adj* goffo(a), impacciato(a)

ungodly [ʌnˈgɒdlɪ] *adj*: **at an ~ hour** a un'ora impossibile

ungrateful [ʌnˈgreɪtful] *adj* ingrato(a)

unhappiness [ʌnˈhæpɪnɪs] *n* infelicità

unhappy [ʌnˈhæpɪ] *adj* infelice; **~ about/ with** (*arrangements etc*) insoddisfatto(a) di

unharmed [ʌnˈhɑːmd] *adj* incolume, sano(a) e salvo(a)

unhealthy [ʌnˈhɛlθɪ] *adj* (*gen*) malsano(a); (*person*) malaticcio(a)

unheard-of [ʌnˈhəːdɒv] *adj* inaudito(a), senza precedenti

unhurt [ʌnˈhəːt] *adj* illeso(a)

uniform [ˈjuːnɪfɔːm] *n* uniforme *f*, divisa ♦ *adj* uniforme

uninhabited [ʌnɪnˈhæbɪtɪd] *adj* disabitato(a)

unintentional [ʌnɪnˈtɛnʃənəl] *adj* involontario(a)

union [ˈjuːnjən] *n* unione *f*; (*also*: **trade ~**) sindacato ♦ *cpd* sindacale, dei sindacati; **U~ Jack** *n bandiera nazionale britannica*

unique [juːˈniːk] *adj* unico(a)

unit [ˈjuːnɪt] *n* unità *f inv*; (*section: of furniture etc*) elemento; (*team, squad*) reparto, squadra

unite [juːˈnaɪt] *vt* unire ♦ *vi* unirsi; **~d** *adj* unito(a); unificato(a); (*efforts*) congiunto(a); **U~d Kingdom** *n* Regno Unito; **U~d Nations (Organization)** *n* (Organizzazione *f* delle) Nazioni Unite; **U~d States (of America)** *n* Stati *mpl* Uniti (d'America)

unit trust (*BRIT*) *n* fondo d'investimento

unity [ˈjuːnɪtɪ] *n* unità

universal [juːnɪˈvəːsl] *adj* universale

universe [ˈjuːnɪvəːs] *n* universo

university [juːnɪˈvəːsɪtɪ] *n* università *f inv*

unjust [ʌnˈdʒʌst] *adj* ingiusto(a)

unkempt [ʌnˈkɛmpt] *adj* trasandato(a); spettinato(a)

unkind [ʌnˈkaɪnd] *adj* scortese; crudele

unknown [ʌnˈnəʊn] *adj* sconosciuto(a)

unlawful [ʌnˈlɔːful] *adj* illecito(a), illegale

unleaded [ʌnˈlɛdɪd] *adj* (*petrol, fuel*) verde, senza piombo

unleash [ʌnˈliːʃ] *vt* (*fig*) scatenare

unless [ʌnˈlɛs] *conj* a meno che (non) +*sub*

unlike [ʌnˈlaɪk] *adj* diverso(a) ♦ *prep* a differenza di, contrariamente a

unlikely [ʌnˈlaɪklɪ] *adj* improbabile

unlisted [ʌnˈlɪstɪd] (*US*) *adj* (*TEL*): **to be ~** non essere sull'elenco

unload [ʌnˈləʊd] *vt* scaricare

unlock [ʌnˈlɒk] *vt* aprire

unlucky [ʌnˈlʌkɪ] *adj* sfortunato(a); (*object, number*) che porta sfortuna

unmarried [ʌnˈmærɪd] *adj* non sposato(a); (*man only*) scapolo, celibe; (*woman only*) nubile

unmistak(e)able [ʌnmɪsˈteɪkəbl] *adj* inconfondibile

unmitigated [ʌnˈmɪtɪgeɪtɪd] *adj* non mitigato(a), assoluto(a), vero(a) e proprio(a)

unnatural [ʌnˈnætʃrəl] *adj* innaturale; contro natura

unnecessary [ʌnˈnɛsəsərɪ] *adj* inutile, superfluo(a)

unnoticed [ʌnˈnəʊtɪst] *adj*: **(to go) ~** (passare) inosservato(a)

UNO [ˈjuːnəʊ] *n abbr* (= *United Nations Organization*) ONU *f*

unobtainable [ʌnəbˈteɪnəbl] *adj* (*TEL*) non ottenibile

unobtrusive [ʌnəbˈtruːsɪv] *adj* discreto(a)

unofficial [ʌnəˈfɪʃl] *adj* non ufficiale; (*strike*) non dichiarato(a) dal sindacato

unpack [ʌnˈpæk] *vi* disfare la valigia (*or* le valigie) ♦ *vt* disfare

unpalatable [ʌnˈpælətəbl] *adj* sgradevole

unparalleled [ʌnˈpærəlɛld] *adj* incomparabile, impareggiabile

unpleasant [ʌnˈplɛznt] *adj* spiacevole

unplug [ʌnˈplʌg] *vt* staccare

unpopular [ʌnˈpɒpjələ*] *adj* impopolare

unprecedented [ʌnˈprɛsɪdəntɪd] *adj* senza precedenti

unpredictable [ˌʌnprɪˈdɪktəbl] *adj*
imprevedibile

unprofessional [ˌʌnprəˈfeʃənl] *adj* poco
professionale

unqualified [ʌnˈkwɒlɪfaɪd] *adj* (*teacher*) non
abilitato(a); (*success*) assoluto(a), senza
riserve

unquestionably [ʌnˈkwestʃənəblɪ] *adv*
indiscutibilmente

unravel [ʌnˈrævl] *vt* dipanare, districare

unreal [ʌnˈrɪəl] *adj* irreale

unrealistic [ˌʌnrɪəˈlɪstɪk] *adj* non realistico(a)

unreasonable [ʌnˈriːznəbl] *adj*
irragionevole

unrelated [ˌʌnrɪˈleɪtɪd] *adj*: **~ (to)** senza
rapporto (con); non imparentato(a) (con)

unreliable [ˌʌnrɪˈlaɪəbl] *adj* (*person,
machine*) che non dà affidamento; (*news,
source of information*) inattendibile

unremitting [ˌʌnrɪˈmɪtɪŋ] *adj* incessante

unreservedly [ˌʌnrɪˈzɜːvɪdlɪ] *adv* senza
riserve

unrest [ʌnˈrest] *n* agitazione *f*

unroll [ʌnˈrəʊl] *vt* srotolare

unruly [ʌnˈruːlɪ] *adj* indisciplinato(a)

unsafe [ʌnˈseɪf] *adj* pericoloso(a),
rischioso(a)

unsaid [ʌnˈsed] *adj*: **to leave sth ~** passare
qc sotto silenzio

unsatisfactory [ˈʌnsætɪsˈfæktərɪ] *adj* che
lascia a desiderare, insufficiente

unsavoury [ʌnˈseɪvərɪ] (*US* **unsavory**) *adj*
(*fig: person, place*) losco(a)

unscathed [ʌnˈskeɪðd] *adj* incolume

unscrew [ʌnˈskruː] *vt* svitare

unscrupulous [ʌnˈskruːpjʊləs] *adj* senza
scrupoli

unsettled [ʌnˈsetld] *adj* (*person*) turbato(a);
indeciso(a); (*weather*) instabile

unshaven [ʌnˈʃeɪvn] *adj* non rasato(a)

unsightly [ʌnˈsaɪtlɪ] *adj* brutto(a),
sgradevole a vedersi

unskilled [ʌnˈskɪld] *adj* non specializzato(a)

unspeakable [ʌnˈspiːkəbl] *adj*
(*indescribable*) indicibile; (*awful*)
abominevole

unstable [ʌnˈsteɪbl] *adj* (*gen*) instabile;

(*mentally*) squilibrato(a)

unsteady [ʌnˈstedɪ] *adj* instabile,
malsicuro(a)

unstuck [ʌnˈstʌk] *adj*: **to come ~** scollarsi;
(*fig*) fare fiasco

unsuccessful [ˌʌnsəkˈsesful] *adj* (*writer,
proposal*) che non ha successo; (*marriage,
attempt*) mal riuscito(a), fallito(a); **to be ~**
(*in attempting sth*) non avere successo

unsuitable [ʌnˈsuːtəbl] *adj* inadatto(a);
inopportuno(a); sconveniente

unsure [ʌnˈʃʊə*] *adj* incerto(a); **to be ~ of
o.s.** essere insicuro(a)

unsuspecting [ˌʌnsəˈspektɪŋ] *adj* che non
sospetta nulla

unsympathetic [ˌʌnsɪmpəˈθetɪk] *adj*
(*person*) antipatico(a); (*attitude*) poco
incoraggiante

untapped [ʌnˈtæpt] *adj* (*resources*) non
sfruttato(a)

unthinkable [ʌnˈθɪŋkəbl] *adj* impensabile,
inconcepibile

untidy [ʌnˈtaɪdɪ] *adj* (*room*) in disordine;
(*appearance*) trascurato(a); (*person*)
disordinato(a)

untie [ʌnˈtaɪ] *vt* (*knot, parcel*) disfare;
(*prisoner, dog*) slegare

until [ʌnˈtɪl] *prep* fino a; (*after negative*)
prima di ♦ *conj* finché, fino a quando; (*in
past, after negative*) prima che +*sub*, prima
di +*infinitive*; **~ he comes** finché *or* fino a
quando non arriva; **~ now** finora; **~ then**
fino ad allora

untimely [ʌnˈtaɪmlɪ] *adj* intempestivo(a),
inopportuno(a); (*death*) prematuro(a)

untold [ʌnˈtəʊld] *adj* (*story*) mai rivelato(a);
(*wealth*) incalcolabile; (*joy, suffering*)
indescrivibile

untoward [ˌʌntəˈwɔːd] *adj* sfortunato(a),
sconveniente

unused [ʌnˈjuːzd] *adj* nuovo(a)

unusual [ʌnˈjuːʒʊəl] *adj* insolito(a),
eccezionale, raro(a)

unveil [ʌnˈveɪl] *vt* scoprire; svelare

unwanted [ʌnˈwɒntɪd] *adj* (*clothing*)
smesso(a); (*child*) non desiderato(a)

unwavering [ʌnˈweɪvərɪŋ] *adj* fermo(a),

incrollabile

unwelcome [ʌn'wɛlkəm] *adj* non gradito(a)

unwell [ʌn'wɛl] *adj* indisposto(a); **to feel ~** non sentirsi bene

unwieldy [ʌn'wiːldɪ] *adj* poco maneggevole

unwilling [ʌn'wɪlɪŋ] *adj*: **to be ~ to do** non voler fare; **~ly** *adv* malvolentieri

unwind [ʌn'waɪnd] (*irreg: like* **wind¹**) *vt* svolgere, srotolare ♦ *vi* (*relax*) rilassarsi

unwise [ʌn'waɪz] *adj* poco saggio(a)

unwitting [ʌn'wɪtɪŋ] *adj* involontario(a)

unworkable [ʌn'wəːkəbl] *adj* (*plan*) inattuabile

unworthy [ʌn'wəːðɪ] *adj* indegno(a)

unwrap [ʌn'ræp] *vt* disfare; aprire

unwritten [ʌn'rɪtn] *adj* (*agreement*) tacito(a); (*law*) non scritto(a)

KEYWORD

up [ʌp] *prep*: **he went ~ the stairs/the hill** è salito su per le scale/sulla collina; **the cat was ~ a tree** il gatto era su un albero; **they live further ~ the street** vivono un po' più su nella stessa strada
♦ *adv* **1** (*upwards, higher*) su, in alto; **~ in the sky/the mountains** su nel cielo/in montagna; **~ there** lassù; **~ above** su in alto
2: **to be ~** (*out of bed*) essere alzato(a); (*prices, level*) essere salito(a)
3: **~ to** (*as far as*) fino a; **~ to now** finora
4: **to be ~** (*depending on*): **it's ~ to you** sta a lei, dipende da lei; (*equal to*): **he's not ~ to it** (*job, task etc*) non ne è all'altezza; (*inf: be doing*): **what is he ~ to?** cosa sta combinando?
♦ *n*: **~s and downs** alti e bassi *mpl*

---

upbringing ['ʌpbrɪŋɪŋ] *n* educazione *f*

update [ʌp'deɪt] *vt* aggiornare

upgrade [ʌp'greɪd] *vt* (*house, job*) migliorare; (*employee*) avanzare di grado

upheaval [ʌp'hiːvl] *n* sconvolgimento; tumulto

uphill [ʌp'hɪl] *adj* in salita; (*fig: task*) difficile ♦ *adv*: **to go ~** andare in salita, salire

uphold [ʌp'həuld] (*irreg: like* **hold**) *vt* approvare; sostenere

upholstery [ʌp'həulstərɪ] *n* tappezzeria

upkeep ['ʌpkiːp] *n* manutenzione *f*

upon [ə'pɔn] *prep* su

upper ['ʌpə*] *adj* superiore ♦ *n* (*of shoe*) tomaia; **~-class** *adj* dell'alta borghesia; **~ hand** *n*: **to have the ~ hand** avere il coltello dalla parte del manico; **~most** *adj* il(la) più alto(a); predominante

upright ['ʌpraɪt] *adj* diritto(a); verticale; (*fig*) diritto(a), onesto(a)

uprising ['ʌpraɪzɪŋ] *n* insurrezione *f*, rivolta

uproar ['ʌprɔː*] *n* tumulto, clamore *m*

uproot [ʌp'ruːt] *vt* sradicare

upset [*n* 'ʌpsɛt, *vb, adj* ʌp'sɛt] (*irreg: like* **set**) *n* (*to plan etc*) contrattempo; (*stomach ~*) disturbo ♦ *vt* (*glass etc*) rovesciare; (*plan, stomach*) scombussolare; (*person: offend*) contrariare; (*: grieve*) addolorare; sconvolgere ♦ *adj* contrariato(a); addolorato(a); (*stomach*) scombussolato(a)

upshot ['ʌpʃɔt] *n* risultato

upside down ['ʌpsaɪd-] *adv* sottosopra

upstairs [ʌp'stɛəz] *adv, adj* di sopra, al piano superiore ♦ *n* piano di sopra

upstart ['ʌpstaːt] *n* parvenu *m inv*

upstream [ʌp'striːm] *adv* a monte

uptake ['ʌpteɪk] *n*: **he is quick/slow on the ~** è pronto/lento di comprendonio

uptight [ʌp'taɪt] (*inf*) *adj* teso(a)

up-to-date *adj* moderno(a); aggiornato(a)

upturn ['ʌptəːn] *n* (*in luck*) svolta favorevole; (*COMM: in market*) rialzo

upward ['ʌpwəd] *adj* ascendente; verso l'alto; **~(s)** *adv* in su, verso l'alto

urban ['əːbən] *adj* urbano(a); **~ clearway** *n* strada di scorrimento (in cui è vietata la sosta)

urbane [əː'beɪn] *adj* civile, urbano(a), educato(a)

urchin ['əːtʃɪn] *n* monello

urge [əːdʒ] *n* impulso; stimolo; forte desiderio ♦ *vt*: **to ~ sb to do** esortare qn a fare, spingere qn a fare; raccomandare a qn di fare

urgency ['əːdʒənsɪ] *n* urgenza; (*of tone*)

insistenza
urgent ['ə:dʒənt] _adj_ urgente; (_voice_)
insistente
urinate ['juərineit] _vi_ orinare
urine ['juərin] _n_ orina
urn [ə:n] _n_ urna; (_also:_ **tea ~**) bollitore _m_ per
il tè
us [ʌs] _pron_ ci; (_stressed, after prep_) noi; _see
also_ **me**
US(A) _n abbr_ (= _United States (of America)_)
USA _mpl_
usage ['ju:zidʒ] _n_ uso
use [_n_ ju:s, _vb_ ju:z] _n_ uso; impiego,
utilizzazione _f_ ♦ _vt_ usare, utilizzare, servirsi
di; **in ~** in uso; **out of ~** fuori uso; **to be of
~** essere utile, servire; **it's no ~** non serve, è
inutile; **she ~d to do it** lo faceva (una
volta), era solita farlo; **to be ~d to** avere
l'abitudine di; **~ up** _vt_ consumare;
esaurire; **~d** _adj_ (_object, car_) usato(a); **~ful**
adj utile; **~fulness** _n_ utilità; **~less** _adj_
inutile; (_person_) inetto(a); **~r** _n_ utente _m/f_;
~r-friendly _adj_ (_computer_) di facile uso
usher ['ʌʃə*] _n_ usciere _m_; **~ette** [-'rɛt] _n_ (_in
cinema_) maschera
USSR _n_ (_HIST_): **the ~** l'URSS _f_
usual ['ju:ʒuəl] _adj_ solito(a); **as ~** come al
solito, come d'abitudine; **~ly** _adv_ di solito
utensil [ju:'tɛnsl] _n_ utensile _m_; **kitchen ~s**
utensili da cucina
uterus ['ju:tərəs] _n_ utero
utility [ju:'tɪlɪtɪ] _n_ utilità; (_also:_ **public ~**)
servizio pubblico; **~ room** _n_ locale adibito
alla stiratura dei panni etc
utmost ['ʌtməust] _adj_ estremo(a) ♦ _n:_ **to do
one's ~** fare il possibile _or_ di tutto
utter ['ʌtə*] _adj_ assoluto(a), totale ♦ _vt_
pronunciare, proferire; emettere; **~ance** _n_
espressione _f_; parole _fpl_; **~ly** _adv_
completamente, del tutto
U-turn ['ju:'tə:n] _n_ inversione _f_ a U

V, v

v. _abbr_ = **verse; versus; volt;** (= _vide_) vedi,
vedere
vacancy ['veikənsi] _n_ (_BRIT: job_) posto
libero; (_room_) stanza libera; **"no
vacancies"** "completo"
vacant ['veikənt] _adj_ (_job, seat etc_) libero(a); (_expression_) assente
vacate [və'keit] _vt_ lasciare libero(a)
vacation [və'keiʃən] (_esp US_) _n_ vacanze _fpl_
vaccinate ['væksineit] _vt_ vaccinare
vaccination [væksi'neiʃən] _n_ vaccinazione _f_
vacuum ['vækjum] _n_ vuoto; **~ cleaner** _n_
aspirapolvere _m inv_; **~ flask** (_BRIT_) _n_
thermos ® _m inv_; **~-packed** _adj_
confezionato(a) sottovuoto
vagina [və'dʒainə] _n_ vagina
vagrant ['veigrnt] _n_ vagabondo/a
vague [veig] _adj_ vago(a); (_blurred: photo,
memory_) sfocato(a); **~ly** _adv_ vagamente
vain [vein] _adj_ (_useless_) inutile, vano(a); (_conceited_) vanitoso(a); **in ~** inutilmente,
invano
valentine ['væləntain] _n_ (_also:_ **~ card**)
cartolina _or_ biglietto di San Valentino;
(_person_) innamorato/a
valet ['vælei] _n_ cameriere _m_ personale
valiant ['væliənt] _adj_ valoroso(a),
coraggioso(a)
valid ['vælid] _adj_ valido(a), valevole; (_excuse_)
valido(a)
valley ['væli] _n_ valle _f_
valour ['vælə*] (_US_ **valor**) _n_ valore _m_
valuable ['væljuəbl] _adj_ (_jewel_) di (grande)
valore; (_time, help_) prezioso(a); **~s** _npl_
oggetti _mpl_ di valore
valuation [vælju'eiʃən] _n_ valutazione _f_,
stima
value ['vælju:] _n_ valore _m_ ♦ _vt_ (_fix price_)
valutare, dare un prezzo a; (_cherish_)
apprezzare, tenere a; **~ added tax** (_BRIT_)
_n_ imposta sul valore aggiunto; **~d** _adj_
(_appreciated_) stimato(a), apprezzato(a)
valve [vælv] _n_ valvola

van [væn] n (AUT) furgone m; (BRIT: RAIL) vagone m

vandal ['vændl] n vandalo/a; **~ism** n vandalismo

vanilla [vəˈnɪlə] n vaniglia ♦ cpd (ice cream) alla vaniglia

vanish ['vænɪʃ] vi svanire, scomparire

vanity ['vænɪtɪ] n vanità

vantage ['vɑːntɪdʒ] n: **~ point** posizione f or punto di osservazione; (fig) posizione vantaggiosa

vapour ['veɪpə*] (US **vapor**) n vapore m

variable ['vɛərɪəbl] adj variabile; (mood) mutevole

variance ['vɛərɪəns] n: **to be at ~ (with)** essere in disaccordo (con); (facts) essere in contraddizione (con)

varicose ['værɪkəʊs] adj: **~ veins** vene fpl varicose

varied ['vɛərɪd] adj vario(a), diverso(a)

variety [vəˈraɪətɪ] n varietà f inv; (quantity) quantità, numero; **~ show** n varietà m inv

various ['vɛərɪəs] adj vario(a), diverso(a); (several) parecchi(e), molti(e)

varnish ['vɑːnɪʃ] n vernice f; (nail ~) smalto ♦ vt verniciare; mettere lo smalto su

vary ['vɛərɪ] vt, vi variare, mutare

vase [vɑːz] n vaso

Vaseline ® ['væsɪliːn] n vaselina

vast [vɑːst] adj vasto(a); (amount, success) enorme

VAT [væt] n abbr (= value added tax) I.V.A. f

vat [væt] n tino

Vatican ['vætɪkən] n: **the ~** il Vaticano

vault [vɔːlt] n (of roof) volta; (tomb) tomba; (in bank) camera blindata ♦ vt (also: **~ over**) saltare (d'un balzo)

vaunted ['vɔːntɪd] adj: **much-~** tanto celebrato(a)

VCR n abbr = **video cassette recorder**

VD n abbr = **venereal disease**

VDU n abbr = **visual display unit**

veal [viːl] n vitello

veer [vɪə*] vi girare; virare

vegan ['viːgən] n vegetaliano(a)

vegeburger ['vedʒɪbɜːgə*] n hamburger m

inv vegetariano

vegetable ['vedʒtəbl] n verdura, ortaggio ♦ adj vegetale

vegetarian [vedʒɪˈtɛərɪən] adj, n vegetariano(a)

vehement ['viːɪmənt] adj veemente, violento(a)

vehicle ['viːɪkl] n veicolo

veil [veɪl] n velo; **~ed** adj (fig: threat) velato(a)

vein [veɪn] n vena; (on leaf) nervatura

velvet ['velvɪt] n velluto ♦ adj di velluto

vending machine ['vendɪŋ-] n distributore m automatico

vendor ['vendə*] n venditore/trice

veneer [vəˈnɪə*] n impiallacciatura; (fig) vernice f

venereal [vɪˈnɪərɪəl] adj: **~ disease** malattia venerea

Venetian [vɪˈniːʃən] adj veneziano(a); **~ blind** n (tenda alla) veneziana

vengeance ['vendʒəns] n vendetta; **with a ~** (fig) davvero; furiosamente

Venice ['venɪs] n Venezia

venison ['venɪsn] n carne f di cervo

venom ['venəm] n veleno

vent [vent] n foro, apertura; (in dress, jacket) spacco ♦ vt (fig: one's feelings) sfogare, dare sfogo a

ventilate ['ventɪleɪt] vt (room) dare aria a, arieggiare; **ventilator** n ventilatore m

ventriloquist [venˈtrɪləkwɪst] n ventriloquo/a

venture ['ventʃə*] n impresa (rischiosa) ♦ vt rischiare, azzardare ♦ vi avventurarsi; **business ~** n iniziativa commerciale

venue ['venjuː] n luogo (designato) per l'incontro

verb [vɜːb] n verbo; **~al** adj verbale; (translation) orale

verbatim [vɜːˈbeɪtɪm] adj, adv parola per parola

verdict ['vɜːdɪkt] n verdetto

verge [vɜːdʒ] (BRIT) n bordo, orlo; **"soft ~s"** (BRIT: AUT) banchine fpl cedevoli; **on the ~ of doing** sul punto di fare; **~ on** vt fus rasentare

veritable ['vɛrɪtəbl] *adj* vero(a)

vermin ['vəːmɪn] *npl* animali *mpl* nocivi; (*insects*) insetti *mpl* parassiti

vermouth ['vəːməθ] *n* vermut *m inv*

versatile ['vəːsətaɪl] *adj* (*person*) versatile; (*machine, tool etc*) (che si presta) a molti usi

verse [vəːs] *n* versi *mpl*; (*stanza*) stanza, strofa; (*in bible*) versetto

version ['vəːʃən] *n* versione *f*

versus ['vəːsəs] *prep* contro

vertical ['vəːtɪkl] *adj* verticale ♦ *n* verticale *m*; **~ly** *adv* verticalmente

vertigo ['vəːtɪgəu] *n* vertigine *f*

verve [vəːv] *n* brio; entusiasmo

very ['vɛrɪ] *adv* molto ♦ *adj*: **the ~ book which** proprio il libro che; **the ~ last** proprio l'ultimo; **at the ~ least** almeno; **~ much** moltissimo

vessel ['vɛsl] *n* (ANAT) vaso; (NAUT) nave *f*; (*container*) recipiente *m*

vest [vɛst] *n* (BRIT) maglia; (: *sleeveless*) canottiera; (US: *waistcoat*) gilè *m inv*

vested interests ['vɛstɪd-] *npl* (COMM) diritti *mpl* acquisiti

vet [vɛt] *n abbr* (BRIT: = *veterinary surgeon*) veterinario ♦ *vt* esaminare minuziosamente

veteran ['vɛtərn] *n* (*also*: **war ~**) veterano

veterinary ['vɛtrɪnərɪ] *adj* veterinario(a); ~ **surgeon** (US **veterinarian**) *n* veterinario

veto ['viːtəu] (*pl* **~es**) *n* veto ♦ *vt* opporre il veto a

vex [vɛks] *vt* irritare, contrariare; **~ed** *adj* (*question*) controverso(a), dibattuto(a)

via ['vaɪə] *prep* (*by way of*) via; (*by means of*) tramite

viable ['vaɪəbl] *adj* attuabile; vitale

viaduct ['vaɪədʌkt] *n* viadotto

vibrant ['vaɪbrənt] *adj* (*lively, bright*) vivace; (*voice*) vibrante

vibrate [vaɪ'breɪt] *vi*: **to ~ (with)** vibrare (di); (*resound*) risonare (di)

vicar ['vɪkə*] *n* pastore *m*; **~age** *n* presbiterio

vicarious [vɪ'kɛərɪəs] *adj* indiretto(a)

vice [vaɪs] *n* (*evil*) vizio; (TECH) morsa

vice- [vaɪs] *prefix* vice...

vice squad *n* (squadra del) buon costume *f*

vice versa ['vaɪsɪ'vəːsə] *adv* viceversa

vicinity [vɪ'sɪnɪtɪ] *n* vicinanze *fpl*

vicious ['vɪʃəs] *adj* (*remark, dog*) cattivo(a); (*blow*) violento(a); ~ **circle** *n* circolo vizioso

victim ['vɪktɪm] *n* vittima

victor ['vɪktə*] *n* vincitore *m*

Victorian [vɪk'tɔːrɪən] *adj* vittoriano(a)

victory ['vɪktərɪ] *n* vittoria

video ['vɪdɪəu] *cpd* video... ♦ *n* (~ *film*) video *m inv*; (*also*: ~ **cassette**) videocassetta; (*also*: ~ **cassette recorder**) videoregistratore *m*; ~ **tape** *n* videotape *m inv*; ~ **wall** *n* schermo *m* multivideo *inv*

vie [vaɪ] *vi*: **to ~ with** competere con, rivaleggiare con

Vienna [vɪ'ɛnə] *n* Vienna

Vietnam [vjɛt'næm] *n* Vietnam *m*; **~ese** *adj, n inv* vietnamita *m/f*

view [vjuː] *n* vista, veduta; (*opinion*) opinione *f* ♦ *vt* (*look at: also fig*) considerare; (*house*) visitare; **on ~** (*in museum etc*) esposto(a); **in full ~ of** sotto gli occhi di; **in ~ of the weather/the fact that** considerato il tempo/che; **in my ~** a mio parere; **~er** *n* spettatore/trice; **~finder** *n* mirino; **~point** *n* punto di vista; (*place*) posizione *f*

vigil ['vɪdʒɪl] *n* veglia

vigorous ['vɪgərəs] *adj* vigoroso(a)

vile [vaɪl] *adj* (*action*) vile; (*smell*) disgustoso(a), nauseante; (*temper*) pessimo(a)

villa ['vɪlə] *n* villa

village ['vɪlɪdʒ] *n* villaggio; **~r** *n* abitante *m/f* di villaggio

villain ['vɪlən] *n* (*scoundrel*) canaglia; (BRIT: *criminal*) criminale *m*; (*in novel etc*) cattivo

vindicate ['vɪndɪkeɪt] *vt* comprovare; giustificare

vindictive [vɪn'dɪktɪv] *adj* vendicativo(a)

vine [vaɪn] *n* vite *f*; (*climbing plant*) rampicante *m*

vinegar ['vɪnɪgə*] *n* aceto

vineyard ['vɪnjɑːd] *n* vigna, vigneto

vintage ['vɪntɪdʒ] n (year) annata, produzione f ♦ cpd d'annata; ~ **car** n auto f inv d'epoca; ~ **wine** n vino d'annata

vinyl ['vaɪnl] n vinile m

violate ['vaɪəleɪt] vt violare

violence ['vaɪələns] n violenza

violent ['vaɪələnt] adj violento(a)

violet ['vaɪələt] adj (colour) viola inv, violetto(a) ♦ n (plant) violetta; (colour) violetto

violin [vaɪə'lɪn] n violino; ~**ist** n violinista m/f

VIP n abbr (= very important person) V.I.P. m/f inv

virgin ['vɜːdʒɪn] n vergine f ♦ adj vergine inv

Virgo ['vɜːgəu] n (sign) Vergine f

virile ['vɪraɪl] adj virile

virtually ['vɜːtjuəlɪ] adv (almost) praticamente

virtual reality ['vɜːtʃuəl -] n (COMPUT) realtà virtuale

virtue ['vɜːtjuː] n virtù f inv; (advantage) pregio, vantaggio; **by ~ of** grazie a

virtuous ['vɜːtjuəs] adj virtuoso(a)

virus ['vaɪərəs] n (also COMPUT) virus m inv

visa ['viːzə] n visto

vis-à-vis [viːzə'viː] prep rispetto a, nei riguardi di

visibility [vɪzɪ'bɪlɪtɪ] n visibilità

visible ['vɪzəbl] adj visibile

vision ['vɪʒən] n (sight) vista; (foresight, in dream) visione f

visit ['vɪzɪt] n visita; (stay) soggiorno ♦ vt (person: US also: ~ **with**) andare a trovare; (place) visitare; ~**ing hours** npl (in hospital etc) orario delle visite; ~**or** n visitatore/trice; (guest) ospite m/f; ~**or centre** n centro informazioni per visitatori di museo, zoo, parco ecc

visor ['vaɪzə*] n visiera

visual ['vɪzjuəl] adj visivo(a); visuale; ottico(a); ~ **aid** n sussidio visivo; ~ **display unit** n visualizzatore m

visualize ['vɪzjuəlaɪz] vt immaginare, figurarsi; (foresee) prevedere

visually-impaired ['vɪzjuəlɪ-] adj videoleso(a)

vital ['vaɪtl] adj vitale; ~**ly** adv estremamente; ~ **statistics** npl (fig) misure fpl

vitamin ['vɪtəmɪn] n vitamina

vivacious [vɪ'veɪʃəs] adj vivace

vivid ['vɪvɪd] adj vivido(a); ~**ly** adv (describe) vividamente; (remember) con precisione

V-neck ['viːnɛk] n maglione m con lo scollo a V

vocabulary [vəu'kæbjulərɪ] n vocabolario

vocal ['vəukl] adj (MUS) vocale; (communication) verbale; ~ **cords** npl corde fpl vocali

vocation [vəu'keɪʃən] n vocazione f; ~**al** adj professionale

vociferous [və'sɪfərəs] adj rumoroso(a)

vodka ['vɔdkə] n vodka f inv

vogue [vəug] n moda; (popularity) popolarità, voga

voice [vɔɪs] n voce f ♦ vt (opinion) esprimere; ~ **mail** n servizio di segreteria telefonica

void [vɔɪd] n vuoto ♦ adj (invalid) nullo(a); (empty): ~ **of** privo(a) di

volatile ['vɔlətaɪl] adj volatile; (fig) volubile

volcano [vɔl'keɪnəu] (pl ~**es**) n vulcano

volition [və'lɪʃən] n: **of one's own** ~ di sua volontà

volley ['vɔlɪ] n (of gunfire) salva; (of stones, questions etc) raffica; (TENNIS etc) volata; ~**ball** n pallavolo f

volt [vəult] n volt m inv; ~**age** n tensione f, voltaggio

voluble ['vɔljubl] adj loquace, ciarliero(a)

volume ['vɔljuːm] n volume m

voluntarily ['vɔləntrɪlɪ] adv volontariamente; gratuitamente

voluntary ['vɔləntərɪ] adj volontario(a); (unpaid) gratuito(a), non retribuito(a)

volunteer [vɔlən'tɪə*] n volontario/a ♦ vt offrire volontariamente ♦ vi (MIL) arruolarsi volontario; **to ~ to do** offrire (volontariamente) di fare

voluptuous [və'lʌptjuəs] adj voluttuoso(a)

vomit ['vɔmɪt] n vomito ♦ vt, vi vomitare

vote [vəut] n voto, suffragio; (cast) voto; (franchise) diritto di voto ♦ vt: **to be ~d**

chairman *etc* venir eletto presidente *etc*; (*propose*): **to ~ that** approvare la proposta che ♦ *vi* votare; **~ of thanks** discorso di ringraziamento; **~r** *n* elettore/trice; **voting** *n* scrutinio

vouch [vautʃ]: **to ~ for** *vt fus* farsi garante di

voucher ['vautʃə*] *n* (*for meal, petrol etc*) buono

vow [vau] *n* voto, promessa solenne ♦ *vt*: **to ~ to do/that** giurare di fare/che

vowel ['vauəl] *n* vocale *f*

voyage ['vɔɪdʒ] *n* viaggio per mare, traversata

V-sign ['viː-] (*BRIT*) *n* gesto volgare con le dita

vulgar ['vʌlgə*] *adj* volgare

vulnerable ['vʌlnərəbl] *adj* vulnerabile

vulture ['vʌltʃə*] *n* avvoltoio

W, w

wad [wɔd] *n* (*of cotton wool, paper*) tampone *m*; (*of banknotes etc*) fascio

waddle ['wɔdl] *vi* camminare come una papera

wade [weɪd] *vi*: **to ~ through** camminare a stento in; (*fig: book*) leggere con fatica

wafer ['weɪfə*] *n* (*CULIN*) cialda

waffle ['wɔfl] *n* (*CULIN*) cialda; (*inf*) ciance *fpl* ♦ *vi* cianciare

waft [wɔft] *vt* portare ♦ *vi* diffondersi

wag [wæg] *vt* agitare, muovere ♦ *vi* agitarsi

wage [weɪdʒ] *n* (*also:* **~s**) salario, paga ♦ *vt*: **to ~ war** fare la guerra; **~ earner** *n* salariato/a; **~ packet** *n* busta *f* paga *inv*

wager ['weɪdʒə*] *n* scommessa

wag(g)on ['wægən] *n* (*horse-drawn*) carro; (*BRIT: RAIL*) vagone *m* (*merci*)

wail [weɪl] *n* gemito; (*of siren*) urlo ♦ *vi* gemere; urlare

waist [weɪst] *n* vita, cintola; **~coat** (*BRIT*) *n* panciotto, gilè *m inv*; **~line** *n* (*giro di*) vita

wait [weɪt] *n* attesa ♦ *vi* aspettare, attendere; **to lie in ~ for** stare in agguato a; **to ~ for** aspettare; **I can't ~ to** (*fig*) non vedo l'ora di; **~ behind** *vi* rimanere (ad

aspettare); **~ on** *vt fus* servire; **~er** *n* cameriere *m*; **~ing** *n*: **"no ~ing"** (*BRIT: AUT*) "divieto di sosta"; **~ing list** *n* lista di attesa; **~ing room** *n* sala d'aspetto *or* d'attesa; **~ress** *n* cameriera

waive [weɪv] *vt* rinunciare a, abbandonare

wake [weɪk] (*pt* **woke**, **~d**, *pp* **woken**, **~d**) *vt* (*also:* **~ up**) svegliare ♦ *vi* (*also:* **~ up**) svegliarsi ♦ *n* (*for dead person*) veglia funebre; (*NAUT*) scia; **waken** *vt, vi* = **wake**

Wales [weɪlz] *n* Galles *m*

walk [wɔːk] *n* passeggiata; (*short*) giretto; (*gait*) passo, andatura; (*path*) sentiero; (*in park etc*) sentiero, vialetto ♦ *vi* camminare; (*for pleasure, exercise*) passeggiare ♦ *vt* (*distance*) fare *or* percorrere a piedi; (*dog*) accompagnare, portare a passeggiare; **10 minutes' ~ from** 10 minuti di cammino *or* a piedi da; **from all ~s of life** di tutte le condizioni sociali; **~ out** *vi* (*audience*) andarsene; (*workers*) scendere in sciopero; **~ out on** (*inf*) *vt fus* piantare in asso; **~er** *n* (*person*) camminatore/trice; **~ie-talkie** ['wɔːkɪ'tɔːkɪ] *n* walkie-talkie *m inv*; **~ing** *n* camminare *m*; **~ing shoes** *npl* pedule *fpl*; **~ing stick** *n* bastone *m* da passeggio; **W~man** ® ['wɔːkmən] *n* Walkman ® *m inv*; **~out** *n* (*of workers*) sciopero senza preavviso *or* a sorpresa; **~over** (*inf*) *n* vittoria facile, gioco da ragazzi; **~way** *n* passaggio pedonale

wall [wɔːl] *n* muro; (*internal, of tunnel, cave*) parete *f*; **~ed** *adj* (*city*) fortificato(a); (*garden*) cintato(a)

wallet ['wɔlɪt] *n* portafoglio

wallflower ['wɔːlflauə*] *n* violacciocca; **to be a ~** (*fig*) fare da tappezzeria

wallow ['wɔləu] *vi* sguazzare

wallpaper ['wɔːlpeɪpə*] *n* carta da parati ♦ *vt* (*room*) mettere la carta da parati in

wally ['wɔlɪ] (*inf*) *n* imbecille *m/f*

walnut ['wɔːlnʌt] *n* noce *f*; (*tree, wood*) noce *m*

walrus ['wɔːlrəs] (*pl* **~** *or* **~es**) *n* tricheco

waltz [wɔːlts] *n* valzer *m inv* ♦ *vi* ballare il valzer

wand [wɔnd] *n* (*also:* **magic ~**) bacchetta

(magica)

wander ['wɔndə*] vi (person) girare senza meta, girovagare; (thoughts) vagare ♦ vt girovagare per

wane [weɪn] vi calare

wangle ['wæŋgl] (BRIT: inf) vt procurare con l'astuzia

want [wɔnt] vt volere; (need) aver bisogno di ♦ n: **for ~ of** per mancanza di; **~s** npl (needs) bisogni mpl; **to ~ to do** volere fare; **to ~ sb to do** volere che qn faccia; **~ed** adj (criminal) ricercato(a); **"~ed"** (in adverts) "cercasi"; **~ing** adj: **to be found ~ing** non risultare all'altezza

WAP n abbr (= wireless application protocol) WAP

war [wɔ:*] n guerra; **to make ~ (on)** far guerra (a)

ward [wɔ:d] n (in hospital: room) corsia; (: section) reparto; (POL) circoscrizione f; (LAW: child: also: **~ of court**) pupillo/a; **~ off** vt parare, schivare

warden ['wɔ:dn] n (of park, game reserve, youth hostel) guardiano/a; (BRIT: of institution) direttore/trice; (BRIT: also: **traffic ~**) addetto/a al controllo del traffico e del parcheggio

warder ['wɔ:də*] (BRIT) n guardia carceraria

wardrobe ['wɔ:drəub] n (cupboard) guardaroba m inv, armadio; (clothes) guardaroba; (CINEMA, THEATRE) costumi mpl

warehouse ['weəhaus] n magazzino

wares [weəz] npl merci fpl

warfare ['wɔ:feə*] n guerra

warhead ['wɔ:hed] n (MIL) testata

warily ['weərɪlɪ] adv cautamente, con prudenza

warlike ['wɔ:laɪk] adj bellicoso(a)

warm [wɔ:m] adj caldo(a); (thanks, welcome, applause) caloroso(a); (person) cordiale; **it's ~** fa caldo; **I'm ~** ho caldo; **~ up** vi scaldarsi, riscaldarsi ♦ vt scaldare, riscaldare; (engine) far scaldare; **~-hearted** adj affettuoso(a); **~ly** adv (applaud, welcome) calorosamente; (dress) con abiti pesanti; **~th** n calore m

warn [wɔ:n] vt: **to ~ sb that/(not) to do/of** avvertire or avvisare qn che/di (non) fare/ di; **~ing** n avvertimento; (notice) avviso; (signal) segnalazione f; **~ing light** n spia luminosa; **~ing triangle** n (AUT) triangolo

warp [wɔ:p] vi deformarsi ♦ vt (fig) corrompere

warrant ['wɔrnt] n (voucher) buono; (LAW: to arrest) mandato di cattura; (: to search) mandato di perquisizione

warranty ['wɔrəntɪ] n garanzia

warren ['wɔrən] n (of rabbits) tana; (fig: of streets etc) dedalo

warrior ['wɔrɪə*] n guerriero/a

Warsaw ['wɔ:sɔ:] n Varsavia

warship ['wɔ:ʃɪp] n nave f da guerra

wart [wɔ:t] n verruca

wartime ['wɔ:taɪm] n: **in ~** in tempo di guerra

wary ['weərɪ] adj prudente

was [wɔz] pt of **be**

wash [wɔʃ] vt lavare ♦ vi lavarsi; (sea): **to ~ over/against sth** infrangersi su/contro qc ♦ n lavaggio; (of ship) scia; **to give sth a ~** lavare qc, dare una lavata a qc; **to have a ~** lavarsi; **~ away** vt (stain) togliere lavando; (subj: river) trascinare via; **~ off** vi andare via con il lavaggio; **~ up** vi (BRIT) lavare i piatti; (US) darsi una lavata; **~able** adj lavabile; **~basin** (US **~bowl**) n lavabo; **~cloth** (US) n pezzuola (per lavarsi); **~er** n (TECH) rondella; **~ing** n (linen etc) bucato; **~ing machine** n lavatrice f; **~ing powder** (BRIT) n detersivo (in polvere)

wash: **~ing up** n rigovernatura, lavatura dei piatti; **~ing-up liquid** n detersivo liquido (per stoviglie); **~-out** (inf) n disastro; **~room** n gabinetto

wasn't ['wɔznt] = **was not**

wasp [wɔsp] n vespa

wastage ['weɪstɪdʒ] n spreco; (in manufacturing) scarti mpl; **natural ~** diminuzione f di manodopera (per pensionamento, decesso etc)

waste [weɪst] n spreco; (of time) perdita; (rubbish) rifiuti mpl; (also: **household ~**) immondizie fpl ♦ adj (material) di scarto; (food) avanzato(a); (land) incolto(a) ♦ vt sprecare; **~s** npl (area of land) distesa desolata; ~ **away** *vi* deperire; ~ **disposal unit** (*BRIT*) *n* eliminatore *m* di rifiuti; ~**ful** *adj* sprecone(a); (*process*) dispendioso(a); ~**ground** (*BRIT*) *n* terreno incolto *or* abbandonato; ~**paper basket** *n* cestino per la carta straccia; ~**pipe** *n* tubo di scarico

watch [wɔtʃ] *n* (*also*: **wrist** ~) orologio (da polso); (*act of watching, vigilance*) sorveglianza; (*guard*: MIL, NAUT) guardia; (*NAUT*: *spell of duty*) quarto ♦ *vt* (*look at*) osservare; (: *match, programme*) guardare; (*spy on, guard*) sorvegliare, tenere d'occhio; (*be careful of*) fare attenzione a ♦ *vi* osservare, guardare; (*keep guard*) fare *or* montare la guardia; ~ **out** *vi* fare attenzione; ~**dog** *n* (*also fig*) cane *m* da guardia; ~**ful** *adj* attento(a), vigile; ~**man** (*irreg*) *n see* **night**; ~ **strap** *n* cinturino da orologio

water ['wɔːtə*] *n* acqua ♦ *vt* (*plant*) annaffiare ♦ *vi* (*eyes*) lacrimare; (*mouth*): **to make sb's mouth** ~ far venire l'acquolina in bocca a qn; **in British** ~**s** nelle acque territoriali britanniche; ~ **down** *vt* (*milk*) diluire; (*fig*: *story*) edulcorare; ~**cannon** *n* idrante *m*; ~**closet** (*BRIT*) *n* water *m inv*; ~**colour** *n* acquerello; ~**cress** *n* crescione *m*; ~**fall** *n* cascata; ~ **heater** *n* scaldabagno; ~**ing can** *n* annaffiatoio; ~ **lily** *n* ninfea; ~**line** *n* (*NAUT*) linea di galleggiamento; ~**logged** *adj* saturo(a) d'acqua; imbevuto(a) d'acqua; (*football pitch etc*) allagato(a); ~ **main** *n* conduttura dell'acqua; ~**melon** *n* anguria, cocomero; ~**proof** *adj* impermeabile; ~**shed** *n* (*GEO, fig*) spartiacque *m*; ~**-skiing** *n* sci *m* acquatico; ~**tight** *adj* stagno(a); ~**way** *n* corso d'acqua navigabile; ~**works** *npl* impianto idrico; ~**y** *adj* (*colour*) slavato(a); (*coffee*) acquoso(a); (*eyes*) umido(a)

watt [wɔt] *n* watt *m inv*

wave [weɪv] *n* onda; (*of hand*) gesto, segno; (*in hair*) ondulazione *f*; (*fig*: *surge*) ondata ♦ *vi* fare un cenno con la mano; (*branches, grass*) ondeggiare; (*flag*) sventolare ♦ *vt* (*hand*) fare un gesto con; (*handkerchief*) sventolare; (*stick*) brandire; ~**length** *n* lunghezza d'onda

waver ['weɪvə*] *vi* esitare; (*voice*) tremolare

wavy ['weɪvɪ] *adj* ondulato(a); ondeggiante

wax [wæks] *n* cera ♦ *vt* dare la cera a; (*car*) lucidare ♦ *vi* (*moon*) crescere; ~**works** *npl* cere *fpl* ♦ *n* museo delle cere

way [weɪ] *n* via, strada; (*path, access*) passaggio; (*distance*) distanza; (*direction*) parte *f*, direzione *f*; (*manner*) modo, stile *m*; (*habit*) abitudine *f*; **which** ~? – da che parte *or* in quale direzione? – da questa parte *or* per di qua; **on the** ~ (*en route*) per strada; **to be on one's** ~ essere in cammino *or* sulla strada; **to be in the** ~ bloccare il passaggio; (*fig*) essere tra i piedi *or* d'impiccio; **to go out of one's** ~ **to do** (*fig*) mettercela tutta *or* fare di tutto per fare; **under** ~ (*project*) in corso; **to lose one's** ~ perdere la strada; **in a** ~ in un certo senso; **in some** ~**s** sotto certi aspetti; **no** ~! (*inf*) neanche per idea!; **by the** ~ ... a proposito ...; **"~ in"** (*BRIT*) "entrata", "ingresso"; **"~ out"** (*BRIT*) "uscita"; **the** ~ **back** la strada del ritorno; **"give ~"** (*BRIT*: *AUT*) "dare la precedenza"

waylay [weɪ'leɪ] (*irreg*: *like* **lay**) *vt* tendere un agguato a; attendere al passaggio

wayward ['weɪwəd] *adj* capriccioso(a); testardo(a)

W.C. ['dʌblju:'siː] (*BRIT*) *n* W.C. *m inv*, gabinetto

we [wiː] *pl pron* noi

weak [wiːk] *adj* debole; (*health*) precario(a); (*beam etc*) fragile; (*tea*) leggero(a); ~**en** *vi* indebolirsi ♦ *vt* indebolire; ~**ling** ['wiːklɪŋ] *n* smidollato/a; debole *m/f*; ~**ness** *n* debolezza; (*fault*) punto debole, difetto; **to have a ~ness for** avere un debole per

wealth [welθ] *n* (*money, resources*) ricchezza, ricchezze *fpl*; (*of details*) abbondanza, profusione *f*; ~**y** *adj* ricco(a)

wean [wiːn] *vt* svezzare

weapon ['wepən] *n* arma

wear [wεə*] *n* (*use*) uso; (*damage through use*) logorio, usura; (*clothing*): **sports/baby** ~ abbigliamento sportivo/per neonati ♦ *vt* (*clothes*) portare; (*put on*) mettersi; (*damage*) consumare ♦ *vi* (last) durare; (rub etc through) consumarsi; **evening** ~ abiti mpl or tenuta da sera; ~ **away** vt consumare; erodere ♦ vi consumarsi; essere eroso(a); ~ **down** vt consumare; (strength) esaurire; ~ **off** vi sparire lentamente; ~ **out** vt consumare; (person) esaurire; ~ **and tear** n usura, consumo

weary ['wɪərɪ] adj stanco(a) ♦ vi: **to ~ of** stancarsi di

weasel ['wiːzl] n (ZOOL) donnola

weather ['wɛðə*] n tempo ♦ vt (storm, crisis) superare; **under the ~** (fig: ill) poco bene; **~-beaten** adj (face, skin) segnato(a) dalle intemperie; (building) logorato(a) dalle intemperie; **~cock** n banderuola; ~ **forecast** n previsioni fpl del tempo, bollettino meteorologico; **~man** (irreg inf) n meteorologo; ~ **vane** n = **~cock**

weave [wiːv] (pt **wove**, pp **woven**) vt (cloth) tessere; (basket) intrecciare; **~r** n tessitore/trice; **weaving** n tessitura

web [wɛb] n (of spider) ragnatela; (on foot) palma; (fabric, also fig) tessuto; **the (World Wide) Web** la Rete

webcam ['wɛbkæm] n abbr (= webcamera) webcamera

webcast ['wɛbkɑːst] n spettacolo cui si può assistere in Internet

website ['wɛbsaɪt] n (COMPUT) sito (Internet)

wed [wɛd] (pt, pp **wedded**) vt sposare ♦ vi sposarsi

we'd [wiːd] = **we had**; **we would**

wedding ['wɛdɪŋ] n matrimonio; **silver** ~ (**anniversary**) n nozze fpl d'argento; ~ **day** n giorno delle nozze or del matrimonio; ~ **dress** n abito nuziale; ~ **ring** n fede f

wedge [wɛdʒ] n (of wood etc) zeppa; (of cake) fetta ♦ vt (fix) fissare con zeppe; (pack tightly) incastrare

Wednesday ['wɛdnzdɪ] n mercoledì m inv

wee [wiː] (SCOTTISH) adj piccolo(a)

weed [wiːd] n erbaccia ♦ vt diserbare; **~killer** n diserbante m; **~y** adj (person) allampanato(a)

week [wiːk] n settimana; **a ~ today/on Friday** oggi/venerdì a otto; **~day** n giorno feriale; (COMM) giornata lavorativa; **~end** n

fine settimana m or f inv, weekend m inv; **~ly** adv ogni settimana, settimanalmente ♦ adj settimanale ♦ n settimanale m

weep [wiːp] (pt, pp **wept**) vi piangere; **~ing willow** n salice m piangente

weigh [weɪ] vt, vi pesare; **to ~ anchor** salpare l'ancora; ~ **down** vt (branch) piegare; (fig: with worry) opprimere, caricare; ~ **up** vt valutare

weight [weɪt] n peso; **to lose/put on ~** dimagrire/ingrassare; **~ing** n (allowance) indennità; ~ **lifter** n pesista m; **~y** adj pesante; (fig) importante, grave

weir [wɪə*] n diga

weird [wɪəd] adj strano(a), bizzarro(a); (eerie) soprannaturale

welcome ['wɛlkəm] adj benvenuto(a) ♦ n accoglienza, benvenuto ♦ vt dare il benvenuto a; (be glad of) rallegrarsi di; **thank you – you're ~!** grazie – prego!

welfare ['wɛlfɛə*] n benessere m; ~ **state** n stato assistenziale

well [wɛl] n pozzo ♦ adv bene ♦ adj: **to be** ~ (person) stare bene ♦ excl allora!; ma!; ebbene!; **as** ~ anche; **as** ~ **as** così come; oltre a; ~ **done!** bravo(a)!; **get** ~ **soon!** guarisci presto!; **to do** ~ andare bene; ~ **up** vi sgorgare

we'll [wiːl] = **we will**; **we shall**

well: **~-behaved** adj ubbidiente; **~-being** n benessere m; **~-built** adj (person) ben fatto(a); **~-deserved** adj meritato(a); **~-dressed** adj ben vestito(a), vestito(a) bene; **~-heeled** (inf) adj agiato(a), facoltoso(a)

wellingtons ['wɛlɪŋtənz] npl (also: **wellington boots**) stivali mpl di gomma

well: **~-known** adj noto(a), famoso(a); **~-mannered** adj ben educato(a); **~-meaning** adj ben intenzionato(a); **~-off** adj benestante, danaroso(a); **~-read** adj colto(a); **~-to-do** adj abbiente, benestante; **~-wisher** n ammiratore/trice

Welsh [wɛlʃ] adj gallese ♦ n (LING) gallese m; **the** ~ npl i Gallesi; ~ **Assembly** n Parlamento gallese; **~man/woman** (irreg) n gallese m/f; ~ **rarebit** n crostino al formaggio

went [wɛnt] *pt of* **go**

wept [wɛpt] *pt, pp of* **weep**

were [wə:*] *pt of* **be**

we're [wɪə*] = **we are**

weren't [wə:nt] = **were not**

west [wɛst] *n* ovest *m*, occidente *m*, ponente *m* ♦ *adj* (a) ovest *inv*, occidentale ♦ *adv* verso ovest; **the W~** l'Occidente *m*; **the W~ Country** (*BRIT*) *n* il sud-ovest dell'Inghilterra; **~erly** *adj* (*point*) a ovest; (*wind*) occidentale, da ovest; **~ern** *adj* occidentale, dell'ovest ♦ *n* (*CINEMA*) western *m inv*; **W~ Germany** *n* Germania Occidentale; **W~ Indian** *adj* delle Indie Occidentali ♦ *n* abitante *m/f* delle Indie Occidentali; **W~ Indies** *npl* Indie *fpl* Occidentali; **~ward(s)** *adv* verso ovest

wet [wɛt] *adj* umido(a), bagnato(a); (*soaked*) fradicio(a); (*rainy*) piovoso(a) ♦ *n* (*BRIT: POL*) politico moderato; **to get ~** bagnarsi; "**~ paint**" "vernice fresca"; **~ suit** *n* tuta da sub

we've [wiːv] = **we have**

whack [wæk] *vt* picchiare, battere

whale [weɪl] *n* (*ZOOL*) balena

wharf [wɔːf] (*pl* **wharves**) *n* banchina

wharves [wɔːvz] *npl of* **wharf**

KEYWORD

what [wɔt] *adj* **1** (*in direct/indirect questions*) che; quale; **~ size is it?** che taglia è?; **~ colour is it?** di che colore è?; **~ books do you want?** quali *or* che libri vuole?
2 (*in exclamations*) che; **~ a mess!** che disordine!
♦ *pron* **1** (*interrogative*) che cosa, cosa, che; **~ are you doing?** che *or* (che) cosa fai?; **~ are you talking about?** di che cosa parli?; **~ is it called?** come si chiama?; **~ about me?** e io?; **~ about doing ...?** e se facessimo ...?
2 (*relative*) ciò che, quello che; **I saw ~ you did/was on the table** ho visto quello che hai fatto/quello che era sul tavolo
3 (*indirect use*) (che) cosa; **he asked me ~ she had said** mi ha chiesto che cosa avesse detto; **tell me ~ you're thinking about** dimmi a cosa stai pensando
♦ *excl* (*disbelieving*) cosa!, come!

whatever [wɔt'ɛvə*] *adj*: **~ book** qualunque *or* qualsiasi libro +*sub* ♦ *pron*: **do ~ is necessary/you want** faccia qualunque *or* qualsiasi cosa sia necessaria/lei voglia; **~ happens** qualunque cosa accada; **no reason ~** *or* **whatsoever** nessuna ragione affatto *or* al mondo; **nothing ~** proprio niente

whatsoever [wɔtsəu'ɛvə*] *adj* = **whatever**

wheat [wiːt] *n* grano, frumento

wheedle ['wiːdl] *vt*: **to ~ sb into doing sth** convincere qn a fare qc (con lusinghe); **to ~ sth out of sb** ottenere qc da qn (con lusinghe)

wheel [wiːl] *n* ruota; (*AUT: also:* **steering ~**) volante *m*; (*NAUT*) (ruota del) timone *m* ♦ *vt* spingere ♦ *vi* (*birds*) roteare; (*also:* **~ round**) girare; **~barrow** *n* carriola; **~chair** *n* sedia a rotelle; **~ clamp** *n* (*AUT*) morsa che blocca la ruota di una vettura in sosta vietata

wheeze [wiːz] *vi* ansimare

KEYWORD

when [wɛn] *adv* quando; **~ did it happen?** quando è successo?
♦ *conj* **1** (*at, during, after the time that*) quando; **she was reading ~ I came in** quando sono entrato lei leggeva; **that was ~ I needed you** era allora che avevo bisogno di te
2 (*on, at which*): **on the day ~ I met him** il giorno in cui l'ho incontrato; **one day ~ it was raining** un giorno che pioveva
3 (*whereas*) quando, mentre; **you said I was wrong ~ in fact I was right** mi hai detto che avevo torto, quando in realtà avevo ragione

whenever [wɛn'ɛvə*] *adv* quando mai
♦ *conj* quando; (*every time that*) ogni volta che

where [wɛə*] *adv, conj* dove; **this is ~** è qui che; **~abouts** *adv* dove ♦ *n*: **sb's**

~abouts luogo dove qn si trova; **~as** *conj* mentre; **~by** *pron* per cui; **wherever** [-'ɛvə*] *conj* dovunque +*sub*; (*interrogative*) dove mai; **~withal** *n* mezzi *mpl*

whet [wɛt] *vt* (*appetite etc*) stimolare

whether ['wɛðə*] *conj* se; **I don't know ~ to accept or not** non so se accettare o no; **it's doubtful ~** è poco probabile che; **~ you go or not** che lei vada o no

---

KEYWORD

which [wɪtʃ] *adj* 1 (*interrogative: direct, indirect*) quale; **~ picture do you want?** quale quadro vuole?; **~ one?** quale?; **~ one of you did it?** chi di voi lo ha fatto?
2: in ~ case nel qual caso
♦ *pron* 1 (*interrogative*) quale; **~ (of these) are yours?** quali di questi sono suoi?; **~ of you are coming?** chi di voi viene?
2 (*relative*) che; (*: indirect*) cui, il (la) quale; **the apple ~ you ate/~ is on the table** la mela che hai mangiato/che è sul tavolo; **the chair on ~ you are sitting** la sedia sulla quale *or* su cui sei seduto; **he said he knew, ~ is true** ha detto che lo sapeva, il che è vero; **after ~** dopo di che

---

whichever [wɪtʃ'ɛvə*] *adj*: **take ~ book you prefer** prenda qualsiasi libro che preferisce; **~ book you take** qualsiasi libro prenda

whiff [wɪf] *n* soffio; sbuffo; odore *m*

while [waɪl] *n* momento ♦ *conj* mentre; (*as long as*) finché; (*although*) sebbene +*sub*; per quanto +*sub*; **for a ~** per un po'; **~ away** *vt* (*time*) far passare

whim [wɪm] *n* capriccio

whimper ['wɪmpə*] *n* piagnucolio ♦ *vi* piagnucolare

whimsical ['wɪmzɪkl] *adj* (*person*) capriccioso(a); (*look*) strano(a)

whine [waɪn] *n* gemito ♦ *vi* gemere; uggiolare; piagnucolare

whip [wɪp] *n* frusta; (*for riding*) frustino; (*POL: person*) capogruppo (*che sovrintende alla disciplina dei colleghi di partito*) ♦ *vt* frustare; (*cream, eggs*) sbattere; **~ped cream** *n* panna montata; **~-round** (*BRIT*)

n colletta

whirl [wə:l] *vt* (*far*) girare rapidamente; (*far*) turbinare ♦ *vi* (*dancers*) volteggiare; (*leaves, water*) sollevarsi in vortice; **~pool** *n* mulinello; **~wind** *n* turbine *m*

whirr [wə:*] *vi* ronzare; rombare; frullare

whisk [wɪsk] *n* (*CULIN*) frusta; frullino ♦ *vt* sbattere, frullare; **to ~ sb away** *or* **off** portar via qn a tutta velocità

whiskers ['wɪskəz] *npl* (*of animal*) baffi *mpl*; (*of man*) favoriti *mpl*

whisky ['wɪskɪ] (*US, IRELAND* **whiskey**) *n* whisky *m inv*

whisper ['wɪspə*] *n* sussurro ♦ *vt, vi* sussurrare

whist [wɪst] *n* whist *m*

whistle ['wɪsl] *n* (*sound*) fischio; (*object*) fischietto ♦ *vi* fischiare

white [waɪt] *adj* bianco(a); (*with fear*) pallido(a) ♦ *n* bianco; (*person*) bianco/a; **~ coffee** (*BRIT*) *n* caffellatte *m inv*; **~-collar worker** *n* impiegato; **~ elephant** *n* (*fig*) oggetto (*or* progetto) costoso ma inutile; **W~ House** *n* Casa Bianca; **~ lie** *n* bugia pietosa; **~ness** *n* bianchezza; **~ paper** *n* (*POL*) libro bianco; **~wash** *n* (*paint*) bianco di calce ♦ *vt* imbiancare; (*fig*) coprire

whiting ['waɪtɪŋ] *n inv* (*fish*) merlango

Whitsun ['wɪtsn] *n* Pentecoste *f*

whittle ['wɪtl] *vt*: **to ~ away**, **~ down** ridurre, tagliare

whizz [wɪz] *vi*: **to ~ past** *or* **by** passare sfrecciando; **~ kid** (*inf*) *n* prodigio

---

KEYWORD

who [hu:] *pron* 1 (*interrogative*) chi; **~ is it?**, **~'s there?** chi è?
2 (*relative*) che; **the man ~ spoke to me** l'uomo che ha parlato con me; **those ~ can swim** quelli che sanno nuotare

---

whodunit [hu:'dʌnɪt] (*inf*) *n* giallo

whoever [hu:'ɛvə*] *pron*: **~ finds it** chiunque lo trovi; **ask ~ you like** lo chieda a chiunque vuole; **~ she marries** chiunque sposerà, non importa chi sposerà; **~ told you that?** chi mai gliel'ha detto?

whole [həʊl] *adj* (*complete*) tutto(a), completo(a); (*not broken*) intero(a), intatto(a) ♦ *n* (*all*): **the ~ of** tutto(a) il(la); (*entire unit*) tutto; (*not broken*) tutto; **the ~ of the town** tutta la città, la città intera; **on the ~, as a ~** nel complesso, nell'insieme; **~ food(s)** *n(pl)* cibo integrale; **~hearted** *adj* sincero(a); **~meal** *adj* (*bread, flour*) integrale; **~sale** *n* commercio *or* vendita all'ingrosso ♦ *adj* all'ingrosso; (*destruction*) totale; **~saler** *n* grossista *m/f*; **~some** *adj* sano(a); salutare; **~wheat** *adj* = **~meal**; **wholly** *adv* completamente, del tutto

---
KEYWORD

whom [huːm] *pron* **1** (*interrogative*) chi; **~ did you see?** chi hai visto?; **to ~ did you give it?** a chi lo hai dato?
2 (*relative*) che, *prep* +il (la) quale (*check syntax of Italian verb used*); **the man ~ I saw/to ~ I spoke** l'uomo che ho visto/al quale ho parlato

---

whooping cough ['huːpɪŋ-] *n* pertosse *f*
whore [hɔː*] (*inf: pej*) *n* puttana

KEYWORD

whose [huːz] *adj* **1** (*possessive: interrogative*) di chi; **~ book is this?, ~ is this book?** di chi è questo libro?; **~ daughter are you?** di chi sei figlia?
2 (*possessive: relative*): **the man ~ son you rescued** l'uomo il cui figlio hai salvato; **the girl ~ sister you were speaking to** la ragazza alla cui sorella stavi parlando
♦ *pron* di chi; **~ is this?** di chi è questo?; **I know ~ it is** so di chi è

---

why [waɪ] *adv, conj* perché ♦ *excl* (*surprise*) ma guarda un po'!; (*remonstrating*) ma (via)!; (*explaining*) ebbene!; **~ not?** perché no?; **~ not do it now?** perché non farlo adesso?; **that's not ~ I'm here** non è questo il motivo per cui sono qui; **the reason ~** il motivo per cui; **~ever** *adv* perché mai
wicked ['wɪkɪd] *adj* cattivo(a), malvagio(a);

maligno(a); perfido(a)
wickerwork ['wɪkəwəːk] *adj* di vimini ♦ *n* articoli *mpl* di vimini
wicket ['wɪkɪt] *n* (CRICKET) porta; area tra le due porte
wide [waɪd] *adj* largo(a); (*area, knowledge*) vasto(a); (*choice*) ampio(a) ♦ *adv*: **to open ~** spalancare; **to shoot ~** tirare a vuoto *or* fuori bersaglio; **~-angle lens** *n* grandangolare *m*; **~-awake** *adj* completamente sveglio(a); **~ly** *adv* (*differing*) molto, completamente; (*travelled, spaced*) molto; (*believed*) generalmente; **~n** *vt* allargare, ampliare; **~ open** *adj* spalancato(a); **~spread** *adj* (*belief etc*) molto *or* assai diffuso(a)
widow ['wɪdəʊ] *n* vedova; **~ed** *adj*: **to be ~ed** restare vedovo(a); **~er** *n* vedovo
width [wɪdθ] *n* larghezza
wield [wiːld] *vt* (*sword*) maneggiare; (*power*) esercitare
wife [waɪf] (*pl* **wives**) *n* moglie *f*
wig [wɪg] *n* parrucca
wiggle ['wɪgl] *vt* dimenare, agitare
wild [waɪld] *adj* selvatico(a); selvaggio(a); (*sea, weather*) tempestoso(a); (*idea, life*) folle; stravagante; (*applause*) frenetico(a); **~erness** ['wɪldənɪs] *n* deserto; **~life** *n* natura; **~ly** *adv* selvaggiamente; (*applaud*) freneticamente; (*hit, guess*) a casaccio; (*happy*) follemente; **~s** *npl* regione *f* selvaggia
wilful ['wɪlfʊl] (US **willful**) *adj* (*person*) testardo(a), ostinato(a); (*action*) intenzionale; (*crime*) premeditato(a)

KEYWORD

will [wɪl] (*pt, pp* **~ed**) *aux vb* **1** (*forming future tense*): **I ~ finish it tomorrow** lo finirò domani; **I ~ have finished it by tomorrow** lo finirò entro domani; **~ you do it? – yes I ~/no I won't** lo farai? – sì (lo farò)/no (non lo farò)
2 (*in conjectures, predictions*): **he ~** *or* **he'll be there by now** dovrebbe essere arrivato ora; **that ~ be the postman** sarà il postino
3 (*in commands, requests, offers*): **~ you be**

quiet! vuoi stare zitto?; **~ you come?** vieni anche tu?; **~ you help me?** mi aiuti?, mi puoi aiutare?; **~ you have a cup of tea?** vorrebbe una tazza di tè?; **I won't put up with it!** non lo accetterò!
♦ *vt*: **to ~ sb to do** volere che qn faccia; **he ~ed himself to go on** continuò grazie a un grande sforzo di volontà
♦ *n* volontà; testamento

willful ['wɪlful] (*US*) *adj* = **wilful**

willing ['wɪlɪŋ] *adj* volonteroso(a); **~ to do** disposto(a) a fare; **~ly** *adv* volentieri; **~ness** *n* buona volontà

willow ['wɪləu] *n* salice *m*

will power *n* forza di volontà

willy-nilly [wɪlɪ'nɪlɪ] *adv* volente o nolente

wilt [wɪlt] *vi* appassire

win [wɪn] (*pt, pp* **won**) *n* (*in sports etc*) vittoria ♦ *vt* (*battle, prize, money*) vincere; (*popularity*) conquistare ♦ *vi* vincere; **~ over** *vt* convincere; **~ round** (*BRIT*) *vt* convincere

wince [wɪns] *vi* trasalire

winch [wɪntʃ] *n* verricello, argano

wind[1] [waɪnd] (*pt, pp* **wound**) *vt* attorcigliare; (*wrap*) avvolgere; (*clock, toy*) caricare ♦ *vi* (*road, river*) serpeggiare; **~ up** *vt* (*clock*) caricare; (*debate*) concludere

wind[2] [wɪnd] *n* vento; (*MED*) flatulenza; (*breath*) respiro, fiato ♦ *vt* (*take breath away*) far restare senza fiato; **~ power** energia eolica; **~fall** *n* (*money*) guadagno insperato

winding ['waɪndɪŋ] *adj* (*road*) serpeggiante; (*staircase*) a chiocciola

wind instrument *n* (*MUS*) strumento a fiato

windmill ['wɪndmɪl] *n* mulino a vento

window ['wɪndəu] *n* finestra; (*in car, train*) finestrino; (*in shop etc*) vetrina; (*also:* **~ pane**) vetro; **~ box** *n* cassetta da fiori; **~ cleaner** *n* (*person*) pulitore *m* di finestre; **~ envelope** *n* busta a finestra; **~ ledge** *n* davanzale *m*; **~ pane** *n* vetro; **~-shopping** *n*: **to go ~-shopping** andare a vedere le vetrine; **~sill** *n* davanzale *m*

windpipe ['wɪndpaɪp] *n* trachea

windscreen ['wɪndskriːn] *n* parabrezza *m inv*; **~ washer** *n* lavacristallo; **~ wiper** *n* tergicristallo

windshield ['wɪndʃiːld] (*US*) *n* = **windscreen**

windswept ['wɪndswept] *adj* spazzato(a) dal vento

windy ['wɪndɪ] *adj* ventoso(a); **it's ~** c'è vento

wine [waɪn] *n* vino; **~ bar** *n* enoteca (*per degustazione*); **~ cellar** *n* cantina; **~ glass** *n* bicchiere *m* da vino; **~ list** *n* lista dei vini; **~ merchant** *n* commerciante *m* di vini; **~ tasting** *n* degustazione *f* dei vini; **~ waiter** *n* sommelier *m inv*

wing [wɪŋ] *n* ala; (*AUT*) fiancata; **~s** *npl* (*THEATRE*) quinte *fpl*; **~er** *n* (*SPORT*) ala

wink [wɪŋk] *n* ammiccamento ♦ *vi* ammiccare, fare l'occhiolino; (*light*) baluginare

winner ['wɪnə*] *n* vincitore/trice

winning ['wɪnɪŋ] *adj* (*team, goal*) vincente; (*smile*) affascinante; **~s** *npl* vincite *fpl*

winter ['wɪntə*] *n* inverno; **~ sports** *npl* sport *mpl* invernali

wintry ['wɪntrɪ] *adj* invernale

wipe [waɪp] *n* pulita, passata ♦ *vt* pulire (*strofinando*); (*erase: tape*) cancellare; **~ off** *vt* cancellare; (*stains*) togliere strofinando; **~ out** *vt* (*debt*) pagare, liquidare; (*memory*) cancellare; (*destroy*) annientare; **~ up** *vt* asciugare

wire ['waɪə*] *n* filo; (*ELEC*) filo elettrico; (*TEL*) telegramma *m* ♦ *vt* (*house*) fare l'impianto elettrico di; (*also:* **~ up**) collegare, allacciare; (*person*) telegrafare a

wireless ['waɪəlɪs] (*BRIT*) *n* (*set*) (apparecchio *m*) radio *f inv*

wiring ['waɪərɪŋ] *n* impianto elettrico

wiry ['waɪərɪ] *adj* magro(a) e nerboruto(a); (*hair*) ispido(a)

wisdom ['wɪzdəm] *n* saggezza; (*of action*) prudenza; **~ tooth** *n* dente *m* del giudizio

wise [waɪz] *adj* saggio(a); prudente; giudizioso(a)

...wise [waɪz] *suffix*: **time~** per quanto

riguarda il tempo, in termini di tempo
wish [wɪʃ] n (desire) desiderio; (specific desire) richiesta ♦ vt desiderare, volere; **best ~es** (on birthday etc) i migliori auguri; **with best ~es** (in letter) cordiali saluti, con i migliori saluti; **to ~ sb goodbye** dire arrivederci a qn; **he ~ed me well** mi augurò di riuscire; **to ~ to do/sb to do** desiderare or volere fare/che qn faccia; **to ~ for** desiderare; **~ful** adj: **it's ~ful thinking** è prendere i desideri per realtà

wishy-washy [wɪʃɪ'wɔʃɪ] (inf) adj (colour) slavato(a); (ideas, argument) insulso(a)
wisp [wɪsp] n ciuffo, ciocca; (of smoke) filo
wistful ['wɪstful] adj malinconico(a)
wit [wɪt] n (also: ~s) intelligenza; presenza di spirito; (wittiness) spirito, arguzia; (person) bello spirito
witch [wɪtʃ] n strega

KEYWORD

with [wɪð, wɪθ] prep 1 (in the company of) con; **I was ~ him** ero con lui; **we stayed ~ friends** siamo stati da amici; **I'll be ~ you in a minute** vengo subito

2 (descriptive) con; **a room ~ a view** una stanza con vista sul mare (or sulle montagne etc); **the man ~ the grey hat/blue eyes** l'uomo con il cappello grigio/gli occhi blu

3 (indicating manner, means, cause): **~ tears in her eyes** con le lacrime agli occhi; **red ~ anger** rosso dalla rabbia; **to shake ~ fear** tremare di paura

4: **I'm ~ you** (I understand) la seguo; **to be ~ it** (inf: up-to-date) essere alla moda; (: alert) essere sveglio(a)

withdraw [wɪθ'drɔ:] (irreg: like draw) vt ritirare; (money from bank) ritirare; prelevare ♦ vi ritirarsi; **~al** n ritiro; prelievo; (of army) ritirata; **~al symptoms** (MED) crisi f di astinenza; **~n** adj (person) distaccato(a)
wither ['wɪðə*] vi appassire
withhold [wɪθ'həuld] (irreg: like hold) vt (money) trattenere; (permission): **to ~ (from)** rifiutare (a); (information): **to ~**

(from) nascondere (a)
within [wɪð'ɪn] prep all'interno; (in time, distances) entro ♦ adv all'interno, dentro; **~ reach (of)** alla portata (di); **~ sight (of)** in vista (di); **~ a mile of** entro un miglio da; **~ the week** prima della fine della settimana
without [wɪð'aut] prep senza; **to go ~ sth** fare a meno di qc
withstand [wɪθ'stænd] (irreg: like stand) vt resistere a
witness ['wɪtnɪs] n (person, also LAW) testimone m/f ♦ vt (event) essere testimone di; (document) attestare l'autenticità di; **~ box** (US **~ stand**) n banco dei testimoni
witticism ['wɪtɪsɪzm] n spiritosaggine f
witty ['wɪtɪ] adj spiritoso(a)
wives [waɪvz] npl of **wife**
wizard ['wɪzəd] n mago
wk abbr = **week**
wobble ['wɔbl] vi tremare; (chair) traballare
woe [wəu] n dolore m; disgrazia
woke [wəuk] pt of **wake**; **woken** pp of **wake**
wolf [wulf] (pl **wolves**) n lupo
wolves [wulvz] npl of **wolf**
woman ['wumən] (pl **women**) n donna; **~ doctor** n dottoressa; **women's lib** (inf) n movimento femminista
womb [wu:m] n (ANAT) utero
women ['wɪmɪn] npl of **woman**
won [wʌn] pt, pp of **win**
wonder ['wʌndə*] n meraviglia ♦ vi: **to ~ whether/why** domandarsi se/perché; **to ~ at** essere sorpreso(a) di; meravigliarsi di; **to ~ about** domandarsi di; pensare a; **it's no ~ that** c'è poco or non c'è da meravigliarsi che +sub; **~ful** adj meraviglioso(a)
won't [wəunt] = **will not**
wood [wud] n legno; (timber) legname m; (forest) bosco; **~ carving** n scultura in legno, intaglio; **~ed** adj boschivo(a); boscoso(a); **~en** adj di legno; (fig) rigido(a); inespressivo(a); **~pecker** n picchio; **~wind** [pl] (MUS): **the ~wind** i legni; **~work** n (craft, subject) falegnameria; **~worm** n tarlo del legno
wool [wul] n lana; **to pull the ~ over sb's**

eyes (fig) imbrogliare qn; **~len** (US **~en**) adj di lana; (industry) laniero(a); **~lens** npl indumenti mpl di lana; **~ly** (US **~y**) adj di lana; (fig: ideas) confuso(a)

word [wəːd] n parola; (news) notizie fpl ♦ vt esprimere, formulare; **in other ~s** in altre parole; **to break/keep one's ~** non mantenere/mantenere la propria parola; **to have ~s with sb** avere un diverbio con qn; **~ing** n formulazione f; **~ processing** n elaborazione f di testi, word processing m; **~ processor** n word processor m inv

wore [wɔː*] pt of **wear**

work [wəːk] n lavoro; (ART, LITERATURE) opera ♦ vi lavorare; (mechanism, plan etc) funzionare; (medicine) essere efficace ♦ vt (clay, wood etc) lavorare; (mine etc) sfruttare; (machine) far funzionare; (cause: effect, miracle) fare; **to be out of ~** essere disoccupato(a); **~s** n (BRIT: factory) fabbrica ♦ npl (of clock, machine) meccanismo m; **to ~ loose** allentarsi; **~ on** vt fus lavorare a; (person) lavorarsi; (principle) basarsi su; **~ out** vi (plans etc) riuscire, andare bene ♦ vt (problem) risolvere; (plan) elaborare; **it ~s out at £100** fa 100 sterline; **~ up** vt: **to get ~ed up** andare su tutte le furie; eccitarsi; **~able** adj (solution) realizzabile; **~aholic** n maniaco/a del lavoro; **~er** n lavoratore/trice, operaio/a; **~force** n forza lavoro; **~ing class** n classe f operaia; **~ing-class** adj operaio(a); **~ing order** n: **in ~ing order** funzionante; **~man** (irreg) n operaio; **~manship** n abilità; **~sheet** n foglio col programma di lavoro; **~shop** n officina; (practical session) gruppo di lavoro; **~ station** n stazione f di lavoro; **~-to-rule** (BRIT) n sciopero bianco

world [wəːld] n mondo ♦ cpd (champion) del mondo; (power, war) mondiale; **to think the ~ of sb** (fig) pensare un gran bene di qn; **~ly** adj di questo mondo; (knowledgeable) di mondo; **~-wide** adj universale; **W~-Wide Web** n World Wide Web m

worm [wəːm] n (also: **earth~**) verme m

worn [wɔːn] pp of **wear** ♦ adj usato(a); **~-**

out adj (object) consumato(a), logoro(a); (person) sfinito(a)

worried ['wʌrɪd] adj preoccupato(a)

worry ['wʌrɪ] n preoccupazione f ♦ vt preoccupare ♦ vi preoccuparsi

worse [wəːs] adj peggiore ♦ adv, n peggio; **a change for the ~** un peggioramento; **~n** vt, vi peggiorare; **~ off** adj in condizioni (economiche) peggiori

worship ['wəːʃɪp] n culto ♦ vt (God) adorare, venerare; (person) adorare; **Your W~** (BRIT: to mayor) signor sindaco; (: to judge) signor giudice

worst [wəːst] adj il(la) peggiore ♦ adv, n peggio; **at ~** al peggio, per male che vada

worth [wəːθ] n valore m ♦ adj: **to be ~** valere; **it's ~ it** ne vale la pena; **it is ~ one's while (to do)** vale la pena (fare); **~less** adj di nessun valore; **~while** adj (activity) utile; (cause) lodevole

worthy ['wəːðɪ] adj (person) degno(a); (motive) lodevole; **~ of** degno di

KEYWORD

would [wʊd] aux vb 1 (conditional tense): **if you asked him he ~ do it** se glielo chiedesse lo farebbe; **if you had asked him he ~ have done it** se glielo avesse chiesto lo avrebbe fatto

2 (in offers, invitations, requests): **~ you like a biscuit?** vorrebbe or vuole un biscotto?; **~ you ask him to come in?** lo faccia entrare, per cortesia; **~ you open the window please?** apra la finestra, per favore

3 (in indirect speech): **I said I ~ do it** ho detto che l'avrei fatto

4 (emphatic): **it WOULD have to snow today!** doveva proprio nevicare oggi!

5 (insistence): **she ~n't do it** non ha voluto farlo

6 (conjecture): **it ~ have been midnight** sarà stato mezzanotte; **it ~ seem so** sembrerebbe proprio di sì

7 (indicating habit): **he ~ go there on Mondays** andava lì ogni lunedì

would-be (*pej*) *adj* sedicente
wouldn't ['wudnt] = **would not**
wound[1] [waund] *pt, pp of* **wind**[1]
wound[2] [wu:nd] *n* ferita ♦ *vt* ferire
wove [wəuv] *pt of* **weave**; **woven** *pp of* **weave**
wrangle ['ræŋgl] *n* litigio
wrap [ræp] *vt* avvolgere; (*pack: also:* ~ **up**) incartare; ~**per** *n* (*on chocolate*) carta; (*BRIT: of book*) copertina; ~**ping paper** *n* carta da pacchi; (*for gift*) carta da regali
wreak [ri:k] *vt* (*havoc*) portare, causare; **to** ~ **vengeance on** vendicarsi su
wreath [ri:θ, *pl* ri:ðz] *n* corona
wreck [rɛk] *n* (*sea disaster*) naufragio; (*ship*) relitto; (*pej: person*) rottame *m* ♦ *vt* demolire; (*ship*) far naufragare; (*fig*) rovinare; ~**age** *n* rottami *mpl*; (*of building*) macerie *fpl*; (*of ship*) relitti *mpl*
wren [rɛn] *n* (*ZOOL*) scricciolo
wrench [rɛntʃ] *n* (*TECH*) chiave *f*; (*tug*) torsione *f* brusca; (*fig*) strazio ♦ *vt* strappare; storcere; **to** ~ **sth from** strappare qc a *or* da
wrestle ['rɛsl] *vi*: **to** ~ (**with sb**) lottare (con qn); ~**r** *n* lottatore/trice; **wrestling** *n* lotta
wretched ['rɛtʃid] *adj* disgraziato(a); (*inf: weather, holiday*) orrendo(a), orribile; (: *child, dog*) pestifero(a)
wriggle ['rigl] *vi* (*also:* ~ **about**) dimenarsi; (: *snake, worm*) serpeggiare
wring [riŋ] (*pt, pp* **wrung**) *vt* torcere; (*wet clothes*) strizzare; (*fig*): **to** ~ **sth out of** strappare qc a
wrinkle ['riŋkl] *n* (*on skin*) ruga; (*on paper etc*) grinza ♦ *vt* (*nose*) torcere; (*forehead*) corrugare ♦ *vi* (*skin, paint*) raggrinzirsi
wrist [rist] *n* polso; ~**watch** *n* orologio da polso
writ [rit] *n* ordine *m*; mandato
write [rait] (*pt* **wrote**, *pp* **written**) *vt, vi* scrivere; ~ **down** *vt* annotare; (*put in writing*) mettere per iscritto; ~ **off** *vt* (*debt, plan*) cancellare; ~ **out** *vt* mettere per iscritto; (*cheque, receipt*) scrivere; ~ **up** *vt* redigere; ~**-off** *n* perdita completa; ~**r** *n* autore/trice, scrittore/trice
writhe [raið] *vi* contorcersi

writing ['raitiŋ] *n* scrittura; (*of author*) scritto, opera; **in** ~ per iscritto; ~ **paper** *n* carta da lettere
written ['ritn] *pp of* **write**
wrong [rɔŋ] *adj* sbagliato(a); (*not suitable*) inadatto(a); (*wicked*) cattivo(a); (*unfair*) ingiusto(a) ♦ *adv* in modo sbagliato, erroneamente ♦ *n* (*injustice*) torto ♦ *vt* fare torto a; **you are** ~ **to do it** ha torto a farlo; **you are** ~ **about that, you've got it** ~ si sbaglia; **to be in the** ~ avere torto; **what's** ~? cosa c'è che non va?; **to go** ~ (*person*) sbagliarsi; (*plan*) fallire, non riuscire; (*machine*) guastarsi; ~**ful** *adj* illegittimo(a); ingiusto(a); ~**ly** *adv* (*incorrectly, by mistake*) in modo sbagliato; ~ **number** *n* (*TEL*): **you've got the** ~ **number** ha sbagliato numero
wrote [rəut] *pt of* **write**
wrought iron [rɔ:t-] *n* ferro battuto
wrung [rʌŋ] *pt, pp of* **wring**
WWW *n abbr* (= *World Wide Web*): **the** ~ la Rete

X, x

Xmas ['ɛksməs] *n abbr* = **Christmas**
X-ray ['ɛksrei] *n* raggio X; (*photograph*) radiografia ♦ *vt* radiografare
xylophone ['zailəfəun] *n* xilofono

Y, y

yacht [jɔt] *n* panfilo, yacht *m inv*; ~**ing** *n* yachting *m*, sport *m* della vela
Yank [jæŋk] (*pej*) *n* yankee *m/f inv*
Yankee ['jæŋki] (*pej*) *n* = **Yank**
yap [jæp] *vi* (*dog*) guaire
yard [jɑ:d] *n* (*of house etc*) cortile *m*; (*measure*) iarda (= *914 mm; 3 feet*); ~**stick** *n* (*fig*) misura, criterio
yarn [jɑ:n] *n* filato; (*tale*) lunga storia
yawn [jɔ:n] *n* sbadiglio ♦ *vi* sbadigliare; ~**ing** *adj* (*gap*) spalancato(a)
yd. *abbr* = **yard(s)**

yeah [jɛə] (inf) adv sì

year [jɪə*] n anno; (referring to harvest, wine etc) annata; **he is 8 ~s old** ha 8 anni; **an eight-~-old child** un(a) bambino(a) di otto anni; **~ly** adj annuale ♦ adv annualmente

yearn [jəːn] vi: **to ~ for sth/to do** desiderare ardentemente qc/di fare

yeast [jiːst] n lievito

yell [jɛl] n urlo ♦ vi urlare

yellow [ˈjɛləu] adj giallo(a)

yelp [jɛlp] vi guaire, uggiolare

yeoman [ˈjəumən] n: **~ of the guard** guardiano della Torre di Londra

yes [jɛs] adv sì ♦ n sì m inv; **to say/answer ~** dire/rispondere di sì

yesterday [ˈjɛstədɪ] adv ieri ♦ n ieri m inv; **~ morning/evening** ieri mattina/sera; **all day ~** ieri per tutta la giornata

yet [jɛt] adv ancora; già ♦ conj ma, tuttavia; **it is not finished ~** non è ancora finito; **the best ~** il migliore, la migliore; **as ~** finora

yew [juː] n tasso (albero)

yield [jiːld] n produzione f, resa; reddito ♦ vt produrre, rendere; (surrender) cedere ♦ vi cedere; (US: AUT) dare la precedenza

YMCA n abbr (= Young Men's Christian Association) Y.M.C.A. m

yoga [ˈjəugə] n yoga m

yog(h)ourt [ˈjəugət] n = **yog(h)urt**

yog(h)urt [ˈjəugət] n iogurt m inv

yoke [jəuk] n (also fig) giogo

yolk [jəuk] n tuorlo, rosso d'uovo

KEYWORD

you [juː] pron 1 (subject) tu; (: polite form) lei; (: pl) voi; (: very formal) loro; **~ Italians enjoy your food** a voi Italiani piace mangiare bene; **~ and I will go** tu ed io or lei ed io andiamo

2 (object: direct) ti; la; vi; loro (after vb); (: indirect) ti; le; vi; loro (after vb); **I know ~** ti or la or vi conosco; **I gave it to ~** te l'ho dato; gliel'ho dato; ve l'ho dato; l'ho dato loro

3 (stressed, after prep, in comparisons) te; lei; voi; loro; **I told YOU to do it** ho detto a TE (or a LEI etc) di farlo; **she's younger**

than ~ è più giovane di te (or lei etc)

4 (impers: one) si; **fresh air does ~ good** l'aria fresca fa bene; **~ never know** non si sa mai

---

you'd [juːd] = **you had**; **you would**

you'll [juːl] = **you will**; **you shall**

young [jʌŋ] adj giovane ♦ npl (of animal) piccoli mpl; (people): **the ~** i giovani, la gioventù; **~er** adj più giovane; (brother) minore, più giovane; **~ster** n giovanotto, ragazzo; (child) bambino/a

your [jɔː*] adj il(la) tuo(a), pl i(le) tuoi(tue); il(la) suo(a), pl i(le) suoi(sue); il(la) vostro(a), pl i(le) vostri(e); il(la) loro, pl i(le) loro; see also **my**

you're [juə*] = **you are**

yours [jɔːz] pron il(la) tuo(a), pl i(le) tuoi(tue); (polite form) il(la) suo(a), pl i(le) suoi(sue); (pl) il(la) vostro(a), pl i(le) vostri(e); (: very formal) il(la) loro, pl i(le) loro; see also **mine**; **faithfully**; **sincerely**

yourself [jɔːˈsɛlf] pron (reflexive) ti; si; (after prep) te; sé; (emphatic) tu stesso(a); lei stesso(a); **yourselves** pl pron (reflexive) vi; si; (after prep) voi; loro; (emphatic) voi stessi(e); loro stessi(e); see also **oneself**

youth [juːθ, pl juːðz] n gioventù f; (young man) giovane m, ragazzo; **~ club** n centro giovanile; **~ful** adj giovane; da giovane; giovanile; **~ hostel** n ostello della gioventù

you've [juːv] = **you have**

Yugoslav [ˈjuːgəuˈslɑːv] adj, n jugoslavo(a)

Yugoslavia [ˈjuːgəuˈslɑːvɪə] n Jugoslavia

yuppie [ˈjʌpɪ] (inf) n, adj yuppie m/f inv

YWCA n abbr (= Young Women's Christian Association) Y.W.C.A. m

---

Z, z

zany [ˈzeɪnɪ] adj un po' pazzo(a)

zap [zæp] vt (COMPUT) cancellare

zeal [ziːl] n zelo; entusiasmo

zebra [ˈziːbrə] n zebra; **~ crossing** (BRIT) n (passaggio pedonale a) strisce fpl, zebre fpl

zero ['zɪərəu] n zero
zest [zɛst] n gusto; (CULIN) buccia
zigzag ['zɪgzæg] n zigzag m inv ♦ vi
  zigzagare
Zimbabwe [zɪm'bɑːbwɪ] n Zimbabwe m
zinc [zɪŋk] n zinco
zip [zɪp] n (also: ~ **fastener**, (US) **~per**)
  chiusura f or cerniera f lampo inv ♦ vt
  (also: ~ **up**) chiudere con una cerniera
  lampo; ~ **code** (US) n codice m di
  avviamento postale

zodiac ['zəudɪæk] n zodiaco
zombie ['zɔmbɪ] n (fig): **like a ~** come un
  morto che cammina
zone [zəun] n (also MIL) zona
zoo [zuː] n zoo m inv
zoology [zuː'ɔlədʒɪ] n zoologia
zoom [zuːm] vi: **to ~ past** sfrecciare;
  ~ **lens** n zoom m inv, obiettivo a focale
  variabile
zucchini [zuː'kiːnɪ] (US) npl (courgettes)
  zucchine fpl

ITALIAN VERBS

1 Gerundio *2* Participio passato *3* Presente *4* Imperfetto *5* Passato remoto *6* Futuro
7 Condizionale *8* Congiuntivo presente *9* Congiuntivo passato *10* Imperativo

andare *3* vado, vai, va, andiamo, andate, vanno *6* andrò *etc* *8* vada *10* va'!, vada!, andate!, vadano!

apparire *2* apparso *3* appaio, appari *o* apparisci, appare *o* apparisce, appaiono *o* appariscono *5* apparvi *o* apparsi, apparisti, apparve *o* apparì *o* apparse, apparvero *o* apparirono *o* apparsero *8* appaia *o* apparisca

aprire *2* aperto *3* apro *5* aprii *o* apersi, apristi *8* apra

AVERE *3* ho, hai, ha, abbiamo, avete, hanno *5* ebbi, avesti, ebbe, avemmo, aveste, ebbero *6* avrò *etc* *8* abbia *etc* *10* abbi!, abbia!, abbiate!, abbiano!

bere *1* bevendo *2* bevuto *3* bevo *etc* *4* bevevo *etc* *8* beva *etc* *9* bevessi *etc*

cadere *5* caddi, cadesti *6* cadrò *etc*

cogliere *2* colto *3* colgo, colgono *5* colsi, cogliesti *8* colga

correre *2* corso *5* corsi, corresti

cuocere *2* cotto *3* cuocio, cociamo, cuociono *5* cossi, cocesti

dare *3* do, dai, dà, diamo, date, danno *5* diedi *o* detti, desti *6* darò *etc* *8* dia *etc* *9* dessi *etc 10* da'!, dia!, date!, diano!

dire *1* dicendo *2* detto *3* dico, dici, dice, diciamo, dite, dicono *4* dicevo *etc 5* dissi, dicesti *6* dirò *etc 8* dica, diciamo, diciate, dicano *9* dicessi *etc 10* di'!, dica!, dite!, dicano!

dolere *3* dolgo, duoli, duole, dolgono *5* dolsi, dolesti *6* dorrò *etc 8* dolga

dovere *3* devo *o* debbo, devi, deve, dobbiamo, dovete, devono *o* debbono *6* dovrò *etc 8* debba, dobbiamo, dobbiate, devano *o* debbano

ESSERE *2* stato *3* sono, sei, è, siamo, siete, sono *4* ero, eri, era, eravamo, eravate, erano *5* fui, fosti, fu, fummo, foste, furono *6* sarò *etc 8* sia *etc 9* fossi, fossi, fosse, fossimo, foste, fossero *10* sii!, sia!, siate!, siano!

fare *1* facendo *2* fatto *3* faccio, fai, fa, facciamo, fate, fanno *4* facevo *etc* feci, facesti *6* farò *etc 8* faccia *etc* facessi *etc 10* fa'!, faccia!, fate! facciano!

FINIRE *1* finendo *2* finito *3* finisco finisci, finisce, finiamo, finite finiscono *4* finivo, finivi, finiva finivamo, finivate, finivano *5* fini finisti, finì, finimmo, finiste, finiron *6* finirò, finirai, finirà, finiremo finirete, finiranno *7* finirei, finirest finirebbe, finiremmo, finireste, fin rebbe *8* finisca, finisca, finisca finiamo, finiate, finiscano *9* finiss finissi, finisse, finissimo, finiste finissero *10* finisci!, finisca!, finite finiscano!

giungere *2* giunto *5* giunsi, giungesti

leggere *2* letto *5* lessi, leggesti

mettere *2* messo *5* misi, mettesti

morire *2* morto *3* muoio, muor muore, moriamo, morite, muoiono morirò *o* morrò *etc 8* muoia

muovere *2* mosso *5* mossi, movesti

nascere *2* nato *5* nacqui, nascesti

nuocere *2* nuociuto *3* nuoccio, nuoc nuoce, nociamo *o* nuociamo, nuocet nuocciono *4* nuocevo *etc 5* nocqu nuocesti *6* nuocerò *etc 7* nuoccia

offrire *2* offerto *3* offro *5* offersi *o* offri offristi *8* offra

parere *2* parso *3* paio, paiamo, paiono parvi *o* parsi, paresti *6* parrò *etc* paia, paiamo, paiate, paiano

PARLARE *1* parlando *2* parlato *3* parlo parli, parla, parliamo, parlat parlano *4* parlavo, parlavi, parlava parlavamo, parlavate, parlavano parlai, parlasti, parlò, parlammo parlaste, parlarono *6* parlerò, parlera parlerà, parleremo, parleret parleranno *7* parlerei, parlerest parlerebbe, parleremmo, parlereste, parlerebbero *8* parli, parli, parli, parliamo, parliate, parlino *9* parlassi, parlassi, parlasse, parlassimo, parlaste, parlassero *10* parla!, parli!, parlate!, parlino!

piacere *2* piaciuto *3* piaccio, piacciamo, piacciono *5* piacqui, piacesti *8* piaccia *etc*

porre *1* ponendo *2* posto *3* pongo, poni, pone, poniamo, ponete, pongono *4* ponevo *etc* *5* posi, ponesti *6* porrò *etc* *8* ponga, poniamo, poniate, pongano *9* ponessi *etc*

potere *3* posso, puoi, può, possiamo, potete, possono *6* potrò *etc* *8* possa, possiamo, possiate, possano

prendere *2* preso *5* presi, prendesti

ridurre *1* riducendo *2* ridotto *3* riduco *etc* *4* riducevo *etc* *5* ridussi, riducesti *6* ridurrò *etc* *8* riduca *etc* *9* riducessi *etc*

riempire *1* riempiendo *3* riempio, riempi, riempie, riempiono

rimanere *2* rimasto *3* rimango, rimangono *5* rimasi, rimanesti *6* rimarrò *etc* *8* rimanga

rispondere *2* risposto *5* risposi, rispondesti

salire *3* salgo, sali, salgono *8* salga

sapere *3* so, sai, sa, sappiamo, sapete, sanno *5* seppi, sapesti *6* saprò *etc* *8* sappia *etc* *10* sappi!, sappia!, sappiate!, sappiano!

scrivere *2* scritto *5* scrissi, scrivesti

sedere *3* siedo, siedi, siede, siedono *8* sieda

spegnere *2* spento *3* spengo, spengono *5* spensi, spegnesti *8* spenga

stare *2* stato *3* sto, stai, sta, stiamo, state, stanno *5* stetti, stesti *6* starò *etc* *8* stia *etc* *9* stessi *etc* *10* sta'!, stia!, state!, stiano!

tacere *2* taciuto *3* taccio, tacciono *5* tacqui, tacesti *8* taccia

tenere *3* tengo, tieni, tiene, tengono *5* tenni, tenesti *6* terrò *etc* *8* tenga

trarre *1* traendo *2* tratto *3* traggo, trai, trae, traiamo, traete, traggono *4* traevo *etc* *5* trassi, traesti *6* trarrò *etc* *8* tragga *9* traessi *etc*

udire *3* odo, odi, ode, odono *8* oda

uscire *3* esco, esci, esce, escono *8* esca

valere *2* valso *3* valgo, valgono *5* valsi, valesti *6* varrò *etc* *8* valga

vedere *2* visto *o* veduto *5* vidi, vedesti *6* vedrò *etc*

VENDERE *1* vendendo *2* venduto *3* vendo, vendi, vende, vendiamo, vendete, vendono *4* vendevo, vendevi, vendeva, vendevamo, vendevate, vendevano *5* vendei *o* vendetti, vendesti, vendé *o* vendette, vendemmo, vendeste, venderono *o* vendettero *6* venderò, venderai, venderà, venderemo, venderete, venderanno *7* venderei, venderesti, venderebbe, venderemmo, vendereste, venderebbero *8* venda, venda, venda, vendiamo, vendiate, vendano *9* vendessi, vendessi, vendesse, vendessimo, vendeste, vendessero *10* vendi!, venda!, vendete!, vendano!

venire *2* venuto *3* vengo, vieni, viene, vengono *5* venni, venisti *6* verrò *etc* *8* venga

vivere *2* vissuto *5* vissi, vivesti

volere *3* voglio, vuoi, vuole, vogliamo, volete, vogliono *5* volli, volesti *6* vorrò *etc* *8* voglia *etc* *10* vogli!, voglia!, vogliate!, vogliano!

VERBI INGLESI

present	pt	pp	present	pt	pp
arise	arose	arisen	feed	fed	fed
awake	awoke	awoken	feel	felt	felt
be (am, is, are; being)	was, were	been	fight	fought	fought
			find	found	found
bear	bore	born(e)	flee	fled	fled
beat	beat	beaten	fling	flung	flung
become	became	become	fly (flies)	flew	flown
begin	began	begun	forbid	forbade	forbidden
behold	beheld	beheld	forecast	forecast	forecast
bend	bent	bent	forego	forewent	foregone
beseech	besought	besought	foresee	foresaw	foreseen
beset	beset	beset	foretell	foretold	foretold
bet	bet, betted	bet, betted	forget	forgot	forgotten
bid	bid, bade	bid, bidden	forgive	forgave	forgiven
bind	bound	bound	forsake	forsook	forsaken
bite	bit	bitten	freeze	froze	frozen
bleed	bled	bled	get	got	got, (US) gotten
blow	blew	blown			
break	broke	broken	give	gave	given
breed	bred	bred	go (goes)	went	gone
bring	brought	brought	grind	ground	ground
build	built	built	grow	grew	grown
burn	burnt, burned	burnt, burned	hang	hung, hanged	hung, hanged
burst	burst	burst	have (has; having)	had	had
buy	bought	bought			
can	could	(been able)	hear	heard	heard
cast	cast	cast	hide	hid	hidden
catch	caught	caught	hit	hit	hit
choose	chose	chosen	hold	held	held
cling	clung	clung	hurt	hurt	hurt
come	came	come	keep	kept	kept
cost	cost	cost	kneel	knelt, kneeled	knelt, kneeled
creep	crept	crept			
cut	cut	cut	know	knew	known
deal	dealt	dealt	lay	laid	laid
dig	dug	dug	lead	led	led
do (3rd person: he/she/it does)	did	done	lean	leant, leaned	leant, leaned
			leap	leapt, leaped	leapt, leaped
draw	drew	drawn			
dream	dreamed, dreamt	dreamed, dreamt	learn	learnt, learned	learnt, learned
drink	drank	drunk	leave	left	left
drive	drove	driven	lend	lent	lent
dwell	dwelt	dwelt	let	let	let
eat	ate	eaten	lie (lying)	lay	lain
fall	fell	fallen	light	lit, lighted	lit, lighted

present	pt	pp	present	pt	pp
lose	lost	lost	spell	spelt, spelled	spelt, spelled
make	made	made			
may	might	—	spend	spent	spent
mean	meant	meant	spill	spilt, spilled	spilt, spilled
meet	met	met			
mistake	mistook	mistaken	spin	spun	spun
mow	mowed	mown, mowed	spit	spat	spat
must	(had to)	(had to)	split	split	split
pay	paid	paid	spoil	spoiled, spoilt	spoiled, spoilt
put	put	put			
quit	quit, quitted	quit, quitted	spread	spread	spread
			spring	sprang	sprung
read	read	read	stand	stood	stood
rid	rid	rid	steal	stole	stolen
ride	rode	ridden	stick	stuck	stuck
ring	rang	rung	sting	stung	stung
rise	rose	risen	stink	stank	stunk
run	ran	run	stride	strode	stridden
saw	sawed	sawn	strike	struck	struck, stricken
say	said	said			
see	saw	seen	strive	strove	striven
seek	sought	sought	swear	swore	sworn
sell	sold	sold	sweep	swept	swept
send	sent	sent	swell	swelled	swollen, swelled
set	set	set			
shake	shook	shaken	swim	swam	swum
shall	should	—	swing	swung	swung
shear	sheared	shorn, sheared	take	took	taken
shed	shed	shed	teach	taught	taught
shine	shone	shone	tear	tore	torn
shoot	shot	shot	tell	told	told
show	showed	shown	think	thought	thought
shrink	shrank	shrunk	throw	threw	thrown
shut	shut	shut	thrust	thrust	thrust
sing	sang	sung	tread	trod	trodden
sink	sank	sunk	wake	woke	woken
sit	sat	sat	waylay	waylaid	waylaid
slay	slew	slain	wear	wore	worn
sleep	slept	slept	weave	wove, weaved	woven, weaved
slide	slid	slid			
sling	slung	slung	wed	wedded, wed	wedded, wed
slit	slit	slit			
smell	smelt, smelled	smelt, smelled	weep	wept	wept
			win	won	won
sow	sowed	sown, sowed	wind	wound	wound
speak	spoke	spoken	wring	wrung	wrung
speed	sped, speeded	sped, speeded	write	wrote	written

I NUMERI

NUMBERS

uno(a)	1	one
due	2	two
tre	3	three
quattro	4	four
cinque	5	five
sei	6	six
sette	7	seven
otto	8	eight
nove	9	nine
dieci	10	ten
undici	11	eleven
dodici	12	twelve
tredici	13	thirteen
quattordici	14	fourteen
quindici	15	fifteen
sedici	16	sixteen
diciassette	17	seventeen
diciotto	18	eighteen
diciannove	19	nineteen
venti	20	twenty
ventuno	21	twenty-one
ventidue	22	twenty-two
ventitré	23	twenty-three
ventotto	28	twenty-eight
trenta	30	thirty
quaranta	40	forty
cinquanta	50	fifty
sessanta	60	sixty
settanta	70	seventy
ottanta	80	eighty
novanta	90	ninety
cento	100	a hundred, one hundred
cento uno	101	a hundred and one
duecento	200	two hundred
mille	1 000	a thousand, one thousand
milleduecentodue	1 202	one thousand two hundred and two
cinquemila	5 000	five thousand
un milione	1 000 000	a million, one million

primo(a), 1º		first, 1st
secondo(a), 2º		second, 2nd
terzo(a), 3º		third, 3rd
quarto(a)		fourth, 4th
quinto(a)		fifth, 5th
sesto(a)		sixth, 6th

I NUMERI

settimo(a)
ottavo(a)
nono(a)
decimo(a)
undicesimo(a)
dodicesimo(a)
tredicesimo(a)
quattordicesimo(a)
quindicesimo(a)
sedicesimo(a)
diciassettesimo(a)
diciottesimo(a)
diciannovesimo(a)
ventesimo(a)
ventunesimo(a)
ventiduesimo(a)
ventitreesimo(a)
ventottesimo(a)
trentesimo(a)
centesimo(a)
centunesimo(a)
millesimo(a)
milionesimo(a)

Frazioni etc

mezzo
terzo
due terzi
quarto
quinto
zero virgola cinque, 0,5
tre virgola quattro, 3,4
dieci per cento
cento per cento

Esempi

abita al numero dieci
si trova nel capitolo sette, a
  pagina sette
abita al terzo piano
arrivò quarto
scala uno a venticinquemila

NUMBERS

seventh
eighth
ninth
tenth
eleventh
twelfth
thirteenth
fourteenth
fifteenth
sixteenth
seventeenth
eighteenth
nineteenth
twentieth
twenty-first
twenty-second
twenty-third
twenty-eighth
thirtieth
hundredth
hundred-and-first
thousandth
millionth

Fractions etc

half
third
two thirds
quarter
fifth
(nought) point five, 0.5
three point four, 3.4
ten per cent
a hundred per cent

Examples

he lives at number 10
it's in chapter 7, on page 7

he lives on the 3rd floor
he came in 4th
scale 1:25,000

L'ORA

THE TIME

che ora è?, che ore sono?

what time is it?

è ..., sono ...

it is ...

mezzanotte	midnight, twelve p.m.
l'una (della mattina)	one o'clock (in the morning), one (a.m.)
l'una e cinque	five past one
l'una e dieci	ten past one
l'una e un quarto, l'una e quindici	a quarter past one, one fifteen
l'una e venticinque	twenty-five past one, one twenty-five
l'una e mezzo *or* mezza, l'una e trenta	half-past one, one thirty
le due meno venticinque, l'una e trentacinque	twenty-five to two, one thirty-five
le due meno venti, l'una e quaranta	twenty to two, one forty
le due meno un quarto, l'una e quarantacinque	a quarter to two, one forty-five
le due meno dieci, l'una e cinquanta	ten to two, one fifty
mezzogiorno	twelve o'clock, midday, noon
l'una, le tredici	one o'clock (in the afternoon), one (p.m.)
le sette (di sera), le diciannove	seven o'clock (in the evening), seven (p.m.)

a che ora?

at what time?

a mezzanotte	at midnight
all'una, alle tredici	at one o'clock
fra venti minuti	in twenty minutes
venti minuti fa	twenty minutes ago